ISBN 978-0-282-41280-7
PIBN 10850821

English
Français
Deutsche
Italiano
Español
Português

www.forgottenbooks.com

Mythology Photography **Fiction**
Fishing Christianity **Art** Cooking
Essays Buddhism Freemasonry
Medicine **Biology** Music **Ancient**
Egypt Evolution Carpentry Physics
Dance Geology **Mathematics** Fitness
Shakespeare **Folklore** Yoga Marketing
Confidence Immortality Biographies
Poetry **Psychology** Witchcraft
Electronics Chemistry History **Law**
Accounting **Philosophy** Anthropology
Alchemy Drama Quantum Mechanics
Atheism Sexual Health **Ancient History**
Entrepreneurship Languages Sport
Paleontology Needlework Islam
Metaphysics Investment Archaeology
Parenting Statistics Criminology
Motivational

ΗΡΟΔΟΤΟΥ ΙΣΤΟΡΙΩΝ

Η, Θ, Ι

ΠΟΛΥΜΝΙΑ ΟΥΡΑΝΙΑ ΚΑΛΛΙΟΠΗ

MACMILLAN AND CO., Limited
LONDON · BOMBAY · CALCUTTA
MELBOURNE

THE MACMILLAN COMPANY
NEW YORK · BOSTON · CHICAGO
ATLANTA · SAN FRANCISCO

THE MACMILLAN CO. OF CANADA, Ltd.
TORONTO

HERODOTUS

THE SEVENTH, EIGHTH, & NINTH BOOKS

4 6 7 2 WITH

INTRODUCTION, TEXT, APPARATUS, COMMENTARY,
APPENDICES, INDICES, MAPS

BY

REGINALD WALTER MACAN, D.Litt.

UNIVERSITY READER IN ANCIENT HISTORY
MASTER (SOMETIME FELLOW AND TUTOR, FORMERLY SCHOLAR) OF
UNIVERSITY COLLEGE, OXFORD

VOL. I—PART II

BOOKS VIII. AND IX. (TEXT AND COMMENTARIES)

MACMILLAN AND CO., LIMITED
ST. MARTIN'S STREET, LONDON
1908

TRIBUS VIRIS ILLUSTRIBUS

HENRICO STEIN
HENRICO VAN HERWERDEN
ALUREDO HOLDER

HOC VOLUMEN

D.D.D.

EDITORIBUS EDITOR

CONTENTS

ΗΡΟΔΟΤΟΥ

ΟΥΡΑΝΙΑ

Οἱ δὲ Ἑλλήνων ἐς τὸν ναυτικὸν στρατὸν ταχθέντες ἦσαν 1
οἵδε, Ἀθηναῖοι μὲν νέας παρεχόμενοι ἑκατὸν καὶ εἴκοσι καὶ

OYPANIA H AB: οὐρανία | ἡροδότου ἱστοριῶν ὀγδόη d **1. 1**
οἱ δὲ: ταῦτα μὲν δὴ οὕτω λέγεται γενέσθαι· οἱ δὲ codd. z (nisi quod R om.
δή, V pro ταῦτα exhib. αὗτα) ‖ ἑλλήνων ἐς a: ἕλληνες BC ‖ τὸ B **2**
ἑπτὰ καὶ εἴκοσι καὶ ἑκατόν B, Holder

---

1. 1. οἱ δὲ Ἑλλήνων ἐς τ. ν. στ. ταχθέντες refers (a) to the colon immediately preceding, ταῦτα μὲν δὴ οὕτω λέγεται γενέσθαι, and now forming the close of the seventh Book (cp. App. Crit.). But (b) if 7. 239 is a late insertion (cp. notes ad l.), the grammatical correspondence may have been originally, and more happily, with the closing words of 7. 238 οἱ μὲν δὴ ταῦτα ἐποίευν τοῖσι ἐνετέτακτο ποιέειν. Yet perhaps (c) the original correspondence lay with the first sentence of 7. 234 οἱ μὲν δὴ περὶ Θερμοπύλας Ἕλληνες οὕτω ἠγωνίσαντο, both Demaratos episodes, as well as 7. 238, which now intervene, being of the second or third redaction. The true contrast and correspondence lies between 'the Hellenes comprised in the naval forces' and 'the Hellenes brigaded at Thermopylai,' and the navy-list which here follows (d) really carries back to the army-list given above 7. 202. The transition between Bks. 7 and 8 is, indeed, abrupt, but the better inference from the abruptness of the transition is not (with Stein²) to a lacuna (Ausfall im Texte) but to an insertion, or to insertions, in the text by author and by interpolator to boot, destructive of the original continuity. The abruptness has been at once emphasized and obliterated by the division into books, made (by some anonymous Alexandrian), naturally enough, just at this point. The result

has been still further to divorce the synchronous and inter-related operations on land and sea, the stories of Thermopylai and of Artemision as narrated by Hdt., on which point see further, Introduction, § 11, Appendix V. Ἑλλήνων is, of course, a partitive genitive. ἐς, not 'against' but 'into'; cp. 7. 21 οἱ δὲ ἐς πεζὸν ἐτετάχατο.

ἦσαν οἵδε. The sources of the Greek navy-lists for Artemision (here) and Salamis (cc. 43–48 infra) cannot be exactly determined; but if Hdt.'s figures are ever to be trusted, it is in these two cases, the rather in view of his omission of all details for the fleet in the following year (c. 131 infra). See further, Introduction, § 10, and the notes on the details below.

2. Ἀθηναῖοι. The order here is determined by the size of the respective contingents, or perhaps by the (Athenian) provenience of the list (in contrast with the list of Salamis, cc. 43–48 infra). To the 127 ships here specified are to be added the 53 supplied in c. 14 infra, besides the 20 manned from Chalkis, just below, making a total of 200 bottoms from Athens, cp. 7. 144. With the use of the middle (παρεχόμενοι) for the war-ships (νέας), manned by the Athenians themselves, cp. the active (παρεχόντων) just below for the ships furnished to the men of Chalkis.

VOL. I PT. II   357   B

ἑπτά· ὑπὸ δὲ ἀρετῆς τε καὶ προθυμίης Πλαταιέες, ἄπειροι
τῆς ναυτικῆς ἐόντες, συνεπλήρουν τοῖσι Ἀθηναίοισι τὰς νέας.
5 Κορίνθιοι δὲ τεσσεράκοντα νέας παρείχοντο, Μεγαρέες δὲ εἴκοσι.
καὶ Χαλκιδέες ἐπλήρουν εἴκοσι, Ἀθηναίων σφι παρεχόντων
τὰς νέας, Αἰγινῆται δὲ ὀκτωκαίδεκα, Σικυώνιοι δὲ δυοκαίδεκα,
Λακεδαιμόνιοι δὲ δέκα, Ἐπιδαύριοι δὲ ὀκτώ, Ἐρετριέες δὲ
ἑπτά, Τροιζήνιοι δὲ πέντε, Στυρέες δὲ δύο, καὶ Κήιοι δύο τε

---

5 τεσσαράκοντα d   6 καλχιδέες B ‖ παρεχόντων σφι BPz
7 δυώδεκα B   9 στυριέες B : τυρέες δ ‖ Κήιοι Stein : κεῖοι a : κίοι B

---

3. **ὑπὸ δὲ ἀρετῆς τε καὶ προθυμίης**:
causal, and of psychological causality;
cp. 1. 85 ὑπὸ δέους τε καὶ κακοῦ ἔρρηξε
φωνήν (where the κακόν is external).
The notice of Plataian valour and zeal
is remarkable, and more generous than
the recognition of their service at
Marathon, 6. 108, 9. 27.

Πλαταιέες . . συνεπλήρουν.
Blakesley argues that the verb implies
more than merely service as ἐπιβάται.
His contention is borne out by the
remark ἄπειροι τῆς ναυτικῆς (sc. τέχνης)
ἐόντες, which would be almost pointless
if referred to ἐπιβάται alone. Cp. also
ἐπλήρουν just below.

5. **Κορίνθιοι** supply but 40 ships,
but are also represented by 400 hoplites
at Thermopylai, 7. 202. Cp. also c. 43
infra.

Μεγαρέες supplying 20 ships still
rank apparently as the fourth naval
power in the confederacy.

6. **Χαλκιδέες.** Are these Athenian
'Kleruchs' (5. 77, 6. 100) ? or natives of
Chalkis ? or both combined ? Blakesley
acutely remarks that 4000 men represent
just the complement for 20 triremes ;
and it is possible that there is a relation
between the 20 here and the 4000 there
(ll.c.). But if so, the 4000 is probably
an inference from the 20, and this passage
is the older of the two (whether Hdt.
himself or his authorities made the
combination and drew the inference).
This observation further strengthens the
suspicion with which the figure 4000 is
to be viewed (cp. my note to 5. 77),
seeing that here the crews of these
triremes may well have been natives of
Chalkis and the Athenian Kleruchs
serving merely, or mainly, as epibatai
(= 600. If the real number of Kleruchs
was only 600, the story in 6. 100 would
be more intelligible).

7. **Αἰγινῆται.** That Aigina sends
only 18 ships to Artemision is curious :
does the item include the ship of
Asonides captured off Skiathos (7. 181) ?
The Aiginetan figure for Salamis is also
perplexing ; cp. c. 46 infra.

Σικυώνιοι are below their full
strength with 12 ships ; cp. c. 43.

8. **Λακεδαιμόνιοι** means, of course,
the Spartan state. Doubtless the crews
were composed of Helots, or at best
Perioikoi ; and perhaps there were few,
if any, Spartiatai on board, except the
Epibatai and officers. The Lakedaimonian contingent looks miserably small
for the hegemonic power ; but the service
at Thermopylai is concomitant. Even
at Salamis the Lakedaimonians muster
only 16 ships, if c. 43 is to be trusted.

Ἐπιδαύριοι, unrepresented at
Thermopylai, raise their contingent from
8 to 10 for Salamis (c. 43), and send
only 800 Hoplites to Plataiai, 9. 28.
Their best days were past (cp. 7. 99), or
in the future, when the ἱερόν of Asklepios
was to rise into oecumenical significance
(cp. R. Caton, The Temples and Ritual
of Asklepios, Cambridge, 1900).

Ἐρετριέες. After their experiences
in 490 B.C. (cp. 6. 101, 119) it is surprising to find men of Eretria in a position
to supply even 7 ships in 480 B.C.
Either the destruction had not been so
complete as Hdt. asserts, or the place
had been reoccupied and reinforced.

9. **Τροιζήνιοι.** Troizen was a small
place, supplying but 5 ships (cp. c. 43) ;
it ranked as the metropolis of Halikarnassos (7. 99), and appears to have been
at this time on especially good terms
with Athens ; cp. c. 41 infra.

Στυρέες. The men of Styra in
Euboia supply 2 triremes. In the
Athenian tribute-lists Styra is assessed
at 100 drachmai.

νέας καὶ πεντηκοντέρους δύο· Λοκροὶ δέ σφι οἱ Ὀπούντιοι 10
ἐπεβοήθεον πεντηκοντέρους ἔχοντες ἑπτά.

Ἦσαν μὲν ὦν οὗτοι οἱ στρατευόμενοι ἐπ' Ἀρτεμίσιον, 2
εἴρηται δέ μοι καὶ ὡς τὸ πλῆθος ἕκαστοι τῶν νεῶν παρείχοντο. ἀριθμὸς δὲ τῶν συλλεχθεισέων νεῶν ἐπ' Ἀρτεμίσιον
ἦν, πάρεξ τῶν πεντηκοντέρων, διηκόσιαι καὶ ἑβδομήκοντα καὶ
μία. τὸν δὲ στρατηγὸν τὸν τὸ μέγιστον κράτος ἔχοντα 5

---

10 νῆας Β   11 ἐπεβώθεον Β, van H.   2. 1 οὖν Β: om. α
2 ὡς τὸ: ὅσον τὸ Reiske: ὅσον τι Schaefer: quot (ὅσας) Valla ‖ verba
εἴρηται . . παρείχοντο suspecta habet van H.   2, 3 νηῶν (bis) Β
4 μία καὶ ἑβδομήκοντα καὶ διηκόσιαι Β, Holder   5 τὸ om. Β ‖
κάρτος ads

Κήιοι. The island of Keos appears in the tribute-lists as assessed for 400 drachmai, though in 480 B.C. it furnishes but 2 pentekonters beyond the Styrean contingent. The assessment probably represents the resources of Keos better than the contingent: the island was the birth-place of Simonides, the poet-laureate of the war. Cp. 7. 228.

10. **Λοκροὶ . . οἱ Ὀπούντιοι**: cp. 7. 203. As they were serving πανστρατιῇ at Thermopylai it is a wonder to find them represented at Artemision even by 7 pentekonters.

σφι might naturally be referred to Κήιοι just before, as σφι up above certainly refer to Χαλκιδέες immediately preceding; but the general sense of the passage suggests a reference here to the fleet as a whole, all the contingents enumerated above, or more vaguely still τοῖς Ἕλλησι. The verb (ἐπεβοήθεον) is varied from the ἐπλήρουν and παρείχοντο preceding, and requires the personal object expressed or understood.

2. 2. εἴρηται δέ μοι καὶ ὡς. As the reference is to the immediate context, and as ὡς appears to be used in a doubtful sense, this whole sentence is naturally suspect. The verb παρείχοντο, too, is unfortunate, repeated, as it is, just below. Yet the μοι makes for authenticity, and there is a sufficient reason for the introduction of the sentence, the purpose of which is evidently to justify the *order* in which the ethnic names have been given, as corresponding to the relative strength of the respective contingents. A. G. Laird in *Class. Rev.* xviii. 1904, 97 ff. suggests, on the analogy of an Ionic inscription *circa* 400 B.C., that Hdt. might have

intended εἴρηται (= εἴρέαται) as a plural; a *corruptela* might seem the simpler alternative. The difficulty in the sentence appears to arise less from the use of ὡς to signify the order of the list than from the presence of καὶ and τὸ (πλῆθος). The sentence would certainly be easier if it ran εἴρέαται δέ μοι ὡς καὶ (τὸ) πλῆθος ἕκαστοι (τῶν) νεῶν παρείχοντο. The article, however, may be referred in the first place to the particular contingents, taken severally, and in the second place to the total fleet; but the words καὶ ὡς, especially in that order, appear suspicious.

3. **ἀριθμός.** The total 271 agrees with the items. Diodoros 11. 12 gives 280 as the total, including, apparently, the 9 pentekonters.

4. **πάρεξ τῶν πεντηκοντέρων.** It is apparently to be understood that the only pentekonters were the two from Keos and the seven from Opuntian Lokris enumerated above. There were some still smaller and lighter boats in commission (cp. c. 21 *infra*), though not included in the navy-list.

5. **τὸν δὲ στρατηγόν.** Each of the distinct contingents enumerated above was presumably under an enchorial strategos: the process, by which the Spartan navarch (ὁ Λάκων) came to be commander-in-chief of the whole fleet, is not quite clearly exhibited by Hdt. The aorist (ἔφασαν) may here have temporally the force of a pluperfect, and the next chapter, not to say the very necessities of the case, will show that the question of the hegemony by sea and by land had been raised and determined before any operations at all were undertaken, probably at the Isthmus

παρείχοντο Σπαρτιῆται Εὐρυβιάδην Εὐρυκλείδεω· οἱ γὰρ
σύμμαχοι οὐκ ἔφασαν, ἢν μὴ ὁ Λάκων ἡγεμονεύῃ, Ἀθηναίοισι
ἕψεσθαι ἡγεομένοισι, ἀλλὰ λύσειν τὸ μέλλον ἔσεσθαι στρά-
3 τευμα. ἐγένετο γὰρ κατ' ἀρχὰς λόγος, πρὶν ἢ καὶ ἐς Σικελίην
πέμπειν ἐπὶ συμμαχίην, ὡς τὸ ναυτικὸν Ἀθηναίοισι χρεὸν εἴη
ἐπιτράπειν. ἀντιβάντων δὲ τῶν συμμάχων εἶκον οἱ Ἀθηναῖοι
μέγα πεποιημένοι περιεῖναι τὴν Ἑλλάδα καὶ γνόντες, εἰ

---

6 εὐρυβιάδεα SV: εὐρνάδεα R ‖ τὸν Εὐρυκλείδεω z, edd. plures ‖ γὰρ:
δὲ R   7 Ἀθηναίοισι: ἄλλοισι Naber   3. 1 καταρχὰς Pz
2 ἐπὶ τὴν B: τὴν ἐπὶ συμμαχίῃ? Kallenberg   3 ἐπιτρέπειν codd.
4 μέγα τε ποιεύμενοι coni. Stein, adm. van H.

---

in the previous year. Cp. further
Appendix III. § 5, and c. 3 *infra*.

6. Σπαρτιῆται: the navarch was
probably elected in the Spartan *Apella*
to hold office for a year, beginning about
the autumnal equinox (cp. Thuc. 5. 36.
1). Though 'Eurybiades son of Eury-
kleides' is the first Spartan navarch
whose name has reached us, we are not
justified in assuming that the office itself
came into existence for and with him.
It may have been of long standing,
though of little importance, before the
Persian war (cp. 3. 39). Eurybiades
was not (perhaps) elected in view of the
Persian war, but in the ordinary course
of business; he is credited, by tradition,
with little aptitude for the post, and in
the two ensuing naval campaigns the
command is entrusted to men of royal
standing, Leotychidas, Pausanias.

7. ἢν μὴ ὁ Λάκων ἡγεμονεύῃ: this
sentence, or else the words Ἀθηναίοισι
ἡγεομένοισι, may be regarded as superfluous; the two conjoined are, indeed,
logically inconsistent. What the allies
declared was that (*a*) they would abandon
the whole undertaking if the Athenians
were to have the leading, (*b*) that they
would join in the undertaking if the
Spartans had the lead. Two further
points may be remarked. (i.) The
question of leading is not necessarily
confined to the naval operations; τὸ
μέλλον ἔσεσθαι στράτευμα has a more
extended reference, actual or potential.
(ii.) That being so ὁ Λάκων need not be
referred specifically to Eurybiades, or
even to the Spartan navarch (whoever
he was, or was to be), but should be
taken to refer generally to 'the Lakonian,'
the man of Lakedaimon.

8. λύσειν τὸ μέλλον ἔσεσθαι στράτευμα: the two-fold, if not triple, future

must place the declaration of the
Symmachoi well before the despatch of
the forces to Thermopylai-Artemision.
στράτευμα is used by Hdt. both for
'expedition' (e.g. 3. 49=στρατεία) and
'forces' (=στρατός 7. 48). Whichever
sense be here preferred, the application
need not, and indeed cannot, be restricted to the navy, for the defence of
Thermopylai and Artemision is a single
undertaking, a single plan.

3. 1. κατ' ἀρχάς: the dating is not quite
precise, even with the additional indication πρὶν ἢ καὶ ἐς Σικελίην πέμπειν. The
question of the *Hegemonia* was doubtless
one of the first to be decided, but it can
hardly have been intercalated between
the mission to Argos, 7. 148 (where, by
the way, the Argives demand ἡγέεσθαι
κατὰ τὸ ἥμισυ), and the mission to Sicily,
7. 153ff. The dispute with the Athenian
must have preceded both the other dis-
putes, the stories of which imply that
the hegemony is vested in Sparta. The
λόγος here recorded, whether speech,
demand, or argument, must have taken
place (ἐγένετο) at the first meeting of the
allies at the Isthmus, in the autumn or
early winter of 481 B.C. The Athenians
themselves (Themistokles?), or some
state friendly to Athens (Plataia?), must
have been its authors. The opposition
of the allies here recorded must be
identical with the opposition of the
allies just above recorded in c. 2.

4. μέγα πεποιημένοι: the whole passage, down to the second εἶκον *infra*,
introduces some obscurity into the argument or narrative, but is in itself clear
enough, the subject οἱ Ἀθηναῖοι being
carried over or resumed apparently, at
least as far as the second εἶκον.

The passive form πεποιημένοι is remarkable as the perfect or pluperfect

στασιάσουσι περὶ τῆς ἡγεμονίης, ὡς ἀπολέεται ἡ Ἑλλάς, ὀρθὰ 5
νοεῦντες· στάσις γὰρ ἔμφυλος πολέμου ὁμοφρονέοντος τοσούτῳ
κάκιον ἐστὶ ὅσῳ πόλεμος εἰρήνης. ἐπιστάμενοι ὦν αὐτὸ τοῦτο
οὐκ ἀντέτεινον ἀλλ' εἶκον, μέχρι ὅσου κάρτα ἐδέοντο αὐτῶν,
ὡς διέδεξαν· ὡς γὰρ δὴ ὡσάμενοι τὸν Πέρσην περὶ τῆς ἐκείνου

---

5 στασιοῦσι Β   6 νοέοντες Β ‖ στάσις . . εἰρήνης damn. Blakesley
‖ τοσοῦτο Β   8 μέχρις οὗ ΒΡ: μέχρι οὗ z   9 δὴ ὡσάμενοι:
διωσάμενοι Bekker, van H. ‖ πέρσεα Βz

---

of ποιέεσθαι. The tense does not appear
to have a merely temporal force. Stein's
emendation would spoil this aspect of
the word.

5. ὀρθὰ νοεῦντες. Hdt. apparently
applauds the patriotic modesty of the
Athenians, and adds a stock *gnome* of
but doubtful application to the case in
question, unless, indeed, the Athenians
had been contemplating actually coming
to blows over the question. The gnome
was hardly meant in the first instance
to be applied to the case of an alliance
or confederacy. 'Civil war (στάσις
ἔμφυλος) is to war conducted by a state
at unity with itself (πόλεμος ὁμοφρονέων)
as war is to peace (εἰρήνη).' The gnome
does not cover the still darker evil of
στάσις and πόλεμος combined (cp. Thuc.
3. 82). The neuter κάκιον is observable.

8. μέχρι ὅσου: sc. χρόνου: but the
phrase might still mean either *dum*
(while, so long as) or *donec* (until the
point when). The exact rendering must
depend upon the sense in which the
words immediately succeeding are taken.

κάρτα ἐδέοντο αὐτῶν. What is the
subject of ἐδέοντο, and to whom does the
word αὐτῶν refer? The exact meaning
of ἐδέοντο may also be in question. If
there is no change of subject, if the
subject of all the final verbs (εἶκον,
ἐδέοντο, διέδεξαν, ἐποιεῦντο, ἀπείλοντο)
is 'the Athenians,' then the passage
contains a distinctly unfavourable judgement upon the conduct of Athens, thereby
conflicting not merely with the general
Atticism of Hdt., but with the immediate
context, wherein their patriotism, their
pan-Hellenism, has been commended.
'The Athenians, however, made these
concessions only so long as they were
badly in need of them (the allies? or
the Lakedaimonians? in preference the
latter); for as soon as they had repulsed
the Persian, and were carrying the war
into the enemy's country, they deprived
the Lakedaimonians of the lead on pre-

text of the violence of Pausanias.' But
there is something to be said for a change
of subject. The repulse of the Persian,
and the war in Ionia or Thrace, were not
simply the doing of the Athenians:
ὡσάμενοι, ἐποιεῦντο, ἀπείλοντο should
hardly be referred exclusively to the
Athenians, but rather to 'the allies,'
or 'the Hellenes'; in which case αὐτῶν
will refer to 'the Athenians,' and the
meaning will be: 'the Athenians gave
way and yielded, until such time as they
(the allies, the Greeks) had sore need
of them (or possibly 'petitioned them'),
as they showed: for the Greeks, after
repulsing the Persian, etc.' The words
ὡς διέδεξαν are in any case against the
alternative rendering of ἐδέοντο, for it
would be intolerably harsh to take 'the
Greeks' as the subject of ἐδέοντο and
ἐποιεῦντο, but resume 'the Athenians'
as the subject of the intercalary διέδεξαν.
If, however, the subject of ἐδέοντο is
οἱ σύμμαχοι, there is some confusion of
thought in the passage, as the allies,
or Hellenes, who deprived the Lakedaimonians of the naval hegemony at
Byzantion in 477 B.C., were quite different
persons and states from the allies who
refused naval hegemony to the Athenians
in 481 B.C. The story of the transfer
is told, from an Attic point of view,
Thucyd. 1. 95, Diodor. 11. 44, Plutarch,
Aristeid. 23, etc. (Cp. G. F. Hill,
Sources, i. 18 ff.)

This passage has a bearing on the
question of the composition, plan, and
completion of the work of Herodotus.
He could hardly have expressed himself
as here, or concluded this prospective
episode with the summary ἀλλὰ ταῦτα
μὲν ὕστερον ἐγένετο, had he been intending to carry his narrative below the
point where it now terminates, viz. the
siege of Sestos in 479-8 B.C. In other
words, this passage supports the view
that the work of Hdt., as we have it,
is finished and complete, according to

10 ἤδη τὸν ἀγῶνα ἐποιεῦντο, πρόφασιν τὴν Παυσανίεω ὕβριν
προϊσχόμενοι ἀπείλοντο τὴν ἡγεμονίην τοὺς Λακεδαιμονίους.
ἀλλὰ ταῦτα μὲν ὕστερον ἐγένετο.

4   Τότε δὲ οὗτοι οἱ καὶ ἐπ᾽ Ἀρτεμίσιον Ἑλλήνων ἀπικόμενοι
ὡς εἶδον νέας τε πολλὰς καταχθείσας ἐς τὰς Ἀφέτας καὶ

10 ἐποιέοντο Β   12 ἐγένοντο C   4. 2 νῆας Β ‖ ἐς τοὺς Β

the author's own idea. Cp. Introduction, § 6.

10. τὴν Παυσανίεω ὕβριν is a remarkable expression, which might point to
this passage being an insertion, cp. 9. 10
infra ; but the phrase may be a current
one, descriptive of the proceedings recorded more fully by Thuc. 1. 94, 95,
and touched by Hdt. himself 5. 32.

4. 1. τότε: in contradistinction to the
ὕστερον just above, or to the κατ᾽ ἀρχάς,
c. 3 *ad init.* ; but the precise date is
still in question, and is to be inferred,
or extracted, from the words immediately
following. The term οὗτοι . . ἀπικόμενοι
denotes undoubtedly the same object as
οἱ στρατευόμενοι ἐπ᾽ Ἀρτεμίσιον of c. 2,
or again οἱ ἐς τὸν ναυτικὸν στρατὸν
ταχθέντες of c. 1; but the τάξις, the
στρατεία, the ἄπιξις ἐπ᾽ Ἀρτεμίσιον, are
successive epochs in the operations of
the fleet, the last of which is here more
precisely defined by the sight of the
enemy's fleet already in position at
Aphetai, albeit whether the occupation
of Artemision by the Greeks here involved precedes or succeeds the occupation of Aphetai by the Persians is not
quite clearly indicated in this context.
A problem at once arises as to the relation of this narrative to the narrative
in Bk. 7. There the occupation, or first
occupation, of Artemision by the Greeks
precedes by some time the appearance
of the Persian ships at Aphetai (cp. 7.
177, 183, 195). The Greek fleet, in fact,
apparently occupies Artemision before
the Persian fleet has quitted Therme,
and actually retreats from Artemision to
Chalkis upon news of the Persian advance
signalled from Skiathos (7. 183). But
the three days' storm detains the Persian
fleet *en voyage*, and not until the fourth
and last day of the storm (7. 191), that
is, the fifth day after leaving Therme,
at earliest, could the Persian fleet have
steered into Aphetai (7. 193). The
Greeks have already resumed their station
at Artemision on the third (or fourth)
day of the storm (7. 192), and conse-

quently it is the Persians on their way
to Aphetai who lose fifteen ships to the
Greeks already stationed, for the second
time, at Artemision (7. 194). To harmonize this passage with that it must
be inferred that the ἄπιξις ἐπ᾽ Ἀρτεμίσιον
here in question is the second occupation
of Artemision by the Greek fleet which
in Bk. 7 precedes, not merely the arrival
of the Persian ships at Aphetai, but
apparently even their departure from
the Magnesian strand. This harmony,
indeed, Hdt. himself has apparently
attempted. Stein finds a proof of this
in the otherwise superfluous καί in this
passage: a still clearer proof lies in the
sentence ἐπὶ αὐτοῖσι παρὰ δόξαν κτλ.,
which clearly resumes the statement in
7. 192, ἐλπίσαντες ὀλίγας τινὰς σφι ἀντι-
ξόους ἔσεσθαι νέας. The attempt is clear;
not so the harmony itself. For (1) the
Greeks here on arriving at Artemision
(for the second time) apparently discover
the Persians before them at Aphetai;
(2) the Greeks at once project a second
retreat. But such a retreat at this point
is out of the question, as inconsistent
with the whole plan of defence for
Thermopylai-Artemision, and also inconsistent with the brilliant success they
have just achieved (according to 7. 194)
in the capture of fifteen of the king's
vessels. The conclusions are forced upon
us that the two passages are in the main
from different sources (the one here probably of European, the other, that in
Bk. 7, of Asianic origin), and that Hdt.
has been ill-advised in his attempt to
harmonize them, especially in his duplica-
tion of the retirement, or supposed retirement, of the Greek fleet from Artemision.
The doubling of his sources has also
apparently doubled the storms, and complicated other episodes in the naval operations, for the reduction of which to the
simpler issues see further, Appendix V.

2. καταχθείσας: κατάγεσθαι is the
proper word for putting into land ; cp.
6. 107 καταγομένας ἐς τὸν Μαραθῶνα τὰς
νέας ὁρμίζε οὗτος.

στρατιῆς ἄπαντα πλέα, ἐπεὶ αὐτοῖσι παρὰ δόξαν τὰ πρήγματα
τῶν βαρβάρων ἀπέβαινε ἢ ὡς αὐτοὶ κατεδόκεον, καταρρωδή-
σαντες δρησμὸν ἐβουλεύοντο ἀπὸ τοῦ Ἀρτεμισίου ἔσω ἐς τὴν 5
Ἑλλάδα. γνόντες δὲ σφέας οἱ Εὐβοέες ταῦτα βουλευομένους
ἐδέοντο Εὐρυβιάδεω προσμεῖναι χρόνον ὀλίγον, ἔστ' ἂν αὐτοὶ
τέκνα τε καὶ τοὺς οἰκέτας ὑπεκθέωνται. ὡς δ' οὐκ ἔπειθον,
μεταβάντες τὸν Ἀθηναίων στρατηγὸν πείθουσι Θεμιστοκλέα
ἐπὶ μισθῷ τριήκοντα ταλάντοισι, ἐπ' ᾧ τε καταμείναντες πρὸ 10
τῆς Εὐβοίης ποιήσονται τὴν ναυμαχίην. ὁ δὲ Θεμιστοκλέης 5
τοὺς Ἕλληνας ἐπισχεῖν ὧδε ποιέει· Εὐρυβιάδῃ τούτων τῶν
χρημάτων μεταδιδοῖ πέντε τάλαντα ὡς παρ' ἑωυτοῦ δῆθεν

---

3 πάντα β   5 ἐβούλευον β, Holder : ἐβούλευον τὸν vel τὸ ?
Kallenberg   8 <τὰ> τέκνα van H. ‖ τε om. β

3. στρατιῆς ἄπαντα πλέα : a reference
to the king's encampment in Melis (7.
198-200) can hardly be excluded from
these words.

αὐτοῖσι : the 'ethical' dative ; the
words ἢ ὡς αὐτοὶ κατεδόκεον are somewhat redundant, for they cannot be
referred to τῶν βαρβάρων as subject.

τὰ πρήγματα : cp. 7. 10 (ll. 34 ff.).

4. ἀπέβαινε has the full imperfect
sense ; and likewise ἐβουλεύοντο just
below.

5. δρησμὸν . . ἔσω ἐς τὴν Ἑλλάδα :
apparently a further and still more
craven flight than their supposed first
move to Chalkis, 7. 182 supra ; the
change of phrase may be intended by
Hdt. to mark the difference of the two
occasions ; but in reality the two were
probably only one and the same, and
the goal was neither the Isthmus, nor
even Chalkis, but probably at most the
bay of Aidepsos ; cp. Appendix V. § 4.

6. οἱ Εὐβοέες : the term might seem
to ascribe a solidarity to the peoples
and cities of the island, which they
certainly did not possess. Rationalistically the word might be interpreted of
the Euboians in loco, chiefly those of
Histiaia (c. 23 infra) : critically viewed,
it rather betrays the bad conscience of
the narrator, or his source, by its
vagueness.

7. ἐδέοντο, 'petitioned,' 'besought' ;
cp. cc. 3 supra, 132 infra.

8. τέκνα τε καὶ τοὺς οἰκέτας ὑπεκθέωνται : the women doubtless come in
somewhere by implication, either with
τέκνα, or with the οἰκέται (οἱ κατὰ τὸν
οἶκον πάντες, Hesychius) ; cp. cc. 36, 41

infra, ὑπεκθέσθαι c. 41 infra, ὑπεκτι-
θέμενοι 5. 65, ὑπέκκειται c. 60 infra,
ὑπεξεκομίσαντο 9. 6. The prepositions
suggest the ideas of secrecy and safety,
the subjunctive their design and intention.

9. μεταβάντες : here perhaps of psychological, as in 7. 73 of local movement.

τὸν Ἀθ. στρατηγόν incidentally
implies a chief commander, although he
must constitutionally have had nine
colleagues. The form of expression
πείθουσι . . ἐπ' ᾧ τε recurs verbatim
5. 65. πρό here is not merely causal,
but locative. The story of the bribing of
Themistokles on this occasion is a transparent scandal ; cp. Appendix V. § 2.

A delightful inconsequence in this
passage lies in the Euboians wanting
Eurybiades to remain 'a little while,'
just till they have cleared their families
out of the island, while Themistokles
gets the Greeks to hold on and fight
three battles (τὴν ναυμαχίην !) on three
successive days.

11. ποιήσονται : the voice, the mood,
the tense, not to say the change of
subject, are all observable, and point
rather to the actual result than to any
implied condition.

5. 2. ἐπισχεῖν, 'to hold on' : a
stronger term than προσμεῖναι or even
καταμεῖναι, connoting a longer time, a
larger purpose.

τούτων τῶν χρημάτων : partitive
genitive, emphasized by μεταδιδοῖ.

3. ὡς παρ' ἑωυτοῦ δῆθεν : so on a subsequent occasion he presents to Eurybiades arguments which are not of his

διδούς. ὡς δέ οἱ οὗτος ἀνεπέπειστο, Ἀδείμαντος γὰρ ὁ Ὠκύτου
5 ὁ Κορίνθιος στρατηγὸς τῶν λοιπῶν ἠσπαιρε μοῦνος, φάμενος
ἀποπλεύσεσθαί τε ἀπὸ τοῦ Ἀρτεμισίου καὶ οὐ παραμενέειν,
πρὸς δὴ τοῦτον εἶπε ὁ Θεμιστοκλῆς ἐπομόσας " οὐ σύ γε
ἡμέας ἀπολείψεις, ἐπεί τοι ἐγὼ μέζω δῶρα δώσω ἢ βασιλεὺς
ἄν τοι ὁ Μήδων πέμψειε ἀπολιπόντι τοὺς συμμάχους." ταῦτά
10 τε ἅμα ἠγόρευε καὶ πέμπει ἐπὶ τὴν νέα τὴν Ἀδειμάντου
τάλαντα ἀργυρίου τρία. οὗτοί τε δὴ πληγέντες δώροισι ἀνα-

---

5. 5 ὁ Κορίνθιος Suidas (sub v. ἠσπαιρεν) cum v.l. Κορινθίων : κόρινθος
C : κορίνθιος ceteri : Κορινθίων Schaefer, van H. ‖ τῶν λοιπῶν om. β :
'fortasse est glossema' van H.   6 ἀποπλώσεσθαί β, van H.   10
νῆα β ‖ τὴν alterum : τοῦ dz   11 πληγέντες βz, Holder, van H., Stein³ :
πάντες a, Stein¹ ²

---

own devising, as though they were his
own, c. 58 infra.

4. ἀνεπέπειστο: the pluperfect here
has its full temporal force; but a shade
of difference enters below, in ἀναπεπει-
σμένοι ἦσαν and ἐκεχάριστο.

Ἀδείμαντος . . ὁ Ὠκύτου: cp.
7. 137 ad f., a passage which in part
might explain the hostility of Athens
to the memory of Adeimantos, were it
not that the stories to the discredit of
Adeimantos are surely far older than
the exploits of Aristeas his son. The
account of the bribery of Adeimantos by
Themistokles at Artemision is, indeed,
not merely absurd in view of the strategic
necessities of the position, and obviously
'pragmatic'—to the discredit of Themistokles too; but it is flagrantly inconsistent with the stories of the relations
between Themistokles and the Korinthian
admiral just before the battle of Salamis.
It is thus doubly significant that the
version of the story followed by Plutarch,
Themist. 7, omits Adeimantos altogether.
If there is any truth in the tradition of
the employment of money by Themistokles to procure a halt, to promote a
battle, the scene must be laid at Salamis,
not at Artemision, where the Peloponnesians could no more have thought of
retreating than the Athenians themselves,
as long as Leonidas was holding Thermopylai. The name and patronymic
of the Korinthian strategos are here
genuine, as the γὰρ would show; cp. c.
59 infra. Aineas, son of Okytos, a
Korinthian, appears among the signa-
tories of the truce of Laches in 423 B.C.,
Thuc. 4. 119. 2. This second Okytos

might well be a son of Adeimantos; the
name is presumably connected with ὠκύς.

5. ἠσπαιρε: like a fish out of water,
cp. 9. 120, or a babe new-born, cp. 1. 111,
or (as Stein suggests, but without a
reference) a bird in the hand of the fowler.

9. Μήδων. Did Themistokles, and
the Athenians of his generation, speak
of the 'Mede' rather than of the
'Persian'? cp. Aristoph., Thuc. The
general colour of the stories of Artemision
is decidedly Attic; Hdt. and the Ionians
for at least a generation before him could
clearly distinguish between Mede and
Persian.

ταῦτά τε ἅμα ἠγόρευε καὶ πέμπει :
the emphatic parataxis and the historic
tenses are observable : 'the words were
hardly out of his mouth before he sends
to the Korinthian admiral's flag-ship
three talents of silver.'

11. πληγέντες. The reading of the
second class for πάντες (cp. App. Crit.),
adopted by Blakesley and Baehr, from
Wesseling, and now by Stein, on the
ground that πάντες is inadmissible for
δύο. Baehr compares Plutarch, Demosth.
25 πληγεὶς ὑπὸ τῆς δωροδοκίας, and other
Plutarchisms more remote; Stein still
thinks of bird-snaring, and cps. Horace,
Od. 3. 16 munera navium Saevos illa-
queant duces. It is easier to understand
πάντες as a corruption of πληγέντες ex
librariorum quibus vulgatum durius
visum ingenio (Wesseling) than vice
versa, or one might be tempted to see in
πάντες a hint of a story of still more far-
reaching corruption than that just related; at any rate, the corruptela was
intended to cover 'all three.'

πεπεισμένοι ἦσαν καὶ τοῖσι Εὐβοεῦσι ἐκεχάριστο, αὐτός τε ὁ
Θεμιστοκλέης ἐκέρδηνε, ἐλάνθανε δὲ τὰ λοιπὰ ἔχων, ἀλλ'
ἠπιστέατο οἱ μεταλαβόντες τούτων τῶν χρημάτων ἐκ τῶν
Ἀθηνέων ἐλθεῖν ἐπὶ τῷ λόγῳ τούτῳ τὰ χρήματα.　　　　　15

Οὕτω δὴ κατέμεινάν τε ἐν τῇ Εὐβοίῃ καὶ ἐναυμάχησαν, 6
ἐγένετο δὲ ὧδε. ἐπείτε δὴ ἐς τὰς Ἀφέτας περὶ δείλην πρωίην
γινομένην ἀπίκατο οἱ βάρβαροι, πυθόμενοι μὲν ἔτι καὶ πρότερον
περὶ τὸ Ἀρτεμίσιον ναυλοχέειν νέας Ἑλληνίδας ὀλίγας, τότε

---

13 ἐκέρδανεν B : ἐκέρδησε d　　　15 Ἀθηνέων Bekker, Stein²³ :
ἀθηναίων codd., Stein¹ ‖ τὰ χρήματα om. B　　6. 1 δὴ om. B　　2
τὰς : τοὺς R　　3 γενομένην Bz ‖ ἀπικέατο Pz　　4 τὸ om. a ‖
νῆας B ‖ τότε . . ἰδόντες om. B

---

13. ἀλλ': as though a negative had
preceded, ἐλάνθανε having indeed a sort
of negative force.

14. ἐκ τῶν Ἀθηνέων: if we transfer the
scene to Salamis we shall be convinced
that the recipients were right in their
opinion ; and the purpose (λόγος, ratio)
was to keep them at Salamis.

6. 1. ἐν τῇ Εὐβοίῃ: the officers and
men were mostly ashore, even if the
ships were not actually beached.

2. ἐπείτε δὴ ἐς τὰς Ἀφέτας: referring back (δὴ) not so much to c. 4
supra, as to 7. 195, or 193.

περί: here of time, as just below
of place.

δείλην πρωίην γινομένην, 'the
early afternoon' ; cp. δείλην ὀψίην γινομένην τῆς ἡμέρης c. 9 infra. The
present participle is more curious with
the πρωίην than with the ὀψίην, as δείλη
itself (whatever its derivation) means
afternoon, in distinction from ἠώς and
μέσον ἦμαρ. Cp. Iliad 21. 111. At what
o'clock exactly we are to place the
arrival (ἀπίκατο 7. 198) is unfortunately
not clear : before 3 P.M. ?

3. πυθόμενοι μὲν ἔτι καὶ πρότερον:
cp. 7. 208. The Persian advance has
been conducted with all due foresight
and circumspection : the number of the
Greek fleet does not apparently exceed
their anticipations.

The construction (and sense) of the
words ἔτι καὶ πρότερον, especially of ἔτι,
is disputable. Are they to be taken
together ? Do they, if so taken, qualify
πυθόμενοι or ναυλοχέειν ? Or are they to
be taken separately, and, if so, do καὶ
πρότερον cohere, or are ἔτι and πρότερον
co-ordinate ? Finally, what is the exact
sense of ἔτι ? Stein takes ἔτι = ἤδη (schon) ;

cp. 5. 62 ἐόντες ἄνδρες δόκιμοι ἀνέκαθεν
ἔτι, 1. 65 τὸ δὲ ἔτι πρότερον τούτων καὶ
κακονομώτατοι ἦσαν, 1. 92 τὴν δὲ οὐσίην
αὐτοῦ ἔτι πρότερον κατιρώσας κτλ., 1. 190
ἐξεπιστάμενοι ἔτι πρότερον τὸν Κῦρον οὐκ
ἀτρεμίζοντα, 3. 64 τῷ δὲ ἔτι πρότερον
ἐκέχρηστο, 6. 38 αὐτοὶ γὰρ Κυζικηνοὶ ἔτι
πρότερον τοῦ Φοινίκων ἐσπλόου τούτου
ἐγεγώνεσαν ὑπὸ βασιλέι. So also c. 69
infra νομίζων ἔτι πρότερον σπουδαίην εἶναι
τότε πολλῷ μᾶλλον αἵνεε. But in no
instance does ἔτι appear used with a
verb simply as = ἤδη, but always as
reinforcing a temporal adverb, generally
πρότερον, and so in its normal (comparative) force of 'still'—the point of departure being the latest date, and the
point of arrival not 'already' but 'still'
and 'still' earlier. In c. 62 infra ἐκ
παλαιοῦ ἔτι, where there is no comparison,
the ἔτι may have its true (temporal)
force. In none of these cases does a καὶ
separate, or connect, the ἔτι πρότερον.
The very peculiar case in 9. 102 ἔτι καὶ
δὴ is now abandoned by Stein (cp. note
ad l. infra). The καὶ here therefore
remains a problem, most simply resolved
by understanding it as intensive 'still
even' (or 'even still') earlier, and
taking the phrase as qualifying πυθόμενοι (c. 69 infra, quoted above, favouring this, as well as the τότε δὲ αὐτοὶ
ἰδόντες). But if ἔτι καὶ πρότερον might
be taken with ναυλοχέειν, then καὶ is
disjunctive ('still as before,' referring
to the reoccupation of the position) ;
but the τότε δὲ αὐτοὶ ἰδόντες seems to
forbid this.

4. τότε δὲ: on their arrival at Aphetai,
or on the way thither ; in either case it
appears here that the Greek fleet is
already in position at Artemision (for

5 δὲ αὐτοὶ ἰδόντες, πρόθυμοι ἦσαν ἐπιχειρέειν, εἴ κως ἔλοιεν
αὐτάς. ἐκ μὲν δὴ τῆς ἀντίης προσπλέειν οὔ κώ σφι ἐδόκεε
τῶνδε εἴνεκα, μή κως ἰδόντες οἱ Ἕλληνες προσπλέοντας ἐς
φυγὴν ὁρμήσειαν φεύγοντάς τε εὐφρόνη καταλαμβάνῃ· καὶ
ἔμελλον δῆθεν φεύξεσθαι, ἔδει δὲ μηδὲ πυρφόρον τῷ ἐκείνων
7 λόγῳ ἐκφυγόντα περιγενέσθαι. πρὸς ταῦτα ὦν τάδε ἐμη-

6 προσπλώειν Βz, van H.　　　　7 εἴνεκε R ‖ κως z : πως a : om. Β ‖
προσπλώοντας Βz, van H.　　　　8 καταλάβῃ Β : καταλάβοι Pz : κατα-
λαμβάνει d　　　　9 φεύξεσθαι Stein(2) 3, van H. : ἐκφεύξεσθαι　　　10
λόχω Β　　　　7. 1 ἐμηχανῶντο Stein² 3, Holder : ἐμηχανέωντο d : ἐμη-
χανέοντο ceteri, Stein¹, van H.

the second time), before the arrival of
the Persians at Aphetai ; but if so, why
did not the Greeks advance upon the
Persians (especially if Aphetai should
be placed within the entrance of the
gulf of Pagasai) ? The Persians do not
advance at once for a frontal attack upon
the Greeks (ἐκ τῆς ἀντίης προσπλέειν) for
fear the Greeks should sail away and
escape, through the Euripos, under
cover of night ; a squadron of 200 sail
is detached to circumnavigate the island
and take the Greeks in the rear, while
the fleet from Aphetai will attack ἐξ
ἐναντίης when the time arrives. The
exposition of the plan ignores the bearing of the naval manœuvres upon the
situation at Thermopylai : had the Greek
fleet desired, and been allowed, to 'fly'
from Artemision, Leonidas and his men
were at the mercy of the Persians. The
squadron detached to circumnavigate
Euboia may have been directed rather
against Thermopylai than against Artemision.

8. εὐφρόνη καταλαμβάνῃ. The noun
is a poetic word for 'night,' cp. 7. 12.
The verb is used in a favourable, or at
least a neutral sense, here ; cp. 3. 139.

9. ἔμελλον δῆθεν φεύξεσθαι seems to
be not the writer's own opinion, but an
idea spread among the Persians ; the
tone of the passage, therefore, hardly
accords with the account of the Greek
panic in c. 4 supra. (ἐκφεύξεσθαι is of
course barely sense, but would accord
better with referring the utterance wholly
to the author.)

ἔδει δὲ μηδὲ πυρφόρον τῷ ἐκείνων
λόγῳ ἐκφυγόντα περιγενέσθαι : ἐκείνων
must refer to the Persians, but τῷ ἐκείνων
λόγῳ cannot be intended to ascribe to
Persian origin the obviously Greek, or
Lakonic, proverb. The Fire-bearer was

a Spartan official, but not perhaps to
be found only at Sparta ; cp. Xenophon,
Laced. resp. 13. 2 θύει μὲν γὰρ πρῶτον
οἴκοι ὦν (sc. ὁ βασιλεὺς) καὶ οἱ σὺν αὐτῷ· ἢν
δὲ ἐνταῦθα καλλιερήσῃ, λαβὼν ὁ πυρφόρος
πῦρ ἀπὸ τοῦ βωμοῦ προηγεῖταί ἐπὶ τὰ ὅρια
τῆς χώρας· ὁ δὲ βασιλεὺς ἐκεῖ αὖ θύεται Διὶ
καὶ Ἀθηνᾷ. ὅταν δὲ ἀμφοῖν τούτοιν τοῖν
θεοῖν καλλιερηθῇ, τότε διαβαίνει τὰ ὅρια τῆς
χώρας· τὸ πῦρ μὲν ἀπὸ τούτων τῶν
ἱερῶν προηγεῖται οὔποτε ἀποσβεννύμενον,
σφάγια δὲ παντοῖα ἕπεται. Cp. Suidas
sub v. who says, ἐν τοῖς οὖν πολέμοις
εἰώθασι τῶν ἱερέων οἱ νενικηκότες φείδεσθαι.
This might be true of Greeks, but would
not hold good for 'barbarians.' Canon
Blakesley, however, denies the sacro-
sanctity of the πυρφόρος, and supposes
only that he would be more likely than
the fighting men to escape.

7. 1. πρὸς ταῦτα ὦν : pleonastic. The
subject of ἐμηχανῶντο is understood, sc.
οἱ στρατηγοὶ τοῦ ναυτικοῦ στρατοῦ : cp. the
(subsequent) conversation previously reported 7. 236. This device (μηχανή), of
detaching a squadron (200 strong) to
circumnavigate Euboia, and take the
Greeks at Artemision (or Thermopylai ?)
in the rear, is here apparently dated
after the arrival of the Persians at
Aphetai. But (1) the direction to sail
ἔξωθεν Σκιάθου ; (2) the previous knowledge of the Persians concerning the
positions occupied by the Greeks ; (3)
the curious introduction of the word
ἀπασέων—i.e. 'while the ships were
still in full force' ; (4) the improbability
of the Persians dividing their fleet, if
they had just suffered the colossal losses
recorded off Magnesia ; (5) the probability
that the storm has been duplicated in
Hdt.'s narrative, and the Persian losses
thereby enhanced ; (6) and last, not least,
the whole strategic development of the

χανῶντο· τῶν νεῶν ἀπασέων ἀποκρίναντες διηκοσίας περιέπεμπον ἔξωθεν Σκιάθου, ὡς ἂν μὴ ὀφθείησαν ὑπὸ τῶν πολεμίων περιπλέουσαι Εὔβοιαν κατά τε Καφηρέα καὶ περὶ Γεραιστὸν ἐς τὸν Εὔριπον, ἵνα δὴ περιλάβοιεν οἱ μὲν ταύτῃ ἀπικόμενοι 5 καὶ φράξαντες αὐτῶν τὴν ὀπίσω φέρουσαν ὁδόν, σφεῖς δὲ ἐπισπόμενοι ἐξ ἐναντίης. ταῦτα βουλευσάμενοι ἀπέπεμπον τῶν νεῶν τὰς ταχθείσας, αὐτοὶ οὐκ ἐν νόῳ ἔχοντες ταύτης τῆς ἡμέρης τοῖσι Ἕλλησι ἐπιθήσεσθαι, οὐδὲ πρότερον ἢ τὸ

---

2 νηῶν B ‖ ἀπασέων R: πασέων aV: πασῶν S ‖ περιέπεμψαν ἔξω 3 ὀφθέωσι(ν V) B, van H.   4 περιπλώουσαι B, van H. ‖ περὶ om. B, van H. ‖ γερεστὸν B   5 μὲν δὴ B   7 ἐξεναντίας B: ἐξ ἀντίης malit van H.   8 νηῶν B   9 ἐπιθέσθαι d

---

operations, itself so superficially conceived by Hdt., make it probable that the squadron commissioned to circumnavigate Euboia was detached from the Persian fleet not at Aphetai, as Hdt. here seems to imply, but off the Magnesian coast, if not already, still earlier, at the start from Therme.

3. ἔξωθεν Σκιάθου: the island formed a channel with the Magnesian main, cp. 7. 176, 183, and was the objective of the Persian navy from Therme, 7. 179, and likewise the station of the three Hellenic cruisers on the outlook, *ibid.*, c. 92 *infra*, and a telegraph station, 7. 182. But from Aphetai, or from Artemision, to sail 'outside Skiathos' would be to sail northward between Skiathos and Peparethos, a mysterious, not to say senseless manoeuvre, which would be fully in view of the Greeks at Artemision.

ὡς ἂν μὴ ὀφθείησαν. There is no need to prefer (with Blakesley, van H., and others) the *v.l.* ὀφθέωσι, as Hdt. uses the optative, with ἄν, after final ὡς, ὅκως, rather freely (cp. Heiligenstaedt, *de enunt. finalium usu*, i. 39).

4. κατά τε Καφηρέα καὶ περὶ Γεραιστόν. Kaphereus and Geraistos are the two headlands at the south-east end of Euboia, Kaphereus being the northern one, Geraistos the southern. Geraistos is mentioned again, 9. 105, as the burial-place of the Athenian pankratiast, Hermolykos, son of Euthoinos, the hero of Mykale, who fell subsequently in the war with the Karystians. The variation of the prepositions is observable: you might sail περὶ Καφηρέα and even κατὰ Γεραιστόν without getting round Euboia into the Euripos; but cp. App. Crit. The narrative here treats all these places

as notorious, perhaps with a touch of Atticism. 7. 182, 5. 77 suggest that the term Euripos is restricted to the straits at Chalkis, though the other passages where the term occurs in Hdt. admit of a more extended reference.

5. ταύτῃ: sc. ἐς τὸν Εὔριπον.

6. αὐτῶν: the Greeks, that is, the Greek fleet; for Hdt. treats the contrivance throughout as directed against Artemision.

τὴν ὀπίσω φέρουσαν ὁδόν: by sea, not by land. τῆς ὀπίσω ὁδοῦ in quite a different connexion, 2. 87.

7. ἐπισπόμενοι ἐξ ἐναντίης: the Greek fleet being assumed to have taken to flight, ἐξ ἐναντίης signifies not so much a 'frontal attack' on the Greeks as an 'advance to meet' their own squadron.

8. τὰς ταχθείσας: i.e. the two hundred.

αὐτοί: i.e. the remainder, or rather the main fleet; if Hdt.'s figures were to be trusted, it would still have numbered upwards of 600 vessels.

ταύτης τῆς ἡμέρης: the day of their arrival at Aphetai, and, as afterwards appears, c. 15 *infra*, the day upon which the frontal attack upon Thermopylai had begun, 7. 210, the first of the great *Triduum*; cp. c. 15 *infra*, Appendix V. § 4.

9. οὐδὲ πρότερον ἢ τὸ σύνθημά σφι: they might have some time to wait for the signal that the circumnavigating squadron had arrived (in the Euripos? or where?). But where was such a signal to come from? No part or point of Euboia was as yet in Persian hands. The signal was to be given from the mainland — an unconscious indication that the circumnavigating squadron was directed rather against Thermopylai than

10 σύνθημά σφι ἔμελλε φανήσεσθαι παρὰ τῶν περιπλεόντων ὡς
ἠκόντων. ταύτας μὲν δὴ περιέπεμπον, τῶν δὲ λοιπέων νεῶν
ἐν τῇσι Ἀφέτῃσι ἐποιεῦντο ἀριθμόν.

8   Ἐν δὲ τούτῳ τῷ χρόνῳ ἐν ᾧ οὗτοι ἀριθμὸν ἐποιεῦντο
τῶν νεῶν, ἦν γὰρ ἐν τῷ στρατοπέδῳ τούτῳ Σκυλλίης Σκιωναῖος δύτης τῶν τότε ἀνθρώπων ἄριστος, ὃς καὶ ἐν τῇ ναυηγίῃ
τῇ κατὰ Πήλιον γενομένῃ πολλὰ μὲν ἔσωσε τῶν χρημάτων
5 τοῖσι Πέρσῃσι, πολλὰ δὲ καὶ αὐτὸς περιεβάλετο, οὗτος ὁ
Σκυλλίης ἐν νόῳ μὲν εἶχε ἄρα καὶ πρότερον αὐτομολήσειν ἐς
τοὺς Ἕλληνας, ἀλλ' οὐ γάρ οἱ παρέσχε ἕως τότε. ὅτεῳ μὲν
δὴ τρόπῳ τὸ ἐνθεῦτεν ἔτι ἀπίκετο ἐς τοὺς Ἕλληνας, οὐκ ἔχω

---

10 περιπλωόντων B, van H.   11 λοιπῶν B ‖ νηῶν ἐπὶ τῇσι(ν V)
ἀφετῆσιν B   12 ἐποιέοντο B ‖ τὸν ἀριθμόν z   8. 1 τούτῳ om. C ‖
ἐν ᾧ: ἐν τῷ edd. nonnulli: ἐν ᾧ.. νεῶν secl. van H. ‖ ἐποιέοντο B   2
νηῶν B   3 ναυαγίῃ d   4 κατὰ τὸ dz   5 τῇσι Bz ‖ περιεβάλετο AR: περιεβάλλετο BSV   6 αὐτομολήσειν.. οἱ om. B
7 ἕως Cobet, van H., Stein³: ὡς

---

against Artemision. This conclusion
supports the theory that 200 ships were
detached from the Persian fleet off the
Magnesian coast—or earlier. The voyage
from Skiathos to the Euripos, round
Kaphereus and Geraistos, could not be
less than 200 (E.) miles; sailing night
and day, under favourable circumstances,
the squadron could hardly arrive at
Chalkis, not to say at Thermopylai, in
less than thirty-six hours (cp. 4. 86, where
a ship is supposed to perform 1300 stades
in a νυχθήμερον; but we have here 200
ships to move together, and a difficult
channel to negotiate). It was, perhaps,
hoped that the flying squadron would
arrive in the rear of Thermopylai in the
course of the third day (assuming it to
have been despatched on the afternoon
or evening of the first day).

10. ἔμελλε φανήσεσθαι is rather
curious, for they must have been intending to await a definite signal, not
merely to wait until a signal was about
to be displayed. The futurity seems to
be purely relative to their intentions at
the moment of despatch, not on the eve
of arrival.

12. ἐν τῇσι Ἀφέτῃσι ἐποιεῦντο
ἀριθμόν. As had been done at Doriskos,
7. 59, 89, 100. Their losses by the
storm were to be computed (cp. 7. 190).
It is possible that some reorganization
of the fleet was now attempted. Documents may have resulted from this
numbering, but there is little to suggest
that Hdt. or his authorities made use
of them.

8. 2. Σκυλλίης Σκιωναῖος: Skyllias
(cp. Σκύλλα, Σκύλλη) of Skione, the city
on Pallene, 7. 123.

3. δύτης τῶν τότε ἀνθρώπων ἄριστος.
Had Hdt. believed the anecdote which
he proceeds to relate he would perhaps
have employed the formula πάντων τῶν
ἡμεῖς ἴδμεν ἄριστος. The term ἀνθρώπων
is introduced perhaps because the water
is not man's native element.

τῇ ναυηγίῃ τῇ κατὰ Πήλιον γενομένῃ: cp. 7. 188–91, and the luck of
Ameinokles, 7. 190. περιεβάλετο, ibid.
ἦν γάρ.. οὗτος shows a slight anacoluthon; the whole anecdote rings with
the vox viva: so ἄρα ('as he afterwards
explained'), ἀλλ' οὐ γάρ οἱ κτλ.

6. καὶ πρότερον, 'even before this';
cp. c. 6 supra.

7. παρέσχε is neuter. ἀνέσχε, just
below, is of course personal, but intransitive; cp. Od. 5. 320 οὐδ' ἐδυνάσθη
Αἶψα μάλ' ἀνσχεθέειν μεγάλου ὑπὸ κύματος
ὁρμῆς.

8. τὸ ἐνθεῦτεν, coming just after τότε,
might appear to be spatial rather than
temporal; but if taken with ἔτι must be
vaguely opposed to καὶ πρότερον just before. ἔτι may be referred (with Stein) to
the man's previous unsuccessful attempts
(not that any are recorded), or more
generally (with Sitzler) to his period of

εἰπεῖν ἀτρεκέως, θωμάζω δὲ εἰ τὰ λεγόμενα ἐστὶ ἀληθέα·
λέγεται γὰρ ὡς ἐξ Ἀφετέων δὺς ἐς τὴν θάλασσαν οὐ πρότερον 10
ἀνέσχε πρὶν ἢ ἀπίκετο ἐπὶ τὸ Ἀρτεμίσιον, σταδίους μάλιστά
κῃ τούτους ἐς ὀγδώκοντα διὰ τῆς θαλάσσης διεξελθών. λέγεται
μέν νυν καὶ ἄλλα ψευδέσι εἴκελα περὶ τοῦ ἀνδρὸς τούτου, τὰ
δὲ μετεξέτερα ἀληθέα· περὶ μέντοι τούτου γνώμη μοι ἀποδε-
δέχθω πλοίῳ μιν ἀπικέσθαι ἐπὶ τὸ Ἀρτεμίσιον. ὡς δὲ ἀπίκετο, 15
αὐτίκα ἐσήμηνε τοῖσι στρατηγοῖσι τήν τε ναυηγίην ὡς γένοιτο,
καὶ τὰς περιπεμφθείσας τῶν νεῶν περὶ Εὔβοιαν. τοῦτο δὲ 9
ἀκούσαντες οἱ Ἕλληνες λόγον σφίσι αὐτοῖσι ἐδίδοσαν. πολλῶν

---

9 εἴται Βα, van H. ‖ θωυμάζω Β, Stein[1]   10 ὡς om. Β   11
ἀνέχειν Β   12 τούτους ἐς om. Β   13 ἴκελλα RV : ἴκελα S,
Bekker, van H.   15 ἀπικέεσθαι R   16 ἐσήμαινε Β, Holder
17 περιπεφθείσας A[1]B[1] ‖ νηῶν Β

suspense and waiting for a favourable
opportunity.

9. **θωυμάζω δὲ εἰ τὰ λεγόμενα ἐστὶ
ἀληθέα**, 'I wonder if the story is true'
—a wonder which, if Hdt. had given
more way to it, might have flooded his
work with shallow rationalism. His
critique of the story of Skyllias is poor,
for he seems to see no alternative between
Skyllias having dived all the way from
Aphetai to Artemision and having come
all the way in a boat.

11. **σταδίους μάλιστά κῃ τούτους ἐς
ὀγδώκοντα.** 80 stades would not cover
the whole distance from Aphetai (wherever it be placed) to Artemision, assuming
that Artemision is east of Aphetai. But
from shore to shore the channel is in
places barely 50 stades, and many a
swimmer nowadays would make little
of it. **τούτους** (omitted by Β) is rightly
taken by Stein as "appositive"; cp. 3.
5 ἐὸν τοῦτο οὐκ ὀλίγον χωρίον.

13. **ἄλλα ψευδέσι εἴκελα**, as perhaps
the story told by Pausanias l.c. infra
of his (and his daughter's) diving down,
in the storm off Pelion, and cutting the
cables, etc., of the Persian ships. **τὰ δὲ
μετεξέτερα ἀληθέα** may be a concession
to Delphi, where was a statue, dedicated
by the Amphiktyones, of Σκύλλις and
of his daughter, Ὕδνα by name, which
Hdt. may have seen (Pausan. 10. 19. 1).
If so, this story would not be of the
original draft; cp. Introduction, § 9.
The dedication attests the reality and
importance of the services of Skyllias,
whatever they were. **μετεξέτερα = ἔνια.**

16. **αὐτίκα ἐσήμηνε τοῖσι στρατη-**

γοῖσι: according to Hdt. Skyllias reported to the Greek admirals (1) the
storm, its origin and effects; (2) the
despatch of the 200 ships round Euboia.
The Greeks knew all about the storm
already, **πάντα τὰ γενόμενα περὶ τὴν
ναυηγίην**, from their scouts, 7. 192, and
they had also, apparently before the
arrival of Skyllias, captured fifteen of
the enemy's vessels, and closely questioned their prisoners, 7. 194 f. It is
possible (with Stein) to emphasize the
construction **ὡς γένοιτο** as referring not
to the fact, the bare fact of a storm
having occurred, but to the course,
circumstances, and results of the storm,
the extent of the Persian losses, etc.
The change or incompleteness of the
construction is observable, a limb co-
ordinate with **ὡς γένοιτο** to follow **τὰς
περιπεμφθείσας τῶν νεῶν** being conspicuous by its absence, though not
grammatically indispensable. Hdt.
seems to make the report on the storm
(off Pelion) the chief point of Skyllias's
communication; while, upon the face of
it, his report on the flying squadron was
newer and more startling and important
tidings for the Greeks. But what did
he report of the 200 ships? Simply
that they had been despatched? Or
that they too had been, must have been,
wrecked? (**ὡς νεναυηγήκασι**).

9. 2. **οἱ Ἕλληνες**: sc. οἱ στρατηγοὶ τῶν
Ἑλλήνων. On learning the despatch of
a squadron round Euboia the Greek
admirals held a council of war (**λόγον
σφίσι αὐτοῖσι ἐδίδοσαν**). So far the statement may be historical; what follows is

δὲ λεχθέντων ἐνίκα τὴν ἡμέρην ἐκείνην αὐτοῦ μείναντάς τε
καὶ αὐλισθέντας, μετέπειτα νύκτα μέσην παρέντας πορεύεσθαι
5 καὶ ἀπαντᾶν τῇσι περιπλεούσῃσι τῶν νεῶν. μετὰ δὲ τοῦτο,
ὡς οὐδείς σφι ἐπέπλεε, δείλην ὀψίην γινομένην τῆς ἡμέρης

9. 5 περιπλωοὔσῃσι β ‖ τοῦτο del. van H.   6 ἐπέπλωε βz, van H.
‖ τῆς ἡμέρης γινομένην S

inconsistent with itself, and unintelligible. The Greeks debate various alternatives (not stated); they decide upon one,
and that one an absurdity, a strategic
inconceivability; and they proceed to
act in defiance of their decision. For
obvious reasons the Greeks at Artemision
could not abandon that position, so long
as Thermopylai was held by Leonidas;
they cannot have determined at this
point to retreat. Nor was any such
move demanded by the Persian *periplous*
of Euboia; a few ships would be sufficient to hold the narrow channel at
Chalkis, and, if that were held, the fleet
at Artemision, the army at Thermopylai,
had little to fear from the *periplous*.
But a real source of anxiety may have
lain in a doubt as to the true objective
of the Persian flying squadron. What
if the 200 vessels were making, not for
Chalkis, but for Oropos, for Phaleron,
for the Isthmos? The storm may have
reassured the Greeks, convinced that
a squadron on the high sea could not
weather it, even if Skyllias had reported
only the despatch of the Persian vessels.
The actual resolution taken by the
Greeks is to be inferred from their
action; they must have decided to remain, and to attack the Persian fleet, or
perhaps the rear-guard thereof. Possibly
the account here of the fighting on the
'first' day, resulting in the capture of
thirty ships, is an unconscious doublet
of the account given in 7. 194 of the
capture of the fifteen ships, that being
from an Asianic, this from a European
source; Kypriotes are concerned in both
stories, and it is extremely hard to find
room otherwise, in the narrative here,
for the episode there recorded; cp.
Appendix V. § 4.
8. ἐνίκα: of a deliberative decision,
6. 101. This decision might be identical
with the one reported in c. 4 *supra*; cp.
next note.
τὴν ἡμέρην ἐκείνην: *prima facie*
this day witnesses (1) the arrival of the
Persian fleet at Aphetai, (2) the arrival
of Skyllias at Artemision, (3) the council

of war, (4) the first engagement at sea,
whether this be, or be not, identical
with (5) the capture of the fifteen ships
described in 7. 194; to these items
must apparently be added (6) the first
day's fighting at Thermopylai, and, as
Hdt. would have us believe, (7) the
despatch of the squadron to circumnavigate Euboia. It is, however, possible
that these events are unduly accumulated.
The despatch of the squadron to circumnavigate Euboia is, as above shown, to
be dated before the Persian fleet passed
Skiathos and the *myrmex*, that is, before
the storm. The interval (ἐν δὲ τούτῳ τῷ
χρόνῳ c. 8 *supra*) between the despatch
of the squadron and the arrival of Skyllias
at Artemision may have comprised not
hours, but days; or again, his arrival
at Artemision may have anticipated the
Persian arrival at Aphetai by some days,
and not, as apparently implied by Hdt.
here, have succeeded it by some hours.
Again, the further chronological indication just below (μετὰ δὲ τοῦτο) is of little
or no value, the interval being entirely
vague. If Skyllias arrived in the Greek
camp before the storm, before the Persians
had passed Skiathos, in fact days before
the capture of the fifteen Persian vessels,
or the first engagements at Artemision
and Thermopylai, then, indeed, the
Greek admirals may have decided, on
the strength of his information, to detach
a portion of their own fleet (cp. c. 14
infra) to guard, or to reinforce the ships
guarding, the Euripos channel, while
themselves remaining on the spot (αὐτοῦ),
as a matter of course, with the larger
part, to cover Thermopylai and the
northern channel (of Oreos) from the
advance of the Persian navy.
6. δείλην ὀψίην γινομένην τῆς ἡμέρης:
prima facie this chronological reference
carries back not merely to τὴν ἡμέρην
ἐκείνην just above, but to the δείλην
πρωίην γινομένην of c. 6 *supra*, the hour
of the arrival of the Persians at Aphetai.
It is, however, possible that these early
and late afternoons are not on the same
day. The arrival of the Persian fleet at

φυλάξαντες αὐτοὶ ἐπανέπλεον ἐπὶ τοὺς βαρβάρους, ἀπόπειραν
αὐτῶν ποιήσασθαι βουλόμενοι τῆς τε μάχης καὶ τοῦ διεκπλόου.
ὁρῶντες δὲ σφέας οἵ τε ἄλλοι στρατιῶται οἱ Ξέρξεω καὶ οἱ 10
στρατηγοὶ ἐπιπλέοντας νηυσὶ ὀλίγῃσι, πάγχυ σφι μανίην
ἐπενείκαντες ἀνῆγον καὶ αὐτοὶ τὰς νέας, ἐλπίσαντες σφέας
εὐπετέως αἱρήσειν, οἰκότα κάρτα ἐλπίσαντες, τὰς μέν γε τῶν
Ἑλλήνων ὁρῶντες ὀλίγας νέας, τὰς δὲ ἑωυτῶν πλήθεί τε 5
πολλαπλησίας καὶ ἄμεινον πλεούσας· καταφρονήσαντες ταῦτα
ἐκυκλοῦντο αὐτοὺς ἐς μέσον. ὅσοι μέν νυν τῶν Ἰώνων ἦσαν

7 ἐπανέπλωον Βz, van H.   8 διεκπλόου Β   10. 1 ὁρέωντες
C: ὁρέοντες R, Stein¹, van H.: ὁρέοντος V   2 ἐπιπλώοντας Βz, van H.
3 ἀνήγαγον Β ‖ ἐλπίσαντές σφεας Stein¹   5 ὁρέωντες C: ὁρέοντες Β,
Stein¹, van H.   6 πολλαπλασίας ΒCPz ‖ πλωούσας Β, van H.

Aphetai, to say nothing of the subsequent
numbering, was not to be accomplished
in the twinkling of an eye ; the only
synchronism to which we may cling
with desperate tenacity is the coincidence of the three days' fightings at
Artemision and at Thermopylai, this
being grounded, though not absolutely,
in the strategic and tactical necessities of
the case. The use of φυλάξαντες is made
clear in c. 14 infra.
Blakesley suggests that the Greeks
timed their attack so as to have the sink-
ing sun full in the eyes of the enemy's
steersmen ; if so, Hdt.'s account will require further revision, for Aphetai is, if
anything, west of Artemision.
7. ἀπόπειραν αὐτῶν ποιήσασθαι βουλόμενοι : verily a laudable curiosity !
That Hdt. should solemnly record a
decision to retreat (and this the third,
cp. c. 4 supra, 7. 182) and immediately
thereupon an assumption of the offensive
by the would-be fugitives, and that out
of experimental curiosity, is fatally
symptomatic of his military motivation,
and must be taken to set the modern
reader free to enforce the Sach-Kritik, or
standard of physical and psychological
probability, with considerable boldness.
8. τῆς τε μάχης καὶ τοῦ διεκπλόου :
with μάχη, manner of fighting, cp. 5.
49, 7. 9. The διέκπλοος was, perhaps,
an Ionian device ; cp. my note to 6. 12,
and c. 11 infra.
10. 1. ὁρῶντες δέ κτλ. There is a
remarkable coincidence between the
language (the sentiment also) of this
passage and the description of the
Persian mind at Marathon, 6. 112 οἱ δὲ
Πέρσαι ὁρέοντες (sic) . . δρόμῳ ἐπιόντας

. . μανίην τε τοῖσι Ἀθηναίοισι ἐπέφερον
καὶ πάγχυ ὀλεθρίην, ὁρέοντες αὐτοὺς ὀλίγους
καὶ τούτους δρόμῳ ἐπειγομένους. If Stein's
readings are correct the Atticism of this
passage—the earlier in order of composition, if my theory (Introduction, §§ 7, 8)
holds—is the more pronounced : as is
natural, on that theory.
4. οἰκότα κάρτα ἐλπίσαντες : for two
reasons, their ships being more numerous,
and better sailers (ἄμεινον πλεούσας) : a
notable admission, perhaps not free from
exaggeration, especially under the circumstances, the Persian ships having been
so long in the water, even if the storm
had not already occurred to damage them.
They had, however, perhaps been carefully overhauled at Doriskos, and at
Therme.
6. καταφρονήσαντες ταῦτα : the verb
has not yet acquired its dyslogistic force ;
cp. 1. 59, 66.
7. ἐκυκλοῦντο αὐτοὺς ἐς μέσον, 'they
attempted to surround them in a circle'
(cp. c. 85 infra), and were apparently
in the first instance successful. This
was a περίπλοος of another sort to that
conducted by τῆσι περιπλεούσῃσι τῶν νεῶν
above : could it be that there is some
confusion up above in the report of the
resolution of the Greeks ἀνανταν τῆσι
περιπλεούσῃσι to front, or attack, the
ships which were surrounding them ?
ὅσοι μέν νυν τῶν Ἰώνων : there
were, then, some of the Ionians in the
Persian ranks well-disposed, loyal (εὔνοοι),
to the 'Hellenic' cause : an important
admission, and indicating a weakness,
with which the Persian admirals just
before have failed to reckon ; cp. 7. 51.

εὔνοοι τοῖσι ῞Ελλησι ἀέκοντές τε ἐστρατεύοντο, συμφορήν τε
ἐποιεῦντο μεγάλην ὁρῶντες περιεχομένους αὐτοὺς καὶ ἐπιστά-
10 μενοι ὡς οὐδεὶς αὐτῶν ἀπονοστήσει· οὕτω ἀσθενέα σφι
ἐφαίνετο εἶναι τὰ τῶν ῾Ελλήνων πρήγματα. ὅσοισι δὲ καὶ
ἡδομένοισι ἦν τὸ γινόμενον, ἅμιλλαν ἐποιεῦντο ὅκως αὐτὸς
ἕκαστος πρῶτος νέα 'Αττικὴν ἑλὼν παρὰ βασιλέος δῶρα
λάμψεται· 'Αθηναίων γὰρ αὐτοῖσι λόγος ἦν πλεῖστος ἀνὰ τὰ
11 στρατόπεδα. τοῖσι δὲ ῞Ελλησι ὡς ἐσήμηνε, πρῶτα μὲν ἀντί-

---

8 τοῖσι ῞Ελλησι, ἀέκοντές Stein[1,2], edd. plerique : virgulam del. van H.,
Stein[3] ‖ ἐστρατεύοντο, συμφορήν : virgulam exhib. Gaisford, Holder, van
H., Stein[3] ‖ τε alterum del. van H.　　　9 ὀρέωντες C : ὀρέοντες β :
ὀρέοντές <τε> van H.　　　10 οὐδείς σφιν ἀπονοστήσειν RS : (ἀπονοστη.
cum σ litt. ult. superscr. V) ‖ σφιν ἀσθενέα S　　　11 τῶν om. S
12 ἐποιέοντο β ‖ ἕκαστος αὐτὸς β　　　13 νῆα β ‖ βασιλέως Cd　　　14
λάμψηται Sz　　　11. 1 ἀντίπρῳροι van H., Stein[3] : volgo sine ι subscr.

---

9. περιεχομένους: imperfect, 'in course
of being surrounded': so τὸ γινόμενον
just below.

ἐπιστάμενοι: the word seems used
by Hdt. in reference to the strength
rather than the truth of their certitude,
not without a touch of irony herein.

11. πρήγματα: c. 4 supra.

ὅσοισι δέ: sc. τῶν 'Ιώνων : or was
it rather the Dorians, and that set?
Artemisia par exemple and the Hali-
karnassians? Or is the reference wider
still, covering all the components of the
fleet, who were pleased with what was
going on, and ambitious, every man of
them, to capture an Attic ship and to
receive rewards from the king therefor?
With the construction cp. ἀσμένοισι c. 14
infra, ἡδομένοισι 9. 46. Blakesley cps.
Tacitus Agric. 18, quibus . . bellum
volentibus erat.

14. 'Αθηναίων γάρ: the unblushing
Atticism of the passage suggests the
ultimate source, if not the channel, of
these reports. There is some slight inconsequence in the rewards offered for
the capture of a Greek, or at least an
Attic ship, and the sure and certain
confidence of victory ; but the rewards
are likely to be historical. The Athenians
had been victors at Marathon ; the
Athenians had supported the Ionic revolt ; Athenian exiles were on the
Persian fleet, or in the king's camp.

ἀνὰ τὰ στρατόπεδα. Stein refers
to the navy, and to the Persian navy
alone, which was of a composite character. στρατόπεδον can certainly denote

a naval force, perhaps especially when
brought to land (cp. 5. 36), but the
mention of the king in the immediate
context, and the considerations urged in
the previous note, justify the extension
of the term here to cover the forces in
front of Thermopylai. The phrase thus
becomes a homage to the solidarity of
the parallel operations.

11. 1. ἐσήμηνε: sc. ὁ σαλπιγκτής :
cp. Aischyl. Pers. 395. The Greek
manœuvres are proceeding with the
utmost coolness and precision ; their
ships are conglobated, and with their
sterns centred on one point (ἐς τὸ μέσον
τὰς πρύμνας συνήγαγον): this position
is assumed at the first signal, for
previously they were rowing forward
(ἐπανέπλεον ἐπὶ τοὺς βαρβάρους c. 9
supra) ; at the second signal (δεύτερα
δὲ σημήναντος) they shot forwards,
although by that time they were surrounded, the περίπλοος, the κύκλωσις of
the enemy's more numerous fleet having
now developed itself : the Greek ships
charged the enemy bow to bow (κατὰ
στόμα). This account looks at first sight
plausible ; reflexion shows it to be
deficient. Was the κύκλωσις indeed
complete? Was the Greek fleet completely surrounded, and the individual
vessels radiating from a centre, like
spokes from a wheel, all round? Could
271 galleys really be arranged for practical or tactical purposes on such a plan?
Or was the formation, perhaps, but in
a crescent or arc? And again, were the
Persian ships advancing κατὰ στόμα, or

πρῷροι τοῖσι βαρβάροισι γενόμενοι ἐς τὸ μέσον τὰς πρύμνας
συνήγαγον, δεύτερα δὲ σημήναντος ἔργου εἴχοντο ἐν ὀλίγῳ
περ ἀπολαμφθέντες καὶ κατὰ στόμα. ἐνθαῦτα τριήκοντα νέας
αἱρέουσι τῶν βαρβάρων καὶ τὸν Γόργου τοῦ Σαλαμινίων 5
βασιλέος ἀδελφεὸν Φιλάονα τὸν Χέρσιος, λόγιμον ἐόντα ἐν
τῷ στρατοπέδῳ ἄνδρα. πρῶτος δὲ Ἑλλήνων νέα τῶν πολεμίων
εἷλε ἀνὴρ Ἀθηναῖος Λυκομήδης Αἰσχραίου, καὶ τὸ ἀριστήιον

---

2 γινόμενοι βPz   3 εἰσήγαγον C   4 νῆας β   5 τῶν
βαρβάρων om. β, Holder   6 βασιλέως C ‖ ἐν om. C   7 ἄνδρα
om. β, Holder ‖ νῆα β: μετὰ C   8 αἰσχραίου αSV: αἰσχρέου R et
reliqui: Αἰσχρέω Bredow, Holder, van H.

---

were they rowing round and round the
Greeks in the attempt to compress them
into a small space? In the first of the two
engagements, afterwards so celebrated,
between Phormion and the Peloponnesians, anno 429 B.C., the Athenian
admiral, with but twenty ships, succeeded in rowing all round a fleet of
47 sail, which the incompetent Knemos
had drawn up in a hollow circle, their
prows outwards, round their tenders and
convoys. If the Peloponnesian ships
on that occasion ἔργου εἴχοντο ἐν ὀλίγῳ
περ ἀπολαμφθέντες, they might have
struck Phormion's ships, but not κατὰ
στόμα, bow to bow, but much more
advantageously, amidships or broadside.
As it was, the result of Phormion's
manœuvre was to compress the fleet of
Knemos into an ever-narrowing space,
and finally to throw it into complete
confusion (Thucyd. 2. 83 f.). But the
case here is different. A vastly superior
force is encircling an inferior number:
possibly in this case the ships advanced
κατὰ στόμα, prow to prow, albeit ramming
on that system was not likely to result
in a Greek victory. Hence the suspicion
arises that there is something confused
and inaccurate in Hdt.'s description of
this engagement: the capture of the
thirty ships by the Greeks certainly
ensues with surprising rapidity. If
these thirty ships were cut off in some
way from the main fleet, the result would
be more intelligible. And again, if the
story (in 7. 194) of the capture of fifteen
ships, owing to a misunderstanding, be
the Asianic version of this first engagement, we have to seek for a tertium quid,
between that account, which reduces the
engagement to a mere contretemps, and
this account, which magnifies it into a

pitched battle and a glorious victory, as
the real event.

4. κατὰ στόμα : ex adverso, a fronte,
Baehr; Bug gegen Bug, Stein, which
seems better than his first idea, und
zwar nur von vorn.

τριήκοντα : just twice as many as
the Asianic tradition (7. 194) allows.

6. Φιλάονα: on Philaon and his family
cp. note to 7. 98. In the fifteen ships
was captured the Paphian Penthylos
(7. 195), as well as Sandokes and
Aridolis.

7. στρατοπέδῳ: doubtless the fleet,
or naval force; cp. c. 10 supra.

8. Λυκομήδης Αἰσχραίου: Plutarch,
Themist. 15, transfers the exploit to
Salamis, which contradicts c. 84 infra,
but at any rate suggests other possible
transferences: πρῶτος μὲν οὖν λαμβάνει
ναῦν Λυκομήδης ἀνὴρ Ἀθηναῖος τριηρ-
αρχῶν, ἧς τὰ παράσημα περικόψας, ἀν-
έθηκεν Ἀπόλλωνι δαφνηφόρῳ Φλυῆσιν.
The last word may be a gloss (cp. Bauer,
Plutarchs Themistokles, 1884, p. 56);
but was not Lykomedes a member of
the clan (γένος) of the Lykomidai, to
which Themistokles certainly belonged
(cp. Plutarch, op. cit. 1)? The names
Αἰσχραῖος, Αἰσχρίων, Αἰσχρων are all
epigraphically attested for Athens (cp.
Pauly-Wissowa, i. 1063 f.), while Αἰ-
σχριωνίη appears 3. 26 as the name of a
φυλή in Samos. A Lykomedes of Phlye
appears on an inscription of 418–17 B.C.
Dittenberger, Sylloge¹, 38; Hicks, Manual²,
70 [53]. He might be grandson of the
one here in the text.

τὸ ἀριστήιον ἔλαβε οὗτος. The
Aristeion is a definite award (cp. c. 93,
9. 71, 105), and this notice may be
historical; yet in view of Plutarch's
statement, touching τὰ παράσημα, a sus-

ἔλαβε οὗτος. τοὺς δ' ἐν τῇ ναυμαχίῃ ταύτῃ ἑτεραλκέως
10 ἀγωνιζομένους νὺξ ἐπελθοῦσα διέλυσε. οἱ μὲν δὴ Ἕλληνες ἐπὶ
τὸ Ἀρτεμίσιον ἀπέπλεον, οἱ δὲ βάρβαροι ἐς τὰς Ἀφέτας,
πολλὸν παρὰ δόξαν ἀγωνισάμενοι. ἐν ταύτῃ τῇ ναυμαχίῃ
Ἀντίδωρος Λήμνιος μοῦνος τῶν σὺν βασιλέι Ἑλλήνων ἐόντων
αὐτομολέει ἐς τοὺς Ἕλληνας, καὶ οἱ Ἀθηναῖοι διὰ τοῦτο τὸ
15 ἔργον ἔδοσαν αὐτῷ χῶρον ἐν Σαλαμῖνι.

12 Ὡς δὲ εὐφρόνη ἐγεγόνεε, ἦν μὲν τῆς ὥρης μέσον θέρος,
ἐγίνετο δὲ ὕδωρ τε ἄπλετον διὰ πάσης τῆς νυκτὸς καὶ σκληραὶ
βρονταὶ ἀπὸ τοῦ Πηλίου· οἱ δὲ νεκροὶ καὶ τὰ ναυήγια ἐξεφέροντο

---

9 τοὺς δὲ CR ‖ ἐν om. C   10 διέλυε C   11 ἀπέπλωον RS,
van H.   15 αὐτῷ om. ß, Holder, van H. ‖ χώραν ß   12. 2
ἄπλετόν τε ß ‖ βρονταὶ σκληραὶ Pdz   3 ναυάγια B ‖ ἐξεφερέοντο
Holder, van H.

---

picion suggests itself of some possible
confusion.

9. **ἑτεραλκέως ἀγωνιζομένους** : cp. 9.
103 ὡς εἶδον αὐτίκα κατ' ἀρχὰς γινομένην
ἑτεραλκέα τὴν μάχην. The word is taken
to mean in Hdt. 'doubtful,' *ancipiti
Marte*, though it is an Homeric word,
and the Homeric meaning is 'decisive.'
An engagement in which one side loses
thirty triremes to the other is hardly
indecisive, or of doubtful issue ; and
the barbarians return to Aphetai πολλὸν
παρὰ δόξαν ἀγωνισάμενοι.

10. **νύξ**: simply prosaic and depersoni-
fied. The movements resulting in the
engagement had started late in the
afternoon ; cp. c. 10 *supra*.

13. **Ἀντίδωρος Λήμνιος**. The name
Antidoros is epigraphically attested for
Athens in the fourth century B.C. (Pauly-
Wissowa, i. 2397, where this Lemnian
does not appear at all). The island of
Lemnos was claimed for Athens in virtue
of the act of Miltiades (cp. 6. 137-140),
and as the Athenians recovered possession
within a few years (cp. Busolt, *Gr. Gesch.*
III. i. 414 f.), it is, perhaps, doubly
remarkable that they settled this
'Lemnian' in Salamis rather than in
his native place. His exact status in
Lemnos, in Salamis, and in Athens, is
not quite clear. Was he an Athenian
citizen ? Had he been so all along ?
Had he been a citizen and forfeited his
rights ? Salamis was not a 'deme,' and
never appears as such: the Athenian
settlers were technically 'Kleruchs'; but
there were doubtless natives also, and
the possession of a χῶρος ἐν Σαλαμῖνι

probably did not carry with it full
citizenship. The word κλῆρος here would
have been less embarrassing.

12. 1. **εὐφρόνη** : cp. c. 6 *supra* ; the
word appears to be used without any
eulogistic intention. The pluperfect,
ἐγεγόνεε, is used perhaps to avoid clashing
with ἐγίνετο just below. ἦν μέν, 'though
the season (ὥρη) was midsummer, yet'
(δέ). With the date cp. 7. 206. ἄ-
πλετος, as in 1. 14 (χρυσός), 4. 53 (ἅλες),
6. 58 (οἰμωγή), etc., 'boundless,' 'no
end of,' 'galore.' σκληραὶ (*bis*) of the
βρονταί denotes perhaps the sharp rattle
of thunder in close proximity ; L. & S.
cp. Vergil's *aridus fragor*, G. i. 357 f.

3. **ἀπὸ τοῦ Πηλίου** : i.e. from the
north, behind them, the scene of the
great storm in Bk. 7. 188 ff., if, indeed,
the two storms be not all one. But is
the phrase here purely locative or quite
void of a suggestion of causality and
generation ? (Cp. τὸ ἀπὸ Ξέρξου c. 15
infra.)

τὰ ναυήγια : are these wrecks, with
the corpses, the product of the storm
itself or of the antecedent battle ?

ἐξεφέροντο ἐς τὰς Ἀφέτας. The
wreckage and corpses were thrown ashore
on the strand at Aphetai: how was
that, if the storm was from Pelion ?
Was it the result of the tide and the
current, or were they carried by a wind
moving against the thunderstorm ? In
any case it is hardly safe to press this
statement into a proof that there was a
great storm from the south immediately
in succession to the three days' storm
from the north, or north-east (in Bk. 7),

ἐς τὰς Ἀφέτας, καὶ περί τε τὰς πρῴρας τῶν νεῶν εἰλέοντο καὶ
ἐτάρασσον τοὺς ταρσοὺς τῶν κωπέων. οἱ δὲ στρατιῶται οἱ 5
ταύτῃ ἀκούοντες ταῦτα ἐς φόβον κατιστέατο, ἐλπίζοντες πάγχυ
ἀπολέεσθαι ἐς οἷα κακὰ ἦκον· πρὶν γὰρ ἢ καὶ ἀναπνεῦσαι
σφέας ἔκ τε τῆς ναυηγίης καὶ τοῦ χειμῶνος τοῦ γενομένου
κατὰ Πήλιον, ὑπέλαβε ναυμαχίη καρτερή, ἐκ δὲ τῆς ναυμαχίης
ὄμβρος τε λάβρος καὶ ῥεύματα ἰσχυρὰ ἐς θάλασσαν ὁρμημένα 10
βρονταί τε σκληραί. καὶ τούτοισι μὲν τοιαύτη ἡ νὺξ ἐγίνετο, 13
τοῖσι δὲ ταχθεῖσι αὐτῶν περιπλέειν Εὔβοιαν ἡ αὐτή περ ἐοῦσα
νὺξ πολλὸν ἦν ἔτι ἀγριωτέρη, τοσούτῳ ὅσῳ ἐν πελάγεϊ φερο-

---

4 πρῴρας van H., Stein³ : volgo sine ι subscr. ‖ καὶ τῶν B ‖ εἰλέοντο
van H., Stein³ : εἰλέοντο   5 ἀπάρασσον Emperius, van H.   7
ἀπολέσθαι B : ἀπολεῖσθαι van H. ‖ ἐς om. C ‖ ἢ om. R   8 γινομένου B
9 καρτερὴ SPdz : κρατερὴ ceteri   10 τε om. B ‖ λάβρος α : λάμβρος
C : καρτερὸς B ‖ ἐς : κατὰ CPz ‖ ὁρμημένα CPdz   13. 1 <ἡ>νὺξ
Schaefer, Stein²³ : νὺξ   2 αὐτέων α ‖ περιπλώειν Bz, van H.

---

a somewhat improbable sequence. Hdt.
says nothing here about the wind, which
first makes its appearance on the 'high
sea,' in the next chapter, as though
the men at Aphetai had not been exposed to it. In this chapter what the
Persians suffer from is rain, thunders
(and lightnings), and all that at night.
The ships apparently were not beached
but in the water, otherwise the corpses
could hardly have been rolling over
round the prows (which slowly move
through the mass of wreckage and dead
bodies), much less have been interfering
with the blades of the oars (τοὺς ταρσοὺς
τῶν κωπέων). This description, indeed,
suggests rather the position off the
Magnesian coast, where the ships spent
the night at sea, than the situation at
Aphetai, to which the Persians have
retired in the previous chapter.

5. οἱ δὲ στρατιῶται οἱ ταύτῃ : a rather
mysterious designation : who are 'the
soldiers, or fighting men, in the place'?
Are they the epibatai of the fleet? Are
they the Persians in Malis? Are they
a corps of Persians still in Thessaly,
and in more immediate touch with the
fleet? Whoever they are, they seem to
be ashore, while the ships and the
oarsmen are still afloat.

6. ἀκούοντες ταῦτα : hearing what?
news of the disaster? Or, more directly,
the thunder and the rain? the wreckage and the corpses? Or is ἀκούοντες
used (like ταῦτα) in a vaguer and more

extended reference = perceiving? The
disappointment of the day (πολλὸν παρὰ
δόξαν ἀγωνισάμενοι c. 11) is followed by
a scare, a panic, at night, when they
expect(ἐλπίζοντες) to be destroyed utterly,
ὅτι ἐς τοιαῦτα κακὰ ἦκον, such was the
evil plight which had befallen them.

7. ἀναπνεῦσαι, to recover breath.
ἐκ, out of, after. The attitude here
indicated is hardly consistent with the
ideas and expectations ascribed to them
in c. 10 supra.

9. ὑπέλαβε ναυμαχίη καρτερή : so
much for the Greek experiment of c. 9.
The ἀπόπειρα has become a ν. καρτερή.
ὑπολαβεῖν, to succeed, to come on, to
overtake ; generally of disasters ; cp. 6.
27 (bis : λοιμός· ναυμαχίη).

10. ὁρμημένα is noticeable, the verb
being seldom used in a really passive
sense, or of merely inanimate objects.

13. 1. τούτοισι μέν : rather vague ;
hardly to be referred strictly to οἱ
στρατιῶται οἱ ταύτῃ above ; rather more
generally to the whole στρατόπεδον at
Aphetai ; still more general is the αὐτῶν
immediately following (cp. Index).

2. τοῖσι δὲ ταχθεῖσι : cp. c. 7 supra.

ἡ αὐτή περ ἐοῦσα νὺξ πολλὸν ἦν
ἔτι ἀγριωτέρη : a somewhat quaint and
helpless turn, especially followed by
ἐπέπιπτε, all the more as νύξ does not
appear to be personified. For ἄχαρις
cp. 7. 190, etc. πέλαγος is here of great
significance ; cp. next two notes.

μένοισι ἐπέπιπτε, καὶ τὸ τέλος σφι ἐγίνετο ἄχαρι. ὡς γὰρ
5 δὴ πλέουσι αὐτοῖσι χειμών τε καὶ τὸ ὕδωρ ἐπεγίνετο ἐοῦσι
κατὰ τὰ Κοῖλα τῆς Εὐβοίης, φερόμενοι τῷ πνεύματι καὶ οὐκ
εἰδότες τῇ ἐφέροντο ἐξέπιπτον πρὸς τὰς πέτρας· ἐποιέετό τε
πᾶν ὑπὸ τοῦ θεοῦ ὅκως ἂν ἐξισωθείη τῷ Ἑλληνικῷ τὸ

---

4 τὸ om. β ‖ ἐγένετο β, Holder   5 πλώουσι(ν V) β, van H. ‖
<ὁ>χειμών van H. ‖ τὸ om. d   7 ἐξεφέροντο β ‖ ἐς τὰς S(V)   8
τοῦ om. z ‖ ἐξισωθῇ C ‖ τὸ περιεὸν β, Valla

---

5. χειμών τε καὶ τὸ ὕδωρ: 'the rain'
is that already described in c. 12; the
thunder is apparently not within hearing, but a 'storm' (χειμών, πνεῦμα) is
blowing on the high seas.

6. κατὰ τὰ Κοῖλα τῆς Εὐβοίης, 'off
the Hollows of Euboia'; cp. περὶ next
chapter, when the ships are dashed ashore,
and cp. c. 7 supra. As Rawlinson
remarks, it is not perfectly certain
what exact reach of Euboian coast is
denoted by 'the Hollows.' Strabo, 445,
makes it the tract between Geraistos
and the Euripos: τῆς Εὐβοίας τὰ Κοῖλα
λέγουσι τὰ μεταξὺ Αὐλίδος καὶ τῶν περὶ
Γεραιστὸν τόπων· κολποῦται γὰρ ἡ παραλία.
The statement would have been more
convincing if the reason had not been
added, for the outer coast of Euboia,
facing the high sea, is also hollowed
(in contrast, for example, with the
Magnesian coast), even if not sculp-
tured into such a remarkable series of
bays as the Paralia from Geraistos to
Chalkis. The Epitomator of Strabo
places the Hollows between Geraistos
and Kaphereus, a location preferred by
Leake (Demi 247); but the absence of
the requisite physical features to justify
such a nomenclature is fatal to this
identification. Not so the extension
of the term to the Paralia between
Kaphereus and the promontory Cherson-
nesos—a coast the general trend of
which is more truly concave than the
line of coast west of Geraistos, which
is, in fact, a convex, broken by a series
of superficial recesses or cavities.
Possibly the term 'Hollows' was applied
to the whole of the southern scimitar-
shaped section of Euboia, and so ships
wrecked on either side might be said
to have come to grief on or off the
Hollows. But if Strabo is right in re-
stricting the term as above explained,
and that not merely for his own day,
in that case Hdt. is almost certainly
wrong in making the Persian ships pass

Geraistos. They would hardly then
have been ἐν πελάγεϊ, and to wreck them
there we must conjure up an improbable
storm from the south or west in the
teeth of the Hellespontias and Boreas
which have been raging (at most a
day or two before) off Pelion. The
ships in Hdt. (pace Strabo) must have
been wrecked long before they rounded
Geraistos, or even Kaphereus, for they
are wrecked during the night following
the day upon which they have been
despatched. As above shown the
squadron of 200 sail, detached to circumnavigate Euboia, was really detached
from the main fleet off the Magnesian
coast on the day or evening before
the great storm, and passing 'outside
Skiathos' rowed south a whole quiet
midsummer's night (7. 188) before being
overtaken by the great storm. Hdt.
has apparently duplicated the storm,
the more easily as the stories there
and here are from different sources:
his chronology, as well as the causal
sequence, being dislocated thereby.

7. ἐποιέετό τε πᾶν ὑπὸ τοῦ θεοῦ,
'everything was being done by the god'
—of thunder, rain, and wind γ probably
Zeus, rather than Boreas, to whom the
Athenians had prayed (7. 189), or the
Anemoi, or Anemos, invoked by the
Hellenes (7. 178).

8. ὅκως ἂν . . δη. For the construction cp. ὡς ἂν μὴ ὀφθείησαν c. 7
supra. The intention of the god was
not, however, effected, if we are to credit
Hdt. himself, c. 66 infra; in other
words, Hdt., at different moments, in
different contexts, following different
sources, thinks nothing of such self-
contradictions or inconsequences. The
further question emerges: were the
numbers of the Persian fleet at Artemision, at Salamis, after all, very much
in excess of the Greek? Perhaps not!
as seems hinted, admitted, in this
curious passage, even though Herodotus

Περσικὸν μηδὲ πολλῷ πλέον εἴη. οὗτοι μέν νυν περὶ τὰ **14**
Κοῖλα τῆς Εὐβοίης διεφθείροντο· οἱ δ' ἐν Ἀφέτῃσι βάρβαροι,
ὥς σφι ἀσμένοισι ἡμέρη ἐπέλαμψε, ἀτρέμας τε εἶχον τὰς
νέας καί σφι ἀπεχρᾶτο κακῶς πρήσσουσι ἡσυχίην ἄγειν ἐν
τῷ παρεόντι. τοῖσι δὲ Ἕλλησι ἐπεβοήθεον νέες πεντήκοντα 5
καὶ τρεῖς Ἀττικαί. αὗταί τε δή σφεας ἐπέρρωσαν ἀπικό-
μεναι καὶ ἅμα ἀγγελίη ἐλθοῦσα, ὡς τῶν βαρβάρων οἱ περιπλέοντες τὴν Εὔβοιαν πάντες εἴησαν διεφθαρμένοι ὑπὸ τοῦ
γενομένου χειμῶνος. φυλάξαντες δὴ τὴν αὐτὴν ὥρην, πλέοντες
ἐπέπεσον νηυσὶ Κιλίσσῃσι· ταύτας δὲ διαφθείραντες, ὡς εὐφρόνη 10
ἐγίνετο, ἀπέπλεον ὀπίσω ἐπὶ τὸ Ἀρτεμίσιον.

---

14. 2 οἱ δὲ β, Holder   3 ἀτρέμας βα : ἀτρέμα ‖ τὰς νέας abesse
velim   4 ἀπεχρέετο βα : ἀπεχρῆτο ceteri   5 ἐπεβώθεον β, van H.
‖ νῆες β ‖ τρεῖς καὶ πεντήκοντα β, Holder, Stein¹², van H.   7 περι-
πλώοντες β, van H.   9 δὲ α ‖ πλώοντες βα, van H.   10 ἔπεσον R
11 ἐγένετο β, Stein¹ ‖ ἀπέπλωον βα, van H.

---

himself retracts the admission in c. 66.
The *Deus ex machina*, here something
of a sporting character, is for making
it a fair match twixt Greek and Persian!
Verily, a trivial Providence. Hdt. lacks
logic, whether that of piety or that of
philosophy, and is neither very devout
nor rational. Cato, the Stoic, went as
far as any man in another direction
when he excused his opposition to the
motion for a *supplicatio* in Cicero's
honour : such a solemnity would seem
to imply (said he) that Mark's victory
was more Heaven's doing than his own :
a simple vote of thanks puts the human
hero in his proper place ; Cicero, *Epp.
ad F.* 15. 5.

14. 3. ἀσμένοισι ἡμέρη ἐπέλαμψε : on
the construction cp. c. 10 *supra*. This
day is the 'second' of the *triduum*—
say Monday. The present in κακῶς
πρήσσουσι is a little remarkable, but
may denote the effects of the defeat on
the previous day, and the inconveniences
and terrors of the past night.

5. ἐπεβοήθεον νέες . . Ἀττικαί. With
these 53 ships the Attic squadron is
raised to 180, or even 200 sail. It is
natural to surmise that this detachment
had been holding the Euripos, whether
left there by the main fleet on its way
north or sent back to bar the channel,
as the result of deliberations at Artemision
(cp. c. 4 *supra*). Nor need we suppose
that Chalkis was left entirely without
guardships ; perhaps the twenty vessels

manned by the Chalkidians (c. 1 *supra*)
were there all the time.

7. ἅμα ἀγγελίη ἐλθοῦσα : the adverb
qualifies ἐπέρρωσαν rather than ἐλθοῦσα :
Hdt. plainly does not suspect that just
the Attic reinforcement brought the
good news from Chalkis, or Geraistos,
to Artemision. Nor could it have done
so, if the Persian ships had been wrecked
on the south-west coast of Euboia the
night before ; the news could hardly
have travelled so far and fast. Hdt.
marks a coincidence—the arrival of this
message so early confirms the view that
the Persian squadron of 200 had been
wrecked off the east coast of Euboia.
But is the message correctly dated ?
Was it on the second day of the fighting
that the Greeks learnt of this fresh
disaster to the Persians ? Had not the
wreck occurred three days ago ? Had
Skyllias already brought the news ? Cp.
c. 8 *supra*.

8. ὑπὸ τοῦ γενομένου χειμῶνος. Though
Hdt. speaks, or seems to speak. in 7. 192
of the storm off the Magnesian coast as
ὁ χειμὼν ὁ πρῶτος, he nowhere speaks of
the storm off Euboia as ὁ χειμὼν ὁ δεύτερος.
But cp. note *ad l.c.*

9. φυλάξαντες δὴ τὴν αὐτὴν ὥρην :
cp. c. 9 *supra* δελην ὀψίην γινομένην τῆς
ἡμέρης φυλάξαντες. The use of the word
ὥρη here comes very near to our 'hour' ;
not as τῆς ὥρης c. 12 *supra*. But why
the Greeks, reinforced and encouraged,
after a victory too the previous day,

15　　Τρίτῃ δὲ ἡμέρῃ δεινόν τι ποιησάμενοι οἱ στρατηγοὶ τῶν
βαρβάρων νέας οὕτω σφι ὀλίγας λυμαίνεσθαι, καὶ τὸ ἀπὸ
Ξέρξεω δειμαίνοντες, οὐκ ἀνέμειναν ἔτι τοὺς Ἕλληνας μάχης
ἄρξαι, ἀλλὰ παρακελευσάμενοι κατὰ μέσον ἡμέρης ἀνῆγον τὰς
5 νέας. συνέπιπτε δὲ ὥστε τὰς αὐτὰς ἡμέρας τάς τε ναυμαχίας
γίνεσθαι ταύτας καὶ τὰς πεζομαχίας τὰς ἐν Θερμοπύλῃσι. ἦν
δὲ πᾶς ὁ ἀγὼν τοῖσι κατὰ θάλασσαν περὶ τοῦ Εὐρίπου,
ὥσπερ τοῖσι ἀμφὶ Λεωνίδην τὴν ἐσβολὴν φυλάσσειν. οἱ μὲν
δὴ παρεκελεύοντο ὅκως μὴ παρήσουσι ἐς τὴν Ἑλλάδα τοὺς

---

15. 1 τι : τε ? Kallenberg　　　　2 νῆας **B** ‖ σφέας **B**　　　　4 παρα-
σκευασάμενοι **B** ‖ ἀνήγαγον τὰς νῆας **B**　　　5 τὰς αὐτὰς ταύτας ἡμέρας (R,
Stein¹) **B** : (τὰς αὐτὰς ἡμέρας R, Stein²) : ταῖς αὐταῖς ἡμέραις **a** etc. probante
Cobet ‖ τε om. **a**　　　8 λεωνίδεα **B**Pz　　　9 παρήσωσι(ν V) **B**

---

should have waited again until late
afternoon before delivering an attack,
is not clear. Possibly the 'Kilikian'
vessels (100 strong originally, 7. 91),
on which they 'fell,' were only now
coming to Aphetai for the first time.

15. 1. τρίτῃ δὲ ἡμέρῃ, 'on the third
day' (say Tuesday); the article omitted
with the ordinal. δεινὸν ποιέεσθαι : cp.
7. 1. τι, if correct, aggravates δεινόν.

οἱ στρατηγοί : Achaimenes, Ariabignes, Prexaspes, Megabazos ; cp. 7.
97, 236. But who was in command of
the flying squadron ?

2. τὸ ἀπὸ Ξέρξεω : an admirable
vagueness invests the phrase with all
the more serious possibilities. But they
were probably acting under the king's
orders.

3. ἔτι : any further, as on the two
days previous, when the Greeks had
been left to take the initiative ; a fact
which supports the view that the real
assault on Thermopylai was postponed
till 'the third day' ; and that the two
engagements at sea, on the first and on
the second afternoons, were little more
than manœuvres, by which the Greeks
cut off straggling or belated squadrons
of the Persian fleet. With the news of
the wreck of the 200 vessels off Euboia
the Persian admirals were driven to
attempt a frontal attack. They opened,
about the time when Hydarnes was
descending the mountain, upon 'the
Middle Gate' at Thermopylai ; cp. 7.
225.

4. On μέσον ἡμέρης cp. c. 23 infra.

5. συνέπιπτε δὲ ὥστε κτλ. Hdt.
apparently treats this essential synchronism as purely fortuitous. He

follows up this oversight by the misconception that the whole and sole
object of the Greek fleet was to defend
the Euripos, as that of Leonidas to hold
the pass. Every one can now see that
the Greeks at Artemision were covering
Leonidas, and that Leonidas was making
it possible, yea, necessary, for the fleet
to remain at Artemision. On which of
the two correlated points the Greeks
desired the more stress to be laid is a
further question, less easy of solution ;
perhaps they were not quite at one on
this matter. So much is clear, that a
really decisive victory off Artemision
might have saved Thermopylai and
Athens to boot. On the first two days,
according to their own account, the
Greek sea-dogs assumed the offensive
(though late in the afternoon !), and won
two victories ; but on the third day,
when the Persian admirals are earlier
on the move, it is the turn of the Greeks
ἀτρέμας ἔχειν. The manœuvres of this
day reproduce to a great extent the
manœuvres reported c. 11 supra of the
first engagement (ναυμαχίη καρτέρη), or,
more probably, the really severe engagement on the third day has been discounted and transferred, in maiorem
gloriam Atheniensium, to the first.

9. παρεκελεύοντο : there is a παρα-
κέλευσις on each side, marking this day's
engagement as the climax and the chief
battle. Is a set speech (παραίνεσις) or
mere casual exhortation to be understood ?

ὅκως μὴ παρήσουσι seems rather
to introduce the purpose or result of
the appeals than their actual contents
or substance, which the infinitive (with-

βαρβάρους, οἱ δ᾽ ὅκως τὸ Ἑλληνικὸν στράτευμα διαφθείραντες 10
τοῦ πόρου κρατήσουσι. ὡς δὲ ταξάμενοι οἱ Ξέρξεω ἐπέπλεον, 16
οἱ Ἕλληνες ἀτρέμας εἶχον πρὸς τῷ Ἀρτεμισίῳ. οἱ δὲ
βάρβαροι μηνοειδὲς ποιήσαντες τῶν νεῶν ἐκυκλοῦντο, ὡς
περιλάβοιεν αὐτούς. ἐνθεῦτεν οἱ Ἕλληνες ἐπανέπλεόν τε καὶ
συνέμισγον. ἐν ταύτῃ τῇ ναυμαχίῃ παραπλήσιοι ἀλλήλοισι 5
ἐγίνοντο. ὁ γὰρ Ξέρξεω στρατὸς ὑπὸ μεγάθεός τε καὶ πλήθεος
αὐτὸς ὑπ᾽ ἑωυτοῦ ἔπιπτε, ταρασσομενέων τε τῶν νεῶν καὶ
περιπιπτουσέων περὶ ἀλλήλας· ὅμως μέντοι ἀντεῖχε καὶ οὐκ
εἶκε· δεινὸν γὰρ χρῆμα ἐποιεῦντο ὑπὸ νεῶν ὀλιγέων ἐς φυγὴν
τράπεσθαι. πολλαὶ μὲν δὴ τῶν Ἑλλήνων νέες διεφθείροντο 10
πολλοὶ δὲ ἄνδρες, πολλῷ δ᾽ ἔτι πλεῦνες νέες τε τῶν βαρβάρων
καὶ ἄνδρες. οὕτω δὲ ἀγωνιζόμενοι διέστησαν χωρὶς ἑκάτεροι.
ἐν ταύτῃ τῇ ναυμαχίῃ Αἰγύπτιοι μὲν τῶν Ξέρξεω στρατιωτέων 17

---

10 δὲ B   11 κρατήσουσι P: κρατήσωσι(ν S) reliqui   16. 1 ἐπέ-
πλωον Bz   3 νηῶν B || ἐκυκλοῦντο Stein²⁸, van H.: ἐκυκλεῦντο Reiske,
Stein¹, Holder: ἐκυκλέοντο B: ἐκυκλεύοντο a etc.   5 συνέσμιγον A
6 ἐγένοντο Bz   7 ταρασσομένων Ad: παρατασσομένων B || νηῶν B
9 χρῆμα del. van H. || ἐποιέοντο BPz || ὀλίγων codd. z, Holder, van H. ||
φυγεῖν B   10 τραπέσθαι codd. z || νέες om. A¹: νῆες B   11
δὲ: τε B   12 ἀγωνισάμενοι Schweighaeuser, van H.

---

out the final conjunction) might express;
cp. App. Crit. Most mss. have κρατή-
σωσι infra.

11. τοῦ πόρου here clearly means the
actual waterway; cp. 7. 36.

16. 1. ταξάμενοι, 'having put themselves in battle-array.' οἱ Ξέρξεω
(unconsciously) suggests the presence of
his majesty, who thus preserves in this,
as in the previous chapter, the sovran
power and command.

3. μηνοειδὲς .. ἐκυκλοῦντο: cp. c. 10
supra ἐκυκλοῦντο αὐτοὺς ἐς μέσον. The
manœuvres are apparently identical.

4. ἐπανέπλεον: just as on the first day
(c. 9 supra), after all, without waiting
to be actually attacked; cp. c. 11 supra.

5. παραπλήσιοι ἀλλήλοισι ἐγίνοντο.
This phrase cannot mean that the Greeks
and Persians had equal forces engaged
(as a result of the efforts of the Deus ex
machina of c. 13 supra), for Hdt. goes
on at once to admit that μέγαθος and
πλῆθος were both conspicuous on the
side of the king's fleet (στρατός). But
if the forces were still unequal, 'they
came to be on an equality,' because the
μέγαθος and the πλῆθος turned rather
to the disadvantage of the barbarians,
as Hdt. explains. The obvious ten-

dency of the passage is apologetic, and
apologetic in the Greek interest, for in
view of their derring deeds of the two
previous days (and, it might be added,
in view of the sequel at Salamis), surely
a crowning victory was now to have
been expected. No such victory could
be claimed for Artemision; but with
great subtilty the argument is converted
into an explanation of the failure of the
larger and more numerous force to effect
the complete discomfiture of the smaller!
(This view seems better than to see in
this passage the intention of an Asianic
source to explain the failure of the king's
fleet.)

7. αὐτὸς ὑπ᾽ ἑωυτοῦ ἔπιπτε: a formula
afterwards enlarged and converted into
the chief rationale of the Persian failure
in the whole war; cp. Thucyd. 1. 69. 5.

8. ἀντεῖχε καὶ οὐκ εἶκε: an unfortunate jingle. δεινὸν χρῆμα ἐποιεῦντο: cp.
c. 15 supra. The plain truth is that
the Persian fleet did not give way,
notwithstanding its cumbrous size and
numbers, but inflicted very heavy losses
upon the Greek. The tense in ἀγωνιζόμενοι is remarkable; cp. τρήσουσι in c.
14, and App. Crit. χωρὶς is pleonastic.

17. 1. Αἰγύπτιοι. It is curious that

ἠρίστευσαν, οἵ ἄλλα τε μεγάλα ἔργα ἀπεδέξαντο καὶ νέας
αὐτοῖσι ἀνδράσι εἷλον Ἑλληνίδας πέντε. τῶν δὲ Ἑλλήνων
κατὰ ταύτην τὴν ἡμέρην ἠρίστευσαν Ἀθηναῖοι καὶ Ἀθηναίων
5 Κλεινίης ὁ Ἀλκιβιάδεω, ὃς δαπάνην οἰκηίην παρεχόμενος
ἐστρατεύετο ἀνδράσι τε διηκοσίοισι καὶ οἰκηίῃ νηί.

18　　Ὡς δὲ διέστησαν, ἄσμενοι ἑκάτεροι ἐς ὅρμον ἠπείγοντο.

---

17. 2 ἔργα μεγάλα β, Holder, van H. ‖ νῆας β　　　5 κλεινίας α ‖
οἰκίην C　　　18. 1 οἱ δὲ ὡς διέστασαν β

---

the 'Egyptians' of all peoples should
most have distinguished themselves in
a sea-fight: perhaps the Egyptian
Aristeia was a compliment to their
Persian admiral Achaimenes (cp. 7. 236),
or that special account was taken of
their prejudices and inexperience !
Diodoros 11. 13. 2 awards the prize
(with more probability) to the Sidonians
(perhaps from Hdt. 7. 44).

στρατιωτέων: cp. c. 12 supra. The
five ships taken, men and all (αὐτοῖσι
ἀνδράσι), were presumably not Athenian,
notwithstanding c. 10 supra, or the
Athenians could hardly have obtained
the ἀριστεῖα on this day among the
Greeks. Cp. Plutarch de malig. Hdti.
34 = Mor. 867 ὁ μὲν Πίνδαρος, οὐκ ἂν
συμμάχου πόλεως, ἀλλὰ μηδίζειν αἰτίαν
ἐχούσης, ὅμως τοῦ Ἀρτεμισίου μνησθεὶς
ἐπιπεφώνηκεν, ὅθι παῖδες Ἀθαναίων ἐβά-
λοντο φαεννὰν κρηπῖδ' ἐλευθερίας. There
are three other citations of the same
Pindaric laud in Plutarch's works, viz.
Themist. 8 ; de glor. Ath. 7 = Mor. 350 ;
de s. num. v. 6 = Mor. 552 c.

5. Κλεινίης ὁ Ἀλκιβιάδεω. This
Kleinias, son of Alkibiades, is, of
course, the father of that better known
Alkibiades, the pupil of Sokrates, and
the author of so much woe to Athens
from 421 B.C. onwards. The name
'Alkibiades' is probably rather a Spartan
than an Athenian favourite (cp. Thuc.
8. 6. 3), and the elder Alkibiades, a
member of the great clan of the
Eurysakidai (Petersen, Hist. Gent. Att.
1880, p. 126), or rather of the Εὐπατρίδαι
(cp. Toepffer, Attische Genealogie, 1889,
pp. 175 ff.), had been at one time Spartan
πρόξενος in Athens, but had renounced
the office (Thuc. 5. 43. 2), perhaps in
consequence of his relations with Kleisthenes and the Alkmaionidai, a daughter
of which house, Deinarete by name, he
espoused, Alkibiades the younger, their
offspring, being thus related to Perikles

the son of Agariste (6. 131) on the
spindle side. The elder Alkibiades
had probably (with Aristeides, Xanthippos, and others) opposed the naval
policy of Themistokles, and had suffered
ostracism (see Appendix III. § 4), but,
if still alive, would have returned with
Aristeides (cp. c. 79 infra): that his
son Kleinias here defrays the expenses,
and more than all the expenses of a
τριηραρχία, seems to show that the father
was no longer alive in 480 B.C. (or that
the son had an independent fortune !).
A further question arises whether the
said Kleinias was alive or dead when
this passage was written by Hdt. But
alas ! this passage is consistent with
either alternative, and cannot be used
as conclusive of the date of composition.
Kleinias fell in the disastrous battle of
Koroneia in 447 B.C. (Plutarch, Alkib.
1), and the fact that his death is not
here mentioned might be taken to prove
that this passage was originally written
during his lifetime (cp. per contra the
case of Sophanes 9. 75); but, on the
other hand, (i.) this record might well
have been taken from a sepulchral
monument; (ii.) the disaster at Koroneia
might better be passed over in silence ;
(iii.) Hdt. might easily have inserted
a reference, had he wished to do so, in
the final revision of his work ; (iv.) he
has not always recorded the deaths of
eminent men, his dramatis personae, e.g.
Aristeides, Themistokles, Xanthippos,
and others.

δαπάνην οἰκηίην· οἰκηίῃ νηί: cp.
5. 47 for a parallel instance. At Athens,
in Hdt.'s time, the state provided the
'trierarch' with the hull, mast, pay and
rations for the men. On the trierarchy
cp. Appendix III. § 4.

18. 1. διέστησαν: without the superfluous χωρὶς of c. 17 supra. This day
had begun, as it ends, with joy, on
both sides ! cp. c. 14 supra. Stein cps.

οἱ δὲ Ἕλληνες ὡς διακριθέντες ἐκ τῆς ναυμαχίης ἀπηλλάχθησαν, τῶν μὲν νεκρῶν καὶ τῶν ναυηγίων ἐπεκράτεον, τρηχέως δὲ περιεφθέντες, καὶ οὐκ ἥκιστα Ἀθηναῖοι τῶν αἱ ἡμίσεαι τῶν νεῶν τετρωμέναι ἦσαν, δρησμὸν δὴ ἐβούλευον 5 ἔσω ἐς τὴν Ἑλλάδα. νόῳ δὲ λαβὼν ὁ Θεμιστοκλέης ὡς εἰ 19

---

2 ἀπαλλάχθησαν ! van H.   3 ναυγίων R : ναυηγέων S : ναυηγίων V   4 τρηχέος R : τρίχεως V   5 ἡμίσεαι z : ἡμίσειαι aPd : ἡμίσεε C : ἡμίσεες B ‖ νηῶν RS(V) ‖ ἐβουλεύοντο Cdz, van H. 19. 1 ὁ om. B, Holder

---

Od. 9. 62 f. ἔνθεν δὲ προτέρω πλέομεν ἀκαχήμενοι ἦτορ, Ἀσμενοι ἐκ θανάτοιο, φίλους ὀλέσαντες ἑταίρους.

2. διακριθέντες. The verb διακρίνειν is used of the physical separation of combatants in all three voices (Homer); cp. also Thuc. 1. 105. 5 μάχης γενομένης ἰσορρόπου . . διεκρίθησαν ἀπ' ἀλλήλων. (So in 3. 11. 2 of voluntary separation, secession, of allies.)

3. τῶν μὲν νεκρῶν καὶ τῶν ναυηγίων ἐπεκράτεον has a suggestion of victory about it, but probably is to be explained by the turn of the tide; cp. c. 12 supra. (May it be assumed that they buried the dead ?)

4. τρηχέως δὲ περιεφθέντες : cp. 5. 1. It is admitted that the Greeks had been very roughly handled in this naumachy; and perhaps the Athenians, to whom the Aristeia were awarded, had borne the brunt of the fray; but that "the half of their ships" (nigh one hundred) were damaged must surely be an exaggeration, in view of their subsequent condition at Salamis. True, they may have had further vessels in reserve, and they had some time to refit before Salamis; but most probably the τραύματα were of every variety, and the half of the ships were only 'more or less' damaged. τετρωμέναι ἦσαν seems to give a somewhat different meaning to ἐτέτρωντο, the ἦσαν not being a mere auxiliary; the ships were there still, though in a damaged condition (τιτρώσκειν of ships, Thuc. 4. 14. 1).

5. δρησμὸν δὴ ἐβούλευον : this would be for the third time, if we could trust c. 4 supra and 7. 182. Placed here the statement amounts to a confession of defeat; but it is even yet hardly credible, before the arrival of the bad news from Thermopylai, after which, indeed, there was no further room for debate or delay; cp. c. 21 infra.

19. 1. νόῳ δὲ λαβών : the dative may

be 'instrumental' or even 'locative'; the verb, which denotes physical action (9. 22, 119 etc.), may also denote a psychological act; cp. 9. 10 (6. 137, 4. 79).

ὁ Θεμιστοκλέης. The article may be taken to refer back to the occurrence of the name in c. 4 supra; cp. also c. 5. This fresh anecdote is less discreditable but hardly more credible, at least in its details and surroundings, than the other. Themistokles here assumes an initiative which belongs to Eurybiades (cp. c. 2 supra). Moreover, he summons the Strategoi to a council, when a council is already sitting (ἐβούλευον just above, cp. c. 21 infra). Further, he treats the question of retreat as settled, though that is just the question at issue—or rather, we may say, though Themistokles cannot have dreamt of retreat, so long as Leonidas held out; nor is it likely that Eurybiades and the Peloponnesian admirals committed themselves blindly to Themistokles. In the speech put into the Athenian's mouth two or three different devices with different objects are confusedly combined, and there is a suggestion of deceit and unscrupulousness imparted to the words and acts of Themistokles, quite in the style of the partisan legend. But that there is something historical at the back of this anecdote is likely enough. After retreat became inevitable, Themistokles and the Athenians perhaps volunteered, or were detailed, to cover the retreat (cp. c. 21). All along Themistokles (and the Athenians) will have been hoping and planning to detach the Ionians from the king's forces, perhaps to foment a new Ionian 'Revolt'; and Themistokles may have made or left appeals, addressed to the Ionians, behind him at Artemision (cp. c. 22 infra). The treatment of the Euboians and their flocks requires no justification; but the fires were not, we may suppose, merely sacrificial or

ἀπορραγείη ἀπὸ τοῦ βαρβάρου τό τε Ἰωνικὸν [φῦλον] καὶ τὸ
Καρικόν, οἷοί τε εἴησαν <ἂν> τῶν λοιπῶν κατύπερθε γενέσθαι,
ἐλαυνόντων τῶν Εὐβοέων πρόβατα ἐπὶ τὴν θάλασσαν ταύτην,
5 συλλέξας τοὺς στρατηγοὺς ἔλεγέ σφι ὡς δοκέοι ἔχειν τινὰ
παλάμην, τῇ ἐλπίζοι τῶν βασιλέος συμμάχων ἀποστήσειν
τοὺς ἀρίστους. ταῦτα μέν νυν ἐς τοσοῦτο παρεγύμνου, ἐπὶ

---

2 βαρβαρικοῦ z || φῦλον secl. Stein³ : post Καρικὸν transt. z   3
ἦσαν C || ἂν add. Werfer, Stein² || γίνεσθαι a, Stein¹   4 cf. comment.
infra || θάλασσαν, ταύτῃ B, Valla, Holder, edd. plerique : ταύτην del. van H.
6 ἐλπίζει Pdz || βασιλέως C : βασιλῆος z   7 τοσοῦτον B

---

culinary, but intended to deceive the Persians into the belief that the Greeks were still encamped at Artemision long after they had cleared out : a common stratagem (cp. Livy 22. 43. 6).

2. τοῦ βαρβάρου Baehr takes as masculine, and refers to the king; Stein, more subtly, as neuter, while admitting that the Attic form would be βαρβαρικοῦ, which is actually read ; cp. App. Crit.

τό τε Ἰωνικὸν [φῦλον] καὶ τὸ Καρικόν : including doubtless the Dorians in Karia, and the neighbouring islands, whom, however, Hdt. does not specify. When Themistokles is represented as calling the Ionio-Karian contingent τῶν βασιλέος συμμάχων τοὺς ἀρίστους, he is made to use language which represents neither the Persian nor the Herodotean view; cp. below.

3. τῶν λοιπῶν κατύπερθε γενέσθαι : the two latter words=κρατῆσαι, cp. cc. 60, 75, 136 etc. The Greek contingents in the Persian fleet amounted all told to some 400 (407) vessels, according to the navy-list in Bk. 7. 89 ff. ; the Ionio-Karian (+Dorian) in the stricter sense to exactly 200. Ariabignes was admiral of this squadron, but whether the Ionio-Karian division strictly corresponded to its title may be questioned. In either case the detachment of these contingents, especially after the losses of the king's fleet in the storm, or storms, would be a very serious blow. Baehr maintains that ἂν is not necessary in this apodosis.

4. ἐλαυνόντων τῶν Εὐβοέων πρόβατα, as usual ; but what the practice, or the phrase, has to say to the context here is anything but obvious. The fate of the sheep has nothing to do with the Ionian question, or the device for detaching the Ionians from the king's fleet. Is it possible that the whole line is a

mere gloss, which has made its way into the text, and at an absurd point ? It would come in more logically after ἔλεγέ σφι ὡς below, or after ἔλεγε in l. 8.

5. συλλέξας τοὺς στρατηγούς : Themistokles could not do that; and they were already collected in council. Hdt. has apparently 'contaminated' two or three different anecdotes : (1) the appeal to the Ionians ; (2) the provisioning of the fleet at the expense of the Euboians ; (3) the ruse by which the Persians were led to believe that the Greek fleet was still at its moorings, and the soldiers still ashore at Artemision.

6. παλάμην=τέχνην, Suidas sub v. The word is Homeric, but not in that meaning, which is, however, frequent in Pindar ; e.g. Ol. 13. 52 Σίσυφον μὲν πυκνότατον παλάμαις ὡς θεόν. Cp. Aristophanes, Wasps 644 f. δεῖ δέ σε παντοίας πλέκειν εἰς ἀπόφυξιν παλάμας. The word is especially appropriate on the lips of Themistokles, a veritable Palamedes.

συμμάχων . . τοὺς ἀρίστους : they are involuntary σύμμαχοι, but the word is used, perhaps, less in the derivative sense, of allies, than in the literal sense, of co-fighters ; 'the most valiant' they could scarce be truly called among the king's fighting men (have not the Egyptians just gained the Aristeia ! c. 17 supra) ; perhaps there is a slight Herodotean irony in the use of the term here.

7. ἐς τοσοῦτο παρεγύμνου, 'so much, and no more, he revealed' of his plan ; cp. 5. 50, 7. 99. With παρεγύμνου cp. 1. 126 ὁ Κῦρος παρεγύμνου τὸν πάντα λόγον.

ἐπὶ τοῖσι κατήκουσι πρήγμασι : pro praesenti rerum statu, Baehr. Cp. 5. 49.

δὲ τοῖσι κατήκουσι πρήγμασι τάδε ποιητέα σφι εἶναι ἔλεγε,
τῶν τε προβάτων τῶν Εὐβοϊκῶν καταθύειν ὅσα τις ἐθέλοι·
κρέσσον γὰρ εἶναι τὴν <σφετέρην> στρατιὴν ἔχειν ἢ τοὺς 10
πολεμίους· παραίνεέ τε προειπεῖν τοῖσι ἑωυτῶν ἑκάστους
πυρὰ ἀνακαίειν· κομιδῆς δὲ πέρι τὴν ὥρην αὐτῷ μελήσειν,
ὥστε ἀσινέας ἀπικέσθαι ἐς τὴν Ἑλλάδα. ταῦτα ἤρεσέ σφι
ποιέειν, καὶ αὐτίκα πυρὰ ἀνακαυσάμενοι ἐτράποντο πρὸς τὰ
πρόβατα. οἱ γὰρ Εὐβοέες, παραχρησάμενοι τὸν Βάκιδος 20
χρησμὸν ὡς οὐδὲν λέγοντα, οὔτε τι ἐξεκομίσαντο οὐδὲν οὔτε
προσεσάξαντο ὡς παρεσομένου σφι πολέμου, περιπετέα τε

8 τῆσι B ‖ εἶναί σφι(ν V) B : 'an σφι delendum ?' Kallenberg 9
εὐβοεικῶν CPz ‖ καταθύειν post ἐθέλοι z ‖ θέλοι B 10 <σφετέρην>
Stein⁽²⁾ ³ 11 ἑωυτοῦ ἕκαστον Cobet, van H. ‖ ἑκάστοις C 12
πυρὰ Cobet, Stein⁽²⁾ ³ : πῦρ codd., Stein¹, Holder, van H. : πυρὴν z ‖ αὐτῶν C
13 ἐς : ἐπὶ z 14 πυρὰ Cobet, van H., Stein² : πῦρ ‖ καυσόμενοι B ‖
ἐτρέποντο a 20. totum caput suspectum habeo 2 οὔτ'
ἐξεκομίσαντο βz, Holder : οὔτε ἐξεκομίσαντο P, van H. ‖ οὐδὲν alterum
delendum vid. nisi τι potius omiseris, aut saltem post προσεσάξαντο
transposueris 3 προεσάξαντο βz, Holder, van H. : προεφυλάξαντο Naber

9. καταθύειν : no doubt the sacrifice
was to be followed by a feast ; the
animals were to be eaten by the fleet.
Themistokles did not expect his men to
fight on an empty stomach.

11. παραίνεέ τε . . πυρὰ ἀνακαίειν :
there seems to be some confusion between
the fires for burning, or roasting, the
meat, and fires left burning, after the
retreat of the Greeks, in order to deceive
the enemy. It is not likely that the
Greeks postponed seizing the sheep until
the moment of their departure.

12. κομιδῆς δὲ πέρι : this sentence treats
the resolution to retreat as already
taken, at least by Themistokles. It
could not have been so, before the
disaster at Thermopylai was known.
τὴν ὥρην : cp. c. 14 supra.

20. 1. οἱ γὰρ Εὐβοέες : Blakesley endorses Schweighaeuser's observation that
the proper place for c. 20 is immediately
after c. 4 supra ; but the displacement
may be as old as Hdt.'s own composition.
In which case, or otherwise, the connexion seems to be that, à propos des
moutons, the question arises : how did
it happen that the sheep were there to
be looted after that fashion ! Why,
because the Euboians had made no preparations for the war, and that although
there was an oracle of Bakis to warn
them. But the authenticity of this
chapter is not above suspicion.

παραχρησάμενοι τὸν Βάκιδος
χρησμόν : παραχρᾶσθαι as in 4. 159, 1.
108 ; cp. 2. 141 τὸν ἐν ἀλογίῃσι ἔχειν
παραχρησάμενον τῶν μαχίμων, and 4. 150
ἀλογίην εἶχον τοῦ χρηστηρίου. The word
as used in 7. 223 has a further application. Βάκις may be connected with
βάζειν, βακ- to say, speak, though the
verb βακίζειν in Aristophanes Peace 1072
is no doubt formed from the proper
name. The word Βάκιδες is associated
with Σίβυλλαι by Aristotle, Probl. 30. 1 =
954 A, in such a way as to suggest that
the ancients themselves regarded the
name rather as a generic term than as
a proper name ; but there were two or
three Βάκιδες of especial fame, to whom
the title was successively appropriated,
a Boiotian, an Attic, an Arkadian. (Cp.
Pauly-Wissowa ii. 2802.) It is probably
the Boiotian of Eleon (cp. 5. 43) that
Hdt. believes himself to be quoting here,
and in cc. 77, 96 infra, and 9. 43.
Special collections of oracles of Bakis,
of Mussaios (cp. 7. 6), and others, had
come much into fashion in the seventh
and sixth centuries B.C. with the development, or revival, of mysteries, orgies,
and other religious consolations ; cp. E.
Rhode, Psyche (1894), pp. 351 ff. ; J. B.
Bury, Hist. of Greece, i. (1902) 335.

3. προσεσάξαντο : cp. 5. 34, 1. 190.
The v.l. προεσάξαντο, from προσάττειν,
is preferred also by Baehr and Sitzler.

ἐποιήσαντο σφίσι αὐτοὶ τὰ πρήγματα. Βάκιδι γὰρ ὧδε ἔχει
5 περὶ τούτων ὁ χρησμός.

　　φράζεο, βαρβαρόφωνος ὅταν ζυγὸν εἰς ἅλα βάλλῃ
　　βύβλινον, Εὐβοίης ἀπέχειν πολυμηκάδας αἶγας.

τούτοισι οὐδὲν τοῖσι ἔπεσι χρησαμένοισι ἐν τοῖσι τότε παρεοῦσί
τε καὶ προσδοκίμοισι κακοῖσι παρῆν σφι συμφορῇ χρᾶσθαι
10 πρὸς τὰ μέγιστα.

21　Οἵ μὲν δὴ ταῦτα ἔπρησσον, παρῆν δὲ ὁ ἐκ Τρηχῖνος
κατάσκοπος. ἦν μὲν γὰρ ἐπ' Ἀρτεμισίῳ κατάσκοπος Πολύας,
γένος Ἀντικυρεύς, τῷ προσετέτακτο, καὶ εἶχε πλοῖον κατῆρες
ἕτοιμον, εἰ παλήσειε ὁ ναυτικὸς στρατός, σημαίνειν τοῖσι ἐν

---

4 αὐτοὶ Stein[3] : αὐτοῖσι　　6 βαρβαρόφωνος Valla (barbarious) :
βαρβαρόφωνον ‖ ὅτ' ἂν A : ἐστὰν B ‖ ἄλλα β　　7 βύβλιον β ‖ πολὺ
μηκάδας SV, van H.　　8 τούτοισι δὲ β, Stein[1], Holder : 'an τούτοισι
δὴ ?' van H.　　9 χρῆσθαι a　　10 πρὸς : ἐς van H.　　21. 4
ἕτοιμον CPdz, van H. : del. Bekker ‖ παλήσιεν β : παλαίσειεν C : ἀπελάσειε
Valla (discessisset) : τι πταίσειε Valckenaer

περιπετέα τε ἐποιήσαντο . . τὰ
πρήγματα: sed res suas ipsi in summum
discrimen adduxerunt, Schweig. followed
by Baehr. περιπετής is used literally of
'falling round' or upon an object (cp.
Soph. Ai. 907, Ant. 1223); metaphorically, of 'falling in with' evil or misfortune. It may be used here with the
further suggestion of a sudden change
or reverse of fortune; but that seems
unnecessary. Rather the word here
appears to come short of its fuller force,
inasmuch as danger rather than actual
disaster appears indicated. At any rate
(as Stein observes), except for the sack
of Histiaiotis c. 23 infra, the Euboians
are not recorded to have suffered ; the
Persian fleet made straight from Histiaia
to Phaleron, c. 66 infra. The Euboians,
indeed, appear to have suffered almost
as much from their friends as from their
enemies.

6. ὅταν ζυγὸν εἰς ἅλα βάλλῃ βύβλινον
appears to be a clear reference to the
bridging of the sea (Hellespont) ; cp. 7.
25, 34, 36 ; though it might conceivably
refer merely to the employment of
byblos-hawsers for ordinary marine or
naval purposes. Cp. c. 77 infra.

7. πολυμηκάς appears to be an ἅπαξ
λεγ.

8. τούτοισι οὐδὲν τοῖσι ἔπεσι χρησαμένοισι. οὐδὲν χρησαμένοισι means
'after utterly neglecting, disregarding' ;
cp. 5. 72 τῇ κληδόνι οὐδὲν χρεώμενος.
The personal subject is supplied by σφι.

This short sentence is a clumsy and
inelegant one ; there are ten words in
the dative in four different constructions :
τούτοισι might be masculine, but for the
belated σφι ; χρησαμένοισι followed by
χρᾶσθαι and παρεοῦσι followed by παρῆν,
and παρῆν again by παρῆν in the next
line (c. 21), are stylistic abortions ; in
short, with the wry setting of the
chapter, and other peculiarities, doubts
as to its authenticity are legitimate.

21. 1. ἔπρησσον Stein takes = ἐποίεον
(cp. 4. 145), Sitzler as = ἔπαθον (sic). It
refers back to ταῦτα ἤρεσέ σφι ποιέειν
c. 19 supra. The μέν and δέ here almost
constitute a parataxis.

ὁ ἐκ Τρηχῖνος κατάσκοπος: the
article is explained by what follows.
That the scout, or aide-de-camp, is
described as ἐκ Τρηχῖνος, a place apparently in the hands of Xerxes, is
observable, but may be explained by
7. 176, where ἡ διὰ Τρηχῖνος ἔσοδος is
apparently used for the pass of Thermopylai, though it probably should have
denoted a different one ; cp. note ad l.c.

2. Πολύας γένος Ἀντικυρεύς. The
man's name seems to be unique. On
Antikyra cp. 7. 198, 213. Polyas was
presumably from the Malian city.

3. πλοῖον κατῆρες, a boat fitted, or
well-fitted with oars : κατήρης perhaps
= εὐήρης. The same stem is seen in
τριήρης etc. Cp. note to 7. 36.

4. παλήσειε : apparently from a verb
παλέω, the Ionic form of παλαίω (πάλη),

Θερμοπύλησι ἐοῦσι· ὡς δ᾽ αὔτως ἦν Ἀβρώνιχος ὁ Λυσικλέος 5
Ἀθηναῖος καὶ παρὰ Λεωνίδῃ ἕτοιμος τοῖσι ἐπ᾽ Ἀρτεμισίῳ
ἐοῦσι ἀγγέλλειν τριηκοντέρῳ, ἤν τι καταλαμβάνῃ νεώτερον τὸν
πεζόν. οὗτος ὢν ὁ Ἀβρώνιχος ἀπικόμενός σφι ἐσήμαινε τὰ
γεγονότα περὶ Λεωνίδην καὶ τὸν στρατὸν αὐτοῦ. οἱ δὲ ὡς
ἐπύθοντο ταῦτα, οὐκέτι ἐς ἀναβολὰς ἐποιεῦντο τὴν ἀποχώρησιν, 10
ἐκομίζοντο δὲ ὡς ἕκαστοι ἐτάχθησαν, Κορίνθιοι πρῶτοι, ὕστατοι
δὲ Ἀθηναῖοι. Ἀθηναίων δὲ νέας τὰς ἄριστα πλεούσας ἐπιλε- 22
ξάμενος Θεμιστοκλέης ἐπορεύετο περὶ τὰ πότιμα ὕδατα,

---

5 ως AB: ὡς Pdz ‖ ἀβρόνιχος B: ἀβρόνυχος d : Αβρώνυχος z
6 λεωνίδην S ‖ ἕτοιμος CPdz, van H.   8 ἀβρόνυχος d : Αβρώνυχος z
‖ ἐσήμηνε B   9 λεωνίδεα Bz ‖ <τε>καί? Kallenberg   10 οὐκ
ἐς ἀμβολὰς Cobet ‖ ἐποιέοντο BPz   11 Κορίνθιοι <μὲν>? Stein²
22. 1 νῆας B ‖ πλωούσας Bz

---

to wrestle, to engage; here obviously a euphemism for 'succumb' or 'encounter a fall.' Hesychius has the gloss παλήσεις· διαφθείρειε (διαφθαρείη Valckenaer). The emendation of the Herodotean text (cp. App. Crit.) is hardly necessary, but Baehr's note is worth consulting.

5. ὡς δ᾽ αὔτως: as in 9. 81 et al.

Ἀβρόνιχος ὁ Λυσικλέος: the same man, doubtless, who reappears in the winter of 479–8 B.C. as colleague of Themistokles and Aristeides in the embassy to Sparta about the fortification of Athens; Thuc. 1. 91. 3. Lysikles was a not uncommon name at Athens; the man here mentioned might be conceivably the grandfather of the well-known Lysikles, who belonged apparently to the entourage of Perikles; cp. Thuc. 3. 19. 1; Aristoph. Knights 765; Plutarch, Perikl. 24.

7. τριηκοντέρῳ: a galley with thirty oars; probably a distinction, without a difference, from πλοῖον κατῆρες supra.

ἤν τι καταλαμβάνῃ νεώτερον: νεώτερον is a familiar euphemism; καταλ., cp. c. 6 supra; but here with a suggestion of evil. Cp. εἰ παλήσειε supra, and for an inverse change of construction cp. 9. 48.

8. τὰ γεγονότα: a strict temporal pluperfect; περί, 'in the case of . .'

10. οὐκέτι ἐς ἀναβολὰς ἐποιεῦντο τὴν ἀποχώρησιν, 'considered the retreat no longer a matter for delay . .' That they could not strategically have retreated before the fall of Leonidas, nor reasonably have delayed afterwards, is not apparent to Hdt. Plutarch de

malig. Hdti. 34 = Mor. 867 puts the connexion more clearly: οὐδὲ γὰρ ἦν ὄφελος ἐνταῦθα καθημένους φρουρεῖν τὴν θάλασσαν, ἐντὸς Πυλῶν τοῦ πολέμου γεγονότος, καὶ Ξέρξου τῶν παρόδων κρατοῦντος.

11. ὡς ἕκαστοι ἐτάχθησαν, 'each contingent in order, as previously posted': these words, perhaps purposely introduced by Hdt., rob the record of the smear at the expense of the Korinthians, which it must otherwise have conveyed, and may have conveyed in its original Attic form. The Herodotean version is clearly acceptable: the retreat was a perfectly orderly proceeding; the Korinthians had apparently occupied the left wing of the fleet; the Athenians, probably at the suggestion of Themistokles, cp. c. 19 supra, remained somewhat in the rear to cover the retreat and to inscribe an appeal to their kinsmen and quondam allies now in the ranks of the Persian. On ὡς cp. c. 2 supra.

22. 2. Θεμιστοκλέης here puts into operation the παλάμη announced in c. 19 supra. The employment of ἐπιλεξάμενος followed by ἐπελέξαντο in a different sense (ἐπιλέγεσθαι eligere 6. 73, 7. 10, etc., legere c. 136 infra, etc.) is not quite happy: an 'unconscious iteration.'

ἐπορεύετο περὶ τὰ πότιμα ὕδατα: he would, of course, have to land in order to do this: what time of day was it? The battle had begun at mid-day, or somewhat later, c. 15 supra; the hour at which it ended has not been specified; but it had been a long and heavy engagement, in which half the Athenian vessels had been damaged (c.

ἐντάμνων ἐν τοῖσι λίθοισι γράμματα, τὰ Ἴωνες ἐπελθόντες τῇ
ὑστεραίη [ἡμέρῃ] ἐπὶ τὸ Ἀρτεμίσιον ἐπελέξαντο. τὰ δὲ
5 γράμματα τάδε ἔλεγε. "ἄνδρες Ἴωνες, οὐ ποιέετε δίκαια ἐπὶ
τοὺς πατέρας στρατευόμενοι καὶ τὴν Ἑλλάδα καταδουλούμενοι.
ἀλλὰ μάλιστα μὲν πρὸς ἡμέων γίνεσθε· εἰ δὲ ὑμῖν ἐστι τοῦτο
μὴ δυνατὸν ποιῆσαι, ὑμεῖς δὲ ἔτι καὶ νῦν ἐκ τοῦ μέσου ἡμῖν
ἔζεσθε καὶ αὐτοὶ καὶ τῶν Καρῶν δέεσθε τὰ αὐτὰ ὑμῖν ποιέειν.
10 εἰ δὲ μηδέτερον τούτων οἷόν τε γίνεσθαι, ἀλλ᾽ ὑπ᾽ ἀναγκαίης
μέζονος κατέζευχθε ἢ ὥστε ἀπίστασθαι, ὑμεῖς δὲ ἐν τῷ ἔργῳ,
ἐπεὰν συμμίσγωμεν, ἐθελοκακέετε, μεμνημένοι ὅτι ἀπ᾽ ἡμέων

3–5 τὰ . . γράμματα om. Β   4 ἡμέρῃ damn. van H., Stein³
5 τάδε ἔλεγε : λέγοντα τάδε Β   7 γίνεσθαι α, 'forsan recte' van H.
8 ὑμέες ΒΡz   9 ἵζεσθε malit van H. : ἔσεσθε Βz ‖ δέεσθαι Β ‖ ταῦτα R :
(ταυτὰ SV)   10 ἀνάγκης μείζονος α   11 ὥστε μὴ ἀπίστασθαι Β ‖
δὲ : γε ΒΡz, Holder   12 συμμίξωμεν d

---

18 supra): then, according to Hdt., a
council was held—the account of which
is obscure. Then, the news of the
disaster at Thermopylai is brought by
Abronichos, and retreat becomes at once
inevitable ; but Themistokles now proceeds to carry out his projected παλάμη.
How many the springs, or fountains, to
which the device was applied Hdt. does
not say.

3. ἐντάμνων ἐν τοῖσι λίθοισι γράμματα.
We are to understand that these inscriptions were incised (and coloured ?) in the
living rocks, or in some cases in the
stones (marble) with which the springs,
or cisterns, were fenced and builded.
These inscriptions were read by the
Ionians on the very next day; cp. c.
23 infra: were they ever read by any
other mortals thereafter ? How many
times the inscription was reproduced by
Themistokles Hdt. does not specify, but
he gives the ipsissima verba, which ' cut
the record,' for argument and rhetoric
in inscriptions, a veritable ' sermon in
stones' ; had Hdt. copied the same ?
Did ' Ionians' remember and report
them at home ? Is the anecdote an Attic
invention ? The appeal reads in any
case more like a letter or an oral address
than like a hastily cut inscription, and
that in duplicate. There was no need
to cut these inscriptions ; they might as
well have been simply written or painted
up.

4. τὰ δὲ γράμματα τάδε ἔλεγε : a
conclusive proof of the use of λέγειν,

λόγοι, et sim. for script. The order of
the words τάδε ἔλεγε is unusual, but
occurs also 2. 136 in a less abrupt form.

5. ἐπὶ τοὺς πατέρας : cp. 7. 51, where
the same point and the same moral are
urged by Artabanos.

7. μάλιστα μὲν . . εἰ δὲ . . μή :
perhaps the earliest instance of the
employment of this rhetorical formula ;
cp. Thuc. 1. 40. 4, Plato Rep. 590 D, etc.

8. ὑμεῖς δέ : a genuine δέ in apodosi ;
the construction is repeated immediately
below ; cp. 7. 50, and Index.

ἐκ τοῦ μέσου ἡμῖν ἔζεσθε, ' assume
a neutral position' ; cp. 4. 118 ὑμεῖς ὧν
μηδενὶ τρόπῳ ἐκ τοῦ μέσου κατήμενοι
περιίδητε ἡμέας διαφθαρέντας. Also 3. 83
and c. 73 infra. ἡμῖν dat. ethicus, ' we
pray you'—

9. τῶν Καρῶν δέεσθε : cp. c. 19 supra ;
and for δέεσθαι cc. 3, 4 supra.

10. εἰ δὲ μηδέτερον τούτων : three
courses are open to the Ionians, more
or less consistent with their duty to
their fathers : (i.) μάλιστα μέν, to desert
the Persian and join the Greeks (πρὸς
Ἑλλήνων γίνεσθαι) ; (ii.) εἰ δὲ μή, to
leave the Persian and assume a neutral
position (ἐκ τοῦ μέσου ἔζεσθαι, κατῆσθαι) ;
(iii.) to play the Persian false in the hour
of battle (ἐν τῷ ἔργῳ ἐθελοκακέειν).

11. μέζονος . . ἢ ὥστε ἀπίστασθαι.
The conjunction ὥστε is not de rigueur
in this construction of the infinitive
after a comparative, but is certainly in
place ; cp. Madvig, G. S. 150 c.

γεγόνατε καὶ ὅτι ἀρχῆθεν ἡ ἔχθρη πρὸς τὸν βάρβαρον ἀπ'
ὑμέων ἡμῖν γέγονε." Θεμιστοκλέης δὲ ταῦτα ἔγραφε, δοκέειν
ἐμοί, ἐπ' ἀμφότερα νοέων, ἵνα ἢ λαθόντα τὰ γράμματα βασιλέα 15
Ἴωνας ποιήσῃ μεταβαλεῖν καὶ γενέσθαι πρὸς ἑωυτῶν, ἢ ἐπείτε
ἀνενειχθῇ καὶ διαβληθῇ πρὸς Ξέρξην, ἀπίστους ποιήσῃ τοὺς
Ἴωνας καὶ τῶν ναυμαχιέων αὐτοὺς ἀπόσχῃ.

Θεμιστοκλέης μὲν ταῦτα ἐνέγραψε. τοῖσι δὲ βαρβάροισι **23**
αὐτίκα μετὰ ταῦτα πλοίῳ ἦλθε ἀνὴρ Ἱστιαιεὺς ἀγγέλλων
τὸν δρησμὸν τὸν ἀπ' Ἀρτεμισίου τῶν Ἑλλήνων. οἳ δ' ὑπ'
ἀπιστίης τὸν μὲν ἀγγέλλοντα εἶχον ἐν φυλακῇ, νέας δὲ ταχέας
ἀπέστειλαν προκατοψομένας· ἀπαγγειλάντων δὲ τούτων τὰ ἦν, 5
οὕτω δὴ ἅμα ἡλίῳ σκιδναμένῳ πᾶσα ἡ στρατιὴ ἐπέπλεε ἀλὴς
ἐπὶ τὸ Ἀρτεμίσιον. ἐπισχόντες δὲ ἐν τούτῳ τῷ χώρῳ μέχρι

---

13 ἀρχῆθεν post ἔχθρη d ‖ ἡ om. B   14 δὲ om. B ‖ ἔγραψε B,
Holder, van H. : ἐνέγραφε? hic idem   16, 17 ποιήσει (bis) B ‖ μετα-
βαλέειν B ‖ ἐπείτε : ἐπεὰν Krueger, van H. ‖ ἀνενεχθῆι AB ‖ ξέρξεα BPz
18 συμμαχιέων z   23. 2 ἱστιεὺς Pd : ἱστιεὺς C : Ἰστιεὺς z   3
δὲ B   4 νῆας Bz ‖ ταχείας codd. z   5 τουτέων a   6 οὕτωι B ‖
ἁμ' CPdz ‖ ἔπλεε P, Holder : ἔπλωε(ν V) Bz, van H. ‖ ἀλὴς a : ἀλλὴς B

---

13. ἀρχῆθεν ἡ ἔχθρη: a parallel argument is addressed to the Athenians by the Spartans c. 142 *infra*. The reference here is, of course, to the Ionian revolt and the part taken by Athens therein; but, as Hdt. 5. 73, 96, 97 clearly shows, the *casus belli* between Athens and Persia was already in existence before Athens espoused the cause of the Ionians, and the participation in the Ionian revolt was the effect and not the cause of the Athenian enmity with Sardes and with Susa.

14. δοκέειν ἐμοί, ἐπ' ἀμφότερα νοέων: was this very obvious design really a discovery of Hdt.'s, or was the double-mindedness of Themistokles other than commendable?

16. μεταβαλεῖν, intransitive; 7. 52.

17. καὶ διαβληθῇ: sc. τὰ γράμματα; a curious phrase, though the meaning of διαβάλλειν cannot be doubtful; cp. 5. 50, 97 etc. But the sentence is rather clumsy, τὰ γράμματα as the subject of τοιήσῃ and of ἀπόσχῃ being harsh.

ἀπίστους, passive; 9. 98.

23. 2. αὐτίκα μετὰ ταῦτα: still at night?

πλοίῳ: the size of this boat is not specified; was the man of Histiaia alone in it? And why is not his proper name

given? The retreat is a δρησμός—is that the man's word, or Hdt.'s?

3. ὑπ' ἀπιστίης: the man evidently went to Aphetai; if the Persian admirals actually disbelieved his report, they can hardly have heard as yet of the capture of Thermopylai. **εἶχον ἐν φυλακῇ**, 'kept under arrest.'

5. τούτων, masculine, of the men on the ships; cp. 7. 179. 4 *supra*. **τὰ ἦν**: the true state of the case, the facts.

6. ἅμα ἡλίῳ σκιδναμένῳ: dawn of the fourth day (say Wednesday); the phrase is peculiar: σκίδναμαι (σκίδνημι), cp. 7. 141 (σκιδναμένης Δημήτερος), here seems to refer to the dispersion of light, the diffusion of rays by the sun. Blakesley cps. Milton's "Morn sowing the earth with orient pearl." Cp. also Aischyl. *Pers.* 502 πρὶν σκεδασθῆναι θεοῦ Ἀκτῖνας. Also *Psalm* 97. 11 (R.V. "Light is sown for the righteous").

πᾶσα ἡ στρατιή: sc. ἡ ναυτική.

ἀλής, without stragglers, and without detaching any scouts, etc., *en masse*.

7. ἐπισχόντες . . μέχρι μέσου ἡμέρης: the hour at which they had moved out to battle on the previous day (c. 15 *supra*, which also shows that μέσου here is neuter). The double omission of

μέσου ἡμέρης, τὸ ἀπὸ τούτου ἔπλεον ἐς Ἰστιαίην· ἀπικόμενοι
δὲ τὴν πόλιν ἔσχον τῶν Ἰστιαιέων, καὶ τῆς Ἑλλοπίης μοίρης
10 γῆς δὲ τῆς Ἰστιαιώτιδος τὰς παραθαλασσίας κώμας πάσας
ἐπέδραμον.

24 Ἐνθαῦτα δὲ τούτων ἐόντων, Ξέρξης ἑτοιμασάμενος τὰ περὶ
τοὺς νεκροὺς ἔπεμπε ἐς τὸν ναυτικὸν στρατὸν κήρυκα, προετοι-
μάσατο δὲ τάδε· ὅσοι τοῦ στρατοῦ τοῦ ἑωυτοῦ ἦσαν νεκροὶ
ἐν Θερμοπύλῃσι (ἦσαν δὲ καὶ δύο μυριάδες), ὑπολιπόμενος

8 ἔπλωον βα, van H. ‖ ἰστιαίην Cd   9 ἰστιαιέων S: ἰστιαίων ‖
ἐλλογίμης B   10 ἰστιαιώτιδος Cd: ἰστιαιητίδος B ‖ τὰς om. B
24. 1 τὰ om. B   2 στρατὸν om. B ‖ προητοιμάσατο a   3 τοῦ
post στρατοῦ om. C   4 καὶ: ὡς Naber ‖ ὑπολειπόμενος C(superscr.) d :
ὑπολοιπόμενος s

the article may be easily understood in
a colloquialism. There is no eagerness
to pursue the Greek fleet ; cp. c. 10 *supra*.
τὸ ἀπὸ τούτου appears to be temporal.

9. τὴν πόλιν ἔσχον: cp. 7. 164 for
the strong ἔχω. They seem to have
had no resistance to encounter. Ἰστιαία
(ἡ) suffered afterwards a worse fate from
the Athenians in 446 B.C., Ἑστιαιᾶς δὲ
ἐξοικίσαντες αὐτοὶ τὴν γῆν ἔσχον, Thuc.
1. 114. 3 ; cp. Hicks, *Manual*,³ p. 65,
though there is no reference to that
catastrophe here. It hardly seems likely
that Histiaia was no more and its place
taken by Oreos (the name which yet
prevails) when Hdt. wrote this passage ;
in other words, the first draft of his
history is appreciably older than the
thirty years' truce ; cp. Introduction, § 9.

τῆς Ἑλλοπίης μοίρης γῆς δὲ τῆς
Ἰστιαιώτιδος: commentators (so Rawlinson, Baehr) have misunderstood the
relation of these terms, and made ἡ
Ἑλλοπίη μοίρη a part of *Histiaiotis* ; as
Stein rightly points out, γῆς δέ is a
"second closer definition," according to
a regular use of δέ, cp. 1. 114. The
Persians did not over-run Euboia, but
only Ellopia, or Hellopia, nor all Hellopia,
but only Histiaiotis, nor yet quite all
Histiaiotis, but only τὰς παραθαλασσίας
κώμας—though not one of those they
spared (πάσας). The Persians did not
venture far from their ships. Hellopia
is no doubt the land of the Ἕλλοπες,
an interesting and surely primitive folk,
in view of their congeners Δρύοπες,
Δόλοπες, Κέκροπες (Κεκροπίδαι), Κύκλοπες
(Κύκλωπες), Πέλοπες (Πελοπίδαι) and
others like. Perhaps Ἕλλοπες is not
far removed from Ἕλληνες itself ; Strabo

445 gives Ἑλλοπία as a name for Euboia,
ἀπὸ Ἕλλοπος τοῦ Ἴωνος. Elsewhere (328)
he quotes Philochoros as saying τὸν περὶ
Δωδώνην τόπον, ὥσπερ τὴν Εὔβοιαν,
Ἑλλοπίαν κληθῆναι (on the authority of
Hesiod) ; and connects Ἑλλοί (Σελλοί)
and Ἕλλοπες.

24. 1. τὰ περὶ τοὺς νεκρούς, the title
of this anecdote, which seems quite
independent of the record in 7. 238.

4. καὶ δύο μυριάδες, 'about (even)
twenty thousand' : of these the king
buried 19,000 and left 1000 unburied,
as a preparation for the ensuing comedy.
The figures and the farce are alike incredible : 20,000 men cannot have fallen
at Thermopylai, still less could 19,000
have been so speedily interred ; nor is
it by any means certain that the Persian
king would have caused them to be interred at all—exposure being perhaps
the Persian custom ; cp. 7. 117—though
doubtless he would have permitted the
various nations concerned each to follow
its own rite. Nor, had the king
attempted such a fraud, could he have
hoped to silence men's tongues, or befool
their eyes. It is likely enough that a
good many of the slain had been interred
before the visitors from the fleet made
their appearance at Thermopylai ; for
the rest, the anecdote seems to be part
of the comic Nemesis which Greek
anecdote-mongers inflicted upon Xerxes
(cp. Introduction, § 11). It forms in
any case a contrast to the Spartan review
of the Persian dead at Marathon, 6. 120
—a truly dignified proceeding. Perhaps
ἐς χιλίους represents about the numbers
of the Persian slain in the third engagement.

τούτων ὡς χιλίους, τοὺς λοιποὺς τάφρους ὀρυξάμενος ἔθαψε, 5
φυλλάδα τε ἐπιβαλὼν καὶ γῆν ἐπαμησάμενος, ἵνα μὴ ὀφθείησαν
ὑπὸ τοῦ ναυτικοῦ στρατοῦ. ὡς δὲ διέβη ἐς τὴν Ἱστιαίην ὁ
κῆρυξ, σύλλογον ποιησάμενος παντὸς τοῦ στρατοπέδου ἔλεγε
τάδε. " ἄνδρες σύμμαχοι, βασιλεὺς Ξέρξης τῷ βουλομένῳ ὑμέων
παραδίδωσι ἐκλιπόντα τὴν τάξιν καὶ ἐλθόντα θεήσασθαι ὅκως 10
μάχεται πρὸς τοὺς ἀνοήτους τῶν ἀνθρώπων, οἳ ἤλπισαν τὴν
βασιλέος δύναμιν ὑπερβαλέεσθαι." ταῦτα ἐπαγγειλαμένου, 25
μετὰ ταῦτα οὐδὲν ἐγίνετο πλοίων σπανιώτερον· οὕτω πολλοὶ
ἤθελον θεήσασθαι. διαπεραιωθέντες δὲ ἐθηεῦντο διεξιόντες τοὺς
νεκρούς· πάντες δὲ ἠπιστέατο τοὺς κειμένους εἶναι πάντας
Λακεδαιμονίους καὶ Θεσπιέας, ὁρῶντες καὶ τοὺς εἵλωτας. οὐ 5

---

6 φυλλάδα A[1] : φυλλάδας S || ἐπιβάλλων B   7 ἱστιαίην Cd
9 ξύμμαχοι z   10 καὶ om. B, Holder || θεήσεσθαι Ask.   12
βασιλέως C : βασιλῆος z || ὑπερβαλέσθαι B : ὑπερβαλεῖσθαι van H.
25. 2 ἐγένετο CP   3 θεήσεσθαι z || ἐθηέοντο SV : ἐθηεῦντο . . δὲ om.
R   4 πάντες : πάντας Cobet || πάντας del. idem   5 καὶ Θεσπιέας
suspecta mihi || ὁρῶντες a : ὁρέωντες C : ὁρέοντες B, etc., Stein[1]

---

5. τάφρους ὀρυξάμενος : cp. τάφρον
μεγάλην ὀρύξαντες c. 28 infra. The king
did not work with is own hands,
ἐπιβαλών notwithstanding.
6. φυλλάδα τε ἐπιβαλὼν καὶ γῆν
ἐπαμησάμενος. Stein takes φ. ἐπιβ. as
a hysteron proteron with γ. ἐπαμ. The
earth would first be filled in, heaped up
(ἐπαμάομαι), and the leaves then strawed
over to conceal the diggings. φυλλάς,
collective, like λιθάς, νιφάς, ἱππάς.
ἵνα μὴ ὀφθείησαν : sc. αἱ τάφροι
rather than οἱ νεκροί. With the construction cp. c. 7 supra.
8. σύλλογον ποιησάμενος : cp. c. 88
infra.
παντὸς τοῦ στρατοπέδου : sc. τοῦ
ναυτικοῦ. He would need an interpreter,
or rather a number of interpreters, to
address the motley array.
9. σύμμαχοι is polite ; cp. c. 19 supra.
10. παραδίδωσι, 'permits, gives leave';
in 6. 103, with a slightly different suggestion, the victor Miltiades παραδιδοῖ
Πεισιστράτῳ ἀνακηρυχθῆναι.
12. ὑπερβαλέεσθαι : superare, 7. 39,
163.
25. 1. ἐπαγγειλαμένου : the king,
through his herald. On the word cp.
7. 1.
2. οὐδὲν ἐγίνετο πλοίων σπανιώτερον :
they went across in small boats, and
the supply was soon exhausted. Their

own πλοῖα were still perhaps at Aphetai,
and only the local stock available.
Some of these might make the passage
more than once ; it must have been a
busy scene, the straits alive with small
craft ; but there is a suspicion of persiflage about Hdt.'s expression.
3. διεξιόντες, between the Greek on
the one hand and the Persian on the
other ; or perhaps, more generally,
passing right through the Greek dead ;
cp. 7. 39. (It is not clear that the
1000 were lying about, scattered where,
ex hypothesi, they had fallen.)
4. ἠπιστέατο, 'were firmly convinced'
—though utterly mistaken. The word
with Hdt. carries no implication of
scientific or accurate knowledge, but can
scarcely be a mere synonym for νομίζειν.
If καὶ Θεσπιέας (cp. 7. 222) be not a
gloss, it is explained by the next words.
Or should it follow ὁρῶντες ?
5. ὁρῶντες καὶ τοὺς εἵλωτας. The
argument is not clear, for Helots were
in a sense 'Lakedaimonians'; did the
sight-seers mistake Helots for Thespians ? But cp. previous note. Except
for 7. 229, this is the only express
indication of the presence of Helots at
Thermopylai. Though the sight-seers
fell into this error about the Greek dead
(a strange error, with the Greeks from
the king's navy among them !), they

μὲν οὐδ' ἐλάνθανε τοὺς διαβεβηκότας Ξέρξης ταῦτα πρήξας
περὶ τοὺς νεκροὺς τοὺς ἑωυτοῦ· καὶ γὰρ δὴ καὶ γελοῖον ἦν·
τῶν μὲν χίλιοι ἐφαίνοντο [νεκροὶ] κείμενοι, οἱ δὲ πάντες ἐκέατο
ἀλέες συγκεκομισμένοι ἐς τὠυτὸ χωρίον, τέσσερες χιλιάδες.
10 ταύτην μὲν τὴν ἡμέρην πρὸς θέην ἐτράποντο, τῇ δ' ὑστεραίῃ
οἱ μὲν ἀπέπλεον ἐς Ἱστιαίην ἐπὶ τὰς νέας, οἱ δὲ ἀμφὶ Ξέρξην
ἐς ὁδὸν ὁρμέατο.

26   Ἧκον δέ σφι αὐτόμολοι ἄνδρες ἀπ' Ἀρκαδίης ὀλίγοι τινές,

---

6 ξέρξης δὲ B   8 νεκροὶ secl. Stein²   9 τέσσαρες Cd : τέσσερες
χιλιάδες del. Heraeus, Holder : (χειλιάδες van H. constanter)   10 δὲ B
11 ἀπέπλωον B ‖ ιστιαίην d ‖ νῆας Bz ‖ ξέρξεα B   12 ὡρμέατο Pdz

---

were not taken in by the (supposed)
trick devised by the king, as above described, in relation to the dead bodies
of his own warriors.

7. καὶ γὰρ δὴ καὶ γελοῖον ἦν: the
comic Nemesis proceeds.

8. τῶν μὲν . . κείμενοι: of the Persian
side a' thousand were to be seen lying
(about on the field, just where they had
fallen !) ; meantime 19,000 had been
collected and buried !

οἱ δὲ . . τέσσερες χιλιάδες. Hdt.
apparently means that the king had
caused all the Greek bodies to be collected
in one place. It is possible that something of the kind had been done ; in
any case the χωρίον, the spot where the
Greek dead would be thickest piled, was
no doubt the hill on which the last
stand had been made ; 7. 225ff. Around
the hill might well be lying the corpses
of the king's men, where they had fought
and fallen. Stein thinks the object (of
the king—or the story-teller !) was to
make it appear that 4000 Greeks had
been slain by 1000 Persians, 4 Greeks
by each Persian (je vier von einem); but,
really, neither Hdt., nor in the last resort
Xerxes, can well have expected any one
to believe that the 4000 dead Greeks had
been slain wholly and solely by the dead
Persians ! The trick was devised, or
supposed to have been devised, to exhibit the proportional losses on each
side. The figure 4000 for the Greek
dead comes no doubt from a misapplica-
tion of the epigram in 7. 228, which
gives 4000 as the number of Peloponnesians who fought, not the number of
Greeks who fell, at Thermopylai. Stein
here seems to overlook ἐκ Πελοποννάσου
there and makes the 4000 include
Thebans and Thespians. 3100 Pelopon-

nesian Hoplites are accounted for in
7. 202 ; but there were probably 1000
'Lakedaimonians' to boot, even not
including the Helots ; or the 4000
might less probably be made up of 3100 +
900 Helots, 3 for each Spartiate. The
actual number of Greek fighting men at
Thermopylai, first and last, far exceeded
4000 : albeit they may not all have
been posted at Thermopylai proper ;
cp. l.c.

10. ταύτην μὲν τὴν ἡμέρην : there has
been no clear indication of a change of
day since the dawn of the ὑστεραίῃ (cp.
cc. 22, 23 supra) of the battle ; but it
seems more natural, considering all that
has taken place in the interval, to reckon
'this day' here as a different one, i.e. at
least the 'fifth' day of the memorable
week : τῇ ὑστεραίῃ would then be the
sixth. The story and journal of the
fleet is here dropped, not to be renewed
till c. 66 infra.

26. 1. ἧκον : i.e. before the Persians
left Thermopylai. These Arkadian
medizers, or mercenaries, were long ago
traced to Karyai (vide Schweighaeuser
in loco) on the strength of Vitruvius 1.
1, who, in explaining the origin of
Caryatides (in architecture), mentioned
that Carya had joined the Persians
against Greece. A medizing movement
in Arkadia might help, with the attitude of Argos, to explain a good deal in
the policy of the Peloponnesians during
the war ; but does this anecdote go
beyond a mercenary adventure ! Even
so, it is significant of the miserable lack
of pan-Hellenic sentiment or loyalty in
the peninsula ; albeit these very men
have a word to say concerning the
Olympiad, a celebration which existed
to emphasize the 'Unity of Hellas' ; cp.

βίου τε δεόμενοι καὶ ἐνεργοὶ βουλόμενοι εἶναι. ἄγοντες δὲ
τούτους ἐς ὄψιν τὴν βασιλέος ἐπυνθάνοντο οἱ Πέρσαι περὶ
τῶν Ἑλλήνων τί ποιέοιεν· εἷς δέ τις πρὸ πάντων ἦν ὁ
εἰρωτῶν αὐτοὺς ταῦτα. οἱ δέ σφι ἔλεγον ὡς Ὀλύμπια ἄγουσι 5
καὶ θεωρέοιεν ἀγῶνα γυμνικὸν καὶ ἱππικόν. ὁ δὲ ἐπείρετο ὅ

26. 2 ἀγαγόντες CP*dz*, van H.   3 τὴν βασιλέως C : τὴν βασιλῆος
z : τῷ βασιλεῖ *d* Paris. 1634 : τῷ βασιλεῖ ἐς ὄψιν Paris. 2933   4 τί :
τὰ (β), van H.   5 εἰρωτῶν *ad*, Stein²³ : εἰρωτέων β, Stein¹ : ἠρωτῶν
C : ἐρωτέων P : ἐρωτῶν *z* || ἄγοιεν β, Holder, van H. : διάγοιεν *z*   6
θεωροῖεν α || καὶ alt. : τε καὶ frag. cod. Paris. || ἐπήροντο ibid.

5. 22. But this whole anecdote is open
to suspicion; it is 'gnomic,' it is told
for the sake of an ἔπος εὖ εἰρημένον,
such as Hdt. loves to close a section
of his narrative withal (cp. my notes
to 4. 143 f.), as here, the story of
Thermopylai - Artemision; and the
chronological implication, strictly interpreted, is neither in itself quite
acceptable nor quite consistent with
7. 206 *supra*.

2. βίου τε δεόμενοι, *victus egentes* : the
word ἐνεργός may mean simply 'employed,' not necessarily 'employed for
hire,' though the word ἐνεργάζεσθαι in
1. 93 certainly connotes filthy lucre,
and the 'hire' here may be taken for
granted. The use of the word in Thuc.
3. 17 does not help us, as the passage
is in every way doubtful; but the use
ap. Xenoph. Platon. *et al.* shows that
the word does not necessarily connote
wages. Was this Arcadian embassy a
political move (ὀλίγοι τινές) or simply a
mercenary adventure?

4. εἷς δέ τις πρὸ πάντων : this circum-
stantiality would hardly belong to Hdt.'s
own method at this stage of the story
if he had not found it in his source;
natural to the isolated anecdote, it is
hardly called for in the body of a work,
which has narrated many interviews
with the Persian king already. The
'one' in question was presumably 'the
son of Artabanos,' named below : πρό,
'on behalf of'; cp. Index.

5. Ὀλύμπια ἄγουσι : the general
synchronism of the invasion with an
Olympiad is indubitable, and a corner-
stone for the chronology of the war;
but the exact coincidence of the festival,
or any of its five (?) days (Pindar, *Ol.*
5. 6), with the defence of Thermopylai
(7. 206), or with the Arkadian application to the king, is very doubtful, all the
more as these two supposed synchron-

isms conflict with each other! Stein's
note, however, on this passage still
remains as written under the exploded
hypothesis that the Olympiad coincided
with the first full moon after the summer
solstice, the last day of the festival in
480 B.C. being June 25. He therefore
transfers the scene of the Arkadian reception to Therme, maintaining its
synchronism with the Olympiad, while
rightly dating the defence of Thermopylai to the end of August or beginning
of September. But if the synchronism
of the Olympiad with the defence of
Thermopylai is to be abandoned as an
anachronism, why is the Olympiad in
this anecdote to be maintained as good
chronology? It is surely much more
probable that the Arkadian application
(assuming the anecdote to have any
truth in it) is correctly located at
Thermopylai, and correctly dated after
the Spartan fiasco there, than that the
very substance of the conversation, including the Olympiad synchronism, is
precisely and exactly reproduced. However that may be, and not to press the
distance from Arkadia to Macedon, the
revised calculation for the Olympiad
celebrations (Unger, *Philol.* 30, 1874,
227 ff.; A. Mommsen, *Ueber die Zeit der
Olympien*, 1891; cp. Busolt, ii.² 708)
makes the approximate synchronism of
Ol. 75, with the scenes laid at Thermopylai, a sufficiently reasonable yet elastic
date to cover both cases. Cp. Appendix
V. § 4.

6. καὶ θεωρέοιεν ἀγῶνα γ. καὶ ἱ. :
a similar change of moods (ἄγουσι·
θεωρέοιεν) in a question is exemplified
5. 13 τίνες .. εἰσί .. καὶ τί .. ἐθέλοντες
ἔλθοιεν, with somewhat less abruptness
than in the answer here. The Olympian
festival was purely athletic and 'hippic'
—not including a 'musical' element
(as did the Pythian).

τι [τὸ ἄεθλον] εἴη σφι κείμενον, περὶ ὅτευ ἀγωνίζονται· οἱ
δ' εἶπον τῆς ἐλαίης τὸν διδόμενον στέφανον. ἐνθαῦτα εἴπας
γνώμην γενναιοτάτην Τιγράνης ὁ Ἀρταβάνου δειλίην ὤφλε
10 πρὸς βασιλέος. πυνθανόμενος γὰρ τὸ ἄεθλον ἐὸν στέφανον·
ἀλλ' οὐ χρήματα, οὔτε ἠνέσχετο σιγῶν εἶπέ τε ἐς πάντας
τάδε. "παπαὶ Μαρδόνιε, κοίους ἐπ' ἄνδρας ἤγαγες μαχησο-
μένους ἡμέας, οἳ οὐ περὶ χρημάτων τὸν ἀγῶνα ποιεῦνται ἀλλὰ
περὶ ἀρετῆς." τούτῳ μὲν δὴ ταῦτα εἴρητο.

---

7 τὸ ἄεθλον secl. Stein² : 'saltem articulus vitiosus est' van H. ‖ προκείμενον z ‖ ὅτεο R : ὅτεω SV (sc. ὅτεῳ, cf. Gaisford et 7. 57 supra)   8
δὲ β ‖ εἶπον : εἶταν van H. ‖ διδόμενον : ᾀδόμενον Valckenaer : ἀοίδιμον
Naber   9 τριτανταίχμης β, Holder, van H. ‖ ὤφλεε β   10
βασιλέως C : βασιλῆος z ‖ πυθόμενος βPz ‖ τὸν ἄεθλον ἐόντα β   11
τε : δὲ β   12 τόδε β   13 τὸν om. β ‖ ἀλλ' ἀρετῆς β, Holder
14 ἤρετο C : εἴρετο d

---

8. τῆς ἐλαίης τὸν διδόμενον στέφανον:
sc. κεῖσθαι, or εἶναι ; the article (bis) and
the present participle mark the notoriety
and the periodicity of this proud yet
paltry prize ; but the Arkadians presumably did not use exactly this phrase, but
simply ἐλαίης or κοτίνου στέφανον. Cp.
Pausanias 5. 15. 8 κατὰ δὲ τὸν ὀπισθό-
δομον μάλιστά ἐστιν ἐν δεξιᾷ πεφυκὼς
κότινος· καλεῖται δὲ ἐλαία καλλιστέφανος,
καὶ τοῖς νικῶσι τὰ Ὀλύμπια καθέστηκεν
ἀπ' αὐτῆς δίδοσθαι τοὺς στεφάνους.
The value of a win is very much
under-stated and under-estimated by this
anecdote, in the interests of the moral ;
an Olympian victor obtained substantial
rewards and advantages from his own
city ; cp. K. F. Hermann, gottesdienst.
Alterth. iii. 50, with reff. (e.g. Plutarch,
Solon 23 ; Plato, Ap. 36 D, Rep. 465 D ;
Thuc. 4. 121, etc.).

9. γνώμην γενναιοτάτην : herein no
doubt the key to the fable, which exists
for the sake of the moral, as fables
always do. These poor men of Arkadia
are come to read the proud Persians a
lesson on the connexion between πενίη
and ἀρετή ; cp. 7. 102. The moralist
has, however, nothing to say on the
amazing spectacle of a nation's amusing
itself at Olympia with the enemy at its
very gates ; the religious associations
prohibit that (but cp. 9. 11) ; nor, again,
of the uselessness of such spectacles and
athleticisms for purposes of war ; it was
left to the Makedonian age to discover
the inferiority of athletes to soldiers ;
cp. Plutarch, Alex. 4, Philopoem. 8.

Τιγράνης ὁ Ἀρταβάνου. The
variant Τριτανταίχμης : many have preferred on the ground, given by Wesseling,
that Tigranes, though well known, is
nowhere (else) described as a son of
Artabanos. But he is described as an
Achaimenid, 7. 62, cp. 9. 95, which is
enough. Hdt. follows his sources without fully co-ordinating, harmonizing,
and relating them. The patronymic
here for Tigranes is in itself a valuable
evidence for the independence of this
anecdote, and of the gnomic source to
which it must be referred ; cp. Introduction, § 10.

δειλίην ὤφλε : cp. αἰσχύνην ὀφλεῖν
Thuc. 5. 101. This well-known Atticism
does not occur elsewhere in Hdt. (nor
indeed in Thucydides either).

11. οὔτε ἠνέσχετο σιγῶν : the participial construction is noticeable, cp. 5.
19 ἀνέχευ ὁρέων τὰ ποιεύμενα, and the
parallel in 1. 206. On the other hand,
7. 139 καταμείναντες ἀνέσχοντο τὸν ἐπιόντα
ἐπὶ τὴν χώρην δέξασθαι is obviously a
different construction.

ἐς πάντας : coram omnibus (Baehr)
= ἐς μέσον.

13. οὐ περὶ χρημάτων . . ἀλλὰ περὶ
ἀρετῆς. χρήματα and ἀρετή are not quite
co-ordinate in this passage ; the slight
inconsequence only sharpens the gnome.
περὶ ἀρετῆς = τοῦ καλοῦ ἕνεκα. Baehr
observes that the speaker utters a
thoroughly Greek sentiment : Stein adds,
one worthy of his sire ! ("spricht ganz
im Geiste seines Vaters "). Such observations, however, go to illustrate not so
much the spread of Hellenic culture and
ethos among the Asiatics as the literary

Ἐν δὲ τῷ διὰ μέσου χρόνῳ, ἐπείτε τὸ ἐν Θερμοπύλῃσι **27**
τρῶμα ἐγεγόνεε, αὐτίκα Θεσσαλοὶ πέμπουσι κήρυκα ἐς Φωκέας,
ἅτε σφι ἔχοντες αἰεὶ χόλον, ἀπὸ δὲ τοῦ ὑστάτου τρώματος
καὶ τὸ κάρτα. ἐσβαλόντες γὰρ πανστρατιῇ αὐτοί τε οἱ

27. 1 ἐπείτε: ἐπεὶ τάχιστα β   2 κήρυκας β   3 ἔχοντες αR :
ἐνέχοντες SVz, van H.

mechanism of Hellenic logography. 'The distinguished foreigner' as a vehicle for national sentiment, whether praise or blame be the object in view, seems to have been a Greek invention ; cp. 4. 77, 142 ; 7. 9, 236, etc.

27. 1. **ἐν δὲ τῷ . . αὐτίκα**, 'meanwhile, immediately after the occurrence of the disaster in Thermopylai'; i.e. before the transactions narrated in cc. 23-26.

2. **Θεσσαλοὶ . . ἐς Φωκέας.** The χόλος between Thessalians and Phokians was even more deadly than the ἔχθρη between Athens and Aigina ; cp. 7. 145, where nothing is said of any attempt to compose this quarrel at the Isthmus. (Hdt. does not co-ordinate his materials fully.) The word χόλος has a more physical and concrete ring in it than ἔχθρη. The antiquity of the feud between Thessalian and Phokian is exhibited in 7. 176 *supra*. That it is less in evidence during the fifth century is perhaps rather an accident of our sources than a proof of mutual goodwill, save that Phokians and Thessalians may have had, to some extent, a common friend in Athens. (In the fourth century the short-lived supremacy of Phokis was in great part maintained by the division of Thessaly against itself ; cp. Bury, *Hist. of Greece*, ii. 281 ff.)

3. **τρώματος** : an awkward iteration after τρῶμα just above, **καὶ τὸ κάρτα**, 'very specially,' 7. 16, 4. 181, etc.

4. **γὰρ** explains and introduces an account of τὸ ὕστατον τρῶμα. The exact date of this affair is not to be extracted from the phrase οὐ πολλοῖσι ἔτεσι πρότερον ταύτης τῆς βασιλέος στρατηλασίης. It would be interesting to know who the σύμμαχοι were, or whether that word points to anything more than τὸ κοινὸν τῶν Θεσσαλῶν. The account in Hdt. is neither quite complete nor perhaps quite accurate. He records two victories of the Phokians over the Thessalians, the more recent one apparently on Parnassos, a τεζομαχία, a νυχτομαχία, and apparently a sortie of a besieged force, resulting in

a great victory, due to a ruse or stratagem devised by their Eleian diviner Tellias. This great victory is commemorated, according to Hdt., by splendid offerings at Delphi and at Abai. The other victory, in the pass by Hyampolis, and at a previous date, where they discomfit the Thessalian cavalry, also by a stratagem or ruse, the authorship of which is not specified (c. 28 *infra*), appears of less moment, and is not especially commemorated at Delphi, or even at Abai, in the immediate neighbourhood ; otherwise, despite Hdt.'s assertion, we might have been tempted to conjecture that the *anathema* at Abai was in reality a commemoration of the victory at Hyampolis.

Polyainos 6. 18 narrates the two Phokian stratagems against the Thessalians in the same order as Hdt., without adding any point, and even omitting the Eleian *mantis*. Pausanias in the *Phokika* (10. 1) gives a much fuller account of these transactions. According to the *Periegete* there were four battles, the second and third of which are not represented by anything in Hdt., while the first and fourth correspond to the two engagements in Hdt., restored to their proper order. Pausanias records first (i.) the battle by Hyampolis, and the disaster to the Thessalian cavalry caused by the concealed jars (c. 28 *infra*). It appears, however, to be an indecisive affair, for (ii.) the Thessalians at once prepare to invade Phokis on a far larger scale (συνελέχθησαν ἀπὸ τῶν πόλεων πασῶν), a project which strikes terror into the Phokians, especially as the cavalry is chiefly in evidence. After consulting the Delphic oracle they despatch, under cover of night, 300 picked men, led by Gelon, to reconnoitre; but this force is trampled and cut to pieces by the Thessalian cavalry. (iii.) This disaster leads to a desperate resolve : the Phokians determine to conquer or to die, after devoting withal their wives, children, and all their properties to the flames. ἀντὶ τούτου μὲν ἅπαντα τὰ

5 Θεσσαλοὶ καὶ οἱ σύμμαχοι αὐτῶν ἐς τοὺς Φωκέας, οὐ πολλοῖσι
ἔτεσι πρότερον ταύτης τῆς βασιλέος στρατηλασίης, ἐσσώθησαν

6 βασιλέως C : βασιλῆος z ‖ ἐσώθησαν B

ἀνάληπτα βουλεύματα ἀπόνοια ὑπὸ Ἑλλήνων ὀνομάζεται Φωκική. The Phokians
march out under two generals, an
Ambrosian named Rhoios and Daiphantes
of Hyampolis, the former in command
of the infantry, the latter of the horse.
This expedition is accompanied by Tellias
of Elis, on whom the hopes of the
Phokians were fixed. The result of their
desperate courage was a brilliant victory,
and the oracle was justified ; but where
exactly the battle took place, and what
service on the occasion Tellias performed,
is not specified. The same story is
told, with some important additions, by
Plutarch, *Mor.* 244 ; see notes to c. 29
infra. (iv.) Subsequently, when the
two armies were laagered opposite each
other, περὶ τὴν ἐς τὴν Φωκίδα ἐσβολήν,
the stratagem of Tellias came off. Taking advantage of a full moon, 500 picked
men, their arms and persons whitened
with chalk, surprised the Thessalians,
and slew an immense number. Pausanias
describes two monuments at Delphi as
records of these events. One he connects
with the great but anonymous Phokian
victory, (iii.) *supra.* ἀπὸ τούτου δὲ τοῦ
ἔργου καὶ ἀναθήματα οἱ Φωκεῖς ἀπέστειλαν
ἐς Δελφοὺς Ἀπόλλωνι Τελλίαν τε τὸν
μάντιν καὶ ὅσοι μαχομένοις ἄλλοι σφίσιν
ἐστρατήγησαν, σὺν δὲ αὐτοῖς καὶ ἥρωας
τῶν ἐπιχωρίων· ἔργα δὲ αἱ εἰκόνες
Ἀριστομέδοντὸς εἰσιν Ἀργείου (10. 1. 10).
Another notice of Phokian *anathemata*
occurs in a different connexion, not
free from ambiguity. εἰσὶ καὶ εἰκόνες
χαλκαῖ Φωκέων ἀναθέντων, ἡνίκα δευτέρᾳ
συμβολῇ τὸ ἱππικὸν ἐτρέψαντο τὸ ἐκ
Θεσσαλίας . . Ἡρακλῆς δὲ καὶ Ἀπόλλων
ἔχονται τοῦ τρίποδος καὶ ἐς μάχην περὶ
αὐτοῦ καθίστανται· Λητὼ μὲν δὴ καὶ
Ἄρτεμις Ἀπόλλωνα, Ἀθηνᾶ δὲ Ἡρακλέα
ἐπέχουσι τοῦ θυμοῦ. Φωκέων καὶ τοῦτό
ἐστιν ἀνάθημα, ὅτε σφίσιν ἐπὶ τοὺς Θεσσαλοὺς Τελλίας ἡγήσατο Ἠλεῖος. τὰ
μὲν δὴ ἄλλα ἀγάλματα Δίυλλός τε ἐν
κοινῷ καὶ Ἀμυκλαῖος, τὴν δὲ Ἀθηνᾶν καὶ
Ἄρτεμιν Χίονίς ἐστι εἰργασμένοι· Κορινθίους δὲ εἶναι φασιν αὐτούς (10. 18. 7).

Assuming that the first group here
mentioned was identical with the *anathema* previously described, there were,
according to Pausanias, at Delphi only
two groups commemorating Phokian

victories over Thessalians. (a) There was
the work of Aristomedon of Argos, which
represented Tellias, Rhoios, Daiphantes,
and possibly other στρατηγοί (Gelon, for
example ?), together with certain local
Phokian heroes. This commemorated
the great victory over the Thessalian
cavaliers, numbered (iii.) above, but not
recorded by Hdt. at all : these figures
were apparently of bronze. (b) There
was the group, various figures in which
had been wrought by Diyllos, Amy-
klaios, and Chionis, all Korinthians, to
commemorate apparently the success
enumerated as (iv.) above, and identical
with the πεζομαχία of Hdt. in which
the ruse of Tellias the Eleian was
brilliantly successful. This anathema
represented a contest between Herakles
and Apollon for possession of the divining stool or tripod, Leto and Artemis
supporting Apollon, and Athena backing
Herakles. To this group Hdt. apparently
refers.

Though Pausanias is more explicit
than Hdt., it by no means follows that
we are to adopt his account of the war
simpliciter ; nor is a partial harmony
between the two out of compass. Hdt.
records two Phokian victories over the
Thessalians and but one Delphian monument, the work apparently of the
Korinthian school, and commemorating
the night battle, which, though he
describes it first, he has previously
introduced as τὸ ὕστατον τρῶμα. On
this point, then, Hdt. and Pausanias
are at one. For the victory which he
records over the Thessalian cavalry Hdt.
mentions no monument. Pausanias,
however, also, on his own showing, is
a monument short, for he records three
Phokian victories over the Thessalians,
two of them victories over the cavalry,
and has but two monuments to describe,
the one commemorating a victory over
the Thessalian cavalry 'in a second
engagement'—plainly the one numbered
(iii.) above — a victory, the story of
which is, on the face of it, as above
indicated, full of improbabilities. The
solution lies near, that Pausanias (or
his source) has duplicated the victory
over the Thessalian cavalry. There was
only one victory over the cavalry, as

ὑπὸ τῶν Φωκέων καὶ περιέφθησαν τρηχέως. ἐπείτε γὰρ
κατειλήθησαν ἐς τὸν Παρνησὸν οἱ Φωκέες ἔχοντες μάντιν
Τελλίην τὸν Ἠλεῖον, ἐνθαῦτα ὁ Τελλίης οὗτος σοφίζεται
αὐτοῖσι τοιόνδε. γυψώσας ἄνδρας ἑξακοσίους τῶν Φωκέων 10
τοὺς ἀρίστους, αὐτούς τε τούτους καὶ τὰ ὅπλα αὐτῶν, νυκτὸς
ἐπεθήκατο τοῖσι Θεσσαλοῖσι, προείπας αὐτοῖσι, τὸν ἂν μὴ
λευκανθίζοντα ἴδωνται, τοῦτον κτείνειν. τούτους ὦν αἵ τε
φυλακαὶ τῶν Θεσσαλῶν πρῶται ἰδοῦσαι ἐφοβήθησαν, δόξασαι
ἄλλο τι εἶναι τέρας, καὶ μετὰ τὰς φυλακὰς αὐτὴ ἡ στρατιὴ 15
οὕτω ὥστε τετρακισχιλίων κρατῆσαι νεκρῶν καὶ ἀσπίδων

8 παρνησὸν ßPε   13 λευκανθίζοντα Α²Pdε: λευκαθίζοντα
(λευκανθέντα malit van H.)   14 πρῶται τῶν Θεσσαλῶν S ‖ ἰδοῦσαι
om. R   15 τέρας mihi suspectum   16 ὥστε καὶ τρισχιλίων ß

described by Hdt. and by Pausanias
himself, (i.) supra; it was in honour
of this victory that the group by Aristomedon of Argos was dedicated, and we
may fairly conjecture that the stratagem
by which the cavalry was discomfited
was due to the ingenuity of Tellias.
The error in Pausanias can even be
explained. As Hdt. had recorded this
engagement without assigning a monument to it, a victory had to be invented
in order to account for the presence of
a second monument at Delphi. The
omission by Hdt. of any mention of
the monument is no doubt a difficulty ;
but a monument there was.

The only crux remaining is the occurrence in Pausanias of the disaster to the
Phokians under Gelon, omitted by Hdt.
This episode has an air of verisimilitude,
and need not be dismissed as merely a
set-off to the victory of the 'Six Hundred.'
Its omission by Hdt. is easily accounted
for by the consideration that he is
merely describing the grievances of the
Thessalians against the Phokians, a list
from which Thessalian victories might
fairly be omitted. A combination, then,
gives a more complete and a more correct
view of the war than either source taken
alone. The war comprised three great
episodes : (i.) A Phokian victory over
the Thessalian cavalry, commemorated
at Delphi by the group above described
as the work of the Argive, Aristomedon.
(ii.) A Thessalian victory over the
Phokians, under Gelon ; probably a
much more extensive affair than the
record suggests. (iii.) A second Phokian
victory, due, like the first, chiefly to

a stratagem devised by Tellias, and
commemorated at Delphi in the group
wrought by the Korinthian school.

7. περιέφθησαν τρηχέωs : c. 18 supra.

8. κατειλήθησαν ἐς τὸν Παρνησόν :
cp. 9. 31 περὶ τὸν Παρνησὸν (sic) κατειλημένοι. Parnassos appears below, c. 32,
as the natural refuge of the Phokians
(from the east and north sides) ; its
position is further defined in c. 35 infra,
and in c. 36 it appears as the natural
refuge for the Delphians (from the south
and west sides), rising indeed immediately over the Holy Place (cp. c. 39).

μάντιν Τελλίην τὸν Ἠλεῖον.
Eleans are in great demand as seers and
diviners ; cp. 9. 37, where a member of
the same clan appears. This divine is
a 'sophist' in a way ; with σοφίζεται
cp. σοφίζεσθαι 3. 111.

10. γυψώσαs : a treatment accorded
in Aithiopia to corpses and warriors, 3.
24 ; cp. 7. 69.

ἑξακοσίουs : Pausanias l.c. cuts
them down to 500.

11. νυκτόs. Pausanias l.c. supplies
the moon, which is necessary for the
due effect. The whitening of the hoplites
had a double purpose : it enabled them
to discriminate friend and foe (often a
difficult matter in night-attacks, cp.
Thucyd. 7. 43) ; and it struck terror
into the Thessalians, who mistook them
for ghosts.

15. τέραs is either exegetical, as though
we read καὶ δὴ καὶ τέρας (cp. 4. 179 ἄλλην
τε ἑκατόμβην καὶ δὴ καὶ τρίποδα), or else
spurious.

16. τετρακισχιλίων : this item is probably authentic, but suggests that the

Φωκέας, τῶν τὰς μὲν ἡμισέας ἐς Ἄβας ἀνέθεσαν τὰς δὲ ἐς
Δελφούς· ἡ δὲ δεκάτη ἐγένετο τῶν χρημάτων ἐκ ταύτης τῆς
μάχης οἱ μεγάλοι ἀνδριάντες οἱ περὶ τὸν τρίποδα συνεστεῶτες
20 ἔμπροσθε τοῦ νηοῦ τοῦ ἐν Δελφοῖσι, καὶ ἕτεροι τοιοῦτοι ἐν
28 Ἄβῃσι ἀνακέαται. ταῦτα μέν νυν τὸν πεζὸν ἐργάσαντο τῶν
Θεσσαλῶν οἱ Φωκέες πολιορκέοντας ἑωυτούς· ἐσβαλοῦσαν δὲ
ἐς τὴν χώρην τὴν ἵππον αὐτῶν ἐλυμήναντο ἀνηκέστως. ἐν
γὰρ τῇ ἐσβολῇ ἥ ἐστι κατὰ Ὑάμπολιν, ἐν ταύτῃ τάφρον
5 μεγάλην ὀρύξαντες ἀμφορέας κενεοὺς ἐς αὐτὴν κατέθηκαν, χοῦν

---

17 ἡμισέας ἀσπίδας Β   19 τοῦ τρίποδος Β   20 ἔμπροσθεν Β
21 ἀνακέεται Β: num genuina sunt verba καὶ . . ἀνακέαται ?   28. 1
εἰργάσαντο CPS   2 πολιορκέοντες z: 'fortasse πολιορκέοντα' Stein[1]
4 ὑάνπολιν a   5 κεινοὺς Β, Holder, van H.

---

attack was not confined to the 500–600 λευκανθίζοντες, but supplemented by the Phokians en masse. Perhaps there were many more shields than corpses; it is not likely that the numbers were identical: τῶν, indeed, refers only to ἀσπίδων.

18. ἡ δὲ δεκάτη: a tithe of the spoil to Delphi, or the gods, was a matter of course—hence the article; cp. 7. 132 δεκατεῦσαι.

τῶν χρημάτων: the shields not included apparently.

19. οἱ μεγάλοι ἀνδριάντες οἱ περὶ τὸν τρίποδα συνεστεῶτες: these words are translated by Rawlinson (iv.³ 280) "the gigantic figures which stand round the tripod"—and so the older commentators, and L. & S. The accusative with περὶ favours this rendering, but on the other hand the meaning given to συνεστεῶτες is highly objectionable: συνεστάναι, συστῆναι meaning with Hdt. constantly stare cum aliquo, sed non ab eadem parte verum a parte opposita, pugnare, contendere cum aliquo (Schweighaeuser, Lexicon). So c. 79 infra, 6. 108; cp. 7. 142; and with more metaphorical sense, 7. 142, 170, c. 74 infra, 9. 89. Further, the description of the work here in question makes it clear that the subject of this group of statuary was a contest between Herakles and Apollon for 'the tripod,' which further proves that the tripod here mentioned is not, for example, the tripod which stood on the τρικάρηνος ὄφις 9. 81 (cp. c. 82 infra), but the Delphian divining stool, represented in the bronze. This mention of the monument suggests the probable source of Hdt.'s digression on the

Thessalo-Phokian war, which is apparently an addition to the first draft of his history, made after his visit to Delphi; cp. Introduction, § 9.

20. ἕτεροι τοιοῦτοι ἐν Ἄβῃσι ἀνακέαται. If this statement is correct, they must have been restorations, or dedications later than the Persian war, for Abai was sacked and destroyed by fire, c. 33 infra.

28. 1. τὸν πεζὸν . . πολιορκέοντας ἑωυτούς: the construction is paralleled 7. 40 στρατὸς . . οὐ διακεκριμένοι, 7. 196 ὁ ναυτικὸς στρατὸς . . ἀπίκοντο ἐς Ἀφέτας. Thuc. 6. 61. 2 στρατιὰ Λακεδαιμονίων . . πρὸς Βοιωτοὺς τι πράσσοντες (Stein). Yet none of these passages is quite so harsh as the present. Was the plural a correction to avoid the hiatus? The reading is found in both families of MSS. ἑωυτούς of course refers to Φωκέες, but is barely correct.

3. ἐλυμήναντο ἀνηκέστως. λυμαίνεσθαι is found c. 15 supra, and both words in 6. 12 λυμαίνεται λύμῃσι ἀνηκέστοισι.

4. τῇ ἐσβολῇ ἥ ἐστι κατὰ Ὑάμπολιν: Hyampolis appears again c. 33 in close connexion with Elateia, Parapotamioi, Abai; see note ad l. The pass here named is undoubtedly the main route from the valley of the Kephisos into Opūs, and so on through Thermopylai. The Persians must have come down through this pass into Phokis and Boiotia, as well as by the pass indicated c. 31 infra.

τάφρον μεγάλην: the author of this device must have been Tellias the Eleian diviner; cp. c. 27 supra.

δὲ ἐπιφορήσαντες καὶ ὁμοιώσαντες τῷ ἄλλῳ χώρῳ ἐδέκοντο τοὺς Θεσσαλοὺς ἐσβάλλοντας. οἱ δὲ ὡς ἀναρπασόμενοι τοὺς Φωκέας φερόμενοι ἐσέπεσον ἐς τοὺς ἀμφορέας. ἐνθαῦτα οἱ ἵπποι τὰ σκέλεα διεφθάρησαν. τούτων δή σφι ἀμφοτέρων 29 ἔχοντες ἔγκοτον οἱ Θεσσαλοὶ πέμψαντες κήρυκα ἠγόρευον τάδε. "ὦ Φωκέες, ἤδη τι μᾶλλον γνωσιμαχέετε μὴ εἶναι ὅμοιοι ἡμῖν. πρόσθε τε γὰρ ἐν τοῖσι Ἕλλησι, ὅσον χρόνον ἐκεῖνα ἡμῖν ἥνδανε, πλέον αἰεί κοτε ὑμέων ἐφερόμεθα· νῦν τε 5 παρὰ τῷ βαρβάρῳ τοσοῦτο δυνάμεθα ὥστε ἐπ᾽ ἡμῖν ἐστι τῆς γῆς ἐστερῆσθαι καὶ πρὸς ἠνδραποδίσθαι ὑμέας. ἡμεῖς μέντοι

---

7 ἐσβάλλοντας A : ἐσβαλόντας B : ἐσβαλέοντας B   8 ἐνέπεσον B
29. 4 ὅμοιοι CPz ‖ πρόσθεν a   5 αἰεί : εἰ B   6 τοσούτω B ‖ ὥστε a : ἐστὲ B (Holder) ‖ ἐστι : ἐστὲ S (Gaisf.)   7 γῆς τε B, Holder, van H. ‖ προσηνδραποδίσθαι CPSz ‖ ἡμεῖς : ἡμέες B

---

6. ἐδέκοντο : a decided imperfect.

7. ὡς ἀναρπασόμενοι : ibidem 9. 60.

8. οἱ ἵπποι τὰ σκέλεα διεφθάρησαν : with the construction (accusative of 'reference,' or limitation) cp. 1. 38 τὸν γὰρ δὴ ἕτερον διεφθαρμένον τὴν ἀκοὴν οὐκ εἶναί μοι λογίζομαι, and Index. But in this case the breaking of the horses' legs must have meant total destruction of horse and man. On this battle see notes to previous chapter.

29. 2. ἔγκοτον : 9. 110, 6. 133. The word is properly an adjective. The substantive κότος is used by Homer and Aischylos, and this word as adj. by the latter.

οἱ Θεσσαλοὶ πέμψαντες κήρυκα resumes the thread of the story from c. 27, for the year 480 B.C.

3. γνωσιμαχέετε μὴ εἶναι ὅμοιοι ἡμῖν, 'recognize your inferiority to us.' The Thessalians themselves appear as γνωσιμαχέοντες (in the king's opinion) 7. 130 ; see note ad l. ὅμοιοι prima facie here in war ; but as there had been a political subordination of the Phokians, for a time at least, to the Thessalians, the connotation of the word may be extended. Plutarch, de mulier. v. 2=Mor. 244, records a rising of the Lokrians against the ἄρχοντες and τύραννοι in their cities who were apparently dependents of the Thessalians, while the Thessalians retorted with the butchery of 250 Phokian hostages, and the invasion of Phokis, which resulted in the Phokian victory at Kleonai, just above Hyampolis, as described by Hdt. in the previous c. and

by Pausanias, as above quoted, c. 27 (i.) and (iii.).

5. ἐκεῖνα=τὰ ἐκείνων : cp. 2. 39 κεφαλῇ κείνῃ=τῇ κείνου, 2. 40 κοιλίην μὲν κείνην τᾶσαν ἐξ ὧν εἷλον, 5. 82 ἱρωτάτας δὴ κείνας νομίζοντες εἶναι (sc. τὰς ἐλαίας τὰς ἐκείνων). With the neuter article cp. τὰ Ἑλλήνων c. 30, τὰ Μήδων c. 34 infra (Stein).

πλέον αἰεί κοτε ὑμέων ἐφερόμεθα : cp. πλέον ἔχειν τινός 7. 168, 211, 9. 70. Stein sees in this phrase a possible reference to the first Sacred War (595-4 to 586-5 B.C.) in which the Thessalians, under Eurylochos the Aleuad, played a prominent part ; the reference would be absolutely unique, for nowhere else in the work of Hdt., not even in the passages on Kleisthenes of Sikyon, the Alkmaionidai, Solon, is there the slightest hint of the great subject. One must ruefully acquiesce in the alternative that the reference is, at most, to the general superiority of the Thessalians to the Phokians in the Delphic or Pylian Amphiktyony—albeit that would unconsciously cover the case of the Sacred War. On Eurylochos the Thessalian cp. Strabo 418.

6. ἐπ᾽ ἡμῖν ἐστι : cp. 7. 10 ἐπ᾽ ἀνδρὶ γε ἑνὶ πάντα τὰ βασιλέος πρήγματα γεγενῆσθαι. ὥστε with the indicative "expresses the actual (or potential ?) result with emphasis" (L. & S.). Cp. 3. 12 αἱ μὲν τῶν Περσέων κεφαλαί εἰσι ἀσθενέες οὕτω ὥστε εἰ θέλεις ψήφῳ μούνῃ βαλεῖν, διατετρανέεις. The passive construction (ἐστερῆσθαι· ἠνδραποδίσθαι) is

τὸ πᾶν ἔχοντες οὐ μνησικακέομεν, ἀλλ᾽ ἡμῖν γενέσθω ἀντ᾽
αὐτῶν πεντήκοντα τάλαντα ἀργυρίου, καὶ ὑμῖν ὑποδεκόμεθα τὰ
30 ἐπιόντα ἐπὶ τὴν χώρην ἀποτρέψειν." ταῦτά σφι ἐπαγγέλλοντο
οἱ Θεσσαλοί. οἱ γὰρ Φωκέες μοῦνοι τῶν ταύτῃ ἀνθρώπων
οὐκ ἐμήδιζον, κατ᾽ ἄλλο μὲν οὐδέν, ὡς ἐγὼ συμβαλλόμενος
εὑρίσκω, κατὰ δὲ τὸ ἔχθος τὸ Θεσσαλῶν· εἰ δὲ Θεσσαλοὶ

---

9 αὐτέων R ‖ ἐπιδεκόμεθα B   10 ἐπιόντα om. B   30. 1
ἐπηγγέλλοντο a   3 ἄλλον R   4 κατὰ : μετὰ C ‖ ἔχθος τὸ :
ἔχθος τῶν S₂

---

remarkable, as well as the highly rhetorical perfect tense.

8. τὸ πᾶν ἔχοντες οὐ μνησικακέομεν
is curious, if not ambiguous. Baehr
takes τὸ πᾶν ἔχοντες together, omnem
potestatem habentes. Cp. 7. 162 οὐδὲν
ὑπιέντες ἔχειν τὸ πᾶν ἐθέλετε. But
Stein's exegesis, τὸ πᾶν ἔχοντες sc. μνησικακῆσαι, suits the present context better,
albeit Demosthenes de cor. 96 (τῶν τότε
Ἀθηναίων πόλλ᾽ ἂν ἐχόντων μνησικακῆσαι
Κορινθίοις), being perfectly simple and
lucid, is not an exact parallel. It is τὸ
πᾶν, rather than the suppression of the
infinitive, which causes the ambiguity
here ; there πολλά is simpler than τὸ
πᾶν and the infinitive after ἔχειν is
expressed.

ἀντ᾽ αὐτῶν, 'in return for what
you have done' ; or perhaps, 'instead of
what you deserve.' For this vague αὐτά
cp. 7. 8, 14 etc.

9. τὰ ἐπιόντα : cp. 7. 138, 157 τὸν
ἐπιόντα. The neuter plural is certainly
more appropriate here.

30. 1. ἐπαγγέλλοντο : simply on their
own account, and not speaking with
any authority from the Persian, but
through their own messenger. Repeated
in ἐπαγγελλομένων just below ; on the
word cp. 7. 1.

2. τῶν ταύτῃ ἀνθρώπων. The phrase
doubtless covers the Lokrians, the
Dorians, and other tribes or peoples of
the neighbourhood ; but Hdt. at least
cannot mean to include the Delphians
under it, though others might be tempted
to do so.

3. ὡς ἐγὼ συμβαλλόμενος εὑρίσκω :
cp. ὡς ἐμοὶ δοκέειν just below. Hdt.
accepts, nay invites, full responsibility
for the very unfavourable verdict on
the Phokians at this crisis, enforcing
it by the disparaging ἀνθρώπων just
before. He wholly discounts, in fact,
and discredits the spirited and patriotic

reply of the Phokians, which he faith-
fully proceeds to report, as he has
previously reported their actual service
on the Greek side, 7. 203, 218, a service
not very efficient, according to his
showing. Hdt.'s attitude towards the
Thessalians appears in contrast strongly
favourable : according to him they, in
the first instance, espoused the Greek
cause, and only afterwards 'medized'
under 'necessity' ; cp. 7. 172. Pausanias 10. 1 contradicts Hdt. by representing the Phokians as in the first
instance compounding with the Persians,
and afterwards reverting to the national
cause. This representation of the case
might be due to an inference from the
conduct of the Thessalians, as reported
by Hdt., coupled with the judgement
of Hdt. in the present passage. Or
could there be any connexion between
the conduct of the Phokians and the
policy and fortunes of Delphi? The
Phokians at least talked big, or reported
themselves as so doing ; but their positive services to the Greek cause are not
very clear. If Delphi escaped their
fate, its escape may have been due to
the very different attitude of the
Thessalians (and other medizing states)
to Phokis and to the Amphiktyonic
shrine. Considering how decidedly Hdt.
'atticizes,' his attitude towards the
Phokians is the more remarkable.
Should it be connected with τὸν ἱερὸν
καλούμενον πόλεμον in 448 B.C. (cp.
Thuc. 1. 112. 5 ; Busolt III. i. 419 ff.)?

4. κατὰ δὲ τὸ ἔχθος τὸ Θεσσαλῶν :
the preposition = οὐ, propter, as in 7.
136 κατὰ ταῦτα ἥκειν, 9. 15 κατὰ ἔχθος
αὐτῶν (just as here), 9. 109 κατ᾽ ἄλλο
μὲν οὐδὲν (as here, above) φοβεόμενος δὲ
Ἄμηστριν μή κτλ. The genitive is
'objective' ; cp. 9. 38 ἐθύετό τε καὶ
προεθυμέετο κατά τε τὸ ἔχθος τὸ Λακεδαιμονίων καὶ κατὰ τὸ κέρδος.

τὰ Ἑλλήνων ηὖξον, ὡς ἐμοὶ δοκέειν, ἐμήδιζον ἂν οἱ Φωκέες. 5
ταῦτα ἐπαγγελλομένων Θεσσαλῶν, οὔτε δώσειν ἔφασαν χρήματα,
παρέχειν τέ σφι Θεσσαλοῖσι ὁμοίως μηδίζειν, εἰ ἄλλως
βουλοίατο· ἀλλ' οὐκ ἔσεσθαι ἑκόντες εἶναι προδόται τῆς
Ἑλλάδος.

Ἐπειδὴ δὲ ἀνηνείχθησαν οὗτοι οἱ λόγοι, οὕτω δὴ οἱ 31
Θεσσαλοὶ κεχολωμένοι τοῖσι Φωκεῦσι ἐγένοντο ἡγεμόνες τῷ
βαρβάρῳ τῆς ὁδοῦ. ἐκ μὲν δὴ τῆς Τρηχινίης ἐς τὴν Δωρίδα

5 αὖξον van H. ‖ δοκέει S, Cobet: δοκεῖ van H.   6 ἔφασαν·
χρήματα α   7 παρέχειν τέ βz: τε παρέχειν ceteri ‖ σφι : σφίσιν
Stein⁽¹⁾², van H.   31. 1 ἐπεὶ δὲ δὴ β   2 φωκεεῦσι α ‖ ἐγίνοντο β
3 τρηχίνης R

7. παρέχειν is impersonal; cp. c. 8
supra; the tense must be at least imperfect: a pluperfect would have been
acceptable.

Θεσσαλοῖσι ὁμοίως μηδίζειν has
the sharper point as a reply to μὴ εἶναι
ὁμοίοι ἡμῖν in the Thessalian message,
c. 29 supra.

ἄλλως, 'on independent grounds';
i.e. it would not in any case have
been for the purpose of conciliating the
Thessalians.

8. οὐκ ἔσεσθαι ἑκόντες εἶναι: the
idiomatic εἶναι in 7. 104, 164, 9. 7, but
here rather odd after ἔσεσθαι.

προδόται τῆς Ἑλλάδος, 'like the
Thessalians', subaud.: a dangerous taunt.
The Phokian language is somewhat
grandiloquent in view of their performance above Thermopylai, 7. 218, and
sits better (if not quite discreetly) on
the lips of Athens later on (c. 144 infra).

31. 1. οὗτοι οἱ λόγοι can only refer to
the short reply, of less than three lines,
just preceding; perhaps that is to be
regarded only as a summary of a longer
reply, or speeches: ἀνηνείχθησαν, were
'reported.'

2. κεχολωμένοι: no doubt specifically
by the title of 'traitors' just flung at
them. Hdt. is rich in terms for the
Thessalo-Phokian feud: ἔχοντες αἰεὶ χόλον
c. 27, ἔχοντες ἔγκοτον c. 29, τὸ ἔχθος
c. 30.

ἡγεμόνες . . τῆς ὁδοῦ: cp. 7. 197
οἱ καθηγεμόνες τῆς ὁδοῦ, where ὁδός is
abstract, or conceptual.

τῷ βαρβάρῳ: sc. τῷ βασιλέι, or τοῖς
Πέρσῃσι.

3. ἐκ μὲν δὴ τῆς Τρηχινίης ἐς τὴν
Δωρίδα: one of the most luminous
hints in the record. The term clearly

implies and only applies to a pass west
of and at right angles to Thermopylai,
and roughly parallel to τῇ ἐσβολῇ ἡ
ἐστὶ κατὰ Τάμπολιν mentioned up above
incidentally, c. 28. This western pass
(running north and south) led over
from the plain of the Spercheios and
the Asopos to the upper plain of the
Kephisos, and so to Delphi, and further.
It has been identified above, 7. 176,
notes, with ἡ διὰ Τρηχῖνος ἔσοδος ἐς τὴν
Ἑλλάδα, a formula which Hdt. himself
apparently (mis)applies to Thermopylai.
However that may be, in the present
context Hdt. undoubtedly carries the
whole Persian land-forces by this route,
and by this route alone, from the banks
of the Spercheios to the banks of the
Kephisos. That is a manifestly absurd
proceeding. One Persian column, of
course, marched by Thermopylai, Kleonai,
Hyampolis, and so forth. But what we
have here to be thankful for is the
clear indication that another column
(probably more lightly equipped) made
its way direct from Trachis into Doris.
The cavalry may all have passed by
the easier route to Hyampolis (cp. the
Thessalian case c. 28 supra). There is
no clear indication of the continued
tripartition of the Persian forces (unless
c. 34 contains it obscurely), but probably the system was maintained (unless
one whole corps d'armée had remained
behind in Makedon and Thrace). Perhaps while one column crossed by the
Asopos-gorge or Trachinian pass, and
another followed the coast-route and
then turned inland to Hyampolis, a
third may have made its way across the
hills, between the two, by the modern
Boudonitsa—then, as now, a sufficiently

ἐσέβαλον· τῆς γὰρ Δωρίδος χώρης ποδεὼν στεινὸς ταύτῃ
5 κατατείνει, ὡς τριήκοντα σταδίων μάλιστά κῃ εὖρος, κείμενος
μεταξὺ τῆς τε Μηλίδος καὶ Φωκίδος χώρης, ἥ περ ἦν τὸ
παλαιὸν Δρυοπίς· ἡ δὲ χώρη αὕτη ἐστὶ μητρόπολις Δωριέων
τῶν ἐν Πελοποννήσῳ. ταύτην ὦν τὴν Δωρίδα γῆν οὐκ
ἐσίναντο ἐσβαλόντες οἱ βάρβαροι· ἐμήδιζόν τε γὰρ καὶ οὐκ
32 ἐδόκεε Θεσσαλοῖσι. ὡς δὲ ἐκ τῆς Δωρίδος ἐς τὴν Φωκίδα
ἐσέβαλον, αὐτοὺς μὲν τοὺς Φωκέας οὐκ αἱρέουσι. οἱ μὲν γὰρ

---

5 τριάκοντα β   6 μηλίδος β: μηλιάδος ‖ καὶ τῆς Sɜ ‖ ἥ: ἧι α:
ἧ β   7 δρυοπίης β   32. 1 δὲ: δ' α

---

easy route (as I found to my own satisfaction in 1899).

4. **τῆς γὰρ Δωρίδος χώρης ποδεὼν στεινὸς ταύτῃ κατατείνει**, 'for there is a narrow neck, or strip, of the Dorian land (Doris) stretching down in this quarter'—to the vale of the Kephisos. Hdt. appears to give an extension to 'Doris' which would make it include not merely the higher ground of the Dorian tetrapolis but the head streams of the upper Kephisos valley. K. O. Mueller, *Orchomenos*[2] (1844) p. 486, observes that Pindos (= Dorion, Aischin. *de f. L.* 286. 2), Boion, Kytinion, Erineon formed the Dorian tetrapolis, properly so called: Lilaia, Karphaia (= Skarphaia), and Dryope, "if there ever was a town of this name," were 'Dorian' in 480 B.C. (Schol. Pindar *Pyth.* 1. 121, Tzetz. *Lyk.* 980), and constitute the στεινὸς ποδεών here described. For ποδεών cp. 2. 121. Stein remarks that the forms Δρυοπαῖος, Δρυπαῖος on Delphian inscripp. implies a township Δρυόπη.

6. **ἥ περ ἦν τὸ παλαιὸν Δρυοπίς.** These words must refer to the whole Δωρὶς χώρη, and have the air of a gloss, which has crept into the text, and at an awkward place: in any case they should follow the Δωρίδος χώρης and not the Φωκίδος χώρης. Cp. c. 43 *infra*.

7. **μητρόπολις Δωριέων τῶν ἐν Πελοποννήσῳ**: a memorable note, marking Dryopis-Doris as the last station in the chart of the Dorian wandering before the invasion of the Peloponnesos and 'the return of the Herakleidai'; cp. c. 43 *infra*. Whether Hdt. is right in bringing all the Dorians in the Peloponnesos from this 'metropolis' (and apparently by one route? at one time?) is a further question, or group of questions, too large to discuss here in

a note. It seems, however, that the Legend of the Return lay completely developed before Hdt. ; cp. 9. 26 *infra*. The fact that the name of the Dorians attaches itself to this Dryopis, and to this place alone on the whole map of Greece, is at least proof of a genuinely Dorian character in the folk of that place. In 457 B.C. the Phokians invaded Δωριᾶς τὴν Λακεδαιμονίων μητρόπολιν Βοῖον καὶ Κυτίνιον καὶ Ἐρινεόν Thuc. 1. 107. 2, and in 426 B.C. ξυνεπρεσβεύοντο δὲ αὐτοῖς (sc. Τραχινίοις) καὶ Δωριῆς ἡ μητρόπολις τῶν Λακεδαιμονίων Thuc. 3. 92. 3. This application led to the foundation of Herakleia, the fortress which commanded the road from Trachis into Doris, used by the Persians in 480 B.C. In Amphiktyonic inscripp. the official title of these Dorians is Δωριεῖς οἱ ἐκ τῆς Μητροπόλεως, Buergel, *Amphic-tyonie* (1887) p. 29.

8. **οὐκ ἐσίναντο ἐσβαλόντες**, 'they entered it, but they did it no harm,' for two reasons: (1) the Dorians 'medized,' (2) the Thessalians disapproved. This patronage or *prostasia* of Thessaly over Doris challenges observation.

32. 1. ἐκ τῆς Δωρίδος ἐς τὴν Φωκίδα: the exact frontier between Doris and Phokis is not very clearly marked by any actual boundary ; the list of town-ships destroyed, in c. 33 *infra*, seems to show that K. O. Mueller, *l.c. supr.*, extended the ποδεών too far in taking it down so as to include Lilaia, though that place, oddly enough, is not included in the list. But Hdt.'s topography of Phokis is not quite all that it might have been (*die Angaben stimmen nicht zur Lokalität*, Stein).

2. **οἱ μέν**: the corresponding term is found in οἱ δὲ πλεῦνες, *infra*. The first term may perhaps be referred to the

τῶν Φωκέων ἐς τὰ ἄκρα τοῦ Παρνησοῦ ἀνέβησαν· ἔστι δὲ
καὶ ἐπιτηδέη δέξασθαι ὅμιλον τοῦ Παρνησοῦ ἡ κορυφή, κατὰ
Νέωνα πόλιν κειμένη ἐπ᾿ ἑωυτῆς· Τιθορέα οὔνομα αὐτῇ· ἐς 5
τὴν δὴ ἀνηνείκαντο καὶ αὐτοὶ ἀνέβησαν.　οἱ δὲ πλεῦνες αὐτῶν

---

3 παρνησοῦ α: παρνησσοῦ ‖ ἀνέβησαν .. Παρνησοῦ om. R　　　4
παρνησοῦ Α: παρνισοῦ Β: παρνησσοῦ　　5 κειμένην ἐπ᾿ αὐτῆς? van H.
‖ τιθωρέα Β ‖ ἐς τὴν διάνηνείκαντο R: ἐς σπάρτην ἀνενείκαντο Eustath.
Od. p. 1604: ἀνηνείκαντό <τε πάντα> καὶ? van H.

---

fighting men, and the second, the
majority, to the non-combatants.

3. τὰ ἄκρα τοῦ Παρνησοῦ need not
necessarily be restricted to just the two
famous topmost peaks, Lykorea and
Tithorea, which earned Parnassos the
title of *biceps*: Ovid, *Metam.* 2. 221; cp.
l. 316 *Mons ibi verticibus petit arduus
astra duobus, Nomine Parnassus*; Lucan,
Phars. 5. 72 *Parnassus gemino petit
aethera colle.* The mountain has many
ἄκρα, like every other large range or
system : ἄκρα (τά) is used by Hdt. for
high ground, as in 6. 100 τὰ ἄκρα τῆς
Εὐβοίης : and the very next sentence
seems to show that Hdt. himself thought
of Parnassos as having only one κορυφή,
though it might have many ἄκρα. But
cp. next note. Pausanias 10. 32. 2
employs the phrase τὰ ἄκρα τοῦ Παρνασοῦ.

4. τοῦ Παρνησοῦ ἡ κορυφή: Parnassos is a mountain with twin peaks,
of which Tithorea was only one; cp.
previous note. Hdt. treats Tithorea
here as the sole summit. In c. 39 *infra*
he names another κορυφή Hyampeia, but
that is in a story from another (a
Delphian) source; and moreover the
word κορυφή there may be used simply
for a peak, cp. c. 37—not as here
obviously for the absolute summit.
This sentence, however, comes in
curiously, and has somewhat the air of
an insertion, from the author's own
hand, for (i.) it postpones the correlative
to οἱ μέν above, and (ii.) it contains a
slight correction of the foregoing statement, as it shows the Phokian minority
gone up not to τὰ ἄκρα generally but to
ἡ κορυφή, that is to Tithorea. Ulrichs
(*l.c. infra*) suggests that the inhabitants
of Neon retired to a large cave, well
supplied with water, and impregnable,
which lies behind *Velitza*.

κατὰ Νέωνα .. Τιθορέα: Bursian,
Geogr. von Griechenl. i. (1862) 166, proves
that there was in later times a township

named Τιθόρρα (inscripp.) or Τιθόρα
(inscripp. and Plutarch, *Sulla* 15), or
(in the mss. generally) Τιθορέα, or (in
Steph. B. erroneously) Τιθόραια, and
asserts that Tithora occupied the site of
the older city Neon. Extensive remains
near the modern village of *Velitza* attest
the site of Tithora, beyond doubt. Cp.
Ulrichs, 'Topographie und Inschriften
von Tithora,' *Rhein. M.* N.F. 2. 544 ff.
(1848), but Ulrichs denies the absolute
identity of the sites of the old Neon and
the new Tithora, and identifies Neon
with a site at *Palea-Fiva* some five miles
north of *Velitza* (Tithora). The name
of Neon, but not that of Tithora, occurs
in the list of the twenty-two members of
the Phokian League given by Pausanias
10. 3. 2. His remarks on the present
passage may be quoted in full : 10. 32. 5
διάφορα ἐς τὸ ὄνομα οἶδα τῆς πόλεως
Ἡροδότῳ τε εἰρημένα ἐν ἐπιστρατείᾳ τοῦ
Μήδου καὶ Βακίδι ἐν χρησμοῖς. Βάκις μὲν
γε Τιθορέας τοὺς ἐνθάδε ἐκάλεσεν ἀνθρώ-
πους· Ἡροδότου δὲ ὁ ἐς αὐτοὺς λόγος
ἐπιόντος φησὶ τοῦ βαρβάρου τοὺς ταύτῃ
οἰκοῦντας ἀναφυγεῖν ἐς τὴν κορυφήν, ὄνομα
δὲ Νέωνα μὲν τῇ πόλει, Τιθορέαν δὲ εἶναι
τοῦ Παρνασοῦ τῇ ἄκρᾳ. ἔοικεν οὖν ἀνὰ
χρόνον πρῶτα μὲν δὴ τῇ ἁπάσῃ χώρᾳ, μετὰ
δὲ ταῦτα, ἐπειδὴ ἀνῳκίσθησαν ἀπὸ τῶν
κωμῶν, ἐκνικῆσαι καὶ ἐπὶ τῇ πόλει Τιθορέαν
μηδὲ ἔτι Νέωνα ὀνομάζεσθαι. Τιθορέα δὲ
οἱ ἐπιχώριοι τεθῆναί φασιν ἀπὸ Τιθορέας
νύμφης, οἵα τὸ ἀρχαῖον λόγῳ τῷ ποιητῶν
ἐφύοντο ἀπό τε ἄλλων δένδρων καὶ μάλιστα
ἀπὸ τῶν δρυῶν. (But what has Tithorea
to do with trees?) Grasberger, *Gr.
Ortnamen*, attempts to connect Τιθορέα
(sic), 'name of one of the heights of
Parnassos,' with τιτθός a 'pap.' The
name Τιθόρεα has a more archaic appearance than Νεών (sic ap. Pausan.), and its
later use was perhaps a revival, although
applied to a fresh site.

5. ἀνηνείκαντο: sc. τὰ ἑαυτῶν: cp.
c. 36 *infra* ; 3. 148 ἀνενεικάμενος τὰ ἔχων
ἐξεχώρησε makes the meaning clear.

ἐς τοὺς Ὀζόλας Λοκροὺς ἐξεκομίσαντο, ἐς Ἄμφισσαν πόλιν
τὴν ὑπὲρ τοῦ Κρισαίου πεδίου οἰκημένην. οἱ δὲ βάρβαροι
τὴν χώρην πᾶσαν ἐπέδραμον τὴν Φωκίδα· Θεσσαλοὶ γὰρ
10 οὕτω ἦγον τὸν στρατόν· ὁκόσα δὲ ἐπέσχον, πάντα ἐπέφλεγον
καὶ ἔκειρον, καὶ ἐς τὰς πόλις ἐνιέντες πῦρ καὶ ἐς τὰ ἱρά.
33 πορευόμενοι γὰρ ταύτη παρὰ τὸν Κηφισὸν ποταμὸν ἐδηίουν
πάντα, καὶ κατὰ μὲν ἔκαυσαν Δρυμὸν πόλιν κατὰ δὲ Χαράδραν

---

7 ἄμφισαν C　　8 κρισσαίου B ‖ οἰκημένην Stein[2], van H. :
κειμένην C: οἰκεομένην ceteri, Stein[1], Holder　　11 πόλιας B: πόλεις C
‖ καὶ ἐς τὰ ἱρά: καὶ ἱστα ἱρά B: καὶ ἕστερα V: καὶ ἕτερα R: κατέκαιον S
33. 1 ταύτη: τά τε ? Stein[2] ‖ παρὰ om. C ‖ κηφισσὸν BPz ‖ ἐδήουν B:
ἐδήουν z　　2 Δρύμον Stein[1] ‖ χαράνδραν C: χαράδρην PRSz (χαρά cum
δρ supersc. V)

---

7. Ὀζόλας Λοκρούς : Hdt. distinguishes from the Ὀπούντιοι Λοκροί :
cp. 7. 203, c. 1 supra. They are the
Western Lokrians in the peninsula, a
primitive, not to say barbarous, folk
even in the days of Thucydides (1. 5. 3),
but useful allies withal on occasion (3.
95. 3). The 'Epizephyrian' Lokri are
also mentioned by Hdt. 6. 23. Pausanias 10. 38 gives five different explanations of the name Ozolai, and
Strabo 427 adds a sixth. Five of these
connect the name with one bad smell or
another (ὄξειν); one traces it to ὄζος, a
branch, shoot, but with a fanciful legend
attached. The latter appears the better
derivation, in the sense that these were
the Branch-Lokri, from the parent stem
in Opûs : but need either alternative be
more than a Volksetymologie ?

Ἄμφισσαν : cp. c. 36 infra. No
doubt the chief city of the Ozolian Lokri,
situate at the inner edge of the ' Krisaian
plain,' on the main route from Delphi to
Thermopylai. The Amphissaians were
not always on good terms with the
Phokians; cp. Thuc. 3. 101. 2. Amphissa
was denounced for sacrilege by Aischines
in 340 B.C., and destroyed by Philip two
years later (cp. J. B. Bury, Hist. of
Greece, ii. 314 ff.), but subsequently restored, as its coinage attests (cp. Head,
Hist. Num. 286).

8. τοῦ Κρισαίου πεδίου : neither
Krisa, nor its port Kirrha, were in
existence when Hdt. wrote; but neither
here, nor elsewhere, has he taken occasion
to refer to the so-called ἱερὸς πόλεμος
which led to their destruction ; cp. note
to c. 29 supra. The old name must
have clung to the fertile landscape, as it

certainly clung to the bay, round which
the landscape lies ; cp. Thuc. 1. 107. 3,
2. 69. 1, etc.

10. οὕτω : sc. ὥστε τὴν χώρην πᾶσαν
ἐπιδραμεῖν.

ὁκόσα δὲ ἐπέσχον : cp. c. 35 infra
ὅσα δὲ καὶ οὗτοι ἐπέσχον τῆς Φωκίδος,
πάντα ἐσιναμώρεον. Whatever places
they touched, reached, overspread, they
devastated. Cp. 1. 104 οἱ δὲ Σκύθαι τὴν
Ἀσίην πᾶσαν ἔσεσχον. It is an abstract
synonym for the more graphic and concrete ἐπέδραμον.

33. 1. τὸν Κηφισὸν ποταμὸν : cp. 7.
178. The river Kephisos had its source
proper in the territory of Lilaia : Pausan.
10. 33. 4 Λίλαιαν δὲ τῶν καλουμένων
Ναΐδων καὶ Θυγατέρα εἶναι τοῦ Κηφισοῦ,
καὶ ἀπὸ τῆς νύμφης τὸ ὄνομα τεθῆναι τῇ
πόλει φασί. It was a day's journey
across Parnassos from Lilaia to Delphi,
ib., i.e. there was a regular path that
way. Lilaia (mod. Agoriani?) was a
regular member of the Phokian League
(Pausan. 10. 3. 2), and no doubt shared
the fate of the other Phokian cities on
this occasion. Pausanias 10. 33. 7 says :
γῆ δὲ διακεκριμένως ἀρίστη τῆς Φωκίδος
ἐστὶν ἡ παρὰ τὸν Κηφισὸν καὶ φυτεῦσαι καὶ
σπείρειν καὶ ἀνεῖναι νομάς· καὶ γεωργεῖται
ταῦτα μάλιστα τῆς χώρας ὥστε κτλ.

2. κατὰ μὲν . . κατὰ δέ : a remarkable tmesis ; cp. 5. 81.

Δρυμὸν πόλιν : no doubt the
Δρυμαία of Pausanias' list l.c., Δρυμία
ap. Steph. B., twenty stades distant from
Tithronion, on the high ground above
left bank of the river.

Χαράδραν : twenty stades east of
Lilaia, that is, on the right (south) side
of the river. The town suffered from

καὶ Ἔρωχον καὶ Τεθρώνιον καὶ Ἀμφίκαιαν καὶ Νέωνα καὶ
Πεδιέας καὶ Τριτέας καὶ Ἐλάτειαν καὶ Τάμπολιν καὶ Παρα-

3 τεθρόνιον **B**: Θρόνιον Eustath. Il. p. 638 ‖ ἀμφίκαια R

want of water, Pausan. 10. 33. 6.
Charadra and Dryonaia may be taken to
represent the frontier townships. Frazer,
Paus. v. 416, gives a plan of the ruins,
and puts the name on his map of Phokis
(vol. vi.).

3. Ἔρωχον: Erochos occurs in Pausanias' list between Daulis and Charadra ;
Leake, *N.G.* ii. 89, regarded its site as
undiscoverable ; Bursian, *op. c.* i. 162,
places it conjecturally between Charadra
and Tithronion ; it appears on Grundy's
and Kiepert's maps on the left side
of the river, between Tithronion and
Elateia. It was probably a small place,
apparently restored after the Phokian
war (in which it had been destroyed
again) ; cp. Frazer, *Paus.* v. 215 (10. 3. 2).

Τεθρόνιον lay on a plain, 15 stades
from Amphikleia, and 20 from Drymaia
(Pausan. 10. 33. 12), apparently on the left
side of the river: παρέχεται δὲ οὐδὲν ἐς
μνήμην, *ibid.* (Tithrone, Plin.; Τιθρώνιον
Steph. B.)

Ἀμφίκαιαν, Pausanias states that
the correct form of the name was
Ἀμφίκλεια, and appeared in the *Dogma*
of the Amphiktyons on the destruction
of the Phokian cities ; but Ἡρόδοτος μὲν
Ἀμφίκαιαν ἐκάλεσεν ἑπόμενος τῷ ἀρχαιο-
τάτῳ τῶν λόγων. Amphikaia was
certainly the epichorian form, as is
proved by the local legend narrated by
Pausanias. This form was associated
with a cult of Dionysos, and cures were
effected δι' ὀνειράτων. The site is identified, apparently, on the hills to the south
of Kephisos, below and east of Lilaia, just
above the modern *Dadi* (Frazer v. 420):
Pausanias' measurements here appear
untrustworthy : Bursian i. 162.

Νέωνα : on the skirts of Parnassos ;
cp. c. 32 *supra.*

4. Πεδιέας καὶ Τριτέας : these names
do not occur in Pausanias' list, nor elsewhere except in this place. Bursian
(i. 163) condemns Leake's conjecture
that Πεδιεῖς represents the township
Λέδων (not mentioned by Hdt.), and
suggests that these two towns never recovered after their destruction by the
Persians in 480 B.C., although a Τριταία
in Ozolian Lokris may, he supposes with
almost equally little reason, be a new
home for the Phokian Τριτεεῖς.

Ἐλάτειαν : the chief city of Phokis
μετά γε τοὺς Δελφούς, Pausan. 10. 34.
Its site is identified (Leake ii. 82, Bursian
i. 163, Frazer v. 425 ff.), commanding
the outlet of the pass of Hyampolis
(c. 28 *supra*). Its strategic importance
becomes more prominent in the fourth
century, and the Makedonian period.
The immortal passage, in which Demosthenes describes the seizure of Elateia
by Philip in 338 B.C. (*de Cor.* 284), is,
or was, known to every schoolboy.

Τάμπολιν : on the main road
from Boiotia and Phokis to Opûs, and
so to Thermopylai ; cp. c. 28 *supra.*
Pausanias 10. 35. 5 records that the
city was a settlement of Ὕαντες from
Thebes, and that the full name of the
city was Ὑάντων πόλις. Kleonai, the
actual scene of the Thessalian defeat
(cp. Plutarch, *l.c.* c. 28 *supra*) a little
higher up the pass, was presumably a
dependency of Hyampolis ; remains of
Hyampolis are identifiable (Leake ii. 167,
Bursian i. 165, Frazer v. 442). The
city would be the first exposed to the
attack of a force coming from Thermopylai, and probably in 480 B.C. (with
Abai) was destroyed, not by the Persian
column which had crossed from Malis
into Doris, and then worked down the
Kephisos valley, spreading ruin and
death wherever it came, but by the
main column, which must have advanced
from Thermopylai along the coast, and
through the pass of Hyampolis.

Παραποταμίους. Parapotamioi
appears in Pausanias' list of the Phokian
League, but the city had never recovered
from its destruction by the Amphiktyons
in the Phokian war. Παραποταμίων μὲν
δὴ οὔτε ἐρείπια ἔτι ἦν, οὔτε ἔνθα τῆς χώρας
ᾠκίσθη ἡ πόλις μνημονεύουσιν (10. 33. 8).
The more careful modern *periegetai* have
improved upon this. The site has been
identified in the narrow strait, between
Mounts Philoboiotos and Hadyleion,
through which the Kephisos passes from
the plain of Elateia to the plain of
Chaironeia (Leake ii. 97, Bursian i. 164,
Frazer v. 418). The order in which Hdt.
names Hyampolis, Parapotamioi and Abai
is not geographical in either direction.
Abai is probably placed last, because
there is a note to add to the name.

5 ποταμίους καὶ Ἄβας, ἔνθα ἦν ἱρὸν Ἀπόλλωνος πλούσιον,
θησαυροῖσί τε καὶ ἀναθήμασι πολλοῖσι κατεσκευασμένον· ἦν
δὲ καὶ τότε καὶ νῦν ἔτι χρηστήριον αὐτόθι. καὶ τοῦτο τὸ
ἱρὸν συλήσαντες ἐνέπρησαν, καὶ τινὰς διώκοντες εἷλον τῶν
Φωκέων πρὸς τοῖσι ὄρεσι, καὶ γυναῖκας τινὰς διέφθειραν
10 μισγόμενοι ὑπὸ πλήθεος.

34   Παραποταμίους δὲ παραμειβόμενοι οἱ βάρβαροι ἀπίκοντο
ἐς Πανοπέας. ἐνθεῦτεν δὲ ἤδη διακρινομένη ἡ στρατιὴ αὐτῶν

---

7 ἔτι: ἔστι B, Holder: 'an ἔτι ἔστι?' van H.   8 συλλήσαντες Bz
‖ τῶν om. α   9 οὔρεσι CPz, van H. ‖ διέφθειρον B   34. 1
παραμειψάμενοι van H.

Hyampolis and Parapotamioi are then in
the order in which they would have been
visited by a force coming from Opûs.
Op. also next chapter.

5. Ἄβας: Abai was plainly situate
lower down the (Assos) valley than
Hyampolis, Pausan. 10. 35. 1. Its
site is clearly identified (Leake ii. 164,
Bursian i. 165, Frazer v. 436 with plans).
Hyampolis, the city of the Hyantes, was
also known as Hya; and it is possible
that Abai was the city of the Abantes:
Abantopolis! But the statement of
Aristotle ap. Strabon. 445 that the old
name of Euboia, viz. Abantis, was traceable to Thrakians, who crossed over into
the island from Abai, in Phokis, is not
convincing. The chief claim of Abai
to renown was no doubt its Apolline
oracle.

6. θησαυροῖσί τε καὶ ἀναθήμασι:
some of them due to the pious liberality
of Kroisos, 1. 46. It is a little remarkable
that Hdt. does not specify this point
here, especially in view of the notice in
c. 35 infra; but perhaps when he wrote
this passage originally he was not yet
acquainted with the story of the Trial
of the Oracles; in other words, his silence
here makes for the earlier composition
of Books 7-9; cp. Introduction, §§ 7, 8.
ἦν δὲ καὶ τότε καὶ νῦν ἔτι: sc. ἔστι.
The χρηστήριον survived the destruction
of the ἱρόν, and was even consulted in
the following winter on behalf of Mardonios, c. 134 infra, a point which
might tempt one to postpone the destruction of Abai till after the Plataian
campaign.

7. τὸ ἱρὸν συλήσαντες ἐνέπρησαν:
Pausanias, 10. 35. 2, says that this was
one of the temples left in ruins as a
witness of the war with the barbarians.

The ruined temple was again fired by
the Thebans in the Phokian war; but
of the twenty-two members of the
Phokian League Abai was the only city
not destroyed and 'di-oikized' by the
Amphiktyons, being, indeed, the only
one not associated in the sacrilegious
attack on Delphi.

9. γυναῖκας τινὰς διέφθειραν: from
the specification it might be inferred that
such atrocities were unknown in Hellenic
warfare.

10. ὑπὸ πλήθεος, prae multitudine, sc.
τῶν μισγομένων (Stein).

34. 1. Παραποταμίους δέ: this re-
version to Parapotamioi, which just above
was mentioned between Hyampolis and
Abai, replaces it in its proper geographical position, at the lower extremity
of the Elateian plain.

2. ἐς Πανοπέας: Panopeus, but twenty
stades from Chaironeia, commanding the
open frontier passage, according to
Pausanias 10. 4. 1, appears in the list
of the Phokian League, though the
periegete is inclined to challenge its title
to be a city at all, so poorly was it
provided with all that doth a city make:
ἀρχεῖα, γυμνάσιον, θέατρον, ἀγορά, κρήνη.
Still the citizens had termini (ὅροι) and
they sent representatives to the Phokian
sanhedrim. He is curiously blind, apparently, to the evidences of its former
greatness and strategic importance; cp.
Leake ii. 110, Bursian i. 168, Frazer
v. 216 ff. Πανοπεύς appears in the
Homeric Catalogue Il. 2. 520 side by
side with Daulis; cp. 17. 307; and in
Od. 11. 581 as on the road to Delphi;
cp. Pausan. l.c. In Thucydides the
name is modified into the form Φανοτεύς,
4. 89. 2; cp. 4. 76. 3 ἔστι δὲ ἡ Χαιρώνεια
ἔσχατον τῆς Βοιωτίας πρὸς τῇ Φανοτίδι τῆς

ἐσχίζετο· τὸ μὲν πλεῖστον καὶ δυνατώτατον τοῦ στρατοῦ
ἅμα αὐτῷ Ξέρξῃ πορευόμενον ἐπ' Ἀθήνας ἐσέβαλε ἐς Βοιωτούς,
ἐς γῆν τὴν Ὀρχομενίων. Βοιωτῶν δὲ πᾶν τὸ πλῆθος ἐμήδιζε, 5

4 ἐπ': ἐς Β ‖ ἐς Βοιωτοὺς καὶ Βοιωτῶν ἐς suspicatur Kallenberg
5 γῆν τῶν Β : τὴν τῶν ᵃ

Φωκίδος. So Strabo (following Homer) 423 after Daulis mentions Πανοπεὺς δ' ὁ νῦν Φανοτεύς, ὅμορος τοῖς περὶ Λεβάδειαν τόποις (of which the insignificant Chaironeia might be one). The Herodotean form of the name is Πανοπέες (-εῖς).

διακρινομένη ἡ στρατιὴ αὐτῶν ἐσχίζετο. Hdt. thinks that at Panopeus there was a new departure. Hitherto the army has advanced, according to him, in a single column, from Thermopylai, via Doris, and the upper valley of the Kephisos, through the pass at Parapotamioi, to Panopeus. At this point, however, a division of the forces takes effect. One column, the smaller one, is detached for service against Delphi; the other, and larger portion of the army, advances with Xerxes into Boiotia, and so to Attika. It has been already shown that from Thermopylai the Persians must have advanced in at least two, and possibly even in three, columns; cp. cc. 28, 31 supra. Two of these columns would naturally have re-united at Parapotamioi, or at Panopeus, unless indeed the left column in the advance crossed the mountain direct by the road from Hyampolis and Abai to Orchomenos (ἡ ἐπὶ Ὀποῦντα λεωφόρος ἡ ἐξ Ὀρχομενοῦ of Pausanias 10. 35. 1). As the main baggage-train and cavalry probably came by the coast route from Thermopylai, this alternative seems the less probable. Parapotamioi, then, may be looked upon as the probable rendezvous of the two columns from Thermopylai, that which devastated upper Phokis, and that which visited Hyampolis and Abai (and possibly other places on Mount Knemis). The columns thus reunited may have passed from Parapotamioi to Panopeus. From Panopeus too a column may have been detached to visit Delphi, as here narrated; but the story of the visit to Delphi is in itself open to the gravest suspicion (see further below), and it is even possible that, if the Persians ever visited Delphi at all, Panopeus was not the point of departure, but the point of reunion, for the forces. The start for Delphi might have been made from

Trachis, or from Doris, and the route followed might have been by Amphissa to Delphi, and from Delphi down to Panopeus. The specification of Amphissa, c. 32 supra, as the chief refuge for the Phokians, is against this hypothesis, though the excellence of the route is in its favour. Or, again, the Persian column, operating in the upper Kephisos valley, might have detached a force at Lilaia—so curiously omitted by Hdt.— to go straight across Parnassos to Delphi. Λίλαια δὲ ἡμέρας μὲν ὁδὸν καὶ ὥρᾳ χειμῶνος ἀπέχει Δελφῶν κατιοῦσι διὰ τοῦ Παρνασοῦ Pausan. 10. 33. 3. The Persian force would then have rejoined the main body at Daulia, or Panopeus. One admission the Herodotean story makes: it shows a vague consciousness that through Central Greece the Persian forces had not moved all along in one single mass, on one single route.

4. ἐς Βοιωτούς, ἐς γῆν τὴν Ὀρχομενίων: the designation of the whole, followed by the designation of the part (cp. c. 23 supra). From Panopeus one road led west to Daulis (cp. next c.) and so to (or from) Delphi; another east to Chaironeia, little more than a couple of miles (twenty stades) distant. The actual frontier between Phokis and Boiotia must be sought in this interval; Bursian (op. cit. i. 167) finds it in the bed of the Μόλος or Μώριος, a small torrent descending from the north-western portion of Helikon and emptying into the Kephisos at the foot of Mount Hadyleion (Plutarch, Sulla, 17, 19). Hdt. does not mention Chaironeia, which was not at this time politically an important place, nor even an independent member of the Boiotian Confederacy (cp. Thuc. 4. 76. 3), but stood, probably, to Orchomenos in much the same relation as that between Kleonai and Hyampolis in Phokis (cp. c. 33 supra). Orchomenos was still no doubt the chief city in the western (or north-western) plain of Boiotia, though fallen from its high estate in 'Minyan' times, and now inferior in political importance to Thebes; cp. further 9. 16, notes.

5. Βοιωτῶν δὲ πᾶν τὸ πλῆθος ἐμήδιζε:

τὰς δὲ πόλις αὐτῶν ἄνδρες Μακεδόνες διατεταγμένοι ἔσφζον
ὑπὸ Ἀλεξάνδρου ἀποπεμφθέντες· ἔσφζον δὲ τῇδε, δῆλον
βουλόμενοι ποιέειν Ξέρξῃ ὅτι τὰ Μήδων Βοιωτοὶ φρονέοιεν.

---

6 πόλιας β || ἔσφζον (bis) van H., Stein³ : ἔσωζον   7 τῇδε om. β,
'et commode abesse potest' van H. || βουλόμενοι δῆλον z

---

the political significance of this statement is ambiguous ; is τᾶν τὸ πλῆθος,
plebs universa, in distinction to the
aristocracy? Or is it merely universa
multitudo, the vast majority, independent of social rank, or political privilege?
Again, what is the force and value of
the contrast between τὸ πλῆθος and τὰς
πόλις? Is the πλῆθος wholly outside the
πόλεις? Is it merely the plebs or multitudo rustica? Or is there any emphasis
on the distinction? Or are the πόλεις
specifically the citadels?

Baehr understands πλῆθος here as
plebs, and takes the point to be that the
rustic population, which was 'plebeian,'
joined the Persians, while the cities, inhabited or held by the upper classes,
were anti-Persian, but were saved from
Persian vengeance by the good offices of
the Makedonians. But this use of τὸ
πλῆθος is hardly Herodotean (even 3.
80, 81 πλῆθος ἄρχον, ἐς τὸ πλῆθος φέρειν
τὸ κράτος not quite justifying the supposed political and social connotation of
the word, as used in this passage). And
again, that interpretation would not
square with the points in the Plataio-
Theban argument in Thuc. 3. 53–67 (ex
hypothesi 427 B.C.), where the Plataians
represent themselves, and that to the
oligarchic Spartans, as the only Boiotians
who had not medized ; while the Theban
reply is not that only the democratic
multitude medized, but that the medism
of Thebes was due to the inner ring of
oligarchy (δυναστεία ὀλίγων ἀνδρῶν 3.
62. 3).

Βοιωτῶν πᾶν τὸ πλῆθος here is, therefore, to be understood 'the Boiotians
without (or with hardly) an exception.'
But Thespiai and Plataia were, of course,
exceptions : perhaps, however, they were
not truly 'Boiotians.'

6. τὰς δὲ πόλις αὐτῶν .. ἔσφζον :
Makedonian garrisons were introduced
into the various Boiotian cities, and
preserved them from the Persians, and
the fate of the Phokian townships.
Hdt. does not enumerate or specify the
Boiotian cities thus preserved, but he
records, c. 50 infra, the destruction of

Thespiai and of Plataiai, and other
Boiotian cities he names incidentally :
Orchomenos (as here), Lebadeia c. 134
infra, Thebes c. 134 infra, et passim,
Tanagra 9. 15 et al., Akraiphia c. 135
infra, and perhaps inferentially Kopai
ibid. Phokis was made more memorable
by its misfortunes than Boiotia by its
immunities.

διατεταγμένοι : distributed, by
order, throughout the cities severally.
'The men of Makedon' were apparently
not single agents, but bodies of soldiers,
garrisons.

7. ὑπὸ Ἀλεξάνδρου ἀποπεμφθέντες :
the absence of the patronymic is to be
observed. Alexander is treated as a
known quantity ; the article is equally
absent, for he has not been named
recently ; but this passage could not be
his first introduction : cp. 7. 173, 175.
These Makedonian garrisons appear to
have been sent on ahead.

τῇδε, 'for this purpose.' Hdt.
ascribes to the men (βουλόμενοι) what
must have been the wish and policy of
their master. This good understanding
between Alexander and the Boiotians,
i.e. primarily the Thebans, throws considerable doubt upon the loyalty of
Thebes and Boiotia to the national cause
in the first instance. But the precautions taken to save them from
pillage, if necessary, would show, either
that the Persian forces were getting out
of hand, or that the Boiotians had really
made a stand at Thermopylai, and
provoked the enemy.

It is, however, quite possible that
here, as elsewhere, while the act is
historical, the motive is fictitious.
Makedonian garrisons may have been
introduced into the Boiotian cities, not
for the purpose of saving them from the
Persians, but for the purpose of saving
the medizing factions from the loyal or
'hellenizing' party. The curious turn
of phrase, ὅτι τὰ Μήδων Βοιωτοὶ φρονέοιεν,
'that there were Boiotians of the Medes'
way of thinking,' may support that view.
With φρονέω cp. 7. 145 ; with τὰ M. cp.
τὰ Ἑλλήνων c. 30 supra.

οὗτοι μὲν δὴ τῶν βαρβάρων ταύτῃ ἐτράποντο, ἄλλοι δὲ αὐτῶν **35**
ἡγεμόνας ἔχοντες ὁρμέατο ἐπὶ τὸ ἱρὸν τὸ ἐν Δελφοῖσι, ἐν
δεξιῇ τὸν Παρνησὸν ἀπέργοντες. ὅσα δὲ καὶ οὗτοι ἐπέσχον
τῆς Φωκίδος, πάντα ἐσιναμώρεον· καὶ γὰρ τῶν Πανοπέων
τὴν πόλιν ἐνέπρησαν καὶ Δαυλίων καὶ Αἰολιδέων. ἐπορεύοντο 5

·⁹ 35. 2 ὁρμέατο CP　　**3** παρνησὸν α : παρνησσὸν　　**5** αἰολίδων
Pz : Λιλαιέων Valckenaer, (Blakesley), van H.

35. 1. ταύτῃ : sc. ἐς Βοιωτούς.
ἄλλοι δὲ αὐτῶν : Hdt. gives
neither the number of the force sent to
Delphi, nor the name of its commander.
ἡγεμόνας : sc. τῆς ὁδοῦ, cp. c. 31 *supra* :
their names, their race, anonymous too !
2. ὁρμέατο has no psychological
suggestion, but is purely mechanical ;
cp. 7. 215 ὁρμέατο δὲ περὶ λύχνων ἅφας
ἐκ τοῦ στρατοπέδου.
τὸ ἱρὸν τὸ ἐν Δελφοῖσι : the
geographical position of Delphi hardly
requires elucidation, in general : situate
on a sloping edge, or shelf of rock, 2000
feet above the sea, backed by sheer cliffs
of Parnassos, with the gorge of the Pleis-
tos immediately below walled in by the
ridge of Kirphis, with the fertile plain of
Amphissa, of Kirrha, beyond, in full view
of the Krissaian bay, and sighting the
Arkadian mountains that tower beyond
the Korinthian gulf, Delphi yields in
natural charms and grandeur of aspect
and prospect to no landscape in Hellas !
It is accessible from three directions :
(i.) The easiest route comes up from the
sea, across the plain, and the steep spurs
of Parnassos, half a day's journey. (ii.)
Behind Delphi, up over the western
heights and glades of Parnassos, runs
the path to Lilaia (*Agoriani*) in the
valley of the Kephisos, cp. c. 33 *supra*.
(iii.) Away to the east goes the better
route, first rising and then descending,
from Delphi to Boiotia, forking after a
while (the σχιστὴ ὁδός !), the right path
running on to Lebadeia, the left to
Daulia, Panopeus, and so on into
Boiotia, cp. l. 4 *supra*. It is by this
last route that Hdt. would have us conceive the Persian column approaching
the shrine. τὸ ἱρόν was of course the
fabric of the Alkmaionidai : 5. 62. On
all that concerns the topography and
archæology of the place cf. Frazer's
Pausanias, v. 234-398 (pending the full
and official publication of the results of
the excavations conducted by the French
School).

ἐν δεξιῇ τὸν Παρνησὸν ἀπέργοντες :
these words would describe their position
ever since they crossed from Trachis
into Doris, and then marched down the
Kephisos. They would also bar out,
if accepted as final, not merely the
advance on Delphi by the Πυθιάς or
sacred road from the north, *via* Amphissa,
but also an advance from Lilaia across
Parnassos, by which the highest points
of Parnassos would still have lain to
the left. Hdt., believing Panopeus to
be the point of departure, naturally says
they marched with Parnassos on their
right, and, he might have added, with
Helikon and Kirphis on their left.
3. ὅσα δὲ . . ἐπέσχον . . ἐσιναμώρεον :
cp. c. 32 *supra*. σιναμωρέειν (cp. 1. 152,
5. 92 σινάμωρος) appears to be a strengthened variant of σίνεσθαι or σινέεσθαι, c.
31 *supra*. The conduct ascribed to them
is irrational, as they would need supplies
on their way back from Delphi—for they
must have intended to return ; and this
statement is, therefore, inconsistent with
the idea that the visitors for Delphi
started on this occasion from Panopeus.
4. Πανοπέων : cp. 34 *supra* ; i.e. after
the main army had gone on into Boiotia
this corps remained behind and destroyed Panopeus ! If the corps detached
for Delphi destroyed Panopeus, then
assuredly it was on the way down from
Delphi, and not before starting. This
inference favours the view that this corps
had marched *via* Lilaia or Amphissa.
5. Δαυλίων, situate a little way up
the ascent of route (iii.), and the last
station apparently on the road to Delphi
(cp. Strabo 423). From Daulis to Delphi
(or *vice versa*) is an easy day's march ;
cp. *Iliad* 2. 520, Thuc. 2. 29. 3.
Αἰολιδέων, unknown and unintelligible as a place-name : does it represent the modern *Arachova* ! i.e.
Anemoreia (cp. Bursian, *op. cit.* i. 170,
Frazer v. 232). Or shall we not
rather accept Valckenaer's conjecture
ΛΙΛΑΙΕΩΝ, approved by Blakesley,

δὲ ταύτῃ ἀποσχισθέντες τῆς ἄλλης στρατιῆς τῶνδε εἵνεκα,
ὅκως συλήσαντες τὸ ἱρὸν τὸ ἐν Δελφοῖσι βασιλέι Ξέρξῃ
ἀποδέξαιεν τὰ χρήματα. πάντα δ᾽ ἠπίστατο τὰ ἐν τῷ ἱρῷ
ὅσα λόγου ἦν ἄξια Ξέρξης, ὡς ἐγὼ πυνθάνομαι, ἄμεινον ἢ τὰ

6 ταύτην α ‖ εἵνεκεν β   7 συλλήσαντες Sz ‖ τὸ ἐν Δελφοῖσι
'moleste repetitum' Kallenberg ‖ Ξέρξῃ del. van H.   8 δὲ ἐπιστέατο
RSV (ἐπίστατο Schaefer, Bekker) ‖ τὰ om. β

and then reverse the route of this corps, and obtain a name which is conspicuous by its absence in the Herodotean catalogue? Διλαιέων would of course be from Διλαιεύς or Δίλαιαι. Lilaia was an important member of the Phokian confederacy, and its omission from Hdt.'s list (which with it contains fifteen of the twenty-one names in the list of Pausanias) is very remarkable. Cp. note to c. 33 supra.

6. τῶνδε εἵνεκα. The political position and relations of the oracle at the time are of vital importance as bearing upon the story of the Persian visitation in 480 B.C. In the Iliad Pytho, or Python, is apparently as much a Phokian city as Daulis or Panopeus, Hyampolis or Lilaia (2. 517 ff.), which proves, inter alia, that the Catalogue is older than the First Sacred War. That war, waged by the 'Amphiktyons' on behalf of the Delphians, raised or secured the pan-Hellenic significance of the oracle, and doubtless emancipated it completely from Phokian leading. Whether an Ionian (Athens-Sikyon) or a Dorian (Sparta) or a Thessalian influence thereafter predominated may be matter of dispute; but the Phokians at least were but one among the Amphiktyonic folks. The war with the Thessalians, οὐ πολλοῖσι ἔτεσι πρότερον ταύτης τῆς βασιλέος στρατηλασίης c. 27 supra, may have had something of the character of a ἱερὸς πόλεμός, although never so described. It cannot, however, be supposed that on the eve of the Persian war the Delphic oracle had sunk again to be a mere member of the Phokian League, or a mere organ of Phokian policy; the continuous notices of the oracle's action and utterances, from the date of the destruction of the temple in 548 B.C. to the Persian war, forbid that hypothesis. Or even if Phokian influence had been predominant, at least as against Thessalian, would the Thessalians have aimed at the destruction of the Amphiktyonic shrine, and not rather

at the re-establishment of their own influence in Delphi, as commissaries and protégés of the Persian? The national Phokian oracle was at Abai; hence its treatment, c. 33 supra. Delphi was the concern of twelve peoples, of whom nine were now on the king's part, the Thessalians imprimis. Clearly the Thessalians cannot have taken the Persians to Delphi ὅκως συλήσαντες τὸ ἱρὸν τὸ ἐν Δελφοῖσι β. Ξ. ἀποδέξαιεν τὰ χρήματα.

8. ἀποδέξαιεν τὰ χρήματα, 'might exhibit, display, the objects of value' (not merely money). The assumption appears to be that they would pillage the temple, bring away the things, and exhibit them to the king—when they had overtaken him. Some of the things would have been rather difficult to transport, especially by that route! And would the king have been content merely to be a spectator of the show? If so, his best way was to go to Delphi in person and see for himself. The phrase might suggest that course as the one actually taken; but as in the sequel the Persians were utterly discomfited and routed, and no such disaster was or could be reported of the king himself, did the Delphic apologist discreetly suppress the visit of the Persian king?

πάντα δ᾽ ἠπίστατο . . ἄξια: this assertion would read less like a gross exaggeration if Xerxes had, indeed, visited Delphi, and seen the temple and its treasures with his own eyes. Otherwise the statement is a frigid absurdity, not made any better by the rationalistic reminder πολλῶν αἰεὶ λεγόντων, nor by the cautious asseveration ὡς ἐγὼ πυνθάνομαι. Where could Hdt. have convinced himself by inquiry of this absurdity if not in Delphi itself? The Delphian visitation is obviously from a Delphian source, and the story of it, a patent apology for the attitude of Delphi in the war, is an obvious insertion in the main draft of the history. Cp. Introduction, §§ 9, 10, Appendix III. § 7.

ἐν τοῖσι οἰκίοισι ἔλιπε, πολλῶν αἰεὶ λεγόντων, καὶ μάλιστα 10
τὰ Κροίσου τοῦ Ἀλυάττεω ἀναθήματα. οἱ Δελφοὶ δὲ πυν- 36
θανόμενοι ταῦτα ἐς πᾶσαν ἀρρωδίην ἀπίκατο, ἐν δείματι δὲ
μεγάλῳ κατεστεῶτες ἐμαντεύοντο περὶ τῶν ἱρῶν χρημάτων,
εἴτε σφέα κατὰ γῆς κατορύξωσι εἴτε ἐκκομίσωσι ἐς ἄλλην
χώρην. ὁ δὲ θεός σφεας οὐκ ἔα κινέειν, φὰς αὐτὸς ἱκανὸς 5
εἶναι τῶν ἑωυτοῦ προκατῆσθαι. Δελφοὶ δὲ ταῦτα ἀκούσαντες
σφέων αὐτῶν πέρι ἐφρόντιζον. τέκνα μέν νυν καὶ γυναῖκας
πέρην ἐς τὴν Ἀχαιίην διέπεμψαν, αὐτῶν δὲ οἱ μὲν πλεῖστοι

---

11 ἀλυάττεω PR   36. 1 οἱ δὲ δελφοὶ β, Holder, van H.   2
ἀρρωιδίην P ‖ ἀπικέατο Pz ‖ δὲ : τε β   4 σφεας β ‖ κατορύξουσι
Pz ‖ εἴτ β ‖ ἐκκομίσουσι Pz   5 σφεας abesse malim ‖ κινεῖν α, Holder,
van H.   7 περιεφρόντιζον BC   8 ἀχαίην R

---

11. **τὰ Κροίσου τοῦ Ἀλυάττεω ἀναθήματα**: there is no reference here to ὁ πρῶτος τῶν λόγων, cp. 5. 36, and the use of the patronymic is noticeable. The observation supports the hypothesis that these Books (7, 8, 9), even in their second or enlarged draft (cp. previous note), were composed and in existence before the earlier Books (and the *Lydian Logoi* of Bk. 1 perhaps before the story of the Ionian Revolt in Bks. 5–6). Cp. Introduction, §§ 7, 8.

36. 1. οἱ Δελφοί: properly the name of the men, the population; not the place, the city. The place-name is Πυθώ, cp. 1. 54 πέμψας αὐτὶς ἐς Πυθὼ Δελφοὺς δωρέεται. The Catalogue, *Iliad* 2. 519, has the form Πυθών, but Πυθώ (Πυθοῖ) in 9. 405 (with the *epitheton constans* πετρηέσσῃ). Pytho would be the holy place and oracular seat itself (hence ἡ Πυθία); the name of the people becomes the designation of the secular city. The native form of the name was Δάλφοι, a point illustrated, though not specified, in Head's *Hist. Num.* p. 288. Whether the name had anything to say to δελφίς, or to δελφύς (was not Pytho the ὀμφαλὸς τῆς γῆς?) is a question for the etymologists.

2 ταῦτα is vague, but may be referred generally to the sentence ἐπορεύοντο . . χρήματα rather than to the sentence πάντα . . ἀναθήματα, which was an aside by Hdt. *in propria persona.*

ἐς πᾶσαν ἀρρωδίην ἀπίκατο: the pl. perf. is rather intensive than strictly temporal, 'were in the depths of despair'; cp. 4. 140 ἐς τ. ἀρρ. ἀπίκοντο. **κατεστεῶτες**: the same phrase 7. 138, and cp. c. 12 *supra.*

3. **ἐμαντεύοντο περὶ τῶν ἱρῶν χρημάτων**: the first anxiety of the good Delphians is not about themselves, but about the holy things. ἐμ. is strictly medial; they would consult the god through the Pythia, although they apparently suggest two out of three possible alternatives: (a) to bury the treasures in the earth somewhere near, (b) to convey them into the Peloponnese. Are all the sacred vessels and offerings in all the 'Treasuries' (Lakedaimonian, Sikyonian, Siphnian, Korinthian, Athenian, Knidian, etc.) here in view?

5. **αὐτὸς ἱκανὸς εἶναι τῶν ἑαυτοῦ προκατῆσθαι**: the construction is strictly idiomatic. With προκατῆσθαι cp. προκατημένους 7. 172, in a more strictly physical sense, and the same infinitive 9. 106. The sentiment is a pious rendering, or anticipation, of the legal or cynical maxim of the Roman emperor, *Deorum iniurias Dis curae*, Tacit. *Ann.* 1. 73. 5.

7. **σφέων αὐτῶν πέρι ἐφρόντιζον**: little expecting a miraculous intervention on their own account, or that the defence and preservation of the ἱρὰ χρήματα would compass their own.

τέκνα . . καὶ γυναῖκας: cp. cc. 4, 40. The οἰκέται are to be understood.

8. **πέρην ἐς τὴν Ἀχαιίην**: no doubt by sea; a better asylum than Amphissa, where the majority of the Phokians had taken refuge, and might now think themselves lucky if they escaped the Persians and Thessalians; see *infra.*

αὐτῶν δέ is emphatically masculine.

ἀνέβησαν ἐς τοῦ Παρνησοῦ τὰς κορυφὰς καὶ ἐς τὸ Κωρύκιον
10 ἄντρον ἀνηνείκαντο, οἱ δὲ ἐς Ἄμφισσαν τὴν Λοκρίδα ὑπεξῆλθον.
πάντες δὲ ὦν οἱ Δελφοὶ ἐξέλιπον τὴν πόλιν, πλὴν ἑξήκοντα
37 ἀνδρῶν καὶ τοῦ προφήτεω. ἐπεὶ δὲ ἀγχοῦ ἦσαν οἱ βάρβαροι
ἐπιόντες καὶ ἀπώρων τὸ ἱρόν, ἐν τούτῳ ὁ προφήτης, τῷ
οὔνομα ἦν Ἀκήρατος, ὁρᾷ πρὸ τοῦ νηοῦ ὅπλα προκείμενα

---

9 παρνησσοῦ β　　10 ἀνηνείκατο C ‖ ἄμφισαν C　　11 ἐξέλειπον B
37. 1 ἐπείτε δὲ ? van H. ‖ ἀγχοῦ τε β, Holder, van H.　　2 ἀπώρεον
CPdₐ

---

9. τοῦ Παρνησοῦ τὰς κορυφάς looks
like 'the twin peaks,' but is probably
used more generally ; cp. 9. 104 σῴζωνται ἐς τὰς κορυφὰς τῆς Μυκάλης.
The Phokians had, some of them, gone
up ἐς τὰ ἄκρα τοῦ Παρνησοῦ c. 32 supra ;
but there was plenty of room on the
heights and peaks of Parnassos for
Phokians and Delphians.

τὸ Κωρύκιον ἄντρον : the Korykian
cavern, an immense hollow in the lime-
stone, but of less extent and mystery
than our own caves in the Peak (καὶ
ἔστιν ἐπὶ πλεῖστον ὁδεῦσαι δι' αὐτοῦ καὶ
ἄνευ λαμπτήρων Pausan. 10. 32. 7), is
reached from Delphi by ascending above
the 'Phaidriades' on a very steep path
into the upper plateau, still well-wooded,
beyond which rises a steep conical and
rocky hill, near the top of which the
entrance to the cavern may be detected.
(A scramble of twenty-five minutes took
me up this hill on April 7, 1899.) It
was sacred to Pan and to the Nymphs,
Pausan. l.c., Strabo 417.

10. ἀνηνείκαντο, ibidem ; c. 32 supra.

ἐς Ἄμφισσαν τὴν Λοκρίδα : there
they would foregather with the mass of
the Phokian refugees ; cp. c. 32 supra.
The absence of any cross reference, and
the repeated yet different description
of Amphissa, confirm the opinion that
this story of the preservation of Delphi
is an independent narrative, from a
different source, and of later composition
and insertion in the main draft of the
work ; cp. c. 35. 8 supra.

11. δὲ ἄν, 'one way or another.'

πλὴν ἑξήκοντα ἀνδρῶν : why 60 ?
Was that t e number of the Delphian
Council, perhaps, at this date, an
aristocratic body, and did it remain,
like the Roman curule magistrates and
senators, at the coming of the Gauls ?
cp. Livy 5. 41. (The political constitu-

tion of the Delphic state is an enigma ;
the history of Delphi is best given by
H. Pomtow ap. Pauly-Wissowa iv. 1901,
2517 ff.)

12. καὶ τοῦ προφήτεω : his name is
supplied just below, Akeratos. It is
a little surprising that the 'prophet'
and not the 'Pythia' is there. The
exact function of the Delphian, or
Pythian, προφήτης is obscure ; he is
presumably at the head of the Delphian
hierarchy, but whether an ἱερεύς or not,
whether a sole official or with a colleague
or colleagues, are questions hardly to be
answered positively, least of all for the
earlier period. The 'prophet' or 'priest'
would be distinct anyway from the five
ὅσιοι mentioned by Plutarch, Mor. 438
(with the προφήτης) and 292 (πέντε δέ
εἰσι Ὅσιοι διὰ βίου καὶ τὰ πολλὰ μετὰ τῶν
προφητῶν (sic) δρῶσιν οὗτοι, καὶ συνιε-
ρουργοῦσιν, ἅτε γεγονέναι δοκοῦντες ἀπὸ
Δευκαλίωνος) ; like them, and the Pythia
herself, the 'prophets' would hold office
for life.

37. 1. ἀγχοῦ ἦσαν . . καὶ ἀπώρων :
a parataxis. Apparently they never
entered the sacred precincts, but just
came within sight of the temple. They
would have to come pretty near to be
in sight, owing to the way in which
the cliffs project on the road from
Arachova. With ἀπώρων cp. ἀπιδόντες
9. 69.

2. ὁ προφήτης, τῷ οὔνομα ἦν Ἀκήρατος,
see note previous chapter. The name is
rare as a proper name, though common
enough as an epithet, a fine one for a
prophet or a priest (integer, pure, un-
mixed, undefiled).

3. ὁρᾷ : graphic present : πρό, very
distinctly of place. The νηός here would
denote the whole structure, including
the peristyle. The arms would have
been lying before the east front of the
temple, in the open space on the terrace

ἔσωθεν ἐκ τοῦ μεγάρου ἐξενηνειγμένα ἱρά, τῶν οὐκ ὅσιον ἦν
ἅπτεσθαι ἀνθρώπων οὐδενί. ὁ μὲν δὴ ἤιε Δελφῶν τοῖσι 5
παρεοῦσι σημανέων τὸ τέρας· οἱ δὲ βάρβαροι ἐπειδὴ ἐγίνοντο
ἐπειγόμενοι κατὰ τὸ ἱρὸν τῆς Προναίης Ἀθηναίης, ἐπιγίνεταί
σφι τέρεα ἔτι μέζονα τοῦ πρὶν γενομένου τέρεος. θῶμα μὲν
γὰρ καὶ τοῦτο κάρτα ἐστί, ὅπλα ἀρήια αὐτόματα φανῆναι

---

4 ἐξενηνεγμένα α ‖ ἱρά : ἀρήια Naber   5 ἀνθρώπῳ Β ‖ ἤιε C   7
προνηίης RV, Holder, van H. : προνοιίης Sα   8 γεγενημένου Βα ‖
τέρεος del. van H. ‖ θῶμα α, Stein², van H. : θώνμα Β : θῶυμα Stein¹,
Holder ‖ μὲν om. β

---

where now are the remains of the Altar
of the Chians (see plan, Frazer v. 258).

4. τῶν οὐκ ὅσιον ἦν: they were
ἀκίνητα ; cp. c. 36 *supra*.

5. ὁ μὲν δὴ ἤιε: he was evidently in
the temple precincts ; the 'sixty' were
elsewhere.

6. τὸ τέρας: a marvel, sign, *in
abstracto* ; cp. c. 98 τέρας ἀνθρώποισι τῶν
μελλόντων ἔσεσθαι κακῶν ἔφαινε ὁ Θεός.
Down below τέρεα seems to be used in a
slightly more concrete sense, of actual
φάσματα, as certainly c. 27 *supra*, if the
reading stand. Similar portents assured
the courage of the Thebans before
Leuktra : Xenophon, *Hell.* 6. 4. 7
ἀπηγγέλλετο δὲ καὶ ἐκ τῆς πόλεως αὐτοῖς
ὡς οἱ τε νεῷ πάντες αὐτόματοι ἀνεῴγοντο,
αἱ τε ἱέρειαι λέγοιεν ὡς νίκην οἱ θεοὶ φαί-
νοιεν. ἐκ δὲ τοῦ Ἡρακλείου καὶ τὰ ὅπλα
ἔφασαν ἀφανῆ εἶναι, ὡς τοῦ Ἡρακλέους
εἰς τὴν μάχην ἐξωρμημένον. Xenophon,
who, though pious, is no friend to
Thebes, adds : οἱ μὲν δή τινες λέγουσιν ὡς
ταῦτα πάντα τεχνάσματα ἦν τῶν προεστη-
κότων.

7. κατά: of place ; in the vicinity of,
in a line with, over against.

τὸ ἱρὸν τῆς Προναίης Ἀθηναίης.
This temple has now been identified by
M. Homolle, and excavated ; see *J.H.S.*
xxi. (1901) 347. It was the last of five
buildings on the left of the road from
Arachova to Delphi, which formed an
important group, or row, outside the
Pythian sanctuary itself, at a spot known
as the *Marmaria*, halfway between the
Logari and the *gymnasium*. The first
of these buildings was in ruins at the
time of Pausanias, the other four he
mentions. The temple of Athene is now
identified, not with the Rotunda or
tholos (as by Laurent), but with a
temple *in antis*, built of local lime-
stone, the last of the five (πεντέλοιπος !)

and therefore rightly πρόναιος, which
agrees with the description of ps.-
Demosth. *Or.* 25. 34 παρὰ τῷ Ἀπόλλωνι
ἐν Δελφοῖς κάλλιστος καὶ μέγιστος νεὼς
εὐθὺς εἰσιόντι εἰς τὸ ἱερόν. That Προναία
(cp. 1. 92, where the same temple is
mentioned) is the official title of the
goddess at Delphi is proved by inscriptions ; albeit προνοία is a frequent variant,
found apparently in Pausanias 10. 8. 7,
and therefore followed by J. G. Frazer,
Pausanias, v. 251.

8. θῶμα: a more generic term than
τέρας, and probably more 'subjective,'
or psychological, at least in 'origin.'
Hdt.'s method of describing the portent,
miracle, apparition, godsend—perhaps in
close loyalty to his source—is remarkable, and suggests some antecedent
challenge, doubt, discussion. (*a*) There
is a *crescendo*, a climax, from τέρας to
τέρεα ἔτι μέζονα, and so on. (*b*) Thrice
is the exact locality of the apparition
indicated, κατὰ τὸ ἱρὸν τῆς Προναίης
Ἀθηναίης (*bis*), ἐν τῷ τεμενέι τ. Π. Ἀ. (*c*)
His grammar becomes slightly disordered,
as not infrequently, at moments of
excitation : οἱ δὲ βάρβαροι . . ἐπιγίνεταί
σφι. (*d*) He urges the case for marvelling
the more : θῶμα μὲν γὰρ . . ἄξια θωμάσαι
μάλιστα. (*e*) He adduces as evidence
confirmatory of the miracle the stones
still lying in the close of Athene. (*f*)
He cites the Persians themselves as
witnesses for ἄλλα θεῖα sc. φάσματα, sc.
θώματα sc. τέρεα. One cannot but
admire the courage with which Delphi,
when censured for its escape in the
Persian war, knew how to defend itself.
It is likely that the critique had been
mainly an Athenian one ; if so, Delphi
called Athene Pronaia herself as chief
witness for the defence, and Athene
Pronaia, or Pronoia, was justified of her
children. Cp. Appendix III. § 4.

10 ἔξω προκείμενα τοῦ νηοῦ· τὰ δὲ δὴ ἐπὶ τούτῳ δεύτερα
ἐπιγενόμενα καὶ διὰ πάντων φασμάτων ἄξια θωμάσαι μάλιστα.
ἐπεὶ γὰρ δὴ ἦσαν ἐπιόντες οἱ βάρβαροι κατὰ τὸ ἱρὸν τῆς
Προναίης Ἀθηναίης, ἐν τούτῳ ἐκ μὲν τοῦ οὐρανοῦ κεραυνοὶ
αὐτοῖσι ἐνέπιπτον, ἀπὸ δὲ τοῦ Παρνησοῦ ἀπορραγεῖσαι δύο
15 κορυφαὶ ἐφέροντο πολλῷ πατάγῳ ἐς αὐτοὺς καὶ κατέβαλον
συχνούς σφεων, ἐκ δὲ τοῦ ἱροῦ τῆς Προναίης βοή τε καὶ
38 ἀλαλαγμὸς ἐγίνετο. συμμιγέντων δὲ τούτων πάντων, φόβος
τοῖσι βαρβάροισι ἐνεπεπτώκεε. μαθόντες δὲ οἱ Δελφοὶ φεύγοντας σφέας, ἐπικαταβάντες ἀπέκτειναν πλῆθός τι αὐτῶν.
οἱ δὲ περιεόντες ἰθὺ Βοιωτῶν ἔφευγον. ἔλεγον δὲ οἱ ἀπονο-

---

11 ἐπιγενόμενα Pz, Stein² : ἐπιγινόμενα α, Stein¹ : γινόμενα β ‖
θωμάσαι α, Stein², van H. : θωυμάσαι β, Stein¹, Holder   12 ἐπείτε ?
van H.   13 προνηίης R, Holder, van H. : προνοιίης SVz   14
παρνησοῦ α : παρνησσοῦ ‖ ἀπορραγῆσαι α   15 κατέβαλον Reiske,
Stein², van H. : κατέλαβον   16 προνηίης β, Holder, van H. :
προνοιίης SVz (νηοῦ add. V)   38. 1 συμμισγέντων C   3 τι :
τε β   4 ἰθὺ βz : εὐθὺ

---

10. δεύτερα, 'next,' but not inferior.

11. διὰ πάντων: in the whole catalogue
(number, series) of . . ; cp. 1. 25 of the
krater of Glaukes the Chian, θέης ἄξιον
διὰ πάντων τῶν ἐν Δελφοῖσι ἀναθημάτων.
Also 7. 83 supra.

13. ἐν τούτῳ: sc. τῷ χρόνῳ.

κεραυνοί: fulmina; thunderbolts,
strictly material and massive (like the
rocks themselves), and not the mere
flashes of lightning (στεροπαί, fulgura)
much less the mere crash or rumble of
thunder (βρονταί, tonitrus). A thunder-
bolt can strike a ship: Od. 14. 305
ἔμβαλε νηὶ κεραυνόν etc.

14. δύο κορυφαί: not αἱ δ. κ. but
simply two 'peaks' or pointed rocks;
cp. τοῦ Παρνησοῦ τὰς κορυφάς c. 36 supra,
which cannot be supposed to have fallen
on the Persians.

16. βοή τε καὶ ἀλαλαγμός, 'war-whoop
and battle-cry '—a distinction without a
difference: βοή is perhaps more generic.
ἀλαλάζειν is to utter a specific cry,
ἀλαλαί. Perhaps this is a cry of victory;
cp. νίκην ὁρμῶντα ἀλαλάξαι Soph. Antig.
133. Pindar uses ἀλαλά (ἀλαλή) Nem.
3. 60, Isth. 6. (7.) 10, which L. & S. render
'the cry with which battle was begun,'
and Rumpel (Lex. Pind. (1883) p. 25)
clamor bellicus. Most remarkable is the
personification Pindar Fr. 78 (225) κλῦθ'
Ἀλαλὰ Πολεμοῦ θύγατερ. The words
ἀλαλάζειν et cog. of course came to be

used for any loud cry, shout, etc.
ἐλελίζειν is to raise the cry ἐλελεῦ, a
battle-cry still, but a thinner, shriller
one than ἀλαλαί, while ὀλολύζειν—the
cry ὀλολύ—is distinctly womanish:
ὠλόλυξαν μὲν αἱ γυναῖκες, ἠλάλαξαν δὲ οἱ
ἄνδρες Heliod. 3. 5.
We cry the cry still in our borrowed
Allelu-jah; but it is only the 'Salvation
Army' which uses it as a 'war-cry.'

38. 1. συμμιγέντων: more forcible
than συμπεσόντων, συνελθόντων. It is
only τὰ μέγονα τέρεα, not τὸ πρὶν γενόμενον τέρας, that could strictly be included
in the μίξις. The new-comers would
not know the miracle of the arms.

φόβος . . ἐνεπεπτώκεε, 'a panic
possessed them': the pluperfect tense
is rather rhetorical and stylistic than
strictly temporal, much less past, in its
effects. The φόβος is of course θεῖόν τι.

2. οἱ Δελφοὶ . . ἐπικαταβάντες: that
is, of course, from the peaks of Parnassos
and the Korykian cavern, c. 36 supra,
but not before the Persians were in
panic-stricken flight.

3. πλῆθός τι: the exact number of
the Persians slain on this occasion
would surely have been noted and
remembered were the episode itself
historical. This numerical vagueness is
another nail in the coffin of this dead
history.

4. ἰθὺ Βοιωτῶν: ex hypothesi by the

στήσαντες οὗτοι τῶν βαρβάρων, ὡς ἐγὼ πυνθάνομαι, ὡς πρὸς 5
τούτοισι καὶ ἄλλα ὥρων θεῖα· δύο γὰρ ὁπλίτας μεζόνως ἢ
κατ᾽ ἀνθρώπων φύσιν ἔχοντας ἔπεσθαί σφι κτείνοντας καὶ
διώκοντας. τούτους δὲ τοὺς δύο Δελφοὶ λέγουσι εἶναι ἐπι- 39
χωρίους ἥρωας Φύλακόν τε καὶ Αὐτόνοον, τῶν τὰ τεμένεα

---

6 μεζόνως: μέζονας codd., Stein, van H.: 'aut μεζόνως legendum aut
μέζονα aut tandem delendum ἔχοντας' Reiske: μεζόνως Holder: μέζονα
ἢ κατὰ ἄνθρωπον Wesseling: ἔχοντας secl. Stein, van H.: ἐόντας pro
ἔχοντας coni. Koen: μέζονας ἢ κατ᾽ ἄνθρωπον ἔπεσθαί vult Cobet: κατὰ
ACs　　　　　39. 1 εἶναι post ἥρωας Pz

---

way they had come, which would bring
them down to Daulia, and so to
Panopeus and to Orchomenos, where
they may have rejoined—or have joined
—the army. Perhaps Xerxes himself
crossed Parnassos from Lilaia to Delphi,
and so to Daulia and Panopeus, and
there rejoined the main body of the
army; cp. c. 34 *supra*.

Ἔλεγον . . οἱ ἀπονοστήσαντες . .
ὡς ἐγὼ πυνθάνομαι. Where did Hdt.
get this information? Was it from
Thersandros of Orchomenos, who seems
to have made it his business to collect,
or to relate (*ex eventu*), the signs of
Persian pessimism and panic in the war
(cp. 9. 16); or was it from the Delphians,
who, of course, could easily have gotten
the information from Greeks in the
Persian camp? The story was certainly
to be heard at Delphi, for the Delphians
interpreted it to Hdt.—and we can hardly
suppose that he first told the facts to
the Delphians and asked for the interpretation.

5. πρὸς τούτοισι καὶ ἄλλα ὥρων θεῖα:
in addition there were other manifesta-
tions of a supernatural order. ὁρᾶν is
used in an extended sense, for there had
been πάταγος, βοή, ἀλαλαγμός, φόβος,
φυγή, τραύματα, besides φάσματα. Even
their experiences with these further
apparitions are not confined to ὄψεις.

7. ἀνθρώπων φύσιν: φύσις is 'growth,'
hence 'stature,' for which φυή is the
more usual term, which, *vice versa*, is
used at times as = φύσις, in the usual
senses. Each exchange is poetic, and
chiefly to be illustrated from Pindar;
cp. Rumpel, *Lexicon, sub vv.* The text
is here in doubt; cp. App. Crit.
Reiske's suggestion, adopted by Holder,
is supported by Isokrates, 9. 21 τὰς μὲν
φήμας καὶ τὰς μαντείας καὶ τὰς ὄψεις τὰς
ἐν τοῖς ὕπνοις γενομένας, ἐξ ὧν μειζόνως
ἂν φανείη γεγονὼς ἢ κατ᾽ ἄνθρωπον,

αἱροῦμαι παραλιπεῖν κτλ., for if we may
say μειζόνως ἢ κατ᾽ ἄνθρωπον γεγονέναι
we may say μειζόνως ἔχειν ἢ κατ᾽ ἀνθρώπων
φύσιν.

καὶ διώκοντας seems rather weak,
but is added to explain why any escaped.

39. 1. Δελφοὶ λέγουσι: it hardly
needs this late indication to prove the
story of the miraculous preservation of
the Delphians, their temple and its
treasures, a local Delphian legend, in
the last resort. The phrase in itself
would not prove that Hdt. had gleaned
information in Delphi, but the context
below points to that conclusion.

2. Φύλακόν τε καὶ Αὐτόνοον: Phylakos
has a significant name (cp. φύλακος 1. 84
et passim), which is also a genuine *pro-
prium*, cp. c. 85 *infra*. In the *Iliad*
(besides a 'Trojan' of the name, 6. 35)
Podarkes, leader of the Thessalians, is
son of Iphiklos, and grandson of Phylakos
(heroic founder of Phylake), 2. 695–705,
and the name reappears in *Od.* 15. 231.
Could the Delphian 'Phylakos' be, after
all, a Thessalian hero, and a further
witness of the early period of Thessalian
predominance in Delphi?

Autonoos, the name of a Danaan slain
by Hektor, *Il.* 11. 301, is also found on
the 'Trojan' side, *ll.* 16. 694 (a hero
slain by Patroklos). But again the name
appears in historic times in Thessaly,
Polyb. 7. 5. 8.

τῶν τὰ τεμένεα: the ''closes' of
these heroes were in the vicinity of the
Pythian sanctuary; that of Phylakos
hard by the road (from Delphi to
Arachova and Daulia) along which the
Persians fled, and so on higher ground
than the temple of Pronaia Athene; that
of Autonoos 'nigh Kastalia, the famous
spring and burn close under the Hyam-
peian peak.' A small building, one of
two discovered in the excavation of the
Marmaria, has been conjecturally identi-

ἐστὶ περὶ τὸ ἱρόν, Φυλάκου μὲν παρ' αὐτὴν τὴν ὁδὸν
κατύπερθε τοῦ ἱροῦ τῆς Προναίης, Αὐτονόου δὲ πέλας τῆς
5 Κασταλίης ὑπὸ τῇ Ὑαμπείῃ κορυφῇ. οἱ δὲ πεσόντες ἀπὸ
τοῦ Παρνησοῦ λίθοι ἔτι καὶ ἐς ἡμέας ἦσαν σόοι, ἐν τῷ τεμένεϊ
τῆς Προναίης Ἀθηναίης κείμενοι, ἐς τὸ ἐνέσκηψαν διὰ τῶν
βαρβάρων φερόμενοι. τούτων μέν νυν τῶν ἀνδρῶν αὕτη ἀπὸ
τοῦ ἱροῦ ἀπαλλαγὴ γίνεται.

4 προνηίης R : προνοιίης SVz   6 παρνησοῦ α : παρνησσοῦ ‖ ἔσαν ℤ
‖ σῶοι CPz ‖ τεμένεϊ AB   7 προνηίης R : προνοιίης SVz ‖ ἀνέσκηψαν B :
ἐνεσκήψαντο B

fied with the Phylakion (*J. H. S.* xxi.
1901, p. 347), which would thus appear
to have been on the same side of the
road as the Athenaion. Pausanias 10.
8. 7 describes the Φυλάκου τέμενος as
πρὸς τῷ ἱερῷ τῆς Προνοίης (*sic*). For
the temenos of Autonoos see next note.
Thirlwall (ii. 326) assumes that these
dedications were made in consequence
of the events of 480 B.C., but there is
nothing in Hdt. to suggest that (cp.
contra 7. 189).

5. Κασταλίης: Pausan. 10. 8. 9 ἐκ
δὲ τοῦ γυμνασίου τὴν ἐς τὸ ἱερὸν ἀνιόντι
ἐστιν ἐν δεξιᾷ τῆς ὁδοῦ τὸ ὕδωρ τῆς
Κασταλίας, καὶ πιεῖν ἡδύ. There has
never been any doubt as to the identification of 'the water of Castaly' (cp.
the exhaustive note in Frazer, *Pausanias*
v. 255); but the shrine of the hero
Autonoos has not yet been certainly
identified, and is not even mentioned
by Pausanias. "Leake thought that
the little chapel of St. John hewn in
the rock above the pool might be the
precinct of the hero Autonoos. . . M.
Foucart prefers to suppose that the
precinct stood on a small platform
between the pool and the road. Bursian
thought he recognised a piece of the
wall which had enclosed the precinct,"
Frazer *l.c.* (Bursian i. 172, says dog-
matically enough : *In der Nähe der
Quelle war das Temenos des Heros
Autonoos, von welchem noch ein Stück
der Umfangsmauer erhalten ist.*)

τῇ Ὑαμπείῃ κορυφῇ : Hyampeia is
the sheer wall of rock rising into a
peaked summit a thousand feet or so
above the road and the spring, and
forming the right or eastern wall of the
gorge or chasm in which the Kastalian
waters arise. A similar peak flanks the
narrow chasm on the other side, but
the ancient name thereof has not been

preserved. It cannot possibly be these
two κορυφαί which earned Parnassos the
title of ' biceps' (cp. c. 32 *supra*), for
they are purely local features in the
Delphian landscape, and can never have
been mistaken for the actual summits of
the mountain, to one of which Hdt. has
already and correctly assigned a name
(c. 32 *supra*, if the passage be not a
gloss); Pape-Benseler's *Wörterbuch,* ii.
1573 *sub v.,* achieves indeed the confusion, or seems to do so (*eine der beiden
Bergspitzen des Parnassos in der Nähe
von Delphi*). Strabo 424 mentions
Hyampeia ἐν τῷ Παρνασσῷ only to
distinguish it from Τάμπολις or Ἴα
(cp. c. 33 *supra*). Plutarch, *Mor.* 557,
reports that the Delphians executed
Aisopos (cp. Hdt. 2. 134) ὤσαντες ἀπὸ
τῆς πέτρας ἐκείνης ἣν Ὑάμπειαν καλοῦσιν.

6. ἔτι καὶ ἐς ἡμέας ἦσαν σόοι, and,
for aught known, to the present day
also : for the ground about there, below
the road, is strewn with λίθοι, large and
smaller, all of which have doubtless
descended from Parnassos. The phrase
has the note of Hdt.'s 'autopsy,' and
the argument the stamp, alas ! of Hdt.'s
logic. He seems to think the stones an
evidence of the truth of the story. It
was, perhaps, the position of these stones
which determined the point reached by
the Persians in their "sacrilegious enterprise."

8. τούτων . . αὕτη . . ἀπαλλαγή : in
sharpest contrast to the usual departure
of good men, even non-Hellenes, who
came to worship, to seek advice and
consolation, to assist at the ἀγών or
other solemn function, and went their
way rejoicing.

9. γίνεται puts us *en rapport* with
the story and the story-tellers, rather
than with the Persians and their *exeunt.*
The story is verily a test one ; it is one

Ὁ δὲ Ἑλλήνων ναυτικὸς στρατὸς ἀπὸ τοῦ Ἀρτεμισίου 40
Ἀθηναίων δεηθέντων ἐς Σαλαμῖνα κατίσχει [τὰς νέας]. τῶνδε

40. 2 κατασχεῖν Β ‖ τὰς νέας secl. Stein[3] : τὰς νῆας Β ‖ τῶνδε : τῶν RS, Schaefer

of the most transparent fictions in Hdt., though one that fully imposed on the good man himself. The early Victorian rationalists made sad work of it, of whom the Rev. Professor Rawlinson may in this case be taken as typical. He (iv.[3] 291) interprets the story as follows :— (1) The fragments of rock "were carefully prepared beforehand," and precipitated by the men on the "peaks." (2) In falling the rocks made a noise, which was mistaken for "thunder." (3) The armour in front of the temple was arranged by a priest. (4) The war-cry was a shout from another priest. (5) The heroes were impersonated by "two men of unusual stature," or (6) may have been "a mere excuse" made to Xerxes by his men. Such is the last word of unhistorical criticism upon uncritical history. It may not be possible to determine exactly what took place at Delphi in 480 B.C., or whether the Persians had any direct relations with Delphi, or ever visited it at all; but two points may here at least be urged. (i.) The story just examined (cc. 35–39) is evidently *apologetic*, i.e. told and devised in order to explain the suspicious escape of Delphi in the war. (ii.) It must not be isolated, and considered merely on its own merits, but must be brought into relation with (a) the evidences in regard to the whole attitude and policy and action of Delphi throughout the great crisis, and even in other similar crises ; (b) the evidences for the policy of the Persians towards the Greeks, and especially towards the 'medizers,' who were as much interested in Delphi as any others ; (c) the accounts preserved in Pausanias (1. 4. 4, 10. 23) of the attack of the Gauls upon Delphi in the year 279 B.C., and the part played by the 'divine' in that second deliverance. For an attempt to appreciate the story from that point of view cp. Appendix III. § 4.

40. 1. ὁ δὲ Ἑλ. ν. στ. ἀπὸ τοῦ Ἀρτεμισίου: the narrative is resumed from c. 21 or 22 *supra*, or even from the words Θεμιστοκλέης μὲν ταῦτα ἐνέγραψε in c. 23. The present tense κατίσχει anticipates much of the intervening narra-

tive, the arrival of the Hellenic fleet "at Salamis" doubtless preceding the advance of the Persian forces from Thermopylai. The Greek fleet might well have arrived at the Salaminian station within forty-eight hours of quitting Artemision. If it left Artemision on Tuesday night (as it were) it might easily have reached Salamis in the course of Thursday morning. The words ἀπὸ τ. Ἀρτ. might be taken loosely to qualify ὁ . . στρατός, or might be loosely constructed with κατίσχει, or might seem to desiderate a participle, e.g. ἀπαχθείς. For κατίσχει cp. 6. 101, and App. Crit.

2. Ἀθηναίων δεηθέντων. It is generally assumed that in the conception of Hdt. and his sources the station at Salamis was no part of the general plan of defence, but an after-thought, and an impromptu. To what extent is this assumption binding? What event called for an improvisation? The failure at Thermopylai? Or the non-appearance of the Peloponnesian forces in Boiotia? Had the full levy of the land-forces been, as was expected, already north of Kithairon, or even of the Isthmos, where better could the Greek fleet have halted than in the straits of Salamis? What appears to have taken the Athenians by surprise was that a situation had been allowed to arise in which the complete evacuation of Attica had become at least an open question. It is here that I would insert the story of the consultation of the Delphic oracle told, anachronistically, 7. 140–143 *supra*.

τῶνδε δὲ εἵνεκα. Hdt.'s motivation in this passage is curious, and perhaps involves a *hysteron-proteron*. He treats the evacuation of Attica as a foregone conclusion, and the problem of the *quid agendum* as only starting from that *fait accompli*. But τὸ ποιητέον ἔσται covers all that and much more (τό, of course, relative). Had the Peloponnesian forces been in Boiotia (as was expected), the evacuation of Attica would not have been in question, but Salamis might still have been the natural halting-place for the fleet, covering, as it would have done, the land-forces in Boiotia from the rear, or flank. But so far from the

δὲ εἵνεκα προσεδεήθησαν αὐτῶν σχεῖν πρὸς Σαλαμῖνα ᾿Αθηναῖοι,
ἵνα αὐτοὶ παῖδάς τε καὶ γυναῖκας ὑπεξαγάγωνται ἐκ τῆς
5 ᾿Αττικῆς, πρὸς δὲ καὶ βουλεύσωνται τὸ ποιητέον αὐτοῖσι
ἔσται. ἐπὶ γὰρ τοῖσι κατήκουσι πρήγμασι βουλὴν ἔμελλον
ποιήσασθαι ὡς ἐψευσμένοι γνώμης. δοκέοντες γὰρ εὑρήσειν
Πελοποννησίους πανδημὶ ἐν τῇ Βοιωτίῃ ὑποκατημένους τὸν
βάρβαρον, τῶν μὲν εὗρον οὐδὲν ἐόν, οἱ δὲ ἐπυνθάνοντο τὸν
10 ᾿Ισθμὸν αὐτοὺς τειχέοντας, ὡς τὴν Πελοπόννησον περὶ πλείστου
τε ποιευμένους περιεῖναι καὶ ταύτην ἔχοντας ἐν φυλακῇ, τὰ

---

4 ἵν᾿ C ‖ αὐτοὶ om. ß   7 ποιήσεσθαι ßPz, Holder, van H.   8
πελοποννησίους R ‖ πανδημεὶ ß, Stein   9 τῶν, οἱ μὲν z   10 ὡς τὴν
Stein², van H.: τὴν α, Stein¹, Holder: καὶ τὴν ß: ἐς τὴν Pz: εἰς τὴν
C ‖ πελοπόννησον R   11 τε post περιεῖναι ß ‖ ποιευμένους R: ποιεο-
μένους ‖ τἄλλα ß: τἆλλα z, Holder: τὰ δὲ ἄλλα van H.

---

complete evacuation of Attica being a
self-obvious necessity, it was even now
not really adopted or fully carried out,
cp. c. 51 *infra*. Moreover, there would
be the question, even in the case of the
women and children (παῖδάς τε καὶ
γυναῖκας, cp. cc. 36 *supra*, 41, 44, 60
infra), to what place or places they were
to be conveyed. These are all matters
for separate deliberation by the Athenians
alone (it is not possible to refer αὐτοὶ
and αὐτοῖσι to different persons); but
they leave the purely strategic plan of
occupying the straits of Salamis untouched.

6. τοῖσι κατήκουσι πρήγμασι (cp. c.
19 *supra*) may cover the evacuation of
Artemision, but refers primarily to the
news that the Peloponnesians, instead of
being in full force beyond Kithairon, are
busy fortifying the Isthmos. This news
required formal deliberation, and the
situation was discussed in Athens by the
βουλή and ἐκκλησία (βουλεύσωνται, βουλὴν
ποιήσασθαι, cp. 9. 5 *infra*). The term
Ἀθηναῖοι in this passage may be somewhat loosely used to merge the στρατηγοί
in the general mass of citizens. One
might suspect that Themistokles was less
taken by surprise (ἐψευσμένοι γνώμης,
n.b. the perfect or pluperfect participle)
than the majority of Athenians.

7. δοκέοντες . . τὸν βάρβαρον: there
must have been good reason for this
expectation; in other words, the plan of
defence must have comprised a second
stand for the protection of Attica, even
if Phokis and Boiotia might have to be
abandoned. The phraseology here in-

volves more than the supposition that
the Peloponnesians might reasonably
have been expected to be on the march
for Thermopylai: εὑρήσειν, πανδημί, ὑποκατημένους, all go beyond that. The
participle here scarcely implies an am-
buscade, but it certainly implies a settlement or resting-place; cp. 7. 27. The
adverb signifies the *levée en masse* such
as afterwards fought at Plataia; the
verb may have an immaterial or purely
psychological force (as εὗρον just below),
i.e. 'to find that the Peloponnesians'
etc., or a less figurative and more
material meaning ('to find the Peloponnesians posted in wait for the barbarian
north of Kithairon'). In either case the
futurity is conditioned by the interval
between the date of the δόκησις and its
realisation or disappointment, and can
hardly be reproduced in English idiom.

9. τῶν μὲν . . οἱ δέ: an inaccurate use
of the antithetical particles, produced by
the emphatic repetition of the subject;
cp. 7. 6 *supra*: the τῶν must be neuter.
αὐτοὺς δέ would have been more in order.

11. τὰ ἄλλα δὲ ἀπιέναι: sc. βουλομένους,
νοεόντας, or some such word, out of περὶ
πλείστου ποιευμένους, a kind of zeugma.
The position of the δέ is emphatic, and
none the less, that μέν has been omitted
(τὴν μὲν Π.). Stein takes ἀπιέναι as co-
ordinate with ἔχοντας ἐν φ. (=ταύτην
μὲν φυλάσσειν) and cps. 5. 15, where,
however, συναλίσθαι καὶ φυλάσσοντας is
far less harsh than the phrase here, for
at least two reasons: (a) πυθόμενοι can be
used regularly with both infinitive and
participle; (b) the copula καί there

ἄλλα δὲ ἀπιέναι. ταῦτα πυνθανόμενοι οὕτω δὴ προσεδεήθησαν
σφέων σχεῖν πρὸς τὴν Σαλαμῖνα. οἱ μὲν δὴ ἄλλοι κατέσχον 41
ἐς τὴν Σαλαμῖνα, 'Αθηναῖοι δὲ ἐς τὴν ἑωυτῶν. μετὰ δὲ τὴν
ἄπιξιν κήρυγμα ἐποιήσαντο, 'Αθηναίων τῇ τις δύναται σῴζειν
τέκνα τε καὶ τοὺς οἰκέτας. ἐνθαῦτα οἱ μὲν πλεῖστοι ἐς
Τροίζηνα ἀπέστειλαν, οἱ δὲ ἐς Αἴγιναν, οἱ δὲ ἐς Σαλαμῖνα. 5
ἔσπευσαν δὲ ταῦτα ὑπεκθέσθαι τῷ χρηστηρίῳ τε βουλόμενοι

---

12 δὴ post ταῦτα ßPz   41. 3 σῴζειν van H., Stein³ : σώιζειν
C : σώζειν   4 τὰ τέκνα ßz, Holder, van H.   6 ὑπεκθέσθαι del.
Gomperz, Holder

makes the co-ordination easier than the
δέ here.

41. 2. τὴν Σαλαμῖνα . . τὴν ἑωυτῶν.
Not but what Salamis was also theirs,
but it was no part of Attica proper, it
never was a 'deme.' (A kleruchy might
be 'Athenian' without being 'Attic';
cp. 6. 139 f.) For the Salaminian settlement cp. my note to 5. 77. 9, and Hicks,
*Manual*² (1901), p. 6.

3. κήρυγμα ἐποιήσαντο. This proclamation will have succeeded the decision
of βουλή and δῆμος to abandon Attica,
which itself will have followed upon the
return of the θεωρία from Delphi (7. 140–
144). The story told c. 51 *infra* makes
it probable that the evacuation of Attica
neither was nor was intended to be complete in a strategic sense. To have
abandoned city and country without
such authorization constituted προδοσία,
and was a capital crime, as the extant
speech of Lykurgos proves—nay, even to
convey out of the country into a place
of safety τέκνα τε καὶ οἰκέτας (cp. c.
Leocrat. 53). Lykurgos' reply on the
case before us is rather rhetorical than
technical : § 69 οὐ γὰρ τὴν πόλιν ἐξέλιπον
ἀλλὰ τὸν τόπον μετήλλαξαν. It is not to
be supposed that the Strategoi by themselves either would or could have issued
such a proclamation. The terms of the
psephism are inaccurately preserved in
7. 144. The psephism there recorded
belongs to a much earlier stage ; cp. note
ad l.

4. οἱ μὲν πλεῖστοι ἐς Τροίζηνα : the
passage is not free from ambiguity. Are
we to understand that an actual majority
of Athenian households were sent across
to Troizen ? Or, merely, that the
number at Troizen was larger than either
the number in Aigina, or the number in

Salamis ? That any should have been
deposited in Aigina at all is remarkable,
in view of the recent war (7. 144) and
the present jealousies (c. 92 *infra*) ;
that any should have remained in
Salamis but fighting men would tend
to show that the Athenians by no means
despaired of victory. The historic connexion between Athens and Troizen
went back to the days when both were
members of the Kalaurian amphiktyony
(Strabo 204), to which Aigina also had
belonged ; and the mythic associations
were no doubt deepened by the Theseus-
legend, which was already fully domiciled
in Attica. No state in Peloponnese
was so closely connected with Athens
as Troizen, which even used the Attic
standard of weight ; there too Athene
and Poseidon had contended for possession and divided the spoil ; cp. Head,
H.N. 371. Yet Troizen, like Aigina,
was Dorian ; cp. 7. 99 *supra*, 9. 28 *infra*.
It is curious that the two vessels on the
look-out with the Attic cruiser in 7. 179 f.
are from Troizen and Aigina.

6. τῷ χρηστηρίῳ can only have been
the response, or responses, recorded
above, 7. 140—which (as I suggest)
were sought and obtained only after
the disaster at Thermopylai. This
passage, ἔσπευσαν δὲ ταῦτα . . τὴν
ἀκρόπολιν, will hardly have been
written before Hdt.'s first visit to
Athens, and may very well be an
insertion in the original draft. It is
obviously not calculated primarily for
an Athenian public : Athenians would
be glad to hear of their fathers' derring
deeds, but would not look to Hdt. for
information on their own current ritual.
This passage, then, probably belongs to
the 'second draft.' Cp. Introduction,
§ 9.

ὑπηρετέειν καὶ δὴ καὶ τοῦδε εἵνεκα οὐκ ἥκιστα. λέγουσι
Ἀθηναῖοι ὄφιν μέγαν φύλακα τῆς ἀκροπόλιος ἐνδιαιτᾶσθαι ἐν
τῷ ἱρῷ· λέγουσί τε ταῦτα καὶ δὴ ὡς ἐόντι ἐπιμήνια ἐπιτε-
10 λέουσι προτιθέντες· τὰ δ' ἐπιμήνια μελιτόεσσα ἐστί. αὕτη
δὴ ἡ μελιτόεσσα ἐν τῷ πρόσθε αἰεὶ χρόνῳ ἀναισιμουμένη τότε
ἦν ἄψαυστος. σημηνάσης δὲ ταῦτα τῆς ἱρείης, μᾶλλόν τι οἱ

---

7 ὑπηρετεῖν Β, Holder, van H. || τοῦδε : τούτου Pz || εἵνεκεν Β, van H.
8 ὄφιν : σφι Β || ἐνδιαιτέεσθαι Β   9 τε : δὲ Β || καὶ δὴ καὶ Β, Holder,
van H. || τελέουσι Paris. 1635, z   10 τὰ δ' : τὰ δὲ R || ἐστι μελι-
τόεσσα Β, Holder : ἐστι del. Kallenberg || αὕτη δὴ ἡ Stein² : αὕτη δ'·(δὲ
R) ἡ   11 πρόσθεν codd., z || ἐναισιμουμένη Β   12 τῆς om. R ||
ἱερείης a, Holder

---

7. λέγουσι Ἀθηναῖοι: there was no
real snake visible ; such is the inevitable
inference from this passage and the still
more explicit phrase below : λέγουσί τε
ταῦτα καὶ δὴ ὡς ἐόντι κτλ., a conclusion
which only adds point to the Aristophanic gibe : Lysistr. 710 ἐξ οὗ τὸν ὄφιν
εἶδον τὸν οἰκουρόν ποτε. The οἰκουρὸς
ὄφις was no doubt sacred to Athene, and
may have been regarded as a symbol,
or a reincarnation, of the earth-born
Erechtheus ; cp. M. P. Nilsson, J.H.S.
xxi. (1901) p. 329 ; but in this case the
only proof of the real presence of the
serpent was the disappearance of the
offering, the divine creature, no doubt,
being thought to reside in the crypt
of the Erechtheion (ἐνδιαιτᾶσθαι ἐν τῷ
ἱρῷ, cp. c. 55 infra). With this story
is naturally compared the tale of Bel
and the Dragon (Apocryph. Vet. Test.
ed. Fritzsche (1871) pp. 86 ff.), in
which, as here, the serpent himself
took the cake. Blakesley (quoting
Valckenaer apparently) adds that at
Alexandria any one might eat the cakes
of Kronos (Athenaeus 110), while the
fish-offerings to Atargatis (at Askalon ?
Athen. 346) were consumed by the
priests as a matter of course, and above
board, like the ἄρτοι προθέσεως of the
Hebrews (cp. προτιθέντες here). The
parataxis τε . . καὶ is observable.

9. ἐπιμήνια ἐπιτελέουσι: sc. ἱερά.
The offering was made once a month
(perhaps at the new moon ; cp. 6. 57),
and in this case took the form of a sweet
cake (μελιτόεσσα, sc. μᾶζα).

12. τῆς ἱρείης : sc. of Athene. The
word σημηνάσης is consciously used of
an official and solemn report ; the thing
reported is here indeed a 'sign.' τῆς
θεοῦ, sc. Athene. The untouched cake

proved the absence of the snake, the
absence of the snake that of the goddess.
But how long had the cake remained
untouched ? Did it generally disappear
immediately on oblation ? The serpent,
as a religious symbol or cult-object, is
found broad-cast in Hellas and the
Mediterranean area ; nor is it confined
to that region ; serpent-myths were
"specially abundant in Egypt and Babylonia " (Encycl. Bibl. iv. 4395), and their
area may safely be extended so as to
include at least India on the one side
and Scandinavia on the other. Whether
it have a chthonian or an autochthonous
reference, embody an oracular mission,
or represent the heroic ancestor, be
intended to convey a phallic suggestion,
or be connected with the charm and
mystery of the lithest and subtlest of
animal forms ; or whether, on the other
hand, it serve, in venomous kind, to
typify the powers of evil and destruction :
whatever its purpose and significance,
the serpent has played a long and
curious rôle in religious legend and
symbolism. Has it not everywhere
gained admission ? Remarkably enough,
the serpent scarcely figures on the
monuments of 'Mykenaean Tree and
Pillar cult' collected by A. J. Evans
(J.H.S. xx. 1900, p. 52), but the
missing link has been recently supplied
(Annual Br. Sch. Ath. ix. 1902-3). At
Knossos snakes are now to be seen
brandished aloft by the Minoan goddess
in her star-chamber (is she not Aphrodite
Urania ? cp. Hdt. 1. 105). At Delphi
the dragon (there, then, an evil being)
was slain, but immortalized, by Apollo.
At Athens the goddess received the
snake into her service ; it curled round
the caduceus of Hermes and the magic

'Αθηναῖοι καὶ προθυμότερον ἐξέλιπον τὴν πόλιν, ὡς καὶ τῆς θεοῦ ἀπολελοιπυίης τὴν ἀκρόπολιν. ὡς δέ σφι πάντα ὑπεξέκειτο, ἔπλεον ἐς τὸ στρατόπεδον.　15

Ἐπεὶ δὲ οἱ ἀπ' Ἀρτεμισίου ἐς Σαλαμῖνα κατέσχον τὰς 42 νέας, συνέρρεε καὶ ὁ λοιπὸς πυνθανόμενος ὁ τῶν Ἑλλήνων ναυτικὸς στρατὸς ἐκ Τροίζηνος· ἐς γὰρ Πώγωνα τὸν Τροιζηνίων λιμένα προείρητο συλλέγεσθαι· συνελέχθησάν τε δὴ πολλῷ

---

13 προθυμότερον: πρότερον α ǁ ἐξέλειπον α　　14 ἀπολελοποίης α
42. 1 ἐπείτε δὲ ¿ van H. ǁ ἀπὸ β ǁ εἰς β, Holder　　2 νῆας συνέρεε β
3 τῶν β　　4 εἴρητο β

---

or medicinal wand of Asklepios. The serpent inspired the oracle of Trophonios at Lebadeia, and dominated the legend of Kadmos at Thebes; appeared in the ritual of Demeter at Eleusis, and contends with the eagle of Zeus on the coins of Elis. The god visited Olympias, the mother of Alexander, in the form of a snake (Plutarch, *Alex.* 2), and twin-snakes led the son safely through the wilderness to the temple of his divine sire (Arrian, *Anab.* 3. 3. 5). The snake-symbol, the ἀγαθὸς δαίμων, preserved the walls of Pompeii (and many another city) from impurity; the serpent figures on the monuments of Mithras, with the bull, the hound, and the scorpion, as a sacred mystery. The bronze serpent which, raised upon a mast, had stayed the plague in the wilderness for the Israelites, was worshipped till a reforming king destroyed the idol, and an idealizing legend identified the serpent's image with the Evil One, who had seduced the mother of mankind beside the tree of knowledge. Henceforth, for Hebrew and for orthodox Christian thought the snake-symbol is *nehustan*; but the earlier associations of tree and serpent were apparently beneficent. As round the world-ash in the *Edda* twines the great snake, Igdrasil, so the Attic serpent may have coiled round the sacred olive of Athene in the Erechtheion; cp. the remarkable representation, reproduced in Baumeister, *Denkmaeler* iii. 1394, fig. 1542.

μᾶλλόν τι . . καὶ προθυμότερον. The phrase betrays the reluctance and opposition to the evacuation of the land and the abandonment of the city, which is more clearly indicated above 7. 142, and c. 51 *infra.*

15. ἐς τὸ στρατόπεδον: at Salamis.

42. 1. οἱ ἀπ' Ἀρτεμισίου: cp. c. 40 *supra,* now including the Athenians.

ἐς Σαλαμῖνα: the sixth occurrence of the phrase since the beginning of c. 40. It is in no wise clear whether Hdt. means 'the island' or the town, or whether he draws any distinction between them. For a moment the Greek naval forces had been in three divisions: (i.) the Athenians in Attica, (ii.) the rest of the fleet from Artemision in Salamis, (iii.) the reserves at Troizen. These three divisions are now united at Salamis, a movement which seems to imply a definite plan to make a stand in the Straits. The harbour of Troizen had been previously specified as the rendezvous for the reserves (προείρητο) by Sparta, or perhaps by the Congress at the Isthmos, and a summons was sent, or at least intelligence conveyed (πυνθανόμενος), from Salamis.

3. Πώγωνα: the 'Beard,' so called, perhaps, with some reference to its shape (εἰς Τροιζῆνα δεῖ βαδίζειν. ἐπὶ τῶν κακογενείων καὶ σπανοπωγώνων εἴρηται. Πώγων γάρ ἐστι λιμὴν εἰς Τροιζῆνα, Suidas), was the well-sheltered and spacious harbour covered by the island Kalauria (mod. *Poros*) on the coast of Argolis, due south from Aigina and Salamis. Troizen itself (a city sacred to Poseidon) was situate inland, some fifteen stades from the sea, Strabo 373. Cp. E. Curtius, *Peloponnesos* ii. (1852) 444, and notes to Pausanias, 2. 32, *ap.* Frazer and Hitzig-Bluemner.

4. πολλῷ πλεῦνες. According to the lists in Hdt. there were 54 more ships at Salamis than at Artemision, and nine states (Hermione, Ambrakia, Leukas, Naxos, Kythnos, Seriphos, Siphnos, Melos, Kroton) are represented at Salamis but not at Artemision: there

5 πλεῦνες νέες ἢ ἐπ' Ἀρτεμισίῳ ἐναυμάχεον καὶ ἀπὸ πολίων
πλεύνων. ναύαρχος μέν νυν ἐπῆν ὡυτὸς ὅσπερ ἐπ' Ἀρτεμισίῳ,
Εὐρυβιάδης ὁ Εὐρυκλείδεω ἀνὴρ Σπαρτιήτης, οὐ μέντοι γένεος
τοῦ βασιληίου ἐών· νέας δὲ πολλῷ πλείστας τε καὶ ἄριστα
43 πλεούσας παρείχοντο Ἀθηναῖοι. ἐστρατεύοντο δὲ οἴδε· ἐκ
μὲν Πελοποννήσου Λακεδαιμόνιοι ἑκκαίδεκα νέας παρεχόμενοι,
Κορίνθιοι δὲ τὸ αὐτὸ πλήρωμα παρεχόμενοι καὶ ἐπ' Ἀρτεμισίῳ·
Σικυώνιοι δὲ πεντεκαίδεκα παρείχοντο νέας, Ἐπιδαύριοι δὲ
5 δέκα, Τροιζήνιοι δὲ πέντε, Ἑρμιονέες δὲ τρεῖς, ἐόντες οὗτοι

---

5 νῆες Β   7 γένεός γε Β, Holder, van H.   8 νῆας Β   9
πλωούσας Βz   43. 1 οἴδε ABR   2 πελοπονήσου R ‖ νῆας Βz
3 παρεχόμενοι τὸ secl. van H. : (τὸ Β, Holder : ὁ α : om. Stein)   4
παρείχοντο secl. van H. : παρέσχοντο Β

---

is one, and only one absentee, the
Opuntian Lokris, which has passed
under the dominion of Persia.

7. **Εὐρυβιάδης ὁ Εὐρυκλείδεω**: cp. c.
2 *supra*. The express renomination,
with the patronymic repeated, marks
less the solemnity of the occasion than
the difference of the source. The description here is, indeed, more specific than
there, more primitive, and may belong
to an older stratum. The data must
be ultimately referable to Sparta. The
technical term **ναύαρχος** is here used, as
against στρατηγὸς ὁ τὸ μέγιστον κράτος
ἔχων *supra*, which has a more Athenian
sound.

8. **νέας δέ**: between the sentence with
μέν and the sentence with δέ there is
here a world of difference and contrast ;
but the latter would have even more
point as the antithesis to the description
of Eurybiades in c. 2, τὸν < μέν > στρατηγὸν τὸν τὸ μέγιστον κράτος ἔχοντα παρείχοντο Σπαρτιῆται. No doubt ἄριστα
πλεούσας covers the merits of the
trierarchs and crew as well as those of
the builder.

43. 1. ἐστρατεύοντο δὲ οἴδε. There
follows the navy-list for Salamis, apparently from a Peloponnesian, perhaps
a Spartan, source. Hdt. apparently
conceives the actual ships in question
to be the very same as fought at
Artemision, the increased total being
due to pure additions ; but some ships
had been lost or completely disabled
off Euboia (cp. cc. 16, 17 *supra*) ; the
additional numbers must in part represent substitutes, and indicate, therefore, all the greater effort on the part
of the Greek states.

2. **Λακεδαιμόνιοι**: 16, an addition of
6, as compared with Artemision.

3. **Κορίνθιοι**: apparently 40. **πλήρωμα**,
used of a single ship, denotes the crew
(Thuc. 7. 4. 6, 12. 3), but of a fleet, or
squadron, as here, and c. 45 *infra*, the
full number, the total.

4. **Σικυώνιοι**: 15, an addition of 3.
Ἐπιδαύριοι: 10, an addition of 2.

5. **Τροιζήνιοι**: 5, the same total.
Ἑρμιονέες: 3, a fresh contingent.
ἐόντες οὗτοι κτλ.: an ethnological
and historical note which can have had
nothing to say to an official navy-list,
and comes, presumably, from a wholly
different source, some logograph's work.
It falls into two parts—a remark upon
the Dorians, a remark upon the Dryopes.
The former invites comparison with the
locus classicus in 1. 56, the latter with
the similar inset, or aside, in c. 31
supra.
There are two marked differences
between this passage and 1. 56. (*a*)
The chart of the Dorian wanderings
is much fuller there than here, both in
point of chronology and in point of
geography, and therewith the historical
aperçu is fuller. (*b*) Pindos here, coupled
as it is with Erineos, plainly denotes
the town in Dryopis, or Doris, of that
name ; in 1. 56 Pindos no less plainly
(*pace* Stein) denotes the great mountain-
range to the west of Thessaly. The
passage in Bk. 1 is also more explicit on
the question of nomenclature, attaching
the 'Makedonian' title to the Pindos-
station, and the 'Dorian' to Dryopis
only.
There is thus a discrepancy between
the two passages, at least upon the

πλὴν Ἑρμιονέων Δωρικόν τε καὶ Μακεδνὸν ἔθνος, ἐξ Ἐρινεοῦ τε καὶ Πίνδου καὶ τῆς Δρυοπίδος ὕστατα ὁρμηθέντες. οἱ δὲ

second point; the phrase just below, ὕστατα ὁρμηθέντες, may be taken to cover the first point implicitly; and if the text is to stand, we must suppose that Hdt. (as not infrequently) lapsed from forgetfulness into a slight inconsequence; for an inconsequence it is, even if Mount Pindos and the town of the same name marked two stations (separated by a considerable interval both spatial and temporal) in the Dorian migration. But are the words Πίνδου καὶ here a gloss, an insertion, a reminiscence, by a mere transcriber of l. 56? Sense and grammar would be complete without them, and the inconsequence would disappear from the author's text. Failing that solution, we might delete καὶ and read Πίνδου τῆς Δρυοπίδος.

The question in any case remains of the repetition, the quasi-dittograph. The composition of the two passages was evidently separated by a considerable interval; but which was the earlier? Probably the fuller and completer passage in Bk. 1 is of later composition in the work of Hdt. Had it stood in its place originally, as it now stands, in relation to this, a reference here backwards would have been natural and sufficient, and in keeping with Hdt.'s practice. This passage, then, distinctly supports the theory that Bks. 7, 8, 9 are of earlier composition than the first and subsequent Books. Cp. Introduction, §§ 7, 8.

6. Δωρικόν τε καὶ Μακεδνόν: etymologizing is hazardous work, yet connexion between Μακεδνός and Μακεδών can scarcely be doubted. In l. 56, where the term is associated with the station of the Dorians on Mount Pindos, in the NW. of Thessaly, a geographical argument for the etymological identification presents itself. This Makedonian station for the Dorians is in truth as far back as the chart or the story of the wandering in l. 56 really carries us; for the previous stages not only involve a pragmatic blunder (the confusion of Histiaiotis with Pelasgiotis, in order to purge the Dorians of all taint of 'barbarism'), but are also obviously designed to bring back the Dorians to the true fold and cradle of Hellenism in Achaia Phthiotis! It is infinitely

more probable that the northern Dorians reached their station on Mount Pindos—within view of Hellas—from Makedonia, than that the ultimate conquerors of the south had been driven out of Phthiotis to start with.

ἐξ Ἐρινεοῦ (τε καὶ τῆς Δρυοπίδος). Erineos is mentioned by Thuc. 1. 107. 2 with Boion and Kytinion, as forming the 'metropolis' of the Lakedaimonians (Pindos is there conspicuous by its absence). Strabo 427 adds Pindos, the old name of which was said to be Akyphas, and makes the tetrapolis μητρόπολιν τῶν ἀπάντων Δωριέων. The Dorian Tyrtaios celebrated windy Erineos as the point of departure (ap. Strabon. 362; Bergk ii.[4] 8, F. 2).

αὐτὸς γὰρ Κρονίων, καλλιστεφάνου πόσις Ἥρης
Ζεὺς Ἡρακλείδαις τήνδε δέδωκε πόλιν·
οἷσιν ἅμα προλιπόντες Ἐρινεὸν ἠνεμόεντα
εὐρεῖαν Πέλοπος νῆσον ἀφικόμεθα.

The name may be compared with Ὄλυνθος and many others derived ἀπὸ φυτῶν. Cp. Grassberger, Ortsnamen, pp. 221 ff. If Pindar, Pyth. 1. 65, describes the Herakleida, or Dorians, as Πινδόθεν ὀρνύμενοι (a phrase which Pindaric commentators—Donaldson, Fennell, Mezger, Gildersleeve—leave severely alone), he will have had not the town, not the river, but the mountain in mind (Aigimios was at home in Thessaly).

7. οἱ δὲ Ἑρμιονέες εἰσὶ Δρύοπες: the people of Hermion (for its site cp. Thuc. 2. 56. 5) no doubt represented a non-Dorian and a prae-Dorian stock in the Peloponnesos, like the people of Asine in Lakonia, c. 73 infra, or like the 'Minyai' of the Lepreatis (ibid. 4. 148); but perhaps no more came from Doris-Dryopis than the Lepreatai from Lemnos, unless, indeed, they came with the Dorians. The people of Kythnos too are 'Dryopians,' c. 46 infra; and there were 'Dryopians' on the Asiatic side (cp. 1. 146). Karystos in Euboia was 'Dryopian,' Thuc. 7. 57. 4, and also perhaps Styra (Pausan. 4. 34. 11, despite Thuc. l.c., who makes them 'Ionian'). Even Kypros—if Diod. 4. 87. 2 were to be believed—contained Dryopians. That the name Dryopis was most clearly attached to the soil in the Oitaian region argues Oita as a real

Ἑρμιονέες εἰσὶ Δρύοπες, ὑπὸ Ἡρακλέος τε καὶ Μηλιέων ἐκ
44 τῆς νῦν Δωρίδος καλεομένης χώρης ἐξαναστάντες. οὗτοι μέν
νυν Πελοποννησίων ἐστρατεύοντο, οἵδε δὲ ἐκ τῆς ἔξω ἠπείρου,
Ἀθηναῖοι μὲν πρὸς πάντας τοὺς ἄλλους παρεχόμενοι νέας
ὀγδώκοντα καὶ ἑκατόν, μοῦνοι. ἐν Σαλαμῖνι γὰρ οὐ συνεναυ-

---

8 ἡρακλέους B   **44. 2** οἶδε δὲ Schweighaeuser, van H., Stein³ ⋅
οἱ δὲ   3 νῆας B

---

seat of the Dryopians, and may help to
explain its 'metropolitan' character.
Busolt i.² (1893) 209 connects Dryops,
'oak-man,' with the Lapith 'Dryas,'
Il. 1. 263, and so takes the Dryopians
back into Thessaly, seeing in the geographical order of the Dryopian stations
—Styra, Karystos, Kythnos—the links
between the Malianh and the Argolic
gulfs. But geograp y is not history,
and the historic inference from geographical distribution is just the fallacy
committed in the Herodotean legend of
the Minyai, 4. 145 ff. The Dryopians,
like the Minyai, the Dolopians, the
Kaukones, the Kekropians, and so on,
put us doubtless face to face with the
primitive, or all but primitive, population
of the Hellenic area. ἐπῴκησαν δὲ καὶ
Ἑρμιόνα ὕστερον Δωριεῖς οἱ ἐξ Ἄργους
Pausan. 2. 34. 5. The date and circumstances of this ἐποίκισις are not given,
but it did not obliterate apparently the
Dryopian character of the town.

8. ὑπὸ Ἡρακλέος τε καὶ Μηλιέων.
The story is told by Diodor. 4. 37, and
by the *Mythographi*; e.g. Apollodoros
2. 7. 7 ; *Appendix Narrationum*, 28. 6,
ed. Westermann (1843). Cp. also Pausan.
4. 35. 6 (for a version told by the
Asinaians, cp. c. 73 *infra*). For the
connexion of Herakles with Malis cp.
7. 176, 216 *supra*.

44. 2. ἐκ τῆς ἔξω ἠπείρου : not merely
have the Peloponnesians precedence in
this navy-list, but the remainder are
enumerated from a Peloponnesian standpoint ; contrast the list for Artemision
c. 1 *supra*.

3. Ἀθηναῖοι μέν : to this μέν may
correspond the δέ in c. 45 *infra*, Μεγαρέες
δέ κτλ., but it looks somewhat 'pendent.'
A kind of contrast is supplied by the
case of the Plataians, but without a δέ,
its place, perhaps, supplied by γάρ ; in
fact the Plataians are resumed with
οὗτοι μέν νυν, to which immediately
corresponds Ἀθηναῖοι δέ. The parenthetical character of the passage, and

especially of the learned parenthesis on
the *origines* of the Athenians, is manifest
even in the style.

πρὸς πάντας τοὺς ἄλλους, 'to set
against, to compare with all the other
peoples.' For this use of πρός Blakesley
cps. 2. 35 πρὸς πᾶσαν χώρην, and 3. 94
φόρον ἀπαγίνεον πρὸς πάντας τοὺς ἄλλους
ἑξήκοντα καὶ τριηκόσια τάλαντα ψήγματος.
Hdt. gives the number of the Athenian
ships at Salamis as 180. He evidently
conceives of the total number available
as 200, 20 being manned by the men
of Chalkis, cc. 1, 14 *supra*. The anonymous Athenian *ap.* Thuc. 1. 74. 1 claims
a little less than two-thirds of 400—
which might be about 250. Cp. 7. 144
supra.

4. μοῦνοι : by themselves alone, i.e.
without the Plataians, as the next sentence explains. There was evidently a
problem : why were the Plataians, who
had assisted to man the Athenian
squadron at Artemision (c. 1 *supra*),
absent from Salamis ? The reason
appears to be somewhat conjectural (διὰ
τοιόνδε τι πρῆγμα). They had landed
opposite Chalkis in order to remove their
households. The fact of the debarkation
is plainly indubitable ; the reason for
the act is more doubtful. It implies
that the complete evacuation of Plataia,
and therefore of Attica, had already been
resolved on. In the light of c. 40 *supra*
it is possible that the Plataians landed
in Boiotia expecting to find the Peloponnesian army ready to cover and
defend Plataia : they would naturally
elect, and indeed be bound, to join the
land-forces under such circumstances.
The removal was then necessitated by
the non-appearance of the Greek army.
But had the Plataians been especially
eager for further service at sea, they
surely might have found a way of re-
joining the Athenians at Salamis. Had
the evacuation of Attica been already
decided on when the Athenians and
Plataians parted at Chalkis, surely

μάχησαν Πλαταιέες Ἀθηναίοισι διὰ τοιόνδε τι πρῆγμα· 5
ἀπαλλασσομένων τῶν Ἑλλήνων ἀπὸ τοῦ Ἀρτεμισίου, ὡς
ἐγίνοντο κατὰ Χαλκίδα, οἱ Πλαταιέες ἀποβάντες ἐς τὴν
περαίην τῆς Βοιωτίης χώρην πρὸς ἐκκομιδὴν ἐτράποντο τῶν
οἰκετέων. οὗτοι μέν νυν τούτους σῴζοντες ἐλείφθησαν. Ἀθη-

· 5 τι om. α　　　 8 πτερίην β: πιερίην V, Valla ‖ χώρην Stein³:
χώρης ‖ κομιδὴν β　　　 9 σῴζοντες van H., Stein³: σώζοντες

Salamis would have been given as the rendezvous. The Plataians did not perhaps escape some censure at Athens; there is some trace of an apologetic note in this passage. Athenian tradition had its revenge: this μοῦνοι became so emphatic that it was sometimes forgotten that the Plataians had fought at Marathon! Cp. 9. 27.

7. τὴν περαίην τῆς Βοιωτίης χώρην, "the Boeotian territory on the opposite shore," Blakesley; "the opposite shore of Boeotia," Rawlinson,. Macaulay (sc. χώρης). The meaning is clear, though the more usual sense would be "the coast opposite Boiotia." The 'Peraia' is looked at from Chalkis, not from Boiotia. Cp. App. Crit.

8. τῶν οἰκετέων must surely include 'wives and children' as in c. 106 infra κομίσαι τοὺς οἰκέτας, at once followed by κομίσαι τὰ τέκνα καὶ τὴν γυναῖκα, or c. 142 infra γυναῖκάς τε καὶ τὰ ἐς πόλεμον ἐχρῆστα οἰκετέων ἐχόμενα πάντα, where it includes τέκνα. Cp. παῖδάς τε καὶ γυναῖκας c. 40 supra (where οἰκέται are not specified), τέκνα τε καὶ τοὺς οἰκέτας c. 41, where γυναῖκας must be included. Add τέκνα καὶ γυναῖκες cc. 36, 60. The use of οἰκέτης as a domestic slave is perhaps something of a euphemism, or meiosis; cp. 7. 170. With ἐλείφθησαν cp. 7. 153 οὐκ ἐλείφθη.

9. Ἀθηναῖοι δέ: as the text now stands this phrase is antithetical to οὗτοι μέν, but there is no true antithesis in the argument. This parenthesis on the Attic origines can hardly have been intended in the first instance for an Attic public, and may very well be an insertion (belonging to the second draft); in which case Μεγαρέες δέ would follow on οὗτοι μέν . . ἐλείφθησαν. But in that case too the antithesis is hardly correct. Perhaps the original text ran Ἀθηναῖοι μὲν πρὸς πάντας . . ἑκατόν, Μεγαρέες δέ κτλ., and the double parenthesis may all be later insertion, and even perhaps not all of the same date and draft (the Attic

origins being of the second, the note on the Plataian desertion of Athens of the third hand, or draft, that revision which took place at Athens after the outbreak of the Peloponnesian war, what time the case of Plataia was doubtless freely and frequently canvassed; cp. Introduction, § 9).

The epitome which follows is the quintessence of primitive Attic history. Hdt. has taken it from some predecessor (possibly Hekataios), though there were perhaps already native Ἀτθιδογράφοι at work, cp. 6. 137. But this passage is hardly of strict Attic provenience, nor does it represent the orthodox Athenian tradition or theory. An Athenian would not have admitted Pelasgianism, nor allowed Κέκροψ a merely secondary place, nor described Ion as στρατάρχης (but rather as πολέμαρχος) of Athens. In this passage, as in 1. 57, the Athenians are Pelasgians, virtually from first to last, for the changes they have undergone are merely, or mainly, nominal—a change of names; but Hdt. does not here go so far as to assert that they had changed their language too, or that time was when the Athenians, yea the Ionians, spake a non-Hellenic tongue. The early history of Attica, or at least of Athens, is resumed in four stages, of which the Ionian (with the Ionian tribes, and so forth) was but the last, and imposed ab extra. Before there were Ionians there had been Athenians; the Athenian is older than the Ionian name—in Attica. But the names of Kekrops and Kekropidai are older still than the Athenian. So far back the stages, the epochs, are marked by proper names, Ion, Erechtheus, Kekrops. Before Kekrops there is a dim Pelasgian prime, and the forbears of the Athenian people, seemingly one tribe or section of the Pelasgian stock, were hight Kranaoi. But here it is the difference rather than the identity between Athenian and Pelasgian that is emphasized.

10 ναῖοι δὲ ἐπὶ μὲν Πελασγῶν ἐχόντων τὴν νῦν Ἑλλάδα καλεομένην ἦσαν Πελασγοί, ὀνομαζόμενοι Κραναοί, ἐπὶ δὲ Κέκροπος

11 οὐνομαζόμενοι Β

---

10. **ἐπὶ μὲν Πελασγῶν ἐχόντων τὴν νῦν Ἑλλάδα.** Hdt., so far as he has one single consistent view on the 'Pelasgian question,' regards the Pelasgoi as the fore-Hellenic and non-Hellenic population of all the continuous area afterwards invaded and occupied by the Hellenes, and so hellenized. Thus (i.) he places Pelasgoi in Peloponnese (1. 146, 2. 171, 7. 94): in Attica (1. 56, 2. 51, 4. 145, 6. 137): N. Greece (2. 52, 56): in the Islands (2. 51, 4. 145, 5. 26, 6. 136, 140): Asia Minor (7. 42, 95); (ii.) he makes Pelasgia the older name of the Hellenic peninsula (2. 56); (iii.) he believes that the Pelasgoi spake a non-Hellenic language (1. 57). On this view many or most of the early tribal names are subdivisions of the Pelasgic stock: Αἰγιαλέες Πελασγοί (7. 94), Κραναοὶ Πελασγοί, and so forth ; the Dorians become the Hellenes κατ᾿ ἐξοχήν, and the area occupied by Hellenic or hellenized tribes in the historic period has, ex hypothesi, been occupied in the prehistoric by non-Hellenic tribes, exterminated or absorbed and hellenized by the invaders, leaving only a few isolated survivals here and there (1. 57). But the case of Athens, where there was no record of a Dorian conquest, is a difficulty on this theory, though Herodotus, the Dorian, nevertheless, or perhaps for that very reason, represents

the Athenians as Pelasgic, without ever explaining their adoption of Hellenism. Thucydides, the Athenian, represents an opposite, or at least a corrective and rival view. He nowhere commits himself to the doctrine of the non-Hellenic character of the Pelasgoi, or the non-Hellenic character of their language. Hellene and Pelasgian are not with him alternative or exclusive terms at any period ; the distinction is merely nominal and verbal. The Pelasgic is indeed older than the Hellenic, but the Pelasgoi are but one, the most considerable, of many tribes inhabiting the potentially Hellenic area (1. 3). The Hellenic name is a matter of fashion, culture, exchange, adoption. The exact relation of Athens to the Pelasgoi is not clear. It is possible that Thucydides did not connect τὸ Πελαργικόν (2. 17) with the Pelasgoi ; but if the words καὶ Ἀθήνας in 4. 109. 4 are authentic (to me they have the air of a gloss), Thucydides admitted Πελασγοὶ Τυρσηνοί as quondam inhabitants (οἰκησάντων) of Athens: an excursion into the rival hypothesis ! In any case he will hardly have regarded the Athenians as Pelasgoi in his own time, much less allowed the Dorian claim to the flower of ' Hellenism.'

Hdt.'s theory in this passage may be diagrammatically exhibited :

'Αθηναῖοι				
i.	ἦσαν / ὀνομάσθησαν	Πελασγοί / Κραναοί	<ἀπ᾿ ἀρχῆς> / ἐπὶ Πελασγῶν	Πελασγῶν ἐχόντων / τὴν νῦν Ἑλλάδα καλεομένην
ii.	ἐπεκλήθησαν	Κεκροπίδαι	ἐπὶ Κέκροπος	βασιλέος
iii.	μετωνομάσθησαν	Ἀθηναῖοι	ἐπ᾿ Ἐρεχθέος	ἐκδεξαμένου τὴν ἀρχήν
iv.	ἐκλήθησαν	Ἴωνες	ἐπ᾿ Ἴωνος	στρατάρχεω γενομένου Ἀθηναίοισι

11. **Κραναοί.** Hdt. knows nothing apparently of the king or hero Kranaos, who is mentioned by Aischylos (παῖδες Κραναοῦ Eumen. 1011 = Athenians), and whose monument (μνῆμα) was to be seen, in the time of Pausanias (1. 31. 3), in the deme of Lamptrai ; yet, on the other hand, he seems to anticipate the later traditions (i.e. theories) in denying the primacy of Kekrops. κρα-ναός may be rightly etymologized (καρ-, κρα-, and ναίειν) as the Dwellers-on-high (Stein : the antithesis to the Δα-ναοί = Ἀργεῖοι

'dwellers below, on the plain' looks daring, though attractive). Aristophanes has Κραναὰ πόλις Ach. 75 for Athens ; cp. Birds 123 (τῶν Κραναῶν πόλιν) and (more specifically for the Akropolis ?) Lys. 481 (μεγαλόπετρον ἄβατον). But Pindar has the word as an epithet not merely of Athens (Nem. 8. 11, Ol. 7. 82, 13. 38) but of Delos, Isth. 1. 4, and with Homer it is the standing epithet of Ithaca (Il. 3. 201, Od. 1. 247). The primitive meaning would seem to be rather ' hard' than ' head' or ' high.'

βασιλέος ἐκλήθησαν Κεκροπίδαι, ἐκδεξαμένου δὲ Ἐρεχθέος τὴν ἀρχὴν Ἀθηναῖοι μετωνομάσθησαν, Ἴωνος δὲ τοῦ Ξούθου

---

12 βασιλέως C : βασιλῆος z ‖ ἐπεκλήθησαν βα, Holder, van H. ‖ ἐρεχθέως β   13 Ἀθηναῖοι : Ἐρεχθηΐδαι coni. Krueger

---

The word is, however, also found as a proper name already in Homer, Il. 3. 445, of an island, variously identified (but in no case Ithaca !) ; cp. Pausan. 3. 22. 1. Perhaps the names Κράνιοι Thuc. 2. 30. 2 etc., Κραννώνιοι 2. 22. 3 may be traced to the same root. Cp. also next note.

Κέκροπος βασιλέος : for Thucydides, at least, Kekrops is apparently the first king in the land, 2. 15. 1, and the only one named by him previous to Theseus, though others are implied. Hdt. here adds Erechtheus, and in 1. 173 supplies the names of Pandion and Aigeus. Whether these four names would have comprised for Hdt. the complete list of Attic, or even of Athenian, kings before Theseus it is not easy to determine. As pointed out in the previous note, Kekrops can hardly be the first king for Hdt. What exact date he would have assigned to Kekrops must also remain an open question ; but here at least the period of the Kekropidai is post-Pelasgian and prae-Ionian, nay, even prae-Athenian !

'Kranaos' appears to be an epithet localized, and then converted into a tribe-name and a tribe-ancestor. The eponym has here been generated from the epithet. Is the case to some extent similar with 'Kekrops' ? The etymology and meaning of Kekrops are, indeed, obscure. G. Curtius connected the word with καρπ-, fruit, fruitful (vid. L. & S.), in which case the Κέκροπες, Κεκρόπιοι, κεκροπίδαι—terms all used = Ἀθηναῖοι— would be the πέδιοι, or πεδιαῖοι, under another aspect (and contrast well with the κραναοί as above explained). But is not κέκροψ a variant of κέρκοψ, κέρκωψ, the beast, or man, with the tail ? (cp. 7. 216 supra). It was under such a form that Kekrops was found and worshipped on the Akropolis ; and the serpentine image was, or became, symbolical of the autochthonous claim ; cp. c. 41 supra. Apollod. 3. 14. 1 probably gives the orthodox Attic theory : Κέκροψ αὐτόχθων, συμφυὲς ἔχων σῶμα ἀνδρὸς καὶ δράκοντος, τῆς Ἀττικῆς ἐβασίλευσε πρῶτος (except that the unification, the synoikism, of the land should be left for Theseus).

12. Ἐρεχθέος : of the true essence of Erechtheus there need be comparatively little doubt ; he is one with Poseidon (cp. c. 55 infra), although, of course, tradition, i.e. early speculation, divided them, and then multiplied Erechtheus by two, or more, into Erechtheus, Erichthonios, in order the better to harmonize discrepant legends. Etymologically he is 'the Render' (cp. ἐρέχθω, Ποσειδῶν ἐρεχθεύς = ἐννοσίγαιος (?), though the connexion with χθών even in Erichthonios is pseudetymology). Like Kekrops, with whom he was sometimes, reasonably enough, identified (cp. Eustath. p. 283, ap. Clinton, Fasti, i. (1834) p. 62a), Erechtheus is in Attic legend αὐτοχθών. But his divinity is even more incontestable, and he had his temple on the Akropolis, in close association with Athene ; cp. above all Homer, Il. 2. 547. This close association accounts for the metonomasia from Κεκροπίδαι to Ἀθηναῖοι here associated with his régime ; not but what Ἐρεχθεῖδαι is found in the poets as an equivalent, Pindar, Isth. 2. 19, cp. Pyth. 7. 10 ; Sophokles, Antig. 969, Aj. 201, etc. etc. Yet it is perhaps a pity that Hdt. did not complete his schematic history of Athenian titles by employing the term ; so would he have had 'Athenians' all through as the common element underlying Pelasgians, Kranaians, Kekropids, Erechtheids, Ionians ! Cp. App. Crit.

13. Ἴωνος δὲ τοῦ Ξούθου. The conventional pedigree of the sons of Hellen, for which our oldest authority is the Boiotian Hesiod (Frag. 25 = Rzach 7), is everywhere presupposed in Hdt., even though the Hellenic character of the Ionians is thus guaranteed, in conflict with his theory (1. 56) of their Pelasgic descent. The insertion of Xuthos does, however, put Ion (and Achaios) one step further from Hellen than Doros (and Aiolos) ; unless, indeed, with Euripides we make Doros also a son of Xuthos. In Attica Ion (and the Ionians) are immigrant, not autochthonous (though Euripides places his birth in one of the holy caves under the Akropolis), and no Attic tradition gave Ion a place in the suc-

στρατάρχεω γενομένου Ἀθηναίοισι ἐκλήθησαν ἀπὸ τούτου
45 Ἴωνες. Μεγαρέες δὲ τώυτὸ πλήρωμα παρείχοντο καὶ ἐπ'
Ἀρτεμισίῳ, Ἀμπρακιῶται δὲ ἑπτὰ νέας ἔχοντες ἐπεβοήθησαν, Λευκάδιοι δὲ τρεῖς, ἔθνος ἐόντες οὗτοι Δωρικὸν ἀπὸ

14 ἀπὸ: ἐπὶ? van H.
παρείχον τὸ a C: παρείχοντο τὸ PRz
ἐπεβώθησαν SV, Gaisford, van H.

45. 1 παρείχοντο SV Marcianus:
2 νῆας B ‖ ἐπεβωήθησαν R:

cession of kings, though he is recognized
here (as in Ἀθην. πολ. l.c. infra) as
war-leader, war-lord. Was there never
an Ionian conquest of or in Attica?
The Ionian elements in Attica seem
closely welded with the native, and yet
distinct (the analogy of Great Britain,
with its Saxons and Britons, is perhaps
admissible). In Attica, however, the
Ionian can hardly have been the aboriginal
element, and the 'Athenian' the immigrant; albeit such complete inversions
of the truth, such hystera protera, are
found in Greek legend (cp. 4. 145). One
thing is clear: there was no 'Norman,'
no Dorian conquest of Attica (cp. 5. 76
and my notes); and the settlement of
population in Attica went back to a
much more primitive date than in Peloponnese, or in the rest of Central Greece;
hence the relative continuity of Attic
history and culture, the priority and
scale of the 'Theseian' synoikism.

14. στρατάρχεω: elsewhere Ion had
been perhaps a king (cp. Pausan. 7. 1.
5 ἐπὶ τῆς Ἴωνος βασιλείας κτλ.), though
Hdt. does not expressly say so in 7. 94.
The 'Aristotelian' theory traced the
origin of the πολεμαρχία, as distinct from
the βασιλεία, to the appointment of Ion:
δεύτερα δὲ ἐπικατέστη πολεμαρχία, διὰ
τὸ γενέσθαι τινὰς τῶν βασιλέων τὰ πολέμια
μαλακούς, ὅθεν καὶ τὸν Ἴωνα μετεπέμψαντο
χρείας καταλαβούσης, Ath. Pol. c. 3. (The
need was the war with Eumolpos of Eleusis.) Something very like this theory, this
story, is already implied in Hdt. Strabo
383 possibly preserves the 'Aristotelian'
version: Ἴων δὲ τοὺς μετ' Εὐμόλπου νικήσας
Θρᾷκας οὕτως ηὐδοκίμησεν ὥστ' ἐπέτρεψαν
αὐτῷ τὴν πολιτείαν. ὁ δὲ πρῶτον μὲν εἰς
τέτταρας φυλὰς διεῖλε τὸ πλῆθος εἶτα εἰς
τέτταρας βίους· τοὺς μὲν γὰρ γεωργοὺς
ἀπέδειξε τοὺς δὲ δημιουργοὺς τοὺς δὲ ἱερο-
ποιοὺς τετάρτους δὲ τοὺς φύλακας· τοιαῦτα
δὲ πλείω διατάξας τὴν χώραν ἐπώνυμον
ἑαυτοῦ κατέλιπεν. This looks like the
πρώτη μετάστασις τῶν ἐξ ἀρχῆς, the κατάστασις Ἴωνος καὶ τῶν μετ' αὐτοῦ συνοικι-

σάντων (or συνοικησάντων Blass)· τότε
γὰρ πρῶτον εἰς τὰς τέτταρας συνενεμήθησαν
φυλάς, καὶ τοὺς φυλοβασιλέας κατέστησαν,
c. 41. 2. Ion, on that showing, is war-
lord and legislator, though not strictly
'king.' The four βίοι ap. Strabon. are,
of course, a rationalization of the tribal
names, as in 5. 66 supra; cp. notes ad
l.c. The tomb of Ion was to be seen,
in Pausanias' time, at Potamoi, Pausan.
1. 31. 3 (n.b. ἐπολεμάρχησε), 7. 1. 5.

45. 1. Μεγαρέες, like the Korinthians,
add nothing to their Artemisian contingent (20), and the same formula is
applied; cp. c. 43 supra. That they
were Dorian 'goes without saying'; unless, indeed, the concluding words of the
chapter be taken to cover the case of
Megara, and to make it a Korinthian
colony. This view would scarcely agree
with 5. 76 supra, where the Dorian
settlement of Megara is expressly recorded. Cp. Busolt i.[2] (1893) 220, who
omits any reference to this passage,
rightly enough. The later tradition
that the Korinthians were especially
concerned in the Dorization of Megara
hardly accords, as Busolt points out,
with the silence of Thucydides (i.e. the
Korinthians ap. Thuc.), or with the
cult of Hera Akraia, in Megara and
in Byzantion, its colony.

2. Ἀμπρακιῶται: for the geographical
position of Ambrakia cp. c. 47 infra.
Ἀμπρακία is the older form of the name:
cp. Oberhummer, Akarnanien, 25, etc.
Their contingent of 7 is a clear addition
to the Artemision list. Ambrakia is
expressly described as a colony from
Korinth by Thuc. 2. 80. 3, and was
plainly a loyal colony. For the coinage
cp. B. Head, Historia Numorum, 270—
none of the many extant varieties (all
of Korinthian type) going back before
the fourth century. The Ambrakiotes
probably came to Pogon and Salamis
out of loyalty to Korinth and at her
summons (ἐπεβοήθησαν).

3. Λευκάδιοι: for the geographical

Κορίνθου. νησιωτέων δὲ Αἰγινῆται τριήκοντα παρείχοντο. 46 ἦσαν μέν σφι καὶ ἄλλαι πεπληρωμέναι νέες, ἀλλὰ τῇσι μὲν τὴν ἑωυτῶν ἐφύλασσον, τριήκοντα δὲ τῇσι ἄριστα πλεούσῃσι ἐν Σαλαμῖνι ἐναυμάχησαν. Αἰγινῆται δὲ εἰσὶ Δωριέες ἀπὸ

---

46. 2 ἔσαν ε ‖ μέν νυν β ‖ ἄλλαι < ι′ = δέκα> Cobet : ἄλλαι <δυοκαίδεκα> van H. ‖ νῆες β : νέες δυοκαίδεκα ? Stein   3 πλωούσῃσι (-ϊν V) β : πλωούσῃσι Palm, van H.

---

position of Leukas cp. c. 47 *infra*. The Leukadian contingent of 3 is a clear addition to the navy-list. Leukas was a Korinthian colony (Thuc. 1. 30. 2), and, like Ambrakia, a loyal colony. Its coinage, of the Korinthian type and standard, reaches back into the fifth century B.C., Head p. 279.

οὗτοι. It is not quite clear whether Hdt. means this word, and the statement which follows, to apply to the Leukadians only, or to Ambrakiotes and Leukadians, or to Megarians, Ambrakiotes, and Leukadians, all three. *Prima facie* it applies to the Leukadians alone. Historically it would be equally true of the Ambrakiotes. Its application to the Megarians would be at least highly questionable in a historic sense; see above.

46. 1. νησιωτέων : the third geographical division : without the article cp. 7. 95. There follow the names and numbers of ten contingents, from eight islands, Aigina, Euboia, Keos, Naxos, Kythnos, Seriphos, Siphnos, Melos, three separate contingents being drawn from Euboia. It is not clear on what principle the order is determined.

Αἰγινῆται, as furnishing the largest contingent, perhaps as having afterwards won the ἀριστεῖα, and as Dorians, have the first place. The contingent of 30 here recorded for Salamis exceeds the Artemisian contingent by 12; whether it includes the ships present at Artemision is not made clear. The statement is that the 30 ships at Salamis did not include all the Aiginetan ships actually in commission (πεπληρωμέναι, the πλήρωμα in this case being the *Mannschaft*; cp. c. 43 *supra*). The ἄλλαι νέες may have comprised all, or some, of the Artemisian contingent of 18, which, after the engagements off Euboia, might no longer be reckoned to τῇσι ἄριστα πλεούσῃσι. So the total of the Aiginetan vessels in commission might be raised

to 48, and yet fall short of the fleet with which they had fought Athens between 487–482 B.C., cp. 6. 92, 93 (which can hardly have numbered less than 50). There is something amiss with the numbering of the Aiginetan fleets. Below, c. 48, Hdt. gives the total figure for the fleet at Salamis as 378, while his items only supply a sum 366. Are the missing 12 to be added to the 30 Aiginetans so as to bring the actual contingent present at Salamis to 42? If so, how did the figure 30 arise? Or are the 12 to be inserted even as the figure for the ἄλλαι (cp. App. Crit.)? But, if so, they should not be reckoned in the Salaminian total *infra*, for they were not at Salamis; moreover, Pausanias 2. 29. 5, rightly or wrongly, makes the Aiginetans second only to the Athenians in the number of their fleet (ἐν τῷ Μηδικῷ πολέμῳ παρασχέσθαι πλοῖα μετά γε 'Αθηναίους πλεῖστα), yet the figure above given for the Korinthian squadron was 40. The figures 30, 18, 12 all come into the reckoning, and all stand in a definite relation to one another : did the Aiginetan fleet in 480 B.C. number less than 60 vessels, of which 42 were present at the battle of Salamis, only 30 being reckoned (αἱ) ἄριστα πλέουσαι, while with 18—possibly those previously at Artemision—τὴν ἑωυτῶν ἐφύλασσον—they were on guard off Aigina!

4. εἰσὶ Δωριέες ἀπὸ 'Επιδαύρου : at the time when Hdt. wrote these words surely the Aiginetans were still in their own island home, and not outcasts in Kynuria, Thuc. 2. 27 (much less victims of extreme Athenian vengeance, Thuc. 4. 57); in other words, this passage is of older composition than 6. 91 *supra*. Cp. Introduction, §§ 7, 8. This note on the origin of the Aiginetans—Dorians from Epidauros—also seems written quite independently of the story in 5. 83, where the early dependence of Aigina

5 Ἐπιδαύρου· τῇ δὲ νήσῳ πρότερον οὔνομα ἦν Οἰνώνη. μετὰ
δὲ Αἰγινήτας Χαλκιδέες τὰς ἐπ' Ἀρτεμισίῳ εἴκοσι παρεχόμενοι καὶ Ἐρετριέες τὰς ἑπτά· οὗτοι δὲ Ἴωνες εἰσί. μετὰ

upon Epidauros is described, though
without any express recognition of the
'metropolitan' character of Epidauros—
a contrast at least compatible with the
hypothesis that this note is of earlier
composition. That Aigina was a Dorian
island in the historic period is indubitable ; e.g. the not very numerous tituli
Aeginetici, Cauer, *Delectus* ² No. 65–70,
E. S. Roberts, *Gk. Epigraphy* i. (1887)
§§ 57–59, and the uniform literary and
historical evidences from Pindar to
Pausanias. The date and circumstances
of its occupation by the Dorians, and
the precise starting-point of the colonists,
are items of doubtful tradition and
speculation. Hdt. here traces the Dorian
colonists no further back than Epidauros ;
in 1. 146 he mixes up Dorians of
Epidauros with the Ionian migration to
Asia Minor; the Dorization of Epidauros
itself he does not record. Pausanias 2.
29. 5 supplies a text : μοῖρα Ἀργείων τῶν
Ἐπίδαυρον ὁμοῦ Δηϊφόντῃ κατασχόντων
διέβη ἐς Αἴγιναν. The Dorians of Aigina
ultimately hailed from Dorian Argos ;
and so more expressly Aigina was sometimes made a colony of Argos : Τριάκων
τις Ἀργεῖος συλλέξας πλῆθος Ἀργείων,
οἱ δὲ Ἀργεῖοι τοῦ Δωρικοῦ γένους, εἰς τὴν
Αἴγιναν ἦλθε καὶ κατῴκησε Schol. Pind.
Ol. 8. 39. Epidauros was perhaps no
more than the port of departure ; and
notwithstanding the air of antiquity
lent to the traditions, we may reasonably
doubt whether the Dorization of Aigina
was much more ancient than the age of
Pheidon, or the dependence of Aigina
on Epidauros (5. 83) more than a
misconception of the relations of the
island to the Argive power under the
last of the Temenid kings of Argolis.

5. τῇ δὲ νήσῳ . . Οἰνώνη. The
statement would suggest that the name
Αἴγινα was of Dorian coinage ; but it
belongs to a class of names (beginning
with Αἰγ-) that go back long before
the coming of the Dorians, and Aigina
was the name of the island apparently
in the days of the Kalaurian Amphiktyony. So, too, the tradition that Zeus
carried the nymph Aigina to the desert
island Oinone, where she became mother
of the first inhabitant Aiakos (Pausan.
2. 29. 2), pushes the proper name back

as far as the earliest population. The
form of the name given by Pindar *Isth.*
7. 23 (telling the same story) is Οἰνοπία
(σὲ δ' ἐς νᾶσον Οἰνοπίαν φέρων ἐκοιμᾶτο
κτλ.), but elsewhere he has Οἰνώνα (*Nem.*
4. 46, 5. 15, 8. 7, *Isth.* 4. (5.) 35). Is
the supposed ancient 'name' of the
island much more than an epithet
deranged? As in the parallel cases of
Καλλίστη Θήρα (4. 147), or Σχερία =
Κόρκυρα (Pausan. 2. 5. 2), the supposed
original is more indubitably Greek, or
at least more transparently significant,
than the name of supposed later origin
—a point fatal to the asserted priority.
'Oinone,' too, is known as a nymph,
the bride of Paris (Apollod. 3. 12. 6 *et
al.*) ; and the syllable οἰν- is as common,
but is it also as ancient, as αἰγ- in the
composition of proper names? The name
Oinone might be connected with the
frequent Οἰνόη (*bis* in Attica, *ter* in
Peloponnese, and elsewhere ; e.g. Ikaria,
Steph. B.), Οἰνοῦς, Οἰνοῦσσαι, Οἰνεών
(Οἰνόανδα), and others—all genuine
place - names, of indubitably vinous
associations. Cp. Grassberger, *Gr. Ortsnamen*, p. 227. This nomenclature looks
Indo-European : can it be primitive *in
loco* ?

6. Χαλκιδέες furnish 20 vessels to the
Salaminian navy-list, and these expressly
the same ships as at Artemision ; but
the list here leaves us to find out for
ourselves by back reference that the
ships, though manned by the men of
Chalkis, were really supplied by Athens
(c. 1 *supra*) ; in fact it might more
accurately have been said of the Chalkidians, τὠυτὸ πλήρωμα παρείχοντο. The
observation confirms the suspicion that
Hdt. is here drawing on a different
source.

7. Ἐρετριέες supply 'the seven,' i.e.
the same as before, at Artemision ; but
these were really their own. The οὗτοι
here refers to the Eretrians, who, though
Ionians, are not ἀπὸ Ἀθηνέων. It might
conceivably refer to both Chalkidians
and Eretrians, but συναμφότεροι οὗτοι
would then have been clearer ; see
below. The 'Chalkidians' are presumably Athenian kleruchs, even though
the crews· in the 20 vessels may have
been natives. Cp. c. 1 *supra*.

δὲ Κήιοι τὰς αὐτὰς παρεχόμενοι, ἔθνος ἐὸν Ἰωνικὸν ἀπὸ
Ἀθηνέων. Νάξιοι δὲ παρείχοντο τέσσερας, ἀποπεμφθέντες
μὲν ἐς τοὺς Μήδους ὑπὸ τῶν πολιητέων κατά περ οἱ ἄλλοι 10
νησιῶται, ἀλογήσαντες δὲ τῶν ἐντολέων ἀπίκατο ἐς τοὺς
Ἕλληνας Δημοκρίτου σπεύσαντος, ἀνδρὸς τῶν ἀστῶν δοκίμου

---

8 κεῖοι αCP, Palm, van H. : κῖοι Βα || ἐὸν om. Β   9 ἀθηναίων ΒΒ,
Stein[1]   10 ἄλλοι Β : ἄλλοι Schaefer, Gaisford, Holder, van H.
11 ἀπίκοντο Β   12 πλεύσαντος Β

---

8. Κήιοι supply 'the same' ships as at Artemision, 2 in number; their Atheno-Ionian origin is expressly specified. The island of Keos is nowhere mentioned *nominatim* by Hdt. (cp. c. 76 *infra*), nor does it appear that he ever landed on it; but he had doubtless seen the Κηίων ἱστιητόριον at Delos (4. 35 *supra*), and he was acquainted with the works of the greatest of all Keians, Simonides; cp. 7. 228 *supra*. Athens claimed 'metropolitan' recognition, of course, from the Ionians of the Kyklades as from the Ionians of Asia; cp. 5. 99, 1. 147.

9. Νάξιοι : the four Naxian triremes are pure gain; the title refers grammatically to the very men on board, who had been despatched by the Commonwealth to join the enemy, their nominal suzerain, but had taken the law into their own hands, and joined the Greek side. This independent action of the Naxian fleet recalls, *mutatis mutandis*, the action of the Samians despatched by Polykrates to serve under Kambyses in Egypt, 3. 45, and anticipates (in a small way) the separate action of the Athenian fleet at Samos in 412–11 B.C., Thucydides 8. 75 f., not to say that of the Ionians at Byzantion in 477 B.C., Thuc. 1. 95, Plutarch. *Arist.* 23. One might suspect that the Naxian fleet on this occasion was more 'democratic,' more Attic, than οἱ πολιῆται. But see l. 12 below.

10. ἐς τοὺς Μήδους : not here, as sometimes, a geographical phrase. The employment of Μῆδος for Πέρσης is not common in these Books, and perhaps belongs to 'the source.'

κατά περ οἱ ἄλλοι νησιῶται : in the Aegean, who, with the exception of Seriphos, Siphnos, Melos, had all given 'earth and water' to 'the barbarian.' Cp. c. 66 below.

11. ἀπίκατο : a pluperfect, with the full temporal significance, referring to a past act rather than to a present result; so, the force of the form is different from the construction with the auxiliary verb, as in ἦσαν τεπληρωμέναι νέες l. 2 above.

12. Δημοκρίτου. Hdt. may owe the name of Demokritos (a popular name!) to an epigram of Simonides, recognized as authentic by M. Hauvette, *de l'authenticité des Épigrammes de Simonide* (1896) p. 53,

Δημόκριτος τρίτος ἦρξε μάχης ὅτε πὰρ
    Σαλαμῖνα
Ἕλληνες Μήδοις σύμβαλον ἐν πελάγει·
πέντε δὲ νῆας ἕλεν δηίων, ἕκτην δ' ὑπὸ
    χειρὸς
ῥύσατο βαρβαρικῆς Δωρίδ' ἁλισκομένην,

preserved by Plutarch, *de malig. Hdti.* 36. His τριηραρχία presumably extended to one only of the four triremes. His position would not be inconsistent with his being a democrat. It is remarkable that Hdt. does not supply his father's name, nor does the epigram. There is no sharp opposition intended between τῶν ἀστῶν and τῶν πολιητέων just above.

On the Athenian origin of the Ionian Naxians cp. l. 8 above. Naxos was and had been a much more important island than Keos, and had been held to Athenian interests in the days of Peisistratos (1. 64). Its rivalry with Miletos at the end of the sixth cent., and party feuds within the island itself, had led indirectly to the conflict between the Ionians and Persia in which Athens had become involved (5. 28, 31); and though Naxos had escaped the first assault upon its liberties from the Asiatic side (5. 33), it had succumbed—with the rest—to Datis and Artaphrenes (6. 95 f.) in 490 B.C. For the decade previous to Salamis its history is a blank; but evidently Naxos had resigned neither its ambitions nor its party feuds.

καὶ τότε τριηραρχέοντος. Νάξιοι δὲ εἰσὶ Ἴωνες ἀπὸ Ἀθηνέων
γεγονότες. Στυρέες δὲ τὰς αὐτὰς παρείχοντο νέας τάς περ
15 ἐπ᾽ Ἀρτεμισίῳ, Κύθνιοι δὲ μίαν καὶ πεντηκόντερον, ἐόντες
συναμφότεροι οὗτοι Δρύοπες. καὶ Σερίφιοι δὲ καὶ Σίφνιοι
καὶ Μήλιοι ἐστρατεύοντο· οὗτοι γὰρ οὐκ ἔδοσαν μοῦνοι
47 νησιωτέων τῷ βαρβάρῳ γῆν τε καὶ ὕδωρ. οὗτοι μὲν ἅπαντες
ἐντὸς οἰκημένοι Θεσπρωτῶν καὶ Ἀχέροντος ποταμοῦ ἐστρα-
τεύοντο· Θεσπρωτοὶ γάρ εἰσι ὁμουρέοντες Ἀμπρακιώτῃσι καὶ

---

13 ἀπ᾽ Β, Holder, van H.   14 γεγονότες secl. Kallenberg ǁ νῆας Β ǁ
τάς περ: τὰς καὶ Β, Holder   15 Κύθνιοι Wesseling: κύνθιοι ΑΒ₂:
κίνθιοι ΒΟ, Marc.   16 δὲ Stein³: τε (πρὸς δὲ τούτοισι καὶ Σερίφιοι ?
Stein²) ǁ σίφνιοί τε Β   47. 1 πάντες Β   3 γάρ εἰσι Stein¹ ǁ
οἱ ὁμουρέοντες Β₂

---

14. **Στυρέες.** Styra, in Euboia, sends
the same ships as to Artemision, two in
number. The Styrians are 'Dryopians';
cp. c. 43 *supra*.

15. **Κύθνιοι.** Kythnos, a small island
due south of Keos, had been unrepresented at Artemision; its modest
contingent, one trireme and one 'pentekonter,' is hardly equivalent to its
later, and apparently fixed, tribute to
Athens of 3 talents, an amount doubled
by the τάξις of 425 B.C.

16. **συναμφότεροι** clears **οὗτοι.**
Σερίφιοι. Seriphos, due south of
Kythnos, appears for the first time, and
with but one pentekonter; c. 48 *infra*.
(It paid Athens afterwards 2 – 1 talents
tribute—the figure for 425 B.C. unfortunately irrecoverable.) Athens counts as
its metropolis, *ib.*
Σίφνιοι. Siphnos, SE. of Seriphos, was a well-to-do island (cp. 3.
57 f.), and afterwards paid 3 talents'
tribute to Athens, a sum trebled by the
τάξις of 425 B.C. Yet it likewise con-
tributes but one pentekonter to the fleet,
c. 48 *infra*. The population is indis-
tinguishable from that of Seriphos, *ib.*

17. **Μήλιοι.** Melos, SW. of Siphnos,
a larger island, and still better known
to fame, but not properly belonging to
the Kyklades (cp. c. 48 *infra*), furnished
two pentekonters, c. 48 *infra*. In
425 B.C. the Athenians assessed Melos
at 15 talents (vid. τάξις φόρου, Hicks's
Manual,² No. 64); but this was probably
a mere excuse for the conquest and
destruction of the island, which was
accomplished in 416 B.C., Thucyd. 5.
84–116 (unless, indeed, it was meant
to recoup the Athenians for the failure

of the previous expedition in the year
before the τάξις, Thuc. 3. 91). The days
of greatest wealth for Melos were in
that primitive period when its beds of
obsidian supplied one of the most valuable staples of the stone age (cp. *Annual
of Br. School at Athens*, Nos. iii., iv., v.);
but the fame of the island in modern
times is more intimately associated with
the marble now standing in the Louvre
and known as the 'Venus of Milo.'
οὗτοι: there is again, and for the
third time in the list, some ambiguity
in the extension of this term, but it
may be restricted to **Μήλιοι.**

47. 2. **ἐντός**, 'east of' this side: a
natural phrase to Hdt. and his eastern
sources, but not one that he would have
used in this connexion while resident in
Italy, or even after familiarity with the
further west. *Pro tanto* the phrase
makes for the early composition of these
Books; cp. Introduction, §§ 7, 8.

3. **Θεσπρωτῶν καὶ Ἀχέροντος
ποταμοῦ:** the same conjunction in 5.
92 ἐς Θεσπρωτοὺς ἐπ᾽ Ἀχέροντα ποταμόν,
the seat of a νεκυομαντήιον. Thesprotia
is given above, 7. 176, as the original
home of the Thessalians, and still more
precisely in 2. 56 as in the neighbourhood
of the oracle of Dodona. The position
of Acheron and Thesprotis is still more
clearly marked by Thucydides, 1. 46. 3
f. ἐπειδὴ δὲ προσέμειξαν τῇ κατὰ Κέρκυραν
ἠπείρῳ ἀπὸ Λευκάδος πλέοντες, ὁρμίζονται
ἐς Χειμέριον τῆς Θεσπρωτίδος γῆς. ἔστι
δὲ λιμήν, καὶ πόλις ὑπὲρ αὐτοῦ κεῖται ἀπὸ
θαλάσσης ἐν τῇ Ἐλαιάτιδι τῆς Θεσπρωτίδος
Ἐφύρη. ἐξίησι δὲ παρ᾽ αὐτὴν Ἀχερουσία
λίμνη ἐς θάλασσαν· διὰ δὲ τῆς Θεσπρωτίδος Ἀχέρων ποταμὸς ῥέων ἐσβάλλει ἐς

Λευκαδίοισι, οἳ ἐξ ἐσχατέων χωρέων ἐστρατεύοντο. τῶν δὲ
ἐκτὸς τούτων οἰκημένων Κροτωνιῆται μοῦνοι ἦσαν οἳ ἐβοήθησαν 5
τῇ Ἑλλάδι κινδυνευούσῃ μιῇ νηί, τῆς ἦρχε ἀνὴρ τρὶς πυθιονίκης Φάυλλος. Κροτωνιῆται δὲ γένος εἰσὶ Ἀχαιοί. οἱ μέν 48

---

4 οἱ om. B ‖ δ' α   5 οἱ ἐβώθησαν B, van H. : οἱ ἐβόθησαν V :
οἱ βοηθήσαντες z   6 νηὶ μιῇ BPz, Holder, van H. ‖ πυθιόνικος B
(πυθόνικος R ap. Stein⁽¹⁾)   7 φάυλος S Valla : Φαῦλος Eustath.
Dion. 308   48. 1 μέν νυν B : μὲν cum νυν superscr. A : μὲν B

αὐτήν, ἀφ' οὗ καὶ τὴν ἐπωνυμίαν ἔχει.
ῥεῖ δὲ καὶ Θύαμις ποταμός, ὁρίζων τὴν
Θεσπρωτίδα καὶ Κεστρίνην, ὧν ἐντὸς ἡ
ἄκρα ἀνέχει τὸ Χειμέριον (where, by the
way, ἐντός = μεταξύ). Cp. Thuc. 1. 30.
3. also 50. 3 ἔστι δὲ τὰ Σύβοτα τῆς Θεσπρωτίδος λιμὴν ἐρῆμος.
Hdt.'s description of Thesprotis as
bordering on Leukas and Ambrakia is
not very precise, and leaves the relative
positions of the two great Korinthian
colonies in doubt. Here again Thucydides supplies fuller and more accurate
topography, both directly and incidentally, e.g. the relation of Leukas to
Kephallenia and its position in Akar-
nania, 2. 30. 2, and narrative passim ;
the site of Ambrakia, on the 'Ambrakian
gulf,' 1. 29. 3 ; and the chorography
presented in the account of the campaign
round Argos Amphilochicum, 2. 68-114,
passim.
Hdt.'s references here do not suggest
autopsy, or any personal acquaintance
with the region. If he ever landed
in those parts (as e.g. for a visit to
Dodona) it was after this passage had
been written, and the passage has been
left unrevised : fresh evidence of the
relatively early date of the composition
of this part of the work.
Acheron must have been notorious
as the principal stream of Thesprotia,
though by no means so considerable a
stream as the Arachthos, on which
Ambrakia was situate. What its relation,
if any, to the subterranean stream of
Homer, Od. 10. 513, is an obscure
problem (but there was necromancy
in the neighbourhood, see above).
5. Κροτωνιῆται : this passage on
Kroton looks as though it might be an
insertion (cp. Introduction, § 9) : the
one trireme from Italy does not affect
the total, which is in any case out of
gear. The addition of any one, after
naming those ἐξ ἐσχατέων χωρέων, is
rather clumsy. The absence of any

reference in Bk. 7 to an invitation to
Kroton further isolates this note. The
Krotoniate name does not figure on the
τρικάρηνος ὄφις. On the other hand, the
notice of Phayllos τρὶς πυθιονίκης makes
it more likely that the service of the
Krotoniate trireme at Salamis was
definitely commemorated in the east, or
the mother-land ; and the passage
presently quoted from Pausanias makes
this conclusion binding. The μοῦνοι
here excludes not merely all other
Italiotes and Sikeliotes, but the Korky-
raians to boot ; cp. 7. 168.
7. Φάυλλος : Phayllos of Kroton was
celebrated throughout Hellas for his
three victories at Pytho, two in the
Pentathlon, one in the foot-race alone.
The inference that all three Pythian
victories were won previously to his
service at Salamis is not binding : it is
enough that they were all ancient history to Herodotus. Φαύλῳ (sic) δὲ Κροτω-
νιάτῃ—Ὀλυμπίασι μὲν οὐκ ἔστιν αὐτῷ νίκη,
τὰς δὲ Πυθοῖ πεντάθλου δύο ἀνείλετο καὶ
σταδίου τὴν τρίτην· ἐναυμάχησε δὲ καὶ
ἐναντία τοῦ Μήδου ναῦν τε παρασκευασάμενος οἰκείαν, καὶ Κροτωνιατῶν ὁπόσοι
ἐπεδήμουν τῇ Ἑλλάδι ἀναβιβάσε—τούτου
ἐστὶν ἀνδριὰς ἐν Δελφοῖς Pausan. 10. 9. 2.
The inscription on this statue is
ultimately at least the source of this
notice in Hdt. A Phayllos is mentioned
by Aristophanes, Acharn. 215, Wasps 1206,
as a proverbially good runner : the
Scholiast calls him an Ὀλυμπιονίκης—
which, if correct, would forbid identification with the man here in question, for
not only does Pausanias expressly guard
against it, but Phayllos of Kroton was
more distinguished as a 'pentathlete,'
and most distinguished for his service at
Salamis. The name, a diminutive of
Φάων, is not uncommon : the most
celebrated bearer was undoubtedly the
brother of Onomarchos, the Phokian,
who plundered Delphi, Pausan. 10. 2. 6
etc. The passage in Pausanias quoted

νῦν ἄλλοι τριήρεας παρεχόμενοι ἐστρατεύοντο, Μήλιοι δὲ καὶ
Σίφνιοι καὶ Σερίφιοι πεντηκοντέρους· Μήλιοι μὲν γένος ἐόντες

---

2 παρέχοντες β (' perperam ' van H.)   3 ἐόντες β : γεγονότες α

---

above suggests to Blakesley that Phayllos
and his comrades were exiles, and that
his participation in the battle of Salamis
was a purely private affair. Had the
Krotoniate by any chance come to try
his fortunes at the 75th Olympiad ?
Κροτωνιῆται δὲ γένος ἐσι 'Αχαιοί.
To Hdt. the prae-Dorian population of
the Peloponnesos was mainly or largely
'Achaian' (cp. 5. 72), a theory no doubt
in part based upon the Homeric poems.
The Achaians of historic Achaia had
apparently concentrated in what was
previously an Ionian province on the
north coast, and expelled the Ionians ;
cp. 1. 145. From that Peloponnesian
Achaia, Achaians had apparently subsequently migrated to southern Italy,
and made of it a great or greater Hellas.
To the Greeks of the fifth century the
Achaians were undoubtedly the most
genuine 'Hellenes' at least of earlier or
prae-Dorian days, and the prae-Dorian
culture, the culture of the Homeric
poems, of the heroic age, was in their
eyes an Achaian culture. The Achaian
name is found actually attached to the
soil of historic Hellas in two places,
south Thessaly and north Peloponnese,
and Achaians are with certainty to be
found in Krete, in south Italy, and even
as far as Kypros. How that could be, if
the Achaians were not Greeks at all,
but 'a small Celtic tribe' (Ridgeway,
Early Age of Greece, i. 1901) merged and
lost in the Hellenic mass, is an enigma.
Prof. Bury, who in his History (1900)
appears somewhat to minimize the
importance of the Achaians, and even of
the Hellenes, in Hellenic culture,
nevertheless proved (to my mind) the
virtual identity of Hellenes and Achaians
originally, and explained thereby the
strange origin of the designation of
'Great Greece' for the south of Italy,
which could only have been so called in
distinction to the lesser Hellas from
which the Achaian colonists had come—
a mere district of Peloponnese, or it may
be of Thessaly ; cp. J.H.S. xv. (1895)
235 ff.

43. 2. τριήρεας . . πεντηκοντέρους.
The 'pentekonter' was a war-galley,
no doubt open throughout, with 50
oars (25 each side), and probably not

less than 100 feet long (120 feet ; cp.
Torr, *Ancient Ships*, p. 21). Its construction in Greece dated to the beginning
of the seventh century if Thuc. 1. 13
is to be trusted (see C. Torr, *op. cit.*
p. 4) ; the Phaiakians, however, in the
Odyssey (8. 34 ff.) had such a vessel.
It was in pentekonters, according to
Hdt. 1. 163, that the Phokaians made
their long voyages in the west, and that
the Theraians crossed to Libya to found
Kyrene in 630 B.C. ; and in pentekonters,
according to Thuc. 1. 13. 6, the Phokaians
defeated the Carthaginians off Massalia
about 600 B.C. Even the Athenian and
Aiginetan navies at the beginning of
the fifth century were mainly composed
of pentekonters, according to Thuc. 1.
14. 3, and he even declares that most
of the vessels in which the Athenians
fought at Salamis were not fully decked,
ib., a statement which ill accords with
the large number of *Epibatai* carried.
He does not, however, expressly deny
that they were triremes.

Triremes were the rule in 480 B.C.,
according to Hdt. in this passage. He
elsewhere reckons 200 men as the crew,
or complement of rowers ; cp. 7. 184
supra. (The actual number of oars used
on the three banks (?) of an Attic trireme
was 170 to 174, cp. Torr, *op. cit.* p. 10 f.,
and there might be thirty in reserve,
or supplement; for the precise allocation
of the oars cp. *op. cit.*) The trireme
was something less than 150 feet long,
and less than 20 feet broad (cp. Torr,
p. 22)—measurements which may not
be quite precise for 480 B.C. Cp. also
M. A. Cartault, *La trière Athénienne*,
1881 ; J. Kopecky, *Die attischen Trieren*,
1890.

**3. Μήλιοι . . γένος ἐόντες ἀπὸ Λακε-
δαίμονος.** Hdt. says the Melians were
from Lakedaimon ; he does not expressly
say that they were Dorian. Thuc. 5.
84, 2. 89, 106, fully recognizes them as
Λακεδαιμονίων ἄποικοι, and seems to give
1116 B.C. as an approximate date for
the colonization in c. 112 (416 + 700).
Judging by the parallel case of Thera
(Hdt. 4. 148), the genuinely 'Dorian'
element in the emigration will have been
very small ; yet, like Thera, Melos used
a 'Dorian' alphabet and dialect (cp.

ἀπὸ Λακεδαίμονος δύο παρείχοντο, Σίφνιοι δὲ καὶ Σερίφιοι
Ἴωνες ἐόντες ἀπ' Ἀθηνέων μίαν ἑκάτεροι. ἀριθμὸς δὲ ἐγένετο 5
ὁ πᾶς τῶν νεῶν, πάρεξ τῶν πεντηκοντέρων, τριηκόσιαι καὶ
ἑβδομήκοντα καὶ ὀκτώ.

     Ὡς δὲ ἐς τὴν Σαλαμῖνα συνῆλθον οἱ στρατηγοὶ ἀπὸ **49**

---

5 Ἀθηνέων Stein[2] : ἀθηναίων   6 νηῶν β || ὀκτὼ καὶ ἑβδομήκοντα
(πεντήκοντα V) καὶ τριηκόσιαι β, Holder, van H.   **49**. 1 στρατηγοὶ
<οἱ> van H.

Roberts, *Greek Epigraphy*, §§ 19–23), a fact which no doubt would favour the 'Lakedaimonian' legend.

6. πάρεξ τῶν πεντηκοντέρων, of which there were all told seven: two from Keos, two from Melos, and one each from Kythnos, Seriphos, and Siphnos.

τριηκόσιαι καὶ ἑβδομήκοντα καὶ ὀκτώ. This total is repeated (virtually) and raised to 380 by the addition of the Tenian vessel which joined at Salamis, and the Lemnian vessel which had joined at Artemision, c. 82 *infra*; the total here is therefore certain. Yet it exceeds the items, which amount only to 366, by 12. There is therefore something wrong with the items. Valckenaer would have read 42 for the Aiginetans, c. 46 *supra*; this agrees with the statement of Pausanias that next to the Athenians the Aiginetans supplied most ships. The repetition of the τριήκοντα need not bar this emendation; if the figure was once corrupted, it would be corrected in the other case in the light of the corruption. Moreover, this bolder emendation is preferable to the insertion of 12 for the ἄλλαι νέες, first because the list is not a list of all the ships in commission, but only of those which fought at Salamis; secondly, because 42 is rather a low figure for the absolute sum of the Aiginetan navy, all told; while if 42 were at Salamis, and 18 in service at home, we get a total of 60 ships in commission, which is a more probable figure for Aigina at this time. If the Aiginetan 30 were to be maintained for Salamis we should have to tinker one or more of the other items. K. O. Mueller, *Aeginetica*, p. 122, suggested reading Σικυώνιοι δὲ πεντεκαίδεκα παρείχοντο πλεῦρας, i.e. 12+15, raising the Sikyonian contingent from 12 (Artemision) to 27, which is less ingenious than Gutschmid's compromise to raise Troizen from 5 to 7, and the Aiginetans from 30 to 40.

Hdt. evidently finds it necessary to account for the smallness of the Aiginetan contingent by the remark that it was by no means all the ships they had in commission; but Rawlinson, in supposing that they had 40 on guard off their own island, while maintaining 30 at Salamis, seems to go too far; the majority of the Aiginetan navy, like that of every other Greek state, was at Salamis. The variant 358 is quite worthless; cp. App. Crit.

With Hdt.'s total of 378 (or 380) for the Greek navy at Salamis is to be compared Aischylos' 300 (*Pers.* 339), Thucydides' 400 (1. 74. 1), Demosthenes' 300 (*de cor.* 238). If Demosthenes did not find this figure in his copy of Thucydides (Stahl; "ex aliquot deterioribus," Hude) the two historians virtually agree as against the poet and the orator. Ktesias (ed. Gilmore, § 57), from the Persian point of view, makes it 700 (of which apparently only 110 are Athenian). Tzetzes' 271 (*ad Lycoph.* 1432) is surely only a confusion with the numbers given by Hdt. for Artemision.

The phrase repeated ἐν Σαλαμῖνι ἐναυμάχησαν suggests that the list is compiled not from documents drawn up for working purposes beforehand, but from memorial lists and commemorative offerings—an inference further supported by the mention of Demokritos and Phayllos.

49. 1. ἐς τὴν Σαλαμῖνα: perhaps the town; cp. c. 42 *supra*.

οἱ στρατηγοὶ ἀπὸ τ. εἰρ. πολίων: including Kroton, 21 πόλιες have been named in the navy-list. It is hardly conceivable that Phayllos, or even Demokritos, was admitted on equal terms with the general, or generals, from Athens and Korinth, to say nothing of Sparta. Probably the six Peloponnesian cities were each represented by a strategos, Eurybiades for Sparta, Adeimantos for Korinth; the

τῶν εἰρημενέων πολίων, ἐβουλεύοντο, προθέντος Εὐρυβιάδεω
γνώμην ἀποφαίνεσθαι τὸν βουλόμενον, ὅκου δοκέοι ἐπιτηδεότατον εἶναι ναυμαχίην ποιέεσθαι τῶν αὐτοὶ χωρέων ἐγκρατέες
5 εἰσί· ἡ γὰρ Ἀττικὴ ἀπεῖτο ἤδη, τῶν δὲ λοιπέων πέρι
προετίθεε. αἱ γνῶμαι δὲ τῶν λεγόντων αἱ πλεῖσται συνεξ-

---

2 εἰρημενέων Stein : εἰρημένων   3 ἐπιτηδεώτατον CPdz ‖ ποιήσεσθαι R (Stein) SV (Gaisf.) ‖ χώρων B : χωρίων z   5 ἀφεῖτο B :
ἀφεῖται Ps ‖ λοιπῶν B ‖ πέρι om. B

---

others are anonymous. The Athenians,
Aiginetans, and Megarians may have
each been represented by one and only
one voice. Ambrakia and Leukas probably were represented by Korinth ; the
position of Chalkis, Eretria, and the rest
is obscure. The Council may not have
comprised more than 9-12 persons. In
the sequel the only *dramatis personae*
are Eurybiades, Adeimantos, Themistokles ; the rest are mutes—unless we
add Mnesiphilos and Aristeides. Themistokles should perhaps be regarded as
protagonist ; but, council or no council,
it is evident that Eurybiades, in virtue
of the Spartan *Hegemonia* and his own
Navarchia, could do as he pleased : if
he puts the question to the vote, it is
merely for his own guidance ; the result
is not obligatory. The first council at
Salamis may be taken to begin here ;
but the passages which follow are not
sharply separated, but are in the nature
of dissolving scenes.

3. ὅκου δοκέοι κτλ. : the question laid
before the council of war is limited to
the selection of a battle-ground ; 'the
previous question,' whether to fight a
sea-battle at all or not, is treated as
closed and determined. It is, however,
assumed that the fleet must rest upon
a friendly shore, and have a harbour to
retire on. τῶν is relative, but χωρέων
is genitive, not by inverse attraction,
but in regular construction with ὅκου,
though it seems to come in rather
epexegetically.

5. ἡ γὰρ Ἀττικὴ ἀπεῖτο ἤδη : this
statement, which may be :conceived as
Hdt.'s own, or as proceeding from
Eurybiades upon the occasion, was not
strictly true, so long at least as the
Akropolis was still held by Athenians.
The obfuscation of the defence of the
Akropolis in the story which presently
follows has perhaps reacted prejudicially
upon the account of the deliberations

at Salamis. The pluperfect force of
ἀπεῖτο is emphasized by ἤδη. The phrase
shows anyway that Salamis was no part
of Attica.

τῶν δὲ λοιπέων : was there any
other conceivable alternative but Salamis
or the Isthmos ?

6. αἱ γνῶμαι δὲ τῶν λεγόντων : the
opinions of the speakers—not the votes
of those present—and, moreover, but a
majority of them. There was a minority
argument, but it is not given here by
Hdt. He reserves it to be produced
on a later occasion. Evidently Themistokles (backed by the Megarians and
Aiginetans) must already at this stage
have used those arguments in favour of
remaining and doing battle at Salamis,
which are put into his mouth by Hdt.
at a later stage—always supposing that
the question of remaining and fighting
at Salamis was still, or ever, an open
one.

συνεξέπιπτον, 'were falling out
together' : sc. ἀλλήλαισι, i.e. were tending to agree, "de sententiis in unum
convenientibus," Baehr, who perhaps
rightly in this place derives the metaphor from casting of lots. Yet the
sense might equally well (especially in
view of the tense) be, 'were tending to
fall (come, work) out to the same conclusion.' As the strategoi who spoke did
not all speak together the tendency and
result was cumulative and not instantaneous. συνεξέπιπτε is, however, used
in 5. 22 of an occurrence which was
single and instantaneous (though it has
there nothing to say either to 'lots' or
'opinions'). In c. 123 *infra* the word
might simply mean 'agreed.' An exact
parallel to the present passage is found
in 1. 206.

The construction of πλέσαντας is
κατὰ σύνεσιν, as though οἱ πλεῖστοι τῶν
λεγόντων had preceded.

ἔπιπτον πρὸς τὸν Ἰσθμὸν πλώσαντας ναυμαχέειν πρὸ τῆς
Πελοποννήσου, ἐπιλέγοντες τὸν λόγον τόνδε, ὡς, εἰ νικηθέωσι
τῇ ναυμαχίῃ, ἐν Σαλαμῖνι μὲν ἐόντες πολιορκήσονται ἐν νήσῳ,
ἵνα σφι τιμωρίη οὐδεμία ἐπιφανήσεται, πρὸς δὲ τῷ Ἰσθμῷ 10
ἐς τοὺς ἑωυτῶν ἐξοίσονται. ταῦτα τῶν ἀπὸ Πελοποννήσου 50
στρατηγῶν ἐπιλεγομένων, ἐληλύθεε ἀνὴρ Ἀθηναῖος ἀγγέλλων
ἥκειν τὸν βάρβαρον ἐς τὴν Ἀττικὴν καὶ πᾶσαν αὐτὴν πυρπολέεσθαι. ὁ γὰρ διὰ Βοιωτῶν τραπόμενος στρατὸς ἅμα

---

7 πλώσαντες z   8 τόνδε: τοῦτον β || εἰ: ἦν βΡz, Baehr, Holder,
van H.   9 μενέοντες β || [ἐν νήσῳ]? van H.   10 οὐδεμία Ρ:
οὐδεμίη βz: οὐδὲ μίη || φανήσεται β   50. 2 ἐληλύθεε Werfer:
ἐλήλυθε

---

7. **πρό** seems to have a double significance, both local and causal. Op.
Index.

8. **ἐπιλέγοντες τὸν λόγον τόνδε**, 'adding this argument, or consideration . .'
But the speech can hardly have been
an ἐπίλογος to the γνῶμαι, containing, as
it does, the pith and marrow of the
arguments for adjourning to the Isthmos:
a defeat at Salamis would mean a
πολιορκία ἐν νήσῳ—and a siege meant
inevitable starvation and surrender.
Themistokles no doubt would have met
such an argument at once with his three
reasons : c. 60 infra.

εἰ νικηθέωσι . . πολιορκήσονται
is doubly remarkable to the grammarian.
(a) εἰ without ἄν with the subjunctive
Stein defends by ref. to 2. 13 εἰ (μή) . .
ἀναβῇ: 4. 172 ὡς . . μιχθῇ: 1. 132 ὡς
ἐθέλῃ: c. 22 supra ἔπειτε ἀνενειχθῇ, and
other temporal clauses (vide Stein's note
to 4. 172). We have εἰ with the subj.
in questions, as in εἰ στρατεύηται 1. 53, εἰ
ἀπέλωνται 2. 52, etc., not exact parallels
to this case. If the reading here is
maintained (vide App. Crit.) the condition may be understood as emphasizing
the probability of defeat ; it is merely a
question of time. (b) πολιορκήσονται is
passive in sense ; cp. c. 70 infra.

11. **ἐς τοὺς ἑωυτῶν ἐξοίσονται**, 'they
will have their own folks to fall back
on' ; the verb perhaps suggesting further
their wrecked and shattered condition ;
cp. ἐξοισομένων c. 76 infra, ἐξενειχθέντα
c. 96 infra.

50. 1. **τῶν ἀπὸ Π. στ. ἐπιλεγομένων** :
the verb means 'pondering, considering' ;
cp. 7. 49, 149, 236, etc. (Contr. the
verb in the active just above.) The local
designation of the doubters is important.

2. **ἐληλύθεε** : whether pluperfect or
not (cp. App. Crit.) his arrival anticipates
the decision of the deliberating generals
in council. This anonymous messenger
reports only what was to be fully
expected, unless indeed the defence of
the Akropolis was more seriously intended
than appears from the subsequent narrative. But with this message, vague in
its form, the narrative breaks off, only
to be resumed in c. 56 infra, where the
Greeks have learnt further of the capture
and destruction of the Akropolis : a
different matter to this first message.

3. **πᾶσαν** cannot be taken here to
cover the destruction of the Akropolis, a
disaster which would have demanded
more precision in the messenger's report.

πυρπολέεσθαι : igne vastare, a word
used (in the active) by Aristophanes
frequently, and by Xenophon (Cyr. 3. 3.
25), and found in Homer, Od. 10. 30,
but not elsewhere in Hdt.

4. **ὁ γάρ κτλ.** introduces what is
virtually a digression, resuming the
narrative of the advance of the Persian
army, from c. 39, or even from c. 34 supra.
There was perhaps a concentration of
the Persians in W. Boiotia (Koroneia ?)
—to which point the centre would have
advanced by Parapotamioi and Chaironeia,
the left wing, from Abai, by Aspledon
and Orchomenos, the right wing, by Lilaia
— Delphi — Panopeus—Chaironeia, or
possibly even by Trachis—Amphissa—
Delphi—Lebadeia.

Thespiai and Plataiai may have been
destroyed by an advance of the column
from Delphi ; or by an excursion from
Thebes, where no doubt the Persian
force was concentrated : the Plataians
serving on the fleet had reached home

5 Ξέρξῃ, ἐμπρήσας Θεσπιέων τὴν πόλιν αὐτῶν ἐκλελοιπότων ἐς
Πελοπόννησον, καὶ τὴν Πλαταιέων ὡσαύτως, ἡκέ τε ἐς τὰς
Ἀθήνας καὶ πάντα ἐκεῖνα ἐδηίου. ἐνέπρησε δὲ Θέσπειάν τε

51 καὶ Πλάταιαν πυθόμενος Θηβαίων ὅτι οὐκ ἐμήδιζον. ἀπὸ δὲ
τῆς διαβάσιος τοῦ Ἑλλησπόντου, ἔνθεν πορεύεσθαι ἤρξαντο
οἱ βάρβαροι, ἕνα αὐτοῦ διατρίψαντες μῆνα ἐν τῷ διέβαινον
ἐς τὴν Εὐρώπην, ἐν τρισὶ ἑτέροισι μησὶ ἐγένοντο ἐν τῇ Ἀττικῇ,

---

5 αὐτῶν : ἐκ τῶν Β : αὐτέων z   6 τὴν : τῶν Β : an τὴν τῶν ?
7 ἐδήου Β : ἐδήου z ‖ δὲ et τε om. Β ‖ θέσπιαν Β : Θεσπεάν z   51. 3
μῆνα om. Β (Holder) : μῆνα διατρίψαντες S (Gaisf.)   4 μήνεσι Β
('iniuria probatum Schaefero et Gaisfordio' van H.)

---

in time to take part in the flitting to
Peloponnesos; cp. c. 44 supra.

Hdt. evidently thinks that the whole
land-forces of Xerxes entered Attica by
one and the same road; cp. c. 113 infra.
This supposition is absurd. From Thebes
into Attica three routes would have
been available. I. Right, or west, by
Eleutherai—Eleusis (detaching a force
against Plataiai ?): probably the best
and easiest route, then as now. II. Central, by Panakton—Phyle—Acharnai:
the most direct, and also the most
difficult. III. Left, or east, by Tanagra
and Dekeleia (cp. 9. 15 infra), a considerable circuit, but a good and much
frequented road. Probably the Persians
used all three, both going and coming;
doubtless also a considerable force was
left behind in Boiotia, and garrisons all
along the king's route to the rear. The
singulars Θέσπεια, Πλάταια are unique
in Hdt.

51. 1. ἀπό: temporal; cp. cc. 54, 55
infra.

2. τῆς διαβάσιος τοῦ Ἑλλησπόντου:
cp. 7. 54-56 supra. The Hellespont is
here, curiously enough, treated as the
starting-point of the march (ἔνθεν πορεύεσθαι ἤρξαντο οἱ βάρβαροι). In Bk. 7
the passage of the Hellespont is a mere
episode on the march from Sardes in 480
B.C., and the start is made from Sardes
with great pomp and circumstance (7.
37-40). Again, in Bk. 7. 56 the passage
of the Hellespont occupies seven days
and seven nights, just a week of our
reckoning: here, a month is spent in
passing the Hellespont (ἕνα αὐτοῦ διατρίψαντες μῆνα ἐν τῷ διέβαινον ἐς τὴν
Εὐρώπην). It might be possible to
'harmonize' the two statements by supposing that the month covers all the
time spent on the Hellespont; but such

a harmony is not convincing. The
month might as well cover all the period
from the start at Sardis: and in any
case the discrepancy remains, and
suggests a difference of source. The
passages in Bk. 7 are probably from
Asianic sources. The passage before us
here is hardly less obviously from the
European side, and presumably from
Attic authority, as the Archontate
suggests. It is important to recognize
the insouciance with which Hdt. writes
down in different contexts different data
from different sources, without troubling
himself to rationalize them; cp. Introduction, § 10. This acceptance of the
local source for all it may be worth is of
the essence of Hdt.'s method, or un-
method; it is half the secret of his
charm, and the chief cause of his value;
the unity of his work is a literary, a
poetic illusion, not a scientific miracle.

4. ἐν τρισὶ ἑτέροισι μησί. The meaning is not so self-evident as might be
wished. How are the 'months' computed ? By the calendar ? Or purely by
the interval between start and arrival ?
Are we to understand that just ninety
days, or rather less, separated Sestos and
Athens on the Persian march ? Or
are the months three months of the
Attic calendar, Skirophorion, Hekatombaion, Metageitnion, for example ?
In either case the three months seems
an underestimate. The battle of Salamis was fought about the 20th of
Boedromion (cp. c. 65 infra), and surely
within a month of the arrival of the
Persians in Athens. The fighting at
Artemision-Thermopylai approximately
synchronized with the Olympiad (7. 206
supra, but cp. c. 26 supra), i.e. could
not at the earliest have fallen before the
Attic new year, which suits the date for

Καλλιάδεω ἄρχοντος Ἀθηναίοισι. καὶ αἱρέουσι ἔρημον τὸ 5
ἄστυ, καί τινας ὀλίγους εὑρίσκουσι τῶν Ἀθηναίων ἐν τῷ ἱρῷ
ἐόντας, ταμίας τε τοῦ ἱροῦ καὶ πένητας ἀνθρώπους, οἳ φραξά-

5 ἐρῆμον CPₐ, van H.　　7 ἱροῦ A, Holder : cf. 55. 8 infra

Salamis and the Archontate. But to suppose that the battle of Salamis took place only ninety days or so after the passage of the Hellespont ascribes extraordinary activity to the Persian advance. Moreover, the start from Sardes will probably have taken place at latest in Elaphebolion (say March), and t e passage of the Hellespont in Thargeliõn (say May). Taking the months here as Attic months, and reckoning exclusively, it might be correct to say that Xerxes reached Athens three months after leaving the Hellespont, i.e. in the fifth month, reckoning inclusively.

There is an exactly parallel case in Xenoph. *Hell.* 1. 4. 21, where Alkibiades is said to have quitted Athens τρίτῳ μηνὶ μετὰ τὸν κατάπλουν (407 B.C.). He had landed on Thargelion 25 (*ib.* § 12) ; he left after Boëdromion 20 (§ 20). This would be at least four months after, reckoning simply from arrival to departure, or in the fifth month, reckoning by Attic months, *nominatim*, or after a clear three months' interval, reckoned exclusively. The word ἑτέροισι here might favour this last method. (But does τρίτῳ μηνὶ in Xenophon perhaps = Βοηδρομιῶνι ?) See further on the chronology Appendix IV. § 2.

5. **Καλλιάδεω ἄρχοντος Ἀθηναίοισι**, i.e. in the course of the year 480–479 B.C. = OL 75. 1. Cp. Clinton, *F. H. ad an.* But as there were twelve months in the year (and sometimes thirteen) this chronological indication, though highly acceptable on many grounds, leaves a good deal to be wished : if but the day of Xerxes' coming had happened to engrave itself upon the records ! Probably it was a day towards the end of Metageitnion (say August) or beginning of Boëdromion (September).

τὸ ἄστυ, here, at least, must be admitted as contradistinguished from ἡ ἀκρόπολις, which they did not find deserted, or take without a struggle. Even in Attica they had picked up some 500 captives, if the story in 9. 99 *infra* be true as it stands, and the men there reported be not the remnant of the Akropolis garrison. The *Asty* was not apparently at this time sufficiently walled, or fortified, to enable it to stand a siege, or we may well doubt whether the Athenians would have evacuated Attica. It was, however, a πόλις τροχοειδής—unless, indeed, that description apply to the Akropolis, 7. 140.

6. **καί τινας ὀλίγους εὑρίσκουσι . . ἐόντας** : they discover a fact, perhaps to their astonishment, viz. that some few men of the citizens of Athens are in the Sacred Place—these words introduce an eminently apologetic and fictitious account of the defence and siege of the Akropolis, which was probably a far more serious and formidable undertaking than the story, devised in the light of events, expressly suggests. The men in the Akropolis were perhaps neither so few, so poor, so abject, so superstitious, nor so deplorable as the story assumes and asserts.

ἐν τῷ ἱρῷ : what temple is meant ? Was this an old Erechtheion (cp. c. 55 *infra*), or was it the old 'Athenaeum' (so to speak) which had been enlarged by Peisistratos ? Did Hdt. know anything of there being more than one temple on the Akropolis of Peisistratos ? Or was there, in fact, more than one ? Cp. Furtwaengler, *Masterpieces* (E.T.) Appendix, pp. 415 ff. ; E. A. Gardner, *Ancient Athens,* c. iii. pp. 78 ff. Baehr would take τὸ ἱρόν here in a wider sense: *de toto loco diis ac potissimum Minervae consecrato in arce.* But its recurrence just below, and in c. 53, is against him.

7. **ταμίας τε . . καὶ πένητας ἀνθρώπους** : *prima facie*, the same persons are meant, but the ταμίαι τοῦ ἱροῦ, or more correctly ταμίαι τῶν ἱερῶν χρημάτων τῆς Ἀθηναίας, for it surely must be these officials that are here intended (cp. G. Gilbert, *Handbuch* i.² 269), would of necessity have been assessed under the highest τίμημα, cp. Ἀθ. πολ. 7. 3, 8. 1. Their existence is demonstrable epigraphically before the middle of sixth cent., *C.I.A.* iv. 8. 373. They were not 'poor,' except in so far as the war had ruined them. ἀνθρώπους too is contemptuous: **φραξάμενοι** is a strict middle,

μενοι τὴν ἀκρόπολιν θύρῃσί τε καὶ ξύλοισι ἠμύνοντο τοὺς
ἐπιόντας, ἅμα μὲν ὑπ' ἀσθενείης βίου οὐκ ἐκχωρήσαντες ἐς
10 Σαλαμῖνα, πρὸς δὲ αὐτοὶ δοκέοντες ἐξευρηκέναι τὸ μαντήιον τὸ
ἡ Πυθίη σφι ἔχρησε, τὸ ξύλινον τεῖχος ἀνάλωτον ἔσεσθαι·
αὐτὸ δὴ τοῦτο εἶναι τὸ κρησφύγετον κατὰ τὸ μαντήιον καὶ
52 οὐ τὰς νέας. οἱ δὲ Πέρσαι ἱζόμενοι ἐπὶ τὸν καταντίον τῆς
ἀκροπόλιος ὄχθον, τὸν Ἀθηναῖοι καλέουσι Ἀρήιον πάγον,

---

9 ἐκχωρήσαντας z   10 δὲ καὶ ß, Holder, van H. ‖ τῷ ἡ malebat
Valckenaer ('inutiliter' Gaisf.)   12 αὐτὸ : καὶ αὐτὸ Sz, van H., aliique :
αὐτὸ γὰρ ! Stein³ ‖ εἶναι : ἔσεσθαι καὶ ß ‖ κατὰ τὸ μαντήιον abesse malit
van H. ‖ καὶ οὐ . . καταντίον om. R   13 νῆας ßz

---

and ἠμύνοντο a strict imperfect : θύραι
not so much 'doors' torn from their
hinges, as 'raft-like structures' (cp. 2.
96, Thuc. 6. 101. 3).

9. ἅμα μὲν . . πρὸς δέ . .: two reasons
are given, one reflecting upon their
material, the other upon their mental
resources : they were poverty-stricken,
deficient in means of livelihood ; yet
they were proud, or conceited enough to
have a private interpretation of the
divine word (αὐτοί) : cp. τοὺς πλέον τι ἐς
τὸν χρησμὸν ἢ Θεμιστοκλῆς εἰδέναι νομίζον-
τας Pausan. 1. 18. 2. These two reasons
are sibi repugnantia (but this was
written before the Lords decided that
the 'Wee Frees' were in the right !) :
anyway everything tends to depreciate
the defenders of the Akropolis, and to
betray the 'pragmatism' of the story !

10. ἐξευρηκέναι τὸ μαντήιον, '(to have
discovered), to understand, the true
meaning of) the response.' The reference
is, of course, to the story told 7. 140-144 ;
cp. especially c. 142, where the justification of the ξύλινον τεῖχος is better
explained than in this passage, which
only suggests the extemporized θύραι
and ξύλα of these poor wretches.

Replaced in its proper perspective,
that is, after the fiasco at Thermopylai,
the story of the Athenian theoria to
Delphi, of the two responses, and the
various interpretations thereof, gains
immensely in point. The defence of the
Akropolis may have been of the nature
of a compromise, a concession, on the
part of Themistokles ; yet it looks by no
means inconsistent with his plan of a
sea-fight at Salamis, and it might have
had the effect of bringing the Peloponnesian army from behind the Isthmos
into Attica to the rescue of the Akro-

polis : in any case, it occupied the
Persian forces, and to some extent
checked and divided them, and made
pro tanto for the safety of Salamis and
the success of the fleet.

11. ἀνάλωτον ἔσεσθαι : these words
might have ended an hexameter, but as
a matter of fact the actual verse ran
ἀπόρθητον τελέθειν. The variation
suggests that Hdt. is here following an
independent story, without reference to
7. 141 supra.

12. τὸ κρησφύγετον : cp. 5. 124.

52. 1. καταντίον : right opposite the
west end, where the ascent and entrance
lay.

2. τὸν Ἀθηναῖοι καλέουσι : a phrase
not taken from an Attic source, nor
intended for an Attic audience.

Ἀρήιον πάγον. πάγος is a rocky
point, or summit, as in Homer, Od. 5.
405 etc. The epithet may rather be
connected with ἀραί than with Ἄρης
originally, as the cult of the Σεμναί was
certainly far more ancient on the spot
than the cult of the war-god (cp.
Aischyl. Eumen. 417, etc.), and it was
with them and their rights that the
Areiopagite court had to do ; though in
the historical period the association
with Ἄρης was fully recognized—perhaps
in consequence of a pseud-etymology—
and a temple to Ares actually stood on
or near the rock : Pausan. 1. 8. 4, with
notes, Frazer ii. 91, Hitzig-Bluemner i.
161 f. The topographical relation of the
Areios rock, or Athenian Ebal, to the
Akropolis fitted it to form a base for
the Persian siege-operations, as once for
the operations of the Amazones against
the Theseian citadel ; so Aischyl. Eumen.
685 ff.—

ἐπολιόρκεον τρόπον τοιόνδε· ὅκως στυππεῖον περὶ τοὺς ὀιστοὺς
περιθέντες ἅψειαν, ἐτόξευον ἐς τὸ φράγμα. . . . ἐνθαῦτα
Ἀθηναίων οἱ πολιορκεόμενοι ὅμως ἠμύνοντο, καίπερ ἐς τὸ 5
ἔσχατον κακοῦ ἀπιγμένοι καὶ τοῦ φράγματος προδεδωκότος·
οὐδὲ λόγους τῶν Πεισιστρατιδέων προσφερόντων περὶ ὁμολογίης
ἐνεδέκοντο, ἀμυνόμενοι δὲ ἄλλα τε ἀντεμηχανῶντο καὶ δὴ καὶ
προσιόντων τῶν βαρβάρων πρὸς τὰς πύλας ὀλοιτρόχους
ἀπίεσαν, ὥστε Ξέρξην ἐπὶ χρόνον συχνὸν ἀπορίῃσι ἐνέχεσθαι 10
οὐ δυνάμενον σφέας ἑλεῖν. χρόνῳ δ' ἐκ τῶν ἀπόρων ἐφάνη 53
δή τις ἔξοδος τοῖσι βαρβάροισι· ἔδεε γὰρ κατὰ τὸ θεοπρόπιον
πᾶσαν τὴν Ἀττικὴν τὴν ἐν τῇ ἠπείρῳ γενέσθαι ὑπὸ Πέρσῃσι.

---

52. 3 ἐπολιορκέοντο β(?) ‖ στυππίον SV (Gaisf.): στυπεῖον CPdz
4 lacunam suspicatur Stein³ 6 τοῦ κακοῦ z ‖ φρήγματος z ‖ προσδεδω-
κότος β 8 ἀντεμηχανῶντο a, Stein²: ἀνεμηχανέοντο β: ἀντεμη-
χανέοντο Stein¹ 9 ὀλοιτρόχους Pz: ὄλοι τροχοὺς RS 10 ξέρξεα
βPz **53.** 1 δὲ β 2 ἔξοδος Gomperz, Stein², van H.: ἔσοδος
codd., Stein¹, Holder 3 τήν γε ἐν? Kallenberg ‖ ἐν: ἐπὶ β

πάγον δ' Ἄρειον τόνδ' Ἀμαζόνων ἔδραν,
σκηνάς θ' ὅτ' ἦλθον Θησέως κατὰ φθόνον
στρατηλατοῦσαι, καὶ πόλιν νεόπολιν
τήνδ' ὑψίπυργον ἀντεπύργωσαν τότε,
Ἄρει δ' ἔθυον, ἔνθεν ἔστ' ἐπώνυμος
πέτρα, πάγος τ' Ἄρειος κτλ.

A passage which could hardly have been
recited to an Athenian audience in 458
B.C. (Philokles) without vividly recalling
the experiences of twenty-two years before
(480, Kalliades). That there was a
regular πολιορκία Hdt. expressly admits.

3. ὅκως . . ἅψειαν, ἐτόξευον : the
construction is observable, the sense is
clear : they wound tow round their
arrows, ignited it, and discharged them
into the fortified enclosure on the
Akropolis. Nor does Hdt. mean that
they discharged any other arrows than
those so treated. ἐτόξευον is used
absolutely (cp. c. 128 infra, where the
construction ὅκως γράψειε κτλ. is more
regular, or logical, than here).

6. ἀπιγμένοι καὶ . . προδεδωκότος is
not quite regular : the καὶ is de trop ;
cp. δ. 127 ἅτε οἰδεόντων . . καὶ ἔχων.
The p. or pl.p. participles mark the
intense and utter certainty of their position. Also the words ὅμως ἠμύνοντο
would more naturally come after καίπερ
κτλ.

7. τῶν Πεισιστρατιδέων : they have
not been heard of since 7. 6 supra,
which does not look as if much of the

intervening matter had come from the
supposed 'Memoirs of Dikaios'; cp.
Introduction, § 10.

9. τὰς πύλας : at the west end, where
afterwards stood (and stand to some
extent) the great Propylaia of Mnesikles
and Perikles ; cp. E. A. Gardner, Ancient
Athens, 224 ff.

ὀλοιτρόχους, ap. oracul. 5. 92 :
no doubt 'round stones' that could be
rolled down on the assailants. Where
did these few poor creatures get these
missiles ! Were there any columns or
pillar-drums lying about ! (These, however, might have needed to have the
gates opened for emission, which would
not have done.)

10. ἐπὶ χρόνον συχνόν might mean
almost any length of time, and is
lamentably vague, but still goes to show
the relative success of the desperate
resistance.

ἀπορίῃσι ἐνέχεσθαι : a common
expression ; 7. 128, 9. 37, 98 etc.

53. 2. ἔξοδος, metaphorical; also a
certain emendation. Cp. App. Crit.

ἔδεε γάρ : that the word of the
god might be fulfilled ! Cp. 7. 141 for
the θεοπρόπιον in question, 5. 33 for the
formula.

3. πᾶσαν τὴν Ἀττικὴν τὴν ἐν τῇ
ἠπείρῳ : a curious qualification, for
where was there any Ἀττική except
ἐν τῇ ἠπείρῳ ! Salamis was no part
of Attica ; cp. c. 49 supra. Cp. also

ἔμπροσθε ὦν πρὸ τῆς ἀκροπόλιος, ὄπισθε δὲ τῶν πυλέων καὶ
5 τῆς ἀνόδου, τῇ δὴ οὔτε τις ἐφύλασσε οὔτ' ἂν ἤλπισε μή κοτέ
τις κατὰ ταῦτα ἀναβαίη ἀνθρώπων, ταύτῃ ἀνέβησαν τινὲς
κατὰ τὸ ἱρὸν τῆς Κέκροπος θυγατρὸς Ἀγλαύρου, καίτοι περ
ἀποκρήμνου ἐόντος τοῦ χώρου. ὡς δὲ εἶδον αὐτοὺς ἀναβε-
βηκότας οἱ Ἀθηναῖοι ἐπὶ τὴν ἀκρόπολιν, οἱ μὲν ἐρρίπτεον
10 ἑωυτοὺς κατὰ τοῦ τείχεος κάτω καὶ διεφθείροντο, οἱ δὲ ἐς τὸ
μέγαρον κατέφευγον. τῶν δὲ Περσέων οἱ ἀναβεβηκότες πρῶτον
μὲν ἐτράποντο πρὸς τὰς πύλας, ταύτας δὲ ἀνοίξαντες τοὺς

---

4 πρὸ om. ß, Holder, van H.   6 ταῦτα : τοῦτο ! Stein², approb.
van H. (' sed κατὰ ταῦτα, quod post τῇ abundat, glossema videtur' van H.)
7 καίπερ ß, Holder, van H.   8 δ' ß   9 ἐπὶ : ἐς ß ‖ ἐπὶ τὴν
ἀκρόπολιν del. Cobet, Holder, (van H.)

---

6. 139.   Perhaps Ἀττική = Ἀθῆναι =
Ἀθηναῖοι.

γενέσθαι ὑπὸ Π. : cp. 7. 11.

4. ἔμπροσθε . . πρὸ τῆς ἀκροπόλιος,
ὄπισθε δὲ τῶν πυλέων καὶ τῆς ἀνόδου:
the position is further defined just below
by the grotto of Aglauros. The place
described is no doubt the north side,
towards the west end. It is curious
that Hdt. does not specify the point of
the compass, or rather the quarter
of the heavens, but Leake asserts that the
north side is spoken of as 'the front'
—so it might appear to the modern
Athenian, the town lying mainly on
the north side; so also to a Greek,
perhaps, of Hdt.'s time, when the larger
quarter of the town was on that same
side; so to invaders, like the Persians,
who had approached, perhaps, from the
north side, or were laagering to a great
extent there. The gates of an ancient
citadel were seldom in 'the front,' but
rather to the side; the case of the
Athenian Akropolis, especially as we
know it, may be peculiar, if not unique;
and even at the time of the Persian
siege the πύλαι may have presented a
very different appearance, and one less
suggestive of a front, or frontage, than
the glorious building of Mnesikles. πρὸ
looks de trop, but is plainly local.

6. ἀνθρώπων : to ascend b that route
one had needs be ἢ θηρίον ἢ θεός !

7. τὸ ἱρὸν τῆς Κέκροπος θυγατρὸς
Ἀγλαύρου : for Kekrops cp. c. 44 supra,
7. 141. Aglauros was one of three
sisters (Herse, Pandrosos); Pausan. 1.
18. 2. Athena entrusted to their charge

an ark, containing Erichthonios, with
strict orders not to look therein ;
Pandrosos obeyed, the other two opened
the ark, went mad, and cast themselves
headlong down from the Akropolis, ἔνθα
ἦν μάλιστα ἀπότομον. There, or there-
under, was no doubt the sanctuary :
ὑπὲρ δὲ τῶν Διοσκούρων τὸ ἱερὸν Ἀγλαύρου
τέμενός ἐστιν, Pausan. l.c. It probably
communicated with the Akropolis by a
flight of steps; Wachsmuth ap. Pauly-
Wissowa i. 1829. Cp. E. A. Gardner,
Anc. Ath. 526. Hdt. seems to think
that the Persians clambered up the
inaccessible cliff ; possibly they ascended
the steps. There were Athenians with
them who might show the way—the
suspicion of a betrayal is hard to resist.

καίτοι περ is a strong expression ;
καίπερ or καίπερ τοι would be less surprising. Hdt. evidently supposes this
party of Persians to have scaled the rock.
Curiously enough the garrison attempts,
according to Hdt., no resistance, some
leaping down from the wall to certain
destruction, others taking refuge in the
Megaron, where they were presently
butchered.

11. τῶν δὲ Περσέων κτλ.: there is some
obscurity or confusion in this passage.
What 'gates' did these Persians open ?
If the gates of the Akropolis, we should
expect them to admit the main force
before slaughtering the suppliants. Did
the suppliants too forgo all resistance ?
A good deal seems left here to the
imagination. Who was there to tell
the story if none of the Athenians
escaped ? Is this story from Athenian
sources ?

ἰκέτας ἐφόνευον· ἐπεὶ δέ σφι πάντες κατέστρωντο, τὸ ἱρὸν
συλήσαντες ἐνέπρησαν πᾶσαν τὴν ἀκρόπολιν.

Σχὼν δὲ παντελέως τὰς Ἀθήνας Ξέρξης ἀπέπεμψε ἐς 54
Σοῦσα ἄγγελον ἱππέα Ἀρταβάνῳ ἀγγελέοντα τὴν παρεοῦσάν
σφι εὐπρηξίην. ἀπὸ δὲ τῆς πέμψιος τοῦ κήρυκος δευτέρῃ
ἡμέρῃ συγκαλέσας Ἀθηναίων τοὺς φυγάδας, ἑωυτῷ δὲ ἑπομένους, ἐκέλευε τρόπῳ τῷ σφετέρῳ θῦσαι τὰ ἱρὰ ἀναβάντας 5
ἐς τὴν ἀκρόπολιν, εἴτε δὴ ὦν ὄψιν τινὰ ἰδὼν ἐνυπνίου
ἐνετέλλετο ταῦτα, εἴτε καὶ ἐνθύμιόν οἱ ἐγένετο ἐμπρήσαντι τὸ
ἱρόν. οἱ δὲ φυγάδες τῶν Ἀθηναίων ἐποίησαν τὰ ἐντεταλμένα.
τοῦ δὲ εἵνεκεν τούτων ἐπεμνήσθην, φράσω. ἔστι ἐν τῇ 55
ἀκροπόλι ταύτῃ Ἐρεχθέος τοῦ γηγενέος λεγομένου εἶναι νηός,

13 οἰκέτας Bz ‖ ἐπείτε δέ van H.   14 πᾶσαν om. B   54. 1
ἔχων δὲ παντελῶς B   3 εὐπραξίην a : εὐταξίην C   7 ἐνετέλλετο
ταῦτα del. Krueger, van H. ‖ ἐμπρήσαντα A¹ C : ἐμπρήσοντα B   55. 2
ἀκροπόλει B

13. κατέστρωντο: 9. 76 infra.

τὸ ἱρόν: there is nothing to distinguish this from τὸ μέγαρον just above,
or to show that Hdt. would have recognized the existence of more than one
temple of Athene ; cp. cc. 41, 51 supra.

54. 1. σχὼν δὲ παντελέως τὰς Ἀθήνας,
'having gained complete possession of
Athens' (but not of the Athenians)—
ταττ., cp. 7. 37 supra, 4. 95 (τ. εἶχε in a
different sense and construction) ; with
σχ. cp. ἔσχε 5. 46, etc. The despatch
to Artabanos is for a dramatic purpose,
perhaps from a dramatic hint, cp. c. 99
infra. Artabanos has been left as major-
domo 7. 52 supra. It is not to be
supposed, in the light of c. 98 infra,
that the one courier rode all the way
from Athens to Susa. ἄγγελον ἱππέα
. . ἀγγελέοντα is a little redundant ;
which noun is adj. may be doubted.
Just below the man is a κῆρυξ.

3. ἀπό: temporal. The audience with
the 'Peisistratidai,' Dikaios, and so
forth, 'the Athenian exiles, those to wit
(δέ) in his suite,' takes place on the next
(δευτέρῃ) day. The behest to offer
sacrifice according to Hellenic ritual on
the Akropolis appears to be entirely in
accordance with Achaimenid policy and
practice, though Hdt. seems to think it
demands special explanation. The wonder
rather was that Xerxes deputed the
duty : probably he 'assisted' at it,
and the sacrifice is made on the king's

behalf. The alternatives εἴτε δὴ ὦν—εἴτε
καί . . are not mutually exclusive.

7. ἐνθύμιον, 'matter of conscience,'
scruple, misgiving ; cp. 2. 175 ; Thuc.
7. 50. 4 (of the lunar eclipse, Aug. 27,
413 B.C.).

τὸ ἱρόν, of Athene ; cp. cc. 51, 53.

55. 1. ἔστι: presumably at the time
of writing ; the νηός referred to is apparently an Erechtheion, or contains the
sacred memorials afterwards associated
with the Erechtheion, Pausan. 1. 26. 5 ff.
That temple was only built or restored,
completely, long after the death of Hdt.
This chapter is not free from ambiguity.
Hdt. does not distinguish between the
temple of Athene and 'the House of
Erechtheus' ; he speaks of the temple
in a way as both existing and not existing—for it had just been burnt down—
even on the day after the burning. It
is quite possible that not merely the
portent of the olive-shoot, but the whole
circumstances of this story as first composed by Hdt., rested upon the authority
of the Athenian Emigrés, at least ultimately, and that this passage may
belong to the draft of these Books
written before Hdt. himself had visited
Athens. Cp. Introduction, § 9.

2. Ἐρεχθέος τοῦ γηγενέος λεγομένου
εἶναι. The Erechtheus, who is the child
of Earth, the nursling of Athene, taken
into her own shrine (ἑῷ ἐν πίονι νηῷ) and
therein worshipped by his people (δῆμος),

ἐν τῷ ἐλαίη τε καὶ θάλασσα ἔνι, τὰ λόγος παρὰ Ἀθηναίων
Ποσειδέωνά τε καὶ Ἀθηναίην ἐρίσαντας περὶ τῆς χώρης
5 μαρτύρια θέσθαι. ταύτην ὦν τὴν ἐλαίην ἅμα τῷ ἄλλῳ ἱρῷ
κατέλαβε ἐμπρησθῆναι ὑπὸ τῶν βαρβάρων· δευτέρῃ δὲ ἡμέρῃ
ἀπὸ τῆς ἐμπρήσιος Ἀθηναίων οἱ θύειν ὑπὸ βασιλέος κελευό-

3 παρὰ : παρ' z : ὑπὸ Β   7 Ἀθηναῖοι οἱ z, vulg. ‖ βασιλέως C :
βασιλῆος z

Iliad 2. 546 ff., is no doubt one and the
same ultimately with Poseidon Erechtheus (op. c. 41 *supra*), as his μαρτύρια,
the θάλασσα, and the σχῆμα τριαίνης
(Pausan. 1. 26. 6) of themselves would
show. A (possibly late) ἱερὸς λόγος
made him son of Athene and Hephaistos,
Apollod. 3. 14. 6. In *Od*. 7. 81 Athene
goes in under the roof of Erechtheus
(perhaps the older view !). Anyway,
the reference in Homer as in Hdt. here
is *prima facie* to an Erechtheion, but
whether the House of Erechtheus had
been absorbed in the Old Temple of
Athene, which was destroyed by the
Persians and never rebuilt, or whether
there was an Erechtheion north of that
temple, and more or less on the site of
the existing building, is a moot point.
Cp. c. 51 *supra*.

3. ἐλαίη τε καὶ θάλασσα : the existing temple comprised three *cellae*, of
which the eastern one, or Erechtheion
proper, contained θαλάσσιον ἐν φρέατι
and also a σχῆμα τριαίνης ἐν τῇ πέτρᾳ . .
ταῦτα δὲ λέγεται Ποσειδῶνι μαρτύρια ἐς
τὴν ἀμφισβήτησιν τῆς χώρας φανῆναι,
Pausan. 1. 26. 5. Hdt. would probably
have mentioned the σχῆμα τριαίνης had
he seen it. In the Erechtheion also
were three altars, one to Poseidon—ἐφ'
οὗ καὶ Ἐρεχθεῖ θύουσιν—one to the hero
Boutes, and one to Hephaistos. The
central shrine was dedicate to the
Polias, and contained, among many
interesting objects, the olive (Pausan. 1.
27. 2, but cp. *l.c.* Apollod. *infra*),
apparently a growing tree. The third,
or western shrine, was dedicate to
Pandrosos (cp. c. 53 *supra*).

λόγος παρὰ Ἀθηναίων : the phrase
suggests that the passage is written for
other than an Athenian audience ; nor
does it involve the inference that Hdt.
had visited Athens before making this
report. Cp. Introduction, § 10.

4. Ποσειδέωνά τε καὶ Ἀθηναίην : the
myth of the ἔρις περὶ τῆς χώρης is given
by Apollodoros 3. 14. 1, the event being
dated to the days of Kekrops : ἐπὶ τούτου,

φασίν, ἔδοξε τοῖς θεοῖς πόλεις καταλαβέσθαι,
ἐν αἷς ἔμελλον ἔχειν τιμὰς ἰδίας ἕκαστος.
ἧκεν οὖν πρῶτος Ποσειδῶν ἐπὶ τὴν Ἀττικὴν
καὶ πλήξας τῇ τριαίνῃ κατὰ μέσην τὴν
ἀκρόπολιν ἀνέφηνε θάλασσαν, ἣν νῦν
Ἐρεχθηίδα καλοῦσι. μετὰ δὲ τοῦτον ἧκεν
Ἀθηνᾶ καὶ ποιησαμένη τῆς καταλήψεως
Κέκροπα μάρτυρα ἐφύτευσεν ἐλαίαν, ἣ νῦν
ἐν τῷ Πανδροσίῳ (*sic*) δείκνυται. γενομένης
δὲ ἔριδος ἀμφοῖν περὶ τῆς χώρας Ἀθηνᾶν
καὶ Ποσειδῶνα διαλύσας Ζεὺς κριτὰς ἔδωκεν,
οὐχ ὡς εἶπόν τινες Κέκροπα καὶ Κραναόν,
οὐδὲ Ἐρυσιχθόνα, θεοὺς δὲ τοὺς δώδεκα,
καὶ τούτων δικαζόντων ἡ χώρα τῆς Ἀθηνᾶς
ἐκρίθη, Κέκροπος μαρτυρήσαντος ὅτι πρῶτον
τὴν ἐλαίαν ἐφύτευσεν. The evidence of
Kekrops was on the showing of this
myth untrue ; the jury of the Twelve
Gods was deceived. The most reasonable interpretation of the myth is the
historical, which sees in it a transfigured
reminiscence of a struggle between two
cults, and the different worshippers
of two deities, Athene - worshippers,
Poseidon - worshippers, in Attica, in
which case, further, the Poseidonians
can be no other than Ionians, and the
Ἀθηναῖοι may well be the natives. Cp.
c. 44 *supra* ; Roscher's *Lexikon* (1884),
688 ; Pauly - Wissowa ii. (1896) 1951 ;
and especially L. R. Farnell, *Cults of the
Greek States*, i. (1896) 270. The association of the olive with Athene marks her
at least in this connexion as an agri-
cultural deity (Roscher *l.c.*) ; the significance of the connexion of Poseidon with
the θάλασσα is self-evident.

5. μαρτύρια θέσθαι : the substantive
is appositive, or predicative.

ἅμα τῷ ἄλλῳ ἱρῷ, as well as the
temple, or 'together with the temple as
well.' The force of ἄλλος in such a
construction is noticeable ; cp. 7. 206. 2,
and c. 65 *infra*, ad *f*. (also 4. 191, 5.
82, 6. 129, etc.).

6. δευτέρῃ δὲ ἡμ. ἀπὸ τῆς ἐμπρήσιος :
cp. c. 54 *supra*, from whence it follows
that the ἔμπρησις τῆς πόλεως and the
πέμψις τοῦ κήρυκος took place on the
same day.

μένοι ὡς ἀνέβησαν ἐς τὸ ἱρόν, ὥρων βλαστὸν ἐκ τοῦ στελέχεος
ὅσον τε πηχυαῖον ἀναδεδραμηκότα. οὗτοι μέν νυν ταῦτα
ἔφρασαν <τῷ βασιλέι>.   10

  Οἱ δὲ ἐν Σαλαμῖνι Ἕλληνες, ὡς σφι ἐξηγγέλθη ὡς ἔσχε 56
περὶ τὴν Ἀθηναίων ἀκρόπολιν, ἐς τοσοῦτον θόρυβον ἀπίκοντο
ὡς ἔνιοι τῶν στρατηγῶν οὐδὲ κυρωθῆναι ἔμενον τὸ προκείμενον
πρῆγμα, ἀλλ' ἔς τε τὰς νέας ἐσέπιπτον καὶ ἱστία ἀείροντο

---

8 ἱρόν : ἱ//ρὸν Α ('Herodotum ubique scripsisse ἱερός et ἱερόν probabile
est propter vetustiores titulos Ionicos' van H.)   9 μὲν ὦν B   10
<τῷ βασιλέι> Stein³   56. 1 ἐξαγγέλθη B, vulg.   2 τὰ περὶ B,
Stein¹², Holder, van H. ‖ Ἀθηνέων Bekker, Holder, alii   3 ὡς : ὥστε
B, Holder, van H.   4 νῆας Βz ‖ <τὰ> ἱστία Jacobitz

---

8. τὸ ἱρόν, as above, cc. 41, 51, 54.

βλαστόν . . ἀναδεδραμηκότα :
obviously a portent, a miracle, under
the circumstances (ὅσον τε does not so
much qualify as emphasize the cubit's
length), explained by Dionys. Halic. 14.
4 as signifying ὅτι ταχέως ἑαυτὴν ἡ πόλις
ἀναλαβοῦσα βλαστοὺς ἀντὶ τῶν παλαιῶν
ἐξοίσει νέους. Pausanias 1. 27. 2 makes
the shoot two cubits length, on the same
day as the burning. Blakesley sees
references to the story in Soph. O.K.
698 ff. ; Eurip. Ion 1433.

56. 1. οἱ δὲ ἐν Σαλαμῖνι Ἕλληνες
shifts the scene back to Salamis, as in
c. 50 supra ; but what of the time ? The
message there is not prima facie identical
with the message here ; and an appreci-
able interval of time might be held to
occur between the news of the Persians'
arrival in Athens and the news of the
destruction of the Akropolis (op. cc. 52,
53). But was it the news of the destruction of the Akropolis, or only the news
of the blockade of the Akropolis, which
reached the Greek camp ? Hdt. does
not here say clearly which. Would the
destruction of the Akropolis have required to be reported ? The conflagration
would have been fully visible from
Salamis. Whether reported or witnessed,
the capture of the Akropolis might form
a ground for reopening the question
whether the Greek fleet should remain
at Salamis or not. Perhaps the error in
Hdt. lies in his having recorded a debate
above, before the news of the Persian
arrival, or the evidence of the Persian
capture of the Akropolis, was conveyed
to Salamis. As long as the Akropolis
stood siege, there might be a hope that
the Peloponnesian army would advance

to its relief ; and so long at least the
Greek fleet would of course remain at
Salamis. Once the Akropolis had been
captured, or surrendered, a new situation
did arise. The anecdote of Mnesiphilos
is transparently apocryphal ; but the
notion that a debate on the next move
arose after the capture of the Akropolis
is not in itself so improbable.

ὡς : the word occurs four times in
as many lines, but may be rendered
differently : 'when—how—that—as.'
But cp. App. Crit.

3. ἔνιοι τῶν στρατηγῶν : these members
of the council of war (c. 49 supra) are to
be supposed to have treated the news
about the Athenian Akropolis as leaving
only one alternative, or at least as
rendering the retreat from Salamis
inevitable. But it had not yet been
decided, when 'they tumbled into their
ships' (ἐσέπιπτον imp.), what the scene
of the naumachy was to be. They may
have intended to wait to hear this. The
θόρυβος was not exactly a panic, it was
a hubbub (they would be all speaking
at the same time now) ; but no one as
yet actually takes to flight, though
ἀποθευσόμανοι seems to expect it (cp.
App. Crit.). It is not very probable that
any actual members of the Synedrion
conducted themselves in this fashion :
subordinate officers and crews may have
made preparations on the safe side.

τὸ προκείμενον πρῆγμα seems to
refer back to the subject of discussion in
c. 49, ὅκου δοκέοι ἐπιτηδεότατον εἶναι κτλ.

4. ἱστία ἀείροντο : the voice is middle
and the tense imperfect : even so, if
they were in such a desperate hurry
to be off, they would surely first get
the oars out.

5 ὡς ἀποθευσόμενοι· τοῖσί τε ὑπολειπομένοισι αὐτῶν ἐκυρώθη
πρὸ τοῦ Ἰσθμοῦ ναυμαχέειν. νύξ τε ἐγίνετο καὶ οἱ διαλυθέντες
57 ἐκ τοῦ συνεδρίου ἐσέβαινον ἐς τὰς νέας. ἐνθαῦτα δὴ Θεμιστοκλέα ἀπικόμενον ἐπὶ τὴν νέα εἴρετο Μνησίφιλος ἀνὴρ
Ἀθηναῖος ὅ τι σφι εἴη βεβουλευμένον. πυθόμενος δὲ πρὸς
αὐτοῦ ὡς εἴη δεδογμένον ἀνάγειν τὰς νέας πρὸς τὸν Ἰσθμὸν
5 καὶ πρὸ τῆς Πελοποννήσου ναυμαχέειν, εἶπε "οὔτ' ἄρα, ἢν
ἀπαείρωσι [τὰς νέας] ἀπὸ Σαλαμῖνος, περὶ οὐδεμιῆς ἔτι πατρίδος

---

5 ἀποπλευσόμενοι Naber || αὐτέων Βz   6 ἐγένετο Β   7 νῆας Βz
57. 1 Θεμιστοκλῆα z   2 νῆα Βz   4 νῆας Βz   5 οὔτ' α:
οὗτοι Β: οὔ τοι Bekker, Holder, van H.: οὐκ Plutarch. Mor. 869   6
ἀπαίρωσι codd. z || τὰς νέας del. Stein²: τὰς νῆας Βz || περὶ οὐδὲ μιῆς AB:
οὐδὲ περὶ μιῆς Plutarch. l.c.

---

5. τοῖσί τε ὑπολειπομένοισι αὐτῶν
ἐκυρώθη: how this decision was arrived
at Hdt. does not clearly indicate; it
might seem by a sheer majority of votes,
but below Eurybiades is treated as
really supreme in the matter. When
the others left the council (was it held
in a building or *sub Iove*?) the Isthmos
was still *ex hypothesi* only one of several
potential stations, cp. c. 49 *supra*. The
decision is still to fight a battle: only
the venue is shifted. This more dignified
section did not 'tumble into their ships,'
but ἐσέβαινον. On πρό cp. c. 49.
The *parataxis* νύξ τε ἐγ. καί is observable: οἱ is doubtless demonstrative.
τὸ συνέδριον marks the meeting decidedly as a regular and formal one; cp.
7. 145 *supra*, cc. 75, 79 *infra*; it was
probably held under cover, in a house on
shore, perhaps occupied by Eurybiades.

57. 1. Θεμιστοκλῆα: not mentioned in
the account of the first council (συνέδριον)
on shore, *chez* Eurybiades; cc. 49 ff.
But, of course, if any such decision arrived
at, Themistokles had been there and
against the making of it.

2. Μνησίφιλος ἀνὴρ Ἀθηναῖος: a
shrewder man than Themistokles, and
one well and significantly named!
Plutarch, *Them.* 2, makes him a demote
of Themistokles, and in *Mor.* 795 an
older man, quite naturally! But more
critically in the *de Hdti. malig.* 37 f.,
Mor. 869, he points out the improbability
of this tale, according to which Themistokles was dishonestly indebted to
Mnesiphilos for the arguments in favour
of giving battle at Salamis. Going
beyond Plutarch, one might suspect

that Mnesiphilos was a pure fiction, the
only evidence of his existence being
this apocryphal anecdote. Of course
Hdt. did not invent him: the story is
part of the Themistoklean legend, and
perhaps among the older elements therein, forming perhaps the reply by some
detractor to the foundation by Themistokles of the ναὸν Ἀριστοβούλης Ἀρτεμίδος
ἐν Μελίτῃ.

3. βεβουλευμένον . . δεδογμένον, 'the
matter of their deliberations,' ' the thing
decided on': both words might seem to
imply a joint decision; yet cp. 7. 12
supra δεδογμένων οἱ.

5. εἶπε: Hdt. and his sources do not
hesitate to reproduce in *oratio recta* the
ipsissima verba of Mnesiphilos to Themistokles: a device which adds nothing to
the probability of the story in the eyes
of a critical reader. Who else was
present at the interview? Did Themistokles report it? Or Mnesiphilos?
οὔτ' ἄρα is answered by ἀπολέεται
τε *infra*. For ἄρα cp. Index.

6. ἀπαείρωσι: cp. c. 60 *infra*.
περὶ οὐδεμιῆς ἔτι πατρίδος ναυμαχήσεις: 'thou wilt no longer have a country
to fight for at sea' might mean one of three
things: (a) that Attica will be lost for
ever—the context and explanation seem
to rule this out as inadequate; (b) that
there will no longer be any country
belonging to any of the Greek peoples
taken severally, to fight for—this would
be far-fetched; (c) that Hellas will no
longer exist to fight for. On the whole
this appears to be the meaning—albeit it
anticipates the second clause, and the
use of πατρίς for the whole of Hellas is
remarkable. The double negative οὔτε

ναυμαχήσεις· κατὰ γὰρ πόλις ἔκαστοι τρέψονται, καὶ οὔτε
σφέας Εὐρυβιάδης κατέχειν δυνήσεται οὔτε τις ἀνθρώπων
ἄλλος ὥστε μὴ οὐ διασκεδασθῆναι τὴν στρατιήν· ἀπολέεταί
τε ἡ Ἑλλὰς ἀβουλίῃσι. ἀλλ᾽ εἴ τις ἐστὶ μηχανή, ἴθι καὶ 10
πειρῶ διαχέαι τὰ βεβουλευμένα, ἤν κως δύνῃ ἀναγνῶσαι
Εὐρυβιάδην μεταβουλεύσασθαι ὥστε αὐτοῦ μένειν." κάρτα 58
τε τῷ Θεμιστοκλέι ἤρεσε ἡ ὑποθήκη, καὶ οὐδὲν πρὸς ταῦτα
ἀμειψάμενος ἤιε ἐπὶ τὴν νέα τὴν Εὐρυβιάδεω. ἀπικόμενος δὲ
ἔφη θέλειν οἱ κοινόν τι πρῆγμα συμμεῖξαι· ὁ δ᾽ αὐτὸν ἐς
τὴν νέα ἐκέλευε ἐσβάντα λέγειν, εἴ τι θέλει. ἐνθαῦτα ὁ 5
Θεμιστοκλέης παριζόμενός οἱ καταλέγει ἐκεῖνά τε πάντα τὰ
ἤκουσε Μνησιφίλου, ἑωυτοῦ ποιεύμενος, καὶ ἄλλα πολλὰ

7 πόλιας ΒΡz   9 οὐ μὴ α   10 καὶ del. van H.   12
εὐρυβιάδεα Β ‖ μεταβαλέσθαι, ὥστ᾽ Β ‖ μενέειν Β, Stein¹   58. 2 τε Β :
δὲ α : δὴ z : 'fortasse τε δὴ' Kallenberg ‖ τῷ om. Β   3 νῆα Βz   4
ἐθέλειν α, Holder, van H. ‖ συμμῖξαι Stein¹² ‖ δὲ Β   5 νῆα Βz ‖
ἐμβάντα ἐκέλευε Β ‖ ἐσβάλοντα Β ‖ θέλοι Β ‖ ὁ om. Β   6 παρεζό-
μενός α ‖ γέ οἱ Β ‖ κεῖνά Βz

. . οὐδεμῆς is purely intensive. The
reading in Plutarch, Mor. 869, οὐκ ἄρα
. . οὐδὲ περὶ μῆς ἔτι πατρίδος ναυμαχήσεις·
κατὰ γὰρ πόλεις ἔκαστοι τρέψονται appears
to mean, the country for which you are
going to fight will no longer be one and
united ; or, you will be fighting for a
country divided into as many sections as
states. The expression is not Herodotean
(Krueger).

9. ὥστε μὴ οὐ διασκεδασθῆναι τὴν
στρατιήν : an instance of a genuinely
idiomatic μὴ οὐ, which follows not merely
the alternative negatives οὔτε . . οὔτε .
but also perhaps the subordinate negation
contained in the word κατέχειν, to re-
strain, prevent, prohibit. Cp. c. 100
infra οὐ γάρ ἐστι Ἕλλησι οὐδεμία ἔκδυσις,
μὴ οὐ δόντας λόγον κτλ., c. 119 ἐν μυρίῃσι
γνώμῃσι μίαν οὐκ ἔχω ἀντίξοον, μὴ οὐκ ἂν
ποιῆσαι βασιλέα τοιόνδε.

11. διαχέαι, to upset, confound, undo.
The verb is used in the literal sense
6. 119.

τὰ βεβουλευμένα=τὰ δεδογμένα.

12. μεταβουλεύσασθαι : cp. 7. 12 supra
μετὰ δὴ βουλεύεαι—there too of a change
of decision, resolve, counsel, by a single
individual ; cp. l. 3 supra.

58. 2. ὑποθήκη : the suggestion ; 6.
52, 1. 156, 211.

οὐδὲν πρὸς ταῦτα ἀμειψάμενος : not
even, for example, that he had pointed
all that out already. The arguments

were irrefutable, and obvious. The
remark has a somewhat unfavourable
suggestion about it, as of an incriminat-
ing silence ! See below.

3. ἤιε : afoot, or in a boat ! It is not
quite clear. As just below he asks
Eurybiades ἐκ τῆς νεὸς ἐκβῆναι, Eurybiades was on board, and his ship
presumably in the water. Moreover, the
strategoi in c. 56 supra have not to
launch their galleys. It seems more
probable that the ships were all afloat.
In c. 83 infra Themistokles addresses a
σύλλογον τῶν ἐπιβατέων on land ; but
that would not show that the ships were
not in the water.

4. κοινόν : of public concern ; e re
publica. συμμεῖξαι, in the sense 'to communicate,' is observable.

6. παριζόμενος : was Eurybiades abed !
καταλέγει ἐκεῖνά τε . . καὶ προστιθείς looks a little irregular. But
the sentence here is complete without
προστιθείς, which is 'epexegetical.' So
too τάξαντες in 9. 10 infra. l. 8 is more
remarkable.

ἐκεῖνά τε πάντα : there had not
been so many points ; practically but one.

7. ἑωυτοῦ ποιεύμενος enforces the unfavourable insinuation above conveyed
in οὐδὲν ἀμειψάμενος, more explicitly.

ἄλλα πολλά : perhaps arguments
—if so, what ! Perhaps only entreaties,
prayers, etc. (χρηζων). In either case

προστιθείς, ἐς ὃ ἀνέγνωσέ <μιν> χρηίζων ἔκ τε τῆς νεὸς
59 ἐκβῆναι συλλέξαι τε τοὺς στρατηγοὺς ἐς τὸ συνέδριον. ὡς
δὲ ἄρα συνελέχθησαν, πρὶν ἢ τὸν Εὐρυβιάδην προθεῖναι τὸν
λόγον τῶν εἵνεκα συνήγαγε τοὺς στρατηγούς, πολλὸς ἦν ὁ
Θεμιστοκλέης ἐν τοῖσι λόγοισι οἷα κάρτα δεόμενος· λέγοντος
5 δὲ αὐτοῦ, ὁ Κορίνθιος στρατηγὸς [Ἀδείμαντος ὁ Ὠκύτου]
εἶπε "ὦ Θεμιστόκλεες, ἐν τοῖσι ἀγῶσι οἱ προεξανιστάμενοι
ῥαπίζονται." ὃ δὲ ἀπολυόμενος ἔφη "οἱ δέ γε ἐγκαταλει-
60 πόμενοι οὐ στεφανοῦνται." τότε μὲν ἠπίως [πρὸς] τὸν
Κορίνθιον ἀμείψατο, πρὸς δὲ τὸν Εὐρυβιάδην ἔλεγε ἐκείνων

---

8 μιν Stein(2)8 || νῆος Βz   9 ἐκβῆναι τὸν εὐρυβιάδεα Βz   59. 2
ἄρα om. Β || εὐρυβιάδεα Βz || προσθεῖναι a || τὸν del. Cobet, van H.
3 πολὺς codd., z   5 Κορινθίων Kallenberg: 'si στρατηγὸς genuinum,
requiro Κορινθίων' van H. : emblema seclusi || ὁ om. Β   6 ὦ om. Β ||
θεμιστόκλεις Β   8 στεφανεῦνται Β   60. 1 τότε: τοῦτο Naber ||
πρὸς del. Krueger, Holder, van H., Stein8   2 ἠμείψατο Β: ἀμείβεται
Krueger : aut πρὸς aut hoc suspectum hab. Stein2 || εὐρυβιάδεα Rz

---

the phrase should not be held to cancel
the insinuations to Themistokles' discredit, albeit somewhat weakening them.
Once started on this line—by Mnesiphilos—he can find further pleas of himself, till finally, at the ensuing council,
he makes a really powerful speech!

9. τὸ συνέδριον : evidently held on
land, but not necessarily sub Iove frigido.

59. 2. συνελέχθησαν : this will be the
second or the third meeting, according
as cc. 49 and 56 are interpreted of one
and the same meeting, or of two different
meetings.

πρὶν ἢ . . τοὺς στρατηγούς : if προθεῖναι τὸν λόγον means 'to give account
of,' 'to explain,' the statement appears
again to be designed to discredit Themistokles ; in any case, the commander-
in-chief must surely have offered some
reason for the extraordinary summons of
this meeting, which is apparently to be
conceived as taking place at night.

3. πολλὸς ἦν . . ἐν τοῖσι λόγοισι : i.e.
π. ἦν λέγων, surely not simply 'made
a long speech,' or even 'said a great
many things,' but rather 'was vehement';
cp. 7. 158 supra, 9. 91 infra. But what,
by the way, could he have said, if Eurybiades had the subject of debate still
in petto?

4. οἷα κάρτα δεόμενος : cp. c. 3 supra.

6. προεξανιστάμενοι : so in the aorist,
9. 62 infra. προ- with the force of

'too soon,' 'prematurely,' 'before they
are bidden.' Competitors are referred to,
not merely spectators, as, indeed, the
answer of Themistokles implies.

7. ῥαπίζονται : by the ῥαβδοῦχοι, who
kept order in the ring. Our athletes
would hardly appreciate this severity.
For the word cp. 7. 35.

ἀπολυόμενος, 'trying to excuse himself,' sc. τὴν αἰτίην, τὴν διαβολήν. He
understood the value of the soft answer,
which, however, failed on this occasion.
Plutarch, Them. 11, substitutes Eurybiades for Adeimantos in this duel of
wit, and adds a second mot by Themistokles to Eurybiades, who raises his
baton to strike : πάταξον μὲν ἄκουσον δέ.
In the Mor. 185 he restores the remark
to the Korinthian.

δέ γε, 'yes, but . .'

ἐγκαταλειπόμενοι, i.e. who get a
bad start, not "longe in cursu post
tergum relicti victique," Wesseling, nor
"qui cunctanter ad certamen prodeunt,"
Sintenis. 2 Cor. 4. 9 διωκόμενοι ἀλλ' οὐκ
ἐγκαταλειπόμενοι does not help us.

60. 1. [πρὸς] τὸν Κορίνθιον ἀμείψατο :
a doubtful construction, not justified by
πρὸς ταῦτα ἀμειψάμενος, c. 58 supra ; cp.
App. Crit.

2. ἐκείνων μὲν . . δ δέ : the subject
expressed and resumed with δέ, cp. 7.
50, etc. ἐκείνων is of course neuter.

μὲν ἔτι οὐδὲν τῶν πρότερον λεχθέντων, ὡς ἐπεὰν ἀπαείρωσι
ἀπὸ Σαλαμῖνος διαδρήσονται· παρεόντων γὰρ τῶν συμμάχων
οὐκ ἔφερέ οἱ κόσμον οὐδένα κατηγορέειν· ὁ δὲ ἄλλου λόγου 5
εἴχετο, λέγων τάδε. " ἐν σοὶ νῦν ἐστὶ σῶσαι τὴν Ἑλλάδα,
ἢν ἐμοὶ πείθῃ ναυμαχίην αὐτοῦ μένων ποιέεσθαι, μηδὲ πειθόμενος τούτων τοῖσι λόγοισι ἀναζεύξῃς πρὸς τὸν Ἰσθμὸν τὰς
νέας. ἀντίθες γὰρ ἑκάτερον ἀκούσας. πρὸς μὲν τῷ Ἰσθμῷ
συμβάλλων ἐν πελάγεϊ ἀναπεπταμένῳ ναυμαχήσεις, [ἐς] τὸ 10
ἥκιστα ἡμῖν σύμφορόν ἐστι νέας ἔχουσι βαρυτέρας καὶ ἀριθμὸν
ἐλάσσονας· τοῦτο δὲ ἀπολέεις Σαλαμῖνά τε καὶ Μέγαρα καὶ
Αἴγιναν, ἤν περ καὶ τὰ ἄλλα εὐτυχήσωμεν. ἅμα δὲ τῷ
ναυτικῷ αὐτῶν ἕψεται καὶ ὁ πεζὸς στρατός, καὶ οὕτω σφέας
αὐτὸς ἄξεις ἐπὶ τὴν Πελοπόννησον, κινδυνεύσεις τε ἀπάσῃ τῇ 15
Ἑλλάδι. ἢν δὲ τὰ ἐγὼ λέγω ποιήσῃς, τοσάδε ἐν αὐτοῖσι
χρηστὰ εὑρήσεις· πρῶτα μὲν ἐν στεινῷ συμβάλλοντες νηυσὶ
ὀλίγῃσι πρὸς πολλάς, ἢν τὰ οἰκότα [ἐκ τοῦ πολέμου] ἐκβαίνῃ,

---

3 ἔτι: οὐκέτι β, Holder, van H. || ἀπαίρωσι codd., z   5 κακηγορέειν
Valckenaer: κακηγορεῖν van H.   7 μένων om. β   8 λόγοισι
Krueger, Stein²: λέγουσι   9 νῆας βz   10 συμβαλὼν RS || ἐς del.
Krueger, Holder, van H., Stein³ || τὸ Struve: ὁ   11 νῆας βz: 'an
ἀνάγειν νέας? Stein¹ ² || βραδυτέρας coni. Stein, recep. van H.: βραχυτέρας
Matthiae   12 ἐλάσσονα α   13 ἤν περ τἄλλα β || δὲ Stein²: γὰρ
14 στρατός om. z   15 αὐτοὺς β   16 ποιῇς α   17 συμ-
βαλόντες β   18 ἐοικότα α || ἐκ τοῦ πολέμου secl. Stein²

---

3. ἀπαείρωσι, as in c. 57 supra.
διαδρήσονται is emphatic, and the δια-
signifies 'in various directions'; the
word is perhaps more contemptuous
than διασκεδασθῆναι, c. 57.

5. οὐκ ἔφερέ οἱ κόσμον οὐδένα, 'it by
no means beseemed him'; cp. κόσμον
φέρον, c. 142 infra.
κατηγορέειν: sc. τί τινος: cp. 7.
205 supra, 2. 113 ; cp. App. Crit.
ἄλλου λόγου εἴχετο: cp. 7. 5
τοιούτου λόγου εἴχετο, λέγων κτλ.

6. λέγων τάδε. The ipsissima verba
of Themistokles in 480 B.C. as of
Miltiades in 490 B.C., 6. 109. The one
speech is modelled on the other as far
as the circumstances admit, but this may
be the prior one in Hdt.'s composition.

7. αὐτοῦ, 'where you are . .'
8. ἀναζεύξῃς: with τὸν στρατὸν 9. 41,
58, 6. 12; but the word is frequently
intransitive, or elliptical, and generally
used of the movements of land-forces ;
cp. App. Crit. ; 'break up and move to
the Isthmos.'

9. ἀντίθες: Themistokles' oratory, in

Hdt.'s conception, runs to antitheses,
cp. c. 88 infra ; and to figures, cp. cc.
109, 111 infra.

πρὸς μέν: the correspondence or
antithesis comes with ἢν δὲ τὰ ἐγὼ λέγω
infra.

10. συμβάλλων: sc. τοῖς ἐναντίοις, or
τῷ βαρβάρῳ, or sim.
π. ἀναπεπταμένῳ: in patenti pelago
(Valla): ἀναπεπταμένους τόπους, Plato
Phaedr. 111 c.

11. βαρυτέρας: were the Greek ships
heavier than the Persian (Phoenician)?
Plutarch Them. 14 says just the opposite.
'Heavier' might be taken to mean 'less
easy to manage' (χεῖρον πλέουσας), and
be referred to the crews and seamanship
rather than to the actual material of the
fleet. But cp. App. Crit.

12. τοῦτο δέ: the τοῦτο μέν has not
preceded. It may be ideally supplied
before ἐν πελάγει ἀναπ. ναυμαχήσεις—
where the proximity of πρὸς μέν might
account for its omission.

18. ἢν τὰ οἰκότα . . ἐκβαίνῃ, πολλὸν
κρατήσομεν. Themistokles, according

πολλὸν κρατήσομεν· τὸ γὰρ ἐν στεινῷ ναυμαχέειν πρὸς
20 ἡμέων ἐστί, ἐν εὐρυχωρίῃ δὲ πρὸς ἐκείνων. αὖτις δὲ Σαλαμὶς
περιγίνεται, ἐς τὴν ἡμῖν ὑπεκκέεται τέκνα τε καὶ γυναῖκες.
καὶ μὴν καὶ τόδε ἐν αὐτοῖσι ἔνεστι, τοῦ καὶ περιέχεσθε μάλιστα·
ὁμοίως αὐτοῦ τε μένων προναυμαχέεις Πελοποννήσου καὶ πρὸς
τῷ Ἰσθμῷ, οὐδὲ σφέας, εἴ περ εὖ φρονέεις, ἄξεις ἐπὶ τὴν
25 Πελοπόννησον. ἢν δέ γε καὶ τὰ ἐγὼ ἐλπίζω γένηται καὶ
νικήσωμεν · τῇσι νηυσί, οὔτε ὑμῖν ἐς τὸν Ἰσθμὸν παρέσονται
οἱ βάρβαροι οὔτε προβήσονται ἑκαστέρω τῆς Ἀττικῆς, ἀπίασί
τε οὐδενὶ κόσμῳ, Μεγάροισί τε κερδανέομεν περιεοῦσι καὶ Αἰγίνῃ
καὶ Σαλαμῖνι, ἐν τῇ ἡμῖν καὶ λόγιον ἐστὶ τῶν ἐχθρῶν κατ-
30 ύπερθε γενέσθαι. οἰκότα μέν νυν βουλευομένοισι ἀνθρώποισι
ὡς τὸ ἐπίπαν ἐθέλει <κατὰ νόον> γίνεσθαι· μὴ δὲ οἰκότα
βουλευομένων οὐκ ἐθέλει οὐδὲ ὁ θεὸς προσχωρέειν πρὸς τὰς
ἀνθρωπηίας γνώμας."

20 αὖθις ϛαλαμὶς Β　　　21 ὑπέκκειται αz, van H. : νῦν ἐγκεῖται Β
22 μὴν : μὲν R, Stein² ‖ περιέχεσθαι ΒΒ　　　23 τε : τῇδε post Krueger
van H. ‖ προναυμαχέεις ABC, Stein³ : προναυμαχήσεις SV, Stein¹², Holder,
van H.: πρὸς ναυμαχήσεις R : προσναυμαχήσεις Marc.　　　25 γε καὶ
om. Β, καὶ tantum Marc., van H.　　　26 ἡμῖν Βz　　　27 ἑκαστέρωι P :
ἑκατέρωι α : ἑκατέρω ΒΟ : ἑκαστέρῳ z　　　31 <κατὰ νόον> Stein³ :
<εὖ> Krueger, Cobet, van H. ‖ μὴ οἰκότα δὲ z　　　32 βουλευομένων
Stein³ : βουλευομένοισι

to Hdt., counts upon victory. Phormio
ap. Thuc. 2. 90 seems to contradict the
tactical principle here enunciated by
Themistokles, but on the understanding
that the smaller fleet is superior in
manœuvring power, which the Greek
fleet at Salamis (νέες βαρύτεραι) was not.

19. πρὸς ἡμέων, 'to our interest,' op. c.
22 supra ; the context also illustrates the
use of πρός with accus. (πρὸς πολλάς supra),
and with dative (πρὸς τῷ Ἰσθμῷ infra).

21. ἐς τήν κτλ.: a pregnant construction. The singular verb is to be noticed.
τέκνα τε καὶ γ. : cp. c. 44 supra.

22. καὶ μήν : introducing a fresh
argument. αὐτοῦ τε μένων . . καὶ πρὸς
τῷ Ἰσθμῷ are co-ordinate alternatives.

περιέχεσθε : most of the address
is in 2nd pers. singular. Themistokles
by the plural here avoids accusing
Eurybiades of partiality. Cp. App. Crit.

23. προ- in προναυμαχήσεις, cp. cc. 56,
57 supra. εἰ . . φρονέεις : sc. εἰ αὐτοῦ
μενέεις, or αὐτοῦ μένων. The words
merely resume the wise course.

27. τῆς Ἀττικῆς grammatically
might be a partitive, or a comparative
gen. ; the context, and the fact asserted
c. 50 supra, favour the comparative.

28. οὐδενὶ κόσμῳ : nullo ordine, c.
117, 9. 56, 65 infra, etc. ἀπίασι has
plainly the future sense. περιεοῦσι, by
its position, combines with Αἰγίνῃ and
Σαλαμῖνι as well as with Μεγάροισι, 'we
shall profit by the immunity of Megara,
Aigina, Salamis.'

29. λόγιον ἐστί perhaps merely refers
to his own interpretation of the lines
ὦ θείη Σαλαμὶς κτλ., 7. 142 supra.
Themistokles is made to conclude with
an apophthegm of heavy calibre (='God
helps those that help themselves,' or
'Put your trust in God and keep your
powder dry').

31. A subject (χρηστά vel sim.) were
wanted for ἐθέλει, but for the emendation : cp. App. Crit.

32. προσχωρέειν πρός : to go to meet,
to accede to, to further, men's plans ;
the construction and meaning are remarkable, and not easy to parallel ; 9.
55 infra ad f. might serve best as commentary.

The speech here put into the mouth

Ταῦτα λέγοντος Θεμιστοκλέος αὖτις ὁ Κορίνθιος Ἀδεί- 61
μαντος ἐπεφέρετο, σιγᾶν τε κελεύων τῷ μὴ ἐστὶ πατρὶς καὶ
Εὐρυβιάδην οὐκ ἐῶν ἐπιψηφίζειν ἀπόλι ἀνδρί· πόλιν γὰρ τὸν
Θεμιστοκλέα παρεχόμενον οὕτω ἐκέλευε γνώμας συμβάλλεσθαι.

61. 1 θεμιστοκλέους ßCz ‖ αὖθις R ‖ Ἀδείμαντος secl. Stein[2], Holder,
van H.　　2 μή ἐστι Stein[1] : μὴ ἔστι Pz　　3 εὐρυβιάδεα ß ‖ ἐὰν ß
‖ ἀπόλιδι ß, van H.　　4 Θεμιστοκλῆα z

of Themistokles is a brief and masterly
résumé of the pros and cons of the case
between Salamis and the Isthmos as
the scene of the sea-fight, which (it is
admitted and agreed) must be fought
somewhere. The argument in the main
is presented in a series of six antithetical
considerations, which may be re-combined
into three antithetical or double-edged
assertions, followed by a peroration (iv.).
i. The narrow water of Salamis is
in favour of the Greeks; the open sea
off the Isthmos would tell in favour of
the Persians.
ii. By moving to the Isthmos they
will certainly lose Megara, Aigina,
Salamis; by remaining where they are
they will probably save them.
iii. They will defend the Peloponnesos
as well, or even better, by remaining at
Salamis; a defeat at the Isthmos will
be final. The reasons for this last assertion are not quite fully given in the
speech; only it is suggested that the
Persian fleet and Persian army will be
brought unduly near to the Peloponnesos,
in which case a defeat would be very
serious; Mnesiphilos above, and Themistokles himself, has taken the still more
alarming view that if they once quit
Salamis no battle will be fought at all.
iv. Finally, Themistokles adds that a
divine promise of victory has been received, though they must not expect it
to be fulfilled if they deliberately choose
the less prudent alternative.
61. 1. αὖτις, 'again,' a second time;
the first time being in c. 59 supra. Cp.
αὖτις δέ c. 60 supra corresponding to
πρῶτα μέν just before.
2. πατρίς, 'a fatherland'; cp. c.
57 supra, where Mnesiphilos regards
Themistokles as possessing actually, or
potentially, a πατρίς so long as the
Greek fleet is kept together at Salamis.
3. Εὐρυβιάδην οὐκ ἐῶν ἐπιψηφίζειν
ἀπόλι ἀνδρί, 'trying to prevent Eurybiades reopening the question (putting
a question to the vote) for the benefit of
(at the request of, to please) a landless

(city-less) man: let Themistokles produce
a city to which he belongs before (said
he) offering us his advice.'
There seems to be no sufficient reason
for abandoning (with Stein) the normal
meaning of ἐπιψηφίζειν so as to make it
mean 'to allow a vote to'—an interpretation which leads him to take
γνώμας συμβάλλεσθαι in the sense 'mit-
zustimmen,' i.e. to vote with (us). In
5. 92 (γνώμας ἀμείνονας συμβαλέσθαι ἢ
περ νῦν) the meaning is clearly 'to
advise.' Against the normal interpretation Stein asks: Warum sollte der
Antrag eines heimatlosen Mannes nicht
Gegenstand einer Abstimmung sein
dürfen? The point of the story as told
by Hdt. appears to be that Adeimantos
wishes to find some pretext on which to
prevent the question being reopened.
He objects to Themistokles, who is now
a landless man, being allowed to propose
a motion or an amendment, as subject
for a vote in the council of war:
he takes exception to a man, who no
longer represents a state, having any
opinion or proposal submitted to a vote.
There· is, indeed, a radical flaw or
inconsequence in the narrative of Hdt.
in that, on the one hand, it implies
that the question of remaining or going
was to be decided by the votes of the
majority, while, on the other hand, it
no less clearly implies that the whole
and sole decision rested with Eurybiades.
But this inconsequence leaves the meaning of ἐπιψηφίζειν unaffected.
Stein quotes two late writers in
support of his interpretation. Lucian
Tim. 44 ἐπεψήφισε τῇ ἐκκλησίᾳ. Diog.
L. 7. 10 ἐκκλησίᾳ κυρίᾳ τῶν προέδρων
ἐπεψήφισεν Ἵππων I should take
ἐκκλησίᾳ κυρίᾳ as a remoter dative, or
even locative, and so too τῇ ἐκκλησίᾳ,
rather than as objectively constructed
with ἐπεψήφισεν, and the verb itself as
absolute. Cp. Thuc. 6. 14. 1 ταῦτα . .
ἐπιψήφιζε καὶ γνώμας προτίθει αὖθις
Ἀθηναίοις, where Nikias is pleading for
'the previous question.'

5 ταῦτα δέ οἱ προέφερε, ὅτι ἡλώκεσάν τε καὶ κατείχοντο αἱ
'Αθῆναι. τότε δὴ ὁ Θεμιστοκλέης ἐκεῖνόν τε καὶ τοὺς Κορινθίους πολλά τε καὶ κακὰ ἔλεγε, ἑωυτοῖσί τε ἐδήλου λόγῳ ὡς
εἴη καὶ πόλις καὶ γῆ μέζων ἤ περ ἐκείνοισι, ἔστ' ἂν διηκόσιαι
νέες σφι ἔωσι πεπληρωμέναι· οὐδαμοὺς γὰρ Ἑλλήνων αὐτοὺς
62 ἐπιόντας ἀποκρούσεσθαι. σημαίνων δὲ ταῦτα τῷ λόγῳ διέβαινε
ἐς Εὐρυβιάδην, λέγων μᾶλλον <ἤδη> ἐπεστραμμένα. "σὺ εἰ
μενέεις αὐτοῦ καὶ μένων ἔσεαι ἀνὴρ ἀγαθός· εἰ δὲ μή, ἀνα-

---

5 προεφέρετο aC || αἱ om. ΒΡ, Holder   6 δὴ: δὲ Β: δὲ δὴ
Valckenaer, van H.   7 καλὰ Β   8 μέζω Β   9 νῆες Β ||
οὐδαμῶς Β   10 ἀποκρούσεσθαι ΒΒ: ἀποκρούεσθαι   62. 2 εὐρυ-
βιάδεα Βz || <ἤδη> Stein³   3 <μὲν> μενέεις Werfer, Holder, van H.

---

5. ἡλώκεσάν τε καὶ κατείχοντο, 'had
been taken and were in the hands of
the enemy': the pl.p. and imp. tenses
are noticeable.

6. τότε δή: a contrast to the former
occasion, and the soft answer; τότε, c.
60 *supra*. Now Themistokles 'lets him
have it.'

**7. ὡς εἴη καὶ πόλις καὶ γῆ . . ἔστ' ἂν
διηκόσιαι νέες σφι ἔωσι π.**: the sequence
is hardly quite regular. The 200
includes the ships lent to Chalkis. On
πεπληρωμέναι cp. c. 46 *supra*. The
formula that 'so long as they have 200
ships fully manned, the Athenians have
both City and Land, greater than
Korinth and Korinthia,' is ruined by
the explanation that 'no Hellenes whom
they attack will be able to resist them.'
Nothing further is heard of the threat
in this sense; and it spoils the beautiful
crescendo of Themistokles' arguments,
being the most direct and brutal, if that
indeed was what he meant. He probably
meant something quite different: 'Stone
walls do not a *city* make.' The scholiast
on Aischyl. *Pers.* 347 cites Alkaios; cp.
Bergk, *P.L.G.* iii.⁴ 156, Fr. 23 ἄνδρες
πόληος πύργος ἀρεύίοι. The passage in
Aischylos runs:

ΑΤ. ἔτ' ἆρ' 'Αθηνῶν ἔστ' ἀπόρθητος πόλις;
ΑΓ. ἀνδρῶν γὰρ ὄντων ἕρκος ἐστὶν ἀσφαλές.

Sophokles formulates the idea still
more explicitly, *Oid. Tyr.* 56 f. ὡς οὐδέν
ἐστιν οὔτε πύργος οὔτε ναῦς ἔρημος ἀνδρῶν
μὴ ξυνοικούντων ἔσω. The Athenians,
far beyond most Greeks of the fifth cent.
B.C., attained the conception of the ideal
and spiritual character of the City,
and its independence of the particular
place and material conditions. Their
invention of the *kleruchy*, in anticipation

of the Roman *colonia civium opt. iur.*, is
an evidence of that. A great stage in
their education was doubtless the evacuation of Attica in 480 B.C., and it bore
fruit sixty-eight years later, when in
412 B.C. the Athenian naval στρατόπεδον
at Samos preserved the continuity of
the Athenian Constitution, and formulated the conception of a polity virtually
independent of place: Thucyd. 8. 76.
It is but natural that the *Nephelo-
kokkygia* of Aristophanes and the
Republic of Plato are products of Attic
genius. Cp. 7. 234. 9 *supra*.

62. 1. σημαίνων δὲ ταῦτα, 'with these
significant hints.' τῷ λόγῳ διέβαινε,
together.

2. μᾶλλον ἐπεστραμμένα: not more
earnestly, vehemently, than he had
spoken to Adeimantos—it could hardly
have been so — but than before to
Eurybiades. ἐπεστραμμένος, p.p. from
ἐπιστρέφειν, seems here to = adj. ἐπι-
στρεφής, where it is not the 'turn' but
the 'attention,' the aim, which is emphasized; cp. ἐπιστρεφέως 1. 30, and Plato
Prot. 342 E ἐνέβαλε ῥῆμα . . συνεστραμ-
μένον ὥσπερ δεινὸς ἀκοντιστής.

εἰ μενέεις . . καὶ ἔσεαι: the expression is hardly in strict grammar,
and an *aposiopesis*, or a lacuna, might
be suspected; and so Baehr approves of
Valckenaer's suggestion to supply mentally σώσεις τὴν Ἑλλάδα. But the
excitement of the moment might account
for some incoherence. Certainly καὶ
μένων is tautologous, and *de trop*. One
might try to force a special point in it:
'You, if you are going to remain—yea,
in remaining (as you are now)—will be
a good man and true.'

3. ἀνατρέψεις τὴν Ἑλλάδα: this might
be described as μᾶλλον ἐπεστραμμένον

τρέψεις τὴν Ἑλλάδα· τὸ πᾶν γὰρ ἡμῖν τοῦ πολέμου φέρουσι
αἱ νέες. ἀλλ' ἐμοὶ πείθεο. εἰ δὲ ταῦτα μὴ ποιήσῃς, ἡμεῖς 5
μὲν ὡς ἔχομεν ἀναλαβόντες τοὺς οἰκέτας κομιεύμεθα ἐς Σῖριν

compared with κινδυνεύσεις ἀπάσῃ τῇ
Ἑλλάδι c. 60 supra.
4. τὸ πᾶν γὰρ ἡμῖν τοῦ πολέμου φ.
αἱ νέες: cp. οὐδὲν πλέον ἐφέροντο 7. 211
supra, πλέον μέντοι ἐφερέ οἱ ἡ γνώμη
κατεργάσασθαι τὴν Ἑλλάδα c. 100 infra,
and more especially ταῦτα μέν νυν ἐπὶ
σμικρόν τι ἐφέροντο τοῦ πολέμου 4. 130.
'The whole fate, or issue, of the war
depends for us on the ships.' ἡμῖν need
not be restricted to the Athenians.
5. ἀλλ' ἐμοὶ πείθεο: cp. Il. 1. 259
ἀλλὰ πίθεσθ', 2. 139 ἀλλ' ἀγεθ' ὡς ἀν
ἐγὼ εἴπω πειθώμεθα πάντες.
εἰ . . ποιήσῃς: cp. c. 49 supra.
6. ὡς ἔχομεν, 'just as we are,' without
more ado.
τοὺς οἰκέτας: cp. c. 41 supra.
Σῖριν τὴν ἐν Ἰταλίῃ: there was
another 'Siris' in Paionia; cp. c. 115
infra; the Italiote Siris was on a
navigable river of the same name, twenty-
four stades distant from the (later)
Herakleia (Strabo 264); it was in the
neighbourhood of this river that Pyrrhus
fought his first engagement with the
Romans 280 B.C., Plutarch Pyrrh. 16.
The foundation legend is given by
Strabo, l.c. Siris, originally a settlement of the Chonians (i.e. native Italians
of that region, but cp. 9. 93 infra), was
occupied by fugitive Trojans after the
fall of Troy (hence the worship of the
winking Athene in the city, Strabo l.c.).
At a later time Ionians flying from
the Lydian conqueror (temp. Gygis?)
occupied the town. The Ionians were
apparently from Kolophon, and under
them the Ionian city, in the midst
of Achaian neighbours, rose to great
prosperity, and rivalled Sybaris and
Kroton in wealth and luxury. (Athen.
523 καὶ οἱ τὴν Σῖριν (sic) δὲ κατοικοῦντες, ἣν
πρῶτοι κατέσχον οἱ ἀπὸ Τροίας ἐλθόντες,
ὕστερον δὲ Κολοφώνιοι, ὡς φησι Τίμαιος
καὶ Ἀριστοτέλης, εἰς τρυφὴν ἐξώκειλαν οὐχ
ἧσσον Συβαριτῶν.) The fertility of its
soil was proverbial: οὐ γάρ τι καλὸς
χῶρος οὐδ' ἐφίμερος οὐδ' ἐρατὸς οἷος ἀμφὶ
Σίριος ῥοάς, Archilochos ap. Athen. l.c.,
Bergk ii.⁴ 389, No. 21. Among the
suitors of Agariste (circ. 570 B.C.) figured
Damasos, son of Amyris, τοῦ σοφοῦ λεγο-

μένου, 6. 127 supra. It must have been
after that epoch, and before the destruction of Sybaris by Kroton (see 5. 44),
that the Achaian colonies, Metapontion,
Sybaris, and Kroton, combined to destroy
Siris (Trogus Pomp. ap. Justin. 20. 2.
3 ff.), and apparently accomplished their
purpose, notwithstanding the alliance of
the Sirites with Lokroi. Siris must have
continued to be inhabited, as 'a member
of the Achaian confederacy' (B. Head,
Historia Numorum, p. 69), and stood in
intimate commercial relation with the
town of Pyxos, a town on the Tyrrhene
sea, probably of Sybarite foundation,
and afterwards, perhaps, involved with
Siris in the ruin of that city 510 B.C.—
a catastrophe not inconsistent with the
dim record of a projected occupation of
Sirite territory by Samian adventurers
(cp. 7. 164 supra), which may have
been an anticipation of the Athenian
project: Σάμιοι, πλεύσαντες εἰς Σύβαριν
καὶ κατασχόντες τὴν Σιρῖτιν χώραν, περ-
δίκων ἀναπτάντων καὶ ποιησάντων ψόφον,
ἐκπλαγέντες ἔφυγον, καὶ ἐμβάντες εἰς τὰς
ναῦς ἀπέπλευσαν, Hegesander of Delphi
ap. Athen. 656=Fr. 44, Mueller iv. 421.
The dream of an Ionian restoration at
Siris was part of the heritage which
Athens accepted in placing, or replacing,
herself at the head of the Ionian race,
after the fall of Miletos; but there
shows no definite trace of an earlier
connexion between Siris and Athens.
The dream was not destined to be fulfilled. Thurioi was, indeed, founded in
443 B.C., but at a considerable distance
from the Siris (330 stades, Strabo l.c.),
nor was Thurioi a successful settlement
from an Athenian point of view (cp.
Busolt, Gr. G. III. i. 518–541). Somewhat later, however (in 431 B.C.),
Tarentum succeeded where Athens had
failed: Ταραντῖνοι τοὺς τὴν Σῖριν καλου-
μένην οἰκοῦντας μετοικίσαντες ἐκ τῆς
πατρίδος καὶ ἰδίους προσθέντες οἰκήτορας,
ἔκτισαν πόλιν τὴν ὀνομαζομένην Ἡράκλειαν.
The new city was founded on healthier
ground than the old, but Siris remained
the port (χρόνῳ δὲ τῆς Ἡρακλείας ἐντεῦθεν
οἰκισθείσης ὑπὸ Ταραντίνων, ἐπίνειον αὕτη
τῶν Ἡρακλεωτῶν ὑπῆρξε, Strabo l.c.);

τὴν ἐν Ἰταλίῃ, ἥ περ ἡμετέρη τε ἐστὶ ἐκ παλαιοῦ ἔτι, καὶ
τὰ λόγια λέγει ὑπ' ἡμέων αὐτὴν δέειν κτισθῆναι· ὑμεῖς δὲ
συμμάχων τοιῶνδε μουνωθέντες μεμνήσεσθε τῶν ἐμῶν λόγων."
63 ταῦτα δὲ Θεμιστοκλέος λέγοντος ἀνεδιδάσκετο Εὐρυβιάδης·
δοκέειν δέ μοι, ἀρρωδήσας μάλιστα τοὺς Ἀθηναίους ἀνεδιδάσκετο, μή σφεας ἀπολίπωσι, ἣν πρὸς τὸν Ἰσθμὸν ἀγάγῃ τὰς
νέας· ἀπολιπόντων γὰρ Ἀθηναίων οὐκέτι ἐγίνοντο ἀξιόμαχοι
5 οἱ λοιποί.   ταύτην δὲ αἱρέεται τὴν γνώμην, αὐτοῦ μένοντας
διαναυμαχέειν.

---

7 τέ ἐστι vulgo   8 δεῖ B: δέον Marc., z   9 τοιούτων Pz
63. 1 θεμιστοκλέους d: Θεμιστοκλῆος z ‖ Εὐρυβιάδης . . ἀνεδιδάσκετο
om. R: ἀνεδιδάσκετο post. 1. del. Cobet, van H.   3 ἀνάγῃ B: ἀνάγῃ
Holder, van H.   4 νῆας Bz   5 δὴ S, Krueger: δὲ ὢν ? Stein

---

though Pliny 3. 15. 3 seems to identify
the two (Heraclia, aliquando Siris voci-
tata). Cp. F. Lenormant, La Grand-
Grèce (1881) i. 201 ff.

8. τὰ λόγια λέγει κτλ. : the formula
is noticeable, as the λόγια in question
were no doubt in writing. This passage
may fairly be taken as evidence of the
antiquity of the idea at Athens of an
extension or colonization in the West.
To see in the speech of Themistokles,
more or less fictitious though it be,
nothing but the reflexion of ideas and
discussions current in Athens about the
date of the foundation of Thurioi is to
ignore the points above adduced as antecedents of that very undertaking itself.
There is also other sufficient evidence
to connect the name of Themistokles
with the conception of an expansive
policy in the West; cp. Thucyd. 1. 136.
1, Plutarch Themist. 32 (names of his
daughters, Italia, Sybaris). Busolt's
defence of the claim of Themistokles in
this connexion against the adverse
critique of Beloch, Hermes 29 (1894), 604,
concedes perhaps too much in sacrificing
the antiquity of these λόγια and seeing
in them mere products of the Θουριο-
μάντεις. Athens had long been nursing
commercial relations with the West
(as Busolt well shows), and, moreover,
Themistokles and the Athenians would
probably have claimed as their own
λόγια which in the first instance might
have been intended to promote relations
between the Ionians and the West (cp. 1.
94, 163–167, 170, 3. 136–138, 4. 152, 5.
(42–47), 106, 6. 2, 21, 23–24, 7. 158, 163,
8. 22). Themistokles, if any man, was
likely to have taken into account the

Ionian precedents in the West. Whether
he used any such threat upon this
occasion, as is here fathered on him by
Hdt., is another question.   It would
not have been easy to carry out, and
the threat of joining the Mede would
have been still more efficacious (cp. 9.
11). But the anecdote implies that
Eurybiades and the Peloponnesians were
on the point of withdrawing from
Salamis, and this implication is hardly
acceptable; cp. Appendix VI. § 1.

63. 1. ἀνεδιδάσκετο Εὐρυβιάδης: the
verb has full middle force: 'allowed
himself better instruction '—changed his
mind (his instructions), 'was converted ';
cp. 4. 95 (ἀναδιδάσκειν, to change the
ideas, beliefs, of others). Materially it
is important to observe that everything
depended on the mind of Eurybiades.

2. δοκέειν δέ μοι. This expression of
personal opinion and judgement by Hdt.
is noticeable, especially for the reason
given, that without the Athenians the
Greeks would have been unable to resist
the Persian successfully; cp. the still
more elaborate statement of the same
verdict, 7. 139 supra. Perhaps that
passage is of later composition than this
straightforward matter-of-course judgement here, though its simple directness
might be ascribed to the very fact that
a more elaborate statement and discussion has preceded.

4. οὐκέτι ἐγίνοντο ἀξιόμαχοι : i.e.
ἐγίνοντο οὐκέτι ἀξιόμαχοι, and ἐγίνοντο
=ἔμελλον γίγνεσθαι, or γενήσεσθαι.

5. αὐτοῦ μένοντας διαναυμαχέειν.
This γνώμη involves two elements—(i.)
αὐτοῦ μένειν, (ii.) διαναυμαχέειν. If the
preceding narrative be correct there was

Οὕτω μὲν οἱ περὶ Σαλαμῖνα ἔπεσι ἀκροβολισάμενοι, ἐπείτε **64**
Εὐρυβιάδῃ ἔδοξε, αὐτοῦ παρεσκευάζοντο ὡς ναυμαχήσοντες.
ἡμέρη τε ἐγίνετο καὶ ἅμα τῷ ἡλίῳ ἀνιόντι σεισμὸς ἐγένετο ἔν
τε τῇ γῇ καὶ τῇ θαλάσσῃ. ἔδοξε δέ σφι εὔξασθαι τοῖσι
θεοῖσι καὶ ἐπικαλέσασθαι τοὺς Αἰακίδας συμμάχους.   ὡς δέ 5

---

64. 1 οὗτοι **B**   3 τε om. **B** ‖ ἐγένετο z ‖ ἐγίνετο B

---

no question about (ii.) ; the only question
was where the battle was to take place :
in which case, the decision now is simply
αὐτοῦ *μένειν*, i.e. αὐτοῦ *διαναυμαχέειν*.
But Mnesiphilos above has been allowed
to point out that the two were one—if
the Peloponnesians left Salamis no battle
would be fought anywhere.

64. 1. ἔπεσι ἀκροβολισάμενοι: *nach
solchem Wortgefecht*, Stein, who cps.
λόγων ὠθισμός c. 78 *infra*. But there is
a difference. ὠθισμός would be for the
heavy-armed, ἀκροβολισμός would be
for the light-armed orators. Moreover,
an ἔπος is a 'winged-word.' The reference seems to be rather back to the
bon-mots in cc. 59, 61 than to the
weighty arguments of Themistokles in
cc. 60, 61 f.

ἐπείτε Εὐρυβιάδῃ ἔδοξε: a decision by Eurybiades was all that was
necessary ; the Spartan navarch had
absolute power in the matter, in virtue
of the Spartan Hegemonia. He might
consult a council of war, but he was
not bound by a majority of votes, or
even bound to put the question to the
vote at all. Naturally, however, he
could not give battle unless assured of
the approval of the Athenians, who
supplied two-thirds of the forces.

3. ἡμέρη τε ἐγίνετο καί: the *parataxis*
is to be observed : not that the sunrise
had of necessity anything to say to 'the
earthquake on land and sea.' The earthquake is, however, surely portentous and
Poseidonian. Seisms are unfortunately
of no use chronologically ; but the day
in question is apparently the very day
before the actual battle, the Persian
fleet is all in sight, at Phaleron, albeit
its arrival has still to be recorded in the
story, cp. c. 66 *infra*. If the introduction of the anecdote in c. 65 as upon
this day may be used for a chronological
indication, conscious or unconscious,
then the date would probably be Boëdromion 20 ; cp. *l.c.*

4. ἔδοξε δέ σφι: the Council again ?
or the Athenians ? or, vaguely, the

whole armament of the Greeks ? A
regrettable obscurity.

εὔξασθαι τοῖσι θεοῖσι: the day
before the battle is largely devoted to
religious exercises ; the earthquake having probably emphasized the natural
instinct of piety at such a crisis. The
Athenians will have felt an especial grief
in their exclusion from Eleusis on this
day ; but their prayers to the goddess
were destined to obtain a rich response
within the year, cp. 9. 101 *infra*. None
of the gods was omitted from the litany
on this occasion.

**5. ἐπικαλέσασθαι τοὺς Αἰακίδας συμ-
μάχους**: Aiakos was a son of Zeus (*Il.*
21. 189 etc.), but in Homer Aiakos is not
yet descended into hell, as Judge of the
Underworld). The best known sons of
Aiakos are Peleus, the father of Achilles,
and Telamon the father of Aias. From
Aias were further descended the Phil-
aidai, and Eurysakidai—two great Attic
clans—through their eponyms, his sons,
Philaios, Eurysakes. But Aiakos had
also a son Phokos (Pausanias 2. 29. 7),
whose tomb was shown in Aigina, where
he had been slain by his half-brother
Telamon, who was in consequence
banished the island. Hence the Greeks,
or Athenians, could invoke Telamon
and Aias in Salamis (where they had
resided), but had to send to Aigina
itself to invoke, or to fetch, Aiakos and
the other Aiakidai. But what others ?
For Peleus and for Achilles they would
surely have had to send to their tombs
in Thessaly (?), in the Troad (*Od.* 24. 80
ff. ; Arrian, *Anab.* 1. 11. 12 ; cp. 5.
94 *supra*). The descendants of Phokos,
too, were to be sought in 'Phokis,'
Pausan. 2. 29. 2. (It seems as if Aiakos
and Phokos were the only 'Aiakids' to
be found in Aigina.) In view of the
story in 5. 80, 81 it may fairly be argued
that this ship was sent to fetch actual
idols (ξόανα), and not merely to perform
an invocation *in loco* ; cp. my notes to
l.c. This ship would have to evade the
Persian fleet and look-out, though that

σφι ἔδοξε, καὶ ἐποίευν ταῦτα· εὐξάμενοι γὰρ πᾶσι τοῖσι
θεοῖσι, αὐτόθεν μὲν ἐκ Σαλαμῖνος Αἴαντά τε καὶ Τελαμῶνα
ἐπεκαλέοντο, ἐπὶ δὲ Αἰακὸν καὶ τοὺς ἄλλους Αἰακίδας νέα
ἀπέστελλον ἐς Αἴγιναν.

65   Ἔφη δὲ Δίκαιος ὁ Θεοκύδεος, ἀνὴρ Ἀθηναῖος φυγάς τε
καὶ παρὰ Μήδοισι λόγιμος γενόμενος τοῦτον τὸν χρόνον,
ἐπείτε ἐκείρετο ἡ Ἀττικὴ χώρη ὑπὸ τοῦ πεζοῦ στρατοῦ τοῦ
Ξέρξεω ἐοῦσα ἔρημος Ἀθηναίων, τυχεῖν τότε ἐὼν ἅμα Δημ-

---

6 ἐποίεον B   7 μὲν om. B ‖ ἐκ Σαλαμῖνος secl. van H. ‖ Αἴαντα
τὸν Τελαμῶνος S, Valla (ap. Gaisf.): τε καὶ: τὸν R: τῶν V (ap. Holder)
8 νῆα SVz: νῆας R   65. 1 Δικαῖος z (bis) ‖ τε: 'an δὲ?' van H.

---

necessity has not yet transpired in the
narrative of Hdt. ; it may therefore be
surmised that it was sent at night, not
in daylight. But, again, if so, it can
hardly have gone and come in one night,
but was probably sent out on the night
preceding, and returned as recorded in
c. 83 *infra*.

ὡς . . καί . . : a *parataxis*, but
not a synchronism, and even an incorrect
parataxis, seeing that either ὡς or καί is
de trop ; cp. εἰ . . καί c. 62 *supra*. The
difference in the tenses ἔδοξε, ἐποίευν
should be marked.

65. 1. ἔφη : the word might perfectly
well be understood of a written authority
or source, cp. 4. 13, 6. 137, and Introduction, § 10. Had Hdt. himself spoken
face to face with his authority, he would
have let his readers know it (cp. 9. 16),
and if he were reporting simply a conversation with others he would scarcely
have named one interlocutor without
at least indicating the presence of the
others. The words with which the anecdote, and the chapter, conclude, ταῦτα
μὲν Δίκαιος ὁ Θεοκύδεος ἔλεγε, Δημαρήτου
τε καὶ ἄλλων μαρτύρων καταπτόμενος, look
more like an appeal to the *vox viva*, but
are hardly conclusive in this respect,
and certainly leave Hdt. himself out of
audible range of Dikaios.

Δίκαιος ὁ Θεοκύδεος : doubtless a
man of some importance in his day, presumably of the Peisistratid party (cp.
cc. 52, 54 *supra*), and on friendly terms
with Demaratos, as the ensuing anecdote
proves. But the romantic hypothesis
which P. Trautwein has woven out of
these few indications plus general probability or possibility, making *The Memoirs
of Dikaios* one of the principal sources
used by Hdt. in his history of the Persian

war, especially in those passages wherein
Demaratos figures, is little more than a
suggestive fancy. Sources, and written
sources, Hdt. doubtless had ; but alas !
we can do little to identify or to reproduce them. Cp. Introduction, § 10.

The names 'Dikaios' and 'Theokydes'
are rare, and almost unparalleled ; but
'Thucydides' implies 'Thucydes' (Θεο-
θου-κύδης), and, if fancy is to be the
order of the day, one might speculate
upon a possible connexion between the
father of Dikaios and the son of Oloros.
What was the name of the father of
Oloros, or Orolos ? Considering the
Thracian connexions of Thucydides,
noting the extremely 'superior' manner
in which he disposes of medism and the
Median question, marking his tolerance
of the Peisistratidai and the Tyrannis at
Athens, one might amuse an idle half-
hour in elaborating the conjecture that
here, in this record of the unpatriotic
rôle played by a more or less distant
relative of his own, the Athenian historian and exile scented a provocation
to the depreciatory estimate, both of
the subject selected and the methods
pursued, by his greatest literary predecessor, of whom he was obviously
more than a little jealous ! Cp. Thuc.
1. 20–23.

2. Μήδοισι rather suggests citation
than free composition by Hdt. himself.
Cp. c. 5 *supra*.

3. ἐπείτε ἐκείρετο : the imperfect has
its proper force, but the statement seems
less important chronologically than causally—as explaining how they came to be
where they were.

4. Δημαρήτῳ τῷ Λακεδαιμονίῳ : cp.
Bk. 7 *passim*. The description was
hardly necessary at this stage in the

ἀρήτῳ τῷ Λακεδαιμονίῳ ἐν τῷ Θριασίῳ πεδίῳ, ἰδεῖν δὲ 5
κονιορτὸν χωρέοντα ἀπ᾽ Ἐλευσῖνος ὡς ἀνδρῶν μάλιστά κῃ
τρισμυρίων, ἀποθωμάζειν τε σφέας τὸν κονιορτὸν ὅτεων κοτὲ
εἴη ἀνθρώπων, καὶ πρόκατε φωνῆς ἀκούειν, καί οἱ φαίνεσθαι
τὴν φωνὴν εἶναι τὸν μυστικὸν ἴακχον. εἶναι δ᾽ ἀδαήμονα τῶν

---

6 ἀπὸ **β**, Holder ‖ κου ABC　　7 ἀποθωμάζειν τε ABC, Stein[2], (τέ) Holder, van H.: ἀποθωϋμάζοντες R: ἀποθωϋμάζοντάς S (Gaisf.): ἀποθωυμάζον τέ V: ἀποθωυμάζειν τέ (σφεας) Stein[1] ‖ σφέας om. B: ‘an transponendum post ἰδεῖν δὲ ?’ van H.

---

continuous story, and comes perhaps from the source. Did the Spartan exile recall his previous visit to Eleusis some thirty years before (5. 75) ?

5. **ἐν τῷ Θριασίῳ πεδίῳ**: mentioned again 9. 7 infra by the Athenian envoy at Sparta as τῆς γε ἡμετέρης ἐπιτηδεότατον μαχέσασθαι u.v. How did Dikaios and Demaratos find themselves there ? Had they come from Athens with a Persian column simply to ravage the plain ? or were they on their way to Athens with the column which had left Boiotia by the pass of Dryos-Kephalai (cp. c. 50 supra)? or, as might seem most probable, were they crossing the Thriasian plain with the Persian force detached to move against the Isthmos, as recorded c. 70 infra ? Or are they to be thought as there by themselves, and for no particular purpose, otherwise how could a cloud of dust surprise them ? The Thriasian plain is a good size ; it is a pity their exact position thereon is not more precisely defined.

6. **κονιορτὸν χωρέοντα ἀπ᾽ Ἐλευσῖνος**. Did Hdt. suppose that the Pomp moved from Eleusis to Athens ? K. O. Mueller accused him ; Baehr defends, by invoking the N. or NW. wind ! Surely the dust-cloud must move from Eleusis, because Persian fleet and Persian army are conceived, in the anecdote, as still to the east of Aigaleos.

ἀνδρῶν μάλιστά κῃ τρισμυρίων: this is the conventional number of Athenian citizens, cp. 5. 97, but the figure can hardly be used here with that reference, as the context clearly asserts that the festival was not confined to Athenians, while on the other hand all Athenian citizens were not initiate.

7. **ἀποθωμάζειν τε . . καί . . ἀκούειν**, ‘they were not done wondering . . when they heard (were hearing)’; the parataxis has force. **πρόκατε**: c. 135 infra.

8. **ἀνθρώπων**: not the Persian army,

nor yet the advancing Peloponnesians (they thought), nor any mortal beings. The doubt is whether it be not superhuman.

καί οἱ φ. τ. φ. εἶναι: Dikaios is not quite sure. If there is any truth in the anecdote (as seems probable) this Athenian exile, himself a mystes, may well have been in an excited frame of mind that evening, Boëdromion 20, that found him once more in his native land, under such unhallowed auspices, to assist on the morrow at the consummation of its ruin, or of his own eternal disgrace. Like the anecdote of Thersandros (9. 16), the story would suggest that there were those in the king's following who viewed with apprehension the struggle at close quarters with the Greeks, and were anything but confident of victory.

9. **τὸν μυστικὸν ἴακχον**: i.e. the cry ‘Iakehos,’ or the hymn in honour of ‘Iakchos’—a specimen of which is perhaps presented by Aristoph. Frogs, 398-413, and which was uttered by the band of pilgrims as they went from Athens to Eleusis on the 19th or 20th Boëdromion ; see further infra. The very day itself was also apparently known by the same name, Plutarch, Camillus 19. Iakchos may be etymologically a reduplicated form of Bakchos (ϜιϜακχος, cp. L. & S.), but, as M. Foucart points out (l'Origine et la Nature des Mystères d'Eleusis, 1895, p. 81), Iakchos was a late comer at Eleusis, and a subordinate personage ; this very passage is the earliest evidence of his association with the mysteries.

ἀδαήμονα: an ‘Epic’ word, not used by Hdt. elsewhere. Stein suggests that it comes, with οἶνος and ἀρίδηλα below, from Hdt.'s ‘source’—a suggestion which further suggests that the source in question was in writing. How far this ignorance on the part of the Spartan

10 ἱρῶν τῶν ἐν Ἐλευσῖνι γινομένων τὸν Δημάρητον, εἰρέσθαι τε
αὐτὸν ὅ τι τὸ φθεγγόμενον εἴη τοῦτο. αὐτὸς δὲ εἰπεῖν
" Δημάρητε, οὐκ ἔστι ὅκως οὐ μέγα τι σίνος ἔσται τῇ βασιλέος
στρατιῇ· τάδε γὰρ ἀρίδηλα, ἐρήμου ἐούσης τῆς Ἀττικῆς, ὅτι
θεῖον τὸ φθεγγόμενον, ἀπ' Ἐλευσῖνος ἰὸν ἐς τιμωρίην Ἀθηναίοισί
15 τε καὶ τοῖσι συμμάχοισι. καὶ ἢν μέν γε κατασκήψῃ ἐς τὴν
Πελοπόννησον, κίνδυνος αὐτῷ τε βασιλέι καὶ τῇ στρατιῇ τῇ
ἐν τῇ ἠπείρῳ ἔσται, ἢν δὲ ἐπὶ τὰς νέας τράπηται τὰς ἐν
Σαλαμῖνι, τὸν ναυτικὸν στρατὸν κινδυνεύσει βασιλεὺς ἀπο-
βαλεῖν. τὴν δὲ ὀρτὴν ταύτην ἄγουσι Ἀθηναῖοι ἀνὰ πάντα

---

10 ἱρῶν BBAcorr., cp. c. 55 || τε om. B   11 τοιοῦτον B || εἶπε B :
εἶπαι z   12 σίνος PRz || βασιλέως C : βασιλῆος z   14 ἀπὸ B,
Holder || ἐὸν Bz   16 βασιλέι AB   17 νῆας Bz   18 ἀπο-
βαλέειν Bz   19 ἀνὰ del. Kallenberg, Holder || πᾶν ἔτος maleb. Krueger,
van H.

---

exile is assumed for dramatic purposes, it is hard to determine. But even if Demaratos is the mere vehicle of Herodotean didactics, it is obvious that Herodotus addresses an audience which had much to learn in regard to the *Eleusinia*. Such a public was hardly to be found in Athens. Whether the author himself was a μύστης does not appear, but, no doubt appropriately, the Athenian exile plays the part of divine or exegete, the Spartan that of politician or diplomat.

τῶν ἱρῶν τῶν ἐν Ἐλευσῖνι γινομένων: in Hdt.'s own day, as in the times of Demaratos and Dikaios, of Peisistratos, and long before. There is surely no need to bring down this whole anecdote to the later draft of Hdt.'s work, or its revision—easily as the chapter might be an insertion—or to connect it merely with the attempted revival, or rather extension, of the Eleusinian Festival after the thirty years' truce, which was to be one of Perikles' consolations for the failure of his more violent attempts to make Athens the head of a great empire, or of his still earlier and more ingenuous plan to win pan-Hellenic recognition for his city by making it the focus of a pan-Hellenic Congress (Plutarch *Perik.* c. 17).

12. οὐκ ἔστι ὅκως οὐ .. ἔσται: there is here an omitted antecedent, and the ellipse, coupled with the double negation, serves to emphasize the assertion, in this case a prediction; cp. Xenoph. *Anab.* 2. 4. 3 οὐκ ἔστιν ὅπως οὐκ ἐπιθήσεται ἡμῖν (sc. βασιλεύς). σίνος (neut.), an ἅπαξ λ.

in Hdt., though the verb σίνεσθαι is to be found *passim* (esp. Bk. 9); cp. l. 9 *supra*.

13. στρατιῇ, as the context proves, embraces both the land and sea forces.
ἀρίδηλα, 'absolutely clear'—also a ἅπαξ λ. in Hdt. ; cp. l. 9 *supra*.

14. ἐς τιμωρίην, assistance, aid, support—as often *ap.* Hdt. The prominence of 'the Athenians' betrays the origin of the anecdote.

15. κατασκήψῃ : for the verb cp. 7. 134, 137 *supra*, passages which would suggest that a μῆνις or νέμεσις was here too in view—although clearly not directed against the Greeks in Peloponnese or in Salamis. The word may be used in a weakened sense, meaning little more than the τράπηται just below. The grammatical subject is obscure : the nearest would be τὸ φθεγγόμενον, but, as that must be taken in the passive, the result is nonsense. Stein suggests νέφος, by anticipation ; κονιορτός from above would be less remote and obscure ; but a vague though self-evident subject, such as τὸ θεῖον τοῦτα, or such like, suggests itself in the immediate context, or even τὸ σίνος τοῦτο, τὸ κακὸν τ.

19. τὴν δὲ ὀρτὴν ταύτην : no feast or festival, strictly speaking, has been described, or even expressly mentioned, but may be taken as implied in τὸν μυστικὸν Ἴακχον *supra*. The reference here is not to an ἀγών, which undoubtedly was held at Eleusis (in strict terminology τὰ Ἐλευσίνια), but to the celebration of the 'mysteries' (τὰ με-

ἔτεα τῇ Μητρὶ καὶ τῇ Κούρῃ, καὶ αὐτῶν τε ὁ βουλόμενος 20
καὶ τῶν ἄλλων Ἑλλήνων μυεῖται· καὶ τὴν φωνὴν τῆς ἀκούεις
ἐν ταύτῃ τῇ ὁρτῇ ἰακχάζουσι." πρὸς ταῦτα εἰπεῖν Δημάρητον
" σίγα τε καὶ μηδενὶ ἄλλῳ τὸν λόγον τοῦτον εἴπῃς· ἢν γάρ
τοι ἐς βασιλέα ἀνενειχθῇ τὰ ἔπεα ταῦτα, ἀποβαλέεις τὴν
κεφαλήν, καί σε οὔτε ἐγὼ δυνήσομαι ῥύσασθαι οὔτ' ἄλλος 25
ἀνθρώπων οὐδὲ εἷς. ἀλλ' ἔχ' ἥσυχος, περὶ δὲ στρατιῆς τῆσδε
θεοῖσι μελήσει." τὸν μὲν δὴ ταῦτα παραινέειν, ἐκ δὲ τοῦ
κονιορτοῦ καὶ τῆς φωνῆς γενέσθαι νέφος καὶ μεταρσιωθὲν
φέρεσθαι ἐπὶ Σαλαμῖνος ἐπὶ τὸ στρατόπεδον τὸ τῶν Ἑλλήνων.

---

20 τῇ δήμητρι **B** : τῇ Δήμητρι Holder, van H. || κούρηι ACP : κόρῃ
21 μυέεται Stein[1]   22 εἶπαι z   24 βασιλῆα z || ἀνενεχθῆι B
26 οὐδὲ εἷς ABC : οὐδείς   27 δὴ om. αC || ἐκ δὴ z   28 μετάρσιον
ἀρθὲν Cobet   29 ἐς τὸ **B**, Holder, van H.

γάλα), which took place annually in Boëdromion (15–23 ?), the 19th and 20th being especially devoted to the Iakchospomp, and the latter of the two known by his name. On the evening which began that calendar day the pilgrims reached Eleusis. During the daylight of the 19th they would have been marching from Athens, and it is, therefore, inferentially to the 19th that the conversation between Dikaios and Demaratos is to be dated, and consequently to the 20th that the actual battle is to be referred. Cp. generally, on the festival, etc., A. Mommsen, *Feste der Stadt Athen* (1898), 179–277.

πρὸς ταῦτα ἔπεα : cp. 7. 106 ἀνὰ τὰν ἔτος.

20. τῇ Μητρὶ καὶ τῇ Κούρῃ : the cult of the mother and the daughter, Demeter and Persephone, was presumably the original nucleus of the Eleusinian τελεταί, but not necessarily, like the *Thesmophoria*, confined to women (cp. 2. 171). The Homeric Hymn to Demeter bears no trace of the exclusion of men. The position of the other deities ('the god' and 'the goddess,' Eubulos, Pluton, Triptolemos, Dionysos) associated with the cult is obscure, but the supposed Egyptian origin of the mysteries (Foucart, *op. cit. supra*) looks like a retrogression in constructive criticism. At some early date, perhaps in connexion with the introduction of a new deity, perhaps as a consequence of the Athenian conquest of Eleusis, the cult obtained more catholic recognition, but the exact point at which 'pan-Hellenic' significance was given to the 'mysteries' is not clear; probably at least as early as the times of Peisistratos, with whose position and policy such ideas were congruous. Even in the age of Peisistratos the enlarged *Eleusinia* may have been represented as a restoration.

22. ἰακχάζουσι : sc. ᾄδουσι (τὸν Ἴακχον), cp. l. 9 *supra*.

23. τὸν λόγον τοῦτον . . τὰ ἔπεα ταῦτα appear to be used here as virtual equivalents ; cp. Index *sub vv.*

24. ἀνενειχθῇ, 'be reported.'

26. οὐδὲ εἷς, 'no, not one !'—a somewhat false, but perhaps idiomatic emphasis ; cp. 9. 80 *infra*.

ἔχ' ἥσυχος : an eminently idiomatic expression ; Larcher cites Eurip. *Med.* 553, *Orest.* 1275 for the adjectival construction with ἔχειν.

στρατιῆς : as above, l. 13.

27. θεοῖσι μελήσει, 'the will of the gods be done.'

ἐκ : perhaps with a double force, material and temporal : 'out of the dust and after the voice' ; for temporal ἐκ cp. 7. 188.

28. μεταρσιωθέν = μετάρσιον γενόμενον : μετάρσιον = μετέωρον, cp. 7. 188. But cp. App. Crit.

29. ἐπί : the uses with genitive (Σαλαμῖνος) and accusative (τὸ στρατόπεδον) illustrated. The cloud could not have reached the Hellenic laager without reaching Salamis. Apparently here the genitive denotes the more general direction, the accusative the more definite.

30 οὕτω δὴ αὐτοὺς μαθεῖν ὅτι τὸ ναυτικὸν τὸ Ξέρξεω ἀπολέεσθαι
μέλλοι. ταῦτα μὲν Δίκαιος ὁ Θεοκύδεος ἔλεγε, Δημαρήτου τε
καὶ ἄλλων μαρτύρων καταπτόμενος.

66 Οἱ δὲ ἐς τὸν Ξέρξεω ναυτικὸν στρατὸν ταχθέντες, ἐπειδὴ
ἐκ Τρηχῖνος θεησάμενοι τὸ τρῶμα τὸ Λακωνικὸν διέβησαν ἐς
τὴν Ἱστιαίην, ἐπισχόντες ἡμέρας τρεῖς ἔπλεον δι' Εὐρίπου,
καὶ ἐν ἑτέρῃσι τρισὶ ἡμέρῃσι ἐγένοντο ἐν Φαλήρῳ. ὡς μὲν

---

30 δὴ Stein², van H. : δὲ ‖ ἀπολέσθαι Β   31 μέλλει ? Krueger
(Marc.) ‖ τε om. αC   32 τῶν ἄλλων Β ‖ καθαπτόμενος α   66. 1
δ' Β ‖ ξέρξεωι Β   3 ἔπλωον Βz ‖ διὰ α

---

30. **οὕτω δή κτλ.** : that this vision of
the souls of the faithful celebrating a
pan-Hellenic festival in a land occupied
by the enemy portended aught but destruction to the barbarian, could not
enter their minds !

31. **Δημαρήτου τε καὶ ἄλλων** : they
were not then *tête-à-tête* ; others were
present to attest the truth of the story.
Or did Dikaios disregard the injunctions
of Demaratos, and communicate their
adventure to other persons on returning
to camp ? **μαρτύρων** is of course used
appositively ; cp. note on ἄλλοι c. 55
supra. **καταπτόμενος** : cp. 6. 88, *ante-
stans, obtestans*, a purely Herodotean
use ; cp. L. & S.

This remarkable anecdote is framed in,
so to speak, at the beginning and the
end, by express reference to the source,
the authority. It comes in strangely
and out of place here, at the close of the
account of events on the Greek side, and
before the account of events on the
Persian side, to which it might rather
seem to belong ; but (i.) the Persian
army has already been introduced into
Attica, cc. 50–55 ; (ii.) chronologically
the event seems to belong to the very day
reached in c. 64.

66. 1. **οἱ δὲ . . ταχθέντες** : cp. οἱ δὲ
Ἑλλήνων . . ταχθέντες c. 1 *supra*.
The narrative is here resumed from c.
25 *ad f.*

2. **τὸ τρῶμα τὸ Λακωνικόν**, 'the
disaster to the Lakonians' they beheld
in seeing the corpse-exhibition, c. 25
supra. The Thespians are not here
taken any account of.

3. **ἐπισχόντες** : they 'halted,' or remained at rest, waited ; cp. ἐπισχών
5. 16.

Six days are here accounted for,
three of which are consumed by the
further halt at Histiaia, and three by

the voyage to Phaleron. These six
days are in succession to two days accounted for in c. 25 *supra*, upon the
second of which the naval forces were
occupied in getting back to Histiaia,
while the land-forces were getting under
way on their march through Phokis and
Boiotia to Athens. The previous day
had been devoted to sight-seeing at
Thermopylai ; the day before that the
king's fleet was occupied in advancing
from Aphetai to Histiaia (c. 23 *supra*).
Thus nine days in all are accounted for.
The first of these nine days is the day
immediately succeeding the fighting off
Artemision, which occupies three days,
exactly synchronizing *ex hypothesi* with
the engagements at Thermopylai : adding these three days it would appear
that the Persian fleet arrived at Phaleron
on the twelfth day after its arrival at
Aphetai, both events included.   The
fleet apparently finds the army in full
possession of Athens, but what interval
separated the arrival of army and of
fleet Hdt. does not specify.   If Xerxes
occupied the Athenian Akropolis in less
than a week after leaving Thermopylai,
having in the meantime ravaged at least
Phokis, and destroyed Plataiai and
Thespiai, his advance was a tolerably
rapid one.   In fact, it is hardly credible.
The log of the fleet may have been accurately preserved ; but the arrival of
fleet and army in Attica may have
synchronized, the apparent interval
being an illusion due to Hdt.'s method
in separating the accounts of synchronous
operations, and completing (relatively)
the story of one series before entering
on that of the other. He himself is here
more concerned with the material mass
than with the temporal motions of the
forces. Cp. Appendix VI. § 2.

4. **ὡς μὲν ἐμοὶ δοκέειν** : the construction

ἐμοὶ δοκέειν, οὐκ ἐλάσσονες ἐόντες ἀριθμὸν ἐσέβαλον ἐς τὰς 5
Ἀθήνας, κατά τε ἤπειρον καὶ τῇσι νηυσὶ ἀπικόμενοι, ἢ ἐπί
τε Σηπιάδα ἀπίκοντο καὶ ἐς Θερμοπύλας· ἀντιθήσω γὰρ τοῖσί
τε ὑπὸ τοῦ χειμῶνος αὐτῶν ἀπολομένοισι καὶ τοῖσι ἐν Θερμοπύλῃσι καὶ τῇσι ἐπ᾽ Ἀρτεμισίῳ ναυμαχίῃσι τούσδε τοὺς τότε
οὔκω ἑπομένους βασιλέι, Μηλιέας καὶ Δωριέας καὶ Λοκροὺς 10
καὶ Βοιωτοὺς πανστρατιῇ ἑπομένους πλὴν Θεσπιέων καὶ
Πλαταιέων, καὶ μάλα Καρυστίους τε καὶ Ἀνδρίους καὶ Τηνίους

5 δοκέει 8z, Cobet ‖ ἐσέβαλλον C   6 ἀπικόμενοι om. β, secl.
van H. ‖ ἐπεί z   10 Μηλιέας τε S, Gaisford, van H.   11
Θεσπιέων τε CPz, Gaisford, van H.

is an *asyndeton*, there is no δέ corresponding to μέν, the infinitive is *pendens*.
The judgement or calculation thus introduced by the historian and claimed as
his own is not to his credit, being flatly
contradicted by his own previous narrative, and in itself irrational. He judges
the forces of Xerxes by sea and by land
to have been as large, when they occupied Attica, before the battle of Salamis,
as they had been at their arrival off
Sepias and at Thermopylai. It is not
quite clear, perhaps, whether Hdt.
means to exclude the losses in the storm
off the Magnesian shore (as Blakesley
suggests); but even so, Blakesley finds
it impossible to conceive Hdt.'s statement as "at all near the truth, unless
enormous exaggeration is to be presumed
in the accounts of the engagements off
Artemision." But the more natural interpretation of this passage would refer
it back to 7. 183 *supra*, where the barbarians ἐξανύουσι τῆς Μαγνησίης χώρης
ἐπὶ Σηπιάδα—a statement at once followed
by the grossly exaggerated estimate of
the king's forces (7. 184–7), which is in
itself one of the greatest stumbling-blocks
in Hdt.'s historiography. His record of
the Persian losses at sea since that point
amount to upwards of 700 triremes: of
his original total 1327, only about 600
remain at this point, according to the
narrative, ἀξιόμαχοι. The notion that
these enormous losses could have been
made good by additions to the fleet
between Artemision and Phaleron is
patently absurd. The alternative presents itself: that the losses, and that
the original numbers themselves, have
been greatly exaggerated. But the
navy-list, though not free from miscalculation, is perhaps approximately

sound (cp. Appendix II. § 5). Hdt.'s
purpose is obvious, to identify the navy-
list for Salamis with the estimate and
lists already given, and so to glorify the
victory. He may have been encouraged
by the fact that Aischylos had given,
virtually, the maximum for Salamis.
Hdt. not merely asserts that all losses
had been made good, but also assumes
that the whole fleet came to Phaleron.
Probably on neither point is he correct.
The case of the army is not identical
with that of the fleet. Losses had been
lighter, and the supplements far greater.
The Hellenic troops in the army of
Mardonios are estimated at 50,000 (9.
32 *infra*). But Hdt. apparently makes
no allowance, in the case of army or of
fleet, for any guards or garrisons left *en
route*, or for the ordinary wear and tear
of warfare. He assumes that the whole
land-forces of the king invaded Attica:
that assumption, if true, would render
more than ever incredible the gross
exaggeration of his estimates, 7. 184 ff.
In any case the deliberate calculation
of Hdt. in this passage, as in 7. 184 ff.,
shows that he takes himself seriously as
a historian, precludes our treating him
merely as an irresponsible *raconteur*,
and goes far to justify the rigid application of *Sachkritik* to his methods and
results.

10. Μηλιέας . . Πλαταιέων: on the
Maliana, Lokrians, Boiotians cp. 7. 132;
on the Dorians 8. 31. For Thespiai and
Plataiai, c. 50 *supra*.

12. Καρυστίους: the geographical
position of Karystos is indicated in 4.
33 and 6. 99; the latter passage shows
that the Karystians had in 490 B.C.
resisted the 'barbarians,' though not
successfully. An attempt was made

τε καὶ τοὺς λοιποὺς νησιώτας πάντας, πλὴν τῶν πέντε πολίων
τῶν ἐπεμνήσθημεν πρότερον τὰ; οὐνόματα. ὅσῳ γὰρ δὴ προ-
15 έβαινε ἐσωτέρω τῆς Ἑλλάδος ὁ Πέρσης, τοσούτῳ πλέω ἔθνεά
οἱ εἵπετο.

67 Ἐπεὶ ὦν ἀπίκατο ἐς τὰς Ἀθήνας πάντες οὗτοι πλὴν
Παρίων (Πάριοι δὲ ὑπολειφθέντες ἐν Κύθνῳ ἐκαραδόκεον τὸν
πόλεμον κῇ ἀποβήσεται), οἱ δὲ λοιποὶ ὡς ἀπίκοντο ἐς τὸ
Φάληρον, ἐνθαῦτα κατέβη αὐτὸς Ξέρξης ἐπὶ τὰς νέας, ἐθέλων
5 σφι συμμεῖξαί τε καὶ πυθέσθαι τῶν ἐπιπλεόντων τὰς γνώμας.

---

13 τε post Τηνίους om. **α**   14 ἐπεμνήσθην **B**, Stein[1], Holder,
van H. ‖ προσέβαινε(ν V) **Bz**   15 ἐσωτέρωι **α**   67. 1 ἐπείτε ?
van H. ‖ ἀπικέατο Pz : ἀπίκετο **B** ‖ οὗτοι om. z   3 ἢ **B** : τῇ z   4
νῆας **Bz** ‖ θέλων **B**   5 συμμεῖξαί van H., Stein[3] : συμμῖξαί ‖ ἐπι-
πλωόντων **B**

---

in 480 B.C. to punish them for their
'medism'; cp. c. 121 infra. They were
afterwards subjected to Athens (cp. 9.
105), and assessed generally at five
talents (cp. Hill, Sources, p. 91).

Ἄνδρίους: for the position of
Andros cp. 4. 33, 5. 31. For the subsequent operations against it, cc. 108 ff.
infra.

Τηνίους: for the position of Tenos
cp. 4. 33, 6. 97; for the subsequent
patriotism of Tenos and its reward, cc.
82 f. infra.

13. τῶν πέντε πολίων: not counting
the Aiginetans or Euboian towns, six
island states have been enumerated in
the Greek navy-list (c. 46 supra), viz.
Keos, Naxos, Kythnos, Seriphos, Siphnos,
Melos; it is the first five, perhaps, which
are here referred to (Stein understands
Keos to be the one omitted). Paros also
has to be excepted, c. 67.

**14. τῶν ἐπεμνήσθημεν πρότερον τὰ
οὐνόματα**: the reference back is to c. 46
supra. The grammatical construction
is remarkable; cp. 6. 136. But the
accusatives, especially οὐνόματα here,
might be taken as of reference or limit,
rather than as directly objective.

προέβαινε ἐσωτέρω τῆς Ἑλλάδος:
cp. c. 60 supra προβήσονται ἑκαστέρω τῆι
Ἀττικῆς. 'Hellas' has here rather more
the appearance of a geographical sense,
even limited to the peninsula.

67. 1. ἀπίκατο ἐς τὰς Ἀθήνας: corrected, both as to time and place, just
below into ἀπίκοντο ἐς τὸ Φάληρον. The
city-name might pass for the country,
cp. 9. 17.

2. Πάριοι had paid dearly for Medism

in 489 B.C.; cp. 6. 133–5. They now
'remained behind' (ὑπολειφθέντες, cp.
5. 61, 9. 53) in Kythnos—itself on the
patriotic side, c. 46 supra—and like the
Korkyreans in the west, ἐκαραδόκεον
τὸν π., cp. 7. 168. This attitude of the
Parians seems to show—like the desertion of the Lemnian and the Tenian—
that the islanders by no means regarded
the triumph of the king as a foregone
conclusion.

3. οἱ δὲ λοιποί: the δέ resumptive,
after a parenthesis; cp. 7. 95 tot. verb.

τὸ Φάληρον, c. 66 supra. In 6.
116 it is described as 'at that time
(490 B.C.) the Athenian arsenal (ἐπίνειον)'
—perhaps because in the narrative there
the remark is of especial point in view
of the threatening pause of the Persian
fleet in the offing; or perhaps because
when Hdt. wrote that passage he had
a personal acquaintance with the Attic
harbours, which he still lacked when
writing this, Introd. §§ 6, 7.

4. κατέβη αὐτὸς Ξέρξης: the king
doubtless rode, or was driven down in
his open chariot or closed carriage (cp.
7. 41 supra); he surely would not be
walking from Athens. But it was an
effort of condescension; for Xerxes
might have summoned the council of
war to Athens if he had merely wished
to take advice. The king had not re-
viewed his fleet properly since Doriskos,
or at least since Therme (cp. 7. 44, 100,
127).

5. σφι: not the ships, but the men,
or their commanders. **τῶν ἐπιπλεόντων**:
cp. 7. 98 supra. With συμμεῖξαι cp.
c. 58 supra.

ἐπεὶ δὲ ἀπικόμενος προΐζετο, παρῆσαν μετάπεμπτοι οἱ τῶν
ἐθνέων τῶν σφετέρων τύραννοι καὶ ταξίαρχοι ἀπὸ τῶν νεῶν,
καὶ ἵζοντο ὥς σφι βασιλεὺς ἑκάστῳ τιμὴν ἐδεδώκεε, πρῶτος
μὲν ὁ Σιδώνιος [βασιλεύς], μετὰ δὲ ὁ Τύριος, ἐπὶ δὲ ὦλλοι.
ὡς δὲ κόσμῳ ἐπεξῆς ἵζοντο, πέμψας Ξέρξης Μαρδόνιον εἰρώτα 10
ἀποπειρώμενος ἑκάστου, εἰ ναυμαχίην ποιέοιτο. ἐπεὶ δὲ περιιὼν 68
εἰρώτα ὁ Μαρδόνιος ἀρξάμενος ἀπὸ τοῦ Σιδωνίου, οἱ μὲν ἄλλοι
κατὰ τὠυτὸ γνώμην ἐξεφέροντο κελεύοντες ναυμαχίην ποιέεσθαι,
Ἀρτεμισίη δὲ τάδε ἔφη. "εἰπεῖν μοι πρὸς βασιλέα, Μαρδόνιε,
ὡς ἐγὼ τάδε λέγω, οὔτε κακίστη γενομένη ἐν τῇσι ναυμαχίῃσι 5
τῇσι πρὸς Εὐβοίῃ οὔτε ἐλάχιστα ἀποδεξαμένη. δέσποτα, τὴν

---

7 ταξιάρχαι R || νηῶν Bz   8 ἐδέδωκε RS: ἐδέσδωκε V   9
βασιλεὺς Stein: del. Cobet, van H.   10 ἠρώτα CPz   11 ποιοῖντο α:
ποιέοιτο C   68. 1 ἐπείτε ? van H.   2 μὲν δὴ B, Holder,
van H. || ἄλλοι B, Wesseling   3 ἐπεφέροντο α   4 εἶπαι z, van H.
|| μοι om. B || βασιλῆα z   5 κακίστην γενομένην α   6 ἀποδεξαμένη
Pz : ἀποδεξαμένην αC : προσδεξαμένη B : πωδεξαμένη Marc. || δέσποτα.
PRz || τὴν δὲ : τήνδε S, Reiske : δὲ del. Valckenaer, van H.

---

6. προΐζετο : sedem altiorem, prae-
cipuam, cepit (occupabat ?), Baehr. The
others ἵζοντο, just infra. Cp. 4. 88
Δαρεῖον ἐν προεδρίῃ κατήμενον, and 7. 44
—the προεξέδρη on which Xerxes sat
(ἵζετο) at Abydos to review the fleet.
Similarly προκατιζόμενος 5. 12, and the
same word in the active 1. 14, 97.
ταξίαρχοι, as in 7. 99.

9. ὁ Σιδώνιος [βασιλεύς]: cp. App.
Crit. Stein defends the βασιλεύς on
account of the proximity of ταξίαρχοι,
in which case Σιδωνίων would be more
usual. Tetramnestos was his name, 7.
98 supra ; the Tyrian's was Mapen, ib.

10. Μαρδόνιον : why is Mardonios,
one of the six field-marshals (7. 82), thus
employed on this occasion, when there
were four admirals, including two 'of
the blood,' who commanded the fleet
(7. 97)? Blakesley replied that much
greater confidence was placed in his
strategic talents, and that he was perhaps regarded as the commander-in-chief
of both services. But Xerxes himself
surely occupies at present this position.
Mardonios figures here perhaps for
literary reasons, because he is one of the
leading dramatis personae, and it is high
time that something more were heard
of him ; he is needed as a foil to
Artemisia ; cp. cc. 100–102 infra. One
must not take this council too seriously ;

the Persian admirals are conspicuous by
their absence.

11. ἀποπειρώμενος ἑκάστου: cp. 6. 48.
68. 2. οἱ μὲν ἄλλοι . . 'Ἀρτεμισίη δέ
. . : cp. 5. 36 οἱ μὲν δὴ ἄλλοι πάντες
γνώμην κατὰ τὠυτὸ ἐξεφέροντο κελεύοντες
ἀπίστασθαι· Ἑκαταῖος δ' ὁ λογοποιὸς κτλ.
On Artemisia 7. 99 supra.

4. τάδε ἔφη, 'made the following
speech.' The very words are given of
the speech, and of a speech within the
speech.

εἰπεῖν μοι, 'prythee, say !'—imper.
infin. (cp. 7. 159 App. Crit.), and dativ.
ethic.

Artemisia claims to have distinguished
herself in the sea-fights off Euboia
(Artemision !), of which claim the sources
followed by Hdt. above apparently know
nothing. He is here, doubtless, drawing
upon his native traditions, and perhaps
composing rather freely.

6. τὴν δὲ ἐοῦσαν γνώμην : the δέ is
peculiar but, as Stein explains, may be
taken to express the antithesis between
the real or genuine (ἐοῦσαν) opinion,
which she expresses, and the unreal
opinions given by the others. But the
antithesis would be more pointed if it
lay between the persons—Artemisia on
the one side, the kings on the other—
than between the opinions. How little
τυγχάνω need connote of 'chance' is well

δὲ ἐοῦσαν γνώμην με δίκαιον ἐστὶ ἀποδείκνυσθαι, τὰ τυγχάνω
φρονέουσα ἄριστα ἐς πρήγματα τὰ σά. καί τοι τάδε λέγω·
φείδεο τῶν νεῶν μηδὲ ναυμαχίην ποιέο. οἱ γὰρ ἄνδρες τῶν
10 σῶν [ἀνδρῶν] κρέσσονες τοσοῦτο εἰσὶ κατὰ θάλασσαν ὅσον
ἄνδρες γυναικῶν. τί δὲ πάντως δέει σε ναυμαχίῃσι ἀνακινδυνεύειν; οὐκ ἔχεις μὲν τὰς Ἀθήνας, τῶν περ εἵνεκα ὁρμήθης
στρατεύεσθαι, ἔχεις δὲ τὴν ἄλλην Ἑλλάδα; ἐμποδὼν δέ τοι
ἵσταται οὐδείς· οἳ δέ τοι ἀντέστησαν, ἀπήλλαξαν οὕτω ὡς
15 κείνους ἔπρεπε. τῇ δὲ ἐγὼ δοκέω ἀποβήσεσθαι τὰ τῶν ἀντιπολέμων πρήγματα, τοῦτο φράσω. ἢν μὲν μὴ ἐπειχθῇς
ναυμαχίην ποιεύμενος, ἀλλὰ τὰς νέας αὐτοῦ ἔχῃς πρὸς γῇ
μένων ἢ καὶ προβαίνων ἐς τὴν Πελοπόννησον, εὐπετέως τοι
δέσποτα χωρήσει τὰ νοέων ἐλήλυθας. οὐ γὰρ οἷοί τε πολλὸν
20 χρόνον εἰσί τοι ἀντέχειν οἱ Ἕλληνες, ἀλλὰ σφέας διασκεδᾷς,
κατὰ πόλις δὲ ἕκαστοι φεύξονται. οὔτε γὰρ σῖτος πάρα σφι
ἐν τῇ νήσῳ ταύτῃ, ὡς ἐγὼ πυνθάνομαι, οὔτε αὐτοὺς οἰκός, ἢν
σὺ ἐπὶ τὴν Πελοπόννησον ἐλαύνῃς τὸν πεζὸν στρατόν, ἀτρεμιεῖν

---

9 νηῶν ΒΡz ‖ ποίεε Β: ποιέεο z ‖ τοί, γάρ z   10 ἀνδρῶν secl.
Stein² ‖ τοσοῦτό αC, Stein¹, Holder, van H.: τοσοῦτον   11 δεῖ
Holder, van H.   12 εἵνεκεν Β, van H. ‖ ὡρμήθης Β, Stein¹   14
ἀνέστησαν : ἀντίσταται Β ‖ οὕτως Β   15 ἐκείνοις z ‖ δ᾽ αΡz ‖ δοκέωι Β
17 ποιεόμενος Β ‖ νῆας Βz   18 ἢ om. Β   21 πόλις δὲ α : δὲ
πόλις Ρz : πόλεις δὲ C : πόλιας δέ τοι Β ‖ σφι Stein : σφίσι   22
αὐτὸς Β   23 ἐλαύνεις R ‖ ἀτρεμέειν ΒΡz

---

illustrated by the context (it has as
much affinity with τέχνη as with τύχη).

9. οἱ γὰρ ἄνδρες . . γυναικῶν: cp. 7.
210 supra, where something nearly as
bad is said of the fighting on land, and
c. 88 infra, where Xerxes remembers
this shrewish mot, with a difference.
Cp. 9. 107, which shows how bitter was
the taunt even to the barbarian. In
vilipending the fleet Artemisia apparently
would make a silent exception for the
Greek contingents ! cp. l. 30 infra.

12. ἔχεις μέν, 'thou art in possession
of . .' ἔχῃς just below, 'keep.'

τῶν περ . . στρατεύεσθαι: cp. 7.
4. Athens is the goal of the expedition.
'The rest of Hellas' was hardly to be
included in the actual possessions of the
king, so long as Peloponnesos, to say
nothing of the West, remained.

15. ἀντιπολέμων = ἀντιπολεμίων : cp.
7. 236, 4. 184, 140.

18. ἢ καὶ προβαίνων ἐς τὴν Πελο-

πόννησον. Artemisia too is credited
with the idea previously ascribed to
Demaratos, 7. 235 supra, of an advance
on the Peloponnesos, but with a difference : she appears to advocate a weak
blockade of Salamis and an advance by
the army (cp. below, ἢν σὺ ἐπὶ τὴν Πελοπόννησον ἐλαύνῃς τὸν πεζὸν στρατόν).
Such an advance, she argues, will dissipate
and scatter the Hellenes—apparently
that is the Hellenic fleet at Salamis,
who are to be allowed and encouraged
to break up κατὰ πόλις. They must be
looking for a ναυμαχίη, as shortage of
provisions would in any case compel them
either to fight or to dissolve. 'Refuse
battle by sea, push on by land,' is
Artemisia's plan—a distinctly inferior
plan to that ascribed to Demaratos l.c.
Artemisia underrates the defensibility of
the Isthmos, which, apart from naval co-
operation, the Greeks could have held for
ever ; the gates into Peloponnesos were
across the water ; cp. cp. 9. 9 infra.

τοὺς ἐκεῖθεν αὐτῶν ἥκοντας, οὐδέ σφι μελήσει πρὸ τῶν Ἀθηνέων
ναυμαχέειν. ἢν δὲ αὐτίκα ἐπειχθῆς ναυμαχῆσαι, δειμαίνω 25
μὴ ὁ ναυτικὸς στρατὸς κακωθεὶς τὸν πεζὸν προσδηλήσηται.
πρὸς δὲ ὦ βασιλεῦ καὶ τόδε ἐς θυμὸν βάλευ, ὡς τοῖσι μὲν
χρηστοῖσι τῶν ἀνθρώπων κακοὶ δοῦλοι φιλέουσι γίνεσθαι, τοῖσι
δὲ κακοῖσι χρηστοί. σοὶ δὲ ἐόντι ἀρίστῳ ἀνδρῶν πάντων
κακοὶ δοῦλοι εἰσί, οἳ ἐν συμμάχων λόγῳ λέγονται εἶναι ἐόντες 30
Αἰγύπτιοί τε καὶ Κύπριοι καὶ Κίλικες καὶ Πάμφυλοι, τῶν
ὄφελος ἐστὶ οὐδέν." ταῦτα λεγούσης πρὸς Μαρδόνιον, ὅσοι 69
μὲν ἦσαν εὔνοοι τῇ Ἀρτεμισίῃ, συμφορὴν ἐποιεῦντο τοὺς
λόγους ὡς κακόν τι πεισομένης πρὸς βασιλέος, ὅτι οὐκ ἐᾷ
ναυμαχίην ποιέεσθαι· οἱ δὲ ἀγεόμενοί τε καὶ φθονέοντες αὐτῇ,
ἄτε ἐν πρώτοισι τετιμημένης διὰ πάντων τῶν συμμάχων, 5

---

24 οὐδὲ Stein[3] (fortuito ?): μελήσειν van H. e Plutarch. Mor. 870
25 ναυμαχῆσαι: ναυμαχέειν β   26 προσδηλήσεται α: προδηλήσεται
P: προδηλήσηται βz   27 βαλέο α   28 φιλοῦσι α   30 δοῦλοί
εἰσι Az, Stein[1] || ἐν om. β || εἶναι om. β   69. 2 ἔσαν z || ἐποιεῦντο β
3 βασιλῆος z || ἐᾶι α: ἐᾶ β: ἔα Reiske, Holder, van H.   4 ἀγεόμενοί
BCSV: ἀγαιόμενοί AR, Holder, van H.   5 τετιμημένη z

---

27. ἐς θυμὸν βάλευ: 7. 51. Cp. *Iliad*
1. 297. The aphorism which follows
is not a very sound one; rather, one
might say, 'Good masters (and still
more good mistresses) make good
servants.' If the slaves and subjects
of Xerxes were indeed such as Artemisia
described them, it was a condemnation
of the master, of the system. Still more
absurd is her converse: The better the
master, the worse the slave! But is
not Hdt. himself aware of all this? Is
not the perverted aphorism, put into
the mouth of Artemisia, a hit at the
tyrant, and the *tyrannis*? Is there not
a little malice at the woman's expense?
The lines quoted by Wesseling from
Naumachios *ap.* Stob. lxxi. p. 438 fin.
are not identical in sentiment with the
Herodotean, but rather a plea for the
via media—

μήτε κακὴ ὁμιόεσσι τεοῖς ἔσο· μήτε μάλ'
ἐσθλή
φαίνεο· ῥηίτεροι γὰρ δεί του πῆμα φέρονται.
θάρσεῖ δειδιότων μάλ' ἐπικρατέουσιν ἄνακτες.

30. ἐν συμμάχων λόγῳ: Artemisia
apparently implies that the only persons
deserving the honourable title of the
king's allies were Hellenes—like herself.
The non-Hellenic members of the fleet—
Egyptians, Kyprians, Kilikians, Pam-

phylians—are born slaves, and naturally
worthless for fighting purposes. But
she does not venture so to taboo the
Phoenicians. Mardonios amends her
list, c. 100 *infra*.

According to the navy-list, 7. 89 ff.,
the Egyptians furnished 200 ships, the
Kyprians 150, the Kilikians 100, the
Pamphylians 30, a total of 480 ships.
This might conceivably represent one
squadron of the whole fleet, if it was
divided *tripartito*; cp. 7. 97.

69. 1. ταῦτα λεγούσης: sc. τῆς γυναικός. She had her friends, and her
enemies, as the context suggests.

2. συμφορὴν ἐποιεῦντο: cp. c. 100
infra, 5. 5.

3. οὐκ ἐᾷ: vetabat, dissuadebat; cp.
cc. 36, 61 *supra*. The opt. (ἐᾴη) would
be in order here but less graphic and
forcible.

5. ἄτε . . τετιμημένης below appears
to be co-ordinate with ὡς πεισομένης
above—the gen. abs. following a dat.
(as often)—except that the one is a
conjecture, the other a matter of fact;
but had Hdt. written τετιμημένη it
would (as Stein observes) have transformed the fact, alleged by the historian,
merely into the motive experienced by
her envious enemies. ἀγεόμενοί τε καὶ
φθονέοντες: cp. 6. 61 φθόνῳ καὶ ἄγῃ

ἐτέρποντο τῇ ἀνακρίσι ὡς ἀπολεομένης αὐτῆς. ἐπεὶ δὲ ἀνηνείχθησαν αἱ γνῶμαι ἐς Ξέρξην, κάρτα τε ἤσθη τῇ γνώμῃ τῇ
Ἀρτεμισίης, καὶ νομίζων ἔτι πρότερον σπουδαίην εἶναι τότε
πολλῷ μᾶλλον αἴνεε. ὅμως δὲ τοῖσι πλέοσι πείθεσθαι ἐκέλευε,
10 τάδε καταδόξας, πρὸς μὲν Εὐβοίῃ σφέας ἐθελοκακέειν ὡς οὐ
παρεόντος αὐτοῦ, τότε δὲ αὐτὸς παρεσκεύαστο θεήσασθαι
ναυμαχέοντας.

70   Ἐπεὶ δὲ παρήγγελλον ἀναπλέειν, ἀνῆγον τὰς νέας ἐπὶ

---

6 ἀνακρίσει **a** : κρίσει **Β** : κρίσι Holder, van H. ‖ ἐπειδὴ **Β** : ἐπείτε ?
van H.   7 ξέρξεα **Βz** ‖ τῆι ἀρτεμισίης AB : τῆς ἀρτεμισίης   9
πλείοσι **Β**   11 παρεσκεύαστο deleto, θεήσεσθαι pos. Naber, van H.
70. 1 ἐπειδὴ **Β**, Holder, van H. ‖ παρήγγελον A¹V : παρήγγελλεν (sic)
Valckenaer, van H. ‖ ἀναπλώειν **Βz** ‖ νῆας **Βz**

χρεώμενος (Demaratos: was he among
Artemisia's rivals here ?).
δι πάντων, as in c. 37 supra.
6. The meaning of ἀνάκρισις—discep-
tatio—appears to be guaranteed by
ἀνακρινομένους 9. 56 infra, otherwise
ἀποκρίσι or κρίσι might rather be
expected here ; cp. App. Crit.
8. ἔτι πρότερον, 'still earlier'—just
as we say, ἔτι being used with any
comparative, to strengthen it—and not
necessarily = ἤδη, though no doubt ἤδη
would give an excellent sense with the
temporal adverb. σπουδαίην, sc. τὴν
γυναῖκα.
10. καταδόξας, as in 3. 27.
ἐθελοκακέειν is imperfect.
ὡς οὐ παρεόντος αὐτοῦ, 'in his
absence,' as matter of fact ; a reason in
Xerxes' mind, though not suggested as
a reason which had been in their minds.
11. τότε δέ, 'but now'—αὐτός, though
in the oratio obliqua—'he had made all
preparations to see them fight at sea.'
παρεσκεύαστο : the pl.p. pass. in
midd. or active sense is remarkable.
Cp. App. Crit.
70. 1. ἐπεὶ δὲ παρήγγελλον : what interval, if any, intervened between the
resolution of Xerxes to do battle and
the ἀνάπλοος of the fleet, does not appear.
The grammatical subject of παρήγγελλον
is also obscure : is it οἱ τῶν ἐθνέων τῶν
σφετέρων τύραννοι καὶ ταξίαρχοι of c. 67
supra, or is it not rather οἱ τοῦ ναυτικοῦ
στρατηγοί (7. 97)? Whatever it is, the
subject of ἀνῆγον is different : those
who issue and those who execute one
and the same order cannot be identical.
Hdt. apparently assumes that the whole
fleet was together at Phaleron.

ἀνῆγον κτλ. : though ἀνῆγον is the
imperfect, παρεκρίθησαν διαταχθέντες is a
perfect aorist, and bars the assumption
that the ἀνάπλοος was not accomplished :
it was for ναυμαχίην ποιήσασθαι that
daylight failed.   The exact position,
however, occupied by the fleet, when
this ἀνάπλοος was carried out completely,
is not clearly defined by the words ἐπὶ
τὴν Σαλαμῖνα. Leake, followed by Grote,
argued that the movement here described
took the Persian ships right into the
straits, and ended in their being drawn
up in battle-array along the Attic shore,
facing the Greeks in the bay of Salamis.
That argument is in so far justified as
it gives point to the statement immediately succeeding, τότε μέν νυν . .
ναυμαχίην ποιήσασθαι, for this statement
seems to imply that the Persians have
reached a position in which they have it
in their power to deliver an attack.
Possibly Hdt. so conceived the situation
(as far as he had any clear and distinct conception in the matter), but
nevertheless Leake's theory cannot be
correct or true to the facts.   For
reasons given elsewhere (cp. Appendix
VI. § 3) it is incredible that the Persian
fleet entered the straits by daylight and
took up a position in order of battle
opposite the Greeks in the bay of
Salamis. Nor do the words of Hdt. in
this passage, which no doubt reproduce
what he had heard or read, of necessity
imply any such absurdity. The Persian
ships moved from Phaleron upon Salamis
to attack the Greeks, and reached a
position in battle-array ; but whether
that position was within or outside the
straits is not expressly stated, nor is

τὴν Σαλαμῖνα καὶ παρεκρίθησαν διαταχθέντες κατ' ἡσυχίην.
τότε μέν νυν οὐκ ἐξέχρησέ σφι ἡ ἡμέρη ναυμαχίην ποιήσασθαι·
νὺξ γὰρ ἐπεγένετο· οἱ δὲ παρεσκευάζοντο ἐς τὴν ὑστεραίην.
τοὺς δὲ Ἕλληνας εἶχε δέος τε καὶ ἀρρωδίη, οὐκ ἥκιστα δὲ 5
τοὺς ἀπὸ Πελοποννήσου· ἀρρώδεον δέ, ὅτι αὐτοὶ μὲν ἐν
Σαλαμῖνι κατήμενοι ὑπὲρ γῆς τῆς Ἀθηναίων ναυμαχέειν μέλλοιεν,
νικηθέντες τε ἐν νήσῳ ἀπολαμφθέντες πολιορκήσονται, ἀπέντες

---

3 (ἐξήρκεσε ? van H.) ‖ ποιέεσθαι z   4 τε γὰρ β ‖ ἐγένετο Pz ‖
εἰς B, Holder   8 ἀφέντες a

---

its orientation given. As the Persians were allowed to carry out this manœuvre without being disturbed, the inference would rather be that, as far as the movement went this day, it was all outside the straits.

2. **παρεκρίθησαν διαταχθέντες κατ' ἡσυχίην**: these words mean that they were allowed to take up a position, squadron by squadron, parallel to, or alongside of, some given line or object. On the διάταξις cp. 7. 34, 124, 178. In 9. 98 *infra* we have πολλὸν δὲ πεζὸν παρακεκριμένον παρὰ τὸν αἰγιαλόν. The foot-soldiers are necessarily on land, but drawn up along-shore. In the present instance παρὰ τὸν αἰγιαλὸν is wanting; and even if it were supplied, the question would arise, what or which shore ? The only indication of direction in this passage is in the words ἐπὶ τὴν Σαλαμῖνα —the παράταξις (so to speak) is *prima facie* παρὰ τὴν Σαλαμῖνα, or secondly παρ' ἀλλήλους—simply in parallel lines, the whole position being indefinite, but presumably outside the straits. If 'Salamis' with the article in Hdt. always denoted 'the town' as distinct from 'the island,' this passage would, indeed, carry them inside the straits ; but no such canon obtains.

It is, however, quite possible that Hdt. has gone too far in reporting for this precise point the occupation of a position, wherever it was, by the Persian fleet, in battle - array ; the ἀνάπλοος may have begun, but παρεκρίθησαν διαταχθέντες may be incorrect and premature. Or, again, the διάταξις, two, may have been complete, and the reason why no battle ensued may be, not that night descended on the Persians, but that the Greek fleet remained ensconced in the bay of Salamis, and would not respond to the challenge, or come out to do battle with the king's fleet in the open waters.

The precise day upon which the ἀνάπλοος took place and battle was offered, but not accepted, by the Greeks, is clearly the day before the actual battle, and as such would apparently coincide with the day in cc. 64, 65 *supra*, of the earthquake by sea and land, and the vision of Dikaios and Demaratos. If an earthquake really took place that morning, it speaks volumes for the courage of the Persians that they were prepared to go out to battle.

4. **οἱ δὲ παρεσκευάζοντο ἐς τὴν ὑστεραίην**: these words can hardly cover a return to land, and a fresh start, so to speak ; rather the implication seems to be that the Persian fleet remained at sea. The δέ is associated with the grammatical subject, iterated for sake of emphasis (cp. 7. 50).

5. **τοὺς δὲ Ἕλληνας**: the scene shifts back to the Greek laager, the time is not changed, the day in c. 64 above coinciding with the day in this, but night has apparently fallen, and the tone of the narrative, the temper of the Greeks, is completely transformed ! There they had decided to do battle (but not for a day or two, not until they can summon, or fetch, the Aiakids from Aigina !) : here they are seized with fear and trembling.

6. **αὐτοὶ μέν**: the antithesis is indirectly supplied below by τῶν δὲ βαρβάρων κτλ. They were likely to be shut up in Salamis, while the Peloponnesos was being invaded by the landforces of the Persians (Artemisia's plan, cp. c. 68). The sequence μέλλοιεν—πολιορκήσονται—ἐπορεύετο is observable. Stein takes the last sentence (τῶν δὲ βαρβάρων κτλ.) as simply explanatory of the words immediately preceding : other editors make it begin a new chapter or paragraph.

8. **νικηθέντες . . πολιορκήσονται**: cp. c. 49 *supra*, εἰ νικηθέωσι τῇ ναυμαχίῃ

I

τὴν ἑωυτῶν ἀφύλακτον. τῶν δὲ βαρβάρων ὁ πεζὸς ὑπὸ τὴν
71 παρεοῦσαν νύκτα ἐπορεύετο ἐπὶ τὴν Πελοπόννησον. καίτοι
τὰ δυνατὰ πάντα ἐμεμηχάνητο ὅκως κατ' ἤπειρον μὴ ἐσβάλοιεν
οἱ βάρβαροι. ὡς γὰρ ἐπύθοντο τάχιστα Πελοποννήσιοι τοὺς
ἀμφὶ Λεωνίδην ἐν Θερμοπύλῃσι τετελευτηκέναι, συνδραμόντες
5 ἐκ τῶν πολίων ἐς τὸν Ἰσθμὸν ἵζοντο, καί σφι ἐπῆν στρατηγὸς
Κλεόμβροτος ὁ Ἀναξανδρίδεω, Λεωνίδεω δὲ ἀδελφεός. ἱζόμενοι

---

71. 2 τὰ δυνατὰ del. Krueger, van H. ‖ ἐμβάλοιεν B : ἐσβάλλοιεν z
4 λεωνίδεα B 5 τὲ ἐκ B 6 ὁ om. α

ἐν Σαλαμῖνι μὲν ἐόντες πολιορκήσονται ἐν
νήσῳ. The Greeks, in fact, are back in
the state of mind before—or perhaps
more truly just after—the capture of
the Akropolis; the resolution of the
preceding night goes for nothing. Artemisia, c. 68 supra, seems to deny the
possibility of their standing a siege in
the island, for lack of provision. There
is no similar suggestion here. She,
however, had advised the king to avoid
battle at sea, and restrict his naval
operations to a blockade. The Greeks
anticipate a defeat.

9. τῶν δὲ βαρβάρων . . ἐπὶ τὴν
Πελοπόννησον : we must suppose this a
fact, even if it is an element in their
fear. Towards nightfall on the day on
which the Persian fleet had moved up
on Salamis, the Persian army was
known to be on the march for the
Isthmos, moving in the cool. The
movement of the army must surely
stand in some relation to the movement
of the fleet; Artemisia had proposed it
as an alternative (c. 68 supra).

Were Dikaios and Demaratos with
this army, or army-column, when they
had their vision, c. 65 supra?

Was there, in fact, any demonstration
by land against the Peloponnesos?
From Eleusis to the Isthmos was some
thirty miles. Was some movement of
the land-forces, designed to enable them
to co-operate with the fleet in the
impending battle, misinterpreted as an
advance on the Peloponnese? Or is the
march quite surely timed? Is it certain
that it took place just on this day, and
at nightfall? There is a considerable
margin of possible error in this assertion.
The comprehension of strategic movements and plans depends upon the nicest
chronological accuracy of days and hours;
and it is risky work reconstructing them
from so casual and haphazard a writer
as Hdt.

ὑπὸ τὴν παρεοῦσαν νύκτα, cp. 9.
58 infra.

71. 1. καίτοι, 'and yet'—they need
not have been so mightily afraid, nor
was their own country ἀφύλακτος—it
had been rendered impregnable, as far
as the land route was concerned: and
they must have known it! There were
three measures of defence: i. The Σκιρωνὶς
ὁδός had been broken up and rendered
impassable. ii. A wall had been built
across the isthmus. iii. Just behind
that wall was laagered a large army,
under command of the Spartan Regent.
Yes, κατ' ἤπειρον Peloponnese was safe.
A movement of the Persian army in
that direction could not have caused
consternation in Salamis. Had the
Persian fleet shown signs of moving in
that direction there would have been
more ground for apprehension; cp. c.
68 supra.

2. ἐμεμηχάνητο : the pluperfect here
has its full temporal force, as also
τετελευτηκέναι just below.

3. ὡς . . τάχιστα, 'as soon as ever'
they knew the fate of Leonidas and
his men. How soon would that have
been? Long before the arrival of the
Persian in Attica, and even before the
arrival of the Greek fleet at Salamis.
What follows might almost seem to be
regarded by Hdt. as a spontaneous, and
so fortuitous, concourse of armed men
to the Isthmos: no doubt the movement
was in response to Spartan command.
But the army may have been under
orders to mobilize, nay, may have been
under way. Was not this the very force
that should have been in Boiotia? Cp.
c. 40 supra.

6. Κλεόμβροτος ὁ Ἀναξανδρίδεω,
Λεωνίδεω δὲ ἀδελφεός. Not much
can be made out of this notice under
the head of Composition; see 7. 205
supra. The mere patronymic would
prove little. Yet this passage may be

δὲ ἐν τῷ Ἰσθμῷ καὶ συγχώσαντες τὴν Σκιρωνίδα ὁδόν, μετὰ
τοῦτο ὥς σφι ἔδοξε βουλευομένοισι, οἰκοδόμεον διὰ τοῦ Ἰσθμοῦ
τεῖχος. ἅτε δὲ ἐουσέων μυριάδων πολλέων καὶ παντὸς ἀνδρὸς
ἐργαζομένου, ἤνετο τὸ ἔργον· καὶ γὰρ λίθοι καὶ πλίνθοι καὶ 10
ξύλα καὶ φορμοὶ ψάμμου πλήρεες ἐσεφέροντο, καὶ ἐλίννον
οὐδένα χρόνον οἱ βοηθήσαντες ἐργαζόμενοι, οὔτε νυκτὸς οὔτε

---

7 σκειρωνίδα β, van H.　　　8 ᾠκοδόμεον z　　　9 μυριάδων ABP :
μυριαδέων　　　10 ἤνετο A¹B : ἤρετο C : ἠνύετο　　　11 ἐσεφορέοντο β,
Holder, van H.

---

of older composition than the other,
as it almost certainly is older than
5. 41. Why does not Hdt. add here
that Kleombrotos was Regent for
Pleistarchos? Cp. 9. 10 infra.

7. τὴν Σκιρωνίδα ὁδόν: between
Megara and Krommyon, and so to the
Isthmos ; Strabo 391 μετὰ δὴ Κρομμυῶνα
ὑπερκεῖνται τῆς †Αττικῆς <ἀκτῆς> αἱ
Σκειρωνίδες πέτραι πάροδον οὐκ ἀπολεί-
πουσαι πρὸς θαλάττῃ· ὑπὲρ αὐτῶν δ'
ἐστὶν ἡ ὁδὸς ἡ ἐπὶ Μεγάρων καὶ τῆς
Ἀττικῆς ἀπὸ τοῦ Ἰσθμοῦ· οὕτω δὲ
σφόδρα πλησιάζει ταῖς πέτραις ἡ ὁδὸς
ὥστε πολλαχοῦ καὶ παράκρημνός ἐστι
διὰ τὸ ὑπερκείμενον ὄρος δυσβατόν τε
καὶ ὑψηλόν: Pausanias 1. 44. 7 (10)
τὴν δὲ ὀνομαζομένην ἀπὸ Σκίρωνος καὶ
ἐς τόδε (ὁδὸν) Σκίρων, ἡνίκα Μεγαρεῦσιν
ἐπολεμάρχει, πρῶτος, ὥς λέγουσιν, ἐποίησεν
ἀνδράσιν ὁδεύειν εὐζώνοις. Ἀδριανὸς δὲ
[ὁ] βασιλεὺς καὶ οὕτως, ὡς καὶ ἦν ἅρματα
ἐναντία ἐλαύνηται, κατέστησεν εὐρυχωρῆ
τε καὶ ἐπιτηδείαν εἶναι. It is described
as it existed in the middle of the last
century, a proverbial Via Mala (Kaki
Skala), in Curtius's Peloponnesos i. (1851),
p. 9, when it was again a mere foot-
path. But Hadrian can hardly have
been absolutely the first to make it
available for vehicles. Perhaps the
Peloponnesians on this occasion were
destroying a road adapted for wheels.
The verb συγχώσαντες implies a made
road or causeway. (σκῖρος perhaps
means 'hard-rock.' Strabo 393 mentions Σκιράς among several old names
for the island of Salamis ; cp. c. 94
infra.) There went at least one (cp.
Blakesley, Rawlinson), if not two, other
roads (Curtius l.c.) through the Megarid
to the Peloponnesos : the Skironian was
the shortest, and, bad as it may have
been, presumably the easiest.

8. ὡς σφι ἔδοξε βουλευομένοισι suggests a formal and deliberate plan,
without precisely dating it. There was
room for discussion : ought they not to
have marched into Boiotia? Cp. c. 40
supra. They substitute the defence of
the Peloponnesos for the defence of
Attica.

οἰκοδόμεον διὰ τοῦ Ἰσθμοῦ τεῖχος.
It was not finished for some time—not
till the summer of 479 B.C., if we may
trust 9. 8 infra. Blakesley remarks that
the wall was not built at the narrowest
point of the isthmus, but further south,
from Lechaeum to Cenchreae (cp. Pausan.
7. 6. 7), "with a view of preventing a
debarkation <immediately> in the rear
of the defending force." E. Curtius,
however, Pelop. i. 14, places the wall at
the narrowest part ; cp. below.

9. μυριάδων πολλέων: a vague but
large estimate, which, if anywhere near
the truth, makes it the more surprising
that the work was still unfinished in the
following summer ; 9. 8 infra.

10. ἤνετο: from ἄνω, 'radic. form of
ἀνύω, ἀνύτω' ; cp. 7. 20 supra ; Il. 18.
473 ὅπως Ἥφαιστός τ' ἐθέλοι καὶ ἔργον
ἄνοιτο. The imperfect tense is here
emphatic. The materials of the wall
are remarkable. λίθοι for foundation ;
πλίνθοι for the superstructure ; ξύλα
for palisading, towers, etc. ; φορμοὶ
ψάμμου, either to be used for filling
holes or the sand for making mortar.
The visible traces of building which
still remain hardly go back to 480 B.C.
The wall seems to have been rebuilt in
279 B.C. (Pausan. l.c. supra), as also by
Valerian 253 A.D., and three centuries
later by Justinian, and in modern times
by the Venetians against the Turk ; cp.
Curtius l.c. ; Baedeker's Greece (1889),
p. 233. The line of wall is immediately
south of the Diolkos (cp. Strabo 335).

11. ἐλίννον: cp. 7. 56 supra.

72 ἡμέρης.　οἱ δὲ βοηθήσαντες ἐς τὸν Ἰσθμὸν πανδημὶ οἵδε ἦσαν
Ἑλλήνων, Λακεδαιμόνιοί τε καὶ Ἀρκάδες πάντες καὶ Ἠλεῖοι
καὶ Κορίνθιοι καὶ Σικυώνιοι καὶ Ἐπιδαύριοι καὶ Φλειάσιοι καὶ
Τροιζήνιοι καὶ Ἑρμιονέες. οὗτοι μὲν ἦσαν οἱ βοηθήσαντες
5 καὶ ὑπεραρρωδέοντες τῇ Ἑλλάδι κινδυνευούσῃ· τοῖσι δὲ

---

72. 1 βωθήσαντες β, van H. ‖ πανδημὶ οἵδε Holder, van H.: πανδημεὶ
οἵδε **α** : πανδημεὶ οἵδε Stein : πανδήμιοι δὲ **β** ‖ ἔσαν z (bis)　　　2 καὶ
πάντες RV　　4 βωθήσαντες β, (ὑπεραρρωδέοντες καὶ βωθήσαντες,
van H.)

---

72. 1. οἱ δὲ βοηθήσαντες . . παν-
δημί: evidently some great credit is
taken for this βοήθεια : in six lines the
title or term is used thrice, the effort
is emphasized (πανδημί), the complete
list of folks represented in the muster
is given *nominatim*, the rest of the
Peloponnesians are stigmatized for their
indifference. Yet, in truth, what the
Spartans and their allies deserved was
a severe censure for broken pledges,
and the selfish abandonment of Attica.
This Isthmian wall was no credit to the
Peloponnesians, and hardly consistent
with Spartan principles (though they
had used the wall at Thermopylai likewise, 7. 176 *supra*). The levy for
Plataia was also πανδημί, i.e. the two-
thirds, or all save οἱ πρεσβύτεροι and οἱ
νεώτεροι, and the figures for Plataia
would give a total here of not less than
22,000 hoplites, while, of course, large
masses of ψιλοί and of slaves would have
been employed upon the actual building.
2. **Λακεδαιμόνιοι.** It is perhaps not
to be assumed that Sparta sent as many
men to the Isthmos in 480 B.C. as to
Plataia in 479 B.C. (supposing the figures
for the latter to be correct, 9. 28).
Ἀρκάδες πάντες. Tegea, Mantineia, Orchomenos would certainly be
included — and probably other places.
The phrase is remarkable, as though
relative to a κοινὸν τῶν Ἀρκάδων. At
Thermopylai the Arcadians are represented by 2120 men, 7. 202. But what
of the medizers, c. 26 *supra* ?
Ἠλεῖοι : no figure is given for their
contingent at Plataia ; cp. 9. 77 *infra*.
They could number at least 1000
hoplites.
3. **Κορίνθιοι,** if they sent 5000 to
Plataia, might certainly send 5000 to
the Isthmos, though they have a squadron at Salamis, and had only sent 400
to Thermopylai ; 7. 202.

Σικυώνιοι had at least fifteen ships
at Salamis (cp. c. 43 *supra*), and sent
3000 hoplites to Plataia.
Ἐπιδαύριοι — like Korinth represented at Salamis, and by ten ships—
sent but 800 hoplites to Plataia.
Φλειάσιοι have a Chiliad at
Plataia in 479 B.C., but only 200 at
Thermopylai, 7. 202 *supra*, and are unrepresented at Salamis.
4. **Τροιζήνιοι** have five ships at
Salamis, and send 1000 men to Plataia
next year.
Ἑρμιονέες have three ships at
Salamis, and were to send 300 hoplites to
Plataia.
This list of nine states named as sending contingents to the Isthmos is curious,
and not on the face of it authoritative.
The figures for each contingent are left
to be inferred or conjectured ; and, what
is worse, there may be omissions in it.
Were not the *Megarians* too, who had
twenty ships at Salamis, and sent 3000
hoplites to Plataia in 479 B.C., also
behind the wall ? The order in which
the contingents are named is odd, the
Phleiasians at least curiously breaking
into the geographical continuity.
5. **καὶ ὑπεραρρωδέοντες** : i.e. they
are more afraid even than their fellow-
citizens at Salamis ! For themselves—
or for the fleet ? Only the latter would
be to their credit : the fate of Hellas
hung on the fleet. If so, the βοήθεια at
the Isthmos must be conceived as
intended to co-operate with the fleet :
perhaps Kleombrotos is counting on the
fleet falling back on the Isthmos.
τοῖσι δὲ ἄλ. Π. ἔμελε οὐδέν : a
sentence which obviously betrays the
apologetic purpose of the passage ; it
must be false, so far as the list is incomplete, and it is hardly likely to have
been strictly true in any case—even of
Argos, etc.

ἄλλοισι Πελοποννησίοισι ἔμελε οὐδέν. Ὀλύμπια δὲ καὶ
Κάρνεια παροιχώκεε ἤδη. οἰκέει δὲ τὴν Πελοπόννησον ἔθνεα 73
ἑπτά, τούτων δὲ τὰ μὲν δύο αὐτόχθονα ἐόντα κατὰ χώρην
ἵδρυται νῦν τε καὶ τὸ πάλαι [οἴκεον], Ἀρκάδες τε καὶ

---

6 ἔμελε P : ἔμελλε α (-ν β)   7 κάρνια βP   73. 2 τουτέων z ‖
αὐτώχθενα B   3 τε : τῇ Schaefer, Stein[1], Holder, van H. : τὴν Koen ‖
οἴκεον secl. Stein[2] (τε redintegrato) ‖ τε om. z

---

6. Ὀλύμπια . . Κάρνεια . . ἤδη
appears to be a clear reference back to
7. 206 supra, and a reference of a kind
which could occur only in a work
intended for a reading public. The
passing of the festivals sets the Peloponnesians free to occupy the Isthmos
πανδημί. But the story has advanced
long past the Olympia : the 'night'
in c. 70 supra is the night of Boëdromion
20. One might perhaps suppose with
safety that as soon as the Olympia were
over, certainly as soon as the news of
the end of Leonidas reached Sparta, the
move to the Isthmos was made — if,
indeed, it was not rather a halt of the
forces which were on their way into
Central Greece, to support Leonidas (cp.
7. 203 supra), or to cover Attica (c. 40
supra).

73. 1. ἔθνεα ἑπτά : Hdt. gives the
ethnography of the Peloponnesos, not
its geographical divisions, which only
partially coincide with the ethnography.
Of the seven ἔθνεα therein, Hdt. regards
two as autochthonous and in occupation
of their original seats, viz. Arkadians
and Kynurians ; a third, the Achaians,
as autochthonous, but migrant within
the Peloponnese itself. The four others
are immigrant, ἐπήλυδα, Dorians, Aitolians, Dryopians, Lemnians ; see further
the notes below. The Homeric Catalogue
may be taken as recognizing six groups
in Peloponnesos (Il. 2. 559–624) : i. οἱ δ'
Ἄργος τ' εἶχον κτλ. (559–568) = Argolis.
ii. οἱ δὲ Μυκήνας εἶχον κτλ. (569–580) =
Achaia. iii. οἱ δ' εἶχον κοίλην Λακεδαίμονα κτλ. (581–590) = Lakonia. iv. οἱ δὲ
Πύλον κτλ. (591–602) = Messenia. v. οἱ
δ' ἔχον Ἀρκαδίην κτλ. (603–614) = Arkadia.
vi. οἱ δ' ἄρα Βουπράσιόν τε καὶ Ἤλιδα
δῖαν ἔναιον κτλ. (615–624) = Elis. Thucyd.
1. 10. 2 may be understood to divide
the Peloponnesos into five equal fractions,
assigning two to the Spartans—a division
which disregards ethnology and geography alike ; unless, indeed, we are to
read it in the light of Pausan. 5. 1. 1—

a passage obviously composed in view of
Thucydides : ὅσοι δὲ Ἑλλήνων Πελοποννήσου πέντε εἶναι μοίρας καὶ οὐ πλείονάς
φασιν, ἀνάγκη σφᾶς ὁμολογεῖν, ὡς ἐν τῇ
Ἀρκάδων οἰκοῦσιν Ἠλεῖοι καὶ Ἀρκάδες,
δευτέρα δὲ Ἀχαιῶν, τρεῖς δὲ ἐπὶ ταύταις
αἱ Δωριέων (sc. Messenia, Lakonia,
Argolis. Thucydides, by the way,
reckons Messenia as part of Lakonia,
in accordance with the political situation
in his own time, which clearly shows
that his 'fifths' are arithmetical fractions,
not geographical). Pausanias continues
(with an obvious reference to this passage
in Hdt.) : γένη δὲ οἰκεῖ Πελοπόννησον
Ἀρκάδες μὲν αὐτόχθονες καὶ Ἀχαιοί. καὶ
οἱ μὲν ὑπὸ Δωριέων ἐκ τῆς σφετέρας
ἀνέστησαν, οὐ μέντοι Πελοποννήσου γε
ἐξεχώρησαν, ἀλλὰ ἐκβαλόντες Ἴωνας νέμονται τὸν Αἰγιαλὸν τὸ ἀρχαῖον, νῦν δὲ ἀπὸ
τῶν Ἀχαιῶν τούτων καλούμενον· οἱ δὲ
Ἀρκάδες διατελοῦσιν ἐξ ἀρχῆς καὶ ἐς τόδε
τὴν ἑαυτῶν ἔχοντες. τὰ δὲ λοιπὰ ἐπηλύδων
ἐστὶν ἀνθρώπων. Κορίνθιοι μὲν γὰρ οἱ νῦν
. . Δρύοπες δὲ καὶ Δωριεῖς, οἱ μὲν ἐκ
Παρνασοῦ, Δωριεῖς δὲ ἐκ τῆς Οἴτης ἐς
Πελοπόννησόν εἰσιν ἀφιγμένοι. τοὺς
Ἠλείους ἴσμεν ἐκ Καλυδῶνος διαβεβηκότας
καὶ Αἰτωλίας τῆς ἄλλης. Pausanias then
specifies—for the Hellenic period—
Arkadians, Achaians, (Ionians), Dorians,
Dryopians, Aitolians. (Could ζ' or η'
have dropped out after γένη δέ ?)

2. κατὰ χώρην ἵδρυται emphasizes
the local fixity of the two autochthonous
ἔθνεα specified.

3. νῦν τε καὶ τὸ πάλαι : the date of
this 'Now' is unfortunately obscure ;
no doubt the remark would hold good
of any day in Hdt.'s whole life, but the
precise date of the composition of this
chapter is a curiosity ; cp. Introduction,
§ 9.

The passage contains five illustrations
of the force of τε καί worth observing :
here, (1) of the absolute continuity of
past and present ; just below, (2) of
Arkadians and Kynurians, as belonging
to one class, and further, (3) of Dorians

Κυνούριοι· ἐν δὲ ἔθνος τὸ Ἀχαιικὸν ἐκ μὲν Πελοποννήσου
5 οὐκ ἐξεχώρησε, ἐκ μέντοι τῆς ἑωυτῶν, οἰκέει δὲ τὴν ἀλλοτρίην.
τὰ δὲ λοιπὰ ἔθνεα τῶν ἑπτὰ <τὰ> τέσσερα ἐπήλυδα ἐστί,
Δωριέες τε καὶ Αἰτωλοὶ καὶ Δρύοπες καὶ Λήμνιοι· Δωριέων

---

4 ἀχαιικὸν A²BP: ἀχαϊκὸν   6 <τὰ> Stein³ ‖ τέσσαρα CR
7 καὶ Δωριέων z

---

and Aitolians, who came in perhaps
together, (4) of Hermion and Asine,
cities of one folk, while (5) in 'the
many famous cities' the conjunction is
so close as to disappear altogether in
our idiom.

Ἀρκάδες: to Hdt. the Arkadians
are Pelasgians, cp. 1. 146, 2. 171, and
βαλανηφάγοι ἄνδρες ap. orac. 1. 66.
Tegea (1. 66 etc.), Mantineia (4. 161 etc.),
Orchomenos (7. 202), Nonakris (6. 74),
Pheneos (ibid.), Phigaleia (6. 83), Trapezûs
(6. 127), Paion (ibid.), Dipaia (9. 35), and
indirectly Stymphalos (6. 76), are mentioned among the cities of Arkadia.
Arkadians are serving on the king's fleet
from Kypros (7. 90), and perhaps as
mercenaries in his army (c. 26 supra).

4. Κυνούριοι, described just below
as Ionians, and nowhere else mentioned
expressly by Hdt. Thuc. 4. 56. 2 enables
us to identify their territory: ἀφικνοῦνται
ἐπὶ Θυρέαν, ἥ ἐστι μὲν τῆς Κυνουρίας γῆς
καλουμένης μεθορία δὲ τῆς Ἀργείας καὶ
Λακωνικῆς: cp. 5. 14. 4, and 41. 2 περὶ τῆς
Κυνουρίας γῆς ἧς αἰεὶ πέρι διαφέρονται
μεθορίας οὔσης (ἔχει δὲ ἐν αὐτῇ Θυρέαν καὶ
Ἀνθήλην πόλιν, νέμονται δ᾽ αὐτὴν Λακεδαιμόνιοι). The great chapter out of the
ἔρις περὶ χώρου καλεομένου Θυρέης is told
above 1. 82; of Kynurian Anthele Hdt.
appears to know nothing; and it is remarkable that in one place he speaks of
Thyrea as the χώρη in debate. All this
does not look as if he had knowledge of
the operations in the district during the
Archidamian war (424 B.C., Thuc. 4. 56,
57) or even of the settlement of the
Aiginetans there after their expatriation
in 431 B.C. (6. 91, Thuc. 2. 27. 2).

τὸ Ἀχαιικόν: what the strict
ethnological relation of the Achaians to
the Pelasgians (Arkadians) and Ionians
of the Peloponnese Hdt. nowhere clearly
indicates. Were they also (in his
opinion) Pelasgians? Topographically he
must place them south of their historic
province, probably in Lakonia. Historic
Achaia, with its Dodekapolis, had been
Ionian before it was Achaian, according
to Hdt. 1. 145. The relation of the

'Achaians' of Peloponnesos to the
'Achaians' of Thessaly is not a problem
about which Hdt. concerns himself; cp.
7. 196 supra.

ἐκ μὲν Πελοποννήσου οὐκ ἐξεχώρησε: is it possible that Hdt. did not
trace the 'Achaian' settlements in Italy
to the Peloponnesos? Or the 'Achaians'
in Krete to the same source (Od. 19.
175)? Or does he merely mean by these
words that the Achaian stock has not
completely evacuated the Peloponnese,
though it has shifted from one place to
another within it? τῆς ἑωυτῶν: sc.
historic Lakonia. τὴν ἀλλοτρίην: sc.
historic Achaia.

7. Δωριέες: the legend of the Dorian
invasion, or of 'the Return of the
Herakleids,' is in part narrated 9. 26
infra, and everywhere presupposed in
Hdt.; cp. c. 31 supra.

Αἰτωλοί: Hdt. apparently is acquainted with a form of the legend, which
made Aitolians accompany or guide the
Dorian invaders from 'Naupaktos'; but
he nowhere expressly refers to the legend
of Oxylos (Pausan. 5. 3. 5).

Δρύοπες: the 'Dryopian' invasion
of the Peloponnesos, which left its mark
in Hermion and Asine, is doubtless conceived by the Greek historians as long
prior to the Dorian, though it started,
according to one story, from the same
quarter or cradle (Strabo 434 τὴν Δρυοπίδα
τετράπολιν γεγονυῖάν ποτε καθάπερ καὶ
τὴν Δωρίδα, μητρόπολιν δὲ τῶν ἐν Πελοποννήσῳ Δρυόπων νομιζομένην). They had
quarrelled with Herakles in their native
Dryopis, and been banished by him to
the South. (Diodoros 4. 37; Strabo,
etc.) The geographical positions of the
Dryopians in historical times (cp. c. 43
supra) suggests a sea-route for the migration—if, indeed, the whole legend be
not a fiction, and the Dryopians of
historic times fragments of a wide-spread
stratum of early population. According
to 'Aristotle' ap. Strabon. 373 Dryops
was an Arkadian.

Λήμνιοι, evidently a consequence
of the legend narrated 4. 145; but

μὲν πολλαί τε καὶ δόκιμοι πόλιες, Αἰτωλῶν δὲ Ἦλις μούνη, Δρυόπων δὲ Ἑρμιών τε καὶ Ἀσίνη ἡ πρὸς Καρδαμύλῃ τῇ Λακωνικῇ, Λημνίων δὲ Παρωρεῆται πάντες. οἱ δὲ Κυνούριοι 10 αὐτόχθονες ἐόντες δοκέουσι μοῦνοι εἶναι Ἴωνες, ἐκδεδωρίευνται

8 πόλις α: πόλεις C   9 ἑρμιων Α¹Β: ἑρμιῶν R: ἑρμηῶν
V: ἑρμιώνη Α²C: ἑρμιόνη P8z   10 παρωραιῆται β(S ?)   11
ἐκδεδωρίευνται Pz: ἐκ δὲ δωρίευνται β: ἐκδεδωριᾶται α: ἐκδεδωρίωνται
Valckenaer, van H.: ἐκδεδωρίδαται Dindorf

'Lemnian' is hardly an ethnic designation. Why does not Hdt. here call them *Minyai*? Does he expect his readers to have that passage in mind ? And is this passage of later composition or insertion ? (Cp. Introduction, § 9.) But see below.

8. **δόκιμοι πόλιες**: e.g. Sparta, Argos, Korinth, Sikyon, Phleiûs, Epidauros, Troizen, *et al*.

Ἦλις μούνη. This phrase can hardly be quoted (as by Blakesley) to prove that the passage is 'a later addition' to the work of Hdt., for even if Strabo 336 were right in saying that the city of Elis did not exist at the time of the Persian war, still it existed before any part of the work of Hdt. But Strabo probably overstates his case. Elis increased owing to a συνοικισμός shortly after the Persian war, Diodor. 11. 54. 1 (471 B.C.) (cp. 4. 148 *supra*), but there was a city of Elis already ; cp. Homer, *Il.* 2. 615, cited above.

9. **Ἑρμιών**, cp. c. 43 *supra*, in the SE. of the Argolis peninsula. It was celebrated as the spot from which there was the shortest cut down to Hades. Strabo 373.

Ἀσίνη: the place here mentioned is on the east coast of Messenia, i.e. on the west side of the Μεσσηνιακὸς κόλπος (Strabo 359), not to be confused with the Asine in Lakonia, in the neighbourhood of Helos, visited by the Athenians in 424 B.C. (Thuc. 4. 54. 4), though possibly identical with the Asine mentioned in two other places in Thucydides (4. 13. 1, 6. 93. 3). It may have derived its name from an older settlement in close proximity to Hermion, *Il.* 2. 560, the inhabitants of which sided with the Spartans in the Messenian and Argive wars, and were expelled by the Argives, but given a new home by the Lakedaimonians, Strabo 373 ; Pausan. 2. 36. 4, 3. 7. 4.

ἡ πρὸς Καρδαμύλῃ: expressly to distinguish it from the one in Argolis, which, if still existing, was a mere village (Strabo *l.c.*). But has Hdt. correctly located it, or can πρός here mean 'opposite' 'over against' ? Kardamyle was in the realm of Menelaos of old : σημεῖον δέ· ἐκ γὰρ τοῦ Μεσσηνιακοῦ κόλπου καὶ τοῦ συνεχοῦς Ἀσιναίου λεγομένου ἀπὸ τῆς Μεσσηνιακῆς Ἀσίνης αἱ ἑπτὰ ἦσαν πόλεις, ἃς ὑπέσχετο δώσειν ὁ Ἀγαμέμνων τῷ Ἀχιλλεῖ " Καρδαμύλην Ἐνόπην τε κτλ." (*Il.* 9. 150, 295) Strabo 359. Bursian (ii. 154) describes it as situate about 5 miles (*zwei Stunden*) N. of Leuktra, and 1 mile (20 min.) from the coast, upon a steep rock, the village still preserving the name, *Skardamyla*.

τῇ Λακωνικῇ: to distinguish it from any other place of the same name, e.g. the city on Chios mentioned by Thucyd. 8. 24. 3.

10. **Παρωρεῆται**: according to 4. 148 the 'Paroreatai' and 'Kaukones' had been driven out of their cities by the Minyai (i.e. the Lemnians); here Hdt. appears to identify the Paroreatai with the Lemnians (i.e. Minyai) or with a part of them. The two passages must be regarded as independent, even though the Lemnian legend underlies this one. The two peoples stood on the same ground. Strabo 346 ἐλέγοντο δὲ Παρωρεᾶται τινὲς τῶν ἐν τῇ Τριφυλίᾳ κατέχοντες ὄρη περὶ τὸ Λέπρειον καὶ τὸ Μάκιστον καθήκοντα ἐπὶ θάλατταν πλησίον τοῦ Σαμακοῦ ποσειδίου. The name no doubt means the inhabitants of the Παρωρεία, which means 'the Highland'—though why L. & S. place this particular Paroreia in 'Arcadia,' unless by confusion with the town mentioned by Pausanias 8. 27. 3, is not obvious. The name is found in Thrace (Livy 39. 27) and even on the Euxine (*C.I.G.* 2058, B 17).

11. **μοῦνοι εἶναι Ἴωνες**: Hdt. appears to think that the 'Kynurians' were Ionians, and the only Ionians remaining in the Peloponnesos. As they occupy their original abode, he must conceive

δὲ ὑπό τε Ἀργείων ἀρχόμενοι καὶ τοῦ χρόνου, ἐόντες Ὀρνεῆται
[καὶ οἱ περίοικοι]. τούτων ὦν τῶν ἑπτὰ ἐθνέων αἱ λοιπαὶ
πόλιες, πάρεξ τῶν κατέλεξα, ἐκ τοῦ μέσου κατέατο· εἰ δὲ
15 ἐλευθέρως ἔξεστι εἰπεῖν, ἐκ τοῦ μέσου κατήμενοι ἐμήδιζον.
74 Οἱ μὲν δὴ ἐν τῷ Ἰσθμῷ τοιούτῳ πόνῳ συνέστασαν ἅτε
περὶ τοῦ παντὸς ἤδη [δρόμου] θέοντες καὶ τῇσι νηυσὶ οὐκ

12 ἀρχόμενοι del. Cobet, van H. ‖ καὶ ὑπὸ τοῦ (participio retento)
Schaefer, Krueger ‖ χρόνου <προϊόντος> Stein³ ‖ ὀρνεᾶται α 13
καὶ οἱ περίοικοι secl. Stein²: οἱ om. β: verba ἐόντες .. περίοικοι mihi
suspecta ‖ τουτέων βPz 14 πόλις α: πόλεις C ‖ ἐκαθέατο α:
ἐκατέατο β 15 εἶπαι z, van H. 74. 2 δρόμου del. Lobeck:
an δρόμον?

the Ionians as originally occupying more
ground in the Peloponnesos than the
historic Achaia.

ἐκδεδωρίευνται, 'they have become'
more Dorian than the Dorians, or, at
least, 'thoroughly dorized.' Cp. App.
Crit. But what to Hdt. were the notes
of Dorism, apart from descent?—dialect,
1. 139; dress, 5. 88; organization, 5.
68; perhaps cult, 5. 72. It is, indeed,
curious how little there is to distinguish
the Dorians as such; but of course to
Hdt. they are the Ἕλληνες κατ' ἐξοχήν:
cp. 1. 56, 5. 88, 7. 93 etc. At the time
Hdt. wrote this passage Thyrea can
hardly yet have been in the hands of
the Aiginetans; in other words, it
makes against the theory of the late
composition of Bks. 7-9 (cp. Introduction, § 9), and even against dating the
composition, or insertion, of this chapter
to the final revision (ibid. § 10).

12. ὑπό τε Ἀργείων ἀρχόμενοι καὶ
τοῦ χ.: the participle is exegetical, after
Argives. χρόνου is in direct regimen
from the preposition, 'by their subjection
to the Argives and by lapse of time.'
Stein's last lection (cp. App. Crit.),
reducing the construction to a simple
genit. absol., waters down a forcible
phrase.

Ὀρνεῆται: Orneai is known to
the Homeric Catalogue, Il. 2. 571, in
the Mykenaian (or Achaian) group (cp.
l. 1 supra); it certainly was not in
Kynuria; cp. Strabo 376, Pausan. 2.
25. 5. If this whole phrase be not (as
I suspect) a gloss (cp. App. Crit.), it
must be inferred, with K. O. Müller
(Dorier² i. 85, 160, etc.), that Orneai
had been reduced by Argos before the
Persian war, or at least before the date
of Hdt.'s composition, and that, like
the Caerites at Rome, the Orneatai gave

their name to a political status—resembling that of the perioikoi in Laconia.
At the battle of Mantineia in 418 B.C.
the Orneatai are described, with the
Kleonaians, as ξύμμαχοι of the Argives
(Thuc. 5. 67. 2), and the reduction and
destruction of Orneai is recorded later,
in 415 B.C. (Thuc. 6. 7. 2). The city
was at that time occupied by Argive
exiles, supported by a Lakedaimonian
garrison (Diodor. 12. 81. 4).

14. πάρεξ τῶν κατέλεξα: the construction is by attraction. The phrase, remarkable as a reference back to c. 72,
might perhaps support the view that c.
73 is a later insertion from the author's
hand; or would not Hdt. have used
the perfect rather than the aorist if cc.
72-73 had been originally written in
einem Flug?

εἰ δὲ ἐλευθέρως ἔξεστι εἰπεῖν. Why
should there be any difficulty about free
speech, free writing? Hdt. has an
audience, or a reading public in view,
which may be offended by his verdict.
Is that public found in the 'Achaian'
colonies of Italy? Or in Athens, at a
time when the alliance with Argos, with
Achaia, might be 'in the air'? The
ethnography of the Peloponnesos might
have had special interest for either
public.

15. ἐκ τοῦ μέσου κατήμενοι ἐμήδιζον.
This verdict appears much more severe
than the apology for the Argives in 7.
152 supra, and might well belong to a
different stratum, a different draft, in
the composition of the work.

74. 1. πόνῳ συνέστασαν: cp. λιμῷ
συνεστεῶτας 7. 170, and ἔχοντι δέ οἱ
τοῦτον τὸν πόνον 1. 206. Baehr observes
that συνέστασαν is plus-quam perfectum
in sense, and compares κατέστησαν 2. 30.

2. περὶ .. θέοντες: cp. 7. 57 περὶ

ἐλπίζοντες ἐλλάμψεσθαι· οἱ δὲ ἐν Σαλαμῖνι ὅμως ταῦτα
πυνθανόμενοι ἀρρώδεον, οὐκ οὕτω περὶ σφίσι αὐτοῖσι δειμαίνοντες ὡς περὶ τῇ Πελοποννήσῳ. τέως μὲν δὴ αὐτῶν ἀνὴρ 5
ἀνδρὶ παραστὰς σιγῇ λόγον ἐποιέετο, θῶμα ποιεύμενοι τὴν
Εὐρυβιάδεω ἀβουλίην· τέλος δὲ ἐξερράγη ἐς τὸ μέσον.
σύλλογός τε δὴ ἐγίνετο καὶ πολλὰ ἐλέγετο περὶ τῶν αὐτῶν,
οἱ μὲν ὡς ἐς τὴν Πελοπόννησον χρεὸν εἴη ἀποπλέειν καὶ
περὶ ἐκείνης κινδυνεύειν μηδὲ πρὸ χώρης δοριαλώτου μένοντας 10

3 ἐλλάμψεσθαι CP : ἐλάμψεσθαι s : ἐνλάμψεσθαι ‖ σαλαμῖνι ἕλληνες
Βz ‖ πυνθανόμενοι ταῦτα Β   5 πελοπονήσω Β(?) ‖ τέως Reiske : ἕως
‖ αὐτέων s   6 θῶμα Pz, Stein¹ ‖ ποιεύμενος z : ποιεόμενος Β
8 αὐτέων s   9 χρεὼν CPdz ‖ ἀποπλώειν Βz, van H.   10 δορυα-
λάτου s

ἑωυτοῦ τρέχων. δρόμον might be better
than δρόμου ; cp. App. Crit.

τῇσι ν. οὐκ ἐλπ. ἐλλάμψεσθαι,
'having no hope (expectation) of success
(glory) at sea.' Cp. 1. 80 τὸ ἱππικόν, τῷ
δή τι καὶ ἐπεῖχε ἐλλάμψεσθαι ὁ Λυδός.
But this despair at the Isthmos is
unworthy (i.) of the previous record and
present position of the fleet ; (ii.) of the
plan to co-operate therewith ; (iii.) of the
misgivings on the other side—probably
not unknown to the Greeks. Moreover,
strategically, it involves an absurdity,
for unless the Greek fleet could hold its
own against the Persian, the wall at the
Isthmos would be worse than useless.

3. οἱ δὲ ἐν Σαλαμῖνι : the scene shifts
back to the time and place of c. 70
supra, but the temper of the Greeks
at Salamis is changed ; there they were
nervous on their own account, primarily
anticipating defeat and blockade in
Salamis, while Peloponnese was left exposed. Now, on hearing of the wall,
the army, and all (ταῦτα πυνθανόμενοι),
they drop their selfish fears and are
terror-struck (ἀρρώδεον, cp. c. 72 and c.
70) on account of the Peloponnesos !
This argument and motivation is not
very good. The ταῦτα might, perhaps,
be referred, or made to include, the
medism in the Peloponnesos—but that
was hardly news (πυνθανόμενοι) to them ;
and in any case the point remains that
'the Greeks' are not really afraid of
the result of a naval battle, but wish
to win it at the Isthmos.

5 ff. τέως μὲν δή, 'for a while'—there
was only silent, or at least private,
criticism (σιγῇ λόγον ἐποιέετο), one man

to another, all expressing their astonishment at the folly of Eurybiades : at last
(τέλος δέ) they could stand it no longer
—things came to a head—the storm
burst openly—a meeting came together,
and the whole question was opened
afresh. (ἐξερράγη, app. impers. ; and cp.
3. 133 of a tumour (φῦμα . . ἐκραγέν)
and 6. 129 ἐκραγῆναι ἔς τινα. ἐς τὸ μέσον,
cp. 7. 152.)

Very graphic, but not quite coherent.
Is this in the night which has come
over the scene in c. 70 supra ? The men
are plainly ashore. Who are the actors,
or speakers ? The general body of
Epibatai, or only the Strategoi ? Is the
σύλλογος a public meeting (cp. c. 83
infra), or is it the Synedrion ? These
points are not clear in the story, or in
the mind of the historian.

8. περὶ τῶν αὐτῶν is rather obscure
and clumsy, even if a reference back to
the discussion reported cc. 59-63.

9. οἱ μέν : sc. λέγοντες, as though
ἔλεγον had immediately preceded ; const.
ad sensum.

These would be the Korinthians, and
perhaps Sikyonians, Epidaurians, etc.
They treat the ἀπόπλοος as still completely
open to them. This could not be the
case if the Persian fleet had, in c. 70,
entered the straits and taken up a
position facing the bay of Salamis.
This party is prepared to fight, but
proposes to change the venue.

10. περί . . πρό : the prepositions have
both local and causal force.

δοριαλώτου : cp. 9. 4. The word
looks poetical but is found in Xenophon
and orators ; cp. ἡ αἰχμή 7. 152 supra.

μάχεσθαι, Ἀθηναῖοι δὲ καὶ Αἰγινῆται καὶ Μεγαρέες αὐτοῦ
75 μένοντας ἀμύνεσθαι. ἐνθαῦτα Θεμιστοκλέης ὡς ἐσσοῦτο τῇ
γνώμῃ ὑπὸ τῶν Πελοποννησίων, λαθὼν ἐξέρχεται ἐκ τοῦ

11 δὲ : τε B   12 μένοντες B ‖ ἀμυνέεσθαι R : ἀμύνασθαι z

12. **ἀμύνεσθαι** rather suggests, though
not quite conclusively, that they expect
attack and are prepared to act on the
defensive. The Athenians, Aiginetans,
Megarians have a common interest, and
pull together; cp. c. 60 *supra*.

75. 1. **Θεμιστοκλέης ὡς ἐσσοῦτο τῇ
γνώμῃ** : a strange phrase to be used of
Themistokles ! cp. 9. 122 *infra*. Themistokles surely had much the best of the
argument, cp. c. 60 *supra* ; and he is
backed by the Aiginetans and Megarians.
The phrase is, indeed, a concession to
the necessities of the false tradition,
which represents the Peloponnesians as
resolved, at all costs, to abandon
Salamis. But ἐσσοῦτο (i.q. ἡσσᾶτο) is
of course imperfect, and therefore, perhaps, not quite conclusive.

2. **λαθὼν ἐξέρχεται ἐκ τ. συνεδρίου.**
This is plainly a meeting of the
Strategoi (cp. c. 78 *infra*), and it would
be at least the third recorded in Hdt.
(cp. cc. 49-56, 59-64 *supra*). It is
apparently being holden at night—like
the previous one !—and the night would
be Boëdromion 20 (by Attic reckoning ;
cp. c. 65. 19), on which the Persian army
was reported or believed to be moving
ἐπὶ τὴν Πελοπόννησον, c. 70 *supra*, while
the Persian fleet had been manœuvring
all, or most of the day previous, with a
view to bringing about a battle : *ibid*.
These manœuvres, these movements, may
well have given rise to fresh debate
among the Greek Strategoi. The question
would be, whether to assume the
offensive, or to await attack : and if the
offensive was to be assumed (as at
Artemision, cp. c. 9 *supra*), at what
particular point : were the Greeks to
advance right out of the straits—as the
Persians appeared to desire—and to
encounter the king's fleet in comparatively open water ! Or were they to
allow, or to induce, the Persian admirals
to enter the narrow waters, and to
expose themselves, in entering, to a
flank attack ?
It is possible that the Peloponnesians
were prepared to go out into the open
waters : the move to the Isthmos, the
selection of the open water there as the
scene of the engagement which (all

agreed) had to be fought somewhere,
might almost justify the suspicion that
the Peloponnesians were now advocating
an advance against the Persian fleet in
the open waters to the S. of Salamis.
But such an hypothesis were rash. To
fight in the open water off the Isthmos,
the bay of Kenchreai, with the Peloponnesos immediately in the rear to fall
back upon, is one thing ; but in the
open water off Salamis, another. The
risk of being shut up and besieged in
Salamis was, indeed, not in that case
inevitable ; they might make good their
escape, if needs were, to the Peloponnese ;
but still, with difficulty, and not without risk of being surrounded and cut off,
which would not be possible, in the bay
of Kenchreai.
To fight at Salamis, and in the narrow
waters between Salamis and the Attic
shore, was clearly the plan of Themistokles. But to procure the realization
of this plan, the Persian fleet should
enter the straits ; and it had not yet
done so (cp. c. 70 *supra*). His problem
was to bring that movement about.
The Persians presumably wished to fight
in the open waters off Salamis : some of
the Peloponnesians perhaps preferred to
fight in the less open, but also less confined, waters of the bay of Kenchreai.
But the plan of Themistokles had
been already endorsed and adopted.
The movement of the Persian army
towards the Peloponnese (if it really
was moving thitherwards) could not
affect that plan. What did affect it
was the clear perception that the Persian
admirals had apparently no intention of
entering the straits : how, indeed, could
they venture to do so, with the Greek
fleet drawn up in the bay of Salamis,
ready to charge them in flank ? A
debate might very well arise among the
Greek Strategoi as to the means of
inducing the Persian fleet to enter the
channel. Such a debate once started,
the previous question may possibly have
been raised again, as to whether the
Greek fleet had not better make for the
Isthmos. A battle had to be fought
somewhere. If the Persians would not
fight in closed waters, the battle must

συνεδρίου, ἐξελθὼν δὲ πέμπει ἐς τὸ στρατόπεδον τὸ Μήδων
ἄνδρα πλοίῳ ἐντειλάμενος τὰ λέγειν χρεόν, τῷ οὔνομα μὲν
ἦν Σίκιννος, οἰκέτης δὲ καὶ παιδαγωγὸς ἦν τῶν Θεμιστοκλέος 5
παίδων · τὸν δὴ ὕστερον τούτων τῶν πρηγμάτων Θεμιστοκλέης

---

75. 4 χρεὸν **a**: χρῆν **B**: χρεών   5 σίκυννος **C**: σίκινος **Bz**
|| θεμιστοκλούς **R**: θεμιστοκλέους **V**: θεμιστοκλῆος **z**   6 τῶν
πρηγμάτων τούτων **B** || τουτέων **z** || ὁ θεμιστοκλέης **B**

---

be fought in the open. The bay of Kenchreai was clearly more favourable to the Greek chances than the open waters off Salamis. The ruse of Themistokles, presently related, undoubtedly led to the battle in the straits ; but it is extremely difficult to believe that in effectuating that ruse he acted without the knowledge and connivance of his colleagues (see below) ; it is, therefore, difficult to believe that at this stage at least the question of retreating to the Isthmos was again seriously debated. The real problem before the council was to devise, or to accept, a plan by which the Persians might be induced at dawn of day to be entering the straits. The plan devised, employed, perhaps expounded, by Themistokles was a bold one, not to be accepted without discussion.

The notion that Themistokles could slip unobserved out of the *Synedrion*, the debate still continuing without him, make his elaborate arrangements, remain outside for hours, until Aristeides arrives to report that the ruse is successful, the Persian fleet already fully surrounding the island, and then reenter the council—still sitting—with the startling news, is simply absurd. Moreover, the reception of the news seems to show that the Greek admirals are not taken by surprise. The story, as told by Aischylos, lends absolutely no support to the tradition that the plan of Themistokles was devised as much against the Greeks themselves, his colleagues, as against the Persians, their enemies.

3. **ἐς τὸ στρατόπεδον τὸ Μήδων.** It is not clear above, in c. 70, whether Hdt. conceives the Persian fleet, after the manœuvres of the day, as remaining at sea, or as returning to Phaleron. This passage seems to imply that the admirals at least are ashore, for τὸ στρατόπεδον can hardly be used consciously for the fleet at sea. From

Salamis to Phaleron it would take a man in a boat some hours to go and return—to say nothing of obtaining his interview with the Persian admirals. The admirals (οἱ στρατηγοὶ τῶν βαρβάρων, cp. c. 67 *supra*) make their appearance here again ; in Aischylos the messenger from the Greek camp has audience of the king himself (*Pers.* 355 f.).

5. **Σίκιννος.** The name is Greek (cp. Σίκινος ἡ, the island), Aischyl. *Pers.* 355 makes the messenger a Greek, and Plutarch *Them.* 12 is probably wrong in calling this man a 'Persian' (cp. c. 110 *infra*), though he was, no doubt, a 'domestic slave,' and 'paedagogue' or tutor. Themistokles had five sons in all, Plutarch *Them.* 32 ; but Polyainos 1. 30. 3 has παιδαγωγὸς τοῦ παιδοῦ—so perhaps he had only two in 480 B.C., or two of age to have a tutor.

6. **τὸν δὴ ὕστερον . . ὄλβιον**: the emancipation, enfranchisement, enrichment of Sikinnos followed, presumably, soon after the battle of Plataiai, and, of necessity, before the ostracism of Themistokles (in 473 or 472 ?). The rebuilding and restoration of Thespiai, by the admission of citizens, was, of course, necessitated by its ruin in the war ; cp. 7. 222 and c. 50 *supra*. The active ἐποίησε is remarkable : was the business actually entrusted to Themistokles ? Thespiai may be expected to have 'atticized' subsequently : but the Thespians in 424 B.C. were severely handled by the Athenians in the battle of Oropos (Delion), Thuc. 4. 96. 3, a misfortune which enabled the Thebans shortly afterwards to demolish the walls ; *ib.* 133. 1. Ten years later there was an abortive *coup d'état* by the atticizing party, Thuc. 6. 95. 3, and the dominant faction sent hoplites to Syracuse to take part in the ruin of the Athenian armada (*ib.* 7. 19. 3, 25. 3). In the next century Thespiai is the chief basis of the Spartan operations against Thebes, during the decade

Θεσπιέα τε ἐποίησε, ὡς ἐπεδέκοντο οἱ Θεσπιέες πολιήτας, καὶ
χρήμασι ὄλβιον· ὃς τότε πλοίῳ ἀπικόμενος ἔλεγε πρὸς τοὺς
στρατηγοὺς τῶν βαρβάρων τάδε. " ἔπεμψέ με στρατηγὸς ὁ
10 Ἀθηναίων λάθρῃ τῶν ἄλλων Ἑλλήνων (τυγχάνει γὰρ φρονέων
τὰ βασιλέος καὶ βουλόμενος μᾶλλον τὰ ὑμέτερα κατύπερθε
γίνεσθαι ἢ τὰ τῶν Ἑλλήνων πρήγματα) ¦φράσοντα ὅτι οἱ
Ἕλληνες δρησμὸν βουλεύονται καταρρωδηκότες, καὶ νῦν
παρέχει κάλλιστον ὑμέας ἔργων ἀπάντων ἐξεργάσασθαι, ἢν

---

7 πολιήτας S: πολίτας　　9 ἔπεμψε ὁ στρατηγὸς a (-ν ὁ C) ‖ ὁ
om. aC　　11 βασιλῆος ✼ ‖ μᾶλλον om. B ‖ κατυπέρτερα B　　12
γενέσθαι Pz　　13 βούλονται B　　14 ἔργον πάντων B✼

---

preceding the battle of Leuktra (Xenoph. *Hell.* Bks. 5 and 6), and suffered accordingly, but must have enjoyed (like Plataia) a second or third resurrection (after the ruin of Thebes), as in the first century Thespiai and Tanagra were the only two flourishing cities in Boiotia: Strabo 403.

9. **τάδε**: the message of Themistokles, by the lips of Sikinnos, as reported by Hdt. differs in several notable respects and circumstances from the anonymous message reported by Aischylos. (i.) In Aischylos the message is despatched and received by daylight: in Hdt. by night. (ii.) In Aischylos it is received by the king: in Hdt. by the admirals. (iii.) In Aischylos the message leads the king to resolve on action, to wit, the advance of the fleet: with Hdt. the king has previously resolved to do or to offer battle. This difference is more apparent than real, as in each case the Persian fleet advances to pursue the Greeks supposed to be in flight—but the effect of the difference is to make the message perhaps even more prominent in Aischylos than in Hdt. (iv.) Far more important, with Aischylos the message in no way compromises the sender or the messenger, and there is nothing to show or to suggest that it was despatched with other than the full knowledge and approbation of the authorities on the Greek side: with Hdt. and the main tradition after his time the message is designed to outwit the Greeks no less than the Persians, nay, rather, to force the hand of the Greeks in the first instance, and compel them, against their will, to do battle at Salamis. (v.) As a further difference, the message in Aischylos reports simply a projected flight of the Greeks: the message in Hdt. proclaims the 'medism' of the sender, and of a great part of the fleet.

The 'flight' *motif* and the 'medism' *motif* might be alternatives, combined in the message as given by Hdt. The flight of the Greeks means that they are not going to battle, but to escape, and that under cover of night. The message as given by Aischylos is thoroughly consistent with itself, and with the time and circumstances of its despatch. The message as given by Hdt. reports instant flight (in the night), but also promises medism if the flight is stayed and a battle forced on. Possibly the 'medism' has been projected back into this message from the later career of Themistokles.

στρατηγὸς ὁ Ἀθηναίων: what of his colleagues? Cp. c. 79 *infra.*

12. **οἱ Ἕλληνες δρησμὸν βουλεύονται καταρρωδηκότες**: this is virtually identical with the message as reported by Aischyl. *Pers.* 357-9. In itself it might have been sufficient to induce the Persians to resolve—not on battle, for you cannot fight a flying enemy—but on pursuit, on a forward movement, which would bring a portion at least of the Persian fleet within the straits. As the Greek fleet by that time would be well under way, the Persians might be expected to overhaul it, and come upon its rear in the bay of Eleusis, or in the narrower waters beyond. As the (fresh?) plan or disposition of the Persian admirals certainly included the stopping of the narrow channel between Salamis and the Megarid, they might be expecting to find the Greek fleet thrown into utter confusion when they came upon it by the Eleusis channel.

μὴ περιίδητε διαδράντας αὐτούς. οὔτε γὰρ ἀλλήλοισι ὁμο- 15
φρονέουσι οὔτε ἀντιστήσονται ὑμῖν, πρὸς ἑωυτούς τε σφέας
ὄψεσθε ναυμαχέοντας τούς <τε> τὰ ὑμέτερα φρονέοντας καὶ
τοὺς μή." ὃ μὲν ταῦτά σφι σημήνας ἐκποδὼν ἀπαλλάσσετο · 76
τοῖσι δὲ ὡς πιστὰ ἐγίνετο τὰ ἀγγελθέντα, τοῦτο μὲν ἐς τὴν
νησῖδα τὴν Ψυττάλειαν, μεταξὺ Σαλαμῖνός τε κειμένην καὶ
τῆς ἠπείρου, πολλοὺς τῶν Περσέων ἀπεβιβάσαντο · τοῦτο
δέ, ἐπειδὴ ἐγίνοντο μέσαι νύκτες, ἀνῆγον μὲν τὸ ἀπ' ἑσπέρης 5

16 οὐκέτι (ἀντιστήσονται) B : οὔτ' ἔτι Schaefer, Holder, van H. ‖ τέ
σφεας AB   17 τούς <τε> Stein, van H.   76. 1 ἀπηλλάσσετο B
2 ἐγένετο z   3 νησῖδα Pz ‖ Ψυττάλειαν, del. Cobet, van H.   4
ἀπεβηβάσαντο B : ἀπεβίβασαν B, Holder, van H.   5 νύκτες μέσαι B
‖ ἀπὸ B

76. 1. σημήνας: it was a 'significant' message, much more than a hint; in what language was it conveyed? The Persians would have done well to have detained Sikinnos!

2. τοῖσι δὲ ὡς κτλ.: for the formula cp. cc. 80, 83 *infra*.

τοῦτο μέν: their first act, on being convinced of the projected flight of the Greeks, was to land a large force of Persians on the island of Psyttaleia. Down below the motive of this action is elaborately explained: the island lay in the thoroughfare, or waterway, of the coming battle, and the men upon it would be useful in dealing with wrecks and men, whether friends or foes. This motivation is obviously a complete misconception, if the island Ψυττάλεια is correctly identified with the island bearing the lighthouse between Peiraieus and Salamis to-day (*Leipsokoutali*)—one Engl. mile long and from 200 to 300 yards broad: Strabo 395, and the moderns, e.g. Leake—for an island in that position could have no bearing on the operation of the Persians now in hand. Even if they were expecting a battle at all, it was surely to take place far to the west of this position: unless indeed they assumed that the Greeks would be driven back and out of the straits eastwards by the ships sent round the island to the Megarid channel. Possibly, however, Hdt. has simply mistimed the occupation of Psyttaleia. If it was the first move of the Persians, then it had been made probably on the previous day, in connexion with the manœuvres recorded in c. 70 *supra*. If it was not made during the day of the

19th Boëdromion, then it was probably only made the next morning, after the sea-fight had begun—where Aischylos might be thought to place it, or admit of its being placed.

In any case, the identification of Psyttaleia is unfavourable to the theory of Leake and Grote, according to which the Persian fleet is supposed to be already by this time inside the straits, and drawn up, in battle-array, backed by the Attic shore, and facing the bay of Salamis. (If any island called for occupation from that position—especially in view of the message of Sikinnos—it would rather be the island of *St. George*, or of Leros?) It is difficult to see how *Lipsokoutali* could be said to be ἐν τόρῳ τῆς ναυμαχίης τῆς μελλούσης ἔσεσθαι, if both forces were inside the straits, and the Persian based on the Attic shore. This passage implies that the battle was to be fought between two forces, one attempting to get out of the straits, and the other attempting to get in.

5. ἐπειδὴ ἐγίνοντο μέσαι νύκτες. On the phrase cp. 4. 181, 9. 51 *infra*. The night is apparently that which fell in c. 70 *supra*, and towards the fall of which the Persian army had moved in the direction of the Peloponnesos, *ibid*. Thereafter has taken place the σύλλογος in c. 74, the συνέδριον in c. 75, the performances of Themistokles and Sikinnos, culminating in the present movement of Persian soldiers and ships. The naval movement which results from the (daylight) message in Aischylos begins at nightfall (*Pers.* 374-9): a consequence of the fundamental discrepancy between our two chief authorities. For Dr. G.

κέρας κυκλούμενοι πρὸς τὴν Σαλαμῖνα, ἀνῆγον δὲ οἱ ἀμφὶ
τὴν Κέον τε καὶ τὴν Κυνόσουραν τεταγμένοι, κατεῖχόν τε

7 Κέον: Λέρον Lolling: Ζέαν Pridek, cf. Bursian. J.-B. 86. 80 ‖
τὴν ante Κυνόσουραν fortasse delendum ‖ κατέχον z: κάτεχον Bekker:
(κατεῖλόν Stein³, oper. err.)

B. Grundy's view of the anachronism in Hdt.'s account op. *Great Persian War*, 377 ff., and Appendix VI. § 3.

ἀνῆγον τὸ ἀπ' ἑσπέρης κέρας: the phrase seems to imply that the ships were already at sea, and in position. This implication is consistent with c. 70 *supra*, where the ships have been left apparently in the water. What, then, was the exact position of 'the western wing': how was the fleet oriented? If the fleet was in the position advocated by Leake (*vide supra*) the western wing would be the right wing; if in a position outside the straits (as appears to be here implied in the immediate context, and is alone consistent with Aischylos), then the western wing might be, and probably was, the left wing. On the former hypothesis the movement here described would have for its purpose the foreclosure of the channel into the bay of Eleusis; on the latter hypothesis (really the only tenable one) the movement is one, imperfectly and obscurely described indeed, but apparently designed to detach a part of the fleet in order to circumnavigate the island, and to bar the western channel, between the island and the Megarid. Such a movement must, indeed, have been undertaken in the course of the Persian manœuvres; to have omitted it would have been a cardinal blunder; it is actually recorded by Diodoros (Ephoros) 11. 17. 2, perhaps not from tradition, but from inference and *Sach-Kritik*; it is at best obscurely hinted, or covered, by Hdt. here and by Aischylos, *Pers.* 368.

6. κυκλούμενοι πρὸς τὴν Σαλαμῖνα: these words would more naturally suggest the first alternative stated in the previous note. Baehr, however, understands it *de insula circumeunda*, and that is the better sense. It may be doubted whether Hdt. himself had a very clear view of the manœuvre; he simply repeats his source. Strategy and tactics are not his *forte*, and he may have written this account before he saw the landscape.

οἱ ἀμφὶ τὴν Κέον τε καὶ [τὴν] Κυνόσουραν τεταγμένοι: *prima facie* this is another squadron, contrasted with τὸ ἀπ' ἑσπέρης κέρας, and it is one squadron, and not two squadrons; it is not = οἱ ἀμφὶ τὴν Κέον τεταγμένοι καὶ οἱ ἀμφὶ τὴν Κυνόσουραν τεταγμένοι. It is, in fact, the other, or eastern wing. Baehr and Rawlinson are right against others and Blakesley in refusing to identify this Keos with the island, and this Kynosura with the well-known promontory by Marathon. Hdt. has brought the whole Persian fleet to Phaleron; and he (still more his sources) would have hesitated to move a squadron from Marathon to Munichia in half a September night, even if the order for moving could have been communicated. Leake identified this Kynosura with the long pointed promontory of Salamis projecting due east, and narrowing the channel between Salamis and Psyttaleia. Keos he wished to place somewhere on Salamis, or on the Attic coast opposite Kynosura, or again proposed to read τὴν νῆσον, i.e. Psyttaleia, which last gives good sense. But Stein more ingeniously identifies Keos with Kynosura, a younger and an elder name, 'Kynosura' being also necessitated by the oracle quoted below c. 77. The name of the island, moreover, was not Κέος but Κέως, hence the inhabitants are Κεῖοι, Κήιοι; cp. cc. 1, 46 *supra*. If the repeated article τὴν is an obstacle to the identification of the two place-names, it may be deleted (*O passi graviora!*), or explained away, as due to Hdt.'s ignorance.

But could οἱ ἀμφὶ τὴν Κέον, so understood, be 'the eastern wing'? They would have, or become so, at least when the western wing had moved off to circumnavigate Salamis. It is possible that the topographical indication represents rather the point of destination than the point of departure. In any case the terms ἀνῆγον μέν — ἀνῆγον δέ refer apparently not to a concentration of the fleet, but to a division and separation into two wings, or squadrons, moving in opposite, or independent, directions. Moreover, each squadron, in carrying out this order, may have undergone a fresh tactical disposition.

7. κατεῖχόν τε μέχρι Μουνιχίης:

μέχρι Μουνιχίης πάντα τὸν πορθμὸν τῇσι νηυσί. τῶνδε δὲ
εἵνεκα ἀνῆγον τὰς νέας, ἵνα δὴ τοῖσι Ἕλλησι μηδὲ φυγεῖν
ἐξῇ, ἀλλ' ἀπολαμφθέντες ἐν τῇ Σαλαμῖνι δοῖεν τίσιν τῶν ἐπ' 10
Ἀρτεμισίῳ ͵ἀγωνισμάτων. ἐς δὲ τὴν νησῖδα τὴν Ψυττάλειαν
καλεομένην ἀπεβίβαζον τῶν Περσέων τῶνδε εἵνεκεν, ὡς, ἐπεὰν
γίνηται ναυμαχίη, ἐνθαῦτα μάλιστα ἐξοισομένων τῶν τε ἀνδρῶν
καὶ τῶν ναυηγίων (ἐν γὰρ δὴ πόρῳ τῆς ναυμαχίης τῆς μελλούσης ἔσεσθαι ἔκειτο ἡ νῆσος), ἵνα τοὺς μὲν περιποιέωσι 15
τοὺς δὲ διαφθείρωσι. ἐποίευν δὲ σιγῇ ταῦτα, ὡς μὴ πυν-
θανοίατο οἱ ἐναντίοι. οἱ μὲν δὴ ταῦτα τῆς νυκτὸς οὐδὲν
ἀποκοιμηθέντες παραρτέοντο.

8 Μουνυχίης Stein¹²: correx. van H. || πάντα: παρὰ αC (pace Holder)
|| δὲ om. β, Holder   9 εἵνεκεν β || νῆας βz || μὴ δὲ φυγεῖν α: μὴ
φυγέειν β: μηδὲ φυγέειν z: μὴ διαφυγεῖν mal. Stein¹   10 τίσι z
11 νησῖδα Pz   12 εἵνεκα αz   13 γένηται βz, Holder, van H.
14 πόρρωι C: πόρρῳ z || τῆς ante ναυμαχίης om. βPz, Holder   15
ἔσεσθαι om. β || περιποιῶσι codd., z, Holder   16 ἐποίεον α

these words, especially the topographical
item, might seem some justification for
Grote's view that Keos and Kynosura
were places somewhere on the Attic
coast between Phaleron and Sunion.
But the phrase applies as much to the
clause ἀνῆγον μὲν τὸ ἀπ' ἑσπέρης κέρας as
to the clause ἀνῆγον δὲ οἱ ἀμφὶ τὴν Κέον:
in other words, it applies primarily to
neither, unless, indeed, Hdt. was ignorant
of the position of Munichia, here alone
mentioned in his work. Μουνιχίη is
undoubtedly and notoriously (i.) the hill
above the Peiraieus, which formed the
citadel of the Athenian port ; (ii.) one of
the three harbours under that hill, the
other two being the Peiraieus and Zea (?) ;
cp. E. A. Gardner, Ancient Athens (1902)
pp. 59, 544, etc. ; (iii.) for aps in early
times applied to the whole ib. p. 549;
Strabo 395 λόφος δ' ἐστὶν ἡ Μουνυχία
κτλ. ὑποτίπτουσι δ' αὐτῷ λιμένες τρεῖς.
It is curious that the roadstead μέχρι
Μουνιχίης should be described as a
πορθμόν, a term properly used of a ferry,
strait, or narrow waterway ; cp. c. 91
infra. The whole phrase here would
better apply to the situation and aspect
of the Persian fleet in the bay of
Phaleron than in the more open waters,
between Salamis (Keos) and Munichia ;
yet it may be taken generally to describe
the position of the Persian fleet, extending from the isle of Salamis across to
Munichia (the hill, λόφος) before it
broke up into two squadrons, one of

which moved west, round the island, to
block the Megarian channel, while the
other closed up towards Keos, to block
the channel between Keos and Psyttaleia,
and doubtless also filled up the space
between Psyttaleia and the Peiraieus (cp.
c. 85 infra).

9. ἵνα δή κτλ.: so Hdt.'s sources
(primarily Ionian ?) reported : there is
here no exception made for those who
might 'medize,' nor any clear prospect
of a set battle, but merely the purpose
to prevent the 'flight'—which is treated
(also in Aischylos) as a foregone conclusion. The inscriptions of Themistokles in the neighbourhood of Artemision (cp. c. 22 supra) held out no
prospect of medism, but the reverse.
τίσιν here = δίκην.

16. ἐποίευν δὲ σιγῇ: this is possible,
cp. c. 74 supra, though the movements
of the ships can hardly have failed to be
observed by Greek watchers on Salamis
(was there not a moon ?). Moreover, if
the Greek vessels were already ex
hypothesi in flight into the bay of
Eleusis, for the Megarid channel, the
object of all this secrecy is not apparent.

17. τῆς νυκτὸς οὐδὲν ἀποκοιμηθέντες:
this statement agrees with that of
Aischylos ; and if the mission of
Sikinnos had had no result beyond
keeping the Persian fleet on the go all
night, it would not have been in vain.
ἀποκοιμᾶσθαι is a remarkable word ; cp.
Aristoph. Wasps 213, Xenoph. Kyrop. 2.

77 Χρησμοῖσι δὲ οὐκ ἔχω ἀντιλέγειν ὡς οὐκ εἰσὶ ἀληθέες,
οὐ βουλόμενος ἐναργέως λέγοντας πειρᾶσθαι καταβάλλειν, ἐς
τοιάδε ῥήματα ἐσβλέψας.

ἀλλ' ὅταν 'Αρτέμιδος χρυσαόρου ἱερὸν ἀκτὴν
5   νηυσὶ γεφυρώσωσι καὶ εἰναλίην Κυνόσουραν

77 incipit verbis οἱ μὲν δὴ κτλ. Stein[1]: a verbo νυκτὸς usque ad
c. 84. 4 οὕτω δὴ om. β: totum cap. (χρησμοῖσι . . ἐνδέκομαι) damn.
Krueger, van H.   3 ῥήματα coni. Stein[2]: πρήγματα   4 χρυ-
σάορον z

4. 22, 'perhaps a military term' L. & S.,
'to take a little sleep,' or to be allowed
off duty, to sleep. Stein's interpretation
'to take sufficient sleep,' to have done
with sleep (ἀπο-, as in 2. 40), will hardly
do.

18. παραρτίοντο: with object (ταῦτα),
'were busily engaged in organizing.'

77. This chapter has been challenged;
it is athetized by Krueger and by van
Herwerden: there are at least seven
arguments against its authenticity. (i.)
The matter is very abruptly introduced,
without any obvious justification in the
context. What has a defence of oracles
to do with the manœuvres of the Persian
fleet on the eve of the battle, or with
the discussions of the Greek Strategoi?
(ii.) There is some doubt whether the
oracle cited originally referred to Salamis
at all; see detailed notes below. (iii.)
The language, not indeed of the oracle,
but of the writer, is peculiar, and
his style somewhat incoherent. Would
Hdt. not have expressed himself somewhat differently? (iv.) We should hardly
expect to find Hdt. taking Bakis, rather
than Delphi, as his point d'appui in his
Apologetic. (v.) The defence might
have been introduced more aptly in c.
96 infra. (vi.) The oracle is a vaticinium
post eventum. (vii.) The passage is omitted
in β. But these objections are incon-
clusive both severally and cumulatively.
Thus (i.) Hdt. makes digressions, and
the description of the Persian fleet as
filling the whole 'ferry' or Fahrweg
might be excuse enough for introducing
an oracle interpreted to refer to this
appearance. (ii.) The correctness of the
reference is neither here nor there; it is
clear that the reference was actually
made: why not by Hdt. if by any one?
(iii.) Hdt. waxes incoherent at times,
especially when excited. (iv.) Bakis
and such seers would stand most in
need of defence: many might impugn

Bakis, who would hesitate to challenge
Delphi. (v.) The reference in c. 96 presupposes this quotation. (vi.) Even if a
vatic. p. event. like many other oracles,
there was time enough between the dates
of Salamis and of Hdt.'s composition for
the invention of the verses. (vii.) The
better class of MSS. have this chapter,
and the inferior omit not merely this
chapter, but a good deal besides; cp.
App. Crit. But this chapter is plainly
an insertion; cp. c. 78 ad init.

Stein, who admits the authenticity
of the chapter, seems to regard the
argument as a reply to the scepticism
current at the beginning of the Peloponnesian war. If so, it would belong
to the third, or final draft of Hdt.'s
history. But the reference in c. 98 is
(I think) in favour of an earlier insertion,
and scepticism was not a novelty in 431
B.C. I should be inclined to regard this
chapter as belonging to the second draft,
and as written after Hdt.'s first visit to
Athens. Cp. Introduction, § 9.

2. καταβάλλειν, in a peculiar sense:
deicere, reicere. The use in 9. 79 is
not quite identical. ῥήματα (cp. App.
Crit.) is an emendation: πρήγματα, if
genuine, would be still more peculiar,
as used apparently for the lines following. Still more peculiar, or at least
incoherent, is the sentence which concludes the chapter. See below.

4. ἀλλ' ὅταν κτλ.: the oracle itself
has a thoroughly genuine ring. The
formula is reproduced by Aristophanes
in his parody: Knights 197 ἀλλ' ὁπόταν
κτλ.

'Αρτέμιδος χρυσαόρου ἱερὸν ἀκτήν.
Hesiod uses ἱερὸν ἀκτὴν (Δημήτερος) in
the sense of 'corn,' Homer uses the word
of 'meal' (cp. L. & S. sub v.). Here, of
course, ἀκτή means 'the strand,' shore.
What strand?

(1) Leake understood it of Salamis, or
a part of Salamis: Pausan. 1. 36. 1 ἐν

ἐλπίδι μαινομένῃ, λιπαρὰς πέρσαντες Ἀθήνας,
δῖα δίκη σβέσσει κρατερὸν κόρον, ὕβριος υἰόν,
δεινὸν μαιμώοντα, δοκεῦντ' ἀνὰ πάντα πίεσθαι.
χαλκὸς γὰρ χαλκῷ συμμείξεται, αἵματι δ' Ἄρης
πόντον φοινίξει. τότ' ἐλεύθερον Ἑλλάδος ἦμαρ   10
εὐρύοπα Κρονίδης ἐπάγει καὶ πότνια Νίκη.

8 ἀναπάντα AB: ἂν ἅπαντα Steger: ἀν' ἅπαντα Stein[1] ‖ πίεσθαι
Duentzer, Stein[2], Holder (πίεσθαι van H. oper. err.): πιθέσθαι AP, Stein[1]:
πειθεσθαι B: τίθεσθαι C: πυθέσθαι z: (ἅμα πάντ' ἐφικέσθαι (sic) Naber)
10 φοινίξῃ z

Σαλαμῖνι δὲ . . τοῦτο μὲν Ἀρτέμιδός
ἐστιν ἱερόν, τοῦτο δὲ τρόπαιον ἕστηκεν
ἀπὸ τῆς νίκης κτλ., and placed it on the
west coast of the bay of Ambelaki: if
this were correct the γέφυρα would seem
to be formed by the Hellenic ships; unless, indeed, the reference were to the
(projected) bridge of boats from Attica
to Salamis, c. 97 infra. But the latter
interpretation would ill suit Κυνόσουρα.
(2) A more famous strand of Artemis
was that by Brauron, on the east coast of
Attica. If that were the strand in view,
then Kynosura would naturally be the
best known promontory of the name
at Marathon; and the reference in the
oracle would rather be to the battle of
Marathon than to the battle of Salamis.
Blakesley, who identifies this Kynosura
with the Marathonian, would place the
Artemisian strand on the Euboian coast,
near Eretria, where was a temple of
Artemis Amarusia, which might give a
better sense for γεφυρώσωσι.
(3) The most obvious identification is
to regard the Ἀρτέμιδος ἱερὸς ἀκτή here
in question as the Attic shore near the
temple of Artemis Munichia (Μουνυχίας
ναὸς Ἀρτέμιδος Pausan. 1. 1. 4), and so
R. Adam de Hdti. ratione historica
(1890) p. 22, Goodwin, and others. The
bridging of the sea from Munichia to
Kynosura in this case, of course, would
simply mean the appearance presented
by the vast numbers of the Persian fleet,
which, extending in line (or rather in
three lines, cp. Aisch. Pers. 866) from
the Peiraieus to Hagia Varvara, might
be taken to present the appearance of
a bridge, or raft, covering the sea.
(4) It has been suggested (J. A. R.
Munro, J.H.S. xx. 1902, p. 306) that
the real reference in this oracle is to the
Artemision at the north end of Euboia,
which has already figured largely in
Hdt. Kynosura he refers to the Mara-

thonian promontory of that name, and
interprets the oracle as having originally
promised a victory to Hellas when her
enemies bridged with their ships the
channels at the north and south ends
of Euboia. But (1) if the reference had
been to the circumnavigation of Euboia,
Chalkis rather than Kynosura would
surely have marked the southern channel.
(2) Even if πότνια Νίκη could have been
predicated or predicted of the sea-fights
off North Euboia, (3) the reference to the
sack of Athens, λιπαρὰς πέρσαντες Ἀθήνας,
as antecedent of the 'bridging,' points
clearly to Salamis, and shows that the
previous solution is the correct one.
But the oracle looks like a vaticinium
post eventum.

χρυσαόρου: gen. . of χρυσάορος = χρυ-
σάωρ, 'with sword of gold,' not a specific
epithet of Artemis, but found (practically) attached to Apollo, Zeus, Demeter,
Orpheus; cp. L. & S. sub v. (Chrysaor,
as proper name, Hesiod, Theog. 280).
6. λιπαράς: a favourite epithet of
Athens, as is plain from Aristophanes,
Acharn. 639 f. etc., and so first in Pindar
Isth. 2. 30, Nem. 4. 18 (unless this oracle
of Bakis were earlier?), but also used by
Pindar of other places, Marathon, Orchomenos, Thebes, Smyrna, Naxos, Egypt.
Cp. Rumpel, Lexikon Pind. sub v., who
makes it = splendidus, nitidus. In reference to Athens it might well carry a
special suggestion of the olive and its
oil; cp. L. & S. sub v.
7. δῖα δίκη κτλ.: the personifications
in this line, and also the alliterations in
this and the following line, should not
be lost, just for want of capitals.
8. ἀνὰ πάντα πίεσθαι, a tmesis:
πίεσθαι, cp. App. Crit., future of πίνω, but
ἀναπίνω is rare, late, and technical; cp.
L. & S. sub v.
10. φοινίξει: perhaps no pun was intended. But are φοινός (φόνος) and Φοῖνξ

[ἐς] τοιαῦτα μὲν καὶ οὕτω ἐναργέως λέγοντι Βάκιδι ἀντιλογίης
χρησμῶν πέρι οὔτε αὐτὸς λέγειν τολμέω οὔτε παρ' ἄλλων
ἐνδέκομαι.

78   Τῶν δὲ ἐν Σαλαμῖνι στρατηγῶν ἐγίνετο ὠθισμὸς λόγων
πολλός· ᾔδεσαν δὲ οὔκω ὅτι σφέας περιεκυκλεῦντο τῇσι νηυσὶ
οἱ βάρβαροι, ἀλλ' ὥσπερ τῆς ἡμέρης ὥρων αὐτοὺς τεταγμένους,
79 ἐδόκεον κατὰ χώρην εἶναι.   συνεστηκότων δὲ τῶν στρατηγῶν ἐξ

---

12 ἐς del. Stein³: idem mihi visum erat (ἐς e verb. ἐς τοιάδε supra
repetitum) || μὲν <ἐσβλέψας> e coni. Stein¹² in text. recep. van H. ||
ἀντιλογίης: ἀντιλογίην Reiske, (van H.): ἀντιλογίας vel potius δι' ἀντιλογίης, cum ἐλθεῖν pro λέγειν, Wesseling approb. van H.: αὐτός τι vel
τολμέω οὐδὲν suspic. Stein (οὔτε τι Stein¹) || τολμέωι B   78. 2
περιεκυκλέοντο a: περικυκλέοντο C: περιεκυκλοῦντο Pz, Holder, van H.

---

not connected etymologically ? Cp. 7.
89 supra.
   12. [ἐς] τοιαῦτα μὲν .. ἐνδέκομαι: an
admittedly difficult passage, and perhaps
corrupt; cp. App. Crit. ἐς is unmean-
ing; it might be dittographed from ἐς
τοιάδε supra. There is no direct object
expressed for λέγειν. ἀντιλογίας might
be supplied with Wesseling, or τι after
αὐτὸς or οὐδὲν after τολμέω with Stein.
Βάκιδι ἀντιλογίης χρησμῶν πέρι is
odd: Stein takes B. ἀντ. together (of
speaking against Bakis) and χρ. πέρι
absolutely, cp. 7. 237 supra. The genitive ἀντιλογίης remains in suspense. On
Bakis cp. c. 20 supra.
   78. 1. τῶν δέ κτλ. corresponds
grammatically with τοιαῦτα μὲν just
before, and that badly; it corresponds
really and well enough with οἱ μὲν δή
κτλ., c. 76 ad f., and thus clearly betrays
c. 77 for an insertion.
   ὠθισμός: cp. 7. 225 supra; they
were not merely skirmishing, or using
light weapons, cp. c. 64 supra.
   2. ὅτι σφέας περιεκυκλεῦντο κτλ.:
these words primarily support the theory
of Leake (cp. Appendix VI. § 3) as to
the position attained by the Persian fleet
in c. 70 supra. The περικύκλωσις as a
manœuvre round the outside of the
island for the purpose of closing the
Megarid channel is not clearly envisaged
or affirmed by Hdt., nevertheless it
probably underlies this and his similar
expressions.
   The verb is here imperfect, but even
so a considerable lapse of time is presupposed and involved in the session of
the Strategoi on this occasion: they are
sitting up all night (the Persian man-

œuvre only began at midnight, c. 76
supra) and will get as little sleep as the
Persian admirals themselves !
   3. ὥσπερ τῆς ἡμέρης ὥρων αὐτοὺς
τεταγμένους: this phrase implies that
the Persian fleet had attained on the
previous day a definite disposition, as in
c. 70 supra, in that position was visible
to the Greeks, and had not returned to
port, or anchorage. Where exactly
was that position ? Probably its lines
presented the 'bridge' from Keos =
Kynosura, to Munichia-Peiraieus, with
Psyttaleia about the centre of the position. The fleet had now, however,
divided, the one wing, the left, moving
away west to block the Megarid channel,
the rest moving up closer into the
channels either side of Psyttaleia,
especially the eastern; other vessels, no
doubt, may have been posted, or cruising
off the SE. coast of Salamis, and others
held in reserve at Phaleron.
   79. 1. συνεστηκότων τῶν στρατηγῶν:
for the verb cp. c. 27 supra. As to the
tense Blakesley renders it, "after the
commanders had come to a direct issue";
but the sense rather demands a present
or imperfect, 'while the generals were
still contesting the matter,' i.e. before
they had come to a decision; and that
suits the material sense of the word.
   ἐξ Αἰγίνης: there is a precision
about this, which is seductive. Had
Aristeides spent his exile in the island
(cp. Ἀθην. πολ. 22. 8), the war with
which was hardly his policy ? Or would
he have been in Aigina at this time, if
the feud with Athens had not been composed (7. 145 supra) ? Or was he there
on the mission to the Aiakidai (c. 64

Αἰγίνης διέβη Ἀριστείδης ὁ Λυσιμάχου, ἀνὴρ Ἀθηναῖος μὲν
ἐξωστρακισμένος δὲ ὑπὸ τοῦ δήμου· τὸν ἐγὼ νενόμικα, πυνθανόμενος αὐτοῦ τὸν τρόπον, ἄριστον ἄνδρα γενέσθαι ἐν Ἀθήνῃσι
καὶ δικαιότατον. οὗτος ὡνὴρ στὰς ἐπὶ τὸ συνέδριον ἐξεκαλέετο 5
Θεμιστοκλέα, ἐόντα μὲν ἑωυτῷ οὐ φίλον ἐχθρὸν δὲ τὰ μάλιστα·
ὑπὸ δὲ μεγάθεος τῶν παρεόντων κακῶν λήθην ἐκείνων ποιεύμενος ἐξεκαλέετο, θέλων αὐτῷ συμμεῖξαι· προακηκόεε δὲ ὅτι

---

79. 6 Θεμιστοκλῆα z   8 συμμίξαι Stein¹², cp. c. 67. 5 || προ-
ακηκόεε Matthiae : προακηκόει van H. : προακήκοε

---

supra)! The trireme despatched for
them appears to return next morning,
c. 83 infra; but see note ad l.

2. Ἀριστείδης ὁ Λυσιμάχου: his first
appearance on the scene in Hdt., hence
the patronymic, which is repeated with
ἀνὴρ Ἀθηναῖος in c. 95 infra, suggesting
that the two passages are from different
sources, and perhaps belong to different
drafts. The anecdote which here follows
is part of the legend of Themistokles.
Lysimachos is a common Greek name;
upwards of twenty men are known to
have borne it. Of the father of Aristeides
nothing more is recorded, but he was
of course, like his son, of the tribe
Antiochis and of the deme Alopeke
(Plutarch Aristeid. 1); no doubt a
man of substance, and perhaps of the
Alkmaionid party. The ostrakism of
Aristeides had taken place in 483 B.C.
obviously to clear the way for the naval
law of Themistokles (cp. Appendix III.
§ 4), and he had been recalled with all
other exiles in 481 B.C. Stein supposes
that the law of amnesty had only just
been passed, otherwise Aristeides would
have appeared sooner in the camp. But
is the texture of the Herodotean historiography so close as to convince us that
this was the actual κάθοδος of Aristeides?
Far more probable is J. B. Bury's idea
(Class. Rev. x. 1896, 414 ff.), that
Aristeides was at this moment one of
the Athenian Strategoi duly elected in the
spring of 480 B.C., otherwise, indeed,
his exploit in c. 95 infra is hardly intelligible. As such he would presumably
have been present at the Synedrion of
Strategoi, unless we are to suppose that
only one Strategos from each state was
present. If the anecdote here given is
anything more than a fable, Aristeides
must have been away on special service;
in which case a mission to Aigina
presents itself as the most plausible

hypothesis to account for his movements.
That mission, if not to invoke the
Aiakidai, may have been for the purpose of convoying Athenian refugees;
cp. c. 41 supra.

3. τὸν ἐγὼ νενόμικα . . δικαιότατον.
This personal judgement is most significant. In the controversy over the rival
merits of Themistokles and Aristeides,
Hdt. definitely takes sides with the
latter: of the moral superiority of
Aristeides he has no doubt; his mind
is absolutely made up once for all on
that question (hence the perfect tense).
Thucydides' celebrated defence of Themistokles (1.138) only affects his intellectual
qualities, and his policy. The reputation
of Aristeides was based probably upon
four leading points, all subsequent to
his ostrakism and restoration : (i.) his
Strategia at Plataia ; (ii.) his full acceptance of the naval destiny of Athens;
(iii.) his great services in connexion with
the foundation of the maritime hegemony, including the τάξις φόρου; (iv.)
his popular reforms of the Constitution.
But, above all, probably his personal
character, honesty, and honour contributed to his apotheosis. See further,
Appendix l.c.

5. στὰς ἐπὶ τὸ συνέδριον, 'presented
himself at the council of generals': perhaps καταστάς (cp. 8. 46, 156) might be
expected ; but he is not yet inside,
actually in the presence of the council.

ἐξεκαλέετο, middle, by means of a
messenger? ὑπό, 'by reason of.' ἐκείνων:
not, of course, τὰ μάλιστα, but more
vaguely, 'their previous quarrels.' συμ-
μίξαι, as in c. 67 supra.

8. προακηκόεε: the pluperfect time
reinforced by the compositum ; how and
where had he heard of the intentions of
the 'Peloponnesians'? Well, it might,
of course, be merely since his arrival in
Salamis, but more is probably intended.

σπεύδοιεν οἱ ἀπὸ Πελοποννήσου ἀνάγειν τὰς νέας πρὸς τὸν
10 Ἰσθμόν. ὡς δὲ ἐξῆλθέ οἱ Θεμιστοκλέης, ἔλεγε Ἀριστείδης
τάδε. "ἡμέας στασιάζειν χρεόν ἐστι εἰ ἐν τεῷ ἄλλῳ καιρῷ
καὶ δὴ καὶ ἐν τῷδε περὶ τοῦ ὁκότερος ἡμέων πλέω ἀγαθὰ
τὴν πατρίδα ἐργάσεται. λέγω δέ τοι ὅτι ἴσον ἐστὶ πολλά τε
καὶ ὀλίγα λέγειν περὶ ἀποπλόου τοῦ ἐνθεῦτεν Πελοποννησίοισι.
15 ἐγὼ γὰρ αὐτόπτης τοι λέγω γενόμενος ὅτι νῦν οὐδ᾽ ἢν θέλωσι
Κορίνθιοί τε καὶ αὐτὸς Εὐρυβιάδης οἷοί τε ἔσονται ἐκπλῶσαι·
περιεχόμεθα γὰρ ὑπὸ τῶν πολεμίων κύκλῳ. ἀλλ᾽ ἐσελθών
80 σφι ταῦτα σήμηνον." ὁ δ᾽ ἀμείβετο τοισίδε. "κάρτα τε

---

9 νῆας z　　　11 χρεόν AB: χρεών ‖ εἰ ἐν τεῷ Stein³ (ἔν τέ τεῳ
Gomperz, Holder, van H.): ἔν τε τῷ (τε om. z)　　　13 τῇ πατρίδι z ‖
τοι om. z ‖ ἴσον d, hic et alibi prob. Cobet: sed cf. van Herwerden vol.
iii. p. vi.　　　80. 1 τοῖσιδε Marc., Stein: τοῖσδε

---

11. στασιάζειν: with such a man even
στάσις turns to good; 'now, if ever, is
the opportunity for us to rival each
other in promoting the good of our
common country.' But the phrase is
rather overstrained in the mouth of the
returned exile, who has merely some
valuable information to communicate to
the commander-in-chief of the forces!
Does Aristeides already foresee his own
performance on the morrow, in c. 95
infra, which was to be magnified into
one of the chiefest episodes of the ἐλεύθερον Ἑλλάδος ἦμαρ! Or is the phrase
more than the formula of a stock de-
bating question, ὁκότερος αὐτῶν (sc. A.
and Th.) πλέω ἀγαθὰ τὴν πατρίδα εἰργα-
σμένος εἴη;

15. ἐγὼ γὰρ αὐτόπτης .. κύκλῳ. If
this announcement referred simply to a
περικύκλωσις by the Persian fleet inside
the straits (as in Leake's theory), the
Greeks themselves in Salamis would
scarcely have failed to perceive it, and
Aristeides' announcement would have
been stale news. Or again, if Aristeides
had merely meant that the Persians had
moved up and blocked the passages right
and left of Psyttaleia, that movement
would not have constituted a περικύκλωσις, and a way of escape by the
Megarid channel would still have been
open to the Peloponnesians. Moreover,
on neither of these hypotheses is it
clear how Aristeides should have reached
Salamis. If the bay of Ambelaki was
blocked, he might have landed somewhere on the sea-front of the island,
and made his way overland to the Greek

laager; but he would not have been
more an autoptes than hosts of others.
If only the eastern ends of the straits
were blocked, he might have come in
by the west—but by the same channel
the Greeks might go out. The only
adequate meaning of the message is
that both ends, that by Psyttaleia or
Kynosura, and that by Megara-Budoron
(Thuc. 2. 94. 4), are closed and held
by Persian ships. Probably every one
knew by this time that such was the
case with the eastern end; the news
Aristeides brings is that there is a
squadron blocking the western outlet.
Coming from Aigina he might have discovered that by crossing the path of
that squadron on its way, or perhaps
by having to fly before it. How his
own ship reached Salamis is not specified; but he may have come in by the
Budoron channel. If there were Persian
ships patrolling the coast of Salamis
towards the open sea, the περικύκλωσις
would be still more effective; but it was
complete, as far as the argument requires, by the closure of both outlets
from the straits.

18. σήμηνον: of important, significant
news; cp. c. 76 supra.

80. 1. ὁ δ᾽ ἀμείβετο: Themistokles
responds, and gives himself completely
away. Had he really been playing the
very dangerous game ascribed to him,
and attempting to outwit not the Persians
but his colleagues, he would have known
how to contain himself in the presence
of his personal enemy. But perhaps
we take the record too seriously, and

χρηστὰ διακελεύεαι καὶ εὖ ἤγγειλας· τὰ γὰρ ἐγὼ ἐδεόμην
γενέσθαι, αὐτὸς αὐτόπτης γενόμενος ἥκεις. ἴσθι γὰρ ἐξ ἐμέο
τὰ ποιεύμενα ὑπὸ Μήδων· ἔδεε γάρ, ὅτε οὐκ ἑκόντες ἤθελον
ἐς μάχην κατίστασθαι οἱ Ἕλληνες, ἀέκοντας παραστήσασθαι. 5
σὺ δὲ ἐπεί περ ἥκεις χρηστὰ ἀπαγγέλλων, αὐτός σφι ἄγγειλον.
ἢν γὰρ ἐγὼ αὐτὰ λέγω, δόξω πλάσας λέγειν καὶ οὐ πείσω,
ὡς οὐ ποιεύντων τῶν βαρβάρων ταῦτα. ἀλλά σφι σήμηνον
αὐτὸς παρελθὼν ὡς ἔχει. ἐπεὰν δὲ σημήνῃς, ἢν μὲν πείθωνται,
ταῦτα δὴ τὰ κάλλιστα, ἢν δὲ αὐτοῖσι μὴ πιστὰ γένηται, 10
ὅμοιον ἡμῖν ἔσται· οὐ γὰρ ἔτι διαδρήσονται, εἴ περ περιεχόμεθα πανταχόθεν, ὡς σὺ λέγεις." ἐνθαῦτα ἔλεγε παρελθὼν ὁ 81
Ἀριστείδης, φάμενος ἐξ Αἰγίνης τε ἥκειν καὶ μόγις <δι>εκπλῶσαι
λαθὼν τοὺς ἐπορμέοντας· περιέχεσθαι γὰρ πᾶν τὸ στρατό-

---

3 'fortasse αὐτὰ ταῦτα αὐτόπτης' van H.   4 τὰ : τάδε Krueger :
ταῦτα Cobet, van H. : <ποιεύμενα> τὰ Naber ‖ ἔθελον Pz   5 παρα-
στήσεσθαι C   8 ὡς . . ταῦτα secl. van H.   10 ταῦτα δὴ τὰ
κάλλιστα secl. Krueger, τὰ tantum Naber, van H.   11 ὅμοιον CPz
81. 1 ἐνθαῦτα Krueger, Stein², van H. : ταῦτα   2 διεκπλῶσαι Naber,
van H., Stein³ : ἐκπλῶσαι

Themistokles, in this private interview,
preserved his discretion, and said to
Aristeides—something quite other than
this report? *A la bonne heure!* But
then, what becomes of any private speech
or conversation reported by Hdt. ?

2. **διακελεύεαι**: referring to the honourable and magnanimous στάσις to which
Aristeides has challenged him. δια-
κελεύεσθαι, 'to encourage one another';
cp. 1. 1, 3. 77. It is also used more
simply, 'to exhort,' 'command,' as in
c. 84 *infra*.

ἐδεόμην, 'I was wanting,' c. 59
supra.

3. **αὐτόπτης**: sc. αὐτῶν or τούτων.
ἐξ ἐμέο is predicative. **ἔδεε**, sc. ἐμέ.
παραστήσασθαι, trans., sc. ἐς μάχην.
ἑκόντες ἤθελον, redundant, for the sake
of the ἀέκοντας to follow. **αὐτά**, 'what
you have said,' 'the news.'

7. **δόξω πλάσας λέγειν**, 'I shall be
thought to have invented what I say.'
Such, alas, was his reputation!

οὐ πείσω, ὡς οὐ ποιεύντων . . ταῦτα,
'I shall not persuade them, as (they
are convinced) the barbarians are not
doing that.' This ὡς has a good deal to
carry, but is eased a little by the δόξω
πλάσας just before. But cp. App. Crit.

9. **παρελθών**: sc. right into the
presence of the Synedrion of generals.

11. **περιεχόμεθα πανταχόθεν**: a stronger
phrase than περιεχόμεθα κύκλῳ *supra*,
and hardly accurate unless the whole
island were surrounded.

81. 1. παρελθὼν ὁ Ἀριστείδης: into
the very presence of the Strategoi ; cp.
c. 79. 5 *supra*.

2. **μόγις <δι> εκπλῶσαι λαθὼν τοὺς
ἐπορμέοντας**: as the vulgate ἐκπλῶσαι
must mean 'to sail out,' Aristeides
appears to report eit er the difficulty
he had had in getting from Salamis
to Aigina, or—as Hdt. does not
conceive him starting in the first instance from Salamis—the difficulty he
had experienced in getting out from
Aigina, in which case τοὺς ἐπορμέοντας
would be a squadron blockading Aigina.
But this interpretation squares ill with
the words which immediately follow,
apparently as justification. It remains
to interpret ἐκπλῶσαι of escaping from a
pursuing squadron. The emendation
διεκπλῶσαι (vid. App. Crit.), though a
bit of rationalism, is rather favoured by
λαθών and by διεκπλεύσας, Plutarch
Aristeid. 8.

3. **περιέχεσθαι γὰρ . . Ξέρξω**: these
words again favour Leake's interpretation of the movements predicated in
co. 70, 76 *supra*, and point to the
conclusion that, so far as Hdt. himself

πέδον τὸ Ἑλληνικὸν ὑπὸ τῶν νεῶν τῶν Ξέρξεω· παραρτέεσθαί
5 τε συνεβούλευε ὡς ἀλεξησομένους. καὶ ὁ μὲν ταῦτα εἴπας
μετεστήκεε, τῶν δὲ αὖτις ἐγίνετο λόγων ἀμφισβασίη· οἱ γὰρ
82 πλεῦνες τῶν στρατηγῶν οὐκ ἐπείθοντο τὰ ἐσαγγελθέντα. ἀπι-
στεόντων δὲ τούτων ἧκε τριήρης ἀνδρῶν Τηνίων αὐτομολέουσα,
τῆς ἦρχε ἀνὴρ Παναίτιος ὁ Σωσιμένεος, ἥ περ δὴ ἔφερε τὴν
ἀληθείην πᾶσαν. διὰ δὲ τοῦτο τὸ ἔργον ἐνεγράφησαν Τήνιοι
5 ἐν Δελφοῖσι ἐς τὸν τρίποδα ἐν τοῖσι τὸν βάρβαρον κατελοῦσι.

---

4 ξέρξεωι B   6 ἀμφισβησίη z ǁ οἱ πλεῦνες γὰρ z   7 ἐξαγγελ-
θέντα z   82. 2 τουτέων z   3 ἀνὴρ Τήνιος ? Stein[1][2]: ἀνὴρ
<τῶν ἐπιφανέων> Schenkl: Τήνιος inser. Krueger (1856): 'Sin minus,
dele ἀνὴρ' van H. ǁ ἔφερε: 'An ἔφαινε ?' van H.   4 ἀληθηίην z ǁ
ἐγράφησαν C

---

has any clear conception of the situation,
he justifies Leake's interpretation. The
result thereby attained is indeed an
absurdity, but if a military expert and
topographer like Leake could swallow it,
why not Herodotus ?

4. παραρτέεσθαι: here strictly middle
and reflexive; cp. c. 76 *supra*.

6. μετεστήκεε, 'withdrew'; the tense
is rather rhetorical than grammatically
exigent. For the meaning cp. Thuc.
5. 111. 6 (μεταστάντων ἡμῶν). λόγων
ἀμφισβασίη: cp. 4. 14—something less
than λ. ὠθισμός c. 78 and more than
the ἀκροβολισμός c. 64. If the περικύκλωσις had been simply in the bay of
Ambelaki the truth could have very
easily been verified. The reputation
of Aristeides for δικαιοσύνη and ἀρετή
does not appear to have been as yet
established, at least in Peloponnesian
circles.

82. 2. ἧκε is perfect in sense, not to say
pluperfect: evidently ἐληλύθεε might
quite well stand here. Cp. c. 83 *infra*.
The participle agreeing with the ship
and not with the men (αὐτομολέουσα)
is piquant; and so it is the trireme that
carries the truth.

Τηνίων. The Tenians have been
mentioned, c. 66 *supra*, as joining the
fleet of Xerxes, apparently after Thermopylai-Artemision. But the nesiote ships
are all probably included in the 17
counted to the navy, 7. 95 *supra*.
Tenos is located in 4. 33, 6. 97 (lying
immediately S. of Andros, and N. of
Mykonos, Delos, Rheneia). The ship
here in question was probably the one
and only Tenian trireme in existence.
Tenos paid (as a rule) 3 talents tribute
to Athens afterwards.

3. Παναίτιος ὁ Σωσιμένεος. Panaitios
is a grand but not an uncommon name,
its chief bearer, son of Nikagoras, of
Rhodes, a celebrated Stoic, the friend of
P. Scipio Aemilianus (Cicero, *proMurena*,
§ 66, etc.). But of the gallant (ἀνὴρ)
Tenian, and his father Sosimenes, nothing
more is known. The desertion of the
Tenians scarcely looks as though the
Greeks on the Persian side despaired of
the good cause. Plutarch by a lapse
writes Tenedos (*Themist.* 12); Diodor.
11. 17. 3 reports a message, sent by the
Ionians and carried by a Samian, to ap-
prise the Greeks of the king's plans and
dispositions, and to promise their own
desertion; this covers the 'Aristeides'
and 'Tenian' episodes in Hdt. Stein
defends ἀνὴρ (cp. App. Crit.) by ref. to
Π. 11. 92 ἕλε δ' ἄνδρα Βιήνορα, Sophokl.
El. 95.

4. ἔργον: a derring deed ! cp. Index.
ἐνεγράφησαν . . ἐς τὸν τρίποδα.
As the inscription is still legible, the
statement of Hdt. can be verified. The
name of the Tenians appears, not strictly
speaking 'on the tripod,' which was of
gold, but on the τρικάρηνος ὄφις, which
was of bronze; cp. 9. 81. It is the
fourth name on the seventh coil (no
other coil has more than three names),
and is inscribed more deeply than the
rest, in Ionic letters, an addition probably made by the Tenians themselves,
'by permission'; cp. Hicks, *Manual*[2],
No. 19 [12], Dittenberger 7 [1], Michel
1118, and Appendix I.

5. ἐν τοῖσι τὸν βάρβαρον κατελοῦσι. Stein thinks that the word
κατελοῦσι must have occurred on the
inscription, and quotes Thuc. 1. 132. 3.
The word there is συγκαθελοῦσαι, and

σύν τε ὦν ταύτῃ τῇ νηὶ τῇ αὐτομολησάσῃ ἐς Σαλαμῖνα καὶ
τῇ πρότερον ἐπ᾽ Ἀρτεμίσιον τῇ Λημνίῃ ἐξεπληροῦτο τὸ
ναυτικὸν τοῖσι Ἕλλησι ἐς τὰς ὀγδώκοντα καὶ τριηκοσίας νέας·
δύο γὰρ δὴ νεῶν τότε κατέδεε ἐς τὸν ἀριθμόν.

Τοῖσι δὲ Ἕλλησι ὡς πιστὰ δὴ τὰ λεγόμενα ἦν τῶν Τηνίων **83**
[ῥήματα], παρεσκευάζοντο ὡς ναυμαχήσοντες. ἠώς τε διέφαινε
καὶ οἱ σύλλογον τῶν ἐπιβατέων ποιησάμενοι, προηγόρευε εὖ
ἔχοντα μὲν ἐκ πάντων Θεμιστοκλέης, τὰ δὲ ἔπεα ἦν πάντα

---

6 σύν τε Stein³ : σὺν δὴ Krueger : σὺν δὲ   8 νῆας z   9 νηῶν z
83. 2 ῥήματα intercl. Stein, Holder, van H. ‖ τε δὴ ἔφαινε AB : τε δὴ
διέφαινε Wesseling, van H.

---

the extant inscription does not support the inference—having merely the title τοῖδε τὸν πόλεμον ἐπολέμεον. But the inscr. is not complete. (This passage might have been added after Hdt.'s visit to Delphi ; cp. Introduction, § 9.)

6. σύν τε ὦν κτλ.: a notices le passage, containing, as it does, two implicit references back to antecedent passages, obvious to steady readers of the work. (1) In c. 48 *supra* Hdt. has given the total of the fleet as 378. (2) In c. 11 *supra ad f.* Hdt. has recorded the glorious desertion of Antidoros of Lemnos. Why has not the Lemnian been included in the navy-list in cc. 42–48 *supra*? Is not the omission due to Hdt.'s method of working from independent sources without co-ordinating the results ?

83. 1. τοῖσι δὲ Ἕλλησι κτλ. Blakesley considers this passage so confused as to be "quite inexplicable on the mere hypothesis of slovenly writing," and rewrites it not very happily. The chapter is confused, and partially corrupt, but the main purport is clear.

2. ἠώς τε . . καὶ: an effective parataxis. The night has apparently been spent by the Greeks, certainly by the Greek Strategoi, no less wakefully than by the enemy. It must be the Strategoi who are referred to in the demonstrative οἱ.

3. σύλλογον τῶν ἐπιβατέων: in c. 74 *supra* there comes a σύλλογος τῶν στρατηγῶν (Plutarch *Aristeid.* 8). The assembly of *Epibatai* must have been held on shore. The ships were in the water, the rowers on board. The battle was not to be so much a question of manœuvring as of hand-to-hand fight-

ing, in the good old style : laying ships alongside, and boarding !

σύλλογον ποιησάμενοι cuts both ways. There was a plurality of conveners, but not necessarily of speakers. It is not quite clear whether each Strategos addressed his own *Epibatai*, or whether Themistokles was the sole speaker, as he is certainly the sole speaker reported. The total number of *Epibatai* is a matter of conjecture or inference, and might have varied with different contingents. Plutarch, *Themist.* 14, says that at Salamis the number was 18 per ship : if correct that estimate would give 6840 for the 380 ships. Hdt. gives 30 men as the number of *Epibatai* on the Persian side, 7. 184 *supra*—by no means a trustworthy figure in itself for the whole fleet, much less directly transferable to the Greek. If so transferred, it would give a total of 11,400. At the battle of Lade, in 494 B.C., there had been 40 Epibatai on each of the Chian vessels (6. 15), a very large allowance. During the Peloponnesian war, a time when ships were themselves the weapon of offence, and more was done by manœuvring and ramming, the normal complement was only 10 (Thuc. 2. 92, 102, 3. 91, 95, 4. 76, 101). It would be fairly safe to say that at Salamis there were from 7000 to 10,000 *Epibatai* on the Greek side.

4. ἐκ πάντων suggests that he was chosen or allowed to speak out of and on behalf of all ; but it might mean that of all who spoke he was the most eminent and successful on the occasion (and so he alone is reported).

τὰ δὲ ἔπεα ἦν: the speech of Themistokles, verily ἔπεα πτερόεντα, may have been addressed solely, or

5 <τὰ> κρέσσω τοῖσι ἥσσοσι ἀντιτιθέμενα, ὅσα δὴ ἐν ἀνθρώπου
φύσι καὶ καταστάσι ἐγγίνεται· παραινέσας δὲ τούτων τὰ
κρέσσω αἱρέεσθαι καὶ καταπλέξας τὴν ῥῆσιν, ἐσβαίνειν ἐκέλευε
ἐς τὰς νέας. καὶ οὗτοι μὲν δὴ ἐσέβαινον, καὶ ἧκε ἡ ἀπ᾽
84 Αἰγίνης τριήρης, ἣ κατὰ τοὺς Αἰακίδας ἀπεδήμησε. ἐνθαῦτα
ἀνῆγον τὰς νέας ἁπάσας Ἕλληνες, ἀναγομένοισι δέ σφι αὐτίκα

---

5 <τὰ> Dobree, Holder, van H., Stein³ ‖ κρείσσω α ‖ ἀντιτιθέμενα
ὅσα δὴ Α²: ἀντιτιθέμενα· ὅσα δὲ (δὴ Holder: δὲ secl. et punctum post
ἐγγίνεται pos. Gomperz, van H.)   6 φύσει καὶ καταστάσει αC ‖ δὲ
BC: δὴ   7 αἱρέσθαι (sic) Α¹ ‖ καταπλήξας C ‖ κρῆσιν Α¹Β ‖ ἐκβαί-
νειν C ‖ ἐκέλευσε α   8 νῆας z ‖ μὲν: τε ? Stein²   84. 2 νῆας z
‖ οἱ Ἕλληνες z, van H.

---

primarily, to an Athenian audience, and
reported from an Athenian source; it
was no doubt a short speech, though
not so short as this brief summary, or
'concept' thereof; but the speaker was
evidently no mean orator. The speech
comprised three heads: (i.) A series of
antitheses, in which the better and the
worse, the noble and the base alternatives in human nature, circumstances,
and also no doubt actions, were contrasted. Hdt. characteristically fails to
distinguish clearly between action and
circumstance (cp. 7. 152 supra). (ii.) An
appeal, or exhortation (παραίνεσις) to his
hearers to choose the better part, liberty,
honour, death, rather than slavery, defeat,
the lash and the tax-collector; and
doubtless to remember that they were
fighting under the eyes of their wives
and children. (iii.) The appeal merged
into a peroration (καταπλέξας τὴν ῥῆσιν),
in which no doubt the gods and heroes
were invoked, and Marathon, 'the
trophies of Miltiades,' even Artemision,
probably were not forgotten. The whole
speech left upon the hearers' minds the
sense of confidence, courage, ability,
intellectual force. One misses from the
brief report two points, which will
hardly have been absent in the actual
harangue: some estimate of the opponents and their chances, and some hints
of the actual tactics to be pursued.

7. ἐσβαίνειν ἐκέλευε ἐς τὰς νέας: doubtless before or after the speech they had
breakfast on shore, and were better off
than the Persians in this respect.

8. οὗτοι μέν: there is no antithetical
δέ unless it be found somewhat incon-
gruously in ἀναγομένοισι δέ below.

ἐσέβαινον καὶ ἧκε: long before

they were done embarking the trireme
from Aigina was come, which had
left the ranks (ἀπεδήμησε, op. c. 41
supra) for the purpose of summoning,
invoking, (and bringing) the Aiakids to
the aid of Hellas (c. 64 supra). Presumably the trireme brought the images.
But at what point exactly did it reappear
in the ranks? If its arrival is to be
dated in the morning, after the speech
of Themistokles, how did it make its
way through the enemy, where Aristeides
had barely got through, even under
cover of night? Is this trireme any
other than the vessel of Aristeides?
Was not he the envoy despatched to
Aigina, from which he returned in c. 79
supra?

84. 2. ἀνῆγον τὰς νέας ἁπάσας:
advanced (or were advancing) their ships
en masse; but before the movement was
complete (ἀναγομένοισι δέ σφι), indeed
while it was little more than begun
(αὐτίκα), they found themselves attacked
by the barbarians (ἐπεκέατο οἱ β.). Our
whole conception of the actual engagement must turn upon the true interpretation of these words. They look simple
enough, but their meaning is obscure.
At first sight they might seem to lend
themselves to Leake's interpretation of
the movements recorded in cc. 70, 76
supra; the Greek fleet advances out of
the bay of Ambelaki, and finds itself at
once involved, front to front, with the
king's fleet, which has also advanced to
attack. But if that were the situation,
the two fleets would have been in full
view of each other all along since the
first streak of dawn; and the element
of surprise, involved in these words, is
inexplicable. The Greeks are taken

ἐπεκέατο οἱ βάρβαροι. οἱ μὲν δὴ ἄλλοι "Ελληνες ἐπὶ πρύμνην
ἀνεκρούοντο καὶ ὤκελλον τὰς νέας, 'Αμεινίης δὲ Παλληνεὺς
ἀνὴρ 'Αθηναῖος ἐξαναχθεὶς νηὶ ἐμβάλλει· συμπλακείσης δὲ 5
τῆς νεὸς καὶ οὐ δυναμένων ἀπαλλαγῆναι, οὕτω δὴ οἱ ἄλλοι

---

3 ἐπὶ del. Bekker, Holder, van H.   4 ἀνέκρουόν τε Eltz ‖ καὶ . .
νέας suspecta hab. Krueger, van H. ‖ ὤκελον z ‖ νῆας z ‖ Παλληνεὺς om.
Marc.: del. Cobet, Holder, van H.   5 συμπλεκείσης A¹BC   6
νῆος z

---

aback: before their own movement is complete they find the barbarians in motion against them. Nothing of that sort could have arisen on Leake's hypothesis. Granted that Hdt. so conceived the matter: but what sense is there in saying of two fleets, moving upon each other, front to front, that the one fleet advanced to the attack, and, while it was advancing, the other fleet attacked it? Such a statement is only intelligible on the supposition of a flank engagement. If the Greek fleet was emerging from the bay of *Ambelaki* just at the same moment as the Persian fleet was entering the straits, such a situation might arise: either the Greek fleet might cut the Persian column, somewhere behind its leading ships, or the head of the Persian column might strike the extreme right of the Greek fleet *en flanc*. If the Persian column were two or three ships abreast, or if there were two or more Persian columns — the one column perhaps pressing in between Psyttaleia and the island of Salamis, the other between Psyttaleia and the Attic mainland—a more complicated situation might easily arise: the extreme right of the Greek wing might be taken *en flanc*, or involved with the left column of the Persian advance, while the right Persian column might have to advance much further before becoming engaged with the Greek left. If such was, indeed, the whole situation adumbrated in this chapter, it is possible that the engagement opened, that actual contact with the enemy was effected, sooner than Themistokles intended or could have wished: he must have desired a large number of the Persian 'vessels to enter the straits before the actual fighting began.

3. οἱ μὲν δὴ ἄλλοι "Ελληνες: other than 'the Athenians,' or other than the one Athenian named? The latter is an absurd supposition: Themistokles and the other Athenian Strategoi knew what they were about, and were not likely 'to back water'—unless, indeed, the action of Ameinias of Pallene was ill-advised and premature. That the Greek right wing backed water (πρύμνην ἀνεκρούοντο), and, of course, by order, is likely enough; the Greeks on the right were much nearer the advancing enemy. That they were actually for beaching their ships (ὤκελλον) is probably a bit of popular (Attic) scandal, started by the man in the street, or the A.B. in the fleet, who did not understand what was going on, or the tactics of the admirals.

4. 'Αμεινίης δὲ Παλληνεύς: this Ameinias was, according to Diodoros 11. 27. 2, the brother of the poet Aischylos (who was an Eleusinian), cp. 6. 114, and according to Plutarch, *Themist.* 14, of the deme of Dekeleia, cp. 9. 73 *infra* (not of Pallene). The deme Pallene (site of the temple of Athene Παλληνίς, cp. 1. 62) belonged to the tribe Antiochis, and lay on the spurs of Hymettos crossed by the road to Marathon. Ameinias is not an uncommon name, and Aischylos, *Pers.* 409, does nothing for his supposed brother's claim, though he supports the Athenian claim by making a Phoenician ship implicated. The addition of the *Demotikon* here, if genuine, without the patronymic, would betray the Attic source, even without the express statement just below, 'Αθηναῖοι μὲν οὕτω λέγουσι, but it rather conflicts with δι. 'Αθ. and may be an interpellation; cp. App. Crit.

5. ἐξαναχθείς: passive in form, middle in force; cp. 7. 194 *supra* (of ships, not of shipmasters); "longius evectus," Baehr. This chapter exhibits the verb ἀνάγειν in all three voices.

νηί might be his own (instrumental) or an enemy's (objective), probably the latter; cp. ἐνέβαλε νηὶ φιλίη, c. 87 *infra.* τῆς νεὸς is his own. οὐ δυναμένων, sc. τῶν τοῦ 'Αμεινίου.

Ἀμεινίη βοηθέοντες συνέμισγον. Ἀθηναῖοι μὲν οὕτω λέγουσι
τῆς ναυμαχίης γενέσθαι τὴν ἀρχήν, Αἰγινῆται δὲ τὴν κατὰ
τοὺς Αἰακίδας ἀποδημήσασαν ἐς Αἴγιναν, ταύτην εἶναι τὴν
10 ἄρξασαν. λέγεται δὲ καὶ τάδε, ὡς φάσμα σφι γυναικὸς ἐφάνη,
φανεῖσαν δὲ διακελεύσασθαι ὥστε καὶ ἅπαν ἀκοῦσαι τὸ τῶν
Ἑλλήνων στρατόπεδον, ὀνειδίσασαν πρότερον τάδε, " ὦ δαιμόνιοι, μέχρι κόσου ἔτι πρύμνην ἀνακρούσεσθε ; "
85   Κατὰ μὲν δὴ Ἀθηναίους ἐτετάχατο Φοίνικες (οὗτοι γὰρ

---

8 γενέσθαι τῆς ναυμαχίης z   11 τὸ στρατόπεδον τῶν Ἑλλήνων z
13 ἀνακρούσεσθε (remos inhibebitis) Valla, Holder, van H., Stein³ : ἀνα-
κρούεσθε

---

8. **Αἰγινῆται δέ**: plainly a rival
tradition. If the Athenians were on the
extreme left, and the Aiginetans on the
right, and the situation was such as
above indicated, each claim may have
been made in good faith, but the Aiginetan was more probably the true one.
Whether it was the ship that had been
away for the Aiakida, which was actually
the first engaged, may be more doubtful :
it is such a happily ominous detail.
The ship in question is clearly assumed
to have been an Aiginetan ; but Aristeides might have taken a berth in it.

10. **λέγεται δὲ καὶ τάδε** comes in well
to remind us on what slender threads
these λόγοι hang ! The **φάσμα** here is
nothing if not superhuman (cp. c. 94
infra) ; her voice alone is enough to prove
that ! Of the actual and living women
and children, who, like enough, were
lining the shores of Salamis and making
the welkin ring, Hdt. says nothing.

11. **διακελεύσασθαι** : cp. c. 80 *supra*.
τὸ τῶν Ἑλλήνων στρατόπεδον
seems here used of the navy alone and
at sea ; but there was a laager on shore
which cannot have been wholly deserted,
and perhaps this λόγος came from that
quarter. Cp. c. 10. 14 *supra*.

12. **δαιμόνιοι**, 'wretches,' 'luckless
wights' ; cp. 7. 48 *supra*.

85. 1. **κατὰ μὲν δὴ Ἀθηναίους** . .
Φοίνικες : the Phoenician vessels were
presumably on the right of the Persian
line—if the Persian fleet was in line
formation in accordance with Leake's
hypothesis—or they were at the head of
the column (probably three ships abreast,
see Appendix VI. § 4), if the Persian
fleet was entering the straits in column
(the only conceivable formation for such
a manœuvre) : in either case they might

be described vaguely as holding **τὸ πρὸς
Ἐλευσῖνός τε καὶ ἑσπέρης κέρας**, albeit
undoubtedly this expression here squares
best with the projection of the battle
lines on Leake's plan. (If there were
not a good deal in the text of Hdt. to
suggest that plan it would never have
been heard of.) It is the eminent merit
of Professor W. W. Goodwin's paper,
Papers Amer. Sch. Ath. i. 1885, 239 ff.
(cp. Appendix VI. § 3) to have shown
that the (natural) identification of **τὸ
πρὸς Ἐλευσῖνός τε καὶ ἑσπέρης κέρας** in
this place with **τὸ ἀπ' ἑσπέρης κέρας** in
c. 76 *supra* is not necessary, and on a
rational conception of the manœuvres of
the Persian fleet is, indeed, impossible.
It by no means follows that Hdt.
intended to distinguish them, or even
clearly and consciously faced the problem
of the identity or difference between
them. Hdt. reported each movement
in terms of his authorities, his sources ;
he had perhaps written a preliminary
sketch or draft of the battle-piece before
he ever saw the landscape : at no time
did he compose an explicit, coherent, or
relatively complete account. It was
inevitable that Goodwin's suggestion
should be challenged and discarded, in
the forlorn hope of rehabilitating Hdt.
as a competent war-correspondent ; see
'Herodotus's Account of the Battle of
Salamis,' by Pres. B. I. Wheeler in *Trans.
Am. Philol. Assoc.* xxxiii. 1902, 127 ff.
That kind of apology is hardly possible
for students of Hdt. who deal with the
work as a whole, and have realized the
relation of Hdt. to his sources and the
canons of his logography.

In strictest accuracy the wing, or
column, towards Eleusis could not be
the west wing : Eleusis is about due

εἶχον τὸ πρὸς Ἐλευσῖνός τε καὶ ἑσπέρης κέρας), κατὰ δὲ
Λακεδαιμονίους Ἴωνες· οὗτοι δ' εἶχον τὸ πρὸς τὴν ἠῶ τε καὶ
τὸν Πειραιέα. ἐθελοκάκεον μέντοι αὐτῶν κατὰ τὰς Θεμι-

85. 2 πρὸς Σαλαμῖνός Loeschke   3 δὲ Β   4 αὐτέων z

north of 'Old Salamis,' and NNW. of
Psyttaleia. But in entering the straits
the Persian fleet would have been steer-
ing almost due west, and Eleusis would
be ahead of it. The description is not
one which should be found fault with
under the circumstances : both its factors
may be strictly true, not in relation to
each other, but in relation to the
Phoenician ships that fine morning—
whether they were heading into the
straits, or lying with their sterns towards
the Attic coast off Mount *Skaramanga*
(Aigaleos) and their stems to the bay of
Salamis.

In either case the Athenians appear
to be on the Greek left. This was the
position which their hoplites occupied
afterwards in the battle of Plataia, and
the right wing was the natural place for
the hegemonic state, or commander, to
occupy (cp. 'the *prytaneia*' of Miltiades,
and the position of the polemarch at
Marathon : 6. 110, 111). The tactics of
land-fighting were naturally transferred
to the naval war. At Artemision, however, the Athenians had occupied
apparently the right. There the
Spartans wished to be in more immediate
touch with Leonidas : the right was
there also the post of danger ; the Attic
ships at Chalkis might be regarded as
holding the extreme left (for the time
being). In their own waters it may
have been galling for the Athenians to
hold the left ; but Themistokles might
gladly acquiesce in the inner station,
which made a retreat for the Peloponnesians doubly difficult. It is,
indeed, conceivable that had the Peloponnesian vessels at any time actually
attempted to fly past the Athenian
station, the barbarians might have
enjoyed the spectacle of the Greeks πρὸς
ἑωυτοὺς ναυμαχέοντας — promised, or
threatened, by Themistokles, *pro bono
publico*, in c. 75 *supra*.

3. τὸ πρὸς τὴν ἠῶ τε καὶ τὸν Πειραιέα.
Why Hdt. here substitutes the Peiraieus
(an ἅπαξ λ. in his work !) for Munichia
in c. 76 *supra* is an obscure problem,
the solution of which might depend on
the complete disclosure of the mystery
of his sources. From the straits of

Salamis (as W. W. Goodwin *l.c.* p. 252 n.
observes) "the harbour of Peiraieus and
all the lower land of the peninsula
almost disappears from view, and the
high hill of Munichia remains a most
conspicuous landmark." The passage
here before us, then, may come from a
source, possibly even an 'Ionian' source,
which was not looking back from the
straits of Salamis, but was outside the
straits, on sea, or even on land, and
thought of Eleusis (quite invisible) and
Peiraieus naturally as lying west and
east.

If the conception above given of the
manœuvres of the Persian fleet during
the night be correct, it will appear
probable that the Ionians in the first
instance occupied the centre of the
Persian lines—a position in which it
would perhaps have been more difficult
for them ἐθελοκακέειν. When the
Persian position was developed, and
altered, the Egyptians on the left being
detached to circumnavigate the island
and to block the Megarian channel,
and the remainder moved up between
Psyttaleia and the island on the one
hand, the Attic shore on the other,
the Ionian contingent may have occupied
the left, or left centre of the Persian lines.
In the morning when the Phoenician
vessels entered the straits in column,
and the Ionians swung round to follow,
they would become the rear of the
advancing column, and might easily
extend back as far as the Peiraieus.
But 'Peiraieus' may be here used almost
as laxly in relation to actual orientation
as 'Eleusis' just above. It would,
however, be absolutely wrong and misleading if the Persian fleet were still
drawn up in battle-array on the lines
from the Attic coast through Psyttaleia
to Keos-Kynosura ; the left would then
have been furthest from Peiraieus, and
the right (i.e. the Phoenicians) furthest
from Eleusis. Of all modern theories
of the battle-lines at Salamis this one
is the most difficult to reconcile with
the authorities, Hdt. included, and with
common sense.

4. τὰς Θεμιστοκλέος ἐντολάς : an
implicit reference back to c. 22 *supra*.

5 στοκλέος ἐντολὰς ὀλίγοι, οἱ δὲ πλεῦνες οὔ. ἔχω μέν νυν
συχνῶν οὐνόματα τριηράρχων καταλέξαι τῶν νέας Ἑλληνίδας
ἑλόντων, χρήσομαι δὲ αὐτοῖσι οὐδὲν πλὴν Θεομήστορός τε τοῦ
Ἀνδροδάμαντος καὶ Φυλάκου τοῦ Ἱστιαίου, Σαμίων ἀμφοτέρων.
τοῦδε δὲ εἴνεκα μέμνημαι τούτων μούνων, ὅτι Θεομήστωρ μὲν
10 διὰ τοῦτο τὸ ἔργον Σάμου ἐτυράννευσε καταστησάντων τῶν
Περσέων, Φύλακος δὲ εὐεργέτης βασιλέος ἀνεγράφη καὶ χώρῃ
ἐδωρήθη πολλῇ. οἱ δ' εὐεργέται βασιλέος ὀροσάγγαι καλέονται
86 περσιστί. περὶ μέν νυν τούτους οὕτω εἶχε· τὸ δὲ πλῆθος
τῶν νεῶν ἐν τῇ Σαλαμῖνι ἐκερατζετο, αἱ μὲν ὑπ' Ἀθηναίων

---

6 νῆας z   7 θεμήστορός Β: θεομίστορός C   9 τοῦδε δὲ Reiske :
τοῦ δὲ ΑΒ: τοῦ, δὲ CPS: τοῦδε Rz ‖ τουτέων z ‖ μόνων Β   11
βασιλῆος z ‖ χώρηι P, Stein², van H.: χώρη ceteri, Stein¹, Holder : χώρη
οἱ z   12 πολλῆι P, Stein², van H. : πολλή ‖ οἱ δ' . . περσιστί.
Nonne glossema delendum ? ‖ τοῦ βασιλῆος z   86. 1 οὕτω : τοῦτο Β
2 νηῶν z ‖ ὑπὸ CRz

---

5. ἔχω μέν νυν . . ἑλόντων: this
remarkable statement seems to support
the suggestion that in this place Hdt.
is not following Athenian or Spartan
sources, but authorities which were to
be found on the Asianic side; the
particulars he gives are of obvious
Samian provenience, perhaps even backed
by a Persian countersign ! **τριηράρχων**
is used without any suggestion of Attic
institutes.

**7. Θεομήστορός τε τοῦ Ἀνδροδά-
μαντος**: his establishment as 'tyrant'
in Samos (cp. case of Koës of Mytilene
5. 11) immediately succeeded his services;
cp. 9. 90 *infra*. The name Theomestor
is rare, perhaps unique, certainly magnificent; his father's name (not noticed
in Pauly, or in Pauly-Wissowa), hardly
less so, is known from Aristotle (*Pol.*
2. 12. 14=1274 B) as that of a legislator
of Rhegion (possibly the same man),
and from Pausanias (2. 6. 6, 7. 6, 12. 6)
as the mythical son of Chthonophyle
(of Sikyon) by Phlias, son of Dionysos !
8. Φυλάκου τοῦ Ἱστιαίου: Phylakos
is the name of a 'Delphian' hero, c. 39
supra, *u.v.*, but is apparently unique
as the name of an historical person.
His father's name, Histiaios, is found in
Hdt. at Termera, cp. 7. 98 *supra*, and
at Miletos, cp. 7. 10 *supra*. If the great
Milesian tyrant had really been a Samian,
or of Samian extraction (so in fifteenth
century Michael Apostolios 16. 81 *ap.*
Pape-Benseler), would Hdt. have failed
to let us know ?

11. εὐεργέτης βασιλέος ἀνεγράφη: no
doubt in the Royal Archives, but the
fact might have stood recorded in an
inscription, and at Samos. Unfortunately Hdt. does not specify where the
man's great landed possessions were
situated. On such rewards cp. 9. 107
infra. On ἀνεγράφη Blakesley well
compares Plato *Gorgias* 132, and Stein
C.I.G. 84, where ἐν στήλῃ λιθίνῃ is added.
**12. οἱ δ' εὐεργέται β. ὀροσάγγαι κ.
περσιστί**. If not a gloss — it has a
great look of one — this remark is evidence in support of the early composition of these Books, for in 3. 140
is an anecdote of a Samian benefactor
to Dareios, where the explanation would
more naturally have come in; and this,
indeed, a glossator might have observed
as well as the author. The word ὀρ.
is interpreted σωματοφύλακες βασιλέως
by Hesych. and Photius, and apparently
used in that sense by Sophokles *Fr.*
185, and Stein has a derivation accordingly, ὀρο=VAR, to keep ('ware')
— σαγγ=*Khshâyata* (Shah !). Sir H.
Rawlinson *ap.* Rawlinson *ad l.* connected
it with *khur*, 'worthy,' *sansa* = Zend
sañgha, 'to praise'; Benfey and Oppert
had other forms.
86. 2. ἐν τῇ Σαλαμῖνι is rather a
curious way of describing the locality ;
it seems to lay the scene at least between
Salamis and the mainland; the battle
has always and everywhere been named
by the Hellenic base.
   ἐκερατζετο: the verb (κερατζειν, cp.

διαφθειρόμεναι αἱ δὲ ὑπ' Αἰγινητέων. ἅτε γὰρ τῶν μὲν
Ἑλλήνων σὺν κόσμῳ ναυμαχεόντων <καὶ> κατὰ τάξιν, τῶν
δὲ βαρβάρων οὔτε τεταγμένων ἔτι οὔτε σὺν νόῳ ποιεόντων 5
οὐδέν, ἔμελλε τοιοῦτό σφι συνοίσεσθαι οἷόν περ ἀπέβη. καίτοι
ἦσάν γε καὶ ἐγένοντο ταύτην τὴν ἡμέρην μακρῷ ἀμείνονες
αὐτοὶ ἑωυτῶν ἢ πρὸς Εὐβοίῃ, πᾶς τις προθυμεόμενος καὶ
δειμαίνων Ξέρξην, ἐδόκεέ τε ἕκαστος ἑωυτὸν θεήσασθαι
βασιλέα. 10

Κατὰ μὲν δὴ τοὺς ἄλλους οὐκ ἔχω [μετεξετέρους] εἰπεῖν 87
ἀτρεκέως ὡς ἕκαστοι τῶν βαρβάρων ἢ τῶν Ἑλλήνων ἠγωνί-

---

4 καὶ addidit Stein[2] ‖ κατὰ τάξιν del. Cobet   5 οὔτε Baiter : οὐ
6 ἤμελλε aβP ‖ τοιοῦτόν β   7 ἔσαν z   9 τε : τοι B ‖ θεήσασθαι
CP : θεήσεσθαι z : θηήσασθαι vel θηήσεσθαι   87. 1 μετεξετέρους
secl. Stein, Holder, van H. ‖ εἶπαι z, van H.   2 ὡς om. C

1. 88, 159, 2. 115, 121) is used rather
(in its Homeric sense) to mean 'plundering' than merely 'destroying' ; but cp.
7. 125 supra. We recur here, with the
Athenians and Aiginetans, to the chief
rival sources of c. 84 above.

3. ἅτε γὰρ τῶν μὲν Ἑλλήνων : the
term is applied here only to those on
the national side (cp. 7. 149 etc., cc.
111, 121, 132 infra) ; cp. Ἑλληνίς c. 87
infra, also Ἑλλήνων c. 89.

4. σὺν κόσμῳ is more or less reproduced just below by σὺν νόῳ, and
κατὰ τάξιν is paralleled by τεταγμένων
ἔτι, the two merits affirmed of the
Greeks, denied of 'the barbarians,'
albeit hitherto the Phoenicians have
been admittedly 'better sailors' ; cp. c.
10 supra, while the exploits of sundry
Greeks on the Persian side, recorded
below, cc. 87, 90, seem to declare a
certain degree of νοῦς. κοσμός Stein
refers to (a) the command of individual
ships, (b) the general discipline of crews,
etc. ; τάξις to manœuvres of divisions,
each ship keeping its own place, etc.,
perhaps a little hypercritically ; κόσμος
particularly need not be denied of the
ensemble.

6. ἔμελλε, 'was bound,' 'was sure' . .
συνοίσεσθαι and ἀπέβη mark a distinction without a difference ; the συμφορά
comes more home than the ἀποβάν, and
the two words denote one and the same
event looked at as it came home to the
person, or as it 'went off' in its natural
order or sequence.

7. ἦσάν γε καὶ ἐγένοντο κτλ. Hdt.
apparently says two things in one sen-

tence : ἦσαν ταύτην τὴν ἡμέρην (acc. of
time ; cp. Index) ἀμείνονες ἑωυτῶν, i.e.
they surpassed themselves, cp. 5. 118 ;
and ἐγένοντο ἀμείνονες ἢ πρὸς Εὐβοίῃ.
2. 25 αὐτὸς ἑωυτοῦ ῥέει πολλῷ ὑποδεέστερος
ἢ τοῦ θέρεος is not an exact parallel, as
there is only one verb in that passage.
But the double redundance here is not
unnatural, and the alternative does not
so much lie between ἦσαν and ἐγένοντο
as between αὐτοὶ ἑωυτῶν and ἢ πρὸς
Εὐβοίῃ—the extra verb rather eases this
alternative. There is a clear though
general reference back to the account of
the sea-fights off Artemision, cc. 6–17
supra, as in the words with which the
chapter concludes back to c. 69 supra.
Such implicit references are natural in
a work composed for a reading public.

9. ἐδόκεέ τε . . : this sentence is co-
ordinate grammatically not with the
preceding participles, but with the principal verbs ἦσάν γε καὶ ἐγένοντο above.
θεήσασθαι : the aorist is observable ;
each was feeling that the king saw him
—the king's eye was on him. (It might
be for a moment—any moment ; but
that would be enough !)

87. 1. κατά : c. 85 supra, l. 1, purely
locative ; there again, l. 4, sequent,
or consequent (κατὰ τὰς ἐντολάς) ; here,
thirdly, respective, quod attinet ad . .

οὐκ ἔχω εἰπεῖν ἀτρεκέως : a confession of the failure of his sources.
What the historian apparently regrets
is the lack of heroic anecdote ; strategic,
tactical details do not much preoccupy
him.

2. ἕκαστοι : not individual men, but,

ζοντο· κατὰ δὲ ᾿Αρτεμισίην τάδε ἐγένετο, ἀπ᾿ ὧν εὐδοκίμησε
μᾶλλον ἔτι παρὰ βασιλέι. ἐπειδὴ γὰρ ἐς θόρυβον πολλὸν
5 ἀπίκετο τὰ βασιλέος πρήγματα, ἐν τούτῳ τῷ καιρῷ ἡ
νηῦς ἡ ᾿Αρτεμισίης ἐδιώκετο ὑπὸ νεὸς ᾿Αττικῆς· καὶ ἡ οὐκ
ἔχουσα διαφυγεῖν, ἔμπροσθε γὰρ αὐτῆς ἦσαν ἄλλαι νέες φίλιαι,
ἡ δὲ αὐτῆς πρὸς τῶν πολεμίων μάλιστα ἐτύγχανε ἐοῦσα,
ἔδοξέ οἱ τόδε ποιῆσαι, τὸ καὶ συνήνεικε ποιησάσῃ· διωκομένη
10 γὰρ ὑπὸ τῆς ᾿Αττικῆς φέρουσα ἐνέβαλε νηὶ φιλίῃ ἀνδρῶν τε
Καλυνδέων καὶ αὐτοῦ ἐπιπλέοντος τοῦ Καλυνδέων βασιλέος

---

4 βασιλῆι z : βασιλεῖ || ἐπεὶ γὰρ z   5 βασιλῆος z   6 ναῦς B
|| νεὼς (νηὸς z) || ἡ B   7 ἔμπροσθεν Bz || ἦσαν z || νῆες z   9
συνήνεγκε a   10 τε : δὲ ? Kallenberg   11 ἐπιπλώοντος van H. ||
βασιλῆος z

---

as always, individual sets of men, contingents, etc.

3. ᾿Αρτεμισίην: Hdt.'s countrywoman,
concerning whom he might naturally
have fuller information, especially of a
personal kind, from the first. There is
a clear implicit reference in μᾶλλον ἔτι
back to c. 69 supra; cp. last chapter.
Note the use of ἔτι with the comparative; it clearly does not stand for ἤδη.

4. ἐς θόρυβον π. ἀπίκετο τὰ β. πρήγματα: θόρυβος, confusion; cp. c. 90
infra. ἐς θ. ἀπίκετο (aor.) = ἐθορυβήθη.
πρήγματα: cp. c. 75 supra.

6. ἐδιώκετο ὑπὸ ν. ᾿Αττικῆς, which
turns out afterwards (c. 93 infra) to be
the ship of Ameinias! (On the Asianic
side they would not have known the
Attic trierarch's name.) ἡ demonstrative: of the lady, not of the ship.

7. ἔμπροσθε γὰρ αὐτῆς ἦσαν ἄλλαι
νέες φ. Had Artemisia already gone
about, and was she in flight, heading
out for Phaleron or the open sea? If
so, her course is embarrassed by the
Persian reserves, which filled all the
fare-way to Munichia; c. 76 infra.
But it is possible that ἔμπροσθε refers
to vessels ahead of her in the Persian
column, i.e. west of her; that the Attic
squadron had partially headed round the
Phoenician ships: and that Ameinias
was driving in upon Artemisia from the
further side, east (or north). Cp. c. 89
infra, ἐς τὸ πρόσθε, etc. By this time
the lines are rather mixed; Artemisia
will have been in the centre originally
(cp. c. 85 supra), and perhaps on the
left, or in the rear, of the Persian line or
column, after the development of the

Persian position; if an Athenian vessel
now pursues her, the Greek left has
already pushed out beyond Psyttaleia;
or, if Ameinias was posted not on the
extreme left, but on the extreme right
of the Athenian position, then he is
attacking Artemisia from the right, i.e.
west side (or south).

8. ἡ δὲ αὐτῆς: sc. νηῦς. The position
here indicated suggests that Artemisia's
ship might just be clear of Psyttaleia;
but Hdt.'s locatives are too vague for
us to credit him with any clear vision
of the situation. The πολέμιοι here must
be the 'Hellenes.'

9. ἔδοξέ οἱ: a change of construction,
anacoluthon, which leaves ἡ οὐκ ἔχουσα
pendens; an exact parallel in 7. 177
supra.

συνήνεικε here carries an unusually
pregnant sense, 'succeeded,' 'turned out
well'; cp. 9. 37 infra, and contr. cc. 88,
90 infra. The success in question is the
remote, not the immediate result of the
manœuvre. (ποιησάσῃ, 'after she had
done it.')

10. φέρουσα ἐνέβαλε νηὶ φιλίῃ: the
principal verb might be used more naturally of the ship (cp. c. 90 infra) than of
the lady, and the active participle (cp.
φερομένη et sim., cc. 90, 91, 9. 102 infra)
is also remarkable: perhaps a compliment
to this careering woman.

11. Καλυνδέων . . Δαμασιθύμου. The
'Kalyndeans' of this passage are hardly
other folk than the 'Kalydnians' of 7.
99 supra (u.v.), nor can Damasithymos,
their Basileus, be other than Damasithymos, son of Kandaules, of 7. 98 supra.
Hdt. might seem, indeed, to have meant

Δαμασιθύμου. εἰ μὲν καί τι νεῖκος πρὸς αὐτὸν ἐγεγόνεε ἔτι
περὶ Ἑλλήσποντον ἐόντων, οὐ μέντοι ἔχω γε εἰπεῖν οὔτε εἰ
ἐκ προνοίης αὐτὰ ἐποίησε, οὔτε εἰ συνεκύρησε ἡ τῶν Καλυνδέων κατὰ τύχην παραπεσοῦσα [νηῦς]. ὡς δὲ ἐνέβαλέ τε 15
καὶ κατέδυσε, εὐτυχίῃ χρησαμένη διπλᾶ ἑωυτὴν ἀγαθὰ ἐργάσατο.
ὅ τε γὰρ τῆς Ἀττικῆς νεὸς τριήραρχος ὡς εἶδέ μιν ἐμβάλλουσαν νηὶ ἀνδρῶν βαρβάρων, νομίσας τὴν νέα τὴν Ἀρτεμισίης
ἢ Ἑλληνίδα εἶναι ἢ αὐτομολέειν ἐκ τῶν βαρβάρων καὶ
αὐτοῖσι ἀμύνειν, ἀποστρέψας πρὸς ἄλλας ἐτράπετο. τοῦτο μὲν 88

---

12 δαμασύθου R   13 εἶπαι z, van H.   15 κατατυχεῖν B ‖
νηῦς secl. Stein³ ‖ ἐνέβαλλέ C   17 νεὼς A : νηὸς z   18 νῆα z

---

two different states, two different
persons; but the variant forms, if both
genuine, may be ascribed to various
sources, and the failure to refer from
the one passage to the other to Hdt.'s
insouciance, his independence in composition. ἐπιπλέοντος: cp. 7. 97 *supra*.

12. εἰ μὲν καί τι νεῖκος κτλ.: this
passage implicitly indicates that some
authorities, some source (Stein says
'some other' *Geschichtschreiber*, logo-
grapher?) had a story of a quarrel
between Artemisia and Damasithymos,
'while the forces were "still" (ἔτι) in
the Hellespontine region,' i.e. just before
the transit of the Hellespont. Perhaps
the locality is not so certain as the suggested date, i.e. before the Persian forces
crossed into Europe. (It is at least
doubtful whether Artemisia and Damasithymos were on the Hellespont at all;
cp. 7. 44, 59.) Hdt. has here lost a
golden chance! What was the cause of
the νεῖκος? Was it a woman's reason—
spretae iniuria formae? Or a man's
ambition? Damasithymos might ill
brook the 'hegemonia' of the Halikarnassian queen! Was the mother anxious
for the succession of her boy? Was the
Karian dynast intriguing against the
Mutter-recht? (cp. p. 126a *supra*). There
are all the elements of a romance, a
tragedy, or at least a melodrama, behind
this passing allusion: had the subject
been already too well handled for Hdt.
to retouch it? He repeats instead his
formula of despair, οὐκ ἔχω εἰπεῖν.

14. ἐκ προνοίης, *de industria*, of set
purpose, deliberately.

αὐτά, 'it,' we should say. Cp. 7.
8 ἐν αὐτοῖσι.

συνεκύρησε: so c. 92 *infra*, συν-

εκύρεον νέες. In a more abstract sense,
9. 90 *infra*.

15. κατὰ τύχην παραπεσοῦσα. Hdt.
has forgotten that the ship of Damasithymos was one of the five ships led by
Artemisia, 7. 99 *supra*; there can have
been very little 'chance' in the fact that
it was stationed close by the queen's
ship, and so came first in her way.
παραπεσοῦσα, cp. Plato *Rep.* 561 B ἡ
παραπίπτουσα ἀεὶ ἡδονή. ἐργάσατο, with
double accus.; cp. c. 79 *supra*.

17. ὁ . . . τριήραρχος: namely,
Ameinias. His views (νομίσας) may be
matter of conjecture. μιν: sc. τὴν
γυναῖκα.

18. ἀνδρῶν βαρβάρων: Karians, to
wit; cp. c. 135 *infra*. ἐκ τῶν βαρβάρων,
more generally.

20. αὐτοῖσι, sc. τοῖσι Ἕλλησι, 'his
countrymen.' Krueger asserts that
ἑωυτοῖσι would be 'more correct'
(*gehöriger*), cp. c. 61 *supra*. Abicht
observes that, owing to the proximity
of τὴν νέα (i.e. as Subject), ἑωυτοῖσι could
only refer to 'the Persians' (i.e. τοῖσι
βαρβάροισι). Stein rules that "Hdt.
employs the Reflexive (pronoun) in regard to the more remote Subject (here
τριήραρχος) only when the nearer Subject
(here τὴν νέα) follows after"; or, as we
might say: *If a fresh subject intervene
between the subject of a sentence and the
verb, Hdt. substitutes the Personal for the
Reflexive pronoun to describe a Reflexive
relation between the main Subject and its
verb;* for the simple reason that (as
Stein elsewhere suggests), the interposition of the fresh Subject would
eclipse, or obscure, the direct relation
of the Reflexive pronoun; cp. 1. 111 ἡ
δὲ γυνὴ (ἐν φροντίδι ἦν) ὅ τι οὐκ ἐωθὼς ὁ

τοιοῦτο αὐτῇ συνήνεικε γενέσθαι <ὥστε> διαφυγεῖν τε καὶ
μὴ ἀπολέσθαι, τοῦτο δὲ συνέβη ὥστε κακὸν ἐργασαμένην ἀπὸ
τούτων αὐτὴν μάλιστα εὐδοκιμῆσαι παρὰ Ξέρξῃ. λέγεται
5 γὰρ βασιλέα θηεύμενον μαθεῖν τὴν νέα ἐμβαλοῦσαν, καὶ δή
τινα εἰπεῖν τῶν παρεόντων " δέσποτα, ὁρᾷς Ἀρτεμισίην ὡς
εὖ ἀγωνίζεται καὶ νέα τῶν πολεμίων κατέδυσε;" καὶ τὸν
ἐπειρέσθαι εἰ ἀληθέως ἐστὶ Ἀρτεμισίης τὸ ἔργον, καὶ τοὺς
φάναι, σαφέως τὸ ἐπίσημον τῆς νεὸς ἐπισταμένους· τὴν δὲ
10 διαφθαρεῖσαν ἠπιστέατο εἶναι πολεμίην. τά τε γὰρ ἄλλα, ὡς
εἴρηται, αὐτῇ συνήνεικε ἐς εὐτυχίην γενόμενα, καὶ τὸ τῶν ἐκ
τῆς Καλυνδικῆς νεὸς μηδένα ἀποσωθέντα κατήγορον γενέσθαι.
Ξέρξην δὲ εἰπεῖν λέγεται πρὸς τὰ φραζόμενα " οἱ μὲν ἄνδρες

88. 2 τοιοῦτον B ‖ ὥστε coni. Stein² ‖ διαφυγέειν codd. z   4 τουτέων z   5 βασιλῆα z : βασιλέα τε ? Stein² ‖ νῆα z ‖ ἐμβαλλοῦσαν C :
ἐμβάλλουσαν Naber   6 εἰπεῖν om. C : εἶπαι z, van H.   7 <ἦ> καὶ
Naber ‖ νῆα z   9 σαφῶς Pz ‖ νεὼς B : νηὸς z   11 συνήνεικε Pz : συνή-
νεικεν ‖ ἐς om. C   12 νηὸς z ‖ ἀπωσθέντα C   13 εἶπαι z, van H.

Ἅρπαγος μεταπέμψαιτο αὐτῆς τὸν ἄνδρα,
1. 146 (σφέων τοὺς πατέρας), 2. 121 (αὐτοῦ
τὴν κεφαλήν). But the plural αὐτοῖσι
here, after the singular subject, resembles
the use of ἑωυτοῖσι l.c. supra.

88. 1. τοῦτο μὲν .. τοῦτο δέ, 'in
the first place .. in the second place ';
cp. Index for reff.

3. κακὸν ἐργασαμένην αὐτὴν μάλιστα
εὐδοκιμῆσαι παρὰ Ξέρξῃ : there is a
dash of malicious humour at the expense
both of the queen and of the king. ἀπὸ
τούτων is superfluous, and the plural
vague ; the preposition here is scarcely
temporal, but rather causal.

4. λέγεται γάρ : Grote questions the
sequel of Artemisia's exploit (ἔργον) ;
Rawlinson fails to see why. There is
reason enough in that Hdt. himself
questions it, as he shows by the three
apologetic references to the source
(λέγεται bis, φασί ad fin.).

6. τινα : hardly a Greek, presumably
a Persian, who knew no better ; but the
τούς below (like τόν demonstrative)
might well refer to Greeks.

9. τὸ ἐπίσημον τῆς νεός : cp. τὸ
σημήιον c. 92 infra. Polyainos, 8. 53. 1,
says Artemisia varied her 'ensigns,'
sometimes showing Greek and sometimes
Persian colours. Rawlinson regards
that as the refinement of a later age,
such ensigns not existing in 480 B.C.,
the figure-head, which could not be
changed at pleasure, being the only

ensign ; cp. 3. 59 (which cannot prove
a negative !). But the admiral's ensign
can hardly have been a figure-head.
"Flags are represented at the sterns of
the Athenian ships of about 500 B.C.,"
Torr, Ancient Ships, p. 100.

ἐπισταμένους, like μαθεῖν just
above, of sensible perception, and so
more than ἐπίστημη, followed by ἠπιστέατο meaning 'believed'—something
less than ἐπιστήμη (a word not used by
Hdt.). The psychological terminology
of Hdt. is in a rudimentary stage ; cp.
his use of the words θυμός, νόος, φρήν,
φρόνημα, ψυχή, διάνοια, μαθεῖν, ἐπί-
στασθαι, etc.

10. ὡς εἴρηται, just above, a reference back but of a few lines. συνήνεικε
ἐς εὐτυχίην γενόμενα recurs through
συνήνεικε γενέσθαι l. 1, to the συνήνεικε
in c. 87 supra, which was used there
with much the same meaning as the
fuller expression here.

12. μηδένα ἀποσωθέντα κατήγορον
γενέσθαι : the participle is here essentially
a part of the predicate ; the meaning
clearly being, not that none of the survivors impeached her, but that there
were no survivors, and so no impeach-
ment.

13. οἱ μὲν ἄνδρες κτλ. : the remark
was borrowed from (or by) Artemisia, cp.
c. 68 supra ; it comes better from the
lips of Xerxes.

γεγόνασί μοι γυναῖκες, αἱ δὲ γυναῖκες ἄνδρες." ταῦτα μὲν
Ξέρξην φασὶ εἰπεῖν.

15

Ἐν δὲ τῷ πόνῳ τούτῳ ἀπὸ μὲν ἔθανε ὁ στρατηγὸς 89
Ἀριαβίγνης ὁ Δαρείου, Ξέρξεω ἐὼν ἀδελφεός, ἀπὸ δὲ ἄλλοι
πολλοί τε καὶ ὀνομαστοὶ Περσέων καὶ Μήδων καὶ τῶν ἄλλων
συμμάχων, ὀλίγοι δὲ τινὲς καὶ Ἑλλήνων· ἅτε γὰρ νέειν
ἐπιστάμενοι, τοῖσι αἱ νέες διεφθείροντο, καὶ μὴ ἐν χειρῶν 5
νόμῳ ἀπολλύμενοι, ἐς τὴν Σαλαμῖνα διένεον. τῶν δὲ βαρβάρων οἱ πολλοὶ ἐν τῇ θαλάσσῃ διεφθάρησαν νέειν οὐκ
ἐπιστάμενοι. ἐπεὶ δὲ αἱ πρῶται ἐς φυγὴν ἐτράποντο, ἐνθαῦτα
αἱ πλεῖσται διεφθείροντο· οἱ γὰρ ὄπισθε τεταγμένοι, ἐς τὸ
πρόσθε τῇσι νηυσὶ παριέναι πειρώμενοι ὡς ἀποδεξόμενοί τι 10
καὶ αὐτοὶ ἔργον βασιλέι, τῇσι σφετέρῃσι νηυσὶ φευγούσῃσι
περιέπιπτον.

Ἐγένετο δὲ καὶ τόδε ἐν τῷ θορύβῳ τούτῳ. τῶν τινες 90

---

89. 2 ἀριβίγνης C ‖ δὲ ἐὼν ? Kallenberg   5 νῆες codd. s ‖ καὶ:
οἱ Krueger, van H.   8 ἐπείτε ? van H. ‖ ἐσφυγεῖν B   9 ὄπισθεν B
10 πρόσθεν B: ἔμπροσθε z   11 βασιλέι AB ‖ <τῇσι> φευγούσῃσι ?
Stein²

---

89. 1. πόνῳ: cp. 6. 114, 7. 224.

ἀπὸ μὲν . . ἀπὸ δέ: a *tmesis*—
well recalling the originally substantive
quality of the preposition; cp. 5. 81
(κατά).

2. **Ἀριαβίγνης**: cp. 7. 97 *supra*; he
was admiral of the Ionio-Karian division.
His mother was a daughter of Gobryas,
so he was not full brother to the king.

3. **τῶν ἄλλων συμμάχων**: τῶν ἄλλων
is appositive, not adjectival; Περσέων,
and even Μήδων, would hardly come
under the head of συμμάχων. The
Persians and Medes furnished *Epibatai*,
cp. 7. 96 *supra*; the Sakai are here not
specified, except so far as covered by
συμμάχων. Ἑλλήνων seems to refer
primarily to the national forces, but
might cover at least some cases on the
barbarian side; cp. c. 86 *supra*.

4. **νέειν ἐπιστάμενοι**: an art, not a
science; cp. 7. 211, and c. 88 *supra*.
The participles refer not to the ὀλίγοι
τινές who perished, but to the implied
majority who survived, even when their
ships were destroyed; but Hdt.'s way
of putting the case is a little clumsy.
τοῖσι, relative.

5. **ἐν χειρῶν νόμῳ**: cp. 9. 48 *infra*;
cominus, hand to hand, with the ships
laid alongside each other (συμπλακεισῶν
τῶν νεῶν, cp. c. 84 *supra*) and the *Epibatai*

fighting almost as on land. These ones
too could have swum, but did not get
the chance; nor, again, was it only
those who lost their ships that knew
how to swim!

6. **ἐς τὴν Σαλαμῖνα διένεον**, 'swam
right in to Salamis'—one might have
expected some of them to have been
picked up on the way. Were there no
Greek ships left between them and the
shore?

8. **αἱ πρῶται**: the vanguard, the
leading ships, the head of the column,
the first line, in distinction to οἱ ὄπισθε
τεταγμένοι the rearward, the second
line, the tail of the column, as the case
may be; falling back upon those behind,
the foremost ships threw everything
into confusion (πόνος, θόρυβος).

10. **τῇσι νηυσί** is a kind of instrumental, circumstantial, or descriptive
dative.

**ὡς ἀποδεξόμενοί τι καὶ αὐτοὶ
ἔργον βασιλέι** seems written in view of
c. 87 and c. 86—but was there really
such keen competition (καὶ αὐτοί)?

11. **τῇσι σφετέρῃσι νηυσί**: just the
ships on their own side, which were not
their own! cp. σφετέρας 7. 194. With
περιέπιπτον cp. περιπ. περὶ ἀλλήλας c.
16 *supra*.

90. 1. τῶν τινες Φοινίκων: a thoroughly

Φοινίκων, τῶν αἱ νέες διεφθάρατο, ἐλθόντες παρὰ βασιλέα
διέβαλλον τοὺς Ἴωνας, ὡς δι' ἐκείνους ἀπολοίατο αἱ νέες, ὡς
προδόντων. συνήνεικε ὦν οὕτω ὥστε Ἰώνων τε τοὺς στρατη-
5 γοὺς μὴ ἀπολέσθαι Φοινίκων τε τοὺς διαβάλλοντας λαβεῖν
τοιόνδε μισθόν. ἔτι τούτων ταῦτα λεγόντων ἐνέβαλε νηὶ
Ἀττικῇ Σαμοθρηικίη νηῦς. ἥ τε δὴ Ἀττικὴ κατεδύετο καὶ
ἐπιφερομένη Αἰγιναίη νηῦς κατέδυσε τῶν Σαμοθρηίκων τὴν
νέα. ἅτε δὲ δὴ ἐόντες ἀκοντισταὶ οἱ Σαμοθρήικες τοὺς ἐπι-

---

90. 2 Φοινίκων H. Stephanus: φοίνικες ‖ νῆες z ‖ διεφθαρέατο codd.
(διεφθειρέατο P) ‖ βασιλῆα z   3 ἀπολλοίατο C ‖ νῆες z ‖ ὡς
προδόντων del. Cobet, van H.   4 οὕτω <γενέσθαι> ὥστε? Stein² :
nonne melius οὕτω secluseris? (cp. van H. in l.)   5 διαβαλόντας z
6 τοιοῦτον z ‖ τουτέων z ‖ νηῖ (sic) B   7 σαμοθραικίη BC :
σαμοθρακίη ASV   8 αἰγινέη Bz ‖ σαμοθρηκῶν B   9 νῆα z
‖ δὲ δὴ Stein³ : δὲ P marg., Krueger, Stein², Holder, van H. : δὴ

Herodotean collocation, cp. 7. 143, 146
supra. The men in question would of
course be of high position, kings or what
not: it is a pity they are anonymous!
Cp. 7. 98.

2. διεφθάρατο: a pluperfect, and with
its full temporal force.

3. δι' ἐκείνους, 'thanks to them.' ὡς
προδόντων seems to be added as an
explanation, not by the Phoenicians,
but by the writer; it were as well away,
and, but for the change of case, might be
bracketed as a gloss. What had the
Ionians done? Was it the Ionians
who had turned tail? Was it not the
Phoenicians who had been leading the
van? Were they angry that the Ionians
had not made way, when they turned
to flight? Or did they suspect the
Ionians of collusion with the enemy,
and of purposely obstructing the passage?
Such questions may seem to treat the
anecdote too seriously. It is in any
case evidence of a rivalry and friction
between Ionian and Phoenician, which
was doubtless one of the elements of
weakness on the Persian side.

4. συνήνεικε: here quite neutral; cp.
c. 88 supra. οὕτω, 'in the following
way'—i.q. ὧδε.

Ἰώνων . . τοὺς στρατηγούς: not
the Persian admirals, but the (subordinate) Greek captains, or generals of
squadrons.

6. μισθόν: ironical; cp. c. 117 infra.
Hdt. is not a lover of the Ionians, but
he prefers them here to Phoenicians;
cp. 7. 23 supra.

ἐνέβαλε νηὶ Ἀττικῇ Σαμοθρηικίη
νηῦς. The verb is naturally used; cp.
c. 87 supra. The involution of Attic,
Samothrakian, and Aiginetan vessels is
remarkable. The Athenian squadron
must have taken up more than half the
Greek lines of battle; the Aiginetans
may have been posted (or had some of
their ships posted) on the extreme left
of the Peloponnesian contingent, or
wing. The Athenian vessel may have
come out left of Psyttaleia, and the
Aiginetan on the right. The dramatic
transaction, which is probably historical,
should take place in the outer, not in the
inner waters: the notion that it occurred
under the very eyes of Xerxes is perhaps
for the sake of the moral, i.e. is fabulous.

The Samothrakians are in this anecdote
regarded as Ionians: the primitive population was Pelasgian, 2. 51; 'Thrakian
Samos' (Homer, Il. 13. 12) was very
naturally believed to have been colonized
by 'Samians,' Schol. ad l.c., Pausan. 7.
4. 3; but the story in Pausanias throws
some doubt on their Ionism. Blakesley
acutely remarks that 'Ionian' was the
common orientalism for Hellene, and
cps. 4. 138, 6. 8, 7. 95 supra.

9. ἀκοντισταί: armed with the ἀκόν-
τιον, the characteristic weapon of Thrace,
of Asia Minor, and the Peltast (cp.
Appendix II. § 4), which here proves
superior to the panoply of the hoplite.
The Samothrakian Peltasts cleared the
deck of the heavy infantry, boarded and
possessed themselves of the Aiginetan
vessel (ἴσχον). The amount of ramming

βάτας ἀπὸ τῆς καταδυσάσης νεὸς βάλλοντες ἀπήραξαν καὶ 10
ἐπέβησάν τε καὶ ἔσχον αὐτήν. ταῦτα γενόμενα τοὺς Ἴωνας
ἐρρύσατο· ὡς γὰρ εἶδε σφέας Ξέρξης ἔργον μέγα ἐργασαμένους,
ἐτράπετο πρὸς τοὺς Φοίνικας οἷα ὑπερλυπεόμενός τε καὶ πάντας
αἰτιώμενος, καί σφεων ἐκέλευσε τὰς κεφαλὰς ἀποταμεῖν, ἵνα
μὴ αὐτοὶ κακοὶ γενόμενοι τοὺς ἀμείνονας διαβάλλωσι. ὅκως 15
γὰρ τινὰ ἴδοι Ξέρξης τῶν ἑωυτοῦ ἔργον τι ἀποδεικνύμενον ἐν
τῇ ναυμαχίῃ, κατήμενος ὑπὸ τῷ ὄρεϊ τῷ ἀντίον Σαλαμῖνος
τὸ καλέεται Αἰγάλεως, ἀνεπυνθάνετο τὸν ποιήσαντα, καὶ οἱ

---

10 νεὼς C : νηὸς z ‖ ἀπήρραξαν z   13 πᾶν z   14 ἐκέλευε
Jacobitz   15 διαβάλωσιν R   17 οὐρεϊ CPz, van H.

---

done is remarkable ; and if the description is correct—and as early as 494 B.C. the Ionians at least were supposed to be competent in that manœuvre, cp. 6. 12, 15—the battle of Salamis was not simply a land-fight on 'wooden wall' or 'boarded' field, but a true sea-fight, in which the ship was itself a weapon, and manœuvres were as much the order of the day as simply jamming the ships alongside, and fighting ἐν χειρῶν νόμῳ, cp. c. 89.

12. ὡς γὰρ εἶδε σφέας Ξέρξης : if this great feat (ἔργον) really took place as described ; if Xerxes with his own eyes saw it ; if he was at that moment sitting somewhere on Mount Aigaleos, or on its skirts (see just below), then the scene of the action would more probably lie west of Psyttaleia. The σφέας is rather vaguely referent to τοὺς Ἴωνας. In any case the royal logic was at fault : even if the Samothrakians were Ionians, or passed as such, other Ionians, from Asia and elsewhere, might have deserved all the bad things the Phoenicians were supposed to have said of them. There can be no doubt that σφέων refers to Φοίνικας. Xerxes did not order the Phoenicians to cut off the heads of the Ionians, and when he turned himself to the Phoenicians the act was mental rather than physical. 'Heading' was a regular formula, cp. 7. 35 supra, and Phoenicians were accustomed to it—in Ionian story. Hdt. below specifies that the king's orders are executed. ἵνα μὴ . . διαβάλλωσι seems to be a motive supplied by the narrator, not a part of the king's doom.

17. κατήμενος ὑπὸ τῷ ὄρεϊ . . Αἰγάλεως. During at least some part of the day Xerxes may have been seated somewhere on a throne, from which he could witness the fight, "the principal officers of his household standing around him, the imperial parasol held by an attendant over his head, and the scribes by his side, writing down the names of those who had distinguished themselves in the action," Leake, Athens and the Demi, ii.² 270. From Mount Aigaleos you can overlook the whole bay, and survey the waters both within and beyond the island of Lipsokutali : what a view !— but hardly from a seat ὑπὸ τῷ ὄρεϊ, 'at the foot of the mountain.' If the seat of Xerxes was down there, or even down on the lower slopes, but little above the shore, not much would have been seen of the details of a battle, even all confined to the straits and bay of Salamis (Ambelaki).

18. The words τὸ καλέεται Αἰγάλεως have a parenthetic, not to say gloss-like appearance, but might easily have been inserted by the author himself, after making acquaintance with the scene. To survey all the possible area of action, to look down into the bay of Eleusis as well as into the bay of Salamis, Xerxes would have needed to ascend high on Mt. Skaramanga : the matter afloat this time was no mere parade, or procession, as in 4. 88, 7. 44 supra. Neither was the king bound to sit still in one spot all the time ! He will have ridden to the foot of the ascent, and have moved up and about the high ground, attended by his aides-de-camp and suite, as the evolutions of the battle proceeded. Surely, had he been fixed to one spot, we should have heard how he sprang up from his seat, thrice and three times thrice, δείσαντα περὶ τῇ στρατιῇ (7. 212 supra). If Xerxes had a throne for this occasion its exact site is hard to define. The ancients themselves are not agreed.

γραμματισταὶ ἀνέγραφον πατρόθεν τὸν τριήραρχον καὶ τὴν

19 τόν τε ? Stein[1]

It first makes its appearance in the poetic source: Aischyl. *Pers.* 465 ff. ἕδραν γὰρ εἶχε παντὸς εὐαγῆ στρατοῦ ὑψηλὸν ὄχθον ἄγχι πελαγίας ἁλός. In these lines ἕδραν is not necessarily even 'a seat,' much less 'his throne' (the ἀργυρόπους δίφρος preserved afterwards in the Akropolis and stolen by Glauketes, Demosth. *c. Timocr.* 24. 129, hence the silence of Pausan. 1. 27. 1). παντὸς στρατοῦ seems to cover army as well as fleet, and some of the army was, if Hdt. is to be trusted, west of Aigaleos (c. 70 *supra*). ὑψηλὸν ὄχθον would at any rate suit Aigaleos, and the top of Aigaleos, but contradicts Hdt.'s ὑπὸ τῷ ὄρεϊ. πελαγίας ἁλός need not be pressed so as to rule out the straits, as though πέλαγος could only mean the high or open seas; but Aischylos is not anyway in strict accord with Hdt. Phanodemos (*ap.* Plutarch. *Themist.* 13) placed the seat of Xerxes ὑπὲρ τὸ Ἡράκλειον—which may be the source of Diodoros 11. 18. 2, so far as the king's position is concerned therein—but how far, how much above the Herakleion? The Herakleion apparently occupied the shore end of the ferry, across the narrowest part of the straits (cp. note to c. 97 *infra*). Akestodoros (Plutarch *l.c.*) located the king far to the west, beyond Eleusis, ἐν μεθορίῳ τῆς Μεγαρίδος ὑπὲρ τῶν καλουμένων Κεράτων. In that position he would have seen nothing at all of the actual battle described in Hdt., though he might have seen something worth seeing (cp. c. 94 *infra*). The tradition in Akestodoros deserves, however, less absolute contempt than it has received: the very fact that it is so remote from the apparent necessities of the case should have obtained for it a careful scrutiny. Considering that the army, or a part of the army, had moved in the night before the battle to the west (c. 70 *supra*); that on the day before the battle Demaratos and Dikaios, eminent members of the king's suite, were on the Thriasian plain (c. 65 *supra*); that a detachment of the Persian fleet had been sent round Salamis to block the Megarian channel (c. 76 *supra*); that the Greeks were (perhaps) believed to be in full retreat through the bay of Eleusis (c. 75 *supra*), a position overlooking the Megarian

Sound might not have seemed ill-chosen for a bird's-eye view of the coming encounters. No one would have suggested it as commanding the actual scene of the battle of Salamis. Given the main facts of the battle, granted the obvious supposition that the king witnessed it, and a place was bound to be provided for him ἐναντίον τῆς Σαλαμῖνος, pity that the authorities could not agree whether that place was at the top or the bottom of the mountain! That Xerxes actually ascended the Kerata is incredible. Even if he was at Eleusis on the morning of the battle, he would have hurried eastwards when the true state of the case was revealed by the early light. The greater part of the battle he may have actually overlooked from the heights of *Skaramanga*. The oddity in Aristodem. 1. 2 (καθεζόμενοι ἐπὶ τοῦ Πάρνηθος ὄρους) is surely a variant for Aigaleos—the whole for the part. Blakesley's ingenious hypothesis that Xerxes began on the top of the mountain and then descended to the neighbourhood of the Herakleion does not really bear out his own conclusion that "all the varying accounts may have some truth in them," for it ignores Akestodoros; nor does it square with the probable course of events: for at what hour did Xerxes start on the top of the mountain? Did he spend the night there? If not, the unexpected course of events in the morning would probably have upset the plan of ascent. In any case, you inevitably start at the bottom, not at the top of a mountain: once up, no doubt you are sure to come down. The traditional site of the *Throne of Xerxes* is on the hill fronting the road to the ferry, a little beyond the supposed site of the Herakleion. Lolling (Baedeker's *Greece* p. 108) suggested the rocky promontory of *Keratópyrgos*, which projects into the bay about three-quarters of a mile beyond the chapel of St. George, as the point from which Xerxes witnessed the battle, commanding as it does an admirable survey of the straits. It is now occupied by a powder magazine. The partial coincidence between the modern name of this promontory and the Kerata, in Akestodoros, is curious.

οἱ γραμματισταὶ ἀνέγραφον: we have seen these historiographers at

πόλιν. πρὸς δέ τι καὶ προσεβάλετο φίλος ἐὼν <Ἴωσι> 20
Ἀριαράμνης ἀνὴρ Πέρσης παρεὼν τούτου τοῦ Φοινικηίου
πάθεος. οἱ μὲν δὴ πρὸς τοὺς Φοίνικας ἐτράποντο.

Τῶν δὲ βαρβάρων ἐς φυγὴν τραπομένων καὶ ἐκπλεόντων 91
πρὸς τὸ Φάληρον, Αἰγινῆται ὑποστάντες ἐν τῷ πορθμῷ ἔργα

---

20 δέ τι Bekker : δ᾽ ἔτι β : δὲ ἔτι ceteri ‖ προσεβάλλετο C : προσελάβετο Reiske, van H. ‖ Ἴωσι coni. Stein, approb. van H. : Ἰώνων ante
ἐὼν Abresch : cp. comment. infra

---

work, under more favourable circumstances, before, 7. 100 *supra*. Possibly
the royal *Anagraphai* may have contained the names of Theomestor and
Phylakos, but Hdt. will scarcely have
consulted them ; cp. c. 85 *supra*.

19. πατρόθεν : cp. 6. 14, but not
necessarily a Greek touch ; the patronymic plays a prominent part in the
Persian lists, e.g. 7. 61 ff. But τὸν
τριήραρχον καὶ τὴν πόλιν sounds
calculated mainly for the case of Greeks ;
what if not a πόλις but an ἔθνος were
concerned ! The whole sentence ὅκως
γάρ . . τὴν πόλιν comes in very curiously
here, and would be better placed at the
end of c. 85 after πολλῇ.

20. πρὸς δέ κτλ. This is a further
explanation of the escape of the Ionians
and of the doom (πάθος) of the Phoenicians, but the phraseology is peculiar,
and the text perhaps corrupt ; cp. App.
Crit. The texts vary between τι and
ἔτι. προσεβάλετο is of doubtful sense
and reading ; see below.

φίλος ἐών is obscure : whose friend
was Ariaramnes ! Ἴωσι is conjectural.
The last clause, too, οἱ μὲν δή κτλ.,
appears incomplete. Does the corruption extend perhaps much further than
hitherto suspected ! See following note.

προσεβάλετο might be a middle,
or a passive, although if Ariaramnes is
its subject it is presumably middle,
and may be interpreted 'contributed
somewhat (τι) to the disaster of the
Phoenicians' ; *contulit ad illam Phoeni-
cum cladem* ; Schäfer ap. Baehr : Stein
compares Eurip. *Med.* 284 συμβάλλεται
(*sic*) δὲ πολλὰ τοῦδε δείματος. Baehr
himself prefers (with Lange) to take
προσεβάλετό τι absolutely, and παρεών
with τούτου . . πάθεος, 'present at this
disaster' (surely wrong !). (Blakesley
reads προσελάβετο and understands
Ariaramnes to have shared the fate of
the Phoenicians.) φίλος has been taken
in three ways : τῶν Ἰώνων (Baehr),

amicus regis (Valla), of the Phoenicians
(Blakesley).

I am inclined to suspect that the
real verb has here disappeared, and that
προσεβάλετο may have come in from
lower down, where τοῖσι προσεβάλετο
αὐτὴ ἡ ἄχαρις τιμή (7. 36 *supra*), or
some similar phrase, seems to have
dropped out after οἱ μὲν δή. Perhaps
the text in this passage ran πρὸς δὲ (ἔτι)
καὶ ἐπελάβετο φίλος ἐὼν κτλ., in which
case Ariaramnes was a friend of the
Phoenicians, and the conjectural Ἴωσι
must be omitted. With ἐπιλαμβάνεσθαι
τινος cp. 1. 127 (προστάτεω), 6. 49
(προφάσιος), 9. 99 (δυνάμιος), though it
must be confessed that πάθεος is not
in the same category.

21. Ἀριαράμνης. His name suggests
that he was an Achaimenid ; cp. 7. 11
supra.

91. 1. τῶν δὲ βαρβάρων covers, no
doubt, Greeks on the Persian side, but
would scarcely be used unless Phoenicians
and other non-Hellenic folks were
included.

ἐκπλεόντων πρὸς τὸ Φάληρον. If
the barbarian lines had been all parallel
with the Attic shore, then, when driven
back and put to flight, the ships would
naturally have run aground under
Mount Aigaleos. The fact that they
make out of the straits for Phaleron,
though not perhaps in itself conclusive,
favours the view that such was the
natural line of retreat. Phaleron, not
Peiraieus, is their goal, or base ; cp. cc.
85, 67 *supra*.

2. Αἰγινῆται ὑποστάντες ἐν τῷ πορθμῷ.
The Aiginetans will have made their
way out of the straits to the right of
Psyttaleia, unless the squadron here
mentioned has come up, during the
action, from home (cp. c. 46 *supra*),
but the vessels here would surely have
been αἱ ἄριστα πλεοῦσαι. ὑποστάντες
suggests their being posted in ambush,
lying in wait, or at least 'waylaying

ἀπεδέξαντο λόγου ἄξια. οἱ μὲν γὰρ Ἀθηναῖοι ἐν τῷ θορύβῳ
ἐκεράιζον τάς τε ἀντισταμένας καὶ τὰς φευγούσας τῶν νεῶν,
5 οἱ δὲ Αἰγινῆται τὰς ἐκπλεούσας· ὅκως δὲ τινὲς τοὺς Ἀθηναίους
92 διαφύγοιεν, φερόμενοι ἐσέπιπτον ἐς τοὺς Αἰγινήτας. ἐνθαῦτα
συνεκύρεον νέες ἥ τε Θεμιστοκλέος διώκουσα νέα καὶ ἡ Πολυ-
κρίτου τοῦ Κριοῦ ἀνδρὸς Αἰγινήτεω νηὶ ἐμβαλοῦσα Σιδωνίη,
ἥ περ εἷλε τὴν προφυλάσσουσαν ἐπὶ Σκιάθῳ τὴν Αἰγιναίην,
5 ἐπ᾽ ἧς ἔπλεε Πυθέης ὁ Ἰσχενόου, τὸν οἱ Πέρσαι κατακοπέντα
ἀρετῆς εἵνεκα εἶχον ἐν τῇ νηὶ ἐκπαγλεόμενοι· τὸν δὴ περιά-
γουσα ἅμα τοῖσι Πέρσῃσι ἥλω <ἡ> νηῦς ἡ Σιδωνίη, ὥστε
Πυθέην οὕτω σωθῆναι ἐς Αἴγιναν. ὡς δὲ ἐσεῖδε τὴν νέα τὴν
Ἀττικὴν ὁ Πολύκριτος, ἔγνω τὸ σημήιον ἰδὼν τῆς στρατηγίδος,
10 καὶ βώσας τὸν Θεμιστοκλέα ἐπεκερτόμησε ἐς τῶν Αἰγινητέων

---

91. 4 νηῶν z   92. 2 νῆες z   3 αἰγινητέων B   5 Ἰσχενόου
H. Stephanus : ἰσχένου   6 νιῆι B, cf. c. 90. 6   7 ἡ add. Stein²
8 νῆα z   9 ἔγνω τε ? Stein²   10, 12 Θεμιστοκλῆα (bis) z

---

the foe,' as they would do if they were
covered by Psyttaleia. ὁ πορθμός might
doubtless refer to the water inside the
straits (W. of Psyttaleia) primarily ;
but it is used, c. 76 supra, distinctly of
the more open water to the east, and
that interpretation seems to give a better
sense ere.

ἔργα ἀπεδέξαντο λ. ἄξ. : cp. 7.
211. These achievements helped to
win them the prize ; cp. c. 93 infra.

3. ἐν τῷ θορύβῳ might almost seem
to be locative, in contrast with ἐν
τῷ πορθμῷ—the Athenians destroying,
ramming (ἐκεράιζον, c. 86 supra) those
within in the mêlée, whether offering
resistance or trying to escape, the
Aiginetans waylaying those who were
getting out, so that if they escaped
(διαφ.) the Athenians inside Psyttaleia,
they fell headlong (φ. ἐσέπ.) among the
Aiginetans ambushed outside.

92. 2. συνεκύρεον : cp. συνεκύρησε c.
87 supra. The anecdote which follows
is remarkable, inter alia, in its bearing
on the problem of Hdt.'s composition.
'Polykritos, son of Krios, an Aiginetan,'
is introduced, without the slightest apparent reference to the story of the
meeting of his father Krios with King
Kleomenes, 6. 50 supra. Perhaps this
is the earlier passage and the earlier
anecdote, the enmity of Polykritos and
Themistokles having revived, or generated, the story of the medism of Krios
10–11 years earlier ; cp. Introduction,

§§ 7, 8. The Sidonian ship must have
been originally on the right of the
Persian line, or at the head of the
Persian column. (By this time the
Greek right has probably all pushed out
well past Psyttaleia, but the Aiginetans
ὑποστάντες, c. 91 supra.)

4. ἥ περ εἷλε . . ἐκπαγλεόμενοι : an
implicit reference back to the story told
7. 181 supra, with close verbal co-
incidences, unintelligible except to a
reader. ὥστε . . οὕτω is one thing,
οὕτω ὥστε another ; cp. c. 90 supra.

9. τὸ σημήιον . . τῆς στρατηγίδος :
i.e. the admiral's flag, or ensign, whatever it was ; cp. τὸ ἐπίσημον τῆς νεὸς
(of Artemisia) c. 88 supra. That the
ship was an Attic ship he would have
known before identif ing it as the
Flag-ship. Themistokles was assuredly
not the only Athenian Strategos at
Salamis ; probably all nine others were
there (δέκατος αὐτός Thuc.), but he was
certainly ἡγεμών—and doubtless had a
thoroughly distinctive and unmistak-
able pennon or crest. K. O. Müller,
Aeginetica p. 125, suggests that Polykritos was commander-in-chief of the
Aiginetans ; if so, he had supported
Themistokles' plans, c. 74 supra. Or
was he perhaps captain of the ship
which had run the blockade to invoke
the Aiakids ?

10. βώσας . . ὀνειδίζων, 'after a loud
cry (perhaps Themistokles' very name)
he reproached Themistokles in bitter

τὸν μηδισμὸν ὀνειδίζων. ταῦτα μέν νυν νηὶ ἐμβαλὼν ὁ
Πολύκριτος ἀπέρριψε ἐς Θεμιστοκλέα· οἱ δὲ βάρβαροι τῶν αἱ
νέες περιεγένοντο, φεύγοντες ἀπίκοντο ἐς Φάληρον ὑπὸ τὸν
πεζὸν στρατόν.

Ἐν δὲ τῇ ναυμαχίῃ ταύτῃ ἤκουσαν Ἑλλήνων ἄριστα 93
Αἰγινῆται, ἐπὶ δὲ Ἀθηναῖοι, ἀνδρῶν δὲ Πολύκριτός τε ὁ
Αἰγινήτης καὶ Ἀθηναῖοι Εὐμένης τε ὁ Ἀναγυράσιος καὶ
Ἀμεινίης Παλληνεύς, ὃς καὶ Ἀρτεμισίην ἐπεδίωξε. εἰ μέν νυν

---

11 <τῇ> νηὶ Reiske, van H.   13 νῆες z   93. 3 Ἀθηναῖος z
‖ ἀναγυρράσιος Β   4 <ὁ> Παλληνεύς van H.: ἀμινίης παληνεύς R ‖
ἐπεδίωξεν Β: ἀπεδίωξε z

---

terms with reference to the charge of medism against the Aiginetans'—a rather clumsy passage, containing an obscure allusion — nothing having previously been said of any charge of 'medism' against Aigina (except the old charge back in 491 B.C., cp. 6. 49 *supra*: had Themistokles a hand in that?). With ἐπικερτόμησε cp. the adj. κέρτομος in 5. 83. One is almost tempted to think that the Attic and Aiginetan ship had collided (νηὶ ἐμβαλών). The emendations do not affect this materially. ἀπέρριψε: cp. 4. 142, 1. 32, 153.

13. ἐς Φάληρον ὑπὸ τὸν πεζὸν στρατόν, 'into Phaleron, under cover of the land-forces'—which cannot, therefore, all have marched westward; cp. c. 70 *supra*. Doubtless the Persian land-forces had lined the whole coast of the straits during the day.

93. 1. ἤκουσαν Ἑλλήνων ἄριστα Αἰγινῆται: i.e. the Aiginetans, among states or contingents, obtained the ἀριστεῖα: cp. c. 122 *infra*. When was the award made? Immediately after the battle? The Athenians (had) obtained the award for Artemision; cp. c. 17 *supra*. For εὖ, κακῶς ἀκούειν cp. 7. 16, 6. 86, 2. 173; and cp. 3. 131. The aid of the Aiakidai may have contributed to the Aiginetan award. It was alleged that the islanders had begun the fight, and with the trireme which had brought that divine aid; cp. c. 84 *supra*. The Athenians perhaps regarded this award as an injustice to themselves; but it was made not for size and weight of vessels, nor for wisdom in the command, nor for the sacrifice of hearth and home, but simply for collective and individual valour in the actual engagement, and we need not assume that it was flagrantly

unfair. Hdt.'s account of the battle does perhaps less than justice to the action of the Greek right. The Athenian orator in Thuc. 1. 74 does not precisely challenge this award, and Themistokles had not much to complain of (cc. 123, 124 *infra*).

2. ἐπὶ: as in cc. 67, 113.

ἀνδρῶν δέ: included in Ἑλλήνων above, which therefore has no μέν.

Πολύκριτος: c. 92 *supra*.

3. Εὐμένης ὁ Ἀναγυράσιος: i.e. Eumenes of the deme of Ἀναγυροῦς (of the tribe Erechtheis, situate to SE. of Hymettos, and comprising the bay and plain of the modern village *Vari*, named from the ἀνάγυρος, *anagyris foetida*, stinking bean-trefoil; cp. L. & S. and Milchhoefer *ap*. Pauly-Wissowa i. 2028). The *Demotikon* shows the official character of the record; but of t is Eumenes nothing more appears to beknown. Is it possible that Hdt. has, c. 84 *supra*, transferred to Ameinias what belongs to Eumenes? Ameinias has enough to his credit without that! cp. c. 87. There is here a clear reference back to that passage.

4. εἰ μέν .. οὐκ ἂν .. πρότερον ἤ .. ἧλε: a very pretty conditional sentence. 'Had he known that Artemisia was aboard, he would not have abandoned the chase until he had captured her or been himself taken prisoner.' ταύτῃ is rather loose, as her ship has not been mentioned; εἰ μέν νυν ἔμαθε, οὐκ ἂν ἐπαύσατο is of course a perfectly normal form of conditional sentence; πλέοι is certainly defensible in the dependent sentence; cp. εἶεν c. 107, and App. Crit. The verbs εἷλε and ἧλε in the indicative appear to be complementary to the construction of the *protasis*. Baehr's notion

5 ἔμαθε ὅτι ἐν ταύτῃ πλέοι Ἀρτεμισίη, οὐκ ἂν ἐπαύσατο πρότερον ἢ εἷλέ μιν ἢ καὶ αὐτὸς ἥλω. τοῖσι γὰρ Ἀθηναίων
τριηράρχοισι παρεκεκέλευστο, πρὸς δὲ καὶ ἄεθλον ἔκειτο μύριαι
δραχμαί, ὃς ἄν μιν ζωὴν ἕλῃ· δεινὸν γάρ τι ἐποιεῦντο γυναῖκα
ἐπὶ τὰς Ἀθήνας στρατεύεσθαι. αὕτη μὲν δή, ὡς πρότερον
10 εἴρηται, διέφυγε· ἦσαν δὲ καὶ οἱ ἄλλοι, τῶν αἱ νέες περιεγεγόνεσαν, ἐν τῷ Φαλήρῳ.

94   Ἀδείμαντον δὲ τὸν Κορίνθιον στρατηγὸν λέγουσι Ἀθηναῖοι

---

5 πλώει ἡ Ἀρτεμισίη z   7 παρακεκέλευστο CPz   8 τοι z
10 εἴρηται 'Plerumque H. addit μοι' van H. ‖ διέφυγε om. C ‖ ἦσαν . .
Φαλήρῳ del. Krueger approb. van H. ‖ ἔσαν z ‖ νῆες z   94. 1
Κορινθίων Naber, van H. ('sed fortasse insiticium est στρατηγὸν')

---

that ἄν has to be mentally supplied is not
happy. The double use of ἤ, comparative, and simply alternative, is noticeable.

6. Ἀθηναίων τριηράρχοισι: the term
τριήραρχοι is used freely of the ship-
captains, or commanders, on both sides,
and of any folk; though at Athens
a special form of the τριηραρχία had
perhaps already been instituted; cp.
Appendix III. § 4.

7 παρεκεκέλευστο: a strict temporal
pl.p. from παρακελεύεσθαι: cp. c. 15
supra, 9. 102 (absolutely).

μύριαι δραχμαί: 100 minai, or
1⅔ talents, say £400, which at the then
value of money might be multiplied by
at least ten to give the equivalent.

8. ὃς ἄν μιν ζωὴν ἕλῃ, (for) 'whoever took her alive.' What did they
intend to do with her? It was hardly
chivalry that prompted the proclamation: yet was not their guardian deity
of the feminine gender? ζωός (sic) 1.
194, 2. 70, 122, 132, 7. 113.

δεινὸν . . στρατεύεσθαι, 'they
took it sorely to heart that a woman
should be on the war-trail against
Athens'—δ. ποιέεσθαι 7. 35 etc. There
was the precedent of the Amazons!
Cp. 9. 27 infra. That war had ended
with a wedding.

9. ὡς πρότερον εἴρηται: an explicit
reference to c. 87 supra. μοι would
make the phrase less like a gloss.

10. ἦσαν δὲ . . ἐν τῷ Φαλήρῳ. This
sentence is a repetition of the concluding
words of c. 92, but with a difference:
ἀπίκοντο is replaced by ἦσαν (action
by condition), τῶν αἱ νέες περιεγένοντο
by τῶν αἱ ν. περιεγεγόνεσαν (aorist by
pluperfect), and ἐς Φάληρον by ἐν τῷ

Φαλήρῳ (motion by rest). Even καὶ οἱ
ἄλλοι adds a point. But cp. App. Crit.

94. 1. Ἀδείμαντον: c. 5 supra, and
cp. 7. 137.

λέγουσι Ἀθηναῖοι: the story here
told from Athenian sources is a transparent bit of scandal, due to the rivalry
and jealousy of Athens and Korinth in
and after the Persian war. It is improbable, if not absurd, in itself; it is contradicted by the Korinthians, who were supported by the rest of Greece: Plutarch
de Hdti. malig. 39 has an easy task in
refuting it, by the evidence of extant
monuments, and epitaphs and stories.
Dio Chrysostom (?) says, Or. 37. 7 (ed.
Teubner ii. p. 295), that the first draft of
Hdt.'s history did not contain the story,
and that Hdt. inserted it to revenge
himself for the refusal of the Korinthians
to give him money. The fact (of composition) and the explanation can here
be distinguished. The explanation is
itself 'malignant,' and (as Plutarch
shows) the anecdote is hardly less to the
discredit of the Athenians than of the
Korinthians—one might indeed say,
more.

The story might well be an addition,
an insertion, by the author, in a second
or third draft; it has the air of an
anecdote, and Hdt. uses below one of
the rare formulae (φάτις ἔχει) which are
most suggestive of oral sources; cp. Introduction, §§ 9, 10. But false as the
story must be, had the Athenians no
excuse, no peg on which to hang the
scandal? If a detachment of the Persian
fleet had been sent to circumnavigate
Salamis, and to bar or to penetrate the
Megarid channel, a squadron of Greek

αὐτίκα κατ᾽ ἀρχάς, ὡς συνέμισγον αἱ νέες, ἐκπλαγεντα τε καὶ
ὑπερδείσαντα, τὰ ἱστία ἀειράμενον οἴχεσθαι φεύγοντα, ἰδόντας
δὲ τοὺς Κορινθίους τὴν στρατηγίδα φεύγουσαν ὡσαύτως οἴχεσθαι. ὡς δὲ ἄρα φεύγοντας γίνεσθαι τῆς Σαλαμινίης κατὰ 5
ἱρὸν Ἀθηναίης Σκιράδος, περιπίπτειν σφι κέλητα θείῃ πομπῇ,

---

2 καταρχὰς AB ‖ νῆες κ   3 τὰ del. Krueger   4 φέρουσαν C
6 τὸ ἱρὸν κ, van H. ‖ σκιρράδος β

---

ships must have been detached to con-
front the 'barbarians' and keep them
out. The 40 Korinthian ships may
have been detached on this service (cp.
the service of the 53 Athenian ships at
Chalkis, c. 14 supra), and may even
have had some fighting to do on their
own account. The Athenian travesty
need not be brought down to the date of
the Archidamian war in 431 B.C.; the
first Peloponnesian war in 458 B.C. would
be a possible occasion; but there was
already friction enough in 480 B.C. for
a deal of mutual scandal to be set afloat.

2. αὐτίκα κατ᾽ ἀρχάς: cp. 7. 88
supra.

συνέμισγον: here of hostile encounter, cp. 1. 166, 4. 127, 6. 14; of
friendly converse, cc. 67, 79 supra, etc.

3. τὰ ἱστία ἀειράμενον: cp. c. 56
supra.

4. τοὺς Κορινθίους: all forty vessels!
c. 43 supra; what of the Amprakiotes,
and Leukadians (making together ten
more, c. 45 supra)? The Athenians
forgot to account for them; but probably
they accompanied the Korinthians for
better or worse.

5. ἄρα: still the Athenian reporter;
the word has a touch of malignity here,
even if it betokens 'an advance in the
action' (Abicht) as in 7. 116, 9. 8.

κατὰ ἱρὸν Ἀθηναίης Σκιράδος.
According to Pausan. 1. 36. 4 the oldest
temple of Athene Skiras was at Phaleron,
and had been founded by a diviner from
Dodona named Σκῖρος, who had fallen
in the war between the Eleusinians and
Erechtheus, and had been buried, by
them, near a torrent, which afterwards,
as well as the place, was known by his
name. The temple here in question
cannot be the one at Phaleron; it is
plainly on Salamis. Strabo 393 gives
Σκιράς as an old name of Salamis, 'from
some hero,' and therefrom derives also
the title of Athene. The Σκιρωνὶς ὁδός
is not far off, cp. c. 70 supra. σκῖρος

means hard, harsh (σκλῆρος), and appears
in the names of rough places, cp. Σκιρῖτις.
The connexion with σκίρον, Σκιροφόρια
(cp. Strabo l.c.) is doubtless based upon
a Volksetymologie. The temple on
Salamis may have had no proper connexion with the temple at Phaleron.
As to its position: (i.) Stein places the
temple of Athene Skiras on the extreme
southern point of the island; the ἄκρον
τὸ Σκιράδιον is mentioned by Plutarch,
Solon 9, as apparently in the neighbourhood of a χηλή τις πρὸς τὴν Εὔβοιαν (sic)
ἀποβλέπουσα, and in Mor. 870 (=de
Hdti. m. 39) this episode is located περὶ
τὰ λήγοντα τῆς Σαλαμινίας—which would
perhaps suit that 'end' of Salamis best.
If this view be correct the line of the
Korinthian flight would lie outside the
island, and be quite inconsistent with
any of the theories of the battle-lines.
(ii.) Leake, Topogr. and Demi, ii.²171 ff.,
identified the spot with "the north-
western promontory of Salamis" now
occupied by a monastery of the Παναγία
φανερωμένη (the Virgin brought to light).
The monastery stands on the site of an
Hellenic building. This position would
suit the argument better; and the continued existence of a sacred building is
in its favour. (iii.) Westermann ad
Plutarch. makes it the extreme western
promontory of Salamis, nearest Megara.
This location suits best with the suggestion above made in regard to the true
services of the Korinthians; moreover,
if one were concerned to rationalize the
incident of the κέλης this position would
be the most intelligible: a message,
carried from the Greek fleet, across the
wasp's waist of Salamis, and then by
boat to Budoron, might easily have
'met' the Korinthians as they made
their way out of the straits.

6. περιπίπτειν, 'encountered,' c. 89
supra.

κέλητα: here inevitably a boat,
cp. 7. 86 supra; θείῃ πομπῇ 4. 152 etc.

τὸν οὔτε πέμψαντα φανῆναι οὐδένα, οὔτε τι τῶν ἀπὸ τῆς
στρατιῆς δὴ εἰδόσι προσφέρεσθαι τοῖσι Κορινθίοισι· τῇ δὴ
συμβάλλονται εἶναι θεῖον τὸ πρῆγμα. ὡς γὰρ ἀγχοῦ γενέσθαι
10 τῶν νεῶν, τοὺς ἀπὸ τοῦ κέλητος λέγειν τάδε. "Ἀδείμαντε,
σὺ μὲν ἀποστρέψας τὰς νέας ἐς φυγὴν ὅρμησαι καταπροδοὺς
τοὺς Ἕλληνας· οἱ δὲ καὶ δὴ νικῶσι ὅσον αὐτοὶ ἠρῶντο
ἐπικρατήσαντες τῶν ἐχθρῶν." ταῦτα λεγόντων ἀπιστέειν γὰρ
τὸν Ἀδείμαντον, αὖτις τάδε λέγειν, ὡς αὐτοὶ οἷοί τε εἶεν
15 ἀγόμενοι ὅμηροι ἀποθνήσκειν, ἢν μὴ νικῶντες φαίνωνται οἱ
Ἕλληνες. οὕτω δὴ ἀποστρέψαντα τὴν νέα αὐτόν τε καὶ τοὺς
ἄλλους ἐπ' ἐξεργασμένοισι ἐλθεῖν ἐς τὸ στρατόπεδον. τούτους
μὲν τοιαύτη φάτις ἔχει ὑπὸ Ἀθηναίων, οὐ μέντοι αὐτοί γε
Κορίνθιοι ὁμολογέουσι, ἀλλ' ἐν πρώτοισι σφέας αὐτοὺς τῆς
20 ναυμαχίης νομίζουσι γενέσθαι· μαρτυρέει δέ σφι καὶ ἡ ἄλλη
Ἑλλάς.

95　Ἀριστείδης δὲ ὁ Λυσιμάχου ἀνὴρ Ἀθηναῖος, τοῦ καὶ

---

7 φάναι C　　8 τῇ δὴ Stein[(2)8] (et Madvig), Holder, van H. :
τῇδε δὲ　　10 νηῶν z ‖ λέγει C　　11 ναῦς ‖ φυγεῖν B ‖ ὥρμησαι ᵬ,
Stein[1]　　12 αὐτοὶ: αὖ ᵬ　　13 ἐπικρατήσαντες Stein[2], van H. :
ἐπικρατῆσαι　　14 καὶ ὡς ! Stein[2] ‖ τε del. Cobet, van H. : 'expectabam
ἕτοιμοι vel ἄρτιοι' van H.　　16 ἀποστρέψαντες z ‖ νῆα z　　　17
ἐπεξειργασμένοισι Cz　　20 μαρτυρεῖ codd. z, Holder, van H.

---

7. τὸν οὔτε .. οὐδένα. 'It was
never discovered that any one had despatched the boat,' rather than 'it was
evident that no one had despatched the
boat'—a ὕστερον would make the point
clearer. But there was apparently
nothing at the moment in evidence to
suggest to the Korinthians the supernatural character of the occurrence.

οὔτε τι .. Κορινθίοισι: the
meaning is clear, but the expression is
involved: 'and the Korinthians whom
it approached knew nothing of the
fortunes of the fleet'; i.e. προσφέρεσθαι
τε τ. Κ. οὐδὲν τῶν ἀπὸ τ. στ. εἰδόσι.
The participle is essentially a part of
the predicate. τὰ ἀπό, as of news
from; cp. 4. 54 τὰ ἀπὸ τούτων τῶν
ποταμῶν.

9. συμβάλλονται: coniiciunt; sc. οἱ
Ἀθηναῖοι, οἱ λέγοντες.

10. τοὺς ἀπὸ τοῦ κέλητος: a false
parallel to τῶν ἀπὸ τῆς στρατιῆς just
above; perhaps an 'unconscious iteration.'

11. ἀποστρέψας apparently means
'having turned tail,' or having turned

aside, cp. c. 87 supra; which shows
that τὰς νέας is here superfluous; cp. 4.
43. The word is repeated below, of the
return from flight.

ἐς φυγὴν ὅρμησαι: the verb is
apparently perf. pass. unaugmented; cp.
App. Crit. καὶ δή = ἤδη 4. 102. κατα-
προδούς: cp. 7. 157, 9. 7, 11 etc.

12. ὅσον αὐτοὶ ἠρῶντο, 'to the
height of their own prayers,' i.e. of the
Greeks.

14. ὡς αὐτοὶ .. ἀποθνήσκειν: i.e. the
men in the boat (their number is not
given) offered to be treated as hostages,
to go bail, for the truth of their statement. Yet Adeimantos lets them depart,
apparently convinced by this generous
offer ! ἀγόμενοι, middle, 'of their own
accord.'

17. ἐπ' ἐξεργασμένοισι ἐλθεῖν: cp. 9.
77 infra.

τὸ στρατόπεδον, the fleet; cp. c.
11 l. 7, c. 84 l. 11 supra.

18. φάτις ἔχει: cp. 7. 3 supra, and
Introduction, § 10.

95. 1. Ἀριστείδης .. Ἀθηναῖος: cp.
c. 79 supra. To have the full description

ὀλίγῳ τι πρότερον τούτων ἐπεμνήσθην ὡς ἀνδρὸς ἀρίστου,
οὗτος ἐν τῷ θορύβῳ τούτῳ τῷ περὶ Σαλαμῖνα γενομένῳ τάδε
ἐποίεε· παραλαβὼν πολλοὺς τῶν ὁπλιτέων οἳ παρατετάχατο
παρὰ τὴν ἀκτὴν τῆς Σαλαμινίης χώρης, γένος ἐόντες Ἀθηναῖοι, 5

95. 2 ἐμνήσθην Pz   4 οἳ: οἱ R: οἳ πολλοὶ z

of the man repeated *totidem verbis* within
a few pages, together with the express
and unusually explicit reference back (τοῦ
. . ἀρίστου), creates a problem in regard
to Hdt.'s composition. It can hardly
be that the two passages belong to one
and the same draft of the Book, and
were written *in einem Flug*. This
passage may belong to the first draft,
that to the second; in which case the
back reference was inserted, apologeti-
cally, without sacrificing the 'patronymic'
and 'ethnic,' which serve to emphasize
the deed of Aristeides. Was Aristeides
in command of all the Athenian hoplites
on shore (amounting to some thousands),
while Themistokles was in command of
the fleet?

3. **τάδε ἐποίεε.** There are three
accounts of the exploit, more or less
differing from each other, but substantially reconcilable: (i.) Aischylos (*Persae*
447 ff.) places the affair late in the day
apparently, when the enemy's fleet has
been beaten, and there is nothing to
prevent the Greeks surrounding the
island with their own ships (Blakesley).
It is not, however, correct to say that
Aischylos represents the assault as made
by the actual crews of the vessels
(Rawlinson); and it is only fair to
observe that in Aischylos Xerxes is still
looking on. (ii.) Herodotus places the
exploit late in his narrative (perhaps in
conformity with Aischylos), but apparently dates the affair earlier on the day
of battle (ἐν τῷ θορύβῳ τούτῳ κτλ. : cp.
c. 91 *supra*). He does not explain how
Aristeides got his men on to the island :
boats may be supposed. A happy thought
apparently occurs to Aristeides while
the battle is raging, and he executes it
instanter. (iii.) Plutarch, *Aristeid.* 9,
of course, goes further. Aristeides
observes that the island is strongly
occupied : puts picked volunteers in
boats, destroys all the Persians, except a
few (whom he sends to Themistokles,
three nephews of the king included, who
were immolated ὠμηστῇ Διονύσῳ), and

occupies the whole shore of the island
with troops in order to assist the men of
the fleet in destroying the enemy. Yet
Plutarch may be substantially right.

The occupation of Psyttaleia by the
Persians on this occasion proved as great
a tactical blunder as the occupation of
Sphakteria by the Spartans in 425 B.C.,
and for the same reason, that the
occupants of the island were involved in
the fate of the fleet. But there was
more excuse for the Persian. The naval
superiority of the Greeks was not a foregone conclusion, and the occupation of
Psyttaleia probably had as its ultimate
object a landing on Salamis, and an
assault upon the Greek forces in the
island. This aspect of the case makes
it not improbable that the Athenian
attack on the island should be placed ἐν
τῷ θορύβῳ τούτῳ with Hdt., with Plutarch,
and even possibly with Aischylos : it
was not a mere afterthought, or sequel
of the battle, but an essential part of it,
concerted, in all probability, between
Themistokles and Aristeides. The
Athenian hoplites remembered Marathon : not a few of them had even
fought there.

4. **τῶν ὁπλιτέων οἳ παρατετάχατο**: he
did not denude Salamis of its defenders.
The παράταξις shows that the generals
perfectly understood the situation : just
at that point, where the Greek right
wing was posted, a success, even
temporary, on the part of the Persians,
would have led to an attempt to land
from Psyttaleia upon Salamis (Kynosura),
from which it would have been difficult
to dislodge the enemy.

5. **τὴν ἀκτὴν τῆς Σαλαμινίης χώρης**
may refer primarily to Keos = Kynosura,
but need scarcely be confined to that
promontory. If Aristeides was in command (στρατηγὸς ἐπὶ τὰ ὅπλα) he would
naturally have been on the right in this
immediate neighbourhood.

γένος ἐόντες Ἀθηναῖοι: this particularity is remarkable : were his volunteers
primarily the Salaminian οἰκήτορες?

ἐς τὴν Ψυττάλειαν νῆσον ἀπέβησε ἄγων· οἳ τοὺς Πέρσας τοὺς
ἐν τῇ νησῖδι ταύτῃ κατεφόνευσαν πάντας.

96 Ὡς δὲ ἡ ναυμαχίη διελέλυτο, κατειρύσαντες ἐς τὴν
Σαλαμῖνα οἱ Ἕλληνες τῶν ναυηγίων ὅσα ταύτῃ ἐτύγχανε ἔτι
ἐόντα, ἕτοιμοι ἦσαν ἐς ἄλλην ναυμαχίην, ἐλπίζοντες τῇσι
περιεούσῃσι νηυσὶ ἔτι χρήσεσθαι βασιλέα. τῶν δὲ ναυηγίων
5 πολλὰ ὑπολαβὼν ἄνεμος ζέφυρος ἔφερε τῆς Ἀττικῆς ἐπὶ τὴν
ἠιόνα τὴν καλεομένην Κωλιάδα· ὥστε ἀποπλησθῆναι τὸν
χρησμὸν τόν τε ἄλλον πάντα τὸν περὶ τῆς ναυμαχίης ταύτης

---

6 νῆσον del. Cobet, Holder, van H.   7 νησῖδι CPz   96. 1
κατερύσαντες CP : κατερρύσαντες z   2 ταύτηι α : ταύτη ἔτι Β
3 ἕτοιμοι CPz ‖ ἔσαν z   4 βασιλῆα z   5 ὑποβαλὼν C ‖ ὁ
ἄνεμος z ‖ ἐξέφερε τοῖς Ἀττικοῖς Lex. Vindob. p. 181   6 ἀποπλησθῆναι Valla (ut impletum sit): ἀποπλῆσθαι Buttmann : ἀποπεπλῆσθαι
Abicht, van H. : ἀποπλῆσαι

---

6. Ψυττάλειαν : c. 76 supra. According to Steph. Byz. the island was named
from Ψύτταλος : but what of him !
  ἀπέβησε ἄγων: he headed the
landing-party. ἀπέβ. is trans. The
last sentence of the chapter denies the
sacrifice, the story of which is preserved
by Plutarch ; see above.
  96. 1. διελέλυτο : pl.p. There is no
more actual fighting going on. Aischylos,
Pers. 428, does not say that the actual
fighting, but that the weeping and
wailing lasted ἕως κελαινῆς νυκτὸς ὄμμ'
ἀφείλετο. Hdt. plainly implies that the
battle was over, in time apparently for
the Greeks to apprehend a fresh attack.
  κατειρύσαντες, to land. In the
Odyssey it is always used of dragging the
vessel down into the sea.
  2. ὅσα ταύτῃ . . ἔτι ἐόντα: i.e. not
yet driven by wind or current to the
Attic coast ; see just below. They
would easily possess themselves of the
wrecks west of Psyttaleia. Evidently at
first they did not realize the magnitude
of their success, or the depression of the
enemy, but expected (ἐλπίζοντες) that
the king would order a fresh attack.
  3. τῇσι περιεούσῃσι νηυσί : not
merely, or so much, those which had
returned to Phaleron (c. 92 supra), as
the squadron which had moved round
the island the night before, and were
still perhaps almost intact, c. 76 supra.
The text may originally have proceeded
Ξέρξης δέ κτλ. c. 97 infra ; the intervening passage has the air of a παρενθήκη
(cp. 7. 171), or προσθήκη (4. 30), added

in his second draft by Hdt. after a visit
to Athens ; cp. Introduction, § 9.
  5. ὑπολαβών : as in 7. 170 supra.
  τὴν ἠιόνα τὴν καλεομένην Κωλιάδα :
Kolias is a cape, or promontory (ἄκρα
ἤτοι ἀκτή, Steph. Byz.), some twenty
stades from Phaleron, cp. Pausan. 1. 1.
5 ἀπέχει δὲ σταδίους εἴκοσιν ἄκρα Κωλιάς·
. . Κωλιάδος δέ ἐστιν ἐνταῦθα Ἀφροδίτης
ἄγαλμα καὶ Γενετυλλίδες ὀνομαζόμεναι
θεαί. Leake's identification of Kolias
with Hagios Georgios (τρεῖς Πύργοι), the
eastern limit of the bay of Phaleron,
is endorsed by Milchhoefer : Strabo
398 places it apparently further south,
in the neighbourhood of Anaphlystos.
Cp. Hitzig - Bluemner, Pausanias, l.c.
ἠιόν, as in 7. 44 supra.
  6. ὥστε . . τὸ εἰρημένον : the structure and argument of the passage are
remarkable : what Hdt. is apparently
concerned to say is that τὸν χρησμὸν
ἀποπλησθῆναι δὲ ἐλελήθεε πάντας τοὺς
Ἕλληνας, sc. τὸ πολλοῖσι ἔτεσι πρότερον
τούτων ἐν χρησμῷ Λυσιστράτῳ Ἀθηναίῳ
ἀνδρὶ χρησμολόγῳ εἰρημένον—but, having
started on the fulfilment of prophecy,
he is led to say a good word in passing
for the much more extensive and less
obscure prophecy of Bakis. When he
started, τὸν χρησμόν may have been
intended for the prophecy of Lysistratos,
but as it is diverted to Bakis, the idea is
resumed in the words τὸ εἰρημένον ἐν
χρησμῷ.
  7. τόν τε ἄλλον πάντα . . Βάκιδι.
On Bakis cp. c. 77 supra. There was
presumably extant in Hdt.'s time a pretty

εἰρημένον Βάκιδι [καὶ Μουσαίῳ], καὶ δὴ καὶ κατὰ τὰ ναυήγια
τὰ ταύτῃ ἐξενειχθέντα τὸ εἰρημένον πολλοῖσι ἔτεσι πρότερον
τούτων ἐν χρησμῷ Λυσιστράτῳ Ἀθηναίῳ ἀνδρὶ χρησμολόγῳ, 10
τὸ ἐλελήθεε πάντας τοὺς Ἕλληνας,
    Κωλιάδες δὲ γυναῖκες ἐρετμοῖσι φρύξουσι.
τοῦτο δὲ ἔμελλε ἀπελάσαντος βασιλέος ἔσεσθαι.
    Ξέρξης δὲ ὡς ἔμαθε τὸ γεγονὸς πάθος, δείσας μή τις τῶν 97

---

8 καὶ Μουσέῳ z : 'fortasse spuria' Stein, seclusi : verba τὸν χρησμὸν . .
ἐξενειχθέντα genuina esse dubit. van H.   9 ἐξενεχθέντα CR   10
τουτέων z   11 λέληθε ? Stein²   12 φρύξουσι Joach. Kuhn :
φρίξουσι   13 ἐπελάσαντος βασιλῆος z   97. 1 τῶν τις Krueger,
van H.

extensive oracular poem ascribed to Bakis,
the reference of which to Salamis was
obvious. Cp. Introduction, § 10. καὶ
Μουσαίῳ is to be removed as a gloss :
otherwise the problem of the authorship
of the poem is hopelessly confused. On
Musaios cp. 9. 43.
    9. πολλοῖσι ἔτεσι πρότερον τούτων :
τούτων referring not to Hdt. and his own
date of composition, still less to Bakis
and Musaios, or the oracles of Bakis, but
to the battle of Salamis, and the circumstances by which the prediction was
fulfilled. The date is unfortunately
vague : does it refer to the times of
Peisistratos, or of Solon, or to still more
ancient days ?
    10. Λυσιστράτῳ cannot of course be
the Athenian, more or less contemporary
with Hdt., who is a frequent subject of
satire to Aristophanes (Acharn. 855,
Knts. 1267, Wsps. 787 ff., 1301, Lysistr.
1105), but might conceivably be an
ancestor of his.
    11. τὸ ἐλελήθεε πάντας τοὺς Ἕλληνας.
Stein⁵ has cancelled his own emendation
λέληθε, and is content to return to the
view that Hdt. is not claiming for himself the first correct application of the
prophecy of Lysistratos, but dates the
true interpretation to the time of Salamis.
But the antiquity of the oracle demands
an earlier occasion ; one might be found
in the great adventure of Solon at Kolias,
narrated in Plutarch, Solon, 8, which,
according to one account, led to the
Athenian capture of Salamis, though it
is easy to understand that the learned
Hellenes, interpreters of prophecy, in
discussing such matters, might gladly
have transferred, before the date of
Hdt.'s composition, the fulfilment of this

chresm to the still grander occasion in
their own times. Solon's adventure was
scarcely remembered outside Athens—
and Megara ! 'The Hellenes' here may
well be writers, even if Hdt. himself is
not claiming to have put them right.
Cp. Introduction, § 10.
    12. Κωλιάδες δὲ γυναῖκες ἐρετμοῖσι
φρύξουσι. 'The women of Kolias' are
probably not so much local residents as
women visiting the place for the cult or
festival of the local Demeter (sic, Plutarch,
Solon, 8), who may have used the oars
(of the Megarians ?) to cook their cakes
with. φρύξουσι, though an emendation,
seems acceptable, and more oracular than
φρίξουσι (cp. φρύξαντες 2. 94). πέλανοι
would be used in the local cult ; or perhaps κριθαὶ πεφρυγμέναι, Thuc. 6. 22.
Applied to the b. of Salamis in 480
B.C., the prophecy must have been
fulfilled 'after the king's departure,'
an event far in the future (ἔμελλε ἔσεσθαι),
in the time of Lysistratos !
    97. 1. ὡς ἔμαθε τὸ γεγονὸς πάθος,
'when he became aware of the extent
of the disaster which had taken place.'
τις τῶν : contr. c. 90 supra.
    δείσας μή . . ἀπολέσθαι : this re-
ported apprehension of Xerxes conveys
potentially a criticism upon the Greek
conduct of affairs at this crisis. The
Greeks failed to utilize their victory to
the full. Had the Persian communications with Asia been cut at this date,
the king might never have returned
alive, a revolt in Asia would certainly
have taken place, Thrace and Macedon
might have used their opportunity, the
battle of Plataia need never have been
fought. It was not the fault of Themistokles that the more daring but, in the

Ἰώνων ὑποθῆται τοῖσι Ἕλλησι ἢ αὐτοὶ νοήσωσι πλέειν ἐς
τὸν Ἑλλήσποντον λύσοντες τὰς γεφύρας, καὶ ἀπολαμφθεὶς ἐν
τῇ Εὐρώπῃ κινδυνεύσῃ ἀπολέσθαι, δρησμὸν ἐβούλευε. θέλων
5 δὲ μὴ ἐπίδηλος εἶναι μήτε τοῖσι Ἕλλησι μήτε τοῖσι ἑωυτοῦ, ἐς
τὴν Σαλαμῖνα χῶμα ἐπειρᾶτο διαχοῦν, γαύλους τε Φοινικηίους

2 ἐπινοήσωσι ? Stein², van H.   4 ἀπολέσθαι κινδυνεύσηι Ccorr.
P : ἀπολέσθαι κινδυνεύσει Cpr.: ἀπολέσθαι κινδυνεῦσαι z ‖ ἐβούλευσε Pz
5 ἐπίδημος B   6 γαυλούς libri, van H.

long run, the more prudent course was
omitted ; cp. c. 108 infra.

3. ἀπολαμφθείς : c. 11 supra.

4. δρησμόν : c. 4 supra.

5. ἐς τὴν Σαλαμῖνα χῶμα ἐπειρᾶτο
διαχοῦν, 'he attempted (more than
'began') to construct a mole right across
to Salamis,' from the mainland. Hdt.
unfortunately does not locate the structure. The time, the place, the nature
of the work, and its purpose, are all in
debate. The likeliest place would be
on the line of the existing ferry, both
because that is the shortest line, and
also because the island of St. George
offers a ready-made pier or point d'appui
for the structure, though not on the
direct line, which would be less than a
mile across. Ktesias, Persica, ed. Gilmore,
§ 57, p. 157, locates the mole, and dates
the attempt before the battle : ὁ δὲ
Ξέρξης αὐτόθεν ἐλθὼν ἐπὶ στεινότατον τῆς
Ἀττικῆς ('Ηράκλειον καλεῖται) ἐχώννυε
χῶμα ἐπὶ Σαλαμῖνα πεζῇ ἐπ' αὐτὴν διαβῆναι διανοούμενος. The attempt is frus-
trated by Themistokles and Aristeides,
who procure archers from Krete ; and its
failure makes a sea-fight necessary. The
place may be right, 'the narrowest part
of Attica' being taken to mean the
narrowest part of the straits between
Attica and Salamis ; the time, or sequence,
appears to be better in Hdt. To construct a mole, or bridge of boats, all
across the straits, while the Greeks were
in possession, and without a naval battle,
was impossible. Moreover, before the
naval battle such a work would have
been inconsistent with the naval tactics.
If it had run (as Stein supposes) from
the Herakleion to Kynosura, it would
(if completed) have kept the king's fleet
out of the straits, and the Greek fleet
inside ! But even running from the
extreme point of Skaramanga to the isle
of St. George, or (and) on to the actual
shore of Salamis, it could not have been
seriously undertaken before a naval
victory had cleared the Greek ships out
of the bay ; and it would have interfered
with any design of circumnavigating
the island freely. Alexander, indeed,
attempted to take Tyre with a mole,
while the Tyrians had command of the
sea, Arrian 2. 18. But the two cases
are not parallel. Tyre was a fortified
island of small dimensions, half a mile
only off the coast, and not in any way
embayed ; moreover, Alexander failed,
until he had secured command of the
sea, to capture the place. (Rawlinson
is wrong on this matter of fact.) Thus
a serious attempt to bridge the channel
to Salamis was absurd and impossible
without an antecedent naval victory ;
after a naval defeat, still more so. It
follows that, if any such attempt at all
was made, it was a feint, or it was some
work completely misunderstood by Hdt.'s
sources and himself. Phoenician round-
ships may have been lashed together,
the beginning of a mole or pier may
have been started, and this work may
have been begun before the naval engagement, in confident anticipation of a
victory. After the naval defeat such
preparations could have deceived nobody,
and must have been abandoned. In
regard to the form of the structure
itself, the χῶμα may have been intended
to serve as a solid pier leading on to
the round-ships, which would support
some sort of roadway, and could be
tugged into position after the Greek
fleet had been disabled. It is noticeable
that, even according to Hdt., preparations for another naval battle are also
on foot ; i.e. command of the sea must
be regained before the connexion with
Salamis could be established, over which
the land-forces might pour into the
island. Is it not also possible that the
projected or attempted structure was
rather of the nature of a wharf or jetty
or pier, for embarkation and so on, and

συνέδεε, ἵνα ἀντί τε σχεδίης ἔωσι καὶ τείχεος, ἀρτέετό τε ἐς
πόλεμον ὡς ναυμαχίην ἄλλην ποιησόμενος. ὁρῶντες δέ μιν
πάντες οἱ ἄλλοι ταῦτα πρήσσοντα εὖ ἠπιστέατο ὡς ἐκ παντὸς
νόου παρεσκεύασται μένων πολεμήσειν· Μαρδόνιον δ' οὐδὲν 10
τούτων ἐλάνθανε ὡς μάλιστα ἔμπειρον ἐόντα τῆς ἐκείνου
διανοίης.

Ταῦτά τε ἅμα Ξέρξης ἐποίεε καὶ ἔπεμπε ἐς Πέρσας 98
ἀγγελέοντα τὴν παρεοῦσάν σφι συμφορήν. τούτων δὲ τῶν
ἀγγέλων ἐστὶ οὐδὲν ὅ τι θᾶσσον παραγίνεται θνητὸν ἐόν·
οὕτω τοῖσι Πέρσῃσι ἐξεύρηται τοῦτο. λέγουσι γὰρ ὡς ὁσέων

---

8 ὁρέωντες C : ὁρέοντες Pz, Stein[1], van H.   9 εὖ deL Krueger
10 παρεσκεύαστο z   11 τουτέων z ‖ ἐόντα om. R   98. 1 τε
om. S   2 παρεοῦσάν Pz : παροῦσαν ‖ τουτέων z   3 ἐστι PRz
4 ὁσέων Stein, van H. : ὅσον A : ὅσων

---

was never intended to reach the opposite
shore ?

9. **εὖ ἠπιστέατο**: i.e. merely 'were
fully convinced,' 'firmly believed'; cp.
c. 88 supra.

ἐκ παντὸς νόου παρεσκεύασται,
(that the king) 'has completely made
up his mind'; the verb, though passive
in form, has obviously a middle force.

10. **Μαρδόνιον**: cp. c. 68 supra.

11. **ἐλάνθανε**: not merely 'escaped,'
but 'deceived'; Mardonios saw through
the king's ruse. He had most knowledge
of the king's mental ways! **διανοίης**:
cp. c. 88 supra.

98. 1. ἔπεμπε: was the postal route
really carried all round the Aegean, from
Athens to the Hellespont, and so on to
Susa ? Was there no system of signalling ? Cp. 9. 3 infra. The parataxis
with τε ἅμα καί may be noticed ; the
need for special emphasis is not obvious.

2. **σφι** would seem to refer primarily
to (ἐς) Πέρσας, where the συμφορή was not,
strictly speaking, παρεοῦσα—at least
until the news arrived. It may be
taken to cover all Persians—those at
home being involved unwittingly in the
disaster to those abroad. The word can
hardly be taken simply with ἀγγελέοντα
—and ἐς Πέρσας is practically rather
locative than ethnical.

3. **ἐστὶ οὐδὲν ὅ τι θᾶσσον παραγίνεται
θνητὸν ἐόν**, 'there is nothing which comes
along so fast—and yet is mortal.' This
saying has almost a touch of autopsis, and
is more forcible than the stereotyped τῶν
ἡμεῖς ἴδμεν. (But cp. 2. 68 for the two
in combination.) There are two points

in which this account of the Persian
postal service has a special interest for
the problem of Hdt.'s composition: (i.)
This passage conflicts with 3. 105 εἶναι
δὲ ταχυτῆτα οὐδενὶ ἑτέρῳ ὅμοιον, οὕτω ὥστε,
εἰ μὴ προλαμβάνειν τοὺς Ἰνδοὺς τῆς ὁδοῦ
ἐν ᾧ τοὺς μύρμηκας συλλέγεσθαι, οὐδένα ἂν
σφέων ἀποσῴζεσθαι. Hdt. must have
forgotten the one passage in writing the
other. (ii.) A more important point :
the Persian postal service is taken for
granted in 3. 126 without description,
and the very term itself—ἀγγαρήιον here
explained—is used. (The substitution
of ἀγγελιηφόρον is the substitution of
the gloss for the text.) This passage,
therefore, would appear to be of earlier
composition than Bk. 3, although one
must admit that the description of the
post has not been introduced at the first
possible occasion even in these Books
(e.g. c. 54 supra). In 1. 216 the horse
is described as πάντων τῶν θνητῶν τὸ
τάχιστον—a statement not inconsistent
with this passage, but in a different
genre.

4. **οὕτω .. ἐξεύρηται τοῦτο**, 'this swift-
ness the Persians have secured by the
invention of those special messengers';
or, perhaps, 'this institution of messengers is a Persian invention for securing
extraordinary rapidity.' Stein renders
οὕτω adeo sollerter, comparing 4. 200
τοῦτο μὲν δὴ οὕτω ἐξευρέθη. But there the
οὕτω may be merely modal, referring to
the method of discovery just previously
described. Others, again, boldly refer
the whole sentence to what follows ; so
Rawlinson, "and this is the method of

5 ἂν ἡμερέων <ἧ> ἡ πᾶσα ὁδός, τοσοῦτοι ἵπποι τε καὶ ἄνδρες
διεστᾶσι, κατὰ ἡμερησίην ὁδὸν ἑκάστην ἵππος τε καὶ ἀνὴρ
τεταγμένος· τοὺς οὔτε νιφετός, οὐκ ὄμβρος, οὐ καῦμα, οὐ
νὺξ ἔργει μὴ οὐ κατανύσαι τὸν προκείμενον αὐτῷ δρόμον τὴν
ταχίστην. ὁ μὲν δὴ πρῶτος δραμὼν παραδιδοῖ τὰ ἐντεταλμένα
10 τῷ δευτέρῳ, ὁ δὲ δεύτερος τῷ τρίτῳ· τὸ δὲ ἐνθεῦτεν ἤδη
κατ' ἄλλον <καὶ ἄλλον> διεξέρχεται παραδιδόμενα, κατά περ
<ἐν> Ἕλλησι ἡ λαμπαδηφορίη τὴν τῷ Ἡφαίστῳ ἐπιτελέουσι.
τοῦτο τὸ δράμημα τῶν ἵππων καλέουσι Πέρσαι ἀγγαρήιον.

---

5 ἧ add. Schaefer, Stein, Holder, van H.   6 ἵπποι B: ἵππος τε
καὶ ἀνὴρ om. z   7 τεταγμένοι z ‖ οὔτε: οὔ τι z, Schaefer: οὐ Cobet
8 ἔργει z ‖ ἑωυτῷ z, van H.: 'An delendum?' idem   11 καὶ ἄλλον
Valla (alium atque alium)   12 ἐν add. Stein² (παρὰ? Stein¹) ‖ λαμπαδι-
φορίη B   13 ἀγγειρήιον R: num verba τοῦτο .. ἀγγαρήιον quasi
glossema sustuleris?

---

it" (which will hardly do). It is unlikely, by the way, that 'the Persians'
invented this courier service, or imperial
post, though Xenophon, *Kyrop.* 8. 6. 17 f.,
ascribes it to Kyros, and Baehr—on
general grounds—to Dareios. The invention may be taken to be centuries
older than either, and to have been
employed by all the great empires and
kingdoms which were now merged in
the Persian. It is substantially one with
the system of the Prairie Post, or *Pony
Express*, described by Mark Twain in
Roughing it, c. viii.

λέγουσι: with this admission we
relapse upon hearsay, or it may be a
previous writer's description (Hekataios?).
ἡ πᾶσα ὁδός, if it referred primarily to
any actual route, would probably be the
Royal Road, described in 5. 52 f., along
which no doubt the Anatolian posts
travelled. But the word is here of
purely generic significance.

6. διεστᾶσι, 'are posted at intervals'—
of a day's journey: in σταθμοί no doubt.

7. τοὺς οὔτε νιφετός κτλ. Cp. Mark
Twain *l.c.* "No matter whether it was
winter or summer, raining, snowing,
hailing, or sleeting, or whether his
'beat' was a level straight road or a
crazy trail over mountain crags and preci-
pices, . . . he must be always ready to
leap into the saddle and be off like the
wind! There was no idling-time for a
pony-rider on duty. He rode fifty
miles without stopping, by daylight,
moonlight, starlight, or through the

blackness of darkness — just as it
happened."

8. μὴ οὐ κατανύσαι: a simple instance
of the idiom, which follows not merely
the express negative οὔτε, but the
implicit negative in ἔργει=κωλύει=οὐκ
ἐᾷ. The repetition of οὔτε by οὐκ is
rhetorical: nearly the same sequence
in 1. 132. αὐτῷ after τούς (relative)
almost=ἑκάστῳ.

11. διεξέρχεται: sc. τὰ ἐντεταλμένα—
presumably tablets, 7. 239 *supra*, or
βυβλία, 3. 128, 5. 14 (in which passage
one ἱππεύς apparently carries the βυβλίον
from sender to recipient).

κατά περ<ἐν>Ἕλλησι ἡ λαμπα-
δηφορίη, 'just like in Greece the torch-
bearing, with which they conclude the
Festival of Hephaistos.' The reference
is to such a performance as that described
by Plato, *Rep.* 328 (in honour of Bendis),
though the λαμπὰς ἀφ' ἵππων is there
treated as a novelty (καινόν γε τοῦτο).
Nor is the point of the comparison in
Hdt. the presence of horses, but the
passing of the torch from one man to
another (λαμπάδια ἔχοντες διαδώσουσιν
ἀλλήλοις). The method described by
Pausanias 1. 30. 2 of the race from the
Akademeia to the Akropolis, in which
each competitor carried a lighted torch
(if he could) all the way, would not
offer a true analogy. In 6. 105 Hdt.
mentions a λαμπάς at Athens in honour
of Pan—probably of the latter type.

13. τοῦτο .. καλέουσι Πέρσαι ἀγγαρήιον has an unfortunately gloss-like

ἡ μὲν δὴ πρώτη ἐς Σοῦσα ἀγγελίη ἀπικομένη, ὡς ἔχοι **99**
Ἀθήνας Ξέρξης, ἔτερψε οὕτω δή τι Περσέων τοὺς ὑπολειφθέντας ὡς τάς τε ὁδοὺς μυρσίνη πάσας ἐστόρεσαν καὶ ἐθυμίων
θυμιήματα καὶ αὐτοὶ ἦσαν ἐν θυσίῃσί τε καὶ εὐπαθείῃσι. ἡ
δὲ δευτέρη σφι ἀγγελίη ἐπεσελθοῦσα συνέχεε οὕτω ὥστε τοὺς 5
κιθῶνας κατηρείξαντο πάντες, βοῇ τε καὶ οἰμωγῇ ἐχρέωντο
ἀπλέτῳ, Μαρδόνιον ἐν αἰτίῃ τιθέντες. οὐκ οὕτω δὲ περὶ
τῶν νεῶν ἀχθόμενοι ταῦτα οἱ Πέρσαι ἐποίευν ὡς περὶ αὐτῷ
Ξέρξῃ δειμαίνοντες.

99. 3 ὡς τάς τε : ὥστε τάς Cobet : ὥστε τάς τε van H. ‖ μυρσίνῃσι z
4 αὐτοὶ secl. van H. ‖ ἔσαν z ‖ θυσίῃσί : εὐθυμίῃσί Naber : θαλίῃσι ?
van H. ‖ εὐπαθίῃσι codd. z   5 ἐπεσελθοῦσα Reiske, Stein², Holder,
van H.: ἐπεξελθοῦσα ‖ τούς τε coni. Stein², recep. van H.   6 κατηρείξαντο Cobet, Holder, van H., Stein³: κατερρήξαντο ‖ καὶ βοῇ coni. Stein¹,
recep. van H. : βοῇ δέ τε ? Kallenberg ‖ ἐχρέοντο P, van H.   7 αἰτίῃσι P
8 νηῶν αBz

appearance, and might easily be an
addition, even if from the author's hand.
The fact remains that the word ἀγγαρήιον
is also to be read 3. 126, naturally
used ; cf. note above. It was familiar
in Greece before the days of Hdt. So
Aischylos, *Agamemnon* 282 φρυκτὸς δὲ
φρυκτὸν δεῦρ' ἀπ' ἀγγάρου πυρὸς ἔπεμπεν
—of the fire-signals crossing the Aegean ;
cp. 9. 3 *infra*. ἀγγαρεύειν is found
in *N.T.*; *angaria* and *angariare* in
Later Latin. Suidas has articles on
ἀγγαρεία, ἄγγαρος (*bis*), ἄγγαροι. οἱ ἐκ
διαδοχῆς γραμματοφόροι. οἱ δὲ αὐτοὶ καὶ
ἀστάνδαι. τὰ δὲ ὀνόματα Περσικά. In
the Roman Empire the words had come
to be used for any compulsory or enforced service. H. C. R. *ap.* Rawl.
derives the word from *hakkâreh*, 'a man
fit for every sort of work,' 'a messenger'
("a slight unmeritable man, meet to be
sent on errands"), and notices that
courier dromedaries are still known
throughout India and Persia as
karhareh.

99. 1. ἡ μὲν δὴ πρώτη ἐς Σοῦσα: cp.
c. 54 *supra*. Hdt. never shows any consciousness that Susa was not a 'Persian'
city ; in his days it plainly counted in the
West as the chief capital of the 'Persian'
empire. τοὺς ὑπολειφθέντας, 'those
who had stayed behind' (cp. 5. 61, c. 67
supra, 9. 58 *infra*). As if there were
but a few of them ! The passage may
be influenced by scenic and dramatic
representations from Phrynichos, or
even Aischylos.

VOL. I   PT. II

3. μυρσίνη, 'myrtle (boughs),' Att.
μυρρίνη, the plant from which not
merely wreaths, but a balsamic juice
(μύρρα) was procurable ; cp. 1. 132, (4.
195), 7. 54.

4. ἦσαν ἐν : ἐν εὐπαθείῃσι occurs 1. 22,
191, ἐν θαλίῃσι 3. 27, but ἐν θυσίῃσι is
unique (Stein). Schweighaeuser defends
ἐν θυσίῃσι here. The conjunction of
θυσίαι and εὐπαθεῖαι is no offence ; cp.
Stallbaum *ad* Plat. *Rep.* 365 a. Aristoph.
Clds. 328 has θεῶν θυσίαι θαλίαι τε.

5. ἐπεσελθοῦσα: cp. 4. 154 of a
stepmother ; less significantly 1. 37.
συνέχεε Stein takes to be the aorist, cp.
ἔτερψε above. (*Il.* 18. 347 ἐν δ' ἄρ' ὕδωρ
ἔχεαν.)

6. κατηρείξαντο: cp. 3. 66, Aischyl.
Pers. 538.

βοῇ . . ἀπλέτῳ: cp. 7. 211 *supra*,
9. 24 *infra*.

7. Μαρδόνιον ἐν αἰτίῃ τιθέντες: not
for anything specially connected with
the ships, but for having urged the king
in the first instance to undertake the
expedition ; the phrase therefore constitutes an implicit reference to 7. 5 ff.
supra.

περὶ τῶν νεῶν . . περὶ αὐτῷ Ξέρξῃ
'it was not grief arising about the ships
(that had been lost), but fear centred on
the king's person (lest he should never
return).' The genitive and dative are
not mere stylistic variations. Just
below, the accusative περὶ Πέρσας is, of
course, purely locative.

M

100 Καὶ περὶ Πέρσας μὲν ἦν ταῦτα τὸν πάντα μεταξὺ χρόνον
γενόμενον, μέχρι οὗ Ξέρξης αὐτός σφεα ἀπικόμενος ἔπαυσε.
Μαρδόνιος δὲ ὁρῶν μὲν Ξέρξην συμφορὴν μεγάλην ἐκ τῆς
ναυμαχίης ποιεύμενον, ὑποπτεύων δὲ αὐτὸν δρησμὸν βουλεύειν
5 ἐκ τῶν Ἀθηνέων, φροντίσας πρὸς ἑωυτὸν ὡς δώσει δίκην
ἀναγνώσας βασιλέα στρατεύεσθαι ἐπὶ τὴν Ἑλλάδα, καί οἱ
κρέσσον εἴη ἀνακινδυνεῦσαι ἢ κατεργάσασθαι τὴν Ἑλλάδα ἢ
αὐτὸν καλῶς τελευτῆσαι τὸν βίον ὑπὲρ μεγάλων αἰωρηθέντα·
πλέον μέντοι ἔφερέ οἱ ἡ γνώμη κατεργάσασθαι τὴν Ἑλλάδα·
10 λογισάμενος ὦν ταῦτα προσέφερέ <οἱ> τὸν λόγον τόνδε.
" δέσποτα, μήτε λυπέο μήτε συμφορὴν μηδεμίαν μεγάλην ποιεῦ
τοῦδε τοῦ γεγονότος εἵνεκα πρήγματος. οὐ γὰρ ξύλων ἀγὼν

---

100. 1 πάντα τὸν vel τὸν πάντα τὸν Krueger   2 γινόμενον
Bekker, van H.: 'an γινόμενα ?' Stein[2] ‖ σφεα van H., Stein[3]: σφεας
3 ὁρέων CPz, Stein[1], van H.   5 Ἀθηναίων CP[1]Rz   6 βασιλῆα z
7 κρεῖσσον ABRSV ‖ ἀνακινδυνεύσαντα ? van H. ‖ ἢ αὐτὸν . . Ἑλλάδα
om. B[1]: eadem bis R   9 πλέων C[1]: πλέω z ‖ οἱ om. B[2] ‖ ἡ
om. β ‖ κατεργάσθαι V: κατεργάσεσθαι Cobet, Holder   10 οἱ add.
Stein[(2)3], van H.   11 μηδεμίην z ‖ ποιέο van H.

---

100. 1. **ἦν ταῦτα . . μέχρι οὗ . .
ἔπαυσε**: Hdt. apparently forgets that
he is going to retain Xerxes at Sardes
a good while; cp. 9. 108 *infra*. This
passage again looks as if it might have
been borrowed from a scene on the
stage. ἦν ταῦτα is a very bald phrase; γενόμενον
is a remarkable tense, and an unnecessary
sense; Stein suggests γινόμενα.

3. **Μαρδόνιος δέ**: this bold analysis
of the motives of Mardonios may be
compared with the account of the motives
of Aristagoras in a somewhat similar
situation, 5. 35. Not that the prior
passage is of earlier composition, though
referring to an earlier date; rather,
perhaps, the flight of final verbs there,
compared with the procession of participles here, suggests a more accomplished
style. Evidently Greek minds were
greatly exercised to account for the commission of Mardonios after the Persian
defeat at Salamis—reading the situation
of September 480 B.C., as they did, too
much in the light of after events.

ἐκ τῆς ναυμαχίης . . ἐκ τῶν Ἀθ.:
the one ἐκ causal, or material, the other
purely local; neither temporal.

4. **δρησμὸν βουλεύειν**: c. 97 *supra*.
Hdt. somewhat artfully calls Mardonios
as a witness for this libel.

5. **δώσει δίκην**, 'he will be called to
account . .'; cp. c. 114 *infra*.

8. **καλῶς τελευτῆσαι τὸν βίον ὑπὲρ
μεγάλων αἰωρηθέντα**: a stately phrase,
exactly descriptive of the actual and,
as it were, subsequent fate of Mardonios,
which is thus prepared with a touch of
tragic irony. Mardonios is, indeed, the
real hero of the story in these Books;
Xerxes is too capricious, too craven, to
incur aught but the comic nemesis,
which has already begun in c. 99. Cp.
Introduction, § 11. αἰωρηθέντα is better
taken with βίον, notwithstanding Dionys.
H. 5. 27. 2 οὐκ ἀξιῶ λαθεῖν ἅπαντας
αἰωρηθεὶς ὑπὲρ μεγάλων.

9. **πλέον . . ἔφερε**: an exact parallel,
3. 77 ἐγένετο οἷόν τι Δαρείῳ ἡ γνώμη
ἔφερε, 'just such an event as Dareios was
expecting.' προσέφερε just below is inelegant (an ' unconscious iteration '), and
ὁ τὸ πᾶν φέρων worse still; cp. c. 62 *supra*.

11. **λυπέο . . ποιεῦ**: the force of the
middle voice should not be missed, nor the
dialectal inconsistency (cp. App. Crit.).

12. **οὐ γὰρ ξύλων κτλ.** Mardonios is
made, rightly enough, to assert the *de
facto* superiority of the Persian land-
forces over the Greek, and the sequel
justifies his anticipation (i.e. the writer
is wise after the event) that no Greek
army would venture to stay his regress.
But two points are omitted in the
argument of Mardonios: (i.) the question
of the commissariat, now the fleet was

ὁ τὸ πᾶν φέρων ἐστὶ ἡμῖν, ἀλλ' ἀνδρῶν τε καὶ ἵππων. σοὶ
δὲ οὔτε τις τούτων τῶν τὸ πᾶν σφίσι ἤδη δοκεόντων κατεργάσθαι ἀποβὰς ἀπὸ τῶν νεῶν πειρήσεται ἀντιωθῆναι οὔτ' 15
ἐκ τῆς ἠπείρου τῆσδε, οἵ τε ἡμῖν ἠντιώθησαν, ἔδοσαν δίκας.
εἰ μέν νυν δοκέει, αὐτίκα πειρώμεθα τῆς Πελοποννήσου· εἰ
δὲ καὶ δοκέει ἐπισχεῖν, παρέχει ποιέειν ταῦτα. μηδὲ δυσθύ-
μεε· οὐ γὰρ ἔστι Ἕλλησι οὐδεμία ἔκδυσις μὴ οὐ δόντας
λόγον τῶν ἐποίησαν νῦν τε καὶ πρότερον εἶναι σοὺς δούλους. 20
μάλιστα μέν νυν ταῦτα ποίεε· εἰ δ' ἄρα τοι βεβούλευται
αὐτὸν ἀπελαύνοντα ἀπάγειν τὴν στρατιήν, ἄλλην ἔχω καὶ
ἐκ τῶνδε βουλήν. σὺ Πέρσας, βασιλεῦ, μὴ ποιήσῃς κατα-
γελάστους γενέσθαι Ἕλλησι· οὐδὲ γὰρ ἐν Πέρσῃσί τοί τι

---

14 τουτέων z ‖ σφίσι Stein, Holder, van H.: σφι ‖ κατεργάσασθαι Bds
18 παρέχειν C ‖ δυσθύμει libri (sic Stein[1])   19 οὐδὲ μία AB: οὐδεμίη z
20 τοὺς B   21 ποιέειν R: ποιέεν SV (Holder: 'Is tamen codex [sc. S]
perspicue habet ποίεεν' Gaisford)   22 ἀπαγαγεῖν B   24 οὐδὲ
Stein[2]: οὐδὲν ‖ Πέρσῃσί τοί τι Valckenaer, Stein[2], Holder: Πέρσῃσί
τοι Stein[1], van H.: Πέρσῃσι τοισῖδε Reiske: Πέρσῃσι τεοῖσι Schweighaeuser: τοῖσι πέρσῃσι B: πέρσῃσι τοῖσι a etc.

---

broken; (ii.) the possibility of an attack
by the Greeks on the bridges. With
the landsman's contempt for ξύλα cp.
Thuc. 4. 11. 4 (of Brasidas) ἐβόα λέγων
ὡς οὐκ εἰκὸς εἴη ξύλων φειδομένους τοὺς
πολεμίους ἐν τῇ χώρᾳ περιιδεῖν τεῖχος
πεποιημένους, and Xenoph. Hell. 1. 1. 24
μὴ ἀθυμεῖν ἕνεκα ξύλων (Pharnabazo loq.
ref. van H.).

14. τῶν τὸ πᾶν σφίσι ἤδη δοκεόντων
κατεργάσθαι: this is 'without prejudice,'
and does not describe the attitude of
the Greeks as recorded above c. 96.
Perhaps the subsequent action—or inaction—of the Greeks provoked the
taunt as a legitimate comment on their
conduct. But in view of the achievement of Aristeides on Psyttaleia
Mardonios could hardly have ventured
upon such a remark.

16. οἵ τε ἡ. ἦν. ἔδοσαν δίκας contains
of course a reference to Thermopylai,
so notorious a story that even the locality
of the affair is taken for granted, and
also to the capture of the Akropolis.
But the reference could hardly have
been made in such unqualified terms.

17. πειρώμεθα τῆς Π.: the alternative
the speaker apparently prefers; yet he
does not adopt it next year, when in
supreme command—and wisely. He will
hardly have proposed it now.

εἰ δὲ καί: an alternative lies in
δέ, an adversative in καί.

19. οὐ γὰρ ἔστι . . οὐδεμία . . μὴ οὐ:
a simple or primary example of the
doubled negative, though ἔκδυσις itself
perhaps conveys something of a negation; still, the idiom would equally
stand with ὁδός, ἐλπίς, or any purely
positive idea. In other words, the
cumulative negation is not attained by
any strict cancelling of one negative
against another, but is a purely idiomatic
result of the sense of accumulation.
λόγον δοῦναι here seems a variant for
δίκην δοῦναι—and might almost suggest
a civil rather than a criminal process!

21. εἰ δ' ἄρα suggests the more probable alternative: καὶ ἐκ τῶνδε, 'also
suitable to this course' (Stein). The
phrase has been taken to mean vel ex
his quomodo tu bene evadas (Baehr), or,
simply of time, post haec.

24. ἐν Πέρσῃσι might mean 'at home
in Persia'—rather a far cry, and what
of all Asia, and the rest of the empire?
Perhaps the words may be taken in the
same sense as the vulgate ἐν τοῖσι Π.:
ubi Persae pugnarunt, Baehr, or Persarum
culpa, Valckenaer, which is supported by
Xerxes' own words c. 101 infra, and
indeed by the immediate context here.

25 δεδήληται τῶν πρηγμάτων, οὐδ' ἐρέεις ὅκου ἐγενόμεθα ἄνδρες
κακοί. εἰ δὲ Φοίνικές τε καὶ Αἰγύπτιοι καὶ Κύπριοί τε καὶ
Κίλικες κακοὶ ἐγένοντο, οὐδὲν πρὸς Πέρσας τοῦτο προσήκει
τὸ πάθος. ἤδη ὦν, ἐπειδὴ οὐ Πέρσαι τοι αἴτιοι εἰσί, ἐμοὶ
πείθεο· εἴ τοι δέδοκται μὴ παραμένειν, σὺ μὲν ἐς ἤθεα τὰ
30 σεωυτοῦ ἀπέλαυνε τῆς στρατιῆς ἀπάγων τὸ πολλόν, ἐμὲ δὲ
σοὶ χρὴ τὴν Ἑλλάδα παρασχεῖν δεδουλωμένην, τριήκοντα
μυριάδας τοῦ στρατοῦ ἀπολεξάμενον."

101 Ταῦτα ἀκούσας Ξέρξης ὡς ἐκ κακῶν ἐχάρη τε καὶ ἥσθη,
πρὸς Μαρδόνιόν τε βουλευσάμενος ἔφη ὑποκρινέεσθαι ὁκότερον
ποιήσει τούτων. ὡς δὲ ἐβουλεύετο ἅμα Περσέων τοῖσι
ἐπικλήτοισι, ἔδοξέ οἱ καὶ Ἀρτεμισίην ἐς συμβουλίην μετα-
5 πέμψασθαι, ὅτι πρότερον ἐφαίνετο μούνη νοέουσα τὰ ποιητέα
ἦν. ὡς δὲ ἀπίκετο ἡ Ἀρτεμισίη, μεταστησάμενος τοὺς

25 ἐρεῖς codd. z, Holder, van H.   29 μὴ om. C ‖ παραμενέειν B ‖
τὰς ἑωυτοῦ (sic) α   30 δέ σοι libri, Holder : δέ τοι van H.   101. 2
ὑποκρινέεσθαι Bredow : ὑποκρινεῖσθαι van H. : ἀποκρινεῖσθαι codd. : ἀπο-
κρινέεσθαι z   3 τουτέων z ‖ ἐβουλεύσατο ? van H.   4 ἐπὶ συμβουλὴν βPz, van H.

. 25. ὅκου ἐγενόμεθα, 'that we Persians
in any case proved . .'
26. Φοίνικες . . Κίλικες: just as in
Artemisia's speech c. 68 supra, except
that Mardonios substitutes 'Phoenicians'
for 'Pamphylians.' This reproduction
is hardly good art or history. A Persian
would more probably have spoken ill
of the 'Ionians'; Hdt. voices Greek
prejudice. Besides, his account of the
battle (cp. c. 90 supra) may have affected
his composition of this speech.
27. οὐδὲν πρὸς Πέρσας . . τὸ πάθος:
yet what of the Epibatai? What of
the Persians on Psyttaleia? Hdt. in
composing this speech for Mardonios
has sacrificed historic probability to the
ethical interest. Mardonios is ultra-
Persian : the Persians are four times
paraded in half a dozen lines!
29. ἤθεα τὰ σεωυτοῦ: cp. 4. 76, 80,
5. 14, 15, etc. Persia might be meant,
or perhaps Asia, more at large.
30. ἐμὲ δὲ σοὶ χρή. The proposal put
into the mouth of Mardonios is no
unreasonable one: he was to get rid
(1) of the king, (2) of the mob (τὴν
στρατιήν), (3) of the fleet, but to have a
large force of picked men wherewith
to effect the conquest of Hellas. The
dismissal of the fleet was, perhaps, a
doubtful expedient, yet probably neces-

sary to cover the Asiatic coast, and to
prevent a movement in Ionia, or the
larger islands. The figure 300,000 is
an over-estimate, unless he retained the
whole land-forces, which is improbable.
Cp. Appendix II. § 5.
101. 1. ὡς ἐκ κακῶν ἐχάρη τε καὶ
ἥσθη : a merely relative joy. Cp. Thuc.
7. 42. 2 τῷ δὲ προτέρῳ στρατεύματι ὡς ἐκ
κακῶν ῥώμη τις ἐγεγένητο (Stein).
2. βουλευσάμενος . . ὑποκρινέεσθαι,
'he will let him know after consultation.'
Or, 'before replying, he must first take
advice'—the participle is predicative.
3. Περσέων τοῖσι ἐπικλήτοισι: the
privy councillors, cp. 7. 8 supra,
Mardonios no doubt among them ; so
too τοὺς συμβούλους Περσέων just below.
ἐβουλεύετο, imperfect. Artemisia was
not present at the Privy Council of
Persians. The Council of War had been
a different matter ; cp. c. 67 supra.
5. ὅτι πρότερον ἐφαίνετο . . ἦν: a
reference to c. 68 supra, an acquaintance
with which is implied. Hdt. writes for
a reading public.
6. μεταστησάμενος : cp. c. 81 supra.
The king pays Artemisia the compliment
of dismissing not merely his councillors,
but his guard of 'Immortals.' Apparently
only Xerxes and Artemisia were present
at this interview, yet Hdt. can report

ἄλλους τούς τε συμβούλους Περσέων καὶ τοὺς δορυφόρους,
ἔλεξε Ξέρξης τάδε. " κελεύει με Μαρδόνιος μένοντα αὐτοῦ
πειρᾶσθαι τῆς Πελοποννήσου, λέγων ὥς μοι Πέρσαι τε καὶ
ὁ πεζὸς στρατὸς οὐδενὸς μεταίτιοι πάθεος εἰσί, ἀλλὰ βουλο- 10
μένοισί σφι γένοιτ' ἂν ἀπόδεξις. ἐμὲ ὦν ἢ ταῦτα κελεύει
ποιέειν, ἢ αὐτὸς ἐθέλει τριήκοντα μυριάδας ἀπολεξάμενος τοῦ
στρατοῦ παρασχεῖν μοι τὴν Ἑλλάδα δεδουλωμένην, αὐτὸν δέ
με κελεύει ἀπελαύνειν σὺν τῷ λοιπῷ στρατῷ ἐς ἤθεα τὰ ἐμά.
σὺ ὦν ἐμοί, καὶ γὰρ περὶ τῆς ναυμαχίης εὖ συνεβούλευσας 15
τῆς γενομένης οὐκ ἐῶσα ποιέεσθαι, νῦν τε συμβούλευσον
ὁκότερα ποιέων ἐπιτύχω εὖ βουλευσάμενος." ὁ μὲν ταῦτα 102
συνεβουλεύετο, ἡ δὲ λέγει τάδε. " βασιλεῦ, χαλεπὸν μὲν

9 ἀποπειρᾶσθαι z   11 ἀπόδιξις A : ἀπόδειξις R   13 ἐμοὶ S
14 λυπῶι Apr.B¹ ‖ τἀμά z   16 τε : ἄγε? Stein   17 ποιέω C

their *tête-à-tête* conversation : from which
had he heard it ? Had Artemisia let it
out in Halikarnassos ?

8. **αὐτοῦ**, locative adverb, 'on the
spot.' **κελεύειν** may be used of the action
of a political inferior ; cp. l. 116.

9. **Πέρσαι τε καί**, 'the Persians, that
is,' cp. c. 100 *supra*. **ὁ πεζὸς στρατός**
includes the cavalry.

10. **ἀλλὰ βουλομένοισί σφι γένοιτ' ἂν
ἀπόδεξις**, 'as they would be glad to have
an opportunity of demonstrating'—viz.
that **οὐδενὸς (μετ)αίτιοι πάθεος εἰσί**—that
'the naval contingents alone were to
blame for any distressing occurrence.'
With the construction cp. c. 14. 3 *supra*.
The **ἀλλά** is adversative, where a relative
might be expected. **ἀπόδεξις** is here
used in a sense approximate to that in
l. 1 (*ἱστορίης ἀπόδεξις*), not to that in l.
207 *ἡμῖν λείπεται ἀπόδεξις ἔργων μεγάλων*
—though had *ἔργων μεγάλων* occurred
here a good sense would have been
obtained.

12. **τριήκοντα μυριάδας**: the second
time this figure is given as the number
of Mardonios' army ; cp. c. 100 *ad f.*
and c. 113 *infra*.

14. **τῷ λοιπῷ στρατῷ**=τῆς στρατιῆς
τὸ πολλόν c. 100 *supra*; cp. 7. 40, 55
supra. **ἤθεα** repeated from c. 100.

16. **οὐκ ἐῶσα**, 'in opposing,' or 'in
trying to prevent.'

νῦν τε . . βουλευσάμενος. Stein
takes exception to **νῦν τε** as an un-Herodotean
in this sense (*nunc quoque* : cp. Thuc.
1. 69. 2 *μόλις δὲ νῦν γε ξυνήλθομεν καὶ
οὐδὲ νῦν ἐπὶ φανεροῖς*), Hdt. generally
using the combination to introduce

begruendete Adhortativ-saetze. But the
sense here is good. The remainder of
the sentence is rather complicated :
'Advise me by doing which of the two I
shall succeed in having been well advised'
—by Mardonios—i.e. which of the alternatives recommended by Mardonios
would you advise me to adopt ? The
word **ἐπιτυγχάνω** appears to be rather a
blot on the expression, used merely as
equivalent to **τυγχάνω**. The sentence
would be complete if it ran **ὁκότερα
ποιέων** (or **ποιήσας**) **ἐπιτύχω**—i.e. *κότερα
ποιήσας ἐπιτεύξομαι* : cp. Xenoph. *Hell.*
4. 5. 19 *ἐκ τούτου δὲ μάλα καὶ τἆλλα
ἐπετύγχανεν Ἰφικράτης* : (*αἱ ἐπιτετευγ-
μέναι πράξεις* successful actions, Polyb. 6.
53. 2). It would perhaps be possible to
take the word here in its fuller force,
and understand *εὖ βουλευσάμενος* as
epexegetical ; but the absence of a copula,
the difference of tense, the whole rhythm
of the sentence, and the repetition of the
formula in c. 103 *infra* (*λέγουσα . .
ἐπετύγχανε*), are against such a construction. In any case **ποιέων** is the
real predicate.

102. 2. **χαλεπὸν μὲν ἐστὶ συμβουλευομένῳ τυχεῖν τὰ ἄριστα ἅπασαν**: "merito
laudant Stephani versionem : *me tibi
consulenti optimum dare consilium
difficile est*," Baehr. But this 'lauded'
version misses the point ; it should have
run : *viro consulenti optimum dare
consilium mulieri difficile est* ! Nor is
there any *me tibi* in the Greek ! Cp. *αἱ
δὲ γυναῖκες ἄνδρες* c. 88 *supra*, and *εἰ καὶ
πάντες καὶ πᾶσαι συνεβούλευον αὐτῷ infra*
c. 103.

ἐστὶ συμβουλευομένῳ τυχεῖν τὰ ἄριστα εἴπασαν, ἐπὶ μέντοι
τοῖσι κατήκουσι πρήγμασι δοκέει μοι αὐτὸν μέν σε ἀπελαύ-
5 νειν ὀπίσω, Μαρδόνιον δέ, εἰ ἐθέλει τε καὶ ὑποδέκεται ταῦτα
ποιήσειν, αὐτοῦ καταλιπεῖν σὺν τοῖσι ἐθέλει. τοῦτο μὲν
γὰρ ἢν καταστρέψηται τὰ φησὶ θέλειν καὶ οἱ προχωρήσῃ τὰ
νοέων λέγει, σὸν τὸ ἔργον ᾧ δέσποτα γίνεται· οἱ γὰρ σοὶ
δοῦλοι κατεργάσαντο. τοῦτο δὲ ἢν τὰ ἐναντία τῆς Μαρδονίου
10 γνώμης γένηται, οὐδεμία συμφορὴ μεγάλη ἔσται σέο τε
περιεόντος καὶ ἐκείνων τῶν πρηγμάτων [περὶ οἶκον τὸν σόν]·
ἢν γὰρ σύ τε περιῇς καὶ οἶκος ὁ σός, πολλοὺς πολλάκις
ἀγῶνας δραμέονται περὶ σφέων αὐτῶν οἱ Ἕλληνες. Μαρδονίου
δέ, ἤν τι πάθῃ, λόγος οὐδεὶς γίνεται, οὐδέ τι νικῶντες οἱ
15 Ἕλληνες νικῶσι, δοῦλον σὸν ἀπολέσαντες· σὺ δέ, τῶν εἵνεκα
τὸν στόλον ἐποιήσαο, πυρώσας τὰς Ἀθήνας ἀπελᾷς."

---

102. 3 τοι τυχεῖν coni. Stein[2], rec. van H.   4 μέν σὲ codd.
5 ἐθέλοι z || ὑποδέδεκται B ('non male' van H.)   6 καταλειπεῖν B
|| τοῦτο . . θέλειν om. R   7 τά σφισι CP || θέλειν A[2]B : θέλει
A[1]CP : ἐθέλει SVz || προχωρήσει Bd: προχωρήσοι z   8 νοέειν? Stein[2]
10 οὐδὲ μία AB : οὐδεμίη z   11 περὶ . . σὸν secl. Stein[2], Holder,
van H.   13 αὐτέων z   16 ἐποιήσω codd. z || ἀπέλασον Naber

---

3. ἐπὶ τοῖσι κατήκουσι πρήγμασι:
cp. c. 19 supra, 5. 49. δοκέει μοι, it seems
to me advisable.

6. σὺν τοῖσι ἐθέλει: sc. σὺν ἐκείνοις
οὓς ἐθέλει (ἀπολέξασθαι, or κατέχειν), i.e.
the 300,000 λογάδες. Cp. τὰ φησὶ θέλειν
just below: sc. καταστρέψασθαι.

τοῦτο μὲν . . τοῦτο δέ: cp. cc. 76,
60 supra.

7. τὰ νοέων λέγει: what he has in
view when speaking — the predicative
participle.

8. σὸν τὸ ἔργον: even on republican
(but religious) principles the same
formula applied to the Roman who won
a victory alienis auspiciis: the victory
was the doing of the Imperator, not
of the legate. The establishment of
Monarchy, of a sole Imperator, tended
in the direction suggested by Artemisia's
too servile flattery. So Japanese victories
are due to the virtues of the Mikado
(cp. Times, April 18, 1904, p. 5), perhaps on some esoteric principle not fully
understood in the individualistic West.

12. ἢν γὰρ σύ τε περιῇς . . οἱ Ἕλληνες:
this prophecy might seem to enforce the
moral, hinted above c. 97, that it was a
vast mistake to have let the king escape
home out of Europe. Had the Greeks
caught the king, and ended the dynasty,

they would have been saved a deal of
subsequent trouble! On the other hand,
the prophecy can hardly be regarded as
altogether happy: Xerxes escaped, but
the Hellenes, after Plataia, can hardly
be said with truth to have had many
bouts to stand, many races or risks to
run, περὶ σφέων αὐτῶν, except what
they incurred by invading the king's
dominions! Is the passage a specimen
of Hdt.'s irony?

13. Μαρδονίου δὲ . . λόγος οὐδεὶς
γίνεται: cp. 4. 135 τῶν ἢν ἐλάχιστος ἀπολ-
λυμένων λόγος. But Mardonios remains
to all time a more interesting and real
figure than Xerxes himself. Cp. Introduction, § 11.

14. οὐδέ τι νικῶντες οἱ Ἕλληνες νικῶσι,
τι with the verb: νικῶντες = ἐὰν νικῶσι,
the participle doing duty for a conditional
sentence. This unfavourable verdict on
Plataia is not the verdict of Hdt., cp. 9.
64 infra. ἀπελᾷς is future, and absolute;
cp. 7. 32 supra, 1. 207 etc.

16. πυρώσας τὰς Ἀθήνας. Neither
Artemisia nor Mardonios have made
any allusion to the assault on Delphi
and its miserable failure: an unconscious
evidence of the good faith of Hdt. and
the fictitious character of that legend;
perhaps, too, of its bearing no part in

Ἥσθη τε δὴ τῇ συμβουλίῃ Ξέρξης· λέγουσα γὰρ ἐπετύγ- 103
χανε τά περ αὐτὸς ἐνόεε. οὐδὲ γὰρ εἰ πάντες καὶ πᾶσαι
συνεβούλευον αὐτῷ μένειν, ἔμενε ἂν δοκέειν ἐμοί· οὕτω
καταρρωδήκεε. ἐπαινέσας δὲ τὴν Ἀρτεμισίην, ταύτην μὲν
ἀποστέλλει ἄγουσαν αὐτοῦ τοὺς παῖδας ἐς Ἔφεσον· νόθοι γὰρ 5
τινὲς παῖδές οἱ συνέσποντο. συνέπεμπε δὲ τοῖσι παισὶ φύλακον 104
Ἑρμότιμον, γένος μὲν ἐόντα Πηδασέα, φερόμενον δὲ οὐ τὰ
δεύτερα τῶν εὐνούχων παρὰ βασιλέι· [οἱ δὲ Πηδασέες οἰκέουσι

103. 1 δὴ om. Β ‖ συμβουλῇ ΒΡz, Holder, van H.　　　2 ἐνόει van
H.: ἐπενόεε z ‖ καὶ πᾶσαι suspecta habet Kallenberg　　　3 μενέειν C
4 καταρρωδήκεε P ‖ ταύτην τὴν Β　　　5 τοὺς om. α　　　6 συνέσποντο
α: συνέποντο C　　　　104. 2 πηδασσέα B　　　3 βασιλεῖ AB ‖ οἱ
δὲ . . Ἑρμότιμος ἦν damn. Valckenaer, secl. Stein, Holder, e textu eiec.
van H.

the original draft of the Books. The
burning of Athens is an incontestable
fact; but cp. 9. 13 *infra*.

103. 1. **ἥσθη τε**. The advice of Artemisia was a positive pleasure to Xerxes;
cp. c. 101 *ad init.*; it squared so exactly
with his own ideas! **λέγουσα γὰρ ἐπετύγχανε**: cp. c. 101 *ad fin.* The **τε** here
has no **καί** following: the parenthetic
expression of Hdt.'s own opinion (**δοκέειν
ἐμοί**), that all the men and women in
creation could not have persuaded Xerxes
to remain, a little deranges the grammar
of his narrative (which should have
run on **καὶ ἐπαινέσας**).

3. **οὕτω καταρρωδήκεε**, 'so utterly was
he overcome with terror'—the pl.p.
is rather intensive than temporal in
character. **οὕτω**: cp. c. 98.

5. **ἐς Ἔφεσον**: the terminal port of
the Royal Road; cp. 5. 54. Artemisia
doubtless went by sea; per aps on the
very night after the battle. h

6. **οἱ**: sc. Ξέρξῃ, as the **αὐτοῦ παῖδας**
just before makes clear. **ἑωυτοῦ** might
have been expected there; Hdt. treats
the king (Stein remarks) as the remoter
of two subjects, and so prefers the
demonstrative to the possessive pronoun;
cp. c. 87 *supra*, where, however, **ἡ δὲ
αὐτῆς** is in a parenthesis.

The only queen-wife of Xerxes was
(so far as we know) Amestris; cp. 7. 61,
114 *supra*, 9. 109 *infra*, by whom he
had four sons (including Artaxerxes his
successor; cp. 7. 106, 151 *supra*) and two
daughters; cp. Rawlinson, iv. 255.
Dareios is the only other son named by
Hdt.; cp. 9. 108. None of these sons
of Xerxes will have been old enough to

serve on this expedition. The fact that
the **νόθοι** were sent home with Artemisia
would suggest, what the probable age
of Xerxes would confirm, that the **παῖδες**
in question were quite young. The
commission was no doubt a mark of
royal favour, and recorded as such; yet
is there no 'malice' in Hdt.'s notice of
this *exit* of Artemisia?

104. 2. **Ἑρμότιμον**: the name is
doubtless formed in honour of the god
Hermes (not the river Hermos), and is
borne by several historical persons
(Aspasia's father, Plutarch, *Per.* 24, a
philosopher of Klazomenai, prior to
Anaxagoras, Aristot. *Metaph.* 1. 3, 984 B,
to say nothing of the later Stoic, who
gives his name to a Dialogue of Lucian's).
γένος, 'by birth' a man of Pedasa (*infra*)
alias Pedasos, or Pedason, 5. 121—
'second to none' of the 'chamberlains'
at the court (or 'in the king's eyes').
φέρεσθαι τὰ δεύτερα, a metaphor from
the race-course, *Iliad* 23. 537 ff.

3. **εὐνούχοι**, 7. 187 *supra*, is a strictly
Hellenic term for a thoroughly un-
Hellenic institution, at least in the
classic period = οἱ τὴν εὐνὴν ἔχοντες.
From the miserable fate of these confidential slaves emasculation was indis-
solubly associated with the word, and
so completely domineered the merely
etymological meaning that Aristotle (no
humorist) applies the term to fruits
without seed (cp. L. & S. *sub voc.*).
Rawlinson's idea that Hermotimos exhibits the first historical instance of the
great position of the Chamberlains, and
that the influence of the *Seraglio* first
made itself felt in the reign of Xerxes,

ὑπὲρ Ἁλικαρνησσοῦ· ἐν δὲ τοῖσι Πηδάσοισι τουτέοισι τοιόνδε
5 συμφέρεται πρῆγμα γίνεσθαι· ἐπεὰν τοῖσι ἀμφικτυόσι πᾶσι
τοῖσι ἀμφὶ ταύτης οἰκέουσι τῆς πόλιος μέλλῃ τι ἐντὸς χρόνου
ἔσεσθαι χαλεπόν, τότε ἡ ἱερείη αὐτόθι τῆς Ἀθηναίης φύει
105 πώγωνα μέγαν. τοῦτο δέ σφι δὶς ἤδη ἐγένετο. ἐκ τούτων
δὴ τῶν Πηδασέων ὁ Ἑρμότιμος ἦν] τῷ μεγίστη τίσις ἤδη
ἀδικηθέντι ἐγένετο πάντων τῶν ἡμεῖς ἴδμεν. ἀλόντα γὰρ

---

4 ἁλικαρνησοῦ a ‖ Πηδασέοισι z ‖ τούτοισι ΒPz, Holder　　5
φέρεται ΒPz, Holder　　7 ἱρέη Β　　105. 1 τουτέων z

---

is not merely contrary to the evidence
of Ktesias, *Pers.* 5, 9, 11, 20 (ed. Gilmore,
§§ 36, 40, 42, 51, etc.), but in itself
improbable. Hdt. himself mentions τῶν
εὐνούχων τοὺς πιστοτάτους at the court
of Astyages 1. 117, and of Amasis 2. 4,
and the large harems of the oriental
kings will have employed these unfortunates in still earlier ages. Xenoph.
Kyrop. 7. 5 (of course) ascribes the
institution to Kyros.

οἱ δὲ Πηδασέες — ἐγένετο. This
passage occurs, or recurs, almost *totidem
verbis* in 1. 175. Are both passages
genuine? If not, which of the two is
genuine? Or are both spurious? Rawlinson accepts them both, seeing no more
difficulty in such a dittograph by
author than by copyist. Valckenaer first
challenged this passage and regarded
the genuine text as having run παρὰ
βασιλέι, τῷ μεγίστη τίσις κτλ. Stein
adopts and develops his arguments: (1)
The notice suits the context better in
Book 1 (where Hdt. is recording the
resistance offered to Harpagos by the
Pedasians). (2) Strabo 611, in citing,
cites from Bk. 1, not from this passage.
(3) The phraseology is not thoroughly
Herodotean, and betrays (Stein adds)
by incorrect turns the amateur of the
Hadrianic age: thus (*a*) for αὐτοῖσί τε
καὶ τοῖσι περιοίκοισι the interpolator here
has τοῖσι ἀμφικτυόσι—leaving out αὐτοῖσί;
(*b*) πᾶσι is an addition, and an exaggeration; (*c*) the preposition is incorrectly
used, with genitive, of place, probably
suggested by the falsified ἀμφικτυόσι; (*d*)
ἐντὸς χρόνου is *de trop* (perhaps suggested
by ἐκὰς χρόνου c. 144 *infra*, Stein);
(*e*) χαλεπόν is the forger's variant for
the Herodotean ἀνεπιτήδειον; (*f*) so too
φύει for ἴσχει; (*g*) συμφέρεται is also
hardly in order. These arguments are
cogent. (*h*) The most remarkable difference between the two passages is that

the miracle has happened δὶς here, in
Bk. 8, as against τρὶς there in Bk. 1.
That is regarded as an oversight: a
curious one. Had the interpolator held
the opinion that the 8th Bk., or the
story of the Persian war, had been composed by Hdt. previously to the composition of the rest of the work, or of
Bk. 1, he could not have forged a better
bit of evidence! Moreover, he has
inserted this note on the Pedasians here
(by that theory at the earliest possible
chance) rather than in Bk. 5. 121, or
Bk. 6. 20, in either of which contexts
the note would be more consonant with
the context. It is impossible to maintain the authenticity of this passage in
view of the objections; the other, on
the testimony of Strabo, is genuine.
This verdict sacrifices on the altar of
truth a telling argument in favour of the
priority of these Books. Fortunately,
enough remains to prove it. Cp. Introduction, §§ 7, 8.

105. 2. τῷ μεγίστη τίσις ἤδη: almost
more forcible than μεγίστη δὴ τίσις—cp.
πάντων ἀνδρῶν ἤδη κτλ. c. 106 *infra.*
The story of this unparalleled τίσις, δίκη,
is in Hdt.'s best manner, or at least in
a thoroughly characteristic vein, with
the moral which he loves. Whether it
originally stood in this place might be
doubted; incidentally the view is fully
endorsed that the king's objective was
"Athens" (cp. c. 106 *ad init.*).

3. τῶν ἡμεῖς ἴδμεν. This formula
occurs five times in these Books, as from
Hdt.'s own pen (7. 20, 8. 105, 124, 9.
37, 64), twice on the lips of his *dramatis
personae* (7. 27 a Persian; 9. 78 an
Aiginetan). Cp. ὅσον ἡμ. ἴδ. 7. 111,
and contrast τῶν ἐγὼ οἶδα 7. 238. It
might well have occurred in 7. 70 οἱ δ'
ἐκ τῆς Λιβύης . . ἀνθρώπων: and again
9. 35 μοῦνοι δὲ . . πολιῆται. Hdt. will
not add ἀνδρῶν here, or even ἀνθρώπων.

αὐτὸν ὑπὸ πολεμίων καὶ πωλεόμενον ὠνέεται Πανιώνιος ἀνὴρ
Χῖος, ὃς τὴν ζόην κατεστήσατο ἀπ' ἔργων ἀνοσιωτάτων· ὅκως 5
γὰρ κτήσαιτο παῖδας εἴδεος ἐπαμμένους, ἐκταμὼν ἀγινέων
ἐπώλεε ἐς Σάρδις τε καὶ Ἔφεσον χρημάτων μεγάλων. παρὰ
γὰρ τοῖσι βαρβάροισι τιμιώτεροι εἰσὶ οἱ εὐνοῦχοι πίστιος
εἵνεκα τῆς πάσης τῶν ἐνορχίων. ἄλλους τε δὴ ὁ Πανιώνιος
ἐξέταμε πολλούς, ἅτε ποιεύμενος ἐκ τούτου τὴν ζόην, καὶ δὴ 10
καὶ τοῦτον. καὶ οὐ γὰρ τὰ πάντα ἐδυστύχεε ὁ Ἑρμότιμος,
ἀπικνέεται ἐκ τῶν Σαρδίων παρὰ βασιλέα μετ' ἄλλων δώρων,
χρόνου δὲ προϊόντος πάντων τῶν εὐνούχων ἐτιμήθη μάλιστα
παρὰ Ξέρξῃ. ὡς δὲ τὸ στράτευμα τὸ Περσικὸν ὅρμα βασιλεὺς 106
ἐπὶ τὰς Ἀθήνας ἐὼν ἐν Σάρδισι, ἐνθαῦτα καταβὰς κατὰ δή

---

4 παιώνιος Β　　5 ζώην C : ζωὴν Β (cum ὁ supersc. R) ‖ κατεκτή-
σατο Cobet, van H.　　6 ἐκταμὼν Reiske, Stein³ : ἐκτάμνων　　7
ἐπώλεε ἀγινέων ? Stein² ‖ σάρδιάς τε καὶ ἐς Β　　9 εἵνεκεν RS : εἵνεκε V
‖ ἐνορχίεων Β : ἐνορχέων Pz　　10 ποιεόμενος Β ‖ τουτέων z ‖ ζώην C
13 μάλιστα ἐτιμήθη παρὰ βασιλέϊ ξέρξῃ (sic) Β　　106. 1 ὥρμα α,
Stein¹ ‖ ὁ βασιλεὺς z　　2 ἐνθαῦτα δὴ (δὶ R) Β

ἀλόντα . . ὑπὸ πολεμίων suggests
prima facie a misfortune of war; the
Ionian revolt (498–494 B.C.) from 15–18
years previous to the date required for
this story seems to offer a likely enough
occasion. Cp. the threats of the barbarians and their recorded fulfilment,
6. 9, 32. (Stein, however, suggests a
piratical kidnapping.)

4. Πανιώνιος ἀνὴρ Χῖος : Panionios,
a man and a Chian. He did not remain
an ἀνήρ. His name is, perhaps, significant of the 'Panionic' ambitions of
the period, which produced the 'Ionic
Revolt': his ethnicon suggests that the
notorious wealth of the Chians was
partly due to slave-trading; cp. Thucyd.
8. 40. 2, and the whole passage on Chios,
Athenaeus 6. 86–91 = 265 ff. (where inter
alia this passage of Hdt. is cited).

5. τὴν ζόην κατεστήσατο : cp. τὸν βίον
κτησάμενε c. 106 infra. Panionios was
not the only Greek that had engaged
in this trade; the Corinthians were
perhaps tarred with the same brush;
cp. 3. 48.

6. εἴδεος ἐπαμμένους, 'possessed of
beauty.' L. & S. give ἐπάπτω as Ionic
for ἐφάπτω. Homer, at least, only contains the aspirated forms of the verb.
The participle is perf. (passive in form,
middle in force).

ἐκταμὼν ἀγινέων : the double
participles are rather awkward, but not

so awkward as if both were in the
present (defensible as indicating repeated
acts ?) ; cp. App. Crit. ἀγινέων is itself
a frequentative of ἄγω (used in the
middle 7. 33 supra) ; here perhaps
especially suitable for 'bringing to
market.'

7. ἐς Σάρδις τε καὶ Ἔφεσον : the
great markets for such wares, from their
position on the Royal Road (vide 5. 52–
54); and also perhaps with a local
demand for the temples of Kybele and
Artemis (Stein).

παρὰ γὰρ τοῖσι βαρβάροισι κτλ. :
the difference between Hellenic and
Asiatic culture is emphatic; the remark
is, however, only intended to apply to
slaves.

8. πίστιος . . τῆς πάσης, faithfulness, fidelity, in all respects. For the
antithesis εὐνοῦχος, ἔνορχις cp. 6. 32
(ὄρχις subst. 4. 109).

106. 1. τὸ στράτευμα τὸ Περσικόν :
the word στράτευμα is used both for
'expedition' and 'army' or 'host';
here perhaps (with ὅρμα) rather in the
latter sense. It was a 'Persian' army,
not merely politically, but in the main
ethnically, while at Sardes in 481–480
B.C. (cp. 7. 26, 40), and this passage is
an undesigned homage to the fact.

2. καταβάς : from inland to the coast.
κατὰ δή τι πρῆγμα, 'on some
(other) business.' — Perhaps Panionios

τι πρῆγμα ὁ Ἑρμότιμος ἐς γῆν τὴν Μυσίην, τὴν Χῖοι μὲν
νέμονται Ἀταρνεὺς δὲ καλέεται, εὑρίσκει τὸν Πανιώνιον ἐνθαῦτα.
5 ἐπιγνοὺς δὲ ἔλεγε πρὸς αὐτὸν πολλοὺς καὶ φιλίους λόγους,
πρῶτα μέν οἱ καταλέγων ὅσα αὐτὸς δι' ἐκεῖνον ἔχοι ἀγαθά,
δεύτερα δέ οἱ ὑπισχνεύμενος ἀντὶ τούτων ὅσα μιν ἀγαθὰ
ποιήσει, ἢν κομίσας τοὺς οἰκέτας οἰκέῃ ἐκείνῃ, ὥστε ὑποδεξάμενον ἄσμενον τοὺς λόγους τὸν Πανιώνιον κομίσαι τὰ τέκνα
10 καὶ τὴν γυναῖκα. ὡς δὲ ἄρα πανοικίῃ μιν περιέλαβε, ἔλεγε
ὁ Ἑρμότιμος τάδε. " ὦ πάντων ἀνδρῶν ἤδη μάλιστα ἀπ'
ἔργων ἀνοσιωτάτων τὸν βίον κτησάμενε, τί σε ἐγὼ κακὸν ἢ
αὐτὸς ἢ τῶν ἐμῶν τις σὲ προγόνων ἐργάσατο, ἢ σὲ ἢ τῶν σῶν
τινα, ὅτι με ἀντ' ἀνδρὸς ἐποίησας τὸ μηδὲν εἶναι ; ἐδόκεές

---

3 μὲν om. ß, Holder   4 ἀταρνέος ß : Ἀταρνεὸς Holder || παιώνιον ß
5 ἔλεγε ἄρα ß   7 τουτέων z   8 ποιήσει ß : ποιήσειεν || κομισά-
μενος ß || οἰκέτας : παῖδας CPz || ἐκεῖ van H. || ἀποδεξάμενον coni. Stein[1],
rec. van H.   9 παιώνιον ß || τά <τε> van H.   12 σε del. Cobet,
Holder, van H.   13 τίς σε CPz, Stein[1][2] : τις ß, Holder, van H. :
τις σε || προγόνων om. ß, Holder, van H.

---

was a reformed character by this time, with a wife and family of his own, and only engaged in lawful trade: all the more terrible the vengeance. But l. 11 *infra* hardly supports this.

3. **γῆν τὴν Μυσίην**: the term is partitive or restrictive, and plainly not used with the same extension as in 7. 42 *supra*, as the next words prove.

τὴν Χῖοι μὲν νέμονται Ἀταρνεὺς δὲ καλέεται. Cp. 1. 160 χῶρος τῆς Μυσίης Λέσβου ἀντίος. The dreadful story of this 'field of blood' is told 1. 160. Cp. 7. 42 *supra*. The specification here was hardly necessary after that passage. The notice here is probably reproduced from the 'Source,' and without any memory of the other passages. The absence of a cross reference is suggestive of Hdt.'s method of work.

4. **εὑρίσκει**: not that he was looking for him ; it is a casual meeting apparently.

5. **ἐπιγνούς**: as Hermotimos 'recognizes' his tormentor he will not have been a mere child at the time of his capture.

6. **καταλέγων**, of a series, or list ; cp. 7. 110.

δι' ἐκεῖνον, 'thanks to him.'

7. **ὑπισχνεύμενος**: Hdt. apparently uses freely both forms ὑπισχνέομαι and ὑπίσχομαι. Cp. 7. 104, 168, 9. 109, 2. 152, etc.

ἀντί, in return for.

8. **τοὺς οἰκέτας**: τὰ τέκνα καὶ τὴν γυναῖκα *infra* ; cp. c. 41 *supra*.

ἐκείνῃ: sc. ἐν τῷ Ἀταρνέι, Stein ; or possibly ἐν Σάρδισι.

ὑποδεξάμενον ἄσμενον: this construction is paralleled in Thuc. 6. 12. 2 ἄρχειν ἄσμενος αἱρεθείς. ἄσμενος is a curious adjective, itself at times almost participially constructed ; cp. c. 14 *supra*.

10. **πανοικίῃ**: 7. 39 *supra*.

περιέλαβε: cp. περιῆλθε ad fin.

11. **ἤδη**: as in c. 105 *supra*.

12. **ἔργων** is here (and there) used perhaps of industrial 'works' (ἔργα καὶ ἡμέραι). The formula τῶν ἡμ. ἐδ. would be very dull here ! Cp. c. 105 *supra*.

τὸν βίον κτησάμενε: a variant on τὴν ζόην κατεστήσατο c. 105.

τί σε ἐγώ κτλ.: a *vendetta* might have justified the cruelty of Panionios to Hermotimos—as it now justifies that of Hermotimos to Panionios.

14. **ὅτι με ἀντ' ἀνδρὸς ἐποίησας τὸ μηδὲν εἶναι**, 'that thou hast made me to be, instead of a man, the merest cipher.' τὸ μηδέν, cp. 9. 58 *infra* οὐδένες ἄρα ἐόντες κτλ. and 1. 32 ἢ δ' ἡμετέρη εὐδαιμονίη οὕτω τοι ἀπέρριπται ἐς τὸ μηδέν . ., neither of which passages is so forcible as this. Contr. Plato *Laws* 716 B πολλοῖς τισὶν ἔδοξεν εἶναί τις.

ἐδόκεές τε θεοὺς λήσειν οἷα ἐμηχανῶ τότε, 'thou wast thinking to

τε θεοὺς λήσειν οἶα ἐμηχανῶ τότε· οἵ σε ποιήσαντα ἀνόσια, 15
νόμῳ δικαίῳ χρεώμενοι, ὑπήγαγον ἐς χεῖρας τὰς ἐμάς, ὥστε
σε μὴ μέμψασθαι τὴν ἀπ' ἐμέο τοι ἐσομένην δίκην." ὡς δὲ
οἱ ταῦτα ὠνείδισε, ἀχθέντων τῶν παίδων ἐς ὄψιν ἠναγκάζετο
ὁ Πανιώνιος τῶν ἑωυτοῦ παίδων τεσσέρων ἐόντων τὰ αἰδοῖα
ἀποτάμνειν, ἀναγκαζόμενος δὲ ἐποίεε ταῦτα· αὐτοῦ τε, ὡς 20
ταῦτα ἐργάσατο, οἱ παῖδες ἀναγκαζόμενοι ἀπέταμνον. Πανιώνιον μὲν νυν οὕτω περιῆλθε ἥ τε τίσις καὶ Ἑρμότιμος.

Ξέρξης δὲ ὡς τοὺς παῖδας ἐπέτρεψε Ἀρτεμισίῃ ἀπάγειν 107
ἐς Ἔφεσον, καλέσας Μαρδόνιον ἐκέλευσέ μιν τῆς στρατιῆς
διαλέγειν τοὺς βούλεται, καὶ ποιέειν τοῖσι λόγοισι τὰ ἔργα
πειρώμενον ὅμοια. ταύτην μὲν τὴν ἡμέρην ἐς τοσοῦτο ἐγίνετο,
τῆς δὲ νυκτὸς κελεύσαντος βασιλέος τὰς νέας οἱ στρατηγοὶ ἐκ 5

escape the eyes of God in such deeds as
thou wast then contriving.'

16. νόμῳ δικαίῳ χρεώμενοι: the
Divine justice to Hdt. is strictly anthropomorphic. Cp. Introduction, § 11.

ὥστε σε μὴ μέμψασθαι, ferocious
irony: 'so that you (should) find no
fault with . .,' 'so that you (should) have
no fault to find with.' Not merely, 'so
that you have no right to complain that
I revenge myself on you!' Cp. Xenoph.
Hell. 6. 2. 34 εἰ δέ τις μὴ ἀκολουθήσει,
προεῖπε μὴ μέμψεσθαι τὴν δίκην: Plato
Laws 716 B ὑποσχὼν τιμωρίαν οὐ μεμπτὴν
τῇ δίκῃ ἑαυτόν τε καὶ οἶκον καὶ πόλιν ἄρδην
ἀνάστατον ἐποίησε. The aorist infinitive
with the future participle is piquant.

20. ἀναγκαζόμενος, passive: no doubt
by torture.

22. περιῆλθε ἥ τε τίσις καὶ Ἑρμό
τιμος: is it possible that Hdt. should
have meant to spoil his grim story with
a pun? Yet be τίσις never so much
personified the phrase seems not quite
happy. Cp. 3. 4 σοφίῃ γάρ μιν περιῆλθε
ὁ Φανῆς· L. & S. render the word here
'came at last upon . .' (περιέλαβε up
above seems the complement), and in c.
6 supra 'surround,' in potestatem habuit
(Baehr). Perhaps the explanation should
be sought not so much in a zeugma

(περιῆλθε) as in a hendiadys (ἥ τε τίσις
καὶ Ἑρμότιμος), 'Vengeance in the person
of Hermotimos laid hands on Panionios.'

107. 1. Ξέρξης δέ: the narrative
resumed from c. 103 supra; the story
of Hermotimos, though a digression, is
hardly an insertion: it will have belonged to the earliest deposits in Hdt.'s
memory and knowledge.

3. διαλέγειν, secernere, to divide the
'sheep and the goats'; cp. c. 113 infra
τοῖσι εἴδεα ὑπῆρχε διαλέγων.

ποιέειν τοῖσι λόγοισι τὰ ἔργα
πειρώμενον ὅμοια: πειρώμενον, a limitation; si fieri posset, Stein. Or, 'so far
as in him lay.'

4. ταύτην μὲν τὴν ἡμέρην. Is this
merely a conventional turn, or does
Hdt. use it with conscious design? No
change of day has been noticed since the
dawn in c. 83 supra. On that showing,
the day here is the day of battle, and
the night is the night of that very day.
There seems no reason to doubt this
result, though it suggests that the battle
was over long before nightfall (perhaps
before noon?)

ἐς τοσοῦτο ἐγίνετο: things went no
further; ἐγίνετο, impers. as in c. 6 supra.

5. οἱ στρατηγοί, the admirals; cp.
c. 75 supra.

τοῦ Φαλήρου ἀπῆγον ὀπίσω ἐς τὸν Ἑλλήσποντον ὡς τάχεος
εἶχε ἕκαστος, διαφυλαξούσας τὰς σχεδίας πορευθῆναι βασιλέι.
ἐπεὶ δὲ ἀγχοῦ ἦσαν Ζωστῆρος πλέοντες οἱ βάρβαροι, ἀνατεί-
νουσι γὰρ ἄκραι λεπταὶ τῆς ἠπείρου ταύτης, ἔδοξάν τε νέας
10 εἶναι καὶ ἔφευγον ἐπὶ πολλόν· χρόνῳ δὲ μαθόντες ὅτι οὐ νέες
εἶεν ἀλλ' ἄκραι, συλλεχθέντες ἐκομίζοντο.

108   Ὡς δὲ ἡμέρη ἐγίνετο, ὁρῶντες οἱ Ἕλληνες κατὰ χώρην

---

6 ταχέως Sz   7 ἔσχεν B ‖ φυλαξούσας B ‖ βασιλῆα z : βασιλεῖ
8 ἔσαν z ‖ πλώοντες BPz   9 τῆς ἠπείρου, ταύτας B : ' An τῆς ἠπείρου
ταύτῃ ?' Kallenberg : 'An ταύτης, ταύτας ?' van H. ‖ νῆας Bz   10 νέες
C : νῆες   108. 1 ἐγένετο CPz ‖ ὁρέωντες C : ὁρέοντες B, Stein¹,
van H.

ἐκ τοῦ Φαλήρου . . ἐς τὸν Ἑλλήσποντον : from out the bay of Phaleron
into the Hellespont—from which they
had come (ὀπίσω). Did they go direct,
or all round by the route they had come
by ? They apparently reached the
Hellespont, cp. c. 117 infra.

6. ὡς τάχεος εἶχε ἕκαστος, 'each one
as fast as he could . .' The picture presented is of a shattered fleet streaming
across the sea in a sauve qui peut style.

7. διαφυλαξούσας . . βασιλέι, "in-
finitivum πορευθῆναι nescio quid durius
habere videtur," Baehr. διαφ. βασ.
ὥστε αὐτὸν πορευθῆναι, Schweighaeuser.
Perhaps πορευθῆναι is rather an exegetical,
or even a telic infinitive after διαφυλαξούσας, and βασιλέι a purely ethical
dative (so B.). Stein cps. 4. 64 χλαίνας
ἐπείνυσθαι τοιεῦσι, and καταβάλλειν 7.
25 supra (a less exact parallel).

8. Ζωστῆρος. Strabo 398 describes
it as a large promontory, next the deme
of Aixone. It is certainly identified
with the three-headed promontory, near
the modern Vari. Pausanias 1. 31. 1
mentions that there was an altar there
Ἀθηνᾶς καὶ Ἀπόλλωνος καὶ Ἀρτέμιδος καὶ
Λητοῦς, and explains the name : τεκεῖν
μὲν οὖν Λητὼ τοὺς παῖδας ἐνταῦθα οὔ φασι,
λύσασθαι δὲ τὸν ζωστῆρα ὡς τεξομένην,
καὶ τῷ χωρίῳ διὰ τοῦτο γενέσθαι τὸ ὄνομα.
The promontory might perhaps be
considered like a ζωστήρ in appearance.

9. ἄκραι λεπταὶ τῆς ἠπείρου ταύτης :
is ταύτης merely graphic=ταύτῃ, or is
Hdt. writing as in Europe ? Stein cps.
7. 201, which does not settle the point.
Zoster itself is a large promontory ;
but its three headlands may be referred
to as ἄκραι λεπταί. Rawlinson, however,
remarks that "it is not very likely they
could have been mistaken by the Persians

(sic) for ships." Theophrastus Charact.
25 has ὁ δειλὸς τοιοῦτός τις οἷος πλέων τὰς
ἄκρας φάσκειν ἡμιολίας εἶναι.

10. ἐπὶ πολλόν, of space, as in 2. 32,
not of time, as in 2. 119.

11. συλλεχθέντες : passive in form,
middle in force. ἐκομίζοντο, 'they
continued their voyage' ; cp. ἐκομίζετο
c. 118 infra.

108. 1. ἡμέρη : apparently the day
after the battle. Hdt. has spent the
night on the Persian side (cc. 97-107).
The Greeks had retired into the bay of
Salamis again (c. 96 supra), quite
ignorant of the magnitude of their
success, and expecting to have the
struggle renewed (as at Artemision)
upon the following day. The illusion
was not dissipated at once even with the
return of the sun : the Persian army was
still visible on the Attic shore, and the
sight created a presumption that the
fleet was not far off. If so, the presumption was ill-founded : the army might
have remained in order to cover the
retreat of the ships. It seems unlikely
that news of the flight of the king's
vessels had not reached the Greeks ;
but it would have been quite impossible
for the Greeks to leave Salamis, while
the king's land-forces were in occupation
of Attica, even if no visible threat of an
assault upon Salamis (cp. c. 97 supra)
was in being. Hdt. has hardly envisaged
or grasped the strategic situation in this
case.

οἱ Ἕλληνες : the Greeks at large,
but more particularly the commanders.

κατὰ χώρην μένοντα τ. στ. τ. πεζόν :
the same army as was marching, on the
night before the battle, to the attack of
Peloponnesos, c. 70 supra. It is, of
course, possible for us, with two or three

μένοντα τὸν στρατὸν τὸν πεζὸν ἤλπιζον καὶ τὰς νέας εἶναι
περὶ Φάληρον, ἐδόκεόν τε ναυμαχήσειν σφέας παραρτέοντό τε
ὡς ἀλεξησόμενοι. ἐπεὶ δὲ ἐπύθοντο τὰς νέας οἰχωκυίας, αὐτίκα
μετὰ ταῦτα ἐδόκεε ἐπιδιώκειν. τὸν μὲν νυν ναυτικὸν τὸν 5
Ξέρξεω στρατὸν οὐκ ἐπεῖδον διώξαντες μέχρι Ἄνδρου, ἐς δὲ
τὴν Ἄνδρον ἀπικόμενοι ἐβουλεύοντο. Θεμιστοκλέης μὲν νυν

---

2 νῆας **Βz**   4 ἐπείτε ? van H. ‖ δ' **B** ‖ νῆας **Βz** ‖ ὠχωκυία R :
ὠχωκυίας SV   5 τὸν μὲν στρατὸν τὸν ξέρξεω R : τὸν μὲν ναυτικὸν
στρατὸν τὸν ξέρξεω SV

---

columns of Persian infantry and cavalry at our disposal, to harmonize the discrepancy ; but it remains a discrepancy on Hdt.'s own showing.

2. **εἶναι περὶ Φάληρον**: whither the survivors had retired on the previous day ;. c. 93 *supra*. Ships at Phaleron, or in the bay, would be invisible to the Greeks at Salamis : a matter of conjecture or speculation (ἤλπιζον).

3. **παραρτέοντο**: cp. c. 81 *supra*.

4. **ἐπεὶ δὲ ἐπύθοντο**: Hdt. fails to specify the exact time, at which, or the means by which, the Greeks were informed of the flight of the king's fleet. If they no sooner learned it than they resolved to pursue (αὐτίκα μετὰ ταῦτα), we might infer that they only learnt the retreat of the fleet after the evacuation of Athens and Attica by the army. But, if the fleet evacuated Phaleron immediately after the battle, it had a long start of the Greeks, who, whatever they might desire or decide to do, could not leave Salamis unprotected, until they were assured that the Persian army too was in full retreat. Was the pursuit of the Persian fleet seriously intended ? It would certainly not have been lightly undertaken, or without ardent debate. Hdt. records just below a debate at Andros ; but the Hellenes can hardly have rowed to Andros, whatever the object of that movement, without a previous council and discussion. Hdt. has assuredly omitted to report a debate at Salamis, after the victory.

6. **μέχρι Ἄνδρου**. The island of Andros, one of the 'Kyklades' (cp. 5. 31), lies between Euboia and Tenos (cp. 4. 33), and is about 80 E. miles voyage from Salamis. It had evidently 'medized,' cp. c. 66 *supra*, and has special reasons for medizing ; cp. 7. 115 *supra*.

7. **ἐβουλεύοντο**: the scene, the speakers, the subject, of this council, or debate,

are all open to challenge. For reasons above given the Greek fleet can hardly have quitted Salamis in pursuit of 'the flying Mede': if the Greeks put into Andros, which was a Persian outpost or stronghold, it must have been with the intention of 'liberating' or gaining the island for the good cause ; the attack on Andros, and the medizing islands, will have been resolved upon before the Greeks left Salamis. Hdt. treats this operation as a matter of course, or as the obvious alternative to a pursuit of the 'barbarian' fleet (c. 111 *infra*) ; but it will have required an express decision, even if covered by the general vow against the medizers (7. 132). Again, Eurybiades here appears as taking part in the debate, and as the opponent of Themistokles ; dramatic, and perhaps constitutional proprieties are better observed above in the accounts of the debates before Salamis, where Korinthian opposes Athenian, or in the variant on this very anecdote, which pits Aristeides against Themistokles (cp. Appendix VII. § 2). The Spartan has perhaps come in as the exponent of the characteristically Lakonian policy, not to pursue a flying foe. The plan ascribed to Themistokles is here expressed in almost self-contradictory terms, or as combining incompatible objects : διὰ νήσων τραπέσθαι· ἐπιδιῶξαι τὰς νέας· πλέειν ἰθέως ἐπὶ τ. Ἑλλ. λύσοντας τὰς γεφύρας (i.e. ἐπὶ τ. Ἑλλ. πλεύσαντας λῦσαι τ. γ.). The first phrase may be ambiguous, covering alike operations against the islands (the Kyklades) in succession, and a passage through them without touching ; but the ideas of pursuing the Persian fleet and of sailing for the Hellespont to destroy the bridges could only be harmonized on the assumption that the Persian fleet had made for the Hellespont ; and even so, the pursuit of the

γνώμην ἀπεδείκνυτο διὰ νήσων τραπομένους καὶ ἐπιδιώξαντας
τὰς νέας πλέειν ἰθέως ἐπὶ τὸν Ἑλλήσποντον λύσοντας τὰς
10 γεφύρας· Εὐρυβιάδης δὲ τὴν ἐναντίην ταύτῃ γνώμην ἐτίθετο,
λέγων ὡς εἰ λύσουσι τὰς σχεδίας, τοῦτ' ἂν μέγιστον πάντων
σφι κακῶν τὴν Ἑλλάδα ἐργάσαιτο. εἰ γὰρ ἀναγκασθείη
ἀπολαμφθεὶς ὁ Πέρσης μένειν ἐν τῇ Εὐρώπῃ, πειρῷτο ἂν
ἡσυχίην μὴ ἄγειν, ὡς ἄγοντι μέν οἱ ἡσυχίην οὔτε τι προ-
15 χωρέειν οἷόν τε ἔσται τῶν πρηγμάτων οὔτε τις κομιδὴ τὸ
ὀπίσω φανήσεται, λιμῷ τέ οἱ ἡ στρατιὴ διαφθερέεται, ἐπιχει-
ρέοντι δὲ αὐτῷ καὶ ἔργου ἐχομένῳ πάντα τὰ κατὰ τὴν
Εὐρώπην οἷά τε ἔσται προσχωρῆσαι κατὰ πόλις τε καὶ κατὰ

---

8 ἐπεδείκνυτο Β   9 νῆας Βz ‖ πλώειν Βz   12 σφέας Β :
σφεῖς z ‖ κακὸν Β ‖ ἐργάσατο R : ἐργάσαιτο SV : ἐργασαίατο Dindorf,
Cobet, Kallenberg, van H.   13 ἐν τῇ εὐρώπῃ μένειν Β : ἐν τῇ Εὐρώπῃ
huc ex fine cap. translata susp. Kallenberg ‖ πειρῷτ' ΑΒz   15 <ἐς> τὸ
Cobet (quod olim impugn. Schweighaeuser)   16 φανέεται ? Krueger ‖
διαφθαρέεται α : διαφθαρεῖται van H. ‖ ἐπιχωρέοντι Β

---

fleet might involve a second engagement,
which might prove an obstacle to
destroying the bridges. Possibly all
three ideas (i. the destruction of the
bridges; ii. the pursuit of the flying
Phoenicians; iii. the visitation of the
medizing islands) were traditionally and
rightly associated with Themistokles;
but they should not have been given to
him in one breath !

10. γνώμην ἐτίθετο : a variant upon
the more common γν. ἀπεδείκνυτο (cp.
just above), perhaps used here out of
regard to the commanding position of
Eurybiades; or perhaps simply from the
analogy of voting, as in c. 123 infra
ἐτίθετο τὴν ψῆφον. The opinion ascribed
to Eurybiades that the destruction of
the bridges would be a national calamity
for Greece is doubly refuted, (i.) by the
apprehension previous ascribed to
Xerxes (in a different anecdote) c. 97
supra; (ii.) by the logic of facts, the
bridges having been destroyed without
injury to Greece; cp. c. 117 infra.

11. τοῦτ' ἂν . . ἐργάσαιτο : as ἐργάσαιτο can scarcely be passive, the construction is with a double acc. after the
verb (c. 79 supra), of which τοῦτο is
subject, σφι being, of course, ethical
dative. Cp. App. Crit.

14. ἡσυχίην μὴ ἄγειν : a curious
equivalent for ἐπιχειρέειν, or ἔργου
ἔχεσθαι (phrases used below), perhaps

suggested by the speaker's desire that
the Persian should ἡσυχίην ἄγειν (Stein).
The argument which follows (ὡς ἄγοντι
μέν οἱ κτλ.) seems far-fetched : the
destruction of the bridges is to compel
the Persian to the conquest of Europe;
the victory at Salamis and the consequent superiorit of the Greeks at sea
are ignored. The whole passage reads
like an estimate of the necessity for
active and offensive measures on the
invader's part before the invasion, or at
least before his defeat, a necessity which
was not conditioned simply by the
existence or non-existence of the bridges;
cp. Appendix IV. § 1.

15. τῶν πρηγμάτων, 'his plans.'
προσχωρῆσαι, 'to succeed' : προσχωρῆσαι
just below comes in rather inelegantly.

κομιδὴ τὰ ὀπίσω : cp. ἡ κομιδὴ
ἡμῖν ἔσται τὸ ὀπίσω 4. 134, and ἡ ὀπίσω
κομιδή c. 120 infra. κ. in a different
sense 9. 78 infra.

18. οἷά τε ἔσται προσχωρῆσαι. The
subject appears to be πάντα τὰ κ. τ.
Εὐρώπην, 'all the parts of Europe,' i.e.
all Europe; but the speaker is perhaps
to be taken only to refer to the Hellenized
portions, though ἔθνεα may cover non-
Hellenic tribes (cp. 7. 1, 110 supra), and
'Europe' is again and again suggested
as the ultimate Persian objective. The
harvests of Hellas would hardly suffice
for the universal conquest of all Europe.

ἔθνεα, ἤτοι ἁλισκομένων γε ἢ πρὸ τούτου ὁμολογεόντων·
τροφήν τε ἕξειν σφέας τὸν ἐπέτειον αἰεὶ τὸν τῶν Ἑλλήνων 20
καρπόν. ἀλλὰ δοκέειν γὰρ νικηθέντα τῇ ναυμαχίῃ οὐ μενέειν
ἐν τῇ Εὐρώπῃ τὸν Πέρσην· ἐατέον ὦν εἶναι φεύγειν, ἐς ὃ
ἔλθοι φεύγων ἐς τὴν ἑωυτοῦ· τὸ ἐνθεῦτεν δὲ περὶ τῆς ἐκείνου
ποιέεσθαι ἤδη τὸν ἀγῶνα ἐκέλευε. ταύτης δὲ εἴχοντο τῆς
γνώμης καὶ Πελοποννησίων τῶν ἄλλων οἱ στρατηγοί. ὡς δὲ 109
ἔμαθε ὅτι οὐ πείσει τούς γε πολλοὺς πλέειν ἐς τὸν Ἑλλήσποντον ὁ Θεμιστοκλέης, μεταβαλὼν πρὸς τοὺς Ἀθηναίους

---

20 τὸν ante τῶν om. β, Holder   21 ἀλλ' οὐ δοκεῖν C ‖ οὐ μενέειν :
μένειν C   22 πέρσεα β : Περσέα z   23 ἔλθη β : ἔλθῃ Stein[1],
Holder   24 ἐκέλευε del. Cobet, van H.   109. 2 πλώειν βz
3 ἔλεγε πρὸς β

---

19. ἢ πρὸ τούτου ὁμολογεόντων :
grammatically the less likely looks politically the more likely alternative ; viz.
that they should come to an agreement
before being taken, or reduced by force.
The (masculine) gen. abs. is noticeable.
With the phraseology of this passage
cp. 7. 139 supra.
20. τὸν ἐπέτειον αἰεὶ τὸν τ. Ἐλ.
καρπόν. The article as in τὸν ναυτικὸν
τὸν Ξέρξεω στρατόν l. 5 supra. Unless
αἰεί might have practically a locative
sense the phrase seems to imply a series
of annual campaigns, though ἐπέτειος
might not perhaps in itself necessitate
a succession of harvests ; cp. 2. 25 δοκέει
δέ μοι οὐδὲ πᾶν τὸ ὕδωρ τὸ ἐπέτειον
ἑκάστοτε ἀποπέμπεσθαι τοῦ Νείλου ὁ
ἥλιος κτλ., 2. 92 τὴν δὲ βύβλον τὴν
ἐπέτειον γινομένην ἐπεὰν ἀνασπάσωσι κτλ.
21. ἀλλὰ δοκέειν γὰρ νικηθέντα κτλ.
Eurybiades the Spartan is represented
as saying—and so say all of the Peloponnesian commanders—that the Persians
would not remain in Europe after the
defeat at Salamis. This prognostication
is abundantly nullified, not merely by
the commission of Mardonios, but even
after Plataia by the remnant in Thrace,
cp. 7. 106, 107 supra. It is, however,
possible that the formula represents
accurately enough the Spartan and
'Peloponnesian' point of view, or hope:
the more plausible, if the Greeks had
already witnessed the evacuation of
Attica by the land-forces of the barbarian.
Even when later the Spartans must have
been convinced that the Persian had
not abandoned Europe, or even Hellas,
in spite of his defeat at Salamis, they
were still hoping to avoid any necessity

for another land-engagement ; cp.
Appendix VII. § 1.
23. περὶ τῆς ἐκείνου ποιέεσθαι ἤδη
τὸν ἀγῶνα : remarkable is the idea of an
aggressive movement upon the king's
possessions thus formulated on the lips
of Eurybiades. Is it an anachronism,
borrowed from the πρόσχημα of the
Delian League in 477 B.C. (cp. Thuc. 1.
96)? Or is it but an anticipation of the
naval programme of Mykale and Sestos,
in the next year (479 B.C.)? Or is it
not rather a testimony to the first and
fundamental principles of Themistoklean
strategy, which had already, and even
before Salamis, advocated an offensive
movement as the best means of relieving
the tension in Greece? After all, 'the
march to Sardis' was an old idea, nay,
a fait accompli, in Athenian quarters ; cp.
5. 97 ff. ; but that a Spartan in 480 B.C.
contemplates a struggle for the possession of the king's own territory (περὶ τῆς
ἐκείνου, causal not locative) is a little
surprising.
24. εἴχοντο with the gen., 'laid hold
of,' 'adhered to'; cp. (with γνώμης)
Thuc. 1. 140. 1, and 6. 94 supra ταύτης
ἐχόμενος τῆς προφάσιος.
109. 2. οὐ πείσει τούς γε πολλούς.
Hdt. here writes as though the movements of the fleet were determined by
a majority of votes; no doubt the
Navarch, Eurybiades, really had the
actual decision ; cp. c. 64 supra.
3. μεταβαλών : cp. 5. 75 Κορίνθιοι . .
μετέβαλλόν τε καὶ ἀπαλλάσσοντο. In
that passage, as in 7. 52 supra, the word
appears to be used, intransitively, of
actual physical change of place ; and
here the words πρὸς τοὺς Ἀθηναίους

(οὗτοι γὰρ μάλιστα ἐκπεφευγότων περιημέκτεον, ὁρμέατό τε
5 ἐς τὸν Ἑλλήσποντον πλέειν καὶ ἐπὶ σφέων αὐτῶν βαλόμενοι,
εἰ οἱ ἄλλοι μὴ βουλοίατο) ἔλεγέ σφι τάδε. " καὶ αὐτὸς ἤδη
πολλοῖσι παρεγενόμην καὶ πολλῷ πλέω ἀκήκοα τοιάδε
γενέσθαι, ἄνδρας ἐς ἀναγκαίην ἀπειληθέντας [νενικημένους]
ἀναμάχεσθαί τε καὶ ἀναλαμβάνειν τὴν προτέρην κακότητα.
10 ἡμεῖς δέ, εὕρημα γὰρ εὑρήκαμεν ἡμέας τε αὐτοὺς καὶ τὴν
Ἑλλάδα, νέφος τοσοῦτο ἀνθρώπων ἀνωσάμενοι, μὴ διώκωμεν

---

4 ὡρμέατό a etc.   5 πλώειν Βz ‖ αὐτέων z ‖ βαλλόμενοι z : βουλόμενοι Β   6 εἰ ὤλλοι Β   7 πλείω Β   8 νενικημένους Stein :
del. Cobet, Holder, van H.   11 τοσοῦτον A ante ras. Βz ‖ ἀνθρώπων
damn. Dobree ‖ ἀνωσάμενοι ΒPz : ἀνασωσάμενοι

---

support a similar interpretation—otherwise a mental conversion might be preferable. *Mutato consilio ad Athenienses
se convertens* (Schweigh. Lex.) seems
unwarrantably to combine both.

4. **περιημέκτεον**: an Herodotean word,
used with the dative, as in 4. 154, and
absolutely, as in 1. 114 μᾶλλόν τι περιημέκτεε, is here used with a sort of
causal genitive (ἐκπεφευγότων). The
meaning is clear ('were aggrieved'), but
the etymology unknown.

ὁρμέατο: the pluperfect passive,
without augment. The tense might
here have its temporal meaning, even
in view of the sequence εἰ οἱ ἄλλοι μὴ
βουλοίατο. The condition predicated is,
of course, purely psychological.

5. **ἐπὶ σφέων αὐτῶν βαλόμενοι**, 'at
their own risk'! 'on their own responsibility'! or 'by themselves'! cp. 5. 78
and 3. 71. The exact metaphor is less
clear than the meaning; the expression
is apparently Herodotean. **καί**, *etiam*.

6. **ἔλεγέ σφι τάδε**. Hdt. does not
shrink from reporting the speeches of
Themistokles; cp. cc. 60, 61 f., 80, 83
supra.

7. **πολλοῖσι παρεγενόμην**: πολλοῖσι is
presumably neuter, as co-ordinate with
πολλῷ πλέω just below. The occasions
referred to, if set out, would have
furnished an interesting chapter of
autobiography. The emphatic co-ordination καί . . καί is observable.

8. **ἀπειληθέντας [νενικημένους]**: the
doubled participles are clumsy though
intelligible; cp. App. Crit. At Andros
(*Mannheim*, Pape-Benseler) the Greeks
have to do with ἄνδρες. Themistokles
does not despise the enemy.

9. **ἀναμάχεσθαί τε καὶ ἀναλαμβάνειν**:
cp. 5. 121 μετὰ δὲ τοῦτο τὸ τρῶμα
ἀνέλαβόν τε καὶ ἀνεμαχέσαντο οἱ Κᾶρες.
(Themistokles can hardly have been
present on that occasion.) ἀναλαμβάνειν
having an object here (κακότητα) is of
simpler construction, and perhaps of
more obvious meaning, cp. 7. 232 *supra*,
but κακότης itself is of disputable
significance. In 2. 128 it appears to
mean 'evil plight,' misery ; and it may
bear the same meaning in 2. 124; so
too, most clearly, in 6. 67, where it is
opposed to εὐδαιμονίη, but in 7. 168
supra it certainly denotes a defect of
character, cowardice or what not (cp.
Thuc. 5. 100 κακότης καὶ δειλία), and it
might bear that interpretation here.

10. **εὕρημα γὰρ εὑρήκαμεν**, 'we have
had a stroke of luck,' cp. 7. 10 l. 43;
the cognate acc. is simple enough, but
the addition of the further accusatives,
ἡμέας τε αὐτοὺς καὶ τὴν Ἑλλάδα, complicates the sentence, and without the
addition of a participle, co-ordinate with
ἀνωσάμενοι, a *constructio ad sensum* is a
trifle violent—as though εὑρ. εὑρήκ.
might form a single verbal idea and construction = ἀναλελαβήκαμεν (sc. ἀνειλή-
φαμεν). ἡμέας τε αὐτοὺς καὶ τὴν Ἑλλάδα
may, however, be taken in apposition to
εὕρημα—a somewhat excited phrase !
Anything were better than· inserting
ἀνασωσάμενοι. Cp. App. Crit.

11. **νέφος τοσοῦτο ἀνθρώπων ἀνωσάμενοι**: the metaphor is superb; the
barbarians are mere ἄνθρωποι from this
point of view (though ἄνδρες φεύγοντες
immediately below). The verb is curious
—cp. App. Crit.—but justified by 7. 139,
a passage perhaps influenced by the
oratory of Themistokles.

ἄνδρας φεύγοντας. τάδε γὰρ οὐκ ἡμεῖς κατεργασάμεθα, ἀλλὰ
θεοί τε καὶ ἥρωες, οἳ ἐφθόνησαν ἄνδρα ἕνα τῆς τε Ἀσίης καὶ
τῆς Εὐρώπης βασιλεῦσαι ἐόντα ἀνόσιόν τε καὶ ἀτάσθαλον·
ὃς τά τε ἱρὰ καὶ τὰ ἴδια ἐν ὁμοίῳ ἐποιέετο, ἐμπιπράς τε καὶ 15
καταβάλλων τῶν θεῶν τὰ ἀγάλματα· ὃς καὶ τὴν θάλασσαν

---

15 τε ante ἱρὰ om. βPz ‖ ἐμπιπρείς α: ἐμπιπρήσας C

---

12. τάδε, of antecedents ; cp. the occasional use of ταῦτα for consequents ; ὅδε
and οὗτος both contrast with ἐκεῖνος, as the
nearer with the more remote ; and with
each other, as the immediate present (or
just coming) with the mediate present
(or just gone).

13. θεοί τε καὶ ἥρωες, 'Gods and Heroes
combined.' The passage refutes incidentally the sneer of Mardonios against the
Greeks as τῶν τὸ πᾶν σφίσι ἤδη δοκεόντων
κατεργάσθαι c. 100 supra (spoken of
course with quite another 'intention'),
for at least it disclaims the victory
as their own work : even Themistokles,
however, appears in the context as over-
rating the effects of the battle of Salamis
(παντελέως ἀπελάσας τὸν βάρβαρον).

οἱ ἐφθόνησαν .. βασιλεῦσαι: the
doctrine of the divine φθόνος appears
here upon the lips of Themistokles in its
simplest form : the gods view with
jealousy one man's lordship of Asia and
Europe combined. Such an excess of
human power is in itself a sufficient
reason for the divine passion. The
words which follow ἐόντα ἀνόσιόν τε καὶ
ἀτάσθαλον may be taken, not as the
justification of the ways of gods to man,
but as a statement of pure matter of fact
—a fact inevitable, since what mortal
invested with such power could avoid
pride, presumption, impiety, sin ! In
the examples which follow (ὃς κτλ.), if
it were worth while to distinguish the
ἀνοσιότης and the ἀτασθαλίη, the destruction of temples and cult-objects might
illustrate the former, and the lashing
and fettering of the sea the latter.

15. ἐν ὁμοίῳ ἐποιέετο, 'made no difference between . .'; cp. 7. 138 supra (in
a somewhat different sense).

ἐμπιπράς τε καὶ καταβάλλων: as
at Abai c. 33 supra, and above all at
Athens c. 53 supra. It is noticeable
that there is no reference to the case of
Delphi (cc. 35-39 supra) ; nor is anything said of the cases in which Xerxes
had shown positive respect for Greek
religion and cult-objects (e.g. at Troy 7.

43 supra, at Halos 7. 197 supra, at
Athens itself c. 54 supra, and of course
at Thebes, not to press the sacrifices at
Nine Ways 7. 114, at Sepias 7. 191).
Athenians naturally made the most of
the point (cp. Aischyl. Pers. 805 f.),
though their own record was not clean
in this respect (cp. 5. 102) ; but it was
left for Cicero to represent the Persians
as Puritan fanatics, indignant with the
Greeks for believing that the gods could
be enclosed 'in temples made with
hands' (de legg. 2. 10. 26 Xerxes
inflammasse templa Graeciae dicitur,
quod parietibus includerent deos, quibus
omnia deberent esse patentia ac libera,
quorumque hic mundus omnis templum
esset et domus). That view is refuted
by what is known of the policy of
Dareios and his successors in Egypt, in
Babylon, in Greece itself—to say
nothing of the acts of Kyros and Kambyses. The invasion of Greece was in
no sense a crusade or religious war, but
the Greeks naturally enough invested
their victory with a religious halo, and
exaggerated the offences against the
national religion committed by the
Persians as incidents of the campaign.
Hence the intensely religious tone of the
Herodotean narrative, little as the great
centres of the national religion did for
Greece in her hour of need. Hence
too the decree, or supposed decree, that
the temples destroyed by the Persian
should remain for ever in ruins (cp. the
forged oath in Lycurgus c. Leocrat. 81,
and Pausan. 10. 35. 2), a decree directly
contravened by the earliest programme
of Perikles (Plutarch, Perikl. 17) inter
alia. But cp. c. 33 supra, 9. 116 infra.

**16. καὶ τὴν θ. ἀπεμαστίγωσε πέδας τε
κατῆκε:** according to the story related
in 7. 35 supra. Themistokles omits the
stigmatization ! If this speech were
authentic, and rightly dated to 480 B.C., it
would be the earliest extant evidence for
the incidents : items of Themistoklean
oratory may be preserved in it, but
hardly this particular sentence, which

ἀπεμαστίγωσε πέδας τε κατῆκε. ἀλλ᾽ εὖ γὰρ ἔχει ἐς τὸ
παρεὸν ἡμῖν, νῦν μὲν ἐν τῇ Ἑλλάδι καταμείναντας ἡμέων
τε αὐτῶν ἐπιμεληθῆναι καὶ τῶν οἰκετέων, καί τις οἰκίην τε
20 ἀναπλασάσθω καὶ σπόρου ἀνακῶς ἐχέτω, παντελέως ἀπελάσας

---

17 τε κατῆκε : τ᾽ ἐγκατῆκε van H.   18 μὲν <ἄμεινον> Stein³
(χρεόν ἐστι ? Stein²) || καταμείναντες Bz   19 αὐτέων aCz || ἐπιμελη-
θῶμεν z   20 ἀναπλασσάσθω z, Eustath. Od. p. 1425 || σπόρους C :
σποράς Eustath. || παντελέως AB : παντελῶς

---

reads in any case rather forcedly.
Perhaps the whole religious parenthesis
(τάδε γὰρ . . κατῆκε) is Herodotean
rather than authentic Themistokles.
ἀπομαστιγῶσαι, 'to flog soundly,' occurs
3. 29.

17. ἀλλ᾽ εὖ γὰρ . . ἡμῖν : cp. 7. 158
ἀλλὰ (sic) εὖ γὰρ ἡμῖν καὶ ἐπὶ τὸ ἄμεινον
κατέστη, Gelone loq. (It can hardly be
argued that the Sikeliote orator preserved
while the Athenian avoided the hiatus :
the variation exhibits the inconstancy
of the MSS., perhaps of the author
himself !)

18. νῦν μὲν . . ἐπιμεληθῆναι. Stein
regards this construction as intolerably
harsh, and emends the text (cp. App.
Crit.) ; but surely the infinitive may
stand as hortative (Madvig, Gk. Syntax,
§ 168), especially here when elucidated
immediately in the very next sentence
by the imperative ἀναπλασάσθω (cp.
Aristoph. Wsps. 108), to say nothing of
the jingle ἄμεινον καταμείναντας. The
form of the verb ἐπιμεληθῆναι, like the
subst. ἐπιμέλεια (6. 105), implies a present
ἐπιμελέομαι—though the form of the
present in use appears to have been
ἐπιμέλομαι ; cp. ἐπιμέλεσθαι 1. 98, ἐπι-
μελομένῳ 2. 2, ἐτεμέλετο 2. 174. (μέλομαι,
I care for, take care of, with gen. ; in
the Tragedians passim.)

19. οἰκετέων : cp. c. 106 l. 8 supra.

20. ἀναπλασάσθω. πλάσσειν is used
properly of soft materials, earth, wax, etc.
σπόρου ἀνακῶς ἐχέτω : cp. l. 24
ἀνακῶς δὲ ἔχειν τῶν πορθμέων. Also
Thuc. 8. 102. 2 ὅπως αὐτῶν ἀνακῶς
ἕξουσιν, ἢν ἐκπλέωσι. The construction
of ἔχειν with the adv. is, of course,
regular enough, but the word ἀνακῶς
itself is a curious one ; cp. Plutarch,
Thes. 33 τιμὰς ἰσοθέους ἔσχον (sc. οἱ
Τυνδαρίδαι) Ἄνακες προσαγορευθέντες, ἢ
διὰ τὰς γενομένας ἀνοχὰς (in Attica), ἢ
διὰ τὴν ἐπιμέλειαν καὶ κηδεμονίαν τοῦ
μηδένα κακῶς παθεῖν στρατιᾶς τοσαύτης

ἔνδον οὔσης· ἀνακῶς γὰρ ἔχειν τοὺς ἐπι-
μελομένους ἢ φυλάττοντας ὁτιοῦν· καὶ τοὺς
βασιλεῖς ἴσως ἄνακτας διὰ τοῦτο καλοῦσιν.
εἰσὶ δὲ οἱ λέγοντες διὰ τὴν τῶν ἀστέρων
ἐπιφάνειαν Ἄνακας ὀνομάζεσθαι· τὸ γὰρ
ἄνω τοὺς Ἀττικοὺς ἀνέκας ὀνομάζειν καὶ
ἀνέκαθεν τὸ ἄνωθεν. The passage contains
an exemplary bit of antique etymologizing, but L. & S. accept the connexion of
ἀνακῶς with ἄναξ. The word was used
by Plato, Com. incert. 24 (ed. Bothe-
Didot) καὶ τὰς (or τᾶς) θύρας ἀνακῶς
ἔχειν : cp. Erotianos p. 66, Ἀνακῶς·
ἐπιμελῶς καὶ περιπεφυλαγμένως. ἔστι δὲ
ἡ λέξις Δωρική. (Is it not rather 'old
Attic,' and so appropriate in the mouth
of Themistokles ?)

παντελέως ἀπελάσας τὸν βάρβαρον. Themistokles appears to share
the illusion (ascribed above to Eurybiades)
that Salamis had put an end to the
presence of the 'barbarian' in Greece.
Stein, indeed, takes the sentence as
conditional, and refers it not to the
battle which has taken place, but to
the land-engagement, which Themistokles
expects to be fought before the winter
(i.e. not "now that we have driven,"
but "as soon as we shall have driven
the barbarian clean away"). This interpretation (i.) ill suits the context,
especially the corresponding passage c.
108 ad fin. ; (ii.) involves Themistokles
in a huge misconception in regard to
the probable action of the Peloponnesians ;
(iii.) makes him treat a great land-battle
immediately to come as a foregone
conclusion, to be mentioned en passant,
sandwiched between the restoration of
Athens and the expedition to the Hellespont ; while (iv.) Hdt. himself declares
the rusé character of Themistokles'
advice to the Athenians ; and although
the purpose he assigns is unacceptable
(see below), the possibility remains open
that the argument of the speaker is a
make-believe. In fact, the words, if

τὸν βάρβαρον· ἅμα δὲ τῷ ἔαρι καταπλέωμεν ἐπὶ Ἑλλησπόντου καὶ Ἰωνίης." ταῦτα ἔλεγε ἀποθήκην μέλλων ποιή-

21 ἑλλήσποντον C   22 ὑποθήκην z ‖ ποιήσασθαι Bβ : ποιήσεσθαι

authentic, may have been used by
Themistokles with his eyes open, and
his participation in the Spartan illusion,
that no land - battle would ever be
necessary, may have been a voluntary
hypothesis, *argumenti causa.* So, too,
the promise to sail to the Hellespont
and Ionia in the spring might at this
point have been rather a concession to
gain the Athenians, and to prevent the
break-up of the fleet, than a deliberate
plan, in view of the utter discomfiture
of the Persian, or in anticipation of
the subsequent policy of reprisals. It
would, however, be a possible preventive
of the re-invasion of Attica, in case the
Persians had not evacuated Europe: as
applicable in the spring as in the present
autumn. The whole discussion (it must
be remembered) can hardly have taken
place until the Persians had evacuated
Attica, and probably did not take place
at Andros, but at Salamis. Whether
Themistokles, when he realized that
Mardonios was still in Greece with an
army, failed to grasp the strategic
aspects of the case, is a further question
(cp. Appendix VII. § 1). It is at least
arguable that the greatest of the
Athenians never had any illusions upon
the point.

22. ταῦτα ἔλεγε ἀποθήκην μέλλων
ποιήσασθαι. This contribution to the
Themistoklean legend represents him as
a traitor from the beginning. The
motivation is plainly an inference from
the event (τά περ ἄν καὶ ἐγένετο), and
is both psychologically and historically
bad. There is an assumption involved
that Themistokles did wrong in dissuad-
ing the Athenians from sailing off by
themselves from Andros (or Salamis ?)
to the Hellespont, and his crime is the
more flagrant seeing that he himself had
advocated the move to the Hellespont
just before. But Themistokles was
neither inconsequent nor disloyal if he
now wrought with the Athenians to
prohibit a schismatic undertaking:
rather might Hdt. have pronounced
such an eulogy upon his act as Thucydides pronounced upon the act of
Alkibiades in retaining the Athenian
fleet at Samos in 411 B.C. from precipi-

tately making for the city (cp. Thuc.
8. 82. 2). Strategically, the separate
adventure of the Athenians must have
been highly precarious; politically, it
might have shattered the Alliance, which
still had work to do: the reduction of
the Kyklades by the confederate fleet
was both strategically and politically
the better investment. In so far as
Hdt. (or his source) ascribes to Themistokles a prevision of possible disaster
to himself in time to come, and sets
him about making provision against a
turn of Fortune's wheel, the bounds of
psychological possibility are not passed,
f'r a Greek and a Themistokles. Of
such reverses, too, he could say: καὶ
αὐτὸς ἤδη πολλοῖσι παρεγενόμην καὶ
πολλῷ πλέω ἀκήκοα τοιάδε γενέσθαι. The
trophies of Miltiades were before his
eyes day and night. But there is no
real relation between his reported advice
on this occasion and his subsequent
'medism'—such as it was. The motivation here depends upon the truth of the
story (in the next c.) of the second
mission of Sikinnos—and that story is
a transparent fraud. Grote, indeed,
credits the view that Themistokles—"a
clever man, tainted with such constant
guilt"—calculated on being one day
detected and punished; i.e. Grote takes
the Themistokles - legend very much at
its own estimation. Blakesley's note is
curiously perverse, amounting to this :
Thucydides is wrong in saying that
Themistokles claimed credit in his letter
to Artaxerxes (1. 187) for having saved
the bridge for Xerxes, while Hdt. is
right in saying that Themistokles,
not knowing that the bridges were
already broken down in 480 B.C. (if
they were; cp. c. 117. 4 *infra*), intended,
on some future occasion, should need
arise, to claim credit with the king for
saving the bridge !

ἀποθήκην . . ποιήσασθαι (=
ἀποθέσθαι, or ἀπόθετον ποιήσασθαι) is
scarcely adequate; cp. 6. 41 χάριτα
μεγάλην καταθήσεσθαι. ἐς here looks
like *apud.* τὸν Πέρσην generalized (for
Ξέρξην) perhaps in the light of the
event, Hdt., of course, knowing that
Themistokles was received by Artaxerxes.

σασθαι ἐς τὸν Πέρσην, ἵνα ἢν ἄρα τί μιν καταλαμβάνῃ πρὸς
Ἀθηναίων πάθος, ἔχῃ ἀποστροφήν· τά περ ὦν καὶ ἐγένετο.

110   Θεμιστοκλέης μὲν ταῦτα λέγων διέβαλλε, Ἀθηναῖοι δὲ
ἐπείθοντο· ἐπειδὴ γὰρ καὶ πρότερον δεδογμένος εἶναι σοφὸς
ἐφάνη ἐὼν ἀληθέως σοφός τε καὶ εὔβουλος, πάντως ἕτοιμοι
ἦσαν λέγοντι πείθεσθαι. ὡς δὲ οὗτοί οἱ ἀνεγνωσμένοι ἦσαν,
5 αὐτίκα μετὰ ταῦτα ὁ Θεμιστοκλέης ἄνδρας ἀπέπεμπε ἔχοντας
πλοῖον, τοῖσι ἐπίστευε σιγᾶν ἐς πᾶσαν βάσανον ἀπικνεομένοισι

---

23 πέρσεα Βz ‖ ἢν : εἰ C ‖ ἀρά τι AB   24 ἔχει Β   110. 1
ταῦτα μὲν z ‖ διέβαλε z   2 σοφός 'fortasse rectius abesset' van H.
3 ἕτοιμοι CPz   4 ἔσαν z ‖ οὗτοι ἀνεγνωσμένη Β ‖ ἔσαν z   5 ὁ
om. Β   6 ἐπίστευσε Β, Holder : ἐπέστελλε z ‖ ἀπικομένοισι(ν V) ΒPz

---

23. ἄρα, "in hypotheticals, to indicate the improbability of the supposition," L. & S. comparing Thuc. 1. 93. 7 τοῖς Ἀθηναίοις παρῄνει (sc. ὁ Θεμιστοκλῆς) ἦν ἄρα ποτὲ κατὰ γῆν βιασθῶσι, καταβάντας ἐς αὐτὸν ταῖς ναυσὶ πρὸς ἅπαντας ἀνθίστασθαι. The particle conveys perhaps a note of irony in the present passage, or perhaps a reference to the mind of Themistokles away from the author's. πάθος = πάθημα, as often.

24. ἀποστροφήν: in somewhat the same sense Thuc. 4. 76. 5 οὔσης ἑκάστοις διὰ βραχέος ἀποστροφῆς (perfugium). In a less literal sense, but more material, Hdt. 2. 13 οὐ γὰρ δή σφι ἐστὶ ὕδατος οὐδεμία ἄλλη ἀποστροφὴ ὅτι μὴ ἐκ τοῦ Διὸς μοῦνον.

110. 1. διέβαλλε: decipiebat, cp. 5. 50. "The expression shows how much prejudiced Herodotus is against Themistokles even in a case where not a shadow of suspicion falls on him," Stein. With the whole phrase cp. 5. 107 Ἱστιαῖος μὲν λέγων ταῦτα διέβαλλε, Δαρεῖος δὲ ἐπείθετο.

2. σοφός: the word in itself is not necessarily commendatory; cp. 5. 23 ὦ βασιλεῦ, κοῖόν τι χρῆμα ἐποίησας, ἀνδρὶ Ἕλληνι δεινῷ τε καὶ σοφῷ δοὺς ἐγκτίσασθαι πόλιν ἐν Θρηίκῃ; but ἀληθέως σοφός τε καὶ εὔβουλος is no faint praise, and admits that the advice of Themistokles to the Athenians was good, however questionable its motive. The contrast between δεδογμένος εἶναι and ἐφάνη ἐών is emphatic, but inappropriate ; the word δεδογμένος is, however, a strong one, and weakens the grammatical or idiomatic antithesis. With the fact cp. c. 124 infra ἐβώσθη τε καὶ ἐδοξώθη εἶναι ἀνὴρ πολλὸν Ἑλλήνων σοφώτατος—a situation which looks almost like the antecedent of the δεδογμένος in this passage ! Wila-

mowitz, Herm. xiv. 183, and Cobet, Mnem. xii. 279, refer to Themistokles the line, σοφὸς μὲν ἀνὴρ τῆς δὲ χειρὸς οὐ κρατῶν (Eupolis Δῆμοι ! van H.).

4. ἀνεγνωσμένοι ἦσαν: this form of construction may be taken to give a really temporal pluperfect, so far as the participle is concerned. It is substantially identical with the construction c. 108 supra ἐπύθοντο τὰς νέας οἰχωκυίας, and in each case the words αὐτίκα μετὰ ταῦτα (emphasizing the tense category) follow immediately. The Herodotean (or Ionic) use of ἀναγιγνώσκειν ('to convince,' 'persuade') is observable ; cp. 7. 10, and passim.

6. τοῖσι ἐπίστευε σιγᾶν. Was Themistokles deceived in his confidential agents, from whose lips tortures were not to wring a confession ! Was one of them, Sikinnos perhaps, the authority for this story ! And who was to torture them—the king ! the Athenians ! To the king they were carrying the message ; he had no need to torture them in order to learn it. The phrase looks as though some of the domestics of Themistokles had been put to the 'question' (say, in 471–70 B.C.) to prove his 'medism'; but whether anything like this anecdote was extracted from them is doubtful ; the phrase might even suggest a negation. Themistokles was, indeed, himself the author of the fiction that Xerxes owed to him the preservation of the Hellespontine bridges (cp. Thuc. 1. 134). The letter of the exiled Athenian to Artaxerxes (in 465 B.C. ?) is the earliest source to which the fiction can be traced : his enemies apparently improved the occasion, and elaborated the version preserved by Herodotus. Cp. Appendix VII. § 3.

τὰ αὑτὸς ἐνετείλατο βασιλέι φράσαι· τῶν καὶ Σίκιννος ὁ
οἰκέτης αὗτις ἐγένετο· οἳ ἐπείτε ἀπίκοντο πρὸς τὴν Ἀττικήν,
οἳ μὲν κατέμενον ἐπὶ τῷ πλοίῳ, Σίκιννος δὲ ἀναβὰς παρὰ
Ξέρξην ἔλεγε τάδε. "ἔπεμψέ με Θεμιστοκλέης ὁ Νεοκλέος, 10
στρατηγὸς μὲν Ἀθηναίων ἀνὴρ δὲ τῶν συμμάχων πάντων
ἄριστος καὶ σοφώτατος, φράσοντά τοι ὅτι Θεμιστοκλέης ὁ
Ἀθηναῖος, σοὶ βουλόμενος ὑπουργέειν, ἔσχε τοὺς Ἕλληνας
τὰς νέας βουλομένους διώκειν καὶ τὰς ἐν Ἑλλησπόντῳ γεφύρας
λύειν. καὶ νῦν κατ' ἡσυχίην πολλὴν κομίζεο." οἳ μὲν ταῦτα 15
σημήναντες ἀπέπλεον ὀπίσω.

---

7 τὰ αὑτὸς : τούτοισιν **B** ‖ βασιλεῖ **AB** ‖ σίκινος **R**   8 ἐπειδὴ
BPz   9 σίκιννος **C**: σίκινος **R**   10 ξέρξεα **Bz**   12 ὅτι :
ὁ **C** ‖ ὁ Ἀθηναῖος del. Kallenberg   13 σοὶ : σὺ **C**: om. **B** ‖ ὑπορηέειν α
14 νήας **Bz**   16 ἀπέπλοον **Bz**

7. **τῶν καὶ Σίκιννος ὁ οἰκέτης αὗτις ἐγένετο**: the reference is to the former mission of Sikinnos reported c. 75 *supra*, which brought about the disastrous movement of the king's navy, and its consequent defeat. The statement (which reappears in Diodor. 11. 19 and Trogus *ap.* Justin. 2. 13) that the same messenger was a second time employed to approach Xerxes, or the Persians, refutes itself, and discredits the whole anecdote. Plutarch, *Them.* 16, and Polyainos 1. 30. 3 follow a more plausible source, which made Arnakes, a eunuch and prisoner, the messenger on this occasion. Blakesley remarks that in the time of Plutarch Themistokles apparently was believed to have purposely hastened the retreat of Xerxes by sending him word of the projected Greek move to the Hellespont, and probable destruction of the bridges. More recent critics have discovered in 'the popular'—or was it the rationalized ?—view of the Plutarchian age the true key to the mystery; cp. Appendix VII. § 2.

8. **τὴν Ἀττικήν**. Hdt. of course assumes that Themistokles is in Andros (c. 108 *supra*), and Xerxes still in Athens; the absurdity of this assumption is noted c. 108 *supra*. Plutarch's story is again more plausible in laying the scene of the debate between Themistokles and Aristeides (*sic*) in Salamis.

10. **ἔλεγε τάδε**. The terms of the message are obviously exaggerated to exhibit the vanity of Themistokles, who iterates his own name and titles, and claims the prize not merely of 'wisdom' but of 'valour' among the Hellenes; the phrase τῶν συμμάχων could not have been used to the king in this connexion; there is no reference to the previous message, which now certainly called for explanation. But if any such message had been sent, it must have run very much in the terms ὅτι Θεμιστοκλέης . . κομίζεο.

13. **ὑπουργέειν**: cp. 7. 38, etc. **ἔσχε**, 'held,' 'stayed'—aor., but why not present tense ? Is it that Sikinnos is in Athens, Themistokles in Andros (*ex hypothesi*), and time has elapsed since the charge was entrusted to the speaker ? Or is the past tense of the essence of the message, Themistokles wishing to suggest a doubt how long the action can be maintained ? Or is the aorist used, 'without prejudice,' but from the speaker's point of view, as simply denoting a particular matter of fact ? But this use would be more proper in a plain narrative than in an authentic message. Perhaps the message here simply preserves one of the charges against Themistokles afterwards formulated in the γραφὴ προδοσίας.

14. **διώκειν . . λύειν**: two different operations, which Themistokles could not assume to involve the same direction for the fleet; cp. c. 108 *supra*, and c. 111 *infra*.

15. **οἳ μὲν . . ὀπίσω**. Had Sikinnos been the messenger he would surely have been retained a prisoner; had Arnakes, he would have regained his position at court: in neither case would the messenger have returned; cp. c. 76 *supra*. On the former occasion Sikinnos had

111   Οἱ δὲ Ἕλληνες, ἐπείτε σφι ἀπέδοξε μήτ' ἐπιδιώκειν ἔτι
προσωτέρω τῶν βαρβάρων τὰς νέας μήτε πλέειν ἐς τὸν
Ἑλλήσποντον λύσοντας τὸν πόρον, τὴν Ἄνδρον περικατέατο
ἐξελεῖν ἐθέλοντες. πρῶτοι γὰρ Ἄνδριοι νησιωτέων αἰτηθέντες
5 πρὸς Θεμιστοκλέος χρήματα οὐκ ἔδοσαν, ἀλλὰ προϊσχομένου
Θεμιστοκλέος λόγον τόνδε, ὡς ἥκοιεν Ἀθηναῖοι περὶ ἑωυτοὺς
ἔχοντες δύο θεοὺς μεγάλους, πειθώ τε καὶ ἀναγκαίην, οὕτω τέ
σφι κάρτα δοτέα εἶναι χρήματα, ὑπεκρίναντο πρὸς ταῦτα
λέγοντες ὡς κατὰ λόγον ἦσαν ἄρα αἱ Ἀθῆναι μεγάλαι τε καὶ

---

111. 2 προσωτέρωι a ‖ νῆας Βz ‖ μήτ' ἐπιπλώειν Β : μήτε πλώειν z
3 περιεκατέατο CPz   4 ἐξελέειν Β   5 Θεμιστοκλέος . . προϊσχομένου om. R ‖ χρήματα ante αἰτηθέντες z   6 τὸν λόγον Β   8
ταῦτα : τάδε Β   9 ἔσαν z ‖ ἄρα ante ἦσαν Β ‖ αἱ om. Β, Holder

---

acted alone; the plurality of messengers here is no argument of the truth of this story. With σημήναντες cp. σημήνας l.c.

111. 1. ἀπέδοξε μήτ': a double negative, the preposition ἀπό in composition having the force of a negation, *displicuit*; cp. ἀπηγόρευε μή c. 116 *infra*. The further pursuit of the 'barbarian' ships, and the voyage to the Hellespont, are here rightly treated as co-ordinate alternatives, not as identical actions.

3. πόρον here seems = γεφύρας, and not the waterway; cp. 7. 36. The object was not to free the passage, but to destroy the crossing.

τὴν Ἄνδρον περικατέατο: is this a maritime or a terrestrial operation? The Greeks were in complete command of the sea, but the actual investment of the city of Andros by land will be here included.

4. πρῶτοι γάρ κτλ.: the rationale is obviously at fault and malicious. The refusal of the Andrians to pay money to Themistokles would be no reason for their being invested by the confederate fleet or forces, unless, indeed, the money was for confederate purposes, a mulct perhaps inflicted on the Andrians for medism; and such is in fact the implication below, c. 112 (ὡς πολιορκέοιτο διότι ἐμήδισε). On the motives of Andrian policy in the Persian war cp. 7. 115. 6 *supra*.

5. προϊσχομένου is imperfect, or at least historical, and is followed by a double construction *in orat. obliq.*: (a) the conjunction with optative (ὡς ἥκοιεν), and (b) accusative with infinitive (δοτέα εἶναι). (κάρτα, by the way, would scarcely have occurred in Attic prose.)

6. λόγον τόνδε, 'a speech, as follows': another speech from Themistokles, in the nature of an apologue, to which the Andrians reply in the same vein. The personification, the apotheosis, of *Peitho* and *Ananke*, Suasion and Necessity, is less piquant or surprising than that of Poverty and Inability (*Penia, Amechania*), especially the latter, as a mere negation. The attitude of the Andrians might come as a fresh case in the experience of Themistokles that Ἄνδρας ἐς ἀναγκαίην ἀπειληθέντας ἀναμάχεσθαί τε καὶ ἀναλαμβάνειν τὴν προτέρην κακότητα, c. 109 *supra*.

περὶ ἑωυτούς, 'about them,' 'in their train'; a well-known Atticism, cp. οἱ περὶ τὸν Πείσανδρον πρέσβεις Thuc. 8. 63. 3. Themistokles is made to speak as though the Athenians were acting independently and alone, a view refuted by the whole context; but perhaps the Andrian apologue was not really uttered on this occasion, in 480 B.C., when Athens was in ruins, but belongs to a later crisis; cp. the reply of the Andrians, below. In fact, the fable of Themistokles and the Andrians reads like a current apologue on the ἀργυρολογία of the Athenians among their allies.

9. κατὰ λόγον ἦσαν ἄρα. The reply of the Andrians is in any case ironical, but doubly so if uttered when Athens itself was in ruins, and Xerxes indeed, *ex hypothesi*, in possession of Attica. But if we may choose between this *mordax ironia* (Schweigh.) and a simple anachronism, let us discount the irony. κατὰ λ., 'proportionately' (to Andros); the imperfect ἦσαν Baehr seems to think refers to the time before the war, and

εὐδαίμονες, καὶ θεῶν χρηστῶν ἥκοιεν εὖ· ἐπεὶ Ἀνδρίους γε 10
εἶναι γεωπείνας ἐς τὰ μέγιστα ἀνήκοντας, καὶ θεοὺς δύο
ἀχρήστους οὐκ ἐκλείπειν σφέων τὴν νῆσον ἀλλ' αἰεὶ φιλο-
χωρέειν, πενίην τε καὶ ἀμηχανίην, καὶ τούτων τῶν θεῶν
ἐπηβόλους ἐόντας Ἀνδρίους οὐ δώσειν χρήματα· οὐδέκοτε γὰρ
τῆς ἑωυτῶν ἀδυναμίης τὴν Ἀθηναίων δύναμιν εἶναι κρέσσω. 15
οὗτοι μὲν δὴ ταῦτα ὑποκρινάμενοι καὶ οὐ δόντες τὰ χρήματα
ἐπολιορκέοντο. Θεμιστοκλέης δέ, οὐ γὰρ ἐπαύετο πλεονεκτέων, 112

---

10 <εἰ> καὶ Steinᵖ: <αἲ> καὶ Stein², Holder, van H. ‖ ἀνδρείους C
11 γεωπείνας B²CPz: γεοπεινίης Krueger: γεωπίνας ‖ μάλιστα PRz
12 χρηστοὺς Β ‖ ἐλείπειν A¹B ‖ ἐμφιλοχωρέειν Naber   13 τουτέων z
14 ἐπηβόλους C: ἐπιβούλους Β ‖ γὰρ <ἀν> Dobree, van H.   16
τὰ χρήματα αC: χρήματα Β etc., Holder, van H.

translates *fuisse*; but it is purely idiomatic, cp. Stallbaum *ad* Plat. *Phaedr.* 35 cited by Baehr himself. Sitzler observes that the imperfect with ἄρα indicates that the speaker has just suddenly become aware of the truth of a proposition, previously ignored. A curious instance is afforded by 4. 64 *supra*: δέρμα δὲ ἀνθρώπου καὶ ταχὺ καὶ λαμπρὸν ἦν ἄρα. The imperfect might then have stood in the *orat. recta.* In any case the ἄρα points the irony.

10. θεῶν χρηστῶν ἥκοιεν εὖ: the sequence ἦσαν . . ἥκοιεν was perhaps eased by the latter's being in a relative sentence (Stein²), unless the optative might express a conditional prediction (cp. 5. 97 ἔλεγε . . ὡς οὔτε ἀσπίδα οὔτε δόρυ νομίζουσι εὐπετέες τε χειρωθῆναι εἶησαν, a fact, and a contingency). Cp. the same combination in the simple *orat. obliq.* 9. 69. 4. Stein, however, simplifies the situation here by a new emendation; cp. App. Crit. With θεῶν χρηστῶν εὖ ἥκειν cp. 1. 30 τοῦ βίου εὖ ἥκοντι (also simply τῆς πόλιος εὖ ἡκούσης just before), and again, 7. 157 *supra* δυνάμιός τε γὰρ ἥκεις μεγάλως. 'Athens, among its many blessings (καί), will be well provided with excellent divinities.'

ἐπὶ Ἀνδρίους γε κτλ, 'the Andrians, on the other hand, in their plentiful lack of real property were unrivalled, and had two divinities, of the 'te kind (χρηστῶν . . ἀχρήστους), pposi never quitted their island but stuck to the spot, Poverty and Inability; with these divinities for their patrons the Andrians must decline to give money; their impotence would always prove too much for the power of the Athenians.'

11. γεωπείνης, 'poor in land' (L. & S.), has nothing (surely) to say to land-hunger; in 2. 6 γεωπείναι are simply contrasted with men of large landed possession, or territory; the word presents a statistical fact, not a personal feeling.

ἐς τὰ μέγιστα ἀνήκοντας: cp. 5. 49 τὰ ἐς τὸν πόλεμον ἐς τὰ μέγιστα ἀνήκετε ἀρετῆς πέρι.

13. πενίην τε καὶ ἀμηχανίην: this pair had already been coupled by Alkaios (Bergk, *Poet. L.* iii.⁴ p. 179, Fr. 92 [65]):

ἀργάλεον πενία κάκον ἄσχετον, ἃ μέγα δάμναις
λᾶον ἀμαχανίᾳ σὺν ἀδελφέᾳ.

Euripides recognizes the divinity of Πενία, but denies it a cult, or at least a temple: Fr. 250 (Nauck) οὐκ ἔστι πενίας ἱερὸν ἐχθίστης θεοῦ.

14. ἐπηβόλους: cp. 9. 94 *infra.*

οὐδέκοτε γὰρ . . κρέσσω: this gnome has already done duty in the mouth of the Thessalians, 7. 172 *supra.* It was probably not original in either connexion.

112. 1. οὐ γὰρ ἐπαύετο πλεονεκτέων: the animus is obvious. Neither the case of the Andrians nor that of the other islanders looks at all like an instance of the private greed of Themistokles. In his previous career the only allegation of corrupt and avaricious practice is the story of his bribery by the Euboians (cc. 4, 5 *supra*), the inconsequence and absurdity of which are self-evident. Rawlinson refers to the well-known lines of Timokreon (Plutarch *Them.* 21) to show that such charges were brought against Themistokles during his lifetime: no doubt —but were they proved? During and

ἐσπέμπων ἐς τὰς ἄλλας νήσους ἀπειλητηρίους λόγους αἴτεε
χρήματα διὰ τῶν αὐτῶν ἀγγέλων, [χρεώμενος τοῖσι καὶ πρὸς
βασιλέα ἐχρήσατο,] λέγων ὡς, εἰ μὴ δώσουσι τὸ αἰτεόμενον,
5 ἐπάξει τὴν στρατιὴν τῶν Ἑλλήνων καὶ πολιορκέων ἐξαιρήσει.
λέγων ταῦτα συνέλεγε χρήματα μεγάλα παρὰ Καρυστίων τε
καὶ Παρίων, οἳ πυνθανόμενοι τήν τε Ἄνδρον ὡς πολιορκέοιτο
διότι ἐμήδισε, καὶ Θεμιστοκλέα ὡς εἴη ἐν αἴνῃ μεγίστῃ τῶν
στρατηγῶν, δείσαντες ταῦτα ἔπεμπον χρήματα. εἰ δὲ δὴ

---

112. 2 αἴτε R   3 αὐτέων z ‖ χρεώμενος tantum del. Cobet,
van H. : totum glossema seclusi : χρεόμενος P ‖ λόγοισι τοῖσι ßPz
4 βασιλέα αC : ἀνδρίους ceteri z, Holder, van H.   5 ἐπάξειν C :
ἀπάξει ß ‖ σφέας ἐξαιρήσει ? van H.   6 λέγων ὂν Schaefer, van H. :
λέγων δὲ Reiske ‖ τε om. ß   8 Θεμιστοκλῆα z ‖ τιμῆ ß

---

after the Persian war they arose and
accumulated. Themistokles was probably a wealthy man, at the time of his
exile (Kritias *ap.* Aelian. *Var. Hist.* 10.
17), but there is no evidence to show
how much, if any, of his fortune was
obtained by illegitimate means ; and it
is quite certain that most of the anecdotes
to illustrate the charge of avarice are
apocryphal. Thucydides 1. 138. 3 neither
condemns nor acquits him ; cp. 2. 65. 8
for the contrasted case of Perikles.

2. ἀπειλητηρίους λόγους : the epithet,
an *Hapaxlegomenon*, is no doubt derived
from ἀπειλή (cp. 6. 32 τὰς ἀπειλὰς τὰς
ἐπηπείλησαν) and has nothing to say to
ἄνδρας ἐς ἀναγκαίην ἀπειληθέντας c. 109
supra !

3. χρεώμενος . . ἐχρήσατο : a manifest
gloss. The reading varies (cp. App.
Crit.). The phrase is an explanation
of τῶν αὐτῶν ἀγγέλων. The motive for
using the same messengers as used
to the king would doubtless be that
they could be trusted to hold their
tongues (cp. c. 110 *supra*), but that
should have been mentioned in connexion
with the message to the Andrians ; and
here, without the elaborate gloss, the
messengers to the Andrians would be
obviously intended. χρεώμενος marks
the gloss ; Hdt. would have been content to write διὰ τῶν αὐτῶν ἀγγέλων τοῖσι
καὶ πρὸς βασιλέα ἐχρήσατο. A perception
of this may have led the inferior scribe to
insert λόγοισι and to alter βασιλέα into
Ἀνδρίους. The gloss thereby becomes
doubly absurd and superfluous, between
ἀπειλητηρίους λόγους and λέγων ὡς κτλ.

5. ἐπάξει τὴν στρατιὴν τῶν Ἑλλήνων.
Themistokles is represented as able to
control the movements and action of the
confederate fleet, at his will and pleasure;
this exaggeration betrays the libel.

6. παρὰ Καρυστίων τε καὶ Παρίων :
the specification of the two places, both
of which had medized at least after
Thermopylai (cp. c. 66 *supra*), among
the general ruck of islanders, might
tempt one to suspect that Karystos and
Paros had at some time or other special
relations with Themistokles. Both
places were of considerable importance
in connexion with the Persian wars and
the *thalattocracy* of Athens. The subsequent reduction of Karystos was of
sufficient interest to obtain an express
notice from Thucydides (1. 98. 3) ; cp.
9. 105 *infra* ; while Paros had already
been visited some ten years previously
by an Athenian squadron for 'medism'
(cp. 6. 132–136 *supra*). But, in fact,
when Andros, Tenos (c. 82 *supra*), Keos,
Naxos, Kythnos, Seriphos, Siphnos (cp.
c. 46 *supra*) have been accounted for,
there is not much left in the neighbourhood of the 'Kyklades' for Themistokles
to exploit, except Paros and Karystos.
(The other Euboian cities, Styra, Eretria,
Chalkis, were on the right side, c. 46
supra.)

8. διότι ἐμήδισε : the conjunction is
perhaps favoured by the oblique or dependent construction. The reason for
the visitation was their medism, not the
avarice of Themistokles.

ἐν αἴνῃ : εἶναι, cp. 9. 16 *infra*, =
ἐπαινετὸς εἶναι. Hdt. uses also the form
αἶνος 7. 107 *supra*.

9. ταῦτα is rather vague, but must
mean the possibility of their being
subjected to a similar visitation.

τινὲς καὶ ἄλλοι ἔδοσαν νησιωτέων, οὐκ ἔχω εἰπεῖν, δοκέω δὲ 10
τινὰς καὶ ἄλλους δοῦναι καὶ οὐ τούτους μούνους. καίτοι
Καρυστίοισί γε οὐδὲν τούτου εἵνεκα τοῦ κακοῦ ὑπερβολὴ
ἐγένετο· Πάριοι δὲ Θεμιστοκλέα χρήμασι ἱλασάμενοι διέφυγον
τὸ στράτευμα. Θεμιστοκλῆς μέν νυν ἐξ Ἄνδρου ὁρμώμενος χρήματα παρὰ νησιωτέων ἐκτᾶτο λάθρῃ τῶν ἄλλων 15
στρατηγῶν.

Οἱ δ' ἀμφὶ Ξέρξην ἐπισχόντες ὀλίγας ἡμέρας μετὰ τὴν 113
ναυμαχίην ἐξήλαυνον ἐς Βοιωτοὺς τὴν αὐτὴν ὁδόν. ἔδοξε

---

10 ἄλλων νησιωτέων ἔδοσαν β ‖ εἶπαι βz, van H.   11 μόνους C
12 γε om. β ‖ οὐδὲν : οὐδὲ Apr. : οὐδεμία? van H. ‖ εἵνεκε β   13 Θεμιστοκλῆα z ‖. ἔφυγον ABC   14 ὁρμεώμενος C : ὁρμεόμενος βPz, Stein[1],
van H.   15 ἐκτᾶτο Merzdorf, Stein, Holder, van H. : ἐκτέατο aC :
ἐκτέετο βP : ἠτέετο z : ἔκτητο Dindorf   113. 1 ξέρξεα βPz ‖ ἡμέρας
ὀλίγας a

---

10. οὐκ ἔχω εἰπεῖν, δοκέω δέ. Hdt.
unfortunately associates himself here
with the scandalmongers. He has not
a scrap of evidence to adduce, but is
willing to supply its place with conjecture.
As above shown, there were not many
places handy, besides Paros and Karystos,
from which to express anything. Delos
would hardly be assailable; Mykonos,
Syros, Gyaros and the rest hardly worth
visiting.

11. καίτοι Καρυστίοισί γε.. ἐγένετο :
grammatically it is not quite clear whether
Hdt. means that there was no postponement of the evil day for Karystos, or that
there was a postponement, though not
procured by their bribes to Themistokles
but by some other means (e.g. the
obstinate resistance of Andros); in other
words, is τούτου εἵνεκα predicative, or is
the predicate simply οὐδὲν τοῦ κακοῦ
ὑπερβολὴ ἐγένετο? The form of the
negative perhaps favours the latter interpretation; and Hdt. records below (c. 121)
that Karystos was 'visited' before the
Greeks returned to Salamis. The final
reduction of the Karystians—evidently
no easy task—was not accomplished
until after the ostrakism, or perhaps the
condemnation, of Themistokles. (Cp.
note to 9. 109 infra.) That observation,
as far as it goes, would suit well enough
their being clients of his, and might
have been cited in support of the scandal,
which is refuted by the fact (if it be a
fact) that Karystos was devastated by
this very expedition. The sense of
ὑπερβολὴ here is unusual, as if from

ὑπερβάλλεσθαι, 7. 206, 9. 51; cp. Polyb.
14. 9. 8.

13. ἱλασάμενοι, generally used of pro-
pitiating gods (1. 50, 67, 4. 7) or
heroes (5. 47), is doubtless used here
with a special intention. Hdt. does not
draw from the visitation of Karystos the
inference that Themistokles had not
been bribed by the Euboians, though
from the escape of Paros—intelligible
enough without it—he infers that the
Parians had bribed the Athenian strategos.

14. Θεμιστοκλῆς μέν κτλ. : the conjecture of four lines back becomes a
precise matter of fact, by repetition : a
frequent fallacy in historiography—and
criticism.

113. 1. οἱ δ' ἀμφὶ Ξέρξην. The scene
shifts back to the Persian camp (cc. 113-
120). It may be true that Attica was
not evacuated for some days after the
naval engagement and the retreat of the
Persian fleet ; but if so, the Greek fleet
must have remained at Salamis. (Is it
even quite certain that the Persian fleet
sped across the Aegean, the day after
the battle ?) Hdt. has now several series
of synchronous movements to co-ordinate
(Persian fleet, Persian army, Greek fleet,
perhaps Greek army) : small wonder if
he fail to adjust them convincingly.

2. τὴν αὐτὴν ὁδόν as that by which
they had come. Hdt. assumes that the
whole Persian force came and went by
one and the same road : unfortunately
he does not specify which of the two or
three possible alternatives (Eleutherai-

γὰρ Μαρδονίῳ ἅμα μὲν προπέμψαι βασιλέα, ἅμα δὲ ἀνωρίη
εἶναι τοῦ ἔτεος πολεμέειν· χειμερίσαι τε ἄμεινον εἶναι ἐν
5 Θεσσαλίῃ, καὶ ἔπειτα ἅμα τῷ ἔαρι πειρᾶσθαι τῆς Πελοποννήσου. ὡς δὲ ἀπίκατο ἐς τὴν Θεσσαλίην, ἐνθαῦτα Μαρδόνιος

---

3 γὰρ καὶ C ‖ βασιλῆα z ‖ ἀνωρίην βPz, Holder : ἀωρίη Cobet, van H.
4 τε : δὲ z 5 Θετταλίῃ z ‖ ἔπειτεν van H. 6 ἀπίκετο βz :
ἀπικέατο P

Eleusia, Panakton - Phyle, Tanagra-Dekeleia). Unless the land-force was very small, no doubt more than one route was followed, but Xerxes and his suite may, of course, have come and gone by the same route, probably the best, via Eleusis (cp. c. 65 *supra*).

δοξε . . **ἅμα μὲν** . . **ἅμα δέ** . . : the verb is used in two senses : 'appeared good' and simply 'appeared,' or 'thought right' and 'thought.' Mardonios might have remained in occupation of Attica, but the season was late for campaigning, supplies probably were difficult to procure so far south, and he wished to see the king well out of Greece. How far Hdt. had any definite information about the motives of Mardonios it is not easy to say ; the intention πειρᾶσθαι τῆς Πελοποννήσου (cp. c. 100 *supra*) was never realized, and the retreat into winter quarters in Thessaly was hardly the best prognostic of it. Attica seems to have been really evacuated ; but it is scarcely likely that Boiotia, Thermopylai, and Central Greece were wholly denuded of Persian troops. At the same time, the naval superiority of the Greeks after Salamis might (had they known how to use it) have made the occupation of Central Greece impracticable. Cp. Appendix VII. § 4.

3. ἀνωρίη appears to be a ἅπαξ λεγόμενον.

4. χειμερίσαι : Hdt. employs χειμερίζειν as = χειμάζειν (to winter) 6. 31, 7. 37, c. 126 *infra*, 9. 130. He has χειμάζειν in its primary sense 7. 191 *supra*. Op. also χειμαίνειν, -εσθαι (to be tempest-tossed) c. 118 *infra*.

5. ἅμα τῷ ἔαρι just after the ἅμα μέν and ἅμα δέ above is not quite happy ('unconscious iteration').

6. ἀπίκατο is a full temporal pl.p.

Μαρδόνιος ἐξελέγετο. The process of selection would take some time : did

the king remain in Thessaly, while Mardonios performed it, and not rather go on immediately, under the escort of Artabazos (cp. cc. 115, 126 *infra*) ! Hdt.'s account of the selection, and of the component elements in the grand army of Mardonios when selected, is far from clear. It is neither quite self-consistent, nor quite consistent with the corresponding lists previously given in Bk. 7, which are apparently here referred to ; and it is scarcely verified in the battle-roll of Plataia, 9. 31, 32 *infra*. Hdt. gives the sum total as 300,000, infantry and cavalry combined. He does not clearly indicate the proportion of the two arms, but the *corps d'armée* under Artabazos is apparently to be included, c. 126 *infra*. Nor does Hdt. treat the thirty myriads as a cadre fixed by the commander, to be filled up by the levies on selection, but as a result, more or less accidental, of the selection of the picked troops (just as at Doriskos the sum total of infantry, 1,700,000, is only discovered as a result of the *levée en masse*, when its numerical aspect is tested and proved !). Mardonios pursues two methods in his selection : certain nations, to wit, Persians, Medes, Scyths, Baktrians, Indians, he selects in full, as they stand ; but of the remaining (42) nations he only takes such individuals as are of obvious value or of made reputation. Probably the five nations named supplied the bulk of the army of Mardonios. The omission of the Kissians, however, is remarkable (were they chiefly in the *corps d'armée* of Artabazos ?).

But we may safely assert that if the total forces left with Mardonios comprised, even nominally, thirty myriads, then there was no selection, he retained the army of Xerxes in full : if there was a real selection, then his forces amounted to nothing like thirty myriads ; cp. further Appendix II. § 5.

ἐξελέγετο πρώτους μὲν τοὺς Πέρσας πάντας τοὺς ἀθανάτους
καλεομένους, πλὴν Ὑδάρνεος τοῦ στρατηγοῦ (οὗτος γὰρ οὐκ
ἔφη λείψεσθαι βασιλέος), μετὰ δὲ τῶν ἄλλων Περσέων τοὺς
θωρηκοφόρους καὶ τὴν ἵππον τὴν χιλίην, καὶ Μήδους τε καὶ 10
Σάκας καὶ Βακτρίους τε καὶ Ἰνδούς, καὶ τὸν πεζὸν καὶ τὴν
ἄλλην ἵππον. ταῦτα μὲν ἔθνεα ὅλα εἵλετο, ἐκ δὲ τῶν ἄλλων
συμμάχων ἐξελέγετο κατ' ὀλίγους, τοῖσι εἰδέα τε ὑπῆρχε διαλέγων καὶ εἰ τεοῖσί τι χρηστὸν συνῄδεε πεποιημένον· ἐν δὲ

7 τοὺς πέρσας πάντας τοὺς a: τοὺς μυρίους πέρσας τοὺς β, Holder:
πέρσας πάντας τοὺς CPz: Πέρσας τοὺς μυρίους τοὺς vel τοὺς μυρίους
Πέρσας πάντας τοὺς van H.   9 λήψεσθαι β ‖ βασιλέως β: βασιλῆος z
11 τε om. βPz   12 ἄλλην om. β, Holder, van H. ‖ εἵλατο β ‖ ἄλλων
om. aC   14 εἰ τέοισί τε Cz: εἴ τι οἱ β ‖ συνῄδεε R: συνείδεε aCSV
‖ ἐν βB²: ἐν AB¹: ἐν reliqui

7. τοὺς Πέρσας πάντας τοὺς ἀθανάτους καλεομένους: these are identical with
the corps described in 7. 83, and apparently in 7. 41, and have been twice seen
in action, 7. 211, and 7. 215. (Whether
they were all strictly speaking 'Persians'
is doubtful, in view of the frieze from
the Apadana now in the Louvre, which
suggests that even the negrito population
of Kissia was admitted to the ranks of
the Immortals. But the heads are
'restored.')

8. Ὑδάρνεος τοῦ στρατηγοῦ: cp. 7.
83. His devotion to the king's person
on this occasion was, perhaps, in part
dictated by an unwillingness to serve
under Mardonios; but for the captain,
stratege, or myriarch of the Immortals to
depart and leave his men behind him is
a strange proceeding. Would the guards
not have seen the king further than
Thessaly? Were the Immortals not
among the king's escort, even if they
returned to take part in the campaign of
479?

9. τῶν ἄλλων Περσέων τοὺς θωρηκοφόρους: this designation is not quite
clear, as all the Persian infantry appear
to have been θωρηκοφόροι, cp. 7. 61, and
there is nothing in 7. 40 and 54 f. to
explain the use of the term here, apparently for a special body of men.

10. τὴν ἵππον τὴν χιλίην: which
chiliad of cavalry is this? The ἱππόται
χίλιοι ἐκ Περσέων πάντων ἀπολελεγμένοι
who headed the procession out of Sardes
7. 40, or the ἵππος ἄλλη χιλίη ἐκ Περσέων
ἀπολελεγμένη who followed the Immortals
on that occasion?

11. καὶ τὸν πεζὸν καὶ τὴν ἄλλην

ἵππον, 'as well infantry, as all the rest
of the cavalry.' The phrase applies to
all the ethnic contingents just previously
named, all of whom figure in the cavalry-
list (7. 84-86). ἄλλην, if not deleted,
may be taken to mean that Mardonios
not only retained the cavalry of these
nations in addition to the chiliad
specified, but all the cavalry. Or is
ἄλλην merely idiomatic, like ἄλλων just
below? Or is it dittographed from
ἄλλων? But cp. App. Crit.

12. ταῦτα: assimilated by ἔθνεα.
τούτων or τούτους might be expected.

13. κατ' ὀλίγους: as in Thuc. 3. 111.
1 ὑπαγῆσαι κατ' ὀλίγους, 4. 11. 3 κατ'
ὀλίγας ναῦς διελόμενοι (Wesseling). The
preposition is distributive in force: 'by
small lots,' in small bodies.

τοῖσι εἰδέα τε ὑπῆρχε διαλέγων:
the copula is not in its strictly correct
place. The plural substantive is
observable, but suggests that there was
a plurality, a variety, of good forms;
Stein cps. μεγάθεα 3. 102 — where
certainly the 'ants' need not all be just
the same size. διαλέγων, as in c. 107
supra.

14. ἐν δὲ πλεῖστον ἔθνος Πέρσας
αἱρέετο seems to mean that the Persians
were the largest unit, the most numerous
national contingent, among those he
was selecting, though Hdt. immediately
adds that the Medes were equally
numerous. There is a parallelism
between this sentence and ταῦτα μὲν
ἔθνεα ὅλα εἵλετο (in spite of the difference
of tense), and πλεῖστον seems to be
attracted to ἔθνος (for πλείστους). ἐν δὲ
would of course be an adverbial use of

15 πλεῖστον ἔθνος Πέρσας αἱρέετο, ἄνδρας στρεπτοφόρους τε καὶ
ψελιοφόρους, ἐπὶ δὲ Μήδους· οὗτοι δὲ τὸ πλῆθος μὲν οὐκ
ἐλάσσονες ἦσαν τῶν Περσέων, ῥώμῃ δὲ ἥσσονες. ὥστε σύμ-
παντας τριήκοντα μυριάδας γενέσθαι σὺν ἱππεῦσι.

114 Ἐν δὲ τούτῳ τῷ χρόνῳ, ἐν τῷ Μαρδόνιός τε τὴν στρατιὴν
διέκρινε καὶ Ξέρξης ἦν περὶ Θεσσαλίην, χρηστήριον ἐληλύθεε
ἐκ Δελφῶν Λακεδαιμονίοισι, Ξέρξην αἰτέειν δίκας τοῦ Λεωνίδεω
φόνου καὶ τὸ διδόμενον ἐξ ἐκείνου δέκεσθαι. πέμπουσι δὴ
5 κήρυκα τὴν ταχίστην Σπαρτιῆται, ὃς ἐπειδὴ κατέλαβε ἐοῦσαν
ἔτι πᾶσαν τὴν στρατιὴν ἐν Θεσσαλίῃ, ἐλθὼν ἐς ὄψιν τὴν
Ξέρξεω ἔλεγε τάδε. "ὦ βασιλεῦ Μήδων, Λακεδαιμόνιοί τέ

---

16 τὸ om. ßPz, Holder, van H.   17 ἔσαν z ‖ ἔσσονες z   **114. 3**
ξέρξεα ßz

the preposition, like ἐπὶ δέ just below;
Stein supports ἐν by Thucyd. 3. 39. 1
μάλιστα δὴ μίαν πόλιν ἠδικηκότας ὑμᾶς:
3. 113. 6 πάθος γὰρ τοῦτο μιᾷ πόλει . .
μέγιστον δὴ . . ἐγένετο: 8. 40. 2 οἱ γὰρ
οἰκέται . . μιᾷ γε πόλει . . πλεῖστοι
γενόμενοι.

15. ἄνδρας στρεπτοφόρους τε καὶ
ψελιοφόρους: curious gear for men!
Cp. 9. 80. The Immortals, par exemple,
χρυσόν τε πολλὸν καὶ ἄφθονον ἔχοντες
ἐνέπρεπον (7. 83).

17. ῥώμῃ: cp. 7. 103.

114. 2. Ξέρξης ἦν περὶ Θεσσαλίην.
Hdt. seems to keep Xerxes waiting all
the while Mardonios was making his
selection—an improbability in itself,
and hardly consistent with the emphasis
laid upon the rapidity of the king's
flight, cc. 115, 120 infra.

χρηστήριον ἐληλύθεε ἐκ Δ. Λ.:
another item in Delphian apologetics;
obviously the anecdote and oracle are
this time at least post eventum. If so, is
it necessary to inquire at what ideal
point of time in 480 B.C. we shall date
the response, or whether the Lakedaimonians had consulted the oracle
concerning the death of their king?
χρηστήριον is here the actual response,
or utterance. The pluperfect appears to
be rhetorical, but not temporarily
incorrect; cp. c. 50 supra. δίκας αἰτέειν
τινά τινος is of course the regular construction, cp. 1. 2 etc.

4. τὸ διδόμενον ἐξ ἐκείνου δέκεσθαι.
De Pauw misunderstood: accipere omen.
Wesseling approved. Baehr corrected:
id quod a Xerxe oblatum esset, accipere.
No doubt δέκομαι can be used of accept-

ing an omen (cp. 9. 91), but also of
accepting anything offered. Stein
follows Baehr (apparently), and for τὸ
διδόμενον cps. 3. 148, 8. 138, 9. 111.
Below, δεξάμενος τὸ ῥηθέν has a slightly
more oracular flavour, and though not
used of accepting an oracle, is used of
accepting something more than human.

5. Σπαρτιῆται is hardly used by
Hdt. in deliberate contrast to Λακεδαιμόνιοι just above, and Λακεδαιμόνιοι
just below, but merely as a literary
variation.

κατέλαβε, deprehendit, overtook;
cp. κατελαμβάνετο 6. 29.

6. πᾶσαν: not merely the select
300,000. Nor is there any hint of any
garrisons south of Othrys.

7. Μήδων: had Sparta or Delphi not
yet perceived the distinction between
Medes and Persians? The use of the
term generally is a kind of recognition,
from the Greek side, of the continuity of
the empires of Astyages, Kyros, Dareios.

Λακεδαιμόνιοί τε . . καὶ Ἡρακλεῖδαι οἱ ἀπὸ Σπάρτης. The demand
is a joint one, on behalf of the state,
and of the royal family—which has
now a blood-feud of its own with the
Achaimenids. The Herakleids of Sparta
—there were other Herakleids elsewhere
—had a longer pedigree than Xerxes
himself; cp. 7. 11, 204, and c. 131 infra.
It can hardly be said that the vendetta
was wiped out by the death of Mardonios,
but it does not figure as real history
afterwards. (Alexander, though an
Herakleid, took a very different line;
cp. Arrian Anab. 3. 22. 1, 30. 1-3, 4. 7.
3 ff.)

σε καὶ Ἡρακλεῖδαι οἱ ἀπὸ Σπάρτης αἰτέουσι φόνου δίκας,
ὅτι σφέων τὸν βασιλέα ἀπέκτεινας ῥυόμενον τὴν Ἑλλάδα."
ὁ δὲ γελάσας τε καὶ κατασχὼν πολλὸν χρόνον, ὡς οἱ ἐτύγχανε 10
παρεστεὼς Μαρδόνιος, δεικνὺς ἐς τοῦτον εἶπε "τοιγάρ σφι
Μαρδόνιος ὅδε δίκας δώσει τοιαύτας οἵας ἐκείνοισι πρέπει."
ὁ μὲν δὴ δεξάμενος τὸ ῥηθὲν ἀπαλλάσσετο, Ξέρξης δὲ 115
Μαρδόνιον ἐν Θεσσαλίῃ καταλιπὼν αὐτὸς ἐπορεύετο κατὰ
τάχος ἐς τὸν Ἑλλήσποντον καὶ ἀπικνέεται ἐς τὸν πόρον
[τῆς διαβάσιος] ἐν πέντε καὶ τεσσεράκοντα ἡμέρῃσι, ἀπάγων

---

8 αἰτέουσα β   9 βασιλῆα z   10 οἱ om. SV ‖ ἔτυχε β
11 τοιγάρ τοι Μαρδόνιος S (Gaisf.)   115. 4 τῆς διαβάσιος del.
van H., Holder, Stein³ ‖ ἐν om. β ‖ τεσσαράκοντα β

---

10. ὁ δὲ γελάσας τε καὶ κατασχὼν
πολλὸν χρόνον : one does not see much
to laugh at (the laugh was soon to be on
the other side) : but perhaps the king
already had his humorous answer ready,
though he must wait some considerable
time to deliver it, until Mardonios is in
evidence.

κατασχών : like another despot,
under sorer provocation, who (6. 129)
κατεῖχε ἑωυτόν, οὐ βουλόμενος ἐκραγῆναι.

11. τοιγάρ σφι Μαρδόνιος . .
πρέπει : the remark is not a reply to the 'herald'
but a witticism addressed to the suite
(but δεικνὺς ἐς τοῦτον, for the benefit of
the Spartan !), unless, indeed, the king
spake Greek, or elaborated his jest
through the medium of an interpreter.
The irony of the anecdote is conspicuous,
and the king's promise, or prophecy, is
fulfilled, to his shame and astonishment,
in 9. 64 ἀποθνῄσκει δὲ Μαρδόνιος ὑπὸ
Ἀειμνήστου ἀνδρὸς ἐν Σπάρτῃ λογίμου.
But if Xerxes himself had fought and
fallen at Plataia, how much more
tragic, more cathartic, had been the
irony ! He would at least have escaped
the comic Nemesis. Mardonios in
death is the more dignified figure.
Even the great Kyros had fallen by a
woman, cp. 1. 214. But that is another
story.

12. πρέπει : sc. διδόναι or δοῦναι : so
L. & S., Krueger, Abicht, Sitzler.
Rawlinson renders 'they deserve to
get' (i.e. δέξασθαι), which gives a more
pregnant and forcible sense, and is,
perhaps, just grammatically possible ad
sensum.

115. 2. ἐπορεύετο κατὰ τάχος ἐς τὸν
Ἑλλήσποντον : considering the time of
year, once it was decided that the king

should not remain in Europe, probably
no time was lost on the march to Asia.
Yet Hdt. has not merely detained the
king 'a few days' in Attica after the
battle (cp. c. 113 supra), but has kept
him waiting in Thessaly, while Mardonios
picks out all the best fighting men,
leaving only the refuse ex hypothesi to
escort the king to the Hellespont ! But
cp. c. 126 infra.

3. τὸν πόρον [τῆς διαβάσιος] : the
πόρος here appears to be the passage from
shore to shore across the strait, by
means of the bridge ; cp. 7. 36 supra.

4. ἐν πέντε καὶ τεσσεράκοντα ἡμέρῃσι :
is this period intended to cover the
march from Thessaly to the Hellespont
only, or the whole course from Athens ?
If the latter, are 'the few days' which
elapsed between the battle and the
move from Athens (c. 113 supra)
included or not ? As forty-five days
would be a longish time to spend over
the march from Thessaly, the latter
alternative, in one form or other, is to
be preferred. In this case the exact
figure would be more convincing if it
did not happen to be exactly half the
time consumed in the advance from the
Hellespont to Athens, c. 51 supra (3
months = 90 days). In 394 B.C. Agesilaos
marched from the Hellespont to Boiotia
in a month, or less (Beloch, Gr. Ges.
ii. 196) ; cp. Xenoph. Ages. 2. 1. But
then he had only a relatively small
force with him : Xenophon does not
give the exact figures. Before the
battle of Koroneia reinforcements had
reached the king, and he was not
inferior in numbers to the allied army
opposed to him, which, a little while
before, at the battle of Korinth, had

5 τῆς στρατιῆς οὐδὲν μέρος ὡς εἰπεῖν. ὅκου δὲ πορευόμενοι
γινοίατο καὶ κατ᾽ οὕστινας ἀνθρώπους, τὸν τούτων καρπὸν
ἁρπάζοντες ἐσιτέοντο· εἰ δὲ καρπὸν μηδένα εὕροιεν, οἱ δὲ
τὴν ποίην τὴν ἐκ τῆς γῆς ἀναφυομένην καὶ τῶν δενδρέων τὸν
φλοιὸν περιλέποντες καὶ τὰ φύλλα καταδρέποντες κατήσθιον,
10 ὁμοίως τῶν τε ἡμέρων καὶ τῶν ἀγρίων, καὶ ἔλειπον οὐδέν·
ταῦτα δ᾽ ἐποίεον ὑπὸ λιμοῦ. ἐπιλαβὼν δὲ λοιμός τε τὸν
στρατὸν καὶ δυσεντερίη κατ᾽ ὁδὸν ἔφθειρε. τοὺς δὲ καὶ
νοσέοντας αὐτῶν κατέλειπε, ἐπιτάσσων τῇσι πόλισι, ἵνα
ἑκάστοτε γίνοιτο ἐλαύνων, μελεδαίνειν τε καὶ τρέφειν, ἐν

---

5 εἶπαι z, van H.   6 τουτέων z ‖ καρπὸν: καρ R   7 ἀναρ-
πάζοντες B ‖ ἐσιτεύοντο C   8 δένδρων B ‖ τόν <τε> coni. Stein, rec.
van H.   9 περιβλέποντες C ‖ τὰ: κατὰ R ‖ καταδιέποντες B   10
ἔλειπον BP: ἔλιπον   11 ταῦτα . . λιμοῦ del. Naber, van H. ‖
ἐποίεεν z ‖ ὑπολαβὼν Cobet, van H. ‖ λιμὸς τότε z   12 διέφθειρε S
13 αὐτέων Bz ‖ κατέλιπε z   14 ἑκάστοθι CR ‖ γίνηται z ‖ τε om. αC

numbered 24,000 hoplites with 1550
cavalry, and numerous light-armed
troops; cp. Xenoph. Hell. 4. 1, 2. 16 ff.,
3. 15 ff.

ἀπάγων τῆς στρατιῆς οὐδὲν μέρος
ὡς εἰπεῖν. He had left (ex hypothesi)
300,000 of the best with Mardonios; he
was escorted by Artabazos with 60,000
of the said 300,000 (cp. c. 126 infra).
The phrase here is apparently intended
to introduce the result of the losses en
route between Thessaly and Sardes; but
these losses are themselves to be heavily
discounted in the light of that authentic
escort. The millions which had accompanied Xerxes into Greece had to be
disposed of somehow: he sheds most of
them on the way home! Have the
flight and sufferings of the survivors of
Plataia been antedated and transferred
to the escort of Xerxes, a year before!
But even in the later disaster, Artabazos
carries a substantial remnant home to
Asia (9. 89). The rectification of the
numbers of the host of Xerxes tends to
adjust the proportion of losses. Bad as
this passage in Hdt. may be, as regards
horrors and exaggerations, he is by no
means the worst offender: his predecessor
Aischylos (Persas 484-516) and Trogus
Pompeius long afterwards (Justin 2. 13)
pile up the agony more unscrupulously
still. Cp. Appendix VII. § 2.

6. καρπόν, Blakesley objects, could
not be the growing harvest, for the
harvest was over; but Hdt. meets that
objection in the next sentence. Nor
need καρπός be restricted to cereals.
There would of course be no hardship
in this, except for the despoiled owners!

7. οἱ δέ: the real hardships are
introduced by δέ in apodosi, with the
subject repeated; cp. 7. 51 supra.

8. ποίην, Att. πόαν (cp. ποιέω, πόεω).

9. φλοιόν: cp. 4. 67. The people of
Petelia ate it, during the siege in the
Hannibalic war, Polyb. 7. 1. 3. περι-
λέπειν is a rare word, Iliad 1. 236, the
only other ref. in L. & S. Baehr,
however, cites Theophrastus, Hist. pl.
6. 4. 10, and Suidas (quoting this passage
sub v. Δρέπου).

11. ὑπό: cp. with genitive prae or
propter; cp. ὑπὸ δέους καὶ κακοῦ 1. 85,
etc.

12. δυσεντερίη: cp. Plato, Tim. 86 A
διαρροίας καὶ δυσεντερίας καὶ τὰ τοιαῦτα
νοσήματα πάντα παρέσχετο. Celsus de
medicin. 4. 22 (15), quoted verbatim by
Baehr, gives a full medical description of
the symptoms and sufferings.

τοὺς δὲ καὶ νοσέοντας κτλ. Xerxes
was at least more careful of the sick than
his father had been beyond the Danube,
according to the story 4. 135.

13. ἵνα, locative; γίνοιτο, "optative of
indefinite frequency," Madvig § 133.

14. μελεδαίνειν: an Ionic word; cp. 7.
31.

Θεσσαλίη τε τινὰς καὶ ἐν Σίρι τῆς Παιονίης καὶ ἐν Μακεδονίη. 15
ἔνθα καὶ τὸ ἱρὸν ἄρμα καταλιπὼν τοῦ Διός, ὅτε ἐπὶ τὴν
Ἑλλάδα ἤλαυνε, ἀπιὼν οὐκ ἀπέλαβε, ἀλλὰ δόντες οἱ Παίονες
τοῖσι Θρήιξι ἀπαιτέοντος Ξέρξεω ἔφασαν νεμομένας ἁρπασθῆναι
ὑπὸ τῶν ἄνω Θρηίκων τῶν περὶ τὰς πηγὰς τοῦ Στρυμόνος
οἰκημένων. ἔνθα καὶ ὁ τῶν Βισαλτέων βασιλεὺς γῆς τε τῆς 116
Κρηστωνικῆς [Θρήιξ] ἔργον ὑπερφυὲς ἐργάσατο· ὃς οὔτε
αὐτὸς ἔφη τῷ Ξέρξῃ ἑκὼν εἶναι δουλεύσειν, ἀλλ᾽ οἴχετο ἄνω
ἐς τὸ ὄρος τὴν Ῥοδόπην, τοῖσί τε παισὶ ἀπηγόρευε μὴ στρα-

---

15 ἐν Σίρι τῆς Παιωνίης . . ἐν Μακεδονίη transponenda vidit Stein², transposuit van H. ‖ παιονίας C   18 ἁρπαχθῆναι codd. z   19 καὶ τῶν περὶ C ‖ πηγὰς om. R   20 οἰκεομένων z   116. 2 κρηστονικῆς R ‖ Θρῆιξ seol. Stein², Holder, van H. (θρῆιξ a : θρῆξ BC : θρήιξ reliqui) ‖ εἰργάσατο z   3 τῷ om. B ‖ ὤιχετο aC   4 οὖρος z : τὸ οὖρος abesse malit van H.

---

15. ἐν Σίρι τῆς Παιωνίης : to avoid confusion with Σίρις ἡ ἐν Ἰταλίη c. 62 supra. Siris in Paionia, the chief town of the Siro- or Siriopaiones (Steph. B. sub v. Σίρις), cp. 5. 15, was situate above Lake Prasias (5. 16), apparently mentioned by Livy 45. 4 Sirae oppidum terrae Odomanticae (Baehr ad 5. 15 suggests that it became 'Odomantian' after the removal of the Siro-paionians to Asia by Dareios). Now Seres, the centre of an important plain, or vale; cp. Hogarth, Nearer East, 89, 101 ; Reclus, Univ. Geogr. E.T. i. 112.

καὶ ἐν Μακεδονίη is strangely out of place, like an afterthought, a correction, a gloss. ἔνθα apparently refers to Siris. But cp. App. Crit.

16. τὸ ἱρὸν ἄρμα : 7. 40 supra. The road west of Siris was presumably too rough. The fact has not been recorded on the outward journey. The two passages are so wholly independent of each other that the chariot-team here is composed of mares (νεμομένας), which there was composed of horses. (Cp. 7. 55 οἵ τε ἵπποι οἱ ἱροὶ καὶ τὸ ἄρμα τὸ ἱρόν, where the horses specified are of course the ten Nesaian, not the eight white horses of 7. 40.)

19. τῶν περὶ τὰς πηγὰς τοῦ Στρυμόνος οἰκημένων. The sources of the Strymon (Struma) appears to have been in the territory of the Agrianes; cp. Strabo 331 (36) ὑπὲρ δὲ τῆς Ἀμφιπόλεως Βισάλται καὶ μέχρι πόλεως Ἡρακλείας, ἔχοντες αὐλῶνα εὔκαρπον, ὃν διαρρεῖ ὁ Στρυμών, ὡρμημένος ἐκ τῶν περὶ Ῥοδόπην Ἀγριανῶν

. . οὐ μόνον δ᾽ ὁ Ἀξιὸς ἐκ Παιόνων ἔχει τὴν ῥύσιν, ἀλλὰ καὶ ὁ Στρυμών· ἐξ Ἀγριάνων γὰρ διὰ Μαίδων καὶ Σιντῶν εἰς τὰ μεταξὺ Βισαλτῶν καὶ Ὀδομάντων ἐκπίπτει. The Agrianes appear to be regarded by Thucyd. (2. 98. 3) as Paionians, though subject (in 429 B.C.) to the suzerainty of the Odrysian monarch.

116. 1. ἔνθα καὶ, repeated from c. 115 l. 16 supra, unless that passage is a later addition.

ὁ τῶν Βισαλτέων βασιλεύς : on the position of Bisaltia cp. Strabo l.c., and 7. 115 supra. γῆ ἡ Κρηστωνική is not immediately north, but higher up, on the sources of the Cheidoros, 7. 124, 127. The king here is anonymous ; but a king named 'Mosses,' dated about 500-480 B.C., is known from the coinage; cp. Head, Hist. Num. p. 179 ; G. Macdonald, Catalogue of Gk. Coins in the Hunterian Collection, i. (1899) p. 269.

2. ἔργον ὑπερφυὲς ἐργάσατο. The epithet here appears to be used in a dyslogistic sense ; in 9. 78 eulogistically ; in a purely matter-of-fact way, 2. 175. The word is not uncommon in the Attic writers.

3. ἑκὼν εἶναι : the substantive verb purely idiomatic, 'at least willingly,' in the negative sentence (Madvig § 151. 2).

4. τὸ ὄρος τὴν Ῥοδόπην : one or other appositive might be a gloss ; Rhodope has not been mentioned before in these Books, but occurs in 4. 49 as a mountain in Paionia. "The main skeleton of the country between the Danube and the Aegean" is well described in Arnold's

5 τεύεσθαι ἐπὶ τὴν Ἑλλάδα. οἱ δὲ ἀλογήσαντες, ἢ ἄλλως σφι
θυμὸς ἐγένετο θεήσασθαι τὸν πόλεμον, ἐστρατεύοντο ἅμα τῷ
Πέρσῃ. ἐπεὶ δὲ ἀνεχώρησαν ἀσινέες πάντες ἐξ ἐόντες, ἐξώρυξε
117 αὐτῶν ὁ πατὴρ τοὺς ὀφθαλμοὺς διὰ τὴν αἰτίην ταύτην. καὶ
οὗτοι μὲν τοῦτον τὸν μισθὸν ἔλαβον, οἱ δὲ Πέρσαι ὡς ἐκ τῆς
Θρηίκης πορευόμενοι ἀπίκοντο ἐπὶ τὸν πόρον, ἐπειγόμενοι τὸν
Ἑλλήσποντον τῇσι νηυσὶ διέβησαν ἐς Ἄβυδον· τὰς γὰρ
5 σχεδίας οὐκ εὗρον ἔτι ἐντεταμένας ἀλλ᾽ ὑπὸ χειμῶνος διαλελυ-
μένας. ἐνθαῦτα δὲ κατεχόμενοι σιτία τε πλέω ἢ κατ᾽ ὁδὸν
ἐλάγχανον, <καὶ οὐδένα τε κόσμον ἐμπιπλάμενοι καὶ ὕδατα
μεταβάλλοντες ἀπέθνησκον τοῦ στρατοῦ τοῦ περιεόντος πολλοί.
οἱ δὲ λοιποὶ ἅμα Ξέρξῃ ἀπικνέονται ἐς Σάρδις.

5 ἀλογίσαντες z   6 θηήσασθαι B ‖ τῷ ξέρξη B   8 αὐτέων Bz
117. 3 θρήκης B   5 οὐχ B ‖ ἐντεταγμένας C ‖ ἀλλὰ a   6 δὴ z ‖
τε om. BPz, Holder   7 <καὶ> Stein² ‖ τε : δὲ (omisso τε post σιτία)?
Kallenberg   8 περιόντος B

note to Thuc. 2. 96. 4 (though Arnold's use of 'Orbelus' is hardly correct). Rhodope is that branch of the fourfold mountain system which runs down to the Aegean, dividing the valleys of the Hebros (Maritza) and Nestos (Kara Su), and breaking away into lower ranges further west, towards the Strymon. Cp. also Hogarth, *Nearer East*, pp. 24 f.

ἀπηγόρευε μή: cp. c. 111 *supra*. This Bisaltian's apparent phil-Hellenism is noticeable: he did not take his cue from Macedon, nor perhaps anticipate the subsequent invasions of his territory by Athenian adventurers.

5. ἀλογήσαντες: c. 46 *supra*.

ἢ ἄλλως .. ἐγένετο: the grammatical co-ordination is not exact. ἄλλως as in 4. 148, εἴ τε δή οἱ ἡ χώρη ἤρεσε, εἴτε καὶ ἄλλως ἠθέλησε τοῦτο ποιῆσαι. But there is not really a true alternative involved.

7. ἀσινέες: cp. c. 19 *supra*. The fact does not support the traditions of the hardships of this campaign.

ἐξώρυξε .. τοὺς ὀφθαλμούς: such a punishment was non-Hellenic, barbarous, as Aelian 5. 11, narrating this anecdote, expressly notices. Cp. 4. 2 *supra*. But Hdt. seems to suggest that they deserved it (τοῦτον τὸν μισθόν). The words διὰ τὴν αἰτίην ταύτην add nothing to the force of the passage, unless it be supposed that there was another view of the motive for the king's inhuman action, e.g. a suspicion of a plot to depose him, or what not.

117. 3. τὸν πόρον: not the bridge, for the bridge was *ex hypothesi* gone, but perhaps the place where the bridge should have been—i.e. the passage across (not adown) the straits; cp. c. 115 *supra*.

4. τῇσι νηυσί: the ships had made for the Hellespont from Salamis διαφυλαξούσας τὰς σχεδίας πορευθῆναι βασιλέι, c. 107 *supra*. But according to this text the bridges were no longer taut (ἐντεταμένας 7. 34, 9. 106, 114), and the ships had to be used to convey Xerxes, and the remnant of his forces, across the Hellespont. Blakesley challenges this tradition: Aischylos takes Xerxes back over the bridge (*Pers.* 725), and the Greeks, a year later, on Hdt.'s own showing, were still ignorant of the supposed destruction of the bridges in the course of the summer or autumn of 480 B.C.

6. κατεχόμενοι: probably passive in force; cp. c. 114 *supra*. ἐμπιπλάμενοι, very distinctly middle.

7. οὐδένα .. κόσμον=ἀκόσμως: this adverbial or modal accusative is observable.

ὕδατα μεταβάλλοντες: they must have been doing so all the way from Attica, and not merely after crossing the Hellespont. Nothing is said of the failure of the rivers on the way back. The mere change of drinking water, if the water in itself was good, could hardly have the effects ascribed to it, *pace* Hippocrat. περὶ ἀέρων κτλ. 2.

9. ἐς Σάρδις: where he remained for a considerable time; cp. 9. 107 *infra*.

Ἔστι δὲ καὶ ἄλλος ὅδε λόγος λεγόμενος, ὡς ἐπειδὴ Ξέρξης 118 ἀπελαύνων ἐξ Ἀθηνέων ἀπίκετο ἐπ' Ἠιόνα τὴν ἐπὶ Στρυμόνι, ἐνθεῦτεν οὐκέτι ὁδοιπορίῃσι διεχρᾶτο, ἀλλὰ τὴν μὲν στρατιὴν Ὑδάρνεϊ ἐπιτράπει ἀπάγειν ἐς τὸν Ἑλλήσποντον, αὐτὸς δ' ἐπὶ νεὸς Φοινίσσης ἐπιβὰς ἐκομίζετο ἐς τὴν Ἀσίην. πλέοντα δέ 5 μιν ἄνεμον Στρυμονίην ὑπολαβεῖν μέγαν καὶ κυματίην. καὶ δὴ μᾶλλον γάρ τι χειμαίνεσθαι γεμούσης τῆς νεός, ὥστε ἐπὶ τοῦ καταστρώματος ἐπεόντων συχνῶν Περσέων τῶν σὺν Ξέρξῃ κομιζομένων, ἐνθαῦτα ἐς δεῖμα πεσόντα τὸν βασιλέα εἰρέσθαι βώσαντα τὸν κυβερνήτην εἴ τίς ἐστί σφι σωτηρίη, καὶ τὸν 10 εἶπαι "δέσποτα, οὐκ ἔστι οὐδεμία, εἰ μὴ τούτων ἀπαλλαγή τις γένηται τῶν πολλῶν ἐπιβατέων." καὶ Ξέρξην λέγεται ἀκούσαντα ταῦτα εἰπεῖν "ἄνδρες Πέρσαι, νῦν τις διαδεξάτω ὑμέων βασιλέος κηδόμενος· ἐν ὑμῖν γὰρ οἶκε εἶναι ἐμοὶ ἡ σωτηρίη." τὸν μὲν ταῦτα λέγειν, τοὺς δὲ προσκυνέοντας 15

118. 1 λεγόμενος λόγος z　　2 ἀθηνέων AP : ἀθηναίων ‖ ἐπ' : ἐς? Kallenberg　　3 ἐνθεῦτεν om. β ‖ διεχρῆτο αC : διεχρέετο　　4 ὑδάρνεϊ ABPz ‖ ἐπιτρέπει libri　　5, 7 νεώς C : νηὸς βa (bis) ‖ πλώοντα β 9 βασιλῆα z　　10 κυβερνίτην B : κυβερνήτεα βa ‖ ἔστι R, van H. ‖ σφι om. P : σφίσι? van H.　　11 εἶπε C ‖ οὐ δὲ μία AB : οὐδεμίη z ‖ εἰ : ἦν β, Holder, van H. ‖ τουτέων z　　12 ξέρξεα βa ‖ λέγεται secl. van H.　　13 εἶπαι RSz, Holder, van H. : εἶπε V　　14 βασιλῆος z ‖ ἔοικεν β ‖ ἐμοὶ εἶναι z ‖ ἡ om. β

118. 1. **ἄλλος ὅδε λόγος λεγόμενος,** 'another story is told, to the following effect . .' The formula does not prove that the variant had not been reduced to writing (cp. Introduction, § 10). If it had been merely an oral tradition perhaps Hdt. would not have been at such pains to refute it.

2. **Ἠιόνα τὴν ἐπὶ Στρυμόνι** : cp. 7. 25.

3. **ὁδοιπορίῃσι** : of journeys by land ; the plural perhaps only idiomatic or rhetorical (like ἀβουλίῃσι c. 97 supra). Cp. 3. 52 ἀλουσίῃσί τε καὶ ἀσιτίῃσι, which Stein regards as Homeric.

4. **Ὑδάρνεϊ** : cp. c. 113 supra. This story coheres with that anecdote, and is contradicted by the story (probably truer) of Artabazos c. 126 infra, though Hdt. misses this argument.

ἐπὶ νεὸς Φοινίσσης : of course ; cp. 7. 128 supra.

6. **ἄνεμον Στρυμονίην.** It was

πνοιαὶ δ' ἀπὸ Στρυμόνος μολοῦσαι
κακόσχολοι, νήστιδες, δύσορμοι,

that detained the fleet of Agamemnon

at Aulis (Aischyl. Ag. 192 f.). Cp. Aristotle, de vent. σ 973 B Θρᾳκίας κατὰ μὲν Θρᾴκην Στρυμονίας, πνεῖ γὰρ ἀπὸ τοῦ Στρυμόνος ποταμοῦ. (It does not, however, figure on the octagonal 'Tower of the Winds' in Athens.) Baehr considers it equivalent to Boreas. 'Strymonian' is presumably a purely geographical expression. Hdt. has suddenly changed into orat. obliq. after having started with ὡς and the recta, as in c. 111 supra.

7. **χειμαίνεσθαι,** cp. c. 113 supra, seems to be a poetical word, an observation not contravened by its (metaphorical) use in Aristotle, Poet. 17. 3. It is not quite plain whether the construction here is transitive (passive) or intransitive (neuter) ; and if transitive, whether τὴν νέα or τὸν βασιλέα should be understood as subject.

13. **διαδεξάτω . . κηδόμενος,** 'may prove his care of . .' ; cp. 3. 72 δεικνύσθω ἐνθαῦτα ἐὼν πολέμιος. With the τις cp. c. 109 supra.

14. **ἐν ὑμῖν** : cp. c. 60 supra.

15. **προσκυνέοντας** : cp. 7. 136 supra. That even in this supreme hour the

ἐκπηδᾶν ἐς τὴν θάλασσαν, καὶ τὴν νέα ἐπικουφισθεῖσαν οὕτω
δὴ ἀποσωθῆναι ἐς τὴν ᾿Ασίην. ὡς δὲ ἐκβῆναι τάχιστα ἐς
γῆν τὸν Ξέρξην, ποιῆσαι τοιόνδε· ὅτι μὲν ἔσωσε βασιλέος
τὴν ψυχήν, δωρήσασθαι χρυσέῃ στεφάνῃ τὸν κυβερνήτην, ὅτι
20 δὲ Περσέων πολλοὺς ἀπώλεσε, ἀποταμεῖν τὴν κεφαλὴν αὐτοῦ.
119 οὗτος δὲ ἄλλος λέγεται λόγος περὶ τοῦ Ξέρξεω νόστου,
οὐδαμῶς ἔμοιγε πιστὸς οὔτε ἄλλως οὔτε τὸ Περσέων τοῦτο
πάθος. εἰ γὰρ δὴ ταῦτα οὕτω εἰρέθη ἐκ τοῦ κυβερνήτεω πρὸς
Ξέρξην, ἐν μυρίῃσι γνώμῃσι μίαν οὐκ ἔχω ἀντίξοον μὴ οὐκ
5 ἂν ποιῆσαι βασιλέα τοιόνδε, τοὺς μὲν ἐπὶ τοῦ καταστρώματος
καταβιβάσαι ἐς κοίλην νέα ἐόντας Πέρσας καὶ Περσέων τοὺς
πρώτους, τῶν δ᾿ ἐρετέων ἐόντων Φοινίκων ὅκως οὐκ ἂν ἴσον
πλῆθος τοῖσι Πέρσῃσι ἐξέβαλε ἐς τὴν θάλασσαν. ἀλλ᾿ ὁ

---

16 ἐκπηδέειν Β ‖ νῆα Rz   18 ξέρξεα Βz ‖ βασιλῆος z   19
χρυσέω στεφάνω Β : χρυσέῳ στεφάνῳ Holder, van H. ‖ κυβερνίτην Β :
κυβερνήτεα Βz   119. 1 ἄλλος Β : ἄλλως ‖ λέγεται ὁ λόγος CPz :
λόγος λέγεται Β   2 ἄλλως Βz : ἄλλος ('ni fuit potius ὁ ἄλλος' Stein)
‖ τὸ post τοῦτο Β   3 οὕτω CPz : οὕτως ‖ ἡρέθη C : ἐρρέθη Β : ἐρρήθη
Pz   4 τὸν ξέρξεα Β : ξέρξεα z ‖ μίην z ‖ ἔχω : ἔξω Krueger, van H. ‖
μὴ om. Β   5 βασιλῆα z ‖ ἐπὶ : ἐκ Β, Holder, van H.   6 νῆα Βz
‖ καὶ τῶν Β   7 δὲ α ‖ ἐρετριέων Β ‖ κῶς Pingel, van H. ‖ ἴσον R
8 θάλασσαν ; (Pingel) van H.

---

forms of Persian court etiquette are not
omitted is a touch not so much of
verisimilitude as of humour.

19. ψυχήν: 7. 39 supra.

20. ἀποταμεῖν τὴν κεφαλήν: on be-
heading, 7. 35 supra; did he wear the
crown at his execution? The anecdote
illustrates the despot's cowardice and
caprice, and the ludicrous loyalty of his
subjects; it is a part of the comic
Nemesis, though a trifle grim.

119. 2. οὐδαμῶς ἔμοιγε πιστός. Hdt.
is no doubt right in discrediting the
story, but the point he emphasizes
against it seems a poor one. Persian
grandees would have been but sorry
hands at the oars compared to the
Phoenician tars; and the process of
pitching a lot of the oarsmen into the
sea, during a raging storm, to make
way for those aristocratic amateurs,
might not have been easy or expeditious.
Hdt. relates a story which he discredits
perhaps on the principle laid down 7.
152.

οὔτε ἄλλως οὔτε τὸ Περσέων τοῦτο
πάθος: reading ἄλλως the construction

seems irregular (which is better, however,
than the very tame ὁ ἄλλος); for is τὸ
πάθος nominative (subject) or accusative
(of reference, limitation)? The latter
seems preferable. ἄλλως itself is simple
enough here ('in other respects'); cp. c.
116 supra. The πάθος is self-inflicted
in this case.

4. ἐν μυρίῃσι γνώμῃσι μίαν . . ἀντίξοον: does Hdt. mean that he had
often discussed the story, and never
found a single person dispute his point?
Or does he merely wish to emphasize his
own conviction by asserting that, if ten
thousand opinions were polled, they
would all be found to agree with him?
ἀντίξοον, cp. 7. 218 supra. The apodosis
in the conditional sentence is not οὐκ
ἔχω, strictly speaking, but οὐκ ἂν ποιῆσαι.
οὐκ ἔχω . . μὴ οὐκ ἂν ποιῆσαι is a clear
case of the idiomatic use of the double
negative μὴ οὐ. Instead of μὴ οὐκ ἂν
ποιῆσαι Hdt. might have written ὅκως
οὐκ ἂν ἐποίησε, as he writes below ὅκως
οὐκ ἂν ἐξέβαλε instead of μὴ οὐκ ἂν
ἐκβαλεῖν. But Pingel's emendation (vide
App. Crit.) is seductive.

6. ἐς κοίλην νέα, 'into the ship's hold.'

μέν, ὡς καὶ πρότερόν μοι εἴρηται, ὁδῷ χρεώμενος ἅμα τῷ
ἄλλῳ στρατῷ ἀπενόστησε ἐς τὴν Ἀσίην. μέγα δὲ καὶ τόδε 120
μαρτύριον· φαίνεται γὰρ Ξέρξης ἐν τῇ ὀπίσω κομιδῇ ἀπικόμενος ἐς Ἄβδηρα καὶ ξεινίην τέ σφι συνθέμενος καὶ δωρησά-
μενος αὐτοὺς ἀκινάκῃ τε χρυσέῳ καὶ τιήρῃ χρυσοπάστῳ. καὶ
ὡς αὐτοὶ λέγουσι Ἀβδηρῖται, λέγοντες ἔμοιγε οὐδαμῶς πιστά, 5
πρῶτον <αὐτοῦ> ἐλύσατο τὴν ζώνην φεύγων ἐξ Ἀθηνέων
ὀπίσω, ὡς ἐν ἀδείῃ ἐών. τὰ δὲ Ἄβδηρα ἵδρυται πρὸς τοῦ
Ἑλλησπόντου μᾶλλον ἤδη τοῦ Στρυμόνος καὶ τῆς Ἠιόνος,
ὅθεν δή μιν φασὶ ἐπιβῆναι ἐπὶ τὴν νέα.

9 μοι om. ΒΡ, Stein¹ || χρεόμενος Ρ, van H.   120 totum caput
necnon c. praeced. a verb. οὔτε ἄλλως suspect. hab. Krueger, Kallenberg
3 ξεινίην Β   4 τε om. Β || τιήρῃ Stein¹², etc.: τιάρῃ Stein³: τιήρῃ Β:
τιήρει a: τριήρει ΟΡ: τριήρει s   5 οὐδαμῶς ἔμοιγε Β: μὲν οὐδαμῶς
ἐμοὶ s   6 <αὐτοῦ> van H., Stein³ || ἀθηναίων ΒΒΟs   7 πρὸς τοῦ
Ἑλλησπόντου δὲ μᾶλλον τὰ Ἀβδηρα ἵδρυται ἢ s   8 ἤδη Stein³: ἢ
(om. Β)   9 νῆα Βs: post hanc voc. λει στι κ̄ (sc. λείπουσι στίχο
εἴκοσι) exhib. Βᵐ

9. ὡς καὶ πρότερόν μοι εἴρηται: the
reference back is but to cc. 115-117 supra.
   ἅμα τῷ ἄλλῳ στρατῷ: a merely
idiomatic ἄλλος without distinct reference
to any division of the army; cp. c. 113
supra.
   120. 1. μέγα δὲ καὶ τόδε μαρτύριον:
the point here made is a convincing one,
the fact being admitted. τόδε is not
merely the exact position of the town,
nor the fact that Xerxes reached it on
his return; for neither of these by itself would prove the point; but more
generally the whole argument which
comprises both items.
   2. φαίνεται . . ἀπικόμενος. No real
proof is given that the visit of Xerxes to
Abdera was ἐν τῇ ὀπίσω κομιδῇ (cp. c. 108
supra); the ξεινίη might have been established, and the gifts presented, on the outward journey, 7. 109 supra; cp. 7. 120.
   4. ἀκινάκῃ: Περσικὸν ξίφος τὸν ἀκινάκην καλέουσι 7. 54 supra.
   τιήρῃ: cp. 7. 61 supra. For
χρυσόπαστος cp. Aischyl. Ag. 776 (769)
τὰ χρυσόπαστα δ' ἔδεθλα.
   5. ὡς αὐτοὶ λέγουσι Ἀβδηρῖται: they
must have been the ultimate authority
for the previous statement which Hdt.
accepts, as much as for the subsequent
statement which he rejects (λέγοντες
ἔμοιγε οὐδαμῶς πιστά). The argument
and sentence are incomplete without the
insertion of ἐς Ἄβδηρα or παρὰ σφέας

ἀπικόμενος or αὐτοῦ: cp. App. Crit. The
statement would be entirely inconsistent
with Hdt.'s own previous narrative (e.g.
c. 114 supra), as well as improbable in
itself; it illustrates the growth of the
legend of Xerxes' flight (φεύγων).
The story of Artabazos also contradicts
it; but Hdt. takes no heed of that.
   6. ἐλύσατο τὴν ζώνην: i.e. changed
his raiment. Stein well cps. the vow of
Histiaios 5. 106 supra. ζώνη was not
an exclusively male article of dress (cp.
L. & S. and l. 51). It has been regarded
as emblematic of virility in the one sex,
and of chastity in the other (cp. Sir R.
Temple in the Cambridge Review, vol.
xxvi. No. 643, p. xxix.).
   8. μᾶλλον ἤδη τοῦ Στρυμόνος. Hdt.
must certainly have meant to say that
Abdera was nearer than Eion to the
Hellespont, not that it was nearer to the
Hellespont than to the Strymon. The
point is necessary to the argument, but
it is only obtained by an emendation.
The substitution of the Strymon for Eion
in the comparison is awkward, and
perhaps led to the corruption. Blakesley,
who obelizes cc. 118, 119 on account of
the weakness of the argument in c. 119,
regards this sentence as a mere gloss;
i.e. a fraud within the fraud. Cp.
App. Crit.
   9. φασί: the authors of the story in
c. 118 supra.

121   Οἱ δὲ Ἕλληνες ἐπείτε οὐκ οἷοί τε ἐγίνοντο ἐξελεῖν τὴν
      Ἄνδρον, τραπόμενοι ἐς Κάρυστον καὶ δηιώσαντες αὐτῶν τὴν
      χώρην ἀπαλλάσσοντο ἐς Σαλαμῖνα. πρῶτα μέν νυν τοῖσι
      θεοῖσι ἐξεῖλον ἀκροθίνια ἄλλα τε καὶ τριήρεας τρεῖς Φοινίσσας,
    5 τὴν μὲν ἐς Ἰσθμὸν ἀναθεῖναι, ἥ περ ἔτι καὶ ἐς ἐμὲ ἦν,
      τὴν δὲ ἐπὶ Σούνιον, τὴν δὲ τῷ Αἴαντι αὐτοῦ ἐς Σαλαμῖνα.
      μετὰ δὲ τοῦτο διεδάσαντο τὴν ληίην καὶ τὰ ἀκροθίνια ἀπέ-
      πεμψαν ἐς Δελφούς, ἐκ τῶν ἐγένετο ἀνδριὰς ἔχων ἐν τῇ

---

121. 1 ἐγένοντο CPz ‖ ἐξελέειν β   2 δηώσαντες β ‖ αὐτέων z
5 ἀναθῆναι C ‖ καὶ om. C   6 δ' ἐπὶ a ‖ 'an αὐτόσε [ἐς Σαλαμῖνα]?'
van H.   7 τοῦτο del. van H. ‖ τὰ om. β ‖ ἔπεμψαν β

---

121. 1. οἱ δὲ Ἕλληνες: the scene shifts back to Hellas (cc. 121–125) and resumes the story dropped in c. 112. The Greeks are foiled at Andros (even as Miltiades had been foiled at Paros, some nine or ten years before, 6. 132 ff.). Karystos is devastated, Rawlinson solemnly remarking that Themistokles seems to have lacked the influence, or the honesty, to keep his bargain with these unfortunates. What is really here disproved is the bargain. αὐτῶν: so. τῶν Καρυστίων.

3. ἀπαλλάσσοντο ἐς Σαλαμῖνα. Had they ever really quitted it ? Are the operations against Andros and Karystos correctly dated, or are they duplicates, by anticipation, of the subsequent operations of the Athenian alliance ? τοῖσι θεοῖσι. Had Polytheism a more vivid sense of the divine presences and operations than our Christendom ? The nations nowadays seldom venture upon particular offerings to the Deity in acknowledgement of victory. Or does our religion dispose us rather to set the higher powers and graces on the losing side ?

4. ἐξεῖλον after ἐξελεῖν just above, in a totally different sense, is not happy, is an 'unconscious iteration.' ἀκροθίνια: a poetical word (but found in the sing., Thuc. 1. 132. 2) and properly an adjective. ἀναθεῖναι appears to be an epexegetical infinitive, nor does it involve the conclusion that these dedications were carried out, or set up, immediately.

5. ἥ περ ἔτι καὶ ἐς ἐμὲ ἦν. It is surely a curious remark for Hdt. to make, that of the three Phoenician triremes dedicated for erection, one at the Isthmos, one at Sunion, and one in Salamis, the first was still in existence

down to his own day. What then of the other two ? Had they disappeared ? Or had Hdt. seen the one at the Isthmos, but not the other two ? Or had he certain information about the first, but not about the others ? It is remarkable that two of these national dedications were to be upon Attic soil, and that of those two Hdt. appears to have no precise knowledge.

6. τῷ Αἴαντι. Hdt. does not specify to whom the dedications at Sunion and the Isthmos were made; presumably to Athene and to Poseidon—by so little were the gods and heroes then distinguished. Aias is of course the Aiakid, op. c. 64 supra. αὐτοῦ, 'on the spot.'

7. μετὰ δὲ τοῦτο: i.e. after the ἐξαίρεσις ἀκροθινίων. 'The' ἀκροθίνια sent to Delphi had presumably been included in the operation, before the division of the spoil; but each state, to whom a share of booty fell, had also to make an offering to Delphi, though the point is not quite clearly put by Hdt. We learn also from Pausanias, l.c. infra, that individual commanders made offerings at Delphi from their shares of the spoil.

8. ἐκ τῶν ἐγένετο: the actual fabrication and erection of this statue, the collective dedication of the Greeks from the victory of Salamis, can hardly have been effected until the victory of Plataia had placed the loyalty and the security of Delphi on a new footing. Hdt. does not specify the subject of the statue. Pausanias 10. 14. 3 (5) is more explicit, without fully describing the type: Ἕλληνες δὲ οἱ ἐναντία βασιλέως πολεμήσαντες ἀνέθεσαν μὲν Δία ἐς Ὀλυμπίαν χαλκοῦν, ἀνέθεσαν δὲ καὶ ἐς Δελφοὺς Ἀπόλλωνα ἀπὸ ἔργων τῶν ἐν ταῖς ναυσὶν ἐπί τε Ἀρτεμισίῳ καὶ ἐν

χειρὶ ἀκρωτήριον νεός, ἐὼν μέγαθος δυώδεκα πηχέων · ἐστήκεε
δὲ οὗτος τῇ περ ὁ Μακεδὼν ᾿Αλέξανδρος ὁ χρύσεος. πέμ- 122
ψαντες δὲ ἀκροθίνια οἱ ῞Ελληνες ἐς Δελφοὺς ἐπειρώτων τὸν
θεὸν κοινῇ εἰ λελάβηκε πλήρεα καὶ ἀρεστὰ τὰ ἀκροθίνια.
ὁ δὲ παρ᾿ Ἑλλήνων μὲν τῶν ἄλλων ἔφησε ἔχειν, παρὰ ·
Αἰγινητέων δὲ οὔ, ἀλλὰ ἀπαίτεε αὐτοὺς τὰ ἀριστήια τῆς ἐν 5
Σαλαμῖνι ναυμαχίης. Αἰγινῆται δὲ πυθόμενοι ἀνέθεσαν ἀστέρας
χρυσέους, οἳ ἐπὶ ἱστοῦ χαλκέου ἑστᾶσι τρεῖς ἐπὶ τῆς γωνίης,
ἀγχοτάτω τοῦ Κροίσου κρητῆρος.

9 χερὶ z ‖ ἀκρωτήριον post ἔχων Β ‖ νεὼς ΒCP : νηὸς z ‖ δυωκαίδεκα a
‖ ἔστηκε RSV, van H. (ἔστηκε Β ap. Holder) 122. 2 ἐπηρώτων
ΒCP : ἐπηρώτεον z 4 ὁ δὲ παλλήνων Α¹ ‖ ἔχει z ‖ παρ᾿ ΒPz 5
ἀλλ᾿ Pz 8 ἀγχοτάτωι aP ‖ κροίσου Pz : χρυσοῦ Β : κροίσεω (Κροι-
σείου coni. Stein², recep. Holder)

Σαλαμῖνι. Apollo had precious little
claim to an offering from Salamis (and
it might have been the god's guilty
conscience which led him to decline the
offering of Themistokles! Pausan. *l.c.*
He could hardly have been wroth with
the Athenian for the defence of the
medizers, Plutarch *Themist.* 20).

9. ἐστήκεε δὲ . . ὁ χρύσεος. To mark
the position of the god's by the man's
image, if both were still *in situ,* is an
odd procedure. [Demosth.] 12. 164
Φιλιπ. ἐπιστ. mentions 'the golden
Alexander' as an offering at Delphi
made] by Alex. I. from the spoil (τῶν
αἰχμαλώτων Μήδων) captured by him
on the site of Amphipolis — a very
questionable item of history. Blakesley
regards ἐστήκεε . . ὁ χρύσεος as the note
of a later editor, on two grounds : (1) a
portrait statue of a living person would
be an anachronism ; (2) a gold statue
seems too rich for the Makedonians of
the period ; and thinks the Alexander
here named was Alex. Magnus. As to
(2), the statue would be bronze gilt, and
Alexander was wealthy, cp. 5. 17. As
to (1), the portrait was probably an ideal,
and the text above cited is some confirmation of Hdt.

122. 1. πέμψαντες δέ. Hdt. seems to
assume that this mission and inquiry
followed at once, and at the same time.
But a more or less considerable interval
is involved (a) in the military situation,
which would make such offerings an
absurdity, while Mardonios was still
about ; (b) in the implicit assumption
that various states had made separate
offerings ; (c) in the time necessary for

the designing and execution of such
dedications. In this 'common inquiry
by the Hellenes' we may fairly see the
hand of the Amphiktyons, at the date
of the attempted revival and development of the League, the rehabilitation
of Delphi, and the reaction against
Athens and the Delian movement ; cp.
7. 228 *supra.*

5. τὰ ἀριστήια τῆς ἐν Σαλαμῖνι
ναυμαχίης, 'the prize of valour for the
sea-fight at Salamis.' The Aiginetans
themselves had obtained the first prize
in the battle (c. 93 *supra*) ; and this
passage has generally been taken to
mean that the god made a special
demand upon the Aiginetans, as the
ἀριστεύσαντες. Stein more subtly interprets the god as claiming for himself
the award, and conjectures that the
Aiginetans had been favoured in the
fight with a propitious sign, such as
befell Lysander at Aigospotami (Plutarch
Lysandr. 12), viz. an apparition of the
Dioskuroi, and of Apollon Delphinios,
a special patron of the Aiginetans—the
three being represented by the stars on
the Aiginetan offering. This explanation is acceptable, and is endorsed by
Busolt ii.² 716. 3. It was a compliment
to the Aiginetans, and a set-back to
Athens : it was also a direct claim, ·
advanced by Delphi, to a credit for
the victory at Salamis. Perhaps the
Aiginetans had already offered the mast
with two stars (at the yard-arm's ends)
(the Dioscuroi), and had only to add a
third, and larger star, above, to represent the sun-god.

7. γωνίης : sc. τοῦ προνηίου 1. 51.

123 Μετὰ δὲ τὴν διαίρεσιν τῆς ληίης ἔπλεον οἱ Ἕλληνες ἐς
τὸν Ἰσθμὸν ἀριστήια δώσοντες τῷ ἀξιωτάτῳ γενομένῳ Ἑλλήνων ἀνὰ τὸν πόλεμον τοῦτον. ὡς δὲ ἀπικόμενοι οἱ στρατηγοὶ
διένεμον τὰς ψήφους ἐπὶ τοῦ Ποσειδέωνος τῷ βωμῷ, τὸν
5 πρῶτον καὶ τὸν δεύτερον κρίνοντες ἐκ πάντων, ἐνθαῦτα πᾶς
τις αὐτῶν ἑωυτῷ ἐτίθετο τὴν ψῆφον, αὐτὸς ἕκαστος δοκέων
ἄριστος γενέσθαι, δεύτερα δὲ οἱ πολλοὶ συνεξέπιπτον Θεμιστοκλέα κρίνοντες. οἱ μὲν δὴ ἐμουνοῦντο, Θεμιστοκλέης δὲ

---

123. 1 ἔπλωον βz, van H.
διέφερον?' van H. ‖ ποσειδέονος B
αὐτέων z: om. β   7 δὲ om. C ‖
8 ἐμουνοῦτο A¹: ἐμυοῦντο C

4 διενέμοντο Pz: ἔφερον β: 'Num
5 κρινέοντες van H.   6
ξυνεξέπιπτον β ‖ Θεμιστοκλῆα z

The *Krater of Kroisos* must be the silver
one, for the gold one was in the Treasury
of Klazomenai ; *ib.* This little chapter
looks very like an addition of the second
hand ; op. Introduction, § 9.

123. 1. μετὰ δὲ τὴν διαίρεσιν τῆς
ληίης : these words, carrying back over
c. 122, show that the Aiginetan episode
just recounted belongs to a later date,
and suggest that the record of it may be
an insertion, not of the first draft ; see
preceding note.

2. ἀριστήια δώσοντες : the prize is
not a mere ideal award, but sufficiently
material to pass from hand to hand ;
op. next c.

3. ἀνὰ τὸν πόλεμον τοῦτον. This
proposal to award the prize for the war
—which is not yet over—is a little premature. Did the Greeks then believe
that the war was over (cp. c. 109 *supra*) ?
Or is this episode at the Isthmos antedated some twelve months ? Or is it
altogether apocryphal ? It has a somewhat fabulous air. Pliny 34. 53 has a
similar anecdote of Polykleitos, presumably plagiarized from this.

οἱ στρατηγοί : apparently of the
fleet : the admirals (but was Aristeides
among them ?). The fleet is all apparently
supposed to have moved to the Isthmos.
The Peloponnesian army too might
still be there ; but its organization was
probably different from that of the fleet,
and in any case its commanders could
hardly be conceived as awarding each to
himself the prize on this occasion.

4. διένεμον τὰς ψήφους ἐπὶ τ. Ποσειδέωνος τῷ βωμῷ : a specially solemn procedure, designed to secure an absolutely
honest decision, as in judicial proceedings

(Plutarch *Perikl.* 32 οἱ δὲ δικασταὶ τὴν
ψῆφον ἀπὸ τοῦ βωμοῦ φέροντες . .
κρίνοιεν). διανέμειν τὰς ψήφους apparently
means to divide the votes among the
(possible) competitors for first and second
place. Cp. διαφέρειν τὴν ψῆφον 4. 138.
φέρειν, τίθεσθαι would be more usual.
How the voting was actually conducted
does not clearly appear. Perhaps there
were two urns upon the altar, into one
of which each strategos put an *ostrakon*,
with the name of his nominee for first
place inscribed upon it, and into the
other that for the second place ; in the
scrutiny it would have been discovered
that in the first urn no two *ostraka* bare
the same name, while in the second
every sherd was inscribed with the name
of Themistokles. (But how did the
Athenian himself vote ?) The shrine of
Poseidon and its contents are described
by Pausanias 2. 1. 7–9, for his own day ;
the temple in 480 B.C. was presumably
the sixth-century edifice, of which
remains have been found ; cp. Frazer
iii. 11.

7. οἱ πολλοὶ συνεξέπιπτον : cp. c. 49
supra ; here (as in 5. 22) the verb is
used with a personal subject, but appears
to have merely the meaning 'coincided,'
agreed ; the fortuitous character of the
agreement may have suggested the use
of the word.

Θεμιστοκλέα κρίνοντες : sc. τὸν
δεύτερον εἶναι. δεύτερα just above is
merely adverbial.

8. οἱ μὲν δὴ ἐμουνοῦντο : they were
left each with one vote only (for first
place). The same remark, however,
applies to Themistokles, so that the
contrast here is not quite complete.

δευτερείοισι ὑπερεβάλλετο πολλόν. οὐ βουλομένων δὲ ταῦτα 124
κρίνειν τῶν Ἑλλήνων φθόνῳ, ἀλλ' ἀποπλεόντων ἑκάστων ἐς
τὴν ἑωυτῶν ἀκρίτων, ὅμως Θεμιστοκλῆς ἐβώσθη τε καὶ
ἐδοξώθη εἶναι ἀνὴρ πολλὸν Ἑλλήνων σοφώτατος ἀνὰ πᾶσαν
τὴν Ἑλλάδα. ὅτι δὲ νικῶν οὐκ ἐτιμήθη πρὸς τῶν ἐν Σαλα- 5
μῖνι ναυμαχησάντων, αὐτίκα μετὰ ταῦτα ἐς Λακεδαίμονα
ἀπίκετο θέλων τιμηθῆναι· καί μιν Λακεδαιμόνιοι καλῶς μὲν
ὑπεδέξαντο, μεγάλως δὲ ἐτίμησαν. ἀριστήια μέν νυν ἔδοσαν
. . Εὐρυβιάδῃ ἐλαίης στέφανον, σοφίης δὲ καὶ δεξιότητος
Θεμιστοκλέϊ καὶ τούτῳ στέφανον ἐλαίης· ἐδωρήσαντό τέ μιν 10
ὄχῳ τῷ ἐν Σπάρτῃ καλλιστεύσαντι. αἰνέσαντες δὲ πολλά,

9 ὑπερέβαλλε B   124. 2 ἀποπλωόντων Bs   3 ἐβοήθη C
4 ἐδοξώσθη z ‖ πολλῶν BCz ‖ Ἑλλήνων del. van H.   5 νικῶν ‘suspectum’ Stein³: φιλονικέων ? Stein⁸   9 ἀνδραγαθίης vel e Plutarch.
Them. c. 17, Mor. p. 871 ἀνδρηίης supplend. cens. Stein et alii   10
τέ : δέ CPz   11 καλλιστεύοντι B, Holder, van H.

9. δευτερείοισι ὑπερεβάλλετο : so. τοὺς ἄλλους στρατηγούς. δευτερεῖα (εὐδαιμονίης) 1. 32 ; ὑπερβάλλεσθαι c. 24 supra; and 1. 61 Θηβαῖοι ὑπερεβάλοντο τῇ δόσι τῶν χρημάτων.

124. 1. οὐ βουλομένων δὲ . . φθόνῳ : the sentence may be taken to refer to the judicial fiasco just recorded. τῶν Ἑλλήνων = τῶν στρατηγῶν. But without much pressing the passage might be taken to refer to a refusal to decide the question on appeal, ἑκάστων (each set and each contingent) just below favouring that too. ἀκρίτων is plainly active, ‘without giving a decision.’

φθόνος is the besetting sin of Greek citizenship, op. 7. 236 supra, and was not eliminated between confederates.

3. ἐβώσθη τε κτλ : cp. 6. 131 οὕτω Ἀλκμεωνίδαι ἐβώσθησαν ἀνὰ τὴν Ἑλλάδα.

7. θέλων τιμηθῆναι : this motivation again betrays animus op. c. 112 supra). The visit of Themistokles to Lakedaimon in the autumn or winter (480–79) was probably by invitation (cp. Plutarch Themist. 17), and may have had deeper political and diplomatic ends in view than the Herodotean historiography has reckoned with.

The honours heaped upon the Athenian in Sparta Diodoros 11. 27 (Ephoros) traces to Spartan apprehensions of reprisals on the part of the Athenians and Themistokles, for the set-back after Salamis ; they may have been intended, at least in part, to promote a naval policy for the

future (cp. c. 108 supra), as well as to reward its past success. They do not appear to have turned his head, much less won Themistokles to sacrifice Athenian to Spartan interests. Within a twelve-month he is in Sparta again, for a very different purpose, and at considerable risk to himself; cp. Thucyd. 1. 89–92. The Themistoklean legend had attempted to discount his services to Athens in Sparta by ignoring the visit after Plataia-Mykale, and caricaturing the visit after Salamis ; Thucydides' record is a part of the Rettung of Themistokles, which he favours. Cp. Appendix VII. § 4.

9. Εὐρυβιάδῃ, who must, according to the antecedent anecdote, have voted the prize to himself at the Isthmos.

σοφίης δὲ καὶ δεξιότητος : the distinction between the ‘ethical’ (ἀνδρηίη, op. App. Crit.) and the ‘intellectual’ virtues, and their rewards, shows that the Spartans had some philosophy in them ! The award is the same in each case, an olive-wreath ; and the co-ordination (which justifies our understanding ἀριστήια before σοφίης) is emphasized by the words καὶ τούτῳ (et ipsi ; cp. καὶ οὗτοι 7. 40, Stein).

11. ὄχῳ τῷ ἐν Σπάρτῃ καλλιστεύσαντι. Stein observes the astonishing use here of the aorist. Perhaps when the chariot reached Athens it was not so much thought of !

αἰνέσαντες might seem grammatically to belong to the τριηκόσιοι, but κατὰ

προέπεμψαν ἀπιόντα τριηκόσιοι Σπαρτιητέων λογάδες, οὗτοι
οἵ περ ἱππέες καλέονται, μέχρι οὔρων τῶν Τεγεητικῶν.
μοῦνον δὴ τοῦτον πάντων ἀνθρώπων τῶν ἡμεῖς ἴδμεν Σπαρτιῆ-
125 ται προέπεμψαν. ὡς δὲ ἐκ τῆς Λακεδαίμονος ἀπίκετο ἐς
τὰς Ἀθήνας, ἐνθαῦτα Τιμόδημος Ἀφιδναῖος τῶν ἐχθρῶν μὲν
τῶν Θεμιστοκλέος ἐών, ἄλλως δὲ οὐ τῶν ἐπιφανέων ἀνδρῶν,
φθόνῳ καταμαργέων ἐνείκεε τὸν Θεμιστοκλέα, τὴν ἐς Λακεδαί-
5 μονα ἄπιξιν προφέρων, ὡς διὰ τὰς Ἀθήνας ἔχοι τὰ γέρεα τὰ
παρὰ Λακεδαιμονίων, ἀλλ᾽ οὐ δι᾽ ἑωυτόν. ὃ δέ, ἐπείτε οὐκ
ἐπαύετο λέγων ταῦτα ὁ Τιμόδημος, εἶπε "οὕτω ἔχει τοι· οὔτ᾽

---

12 ἀνιόντα Pz   13 οὔρων B²z   125. 2 ἀθηναῖος B ‖ μὲν
om. B   3 ἀνδρῶν om. R   4 καταμαρπτέων aCz (γρ. μαρπτέων
Pᵐ) ‖ Θεμιστοκλῆα z ‖ σπάρτην B   5 ἔχει z   6 ἑωυτῶν B ‖
ἐνέκειτο καὶ οὐκ z   7 ταῦτα λέγων z ‖ οὕτως R

σύνεσιν, a reference to the previous subject (Λακεδαιμόνιοι) seems more pointed
and natural. The αἶνος perhaps took
the form of songs or orations in his
honour; cp. Thuc. 2. 25. 2. It is followed
by the 'pomp,' or escort, to the frontier.

12. τριηκόσιοι Σπαρτιητέων λογάδες:
perhaps the royal body-guard, οἱ τριακόσιοι
ἱππῆς καλούμενοι Thuc. 5. 72. 4 (but
cp. 6. 56, 7. 205 supra), apparently
identical with the corps d'élite of hoplites,
described by Xenophon, Laced. Rep. 4, as
chosen by the three Hippagretai, each
choosing 100 men, the Hippagretai
themselves having been selected by
the Ephors; the corps would then be
annually recruited, and a fresh levy may
have been made since Thermopylai.
There were no real riders in the Spartan
army of this date, but the title was an
interesting survival. Cp. 1. 67, a passage
which suggests that the corps of Hippeis
at Sparta was partially recruited every
year, the thirty seniors perhaps taking
their discharge (and furnishing the five
Ἀγαθοεργοί), while thirty juniors would
be admitted to the corps, the whole
being thus normally renewable every
decade. But provision must, of course,
have been made for occasional vacancies.

14. μοῦνον δὴ τοῦτον π. ἀνθ. τ. ἡμεῖς
ἴδμεν: cp. Athenian orator ap. Thuc. 1.
74. 1 καὶ αὐτὸν διὰ τοῦτο ὑμεῖς ἐτιμήσατε
μάλιστα δὴ ἄνδρα ξένον τῶν ὡς ὑμᾶς
ἐλθόντων. On the Herodotean formula
cp. c. 105 supra. The asyndeton is
observable; cp. 9. 35 μοῦνοι δὲ δὴ πάντων
κτλ.

125. 1. ἐς τὰς Ἀθήνας seems to assume

that the Athenians had reoccupied the
city; cp. c. 109 supra.

2. Τιμόδημος Ἀφιδναῖος: on the deme
of Aphidnai cp. 9. 73 infra. Pindar
composed an Ode (Nem. 2) for the victory
of Timodemos, son of Timonoos, of
Acharnai, in the Pankration, about Ol.
75, a man, too, with a Salaminian connexion (op. c. 20), but the only apparent
glory of the Aphidnian was that he
belonged to the well-defined group of
τῶν ἐχθρῶν τῶν Θεμιστοκλέος. The
anecdote is transferred by Plato Rep.
329, followed by Plutarch Them. 18,
to an anonymous Seriphian: had the
aristocratic tradition in Athens grown
sensitive of the fame of Timodemos?

3. ἄλλως, in its simplest meaning.

τῶν ἐπιφανέων: the word appears
used in a party sense in [Aristot.] Ἀθ.
πολ. 28 τῶν μὲν ἐπιφανῶν προειστήκει
Νικίας, but in an entirely unpolitical
sense in Thuc. 2. 43. 3 (ἀνδρῶν γὰρ
ἐπιφανῶν πᾶσα γῆ τάφος). The meaning
here is between the two; cp. 2. 89, 172.

4. φθόνῳ here appears in its proper
place as the characteristic Republican
vice; cp. c. 124 supra. The man here
is mad with it. καταμαργέων: cp. 6.
75 (ὑπέλαβε μανίη νοῦσος ἐόντα καὶ πρότερον
ὑπομαργότερον of Kleomenes).

5. προφέρων: obiciens, exprobrans;
cp. c. 61 supra. The participles καταμαργέων and προφέρων are piled on without copula (Asyndeta).

τὰ γέρεα: to wit, the Olive-wreath,
the Chariot, the Encomium, and the
Escort, enumerated in the previous
chapter.

ἃν ἐγὼ ἐὼν Βελβινίτης ἐτιμήθην οὕτω πρὸς Σπαρτιητέων, οὔτ᾽ ἃν σὺ ὤνθρωπε ἐὼν ᾿Αθηναῖος." ταῦτα μέν νυν ἐς τοσοῦτο ἐγένετο.   10

᾿Αρτάβαζος δὲ ὁ Φαρνάκεος ἀνὴρ ἐν Πέρσῃσι λόγιμος 126 καὶ πρόσθε ἐών, ἐκ δὲ τῶν Πλαταιικῶν καὶ μᾶλλον ἔτι γενόμενος, ἔχων ἐξ μυριάδας στρατοῦ τοῦ Μαρδόνιος ἐξελέξατο, προέπεμπε βασιλέα μέχρι τοῦ πόρου. ὡς δὲ ὁ μὲν ἦν ἐν τῇ

---

8 καὶ ἐὼν Valla (etiam **s**) ‖ πρὸ Α¹ ‖ οὔτε σὺ Β   9 νυν om. αC ‖ τοσοῦτον Βz   126. 2 πρόσθεν Βz ‖ γενησόμενος ? van Η.   3 τοῦ: ὃν z   4 βασιλῆα z ‖ ἦν om. αC

---

8. ἐὼν Βελβινίτης . . ἐὼν ᾿Αθηναῖος. The Βέλβινα here referred to is no doubt the small island of that name (Strabo 375, 398), identified with St. George (*San Giorgio d' Arbore*) about 12 m. due S. of Sunion. It appears once on the Athenian tribute-lists (*C.I.A.* 37, i.e. τάξις φόρου of 425 B.C.) with an assessment of 300 drachmai: perhaps a gross imposition. The first ἐών is obviously hypothetical: why not the second too ? In which case the retort of Themistokles has the added sting of insinuating ξενία against this ἄνθρωπος.

9. ἐς τοσοῦτο, 'no further'; cp. 5. 50.

126. 1. ᾿Αρτάβαζος δὲ ὁ Φαρνάκεος has been already mentioned, 7. 66, as commander (ἄρχων) of the Parthians and Chorasmians. He has not been mentioned above, in the story of the return of Xerxes (cc. 115–17), where his presence is urgently called for. The omission points to the mutual independence of the various sources employed by Hdt., and also to his failure to fuse them into a consistent whole; cp. Introduction, § 10. The story here told of Artabazos reduces even the comparatively unexaggerated record of the 'flight' of Xerxes given by Hdt. above to an absurdity. Stein remarks that Hdt. speaks with such transparent good-will and such special knowledge of Artabazos that we may infer personal relations between the historian and the man's family, or even the man himself. Artabazos became satrap of Daskyleion in 476 B.C. in order to further the treason of Pausanias, Thuc. 1. 129. 1. Pharnakes, son of Pharnabazos (Thuc. 2. 67. 1), plainly a near relative, is found there 431–414 B.C., and was in turn succeeded by his own son, Pharnabazos, 413–388 B.C. (Thuc. 8. 6. 1). An Artabazos appears again in possession of the same satrapy (360–53 B.C.) ; cp. Krumbholz, *de Asiae min. Satrapis* (1883), p. 73. Stein regards Tritantaichmes, son of 'Artabazos,' the satrap of Babylon (1. 192), as another of his sons (but cp. notes to 7. 82, 121 *supra*), and apparently thinks that Hdt. found him as satrap in Babylon. (But Hdt.'s visit to Babylon has still to be proved.) Cp. further, 9. 89.

2. ἐκ δὲ τῶν Πλαταιικῶν καὶ μᾶλλον ἔτι γενόμενος: a clear anticipation of the story in Bk. 9. 41, etc. The participle, γενόμενος, is used from the writer's point of view, and date. Hdt. throughout treats the main events as notorious ; but in the πρόσθε ἐών just before the reference is to the date of the events in the narrative, and might lead us to expect γενησόμενος. How τὰ Πλαταιικά could redound to the credit of Artabazos is not obvious in the narrative of those events, even with this *praeiudicium* to guide us.

3. ἔχων ἐξ μυριάδας στρατοῦ τοῦ Μ. ἐξελέξατο: that would be, strictly speaking, one-fifth of the army of Mardonios. He presumably had some cavalry—say, one myriad : that would give him five myriads of infantry. If the army of Mardonios (Xerxes ?) numbered all told nominally 300,000, it may have been composed of five divisions, each comprising 50,000 infantry and 10,000 cavalry—Artabazos being the commander of one of these divisions. In Bk. 9, indeed, Artabazos appears as almost of co-ordinate authority with Mardonios. If that was the true state of the case, their total forces combined may but have amounted to 120,000 men (nominal). Cp. further, Appendix II. § 5.

4. τοῦ πόρου : cp. c. 115 *supra*. The story, of course, conflicts directly with both the stories previously told and discussed (cc. 115–17, 118–20), and is more moderate than either.

5 Ἀσίη, ὃ δὲ ὀπίσω πορευόμενος κατὰ τὴν Παλλήνην ἐγίνετο,
ἅτε Μαρδονίου τε χειμερίζοντος περὶ Θεσσαλίην τε καὶ Μακεδονίην καὶ οὐδέν κω κατεπείγοντος ἥκειν ἐς τὸ ἄλλο στρατόπεδον, οὐκ ἐδικαίου ἐντυχὼν ἀπεστεῶσι Ποτειδαιήτῃσι μὴ οὐκ
ἐξανδραποδίσασθαι σφέας. οἱ γὰρ Ποτειδαιῆται, ὡς βασιλεὺς
10 παρεξεληλάκεε καὶ ὁ ναυτικὸς τοῖσι Πέρσῃσι οἰχώκεε φεύγων
ἐκ Σαλαμῖνος, ἐκ τοῦ φανεροῦ ἀπέστασαν ἀπὸ τῶν βαρβάρων·
127 ὡς δὲ καὶ οἱ ἄλλοι οἱ τὴν Παλλήνην ἔχοντες. ἐνθαῦτα δὴ
Ἀρτάβαζος ἐπολιόρκεε τὴν Ποτείδαιαν. ὑποπτεύσας δὲ καὶ
τοὺς Ὀλυνθίους ἀπίστασθαι ἀπὸ βασιλέος, καὶ ταύτην ἐπο-

---

5 ἐγένετο z   8 Ποτειδαιήτῃσι van H., Stein³: Ποτιδαιήτῃσι
Stein¹ ², Holder (et sic passim)   11 ἐκ τῆς Σαλαμῖνος z, van H. ‖
ἀπέστησαν C   12 ὡς ABRz: (ὡς van H.) ‖ ὤλλοι β: ὄλλοι Holder,
van H.   127. 2 ὁ Ἀρτάβαζος C ‖ Ποτείδαιαν van H., Stein³:
ποτίδαιαν α, Stein¹ ², Holder: ποτιδαίην βz   3 βασιλῆος z

---

5. **ὀπίσω πορευόμενος κατὰ τὴν
Παλλήνην ἐγίνετο.** Artabazos apparently experiences no difficulty in marching backwards and forwards in Makedonia
and Thrace. Is it possible after all that
Artabazos did not escort the king to
the Hellespont, but simply went from
Thessaly to operate against Poteidaia?
Or is it even possible that he had been
safeguarding the king's route all along,
and never was south of Thessaly until
he joined Mardonios in the spring of
479 B.C.? On Pallene op. 7. 123 supra.

6. **χειμερίζοντος**: op. c. 113 supra;
by this time it was winter. Mardonios'
men were partly in **Μακεδονίη.**

7. **καὶ οὐδέν κω κατεπείγοντος ἥκειν,**
'Mardonios was not yet pressing his
coming . .,' i.e. that Artabazos should
join him. κατεπείγειν is an ἅπαξ λεγόμενον in Hdt. ἐπείγειν is frequent (e.g.
c. 68 supra, bis).

8. **οὐκ ἐδικαίου . . μὴ οὐκ ἐξανδραποδίσασθαι σφέας**: a true instance of
the idiomatic double negative μὴ οὐ:
op. c. 119 supra.

10. **παρεξεληλάκεε . . οἰχώκεε**: both
verbs are strict temporal pluperfects;
but the acts were neither synchronous,
nor are they mentioned in the historical
order — unless, indeed, the fleet was
accompanying the king on his way back
(as the apocryphal story in c. 118 supra
might be held to imply).

12. **ὡς δὲ καὶ οἱ ἄλλοι . . ἔχοντες.**
The revolt of all the towns on Pallene

appears as a direct result of the battle
of Salamis. As they were the first to
disown the Persian yoke, so were they
probably among the first to enter the
Delian League (op. Thuc. 5. 18. 5). The
proximity of Makedon, and its relations
with the Persian, were calculated to
stimulate their Hellenic sympathies.
The complete absence of any reference
in the story of the siege of Poteidaia in
480-79 B.C. which follows, to the siege
of Poteidaia in 432 B.C. and the following
years (Thucyd. i. 58, etc.), is observable,
and makes against the theory that Hdt.
was composing these Books for the first
time about the time of the outbreak of
the Peloponnesian war. This story may
well belong to the first draft of the
work, and he has not inserted into this
context any late reference; the latest
hint of the final revision of these Books
occurs above in 7. 137. Perhaps Hdt.
was not aware of the fall of Poteidaia in
the winter of 430-29 B.C., Thuc. 2. 70,
though he can hardly have been ignorant
of the Athenian blockade, and may have
avoided express reference to its prolonga-
tion out of respect for Athenian suscepti-
bilities. But the argumentum a silentio
does not carry us very far; op. Introduction, § 7.

127. 3. **τοὺς Ὀλυνθίους . . καὶ ταύτην**:
sc. τὴν Ὄλυνθον. Cp. c. 121 supra for
the reverse process. On Olynthos op.
7. 122. For the Βοττιαῖοι op. 7. 123,
Θ. κόλπου 7. 121.

ἀπίστασθαι: imperfect.

λιόρκεε· εἶχον δὲ αὐτὴν Βοττιαῖοι ἐκ τοῦ Θερμαίου κόλπου
ἐξαναστάντες ὑπὸ Μακεδόνων. ἐπεὶ δὲ σφέας εἷλε πολιορκέων, 5
κατέσφαξε ἐξαγαγὼν ἐς λίμνην, τὴν δὲ πόλιν παραδιδοῖ
Κριτοβούλῳ Τορωναίῳ ἐπιτροπεύειν καὶ τῷ Χαλκιδικῷ γένεῖ,
καὶ οὕτω Ὄλυνθον Χαλκιδέες ἔσχον. ἐξελὼν δὲ ταύτην ὁ 128
Ἀρτάβαζος τῇ Ποτειδαίῃ ἐντεταμένως προσεῖχε· προσέχοντι
δέ οἱ προθύμως συντίθεται προδοσίην Τιμόξεινος ὁ τῶν
Σκιωναίων στρατηγός, ὅντινα μὲν τρόπον ἀρχήν, ἔγωγε οὐκ
ἔχω εἰπεῖν (οὐ γὰρ ὦν λέγεται), τέλος μέντοι τοιάδε ἐγίνετο· 5
ὅκως βυβλίον γράψειε ἢ Τιμόξεινος ἐθέλων παρὰ Ἀρτάβαζον
πέμψαι ἢ Ἀρτάβαζος παρὰ Τιμόξεινον, τοξεύματος παρὰ τὰς

---

4 οἱ ἐκ Βz, Holder   7 Τορωναίῳ om. αC ‖ ἐπιτρέπειν αC
128. 3 συνετίθετο z ‖ τιμόξενος Β   4 τρόπων Apr.   5 εἶπαι z,
van H.   6 βιβλίον Pz ‖ γράψοιεν S (Gaisf.) ‖ τιμόξενος θέλων Β
7 τιμόξενον Β ‖ παρά : περὶ Valckenaer, Gaisford, ex Aenea tact. 31

5. ἐξαναστάντες ὑπὸ Μακεδόνων,
'driven out by the Makedonians,' or
'retired before the M.' ὑπό with the
neuter, or intrans. verb, cps. with
θνήσκειν, ἐκπεσεῖν, etc.

6. κατέσφαξε . . ἐς λίμνην: he apparently butchered the inhabitants
(Bottiaians) and threw their bodies
into the lake, prob. the Bolyca Lagoon,
a little E. of the city, Leake, N. Gr.
iii. 155 (ἡ Βολική λίμη, Athenaeus).
The commentators, however, generally
take ἐς λίμνην merely with ἐξαγαγών:
if Hdt. had intended that, would he not
have placed the words differently ? The
Persians worshipped rivers, running
water, 1. 138.

παραδιδοῖ . . ἐπιτροπεύειν: the
first verb is in the historic present—
the rather, perhaps, as the result is
permanent, and obtains at the time of
writing ; the second is epexegetical, and
refers only to the position of Kritoboulos.

7. Κριτοβούλῳ Τορωναίῳ . . καὶ τῷ
Χαλκιδικῷ γένεῖ. Nothing more seems
known of this Kritoboulos: the name
is a common one (cp. 2. 181). Torone
(cp. 7. 122) was presumably a colony
from Chalkis. The Bottiaioi were not exterminated by this massacre at Olynthos,
as they appear in Thucydides again and
again, e.g. 1. 58. The great Chalkidic
synoikism of Olynthos took place in
432 B.C., Thuc. l.c. To it there seems
no reference made by Hdt. Olynthos
thus appears to have passed through at
least three stages of development before
the Peloponnesian war: (i.) primitive

settlement; (ii.) Bottiaian ; (iii.) Chalkidic, in two degrees ; in each of which
the Chalkidic ' race' is the protégé of the
foreigner, Persian, Makedonian.

128. 2. ἐντεταμένως προσεῖχε: sc. τὸν
νοῦν: the adv. from the pass. part. perf. is
observable, cp. 7. 53 supra. προθύμως
just below reproduces the sense.

3. Τιμόξεινος ὁ τῶν Σκιωναίων στρατηγός. The name (Timoxenos) is
common, but this Skionaian is only
mentioned again by Polyainos, 7. 33. 1,
in reproducing this very anecdote. On
Skione cp. 7. 123 supra. The towns
on Pallene had not merely all revolted
(c. 126 supra ad f.) but were all in
alliance ; cp. infra παρὴν δὲ καὶ τῶν
ἄλλων Παλληναίων συμμαχίη.

4. ἀρχήν . . τέλος: both words are
adverbial ; ab initio . . ad extremum.
The correspondence of μέν and μέντοι
is en règle ; cp. Madvig § 254.

ἔγωγε οὐκ ἔχω εἰπεῖν (οὐ γὰρ ὦν
λέγεται): both statements are genuine
Herodotus, he never deliberately in-
vents ; but neither implies that he had
made inquiries in loco: his source might
be literary.

6. ὅκως . . γράψειε, opt. of indefinite
frequency ; cp. c. 52 supra. It is not
likely that any of these interesting
documents were preserved, much less
that Hdt. had seen them.

7. τοξεύματος παρὰ τὰς γλυφίδας:
τόξευμα of the arrow itself, as in 4. 132
(τῶνδε τῶν τοξευμάτων = διστοὺς πέντε c.
131). The γλυφίδες have been variously
interpreted: (i.) of "the notched end of

γλυφίδας περιειλίξαντες καὶ πτερώσαντες τὸ βυβλίον ἐτόξευον
ἐς συγκείμενον χωρίον. ἐπάιστος δὲ ἐγένετο ὁ Τιμόξεινος
10 προδιδοὺς τὴν Ποτείδαιαν· τοξεύων γὰρ ὁ 'Αρτάβαζος ἐς τὸ
συγκείμενον, ἁμαρτὼν τοῦ χωρίου τούτου βάλλει ἀνδρὸς
Ποτειδαιήτεω τὸν ὦμον, τὸν δὲ βληθέντα περιέδραμε ὅμιλος,
οἷα φιλέει γίνεσθαι ἐν πολέμῳ, οἳ αὐτίκα τὸ τόξευμα λαβόντες
ὡς ἔμαθον τὸ βυβλίον, ἔφερον ἐπὶ τοὺς στρατηγούς· παρῆν
15 δὲ καὶ τῶν ἄλλων Παλληναίων συμμαχίη. τοῖσι δὲ στρατηγοῖσι ἐπιλεξαμένοισι τὸ βυβλίον καὶ μαθοῦσι τὸν αἴτιον τῆς
προδοσίης ἔδοξε μὴ καταπλῆξαι Τιμόξεινον προδοσίῃ τῆς
Σκιωναίων πόλιος εἵνεκα, μὴ νομιζοίατο εἶναι Σκιωναῖοι ἐς
129 τὸν μετέπειτα χρόνον αἰεὶ προδόται. ὁ μὲν δὴ τοιούτῳ τρόπῳ
ἐπάιστος ἐγεγόνεε· 'Αρταβάζῳ δὲ ἐπειδὴ πολιορκέοντι ἐνεγε-

---

8 γλαφίδας R ‖ βιβλίον Pz   9 ἐγίνετο aC ‖ τιμόξενος Β   10
Ποτείδαιαν van H., Stein³ ‖ ὅ om. Β   12 Ποτειδαιήτεω van H., Stein³
14 βιβλίον Pz ‖ παρῆσαν A (= M), Gronovius   15 συμμαχίηι Β
16 βιβλίον Pz ‖ μαθοῦσα R ‖ τὸ αἴτιον S (Gaisf.), Marc.   17 καταπλέξαι τιμόξενον Β   129. 2 ἐγένετο Pz

---

an arrow-shaft," i.e. notched for the bow-string (but why, then, the plural ? idiomatic, perhaps: besides, you would make the notch with two cuts). (ii.) Stein understands notches (*Kerben*) cut in the arrow for the first and second fingers to draw; but such notches are superfluous. (iii.) Schweighaeuser suggests four notches, or slits for the insertion of the feathers: four is too many (Eurip. *Orest.* 273 f. is not conclusive: οὐχ ὁρᾷθ' ἐκηβόλων Τόξων πτερωτὰς γλυφίδας ἐξορμωμένας; much less *Od.* 21. 419): L. & S. seem to approve. (iv.) Blakesley boldly understands 'barbs,' rather topsy-turvily; it is clearly the upper end of the arrow that is referred to, and γλυφίδες could scarcely mean the (notched) barb: arrows were not always barbed, and barbs were not always notched.

13. οἷα φιλέει γίνεσθαι ἐν πολέμῳ. Had Hdt. seen any fighting, or is this graphic touch from his literary source ? ὅμιλος . . οἳ is κατὰ σύνεσιν.

14. ἔμαθον, 'perceived'—they did not all, or any, read it. (Cp. ἐπιλεξαμένοισι below.)

τοὺς στρατηγούς: of the Poteidaiatai ? or of the allies generally ? In the latter case Timoxenos himself would have been included. If by reading the document they were able to detect the traitor, it must have been written in

Greek and addressed to him ('Αρτάβαζος Τιμοξείνῳ): a gratuitous imprudence.

15. συμμαχίη = σύμμαχοι, abstract for concrete. The list would comprise Aphytis, Neapolis, Aige, Therambos, Skione, Mende, Sane ; cp. 7. 123 *supra*.

17. ἔδοξε μὴ καταπλῆξαι Τ. προδοσίῃ : a formal resolution of the Council of War : προδοσίῃ *proditione*, i.e. *proditionis crimine* ; καταπλῆξαι, if it is to stand (cp. App. Crit.), 'to dumb-founder.' καταπλέξαι would be 'to involve,' entwist ; but the meaning, c. 83 *supra*, is not parallel.

τῆς Σκιωναίων πόλιος εἵνεκα : a strange degree of consideration ! Timoxenos must have been all-powerful in Skione, and Skione in the peninsula. In 423 B.C. Skione revolted from Athens, after the conclusion of the Twelvemonths' Truce (Thuc. 4. 120), for which revolt it afterwards dearly paid (Thuc. 5. 32. 1) ; but there appears to be no reference whatever in Hdt. to those later events.

129. 2. ἐγεγόνεε . . ἐνεγόνεσαν : the tense does not seem of much importance in either case, but has its full temporal value at least in the second ; the 'unconscious iteration,' duplicated by γίνεται and γενόμενον, all within four lines, marks a certain poverty of style. The three months' siege of Poteidaia will have filled the winter of 480-79 B.C.

γόνεσαν τρεῖς μῆνες, γίνεται ἄμπωτις τῆς θαλάσσης μεγάλη
καὶ χρόνον ἐπὶ πολλόν. ἰδόντες δὲ οἱ βάρβαροι τέναγος
γενόμενον παρήισαν ἐς τὴν Παλλήνην. ὡς δὲ τὰς δύο μὲν 5
μοίρας διοδοιπορήκεσαν, ἔτι δὲ τρεῖς ὑπόλοιποι ἦσαν, τὰς
διελθόντας χρῆν εἶναι ἔσω ἐν τῇ Παλλήνῃ, ἐπῆλθε πλημμυρὶς
τῆς θαλάσσης μεγάλη, ὅση οὐδαμά κω, ὡς οἱ ἐπιχώριοι
λέγουσι, πολλάκις γινομένη. οἱ μὲν δὴ νέειν αὐτῶν οὐκ ἐπιστάμενοι διεφθείροντο, τοὺς δὲ ἐπισταμένους οἱ Ποτειδαιῆται 10
ἐπιπλώσαντες πλοίοισι ἀπώλεσαν. αἴτιον δὲ λέγουσι Ποτειδαιῆται τῆς τε ῥηχίης [καὶ τῆς πλημμυρίδος] καὶ τοῦ Περσικοῦ
πάθεος γενέσθαι τόδε, ὅτι τοῦ Ποσειδέωνος ἐς τὸν νηὸν καὶ
τὸ ἄγαλμα τὸ ἐν τῷ προαστείῳ ἠσέβησαν οὗτοι τῶν Περσέων
οἵ περ καὶ διεφθάρησαν ὑπὸ τῆς θαλάσσης· αἴτιον δὲ τοῦτο 15

5 παρῆσαν codd.: παρίεσαν z ‖ μὲν δύο β, Holder   6 διω-
δοιπορήκεσαν Pz ‖ ἔσαν z   7 ἔσω εἶναι βz, Holder   8 ὅσην β ‖
ὡς om. S   9 γενομένης RS: (γινομένης V): γενομένη z ‖ αὐτέων z
10 δ' α, van H. ‖ οἱ om. βPz, Holder, van H. ‖ Ποτειδαιῆται (bis) van H.,
Stein² : ποτιδαιῆται (ποτιδεῆται V)   12 καὶ τῆς πλημμυρίδος del.
Valckenaer, Stein², Holder, van H.   13 ἐς post ὅτι β ‖ νεὸν B
14 τὸ ἐν τῷ προαστείῳ om. β ‖ ἐσέβησαν AB   15 τοίπερ z

3. **ἄμπωτις**, 'ebb,' cp. 7. 198 *supra.*
The words χρόνον ἐπὶ πολλόν are vague ;
it is impossible to say whether Hdt.
means a matter of hours, or of days.
5. **τὰς δύο μέν** κτλ., a curious particularity : at any rate, they had not got
quite half-way. **ὑπόλοιποι**, cp. 7. 171 and
ὑπολειφθέντες c. 67 *supra.*
7. **πλημμυρίς**, 'flood,' flood-tide : the
reverse of ἄμπωτις just above ; this was
the largest on record, or in memory.
The reference, however, in πολλάκις
γινομένη cannot be to normal tidal
phenomena such as he has recorded in
7. 198. This passage and that, from
different sources, are apparently written
without reference to each other. But
Hdt. can hardly be taken in this passage
to be referring to the great tidal disturb-
ances recorded in Thuc. 3. 89. 2 ff. for
the summer of 426 B.C. He has not
been working at his composition so late
as that ; cp. Introduction, § 9.
8. **ὡς οἱ ἐπιχώριοι λέγουσι** : the
authority (not necessary *viva voce*) is
adduced for a statement which Hdt.
merely gives ' for what it is worth ' ; so,
too, just below, **αἴτιον δὲ λέγουσι**
Ποτειδαιῆται. These citations of sources
do not, and are not intended to,
guarantee the statements, much less to
show that Hdt. has cross-questioned the
natives. Cp. Introduction, § 10. αἴτιον
is used here in a less physical sense than
in 7. 125 *supra.*
12. ῥηχίη is plainly identical with
πλημμυρίδος (cp. 2. 11, 7. 198).
15. **αἴτιον δὲ τοῦτο λέγοντες εὖ λέγειν**
ἔμοιγε δοκέουσι. If just the very
' Persians ' (were they all Persians ?),
neither more nor fewer, who perished,
had been guilty of the sacrilege in the
temple of Poseidon, the coincidence
would, indeed, have been remarkable :
but was not the guilt to some extent
inferred from the doom, on the well-
established canon which condemned the
Galileans on whom the tower in Siloam
fell as sinners above all Galileans ?
Hdt. is less of a critic in this passage
than in his rationale of Poseidonian
action at Tempe, 7. 129 *supra.* Perhaps
the direct intervention of the deity was
more intelligible to him, in a case of
human ἀσέβεια, than in the case of a
natural object. Hdt. does not indeed
here actually specify the personal action
of the outraged god ; but he must be
supposed to have taken it for self-evident,
between the ἀσέβεια and the ῥηχίη.
Poteidaia is, of course, a city of Poseidon :
Poseidon Hippios appears on its coinage,

λέγοντες εὖ λέγειν ἔμοιγε δοκέουσι. τοὺς δὲ περιγενομένους
ἀπῆγε Ἀρτάβαζος ἐς Θεσσαλίην παρὰ Μαρδόνιον. οὗτοι μὲν
οἱ προπέμψαντες βασιλέα οὕτω ἔπρηξαν.

130 Ὁ δὲ ναυτικὸς ὁ Ξέρξεω περιγενόμενος ὡς προσέμειξε τῇ
Ἀσίῃ φεύγων ἐκ Σαλαμῖνος καὶ βασιλέα τε καὶ τὴν στρατιὴν
ἐκ Χερσονήσου διεπόρθμευσε ἐς Ἄβυδον, ἐχειμέριζε ἐν Κύμῃ.
ἔαρος δὲ ἐπιλάμψαντος πρώιος συνελέγετο ἐς Σάμον· αἱ δὲ
5 τῶν νεῶν καὶ ἐχειμέρισαν αὐτοῦ· Περσέων δὲ καὶ Μήδων οἱ
πλεῦνες ἐπεβάτευον. στρατηγοὶ δέ σφι ἐπῆλθον Μαρδόντης

---

16 ἐμοὶ S   18 βασιλῆα ℵ ‖ οὕτω ἔπρηξαν om. α   130. 1
ναυτικὸς στρατὸς ℵ ‖ ὁ περιγενόμενος Krueger, van H. : στρατὸς ὁ περιγενόμενος Stourač, cf. Bursian J.b. 86. 54 ‖ προσέμειξε van H., Stein³ :
προσέμιξε   2 βασιλῆα ℵ ‖ τε om. β   3 χερρονήσου β : χερρονήσου C ‖ διεπόρθμευεν β ‖ ἐχειμέρισε Pℵ   4 δ᾽ α, van H. ‖ πρῶτον β
5 νηῶν βℵ   6 καὶ στρατηγοὶ S ‖ δὲ ἐπῆλθόν σφι C ‖ μαρδόνης Marc.

---

and Head (*Hist. Num.* p. 188) regards
the type of the tetradrachm as "doubtless suggested by the sacred image of
Poseidon, which Herodotus mentions as
standing in front of the city, ἐν τῷ
προαστείῳ." The city itself appears to
have been situate astride the isthmus,
fortified north and south by two parallel
walls, and protected east and west by
the sea. The object of the Persians was
to enter the city round the sea end of
the wall (just as Aristeus did in 432 B.C.,
Thuc. 1. 53). Stein's idea that Poteidaia
was not fortified on the S. side appears
to arise from a misinterpretation of
the words in Thuc. 1. 54. 2 τὸ δ᾽ ἐς τὴν
Παλλήνην ἀτείχιστον ἦν, which refer to
the absence of Athenian siege-works on
the south side. As a matter of fact the
Athenians had demanded the dismantling
of the south wall, τὸ ἐς Παλλήνην τεῖχος
Thuc. 1. 54. 2, a demand compliance
with which would have placed the town
at the mercy of the sea-power.

16. τοὺς περιγενομένους: he has 40,000
men in 9. 66 *infra* against 60,000 in
c. 126 *supra*.

130. 1. ὁ δὲ ναυτικὸς ὁ Ξέρξεω: the
narrative shifts to the Persian navy, cp.
c. 117 *supra*. στρατός is omitted, cp.
next c. l. 3. The article is repeated as in
7. 196, and often ; contr. 7. 124 etc.

3. ἐχειμέριζε ἐν Κύμῃ. On Kyme cp.
7. 194 *supra*. The position was well
chosen, in relation to Sardes, to the
northern portion of Ionia and Aiolis,
and to the Hellespont. It appears,
however, immediately that some of the

vessels had wintered at Samos : had
these not been to the Hellespont, after
Salamis ? It is remarkable that Samos,
not Kyme, is the rendezvous in the
spring. χειμερίζειν, cp. c. 118 *supra*.
ἐπιλάμψαντος = ἀρχομένου, a metaphor
from the day transferred to the year
(Sitzler). πρώιος keeps up the metaphor
(Stein). αὐτοῦ, the adv. of place, 'on
the spot.'

5. Περσέων δὲ καὶ Μήδων οἱ πλεῦνες
ἐπεβάτευον. The literal meaning of
these words is : 'Of Persians and Medes
the majority were *Epibatai*.' Not
absolutely, of course, but in relation to
the Strategoi. This appears to give a
very poor antithesis. 'Of Persians and
Medes, serving on the fleet, very few
were other than *Epibatai*.' But perhaps Hdt. meant to say that on the fleet
the majority of *Epibatai* were Medes and
Persians : 'the majority of those serving
as *Epibatai* were of Persians and Medes,'
οἱ πλεῦνες being the predicate : the
genitive remains problematic. He can
hardly mean that the majority of the
Medo-Persian *Epibatai* originally mentioned (7. 96) were still serving on board :
the allusion would be far-fetched. In
any case the expression is wanting in
style and lucidity.

6. στρατηγοὶ δέ. There are three
new admirals, or commanders, for a
fleet of 300 ; but it appears afterwards
that one of the three (Mardontes) is in
command of the *Epibatai*, and the other
two in command of the fleet ; cp. 9.
102.

τε ὁ Βαγαίου καὶ ᾿Αρταΰντης ὁ ᾿Αρταχαίεω· συνῆρχε δὲ
τούτοισι καὶ ἀδελφιδέος αὐτοῦ ᾿Αρταΰντεω προσελομένου
᾿Ιθαμίτρης. ἅτε δὲ μεγάλως πληγέντες, οὐ προήισαν ἀνωτέρω
τὸ πρὸς ἑσπέρης, οὐδ᾿ ἐπηνάγκαζε οὐδείς, ἀλλ᾿ ἐν τῇ Σάμῳ 10
κατήμενοι ἐφύλασσον τὴν ᾿Ιωνίην μὴ ἀποστῇ, νέας ἔχοντες
σὺν τῇσι ᾿Ιάσι τριηκοσίας. οὐ μὲν οὐδὲ προσεδέκοντο τοὺς
῞Ελληνας ἐλεύσεσθαι ἐς τὴν ᾿Ιωνίην ἀλλ᾿ ἀποχρήσειν σφι τὴν
ἑωυτῶν φυλάσσειν, σταθμεύμενοι ὅτι σφέας οὐκ ἐπεδίωξαν
φεύγοντας ἐκ Σαλαμῖνος ἀλλ᾿ ἄσμενοι ἀπαλλάσσοντο. κατὰ 15
μέν νυν τὴν θάλασσαν ἐσσωμένοι ἦσαν τῷ θυμῷ, πεζῇ δὲ

---

7 ἀρταβύτης ibid. : ἀρταΰτης C ‖ ᾿Αρταχαίεω Stein, van H. : ἀρτα-
χαίου   8 τοῖσδε aC, Stein¹ ‖ ἀρταΰντεωι B : ἀρταΰτεω C : ἀρτα-
βύτεω Marc. ‖ προελομένου B   9 ᾿Ιθαμίτρης Wesseling : ὁ ἀμίτηρ R :
ὁ ἀμίτρης ceteri ‖ προήισαν a : προιέσαν βP : προσῆσαν C : προιέσαν z ‖
ἀνωτέρωι aP   10 τό : τὰ βPz ‖ οὐδὲ εἰς β, Holder ('forsan recte'
van H.)   11 νῆας βz   12 μὴν aC, Holder   13 προσελεύσεσθαι z :
πλεύσεσθαι¦ Stein² ‖ τὴν om. β   14 ὅτί σφεας A   15 φεύγοντες C   16 ἐσσώμενοι ἔσαν z

---

Μαρδόντης τε ὁ Βαγαίου has
appeared already as ἄρχων τῶν νησιωτέων
τῶν ἐκ τῆς Ἐρυθρῆς θαλάσσης 7. 80 supra.
He might know something of sea-faring,
but, as a matter of fact, commands the
men-at-arms ; cp. previous note.

7. ᾿Αρταΰντης ὁ ᾿Αρταχαίεω: the
Artachaies, no doubt, who was an
Achaimenid giant, with a colossal voice,
and had been one of the Commandants
of the Canal (cp. 7. 22, 117). One
Otaspes, brother of Artayntes, had
apparently been ἄρχων of the Assyrians,
7. 63 supra.

9. ᾿Ιθαμίτρης was presumably son of
the Otaspes just referred to. The ἄρχων
of the Πάκτυες, however, was one
᾿Αρταΰντης ὁ ᾿Ιθαμίτρεω, 7. 67 supra.

μεγάλως πληγέντες : at Salamis ;
the expression need not be restricted to
the Strategoi. ἀνωτέρω τὸ πρὸς ἑσπέρης
seems to be used as an 'orientation'
simply from the point of view of the
narrative, or dramatis personae, and can
hardly be cited as proof that Hdt. composed this part of his narrative in Asia.

10. ἐν τῇ Σάμῳ κατήμενοι ἐφύλασσον.
Samos was probably the best basis of
naval operations against an Ionia in
revolt, as the Athenians discover in 412
B.C. But the Persians in 479 B.C. are
in full possession of the Hinterland as
well, and the prospect of a merely local
revolt might well look almost hopeless.

12. οὐ μὲν οὐδέ, 'yet also not,' a double
negative, the elements of which, simple
and composite, do not cancel but confirm
each other (Madvig § 209). The opinion
here predicated of the Persians proved
ill-founded, a strategic miscalculation ; if
entertained, it was based perhaps more
on the presence of Mardonios in Greece
than upon the non-pursuit of the
previous year ; but the conjecture put
forward by Hdt. constitutes a justification of the project of Themistokles (c.
108 supra), and condemns pro tanto the
failure of the Greeks to follow up their
victory. The Persian reflexion takes no
account of the pursuit as far as Andros.

14. σταθμεύμενοι : the form σταθμώ-
μενος occurs 7. 237 supra ; σταθμεύμενοι is
found 2. 150. Are we to conclude that
Hdt. used three different forms of one
participle? Or that the MSS. variants are
responsible for the discrepancies? σταθ-
μάομαι, σταθμέομαι, σταθμώομαι are all
possible Ionica (cp. L. & S. sub vv., and
Weir Smyth § 688, p. 570).

15. ἀπαλλάσσοντο : middle (even the
active is used intransitively).

16. ἐσσωμένοι ἦσαν : the imperfect
final verb here is as important as the
perfect participle for describing their
condition, and the combination, so far
from resulting in a plusquam perfectum,
as a thing of the past, denotes an
enduring state of things, or rather of

ἐδόκεον πολλῷ κρατήσειν τὸν Μαρδόνιον. ἐόντες δὲ ἐν Σάμῳ
ἅμα μὲν ἐβουλεύοντο εἴ τι δυναίατο κακὸν τοὺς πολεμίους
ποιέειν, ἅμα δὲ καὶ ὠτακούστεον ὅκῃ πεσέεται τὰ Μαρδονίου
20 πρήγματα.

131   Τοὺς δὲ Ἕλληνας τό τε ἔαρ γινόμενον ἤγειρε καὶ
Μαρδόνιος ἐν Θεσσαλίῃ ἐών. ὁ μὲν δὴ πεζὸς οὔκω συνελέγετο, ὁ δὲ ναυτικὸς ἀπίκετο ἐς Αἴγιναν, νέες ἀριθμὸν δέκα
καὶ ἑκατόν. στρατηγὸς δὲ καὶ ναύαρχος ἦν Λευτυχίδης ὁ
5 Μενάρεος τοῦ Ἡγησίλεω τοῦ Ἱπποκρατίδεω τοῦ Λευτυχίδεω

---

17 πολλὸν B   18 ἐβουλεύσαντο B ‖ δυνέατο Marc. : δύναιντο z
19 καὶ om. BSV ‖ ὅκηι A : ὅση C : ὅκη ceteri   131. 1 γενόμενον
BPz   2 ὅκου C   3 νῆες aBz   4 λεωτυχίδης Aᵐ (bis)   5
μενάριος C ‖ ἠσίλεω B

---

feelings: no doubt in this case τῷ θυμῷ
helps materially to establish the true
aspect of the verb. They had no
stomach for fighting at sea: at the same
time they are described as planning at
Samos how they may injure the enemy
—a fruitless quest, if they were not
prepared to move at sea. The hopes and
attention concentrated on Mardonios
suggest that the fleet was to be prepared
to act, at least on the receipt of good
news, and possibly upon the receipt of
bad news. Though now far apart, the
fortunes and acts of fleet and of army
could not be matters of indifference,
even strategically, one to the other.
Hdt.'s motivations are seldom quite
adequate or satisfactory; but in regard
to the movements, and even the mind
of the naval forces on the Persian side,
he probably had access to Ionian sources,
both narrative and critical, worth something. Cp. Introduction, § 10.

19. ὠτακούστεον ὅκῃ πεσέεται: cp.
καραδοκέοντες . . τῇ πεσέεται 7. 168
supra. The substantive ὠτακουστής occurs
in Aristot. Pol. 8. 11. 7 = 133 B of spies,
'eavesdroppers,' employed by Hieron:
the verb is used by Xenophon and
others.

131. 1. τό τε ἔαρ γινόμενον κτλ., 'the
approach of spring, and the presence of
Mardonios in Thessaly' (cp. c. 113 supra,
133 infra). ἤγειρε, excitabat: not yet
sufficiently, however, to bring an army
together; it was only the ships which
were under way. Aigina is the port of
rendezvous; the fleet is counted at 110;
its composition and the provenience of the
various contingents are left as matters
of inference and conjecture, no less than

the respective numbers of Ionian and
other vessels in the Persian fleet at
Samos, c. 130 supra.

4. στρατηγὸς δὲ καὶ ναύαρχος, 'commander-in-chief and navarch' (primarily
a Spartan title?). Cp. cc. 2 (στρατηγός)
and 42 (ναύαρχος). The investment of a
king with the 'navarchy' is remarkable:
barring Pausanias, the Regent, such a
commission is unparalleled in the fifth
century B.C. After the ὕβρις of Pausanias
(c. 3 supra) there is a long interval to the
appointment of Agesilaos in 395–94 B.C.,
Xenoph. Hell. 3. 4. 27, and Agesilaos
appointed a deputy.

Λευτυχίδης: Leotychidas here
introduced with an immense flourish of
trumpets is an old acquaintance, as the
work now stands; cp. 6. 71 etc. However weak the argument from the
patronymic, the two Herakleid pedigrees
in these Books must be regarded as good
evidence of the earlier composition of
Bks. 7–9. It seems very unlikely that
Hdt. would have reserved these pedigrees
throughout his work for the sake of
especially glorifying Leonidas and Leotychidas at the end, the latter of whom
had little claim to any special honour.
The pedigree of Leotychidas is interesting
as proving the distinction between
generations and reigns, owing to the
especial circumstances of the succession
in his case: one has to go back eight
generations (inclusive) from Leotychidas
to find the king (Theopompos, 13th from
Herakles) whose eight ancestors are
all kings of Sparta.

5. Μενάρεος: Menares (6. 65, 71), the
20th from Herakles, belongs apparently
to the same 'generation' as Demaratos

τοῦ ’Αναξίλεω τοῦ ’Αρχιδήμου τοῦ ’Αναξανδρίδεω τοῦ
Θεοπόμπου τοῦ Νικάνδρου τοῦ Χαρίλεω τοῦ Εὐνόμου τοῦ

---

7 Χαρίλεω Stein, Holder : χαρίλλου β, van H. : χαρίλου ‖ τοῦ
ἡρακλέος τοῦ εὐνόμου C

---

the son of Ariston, whose complete
pedigree is recoverable from Pausanias,
3. 7, and the antecedent names in the
two Eurypontid pedigrees run back in
pairs, neck and neck, to Theopompos.
'Ηγησίλεω: this Hegesileos (Agesilas, Agesilaos) appears in 6. 65 *supra*
as Agis, which may be regarded as the
hypokoristic, or diminutive, but shows
the independence of Hdt.'s sources, and
how little he is at pains to harmonize
them. This Agesilas is 19th from
Herakles, and corresponds with Ariston
in the pedigree of Damaratos (7. 3 *supra*,
etc.).
'Ιπποκρατίδεω. An Hippokratidas
is credited in Plutarch (*Mor.* 222) with
a couple of apophthegms, but as one
is addressed to a satrap of Karia, its
author can hardly be this man. Names
compounded with Ἱππο- are not common
in Sparta, where ἱπποτροφία was comparatively rare ; cp. c. 124 *supra*. Hippokratidas, as 18th from Herakles, ranges
with Agesikles in the parallel pedigree.
Λευτυχίδεω : Leotychidas ὁ πρῶτος
is distinguished by Plutarch (*Mor.* 224)
from Leotychidas son of Ariston (*sic*),
and credited with four smart apophthegms (on Opportunism, Economics,
Education, Sobriety). Leotychidas is
17th from Herakles, ranging with
Archidamos I. (On the form of the
name Λευ- = Λεω- [Λα-?] cp. Weir Smyth,
§ 287, p. 254.)
6. ’Αναξίλεω. This Anaxilas, the
16th from Herakles (= Anaxidamos in
the parallel line), may be the author
of the apophthegm preserved in Plutarch
Mor. 217 on the Ephoralty, and might
just possibly be identified with the man
who sat in judgement on the Atheno-
Megarean question, Plutarch *Solon* 10.
The name was not common at Sparta,
and was never borne by a king; the
Anaxilaos of Xenoph. *Hell.* 1. 3. 19 is
Βυζάντιος καὶ οὐ Λακεδαιμόνιος.
’Αρχιδήμου. Archidamos, the
15th from Herakles in the pedigree of
Menares (= Zeuxidamos in the parallel
list), bears a name which was not uncommon in the reigning house of
Eurypontids (Prokleids), though never
borne by an Agid (Eurysthenid) king.

Thus this grandson of Theopompos may
have been named from his uncle (through
whom the sceptre descended), and no
less than five kings in all bore the name,
of whom the best known was Hdt.'s contemporary, who succeeded Leotychidas.
’Αναξανδρίδεω: the name Anaxandridas is familiar as that of the (15th)
Agid king, son of Leon, and father of
Kleomenes, as of Dorieus, Leonidas, and
Kleombrotos ; cp. 7. 204 *supra*. This
Anaxandridas, 14th in descent from
Herakles, is not otherwise known to
fame than as the founder of the cadet
branch of the Eurypontids (Prokleids).
His name corresponds with that of his
brother Archidamos in the now elder
branch of the House. This Archidamos
was never king ; Theopompos was
succeeded by his grandson Zeuxidamos
(Pausan. 3. 7. 5). It is rather odd that
the Eurypontid (Prokleid) succession in
the eighth century B.C. should thus anticipate, with so nice a difference, the
succession in the fifth century B.C., when
Zeuxidamos, son of Leotychidas, predeceased his father, leaving an Archidamos to succeed ; cp. 6. 71 *supra* ; the
story preserved in Pausanias looks like
fiction modelled on the facts of the fifth
century. The Eurypontid line of kings
would seem to be longer-lived, or longer-
reigned, than the Agid, for Leotychidas
is but the 16th king, and in the 16th
generation, from Aristodamos, while
Leonidas is the 18th king in the elder
House ; and this discrepancy is rather
increased than diminished subsequently;
but then the lists of kings, and even the
genealogies, are not above suspicion.
With Hdt. Leonidas and Leotychidas
are in the same generation (21st) from
Herakles.
7. Θεοπόμπου: on Hdt.'s own showing (see below) Theopompos is the 9th
king of Sparta (Aristodamos included),
and the 13th generation from Herakles
included, corresponding to Teleklos in
the pedigree of Leonidas, 7. 204 *supra*.
This is the only passage in which the
name of this king—of whom later writers
have so much to tell us—occurs in the
work of Hdt. A great external crisis,
the ‘first’ Messenian war (Pausan. 4.

Πολυδέκτεω τοῦ Πρυτάνιος τοῦ Εὐρυφῶντος τοῦ Προκλέος

8 Πολυδέκτεω Valckenaer: πολυδέκτεος ‖ τοῦ πρυτάνιος om. C ‖
Εὐρυπῶντος Valckenaer, van H., deinde <τοῦ Σόου>, sed vide comment.
infra

4. 3), and a great internal development,
the institution of the Ephors (Aristot.
Pol. 8. 11. 2=1313 A), were dated to his
reign. The story of the Messenian wars
is virtually a lost chapter in Spartan
history to Hdt. (cp. 3. 47, the sole
articulate reference in the work): the
Ephoralty he expressly ascribes to
Lykourgos, 1. 65. The importance of
King Theopompos dates apparently from
the Delphic researches of the (Agid)
King Pausanias early in the fourth
century B.C. Cp. Ed. Meyer, Forschun-
gen, i. (1892) 211 ff.

Νικάνδρου: Nikandros is 8th
king in Sparta and 12th descendant
of Herakles (corresponding thereby to
Archelaos in the pedigree of Leonidas,
7. 204 supra). The later writers have
something to say of him: Plutarch Mor.
250 records three apophthegms (one of
them addressed to an Athenian, and
assuredly not earlier than the fifth
century); Pausanias 2. 36. 5, 3. 7. 4
associates his name especially with the
invasion of Argolis.

Χαρίλεω: Charilaos is 7th king
of Sparta, and 11th descendant of
Herakles (corresponding thereby to
Agesilaos in the pedigree of Leonidas,
7. 204 supra). The name appears in
the Politics of Aristotle in two forms,
Χάριλλος (2. 10. 2=1271 B) and Χαρίλαος
(8. 12. 12=1316 A); and later tradition had something to say of him,
making him out a 'tyrant,' yet also
the nephew and ward of Lykourgos,
and associated in his Reforms (Plutarch
Lykourg. 5). This latter point is in
direct conflict with Hdt. 1. 65, where
Lykourgos appears associated with the
elder House, two (or, as the Greeks
would have said, three) generations
earlier. Pausanias (2. 36. 5, 3. 7. 3,
4. 4. 3), who gives the father's name as
Polydektes (not Eunomos), reversing the
Herodotean order, represents Charillos as
engaged in war especially with Argos
and with Tegea (ll.c.), and as taken
prisoner by the Tegeatai (8. 5. 6) but
liberated after swearing that the Lakedaimonians should never again invade
Argolis, an oath soon broken (8. 48. 5).
Hdt. can hardly have been acquainted

with this story (obviously an Argive
tale) when he wrote 1. 66.

Εὐνόμου: Eunomos is 6th king
of Sparta and 10th descendant of
Herakles, corresponding thereby with
Doryssos in the pedigree of Leonidas,
7. 204 supra; his name is perhaps
suspiciously significant, coming about
the time of Lykourgos, and none the
less so in view of the Εὐνομία of Tyrtaios
(Aristot. Pol. 8. 7. 3=1306 B), and the
fact that Lykourgos was made his son,
in the fourth century theory (cp. Plutarch
Lykourg. 2); but the name is not an uncommon one in the historical period (e.g.
Xenoph. Hell. 5. 1. 5). More suspicious
is the fact that the lists followed by
Pausanias reversed the order of the
names Eunomos and Polydektes, and
that even Pausanias has nothing to tell
us of Eunomos but that he was son of
Prytanis, and that in his reign, and in
his son's, 'the land had rest,' ἐν εἰρήνῃ
διετέλεσεν οὖσα ἡ Σπάρτη (3. 7. 2). According to Plutarch (l.c. supra) he came
to a violent end, being struck down
with a cleaver, in the praiseworthy
attempt to terminate a brawl.

8. Πολυδέκτεω: Polydektes is the
5th king of Sparta and the 9th
descendant of Herakles, corresponding
thereby with Labotas in the pedigree
of Leonidas, 7. 204 supra. Curiously
enough, the name Polydektes is otherwise only associated with mythical
characters, viz. (1) as an epithet of Hades,
Hymn to Demeter, 9 ; (2) as king of
Seriphos, son of Magnes, brother of
Dictys, changed into a stone, Pindar,
Pyth. 12. 24, Pausan. 1. 22. 7, Arrian,
Anab. 3. 3. 1 etc.

Πρυτάνιος: Prytanis is the 4th
king in Sparta, and the 8th descendant of Herakles: corresponding thereby
with Echestratos in the pedigree of
Leonidas, 7. 204 supra. The name is of
course significant, and as a magisterial
title (though not apparently in actual
use at Sparta) somewhat suspicious ;
but historical examples of its use as a
proper name are forthcoming (the earliest,
a Lykian, Iliad 5. 678, also a boxer
from Kyzikos, Pausan. 5. 21. 3, and
others). The statement of Pausan. 3.

τοῦ Ἀριστοδήμου τοῦ Ἀριστομάχου τοῦ Κλεοδαίου τοῦ Ὕλλου τοῦ Ἡρακλέος, ἐὼν τῆς ἐτέρης οἰκίης τῶν βασιλέων. 10 οὗτοι πάντες, πλὴν τῶν ἑπτὰ τῶν μετὰ Λευτυχίδεα πρώτων

11 ἑπτὰ Paulmier: δυῶν (δυῶν z: cum τῶν om. R)

---

7. 2 that the quarrel between Sparta and Argos began in his reign is worth very little, even if it be not contradicted by the next words, that the Spartans had previously made war on the Kynurians.

τοῦ Εὐρυφῶντος: the aspirate in the word is observable; the usual form is Εὐρυτῶν, for which the variant Εὐρυτίων (a more intelligible proper name) occurs, as in Plutarch *Lykourg.* 2 where Valckenaer's emendation Εὐρυτῶντα (and Εὐρυτωντίδας) is now accepted. (So too in Polyain. 2. 13.) This Eurypon is 3rd king in Sparta, and 7th descendant of Herakles, corresponding thereby with Agis, in the pedigree of Leonidas, 7. 204 *supra.* Pausanias (3. 7. 1) only tells us of him that he attained such glory that the House was called Eurypontidai after him, Προκλείδας ἐς ἐκεῖνον καλουμένους. Plutarch *Lykourg.* 2 gives as the reason, ὅτι δοκεῖ πρῶτος Εὐρυτῶν τὸ ἄγαν μοναρχικὸν (sic) ἀνεῖναι τῆς βασιλείας, δημαγωγῶν καὶ χαριζόμενος τοῖς πολλοῖς. That speculation might provoke further speculation: was it really Eurypon who established the 'younger' House, or obtained recognition for it, in the constitution of Sparta, the dual royalty only dating from his day? Polyainos (*l.c. supra*) has a strange story of the ruse by which Eurypon obtained possession of the city of Mantineia for the Lakedaimonians, a story which suffers under a double anachronism, in crediting Mantineia with a democracy, and the democracy with surrendering the city to Eurypon. Stein² wished to insert τοῦ Σόου after Εὐρυφῶντος. This project was for the purpose of harmonizing Hdt. with Pausanias and with himself (1. 65, 67), as Stein⁵ avers. But in reality it would have the effect of dislocating Hdt. himself, whose pedigrees of the two Houses correspond generation by generation, and king for king, as above shown. Hdt. is plainly of a different opinion to Pausanias, 3. 1. 7, in regard to the correspondences.

Πρόκλεος: the 2nd king in Sparta (reckoning Aristodemos), the 6th descendant of Herakles, the twin-brother of Eurysthenes, and the apparent,

though not the nominal founder, not the Eponym, of the younger House; cp. previous note. With Prokles we pass on to ground already familiar, cp. 6. 52, 4. 147 *supra.* The legend of the twins is, of course, an aetiological fiction. Pausanias has nothing to add to the stories in Hdt., but Polyainos again (1. 10) opposes the 'Herakleid' Prokles to the 'Eurystheids' who were in possession of Sparta, and has him win a victory over them, thanks to his pipers. This sporadic tradition is perhaps the most suggestive, the most historic-looking fossil, in the legendary records of Sparta. The name Prokles is borne by many historical personages, cp. 3. 50 (an Epidaurian), Xenoph. *Hell.* 8. 1. 6 (cp. note to Hdt. 6. 70), 6. 5. 38 (a Phleiasian) etc.

9. Ἀριστοδήμου: with this name the dual pedigree, and the dual royalty, cease; Aristodemos is monarch, in or out of Sparta, and 5th descendant of Herakles; cp. note to 7. 204 *supra.* It is possible that Aristodemos is a genuine ancestor in the pedigree of the 'younger,' the true Herakleid, and perhaps Dorian, House: the legend of the Twins has inserted him also as ancestor of the Agid, i.e. Eurysthenid or Eurystheid, House, which was already in possession, and with him his legendary ancestors Kleodaios, Hyllos, Herakles. On these names see further notes to 7. 204 *supra*; and on the still earlier and mythological stages of the pedigree, 6. 53 f.

10. τῆς ἑτέρης οἰκίης τῶν βασιλέων: these words appear to contain an implicit reference back to the pedigree of the other House in 7. 204 *supra.* Such references imply the solidarity of these three Books.

11. πλὴν τῶν ἑπτὰ τῶν μετὰ Δ. πρώτων: ἑπτά is a certain emendation; cp. App. Crit. Hdt. might seem to have fallen into the vulgarism 'seven first' instead of 'first seven'; but πρώτων is to be taken predicatively with καταλεχθέντων. It is a material inaccuracy to reckon the heroes before Aristodemos as 'kings of Sparta,' unless indeed Hdt. means titular or pretendant; but he should not be charged with reckoning

καταλεχθέντων, οἱ ἄλλοι βασιλέες ἐγένοντο Σπάρτης. Ἀθη-
132 ναίων δὲ ἐστρατήγεε Ξάνθιππος ὁ Ἀρίφρονος. ὡς δὲ
παρεγένοντο ἐς τὴν Αἴγιναν πᾶσαι αἱ νέες, ἀπίκοντο Ἰώνων
ἄγγελοι ἐς τὸ στρατόπεδον τῶν Ἑλλήνων, οἳ καὶ ἐς Σπάρτην
5 ὀλίγῳ πρότερον τούτων ἀπικόμενοι ἐδέοντο Λακεδαιμονίων
ἐλευθεροῦν τὴν Ἰωνίην· τῶν καὶ Ἡρόδοτος ὁ Βασιληίδεω
ἦν· οἳ στασιῶται σφίσι γενόμενοι ἐπεβούλευον θάνατον
Στράττι τῷ Χίου τυράννῳ, ἐόντες ἀρχὴν ἑπτά· ἐπιβουλεύοντες

---

12 βασιλήες z   132. 2 νήες z   3 ἐς τὴν z   4 τουτέων z
6 στασιῶται C: στασιῶταί ‖ σφίσι C: σφισι ad : σφι βPz   7 στάττι
β : στράττί cum η lit. ult. superscr. C : στράντη Marc.

'Archidemos son of Theopompos,' who predeceased his father, among the βασιλέες Σπάρτης (Stein⁸). Hdt. nowhere even mentions him. Cp. note p. 561b supra.

18. Ξάνθιππος ὁ Ἀρίφρονος: the patronymic, though he has been mentioned 7. 33 supra, is not surprising, even if that passage be not of later insertion ; cp. 6. 131, 136. Xanthippos was one of the returned exiles, cp. c. 79 supra, and may, like Aristeides, have already been elected one of the Strategoi for 480-79 B.C.

132. 2. Αἴγιναν: a relatively advanced post, which would have left Salamis exposed, if all the Greek ships had been taken so far ; we may reasonably doubt whether Salamis was thus exposed during the reoccupation of Attica. 110 ships would not account even for the Athenian fleet.

Ἰώνων ἄγγελοι = πρέσβεις 'L. (cp. 7. 1 supra): six in number ; see below. The genitive is observable ; they were apparently all Chians, but they act in the general interest, and with authority, for they demand the liberation of 'Ionia.' The story is curious and probably incomplete.

4. ὀλίγῳ πρότερον τούτων: the chronological indication leaves something to be desired, but suggests the winter or spring of 480-79, and even a point after the rendezvous of the fleet at Aigina.

ἐδέοντο : Stein remarks on this as a surprising use of the imperfect ; but explains it (in a note on ἐφέροντο 1. 66) by two considerations : (a) the extremely free use made of the imperfect by Hdt. (wie wohl kein anderer Autor), not so much with strict temporal reference, as with regard to the importance or energy of the action ; (b) and especially in

relative or secondary sentences, where it is freely so used without regard to the temporal relation of the verb to the main sentence and its predicate. As a specially characteristic case he cites 5. 21 καὶ οὗτοι . . διεφθάρησαν . . εἴπετο γάρ κτλ. (a passage in which immediately afterwards the pl. p. ἠφάνιστο occurs) ; cp. also 7. 195 ἦγε, etc.

5. Ἡρόδοτος ὁ Βασιληίδεω. Baehr approves Dahlmann's supposition that the author would not have named his namesake unless they had also been relatives ; but surely the coincidence in their names (and their fortunes, each opposing the 'tyrannis' in his native place) might be reason enough. Herodotos, son of Basileides, the Chian, is not otherwise known to fame. Baehr, vol. iv. p. 401 ff., has compiled a list of about a score of men bearing the name of Herodotos, the majority late-comers. Cp. also Pape-Benseler. The Chian, and the Theban for whom Pindar wrote Isthm. 1, are the only ones contemporary with or prior to our author. (An old Chian inscrip., however, has Ἀθηναγόρης Ἡροδότου C.I.An. 382, Stein.) Basileides, too, is a not uncommon name attested for Athens, Kos, Rhodes, etc. Pape-Benseler, i. 199 sub v.

6. στασιῶται σφίσι γενόμενοι: σφίσι = ἀλλήλοις. Stein takes the phrase as implying that the conspirators came together from various cities (or townships), six or seven of which can just be discovered in Chios ; cp. Forbiger, Alt. Geogr. ii. 199 (Chios, Delphinion, Bolissos, Kaukasa, Polichne, Leukonion, 'the Hollows') : but why should not all the cabal have been resident in the capital ? For the figure 'seven' there was ͪigh precedent ; cp. 3. 70.

7. ͪΣτράττι. A Strattis is named in

δὲ ὡς φανεροὶ ἐγένοντο, ἐξενείκαντος τὴν ἐπιχείρησιν ἑνὸς
τῶν μετεχόντων, οὕτω δὴ οἱ λοιποὶ ἐξ ἐόντες ὑπεξέσχον
ἐκ τῆς Χίου καὶ ἐς Σπάρτην τε ἀπίκοντο καὶ δὴ καὶ τότε 10
ἐς τὴν Αἴγιναν, τῶν Ἑλλήνων δεόμενοι καταπλῶσαι ἐς τὴν
Ἰωνίην· οἱ προήγαγον αὐτοὺς μόγις μέχρι Δήλου. τὸ γὰρ
προσωτέρω πᾶν δεινὸν ἦν τοῖσι Ἕλλησι οὔτε τῶν χώρων
ἐοῦσι ἐμπείροισι, στρατιῆς τε πάντα πλέα ἐδόκεε εἶναι, τὴν

8 ἐγίνοντο αC   9 οὕτω δὴ: οὗτοι B ‖ ἐξ ἐόντες abesse malit
van H.   10 τε om. ßPz   12 προήγαγον δὲ sine οἱ B   13
προσωτέρωι α : προτέρω B

4. 138 as one of the Ionian 'tyrants' on
the Danube in 512 B.C., i.e. 33 years or
so before the date here reached : is this
the same man, or his descendant ? And
at what date was the plot actually
hatched ? ἀρχήν, as in c. 128 *supra*.

8. ἐξενείκαντος τὴν ἐπιχείρησιν: one
of the participants published, or betrayed,
the plot ; for this meaning of ἐκφέρειν
cp. 3. 71, 74.

9. ὑπεξέσχον, as in 5. 72, 'made their
way out secretly.'

10. καὶ δὴ καί, a phrase perhaps not so
common in these Books ; cp. c. 134. 4.

τότε seems to separate somewhat
the visit to Aigina from the visit to
Sparta ; otherwise it might be supposed
that they had been referred by the home
government to the King Navarch at
Aigina.

12. προήγαγον αὐτοὺς μόγις μέχρι
Δήλου, 'with difficulty the Ionian
ambassadors persuaded the Hellenic
admirals to move forwards as far as
Delos.' There follows the motivation,
or rationale, of this reluctance in the
form of two reasons : first, ignorance
of the topography, a point further
emphasized by the remark upon Samos
and the pillars of Herakles ; and secondly,
apprehension of encountering resistance,
that is, of course, in the shape of the
Persian fleet. Hdt. does not suggest
that the naval movements were in any
degree dependent on the operations of
Mardonios and the Persian forces behind
them in Greece. In his scheme of
presenting the facts Mardonios has not
yet been brought into Central Greece,
but is wintering in Thessaly. Literary
methods here help to obscure the real
sequence and nexus of events.

14. τὴν δὲ Σάμον ἐπιστέατο δόξῃ καὶ
Ἡρακλέος στήλας ἴσον ἀπέχειν. At
Delos they were considerably more than
half-way from Aigina to Samos. This is
the only passage in these Books in which
'the Herakleian Pillars' are mentioned :
indeed, save for the mention of them in
2. 33, they are only mentioned in Bk. 4
(and therein seven times, cc. 8, 43, 152,
181, 185, 196), a striking illustration of
the 'Western' interest in that Book.
The form of the designation in Hdt. is
always adjectival (never Ἡρακλέοι στῆλαι,
as in Strabo 169), and the passages cited
leave no room for doubt as to its
geographical significance (=straits of
Gibraltar), but Hdt. nowhere indicates
exactly what he understands by the
phrase. His contemporary Euktemon,
of Athens, apparently understood the
expression to apply to two Islands, 30
stades distant from each other, covered
with wood, and inaccessible for large
vessels, and each provided with a temple
and an altar of Herakles : Euktemon *ap.*
Avienum, *Or. maritim.* ed. A. Holder (cp.
Berger, *Gesch. d. Wissensch. Erdkunde,*
ii. 67). Pomponius Mela (temp.
Claudii), a native of the region, considered the Pillars, or Columns, to be the
two mountains, Calpe (*Gibraltar*) and
Abyla ('Αβύλυκα, Strabo 170 : *Ceuta*),
rising on the European and African side
of the straits respectively (2. 6. 96 ; cp.
Bunbury, *Anc. Geogr.* ii. 358). Poseidonios, however, his predecessor, who
spent a considerable time at Gades
(Strabo 174), believed that the Pillars
were literally Pillars, to wit, the bronze
Pillars 8 cubits (12 feet) high in the
Herakleion at Gades ; cp. Strabo 170,
where the various alternatives (including
that afterwards favoured by Mela) are
set out and discussed, Strabo himself
finally inclining to the metaphorical
meaning (but not deciding between
'islands' and 'mountains'). Our
clearer knowledge of the early import-

15 δὲ Σάμον ἐπιστέατο δόξῃ καὶ Ἡρακλέας στήλας ἴσον ἀπέχειν. συνέπιπτε δὲ τοιοῦτο ὥστε τοὺς μὲν βαρβάρους τὸ πρὸς ἑσπέρης ἀνωτέρω Σάμου μὴ τολμᾶν καταπλῶσαι καταρρωδηκότας, τοὺς δὲ Ἕλληνας, χρηιζόντων Χίων, τὸ πρὸς τὴν ἠῶ κατωτέρω Δήλου. οὕτω δέος τὸ μέσον ἐφύλασσε σφέων.

133 Οἱ μὲν δὴ Ἕλληνες ἔπλεον ἐς τὴν Δῆλον, Μαρδόνιος δὲ

---

15 ἠπιστέατο Pz ‖ δόξῃ secl. van H. 16 τοιοῦτον Β : τοιούτῳ z
17 ἀνωτέρωι a ‖ καταπλῶσαι : ἀναπλῶσαι ? Stein : πλῶσαι van H. ‖
καταρρωιδηκότες P 18 verba χρηιζόντων τῶν Χίων suspecta habet
van H. : χρηιζόντων Apr. : τῶν χίων Β 19 κατωτέρωι aP : κατώτερον
Marc. ‖ δέος ΒΡz : δὲ ἐς ‖ ἐφύλασσέ σφεων Stein¹, Holder, van H. : (ἐφύ-
λασσόν z) 133. 1 ἔπλωον Βz, van H.

---

ance of Pillar-worship (cp. A. J. Evans, *Mycenaean Tree and Pillar Cult*, 1901), and its undoubted association with the Tyrian Herakles (cp. Hdt. 2. 44) might incline us to take the western 'Pillars of Herakles' as really marking the limits of Phoenician navigation, and the meta-phorical application as an afterthought ; but such phrases as δι᾽ Ἡρακλέων στηλέων ἐκπλέειν, διεκπερᾶν .(4. 42, 43, 152) suggest that Hdt. uses the phrase with the metaphorical reference, and would have set the pillars either side the strait. The statement that "the Greeks at Delos (in 479 B.C.) believed (ἐπιστέατο δόξῃ, an interesting collocation) Samos as far off (ἀπέχειν, cp. 9. 52 *infra*) as Gades" is characterized by Rawlinson as "perhaps the grossest instance in Hdt. of rhetorical exaggeration" (5. 97 runs it close). But it should not be put down primarily to Hdt., least of all with the object, "by an imaginary effect of contrast, to place in a more striking light the rapid increase during his own time of nautical power and enterprise among his European fellow-countrymen" (Mure, quoted by Blakesley *ad l.*). Nor is it to be treated (so by Blakesley himself) as a serious record of real matter of fact, or feeling, explicable by the evil associations which had gathered at Sparta round "the voyage to Samos" (cp. 3. 56). The case is really much simpler. The phrase reproduces the impatience of Hdt.'s Ionian source with the cautious policy of the Spartan navarch (for which there were good grounds enough) ; or perhaps it even reflects the scornful witticisms of a period, the *Pentekontaëteris*, when Athenian policy had practically made the Aegean a *mare clausum* to Peloponnesian long-

ships. At Delos the Hellenic fleet was in sight of Samos on a clear day, and before very long, in this very same year, crossed boldly to that bourne (9. 90 ff.). Hdt.'s device of projecting this account of the naval movement into the record of the previous winter and early spring has softened the inconsequence. What kept the Greek fleet at Delos was, first, that they demanded further assurances from the Ionians, and secondly, that they had to consider the situation behind them in Greece. Cp. Appendix IV. § 9, VII. § 7.

16. συνέπιπτε . . ὥστε : cp. c. 15 *supra* ; there of a strictly formal coincidence, here of a rather more material one.

17. καταπλῶσαι Stein regards as a slip on a copyist's part for ἀναπλῶσαι, cp. καταπλῶσαι ἐς τὴν Ἰωνίην just above, but καταπλῶσαι would then need to be supplied with κατωτέρω Δήλου, so the passage is not quite precisely composed ; hence van Herwerden's suggestion is preferable ; cp. App. Crit.

18. χρηιζόντων Χίων : the six Chians had presented themselves at Sparta, at Aigina, as Ἰώνων ἄγγελοι, but they were really or primarily mere στασιῶται, and their credentials may have been incomplete : the fleet advances on the advent of a Samian embassy, 9. 90 *infra*.

19. τὸ μέσον, 'the intervening space,' i.e. mutual fear kept them apart. Cp. 7. 11 *supra*.

133. 1. ἔπλεον : on this imperfect cp. c. 132 *supra*. Here it seems to be calculated rather with regard to what follows—the account of Mardonios, whose actions preceded in temporal order the move to Delos, or even the move to Aigina.

περὶ τὴν Θεσσαλίην ἐχείμαζε. ἐνθεῦτεν δὲ ὁρμώμενος ἔπεμπε
κατὰ τὰ χρηστήρια ἄνδρα Εὐρωπέα γένος, τῷ οὔνομα ἦν
Μῦς, ἐντειλάμενος πανταχῇ μιν χρησόμενον ἐλθεῖν, τῶν οἱά
τε ἦν σφι ἀποπειρήσασθαι. ὅ τι μὲν βουλόμενος ἐκμαθεῖν 5
πρὸς τῶν χρηστηρίων ταῦτα ἐνετέλλετο, οὐκ ἔχω φράσαι·
οὐ γὰρ ὦν λέγεται· δοκέω δ' ἔγωγε περὶ τῶν παρεόντων
πρηγμάτων καὶ οὐκ ἄλλων πέρι πέμψαι. οὗτος ὁ Μῦς ἔς 134

---

2 ἐχειμέριζε? Krueger, van H. ‖ ὁρμεόμενος ΒΡ, Stein[1], van H. :
ὁρμεώμενος Cz   3 τὰ om. Β ‖ Εὐρωμέα emend. Stein, recep. Holder,
van H.   4 χρησάμενον αCP, Stein[1]   5 ἐκμαθέειν z   7 δὲ Β
8 περιπέμψαι Β

---

2. περὶ τὴν Θεσσαλίην ἐχείμαζε: cp.
c. 113 supra. The word χειμάζειν here
(=Hdtn. χειμερίζειν) is observable ; cp.
7. 191.

ἐνθεῦτεν δὲ ὁρμεόμενος : has the participle any real force ? Does it mean ' as
he was starting,' i.e. before leaving ; or
simply ' from headquarters there ' (op.
c. 112 ἐξ Ἄνδρου ὁρμώμενος, where the
phrase is not quite so much atrophied) ?

3. κατὰ τὰ χρηστήρια : the preposition is observable, and appears to be
used locally and distributively rather
than of the object or purpose of the
mission (i.e. not ad consulenda oracula) ;
Stein ops. 1. 30 τὸν Σόλωνα θεράποντες
περιῆγον κατὰ τοὺς θησαυρούς.

Εὐρωπέα γένος, τῷ οὔνομα ἦν Μῦς,
'a man of Europos by name Mys.'
Europos as a place-name or town (fem.)
is found in several quarters, notably in
Makedonia, Thuc. 2. 100. 3. (The towns
of this name in further Asia were probably
Makedonian foundations ?) The man
here named was evidently a Karian, cp.
c. 135 infra : Steph. B. sub v. ἔστι καὶ
ἄλλη Καρίας, τὴν Ἰδριάδα, ἀπὸ Ἰδρίος τοῦ
Χρυσάορος (sc. ὀνομάζουσι). On Ἰδριάς
cp. 5. 118. Oddly enough Steph. B.
also has sub v. Εὐρώμος· πόλις Καρίας,
ἀπὸ Εὐρώμου τοῦ Ἰδριέως Καρός. τὸ
ἐθνικὸν Εὐρωμεύς. Of Europos he gives
the ethnikon as Εὐρώπιος. Stein[2] suggested
Εὐρωμέα as the true reading here, and
Stein[5] suggests that Εὐρωπέα is an
ancient error for Εὐρωμία (sic), i.e. from
the small Karian town of Εὔρωμος (also
Τρωμος). Blakesley (overlooking the
Karian utterance of the Pythia below)
makes Mys a Makedonian, and (observing
that Europe was a surname of Demeter
in the cult of Trophonios, Pausan. 9.

39. 5), an 'Achaian' to boot. Mys
(mouse, 2. 141) as a proper name
is curious, but genuine ; there are
several later instances, e.g. Pausan. 1.
28. 2 (a celebrated artist, possibly
contemporary with Pheidias, as he is
said to have executed the reliefs on the
shield of the Promachos) : a boxer, of
Tarentum, Suidas sub v. etc.

4. τῶν οἱά τε ἦν σφι ἀποπειρήσασθαι :
notwithstanding its plural form, οἱα does
not refer to χρηστήρια, but=ποῖε or fas
esset : one relative is enough ! The
ἀπόπειρα of the Oracles by Mardonios, or
Mys, is a genuine consultation, not a
trial (διάπειρα 1. 47) or testing, like that
of Kroisos 1. 46. On the contrary, it is a
remarkable homage on the part of the
Persian to the Greek religion. Delphi
is apparently not one of the centres it is
possible for him to consult !

6. οὐκ ἔχω φράσαι· οὐ γὰρ ὦν λέγεται·
δοκέω δ' ἔγωγε . . Hdt. s conjecture
appears eminently reasonable, and is
confirmed pro tanto by the anecdote in
9. 42 infra : it is, however, remarkable that Hdt. had not been able to
discover the purport of Mardonios'
inquiries—in other words, he had not
been able to obtain any of the answers
given to Mys. This circumstance
certainly does not enhance the credit of
the story, and taken in conjunction with
the conspicuous absence of the Pythia,
suggests the suspicion that the whole
story may be a part of the Rettung of
Delphi. But it has a bona fide air
withal, and reads like a Boiotian
memory. Was it, perhaps, one of the
tales told Hdt. by his Boiotian friend
Thersander of Orchomenos ? Cp. 9. 16,
and Introduction, § 10.

τε Λεβάδειαν φαίνεται ἀπικόμενος καὶ μισθῷ πείσας τῶν
ἐπιχωρίων ἄνδρα καταβῆναι παρὰ Τροφώνιον, καὶ ἐς Ἄβας
τὰς Φωκέων ἀπικόμενος ἐπὶ τὸ χρηστήριον· καὶ δὴ καὶ ἐς

---

134. 2 λαβάδειαν C || ἀπικόμενος φαίνεται z   3 ἀνδρῶν ἄνδρα
Marc.   4 δὴ καί : δὴ B

---

134. 2. Λεβάδειαν: though the oracle
is mentioned 1. 46, this is the only
passage in Hdt. where the name of the
city occurs, the modern *Livadia*, a place
of more importance in Roman and
Turkish than in ancient times. Plutarch
Lys. 52 mentions its capture and sack by
Lysander ; Strabo 414 marks its position : Λεβάδεια δ' ἐστίν, ὅπου Διὸς Τροφωνίου μαντεῖον ἱδρυται, χάσματος ὑπονόμου
κατάβασιν ἔχον, καταβαίνει δ' αὐτὸς ὁ
χρηστηριαζόμενος· κεῖται δὲ μεταξὺ τοῦ
Ἑλικῶνος καὶ τῆς Χαιρωνείας, Κορωνείας
πλησίον. Pausanias 9. 39, 40 describes
the ritual from his own experience, and
gives the story of the origin of the
oracle. The process of consultation was
extremely awful, and expensive, and
apparently could not be carried on
properly by a deputy, or deputy's
deputy (as contemplated in this case).
The oracle was, of course, chthonian,
and τροφώνιος perhaps originally an
epithet of Zeus.

3. καταβῆναι παρὰ Τροφώνιον: the
grove (ἄλσος) of Trophonios was situate
beyond the river Herkyna, which rose
out of a cave in a gorge on Helikon.
The worshipper crossed the stream and
ascended through the grove (ἀναβᾶσι δὲ
ἐπὶ τὸ μαντεῖον Pausan. *l.c.*) to the cave
in which the actual rite took place.
Several days' preparation and initiation were necessary before the votary
was permitted 'to descend' (ἐς τοῦ
Τροφωνίου κατιέναι), and the privilege
was reserved for the male sex (cp. ἄνδρα
here, and ἀνδρὶ Pausanias *l.c.*). Purifica-
tions, divinations, sacrifices, are the
order of the day, culminating in the
offering of a ram on the night of the
actual descent. You are first washed in
the Herkyna, and anointed, by two
acolytes, or 'Hermai'; the priests then
take you in hand, give you to drink of
the waters of Oblivion and of Remembrance, display to your adoring gaze the
ancient image, and invest you with
proper garb, for the dire ordeal. You
then essay 'the descent' into the house
of Trophonios. In the oracular chamber
is a mysterious opening, or well, care-

fully built round and over, about six
feet in diameter, and some twelve feet
in depth, looking like an oven. Into
this pit you descend by a light ladder,
introduced for the purpose, taking some
honey-buns with you (cp. Aristoph.
Clouds 507 f.). Arrived at the bottom,
you find a small opening at one side, just
large enough to admit you feet foremost :
you lie down on your back and work
through it ; and no sooner have your
knees passed the aperture than you find
yourself suddenly and irresistibly drawn
or sucked down into the Holy of holies.
There the secrets of the future are
revealed to you in a way over which
Pausanias somewhat abruptly drops the
curtain. The exit has to be effected by
the same entrance (στόμα τὸ ἱερόν), and
again feet foremost. By this time you are
more dead than alive, but the ordeal is
not over. The priests set you on the
seat of Remembrance, and question you
on what you have seen and heard below :
after they have obtained the requisite
information, they return you to your
anxious relatives or attendants, who
convey you, in a state of trance or
unconsciousness, back to your apart-
ment at the sign of 'Good Luck and the
Daimon.' But do not despair : no
proper consultant has ever been known
to expire under the ordeal, and some
have lived to smile again after it.

ἐς Ἄβας : it required some effron-
tery on the part of the Persian to consult
this oracle of Apollon ; cp. c. 33 *supra* !
Blakesley tries to get over the difficulty
by supposing that the sack of the shrine
was not the work of the division of the
army commanded by Mardonios—but
according to Blakesley himself Mardonios
was commander-in-chief all along ; and
again, that compensation was now made
—of which Hdt. says nothing. The
important point is that Hdt. is unconscious of the difficulty, so completely
independent are his various stories one
of another.

4. καὶ δὴ καί : c. 132 *supra*.

ἐς Θήβας may be taken in a wide
sense to cover all the territory subject

Θήβας πρῶτα ὡς ἀπίκετο, τοῦτο μὲν τῷ Ἰσμηνίῳ Ἀπόλλωνι 5
ἐχρήσατο· ἔστι δὲ κατά περ ἐν Ὀλυμπίῃ ἱροῖσι αὐτόθι
χρηστηριάζεσθαι· τοῦτο δὲ ξεῖνον τινὰ καὶ οὐ Θηβαῖον χρήμασι πείσας κατεκοίμησε ἐς Ἀμφιάρεω. Θηβαίων δὲ οὐδενὶ
ἔξεστι μαντεύεσθαι αὐτόθι διὰ τόδε· ἐκέλευσε σφέας ὁ Ἀμφιά-

5 ἰσμινίῳ B　　　　6 κατά: καὶ τὰ B　　　　8 κατεκοίμωσε aPz ‖
ἀμφιάρεωι B: ἀμφιάραον Paris. 1635, z　　　9 ἐκέλευσέ σφεας Stein[1],
van H.: ἐκέλευέ σφεας CPz, Holder ‖ ἀμφιάρεος B: Αμφιάραος z

to Thebes (so Baehr): the temple of Amphiaraos was not in Thebes proper. πρῶτα is rather puzzling; nothing is said of a second visit, though doubtless he had been to Thebes in passing through with the army to and from Athens, and doubtless visited it again in company with Mardonios (cc. 34, 50, 113 supra, 9. 2, 15 etc. infra). The meaning is complicated by τοῦτο μέν· τοῦτο δέ (in the first place, in the second place) immediately following. Stein suggests that πρῶτα ὡς ἀπίκετο equals πρῶτα ἀπίκετο, ἀπικόμενος δέ, but adds that Thebes was the first place he visited (coming from Mardonios in Thessaly?). Could Hdt. have meant ὡς πρῶτα ('as soon as he reached Thebes')? Cp. ὡς τάχιστα 1. 65.

5. τῷ Ἰσμηνίῳ Ἀπόλλωνι: cp. 5. 59, a passage which proves that Hdt. himself had at some time visited this shrine. It was perhaps subsequently, and after his visit, that he added the gloss-like note immediately succeeding ἔστι δὲ . . χρηστηριάζεσθαι. The procuration of a χρηστήριον by 'pyromancy' appears to be a special form of Divination, developed by the Iamidai (cp. 9. 33 infra) of Elis ; Pindar Ol. 8. 2 μάντιες ἄνδρες ἐμπύροις τεκμαιρόμενοι παραπειρῶνται Διὸς ἀργικεραύνου. Cp. Bouché-Leclerq ap. Darenberg et Saglio, Dict. ii. 298, 299. It was practised also in Thebes ; cp. Sophok. O.T. 21 ἐπ' Ἰσμηνοῦ τε μαντεία σποδῷ.

7. ξεῖνον τινὰ . . κατεκοίμησε: Plutarch Aristeid. 19 reports the actual dream which visited the 'Lydian,' and which exactly prefigured the death of Mardonios.

8. ἐς Ἀμφιάρεω: this oracle too figures in the list of Kroisos (cp. 1. 46, 49, 52), who, πυθόμενος αὐτοῦ τήν τε ἀρετήν καὶ τὴν πάθην, made presents to him, which in Hdt.'s time had been transferred to the temple of Ismenian Apollo (1. 52), perhaps to prevent their passing under

Athenian dominion. The actual shrine of Amphiaraos himself was at Oropos, Pausan. 1. 34. His valour had been shown in his slaughter of Melanippos (in return for the deaths of Mekisteus and Tydeus; cp. 5. 67); his 'passion' in his terrible fate, the earth opening and swallowing him up, chariot and all, Pindar Nem. 9. 24, Aischyl. Septem 568 ff. The cult was confined practically to Peloponnesos and Central Greece, especially Boiotia (Bethe ap. Pauly-Wissowa, i. 1887), and the departed seer is really 'a chthonian deity of praehistoric Greece,' who, in the person of his son Amphilochos (cp. Thuc. 2. 68. 3), draws one step nearer to historic verisimilitude. The oracle was a dream-divination (Pausanias 1. 34. 5): the consultant, after due purification and sacrifice, sacrifices also a ram, goes to sleep upon its fell, and awaits a dream-revelation (ἀναμένοντες δήλωσιν ὀνείρατος). Amphiaraos is in some respects a replica of Trophonios (both being also distinctly of the Asklepios-type), perhaps because both are forms of chthonian Zeus.

Θηβαίων δὲ οὐδενὶ ἔξεστι: this taboo, or excommunication, is interesting. Was it restricted to Oropos (αὐτόθι bis), or were Thebans universally excluded from the cult of Amphiaraos? There was another Boiotian shrine of Amphiaraos near Potniai (Pausan. 9. 8. 3), but Pausanias does not record any divination there ; at Harma, however, near Mykalessos, there was a temple (Strabo 404) in which, at least in later times, oracles were to be had (Bethe, l.c. supra). The context here might seem to imply that Thebans had once had oracles, or at least one response, of their ally.

9. διὰ τόδε: the taboo is obviously a much more certain fact than the reason given for it. The true reason might perhaps be sought in the difference of race between the Boiotians of Thebes

10 ρεως διὰ χρηστηρίων ποιεύμενος ὁκότερα βούλονται ἑλέσθαι
τούτων, ἑωυτῷ ἢ ἅτε μάντι χρᾶσθαι ἢ ἅτε συμμάχῳ, τοῦ
ἑτέρου ἀπεχομένους· οἱ δὲ σύμμαχόν μιν εἵλοντο εἶναι. διὰ
τοῦτο μὲν οὐκ ἔξεστι Θηβαίων οὐδενὶ αὐτόθι ἐγκατακοιμηθῆναι.

135 τόδε δὲ θῶμά μοι μέγιστον γενέσθαι λέγεται ὑπὸ Θηβαίων·
ἐλθεῖν ἄρα τὸν Εὐρωπέα Μῦν, περιστρωφώμενον πάντα τὰ
χρηστήρια, καὶ ἐς τοῦ Πτῴου Ἀπόλλωνος τὸ τέμενος. τοῦτο
δὲ τὸ ἱρὸν καλέεται μὲν Πτῷον, ἔστι δὲ Θηβαίων, κεῖται δὲ
5 ὑπὲρ τῆς Κωπαΐδος λίμνης πρὸς ὄρεῖ ἀγχοτάτω Ἀκραιφίης

---

11 τουτέων z || μάντει a || χρῆσθαι ad : χρέεσθαι reliqui   13
κατακοιμηθῆναι βPz   135. 1 τόδε Wesseling, van H., Stein³ :
τότε || θῶυμά CPz, Stein¹   2 ἄρα : γὰρ ? van H. || Εὐρωμέα Holder,
van H., cf. c. 133 supra || Μῦν del. van H. || τὰ om. β   3 πτώιου A :
πτώου   4 καλέεται . . ἱρὸν om. R || πτώιον a : πτῷον || κέεται PSV,
Stein¹   5 κοπαΐδος A || ὄρει A¹BS : οὐρεῖ || ἀγχοτάτωι aP : ἀγχοτάτῳ z
|| ἀκραιφνίης C

---

and the pre-Boiotian population to the
south, and on the Attic border. Cult
is stiffer than myth : the Boiotians of
Thebes might appropriate the story of
Amphiaraos and make him their friend
and ally, but they could not get rid of
the religious interdict. They then
invented this reason to account for the
fact.

10. διὰ χρηστηρίων ποιεύμενος : per
oraculum cum iis agens, Baehr : apparently a spontaneous act. τούτων
refers irregularly to the following alternatives.

12. ἀπεχομένους is strong middle.
ἐγκατακοιμηθῆναι = μαντεύεσθαι supra.

135. 1. τόδε : cp. App. Crit. τότε
would mean in 479 B.C.

θῶμά μοι μέγιστον : μοι, à mon avis
(Larcher) ; but not exactly maxime
mirum (Baehr), rather miraculum, me
judice, maximum.

γενέσθαι, 'to have taken place.'

λέγεται ὑπὸ Θηβαίων : the citation
of the source seems to suggest a doubt,
or at least to decline a responsibility.
ἄρα continues the note of admiration,
or marks an advance, a heightening, of
the action. (Cp. Index sub v.)

2. περιστρωφώμενον πάντα τὰ χρ. :
περιστρωφάομαι, a frequentative of περι-
στρέφομαι, itself a word suggesting a
rather hurried procedure, is perhaps
hardly complimentary to Mys, whose
methods all through are somewhat
summary : is the word supplied by the

'Theban' source ? The construction
resembles περιπλέοντες τὰς νήσους 6. 99.
Should not πάντα include Delphi ?

3. τοῦ Πτῴου Ἀπόλλωνος τὸ τέμενος,
'the close of Ptoian Apollon,' i.e. the
Apollo of Mount Ptous, the god being
apparently named from the mount, not
the mountain from the god. Mytho-
logically Ptoos was a son of Athamas
and Themisto (Asios ap. Pausan. 9. 23. 6),
perhaps an afterthought. On the connexion of Athamas with this district
cp. 7. 197 supra. The meaning of the
word is obscure : Grasberger (Gr. Ortsnamen, p. 279) suggests 'Schreckenberg'
(cp. Schreckhorn in Bernese Oberland) ;
cp. Φρίκιον < Φρίκωνις ? >, etc. Hdt.'s
precise description of the site in the
quasi-note τοῦτο δὲ . . πόλιος suggests
autopsy ; the note may be an addition.
The force of the antithesis καλέεται μὲν
. . ἔστι δέ is not obvious, but perhaps
the sense that the name was older than
the Theban (Boiotian) invasion and
conquest underlies it.

5. τῆς Κωπαΐδος λίμνης : this is the
only express mention in Hdt. of the
Kopaic lake which occupied so large a
space in W. Boiotia, at least in the
winter months. The Κωπαῆς or men
of Κῶπαι, the township which gave its
name to the lake, are mentioned by
Thucyd. 4. 93. 4. Strabo 410-11 says
that the lake had been called partially
after the various cities on its edge until
the name of (the insignificant) Kopai

πόλιος. ἐς τοῦτο τὸ ἱρὸν ἐπείτε παρελθεῖν τὸν καλεόμενον
τοῦτον Μῦν (ἕπεσθαι δέ οἱ τῶν ἀστῶν αἱρετοὺς ἄνδρας τρεῖς
ἀπὸ τοῦ κοινοῦ ὡς ἀπογραψομένους τὰ θεσπιεῖν ἔμελλε), ...
καὶ πρόκατε τὸν πρόμαντιν βαρβάρῳ γλώσσῃ χρᾶν. καὶ τοὺς
μὲν ἑπομένους τῶν Θηβαίων ἐν θώματι ἔχεσθαι ἀκούοντας 10
βαρβάρου γλώσσης ἀντὶ Ἑλλάδος, οὐδὲ ἔχειν ὅ τι χρήσωνται
τῷ παρεόντι πρήγματι· τὸν δὲ Εὐρωπέα Μῦν ἐξαρπάσαντα
παρ' αὐτῶν τὴν ἐφέροντο δέλτον, τὰ λεγόμενα ὑπὸ τοῦ
προφήτεω γράφειν ἐς αὐτήν, φάναι δὲ Καρίῃ μιν γλώσσῃ
χρᾶν, συγγραψάμενον δὲ οἴχεσθαι ἀπιόντα ἐς Θεσσαλίην. 15

7, 8 (ἕπεσθαι . . ἔμελλε) cancellos pos. Stein³ ‖ δέ om. ßz, Holder,
van H. ‖ θεσπιέειν ß, Stein¹ ² ‖ lacunam indic. Stein³   9 τὴν z ‖
μάντιν Ppr.S   10 θωῦματι ß, Stein¹, Holder ‖ ἐνέχεσθαι Krueger
11 οὐδ' ß ‖ χρήσωνται aPcorr.: χρήσονται   12 χρήματι C ‖ Εὐρωμέα? vide 2 supra ‖ Μῦν del. van H.   13 αὐτέων z   14 γράφην B
‖ γλώσσῃ : φωνῇ ß

---

prevailed: κοιλότατον γὰρ τοῦτο τὸ χωρίον,
that place being deepest in the vale (and
so never dry).

'Ακραιφίης: Akraiphia ('Ακραίφνιον
Pausan. 9. 23. 5) was apparently an
unimportant township belonging to
Thebes (though to judge by the coinage
"it must have enjoyed intervals of
autonomy," Head, *Hist. Num.* p. 292),
and is described by Pausanias (*l.c.*) as
standing some fifteen stades to the left
of the temple. Dr. Frazer's note
(*Pausanias* v. 97 ff.) deals with the whole
situation fully from personal observation. The precise site of the temple
(which has been archaeologically ex-
plored) is described (*ib.* p. 100) as a
steep slope, elaborately terraced, high
up on the chief mountain in the Ptoan
range. On the highest or sixth terrace
there is a spring; the temple actually
stood on the fifth; lower down the hill
is an artificial cavern, connected with
the spring above by an earthenware
conduit; the oracles were perhaps
delivered in this cavern by the prophet,
who had previously drunk of the water
of the spring (an act paralleled by the
procedure of the prophet of the Clarian
Apollo, Frazer *l.c.*).

6. ἐπείτε παρελθεῖν: the *oratio obliqua*
is resumed for the Theban narrative,
after the interposed note in Hdt.'s own
person. One must understand that the
Theban government had appointed three

commissioners to wait upon Mys. The
subject of ἔμελλε must be ὁ θεός.

9. καὶ πρόκατε: there is an apparent
parataxia, but if the text is correct, Hdt.
must have forgotten the ἐπείτε above,
and the result is an anakoluthon.
Stein⁵ supposes some words to have
fallen out, e.g. ἵζεσθαί τε ἐς τὸ μέγαρον.
The seer is here a man (τὸν πρόμαντιν),
not a woman as at Delphi.

χρᾶν: as in 1. 55, 4. 155.

10. ἐν θώματι ἔχεσθαι, 'were spell-
bound'; cp. below.

11. Ἑλλάδος: (as always) an adjective.
οὐδὲ ἔχειν, 'were at a complete
loss'; cp. 5. 12.

13. τὴν ἐφέροντο δέλτον: on the
imperf. cp. note c. 182 *supra*.

τὰ λεγόμενα ὑπὸ τοῦ προφήτεω
γράφειν: it is tantalizing to think that
this precious tablet was carried off by
Mys to Thessaly, without even a copy
being left behind! Nor does it appear
that Hdt. had seen the original. There
is no hope of recovering it now.

14. Καρίῃ μιν γλώσσῃ χρᾶν: sc. τὸν
προφήτην = τὸν πρόμαντιν. Unless Mys
was a Karian the selection of the Karian
language would have been rather pointless. The story may be substantially
true; it would not have been difficult
to arrange that the prophet should
babble a few words of Karian to the man
of Euromos, or Europos. One need not

136 Μαρδόνιος δὲ ἐπιλεξάμενος ὅ τι δὴ λέγοντα ἦν τὰ χρηστήρια, μετὰ ταῦτα ἔπεμψε ἄγγελον ἐς Ἀθήνας Ἀλέξανδρον
τὸν Ἀμύντεω ἄνδρα Μακεδόνα, ἅμα μὲν ὅτι οἱ προσκηδέες
οἱ Πέρσαι ἦσαν· Ἀλεξάνδρου γὰρ ἀδελφεὴν Γυγαίην, Ἀμύντεω
5 δὲ θυγατέρα, Βουβάρης ἀνὴρ Πέρσης ἔσχε, ἐκ τῆς οἱ ἐγεγόνεε
Ἀμύντης ὁ ἐν τῇ Ἀσίῃ, ἔχων τὸ οὔνομα τοῦ μητροπάτορος,
τῷ δὴ ἐκ βασιλέος τῆς Φρυγίης ἐδόθη Ἀλάβανδα πόλις

136. 1 ἦν λέγοντα Pᴢ   3 οἱ R   4 ἔσαν z   6 τὸ om. C
‖ ὄνομα van H. ‖ τοῦ: τὸ ßP: 'fortasse ἔχων ὄνομα τὸ τοῦ' van H.
7 τῷ: τὸ ß ‖ Ἀλάβαστρα Steph. Byz. quod verum opin. Stein, in text. rec.
Holder: cf. comment. infra

summon up the 'subliminal consciousness' to explain this miracle.
136. 1. ἐπιλεξάμενος ὅ τι δὴ λέγοντα
ἦν τὰ χρηστήρια, 'after reading what
the oracles were saying, whatever it was,'
a good illustration of the deceptive
character of the *formulae* of the *vox viva*
when used to establish the nature of
Hdt.'s sources ; cp. Introduction, § 10.
2. μετὰ ταῦτα : i.e. 'after doing so.'
ἄγγελον = πρεσβέα (cp. 7. 1), and is
predicative.
Ἀλέξανδρον τὸν Ἀμύντεω ἄνδρα
Μακεδόνα : the mere occurrence of the
patronymic would not surprise, even
though Alexander has been introduced
at great length in Bk. 5, and mentioned
before in these Books ; but the precise
repetition of the formula of 7. 173 *supra*
is a little perplexing, and that formula
is in itself remarkable. The repetition
is, perhaps, to be explained by the hypothesis that the present passage is of
earlier composition, and the passage in
Bk. 7 a later insertion. The peculiar
formula itself, which ignores the fact
that Alexander was at this time king in
Makedonia, is more difficult to away
with. Blakesley suggests that "out of
delicacy to democratic feelings" Hdt.
omits reference to Alexander's true
position—an explanation which sounds
a little thin : more probably Hdt. takes
over the phrase from his source, whatever it was ; an explanation which, it
must be admitted, only puts the
difficulty one step backwards : perhaps
the recognition of this passage as
relatively early in Hdt.'s composition
may ease his apparent oversight. The
complete independence of the present
passage is shown by a reference to c. 34
supra, where Alexander is acting as
king or commander of ἄνδρες Μακεδόνες.

3. Hdt. gives two co-ordinate reasons
(ἅμα μὲν .. ἅμα δέ) for the selection of
Alexander as ambassador to Athens :
(i.) his special relation to the Persians on
the one side ; (ii.) his special relation to
the Athenians on the other.
προσκηδέες : *affinitate coniuncti*, cp.
Pollux 3. 5 ff. (ὅσοι τὴν οἰκειότητα τὴν πρὸς
ἡμᾶς ἐκ συνθήκης ἀλλ' οὐκ ἐξ ἀνάγκης
ἔχουσι ib. 6 ; προσκηδεῖς καθ' Ἡρόδοτον
ib. 30).
4. Γυγαίην .. Βουβάρης .. ἔσχε,
'had to wife' (cp. 7. 61. 13). The story
of this marriage is told in Bk. 5. 21.
This match was a precedent for the
Great Alexander, had he needed one.
The absence of an reference here to that
passage is significant for the problem of
composition, and points to the priority
of the present passage. Cp. Introduction, §§ 7, 8. The name Γυγαίη in
Makedonia (cp. 1. 93 for Lydia) is remarkable ; cp. c. 138 *infra*. On Bubares
cp. 7. 22 *supra*.
5. ἐγεγόνεε Ἀμύντης : this Amyntas,
son of Bubares and Gygaia, had no doubt
long been born (ἐγεγόνεε) in 480 B.C., the
marriage of his parents having taken
place at least a quarter of a century
before ; but the date of his establishment
as a boy or grandee in Asia Minor is not
so clear, nor whether it was due to
Dareios or to Xerxes : probably the
latter.
6. μητροπάτορος : 6. 131.
7. τῆς Φρυγίης .. Ἀλάβανδα : there
is a double difficulty here : (i.) Alabanda
was under a native tyranny apparently,
cp. 7. 195. But as the tyrant was taken
by the Greeks in 480 B.C. (*l.c.*) Amyntas
might have been appointed to succeed
him. (ii.) But Alabanda was, and is there
correctly described as being, in Karia.
Rawlinson observes that geographical

μεγάλη νέμεσθαι· ἅμα δὲ ὁ Μαρδόνιος πυθόμενος ὅτι πρόξεινός
τε εἴη καὶ εὐεργέτης ὁ Ἀλέξανδρος ἔπεμπε. τοὺς γὰρ Ἀθηναίους οὕτω ἐδόκεε μάλιστα προσκτήσεσθαι, λεών τε πολλὸν 10
ἄρα ἀκούων εἶναι καὶ ἄλκιμον, τά τε κατὰ τὴν θάλασσαν

---

8 δὲ Wesseling e cod. Ask.: τε ‖ πρόξενός codd. z   9 εὐεργέτης
Ἀθηναίων Reiske: 'an σφι εἴη?' Stein², van H.   10 ἐδόκει van H. ‖
προσκτήσασθαι BPpr. ‖ ληόν van H.

---

limits were not always strictly defined;
still, it would be rather curious to find
Hdt. putting a large city into Karia in
one Book, and into Phrygia in the next,
without a word of explanation; though
the difference of sources, and the
historian's indifference to their dis-
harmony, will doubtless account for a
good deal; cp. Introduction, § 11. Stein
approves of Steph. B. Ἀλάβαστρα, πόλις
Φρυγίας. Ἡρόδοτος. But unfortunately
the other authorities, Ptolemy 4. 5. 59,
Pliny 5. 9. 61, place Alabastra in Egypt
(cp. 3. 20).

8. νέμεσθαι: epexegetical infinitive.
πρόξεινός τε . . καὶ εὐεργέτης: on
the προξενία cp. 6. 57, 9. 85. What
beneficium Alexander conferred, or can
have conferred on the Athenian democracy before 480 B.C. (unless his action
recorded 7. 173 supra were to be so
accounted), is unknown: Blakesley
suggested that the connexion was with
the Peisistratids, not with the Athenian
democracy; cp. 5. 94. But there may
have been some approximation during
the period of the Ionian Revolt. The
story here is doubtless tinged with afterthought and anachronism; following
the Persian war there must have been
friendly relations between Athens and
Makedon for a time, or off and on, during
Alexander's reign. Athenian aggression
in the north, culminating in the foundation of Amphipolis in 436 B.C. (Busolt
III. i. 558), must have strained these
relations; and it is quite clear from
Thucydides that the hostility of Perdikkas, son of Alexander, precipitated
the (so-called) 'Peloponnesian' war
(Thuc. 1. 56. 2, 57. 2 etc.).
The structure of the passage Μαρδόνιος
δὲ . . ἔπεμπε is not elegant or quite
correct: oratio turbata, Baehr. It runs:
Μαρδόνιος δὲ ἐπιλεξάμενος . . ἔπεμπε . .
ἅμα μὲν ὅτι . . long parenthesis . . ἅμα
δὲ ὁ Μαρδόνιος πυθόμενος ὅτι εἴη . . ἔπεμπε.
Perhaps it marks Hdt.'s less accomplished
and earlier style.

9. τοὺς γὰρ Ἀθηναίους: his object
was to obtain the alliance, or the
allegiance, of the Athenians, whereto his
motive was simply the desire to win
command of the sea.
Hdt. fully endorses this calculation
(τά περ ἂν καὶ ἦν): alliance with Athens
would have given Mardonios, and Persia,
a vast superiority at sea.
Mardonios can hardly have failed to
understand (what Hdt. appears in this
place to miss) that the predominance at
sea would ipso facto carry predominance
by land too—not merely by withdrawing
the Athenian land-force from the confederate army, and completely localizing
resistance in the Peloponnese, but by
opening wide the doors into the Peloponnese itself—as Hdt. elsewhere and
afterwards implies (9. 9 infra, cp. 7. 139
supra). In this passage command of
the sea is treated as a purely negative
condition, however important, and
Mardonios having obtained it, by
alliance with Athens, is to finish the
struggle on land simply with his own
land-forces.
The passage also runs into a somewhat
verbose testimonial to Athenian prowess,
ex hypothesi apparently now conveyed
to Mardonios by word of mouth (ἀκούων)
for the first time. As a matter of fact
Mardonios must long have known all
this and much more about the Athenians,
cp. 7. 6 supra. Hdt. is here perhaps the
victim of his Attic sources.
11. ἄρα, 'to his surprise' (rather
than 'of course'): perhaps there is a
touch of irony in the word.
τά τε κατὰ θάλασσαν . .
ἠπίστατο. The verb is co-ordinate with
ἐδόκεε, and in its Herodotean use not of
much stronger import (cp. c. 132 supra):
the co-ordinate sentence, however, extends from τοὺς γάρ to καὶ ἄλκιμον, and
the material considerations in the mind
of Mardonios are, ex hypothesi, (i.) the
number and valour of the Athenians, (ii.)
their recent achievements at sea.

συντυχόντα σφι παθήματα κατεργασαμένους μάλιστα Ἀθηναίους
ἐπίστατο. τούτων δὲ προσγενομένων κατήλπιζε εὐπετέως τῆς
θαλάσσης κρατήσειν, τά περ ἂν καὶ ἦν, πεζῇ τε ἐδόκεε πολλῷ
15 εἶναι κρέσσων, οὕτω τε ἐλογίζετο κατύπερθέ οἱ τὰ πρήγματα
ἔσεσθαι τῶν Ἑλληνικῶν. τάχα δ' ἂν καὶ τὰ χρηστήρια
ταῦτά οἱ προλέγοι, συμβουλεύοντα σύμμαχον τὸν Ἀθηναῖον
ποιέεσθαι· τοῖσι δὴ πειθόμενος ἔπεμπε.

137   Τοῦ δὲ Ἀλεξάνδρου τούτου ἕβδομος γενέτωρ Περδίκκης

---

12 σφίσι? van H.   13 ἐπιστέατο Β : ἠπίστατο z ‖ τουτέων z
14 ἂν : ἦν z ‖ ἐδόκει van H.   15 κρείσσων Β   16 τῶν om. C ‖
ἑλλήνων. τάχα δὲ τὰ Β   17 προλέγουσι Β : προλέγει z   18
ποιεῖσθαι van H. : οἱ ποιήσασθαι Β   137. 1 περδίκης ΒCΒ

---

12. The παθήματα may include Artemision as well as Salamis (but hardly
the disasters due to the storm !): in
any case the view ascribed to Mardonios
differs from the official Greek view, c. 93
supra, though it represents exactly the
Athenian view, cp. Thucyd. 1. 74.

15. κατύπερθε . . ἔσεσθαι: cp. c. 19
supra.

16. τάχα δ' ἂν καὶ τὰ χρηστήρια
ταῦτά οἱ προλέγοι: Hdt. opines that
Mardonios may have been urged to the
above course (ταῦτα) by the oracles
(consulted by Mys). Rawlinson observes
that the Theban "and Phokian" oracles
may very well have done so (well,
hardly Abai, cp. c. 134 supra—but
perhaps Delphi ?). The ἀκούων above
suggests that Mardonios was being
worked upon : his Theban advisers below
(9. 2) have still a card in reserve. The
construction with the opt. present (and
a suppressed protasis) is observable : the
explanation by the res praeterita which
is diuturnior vel saepius repetita (Baehr)
is hardly applicable : Stein calls it ' a
potential present' and cps. 1. 70 τάχα δὲ
ἂν καὶ οἱ ἀποδόμενοι λέγοιεν κτλ., certainly
a more difficult case, for here the opt.
pres. might seem to accord with the
phrase used above, ἐπιλεξάμενος ὅ τι δὴ
λέγοντα ἦν τὰ χρηστήρια.
137. 1. τοῦ δὲ Ἀλεξάνδρου τούτου
ἕβδομος γενέτωρ. An excursus follows
(cc. 137-139) on the origin of the Makedonian monarchy. That this story is
given in these Books rather than in Bk.
5. 22, yea, actually there promised, is
strong evidence in favour of the hypothesis that Bks. 7, 8, 9 are of earlier composition ; cp. Introduction, §§ 7, 8 : that
it is given here rather than at 7. 173

is perhaps in favour of regarding that
passage as of later insertion ; cp. Introd.
§ 9.
The Makedonian pedigree could hold
its own with the Achaimenid (7. 11
supra), to say nothing of its affiliation,
through Temenos, with Herakles (cp. c.
139 infra). The 'seven' are reckoned
inclusively, notwithstanding γενέτωρ
(pro-genitor : an hapaxlegomenon in
Hdt.).
Περδίκκης. Did Alexander himself emphasize the founder's name by
giving it to his own son and successor
(c. 454 B.C.) ? Is the legend, in its Herodotean form, older than the accession
of Perdikkas II. (c. 454 B.C.) ? See
below. In any case Hdt. was hardly
the first author to reduce it to writing,
or even to prose : that had surely
been done already at the Makedonian
Court. Thucydides in 2. 99. 3 asserts
the Argive and Temenid descent, in 2.
100. 2 gives the same number of kings
(without the names), adding Perdikkas
and Archelaos his own contemporaries ;
and in 5. 80 supplies a practical illustration of the force of the Argive claim
(alliance in 417 B.C.). Another and
perhaps later saga made Karanos
(Κάρανος), son or brother of Pheidon of
Argos, found the dynasty, to be succeeded
by Κοῖνος, Τυρίμμας, Περδίκκας. This
version was first given vogue by
Theopompos ; cp. Vell. Pat. 1. 6. 5
Circa quod tempus (sc. Carthag. cond.)
Caranus, vir generis regii, sextus decimus
ab Hercule (?), profectus Argis, regnum
Macedoniae occupavit : a quo magnus
Alexander quum fuerit septimus decimus,
iure materni generis Achille auctore,
paterni Hercule gloriatus est. Cp.

ἐστὶ ὁ κτησάμενος τῶν Μακεδόνων τὴν τυραννίδα τρόπῳ
τοιῷδε. ἐξ Ἄργεος ἔφυγον ἐς Ἰλλυριοὺς τῶν Τημένου
ἀπογόνων τρεῖς ἀδελφεοί, Γαυάνης τε καὶ Ἀέροπος καὶ
Περδίκκης, ἐκ δὲ Ἰλλυριῶν ὑπερβαλόντες ἐς τὴν ἄνω 5
Μακεδονίην ἀπίκοντο ἐς Λεβαίην πόλιν. ἐνθαῦτα δὲ ἐθήτευον
ἐπὶ μισθῷ παρὰ τῷ βασιλέι, ὃ μὲν ἵππους νέμων, ὃ δὲ βοῦς,

---

3 ἰλλυρικοὺς β　　5 περδίκης CS ‖ ἰλλύρων R ‖ ὑπερβαλλόντες BV
6 δὲ: καὶ z　　7 βασιλεῖ AB

Pompeius Trogus 7. 1. 7 ff., Theopompus
Frag. 29, 30 (Mueller i. 283). A third
variant was supplied by Euripides'
Ἀρχέλαος, cp. Nauck[1] p. 339, Hyginus
Fab. 219 (quoted in full by Nauck
and by Stein). This story was more
romantic. Archelaos, a son of Temenos,
exiled by his brethren, took refuge in
Makedonia, and having won a victory
for the king, demanded his promised
reward (regnum et filiam): the king,
however, sought his benefactor's life:
the plot was betrayed: Archelaos took
his would-be slayer in the pit prepared
for him: inde profugit ex responso
Apollinis in Macedoniam capra duce
oppidumque ex nomine caprae Aegas
constituit. As this story was obviously
adopted by Euripides in compliment to
the reigning Archelaos, so the version
in Hdt. is probably a compliment to
Perdikkas, devised on his accession
(the precise circumstances of which are
obscure; cp. Busolt, III. i. 558, ii. 792).

2. τῶν Μακεδόνων τὴν τυραννίδα: the
phrase is remarkable: had Hdt. not
yet acquired his horror of the τυραννίς,
or does he mean to condemn Perdikkas
I. and his whole descent, or does he take
the phrase over from his source, or does
he design to prepare the way for the
Spartan epigram (c. 142 infra), or does
calling the Makedonian principality a
tyranny assimilate it to Greek conditions, or is τυραννίς used here as it
might be of the Lydian, or any foreign
monarchy? Cp. 7. 52 supra.

3. ἐξ Ἄργεος. There existed an
Ἄργος Ὀρεστικόν in the Orestis (cp.
Thuc. 2. 80. 6), a district round the
sources of the Haliakmon, in Upper
Makedonia; Strabo 326 reckons the
Orestis to Epeiros, and records the
foundation of this Argos by Orestes:
obviously an etymological fallacy. Probably the Makedonian royal house had
as little real connexion with Peloponnesian Argos as had Orestes with

the Orestis in Upper Makedonia. ἐς
Ἰλλυριούς perhaps gives the real ὅθεν
ὁρμώμενοι. Cp. l. 5 infra.

4. Γαυάνης: Stein takes the name as
= βουκόλος, cp. Sansk. gō = βοῦς, γῆ.
If so, Hdt. has got the translations or
interpretations just below in reverse
order.

Ἀέροπος: the name appears in its
Ionic form 9. 26 infra; the preservation of the proper form here will be due
to the source. The name might perhaps
be applicable to the herder of horses,
'swift as air,' but there was a mountain
bordering on the Aous of that name,
Livy 32. 5. 11, and Hesychios has the
gloss Ἀέροπος, ἐν Μακεδονίᾳ γένος τι, an
indication of the real significance of the
three names as divisions of the Makedonian folk, or perhaps of the Ἀργεάδαι,
Strabo 329 (cp. the tripartition of the
Skyths 4. 5 etc.) (Stein). The name
Aeropos as a proper name recurs, however, in the list of Makedonian kings in
the fourth century B.C. Cp. c. 139.

5. Περδίκκης: he looks after τὰ λεπτὰ
τῶν προβάτων, a true shepherd, or goat-
herd. The expression suggests that
Hdt. might use πρόβατα of larger
animals; cp. 9. 93 infra.

ἐκ δὲ Ἰλλυριῶν ὑπερβαλόντες
looks like a genuine reminiscence of the
origin of the Makedonian Ἀργεάδαι.
The route indicated would be over Mt.
Skardos, presumably by the line of the
later Egnatian Way. ὑπερβ. 7. 168 in
a somewhat different sense.

ἐς τὴν ἄνω Μακεδονίην: cp. 7. 128.
Λεβαίη is nowhere else mentioned, nor
identifiable: a problem of the same
order as Kritalla, 7. 26.

6. ἐθήτευον ἐπὶ μισθῷ: Homeric (not
to say feudal); cp. Od. 4. 644. The
μισθός included board and lodging.

7. παρὰ τῷ βασιλέι: Pausan. 9. 40.
8 gives his name as Κισσεύς. So too
Hyginus (Euripides); cp. note, l. 1
supra.

ὁ δὲ νεώτατος αὐτῶν Περδίκκης τὰ λεπτὰ τῶν προβάτων.
ἡ δὲ γυνὴ τοῦ βασιλέος αὐτὴ τὰ σιτία σφι ἔπεσσε· ἦσαν
10 γὰρ τὸ πάλαι καὶ αἱ τυραννίδες τῶν ἀνθρώπων ἀσθενέες
χρήμασι [οὐ μοῦνον ὁ δῆμος]. ὅκως δὲ ὀπτῴη, ὁ ἄρτος τοῦ
παιδὸς τοῦ [θητὸς] Περδίκκεω διπλήσιος ἐγίνετο αὐτὸς ἑωυτοῦ.
ἐπεὶ δὲ αἰεὶ τὠυτὸ τοῦτο ἐγίνετο, εἶπε πρὸς τὸν ἄνδρα τὸν
ἑωυτῆς· τὸν δὲ ἀκούσαντα ἐσῆλθε αὐτίκα ὡς εἴη τέρας καὶ
15 φέροι μέγα τι. καλέσας δὲ τοὺς θῆτας προηγόρευέ σφι
ἀπαλλάσσεσθαι ἐκ γῆς τῆς ἑωυτοῦ. οἱ δὲ τὸν μισθὸν ἔφασαν
δίκαιοι εἶναι ἀπολαβόντες οὕτω ἐξιέναι. ἐνθαῦτα ὁ βασιλεὺς
τοῦ μισθοῦ πέρι ἀκούσας, ἦν γὰρ κατὰ τὴν καπνοδόκην ἐς
τὸν οἶκον ἐσέχων ὁ ἥλιος, εἶπε θεοβλαβὴς γενόμενος " μισθὸν
20 δὲ ὑμῖν ἐγὼ ὑμέων ἄξιον τόνδε ἀποδίδωμι," δείξας τὸν ἥλιον.

---

8 αὐτέων z ‖ περδίκης CS   9 ἡ δὲ . . ἔπεσσε sedem hab. infra
post δῆμος, huc retrax. Stein ‖ βασιλέως R : βασιλῆος z ‖ σφι τὰ σιτία S
‖ ἔσαν z   10 γὰρ : δὲ B, Holder, van H. : verba ἦσαν . . δῆμος
ut emblema a sciolo quodam addito del. van H.: οὐ μοῦνον ὁ δῆμος damn.
Stein¹ ³, Holder. Nonne verba ἦσαν γὰρ . . χρήμασι inter βασιλέος et
αὐτὴ potius inserenda ?   11 μοῦνον a : μόνον ‖ ὀπτώιη AB : ὀπτῴτο
(Holder, van H.)   12 τοῦ θητὸς Περδίκκεω damn. Stein¹, secl. van H. :
θητὸς tantum Stein³ : τοῦ περδίκκεω Pz, Holder, van H. : τοῦ περδίκεω B
‖ ἑωυτῷ z   13 ἐπείτε ? van H. ‖ ἐγένετο R ‖ τὸν ante ἑωυτῆς om. z
14 ὡς δὲ ἤκουσε Paris. 1635 z ‖ ἐπῆλθέ οἱ z   15 φέροι ἐς Bz
16 γῆς om. Bd ‖ ἔφασαν τὸν μισθὸν B   17 δίκαιοι AC : δίκαιον ‖
εἶναι post μισθὸν B ‖ ἀπολαβόντας Rz ‖ οὕτως B   20 τόδε C ‖ δέξας
Holder, van H. ‖ <ἐς> τὸν ? Stein⁽²⁾, van H.

---

9. ἡ δὲ γυνή : was the ἀρτοκόπος of
Kroisos a queen, 1. 51 ? Hardly ; the
circumstances here are more primitive.
Cp. the story of the Molossian queen,
Thuc. 1. 136.

ἦσαν γὰρ . . χρήμασι : a note
worthy of Thucydides' *Archaiologia* !
The use of αἱ τυραννίδες after βασιλεύς
(*bis*) is significant ; cp. l. 2 *supra*. For
textual critique cp. App. Crit. Does
the note explain why the queen was
cook, or why the herds were provided
for in the house (or both) ? The story
is all in one genre, making it easier for
the herd to turn king, that he has had
a queen a-baking for him. Blakesley
cites Nausikaa a-washing (*Od.* 6) and
the brothers of Andromache tending
herds, *Il.* 6. 422. Cp. *Psalm* 78, *elegit
David servum suum et sustulit eum de
gregibus ovium.*

11. ὁ ἄρτος . . διπλήσιος . . αὐτὸς

ἑωυτοῦ, 'the loaf of the laddie became
twice its own proper size.' The 'double
portion' was a portent (τέρας) indicating
kingship ; cp. 6. 57, 7. 103. διπλήσιος is
treated as a comparative ; cp. also 2. 25.

15. φέροι μέγα τι : of great significance,
portentous.

17. οὕτω : i.e. ἀπολαβόντες : they declined to depart until they had received
their wages ; the nominatives δίκαιοι . .
ἀπολαβόντες are nicely idiomatic. κατά,
'down.'

18. καπνοδόκη : cp. 4. 103, probably
a simple aperture in the roof, or dome.
The construction of the Balkan house or
palace is in question ! It had only a clay
floor. Was it more than a domed hut !

19. ἐσέχων, 'streaming in,' yet not
quite like one river into another, as in
1. 193, nor as a canal into a sea, 2. 158,
nor as a bay of the sea into the land,
2. 11. But cp. ἀρυσάμενος *infra*.

ὁ μὲν δὴ Γαυάνης τε καὶ ὁ Ἀέροπος οἱ πρεσβύτεροι ἔστασαν
ἐκπεπληγμένοι, ὡς ἤκουσαν ταῦτα· ὁ δὲ παῖς, ἐτύγχανε γὰρ
ἔχων μάχαιραν, εἴπας τάδε " δεκόμεθα ὦ βασιλεῦ τὰ διδοῖς,"
περιγράφει τῇ μαχαίρῃ ἐς τὸ ἔδαφος τοῦ οἴκου τὸν ἥλιον,
περιγράψας δέ, ἐς τὸν κόλπον τρὶς ἀρυσάμενος τοῦ ἡλίου, 25
ἀπαλλάσσετο αὐτός τε καὶ οἱ μετ' ἐκείνου. οἳ μὲν δὴ 138
ἀπήισαν, τῷ δὲ βασιλέι σημαίνει τις τῶν παρέδρων οἷόν τι
χρῆμα ποιήσειε [ὁ παῖς] καὶ ὡς σὺν νόῳ κείνων ὁ νεώτατος
λάβοι τὰ διδόμενα. ὁ δὲ ταῦτα ἀκούσας καὶ ὀξυνθεὶς πέμπει
ἐπ' αὐτοὺς ἱππέας ἀπολέοντας. ποταμὸς δὲ ἐστὶ ἐν τῇ χώρῃ 5
ταύτῃ, τῷ θύουσι οἱ τούτων τῶν ἀνδρῶν <τῶν> ἀπ' Ἄργεος
ἀπόγονοι σωτῆρι· οὗτος, ἐπείτε διέβησαν οἱ Τημενίδαι, μέγας
οὕτω ἐρρύη ὥστε τοὺς ἱππέας μὴ οἵους τε γενέσθαι διαβῆναι.
οἳ δὲ ἀπικόμενοι ἐς ἄλλην γῆν τῆς Μακεδονίης οἴκησαν πέλας
τῶν κήπων τῶν λεγομένων εἶναι Μίδεω τοῦ Γορδίεω, ἐν τοῖσι 10

---

21 καὶ Ἀέροπος B, Holder ‖ οἱ πρεσβύτεροι del. van H., Holder : οἱ
πρεσβύτατοι B   23 ὧδε δεχόμεθα aC ‖ βασιλεὺς C   24 τοὐδαφος z
25 ἀφυσάμενος van H.   26 ἐκείνω B : αὐτοῦ z   138. 2 ἀπῆσαν
C : ἀπήεσαν P : ἀπίεσαν Bz ‖ βασιλεῖ AB ‖ σημαίναι S ‖ τῶν τις Krueger,
van H.   3 ὁ παῖς secl. Stein³ ‖ συνόωι C : συνόω B ‖ ἐκείνων BPz :
κακείνων C : ἐκείνων ὁ νεώτατος secl. van H.   4 δεδομένα Pz
<ὡς> ἀπολέοντας Naber   6 τουτέων z ‖ <τῶν>? van H., Stein³ ‖
ἀπ' Ἄργεος : ἀπ' ἀρχῆς Krueger : nonne potius cum van H. deleveris ?
7 σωτήρια z   8 οὕτως a ‖ τε om. B   10 τούτοισι B

---

22. ἐτύγχανε .. ἔχων μάχαιραν :
how did he come by it ? If the truth
were told, probably this μάχαιρα had a
good deal to say to the sequel ! Was it
of iron ? Was it a claymore ? Or
merely a serving man's dirk ?

23. δεκόμεθα ὦ βασιλεῦ τὰ διδοῖς :
exactly the same motif appears in the
anecdote, c. 114 supra; and with the
corresponding motifs οἷας ἐκείνοισι πρέπει,
ὑμέων ἄξιον.

25. τρὶς ἀρυσάμενος, 6. 119, as though
it had been water, a symbolical action,
repeated, symbolically, thrice : for
' three' and its multiples are significant
numbers ; cp. 1. 86, 5. 105, and countless illustrations in all literatures, rituals,
games and formulae.

138. 2. παρέδρων : i.e. ' councillors,'
as in 7. 147, rather than boon-com-
panions, as in 5. 18. ἱππέας, 'horsemen.'
The political and military institutions
of this king seem more advanced than
the domestic.

3. σὺν νόῳ, 8. 86.   The Sun-rite

appears to have more than a single
purpose : Perdikkas symbolically takes
possession of the Hearth and Home of
the giver, and takes the Sun to witness
his claim. Stein quotes Grimm, Rechts-
alt. 278, on the Sun as the source of real
property : the story of Dareios' accession
is also to be cited, 3. 86. Cp. also 7.
8, ll. 37 ff. supra.

5. ποταμὸς δὲ ἐστὶ .. σωτῆρι : the
name of the river is unfortunately not
given ; it could hardly have been missing if Hdt. had himself culled this story
at the Makedonian court. It would probably be the Erigon or Haliakmon ; Stein
prefers the former, as Hdt. nowhere
mentions it by name, though he has the
Axios (of which it is a tributary) and
the Haliakmon. σωτήρια would be very
agreeable ; cp. App. Crit. Stein thinks
ἔτι καὶ νῦν has dropped out after θύουσι.

9. ἐς ἄλλην γῆν τῆς Μακεδονίης : no
doubt Μακεδονίς proper, cp. 7. 127.

10. τῶν κήπων .. Μίδεω τοῦ Γορδίεω.
Midas, son of Gordias, is, of course, a

φύεται αὐτόματα ῥόδα, ἓν ἕκαστον ἔχον ἑξήκοντα φύλλα,
ὀδμῇ τε ὑπερφέροντα τῶν ἄλλων. ἐν τούτοισι καὶ ὁ Σιληνὸς
τοῖσι κήποισι ἥλω, ὡς λέγεται ὑπὸ Μακεδόνων. ὑπὲρ δὲ τῶν
κήπων ὄρος κέεται Βέρμιον οὔνομα, ἄβατον ὑπὸ χειμῶνος.

---

12 ἄλλων <καὶ χροιῇ> ? Stein[2] ‖ σίληνος R: σηληνὸς S: σήληνὸς
V: δηλινὸς Paris. 1635   13 τοῖσι κήποισι deL Cobet   14 οὖρος
CPz ‖ κεῖται a, van H. ‖ βέρβιον B ‖ ὄνομα van H.

'Phrygian' (cp. 1. 14, 35), and 'Silenos'
has already met us on the Marsyas, cp.
7. 26 supra, but it does not therefore
follow that the Midas and Silenos myths
have been transported from Asia, from
Phrygia, into Europe, into Makedonia.
Did not the Bryges, or Phryges, go from
the Axios to the Marsyas? Do they
not represent a folk perhaps pressed out
by the advancing 'Makedonians' or
even the antecessors of the Makedonians?
Cp. 7. 73 supra.

11. ἓν ἕκαστον: in apposition to ῥόδα.
Hdt. nowhere else mentions the rose.

φύλλα: apparently here 'petals'
—the roses must have been 'double':
do such grow wild (αὐτόματα)? And
have any wild roses such a perfume?
Did the Greeks greatly affect flower-
gardens? Were their views on cultiva-
tion not rather utilitarian, apter auctumno
carpere poma, than vere rosam? The
garden of Alkinoos grew mainly fruit-
trees; the rose is used by Homer but to
paint the fingers of the Morn (ῥοδο-
δάκτυλος Ἠώς), or to preserve the corpse
of Hektor withal (Il. 23. 186): a utility.
The simple word first occurs in the
Hymn to Demeter, 6.

12. ὑπερφέροντα: cp. c. 44 supra, 9.
96 infra.

ὁ Σιληνὸς . . ἥλω: cp. 7. 26
supra; the article here might possibly
be in reference to the 'Silenos' of that
passage, but is more probably used on
more general grounds, 'the notorious.'
The 'capture' this time is not made by
Apollo, but by Midas, who caught
Silenos and conversed with him (Plutarch
l.c.). Theopompos ap. Aelian, V.H. 3. 18,
puts a long fable on the Happy Land
into the mouth of Silenos; Aristotle
represented him as something of a
pessimist (Plutarch Mor. 115) and very
reluctant to answer the question of
Midas, τί ποτέ ἐστι τὸ βέλτιον τοῖς ἀνθρώ-
ποις; Cp. Cicero, Tusc. Dist. 1. 48
Affertur etiam de Sileno fabella quaedam:
qui quum a Mida captus esset, hoc ei

muneris pro sua missione dedisse
scribitur; docuisse regem non nasci
homini longe optimum esse; proximum
autem quam primum mori. That
melancholy doctrine was 'Trausic' or
'Thracian' according to Hdt. 5. 4 (cp.
my note ad l.).

13. ὡς λέγεται ὑπὸ Μακεδόνων. The
citation of the authority, or source,
implies a misgiving, but does not prove
that Hdt. had the story from headquarters, or was not drawing on literature. The version given was obviously
'Makedonian' in origin; cp. 7. 73.

ὑπέρ: higher up the country,
further inland.

14. ὄρος . . Βέρμιον: cp. Strabo 330
(Z 25) τὸ Βέρμιον ὄρος ὃ πρότερον κατεῖχον
Βρίγες Θρακῶν ἔθνος ὧν τινες διαβάντες εἰς
τὴν Ἀσίην Φρύγες μετωνομάσθησαν. ib.
26 ἡ Βέροια πόλις ἐν ταῖς ὑπωρείαις κεῖται
τοῦ Βερμίου ὄρους. The wealth of Midas
is traced (Strabo 680) to the mines περὶ
τὸ Β. ὄ. The mountain is identified
with the range between the Haliakmon
and the Lydias, the highest point of
which now bears the name of Dhoxd.
The exact position of the Rose Garden is
more in dispute. Hdt. here places it in
the neighbourhood of the city of Beroia
(without naming it); i.e. in Makedonia
proper, 7. 127. Abel (Makedonien, pp.
110 ff.) would place it further north, in
the neighbourhood of Edessa, or Aigai,
the more ancient cradle of the Makedonian folk. Kortüm (ap. Baehr ad l.)
very happily relegates the Rose Garden to
the same mythical region as Kriemhilt's
Rosengarten zu Worms am Rhin (Rin),
but instead of Kriemhilt and Brunhilt,
Gunther and Siegfrid, we have here
only Midas and Silenos—the romantic
interest is wanting!

ἄβατον ὑπὸ χειμῶνος, 'inaccessible
by reason of the climate'—the which
notwithstanding it was ascended, "in
defiance of the assertion of Herodotus,"
by Leake (cp. Northern Greece, iii.
295 f.), who indeed describes it as an im-

ἐνθεῦτεν δὲ ὁρμώμενοι, ὡς ταύτην ἔσχον, κατεστρέφοντο καὶ 15
τὴν ἄλλην Μακεδονίην. ἀπὸ τούτου δὴ τοῦ Περδίκκεω 139
Ἀλέξανδρος ὧδε ἐγένετο· Ἀμύντεω παῖς ἦν Ἀλέξανδρος,
Ἀμύντης δὲ Ἀλκέτεω, Ἀλκέτεω δὲ πατὴρ ἦν Ἀέροπος, τοῦ
δὲ Φίλιππος, Φιλίππου δὲ Ἀργαῖος, τοῦ δὲ Περδίκκης ὁ
κτησάμενος τὴν ἀρχήν. 5

15 ὁρμεώμενοι Cz : ὁρμεόμενοι Stein[1], van H. ‖ ὡς ταύτην ἔσχον del.
Cobet　　139. 1 περδίκεω SV : περδίκαιω R　　2 διδε P ‖ ἐγεγόνεε
Βz ‖ Ἀλέξανδρος . . ἦν om. R　　4 ἀργαῖος Β : ἀραῖος Paris. 1635 s :
ἀρουραῖος Marc. : αρραιος Α : ἀρραῖος ‖ περδίκης ΒΒ : περιδίκης C

portant pass between Lower and Upper
Macedonia.

15. **ἐνθεῦτεν δὲ ὁρμώμενοι**: three or
rather four stages in all are indicated in
the advance of the Makedonians, or
Argeadai.　I.　Argos (Orestikon) or
Orestis may be taken as the starting-
point, or cradle, far up the Haliakmon,
and about its sources, Upper Makedonia,
the (unknown) city of Lebaia. II. The
parts under Mount Bermion, Edessa,
Beroia, the **ἄλλη γῆ τῆς Μακεδονίης**,
near the Rose-gardens of Midas ; which
might be called Middle Makedonia, as
no part of it touches the sea, but is
generally included in Lower Makedonia.
III. Lower Makedonia, **τὴν ἄλλην Μακεδονίην**, down to the sea ; cp. 7. 127
supra: **τὴν παρὰ θάλασσαν νῦν Μακεδονίαν**
Thuc. l.c. Thucydides 2. 99 gives a
more matter-of-fact account of the process, and in a somewhat different
stratification, including the further
stage, the advance to the Strymon : the
two representations are not at hopeless
variance.　I. The tribes of the first
region, the Lynkestai, Elimiotai (+
Orestai 2. 80. 6) and others **ἐπάνωθεν**,
high up the country, were under native
kings or chiefs, though owning the
suzerainty of the 'Temenids.' II. III.
This overlordship was perhaps only
acquired, or reasserted by Perdikkas, the
son of Alexander ; cp. Thuc. 4. 83.
(Aigai, Beroia,) Pieria, Bottia, were
the especial acquisition of the Temenids,
and the strip of Paionia along the
Axios, as well as Eordaia, Almopia:
in short, all the territory between the
Haliakmon and the Axios, together with
the sea-coast. IV. Mygdonia and the
territory of the Edonians, as far as the
Strymon. This region is not yet 'Makedonian' in Hdt. and was the especial
acquisition of Alexander I. Cp. further,
notes to 7. 127. 5 supra.

139. 2. **Ἀλέξανδρος ὧδε ἐγένετο**, 'the
generation of Alexander was on this
wise.' The pedigree of Alexander compares favourably with the Achaimenid,
Perdikkas the founder ranging exactly
with Achaimenes, while by the affiliation
on to the Temenid and Herakleid
genealogies it leaves the Achaimenid
far behind. If the Makedonian genealogy be placed side by side with that
of the Spartan Herakleids, Perdikkas
appears almost contemporary with the
kings Polydoros (Agid) and Theopompos
(Eurypontid), at the epoch of the Messenian war, or circa 730 B.C. (7 names = circa
230 years). Eusebius (Chron. p. 169 =
Diodor. 7. 16) gives only 199 years from
the accession of Perdikkas to the death
of Amyntas, but prefixes 101 years for
the three predecessors of Perdikkas, and
so reaches about 800 B.C. as the epoch
of the Makedonian monarchy instead
of 700 B.C. ; see below. The figures in
Clinton Fasti ii.[3] 274 work out rather
differently.

Ἀμύντεω: cp. 5. 17 supra, where
Amyntas I. has something of a distinctive
character, in contrast to his hot-headed
son. Before him the kings, back to Perdikkas, are mere names. He is given
a reign of 49 years : ob. circa 498 B.C.

3. **Ἀλκέτεω**: the name (Ἀλκέτας,
Ἀλκέτης) appears Greek enough, and is
not confined to the Makedonian pedigree,
in which it frequently recurs ; a Lakedaimonian of the name in Xenoph. Hell.
5. 4. 56. The king is given a reign of
18 years.

Ἀέροπος: on the name cp. c. 137
supra. He is given a reign of 20 years
by the Chronicon. The name recurs as
that of a reigning king in the fourth
century, who, according to Polyain. 2. 1.
17, attempted to bar the return of
Agesilaos (in 394 B.C.).

4. **Φίλιππος** is given a reign of 33

140 Ἐγεγόνεε μὲν δὴ ὧδε ὁ Ἀλέξανδρος ὁ Ἀμύντεω· ὡς δὲ
ἀπίκετο ἐς τὰς Ἀθήνας ἀποπεμφθεὶς ὑπὸ Μαρδονίου, ἔλεγε
τάδε. "ἄνδρες Ἀθηναῖοι, Μαρδόνιος τάδε λέγει. ἐμοὶ
ἀγγελίη ἥκει παρὰ βασιλέος λέγουσα οὕτω. ''Ἀθηναίοισι τὰς
5 ἀμαρτάδας τὰς ἐς ἐμὲ ἐξ ἐκείνων γενομένας πάσας μετίημι. νῦν

---

140. 1 ὧδε: οὕτω? van H. ‖ ὁ ante Ἀλέξανδρος om. Apr. **βz**, Holder,
van H.   2 πεμφθεὶς z   4 παρὰ βασιλέος ἥκει S ‖ ἥκε z ‖
βασιλῆος z ‖ οὕτως **β**: ὧδε? van H.   5 ἐξ ἐκείνων ἐς ἐμὲ **βz**, Holder
‖ μετίειμι C

---

years. The name occurs in the family
during the fifth century, cp. Thuc. 1. 57.
3 etc. (a son of Alexander), and was
not uncommon elsewhere (cp. 5. 47).
In the fourth century it was destined to
be eclipsed only by the name Alexander
itself.

Ἀργαῖος is given a reign of 31
years (Euseb. l.c.). The name is Greek
enough, and comes near the Ἀργεάδαι,
Ἀργαῖοι, or Ἀργεῖοι, who play so important a part in the whole story (cp. c.
137 supra). It recurs as the name of an
authentic king in the fourth century:
Diodor. 14. 92. 4 ἔνιοι δέ φασι μετὰ τὴν
ἔκπτωσιν τοῦ Ἀμύντου (383 B.C.) διετῆ
χρόνον Ἀργαῖον βασιλεῦσαι τῶν Μακεδόνων, τότε δὲ Ἀμύνταν ἀνακτήσασθαι τὴν
βασιλείαν.

Περδίκκης: on the name cp. c. 137
supra. He is given a reign of 48 years,
which would make the epoch of the
kingdom 697 B.C., or circa 700 B.C.
To this date the Chronicon, following
the story as given in Theopompos (see
c. 137 supra), adds 101 years (=798 B.C.,
or circa 800 B.C.), allowing Tyremmas
43 years, Koinos 28, and Karanos, the
founder according to that story, 30. The
pedigree here given is doubtless official,
and was, perhaps, constructed for
Alexander I., though the prominence of
the name Perdikkas might tempt one to
depress the genealogical essay to a
date after the accession of Perdikkas II.
The pedigree may, nevertheless, be
authentic, at least in its later members.
Alexander must have produced a pedigree before he was admitted to compete
at Olympia (cp. my notes to 5. 22), not
later than 500 B.C. But the legendary
apotheosis of Perdikkas may be an afterthought; or else Alexander gave his
(eldest?) son the name of the reputed
Founder of the House, in order the
better to publish his claims.

140. 1. ἐγεγόνεε practically = ἐγένετο
c. 139 supra.

2. ἐς τὰς Ἀθήνας: Hdt. throughout
represents the Athenians as having reoccupied the city during the winter of
480–79 B.C.

ἔλεγε τάδε: it is not quite clear
whether the scene is laid in the Ekklesia
or in the Boule; but the ambassador
will have addressed Council before
addressing Assembly. The different
meanings, or shades, in ἔλεγε (of the
actual audible speech), λέγει (of the sense,
or message conveyed by the speaker, at
second hand), and λέγουσα (of the
substance of a despatch or letter), are
noticeable; add λέγω below where
Mardonios speaks in person by the lips
of Alexander. ἀγγελίη is no doubt in
this case a written despatch; cp.
ἀγγελιηφόρος.

4. τὰς ἀμαρτάδας . . μετίημι: there
is a distinctly oriental, not to say
sacerdotal ring about this phrase, and
indeed the whole letter. The offer
comprises six items: (i.) forgiveness, i.e.
no (further) penalties or reprisals against
Athens; (ii.) restoration of their land,
i.e. secure tenure; (iii.) additional
territory (at the expense of the Peloponnesians?); (iv.) αὐτονομία—no restoration of tyrants; (v.) rebuilding of the
temples; (vi.) alliance (ὁμολογέειν: cp.
ὁμαιχμίην ἄνευ τε δόλου καὶ ἀπάτης infra;
and φίλος).

Whether any such despatch had been
received by Mardonios or not is another
question. Up above he has been represented as acting on his own initiative,
or by the advice of oracles. Again,
whether Alexander really delivered just
this (τάδε) speech, or anything like it,
is questionable. Baehr, while regarding
the mission of Alexander as historical,
says that the speeches, as reported, e
rhetorum atque sophistarum fluxisse
scholis; cp. 3. 40, 3. 80 etc.

5. μετίημι: cp. 6. 59 ἐν αὖ δ' αὖ Πέρσῃσι
ὁ κατιστάμενος βασιλεὺς τὸν προοφειλό-
μενον φόρον μετιεῖ. But ἀμαρτάδες are

τε ὧδε Μαρδόνιε ποίεε· τοῦτο μὲν τὴν γῆν σφι ἀπόδος, τοῦτο
δὲ ἄλλην πρὸς ταύτῃ ἑλέσθων αὐτοί, ἥντινα ἂν ἐθέλωσι,
ἐόντες αὐτόνομοι· ἱρά τε πάντα σφι, ἣν δὴ βούλωνταί γε
ἐμοὶ ὁμολογέειν, ἀνόρθωσον, ὅσα ἐγὼ ἐνέπρησα.' τούτων
δὲ ἀπιγμένων ἀναγκαίως ἔχει μοι ποιέειν ταῦτα, ἢν μὴ   10
τὸ ὑμέτερον ἀντίον γένηται. λέγω δὲ ὑμῖν τάδε. νῦν τί
μαίνεσθε πόλεμον βασιλέι ἀειρόμενοι; οὔτε γὰρ ἂν ὑπερβάλοισθε οὔτε οἷοί τε ἐστὲ ἀντέχειν τὸν πάντα χρόνον.
εἴδετε μὲν γὰρ τῆς Ξέρξεω στρατηλασίης τὸ πλῆθος καὶ τὰ
ἔργα, πυνθάνεσθε δὲ καὶ τὴν νῦν παρ' ἐμοὶ ἐοῦσαν δύναμιν·   15
ὥστε καὶ ἢν ἡμέας ὑπερβάλησθε καὶ νικήσητε, τοῦ περ ὑμῖν
οὐδεμία ἐλπίς εἴ περ εὖ φρονέετε, ἄλλη παρέσται πολλαπλησίη. μὴ ὦν βούλεσθε παρισούμενοι βασιλέι στέρεσθαι

---

6 μαρδόνιε ὧδε B ‖ ποίεε V (S): ποίε R: ποίει α, Holder, van H.
7 θέλωσι(ν V) B   9 τουτέων z   11 ἀντίον Valckenaer, Holder,
van H., Stein³: αἴτιον ‖ τάδε νῦν· τί Bekker, van H.   12 βασιλέι
αB ‖ ἀνταειρόμενοι Bz, Holder, van H. ‖ οὗτοι γὰρ ἂν ὑπερβάλλοισθε C
14 τό <τε> πλῆθος coni. Stein¹², adsc. van H.   15 παρ' ἐμοὶ ἐοῦσαν
P: παρεοῦσάν μοι Paris. 1635 z: παρ' ἐμὲ ἐοῦσάν τε καὶ ! Stein¹ ‖ καὶ
νικήσητε del. Cobet, van H.   16 τοῦ z: τό   17 οὐδεμίη z ‖
φρονέοιτε z ‖ <ἀλλ'> ἄλλη Cobet, Holder ‖ παρέστε B ‖ παραπλησίη S
18 βούλεσθαι B: βούλησθε Pz ‖ παρισεύμενοι B ‖ βασιλέι AB ‖ ἐστερῆσθαι maleb. van H.

---

not exactly equivalent to arrears of
tribute ! The debt-metaphor does not
quite work: but the king 'remits' the
penalties owing to him; and from the
remission of penalties to the remission of
'sins' the transition is easy.

9. τούτων: sc. ἀγγελιῶν, ἐπιστολῶν,
ἐντολῶν, or rather, in the neuter abstract,
referring back generally to the king's
orders: just like ταῦτα immediately
below.

10. ἀναγκαίως ἔχει μοι, 'necessity is
laid on me'—Mardonios.

ἢν μὴ τὸ ὑμέτερον ἀντίον γένηται,
'unless you should interpose an obstacle':
in which case ἀντίον is predicative. But
cp. App. Crit. The vulgate αἴτιον has,
perhaps, been too lightly discarded:
it would mean 'unless you should
cause me to fail in my endeavour.' The
predicative force of the possessive, and
the idiomatic use of αἴτιον (cp. c. 7.
125. 5 supra) would then be noticeable.

11. λέγω δέ: Mardonios is still the
speaker, reported by Alexander.

12. πόλεμον βασιλέι ἀειρόμενοι: τ.
ἀείρεσθαι, cp. 7. 132, 156—in both places

with a dative. The tense here is remarkable: is the fresh campaign regarded as a fresh war, or warfare ! Is
not the door diplomatically opened for
the Athenians to drop their arms, by
the insinuation that they have not yet
quite concluded taking them up !

ὑπερβάλοισθε, 'prove superior';
7. 163, 168, c. 24 supra.

13. ἀντέχειν κτλ, 'to withstand'—
hold out against—'for ever.'

τὸν πάντα χρόνον: here future,
cp. 3. 65, (4. 187, 9. 73, 106): in some
cases the past, 6. 123, 9. 27 (Stein).

14. τῆς Ξέρξεω στρατηλασίης τὸ
πλῆθος καὶ τὰ ἔργα: στρατηλασίης appears to =στρατοῦ. The στρατηλασίη of
Xerxes is one thing, that of Mardonios
another. Mardonios may be supposed
to be referring to Thermopylai, and the
destruction of Athens by Xerxes: he
cannot be supposed to have in view the
naval στρατός. He apparently compares
the immense size, and success, of Xerxes'
army (πεζὸς στρατός) with his own reduced numbers and possible, though not
probable, defeat.

μὲν τῆς χώρης, θέειν δὲ αἰεὶ περὶ ὑμέων αὐτῶν, ἀλλὰ
20 καταλύσασθε· παρέχει δὲ ὑμῖν κάλλιστα [καταλύσασθαι],
βασιλέος ταύτῃ ὁρμημένου· ἔστε ἐλεύθεροι, ἡμῖν ὁμαιχμίην
συνθέμενοι ἄνευ τε δόλου καὶ ἀπάτης. Μαρδόνιος μὲν ταῦτα
ὦ Ἀθηναῖοι ἐνετείλατό μοι εἰπεῖν πρὸς ὑμέας· ἐγὼ δὲ περὶ
μὲν εὐνοίης τῆς πρὸς ὑμέας ἐούσης ἐξ ἐμεῦ οὐδὲν λέξω, οὐ
25 γὰρ ἂν νῦν πρῶτον ἐκμάθοιτε, προσχρηίζω δὲ ὑμέων πείθεσθαι
Μαρδονίῳ. ἐνορῶ γὰρ ὑμῖν οὐκ οἵοισί τε ἐσομένοισι τὸν
πάντα χρόνον πολεμέειν Ξέρξῃ· εἰ γὰρ ἐνώρων τοῦτο ἐν ὑμῖν,
οὐκ ἄν κοτε ἐς ὑμέας ἦλθον ἔχων λόγους τούσδε· καὶ γὰρ
δύναμις ὑπὲρ ἄνθρωπον ἡ βασιλέος ἐστὶ καὶ χεὶρ ὑπερμήκης.
30 ἢν ὦν μὴ αὐτίκα ὁμολογήσητε, μεγάλα προτεινόντων ἐπ᾽ οἷσι
ὁμολογέειν ἐθέλουσι, δειμαίνω ὑπὲρ ὑμέων ἐν τρίβῳ τε

---

19 ἑωυτέων z   20 καταλλάσσεσθε z ‖ καταλύσασθαι secl. Stein², Holder, van H.: καταλύσασθε V   21 . βασιλέος P: . βασιλῆος z ‖ ὡρμημένου CPz ‖ , ἐστὲ Pz: . ἐστὲ R   22 δόλου τε van H.   23 εἶπαι z, van H.   24 ἐξ ἐμεῦ ἐούσης Β   25 προσχρηίζω aP: προσχρήζω ΒC: προσχρῄζω z   26 ἐνορῶ ACP, Stein², Holder: ἐνορέω Βz, Stein¹, van H.: ἐνορῶν Β¹: ἐνορῶν Β²   27 ἐνόρων S: ἐνώρεον van H. ‖ [τοῦτο ἐν ὑμῖν]? van H. ‖ ἐν: ἐνὸν z   28 τοιούσδε z   29 βασιλῆος z   30 ὦν: οὖν C: om. Β ‖ ἐπ᾽ οἷσι: ἐποίσει Β

---

19. θέειν: cp. πολλάκις ἀγῶνας δραμέονται c. 102 supra.

21. ταύτῃ ὁρμημένου, 'having taken the initiative in that way,' as aforesaid. (Cum haec regis sit voluntas, Baehr.)

ὁμαιχμίην: cp. 7. 145 supra. The offer is of distinct alliance, with liberty intact (ἔστε ἐλεύθεροι).

22. ἄνευ τε δόλου καὶ ἀπάτης: a standing formula of Hellenic or international diplomacy; cp. 1. 69, and in actual treaty texts ap. Thuc. 4. 118. 1 (ἀδόλως καὶ ἀδεῶς κατὰ τοὺς πατρίους νόμους); 5. 18. 9 (δικαίως καὶ ἀδόλως); 5. 23 bis (δικαίως καὶ προθύμως καὶ ἀδόλως); 5. 47. 8 (δικαίως καὶ ἀβλαβῶς καὶ ἀδόλως). δόλος must be the same word as the Latin dolus; cp. L. & S. The proceedings for 'striking a treaty' as reported in Livy 1. 24 (sine fraude mea, sine dolo malo, etc.) might suggest that the formula was very ancient.

23. ἐγὼ δέ: Alexander, propria persona.

24. εὐνοίης: a thoroughly Attic formula; cp. complimentary decrees passim.

οὐ γὰρ ἂν νῦν πρῶτον ἐκμάθοιτε must mean, not 'I have often spoken of it before,' but 'you have had many

practical proofs of it.' As to the fact cp. note above, c. 136.

26. ἐνορῶ γὰρ ὑμῖν: the construction appears to be determined by the preposition; cp. just below εἰ γὰρ ἐνώρων τοῦτο ἐν ὑμῖν. Cp. συνειδέναι.

29. χεὶρ ὑπερμήκης: the youngest son, the successor of Xerxes, was known to later tradition as μακρόχειρ, i.e. the word is found in Plutarch Artax. 1 μακρόχειρ ἐπεκαλεῖτο τὴν δεξιὰν μείζονα τῆς ἑτέρας ἔχων. But the statement perhaps rests merely on a metaphor misunderstood: χεὶρ = δύναμις, e.g. 4. 155. Ovid Her. 17. 166 an nescis longas regibus esse manus? Pollux 2. 151 ἑκατόγχειρ, μακρόχειρ, εἴτε κατὰ Πολύκλειτον ὁ Ὑστάσπου Δαρεῖος, εἴτε κατὰ Ἀντιλέοντα Ξέρξης, εἴτε κατὰ τοὺς πλείστους Ὦχος ὁ ἐπικληθεὶς Ἀρταξέρξης ἤτοι τὴν δεξιὰν ἔχων προμηκεστέραν ἢ τὴν ἀριστερὰν ἢ ἀμφοτέρας· οἱ δὲ ὅτι καὶ τὴν δύναμιν ἐπὶ πλεῖστον ἐξέτεινεν.

30. μεγάλα, 'advantageous to you.'

προτεινόντων: sc. τῶν Περσέων.

31. ἐν τρίβῳ τε κτλ. Alexander is made to describe the Athenians as (i.) dwelling on the highway (ἐν τρίβῳ), that is, in the most exposed situation; (ii.)

μάλιστα οἰκημένων τῶν συμμάχων πάντων αἰεί τε φθειρομένων
μούνων, ἐξαίρετον μεταίχμιόν τε τὴν γῆν ἐκτημένων. ἀλλὰ
πείθεσθε· πολλοῦ γὰρ ὑμῖν ἄξια ταῦτα, εἰ βασιλεύς γε ὁ
μέγας μούνοισι ὑμῖν Ἑλλήνων τὰς ἁμαρτάδας ἀπιεὶς ἐθέλει 35
φίλος γενέσθαι."

Ἀλέξανδρος μὲν ταῦτα ἔλεξε. Λακεδαιμόνιοι δὲ πυθόμενοι 141
ἥκειν Ἀλέξανδρον ἐς Ἀθήνας ἐς ὁμολογίην ἄξοντα τῷ
βαρβάρῳ Ἀθηναίους, ἀναμνησθέντες τῶν λογίων ὡς σφεας

---

33 μοῦνον C: 'post hoc in libris non dividitur' Stein || ἐξαίρετον
μεταίχμιόν τε CV, Stein, Holder: ἐξαίρετον· μεταίχμιόν τε ABP: ἐξαί-
ρετον· τὲ μεταίχμιον R: ἐξαίρετον, μεταίχμιόν τε S: μεταίχμιον tantum
Marc.: ἐξαίρετόν τι μεταίχμιον z, van H. || ἐκτημένων z: κεκτημένων
34 πίθεσθε Cobet   35 ἀφιεὶς P: ἀφεὶς αC || θέλει β   141. 1
τοσαῦτα β   2 ἐς Ἀθηναίους C   3 ὡς σφέας R, van H.

---

bearing (or likely to bear) all the brunt
of the war alone; (iii.) their territory
being the natural battle-field, or debat-
able ground, between the contending
armies (Persian, Peloponnesian). The
description applies fairly well to Attica,
which during this war was twice invaded and devastated, and had been the
scene of the great naval battle, to say
nothing of Marathon, ten years earlier;
but in a general way, and throughout
Greek history, Boiotia would better
answer to the description (cp. 9. 2. 3
infra), and even in this war it was north
of Kithairon that the ἐξαίρετον μεταίχμιον
was to be found. The phrase here perhaps expresses the Athenian sense of
their special sufferings in the common
cause (τῶν συμμάχων πάντων).

33. ἀλλά: with the imperative, to
cut short the question; cp. L. & S. sub
v. II. 2.

34. ταῦτα might seem to refer to what
follows (εἰ βασιλεύς γε κτλ.), which, however, reproduces the preceding offers.
ὁ μέγας is an unusual addition, but a
(lesser) king is speaking.

141. 1. Λακεδαιμόνιοι δέ κτλ. If any
part of the story of Alexander's embassy
could have come from other than an
Athenian source, it is not this chapter,
which positively reeks Atticism. The
solidarity of the story as a whole carries
the Attic source for every part.

πυθόμενοι: who let them know?
Their friends in Athens? Themistokles?

2. τῷ βαρβάρῳ with ὁμολογίην.
Baehr ops. 7. 169 τὰ Μενελέῳ τιμωρήματα.

3. ἀναμνησθέντες τῶν λογίων: what
oracles were these which they now

recalled to mind? Blakesley detects
herein the oracles found by Kleomenes
in the Akropolis (in 511 B.C.) 5. 90, and
further suggests that they were fabrica-
tions by Onomakritos (cp. 7. 6 supra).
But such a prediction, as is here
reported, likely to have been formulated
so early as that? Or is the added motive,
based upon these supposed oracles, required to account for the action of the
Lakedaimonians on this occasion?
Onomakritos may have been the author
of these λόγια, but, if so, their fabrication
was probably of later date, and they
were perhaps part of the artillery
brought to bear upon the Athenians to
procure their medism, not Lakedaimonian reminiscences of discoveries
thirty years old.

In any case this prediction is precious:
prophecies fulfilled are sweet, but those
unfulfilled are sweeter, to the historian;
their authenticity is so much more
obvious. The unfulfilled prediction,
besides, makes room for some fulfilment
of prediction. The extreme precision
of the present instance raises it to the
level of a maxim of policy, cp. c. 62
supra.

The expulsion of the Lakedaimonians
and all the other Dorians to boot from
the Peloponnesos by the Medes and
Athenians, i.e. the complete reversal of
the Dorian conquest and its effects, was
not a bad idea to conjure with, and has
rather a Themistoklean touch about it:
perhaps it was not an offer made by
Mardonios to attract the Athenians, but
a bogle devised in Athens to terrify the
Spartans. It might at least suggest

χρεόν ἐστι ἅμα τοῖσι ἄλλοισι Δωριεῦσι ἐκπίπτειν ἐκ Πελο-
5 ποννήσου ὑπὸ Μήδων τε καὶ Ἀθηναίων, κάρτα τε ἔδεισαν μὴ
ὁμολογήσωσι τῷ Πέρσῃ Ἀθηναῖοι, αὐτίκα τέ σφι ἔδοξε
πέμπειν ἀγγέλους. καὶ δὴ συνέπιπτε ὥστε ὁμοῦ σφεων
γίνεσθαι τὴν κατάστασιν· ἐπανέμειναν γὰρ οἱ Ἀθηναῖοι
διατρίβοντες, εὖ ἐπιστάμενοι ὅτι ἔμελλον Λακεδαιμόνιοι
10 πεύσεσθαι ἥκοντα παρὰ τοῦ βαρβάρου ἄγγελον ἐπ' ὁμολογίῃ,
πυθόμενοί τε πέμψειν κατὰ τάχος ἀγγέλους. ἐπίτηδες ὦν
ἐποίευν, ἐνδεικνύμενοι τοῖσι Λακεδαιμονίοισι τὴν ἑωυτῶν
142 γνώμην. ὡς δὲ ἐπαύσατο λέγων Ἀλέξανδρος, διαδεξάμενοι
ἔλεγον οἱ ἀπὸ Σπάρτης ἄγγελοι "ἡμέας δὲ ἔπεμψαν Λακεδαιμόνιοι δεησομένους ὑμέων μήτε νεώτερον ποιέειν μηδὲν κατὰ
τὴν Ἑλλάδα μήτε λόγους ἐνδέκεσθαι παρὰ τοῦ βαρβάρου.
5 οὔτε γὰρ δίκαιον οὐδαμῶς οὔτε κόσμον φέρον οὔτε γε ἄλλοισι
Ἑλλήνων οὐδαμοῖσι, ὑμῖν δὲ δὴ καὶ διὰ πάντων ἥκιστα
πολλῶν εἵνεκα. ἠγείρατε γὰρ τόνδε τὸν πόλεμον ὑμεῖς οὐδὲν

---

4 χρεών CPz, van H. ‖ ἐκ: ἀπὸ Β　　5 τε post κάρτα om. S(V)
6 δέ σφι(ϊν V) Β ‖ ἔδοξεν AB ap. Stein¹: ἔδοξε α: ἔδοξε Β ap. Holder
7 σφέων BCz　　10 ἐπομολογίην C　　11 πειθόμενοί R　　142. 5
φέρων R ‖ οὔτι γε Werfer: γε om. Β ('locus vix sanus' van H.)　　6 δὴ
om. S　　7 ἐγείρατε z ‖ τὸν πόλεμον τόνδε Β: (πόλεμον τόνδε absque
τὸν S ap. Gaisf.) ‖ ἡμεῖς οὐδὲν ὑμέων C

---

possibilities in the future : but what of Argos as the king's best friend ! 7. 150 ff. Perhaps the whole notion really belongs to the later date, and the time of Themistokles' medism. The patriotic (i.e. Attic) aspects of that *gran rifiuto* were never allowed to emerge in the Themistoklean legend ; and Athenian tradition was quite capable of ignoring the true and original connexion of this prophecy, and utilizing it in the present connexion, where it is materially and even grammatically *de trop*.

6. **ἔδοξε**: here of a formal decision.

7. **ἀγγέλους** = πρέσβεις : cp. 7. 1.

καὶ δή : each particle has its full and ordinary sense.

συνέπιπτε ὥστε : cp. c. 15 *supra*; it was a coincidence, but not an un-designed one : **ἐπίτηδες ἐποίευν** just below. This latter verb may represent ἐπανέμειναν (so Stein), an abstract idiom, corresponding to the use of our verb 'do,' 'did' (which would, however, require an express object, however abstract : 'this they were doing ').

8. **κατάστασιν** : in the same sense 3. 46 ; in a different one, c. 83 *supra*.

12. **ἐνδεικνύμενοι**, 'displaying' ; cp. Thuc. 4. 126. ὁ τὸ εὔψυχον ἐν τῷ ἀσφαλεῖ ὀξεῖς ἐνδείκνυνται.

142. 1. **διαδεξάμενοι** : exactly as in Plato *Rep.* 576 Β Ἀνάγκη, ἔφη διαδεξά-μενος τὸν λόγον ὁ Γλαύκων. Cp. διάδοχος, διαδοχή.

2. **ἡμέας δέ** : the conjunction is notice-able ; here it might almost suggest a suppressed clause : Ἀλέξανδρον μέν κτλ. Cp. 5. 109 ἡμέας δὲ ἀπέπεμψε.

3. **νεώτερον ποιέειν** (τι 5. 35), to do something newer, too new, outrageous, etc., perhaps not a mere euphemism, but an implicit plea for the maxim *stare super antiquas vias* ; and so probably in the first instance referring not to foreign but to domestic affairs. Its use here might be taken to hint that a schism in the Greek ranks would be of the nature of στάσις (cp. c. 3 *supra*).

4. **λόγους ἐνδέκεσθαι** : 7. 236 *supra*.

5. **κόσμον φέρον** : cp. c. 60 *supra*.

6. **διὰ πάντων** : cp. c. 37 *supra*.

7. **ἠγείρατε . . οὐδὲν ἡμέων βουλο-μένων** : a statement quite inconsistent with the alleged outrage at Sparta upon the Persian heralds, 7. 133 *supra*. If

ἡμέων βουλομένων, καὶ περὶ τῆς ὑμετέρης ἀρχῆθεν ὁ ἀγὼν
ἐγένετο, νῦν δὲ φέρει καὶ ἐς πᾶσαν τὴν Ἑλλάδα· ἄλλως τε
τούτων ἁπάντων, αἰτίους γενέσθαι δουλοσύνης τοῖσι Ἕλλησι 10
Ἀθηναίους οὐδαμῶς ἀνασχετόν, οἵτινες αἰεὶ καὶ τὸ πάλαι
φαίνεσθε πολλοὺς ἐλευθερώσαντες ἀνθρώπων. πιεζευμένοισι
μέντοι ὑμῖν συναχθόμεθα, καὶ ὅτι καρπῶν ἐστερήθητε διξῶν

---

8 βουλευομένων AB ap. Stein[1] : βουλομένων α : βουλευομένων B ap.
Holder ‖ ἀρχῆθεν Wesseling, Stein[2], Holder, van H. : ἀρχὴν Schaefer :
ἀρχῆς   9 ἄλλως τε : ἄλλως τε ἄνευ Reiske : πάρεξ τε vel χωρίς τε coni.
Stein[2] : αἰτίους, αἰτίους de Pauw : 'An delenda verba τούτων ἁπάντων?' van H.
10 τουτέων Bz ‖ πάντων B : ἀπαντώντων Schaefer, Schweighaeuser   11
καὶ : κατὰ z   12 πιεζομένοισι BCz, van H.   13 ἐστέρησθε z

---

we are to go back to the Athenian
challenge in 5. 96, why not to the
Spartan 'Hands off' message in 1. 152?

8. περὶ τῆς ὑμετέρης ἀρχῆθεν ὁ ἀγὼν
ἐγένετο : sc. γῆς. Cp. the words of Themistokles to the Ionians c. 22 supra :
ἀρχῆθεν ἡ ἔχθρη πρὸς τὸν βάρβαρον ἀπ'
ὑμέων ἡμῖν γέγονε. The Athenian responsibility is probably conceived as going
back to 498 B.C. and the despatch of
the twenty ships to Sardes, which were
ἀρχὴ κακῶν Ἕλλησί τε καὶ βαρβάροισι 5.
97. The beautiful anachronism ἀρχῆς
can hardly be maintained, or it would be
extremely serviceable. Blakesley and
Rawlinson indeed would maintain it on
the ground that one anachronism is
already involved in ascribing to the
Athenians in 479 B.C. such services
on behalf of freedom as are predicated
of them in the context : "up to this
time they had never taken any part
in liberating any nation." But the
Athenians would have cited the cases
of (1) Plataia, (2) the Ionians, (3)
Marathon, to say nothing of more
legendary exploits. Cp. 9. 27 infra ;
and αἰεὶ καὶ τὸ πάλαι in any case refutes
R.'s argument. Baehr also defends
ἀρχῆς, quod ipsa sententia loci requirere
. . videtur. Cp. App. Crit. If maintained, it would of course be an afterthought tending to bring down the
composition of this speech after the
Thirty Years' Truce : a date before which
the term ἀρχή will hardly have been
used of the Athenian Symmachia.

9. φέρει . . ἐς, reaches, is threatening,
concerns, affects.

ἄλλως τε τούτων ἁπάντων : a
desperate crux. Stein[2] boldly takes
ἄλλως as = χωρίς, though such a use of
ἄλλως (he admits) is unprecedented ; in

3. 8 (which he cites) ἀμφοτέρων αὐτῶν
seems to be constructed with ἐν μέσῳ
rather than with ἄλλος. For the various
emendations, none of them satisfactory,
cp. App. Crit. If the prepositional use
of ἄλλως is rejected, τούτων ἁπάντων
might be taken 'of all Hellenes' (that
the Athenians, etc.), τούτων referring to
πᾶσαν τὴν Ἑλλάδα just before ; but τοῖσι
Ἕλλησι just after rather militates against
this rendering. The repetition of
αἰτίους is very neat ; but τούτων ἁπάντων would involve tasteless exaggeration
in that case. ἀπαντώντων makes a very
poor sense. The insertion of ἄνευ or
χωρίς (as in 9. 26, 3. 82) gives a good
sense, and an Herodotean formula, but
the omission is not easy to account for
palaeographically.

11. ἀνασχετόν : cp. 7. 163, and
ἀνέχεσθαι tolerare 7. 87, 149 etc. οἵτινες
causal, 'seeing that ye . .'

12. ἀνθρώπων is here used 'without
prejudice' ; for instances see 8 above.

13. συναχθόμεθα, 'we sympathize with';
the word is common in Xenophon and the
orators of the fourth century, but this
appears to be the only place where it is
found in any earlier writer. The double
καὶ ὅτι gives an air of precision to the
statements, which are not in reality exact
co-ordinates ; cp. below.

καρπῶν ἐστερήθητε διξῶν ἤδη.
This assertion raises a slight chronological difficulty : the scene is laid at
Athens in the winter or early spring of
479 B.C. How have the Athenians
already lost two harvests? Are they
the harvests of two years, or the
two harvests of one year? Presumably the former : but if so, the years
being 480, 479 B.C., how had the
Athenians already lost the harvest

ἤδη καὶ ὅτι οἰκοφθόρησθε χρόνον ἤδη πολλόν. ἀντὶ τούτων
15 δὲ ὑμῖν Λακεδαιμόνιοί τε καὶ οἱ σύμμαχοι ἐπαγγέλλονται
γυναῖκάς τε καὶ τὰ ἐς πόλεμον ἄχρηστα οἰκετέων ἐχόμενα
πάντα ἐπιθρέψειν, ἔστ' ἂν ὁ πόλεμος ὅδε συνεστήκῃ. μηδὲ
ὑμέας Ἀλέξανδρος ὁ Μακεδὼν ἀναγνώσῃ, λεήνας τὸν
Μαρδονίου λόγον. τούτῳ μὲν γὰρ ταῦτα ποιητέα ἐστί·
20 τύραννος γὰρ ἐὼν τυράννῳ συγκατεργάζεται· ὑμῖν δὲ οὐ

---

14 τουτέων z   15 οἱ λοιποὶ σύμμαχοι B   16 γυναῖκάς
τε καὶ secl. van H. ‖ πάντα οἰκετέων ἐχόμενα P¹   17 εστὰν AB ‖
συνέστηκε S ‖ μὴ δὲ libri   20 <ἀρχὴν> συγκατεργάζεται ? van H.
‖ δὲ: δέ γε B, Holder

---

of 479? Had they failed to follow the
directions of Themistokles σπόρου ἀνακῶς
ἔχειν c. 109 supra, and so lost a harvest
by anticipation? Or is not the expression here really a slight anachronism,
the two harvests which the Athenians
ultimately lost, one in 480 B.C. by the
devastation of Xerxes, the other in 479
B.C. by the devastation of Mardonios,
having been 'telescoped' by the writer
(or his source) in the light of later
events, from the point of view of the
hypothetical orator? (The anachronism
remains the same if Archontic years are
understood; or, for that matter, Spartan.)
The apparent co-ordination of the aorist
(ἐστράφθητε) and the perfect (οἰκοφθόρησθε) is grammatically interesting;
yet a shade of difference belongs to them.
The καρπῶν στέρησις is a precise and
limited fact; the οἰκοφθορία is a process,
which, though now perfectly complete,
has been a long time going on. Thus
the tenses of the two verbs here could
not be simply interchanged without a
loss of significance.

14. ἀντὶ τούτων δέ: the δέ is emphatic;
cp. l. 2 supra, 'in return therefor'—to
compensate or console you.

15. Λακεδαιμόνιοί τε καὶ οἱ σύμμαχοι:
i.e. the Peloponnesians; it may include
Aigina and Megara, but at least the
Athenians are conceived as excluded
from the title: this is a symmachy
within the symmachy ἐπὶ τῷ Μήδῳ.

ἐπαγγέλλονται, 'make you this
offer'; cp. 7. 1.

16. γυναῖκάς τε καὶ . . οἰκετέων
ἐχόμενα: οἰκ. ἐχ. = οἰκέτας c. 144 infra;
cp. cc. 44, 106 supra. This phrase here
is an elaborate periphrasis; cp. 1. 120,
193. The children are of course included,
as ἐπι-θρέψειν would also suggest.

17. ἔστ' ἂν ὁ πόλεμος ὅδε συνεστήκῃ:
for the phrase (συστῆναι) cp. 7. 144, 225,
'while, so long as, this war obtain.'
The perfect subjunctive is noticeable,
but the word is only 'perfect' in
grammatical form, and practically present,
or rather aoristic, in sense.

18. λεήνας: cp. 7. 10 supra.

20. τύραννος γὰρ ἐὼν τυράννῳ συγκατεργάζεται: an obvious gnome, probably much older than the ostensible
occasion, and perhaps even inherited
from 'the age of the Despots.' Not but
what tyrant at times would work not
with but against his fellow. 'Birds of
a feather fly together,' 'thieves work in
pairs,' etc. etc., were proverbs a little
hard on Alexander and Mardonios.
Alexander was not a 'tyrant' in the
proper sense (cp. c. 137 supra), and
Mardonios was not technically a 'tyrant'
at all. The gnome might have worked
better, especially as illustrating the
co-operation of the tyranny and the
Mede, if applied to the Ionians on the
Ister (4. 137 f.), or Hippias at Sardes
(5. 96), or the Greek exiles in the train of
Xerxes (7. 6 supra). The point here,
however, put forward is not primarily
the connexion of 'medism' and 'tyranny,'
but the tendency of tyrant to stand by
tyrant against the Republics. The
Republics, Sparta herself, did not go
into this matter with clean hands: she
had worked for the restoration of
Hippias (5. 91), she would have accepted
the aid of Gelon upon conditions (7.
157 supra), as she was afterwards glad to
accept the aid of Dionysios, or for that
matter of Persia itself. But there is a
certain amount of truth in the solidarity
of constitutional sentiment. All states
are forced from time to time into strange

ποιητέα, εἴ περ εὖ τυγχάνετε φρονέοντες, ἐπισταμένοισι ὡς βαρβάροισι ἐστὶ οὔτε πιστὸν οὔτε ἀληθὲς οὐδέν." ταῦτα ἔλεξαν οἱ ἄγγελοι.

Ἀθηναῖοι δὲ πρὸς μὲν Ἀλέξανδρον ὑπεκρίναντο τάδε. 143 " καὶ αὐτοὶ τοῦτό γε ἐπιστάμεθα ὅτι πολλαπλησίη ἐστὶ τῷ Μήδῳ δύναμις ἤ περ ἡμῖν, ὥστε οὐδὲν δέει τοῦτό γε ὀνειδίζειν. ἀλλ᾽ ὅμως ἐλευθερίης γλιχόμενοι ἀμυνεύμεθα οὕτω ὅκως ἂν καὶ δυνώμεθα. ὁμολογῆσαι δὲ τῷ βαρβάρῳ μήτε σὺ ἡμέας πειρῶ 5 ἀναπείθειν οὔτε ἡμεῖς πεισόμεθα. νῦν τε ἀπάγγελλε Μαρδονίῳ [ὡς Ἀθηναῖοι λέγουσι], ἔστ᾽ ἂν ὁ ἥλιος τὴν αὐτὴν ὁδὸν ἴῃ τῇ

---

21 τυγχάνεται R : τυγχάνεσθε P   22 βαρβάροισι ἐστὶ P, Stein² : βαρβάροισί ἐστι a, Stein¹, Holder, van H. : βαρβάροισιν ἔστιν R (βαρβάροισιν ἐστιν β ap. Holder)   143. 1 τοιάδε β   2 γε om. R ‖ τῶν μήδων β   4 ἐλευθερίην σκεπτόμενοι βP (in marg. corr.) ε ‖ ἀμύνεσθαι C ‖ οὕτως AB ap. Stein : οὕτω a : οὕτως β ap. Holder ‖ καὶ om. β   6 ἡμέες ε ‖ τε : δὲ RSV   7 ὡς Ἀθηναῖοι λέγουσι del. Cobet, Holder, van H., Stein³ ‖ εστὰν AB ‖ τῇ : τὴν Cobet, van H.

---

or unnatural alliances by necessity or interest : nor is identity of constitution between neighbours any great security for peace. Monarchy will war against Monarchy, Republic against Republic, for the sake of territory, or commerce, or honour, or adventure, or existence, and will seek or accept any alliance that may serve its turn ; but still all the same one form of constitution has an ' elective affinity ' for its like, and other things being equal, tolerates or co-operates with it more easily. A *Bundesstaat* could never arise between states of diverse constitution, and it may be doubted whether diversely constituted units can permanently maintain a *Staaten-Bund*.

22. βαρβάροισι ἐστὶ οὔτε πιστὸν οὔτε ἀληθὲς οὐδέν. Is this monstrous utterance in place here as a common Hellenic sentiment ? Or is it put into the mouth of the speaker as a satirical sample of Spartan philosophy ? Does it simply prepare the way for the magnificent pan-Hellenism of the Athenian reply ? Does it reflect upon the subsequent duplicity and bad faith of the Spartans themselves ? It is certainly not the opinion of the historian, whether he has taken it over from his source or dramatically devised it to give point to the piece : his whole work belies it, and in particular his account of Persian παιδεία, 1. 136.

143. 3. οὐδὲν δέει, 'thou needest not . .' The form (midd. indic. pr. 2nd person) is not noticed by L. & S.

4. γλιχόμενοι : cp. γλίχεαι (ὡς . .) 7. 161 ; γλιχομένοισι περὶ τῆς ἐλευθερίης 2. 102. The participial construction is here equivalent to a dependent sentence : *quia* etc.

ἀμυνεύμεθα is, of course, future ; ὅκως ἂν after οὕτω appears not as a final but rather as a relative, to which οὕτω is antecedent. The correlation is "frequent in poetry, but less so in prose," Madvig § 810. Cp. Plato *Phaed.* 115 c ταῦτα μὲν τοίνυν προθυμηθησόμεθα, ἔφη, οὕτω ποιεῖν· θάπτωμεν δέ σε τίνα τρόπον; "Οπως ἄν, ἔφη, βούλησθε, ἐάνπερ γε λάβητέ με καὶ μὴ ἐκφύγω ὑμᾶς.

5. μήτε . . οὔτε : the forms of the negative are determined by the moods ; so below μήκοτε follows the imperative.

7. ἔστ᾽ ἂν ὁ ἥλιος τὴν αὐτὴν ὁδὸν ἴῃ τῇ περ καὶ νῦν ἔρχεται : is the path from east to west (and *vice versa*) or from south to north (and *vice versa*), or, more generally, both the daily and annual paths intended ? When Hdt. came to write ' the Egyptian *Logoi* ' he had ceased to regard the sun as a safe fixture, and could hardly have taken its annual course as a symbol of τὰ μὴ ἐνδεχόμενα ἄλλως ἔχειν. Cp. 2. 24-26. He would rather, perhaps, have taken the rising and setting of the sun as a perfect certainty ; yet cp. 2. 142. In any case,

περ καὶ νῦν ἔρχεται, μήκοτε ὁμολογήσειν ἡμέας Ξέρξῃ· ἀλλὰ
θεοῖσί τε συμμάχοισι πίσυνοί μιν ἐπέξιμεν ἀμυνόμενοι καὶ
10 τοῖσι ἥρωσι, τῶν ἐκεῖνος οὐδεμίαν ὄπιν ἔχων ἐνέπρησε τούς τε

---

8 περ om. aC   9 πίσυνοί B   10 οὐδὲ μίαν ὄπιν a : ὄπιν
οὐδεμίην B : οὐδεμίην ὄπιν z ‖ ἐνέπρησέ τε τοὺς S

---

however, this proverbial appeal to the Uniformity of Nature would remain dramatically available : Hdt. is not speaking *propria persona.* Stein⁵ happily cps. Sophokl. *Philokt.* 1329 ff. :

> καὶ ταῦλαν ἴσθι τῆσδε μή ποτ' ἐντυχεῖν
> νόσου βαρείας, ὡς ἂν αὐτὸς ἥλιος
> ταύτῃ μὲν αἴρῃ, τῇδε δ' αὖ δύνῃ πάλιν—

and as another symbol of eternal fixity, the relative position of earth and stars, from Euripides, *Fr.* 688 (Nauck) :

> πρόσθε γὰρ κάτω
> γῆς εἰσιν ἄστρα, γῆ δ' ἄνεισ' ἐς αἰθέρα
> πρὶν ἐξ ἐμοῦ σοι θῶπ' ἀπαντῆσαι λόγον.

Herodotus makes a Korinthian orator employ a less dignified symbol, with a similar point, 5. 92.

This grand boast of the Athenians belongs to the pre-Periklean period : it would have sounded rather silly within sight of 'the Treaty of Kallias,' cp. 7. 151 *supra,* even though that ὁμολογία was not concluded with Xerxes, or not concluded at all. War *à outrance* is still the *mot d'ordre* of the day when Hdt. first drafted this history ; cp. 7. 11 *supra.*

9. θεοῖσί τε συμμάχοισι . . καὶ τοῖσι ἥρωσι : not the Spartans, etc. (συμμάχοισι predicative). The gods and heroes figure but to a small extent in the actual story of the Great Invasion. The legend of Marathon was more deeply saturated with the supernatural *motif,* or at least with its symbolical outcome in actual epiphanies (cp. Hdt. IV.–VI. App. X.). No doubt at the time the Athenians looked for divine assistance, according to their lights (cp. 7. 140, 189, c. 64 *supra*), and afterwards believed themselves to have received it in large measure (cc. 13, 65, 109, 121 *supra*) ; but the actual battles of the war go off without much active interposition (c. 94 *supra* unique) from above : the great gods of Themistokles were Persuasion and Force (c. 108 *supra*) ; the supernatural machinery of the story, so far as it exists, is mainly an afterthought (7.

12 etc.), or an apology (cc. 35 ff. *supra*). Cp. Introduction, § 11.

μιν ἐπέξιμεν ἀμυνόμενοι. Is μιν acc. with the participle (as Stein and Sitzler take it) or with the primary verb ? The construction of ἐπέξειμι is very various. ἐπεξήισαν 7. 223 *supra* is used absolutely : where a personal object is expressed it is usually in the dative, whether the verb be used in the martial or in the legal sense, but an accus. of the person is found e.g. Antiphon 1. 11 ἀπηγγέλθη ὅτι ἐπέξοιμι τοῦ πατρὸς τὸν φονέα, cp. also Eurip. *Androm.* 735 τῇδ' (sc. πόλιν) ἐπεξελθεῖν θέλω, and therefore cannot be pronounced impossible here. The *accus. rei* is more common ; e.g. Hdt. 1. 5 ὁμοίως σμικρὰ καὶ μεγάλα ἄστεα ἀνθρώπων ἐπεξιών : Plato *Rep.* 437 πάσας τὰς τοιαύτας ἀμφισβητήσεις ἐπεξιόντες (Thuc. 1. 84. 3, 3. 82. 8 are not conclusive). A sole reference of μιν to the participle here is harsh, considering the order of the words ; but the participle and verb may be conceived as coalescing into a single idea ('we shall resolutely resist him'), and the accus. may be taken as governed by the whole verbal phrase. Strictly speaking ἐπέξ. ἀμ. is an *oxymoron,* or a precise formula for 'the offensive defensive.'

10. τῶν .. τὰ ἀγάλματα. The relative τῶν may be constructed both with ὄπιν and with οἴκους κτλ. ὄπις, a strictly poetic word, recurs 9. 76 *infra.* (Homer uses the word only of the divine action, vengeance, punishment, θεῶν, more frequently in the *Od.,* and even absolutely, *bis,* 14. 82, 88.) Pindar employs the word for the favourable regard of the gods for man (*Pyth.* 8. 101), but also for human regard (not for the gods but for humanity), *Ol.* 2. 6, *Isth.* 4. (5.) 58. The acc. ὄπιδα is also found (e.g. *Od.* 20. 215).

On the Persian destruction of holy places and objects cp. cc. 33, 35, 53, 109 *supra* ; the Athenians were naturally very sore on this subject (though their losses turned out a blessing in disguise),

οἴκους καὶ τὰ ἀγάλματα. σύ τε τοῦ λοιποῦ λόγους ἔχων
τοιούσδε μὴ ἐπιφαίνεο Ἀθηναίοισι, μηδὲ δοκέων χρηστὰ
ὑπουργέειν ἀθέμιστα ἔρδειν παραίνεε· οὐ γὰρ σὲ βουλόμεθα
οὐδὲν ἄχαρι πρὸς Ἀθηναίων παθεῖν ἐόντα πρόξεινόν τε καὶ
φίλον." πρὸς μὲν Ἀλέξανδρον ταῦτα ὑπεκρίναντο, πρὸς δὲ **144**
τοὺς ἀπὸ Σπάρτης ἀγγέλους τάδε. "τὸ μὲν δεῖσαι Λακεδαιμονίους μὴ ὁμολογήσωμεν τῷ βαρβάρῳ, κάρτα ἀνθρωπήιον ἦν·
ἀτὰρ αἰσχρῶς γε οἴκατε ἐξεπιστάμενοι τὸ Ἀθηναίων φρόνημα
ἀρρωδῆσαι, ὅτι οὔτε χρυσός ἐστι γῆς οὐδαμόθι τοσοῦτος οὔτε 5
χώρη κάλλεϊ καὶ ἀρετῇ μέγα ὑπερφέρουσα, τὰ ἡμεῖς δεξάμενοι
ἐθέλοιμεν ἂν μηδίσαντες καταδουλῶσαι τὴν Ἑλλάδα. πολλὰ

---

12 μὴ δὲ ABPz   13 ἀθέμιτα Marc. ‖ ἔρδειν A : ῥέζειν B : ἔρδειν z,
van H.   14 παθέειν B   **144.** 1 ὑπεκρίνατο RV   3 κάρτα
μὲν B   4 γε om. Apr.   6 χώρηι B ‖ κάλλει AB ‖ μεγάλῃ S

---

and take no account of the offer to restore
at the king's expense.

11. τοῦ λοιποῦ: sc. χρόνου.

13. ὑπουργέειν: sc. ἡμῖν, cp. c. 110
supra, and 7. 38.

ἀθέμιστα ἔρδειν has a poetical
ring; cp. 7. 33 supra. ἄχαρι, an
Herodotean euphemism, cp. 7. 36.

14. πρόξεινόν τε καὶ φίλον: cp. c.
136 supra. The phrase here has, of
course, no more evidential value than
there. It would be odd for the Athenians
to be recognizing not merely the προξενία
but the φιλία of Alexander under such
circumstances. The φιλία probably
dated after the war, when Alexander
turned against the Persians (ps.-Dem.
12. 21). But Lykurgos, the orator,
c. Leocr. § 71, in representing Alexander
on this occasion as having narrowly
escaped death by stoning at the hands
of the Athenians, has confused this affair
with that of Lykidas 9. 4 infra.

144. 3. ἦν: the imperfect here is idiomatic. ἐστί would obviously be admissible.

4. ἀτάρ, or αὐτάρ (Homer), a strong
adversative: comparatively rare in prose,
outside Hdt. (Xenoph., Plato). In 4.
188, 5. 66, as here, it answers to a preceding μέν.

αἰσχρῶς with ἀρρωδῆσαι, and ὅτι
after φρόνημα. The further construction
is not quite regular: τοσοῦτος would
naturally be accompanied by οὕτω (ἀρετῇ
ὑπερφέρουσα) and followed by ὥστε, with
infinitive. The place of the final
sentence is taken by the relative (τά)
and conditional (ἂν). The neuter

relative is also observable, the antecedents being χρυσός and χώρη. κάλλος
and ἀρετή of the land refer to its
appearance and its inherent virtues; cp.
7. 5 supra. In Plato Charm. 157 E
the same collocation of words referring
to an οἰκία (family) is based upon the
beauty and valour of the members. It
would have been interesting to have had
κάλλος here more fully defined.

6. ὑπερφέρουσα, 'surpassing'; cp. c.
138 supra. μέγα, adverbial ('far').

7. μηδίσαντες καταδουλῶσαι τὴν
Ἑλλάδα: there is only too much point
in the participle; the Athenian ἀρχή
was originally based upon opposition to
Persia, but opposition to Persia did not
preclude καταδουλῶσαι τὴν Ἑλλάδα—
rather it furnished the means and excuse
therefor. This passage reads so naïvely
that it looks early; not like an apology
on the part of the τυραννὸς πόλις of the
age of Perikles, but rather like a bid for
the hegemony of a free Hellas. According to Plutarch (Aristeid. 10) it was
Aristeides who dictated this answer;
the ascription is at least ben trovato.
Themistokles would hardly have 'given
away' the actual situation so completely.
He is, indeed, conspicuous by his absence
on this occasion. He would hardly
have dismissed the Spartans with an
official inventory of τὰ διακωλύοντα and
a simple request στρατιὴν ὡς τάχιστα
ἐκπέμψαι. Plutarch (l.c.) also records a
further act of Aristeides calculated to
make Sparta's assurance doubly sure:
ἔτι δὲ ἀρὰς θέσθαι τοὺς ἱερεῖς ἔγραψεν, εἴ
τις ἐπικηρυκεύσαιτο Μήδοις ἢ τὴν συμμα-

τε γὰρ καὶ μεγάλα ἐστὶ τὰ διακωλύοντα ταῦτα μὴ ποιέειν
μηδ' ἢν ἐθέλωμεν, πρῶτα μὲν καὶ μέγιστα τῶν θεῶν τὰ
10 ἀγάλματα καὶ τὰ οἰκήματα ἐμπεπρησμένα τε καὶ συγκεχωσμένα, τοῖσι ἡμέας ἀναγκαίως ἔχει τιμωρέειν ἐς τὰ μέγιστα
μᾶλλον ἤ περ ὁμολογέειν τῷ ταῦτα ἐργασαμένῳ, αὖτις δὲ τὸ

9 μὴ δ' ABP ‖ θέλωμεν S ‖ τά τε ? coni. Stein¹ ², adsc. van H.   10
ἐμπεπρημένα aC ‖ τε καὶ συγκεχωσμένα om. Marc.   11 μάλιστα
Marc.   12 τοῖσι ταῦτα ἐργασαμένοισιν B

χίαν ἀπολίποι τῶν Ἑλλήνων. That act
might be held to regularize the 'lynching
of Lykidas,' cp. 9. 5.

9. πρῶτα μέν: the first place is
assigned to the κώλυμα θεῶν (cp. Thuc.
5. 30. 1), arising from the sacrilegious
destruction of holy places and objects.
The constant recurrence to this consideration assures us that this grievance
bulked very largely in Athenian memories
and may have deeply affected their feelings at the time, cp. c. 143 supra; it
also supports a relatively early date for
the speech: after the glories of Periklean
Athens had more than restored the
works destroyed by the Mede, the sharp
edge of these feelings was abated. But
the further inference that the Persian
war was in any special sense a religious
war, or that the Persians were inflamed
by puritanical and iconoclastic zeal
against the idolatry of Hellas, is an
exaggeration; cp. c. 109 supra. τὰ
ἀγάλματα καὶ τὰ οἰκήματα: cp. τούς τε
οἴκους καὶ τὰ ἀγάλματα c. 143. It is a
question whether the Persian incendiaries
or the Athenian restorers wrought the
more havoc on the old Akropolis and
its contents: the ancient wooden image
of Athena, still to be seen in the days of
Pausanias (1. 26. 6), had been transported to Salamis (Plutarch Themist.
10) and so preserved. Cp. Frazer ii.
340 f.; Hitzig-Bluemner, note ad l.c.
It is tolerably certain that the actual
destruction by the Persians was exaggerated afterwards: in any case, at the
ostensible date of this speech, their
work of destruction was not yet fully
accomplished; cp. 9. 13 infra. Blakesley
remarks that after the battle of Plataia
it became the popular view at Athens
that the war had been waged against
the Persians in revenge for the destruction of Hellenic temples: it is a far cry
from the field of Plataia to the (fictitious)
oath, which according to Lykurgos (c.
Leocr. 82) was taken by the collective

allies just before the battle of Plataia;
cp. 7. 132 supra. But that the Athenian
legend was well under way in the generation after the battle is proved by this
very passage. (Cp. Plutarch Perikl.
17, and note to c. 109 supra.)

11. τοῖσι ἡμέας ἀναγκαίως ἔχει τιμωρέειν ἐς τὰ μέγιστα. This formula goes
beyond the case of merely defensive
warfare, and anticipates, or reproduces,
the πρόσχημα of the Delian alliance (Th.
1. 96.). τοῖσι is masc. The Athenian
view differs from the Delphian, cp. c. 36
supra (both no doubt ex post facto), as
also from the 'vengeance is mine' of the
Hebrew God (cp. Romans 12. 19 and reff.).
But then Delphi had not been destroyed
by the Persians.

12. αὖτις δέ: the second κώλυμα is
'political,' in the highest sense; it is
the unity and solidarity of Hellenic
culture, and what is perhaps implied
rather than stated, its superiority to
barbarism, the obligation to defend and
to preserve it, the iniquity of betraying
it: 'the cause of civilization itself is at
stake.' The passage is, indeed, the locus
classicus on 'the unity of Hellas,' and
Curtius' great chapter under that title,
Gr. Gesch. i.⁶ (1887) pp. 458-551, Die
griechische Einheit, a brilliant commentary thereon.

τὸ Ἑλληνικόν: sc. ἔθνος, γένος, or
simply a collective neuter=οἱ Ἕλληνες,
in their potential union. Undoubtedly
in the historic period, and for a good
while before the fifth century, over the
Greek peninsula, and around the Aegean
coasts, to say nothing of Greater Greece
and the outlying colonial regions,
there was spread a dominant population,
more or less homogeneous and national
in character, and with a distinctive
type of civilization of its own. Divided
under various ethnic or tribal names
(chiefly Aiolian, Dorian, Ionian, Achaian,
cp. Hdt. 1. 56-58, 142-151); divided
geographically into distinct territorial

'Ελληνικὸν ἐὸν ὅμαιμόν τε καὶ ὁμόγλωσσον, καὶ θεῶν ἱδρύματά

13 ἐὸν om. Pz

units (Thessalians, Boiotians, Athenians, Peloponnesians, Italiotes, Sikeliotes, etc. etc.); divided politically into separate and independent city-states innumerable; yet all claiming and recognizing each other as belonging to one communion, one organic system, one people—Greeks, as we say; Hellenes, as they preferred to name themselves.

Non-Hellenic elements were not unknown, or unrecognized, within the Hellenic area. There were sects, or strata, on the borders or even in the midst of Hellas, whose character was doubtful or even non-Hellenic, e.g. Aitolians, Epirotes, Makedonians, Pelasgoi, Leleges, Kaukones, etc. There were perhaps foreign intruders (Phoenician, etc.). There were more certainly survivals from a pre-Hellenic population. But these elements were in the main overcome, absorbed, assimilated, expelled, or reduced to insignificance, albeit their presence must be reckoned with, partly as enriching, partly as disturbing, the ideal homogeneity of the Hellenic type. The Hellenic name apparently originated in Thessaly (Homer, *Il.* 2. 683, 9. 395), and spread with the Achaians (or, less probably, the Dorians) over the whole aggregate (cp. J. B. Bury, ' History of the names Hellas, Hellenes,' *J.H.S.* xv. (1895) pp. 217 ff.). The Greek name, in itself every bit as ancient and authentic, originated in Italy as a collective name, having been brought thither by the Chalkidic colonies (cp. Busolt 1.² 198; Ed. Meyer, *G.d.A.* ii. (1893) 302), or more probably—as giving an earlier date —from Epeiros and that neighbourhood (Helbig in *Hermes* xi. (1876) 257); cp. Aristot. *Meteor.* 1. 353 A αὕτη δ' (sc. ἡ Ἑλλὰς ἡ ἀρχαία) ἐστὶν ἡ περὶ Δωδώνην καὶ τὸν Ἀχελῷον · . . ᾤκουν γὰρ οἱ Σελλοὶ ἐνταῦθα καὶ οἱ καλούμενοι τότε μὲν Γραικοὶ νῦν δ' Ἕλληνες.

13. **ὅμαιμον**, 'of one blood.' The expression here, this ' note ' or ' test ' of Hellenism, assumes the national pedigree, which traced the four main divisions of the Hellenic aggregate to the three sons of Hellen, Aiolos, Doros and Xuthos (through his sons Ion and Achaios). This pedigree cannot be much older than Hesiod, in whom it first meets us (*Frag.* 25 = Rzach 7: an entirely different ethnology rules in the

Homeric poems), but its existence is implied in Herodotus (1. 56, 7. 94, 8. 44) and Thucydides (1. 3), and is fully given (from the logographs, etc.) in Strabo 383, 397, Apollodoros 1. 7. 3. In point of fact this note or test of Hellenism is but an explanation, in ethnological terms, of the historic fact of nationality, and is not itself a datum to start from, but a theorem to be proved. For it plainly means, not that in course of time by intermarriage there was brought about such a fusion in the aggregate that all Hellenes might be regarded as related to one another (in any case a highly disputable theorem): but it means that there really was a strict descent and genealogy in the Hellenic stock, *ab initio.* The pedigree in any case took little or no account of women : the theory belongs to a strictly ' patriarchal ' stage or type of culture. A dominant race, a dominant strain, and that ultimately of ' Aryan ' or ' Indo-European ' origin, in the Hellenic aggregate, is proved by the remaining tests, and by the further one, the physical type, of which Hdt. takes here no specific account; but a veritable fusion and confusion of races and stocks probably underlies the Hellenic nationality.

ὁμόγλωσσον, ' of one tongue.' Language, including literature, is undoubtedly a strong mark of racial identity, especially in the earlier stages of a nation's evolution. The prevalence of the Greek language (and its purity) is perhaps the most remarkable fact, and coefficient, in the Hellenic communion. But language is in itself by no means a certain test of nationality, or of race, nor are those who speak one and the same language to be regarded as descendants of one and the same stock (the cases of Latin, of English, of Greek itself are evidential). But the predominance of a language in a given area proves certain conclusions, applicable to the case of the prevalence of Greek in the Hellenic area. (i.) The presence and prevalence (numerical, or political, or both) of the people whose language it is. Moreover, the relative purity of the Greek language points to the early and effective occupation of the given area by Hellenic tribes or folks.

τε κοινὰ καὶ θυσίαι ἤθεά τε ὁμότροπα, τῶν προδότας γενέσθαι

14 τῶν Β: ὃν καὶ z: ὃν

(ii.) Philology proves that the people whose native language was Greek belonged to the Indo-European (or Eurasian) stock, an observation which makes it certain that the Greeks themselves were immigrants into the region which became the theatre of Hellenic history. There is some evidence, however, of the persistence of non‑Hellenic tongues within the Hellenic area, e.g. Hdt. 1. 57, and the non-Hellenic inscriptions (in Greek characters) found in Lemnos and in Krete. Perhaps also the varieties of Greek dialect may have been encouraged by the presence of pre‑Hellenic elements in the population. The linguistic frontier is tolerably well defined round Greece proper: in the East, Karian is a foreign language, c. 135 supra, and the same is true of the Asianic languages generally. In the West the Epeirote and Illyrian are non‑Hellenic (in the historic period), Thuc. 2. 68, 80, 81. In the North the position of Makedonian is rather doubtful, but though akin to Greek, it differs by more than merely dialectal variation, while Thrakian is distinctly 'barbarous.' In the South the Kretans of historic times speak Greek, but the non‑Hellenic tongue survives in the east of the island (cp. 7. 171 supra).

θεῶν ἱδρύματά τε κοινὰ καὶ θυσίαι, 'common foundations, common sacrifices to gods'—that is, a common religion: common cults, a common theology. The great national centres of religion, with their cults, oracles, and festivals— Olympia, Delphi, Dodona (perhaps Delos), Eleusis—must be chiefly in the speaker's (or writer's) mind: the theology is not expressly mentioned, but may be assumed; cp. 2. 53. Perhaps nothing would more clearly show the genetic or non-primitive character of the Hellenic national communion than the history of Hellenic religion. The Hellenic and pan-Hellenic significance of Olympia and of Delphi (to take the most conspicuous examples) was comparatively recent. The pan-Hellenic Agon of Delphi has the year 585 B.C. as its epoch, and it was established by Kleisthenes of Sikyon and Solon of Athens (cp. J. B. Bury, The Nemean Odes of Pindar, 1890, Appendix D). The Olympian Agon was dated conventionally two centuries earlier (776

B.C.), but this is a 'prochronism'; the founder of the Agon was Pheidon of Argos, and the date of the foundation was probably 668 B.C. (Ol. 28; op. Hdt. IV.–VI. i. 383, note to 6. 127). Delphi gave up to mankind what was intended for Hellenes; but the Hellenic character of the Olympian Agon is attested by two striking facts: (a) the title of the stewards, Ἑλλανοδίκαι, which must be associated with the establishment by Pheidon (the same title was used at Nemea). The adoption of this title presupposes the extensive recognition of 'Hellenes,' and 'Hellas.' (b) The inclusion of all Hellenes (2. 160) and the exclusion of 'barbarians' (5. 22) in the competition, which give it a truly 'national' character. But the common theology (θεοὶ κοινοί 9. 90 infra, θεοὶ οἱ Ἑλλήνιοι 5. 49) carries back further than the great festivals. There is apparent in Greece, even in the historic period, a wondrous variety of local cults and of local myths; but there is also apparent a large community of belief and worship: of this community the Homero-Hesiodic 'theology' (including the Hymns) may be taken as typical. This theology is, indeed, comparatively late (cp. Hdt. 2. 53), but its middle and latest ages imply a long past, a long process, a genesis; and the systematization, the general reception of the Homeric Pantheon, imply a large common stock of ideas and of practices, original or acquired, which in turn implies a long history, a long occupation of the area, over which this religious complex is recognizable.

14. ἤθεά τε ὁμότροπα, 'a uniform moral and political culture.' Under this head might be comprised: (i.) the city-state, with its republican constitutions of one kind or another; (ii.) the family and domestic institutions, marriage, paternal descent, etc.; (iii.) the usages in peace and war, προξενία, κήρυκες, etc.; (iv.) the ethical ideals in the fullest sense. But no one knew better than the Athenian Thucydides that this culture was itself a gradual growth, and not a primitive or intrinsic possession of the Hellenes: that primitive 'Hellas' was itself barbarous (τὸ παλαιὸν Ἑλληνικὸν ὁμοιότροπα τῷ νῦν βαρβαρικῷ διαιτώμενον 1. 6. 6).

Ἀθηναίους οὐκ ἂν εὖ ἔχοι. ἐπίστασθέ τε οὕτω, εἰ μὴ πρό- 15
τερον ἐτυγχάνετε ἐπιστάμενοι, ἔστ' ἂν καὶ εἰς περιῇ Ἀθηναίων,
μηδαμὰ ὁμολογήσοντας ἡμέας Ξέρξῃ. ὑμέων μέντοι ἀγάμεθα
τὴν προνοίην τὴν πρὸς ἡμέας ἐοῦσαν, ὅτι προείδετε ἡμέων
οἰκοφθορημένων οὕτω ὥστε ἐπιθρέψαι ἐθέλειν ἡμέων τοὺς
οἰκέτας. καὶ ὑμῖν μὲν ἡ χάρις ἐκπεπλήρωται, ἡμεῖς μέντοι 20

---

15 μὴ καὶ β, van H.   17 μηδαμᾶ Rz   18 πρὸς : εἰς R,
Holder : ἐς SV, Gaisford, van H. ‖ ὑμέας B¹ ‖ ἔχουσαν β, Holder, van H.
19 οἰκοφορημένων R ‖ ἡμῖν S marg.   20 ἡμέες Bz

It is not the business of the speaker in this passage to qualify or to correct the extreme and enthusiastic assertion of 'the unity of Hellas'; but it is worth while for us to observe that under each of the four great tests, or factors, of Hellenism here propounded, history has significant exceptions and contrary instances to notice. Blood, Dialect, Religion, Ethos, were dividing lines in Hellas, though space here precludes further illustration.

16. ἔστ' ἂν καὶ ἐς . . Ξέρξῃ: this dotting of i's and crossing of t's (if it took place) was very unwise from a diplomatic point of view; to give such assurances to Alexander (c. 143 supra) was bad enough; to pledge themselves thus to Sparta was almost suicidal. It looks downright foolish in the light of the sequel: not alone the γνώμη of Lykidas (9. 5), who was one Athenian, but the formal declaration of Athenian representatives in Sparta, ὅτι σύμμαχοι βασιλέος γινόμεθα (9. 11). Hdt. appears quite unconscious of the satire he thus levels against Athens. The two narratives are from independent sources, and more suo he gives them both, without adjustment, for what they are worth.

17. ὑμέων μέντοι. Hitherto they have been speaking of themselves. The position of the words is emphatic. ἀγάμεθα appears to be used in a good sense, as in 4. 46, rather than in an ironical sense, as in 4. 157. Stein⁸ detects, indeed, a politely satirical (höflich hönisch) tone in this speech, and finds in that tone, and in the large scale on which the whole story of the negotiations is narrated, evidence for two conclusions: (i.) that it was committed to writing at the beginning of the Peloponnesian war (i.e. 431 B.C.), and (ii.) that Hdt. takes sides with Athens against her ungrateful foes. As to the first point: (a) it assumes (as is too often assumed) that Sparta and Athens

quarrelled for the first time in 431 B.C. As a matter of fact the direct feeling between Sparta and Athens was probably not so bitter in 431 B.C. as it had been in 446 B.C. or in 461 B.C.; (b) it ignores the bearing of the Makedonian question. The war in 431 B.C. was largely brought about by Perdikkas, who seems to have had a genuine and legitimate grievance against Perikles and Athens (cp. Thuc. 1. 57). It would be a strange way of taking sides with Athens at the outbreak of the war in 431 B.C. to make so much of the εὔνοια, εὐεργεσίαι, προξενία, φιλία of Alexander of Makedon. Possibly Hdt. sympathizes with Athens rather than with Sparta in this passage, but if so, it is an ideal sympathy, projected into the situation of 479 B.C., not an obscure and partisan commentary upon the outbreak of hostilities in 431 B.C. The Atticizing tone of the whole passage may be due to the Attic or phil-Athenian sources, from which Hdt. has drawn it. So far as Atticism illuminates the problem of composition, the passage is most easily intelligible as belonging to the earlier, perhaps to the earliest, draft of these Books. The slight suspicion of persiflage is, perhaps, misleading, for it ill accords with the heroics of the immediate context. The Spartan offer bore, indeed, rather too near a resemblance to inviting a colossal pledge, or hostage, from the Athenians; but an Athenian migration to Sparta had not been suggested; probably only Peloponnesos was intended, and for that move there was a precedent (cp. cc. 41 and 36 supra).

18. προνοίην . . ὅτι προείδετε, 'providence,' provision, provide; op. προνοίη in a different sense, c. 87 supra. The verb in this sense is more generally in the middle (L. & S. sub v. προείδον).

19. τοὺς οἰκέτας: cp. c. 142 supra.

20. ἡ χάρις ἐκπεπλήρωται, 'your

λιπαρήσομεν οὕτω ὅκως ἂν ἔχωμεν, οὐδὲν λυπέοντες ὑμέας.
νῦν δέ, ὡς οὕτω ἐχόντων, στρατιὴν ὡς τάχιστα ἐκπέμπετε.
ὡς γὰρ ἡμεῖς εἰκάζομεν, οὐκ ἑκὰς χρόνου παρέσται ὁ βάρβαρος
ἐσβαλέων ἐς τὴν ἡμετέρην, ἀλλ᾽ ἐπειδὰν τάχιστα πύθηται τὴν
25 ἀγγελίην ὅτι οὐδὲν ποιήσομεν τῶν ἐκεῖνος ἡμέων προσεδέετο.
πρὶν ὦν παρεῖναι ἐκεῖνον ἐς τὴν Ἀττικήν, ἡμέας καιρός ἐστι
προβοηθῆσαι ἐς τὴν Βοιωτίην." οἱ μὲν ταῦτα ὑποκριναμένων
Ἀθηναίων ἀπαλλάσσοντο ἐς Σπάρτην.

21 λιπαρήσωμεν Marc.　　　23 ἡμέες Β ‖ οἰκάζομεν Marc. ‖ ἑᾶις
χρόνον C　　24 ἐσβαλέων Naber, Stein⁸ : ἐσβαλὼν ‖ ἐπειδὰν : ἐπεὰν
Abicht, Holder ‖ ἐπειδὰν πύθηται τάχιστα malit van H.　　25 προσ-
εδέκετο C　　26 ὑμέας Wesseling, van H.　　27 προβωθῆσαι R,
van H.: προσβωθῆσαι SV, Gaisford ‖ οἱ . . Σπάρτην in principio libri
noni Pʀ : utroque ceteri　　ΗΡΟΔΟΤΟΥ Ḣ | ΧΧΗΗΗΔΔΙΙ α:
ἡροδότου ἱστοριῶν η´ CR : τέλος ἡροδότου ἱστοριῶν ὀγδόης Marc.

kindness leaves nothing to be desired'
—is full to overflowing—is far more
than we had any right to expect. χάρις
is here better taken as the 'gracious
act' (an offer) on the part of Sparta
than as 'the feeling of gratitude' on
the part of Athens. The perf. pass. is
not so much temporal as qualitative in
significance.

ἡμεῖς μέντοι: contr. ὑμέων μέντοι
just above.

21. λιπαρήσομεν, 'we shall continue
to hold out'; cp. 9. 45 (μένοντες), 5. 19
(τῇ πόσει).

οὕτω ὅκως ἂν ἔχωμεν, 'as best we
may'; cp. c. 143 supra. λυπέοντες,
'causing annoyance to.'

22. στρατιὴν ὡς τάχιστα ἐκπέμπετε:
the conference at Athens is quite at the
end of the winter. Mardonios is, however, represented as still in Thessaly
9. 1. If the story just told, the speeches
reported, be true, or anywhere near the
truth, the Athenians had themselves to
thank for the Spartan delay in respond-
ing to this demand; they have given
away their diplomatic weapons in a fit
of pan-Hellenic generosity.

23. οὐκ ἑκὰς χρόνου, 'before long.'
ἑκάς is generally a local adverb; it is,
however, used absolutely of time, Pindar
Pyth. 2. 98 (54), Aischyl. Agam. 1650.
For the use of the adv. with the generic
genitive Stein compares Aischyl. Suppl.
597 εἰσόπιν χρόνου.

25. προσεδέετο: like the simple verb,
constructed with the double genitive,
pers. et rei, τῶν . . ἡμέων, cp. cc. 3. 8,
26. 2 supra. (Stronger than taking τῶν
as genitive by attraction = τούτων ἅ, 6. 35
notwithstanding; cp. 5. 40. σευ τῆς
ἐξέσιος, 3. 157 ἐπιτράπεσθαι ἕτοιμοι ἦσαν
τῶν ἐδέετο σφέων.)

26. ἡμέας, 'you and us,' us both. So
Schweighaeuser.

27. ἐς τὴν Βοιωτίην: this rendezvous
could not be thus treated as a matter of
course, except as the result of preliminary
deliberations and a definite plan of
campaign, perhaps the original one; cp.
c. 40 supra.

οἱ μέν κτλ. The corresponding
sentence opens the ninth Book: there
is no grammatical break. Cp. the
transition between Bks. 7 and 8.

ΗΡΟΔΟΤΟΥ

ΚΑΛΛΙΟΠΗ

Μαρδόνιος δέ, ὡς οἱ ἀπονοστήσας Ἀλέξανδρος τὰ παρὰ 1
Ἀθηναίων ἐσήμηνε, ὁρμηθεὶς ἐκ Θεσσαλίης ἦγε τὴν στρατιὴν
σπουδῇ ἐπὶ τὰς Ἀθήνας. ὅκου δὲ ἑκάστοτε γίνοιτο, τούτους
παρελάμβανε. τοῖσι δὲ Θεσσαλίης ἡγεομένοισι οὔτε τὰ πρὸ
τοῦ πεπρηγμένα μετέμελε οὐδὲν πολλῷ τε μᾶλλον ἐπῆγον τὸν 5
Πέρσην, καὶ συμπροέπεμψέ τε Θώρηξ ὁ Ληρισαῖος Ξέρξην

ΚΑΛΛΙΟΠΗ Θ Α : ΚΑΛΛΙΟΠΗ Β : καλλιόπη θ′ C : καλλιόπη R :
καλλιόπη ἡροδότου ἱστοριῶν ἐννάτη Marc.   1. 1 παρ′ Β   5
μετέμελλεν Β   6 τε : τῶ R : om. CP ‖ ληρισσαῖος ΒΡz ‖ ξέρξεα Βz

---

1. 1. **Μαρδόνιος δέ**, corresponding with
οἱ μέν in the preceding sentence, the
last of Bk. 8. There is not merely no
material break between Bks. 8 and 9,
but not even a formal or grammatical
division. ἀπονοστέειν, 8. 38 etc.

τὰ παρ′ Ἀθηναίων, 'the Athenian
answer,' an ellipse of ἔπη or λεχθέντα :
cp. Thuc. 8. 48. 8 τὰ ἀπὸ τοῦ Ἀλκιβιάδου.

2. ὁρμηθείς, of a physical act ; cp.
ὅρμα 8. 106. ἐκ Θεσσαλίης : that
Mardonios wintered in Thessaly seems
a fairly well-established fact (cp. 8. 113 f.,
131), but does not involve the supposition that he abandoned all hold on
Central Greece : were not the Makedonian
garrisons, perhaps, in occupation of
Boiotia throughout the winter ? Cp. 8.
34.

3. ὅκου . . παρελάμβανε : for the
constr. cp. 8. 115. The statement prepares us for the estimate in c. 32 *infra*
of 50,000 Greeks under arms in the
forces of Mardonios. Diodor. 11. 28
raises the figure to 500,000 by levies on

Thrakians, Makedonians and Greeks !
Cp. Appendix VIII. § 2 (iv.).

4. τοῖσι . . Θεσσαλίης ἡγεομένοισι :
the Aleuadai, cp. 7. 6, 130, their chief
man being Thorax of Larisa, named
just below. The victory of Salamis had
apparently done little to convince the
Thessalian cavaliers that the Greek was
the winning side. Stein observes that
Hdt. sees in the Aleuadai the most active
promoters of the war, and is glad to
emphasize their guilt (cp. 7. 130, 172).
παρῆκε here in particular involves a
gross exaggeration : the roads and passes
were not in the hands of Thorax ; Thermopylai, for example, was doubtless held
by a Persian force ; and so on. Demaratos and the Athenian exiles cut no
figures in the camp of Mardonios : have
they retired in the king's suite ?

6. Θώρηξ is named again in c. 58 *infra*
with his brethren ; before the end of the
sixth century he had given a commission
to Pindar, evidence of which we have
in the poet's earliest extant work (*Pyth.*
10, *anno* 502 B.C.), in which also Thorax

φεύγοντα καὶ τότε ἐκ τοῦ φανεροῦ παρῆκε Μαρδόνιον ἐπὶ
2 τὴν Ἑλλάδα. ἐπεὶ δὲ πορευόμενος γίνεται ὁ στρατὸς ἐν
Βοιωτοῖσι, οἱ Θηβαῖοι κατελάμβανον τὸν Μαρδόνιον καὶ συνεβούλευον αὐτῷ λέγοντες ὡς οὐκ εἴη χῶρος ἐπιτηδεότερος
ἐνστρατοπεδεύεσθαι ἐκείνου, οὐδὲ ἔων ἰέναι ἐκαστέρω, ἀλλ'
5 αὐτοῦ ἱζόμενον ποιέειν ὅκως ἀμαχητὶ τὴν πᾶσαν Ἑλλάδα
καταστρέψεται. κατὰ μὲν γὰρ τὸ ἰσχυρὸν Ἕλληνας ὁμο-

---

7 παρεῖκε z   2. 1 ἐπείτε? van H.   2 τὸν om. Β ‖ καὶ
συνεβούλευον αὐτῷ del. Cobet, van H.   3 ἐπιτηδεώτερος CPz, van H.
4 ἐνστρατεύεσθαι C ‖ ἐκαστέρωι a : ἐκατέρω Β   6 καταστρέψεται
Steger : καταστρέψηται codd. : καταστρέψητε z

---

is named (1. 64). Thorax may have been
Tagos of Thessaly : whether the Skopadai
(cp. 6. 127) were acquiescent or co-operating is not quite clear ; cp. 7. 172.

7. φεύγοντα: Xerxes' νόστος is a φυγή;
cp. 8. 97, 103, 115, 120.

2. 2. οἱ Θηβαῖοι κατελάμβανον τὸν
M., 'the Thebans tried to stay Mardonios . .'

3. οὐκ εἴη χῶρος κτλ. : these representations were not ultimately lost
upon Mardonios, who had at least no
intention of risking a pitched battle in
Attica. The physiographical merits of
Boiotia, from a military point of view,
made it again and again the scene of
important battles both in Greek and in
Roman times (Plataia, Tanagra, Delion,
Haliartos, Koroneia, Leuktra, Orchomenos, Chaironeia); but it was apparently not so much on its advantages as
fighting ground that the Thebans laid
stress, as on the advantages it offered (1)
for supplies, (2) as a headquarters and
base of negotiations. He was to halt
there (αὐτοῦ) and work for obtaining
possession of Greece ἀμαχητί. ἀμαχητί
by itself would not necessarily imply that
the Thebans apprehended a Persian defeat in the event of battle : the Persian
conqueror stood to lose by the losses he
might inflict, as well as by those he
incurred ; but the next sentence suggests
the graver alternative. συνεβούλευον
must be repeated after ἀλλά (brachylogy).

4. οὐδὲ ἔων ἰέναι ἐκαστέρω, 'and were
for hindering his further advance.' The
two reasons given for their advice are
scarcely cognate, the one suggesting an
appeal to arms, the other a recourse to
intrigue ; but cp. next note.

6. κατὰ μὲν γὰρ .. ἅπασι ἀνθρώποισι:

a remarkable sentence both in a material
and in a formal sense. Materially it
recognizes the power of a united Hellas
especially for resistance ; cp. Hdt.'s own
judgement upon 'a united Thrace,' 5. 3,
or Aristotle's upon the Greek race, *Pol*.
4(7). 7. 3 = 1327 Β δυνάμενον ἄρχειν πάντων
μιᾶς τυγχάνον πολιτείας. Formally there
are some disputable points in the sentence : (a) κατὰ τὸ ἰσχυρόν is taken by
Baehr (followed by Stein) νί στινισque ;
cp. 1. 76 ἐπειρῶντο κατὰ τὸ ἰσχυρὸν
ἀλλήλων ('they made trial of each
other in respect of strength'; or 'they
made trial of each other with might and
main'?) The words might be taken (as
by Gail) with ὁμοφρονέοντας ('united
heart and soul') : Blakesley, again,
renders, 'in point of actual force,' taking
them as qualifying the whole sentence.
(b) οἱ περ καὶ πάρος ταὐτὰ ἐγίνωσκον
may refer to the actual members of the
Hellenic *Symmachy*, 'those, to wit, who
were previously of one mind,' or, more
generally, those who should agree previously (before being attacked). πάρος
does not occur elsewhere in Hdt. (c) For
the reading χαλεπούς see App. Crit. (d)
περιγίνεσθαι, not so much 'to survive'
as 'to get the upper hand'; the construction is curious, as the verb seems
to govern the accusative. (e) Ἕλληνας
ὁμοφρονέοντας, as though περιγ. = νικᾶν.
But the acc. may better perhaps be
taken as an *acc. pendens* (with Baehr).
Blakesley explains the *anacoluthon* as
due to the difficulty of expressing the
sentiment politely (a difficulty not
arising from Boiotian stupidity, but
from the nature of the case!). (f) καὶ
ἅπασι ἀνθρώποισι is collective, 'even
all the world together,' not distributive,
'any men in existence.' A united

φρονέοντας, οἵ περ καὶ πάρος ταὐτὰ ἐγίνωσκον, χαλεποὺς
εἶναι περιγίνεσθαι καὶ ἅπασι ἀνθρώποισι· "εἰ δὲ ποιήσεις τὰ
ἡμεῖς παραινέομεν," ἔφασαν λέγοντες, "ἕξεις ἀπόνως ἅπαντα
τὰ ἐκείνων ἰσχυρὰ βουλεύματα· πέμπε χρήματα ἐς τοὺς δυνα- 10
στεύοντας ἄνδρας ἐν τῇσι πόλισι, πέμπων δὲ τὴν Ἑλλάδα
διαστήσεις· ἐνθεῦτεν δὲ τοὺς μὴ τὰ σὰ φρονέοντας ῥηιδίως
μετὰ τῶν στασιωτέων καταστρέψεαι." οἱ μὲν ταῦτα συν- 3
εβούλευον, ὃ δὲ οὐκ ἐπείθετο, ἀλλά οἱ δεινὸς ἐνέστακτο ἵμερος

---

7 ταῦτα RV ‖ χαλεποὺς coni. Stein², van H.: χαλεπὰ ('quod ferri
nequit, nisi forte ante περιγίνεσθαι exciderunt verba νικᾶν τε καὶ' van H.:
haec eadem in textum recep. Holder)   8 περιγενέσθαι β ‖ ποιήσειας z
9 ἕξεις: 'an σχίσεις?' Kallenberg ‖ πάντα aCP, Stein²   10 κείνων z
‖ ἰσχυρὰ om. aC, van H.   13 μετὰ στρατιωτέων β ‖ κατάστρεψαι βC
3. 2 ἐπίθετο R ‖ δεινός τις β, Holder, van H.

Hellas, which knew its own mind (even
if only comprising the actually existing confederacy), could hold its own
against a world in arms.

9. ἕξεις, 'thou shalt be in possession
of . .' If ἰσχυρά were to stand, it
would favour taking κατὰ τὸ ἰσχυρόν just
above with ὁμοφρονέοντας. But cp.
App. Crit.

10. πέμπε χρήματα ἐς τοὺς δυναστεύοντας . ., 'divide Hellas by bribery
—of the men in power in the cities.'
Prima facie this might be taken to
imply that the masses, the δῆμος, are
more anti-Persian than the 'dynasts,' the
δυνατοί. Something of that sort is urged
by the Theban orator in Thucydides, 3.
62. 3, and the term δυναστεύοντας here
is illuminated by the words there used
to describe the condition of Thebes in
480 B.C.: δυναστεία ὀλίγων ἀνδρῶν εἶχε
τὰ πράγματα. But perhaps Athens is
not included in the Theban programme,
and Sparta with the Peloponnesian cities
may be mainly in view (cp. Diodor. l.c.
infra). The proposal is not so much
to overthrow democracies by medizing
oligarchs, as to divide the Hellenic
confederacy, separating the partisans of
Persia (τῶν στασιωτέων, 'your partisans')
from τοὺς μὴ τὰ σὰ φρονέοντας. The
two points are not perhaps clearly distinguished in this passage; and even
among the Athenians (it must be admitted), just before Plataia, there was
a strong medizing faction, if the story
told by Plutarch, Arist. 13, is true. Cp.
Appendix VIII. § 2 (iii.).

11. τὴν Ἑλλάδα διαστήσεις, 'thou

shalt divide Hellas against itself'; cp.
διαστάντας 4. 11, 'dividing into two
bodies'—κατὰ πόλεις δὲ διέσταμεν Thuc.
4. 61. 1. The advice is repeated by
Artabazos c. 41 infra.

3. 2. ὃ δὲ οὐκ ἐπείθετο: yet just
below, c. 5, Hdt. himself suggests that
Lykidas, the Athenian, had perhaps
received money from Mardonios. Diodor.
11. 28. 3 asserts that Mardonios τῶν
ἐν Πελοποννήσῳ πόλεων ἐπειρᾶτό τινας
ἀφιστάνειν, χρήματα διαπεμπόμενος τοῖς
προεστηκόσι. He was, of course, en
rapport with Argos; cp. c. 12 infra.
The mission of Arthmios of Zela
(Plutarch, Themist. 6) cannot be referred with confidence to this precise
point (as by Duncker vii.⁵ 318), but it
is hardly likely that Mardonios omitted
to employ so obvious a weapon as
bribery. Rawlinson points out (iv.³
374) that Mardonios was very late in
reoccupying Athens, and thinks that
he spent the spring in efforts to win
over some of the Greek states by bribery.
The Atticizing source speaks in the next
words of Hdt. and accounts for the
supposed folly of Mardonios.

ἀλλά: i.e. δεινὸς γάρ οἱ κτλ. ἐνέστακτο: the simple verb occurs 6. 74,
and in the literal sense; and with the
preposition uncompounded, Pindar, Pyth.
9. 110 νέκταρ ἐν χείλεσσι καὶ ἀμβροσίαν
στάξαισι. Here, of course, as there, it is
a brilliant metaphor (as of poison?), the
pluperfect pointing rather to the depth
than to the date of his passion. This
passage is, however, more probably a
reminiscence of Od. 2. 271 εἰ δή τοι σοῦ

τὰς Ἀθήνας δεύτερα ἑλεῖν, ἅμα μὲν ὑπ' ἀγνωμοσύνης, ἅμα δὲ
πυρσοῖσι διὰ νήσων ἐδόκεε βασιλέι δηλώσειν ἐόντι ἐν Σάρδισι
5 ὅτι ἔχοι Ἀθήνας· ὃς οὐδὲ τότε ἀπικόμενος ἐς τὴν Ἀττικὴν
εὗρε τοὺς Ἀθηναίους, ἀλλ' ἔν τε Σαλαμῖνι τοὺς πλείστους
ἐπυνθάνετο εἶναι ἔν τε τῇσι νηυσί, αἱρέει τε ἔρημον τὸ ἄστυ.
ἡ δὲ βασιλέος αἵρεσις ἐς τὴν ὑστέρην τὴν Μαρδονίου ἐπι-
στρατηίην δεκάμηνος ἐγένετο.

4 Ἐπεὶ δὲ ἐν Ἀθήνῃσι ἐγένετο ὁ Μαρδόνιος, πέμπει ἐς
Σαλαμῖνα Μουρυχίδην ἄνδρα Ἑλλησπόντιον φέροντα τοὺς

---

3 ἐλέειν V, Schaefer, Gaisford   4 βασιλέι AB ‖ δηλώσει R :
δηλω cum σ superscr. V   5 τὰς Ἀθήνας β ‖ ὃς: ὁ δὲ Stein(2)   7
τε post ἐν om. β ‖ ἐρῆμον CPz   8 βασιλῆος z ‖ ὑστεραίην CPz ‖ τὴν :
τοῦ Marc.   4. 1 ἐπείτε? van H. ‖ ἐν om. β ‖ ὁ om. z   2
βουργίδην C : μουριχίδην Rz

πατρὸς ἐνέστακται μένοι ἠύ (a passage
which might have suggested to Pindar
the use of the simple verb in *Nem.* 10.
82).

3. δεύτερα, 'a second time'; not τὸ
δεύτερον—for Mardonios had not 'captured' it the first time ; cp. c. 4 *infra*.

ἅμα μὲν .. ἅμα δέ: the two *cola*
are not strictly correlative. ἀγνωμοσύνη,
vanity, arrogancy, obstinacy—cause for
effect ; cp. c. 41 *infra*: the same word is
used of the Athenians c. 4 *infra*.

4. πυρσοῖσι διὰ νήσων: cp. 7. 183
on this method of signalling, and the
opening of the immortal *Agamemnon*,
which Stein suggests was a grand anachronism, based upon this historic Mar-
doniograph. But Mardonios did not at
this time control the 'islands'; his only
line of communication was by the mainland. The king is in Sardes ; cp. c. 108
infra. Perhaps then Hdt. has borrowed
from Aischylos (the *Oresteia* was presented in 458 B.C.).

6. ἔν τε Σαλαμῖνι: was there in truth
a second complete evacuation of Attica
and Athens ? i.e. had the Athenians in
fact reoccupied their city and houses ?
Had they already begun the rebuilding
to which Themistokles exhorted them
8. 109 *supra*? They may have attempted to raise a harvest, perhaps, in
Attica, or in the parts nearest Salamis ;
but there is fair room for doubt whether
they undertook the rebuilding of the
city until they were assured that they
should not see the Persian army any
more in the land. Hdt. is, indeed,
explicit on the point c. 6 *infra* ; but
he might have been mistaken. A large

number of the Athenians may have
wintered in Salamis. Their occupation,
or reoccupation, of the island implies
a confidence in their superiority by sea.

7. ἔν τε τῇσι νηυσί: the only Attic
ships for which Hdt. accounts at this
time are those with the Hellenic fleet
at Aigina, which numbers but 110 in
all ; 8. 131 *supra*. Where were the
rest? Had they been left on the Attic
side Mardonios would certainly have
used or have destroyed them. A goodly
Attic fleet must have been in and around
Salamis itself, and have counted for
something in the whole plan of campaign,
though completely ignored by Hdt.

9. δεκάμηνος : ten—or rather nine—
months earlier. This date is doubtless
correct, and reckoned by the Attic
Calendar, but unfortunately it is only
approximate. Rawlinson places the reoccupation of Athens in June, and
remarks even so upon the waste of time
(above accounted for) : this chronology
would allow both occupations to the
same Archontic year. Stein brings
Mardonios to Athens "after the middle
of July " (Xerxes having reached Athens
"after the middle of September"), that
is, places the two events in different
Archontic years. Busolt ii.² 722 f. dates
the event to the second half of June (in
Skirophorion). Hdt.'s term, if anything, favours the view that the two
events belong to the same official year ;
otherwise, too, he would perhaps have
added the Archon ; cp. 8. 51.

4. 2. Μουρυχίδην ἄνδρα Ἑλλησπόντιον. The proper name appears in
Attic as Μορυχίδης and Μυριχίδης ; cp.

αὐτοὺς λόγους τοὺς καὶ Ἀλέξανδρος ὁ Μακεδὼν τοῖσι
Ἀθηναίοισι διεπόρθμευσε. ταῦτα δὲ τὸ δεύτερον ἀπέστελλε
προέχων μὲν τῶν Ἀθηναίων οὐ φιλίας γνώμας, ἐλπίζων δὲ 5
σφέας ὑπήσειν τῆς ἀγνωμοσύνης ὡς δοριαλώτου ἐούσης τῆς
Ἀττικῆς χώρης καὶ ἐούσης ὑπ' ἑωυτῷ. τούτων μὲν εἴνεκα 5
ἀπέπεμψε Μουρυχίδην ἐς Σαλαμῖνα, ὃ δὲ ἀπικόμενος ἐπὶ τὴν

---

3 οὓς aC   5 προέχων: προσδοκῶν Krueger: (προσδοκέων ? van H.)
‖ ἐλπίσας B ‖ δὲ σφέας R, Stein²: δέ σφεας   6 δορυαλώτου z ‖ πάσης
τῆς RSV, Gaisford, Holder   7 καὶ ἐούσης ἤδη RSV, Gaisford, Holder:
καὶ .. ἑωυτῷ secl. van H.   5. 1 τουτέων z ‖ ἕνεκα aC: εἵνεκεν B
2 Μουριχίδην z

Μορυχίων and Μόρυχος, a tragic poet,
the butt of sundry Aristophanic gibes
(Acharn. 887, Wasps 506, 1142, Peace
1008). Μόρυχος was also an epithet of
Dionysos, 'in Sicily,' his face 'soiled'
with wine-lees (cp. μορύσσειν), and there
was a proverb μωρότερος Μορύχου or
Μωρύχου (Photius, Lex., et al.). This
Hellespontine with his proposals was
surely 'a son of the foul fiend' to
Athens ! There is a want of precision
about his habitat ; Ἑλλησπόντιοι have,
indeed, been mentioned collectively as
furnishing 100 ships to the Persian fleet
(7. 95), and an anonymous 'Helles-
pontian' is credited with a crude remark,
7. 56 ; was this Morychides the man ?
How does a 'Hellespontine' come to
be with Mardonios ? Was he the nearest
thing to an 'Ionian,' or an Athenian,
that the Persian could employ ? Was
he perhaps an ex-Athenian Kleruch ?

φέροντα τοὺς αὐτοὺς λόγους κτλ. :
cp. 8. 140. Some of the λόγοι would
suit the present situation better than
the former ; e.g. the order from the
king τὴν γῆν σφι ἀπόδος κτλ., which
have a direct bearing on Mardonios'
fiery message ὅτι ἔχω Ἀθήνας c. 3 supra.
φέροντα is but slightly metaphorical ;
indeed, if the λόγοι were in writing
(a despatch), not even slightly. διεπόρθμευσε is very highly metaphorical,
though less highly if the Athenians
had already been in Salamis when
'Alexander the Makedonian' visited
them. The word is elsewhere by Hdt.
always used of actually crossing water ;
cp. 8. 130 supra, 1. 205, 4. 141, 5. 52.

4. τὸ δεύτερον : cp. c. 3 supra.
5. προέχων μὲν τῶν Ἀθηναίων οὐ
φιλίας γνώμας, 'though already in
possession of the hostile mind (or
resolutions) of the Athenians' (against

himself). This simple use of προ- in
comp. (=πρότερον, so Wesseling) is
observable ; cp. προοφειλομένη in 5. 82.
Blakesley somewhat perversely takes
προέχων as 'putting forward.' φίλιος
(λόγος) 7. 163, and in the comparative
7. 151.

6. ὑπήσειν τῆς ἀγνωμοσύνης : the
verb used intrans. as in 1. 156 ὑπεὶς τῆς
ὀργῆς (cp. also 7. 162 supra abs.) ; in
the middle vid. 2. 121, 4. 181. The
substantive as in c. 3 supra ; here used
from Mardonios' point of view (ἐλπίζων,
not, by the way, 'hoping,' but 'expecting'). δοριαλώτου, as in 8. 74 supra.

7. ἐούσης ὑπ' ἑωυτῷ : the preposition
with t e dat. is no doubt very strong,
but thh participle, especially in repetition, is rather thin ; it would be
strengthened by omission the first time.
Cp. App. Crit.

5. 2. ἀπικόμενος ἐπὶ τὴν βουλήν. The
Athenian βουλή, the Athenian ἐκκλησία,
are working in Salamis ; this is a
'record' in its way—for Salamis was not
strictly a part of Attica (cp. 8. 11. 13
supra) ; it marks again a stage in the
education of the Athenians, who grasp
the principle that where the Athenians
are there is Athens. It is especially
remarkable that the probouleutic office .
is discharged by the Boule of 500 (not
by the Strategoi, for example, as at
Samos in 412 B.C.) notwithstanding the
state of war. It is just, however,
conceivable that the Boule here in
action was not the 500 but the
Areiopagos which performed some vague
services in the Persian war ; cp. Aristotle, Pol. 8. 4. 8=1304 A, Ἀθ. π. 23,
Plutarch, Them. 10. ἐπελθών (cp. c. 7
infra) or παρελθών (cp. 8. 81) might
have been expected here in place of the
less technical ἀπικόμενος.

βουλὴν ἔλεγε τὰ παρὰ Μαρδονίου. τῶν δὲ βουλευτέων
Λυκίδης εἶπε γνώμην ὡς ἐδόκεε ἄμεινον εἶναι δεξαμένους τὸν
5 λόγον, τόν σφι Μουρυχίδης προσφέρει, ἐξενεῖκαι ἐς τὸν δῆμον.
ὁ μὲν δὴ ταύτην τὴν γνώμην ἀπεφαίνετο, εἴτε δὴ δεδεγμένος
χρήματα παρὰ Μαρδονίου, εἴτε καὶ ταῦτά οἱ ἐάνδανε· Ἀθηναῖοι
δὲ αὐτίκα δεινὸν ποιησάμενοι οἵ τε ἐκ τῆς βουλῆς καὶ οἱ
ἔξωθεν ὡς ἐπύθοντο, περιστάντες Λυκίδην κατέλευσαν βάλλοντες,

5 Μουριχίδης z ‖ προσφέρει Krueger, Cobet, van H., Stein³ : προφέρει ‖
ἐξενεῖκεν β   7 οἱ ante καὶ z   9 λυκίδεα βz ‖ βάλλοντες del.
van H.

4. Λυκίδης εἶπε γνώμην, 'Lykidas
moved a resolution . .' The phrase is
technically correct, γνώμην being generally dropped in the documents. Hdt.
does not know, or at least does not give,
the man's patronymic or Demotikon.
The name Lykidas was, or became, very
rare in Athens ; it occurs twice in
Demosthenes, (1) of a slave belonging
to Chabrias, (2) of a miller (cp. Orat.
Att., Baiter and Sauppe, Index ii. 91).
The odd thing is that Demosthenes, de
Coron. 204, tells this story, but with two
important variations : (1) the traitor's
name is Kyrsilos, (2) the date is before
Salamis ; cp. Cicero de Off. 3. 11. 2.
Thirlwall (ii. 363 n.) attempts to
harmonize by supposing Kyrsilos a
nickname of Lykidas ; but Kyrsilos is
a good proper name ; cp. Strabo, 530
(a Pharsalian), and C.I.G. ii. 2347 (a
Naxian). Moreover, the discrepancy of
date remains. Rawlinson reconciles the
two stories by accepting them both as
true ! Grote (iv. 249 n.), while recognizing the Herodotean as the more
probable of the two stories, shows
the improbability of both being true ;
it would indeed be easier to believe
that they are both fictitious—an hypothesis more creditable to the constitutional morality of the Athenians and
the common humanity of their wives.
The proposal ascribed to Lykidas would
be 'accursed' (anathema) under the act
of Aristeides above cited ; cp. notes to
8. 144.

ἐδόκεε ἄμεινον εἶναι, 'it seemed
good . .' (not ἔδοξε, 'it was decided.'
But Hdt.'s imperfects are not always to
be rigidly pressed).

δεξαμένους : cp. 8. 115 supra.

5. προσφέρει, not like the Pythia, cp.
4. 151, 5. 63 (a divine revelation or
behest), still less like the Persian writers,

1. 3 (a reproach), but more simply,
'brings forward . .' But cp. App. Crit.

ἐξενεῖκαι ἐς τὸν δῆμον : i.e. 'lay
before the Ekklesia,' exactly as in 5. 79.

6. εἴτε δὴ δεδεγμένος χρήματα, the
more plausible alternative, εἴτε καὶ the
less. δεδεγμένος, perhaps merely to avoid
repeating δεξάμενος (from just above),
albeit δεδεγμένους could not be used
above without a change of sense. (The
passive form of p.p. with middle sense
is noticeable.) Does Hdt. overlook the
inconsistency of this alternative with
his own statement, cc. 2, 3 supra ? or
has Mardonios now, being in possession
of Athens, thought better of the Thebans'
advice ?

7. ἐάνδανε : cp. c. 19 infra.

8. οἵ τε ἐκ τῆς βουλῆς καὶ οἱ ἔξωθεν :
these two classes, or groups, are comprised in Ἀθηναῖοι just before. By οἱ
ἐκ τῆς βουλῆς Hdt. might have meant
simply οἱ βουλευταί, 'the members of
the Council.' Baehr's senatores qui e
senatu egressi etc. goes beyond the
necessary meaning of the words (though
perhaps not beyond the actual facts of
the case). Nor need οἱ ἔξωθεν mean
'those outside the Council-chamber,'
but only those outside the Bar (δρύφακτοι),
exactly described by Demosthenes : l.c.
τοὺς περιεστηκότας ἔξωθεν καὶ ἀκροωμένους,
i.e. persons within hearing of the proceedings in the Council (Baehr unfortunately equates ἀκροωμένους there
with ὡς ἐπύθοντο here !). Hdt. himself,
indeed, by adding ὡς ἐπύθοντο (which of
course refers only to οἱ ἔξωθεν) shows
that he does not understand the Attic
source, which intended οἱ ἔξωθεν περιστάντες to be taken together.

9. Λυκίδην κατέλευσαν βάλλοντες :
to Hdt. this execution is apparently a
wild act of irregular justice, an instance
of 'Lynch-law.' On the face of it this

τὸν δὲ Ἑλλησπόντιον Μουρυχίδην ἀπέπεμψαν ἀσινέα. γενο- 10
μένου δὲ θορύβου ἐν τῇ Σαλαμῖνι περὶ τὸν Λυκίδην, πυνθάνονται
τὸ γινόμενον αἱ γυναῖκες τῶν Ἀθηναίων, διακελευσαμένη δὲ
γυνὴ γυναικὶ καὶ παραλαβοῦσα ἐπὶ τὴν Λυκίδεω οἰκίην ἤισαν
αὐτοκελέες, καὶ κατὰ μὲν ἔλευσαν αὐτοῦ τὴν γυναῖκα κατὰ δὲ
τὰ τέκνα. 15
Ἐς δὲ τὴν Σαλαμῖνα διέβησαν οἱ Ἀθηναῖοι ὧδε. ἕως 6
μὲν προσεδέκοντο ἐκ τῆς Πελοποννήσου στρατὸν ἥξειν
τιμωρήσοντά σφι, οἳ δὲ ἔμενον ἐν τῇ Ἀττικῇ· ἐπεὶ δὲ οἱ μὲν
μακρότερα καὶ σχολαίτερα ἐποίεον, ὁ δὲ ἐπιὼν καὶ δὴ ἐν τῇ

---

10 μουριχίδεα RV : μουρυχίδεα S : Μουριχίδην z : del. van H.   11
ἐν .. Λυκίδην del. van H. ‖ λυκίδεα BPz   12 τῶν Ἀθηναίων αἱ γυναῖκες
τὸ γινόμενον z   13 ἤισαν a : ἤεσαν BPz : ἦσαν C   6. 1 οἱ om.
Pz ‖ ὧιδε CP   2 τὸν ἐκ z   3 σφι : σφίσι ? van H.   4 τε
καὶ z ‖ σχολαιότερα S ‖ ἐς τὴν βοιωτίην BPz

view is unsatisfactory. Was the execution of Lykidas an instance of that summary jurisdiction which the *Boule* formerly possessed (cp. 'Αθ. π. 41. 2, 45), or was the *Boule* here in question the Areiopagos? Was Lykidas stoned as 'Anathema' under the psephism of Aristeides (cp. 8. 144, and c. 2 *supra*), or, again, was there a formal psephism condemning the traitor? Lykurg. *contr. Leocrat.* 122 ἄξιον τοίνυν ἀκοῦσαι καὶ τοῦ περὶ τοῦ ἐν Σαλαμῖνι τελευτήσαντος γενομένου ψηφίσματος, ὃν ἡ βουλή, ὅτι λόγῳ μόνῳ ἐνεχείρει προδιδόναι τὴν πόλιν, περιελομένη τοὺς στεφάνους αὐτοχειρὶ ἀπέκτεινεν. Or was this psephism passed *ex post facto*, to whitewash and justify the illegal execution? (Of all the orators Lykurgos is the worst as a historical authority: he even by anticipation makes the mistake, not uncommon nowadays, of confounding Pausanias 'the King' with Pausanias 'the Regent'; cp. c. 128 *infra*.)
κατέλευσαν, c. 120 *infra*.
10. τὸν δὲ .. ἀσινέα: a remarkable illustration of their respect for law, the law of nations; cp. 7. 133 *supra*.
12. αἱ γυναῖκες τῶν Ἀθηναίων: the only record of any active service by the Attic women in the war, who appear in general passive as sheep, shipped and shifted about from one place to another. It recalls the action reported on another occasion, 5. 87, of which Hdt. records: Ἀθηναίοισι δὲ ἔτι τοῦ πάθεος δεινότερόν τι δόξαι εἶναι τὸ τῶν γυναικῶν ἔργον.
διακελευσαμένη: cp. 7. 16 *supra*.
13. παραλαβοῦσα: sc. γυνὴ γυναῖκα,

cp. παρελάμβανε c. 1. *supra*. The whole construction is a kind of σχῆμα καθ' ὅλον καὶ μέρος.
τὴν Λυκίδεω οἰκίην: the scene is laid in Salamis: had Lykidas the Councillor a house there? Or was his house in Athens, or in Attica, and is this a slip? Should the scene have been laid in Athens, and earlier? Or, in fact, is Demosthenes right that the scene was before the battle of Salamis? It would be easier to account for the 'Hellespontine' in that case. But the whole story is unsatisfactory. Within a few days of this heroic scene—with its 'No surrender' and 'As long as the Sun keeps his path in Heaven, or one single Athenian citizen survive'—the Athenians sent to Sparta threatening to make terms with the king, cc. 6, 11 *infra*.
14. αὐτοκελέες is an *Hapaxlegomenon* = αὐτοκέλευστοι (L. & S.).
κατὰ μὲν .. κατὰ δέ, a violent tmesis; cp. 8. 33.
6. 1. ὧδε gives the material, or rather ideal grounds, for the move, not the physical method or means (e.g. νηυσί).
ἕως μέν is answered by ἐπεὶ δέ ..
3. τιμωρήσοντα, to support, to assist; cp. 8. 169.
οἳ δέ presents a δέ in *apodosi*, and also with resumed subject; cp. 7. 51.
οἱ μέν: sc. οἱ Πελοποννήσιοι.
4. ἐποίεον, 'were acting, behaving in too long and leisurely a fashion'; cp. δεινότερα ἐποίεε 7. 1 *supra*.
ὁ δέ: sc. ὁ Πέρσης.
καὶ δή = ἤδη. Cp. Index.

5 Βοιωτίη ἐλέγετο εἶναι, οὕτω δὴ ὑπεξεκομίσαντό τε πάντα καὶ
αὐτοὶ διέβησαν ἐς Σαλαμῖνα, ἐς Λακεδαιμονά τε ἔπεμπον
ἀγγέλους ἅμα μὲν μεμψομένους τοῖσι Λακεδαιμονίοισι ὅτι
περιεῖδον ἐμβαλόντα τὸν βάρβαρον ἐς τὴν Ἀττικὴν ἀλλ᾽ οὐ
μετὰ σφέων ἠντίασαν ἐς τὴν Βοιωτίην, ἅμα δὲ ὑπομνήσοντας
10 ὅσα σφι ὑπέσχετο ὁ Πέρσης μεταβαλοῦσι δώσειν, προεῖπαί
τε ὅτι εἰ μὴ ἀμυνεῦσι Ἀθηναίοισι, ὡς καὶ αὐτοί τινα ἀλεωρὴν
7 εὑρήσονται. οἱ γὰρ δὴ Λακεδαιμόνιοι ὅρταζόν τε τοῦτον τὸν
χρόνον καί σφι ἦν Ὑακίνθια, περὶ πλείστου δ᾽ ἦγον τὰ τοῦ

---

5 τε: τότε P   6 ἐς Σαλαμῖνα del. Cobet ‖ ἔπεμψαν S, Schaefer,
Bekker   7 μεμψομένους **B**: μεμφομένους   8 ἐσβάλλοντο C:
ἐσβαλόντα z   10 σφι: σφίσι? van H. ‖ προεῖπέ τε C: προειπέται R
11 ὡς del. van H.   7. 1 ὥρταζόν CPz   2 δὲ **B**

---

5. **ἐλέγετο**, 'was being reported';
the evacuation of Attica might seem to
have commenced as soon as Mardonios
reached Chaironeia (the frontier town of
Boiotia; cp. Plutarch, *Kimon* 1). But
Mardonios may have negotiated from
Thebes. In any case there is a chronological return in this c. to a point before
that reached in c. 3 *supra*.

οὕτω δή, *tum demum*.

ὑπεξεκομίσαντο: cp. 8. 4 ὑπεκτί-
θεσθαι, 8. 41, 60 ὑπεκκέεσθαι.

6. **ἐς Λακεδαιμονά τε ἔπεμπον**,
'sending at the same time to L. . .'

7. **ἅμα μὲν . . ἅμα δέ**, strictly
correlative; but **προεῖπαί τε** follows,
with a change of construction (*anacoluthon*): (ἔπεμπον) ἀγγέλους προεῖπαι
= ἀγγελέοντας.

8. **περιεῖδον**: cp. c. 41 *infra*, 7. 16 *supra*.
ἀλλ᾽ οὐ, 'instead of . .'

10. **ὑπέσχετο** must be from ὑπέχειν,
ὑπέχεσθαι or ὑπίσχεσθαι, cp. ὑπίσχοντο
7. 168, though Hdt. also uses the forms
from ὑπισχνέομαι as in c. 109 *infra*; cp.
ὑπέσχε 2. 151, ὑπέχουσι 4. 72, ὑπίσχομαι
7. 104, and ὑπέσχετο 2. 28 in a somewhat
different and stricter sense.

μεταβαλοῦσι, 'if they changed
sides': predicative and conditional
participle.

11. **ὅτι . . ὡς**, "quarum altera
abundat," Baehr; cp. 3. 71. Cp. App.
Crit.

ἀλεωρή: found in Homer both of
an act (*Il.* 24. 216) and of an object (21.
57, 15. 533); and in Aristophanes in
the latter sense, *Wasps* 615.

7. 2. Ὑακίνθια: a three days' celebration, apparently common like the
Karneian, to all Dorians, but certainly
of pre-Dorian origin in the Peloponnese:
Schoemann - Lipsius ii. (1902) 473.
For the texts bearing upon the festival
see Wide, *Lakonische Kulte* (1893) 285 ff.
The feast was held during the Lakonian
month Hekatombeus (Hesych. *s. v.*
Ἑκατομβεύς) (not necessarily = Attic
Hekatombaion: perhaps = Thargelion,
reff. *ap.* Busolt ii.² 722). The cult
implies a spring festival. The celebration lasted three days: on the first day
the death of Hyakinthos was bewailed
(Pausan. 3. 19. 3); on another day the
women of Sparta brought a *Chiton* as an
offering to the god of Amyklai (Pausan.
3. 16. 2); on another day (Athenaeus
189 τῇ δὲ μέσῃ τῶν τριῶν ἡμερῶν—but,
if so, he omits to say what was done on
the third) there was a great and joyous
festival, with songs and dances, with
sacrifice and banquet: presumably in
honour of the apotheosis of Hyakinthos
(τὸν θεὸν ᾄδουσιν), whom by that time
it was very difficult to distinguish from
his destroyer (Apollon). (Rawlinson
seems to think the Hyakinthia lasted
only one day, and that Midsummer-day.)
Thucyd. 5. 23. 4 might favour an earlier
date, in spring; but that would quite
discredit the chronology of this story in
Hdt., not indeed in itself a very strong
objection. Busolt *l.c.* argues from
Xenophon *Hell.* 4. 5. 1 ff. that the
Hyakinthia were celebrated 'a few
weeks at most' after the Isthmia, which
he places in Μουνυχιών (tenth Attic
month); but Xenophon's intervals are
very ill-reckoning, nor does he say how
long after the Isthmia or how long before

θεοῦ πορσύνειν· ἅμα δὲ τὸ τεῖχός σφι <ἤνετο>, τὸ ἐν τῷ
Ἰσθμῷ ἐτείχεον, καὶ ἤδη ἐπάλξις ἐλάμβανε. ὡς δὲ ἀπίκοντο
ἐς τὴν Λακεδαίμονα οἱ ἄγγελοι οἱ ἀπ᾿ Ἀθηνέων, ἅμα ἀγόμενοι 5
ἔκ τε Μεγάρων ἀγγέλους καὶ ἐκ Πλαταιέων, ἔλεγον τάδε
ἐπελθόντες ἐπὶ τοὺς ἐφόρους. "ἔπεμψαν ἡμέας Ἀθηναῖοι
λέγοντες ὅτι ἡμῖν βασιλεὺς ὁ Μῆδων τοῦτο μὲν τὴν χώρην
ἀποδιδοῖ, τοῦτο δὲ συμμάχους ἐθέλει ἐπ᾿ ἴσῃ τε καὶ ὁμοίῃ
ποιήσασθαι [ἄνευ τε δόλου καὶ ἀπάτης], ἐθέλει δὲ καὶ ἄλλην 10
χώρην πρὸς τῇ ἡμετέρῃ διδόναι, τὴν ἂν αὐτοὶ ἑλώμεθα.

---

3 <ἤνετο> Stein³   4 ἤδη: δὴ Schaefer, van H. ‖ ἐπάλξις α:
ἐπάλξεις   5 Ἀθηνέων αP, Stein², Holder, van H.: ἀθηναίων   7 ἐς
τοὺς β   10 ἄνευ . . ἀπάτης secl. Stein, repugn. Cobet, van H., Holder

---

the Hyakinthia the Amyklaians started
home for the latter celebration in 390
B.C. (al. 392).

περὶ πλείστου δ᾿ ἦγον, 'they considered it of utmost importance'; cp. ἄξω
(μέζονος) 7. 150 supra. Cp. 5. 63 τὰ
γὰρ τοῦ θεοῦ πρεσβύτερα ἐποιεῦντο (ἢ τὰ
τῶν ἀνδρῶν). The Hyakinthia again
and again brought Spartan armies, or
regiments, home from the field; cp.
Xenoph. Hell. 4. 5. 11, Pausan. 3. 10.
1, 4. 19. 4.

3. πορσύναν [*πόρω or πόρσω = πρόσω,
to 'further' ?]: an epic, poetic, and solemn
word; 'never found in comedy,' L. & S.
The god is of course Hyakinthos, or
Apollon.

ἅμα δέ: there is no antecedent ἅμα
μέν to correspond; but the phrase,
echoing as it does the terms of the
Athenian message just above, makes a
humorous appearance, perhaps undesigned.

τὸ τεῖχος. This wall at the Isthmos
has been a most unconscionable time
a-building, if it is only now, about
midsummer, receiving the finishing
touches, in the shape of its battlements
(ἐπάλξις). Cp. 8. 71 supra. It had
been begun immediately after (if not
before) the disaster of Thermopylai, and
the work had been pushed on at high
pressure. It could not have taken
longer to finish than the double wall all
round Plataia, with battlements and
towers to boot, erected in 429 B.C. in the
course of the summer (Thuc. 2. 78, 3.
21). Had the Peloponnesians left this
wall unfinished, on the retirement of the
Persians, and only renewed and completed it on the advance of Mardonios in
the spring of 479 B.C. ?

5. οἱ ἀπ᾿ Ἀθηνέων: an inaccuracy, or
perhaps again an undesigned indication
that this embassy is dated too late, if
placed after the reoccupation of Athens
by Mardonios. We can hardly discriminate by aid of the prepositions ἀπό
and ἐκ: the Megarians and Plataians
were doubtless in Salamis with the
Athenians, or at any rate not at home in
their own cities; or, if they were, then
this embassy to Sparta took place in the
early spring.

7. ἐπελθόντες ἐπὶ τοὺς ἐφόρους: ἐπελ-
θεῖν the correct term; cp. c. 5 supra.
If they address the Ephors it is because
the question is not of alliance, of peace
or war, but merely a question of the
mobilization, apparently a function of
the Ephoralty; cp. Xenoph. Hell. 3. 2.
23, etc. At the same time the Ephors
were the presidents both of the Gerousia
and of the Apella, and no doubt our
authorities, Hdt. imprimis, may speak
sometimes of the Ephors acting, where
they acted really with Senate or
Assembly; cp. Xenoph. l.c. Leotychidas,
by the way, would appear to have been
by this time at Aigina, or even Delos (8.
131-183), unless, indeed, it was in
response to this spring embassy that the
fleet was mobilized.

8. βασιλεὺς . . ἀποδιδοῖ κτλ.: this
suits the early message of Mardonios
8. 140 supra, and would have been no
news to the Spartans. If it is supposed
to refer to the same offer, repeated by
Morychides, c. 5 supra, Athens had rejected it again. But this repetition of
the terms from 8. 140 is very tell-tale
and inconsequent.

τοῦτο μὲν . . τοῦτο δέ: cp. Index.

ἡμεῖς δὲ Δία τε Ἑλλήνιον αἰδεσθέντες καὶ τὴν Ἑλλάδα δεινὸν
ποιεύμενοι προδοῦναι οὐ καταινέσαμεν ἀλλ' ἀπειπάμεθα,
καίπερ ἀδικεόμενοι ὑπ' Ἑλλήνων καὶ καταπροδιδόμενοι,
15 ἐπιστάμενοί τε ὅτι κερδαλεώτερον ἐστὶ ὁμολογέειν τῷ Πέρσῃ
μᾶλλον ἤ περ πολεμέειν· οὐ μὲν οὐδὲ ὁμολογήσομεν ἑκόντες
εἶναι. καὶ τὸ μὲν ἀπ' ἡμέων οὕτω ἀκίβδηλον νέμεται ἐπὶ
τοὺς Ἕλληνας· ὑμεῖς δὲ ἐς πᾶσαν ἀρρωδίην τότε ἀπικόμενοι
μὴ ὁμολογήσωμεν τῷ Πέρσῃ, ἐπείτε ἐξεμάθετε τὸ ἡμέτερον
20 φρόνημα σαφέως, ὅτι οὐδαμὰ προδώσομεν τὴν Ἑλλάδα, καὶ
διότι τεῖχος ὑμῖν διὰ τοῦ Ἰσθμοῦ ἐλαυνόμενον ἐν τέλεΐ ἐστί,
καὶ δὴ λόγον οὐδένα τῶν Ἀθηναίων ποιέεσθε, συνθέμενοί τε
ἡμῖν τὸν Πέρσην ἀντιώσεσθαι ἐς τὴν Βοιωτίην προδεδώκατε,

---

13 ἀλλὰ πάντα τε z   14 ὑπὸ B   15 πέρσει R   16 εἴπερ C
17 ἀπ' ἡμέων: ἡμέτερον Pz ‖ ἀκίβδηλον ἐὸν CPz   19 ἐμάθετε R
20 οὐδαμᾶ Rz   21 ὅτι B, Holder, van H. ‖ τὸ διὰ? Stein¹² ‖ ἐν
τέλεΐ ἐστι Stein¹: ἐν τέλει ἐστὶ AB: ἐντελές ἐστι z   22 δὴ: δεῖ C
23 τῷ Πέρσῃ Reiske: τὸν Πέρσην del. Krueger, Holder, van H.

12. **Δία . .** Ἑλλήνιον looks rather
like an anachronism : the Zeus Hellenios
or Panhellenios known at this period is
the Aiginetan ; cp. Pindar, *Nem.* 5. 15
(composed before the date of the battle
of Salamis, cp. Mezger, *Pindars Siegers-
lieder,* p. 332). Were the Aiginetans
represented in this embassy too (cp. 8.
60 *supra*), or have the Athenians gener-
ously adopted the Aiginetan title ! cp.
Farnell, *Cults,* i. (1896) 63. Anyway,
the appeal from the local or Dorian cult
to a pan-Hellenic deity (cp. 8. 144) is
effective.

αἰδεσθέντες: cp. 7. 141 *supra.*

13. **οὐ καταινέσαμεν ἀλλ' ἀπειπάμεθα,**
' we did not consent but refused '—a sort
of *Hendiadys* ! καταινέειν, cc. 33, 34
infra. ἀπείρασθαι, 7. 14 *supra.*

15. **κερδαλεώτερον,** in earlier Ionic
'shrewd,' 'crafty' (Homer, Archilochos);
in Attic (Aristoph., Thucyd.), as here,
'advantageous,' 'profitable' (cp. L. & S.).
μᾶλλον is *de trop.* The sentiment
expressed is observable : the Athenians
are still in heroic mood.

16. **οὐ μὲν οὐδέ,** ' not indeed that . .'
ἑκόντες εἶναι: cp. 7. 164 *supra.*

17. **τὸ μὲν ἀπ' ἡμέων,** ' our conduct,
our policy.' **ὑμεῖς δέ** supplies the contrast. κίβδηλος, 1. 66, 75, 5. 91, of
oracles (Delphic), not as ' spurious ' but
as ' misleading,' deceitful.

νέμεται ἐπὶ τοὺς Ἕλληνας, ' is
(being) exercised, conducted, towards

the Hellenes ' (with perfect honesty,
without ambiguity) ; or ἐπί, distinctly
locative, as in c. 95 *infra,* 'throughout
Hellas ' ; or *coram,* 8. 79, cp. ἐπὶ τοὺς
ἐφόρους *supra.*

18. **τότε** *prima facie* refers back to
the scene laid at Athens in 8. 140-144,
when the Lakedaimonians κάρτα ἔδεισαν
μὴ ὁμολογήσωσι τῷ Πέρσῃ Ἀθηναῖοι.

20. **καὶ διότι** gives a further reason,
parallel to ἐπείτε just above.

21. **ἐν τέλεΐ,** 'complete,' or ' near completion ' ; cp. πρὸς τέλεΐ c. 8 *infra* (and
contr. ἐν τέλεΐ c. 106 *infra*).

22. **καὶ δή**: Stein follows Baehr in
remarking that these words introduce
the apodosis : no doubt—but why not
= ἤδη (with Krüger) ! Cp. c. 6 *supra.*
λόγον οὐδ. π.: cp. 7. 13, 57, 218
supra.

συνθέμενοι . . τὴν Βοιωτίην: an
express agreement (σύνθημα or συνθήκη)
to this effect has not been actually
recorded, but has been taken for granted ;
cp. 8. 144 *ad f.*

23. **προδεδώκατε** is rather strong
language, both in matter and tense : a
perfect, the effects of which are not past.
περιεῖδετε: a particular act, on a particular
occasion, the occasion being apparently
the present invasion of Attica by Mardonios (not the previous occupation by
Xerxes, to which the remark might have
applied, cp. 8. 40 *supra*). These
Athenian ambassadors, however, have

περιείδετέ τε προεσβαλόντα ἐς τὴν Ἀττικὴν τὸν βάρβαρον.
ἐς μέν νυν τὸ παρεὸν Ἀθηναῖοι ὑμῖν μηνίουσι· οὐ γὰρ 25
ἐποιήσατε ἐπιτηδέως. νῦν δὲ ὅτι τάχος στρατιὴν ἅμα ἡμῖν
ἐκέλευσαν ὑμέας ἐκπέμπειν, ὡς ἂν τὸν βάρβαρον δεκώμεθα
ἐν τῇ Ἀττικῇ· ἐπειδὴ γὰρ ἡμάρτομεν τῆς Βοιωτίης, τῆς γε
ἡμετέρης ἐπιτηδεότατον ἐστὶ μαχέσασθαι τὸ Θριάσιον πεδίον."
ὡς δὲ ἄρα ἤκουσαν οἱ ἔφοροι ταῦτα, ἀνεβάλλοντο ἐς τὴν 8
ὑστεραίην ὑποκρινέεσθαι, τῇ δὲ ὑστεραίῃ ἐς τὴν ἑτέρην· τοῦτο

---

24 προεσβαλόντα Stein: ἐσβαλόντα ΒPz, Holder, van H.: προσ-
βαλόντα α: προσβάλλοντα C　　28 ἐπεὶ γὰρ C　　29 ἐπιτηδεό-
τατόν α: ἐπιτηδέστατόν Β: ἐπιτηδεώτατόν ceteri ‖ ἐμμαχέσασθαι Β, Holder,
van H.　　8. 1 ἄκουσαν z ‖ ἀνεβάλοντο ΒCP, Holder　　2 ὑποκρινέεσθαι Cobet, Stein³: ὑποκρινεῖσθαι van H.: ὑποκρίνασθαι ΒCPz,
Stein¹ ², Holder: ὑποκρίνεσθαι α

---

left Athens (or Salamis) for Sparta before
Mardonios had actually entered Attica
(cp. c. 6 *supra*); and if they here
rhetorically treat the invasion of Attica
by Mardonios as a *fait accompli*, it is
rhetoric, not strict history: how else
could they proceed to call upon the
Spartans to send an army back with
them ὡς ἂν τὸν βάρβαρον δεκώμεθα ἐν τῇ
Ἀττικῇ, to 'receive' the barbarian
in Attica!

25. ἐς μέν νυν τὸ παρεὸν . . νῦν δέ:
the antithesis between τὸ παρεόν and νῦν
is not *prima facie* a sharp one; but νῦν
is purely temporal, τὸ παρεόν is circumstantial. Again, ἐς might be taken
'down to' the present = ἐς τὸ νῦν (cp. ἐς
τόδε 7. 29, but ἐς τὸ παρεόν *ibid.* not so):
νῦν δέ is then distinct. νῦν qualifies
ἐκπέμπειν rather than ἐκέλευσαν.

μηνίαν: cp. 7. 229.

26. (οὐκ) ἐπιτηδέως is a *meiosis*; *leniter
dicta* (Schweighaeuser).

ὅτι τάχος = ὡς τάχος 5. 106. Cp.
Thuc. 7. 42. 3.

ἅμα, *simul, simul cum* = σύν but
stronger.

27. δεκώμεθα: cp. 8. 28 *supra*.

28. ἡμάρτομεν τῆς Βοιωτίης: they
were too late to 'receive' him in Boiotia,
but there was still time to 'receive' him
in the Thriasian plain. This argument
likewise points to an earlier date for the
embassy.

29. τὸ Θριάσιον πεδίον: cp. 8. 65
supra. If Mardonios was already at
Athens the Peloponnesian forces could
not count on getting into the Thriasian
plain, for Mardonios would doubtless be
in possession of Eleusis; unless, indeed,
he had entered Attica by Dekeleia or
Phyle, and omitted to use or occupy the
pass of Dryoskephalai: not a very probable hypothesis.

The advantages of the Thriasian plain
as a battle-field, from the Peloponnesian
point of view, are open to discussion: if
the Greeks could have encountered
Mardonios as he emerged from the pass
of Eleutherai-Eleusis they might have
scored a local success, but they would have
had to hold the sacred way by Daphne
and the route between Aigaleos and
Parnes (crossed by Archidamos in 431
B.C., Thuc. 2. 19. 2), while on the plain
itself the Persian cavalry would have
ridden round them. This plain was
never one of the great battle-fields of
Greece. The Greek fleet could not have
been of much service in the case.

8. 1. ἄρα, 'well,' not without surprise;
cp. Index. Abicht regards the particle
here as marking an advance in the
action (or inaction !).

ἀναβάλλεσθαι, *differre*, 6. 86 etc.

2. τοῦτο καὶ ἐπὶ δέκα ἡμέρας ἐποίεον:
i.e. for a whole (Greek) week; cp. c.
40 *infra*. There is an *Asyndeton*. The
next words, ἐξ . . ἀναβαλλόμενοι, are
not otiose (*pace* Stein), for, without
them, the sentence might mean (in
spite of the imperf. ἐποίεον) that they
postponed the answer 'for a week' (i.e.
twelve days in all). Meanwhile they
were working away at the wall across
the Isthmos; cp. c. 7 *supra* (*bis*), which
is even yet not quite finished! If
πάντες Πελοποννήσιοι (i.e. Π. πανδημί)

καὶ ἐπὶ δέκα ἡμέρας ἐποίεον, ἐξ ἡμέρης ἐς ἡμέρην ἀναβαλλόμενοι. ἐν δὲ τούτῳ τῷ χρόνῳ τὸν Ἰσθμὸν ἐτείχεον σπουδὴν
5 ἔχοντες πολλὴν πάντες Πελοποννήσιοι, καί σφι ἦν πρὸς
τέλεϊ. οὐδ' ἔχω εἰπεῖν τὸ αἴτιον διότι ἀπικομένου μὲν
Ἀλεξάνδρου τοῦ Μακεδόνος ἐς Ἀθήνας σπουδὴν μεγάλην
ἐποιήσαντο μὴ μηδίσαι Ἀθηναίους, τότε δὲ ὥρην ἐποιήσαντο
οὐδεμίαν, ἄλλο γε ἢ ὅτι ὁ Ἰσθμός σφι ἐτετείχιστο καὶ
10 ἐδόκεον Ἀθηναίων ἔτι δέεσθαι οὐδέν· ὅτε δὲ Ἀλέξανδρος
ἀπίκετο ἐς τὴν Ἀττικήν, οὔκω ἀπετετείχιστο, ἐργάζοντο δὲ
9 μεγάλως καταρρωδηκότες τοὺς Πέρσας. τέλος δὲ τῆς τε
ὑποκρίσιος καὶ ἐξόδου τῶν Σπαρτιητέων ἐγένετο τρόπος
τοιόσδε. τῇ προτεραίῃ τῆς ὑστάτης καταστάσιος μελλούσης
ἔσεσθαι Χίλεος ἀνὴρ Τεγεήτης, δυνάμενος ἐν Λακεδαίμονι
5 μέγιστον ξείνων, τῶν ἐφόρων ἐπύθετο πάντα λόγον [τὸν

6 εἶπαι ßz, van H.   8 ὥρην CPz   9 οὐδὲ μίαν a : οὐδὲ μίην ß :
οὐδεμίην z   10 δεῖσθαι aCPz, Holder, van H. ‖ οὐδενός ß ‖ ὁ ἀλέξανδρος CPz   11 οὐκ ἔχω εἰπεῖν εἰ ἐτετείχιστο Marc.   9. 4
χίλεως Marc.: Χείλεως Plutarch. Mor. 871 : Χίλεος οὐνόματι z ‖ τεγεήτϊς R
5 ἐφόρων ἔνα z ‖ τὸν . . ἔλεγον secl. Stein², Holder

were at the Isthmos, building or no
building, they surely had arms with
them. The building operations at this
point may be put down to Hdt. They
are not required to keep the Peloponnesians at home, but he seems to think
the action of the Peloponnesians to have
been determined simply by the state of
the building.

6. οὐδ' ἔχω εἰπεῖν τὸ αἴτιον διότι κτλ.,
'I cannot state the reason why . .'
αἴτιον : cp. 7. 125.

8. ὥρη here is plainly = σπουδή (cp.
1. 4, 3. 155), a poetic word ; cp. ὀλίγωρος,
ὀλιγωρία.

9. ἐτετείχιστο : a strictly temporal
pluperfect, reinforced in ἀπετετείχιστο.

10. δέεσθαι οὐδέν, 'to have no need
of . .' (μηδέν was possible here, but
not obligatory, as the governing verb
is not itself in a form or construction
which requires μή for its negation,
Madvig § 205.)

12. μεγάλως καταρρωδηκότες: the abject and utter terror of the Peloponnesians
is expressed in fourfold fashion : (a) by
the strong word ὀρρωδέω (ἀρρ-) ; (b) by
the preposition in comp. ; (c) by the
'perfect' tense; (d) by the adverb.
Probably Hdt. found all this in the
Attic Sources.

9. 1. τέλος δέ : adverbial, 'at last.'

2. ὑπόκρισις = Attic ἀπόκρισις ; cp. 1.

116. Aristot. *Eth. N.* 3. 10. 4 = 1118 A
clearly shows the Attic meaning. Hdt.
never uses the word ὑποκρίτης.

ἔξοδος is practically a technical
military term ; cp. cc. 19, 26 *infra*, 7.
223 *supra* ; Thuc. 2. 10. 1, Xenoph.
Hell. 1. 2. 17.

ἐγένετο τρόπος τοιόσδε, 'took the
following turn,' 'occurred on this wise.'

3. κατάστασις : as in 3. 46, not as in
8. 141 *supra*.

4. Χίλεος : the name appears in
Plutarch *de Hdti. m.* 41 (Mor. 871),
Themist. 6, as Χείλεως, in Polyain. 5. 30
as Χίλιος, a form (Chilius) used by
Cicero (*ad Att.* 1. 9. 2, 12. 2, 16. 15)
of a later poet.   What Chileos was
doing in Sparta neither Hdt. nor Plutarch
nor Polyainos reports.   His critique of
the ephoral policy was notorious ; but
who first let it out ?   The situation
demanded is really a meeting of the
Symmachoi at Sparta—there may very
well have been one in the winter or
spring, or about the Feast of the
Hyakinthia—and the remarks of Chileos
were made in that Synod ; if the Ephors
were specially addressed, it was merely
as the presiding magistrates.

δυνάμενος : of power, influence ;
cp. 7. 5 *supra*.

5. ξείνων : not used in the Spartan
sense, given c. 11 *infra*.

δὴ οἱ Ἀθηναῖοι ἔλεγον]· ἀκούσας δὲ ταῦτα ὁ Χίλεος ἔλεγε
ἄρα σφι τάδε. "οὕτω ἔχει, ἄνδρες ἔφοροι· Ἀθηναίων ἡμῖν
ἐόντων μὴ ἀρθμίων τῷ δὲ βαρβάρῳ συμμάχων, καίπερ τείχεος
διὰ τοῦ Ἰσθμοῦ ἐληλαμένου καρτεροῦ, μεγάλαι κλισιάδες
ἀναπεπτέαται ἐς τὴν Πελοπόννησον τῷ Πέρσῃ. ἀλλ' ἐσακού- 10
σατε, πρίν τι ἄλλο Ἀθηναίοισι δόξαι σφάλμα φέρον τῇ
Ἑλλάδι." ὁ μέν σφι ταῦτα συνεβούλευε· οἱ δὲ φρενὶ 10
λαβόντες τὸν λόγον αὐτίκα, φράσαντες οὐδὲν τοῖσι ἀγγέλοισι
τοῖσι ἀπιγμένοισι ἀπὸ τῶν πολίων, νυκτὸς ἔτι ἐκπέμπουσι
πεντακισχιλίους Σπαρτιητέων καὶ ἑπτὰ περὶ ἕκαστον τάξαντες

---

6 ταῦτα om. βPz, Holder, van H. ‖ ὁ Χίλεος del. van H., Holder
7 οὕτως α ‖ ἡμῖν <μὲν> van H., Holder   8 μὴ ἐόντων β ‖ τῶδε τῶ
βαρβάρῳ R: (τῷδε τῷ β. S: τῷ δὲ τῷ β. V ap. Gaisf.)   9 κρατεροῦ z
10 ἀναπεπταίαται A¹B ‖ ἐσακούσετε B   11 πρὶν <ἢ> τι van H. ‖ τῇ
ἑλλάδι φέρον Pz   10. 1 ἐν φρενὶ βz   3 ἀπηγμένοισι B   4
πεντακισχιλίων β ‖ καὶ . . εἱλώτων om. β, expung. Wesseling, van H.

πάντα λόγον, 1. 21.
7. ἄρα: much to their surprise; cp.
c. 8 supra.
8. ἐόντων μὴ ἀρθμίων: cp. 7. 101 (tot.
verb.), and καὶ ἐὼν μὴ Μηλιεύς 7. 214.
9. μεγάλαι κλισιάδες ἀναπεπτέαται,
'(the) doorways stand wide open'—lit.
large 'shutters' have been unfolded;
μ. may well be predicative; the tense is,
of course, without temporal prejudice,
and essentially present. The verb occurs
with gates, gateways of the Samian
akropolis, 3. 147 ἀναπετάσας τὰς πύλας,
and of Babylon 3. 158, and well describes
the operation of opening double or fold-
ing doors, gates. Cp. Iliad 12. 120 ff.
where (πύλῃσιν) σανίδες ἀναπεπταμέναι are
contrasted with ἐπικεκλιμέναι. In 21.
531 the simple verb occurs (πεπταμένας
πύλας ἔχετε). κλισιάδες, or κλεισιάδες,
might be street-doors (as in Plutarch,
Poplic. 20) or chamber-doors, like the
κλησταὶ σανίδες πυκινῶς ἀραρυῖαι δικλίδες
in the ὑψόροφος θάλαμος of Odysseus
(Od. 2. 344). The significance of the
metaphor ('the Open Door') here is
obvious, its force undeniable. Blakesley
points out that Plutarch copies it three
times (Aristeid. et Cat. Comp. 2, Alcibiad.
10, de Isid. 23 = Mor. 360 A), as St. Paul
twice, 1 Cor. 16. 9, 2 Cor. 2. 12.
10. ἐσακούειν, c. 60 infra. ἀλλό is
euphemistic. σφάλμα φ., cp. 7. 6.
δόξαι, 'be decreed.'
As Rawlinson points out, there is
nothing new in the remarks of Chileos

to the Ephors (except the metaphor!);
the Athenians themselves have more
than hinted it above, c. 7. Placed in
the high summer of 479 B.C. the remarks
of Chileos are sadly belated; but placed
at a meeting either of the Spartan
Symmachy in the winter 480–79 or
even at the Hyakinthia in the (late)
spring, they are much to the point,
as giving an Arkadian's view of the
relative value of the wall at the Isthmos
and the alliance of the chief sea-power.
10. 1. φρενὶ λαβόντες τὸν λόγον: cp.
νόῳ λαβών 3. 41. φρήν (or φρένες) is
unusual in prose; in 8. 134 Hdt. directly
contrasts αἱ φρένες with τὸ σῶμα.
2. αὐτίκα . . νυκτὸς ἔτι: their ἔξοδος
by night appears to be treated as part
of the sudden and secret change of policy;
it is more likely to have been a wise
precaution to get over as much ground
as possible in the cool (hardly to get
start of the Argives; but cp. c. 11 infra).
3. ἀπιγμένοισι, 'still in Sparta.'
τῶν πολίων: sc. ἀπ' Ἀθηνέων, ἐκ
Μεγάρων, ἐκ Πλαταιέων c. 7 supra; yet
the 'cities' are ex hypothesi in the hands
of Mardonios. But ubi cives ibi civitas!
Cp. c. 5 supra.
4. πεντακισχιλίους Σπαρτιητέων:
5000 did not exhaust the total available
citizen-force; cp. 7. 234 supra; but it
is virtually the levy πανδημί, of two-
thirds (from twenty to forty-five years
of age). The figure here is no doubt
a round one, but may be accepted as

5 τῶν εἱλώτων, Παυσανίῃ τῷ Κλεομβρότου ἐπιτάξαντες ἐξάγειν.
ἐγίνετο μὲν ἡ ἡγεμονίη Πλειστάρχου τοῦ Λεωνίδεω· ἀλλ' ὁ
μὲν ἦν ἔτι παῖς, ὁ δὲ τούτου ἐπίτροπός τε καὶ ἀνεψιός.
Κλεόμβροτος γὰρ ὁ Παυσανίεω μὲν πατὴρ 'Αναξανδρίδεω δὲ

---

5 ἐπιτρέψαντες **β**, Holder, van H.   6 ἐγένετο **α**, Stein[1] || μέν νυν
ἠ **β**, Holder, van H.   7 ἀνεψιὸς κλεόμβροτος· κλεόμβροτος γὰρ R
8 Παυσανίῳ van H.

---

substantially correct; what cannot be allowed to pass is the assertion that they took 35,000 Helots with them, seven Helots in attendance on (περί) each Spartiate, by special order (τάξαντες). There may be some sense in this figure, but not as here stated. Pausanias was not well-supplied with ψιλοί, cp. c. 60 infra (but cp. c. 28 infra), so these Helots are probably not fighting men, badly as such were wanted; doubtless large numbers of Helots were employed on the commissariat service, cp. c. 39 infra—roughly speaking some 30,000—and this *Army Service Corps* is here represented as all accompanying the citizen-militia. Or, again, the figure may represent an estimate of the total number of Helots employed in any capacity during the campaign, or during the war (in ships etc.), which Hdt. has misunderstood and misapplied; cp. Appendix VIII. § 2 (iv.).

5. **Παυσανίῃ τῷ Κλεομβρότου**: the question of command was not settled by the Ephors but by the Apella; cp. Xenoph. *Hell.* 4. 2. 9. Pausanias, son of Kleombrotos (mentioned 8. 3 *supra* without patronymic; perhaps therefore in a passage added afterwards; but cp. note *ad l.*), cannot have been an old man at this time; but the fact that he is of age to be Regent, and to command a Spartan army in the field, rather supports the view that his father, Kleombrotos, and his uncle, Leonidas, were twins; cp. 7. 205 *supra* and note to l. 8 *infra*. The relationship of the persons here mentioned may be accurately exhibited:—

Dorieus   Leonidas   Kleombrotos
  | | |
Euryanax Pleistarchos Pausanias

Dorieus, Leonidas and Kleombrotos being full ἀδελφοί and being the younger brothers of Kleomenes, the son of their father's (Anaxandridas) second wife; cp. *l.c. supra.*

6. **ἐγίνετο μὲν ἡ ἡγεμονίη**: i.e. by custom or prescriptive right the actual king would have had the command, the leading. Leotychidas was already in command of the fleet; cp. 8. 131 *supra*; if Pleistarchos had been in command of the army, the arrangement would apparently have conflicted with the 'law' reported by Hdt. 5. 75, albeit the 'law' might refer to one and the same force only, and even so, was hardly quite strictly observed (cp. Xenoph. *Hell.* 5. 3. 10). But Hdt. in this passage is not concerned with any such scruples, and Bk. 5 is probably of later composition than this passage; cp. Introduction, §§ 7, 8.

Πλειστάρχου τοῦ Λεωνίδεω: Pleistarchos was the son of Leonidas and Gorgo, and so the grandson of Kleomenes on the spindle side. Anaxandridas was both his grandfather and his great-grandfather. His exact age is a matter of doubt, but he was still apparently a minor at the time of the fall of Pausanias = 472-1 B.C., Thuc. 1. 132. 1.

7. **ἐπίτροπός τε καὶ ἀνεψιός**: Baehr has here made a curious blunder from mis-understanding Pausan. 3. 5. 1; he says, *successerat nimirum Pleistoanax Pleistarcho qui regno initio abierat.* Why, Pleistoanax was the son of Pausanias, and could only succeed in his father's right ! Pausanias himself was never king (nor is he called so by Aristotle, *pace* Clinton *Fasti* ii.[3] 261, though so described sometimes by orators, lexicographers, and modern scholars; cp. c. 5 *supra*). Pleist-archos was still king in 472 B.C.; cp. previous note. ἐπίτροπος, cp. 7. 170 *supra*, and for the meaning here l. 65. ἀνεψιός, 'first cousin' here; cp. 7. 82.

8. **Κλεόμβροτος . . ἀπέθανε**, 'Kleom-brotos (had) died shortly after leading home the army which (had) built the wall at the Isthmos.' He was no doubt in the first instance 'Regent,' or guardian to Pleistarchos. The much debated wall here appears as a *fait accompli* before

παῖς οὐκέτι περιῆν, ἀλλ᾽ ἀπαγαγὼν ἐκ τοῦ Ἰσθμοῦ τὴν
στρατιὴν τὴν τὸ τεῖχος δείμασαν μετὰ ταῦτα οὐ πολλὸν 10
χρόνον τινὰ βιοὺς ἀπέθανε. ἀπῆγε δὲ τὴν στρατιὴν ὁ
Κλεόμβροτος ἐκ τοῦ Ἰσθμοῦ διὰ τόδε· θυομένῳ οἱ ἐπὶ τῷ
Πέρσῃ ὁ ἥλιος ἀμαυρώθη ἐν τῷ οὐρανῷ. προσαιρέεται δὲ
ἑωυτῷ Παυσανίης Εὐρυάνακτα τὸν Δωριέος, ἄνδρα οἰκίης
ἐόντα τῆς αὐτῆς.   15
Οἳ μὲν δὴ σὺν Παυσανίῃ ἐξεληλύθεσαν ἔξω Σπάρτης· οἱ 11
δὲ ἄγγελοι, ὡς ἡμέρη ἐγεγόνεε, οὐδὲν εἰδότες περὶ τῆς ἐξόδου

10 τὴν om. BC ‖ πολλόν τινα χρόνον B, Holder, van H. : ἔτι coni.
Stein   11 ἀπήγαγε Cobet, van H.   13 προσερέεται B   14
ὁ παυσανίης B ‖ ἄνδρα del. van H.   11. 1 ἐξεληλύθησαν Cs
2 ἰδόντες C

Kleombrotos returned to Sparta in 480
B.C. ! In c. 8 *supra* it is still being
hurried on in the spring—or, as some
would have it, after midsummer of 479
B.C. See note *ad l.*
13. ὁ ἥλιος ἀμαυρώθη ἐν τῷ οὐρανῷ.
Zech attempted to make out that
ἀμαυρώθη did not imply an eclipse.
Nothing short of an eclipse (not necessarily total) would account for the act
of Kleombrotos. Plutarch, *Caesar* 69,
uses ἀμαύρωμα similarly. Petavius dated
this eclipse 2nd Oct. 480; Hoffmann and
Lamp *ap.* Busolt ii.² 715 n. 1 agree in
the date, and time the maximum obscura-
tion at Korinth to 2.20 P.M. (a partial
eclipse). Stein very ingeniously suggests
that the θυσίη was made, after Salamis,
on the question of intercepting the retreat of the Persian land-forces from
Attica.
With οὐ πολλὸν χρόνον τινὰ βιούς
cp. 5. 48 οὐ (γάρ) τινα πολλὸν χρόνον ἦρξε
ὁ Κλεομένης. The sense best taken is
that Kleombrotos died comparatively
young. He can hardly have been less
than fifty, or his son could scarcely have
succeeded him as ἐπίτροπος and ἡγεμών.
But the statement suggests that Pausanias was about as juvenile as a Regent
could be.
προσαιρέεται δὲ ἑωυτῷ: there is
something very curious in this arrangement. The Spartans will scarcely have
allowed the ἡγεμών to select a colleague
at his own free will. Perhaps Pausanias
was barely of age to assume the great
responsibilities of his position, and an
older man, of the Herakleid lineage, was
associated with him in virtual command,
though nominally Pausanias had the
supreme honours; perhaps the great

victory, for which Pausanias claimed
(Thuc. 1. 132. 2) and obtained (c. 64
infra) all the credit, was more due to
the intelligence of his cousin ; if, indeed,
there was not a still greater intelligence
in the background. Cp. Appendix VIII.
§ 9.
14. Εὐρυάνακτα τὸν Δωριέος appears
again in cc. 53, 55 ; as Dorieus was the
eldest of the three brothers, Euryanax
was probably senior to Pausanias. Why
had he not succeeded Leonidas, or, for
that matter, Kleomenes, as son of the
next eldest son ! Dorieus may have
renounced, or forfeited, the right of
succession ; or a king's son (Leonidas,
Pleistarchos) may have succeeded in
preference to a *privatus*; cp. 7. 3, where
Demaratos lays down a law, which may
be illustrated by, or generalized from,
the case of Euryanax.
Rawlinson has an erroneous but very
instructive note on this passage. He
attempts to prove that the Dorieus here
mentioned cannot be Dorieus son of
Anaxandridas for two reasons : (1) Had
Dorieus left a son in Sparta "he would
undoubtedly have succeeded to the
throne"—but no ! see above.   (2) "The
words of Hdt. imply a more distant
relative." Nay, the saddle is on the
wrong horse ! Hdt. in Bks. 5 and 9
follows different sources ; had he known
the story of Dorieus when he wrote this
passage he must have guarded his readers
against the error into which Rawlinson
has fallen ; in other words, this passage
makes strongly for the *earlier composition
of Bks.* 7, 8, 9. Cp. Introduction, §§ 7, 8.
11. 1. ἐξεληλύθεσαν : before any one,
the Athenians for example, knew of it.
2. ἐγεγόνεε : not until after daybreak.

ἐπῆλθον ἐπὶ τοὺς ἐφόρους, ἐν νόῳ δὴ ἔχοντες ἀπαλλάσσεσθαι
καὶ αὐτοὶ ἐπὶ τὴν ἑωυτοῦ ἕκαστος· ἐπελθόντες δὲ ἔλεγον τάδε.
5 " ὑμεῖς μὲν ὦ Λακεδαιμόνιοι αὐτοῦ τῇδε μένοντες Ὑακίνθιά τε
ἄγετε καὶ παίζετε, καταπροδόντες τοὺς συμμάχους· Ἀθηναῖοι
δὲ ὡς ἀδικεόμενοι ὑπὸ ὑμέων χήτεί τε συμμάχων καταλύσονται
τῷ Πέρσῃ οὕτω ὅκως ἂν δύνωνται· καταλυσάμενοι δέ, δῆλα
γὰρ ὅτι σύμμαχοι βασιλέος γινόμεθα, συστρατευσόμεθα ἐπ' ἣν

---

4 ἐπὶ τῆς Pz   7 χήτεί z: χήτει aR: χήτι CPSV, van H. ‖ τε
om. B   8 οὕτως a   9 γὰρ δὴ z ‖ ὅτι εἰ S ‖ βασιλῆος z ‖
γενόμεθα BC ‖ ἐπ' ἣν: ἐπὶ ἣν ABC: ἐπὶ τὴν PRVz, Holder, van H.

These pluperfects are temporal. The
ambassadors, or convoys, must include
those from Megara and Plataia; but the
spokesman is plainly Athenian.

3. **ἐπῆλθον**: cp. c. 7 *supra.*

ἐν νόῳ δὴ ἔχοντες, 'intending at
last' (Blakesley).

4. **καὶ αὐτοί** as well as the army,
though of its departure they knew nothing; or, as well as the representatives
of the various allies assembled in Sparta,
Chileos, and the rest!

ἐπὶ τὴν ἑωυτοῦ ἕκαστος: was there
only one ambassador from each city?
Plutarch (*Arist.* 10) makes Aristeides
the Athenian one, but gives very good
evidence ('the psephism of Aristeides')
that Athens had three representatives,
Kimon, Xanthippos, Myronides. The
mention of Xanthippos dates the embassy before the muster of the fleet at
Aigina, 8. 131.

5. **αὐτοῦ τῇδε**, 'here on the spot.'
Ὑακίνθιά τε ἄγετε καὶ παίζετε.
The title of the festival is anarthrous,
idiomatically; cp. Κάρνεια 7. 206, Ὀλύμπια
δὲ καὶ Κάρνεια 8. 72. ἄγειν *celebrare* 8.
26, etc. παίζειν here can hardly be used
as a scoff (cp. 4. 77), but as in Pindar
Ol. 13. 86 ἐνόπλια χαλκωθεὶς ἔπαιζεν
(orchestic); or *Ol.* 1. 16 μουσικᾶς ἐν ἀώτῳ,
οἷα παίζομεν. Cp. Aristoph. *Frogs* 407
παίζειν τε καὶ χορεύειν, 442 παίζοντες οἷς
μέτουσία θεοφιλοῦς ἑορτῆς etc.; cp. 5. 4
supra.

7. **ὡς** *quippe*, 7. 22 *supra.*

χήτεί, from χῆτος (the form χῆτις,
χῆτι also read), a strictly Homeric word;
cp. χατέω, χατίζω.

**καταλύσονται τῷ Π. οὕτω ὅκως ἂν
δύνωνται**: for καταλύεσθαι cp. 7. 6, 8.
140 *supra.* Even in such phrases as
these the reference of οὕτω is not of
necessity forwards, but might rather be
carried backwards. The sequence here,

future indic. followed by pres. subj., is
observable. Cp. just below συστρατευσόμεθα . . ἂν ἐξηγέωνται . . μαθήσεσθε . .
ἂν ἐκβαίνῃ, the last of which is the most
remarkable; the construction is perhaps
attracted by the preceding instances.

9. **σύμμαχοι βασιλέος γινόμεθα** (N.B.
the tense). This threat and announcement comes with startling rapidity after
the 'lynching of Lykidas' in c. 4 *supra*,
and puts both the Athenians and the
Spartans in a very unfortunate and
probably false position. The notion
that the Peloponnesian forces were only
mobilized at the eleventh hour under
threat of 'medism' on the part of
Athens is highly improbable. (i.) If
Mardonios is in Attica, or even in
Boiotia, then in all probability a
Spartano-Peloponnesian force is already
at the Isthmos—if only to defend the
wall. (ii.) The threat here is entirely
subversive of the heroics in 8. 144, and
even in c. 7 *supra.* (iii.) The more probable date of the Hyakinthia, in spring,
militates against this *ultimatum.* (iv.)
The subsequent relations of Athenians
and Spartans during the campaign are
against it. (v.) The ultimatum is in
itself an absurdity: the point at issue is
really one of detail, as to the exact
modus operandi; the Athenians could
not doubt the substantial *bona fides* of
the Spartans, with the king in command
of the fleet at Aigina. (vi.) The notion
is too comic that 5000 Hoplites and
35,000 Helots had mobilized and marched
without any of the Athenian, Plataian,
or Megarian envoys getting wind of it,
or having a single friend in Sparta
to inform them. Probably there was a
good deal of friction and misgiving
between Athens and Sparta during the
winter and spring after Salamis and
before Plataia: it cannot be said that

ἂν ἐκεῖνοι ἐξηγέωνται. ὑμεῖς δὲ τὸ ἐνθεῦτεν μαθήσεσθε ὁκοῖον 10
ἄν τι ὑμῖν ἐξ αὐτοῦ ἐκβαίνῃ." ταῦτα λεγόντων τῶν ἀγγέλων,
οἱ ἔφοροι εἶπαν ἐπ' ὅρκου καὶ δὴ δοκέειν εἶναι ἐν Ὀρεσθείῳ
στείχοντας ἐπὶ τοὺς ξείνους. ξείνους γὰρ ἐκάλεον τοὺς
βαρβάρους. οἳ δὲ ὡς οὐκ εἰδότες ἐπειρώτων τὸ λεγόμενον,
ἐπειρόμενοι δὲ ἐξέμαθον πᾶν τὸ ἐόν, ὥστε ἐν θώματι γενόμενοι 15
ἐπορεύοντο τὴν ταχίστην διώκοντες, σὺν δέ σφι τῶν περιοίκων

---

10 ἐξηγέονται Β   11 ἐκβαίνει C : ἐκβαίη β ‖ ταῦτα δὲ β   12
ἐφόρκου a ‖ ὀρεστῖω R : ὀρεστείω SV : ὀρεστείῳ Marc. z   13 στί-
χοντας β ‖ ξείνους . . . βαρβάρους. nonne tollenda ? cf. comment. ‖ ἐκάλουν
β   14 οἱ δὲ Stein¹ : om. C ‖ ἐπειρώτων a, Stein², Holder : ἐπειρώτεον
β, Stein¹, van H. : ἐπηρώτων CP : ἐπηρώτεον z   15 ἐπηρόμενοι (C)z ‖
θώματι (C)S, Stein², van H. : θώματϊ V : θώυματι aR, Stein¹, Holder

---

either party comes very well out of this story, which is told more or less at the expense of both parties, perhaps by this or that ally — Arkadian, Epidaurian, Megarian, Aiginetan, or so forth ! Cp. further Appendix VIII. § 3.

10. **ἐκεῖνοι**: sc. οἱ Πέρσαι.

11. **ἐξ αὐτοῦ**: sc. βασιλέος ! But, as ἐκεῖνοι has intervened, perhaps αὐτοῦ is used more vaguely ' thereout' : sc. of our alliance with the Persian.

ταῦτα λεγόντων τῶν ἀγγέλων: the speech just delivered only takes account of the case of Athens ; Plataia and Megara being ignored—as also the mobilization of the fleet !

12. **ἐπ' ὅρκου** = σὺν ὅρκῳ very unusual ; and the more remarkable as ἐπιορκεῖν means 'to forswear' (4. 68), though ἐπομνύναι (8. 5) not so.

καὶ δὴ δοκέειν εἶναι: the subject of εἶναι will be τοὺς σφετέρους ἄνδρας or sim. καὶ δή with εἶναι = ἤδη. Cp. c. 6 supra. στείχειν is an eminently Ionic, or Epic, or poetic word.

ἐν Ὀρεσθείῳ. Pausanias 8. 3. 2 gives Ὀρεσθάσιον as the original name of this place, Ὀρέστειόν τε ἀπὸ Ὀρέστου κληθεῖσα τοῦ Ἀγαμέμνονος. The change of name may belong to the same ' movement' and date as discovered the bones of ' Orestes' in Tegea for the benefit of the Spartans, 1. 67 f. Orestes was henceforward the canonized founder of 'Oresteion' (cp. Eurip. Orest. 1647, Electr. 1273). In reality Oresthasion was the capital town or village of the Oresthis (cp. Thuc. 4. 134. 1), itself a portion of the Mainalia (Thuc. 5. 64. 3 ; cp. Pausan. 8. 27. 3) or mountainous region between the plains of Tegea and

the later Megalopolis, the watershed between Alpheios and Eurotas. The remains of the city lay to the right of the route from Megalopolis to Tegea (Pausanias 8. 44. 2), and quite off the direct road from Sparta to the Isthmos (via Tegea, Mantineia, etc.). Rawlinson suggests that this roundabout route was selected in order to effect a junction with a contingent from the Lepreatis, surely an unnecessary arrangement. Perhaps all the forces from Sparta did not take one and the same route : those that started first may have been sent by the longer road. Or could it be that they took the longer way round to avoid the Argives ! Cp. next c. (In days of yore the Oresthasioi had done ' yeoman's' or rather ' heroic service ' in the wars between Arkadia and Sparta ; cp. Pausan. 8. 39. 3 ff., 41. 1.)

13. **ξείνους γὰρ ἐκάλεον τοὺς βαρβάρους**. This appears to me to be a gloss, introduced from c. 55 infra : the imperfect ἐκάλεον suits. Stein observes that the Spartans applied the term not merely to βάρβαροι but to all foreigners (cp. ξενηλασία), as the Romans hostis.

14. **ἐπειρώτων τὸ λεγόμενον**, 'inquired their meaning . . ,' cp. 3. 22. εἰρωτᾶν, εἴρεσθαι are the Ionic forms ; cp. ἐπειρώτησις c. 44 infra.

15. **πᾶν τὸ ἐόν** : 7. 209 supra. **ὥστε . . ἐπορεύοντο**, Madvig § 166.

ἐν θώματι γενόμενοι, 'after recovering from their astonishment.' (The aorist seems to have almost perfect or pl. p. force.)

16. **ἐπορεύοντο τὴν ταχίστην διώκοντες** : cogn. acc. Their object was to overtake the Van ; they were accompanied

Λακεδαιμονίων λογάδες πεντακισχίλιοι ὁπλῖται [τὠυτὸ τοῦτο
ἐποίεον].

12 Οἱ μὲν δὴ ἐς τὸν Ἰσθμὸν ἠπείγοντο· Ἀργεῖοι δὲ ἐπείτε
τάχιστα ἐπύθοντο τοὺς μετὰ Παυσανίεω ἐξεληλυθότας ἐκ
Σπάρτης, πέμπουσι κήρυκα τῶν ἡμεροδρόμων ἀνευρόντες τὸν
ἄριστον ἐς τὴν Ἀττικήν, πρότερον αὐτοὶ Μαρδονίῳ ὑποδεξά-
5 μενοι σχήσειν τὸν Σπαρτιήτην μὴ ἐξιέναι· ὃς ἐπείτε ἀπίκετο
ἐς τὰς Ἀθήνας ἔλεγε τάδε. "Μαρδόνιε, ἔπεμψάν με Ἀργεῖοι

---

17 Λακεδαιμονίων del. van H., Holder ‖ ὁπλῖται om. ß, Holder, van H.
‖ τὠυτὸ τοῦτο ἐποίεον secl. Stein, Holder, van H.   12. 4 αὐτῷ ß
5 ἐπείτε : ἐπεὶ ß : om. C

---

by 5000 picked hoplites of the Lakedaimonian Perioikoi, who tried to keep up
with them and overtake the Van.

17. τὠυτὸ τοῦτο ἐποίεον — rather a
bathos ! Cp. App. Crit.

It is not asserted that the Rear
overtook the Van at Orestheion : probably not, for they would go the shorter
and more direct route (τὴν ταχίστην
supra).

12. 1. Ἀργεῖοι δέ. The medism of the
Argives was a serious matter for Sparta,
and helps to account for the apparent
weakness of her policy and action in this
campaign. It cannot, however, have
been very ardent, or the Argives would
have made more of their opportunity,
when the Spartans actually did leave the
Peloponnesos ; cp. 8. 73 supra. It was
even a service in disguise to Greece,
sealing the Spartans more surely to the
good cause !

ἐπείτε τάχιστα ἐπύθοντο : how soon
was that ! Had they Proxenoi, or friends
in Sparta, to inform them, or was it
only when the Spartan army was
marching past their own borders !
ἐξεληλυθότας ἐκ Σπάρτης might perhaps
mean 'had crossed the border' ; cp. c.
17 infra.

2. τοὺς μετὰ Π., 'Pausanias and his
men.'

3. κήρυκα (not ἄγγελον, cp. 7. 1).

ἡμεροδρόμων : cp. 6. 105. The
story would be more convincing if the
name of this crack runner had been
preserved ; cp. 6. 105.

4. ἐς τὴν Ἀττικήν . . ἐς τὰς Ἀθήνας :
while the Athenian, Plataian, and
Megarean envoys have been kicking their
heels in Sparta. Mardonios has ex
hypothesi reoccupied Athens, c. 3 supra.

πρότερον αὐτοὶ Μαρδονίῳ ὑποδεξά-

μενοι : according to this story the
Argives were pledged to Mardonios to
keep the Spartans at bay. If true, this
pledge implies previous negotiations
between the Persian and the Argives, of
which nothing further has transpired.
It was a very pretty plan, or a very
pretty commentary on a want of plan.
Had the Argives really been co-operating
with the Persian to that extent they
might have made it impossible for
Sparta to send 10,000 Hoplites and
40,000 Helots beyond the Isthmos.
Argos observed neutrality, perhaps a
neutrality benevolent towards the ' barbarian' ; but Sparta must have been
well assured that a real neutrality
would be observed before she denuded
Lakonia of fighting men. A forgotten
chapter in Greek diplomacy might
have recorded the pourparlers between
Athens, Argos and Sparta during the
winter, or spring, which convinced the
Greeks that they had no active hostility
to expect from Argos : Salamis made a
deeper impression upon Argos than upon
Thessaly and Boiotia, powers which took
their cue from the fiasco at Thermopylai.
The embassy, whose absurd and pitiful
record has just been given above, may
have been better employed in squaring
Argos than in denouncing Sparta.

αὐτοί may best be taken with
σχήσειν.

6. ἔλεγε τάδε. How this ἡμεροδρόμος
got past the Isthmos wall, which was no
doubt guarded from sea to sea, Hdt.
does not say : the problem does not
exist for him. The message is desperate :
Mardonios would have had something
to say in reply, before he allowed the
messenger to depart, on Argive impotence and breach of faith ; except, indeed,

φράσοντά τοι ὅτι ἐκ Λακεδαίμονος ἐξελήλυθε ἡ νεότης, καὶ
ὡς οὐ δυνατοὶ αὐτὴν ἔχειν εἰσὶ Ἀργεῖοι μὴ οὐκ ἐξιέναι.
πρὸς ταῦτα τύγχανε εὖ βουλευόμενος." ὁ μὲν δὴ εἴπας ταῦτα 13
ἀπαλλάσσετο ὀπίσω, Μαρδόνιος δὲ οὐδαμῶς ἔτι πρόθυμος ἦν
μένειν ἐν τῇ Ἀττικῇ, ὡς ἤκουσε ταῦτα. πρὶν μέν νυν ἢ
πυθέσθαι ἀνεκώχευε, θέλων εἰδέναι τὸ παρ' Ἀθηναίων, ὁκοῖόν
τι ποιήσουσι, καὶ οὔτε ἐπήμαινε οὔτε ἐσίνετο γῆν τὴν Ἀττικήν, 5
ἐλπίζων διὰ παντὸς τοῦ χρόνου ὁμολογήσειν σφέας· ἐπεὶ δὲ
οὐκ ἔπειθε, πυθόμενος πάντα λόγον, πρὶν ἢ τοὺς μετὰ

---

7 σοι aC (τε S) ‖ ἐλήλυθεν C   8 αὐτοὶ B ‖ ἴσχειν B, Holder,
van H.: σχεῖν? Stein ‖ Ἀργεῖοι secl. van H.   13. 3 ἤκουε C ‖
μὲν γὰρ? van H. ‖ ἢ om. BPx: ἢ a   4 ἀνοκώχευε van H. ‖ παρὰ a
5 ἐπήμαινε <αὐτοὺς> van H. ‖ ἐσινέετο B   6 τοῦ χρόνου del. Cobet,
van H.   7 τὸν πάντα BP, Stein¹, Holder, van H. ‖ πρινὴ ABR : πρηνὶ S

---

that Mardonios' chief wish must have
been to draw the Peloponnesians into
Boiotia, which is not the point of view
of the anecdote.

7. **ὅτι ἐκ Λακεδαίμονος ἐξελήλυθε ἡ
νεότης**, 'the Lakedaimonian militia has
crossed the border'—a frequent formula,
perhaps, in Peloponnese! νεότης, a
collective term, here apparently includes
all men liable for service abroad; cp.
Thuc. 2. 8. 1 etc. and 7. 13 supra.

8. **ὡς οὐ δυνατοὶ αὐτὴν ἔχειν . . μὴ
οὐκ ἐξιέναι**: a genuine example of the
double negative μὴ οὐ; cp. Index. ἔχειν
(the strong) = 'hold,' 'with - hold,'
'prevent' (cp. Index), itself a negation! just before, σχήσειν . . μὴ ἐξιέναι,
where, however, the action is contingent
and future, while here it is present, or,
indeed, if the Argive would only confess
it honestly, past: a consideration which
may help to account for the positive οὐκ.

9. **τύγχανε εὖ βουλευόμενος**, 'hit
upon a good plan (by yourself!)': if true,
could any message be more fatuous,
under the circumstances? With the
expression cp. 8. 101 ὁκότερα ποιέων
ἐπιτύχω εὖ βουλευσάμενος. The imperative
here is a rude or peremptory optative.

13. 2. **Μαρδόνιος δὲ** had no mind to
stay in Attica once he was assured that
the Peloponnesians would cross the
Isthmos; that assurance can hardly
have been conveyed to him by the
Argives, unless, indeed, the Spartans
had taken them into the secret; he
convinced himself, perhaps, by becoming
aware of movements from the Isthmos
(cp. c. 14 infra), perhaps by pourparlers

with the Athenians, perhaps by information obtained through Greeks in his
camp, that a large force was under
arms; and he apparently retired in
hopes that the Greeks would follow him
into Boiotia, where the ground was
more favourable to cavalry, his base
nearer, and an attack on the Greeks,
as they emerged from the passes into
the plain, feasible. He may, not to
say must, have made sure of their debouching by the pass of Dryoskephalai.

3. **πρὶν . . ἢ πυθέσθαι ἀνεκώχευε**:
πρὶν ἢ with infin. just below again, as
in c. 68 infra; without ἢ 8. 144 supra,
c. 101 infra. ἀνακωχεύειν is used trans.
7. 36 supra (of ropes), 6. 116 (of ships);
here apparently intransitively: 'stayed,
held his hand,' or possibly 'refrained
from acts of hostility'='observed an
armistice'; cp. Thuc. 1. 40. 4 Κορινθίοις
μέν γε ἔνσπονδοί ἐστε, Κερκυραίοις δὲ οὐδὲ
δι' ἀνοκωχῆς πώποτ' ἐγένεσθε, 5. 32. 7
Κορινθίοις δὲ ἀνοκωχὴ ἄσπονδος ἦν πρὸς
Ἀθηναίους, 5. 25. 3 μετ' ἀνοκωχῆς οὐ
βεβαίου ἔβλαπτον ἀλλήλους τὰ μάλιστα.

4. **εἰδέναι . . ὁκοῖόν τι ποιήσουσι**:
the normal prose construction; cp. c. 11
supra.

τὸ παρ' Ἀθηναίων: ellipse; cp.
c. 7 supra.

5. **οὔτε ἐπήμαινε οὔτε ἐσίνετο**: the
former word is poetical, the latter prosaic.

7. **πάντα λόγον**: cp. c. 9 supra.
πρὶν ἢ . . ἐσβαλεῖν looks like an approximately precise date. Hdt. seems
to assume that the wall was unde-
fended, the Isthmos ungarrisoned—that
is incredible. If Mardonios retired

Παυσανίεω ἐς τὸν Ἰσθμὸν ἐσβαλεῖν, ὑπεξεχώρεε ἐμπρήσας τε
τὰς Ἀθήνας, καὶ εἴ κού τι ὀρθὸν ἦν τῶν τειχέων ἢ τῶν
10 οἰκημάτων ἢ τῶν ἱρῶν, πάντα καταβαλὼν καὶ συγχώσας.
ἐξήλαυνε δὲ τῶνδε εἵνεκεν, ὅτι οὔτε ἱππασίμη ἡ χώρη ἦν ἡ
Ἀττική, εἴ τε νικῷτο συμβαλών, ἀπάλλαξις οὐκ ἦν ὅτι μὴ

---

8 ἐσβαλεῖν β, Stein², Holder, van H.: ἐμβαλεῖν ‖ τε: δὲ Apr. C
11 δὲ om. aCz ‖ εἵνεκα z ‖ ἡ post ἦν om. C

---

before Pausanias reached the Isthmos,
it was perhaps inferred that he retired
because he had heard that Pausanias
was on the march, and so, again, that
the Argives must have told him.

8. ὑπεξεχώρεε: sc. αὐτοῖς: he went
out of Attica to avoid them; cp. Plato,
Phaid. 103 D προσιόντος τοῦ θερμοῦ ἢ
ὑπεκχωρήσειν αὐτῷ ἢ ἀπολεῖσθαι (sc. τὴν
χιόνα).

ἐμπρήσας τε . . καὶ . . πάντα
κτλ., 'but not until he had fired Athens,
and thrown down and demolished (συγχώσας, cp. 7. 225) every morsel whether
of the (city) walls, the (private) houses,
or the (holy) temples, which was still
standing upright'—i.e. plainly after the
previous demolition by Xerxes, 8. 50–53
supra; for ὀρθόν cp. Thuc. 5. 42. 2.
Hdt. says nothing of any rebuilding in
the meanwhile. τῶν τειχέων might be
taken to support the view that Athens
was a walled town in 480 B.C. (cp. E.
Gardner, Ancient Athens (1902) pp. 46 ff.,
who does not, however, cite this
instance); but of course it only proves
at most that Hdt. thought so; nor does
it even prove that, for 'the walls'
here might be those of the Akropolis;
or even if the city-walls, would not
prove that the circuit was complete
in 480 B.C. or that a siege of Athens
was a military possibility; cp. further
Appendix VI. § 1.

Rawlinson well remarks that this
account of the destruction of Athens by
Mardonios is exaggerated; Thuc. 1. 89.
3 leaves some of the houses (οἰκίαι)
standing, and even portions of the city-
wall (τοῦ περιβόλου βραχέα). Pausanias
(1. 18. 1, 20. 2) mentions temples older
than the Persian war. Col. Leake
(Athens and the Demi, i. 12) points out
the great difficulties of such total destruction as Hdt. asserts. More recent
excavations have shown that even on
the Akropolis a good deal was left
standing when the Persians departed.
Mardonios had neither time nor zeal

for such wholesale annihilation; it was
only a 'Restoration' that could make
away with the past so utterly! Cp. 8.
50–53 supra.

11. τῶνδε εἵνεκεν. Hdt. surpasses himself, and gives the military reasons for
the evacuation of Attica with the
precision of a professor of the Sach-
Kritik! The reasons are three in
number, and admit of development.
(i.) The Persian's strength lay in his
cavalry; Boiotia was better adapted than
Attica to cavalry operations (Hdt. says
nothing of a great superiority in infantry).
(ii.) Attica was difficult to evacuate
in case of defeat. The point is not
fully or very clearly put; but at any
rate Mardonios is not counting on success
as a foregone conclusion.
(iii.) He wished to be nearer his base
in Thebes. The reason is not quite
clearly put; speaking generally it is
better to fight in your enemy's than in
your friend's territory. Mardonios,
however, was thinking of his commissariat, and also perhaps of the loyalty,
or potential disloyalty, of Greece in his
rear; in case of defeat a position north
of Kithairon was better from this point
of view. Artabazos might never have
effected his masterly retreat (c. 89 infra)
if the great battle had been fought on
the Thriasian or even on the Athenian
plain. The argument as a whole was
purely strategic, and Hdt. does well not
to ascribe to Mardonios the policy of
limiting the Persian frontier of the
Hellenic satrapy in posse to the Kithairon-
Parnes line (pace G. B. Grundy, Great
Persian War, p. 450).

ἦν: the tense carries back to the
historic situation.

12. εἴ τε νικῷτο . . οὐκ ἦν, 'should he
be defeated . . there was no . .' The
construction is irregular but clear, and
even more forcible than stricter grammar
would have been.

ἀπάλλαξις is very rare; Hdt. uses

κατὰ στεινόν, ὥστε ὀλίγους σφέας ἀνθρώπους ἴσχειν. ἐβουλεύετο
ὧν ἐπαναχωρήσας ἐς τὰς Θήβας συμβαλεῖν πρὸς πόλι τε
φιλίη καὶ <ἐν> χώρῳ ἱππασίμῳ.   15

Μαρδόνιος μὲν δὴ ὑπεξεχώρεε, ἤδη δὲ ἐν τῇ ὁδῷ ἐόντι 14
αὐτῷ ἦλθε ἀγγελίη πρόδρομον ἄλλην στρατιὴν ἥκειν ἐς
Μέγαρα, Λακεδαιμονίων χιλίους· πυθόμενος δὲ ταῦτα ἐβουλεύετο
[θέλων] εἴ κως τούτους πρῶτον ἕλοι. ὑποστρέψας δὴ τὴν

13 καὶ ὀλίγους ßz, Holder, van H.   15 ἐν Schweighaeuser, van H.,
Stein³ ‖ χώρῳ Stein⁽¹⁾, van H., Stein³ : χώρῃ   14. 1 ὑπεχώρεεν β
‖ τῇ abesse malit van H.   2 πρόδρομον Schweighaeuser : πρόδρομος
4 θέλων om. cod. unus et alter, del. Reiske, Schaefer, Cobet, van H., Stein³ ‖
δὴ Stein³, Holder : δὲ

ἀπαλλαγή in 7. 207, 8. 39, 118 supra,
'(means of) getting away.'

ὅτι μὴ κατὰ στανόν, except by
a strait, a narrow pass. There are really
three passes from Attica into Boiotia:
(1) Dekeleia-Oropos, (2) Phyle-Panakton,
(3) Eleusis-Eleutherai-Erythrai. Taking in the whole Boiotian frontier from
sea to sea, two further passes may be
added : (4) the direct road or route from
Megara to Plataia, and (5) the route
round the end of Kithairon via Aigo-
sthena-Kreusis. Op. Grundy, G.P.W. pp.
445 ff., and 8. 113. 2 supra. The route
by Eleutherai has a fork, the left prong
of which goes to Plataia, so that from
the Boiotian side the number of apparent
passes would be raised to six. This fact
is of importance on the battle-field of
Plataia ; but, if defeated in the Thriasian
plain, the invaders could not use (3) at
all, and if defeated east of Aigaleos could
only use (1). In any case (2) was very
difficult ; cp. Xenoph. Mem. 3. 5. 25
ὅτι πρόκειται τῆς χώρας ἡμῶν ὄρη μεγάλα,
καθήκοντα ἐπὶ τὴν Βοιωτίαν, δι' ὧν εἰς τὴν
χώραν εἴσοδοι στεναί τε καὶ προσάντεις εἰσί,
καὶ ὅτι μέση διέζωσται ὄρεσιν ἐρυμνοῖς.
13. ἀνθρώπους, not even ἄνδρας.
15. ἱππασίμῳ refers merely to the
space for evolutions (not to the grass
for fodder) ; cp. 2. 108.
14. 2. ἦλθε ἀγγελίη : who brought
this intelligence ? Doubtless his own
scouts and cavalry. Probably the arrival
of this information, or perhaps an in-
effectual attempt to capture Megara—no
doubt a well-walled city—encouraged
Mardonios to hope that the Greeks would
follow him into Boiotia ; the next news,
that they were in full force at the
Isthmos, convinced him.
πρόδρομον ἄλλην στρατιὴν ἥκειν

ἐς Μέγαρα Λακεδαιμονίων χιλίους. This
may not have been the whole force ;
there had been but 300 'Spartans' at
Thermopylai ; perhaps this was really
the avant-garde of the whole army, and
Mardonios would feel that unless he
was prepared to do battle in Attica,
the time had come to retire. πρόδρομον
and ἄλλην are not quite consistent ;
ἄλλην is relative to the previous message
of the Argives ; πρόδρομον is a bit of
information which might or might not
have been reported to Mardonios, but
at any rate shows that the force at
Megara was not a tertium quid, but a
portion of the levée en masse. See,
however, App. Crit. Mardonios is next
credited with a wish, a plan, and an
attempt to catch or capture this force
(ἕλοι, Homeric ; cp. Il. 2. 37 Πριάμου
πόλιν, 13. 42 νῆας Ἀχαιῶν, 21. 102
πολλοὺς ζωούς). To do so he returns
apparently on his tracks (ὑποστρέψας)
and leads his whole force against
Megara. Such conduct is inconsistent
with his deliberate intention to withdraw into Boiotia, for the good and
sufficient reasons set forth in the
previous chapter. Possibly Mardonios
fought a 'rear-guard action,' or sought
to retard the advance of the Peloponnesians, while he evacuated Attica. He
could not view with equanimity the
penetration of Boiotia by the Peloponnesian army (via Dryoskephalai) before
he had evacuated Attica, even though
Thebes was probably held, and held
strongly, by a Persian (or Makedonian)
garrison ; nor did he desire to fight the
great battle in Attica at all. His cavalry,
or a few squadrons of cavalry, employed
in harrying the Megarid, doubtless
retired either by Dryoskephalai or even

5 στρατιὴν ἦγε ἐπὶ τὰ Μέγαρα· ἡ δὲ ἵππος προελθοῦσα
κατιππάσατο χώρην τὴν Μεγαρίδα. ἐς ταύτην δὴ ἑκαστάτω
τῆς Εὐρώπης τὸ πρὸς ἡλίου δύνοντος ἡ Περσικὴ αὕτη στρατιὴ
15 ἀπίκετο. μετὰ δὲ ταῦτα Μαρδονίῳ ἦλθε ἀγγελίη ὡς ἀλέες
εἴησαν οἱ Ἕλληνες ἐν τῷ Ἰσθμῷ. οὕτω δὴ ὀπίσω ἐπορεύετο
διὰ Δεκελέης· οἱ γὰρ βοιωτάρχαι μετεπέμψαντο τοὺς προσ-

---

5 προελθοῦσα β : προσελθοῦσα   6 δὲ β ‖ ἑκαστάτωι αP   7
στρατιὴ αὕτη α   15. 1 ταῦτα del. van H. ‖ ἧκε Pz   3 δεκελέης
RS : δεκελείης ‖ βοιώταρχοι? van H.

---

by Aigosthena into Boiotia, while the
main column marched by the eastern
pass or passes; see next chapter.

5. ἐπὶ τὰ Μέγαρα: apparently Megara,
unlike Athens, was fully fortified, and
strongly held. No previous attack upon
it has been mentioned; and the Megarid
had escaped a Persian visitation in the
previous year, improbable as such immunity may in itself appear, cp. 8. 70.
The loss of Megara was treated by
Themistokles, 8. 60, as the certain consequence of the evacuation of Salamis:
per contra, the victory at Salamis may
have saved the city. Even now only
the χώρα suffers. That would practically
be the plain lying between the Kerata,
Geraneia, and the two seas. The city
itself possessed two citadels (Pausan. 1.
39. 5, 42. 1): hence perhaps the plural
form of the name.

6. ἐς ταύτην δὴ . . ἀπίκετο. "Here
was the furthest point in Europe towards
the setting sun to which this Persian
army ever penetrated," Rawlinson.
"This was the furthest point [not 'the
westernmost'] of Europe, looking westward, which was reached" (by this army
of Persians), Blakesley. "This was the
furthest land in Europe towards the
sun-setting to which this Persian army
came," Macaulay. Blakesley is no doubt
right in saying that the emphasis is not
on the exact orientation, but on the
distance; nevertheless the orientation
is given, and involves Hdt., or his
cartographer, unwittingly in error. Hdt.
evidently conceives of Central Greece as
running approximately north and south
(cf. his orientation of Thermopylai 7.
176). It did not occur to him, when he
wrote this passage, that not merely was
Delphi (visited ex hypothesi by the
Persians, 8. 35) far to the west of the
Megarid, but that the whole route of
the Persian forces in Central Greece,

Mardonios' march from Thessaly in this
very spring, had lain west of the point
here marked as the furthest point of
Europe in the west reached by the
Persian arms. The orientation, then,
breaks down equally whether Hdt.
meant by the words αὕτη στρατιὴ the
army (cp. 6. 12 where it is used absolutely
for πεζὸς στρατός) of Xerxes or the
army of Mardonios; and this passage
evidently belongs to a composition to be
dated before Hdt.'s own visit to Europe,
to Delphi, Thebes and Central Greece,
and was left standing, perhaps by oversight, after he must have known better
(perhaps like the Thermopylai orientation). Cp. Introduction, § 9. Hdt.
certainly did not mean that another
Persian army had penetrated further,
i.e. further westwards, into Europe;
but he may have had in his mind the
possibilities that other Persian armies
had penetrated further into Europe, to
wit, northward, or north-eastwards
(having regard to his conception of the
continent); and he probably has no
special intention of distinguishing here
the army of Mardonios from the army
of Xerxes.

15. 1. ἦλθε ἀγγελίη: counting the
Argive in c. 12, this is the third express
message that reaches Mardonios; his
own intelligence department, or the
medizing Greeks, will have procured it.
This message is not quite correct: the
Athenians only joined the 'Hellenic'
army at Eleusis c. 19 infra; but it
marks probably the union of the rest of
the Peloponnesians with the Spartans
(ib.) or vice versa.

3. διὰ Δεκελέης. Dekeleia (δῆμος τῆς
Ἱπποθοωντίδος φυλῆς Steph. B. sub v.)
is placed by Thuc. 7. 19. 2 at 120 stades
from Athens, and a very little more
from Boiotia: its position is further
defined by this passage, as on the eastern

χώρους τῶν Ἀσωπίων, οὗτοι δὲ αὐτῷ τὴν ὁδὸν ἡγέοντο ἐς
Σφενδαλέας, ἐνθεῦτεν δὲ ἐς Τάναγραν· ἐν Τανάγρῃ δὲ νύκτα 5
ἐναυλισάμενος, καὶ τραπόμενος τῇ ὑστεραίῃ ἐς Σκῶλον, ἐν γῇ

---

5 ἐς τανάγρην RSV, Gaisford, Palm ‖ ἐν ταναγόρηι C   6 κῶλον
Paris. 1635, z

---

road from Athens into Boiotia, and its
exact position (modern *Tatói*) is proved
by Inscripp. and by remains *in situ*. A
chapter in its legendary history is given
below, c. 78.

βοιωτάρχαι: this is the earliest
express mention of the 'Boiotarchs,' a
body which reappears in Thucydides
(4. 91. 1, cp. 2. 2. 1), Xenophon (*Hell.*
3. 4. 4 βοιώταρχοι, *sic*), and the later
writers. They were evidently important,
probably superior officers of the Boiotian
League, and their existence is synchronous therewith : the number of the
Board is doubtful (Eleven in Thuc.
l.c., Seven in Diodor. 15. 52, =371 B.C.
Leuktra, etc.) and may have varied
at different times ; they were elected
annually (entering on office in winter).
Cp. G. Gilbert, *Gr. Staatsalt.* ii. (1885)
54 f., to which later efforts (e.g. Pauly-
Wissowa *sub v.*) have added little.
These officers, or some of them, were
now in attendance on Mardonios, as
they 'sent for' men from the Asopos
valley to act as guides (Athenians were
either not to be found, or not to be
trusted: the Athenian *émigrés* were
apparently not with Mardonios). Guides
might have been needful on the Phyle-
Panakton route : were they needed for
the routes by Dekeleia and by Eleutherai?
And how had Mardonios and his men
found their way into Attica? Or had
they learnt nothing of the routes in the
previous year?

4. Ἀσώπιοι: an *Hapaxlegomenon*?=
Παρασώπιοι, Strabo 409, who also uses
the term Παρασωπία for the land either
side the upper and middle Asopos (cp.
infra), but does not appear to carry
the term so far down as Tanagra.

5. Σφενδαλέας: Steph. B. *sub v.*
Σφενδάλη. δῆμος Ἱπποθοωντίδος φυλῆς.
ὁ δημότης, Σφενδαλεύς. Sphendale does
not play much part in Attic history,
and its exact position has been disputed.
Leake (*Athens and the Demi*, ii. 123)
placed it "near" Hagios Merkurios, but
"at" *Malakasa*, on the road from Aphidna
to Tanagra, apparently in agreement
with Finlay, cp. *op. c.* p. 124 n. Pauly,

R.E. vi. (1852) i. 1375, appears to
be in error on this point. Bursian i.
(1862) 336, "near *Kakosialesi*" (which
Leake *l.c.* describes as "the only site
that could compete with Malakasa as
the site of Sphendale") "at the foot
of an isolated and extensive hill, the
Hyakinthos (now *Kotroni*), on which
the Ἱακινθίδες παρθένοι (cp. Suidas *s.v.*
Παρθένοι) were worshipped, Attic maidens
who had voluntarily taken their own
lives to secure victory for Athens against
Boiotia." (This position Leake regards
as beyond the Attic frontier.)

Τάναγραν: the position of Tanagra,
on the left bank of the Asopos, near the
junction of the Thermodon (c. 43 *infra*)
is quite certain ; Leake, *N.G.* ii. 463,
Bursian i. 222. Some of the natives
believed the old name of the city to be
Graia, cp. Hom. *Il.* 2. 498, until the
still older name was 'restored' to it ;
cp. Strabo 404, Pausan. 9. 20. 2, Steph.
B. *sub v.*, who also gives Ποιμανδρία as
a former name. The population was
'Gephyraian,' cp. 5. 57, and was never
perhaps wholly 'Boiotized' : are not the
charming terra-cottas, that have popularized the city's name in our day, rather
Ionic than 'Boiotian'? After the
humiliation of Thebes Tanagra apparently
"aspired for a time to the leadership of
the Boiotian confederacy," B. Head,
Hist. Num. 295 ; cp. *Coinage of Boiotia*,
p. 20. That ambition was foiled by
the restoration of Thebes after the great
battle in 457 B.C., Thuc. 1. 108. 1–3 ;
but Tanagra survived most of the
members of the Boiotian League, cp.
Strabo 410.

νύκτα ἐναυλισάμενος: 1. 181.

6. τραπόμενος τῇ ὑστεραίῃ ἐς Σκῶλον:
cp. Strabo 408 ἐστὶ κώμη τῆς Παρασωπίας
ὑπὸ τῷ Κιθαιρῶνι, δυσοίκητος τόπος καὶ
τραχύς, ἀφ' οὗ καὶ ἡ παροιμία εἰς Σκῶλον
μήτ' αὐτὸς ἴναι (ἴμεν) μήτ' ἄλλῳ ἔπεσθαι.
Its ruins were seen (?) by Pausanias (9.
4. 4) "about 40 stades" below the bridge
across the Asopos. The town is named in
the Catalogue (*Il.* 2. 47, 496), and figures
in the Spartano-Theban wars of the fourth
century ; Xen. *Hell.* 5. 4. 49, *Ages.* 2. 22.

τῇ Θηβαίων ἦν. ἐνθαῦτα δὲ τῶν Θηβαίων καί περ μηδιζόντων
ἔκειρε τοὺς χώρους, οὔτι κατὰ ἔχθος αὐτῶν ἀλλ᾽ ὑπ᾽ ἀναγκαίης μεγάλης ἐχόμενος ἔρυμά τε τῷ στρατοπέδῳ ποιήσασθαι,
10 καὶ ἦν συμβαλόντι οἱ μὴ ἐκβαίνῃ ὁκοῖόν τι ἐθέλοι, κρησφύγετον τοῦτο ἐποιέετο. παρῆκε δὲ αὐτοῦ τὸ στρατόπεδον

---

7 Θηβαίω ἦν Β   8 οὔτε Bekker ‖ αὐτέων z   9 ἐχόμενος
βουλόμενος ΒΡᵐz, Holder : βουλόμενος Cobet, van H. ‖ στρατῶι Β²CP
10 οἱ : οὐ C ‖ θέλη Β : ἐθέλει z   11 τοῦτο ἐποιέετο del. Cobet, van H.

Strabo 409 reckons all the Παρασώπιοι (to wit, the men of Σκῶλος, Ἐτεωνός, Ἐρύθραι, Ὑσιαί) as subject to Thebes; in that sense, when Mardonios turned (if he did turn) up the river, and recrossed it to Skolos, he would there be ἐν γῇ τῇ Θηβαίων. Hdt., however, does not keep him long at Skolos, but passes him on to the camp or *Laager* described below, which was not at Skolos, nor even on the same side of the river as Skolos. Possibly there is some error or confusion in the account of the retirement of Mardonios from Attica; or rather, is it possible there should not be? Hdt. apparently assumes that Mardonios takes all his forces into Attica—not a probable assumption—and that Mardonios takes them all in, and all out, by one route, and one route only—a still less probable assumption (cp. 8. 113). Skolos evidently lies at the Boiotian end of the middle or direct route from Athens to Thebes. If Mardonios found himself at Skolos it was probably because he himself came out of Attica by this route. More than one, perhaps all three routes out of Attica, may have been used—not to say the route by Aigosthena from Megara, c. 14 *supra*. That the 'Asopioi' acted as guides favours this suggestion. If Mardonios himself came by the easier route from Dekeleia to Tanagra, he probably went on to Thebes, or else to the Laager, by the left bank. The only diarial hint for the march is the night spent in Tanagra, and the next day. Probably nights were also spent at Dekeleia (12 miles from Athens), at Sphendale (7–8 miles from Dekeleia), as well as at Tanagra (11–12 miles from Sphendale). (Skolos would be about 9 miles up the Asopos.)

7. τῶν Θηβαίων . . ἔκειρε τοὺς χώρους: probably not the Thebais proper, but the 'places' on the Asopos, the Parasopia, *in ditione Thebanorum*; cp. *supra.* "Agros Thebanorum vastavit," Schweig-

haeuser ; so too Stein, cp. 3. 58. κείρειν, 7. 131, 8. 32, 65 *supra.*

8. ὑπ᾽ ἀναγκαίης μεγάλης ἐχόμενος, 'with absolutely no free will in the matter.' The construction at this point is a little faulty. Stein apparently takes ποιήσασθαι as dependent on ὑπ᾽ ἀναγ. ἐχόμενος = ἀναγκαζόμενος. Some inf. codd. (followed by some editors ; cp. App. Crit.) insert βουλόμενος—a very sorry device. I should be inclined to take the infinitive as pendent, or telic, or exegetical (cp. Index, for parallels) ; in any case the transition to ἐποιέετο is harsh, and perhaps the omission of ποιήσασθαι would be the simplest remedy. ἐποιέετο is repeated below in a different construction and sense ; here middle ('was having made,' or perhaps 'looked upon,' 'considered') : there passive ('was being constructed ').

9. ἔρυμα : cp. 7. 223 *supra.*

10. ἦν . . μὴ ἐκβαίνῃ ὁκοῖόν τι ἐθέλοι τοῦτο ἐποιέετο : a notable sequence for a conditional sentence. The apprehension of a disaster has already received expression c. 13 *supra.*

κρησφύγετον : 5. 124. The actual construction of this Laager is not so precisely described as that of the ἔρκος and τεῖχος at Mykale, cc. 97, 102 *infra.*

11. τὸ στρατόπεδον: plainly the Laager, which was much more extensive than the τεῖχος, ἔρυμα, κρησφύγετον. 'This Laager reached (παρῆκε) from Erythrai (where it began) along past Hysiai, and extended (κατέτανε, cp. 8. 31) into the territory of Plataiai, stretching (or 'posted' if τεταγμένον be retained) along the Asopos river. The fortified part of it was of less extensive construction, being about ten stades to each front.' This passage makes it clear that the Laager was much larger than the fortified *Praetorium*, and that the fortified portion had a measurement of upwards of a square mile ; but the exact size

ἀρξάμενον ἀπὸ Ἐρυθρέων παρὰ Ὑσιάς, κατέτεινε δὲ ἐς τὴν
Πλαταιίδα γῆν, παρὰ τὸν Ἀσωπὸν ποταμὸν τεταμένον. οὐ

12 Ἐρυθραίων z   13 περὶ τὸν z   ‖   τεταμένον Reiske, Holder,
van H., Stein³: τεταγμένον

and appearance of the camp are not
described, and a large number of other
problems are left unresolved.
(1) Was the τεῖχος square? Hdt. may
perhaps mean this, for otherwise he
should have given the measurements of
the other sides, or flanks; and *prima
facie* each side of a fort is a μέτωπον.
Elsewhere in similar cases he is more
particular to specify quadrature, e.g. of
Babylon, 1. 178 ἐοῦσα μέτωπον ἕκαστον
εἴκοσι καὶ ἑκατὸν σταδίων ἐούσης τετραγώνου : 2. 124 of a pyramid, τῆς ἐστὶ
πανταχῇ μέτωπον ἕκαστον ὀκτὼ πλέθρα
ἐούσης τετραγώνου.
(2) Was the Laager on one side, or
on both sides the Asopos; and in what
part of the Laager was the Fort? The
Fort was on the left bank of the Asopos,
for the Persians cross the river to reach
the Greeks c. 59 *infra*; and the wooden
Fort is ἐν μοίρῃ τῇ Θηβαῖδι, c. 65 *infra*
u.v.; but cp. l. 6 *supra*. Stein⁵ places
the Fort south of Asopos in the neighbourhood of Skolos, but Skolos has
nothing to say to the camp as described
by Hdt. nor to the battle; the mention
of Skolos above is to be otherwise
accounted for. Probably the fortified
camp was close to the river, and to the
bridge across the Asopos, the *tête du pont*
on the south side being no doubt strongly
fortified and held; the rest of the Persian
lines would lie behind, and away from
the river, and no part of the Laager
proper would be on the right bank of
the river. The main road to Thebes
will have passed through the camp,
possibly dividing it in half; the 10
stades may be the measurement of the
river front, which was all palisaded;
the palisading probably went all round
the 'Fort,' and the Fort may have been
square.
(3) It is quite certain that no part of
Mardonios' Laager or Fort actually
touched the towns of Erythrai and
Hysiai, for these places are presently
in possession of the Greeks cc. 19, 25
infra. The description here given of
the extent of the Persian camp must
be understood either (a) to be based upon
a report of the appearance of the Persian
camp as seen from the Greek lines above,

which enclosed Erythrai, and afterwards
Hysiai; or (b) to mean that the Laager
(though north of Asopos) occupied ground
belonging to the two townships named,
and extended further into Plataian territory north of Asopos. But for two reasons
the former explanation is to be preferred:
(1) the contrast here between the names
of the towns and the specification of
Πλαταιὶς γῆ : (2) the doubt whether the
territory of Erythrai and Hysiai did
extend to the further bank of the stream,
which was probably all Theban. The
first reason may be further enforced by
the supposition that the name of Plataiai
is avoided because Plataiai was in ruins;
the second, by the observation that the
Thebans had only been driven across
the Asopos by the Athenians in or about
509 B.C., the river being then made the
frontier between the Thebais on the one
side and the Plataiis and Hysiatis on
the other; 6. 108 *supra*.
12. ἀπὸ Ἐρυθρέων παρὰ Ὑσιάς: there
is little room for doubt that Leake, *N.G.*
ii. 329, located these towns much too far
east, and that they occupied sites in
close proximity to the main roads from
Eleusis - Eleutherai to Thebes and to
Plataia; Erythrai probably commanded
the main road to Thebes, while Hysiai,
about a mile further west, commanded
the branch to Plataia; cp. cc. 22, 25
infra, and G. B. Grundy, *G.P.W.* pp.
458 ff.
13. τὸν Ἀσωπὸν ποταμόν: to be
distinguished from the Malian stream
of the same name (7. 199, etc.), as also
from a river by Sikyon (Ἀσωπὸς ὁ παρ-
αρρέων τὴν Σικυῶνα καὶ ποιῶν τὴν Ἀσωπίαν
χώραν, μέρος οὖσαν τῆς Σικυωνίας, Strabo
382). There was also an Asopos in
Paros, *ibid.* The Boiotian Asopos rises
near Leuktra and flows eastwards into the
sea near Oropos (ὁ παρὰ Θήβας ῥέων καὶ
Πλαταιὰς καὶ Τάναγραν, Strabo, *ib.*) along
the skirts of Kithairon (Strabo 409), a
relatively large and fertilizing stream
(Ἀσωπὸν δ' ἵκοντο βαθύσχοινον λεχεποίην
Il. 4. 388) liable to sudden floods in
spring (ὁ γὰρ Ἀσωπὸς ποταμὸς ἐρρύη μέγας
καὶ οὐ ῥαδίως διαβατὸς ἦν Thuc. 2. 5. 2),
for ever a φίλον πίασμα Βοιωτῶν χθονὶ
(Aischyl. *Pers.* 806).

μέντοι τό γε τεῖχος τοσοῦτο ἐποιέετο, ἀλλ᾽ ὡς ἐπὶ δέκα
15 σταδίους μάλιστά κη μέτωπον ἕκαστον.

16　Ἐχόντων δὲ τὸν πόνον τοῦτον τῶν βαρβάρων, Ἀτταγῖνος
ὁ Φρύνωνος ἀνὴρ Θηβαῖος παρασκευασάμενος μεγάλως ἐκάλεε
ἐπὶ ξείνια αὐτόν τε Μαρδόνιον καὶ πεντήκοντα Περσέων τοὺς
λογιμωτάτους, κληθέντες δὲ οὗτοι εἵποντο· ἦν δὲ τὸ δεῖπνον
5 ποιεύμενον ἐν Θήβῃσι. τάδε δὲ ἤδη τὰ ἐπίλοιπα ἤκουον
Θερσάνδρου ἀνδρὸς μὲν Ὀρχομενίου, λογίμου δὲ ἐς τὰ πρῶτα

---

14 τοσοῦτον CPz: οὕτω R　　　16. 2 μεγαλωστὶ malit van H.
4 εἵποντο z　　5 τὰ δὲ δὲ δὴ R: τὰ δὲ ἤδη SVz　　6, 7 'Ἐρχο-
μενίου et Ἐρχομένῳ suadent tituli' van H.

---

16. 1. ἐχόντων δὲ τὸν πόνον τ.: i.e.
while engaged on the labour of making
the fortified camp.

Ἀτταγῖνος ὁ Φρύνωνος: of the
father, Phrynon, nothing is recorded;
the name was not very uncommon: at
Athens it appears in the war with
Mytilene for Sigeion in the days of
Pittakos, cp. Plutarch, de Hdt. Malig.
15 = Mor. 858, cp. 5. 95 supra.
Attaginos reappears in c. 86 infra, without patronymic, as one of the leading
'dynasts' of Thebes, whose extradition
was demanded by the Hellenes after their
victory. This observation supports the
view that the present passage belongs to
the original draft of the work; see lower
down. According to Plutarch (op. c.
31) he was a hospes of Demaratos, and
had by him been introduced to the king
during the previous year: Δημάρατος ὁ
Σπαρτιάτης διὰ ξενίαν εὔνους ὢν Ἀτταγίνῳ
τῷ προεστῶτι τῆς ὀλιγαρχίας, διεπράξατο
φίλον βασιλέως γενέσθαι καὶ ξένον. (The
name is curious: from ἀτταγᾶς, a
partridge; Aristoph. Bds. 247, 761;
while φρύνη, φρῦνος, is a toad; cp.
Φρύνιχος, Kuropatkin, etc.)

2. μεγάλως, magno apparatu; cp. 6.
70 (ὑποδέχεσθαι), 1. 167 (ἐναγίζειν) etc.

ἐκάλεε ἐπὶ ξείνια, 'invited (or, was
inviting) to a banquet'; cp. 5. 18.
πεντήκοντα: perhaps 'covers were laid'
for 100 in all, or else for 102. λογιμωτάτους, cc. 24, 37 infra: λόγιμος c. 64
infra. κληθέντες δὲ οὗτοι εἵποντο: this
specific record of the acceptance of the
invitation is curious: is it matter of
surprise that Persian grandees should
accept the invitation of a Greek? Or
was Theban cookery of ill repute?
Athenaeus, p. 148 E, reconstructs the
menu: θρῖα, καὶ ἑψητούς, καὶ ἀφύας, καὶ

ἐγκρασικόλους, καὶ ἀλλᾶντας, καὶ σχελίδας
καὶ ἔτνος—very paltry fare, and enough
to account for the defeat of the Persians,
ἀπολωλότες ἤδη ὑπὸ τῶν τοιούτων τροφῶν,
but still luxury compared with the
Λακωνικὸν δεῖπνον c. 82 infra.

4. ἦν . . ποιεύμενον ἐν Θήβῃσι: not
in the Persian camp, cp. infra; the
difference between ἦν ποιεύμενον and
ἐποιέετο is rather fine.

5. τάδε δὲ ἤδη τὰ ἐπίλοιπα ἤκουον.
The 'banquet of Attaginos' was apparently celebrated, and a part of general
tradition; Hdt. has, however, a particular
anecdote to relate about it, which he
owes to a special source of information—
a source full of possibilities! Probably
the general report in regard to the
banquet was very different from the
pessimism of this anecdote, which Hdt.
had apparently heard not once, but
again and again (ἤκουον, cp. ἤκουσα 7. 55).

6. Θερσάνδρου . . Ὀρχομενίου. Why
does not Hdt. give a patronymic to this
prince of Orchomenos? Thersandros
occurs as the name of the son of Polyneikes 4. 147, 6. 52. The Orchomenos
here named is of course the Boiotian;
cp. 8. 34. (On the coinage the all but
constant form of the name is Erchomenos;
cp. Head, H.N. 294 and c. 28 infra.)
Had this Orchomenian paid for his
medism with exile? Had Hdt. as a boy
heard the story from the exile's lips?
Where or when had they met? Perhaps
in Hdt.'s own Halikarnassian home.
The Orchomenian will not have been
quite a young man in 479 B.C., and there
is not the slightest necessity to delay
the intercourse between Thersandros and
Hdt. until the latter's visit to Boiotia (of
which we have conclusive evidence in 5.
59): the imperfect ἤκουον also militates

ἐν Ὀρχομενῷ. ἔφη δὲ ὁ Θέρσανδρος κληθῆναι καὶ αὐτὸς ὑπὸ
Ἀτταγίνου ἐπὶ τὸ δεῖπνον τοῦτο, κληθῆναι δὲ καὶ Θηβαίων
ἄνδρας πεντήκοντα, καί σφεων οὐ χωρὶς ἑκατέρους κλῖναι,
ἀλλὰ Πέρσην τε καὶ Θηβαῖον ἐν κλίνῃ ἑκάστῃ. ὡς δὲ ἀπὸ 10
δείπνου ἦσαν, διαπινόντων τὸν Πέρσην τὸν ὁμόκλινον Ἑλλάδα
γλῶσσαν ἱέντα εἰρέσθαι αὐτὸν ὁποδαπός ἐστι, αὐτὸς δὲ
ὑποκρίνασθαι ὡς εἴη Ὀρχομένιος. τὸν δὲ εἰπεῖν " ἐπεὶ νῦν
ὁμοτράπεζός τέ μοι καὶ ὁμόσπονδος ἐγένεο, μνημόσυνά τοι
γνώμης τῆς ἐμῆς καταλιπέσθαι θέλω, ἵνα καὶ προειδὼς αὐτὸς 15
περὶ σεωυτοῦ βουλεύεσθαι ἔχῃς τὰ συμφέροντα. ὁρᾷς τούτους
τοὺς δαινυμένους Πέρσας καὶ τὸν στρατὸν τὸν ἐλίπομεν ἐπὶ

7 κλιθῆναι Reiske, van H.: κλινῆναι Dindorf   11 ἔσαν z   12
ἱέντα Cz ‖ ποδαπός B : ὀκοδαπός Bekker   13 εἶπαι z, van H. ‖ Ἐπεί
νυν van H.   14 ἐγένετο R ‖ τοι : τε CS   15 ἐθέλω B   16
ἑωυτοῦ C   17 τοὺς om. A¹C

against that. Thersandros is memorable as one of the three men whom Hdt. actually names among his informants (cp. 3. 55, 4. 76—the scribe at Sais is anonymous 2. 28). The pseudo-antithesis ἀνδρὸς μὲν Ὀρχομενίου, λογίμου δὲ ἐν Ὀρχομενῷ is curious; or, perhaps, in contrast to his position as an exile in Asia: otherwise it were a stylistic infelicity. Was the exile of Orchomenos reduced to keeping a school, like Διονύσιος ἐν Κορίνθῳ (Cicero ad A. 9. 9. 1, ad F. 9. 18. 1)? Was he one of Hdt.'s tutors? His doctrine is thoroughly Herodotean !

τὰ πρῶτα : cp. c. 78 infra, 7. 134 supra ; rather differently in 7. 13.

8. Θηβαίων. Rawlinson understands 'Boiotians' generally : there would be more Thebans perhaps than from any other city, but probably all the cities of the Boiotian Confederacy would be represented. Was the banquet rigidly confined to 'Boiotians' and 'Persians'? Were no Makedonians, no Medes, no Thessalians present?

9. οὐ χωρὶς ἑκατέρους κλῖναι. Attaginus hospes (dicitur) κλῖναι, cp. 1. 126 τοὺς Πέρσας κατακλίνας ἐς λειμῶνα εὐώχεε. Quare haud opus scribere κλινῆναι (Baehr). Cp. App. Crit. ἑκατέρους, each set, both sets, i.e. Greeks and 'barbarians.' A Greek couch held two, a Roman three persons. Attaginos evidently wished the 'Thebans' and 'Persians' to fraternize.

10. ὡς δὲ ἀπὸ δείπνου ἦσαν : when they were done eating ; cp. ἀπὸ δ. ἐγίνοντο 6. 129, 5. 18. Thersandros and his companion seem to have preserved silence

during the eating, and only thawed on the arrival of the wine : διαπίνειν l.c. supra. The 'Persian' could speak Greek Ἑλλάδα γλῶσσαν ἱέντα, cp. 1. 57.

12. ὁποδαπός : qua ex terra, cuias ; 5. 13, 7. 218. The Orchomenian does not appear to have emulated the curiosity of his ὁμόκλινος (an Hapaxlegomenon). The idea is, perhaps, that the Persian would not have been so frank to a 'Theban' proper.

14. ὁμοτράπεζος . . ὁμόσπονδος : the one referring to eating, the other to libations ; the tables had no doubt been taken away before the drinking began ; ὁμοτρ. 3. 132.

ἐγένεο : a perfect might have been expected ; but the aorist emphasizes the fact that they were ἀπὸ δείπνου and that the σπονδαί had taken place.

μνημόσυνα, 6. 109. The Persian speaker apparently treats his own death as a foregone conclusion, though he assumes that his boon-companion will survive (ὄψεαι infra) ; his γνώμη is to be found less in his prophecy than in his philosophy. The word γνώμη is used here in the more abstract sense, unusual with Hdt.

15. ἵνα . . ἔχῃς : Thersandros might have acted on this hint at once ; perhaps afterwards he wished that he had done so. ἔχειν is here 'to be able.'

16. ὁρᾷς . . τὸν ἐλίπομεν : only possible to 'the mind's eye' ; so that there is a kind of zeugma.

17. δαινυμένους, middle, 'to have a

τῷ ποταμῷ στρατοπεδευόμενον · τούτων πάντων ὄψεαι ὀλίγου
τινὸς χρόνου διελθόντος ὀλίγους τινὰς τοὺς περιγενομένους."
20 ταῦτα ἅμα τε τὸν Πέρσην λέγειν καὶ μετιέναι πολλὰ τῶν
δακρύων. αὐτὸς δὲ θωμάσας τὸν λόγον εἰπεῖν πρὸς αὐτὸν
" οὐκῶν Μαρδονίῳ τε ταῦτα χρεόν ἐστι λέγειν καὶ τοῖσι μετ᾽
ἐκεῖνον ἐν αἴνῃ ἐοῦσι Περσέων ; " τὸν δὲ μετὰ ταῦτα εἰπεῖν
" ξεῖνε, ὅ τι δεῖ γενέσθαι ἐκ τοῦ θεοῦ ἀμήχανον ἀποτρέψαι
25 ἀνθρώπῳ · οὐδὲ γὰρ πιστὰ λέγουσι ἐθέλει πείθεσθαι οὐδείς.
ταῦτα δὲ Περσέων συχνοὶ ἐπιστάμενοι ἑπόμεθα ἀναγκαίῃ

---

18 ἐστρατοπεδευμένον malit van H. ‖ τουτέων z   19 τοὺς del.
Cobet, van H.   20 ταῦτά τε ἅμα Β, Holder, van H. ‖ πολλοὺς z
21 θωυμάσας Pz, Stein[1] ‖ εἶπαι z, van H.   22 χρεών ΒPz, van H. ‖
μετὰ α   23 εἶπαι z, van H.   25 πείθεσθαι θέλει Β

---

feast prepared for one'; cp. 1. 211;
active, 1. 162—a poetic word.
18. ὄψεαι .. ὀλίγους τινάς, predicative, 'few will be the survivors thou
shalt see.'
20. ἅμα τε .. καί: a strong parataxis.
μετιέναι πολλὰ τῶν δακρύων,
emittere; cp. γλῶσσαν μετεὶς 6. 29 (elsewhere demittere, dimittere, omittere,
remittere; cp. Schweig. Lex.) 'his tears
were many'—though his words were
few. This lachrymose gentleman is a
faithful copy, or perhaps model, of the
weeping despot at Abydos, 7. 46, but
he combines in his own person the
weeping of Xerxes with the wisdom of
Artabanos ! Thersander's instructions
were not lost on Herodotus ; this
anecdote appears to be the nucleus of
that more elaborate and rhetorical scene.
22. οὐκῶν Μαρδονίῳ τι κτλ. The
astounding naïveté of this remark leads
one to doubt whether Thersander, or
Herodotus, has reported the conversation quite fully. Stein indeed suggests
that the Persian must have known of
the treacherous intrigues against Mardonios headed by Artabazos ; cp. c. 66
infra : but are they proven ?
τοῖσι μετ᾽ ἐκεῖνον ἐν αἴνῃ ἐοῦσι
Η. would include Artabazos imprimis,
to whom it would be useless or dangerous
to say much ! ἐν αἴνῃ εἶναι 8. 112;
Περσέων with τοῖσι.
24. ὅ τι δεῖ γενέσθαι ἐκ τοῦ θεοῦ κτλ.
This Persian not only speaks good Greek
but has drunk deeply—at the wells of
Greek wisdom. In a less pious expression the same fatalism appeals to Amasis
as the moral of the story of Polykrates'

Ring, 3. 43 ; in a still higher region it
rules the gods themselves, as the Pythia
informed Kroisos 1. 91 τὴν πεπρωμένην
μοῖραν ἀδύνατα ἐστὶ ἀποφυγεῖν καὶ θεῷ.
There is no such pessimistic quietism
on the Achaimenid monuments, which
breathe glad confidence in the patronage
and providence of Ahura-mazda (τοῦ
θεοῦ); but it must be admitted that
Mazdeism sought to overcome its inherent dualism by tracing Good and
Evil to a common Antecedent, Space,
Time, Fate, or such-like. Such monism
existed in the fourth century, if not
in the fifth ; though if Darmesteter be
right, no direct trace of such a system is
to be found in the Avesta (cp. Sacred Bks.
of the East, IV. p. lxxxii.). But surely
fatalism as a belief, or sentiment, the
recognition of the unappeasable Power
behind the benignant Person, is not the
special product of any nation, or of any
creed, but allgemein menschlich. It is
less Hebraic than Hellenic, less Persian
than Anglian. Boiotian Hesiod and
Wessex Hardy are as deeply tinged
therewith as Ecclesiastes or Omar Khay-
yam ; and the Greek are here the older
sources. Cp. 5. 4 with my notes ad l.
26. ταῦτα δὲ Περσέων συχνοί κτλ. :
not so much the pious generalization,
which has immediately preceded, as
(a) the approaching destruction of the
army, (b) the uselessness of addressing
Mardonios and those in authority. This
anecdote may perhaps be taken for
evidence that a Persian victory was by
no means regarded in the Persian camp
as a foregone conclusion ; many other
hints point to the same inference : (1)

ἐνδεδεμένοι. ἐχθίστη δὲ ὀδύνη ἐστὶ τῶν ἐν ἀνθρώποισι· αὕτη, πολλὰ φρονέοντα μηδενὸς κρατέειν." ταῦτα μὲν τοῦ Ὀρχομενίου Θερσάνδρου ἤκουον, καὶ τάδε πρὸς τούτοισι, ὡς αὐτὸς αὐτίκα λέγοι ταῦτα πρὸς ἀνθρώπους πρότερον ἢ γενέσθαι ἐν 30 Πλαταιῆσι τὴν μάχην.

Μαρδονίου δὲ ἐν τῇ Βοιωτίῃ στρατοπεδευομένου, οἱ μὲν **17** ἄλλοι παρείχοντο ἅπαντες στρατιὴν καὶ συνεσέβαλον ἐς Ἀθήνας

---

27 ἐστὶ del. Holder : om. P : ἔστιν post ἀνθρώποισιν Β   28 κρατεῖν C, van H. ‖ τοῦ ὀρχομενίου Βz, Holder, van H., Stein³ : ὀρχομενίου 29 Θερσάνδρου secl. van H., Holder   30 ἀνθρώπους : ἄλλους Valckenaer ‖ : ἐν om. R   31 πλαταίῃσι ΑΒ : πλαταιῆσι R   17. 1 στρατευομένου Β : ἐστρατοπεδευμένου malit van H.   2 συνέβαλον C : συνέβαλλον PS : συνεσέβαλλον Pᵐ (συνέβαλον Β ap. Holder) ‖ ἐς Ἀθήνας secl. Krueger, van H.

---

the advice of the Thebans, c. 2 *supra* ; (2) the repeated efforts of Mardonios to win over the Athenians, cp. c. 4 *supra*, 8. 136 ; (3) the probable tampering with the Peloponnesians, cp. cc. 12 f. *supra* ; (4) the evacuation of Attica and the reasons therefor, c. 13 *supra* ; (5) the formation of the fortified camp, c. 15 *supra* ; (6) the other suggestions in this very anecdote ; (7) these indications are reinforced later, cp. c. 42 *infra*.

ἀναγκαίῃ ἐνδεδεμένοι : cp. 1. 11 ἀναγκαίῃ ἐνδέειν of a choice—of evils ! Cp. ὑπ' ἀναγκαίης ἐχόμενοι 7. 233, and c. 15 *supra* ; (κατεζευγμένοι) 8. 22. The compulsion is ideal and in the present case would arise from (a) loyalty, (b) military discipline, (c) the double certitude of disaster in case of στάσις, (d) cowardice, or faintheartedness.

27. ὀδύνη : a poetical word for pain of body as well as of mind, and frequently in the plural. (Found also in Xenoph., Plato.)

τῶν ἐν ἀνθρώποισι : sc. ὀδυνῶν, or, perhaps, more generally, 'in the wide world.'

28. πολλὰ φρονέοντα μηδενὸς κρατέειν, 'to have much wit and little weight'; cp. Sophokles *O. T.* 316 (Teiresia loq.) φεῦ φεῦ φρονεῖν ὡς δεινὸν ἔνθα μὴ τέλη λύει φρονοῦντι. The two passages are hardly independent. Sophokles owes something, perhaps, to Hdt. Cp. Baehr, *Commentatio* § 5 (iv.³ 416 ff.). The poet, however, has a more genial word in store, *Antig.* 1347 πολλῷ τὸ φρονεῖν εὐδαιμονίας πρῶτον ὑπάρχει κτλ., and also a useful *caveat* for any would-be Cassandra, *Aias* 1418 ἢ πολλὰ βροτοῖς ἐστιν

ἰδοῦσιν γνῶναι· πρὶν ἰδεῖν δ' οὐδεὶς μάντις τῶν μελλόντων ὅ τι πράξει.

29. ἤκουον : as above. Orchomenian Thersander used to add that he (had) made no secret of the matter at the time, but mentioned it to several persons (ἀνθρώπους : his wife, perhaps, among others ?) before the fulfilment of the Persian's dismal boding in the battle of Plataia. It is plain that Thersander, and Herodotus, were much concerned to refute criticism of this anecdote as a *vaticinium post eventum*. But were any of these persons ever produced as witnesses ? How much of the anecdote as here related is Thersander's, and how much is due to the art and language of Hdt. ? Or was the Orchomenian one of Hdt.'s mentors ? Cp. l. 6 *supra*.

30. ἐν Πλαταιῆσι : as the battle certainly did not take place in the city of Plataia, which had been destroyed (8. 50), and the site of which was at some distance from the actual battlefield, cc. 52 ff. *infra*, it is clear that ἐν Πλαταιῆσι here = ἐν τῇ Πλαταιΐδι.

17. 1. ἐν τῇ Βοιωτίῃ = ἐν τῇ Θηβαΐδι, but here used probably from the reference to Attica on the one side and to Phokis on the other.

2. καὶ συνεσέβαλον ἐς Ἀθήνας : not content with taking all the 'Persian' forces into Attica (cp. 8. 50) Hdt. here takes about 50,000 Greek soldiers in also. Hdt.'s strategy is like some modern Political Economy ; it assumes the infinite mobility of Labour (and Capital) ! τὴν ταύτῃ εἰκημένων excludes probably those in Peloponnesos, Asia, the islands, etc. The next sentence as

ὅσοι περ ἐμήδιζον Ἑλλήνων τῶν ταύτῃ οἰκημένων, μοῦνοι δὲ
Φωκέες οὐ συνεσέβαλον (ἐμήδιζον γὰρ δὴ σφόδρα καὶ οὗτοι)
5 οὐκ ἐκόντες ἀλλ' ὑπ' ἀναγκαίης, ἡμέρῃσι δὲ οὐ πολλῇσι μετὰ
τὴν ἄπιξιν τὴν ἐς Θήβας ὕστερον ἦλθον αὐτῶν ὁπλῖται
χίλιοι, ἦγε δὲ αὐτοὺς Ἁρμοκύδης ἀνὴρ τῶν ἀστῶν δοκιμώτατος. ἐπεὶ δὲ ἀπίκατο καὶ οὗτοι ἐς Θήβας, πέμψας ὁ
Μαρδόνιος ἱππέας ἐκέλευσε σφέας ἐπ' ἑωυτῶν ἐν τῷ πεδίῳ
10 ἵζεσθαι. ἐπεὶ δὲ ἐποίησαν ταῦτα, αὐτίκα παρῆν ἵππος ἡ
ἄπασα. μετὰ δὲ ταῦτα διεξῆλθε μὲν διὰ τοῦ στρατοπέδου

---

4 συνέβαλον S: συνέβαλλον Marc.: συνεσέβαλλον PR (συνεσέβαλλον
β ap. Holder) ‖ γὰρ σφόδρα βC: γὰρ μεγάλως z: σφόδρα del. Letronne,
Holder: γὰρ ἤδη σφόδρα? Stein[2]   5 οὐ <σφόδρα> ἐκόντες Gomperz,
Holder   6 αὐτέων βz   7 δυνατώτατος αC   8 ἐπείτε? van H.
‖ ἀπίκατο Pz ‖ ἐς τὰς β   9 ἱππέας ὁ Μαρδόνιος ἐκέλευε β, Holder ‖
ἱππέας secl. Kallenberg, Holder ‖ ἀπ' β   10 ἐπεὶ: ὡς β, Holder,
van H. ‖ ἡ ἵππος ἄπασα β, Holder, van H.   11 ταῦτα del. van H.

---

it stands is not clear; σφόδρα makes
the difficulty; it would go better with
the preceding ἐμήδιζον, or out altogether;
Stein makes the sentence: μοῦνοι δὲ
Φωκέες οὐ συνεσέβαλον . . οὐκ ἐκόντες
ἀλλ' ὑπ' ἀναγκαίης, perhaps intending
the last five words to be taken with the
first καὶ συνεσέβαλον ἐς Ἀθήνας—rather
a remote reference. And would it have
been true that the Thebans, for example,
invaded Attica οὐκ ἐκόντες? (Yes,
perhaps, in view of c. 2 supra.)

5. ἡμέρῃσι δὲ οὐ πολλῇσι. Hdt.'s
conventionalized journal of Plataia has
not yet begun; if the arrival of the
Phokians at the Persian camp preceded
the arrival of the Hellenes at Erythrai
(c. 19 infra) the Greeks were rather slow
in crossing Kithairon.

6. τὴν ἄπιξιν τὴν ἐς Θήβας: not the
visit to Thebes for the banquet of
Attaginos, c. 16 supra, but the arrival
of the forces out of Attica at the Laager,
c. 15 supra. The name of the city is
put for the name of the country, as ἐς
Ἀθήνας just above; cp. ἐν Πλαταιῇσι c.
16 supra.

7. χίλιοι: the same number had served
in the army of Leonidas 7. 203, 212,
217 f., and no doubt very much the
same men. The anecdote here has the
'tendency,' the intention, to whitewash
the Phokian Chiliad, whose reputation
had been somewhat blasted by the
Spartan (Peloponnesian) story of Thermopylai.

Ἁρμοκύδης: the name appears to
be unique; no patronymic is given;

the leader's name at Thermopylai is
suppressed.

It is not easy to establish much
difference between δοκιμώτατος (δέχομαι)
and λόγιμος ἐς τὰ πρῶτα or λογιμώτατος
(c. 16), but perhaps δόκιμος is less
obviously relative also to posterity.

8. ἀπίκατο . . ἐς Θήβας, pl.p., 'were
come' = ἦσαν ἀπιγμένοι. ἐς Θ. = ἐς τὴν
Θηβαΐδα: cp. above.

9. ἐπ' ἑωυτῶν ἐν τῷ πεδίῳ ἵζεσθαι:
the active ἵζειν is used of the act of
sitting, literally understood, 5. 25, 6.
57—so is the middle, 5. 18—which is,
however, constantly used of this military
operation, 8. 71, c. 2 supra, c. 26 infra,
etc.

ἐπ' ἑωυτῶν, 'by themselves,' separately; cp. c. 38 supra. This use of
ἐπί is primarily locative, as ἐπὶ τῆς
γωνίης, 1. 51, 'in the corner'; cp. 8.
32 ἡ κορυφὴ κατὰ Νέωνα πόλιν ἐπ' ἑωυτῆς
—differing from the temporal force in
ἐπ' ἐμεῦ, ἐπὶ Ξανθίππου, etc.; 'on the
plain' need not be taken to imply that
any part of the forces, or the camp, was
on the mountain, it merely prepares
the way for the ensuing cavalry development.

10. αὐτίκα παρῆν ἵππος ἡ ἄπασα:
the exact number of chiliads, or myriads,
would here be acceptable; but the phrase
will in any case be an over-statement—
unless, indeed, there were far fewer of
the cavalry than Hdt. seems throughout
to assume.

11. διεξῆλθε μὲν . . φήμη: there
seems to be nothing supernormal in this

τοῦ Ἑλληνικοῦ τοῦ μετὰ Μήδων ἐόντος φήμη ὡς κατακοντιεῖ
σφέας, διεξῆλθε δὲ δι' αὐτῶν Φωκέων τὠυτὸ τοῦτο. ἔνθα δή
σφι ὁ στρατηγὸς Ἁρμοκύδης παραίνεε λέγων τοιάδε. "ὦ
Φωκέες, πρόδηλα γὰρ ὅτι ἡμέας οὗτοι οἱ ἄνθρωποι μέλλουσι 15
προόπτῳ θανάτῳ δώσειν, διαβεβλημένους ὑπὸ Θεσσαλῶν, ὡς
ἐγὼ εἰκάζω· νῦν ἄνδρα πάντα τινὰ ὑμέων χρεόν ἐστι γενέσθαι
ἀγαθόν· κρέσσον γὰρ ποιεῦντάς τι καὶ ἀμυνομένους τελευτῆσαι
τὸν αἰῶνα ἤ περ παρέχοντας διαφθαρῆναι αἰσχίστῳ μόρῳ.
ἀλλὰ μαθέτω τις αὐτῶν ὅτι ἐόντες βάρβαροι ἐπ' Ἕλλησι 20
ἀνδράσι φόνον ἔρραψαν." ὃ μὲν ταῦτα παραίνεε· οἱ δὲ 18
ἱππέες ἐπεί σφεας ἐκυκλώσαντο, ἐπήλαυνον ὡς ἀπολέοντες,
καὶ δὴ διετείνοντο τὰ βέλεα ὡς ἀπήσοντες, καί κού τις καὶ

---

12 Μήδον S   13 σφεας ABz: σφέας || αὐτέων z || Φωκέων om. S
|| ταυτὸ τοῦτο C || δέ S   14 Ἁρμοκύδης del. van H. || τάδε B   16
προδώσειν Suidas s.v. προόπτος   17 νῦν ὦν B, Holder || ἄνδρα πάντα
τινά a: πάντά τινα ἄνδρα B, (Holder): ἄνδρα τινὰ πάντα CPz: ἄνδρα post
ἐστι transpos. Cobet, van H. || χρέων CPz, van H. || γίνεσθαι B   20
αὐτέων z   18. 1 μὲν <ὦν> H. Stephanus, van H.   2 ἐπείτε
Holder, van H.: ἐπεί τέ B || ἀπολεύντες B   3 δὴ: δὴ καὶ B: om. C ||
ἀφήσοντες aC

φήμη (cp. c. 100 infra), even when it,
or one to exactly the same effect, passes
right through the Phokians themselves.

στρατοπέδου here apparently =
στρατοῦ or στρατιῆς. Cp. c. 51 infra etc.

12. μετὰ Μήδων. This story (τὰ περὶ
Φωκέων), which is in the nature of a
Rettung, will hardly have come from a
Peloponnesian or from a 'medized'
source. It might be of Phokian or of
Attic origin. Hdt., who distinguishes
Medes and Persians from the first, will
probably have taken over the phraseology
of his source.

κατακοντιεῖ (κατακοντίζειν): sc. ἡ
ἵππος. The weapon is noticeable, and
implies close proximity.

13. τὠυτὸ τοῦτο: sc. ὡς κ. σφεας.
Baehr cps. Thuc. 8. 108. 4 for the story
of the fate of the Delian exiles in Atra-
myttion, who were treacherously surrounded and shot down at their morning
meal by Arsakes the Persian, Sept. 411
B.C. (So too Stein.)

15. πρόδηλα: this pl. is a favourite
construction with Hdt.; cp. 1. 91
ἀδύνατα, 8. 35 δῆλα, 3. 109 βιώσιμα,
etc. Kuehner, Ausf. Gramm. § 366, explains it as derived from the use of the
abstract pl. demonstrative ταῦτα, τάδε
etc. to denote one idea, or thing.

ἄνθρωποι, of course contemptuous

(cp. 7. 210) and making ἄνδρα just below
more significant.

16. διαβεβλημένους ὑπὸ Θεσσαλῶν:
cp. 8. 27–31, for the Thessalo-Phokian
feud.

17. πάντα τινά with the second
person, Kuehner op. c. § 371. 4 γ. The
subject is indefinite, yet conceived as
present, and capable of being addressed
directly.

18. κρέσσον γάρ κτλ. It is a pity
these worthy sentiments had not inspired
the Phokians on the mount above Thermopylai; cp. 7. 218. But that was
another (a Peloponnesian) story!

19. τὸν αἰῶνα, 'life'; cp. 7. 46.

παρέχοντας, 'without opposition,'
like our 'yield.' There is perhaps an
ellipse (ἑαυτούς); cp. L. & S. sub v. II.
2 and passages there quoted, which
show (as Stein observes) that the word
is used of submitting to medical examina-
tion, surgical operations, etc. (Xenophon,
Plato).

20. ἐπ' Ἕλλησι ἀνδράσι: Ἕλλην adj.
(φόνον) ῥάπτειν is poetic; not as in 6. 1.
Cp. Od. 16. 379 φόνον αἰπὺν ἐράπτομεν.
But the metaphor here is rather pointless, unless it were referred to the διαβολή
of the Thessalians, whom the Phokian
could not mean to describe as βάρβαροι.

18. 3. καὶ δὴ διετείνοντο τὰ βέλεα ὡς

ἀπῆκε. καὶ οἱ ἀντίοι ἔστασαν πάντῃ συστρέψαντες ἑωυτοὺς
5 καὶ πυκνώσαντες ὡς μάλιστα. ἐνθαῦτα οἱ ἱππόται ὑπέ-
στρεφον καὶ ἀπήλαυνον ὀπίσω. οὐκ ἔχω δ' ἀτρεκέως εἰπεῖν
οὔτε εἰ ἦλθον μὲν ἀπολέοντες τοὺς Φωκέας δεηθέντων Θεσσαλῶν,
ἐπεὶ δὲ ὥρων πρὸς ἀλέξησιν τραπομένους, δείσαντες μὴ καὶ
σφίσι γένηται τρώματα, οὕτω δὴ ἀπήλαυνον ὀπίσω· ὡς γάρ
10 σφι ἐνετείλατο Μαρδόνιος· οὔτ' εἰ αὐτῶν πειρηθῆναι ἠθέλησε
εἴ τι ἀλκῆς μετέχουσι. ὡς δὲ ὀπίσω ἀπήλασαν οἱ ἱππόται,
πέμψας Μαρδόνιος κήρυκα ἔλεγε τάδε. "θαρσέετε ὦ Φωκέες·
ἄνδρες γὰρ ἐφάνητε ἐόντες ἀγαθοί, οὐκ ὡς ἐγὼ ἐπυνθανόμην.
καὶ νῦν προθύμως φέρετε τὸν πόλεμον τοῦτον· εὐεργεσίῃσι
15 γὰρ οὐ νικήσετε οὔτ' ὦν ἐμὲ οὔτε βασιλέα." τὰ περὶ Φωκέων
μὲν ἐς τοσοῦτο ἐγένετο.

19   Λακεδαιμόνιοι δὲ ὡς ἐς τὸν Ἰσθμὸν ἦλθον, ἐν τούτῳ

---

4 ἀφῆκε aC : ἀπήκετο z ‖ καὶ οἱ Az : καὶ οἱ BCP(SV) : καὶ R ‖
ἔστασαν Pz, van H., Stein³ : ἔστασαν C, Marc. : ἔστησαν ‖ πάντες S ‖
στρέψαντες aC   5 κυκλώσαντες B   6 δὲ B ‖ εἶται z, van H.
7 εἰ om. CR   8 ἑώρων aC   9 τρῶμα Naber ‖ ὡς ABC : ὃς R
10 οὔτε B ‖ αὐτέων z   11 ἔχουσι duo Paris. prob. Valckenaer   15
οὔτε ἐμὲ οὔτε βασιλῆα z   16 τοσοῦτον Bz

ἀπ.: καὶ ἤδη δ. τὰ τόξα ὡς ἀπήσοντες τὰ
βέλεα would be more correct.
4. πάντῃ συστρέψαντες ἑωυτούς: cp.
Livy 8. 11. 5 cum se in unum conglo-
bassent (Valckenaer). But the tactical
manœuvre here described is really at
closer quarters; just as 1. 101 Δηιόκης
τὸ Μηδικὸν ἔθνος συνέστρεψε is on a larger
scale. Cp. συστροφή 7. 9, συστραφέντες
6. 6. ὑποστρέφειν just below gives a
different result; cp. ὑποστροφή c. 22
infra.
6. οὐκ ἔχω δ' ἀτρεκέως εἰπεῖν. Hdt.
thinks that if the intention really was
to destroy the Phokians, it must have
been dictated by the Thessalians; and
this view is evidently a datum of his
source or authority; but he himself
suggests another alternative, viz. that
Mardonios merely meant to put their
mettle to the proof (ἀλκή, cp. cc. 70, 102
infra). A third alternative he does
not face, viz. that the whole story was
an exaggeration, or even based upon a
misunderstanding, of what was intended
for a complimentary reception !
7. οὔτε is, of course, the idiomatic
doubling of the negative, after οὐκ ἔχω.
εἰ ἦλθον . . εἰ ἠθέλησε . . : the two
alternatives put as strict co-ordinates.
8. πρὸς ἀλέξησιν τραπομένους: cp.

πρὸς ἀλκὴν τραπέσθαι c. 102 infra and
Hesych. sub v. ἀλκή· δύναμις ἰσχὺς ἡ
ἀλέξησις ἡ μάχη. The word is an ἅπαξ
λ. in Hdt., and Schweighaeuser overlooked this passage in his Lexicon.
9. ὥς = οὕτω, as often with δὲ καὶ but
only here with γάρ (Krueger).
13. ἐπυνθανόμην: of course from the
Thessalians.
14. π. φέρετε: cp. c. 40 infra: like
the Thebans.
15. ὦν emphasizes his own case.
16. ἐς τοσοῦτο ἐγ., 'went no further.'
19. 1. Λακεδαιμόνιοι δέ: if τὰ περὶ
Φωκέων, cc. 17, 18, should be judged an
addition, second hand (cp. Introduction,
§ 9), these words would correspond with
ταῦτα μὲν Ὀρχομενίου κτλ. at the end of
c. 16. The exact point of time at
which 'the Lakedaimonians' reached the
Isthmos has not been previously indicated. The 5000 'Spartiates' have
started in c. 10, followed by 5000
Perioikoi in c. 11; these forces are under
way in c. 12; but the Spartiatai have
not reached the Isthmos in c. 13 when
Mardonios decided and began to evacuate
Attica (πρὶν ἢ τοὺς μετὰ Παυσανίεω ἐς
τὸν Ἰσθμὸν ἐσβαλεῖν). The arrival of
1000 'Lakedaimonians,' apparently an
advanced guard, at Megara is recorded

ἐστρατοπεδεύοντο. πυνθανόμενοι δὲ ταῦτα οἱ λοιποὶ Πελοποννήσιοι τοῖσι τὰ ἀμείνω ἑάνδανε, οἳ δὲ καὶ ὁρῶντες ἐξιόντας
Σπαρτιήτας, οὐκ ἐδικαίευν λείπεσθαι τῆς ἐξόδου [Λακεδαιμονίων].
ἐκ δὴ ὦν τοῦ Ἰσθμοῦ καλλιερησάντων [τῶν ἱρῶν] ἐπορεύοντο 5
πάντες καὶ ἀπικνέονται ἐς Ἐλευσῖνα· ποιήσαντες δὲ καὶ
ἐνθαῦτα ἱρά, ὥς σφι ἐκαλλιέρεε, τὸ πρόσω ἐπορεύοντο,

---

19. 2 λοιποὶ om. S 3 ὀρέοντες CPz, Stein[1], van H. 4
ἐδικαίουν van H. ‖ nomen secl. Stein 5 τῶν ἱρῶν secl. Krueger, Stein[2],
Holder, van H. 7 ἐκαλλιέρεε, τὸ Suevern : ἐκαλλιρέετο, R :
ἐκαλλιερέετο ‖ ἐπορεύετο R

---

in c. 14, and Mardonios is apparently
still in Attica; in c. 15 intelligence
reaches Mardonios that ἀλέες εἴησαν οἱ
Ελληνες ἐν τῷ Ἰσθμῷ. Only then does
he finally clear out of Attica. οἱ Ελληνες
there covers more than Λακεδαιμόνιοι here
(esp. ἀλέες), and anticipates the junction
of οἱ λοιποὶ Πελοποννήσιοι τοῖσι τὰ ἀμείνω
ἑάνδανε with the Lakedaimonians, which
is recorded here immediately below.
The position of the πρόδρομος στρατιή,
Λακεδαιμονίων χίλιοι (c. 14) at Megara is
a little obscure; but there is a moment
apparently before Mardonios has evacuated Attica when 1000 Lakedaimonians
are in Megara, and some 9000–10,000
at the Isthmos, or on the way thither,
to say nothing of the Helots. At the
Isthmos they are joined by the rest of
the confederate forces from Peloponnese,
but only after Mardonios has heard of
this mobilization and concentration does
he evacuate Attica; and only after he
has evacuated Attica do the confederate
forces advance to Eleusis. It is just
conceivable that the arrival of the πρόδρομος στρατιή in Megara is not quite
correctly chronologized in c. 14, and that
it was not separated by so large an
interval as is there implied from the
advance of the confederate forces from
the Isthmos to Eleusis. Probably the
last of the Persian cavalry had ridden
down the northern slopes of Kithairon,
and the construction of the camp on the
Asopos was reported at Eleusis, before
the sacrifices proved favourable to an
advance into Boiotia.
3. τοῖσι τὰ ἀμείνω ἑάνδανε, 'which
were (being) pleased with the better'—
part, or policy? Is it the same as οἱ
τὰ ἀμείνω φρονέοντες (cp. 7. 145)? Cp.
8. 29. The ones unrepresented were
Argives, and some of the Achaian and
Arkadian towns; with the exception of

the Lepreatai all the states enumerated
below, c. 28, had sent men to Thermopylai and Salamis (7. 202, 8. 1, 43).
οἱ δὲ καὶ ὁρῶντες ἐξ. Σπ. seems
to be a qualification of the immediately
preceding, 'but only when they saw'
—or even perhaps but 'some of them
only when they saw . .' Others may
have been at the Isthmos before, or all
along. The 'seeing' is not perhaps to
be taken quite literally; cp. c. 16 supra.
4. ἐδικαίευν: cp. 8. 126.
λείπεσθαι, to miss, remain behind;
cp. 7. 168, 8. 44, 113.
5. καλλιερησάντων: for the constr.
cp. 7. 134. In the previous year the
sacrifices had proved unfavourable, cp. c.
10 supra, and the Peloponnesians had
not advanced beyond their wall. Even
now, they are only favourable when
Mardonios is already out of reach, or
clearly not remaining in Attica; or at
least not in occupation of the Thriasian
plain.
7. ὥς σφι ἐκαλλιέρεε: why was there
a fresh sacrifice? There was a fresh
frontier to be crossed. Even if the
sacrifice at the Isthmos might have
carried the Peloponnesians to Erythrai
(no express sacrifice is recorded in the
Megarid, but there may have been one)
there were the Athenians to be considered.
Had Mardonios remained about Athens
there could have been no fresh διαβατήρια,
but no doubt there would have been
daily θυσίαι ἐπὶ τῷ Πέρσῃ until the
opportune moment arrived for forward
action; cp. cc. 33, 36, 61 f. infra.
Is it at all likely that the Peloponnesians expected to find the Persians
on the Thriasian plain (as Stein suggests)?
The Athenians in Salamis, to say nothing
of their own πρόδρομοι and ἡμεροσκόποι,
will have kept them better informed
than that. It appears, on the contrary,

Ἀθηναῖοι δὲ ἅμα αὐτοῖσι, διαβάντες μὲν ἐκ Σαλαμῖνος,
συμμιγέντες δὲ ἐν Ἐλευσῖνι. ὡς δὲ ἄρα ἀπίκοντο τῆς
10 Βοιωτίης ἐς Ἐρυθράς, ἔμαθόν τε δὴ τοὺς βαρβάρους ἐπὶ τῷ
Ἀσωπῷ στρατοπεδευομένους, φρασθέντες δὲ τοῦτο ἀντετάσ-

---

11 ἐστρατοπεδευμένους expectaret van H. ‖ δὲ: τε Schaefer, van H.

---

obvious that the sacrifices became favourable to an advance only when the road
was known to be clear.

9. ὡς δὲ ἄρα ἀπίκοντο τῆς Βοιωτίης
ἐς Ἐρυθράς: there was something a
little surprising in this movement, which
certainly marks a new departure in the
action (ἄρα); nothing like it has been
attempted on land since the fiasco at
Thermopylai; and the Persians might
have been holding the pass. No doubt
the junction with the Athenians is the
decisive factor, and the Athenians are the
driving force, in the advance into Boiotia.
The advance to Eleusis was not definitely
what the move into Boiotia is, a resumption of the offensive: perhaps at the
same time the fleet leaves Salamis for
Aigina, or Aigina for Delos, not to say
Delos for Ionia.

Erythrai has been given, c. 15 supra,
as the terminus a quo for the construction or measurement of the Persian
στρατόπεδον. If the Persians were really
at Erythrai, the Greeks could not have
arrived there without first clearing the
Persians out: that would have entailed
a fight. Stein says there must here be
a gap in Hdt.'s narrative. The Hellenes
must have forced the pass of Eleutherai,
and driven the enemy eastward on to
the fortified camp at Skolos, and north,
into the plain. But is that convincing?
The forcing of the pass of Eleutherai-
Erythrai, i.e. Dryoskephalai, would
have been a colossal affair; imagine its
having made not the faintest impression
upon the traditions of the Persian war!
The holding of the pass would not have
been good strategy on Mardonios' part,
nor in accord with his general plan, as
given in c. 13 supra. Moreover, as
above shown, the fortified camp was not
at Skolos, and had it been so, the sight
presented to the Greeks, when they
took up their quarters at Erythrai, would
not have been that described in this
chapter. Finally, Erythrai was not included in the Persian lines, cp. notes to
c. 15 above.

The position of Erythrai has been
determined by G. B. Grundy against
Leake, cp. The Great Persian War
(1901) pp. 458 ff. It is on the higher
ground, above Kriekouki, in the gorge
through which issued the direct road
from Eleutherai to Thebes: ἐπὶ τῆς
ὑπωρέης τοῦ Κιθαιρῶνος. The exact site
of the town matters little, as the name
is here doubtless used for the χώρα, cp.
c. 17 supra.

10. ἔμαθόν.. τοὺς β. ἐπὶ τῷ Ἀσωπῷ
στ.: the whole army would, on arriving
at Erythrai, and taking up its position
in the Erythraïs, see the Persian encampment below; but of course the
generals at least knew what to expect
before they sighted it. The building
of a huge fortified camp, and the settlement of the Persian lines in front of the
Erythraian, Hysian, and (in part) Plataian
ὑπωρέη, were doubtless reported at Eleusis
before the Greek army advanced up the
pass. ἐπὶ τῷ Ἀσωπῷ would be an appropriate expression whether the camp
was all in front of the river, or all
behind the river, or partly on one side
and partly on the other. The third
alternative is to be preferred, but not to
the extent of putting the τεῖχος far
away to the east, on the S. side of the
river, at Skolos. The object of Mardonios
was to bring the Greeks down on to the
lower ground, and even to draw them
across the river; but in the first instance
at least he would probably retain at
least the tête du pont on the Erythraian
side of the bridge.

Stein's text gives an anakoluthon
ἔμαθόν τε δὴ.. φρασθέντες δέ κτλ.
which he defends as an Herodoteanism,
referring to 1. 108 οὔτε.. παρεῖδες..
φυλασσόμεθα δέ (instead of τε). 153 ἐπ'
οὗτε ἐπεῖχέ τε στρατηλατέειν αὐτός, ἐπὶ
δὲ Ἴωνας ἄλλον πέμπειν στρατηγόν. 2.
126 τὴν δὲ τά τε.. πρήσσεσθαι ἰδίη δὲ
κτλ. 3. 38 πολλοῖσί τε.. ἐν δὲ δὴ καὶ
τῷδε. 4. 76 μήτε τεων ἄλλων Ἑλληνικοῖσι
δὲ καὶ ἥκιστα. 8. 142 οὔτε γε ἀλλοῖσι
.. ὑμῖν δὲ δὴ καὶ διὰ πάντων ἥκιστα.

σοντο ἐπὶ τῆς ὑπωρέης τοῦ Κιθαιρῶνος. Μαρδόνιος δέ, ὡς οὐ **20**
κατέβαινον οἱ ῞Ελληνες ἐς τὸ πεδίον, πέμπει ἐς αὐτοὺς πᾶσαν
τὴν ἵππον, τῆς ἱππάρχεε Μασίστιος εὐδοκιμέων παρὰ Πέρσῃσι,

12 ὑπωρείης codd. z　　　20. 2 ἐπ᾽ αὐτοὺς Marc. z　　　3 ἱππάρχε R

12. **Κιθαιρῶνος**: the mighty mountain
chain which divides Attica from Boiotia,
Parnes being but an eastward extension,
while a southern ridge (῞Ονεια), terminating in the Κέρατα, divided Attica from
Megaris ; cp. 7. 141 *supra* and Strabo 380
(the view from the Akrokorinthos), 393
(the ῞Ονεια), 405 (the western eud, above
the Krisaian gulf, and the continuity of
Kithairon, the Megaric and the Attic
mountains), 408-9 (the relation of
Kithairon to the Asopos and the
Parasopia), 411 (Plataia). But after all
the identity of Kithairon is sufficiently
attested by this very Book.

Hdt. takes the Greek forces over
Kithairon in this chapter rather easily.
No doubt the main body will have
marched by the Eleutherai road ; but
some may have found their way over by
the pass from Megara, cp. c. 13 *supra*, or
even by the Aigosthena route ; cp. *ibid.*
The Hellenes are now in ʻthe first position,ʼ or busily engaged in getting into
it (ἀντετάσσοντο ἐπὶ τῆς ὑπωρέης τοῦ
Κιθαιρῶνος) ; but in what order they
deploy thereinto, by what manœuvres
the various contingents take up their
stations, what their line of battle, or of
encampment, opposite the Persian, Hdt.
does not describe, or indicate ; but
presently the Megarians are exposed to
the brunt of the cavalry attack : they
were therefore perhaps athwart the
main road. In the absence of further
positive indications we must either (i.)
carry back the line of battle, described
below for ʻthe second position,ʼ and
make it hold good for the first also ; or
else (ii.) post the Megarians simply at
the head of the marching column, with
the Athenians immediately behind them,
so naturally coming to their support,
while the Peloponnesians bring up the
rear of the *agmen*. Cp. Appendix VIII.
§ 7.

20. 1. **ὡς οὐ κατέβαινον οἱ ῞Ελ. ἐς τὸ
πεδίον.** Mardonios wished to induce
the Greeks to come down from the
higher ground about or above Erythrai,
and Hysiai, on to the lower ground
nearer the Asopos. Later on they did
so, with disastrous results to themselves
in the first instance.

2. **πᾶσαν τὴν ἵππον τῆς ἱππάρχεε
Μ.**, ʻall the cavalry commanded by
Masistiosʼ is not of necessity all the
cavalry in Laager, nor necessarily
identical with ἵππος ἡ ἅπασα of c. 17
supra. But it is arguable that Masistios
was in fact supreme Hipparch in the
corps d'armée of Mardonios, and commanded a myriad of mounted men. In
the army of Xerxes there had been three
ʻhipparchsʼ (one for each *corps d'armée*?
cp. 7. 88), of whom Masistios was
certainly not one. Had the cavalry
now on service in Greece under Mardonios been cut down to one-third, and
a new hipparch appointed ? Or is he
one hipparch of two, or three, in the
whole forces of Mardonios ? Cp. c. 69
infra.

3. **Μασίστιος . . τὸν ῞Ελληνες
Μακίστιον καλέουσι.** What Hellenes
are these ? Stein answers, Greek authors,
writers ; cp. 1. 7, 216, 2. 16. The
sentence, unless athetized as a gloss, is
good evidence that Hdt. had some
written authorities before him for the
history he is writing. But these authors
are hardly poets, Simonides, (still less)
Choirilos, as Stein suggests, but probably prose writers, such as Dionysios
of Miletos, and possibly others ; cp.
Introduction, § 10.

A Μασίστιος ὁ Σιρομίτρεω appears 7.
79 as ἄρχων of the ᾽Αλαρόδιοι and
Σάσπειρες. He may be the same man
on promotion ; but Hdt. is evidently
unconscious of any such identity. This
was a clear case for a patronymic, but
none is forthcoming. Why did Greek
authors call him Makistios if his name
was Masistios ? Was it to distinguish
him from the son of Siromitres ? Or
was it to guard against that very confusion of Μασίστιος with Μασίστης, the
full brother of Xerxes and one of the
six chief Strategoi, 7. 82 (cp. c. 107 *infra*),
into which Tzetzes actually fell ; cp.
Wesseling *ad l.* Or were the Greek
authors perhaps right ? Oddly enough
Μακίστιος was an Eleian ἐθνικόν (cp.
Μάκιστον 4. 148), and this Masistios was
μάκιστος (as they might say in Elis, and
elsewhere, for μήκιστος) ; his corpse even
ἦν θέης ἄξιος μεγάθεος εἵνεκα c. 25 *infra*.

τὸν "Ελληνες Μακίστιον καλέουσι, ἵππον ἔχων Νησαῖον
5 χρυσοχάλινον καὶ ἄλλως κεκοσμημένον καλῶς. ἐνθαῦτα ὡς
προσήλασαν οἱ ἱππόται πρὸς τοὺς "Ελληνας, προσέβαλλον
κατὰ τέλεα, προσβάλλοντες δὲ κακὰ μεγάλα ἐργάζοντο καὶ
21 γυναῖκας σφέας ἀπεκάλεον. κατὰ συντυχίην δὲ Μεγαρέες

---

4 Μακίστιον z ‖ νισαῖον Marc.　　　　5 καὶ cum τε supersc. P : τε καὶ βz,
Holder, van H.　　6 τοὺς om. C ‖ προσέβαλον βP　　　7 προσβάλλοντες V : προσβαλόντες

---

4. ἵππον ἔχων Νησαῖον: riding—
having under him—a Nesaian horse;
cp. 7. 40.

5. ἄλλως, even apart from the gold
bridle; in fact, 'in all respects.'

6. προσήλασαν . . προσέβαλλον:
two distinct manœuvres are indicated.
The whole cavalry under Masistios—
perhaps a myriad, nominal—advanced
together, and then (having halted)
delivered a succession of charges κατὰ
τέλεα, squadron by squadron, perhaps
chiliads, nominal; cp. c. 22 infra.
These attacks inflicted considerable
damage upon the Greek ranks. An
ἱππομαχία is quite en règle as a
preliminary to hoplite or infantry engagements; cp. c. 49 infra, and 1. 80
(Sardes 547 B.C.), 5. 63 (Phaleron 512 B.C.),
Xenoph. Hell. 3. 4. 22 ff. (Paktolos
395 B.C.), 6. 4. 10 ff. (Leuktra 371 B.C.),
Arrian, Anab. 1. 14. 5 ff. (Granikos,
334 B.C.), etc. But at Plataia in 479 B.C.
the Greeks had no cavalry, and therefore
the fighting was not a true ἱππομαχία.

8. γυναῖκας σφέας ἀπεκάλεον: they
added insult to injury by calling them
'women,' cowards! (for not coming down
into the plain); this was the poisoned
arrow in a Persian's quiver! cp. c. 107
infra. Had these riders learnt to speak
Greek? or just picked up the word
wanted? Or did they speak their own
language? ἀποκαλέειν 3. 53, 'to recall';
here 'to reproach'; cp. Plato Gorg.
512 C, Aristot. Eth. N. 9. 8. 1=1168 b
30, but without dyslogism; ib. 2. 9. 7=
1109 b 18.

21. 1. κατὰ συντυχίην δὲ Μεγαρέες.
Hdt. apparently treats the Megarians
as occupying a post in line with the
rest of the forces, which by this time,
according to him, are perhaps drawn up,
or drawing up, along the ὑπωρέη of
Kithairon; but he is not explicit upon
the point, and gives no account of
the respective positions of the various

contingents. ἀντετάσσοντο above may
well be an imperfect of the veriest type
('were falling into line,' or 'were taking
up positions'). Hdt. first describes the
line formation of the Greeks for the
second position below, when there is
even a dispute over a question of precedence, which must have been settled
for the first position, if in the first
position the Greeks were in line formation. I therefore suggest that in this
first position the Greeks were still in
column, emerging down the pass, headed
by the Megarians (and Athenians?),
who were to hold Erythrai and the roadway, which it commanded, while the
remainder of the forces deployed from
behind them only or mainly to the left,
so as to take up positions ἐπὶ τῆς ὑπωρέης τοῦ Κιθαιρῶνος, the Spartans to the
right (but cp. l. 12 infra), the Athenians
to the left, towards Hysiai and Plataia.
This development may or may not have
been finally accomplished; meanwhile
Mardonios attacks the head of the
column as it emerges from the pass.
(Perhaps, if the Athenians headed the
column, they had already deployed on
to the ground to the left.) He seems
to have struck a little too soon, though
not, perhaps, until convinced that the
Greeks were not coming down into the
plain. How it happened that 'the
Megarians,' 3000 strong, were at the
head of the column, if that was their
position, who can say? Possibly the
Lakedaimonian χίλιοι (c. 14 supra) were
still with them, though the strongly
'atticizing' tradition forgets them; they
may have headed the column from
Megara to Eleusis, and so onwards; or
they may even have come across Kithairon
by the direct route from Megara, and so
arrived at the head of the forces, while
the Athenians may have led the column
from Eleusis by Eleutherai. Of course
there was no accident in the matter;
all had been arranged.

ἔτυχον ταχθέντες τῇ τε ἐπιμαχώτατον ἦν τοῦ χωρίου παντός,
καὶ πρόσοδος μάλιστα ταύτῃ ἐγίνετο τῇ ἵππῳ. προσβαλλούσης ὦν τῆς ἵππου οἱ Μεγαρέες πιεζόμενοι ἔπεμπον ἐπὶ
τοὺς στρατηγοὺς τῶν Ἑλλήνων κήρυκα, ἀπικόμενος δὲ ὁ 5
κῆρυξ πρὸς αὐτοὺς ἔλεγε τάδε. "Μεγαρέες λέγουσι· ἡμεῖς,
ἄνδρες σύμμαχοι, οὐ δυνατοί εἰμεν τὴν Περσέων ἵππον
δέκεσθαι μοῦνοι, ἔχοντες στάσιν ταύτην ἐς τὴν ἔστημεν ἀρχήν·
ἀλλὰ καὶ ἐς τόδε λιπαρίῃ τε καὶ ἀρετῇ ἀντέχομεν καί περ
πιεζόμενοι. νῦν τε εἰ μή τινας ἄλλους πέμψετε διαδόχους 10
τῆς τάξιος, ἴστε ἡμέας ἐκλείψοντας τὴν τάξιν." ὃ μὲν δή
σφι ταῦτα ἀπήγγελλε, Παυσανίης δὲ ἀπεπειρᾶτο τῶν Ἑλλήνων

---

21. 2 τῇ τε Bekker : ἦ τε B : ἦι τὸ aCPz   3 καὶ ἡ B ǁ προσβαλλούσης a : προσβαλούσης   6 τάδε. <ὧδε> Μεγαρέες Schenkl,
Holder : ἔλεγε· Τάδε vel ἔλεγε τάδε. Τάδε? van H.   8 στάσιν : aut
τάξιν scribend. aut ἐς versu sq. delend. censet van H. ǁ ἐς τὴν : ἐπ' ἦν B
9 ἀντέσχομεν Naber   10 πιεζεύμενοι B ǁ διαδόχους πέμψητε B   11
τῆς τάξιος del. van H.   12 ἀπήγγειλε Cz : ἀπήγγελε V, Marc.

---

2. τῇ τε ἐπιμαχότατον . . τῇ ἵππῳ.
This description would apply to the
roadway running up the pass ; of course,
even so, the position, τὸ χωρίον, was
not as much exposed as 'the second
position,' c. 25 infra, and the cavalry
could not attack en masse, but only on
a narrow front, κατὰ τέλεα : ἐπίμαχος,
cp. 1. 84, 6. 133 (in both places of
fortifications, liable to assault) ; πρόσοδος, as in 7. 212, 223.

5. τοὺς στρατηγοὺς τῶν Ἑλλήνων.
Where were they? and were they all
together in one place? Are only Pausanias and Euryanax (c. 10 supra)
covered by the term? Below, as the
result of the message, Pausanias appears
in sole authority. The message seems
to imply a standpoint for the Strategoi,
or Strategos, at some distance, and
hardly in sight of the situation, which
could hardly have been the case if the
Greek lines had been already deployed
ἐπὶ τῆς ὑπωρέης. The Megarian message
was carried back up the pass ; they call
for support and relief. μοῦνοι denies the
presence of any other contingent (so the
Athenians ignored the presence of the
Plataians at Marathon c. 27 infra).
ἔχοντες στάσιν . . ἀρχήν suggests an
advanced post, or post some time in
occupation. στάσις, 'station'; cp. c. 26
infra. ἀρχήν, adv., 'to begin with,'
'in the first instance'; cp. 7. 220, 8. 128.

9. λιπαρίῃ τε καὶ ἀρετῇ : cp. c. 70
infra, a sort of hendiadys ; for the
verb λιπαρέειν, perseverare, cp. cc. 45,
111 infra, 8. 144 supra.
ἀντέχειν, resistere, abs., 8. 68.

10. διαδόχους τῆς τάξιος, 'to take our
post,' to succeed us in our position.
ἐκλείπειν τ. τ., cp. 8. 24. In actual
battle λιποταξία (-ιον) was a capital crime ;
and mere failure to serve, λιποστρατία
(-ιον), might have serious consequences
(cp. 5. 27, Thuc. 1. 99. 1, 6. 76. 3).

12. Παυσανίης δὲ ἀπεπειρᾶτο. This
ἀπόπειρα (cp. 8. 9) τῶν Ἑλλήνων, in
which they all prove wanting but the
Athenians, is a transparent Atticism.
The first brush with the Barbarians is
presented as a forlorn hope, calling
for valiant volunteers ; Thermopylai is
forgotten, or only remembered to be
eclipsed ; instead of sending forward
some of his own men, out of his 10,000
hoplites and 40,000 light-armed, Pausanias asks for volunteers ; and Athenians,
a bare 300, step lightly forward into the
breach : it is enough!—300 Athenians
save the situation at Erythrai ; 300
Spartans at Thermopylai could only
die! Probably the Athenians were next
to the Megarians, whether in the column
or in the line, and were ordered forwards
as a matter of course, especially as they
had a corps of archers. The Megarians

εἴ τινες ἐθέλοιεν ἄλλοι ἐθελονταὶ ἰέναι τε ἐς τὸν χῶρον
τοῦτον καὶ τάσσεσθαι διάδοχοι Μεγαρεῦσι. οὐ βουλομένων
15 δὲ τῶν ἄλλων Ἀθηναῖοι ὑπεδέξαντο καὶ Ἀθηναίων οἱ
τριηκόσιοι λογάδες, τῶν ἐλοχήγεε Ὀλυμπιόδωρος ὁ Λάμπωνος.
22 οὗτοι ἦσαν οἵ τε ὑποδεξάμενοι καὶ οἱ πρὸ τῶν ἄλλων τῶν
παρεόντων Ἑλλήνων ἐς Ἐρυθρὰς ταχθέντες, τοὺς τοξότας
προσελόμενοι. μαχομένων δὲ σφέων ἐπὶ χρόνον τέλος τοιόνδε
ἐγένετο τῆς μάχης. προσβαλλούσης τῆς ἵππου κατὰ τέλεα,
5 ὁ Μασιστίου προέχων τῶν ἄλλων ἵππος βάλλεται τοξεύματι

---

14 μεγαρεεῦσι (C)   16 λάμπονος R   22. 1 ἔσαν z ‖ τε om. ß
3 προσελόμενοι B   4 ἐγένετο ßPz: ἐγίνετο ἐπὶ αC: ἐγένετο ἐπὶ Pᵐ,
Marc. ‖ προσβαλλούσης αC: προσβαλούσης

(with the 1000 Spartans perhaps) presumably remained at their post; even
among the Athenians, it was probably
not the 300 hoplites but the archers—
'perhaps 3000 in number' (Rawlinson)—
who kept the Persian cavalry at bay;
meanwhile the rest of the Greek column
was passing forward, behind Erythrai,
westwards towards Hysiai and Plataia,
deploying to the left. When this
manœuvre was accomplished, the
Athenians, Megarians (and Lakedaimonian Chiliad?) might be on the
extreme right of the Greek line, and
the Lakedaimonian main body on the
extreme left, towards Plataia.

15. ὑπεδέξαντο: sc. ἰέναι τε κτλ.

οἱ τριηκόσιοι λογάδες: this corps
d'élite in the Athenian army is remarkable. At this time Athens had little
or no cavalry: does this body constitute
the aristocratic nucleus of the later
institution? Are they like οἱ καλούμενοι
ἱππεῖς at Sparta? (Cp. 8. 124.) These
men are plainly hoplites; 30 from each
tribe? 10, perhaps, from each Trittys?
under a λοχαγός (hardly an Attic term;
cp. c. 53 infra).

16. Ὀλυμπιόδωρος ὁ Λάμπωνος: (1)
a Samian Lampon meets us in c. 90
infra; (2) a better known Aiginetan in
c. 78 infra; (3) the Athenian here
named may be conjecturally regarded as
the grandfather of Lampon the diviner
(Plutarch, Perikl. 6), who was concerned
in the foundation of Thurioi (Diodor. 12.
10. 3), figures as author of a rider in the
celebrated Eleusinian Decree (C.I.A. iv.
276, Dittenberger¹ No. 13, Michel No.
71), and was something of a butt for the
Old Comedy (Aristoph. Bds. 521 Λάμπων
δ' ὄμνυσ' ἔτι καὶ νυνὶ τὸν χῆν' ὅταν ἐξαπατᾷ

τι): his patronymic is not preserved,
but Olympiodoros may have been his
father (or his uncle). Of this Olympiodoros (a high-sounding but not uncommon name) nothing further is known.
Hdt. might have read or heard of his
fame long before joining the colony at
Thurioi, and there is nothing in this
passage to lead us to postdate its composition. The story is an integral
portion of the Attic legend of Plataia.

22. 1. πρό in double sense, local and
causal, 'in front of,' 'in defence of'
(ὑπέρ), and almost 'instead of' (ἀντί),
cp. 7. 152; quite an Athenian formula,
cp. c. 27 infra.

τῶν παρεόντων is remarkable, and
looks rather like a gloss. There is not
much point here in a reference to medizing Greeks; and for those on the right
side, wherever they were, the Athenians
were fighting. If genuine, the words
might convey an unconscious hint that
the whole army was not yet 'present,'
i.e. in position; bearing out the hypothesis above formulated.

2. ἐς Ἐρυθράς: not necessarily, or
only, the actual town; cp. c. 16 supra.

τοὺς τοξότας προσελόμενοι: these
'Archers' are an important element in
the Athenian forces; cp. c. 60 infra.
Rawlinson places their number at 'per-
haps 3000.' But cp. c. 29 l. 5 infra.
It was no doubt they and not the 300
Heavies that proved a match for the
Persian cavalry (cp. τοξεύματι just below).

5. προέχων: perhaps literally 'in
advance of'; cp. προέχοντας τῶν Περσέων
4. 120; prae aliis longius provectum,
Wesseling. But the horse of Masistios
was no doubt conspicuous not merely
as leading, but as of superior excellence

τὰ πλευρά, ἀλγήσας δὲ ἵσταταί τε ὀρθὸς καὶ ἀποσείεται τὸν
Μασίστιον· πεσόντι δὲ αὐτῷ οἱ Ἀθηναῖοι αὐτίκα ἐπεκέατο.
τὸν δὴ ἵππον αὐτοῦ λαμβάνουσι καὶ αὐτὸν ἀμυνόμενον
κτείνουσι, κατ' ἀρχὰς οὐ δυνάμενοι. ἐνεσκεύαστο γὰρ οὕτω·
ἐντὸς θώρηκα εἶχε χρύσεον λεπιδωτόν, κατύπερθε δὲ τοῦ 10
θώρηκος κιθῶνα φοινίκεον ἐνεδεδύκεε· τύπτοντες δὲ ἐς τὸν
θώρηκα ἐποίευν οὐδέν, πρίν γε δὴ μαθών τις τὸ ποιεύμενον
παίει μιν ἐς τὸν ὀφθαλμόν. οὕτω δὴ ἔπεσέ τε καὶ ἀπέθανε.
ταῦτα δέ κως γινόμενα ἐλελήθεε τοὺς ἄλλους ἱππέας· οὔτε

6 τε om. ΒPz   7 ἀπεκέατο R   8 τὸν δὴ aC : τόν τε δὴ R,
Holder, van H. : τὸν δὲ Pz (τὴν δὲ δὴ S ap. Gaisford : τήν τε δὴ V ap.
Holder)   9 καταρχὰς Pz ‖ ἐσκεύαστο ? van H. ‖ οὕτως Β   11
χιτῶνα Β ‖ ἐνεδεδύκεε Β   12 θώρηκα αὐτοῦ z

(προέχειν 1. 1, 56, 2. 136, 3. 82). προέχειν
in different senses, c. 4 supra, c. 27
infra. τὰ πλευρά, accus. of reference, or
limitation, cp. Index : the plural = 'his
side.'

6. Ἵσταταί τε ὀρθὸς καὶ ἀποσείεται :
cp. 7. 88 στὰς ὀρθὸς ἀπεσείσατο τὸν
Φαρνούχεα (his predecessor ?).

8. ἀμυνόμενον, an imperfect, 'trying
to defend himself.'

9. οὐ δυνάμενοι : sc. κτείνειν μιν.

ἐνεσκεύαστο . . οὕτω : the pluperfect here has no particular temporal
force ; nor again just below ἐνεδεδύκεε,
which looks a little poetic : the action
for the state.

οὕτω referring to what follows =
ὧδε : cp. 8. 98. 4, 109. 12 supra.

10. εἶχε, 'he was wearing,' he had on :
(1) a scarlet tunic ; cp. 7. 61 (φ. 7. 76) ;
(2) underneath, just such a cuirass as
is given to all the Persian cavalry (7.
76) except that his was (not plain steel
rings but) gilt. Hdt. unfortunately
omits to describe his headgear (perhaps
his fez fell off, when he slipped from
his horse !) The omission has serious
consequences, for Plutarch (Ephoros ?)
Aristeid. 14 invests him with a helmet,
and the blow that ends him is dealt
through the eye-hole ! The cuirass of
Masistios was still to be seen among the
ἀναθήματα in the shrine of the Polias,
on the Akropolis, in the days of Pausanias, 1. 27. 1. (Its genuineness would
be more indubitable if it had not been
associated with the ἀκινάκης of Mardonios
—the acquisition of which by Athens
naturally puzzled Pausanias. He might
have been still more puzzled had he
remembered that the ἀκινάκης had been

stolen in the days of Demosthenes, cp.
c. Timocrat. 129 ; it was then valued at,
or 'weighing,' L. & S., 300 darics.) Hdt.
shows no sign in this passage of having
seen these σκῦλα Μηδικά (Thuc. 2. 13. 4)
before writing this passage ; which thus
appears of early composition.

11. τύπτοντες δὲ . . ἐποίευν οὐδέν,
'their blows on the cuirass were un-
availing, till some one perceives the
reason (τὸ ποιεύμενον) and gives him a
prod in the eye.' There is a distinct
difference between τύπτειν and παίειν,
the latter corresponding to the Homeric
πλήσσειν (πληγή) ; cp. J. H. H. Schmidt,
Synonymik i. (1879), 283. An exact
illustration of this incident is to be
found on the slab in the left corner of
the frieze, south-side temple of Athene
Nike, on the Akropolis ; Furtwaengler,
Masterpieces, p. 446, Fig. 181.

13. οὕτω δὴ ἔπεσε : he had fallen from
his horse once already (πεσόντι supra) ;
this is a fresh and final fall ; he must
have risen from the ground, and defended
himself awhile, till the nameless one
smote him in the eye (which eye ? Hdt.
does not say ; and the state of the
monument, which he, of course, could
not have seen, does not enable us to say
for certain : probably the right).

14. ἐλελήθεε : it was all over before
any of the Persians discovered it ; they
saw neither the fall from his horse
(πεσόντα), nor the death-wound being
dealt ; nor when they retired and then
turned (ὑποστροφή, cp. c. 14 supra) did
they perceive what was happening (τὸ
γινόμενον) ; it was only when they halted
(ἔστησαν, cp. c. 28 infra ἀποστήσαντες,
which supports 1st aor., sc. τοὺς ἵππους)

15 γὰρ πεσόντα μιν εἶδον ἀπὸ τοῦ ἵππου οὔτε ἀποθνῄσκοντα,
ἀναχωρήσιός τε γινομένης καὶ ὑποστροφῆς οὐκ ἔμαθον τὸ
γινόμενον. ἐπείτε δὲ ἔστησαν, αὐτίκα ἐπόθεσαν, ὡς σφεας
οὐδεὶς ἦν ὁ τάσσων· μαθόντες δὲ τὸ γεγονός, διακελευσάμενοι
ἤλαυνον τοὺς ἵππους πάντες, ὡς ἂν τὸν νεκρὸν ἀνελοίατο.
23 ἰδόντες δὲ οἱ Ἀθηναῖοι οὐκέτι κατὰ τέλεα προσελαύνοντας
τοὺς ἱππέας ἀλλ' ἅμα πάντας, τὴν ἄλλην στρατιὴν ἐπεβώσαντο. ἐν ᾧ δὲ ὁ πεζὸς ἅπας ἐβοήθεε, ἐν τούτῳ μάχη ὀξέα
περὶ τοῦ νεκροῦ γίνεται. ἕως μέν νυν μοῦνοι ἦσαν οἱ
5 τριηκόσιοι, ἐσσοῦντό τε πολλὸν καὶ τὸν νεκρὸν ἀπέλειπον· ὡς
δέ σφι τὸ πλῆθος ἐπεβοήθησε, οὕτω δὴ οὐκέτι οἱ ἱππόται

---

17 γινάμενον R: γενόμενον Gaisford ‖ ἔστησαν Marc., z   18
τάξων ? van H.   19 τόν γε β, Holder, van H.   23. 2 ἀλλ' ἅμα
β, Holder, van H., Stein³: ἀλλὰ   3 ἐβώθεε(ν V) β: ἐπεβώθει van H.
‖ ὀξεῖα codd. z   4 ἐγίνετο β ‖ ἔσαν z   5 ἀπέλιπον z   6 ἐπε-
βώθησε van H.

---

that they missed him at once, when
there was no one to dress them; then
they perceived what had taken place,
and with a shout to encourage each
other, they all put spurs to their horses
and charged to recover the dead body.

17. ἐπόθεσαν Blakesley regarded as
corrupt; cp. ἐπόθησε 3. 36, ἐπιποθήσειν
5. 93, but the variants ἐπόθεσα, ποθέ-
σομαι are admissible; cp. Goodwin Gr.
Gr. p. 352, L. & S. sub v.

ὡς σφεας οὐδεὶς ἦν ὁ τάσσων:
this might be taken to imply that the
cavalry unit commanded by Masistios
was a very small one, or a very large
one: very small, if there was no officer
in command but Masistios; very large,
if no provision existed to fill a vacancy
in the supreme command. If Masistios
was sole Hipparch, or even one of two
or three, there must have been many
subordinate officers in his division: did
none of them pro tempore assume the
command?

19. ἐλαύνειν of 'riding' is not common
in Hdt.; but cp. 5. 111.

ὡς ἄν, like ὅκως ἄν, followed by
the optative is frequent in Hdt. (In
Homer the opt. with ἵνα and ὅπως is
always pure; with ὡς it takes ἄν in a few
places "where there is clear reference to
a single occasion," Monro, Hom. Gram.
§ 306.)

23. 1. οὐκέτι κατὰ τέλεα .. ἀλλ' ἅμα
πάντας: there is a development in the
tactics of the Persian cavalry, not necessarily for the better; it is indeed a
result of 'there being no one to order
them.' The phrase can hardly mean
that the distinction of τέλεα was disregarded, the horsemen charging simply
pêle-mêle; but rather that now all the
τέλεα charged together. Nor, again,
does this involve a more extended formation, or front; they may have charged
en masse, almost in column. In any
case the description tends to reduce the
actual numbers engaged.

2. ἐπεβώσαντο: the Megarians, a while
before in somewhat similar straits, had
to send a message; the Athenians have
only to call, to cry aloud, for support.
But to whom do they call? In c. 25
below οἱ Ἕλληνες appear to be given the
credit of the victory in the ἱππομαχίη,
but even there the phrase is not un-
ambiguous, while here it is not made
quite clear that τὴν ἄλλην στρατιήν and
ὁ πεζὸς ἅπας refer to more than the
Athenian forces, which in any case
would presumably be nearest at hand.
However that may be, there is here
distinctly a second tactical moment, or
development, in the Greek position,
finally culminating in the retirement of
the Persian cavalry, leaving the body of
Masistios in the hands of the Athenians.

4. ἕως μέν νυν μοῦνοι ἦσαν οἱ τριηκόσιοι: if the τοξόται can be ignored
in this fashion, why not the Megarians,
Lakedaimonians, and others? In any
case τὸ πλῆθος could not come up as one
man, and least of all if it means not
merely τῶν Ἀθηναίων but τῶν Ἑλλήνων.

ὑπέμενον οὐδέ σφι ἐξεγένετο τὸν νεκρὸν ἀνελέσθαι, ἀλλὰ πρὸς
ἐκείνῳ ἄλλους προσαπώλεσαν τῶν ἱππέων. ἀποστήσαντες ὦν
ὅσον τε δύο στάδια ἐβουλεύοντο ὅ τι χρεὸν εἴη ποιέειν, ἐδόκεε
δέ σφι ἀναρχίης ἐούσης ἀπελαύνειν παρὰ Μαρδόνιον. ἀπικο- 24
μένης δὲ τῆς ἵππου ἐς τὸ στρατόπεδον πένθος ἐποιήσαντο
Μασιστίου πᾶσά τε ἡ στρατιὴ καὶ Μαρδόνιος μέγιστον, σφέας
τε αὐτοὺς κείροντες καὶ τοὺς ἵππους καὶ τὰ ὑποζύγια οἰμωγῇ
τε χρεώμενοι ἀπλέτῳ· ἅπασαν γὰρ τὴν Βοιωτίην κατεῖχε ἠχὼ 5

---

7 ἐπέμενον z   8 προσαπόλεσαν B ‖ τῶν ἱππέων del. van H.,
Holder ‖ ἀποστάντες Reiske, Cobet, van H.   9 δύο : δέκα ? Krueger ‖
χρεὼν CPz, van H.   24. 2 ἐποιήσατο R   5 χρεόμενοι P, van H.

7. ἐξεγένετο : cp. 5. 51.

8. ἀποστήσαντες : they halted (their horses) at a distance ; cp. 5. 51 ἀποστάς 'he retired'—passages which might tempt the inference that even the aor. 1. of ἵστημι came dangerously near being used intransitively. Blakesley regarded this use of ἀποστῆσαι as quite 'technical' ; Kuehner, Ausf. Gramm. p. 1069, as simply a case of brachylogy, where a substantive is to be understood "out of a cognate substantive, or adjective, or adverb, or out of the general context" (aus dem Zusammenhange der Rede); cp. also App. Crit. and l. 14 supra.

9. ὅσον τε δύο στάδια, 'about four hundred yards'—say, quarter of a mile ; this halt might leave them still a couple of miles from the tête du pont on the Asopos.

ἐβουλεύοντο : the officers, of course. Each τέλος must have had a leader, to say nothing of dekarchs, etc. But as far as Hdt. is concerned the consultation might be conducted by the entire number, rank and file.

ἐδόκεε might surely be ἔδοξε, but cp. c. 5 l. 4 supra.

10. ἀναρχίης ἐούσης : their ἄρχων was gone—they had no commander, for which reason they decided to ride back (ἀπελαύνειν) to headquarters (παρὰ Μαρδόνιον). These statements will have been based rather on the observations and inferences made on the Greek side than on authorities (Greek or other) in the Persian camp (Thersander, for example, c. 16 supra).

24. 2. πένθος ἐποιήσαντο Μασιστίου .. μέγιστον, 'made a very great mourning for Masistios' ; cp. 2. 1 τῆς .. Κύρου αὐτὸς τε μέγα πένθος ἐποιήσατο καὶ τοῖσι ἄλλοισι προεῖπε πᾶσι τῶν ἦρχε πένθος

ποιέεσθαι. Their grief would be increased by their failure to recover the body. It was shown partly by the shaving and hair-cutting of man and beast, and partly by wailing, the sound of which was heard throughout the length and breadth of the land.

Was there anything especially 'barbarous' in this style of mourning (τρόπος ὁ σφέτερος c. 25) ? Just in like manner the Lakonians bewailed the death of a king 6. 58 ; cp. οἰμωγῇ διαχρέωνται ἀπλέτῳ ib.; though that, indeed, Hdt. regards as Asiatic and barbarous ; cp. also 8. 99 supra, 8. 66. Hair-cutting as a sign of grief Hdt., 2. 36, reports as a custom to which Egypt supplies the only exception. Blakesley quotes Eurip. Alk. 428 to prove that cutting the manes of the horses was a Thessalian practice ; Larcher shows that it was done by Greeks, and it is recorded in the case of the death of Pelopidas (Plutarch Pelop. 33), but perhaps the higher culture tended to discountenance it. Aischylos in the Persai (1055) seems to mark it as 'barbarous,' like Hdt. ; and Alexander Magnus was evidently much censured for the extravagance of his grief and mourning (πένθος) for Hephaistion ; cp. Arrian, Anab. 7. 14. 2. But letting the hair grow abnormally may have much the same significance, though it takes longer to operate ; cp. Suetonius, Julius 67.

5. κατεῖχε ἠχώ. Blakesley rationalistically understands this to mean merely that wailing was heard wherever troops were posted. That is hardly adequate to the phrase : Boiotia echoed with the sound of lamentation, and mourning and woe. L. & S. is prosier still : 'all Boeotia rang with the news !' (ὡς ?)

ὡς ἀνδρὸς ἀπολομένου μετά γε Μαρδόνιον λογιμωτάτου παρά
τε Πέρσῃσι καὶ βασιλέι.

25   Οἱ μέν νυν βάρβαροι τρόπῳ τῷ σφετέρῳ ἀποθανόντα
ἐτίμων Μασίστιον· οἱ δὲ Ἕλληνες ὡς τὴν ἵππον ἐδέξαντο
προσβάλλουσαν καὶ δεξάμενοι ὥσαντο, ἐθάρσησάν τε πολλῷ
μᾶλλον καὶ πρῶτα μὲν ἐς ἄμαξαν ἐσθέντες τὸν νεκρὸν παρὰ

---

6 γε om. Β   7 βασιλέι ΑΒ   25. 1 ἐτίμων ἀποθανόντα Β
3 προσβαλοῦσαν SV : προβαλοῦσαν R ‖ ἐθάρρησάν Pz ‖ τε om. punct.
post μᾶλλον pos. Β, Holder, van H., alii   4 ἄμαξαν R

---

6. ὡς ἀνδρὸς . . βασιλέι. That
Masistios, son of Siromithres, took precedence of every one save Mardonios
(Artabazos, for example) in the king's
eyes might support the error of Tzetzes,
op. c. 20 *supra*; but it is not conceivable that Hdt. should not have known
it had Masistios been an Achaimenid,
or nearly related to the king.   His
value to the king is perhaps but an
inference from his position in the army
and the mourning made for him. It
also heightens the Athenian achievement; cp. c. 64 *infra*.
    25. 2. οἱ δὲ Ἕλληνες. This sentence
appears to give credit to 'the Hellenes'
for repulsing the cavalry, i.e. to interpret
τὸ πλῆθος, ὁ πεζὸς ἅπας in c. 23 *supra* as
meaning the whole army.   Even if that
were the intention of Hdt. the fact
would still be disputable : the idea that
the whole forces available upon the
Greek side were deployed and brought
into action before the cavalry skirmish
round the body of Masistios was terminated in favour of the Greeks is on the
face of it improbable ; nor is it easy to
understand how such forces could have
operated in the given position and
locality.   But (i.) *quod facit per alium
facit per se*; (ii.) the advantage benefited
the Greek side as a whole ; (iii.) the
Greeks had repulsed the Persian cavalry,
even if only the Athenians, the Megarians,
and possibly the Lakedaimonian πρόδρομοι were actually engaged in what was
an affair of *Vorposten*, or, at most, of
the head of the column, debouching
through the pass.
    4. πρῶτα μὲν . . παρὰ τὰς τάξις
ἐκόμιζον.   This proceeding seems to
imply (1) that there was a road along
which the wagon was drawn by horses
(oxen, or mules) ; (2) that the Greek
army was posted in tactical array of
some kind.   Only one of two roads can

well be in question : (a) the road from
Erythrai past Hysiai to Plataia ; (b) the
road up the Pass to Eleutherai, etc.   If
the Greek army was already in extended
formation, in lines running east and
west, as is apparently assumed by
Plutarch, *Aristeid.* 11 *ad init.*, and
universally assumed for 'the first
position' by modern authorities, the
Megarians and Athenians would apparently occupy the extreme right wing,
and the rest of the army would be to
the left of them towards Hysiai and
Plataia ; or else the Athenians are already
on the left wing, the rest of the forces
having debouched to the right of them.
Two considerations appear to me to
favour the former supposition :—(i.) Had
the Athenians already been in occupation of the left wing, the question so
hotly disputed in the next chapter could
hardly have arisen at that point.   (ii.)
Strategically and tactically the debou-
chure of the army towards the west is
the natural one.   If Erythrai was at
the foot, or near the foot of the pass,
the Greek van would seize on that
position, and hold it, while the rest
of the army moved from behind out of
the pass.   There is hardly room for such
a development towards the east side,
where the pass is flanked by the great
mass of rock named by Dr. Grundy
'The High Bastions'; moreover, such
a movement would have thrown the
Greek front away to the east of the
Persian encampment, down stream,
exposing them to be outflanked (on
their left) by the Persian cavalry.
Again, the development of the Greek
first position westwards accords with
the subsequent movement reported in
this chapter, and also places the rear of
the column, when developed, in front
of the two other roads, or passes, crossing Kithairon (to Eleutherai and to

τὰς τάξις ἐκόμιζον· ὁ δὲ νεκρὸς ἦν θέης ἄξιος μεγάθεος εἵνεκα 5
καὶ κάλλεος, τῶν δὴ εἵνεκα καὶ ταῦτα ἐποίευν· ἐκλείποντες
τὰς τάξις ἐφοίτων θεησόμενοι Μασίστιον. μετὰ δὲ ἔδοξέ σφι

---

5 τάξεις C ‖ ἐκομίζοντο Β ‖ ἔην z ‖ μεγάθεός τε coni. Stein, adm.
van H. 6 τῶν δὴ Krueger, Stein², Holder, van H.: τῶν δὲ codd.,
Stein¹: τῶνδε z ‖ ταῦτα ἐποίευν· del. Krueger, van H. (ἐποίεον PRSz)
‖ ἐκλιπόντες Β, van H. 7 τάξεις BC ‖ ἐφοίτεον Β, Stein¹, van H.:
καὶ ἐφοίτων z

Megara). Finally, as, upon the above supposition, the Lakedaimonians in the first position come to stand on the extreme left, and the Athenians on the right, not only is there some excuse for the controversy in the next chapter, when the army moves down-hill to 'the second position,' but also a clue is perhaps found to the real or recorded exchange of positions between the Athenians and the Lakedaimonians in the second position (cc. 46, 47 infra), though for that exchange, or supposed exchange, other fair explanations may also be forthcoming. It is possible, then, that the body of Masistios was conveyed upon a wagon along the road running from Erythrai towards Plataia, no doubt mostly behind the Greek lines, as finally developed in 'the first position.' It is also, however, possible that the wagon was taken simply up the road through the pass to the rear, the sight of it mightily encouraging the rear ranks of the column, which had not yet fully emerged on to the ὑπωρέη. What the ultimate destination of the wagon, or what became of the corpse, Hdt. unfortunately does not inform us; presumably he did not know. The θώρηξ found its way to Athens; cp. c. 22 supra.

5. ὁ δὲ νεκρὸς ἦν θέης ἄξιος. Hdt. writes as though he had seen it; but of course he had not. Tall and comely as the corpse was, Masistios does not seem to have been 'heroized' like Artachaies at Akanthos, 7. 117, or Philip of Kroton at Segesta, 5. 47. Cp. c. 20 supra. Hdt. also omits to specify what became of his noble Nesaian charger: was he led to his master's grave, and perhaps sacrificed thereon? Or did he escape with the squadron, after his master's fall? Or die of his wound on the field?

6. ταῦτα ἐποίευν. The difficulty may

be surmounted (a) by deleting ταῦτα ἐποίευν with Krüger; (b) by bracketing ἐκλείποντες . . Μασίστιον as a gloss; (c) by understanding, with Stein, ταῦτα = τάδε. Cp. οὕτω = ὧδε c. 22 supra.

7. ἔδοξέ σφι ἐπικαταβῆναι ἐς Πλαταιάς: this is a formal decision of the council of war, cp. c. 51 infra, or of the commander-in-chief. That it was taken at this moment may not be strictly correct. Hdt. does not say for how long the Greeks occupied 'the first position,' whether for days, or only for hours. The process by which the advance was effected may have been as follows:—The Megarians (or perhaps οἱ ἀμφὶ Μεγαρέας κτλ., cp. c. 69) had seized and occupied Erythrai, until relieved by the Athenians, who in their turn have been supported by more and more of the forces, until ὁ πεζὸς ἅπας has gradually arrived on the scene. The Athenians and Megarians may have moved out of Erythrai, westwards towards Hysiai first, and then beyond, Erythrai being occupied in succession by the various contingents, without further fighting, and the position being constantly developed westwards, until finally the Athenians and Megarians have pushed along the ὑπωρέη far enough to the west to allow of the Lakedaimonians in the rear occupying Erythrai on the extreme right of the position. If this was the process, then the question of precedence between the Athenians and Tegeatai was virtually settled beforehand. But it seems more probable that, as above suggested, the head of the column, composed of the Megarians (and the Spartan Chiliad?) supported by the Athenians continued to hold Erythrai, while the rest of the army deployed behind Erythrai to the west, along the high ground, in front of Hysiai and towards Plataia. This movement would be facilitated by the

ἐπικαταβῆναι ἐς Πλαταιάς· ὁ γὰρ χῶρος ἐφαίνετο πολλῷ ἐὼν
ἐπιτηδεότερός σφι ἐνστρατοπεδεύεσθαι ὁ Πλαταιικὸς τοῦ Ἐρυ-
10 θραίου τά τε ἄλλα καὶ εὐυδρότερος. ἐς τοῦτον δὴ τὸν χῶρον
καὶ ἐπὶ τὴν κρήνην τὴν Γαργαφίην τὴν ἐν τῷ χώρῳ τούτῳ
ἐοῦσαν ἔδοξέ σφι χρεὸν εἶναι ἀπικέσθαι καὶ διαταχθέντας
στρατοπεδεύεσθαι. ἀναλαβόντες δὲ τὰ ὅπλα ἤισαν διὰ τῆς
ὑπωρέης τοῦ Κιθαιρῶνος παρὰ Ὑσιὰς ἐς τὴν Πλαταιίδα γῆν,

9 ἐπιτηδεώτερος CPz, van H. ‖ πλαταϊκὸς a   10 εὐυδρότερος <ἐών>
Krueger   12 χρεὼν Pz, van H.   14 ὑπωρίης V: ὑπωρείης ‖ περὶ z
‖ ὑασιὰς R

existence of the roads from Erythrai to
Plataia, and from Dryoskephalai to
Plataia.

8. **ἐπικαταβῆναι** gives two character-
istics of the movement: (a) it was down-
hill, from higher to lower ground ; (b)
it was a forward, or offensive movement;
cp. 8. 38. **ἐς Πλαταιάς** gives a third:
(c) it was into Plataian territory (cp. c.
16 supra). This might involve not
merely a northerly, but a north-westerly
direction ; that it was not due west, or
on to Plataia itself, or its ruins, is
abundantly clear both from the immediately ensuing topography, and from
the subsequent narrative (cp. c. 52 infra).

ὁ γὰρ χῶρος κτλ. The reasons
given for the move are admittedly incomplete (τά τε ἄλλα καί) ; the only one
emphasized is the water supply, no
doubt a reason of supreme importance,
especially with a view to encamping
(ἐνστρατοπεδεύεσθαι), less important, however, with a view to pure fighting
(ἐμμαχέσασθαι c. 7 supra) which must
have been under consideration. If the
Greeks did not want to provoke a battle
they would have remained in their first
position, or moved at once to the
'Island' (c. 51 infra). The fact that
the battle was not finally fought exactly
in the second position has, perhaps, led
to the 'offensive' or at least provocative
character of this forward movement being
ignored. Any one could appreciate the
reason given, which was manifest to the
merest tiro (ἐφαίνετο ἐών). **τὴν Γαργαφίην**, see below.

12. **διαταχθέντας στρατοπεδεύεσθαι**:
before the new position was occupied,
before the Laager there was formed, and
presumably either in the first position
itself, or in the process of moving from
the first position to the second, a διάταξις
was to be effected, i.e. the existing

arrangement and order of the τάξεις was
to be modified, or at any rate the army
was to be put in battle-array ; it had
not therefore previously been in battle-
array, but in marching order, or at least
not in the order of battle approved by
the commanders. (Cp. 8. 70 παρεκρίθησαν
διαταχθέντες, of the movement of the
Persian fleet into line of battle ; διέτασσε
6. 107, ὡς δέ σφι διετέτακτο 6. 112 acie
ordinata ; cp. also 1. 80 ὡς δέ οἱ πάντες
διετετάχατο with the context.) But
perhaps Hdt. is getting a little out of
his depth here ; the Greeks can hardly
have intended to encamp for any length
of time on the advanced position 'on the
Asopos.'

13. **ἀναλαβόντες δὲ τὰ ὅπλα**: cp. cc.
53, 57 infra. The heavy arms (shields,
etc.) were piled for the halt, or in camp.
and 'taken up' again before moving.
The army had probably bivouacked at
least one night in the position at Erythrai
—though Hdt. does not actually say so.

**ἤισαν διὰ τῆς ὑπωρέης τοῦ Κιθαι-
ρῶνος**: nothing in these words proves
this a down-hill march ; that idea must
be borrowed from the ἐπικαταβῆναι above,
and from the real topography or chorio-
graphy ; otherwise the words might
describe the movement of a column
direct on Plataia, or of a series of contingents extending themselves en échelon
in that direction.

14. **παρὰ Ὑσιάς**. Strabo 404 ἔνιοι δὲ
τὰς Ὑσιὰς Ὑρίην λέγεσθαί φασι, τῆς
Παρασωπίας οὖσαν ὑπὸ τῷ Κιθαιρῶνι
πλησίον Ἐρυθρῶν ἐν τῇ μεσογαίᾳ. It was
'a little to the right' of the road from
Eleutherai to Plataia ; Pausan. 9. 2. 1.
There was a road running from Thebes
to Eleutherai via Hysiai (or rather via
Erythrai !), Pausan. 9. 1. 6, by which
the Thebans circumvented the Plataians
in 373 B.C. The position of Hysiai was

ἀπικόμενοι δὲ ἐτάσσοντο κατὰ ἔθνεα πλησίον τῆς τε κρήνης 15

plainly west of Erythrai and east of Plataia; cp. c. 15 *supra ad f.*; but whether Hysiai was higher up hill, or on lower ground than Erythrai, is not so evident. Tradition (cp. G. B. Grundy, *G.P. W.* p. 464) identifies the site with that of the existing village of *Kriekouki*: Dr. Grundy himself places it outside the area of the existing village, and higher up the hill to the south. I think it probable that just as Erythrai commanded the Dryoskephalai Pass, and the direct road from Thebes to Eleutherai-Eleusis-Athens, so Hysiai commanded the loop-road from Plataia which struck into the main road behind the ridge, by a second pass; while Plataia itself might be taken to command the third road and pass across the ridge of Kithairon, that leading direct to Megara. These three passes cross the ridge at intervals of about a mile (roughly); but Plataia lay somewhat further in advance (and to the west) of Pass III. than Hysiai and Erythrai of Passes II. and I. respectively.

ἐς τὴν Πλαταιίδα γῆν. The territory of Plataia extended northwards right down to the Asopos (cp. c. 15 *supra*); how far it extended eastwards is not so clear. Hysiai (Strabo 404) and Erythrai (Strabo 409) were both in the Παρασωπία, and their territories (whether independent or not) reached down to the river-course. It may be conjectured that the whole water-system of the Oëroë (c. 51 *infra*) belonged to Plataia, while lower down, and to the north, stream A. 4 among the tributaries of the Asopos, descending from Kithairon, may have formed a boundary between the Πλαταιίς and t e 'Τσιαίς. This would place Gargaphia, on every theory, within the *Plataiis*, as also the Heroon of Androkrates; it would leave the Demetrion (c. 62 *infra*) and the 'Long Ridge' in the *Hysiaiis*. The boundary between the territory of Hysiai and that of Erythrai might perhaps be found in the considerable stream A. 6 which Dr. Grundy conjecturally identifies with the Moloeis (c. 57 *infra*). This identification would suit the position suggested above, on the Plataia-Athens pass, for the site of Hysiai very well, and would lead to the inclusion of the Argiopion (c. 57 *infra*) in the territory of Hysiai.

15. **ἀπικόμενοι δὲ ἐτάσσοντο κατὰ ἔθνεα.** This assertion generates two difficulties. (1) Were not the Greeks already τεταγμένοι κατ' ἔθνεα? Most certainly, the various τάξεις, the various contingents in the first position, Megarians, Athenians, etc., were 'ethnic.' (2) Did the Greeks all arrive at the new position and then proceed to the διάταξις? Such an operation is practically incredible. The order in which the ethnic τάξεις should stand, or laager, in the new (i.e. 'second,' or more strictly third) position must have been determined, in the main, before the position was occupied; the Greeks could neither have arrived there in a confused mass, with all the various ἔθνη indiscriminately mixed up, as though the proceeding were a pêle-mêle flight, not a forward movement in the face of the enemy; nor, again, could the various ethnic contingents, each in itself compact, have advanced and taken up a station at random round the fountain of Gargaphia. Whatever the order in which the Greeks had bivouacked in the first position, by Erythrai (or in the second position, west thereof), the order of battle, and the order of the stations in the Asopos position, must have been decided before the forces moved forward to occupy it. But if, as above suggested, the Athenians, in the final development of the first position, occupied the extreme right, at Erythrai, while the Tegeatai were on the left, next the Spartans, there might be a question whether, when the Spartans moved forward to the right, the Tegeatai should follow them, or simply move forward into position so as to form the extreme left of the Greek line in 'the second (i.e. third) position.'

πλησίον τῆς τε κρήνης τῆς Γαργαφίης: the position and identity of Gargaphia have been disputed. (i.) It was identified by Squire (*ap.* Walpole, *Memoirs*, 338 ff.) and by Clarke (*Travels*, ii. 3, p. 83) with the spring now called *Vergutiani*. Blakesley unfortunately acquiesced in this identification, which is quite hopeless, Vergutiani being high up on the ὑπωρέη, and belonging to the water-system of the Oëroë. (The apparent 'second' position of the Greeks is described below, c. 30, as ἐπὶ τῷ Ἀσωπῷ. Perhaps in the true second position Vergutiani was within, or just behind, their lines.) (ii.) Leake (*N.G.* ii. 332, 343) and Vischer (*Erinnerungen*, p. 549) accept the traditional identification of Gargaphia with a spring now known as *Apotripi*,

τῆς Γαργαφίης καὶ τοῦ τεμένεος τοῦ Ἀνδροκράτεος τοῦ ἥρωος,
διὰ ὄχθων τε οὐκ ὑψηλῶν καὶ ἀπέδου χώρου.

17 δι᾽ PRz ‖ χωρίου CPz, Gaisford, alii

just north of and below the (ruined)
Church of St. John on the 'Asopos
Ridge': the head-waters in fact of
stream A. 1 in G. B. Grundy's Maps.
This identification is *prima facie* valid.
(iii.) Grote (followed by Rawlinson
and Stein) regarded Gargaphia as non-
existent at the present day, or, what
comes to the same thing, unidentifiable.
Grote unfortunately never visited the
scenes with which his great work is
concerned. No one who has actually
seen the battle-field of Plataia, or
considered its problems *in loco*, will
easily acquiesce in this *non possumus*.
(iv.) Dr. G. B. Grundy identifies the
spring of Gargaphia with an extant
spring some three-quarters of a mile, or
less, east (slightly by north) of Apotripi,
and virtually in the same hollow ground,
or trough, as Apotripi, surrounding the
Asopos Ridge. This spring is one of
the head-waters of the stream A. 4
forming the east boundary of the Asopos
Ridge, and possibly, as above suggested,
the frontier between the Plataiis and
the Hysiaiis. Not much is gained by
this shift of Gargaphia one-half to three-
quarters of a mile eastward: as a matter
of fact both springs in question will
have been within the Greek lines; but
Dr. Grundy's suggestion tends to put
the spring on the extreme right of the
Greek army, which might appear an
advantage, especially to those who take
Gargaphia and the Androkrateion as
making two termini; see next note.
Hdt. himself makes Gargaphia 10
stades from the Island, c. 51 *infra*, and
20 stades from the Heraion, c. 52 *infra*.
These measurements are obviously mere
round numbers, and of very little value
except as making (i.) *supra* more than
ever impossible. The distance to the
'Island' (as identified by Dr. Grundy)
would suit either spring; the distance
to the Heraion (whatever its exact site)
is in either case an over-estimate. If the
Island had been where Leake and Vischer
put it, the distance would have suited
Apotripi better than the alternative.
(v.) Goettling, *Gesam. Abh.* p. 136,
identified Gargaphia with a spring near
Plataia: the same objections are fatal to
this proposal as to (i.). The name Gar-

gaphia = *Platanisti*, 'Poplar-well.' γάργα
= αἴγειρος, Hesych. γάρκα, 'Macedonian,'
a rod, *ib.* We may suppose the well-
head shaded with a grove of poplars, or
plane-trees.
16. τοῦ τεμένεος τοῦ Ἀνδροκράτεος
τοῦ ἥρωος. Thuc. 3. 24. 1 places τὸ τοῦ
Ἀνδροκράτους ἡρῷον on the right of the
direct road from Plataia to Thebes; cp.
Plutarch, *Aristeid.* 11 αὐτοῦ δ᾽ ἦν καὶ
τὸ τοῦ Ἀνδροκράτους ἡρῷον ἐγγὺς ἄλσει
πυκνῶν καὶ συσκίων δένδρων περιεχόμενον.
These, with Hdt., are the only authorities
on the exact site, and they leave much
to be desired. αὐτοῦ in Plutarch does
not mean (*pace* Rawlinson) ἐν τῷ πεδίῳ
but simply ἐν τῇ Πλαταιΐδι. As far as
Thucydides goes, the Heroon is anywhere, within reach, on the right of the
road from Plataia to Thebes. There is
no evidence that Thucydides himself
ever visited Plataia, and the '5 or 6
stades' mentioned in the context need
not be used to prejudice the position of
the Hero's house. Little is known of
Androkrates, but he was plainly the
greatest of the local Heroes of Plataia,
of the ἀρχηγέται Πλαταιέων, seven in
number, mentioned in the 'oracle' *ap.*
Plutarch, *Aristeid.* 11; cp. Rohde, *Psyche*
(1890) p. 161. A conspicuous site may
be posited for his Heroon. If such a
site is forthcoming, and fits in well with
'the second (i.e. third) position' of the
Greeks before Plataia in 479 B.C., it
cannot be sacrificed to an *obiter dictum*
in Thucydides. I have therefore no
hesitation in accepting the Church of
St. John (first proposed by W. J. Wood-
house, *J.H.S.* xviii. (1898) 38 ff.) as
marking the Androkrateion as surely
as the Church of St. Demetrion on the
neighbouring ridge to the east marks one
of the temples of Eleusinian Demeter
(as proposed by Dr. Grundy; cp. c. 57
infra).
There is nothing to show that Hdt. in
this passage conceived Gargaphia as
marking the extreme right of the Greek
position, and the Androkrateion as
marking the extreme left, a point on
which Rawlinson rightly demurs to
Grote. The Church of St. John occupies
the lower of two summits (300 and 360
ft. respectively above the Asopos Bridge)

Ἐνθαῦτα ἐν τῇ διατάξι ἐγένετο λόγων πολλῶν ὠθισμὸς **26**
Τεγεητέων τε καὶ Ἀθηναίων· ἐδικαίευν γὰρ αὐτοὶ ἑκάτεροι
ἔχειν τὸ ἔτερον κέρας, καὶ καινὰ καὶ παλαιὰ παραφέροντες

---

26. 1 διατάξι Pz : διατάξει ‖ πολλὸς β, Holder, van H.   2
ἐδικαίουν α, van H. ‖ αὐτέων z

---

which are both alike comprised in the 'Asopos Ridge.' The Greeks, now offering battle, will have occupied both these summits, directly in advance of the two springs, or well-heads, (ii.) and (iv.) above, which dispute the name Gargaphia, and both sources will have been used by the troops : Dr. Grundy's Gargaphia by the right wing, Apotripi by the centre, while the Athenians and left wing may have had to draw from the stream A. 1 (not wholly dependent on Apotripi for its water). This position suits the description διὰ ὄχθων τε οὐκ ὑψηλῶν καὶ ἀπέδου χώρου. It was an ἄπεδος χῶρος though not a πεδίον. Dr. Grundy places the Greeks to the south, just above the trough between streams A. 1 and A. 4 and with the wells in front of them.

26. 1. ἐνθαῦτα ἐν τῇ διατάξι. If Hdt. means that the dispute between the Tegeatans and Athenians took place in the Asopos position, and before the forces are disposed in position, he means what is manifestly absurd. What then does he suppose the order to have been in the previous position ? Hdt. has not concerned himself to realize the conditions of his own story ; but the story, however fantastic, doubtless has some ground in actual occurrences. Some time or other, at some place or other, it was discussed and decided what the order of battle should be on the Greek side. In Attica the Athenians might conceivably have claimed the post of honour on the right wing, though such a claim had hardly been consistent with the *Hegemonia* of the Spartans ; but it appears that the Athenians with the Megarians actually formed the head of the marching column (*agmen*) from Eleusis to Erythrai. In a Spartan army the king commanded from the centre ; cp. Thuc. 5. 72. 4 (but Kleombrotos apparently commanded the right wing at Leuktra, Plutarch, *Pelop.* 23). It is conceivable that the question of the exact order of battle was not fully resolved before the Greeks reached Erythrai ; or, again, that the turn taken by the 'Hippomachy,' and the development of the first Greek position, brought

about an order and a situation which had not been distinctly foreseen. The Greek ethnic contingents must have extended along the ὑπωρέη in some definite order, whether the Athenians were then on the extreme left or on the extreme right. In the latter case the manœuvre described below in c. 46 may have taken place, or have been anticipated, and so brought the Athenians on to the left wing, the Lakedaimonians on to the right ; or this result may have been obtained by an advance *en échelon* down the ὑπωρέη and on to the Asopos Ridge. If (as appears to me less probable) the Athenians had evacuated Erythrai and moved to the left, along the ὑπωρέη, making room for the remainder of the marching column to form up in line, the Lakedaimonians being on the extreme right ; then, this order had probably been already decided on, and it was too late for the Tegeatai to enter a claim ; but the story of the dispute may come to have been associated with the transition from the *agmen* to the *acies*, and that transition itself to be confounded with the advance on to the Asopos. Hdt., for whom the problem of the conversion of the marching column, or columns, into the fighting line simply does not exist, has placed the record as an appendix to a description of the (second) position, in which the disposition of the forces in fighting array, in actual line of battle, was effected, or made effective.

λόγων πολλῶν ἀθισμός: cp. 8. 78.

2. Τεγεητέων τε καὶ Ἀθηναίων: 500 Tegeatai had been in the army of Leonidas, 7. 202 ; there are 1500 present on this occasion. (The city has been mentioned 7. 170, but in a passage of later composition.)

ἐδικαίευν: cp. 8. 126.

αὐτοὶ ἑκάτεροι: Baehr cps. 3. 82 αὐτὸς γὰρ ἕκαστος κτλ., 5. 13 αὐτὰ ἕκαστα (*v.l.* ταῦτα). For the plural cp. 7. 1. 7.

3. ἔχειν τὸ ἔτερον κέρας: a strong ἔχειν. Rawlinson's translation is right, ' one of the wings,' following Schweighaeuser, who refuted Valckenaer's interpretation of the term as a euphemism

ἔργα. τοῦτο μὲν οἱ Τεγεῆται ἔλεγον τάδε. "ἡμεῖς αἰεί κοτε
5 ἀξιεύμεθα ταύτης τῆς τάξιος ἐκ τῶν συμμάχων ἀπάντων, ὅσαι
ἤδη ἔξοδοι κοιναὶ ἐγένοντο Πελοποννησίοισι καὶ τὸ παλαιὸν
καὶ τὸ νέον, ἐξ ἐκείνου τοῦ χρόνου ἐπείτε Ἡρακλεῖδαι ἐπειρῶντο

---

4 ἀεί β, Holder　　　5 τάξιος . . ἐγένοντο om. R: στάσιος s　　6
ἔξοδοι ἤδη α ‖ πάλαι β, van H.　　7 ἐπεὶ Paris. 1635 s ‖ ἐπειρέοντο
van H.

---

for sinistrum cornu ; cp. infra : ὀκότερον
βούλεσθε κέρεος ἄρχειν παριεμεν. The
Lakedaimonians were, of course, sure to
take the right.

παραφέροντες : used literally, of
more material arguments, 3. 130 μάστιγάς
τε καὶ κέντρα παραφέρειν ἐς τὸ μέσον.

4. τοῦτο μέν has here no τοῦτο δέ following, but the antithesis is supplied in
more extended terms at the beginning
of the next chapter.

6. ἔξοδοι κοιναί : i.e. 'expeditions of
the confederacy'; cp. c. 11 supra ; this,
which is the antecedent, has been placed
within the relative clause, and then
attracted into the same case as ὅσαι.

καὶ . . καί: the strong co-ordination
occurs three times in this c., ll. 3, 25.

7. τὸ νέον, more usual without the
article ; cp. τὰ νεώτερα 6. 35.

Ἡρακλεῖδαι ἐπειρῶντο . . κατιόντες.
'The sons of Herakles attempted to effect
their return from exile . .' πειρᾶσθαι
with participle, as 7. 139. 7 supra.
Hdt., by the mouth of the Tegeatai, here
makes reference to the all-important
legend of the Expulsion, or Banishment,
and Return of the Herakleids (ἡ κάθοδος
τῶν Ἡρακλειδῶν), the sobriquet in the
fifth century, as this passage among
others proves, for the Dorian Conquest.
One important chapter in the story of
'the Restoration' Hdt. elsewhere (6. 55)
declines to narrate, on the ground that
it has already been put on record by
other writers. That reason has not
operated with him here to preclude his
telling the story of the duel between
Hyllos and Echemos, and the failure of
the first attempt of the 'exiles' to
return. (Cp. Introduction, §§ 7, 8.)

The antecedents of the story of the
Duel are supplied in part by the speech of
the Athenians in c. 27, in part by Thucyd.
1. 9. 2 (cp. Apollod. Biblioth. 2. 8).
The story was that the 'Herakleids' or
'Perseids,' as they were in the last resort (cp. 6. 53), had been deposed by
the 'Pelopids' (the Egyptian by the

Asiatic !), Eurystheus, himself a Perseid,
having first expelled the Herakleids and
then perished in Attica, warring against
them, leaving Atreus (the Pelopid) in
possession at Mykenai.

To this 'fytte' succeeds the Duel of
Hyllos and the 'Arkadian' king recorded
in this place by Hdt. Thereafter for
three generations, a century, the Herakleids abandon the attempt to 'return,'
until, as leaders of the Dorians, and led
by the one-eyed Aitolian Oxylos, they
cross from Naupaktos, and effect the
conquests of the three great districts,
Argolis, Laconia, Messenia.

The subjection of Herakles to Eurystheus appears in Homer (Il. 15. 639 f.),
where the Hero is despatched to Hell to
fetch the Hound (Il. 8. 363 ff., Od. 11.
617–627). Herakles also figures as the
enemy of the Neleids (Il. 11. 689 ff.).
Is this a Dorian Herakles ! The Iliad
of course will know nothing of Dorians
as such. How old the 'Herakleid'
legend is one can hardly say ; Tyrtaios,
Fr. 2, in which it appears (though
not explicitly as a 'Return'), even if
genuine, is not older than the middle of
the seventh century B.C. The expedition of Eurystheus into Attica against
Hyllos and the Herakleids was narrated
by Hekataios, cp. Longinus 27. 2 (ed.²
Vahlen p. 41) and Pherekydes (Anton.
Lib. Metam. c. 33, Mythogr. Gr. ed.
Westermann p. 230). Cp. Diodor. 4. 38.
Such elder writers as these are covered
by Thucydides' remarkable phrase : αἱ
τὰ σαφέστατα Πελοποννησίων μνήμῃ παρὰ
τῶν πρότερον δεδεγμένοι l.c. Before Hdt.
wrote this passage there was undoubtedly
a rich prose literature on Herakles and
the Herakleids, to say nothing of the
poetic development attested by Hesiod,
Pindar, and the dramatists ; and in
regard to Hdt. it is especially to be
remembered that his uncle Panyasis had
composed an epic on Herakles in 9000
verses ; Suidas s.v. Πανύασις. Cp.
Introduction, § 10.

μετὰ τὸν Εὐρυσθέος θάνατον κατιόντες ἐς Πελοπόννησον· τότε
εὑρόμεθα τοῦτο διὰ πρῆγμα τοιόνδε. ἐπεὶ μετὰ Ἀχαιῶν καὶ
Ἰώνων τῶν τότε ἐόντων ἐν Πελοποννήσῳ ἐκβοηθήσαντες ἐς 10
τὸν Ἰσθμὸν ἱζόμεθα ἀντίοι τοῖσι κατιοῦσι, τότε ὦν λόγος
Ὕλλον ἀγορεύσασθαι ὡς χρεὼν εἴη τὸν μὲν στρατὸν τῷ
στρατῷ μὴ ἀνακινδυνεύειν συμβάλλοντα, ἐκ δὲ τοῦ Πελο-
ποννησίου στρατοπέδου τὸν ἂν σφέων αὐτῶν κρίνωσι εἶναι
ἄριστον, τοῦτόν οἱ μουνομαχῆσαι ἐπὶ διακειμένοισι. ἔδοξέ τε 15
τοῖσι Πελοποννησίοισι ταῦτα εἶναι ποιητέα καὶ ἔταμον ὅρκιον
ἐπὶ λόγῳ τοιῷδε, ἢν μὲν Ὕλλος νικήσῃ τὸν Πελοποννησίων
ἡγεμόνα, κατιέναι Ἡρακλείδας ἐπὶ τὰ πατρώια, ἢν δὲ νικηθῇ,
τὰ ἔμπαλιν Ἡρακλείδας ἀπαλλάσσεσθαι καὶ ἀπάγειν τὴν
στρατιὴν ἑκατόν τε ἐτέων μὴ ζητῆσαι κάτοδον ἐς Πελο- 20

---

8 μετ' ΒΡz ‖ εὐρυσθένεος S, Marc.   9 ἐπείτε! van H.   10
πελοπονήσω Β ap. Holder ‖ ἐκβωθήσαντες van H.   11 ἀντίον Β
12 ἀγορήσασθαι C, Grashof, van H. ‖ χρεὼν CPz, van H.   13 συμ-
βαλοντα (sic) α   14 ἂν σφεων Αz ‖ αὐτέων z ‖ εἶναι om. Ρ   16
ὅρκια ΒC, Schaefer   17 τῶν S   18 ἐπὶ . . Ἡρακλείδας om. Β
‖ πατρῶια ΑΒ : πατρῶα C : πατρῷα z

---

9. **εὑρόμεθα** : cp. c. 6 supra, and 3.
148 εὑρήσεται τιμωρίην—neither passage,
however, is quite exactly parallel with
this, ἀλεωρή, τιμωρίη, being more concrete than τοῦτο. Cp. l. 24 infra.

μετὰ Ἀχαιῶν. Hdt. fully shares
the fifth-century theory that the Achaians
were to be found in the Peloponnesos
long before the Dorians ; cp. 8. 73.

10. **Ἰώνων τῶν τότε ἐόντων ἐν Πελοποννήσῳ** : cp. 8. 73 ; most of the Ionians
were supposed to have migrated into
Asia via Athens, cp. 1. 145. (Blakesley's
idea that the Megarians are here intended
is unfortunate.)

ἐς τὸν Ἰσθμόν : the scene is laid
by Pausanias also (1. 44. 10 ad f.) on
the frontiers of Korinthia and Megaris.

12. **Ὕλλον** : the son of Herakles, cp.
7. 204, as here ' goes without saying.'

ἀγορεύσασθαι : a unique instance
of the middle use in this verb; edicendum
curasse, Baehr ; but cp. App. Crit.

14. **στρατοπέδου**=στρατιᾶς, στρατοῦ.

15. **μουνομαχῆσαι**, to engage in a
μονομαχία, or ' single combat ' ; cp. 5. 1,
7. 104 ; in c. 27 infra the word is used
in a somewhat different sense (if the
reading is correct).

ἐπὶ διακειμένοισι : cp. ἐπὶ λόγῳ
τοιῷδε just below ; συγκειμένοισι would be
more in accord with usage ; cp. 3. 58, c.

52 infra, etc.   Hesiod, Scut. Her. 20 ὣς
γάρ οἱ διέκειτο θεοὶ δ' ἐπιμάρτυροι ἦσαν.

ἔδοξε : a decision, decree.

16. **ἔταμον ὅρκιον** : ὅρκιον is properly
the neut. adj. ; cp. L. & S., ' to slay the
sacrificial animal for the treaty '=' to
make a solemn agreement.' So ὅρκιον,
ὅρκια come to stand for the treaty itself,
in such phrases as ὅρκιον ποιεῖσθαι 1. 141,
etc. μένειν τὸ ὅρκιον κατὰ χώρην in
immediate juxtaposition with τάμνοντες
ὅρκια 4. 201.

17. **τὸν Πελοποννησίων ἡγεμόνα**
turns out to be not Atreus but the
Arkadian king Echemos! The term
' Peloponnesian ' in any case involves no
anachronism : ex hypothesi the Pelopids
are in possession and the name of Pelops
given to the peninsula, cp. Thuc. l.c.

18. **τὰ πατρώια**, sc. γέρεα.

19. **τὰ ἔμπαλιν**: 1. 207 ἔχω γνώμην
. . τὰ ἔμπαλιν ἢ οὗτοι, cp. 56 infra
Ἀθηναῖα δὲ . . ἦισαν τὰ ἔμπαλιν ἢ
Λακεδαιμόνιοι, seem to show that Schweighaeuser's e contrario, vicissim, is right
(Stein takes it here=ὀπίσω with ἀπαλλάσσεσθαι—which is strong enough in
itself : the position also favours the
former rendering).

20. **ἑκατόν τε ἐτέων**: i.e. three generations, 2. 142, cp. 7. 171 (Hyllos)—(1)
Kleodaios ; (2) Aristomachos ; (3) his

πόννησον. προεκρίθη τε δὴ ἐκ πάντων τῶν συμμάχων ἐθελοντὴς
Ἔχεμος ὁ Ἠερόπου τοῦ Κηφέος στρατηγός τε ἐὼν καὶ βασιλεὺς
ἡμέτερος, καὶ ἐμουνομάχησέ τε καὶ ἀπέκτεινε Ὕλλον. ἐκ
τούτου τοῦ ἔργου εὑρόμεθα ἐν Πελοποννησίοισί γε τοῖσι τότε
25 καὶ ἄλλα γέρεα μεγάλα, τὰ διατελέομεν ἔχοντες, καὶ τοῦ
κέρεος τοῦ ἑτέρου αἰεὶ ἡγεμονεύειν κοινῆς ἐξόδου γινομένης.
ὑμῖν μέν νυν ὦ Λακεδαιμόνιοι οὐκ ἀντιεύμεθα, ἀλλὰ διδόντες
αἴρεσιν ὁκοτέρου βούλεσθε κέρεος ἄρχειν παρίεμεν· τοῦ δὲ
ἑτέρου φαμὲν ἡμέας ἱκνέεσθαι ἡγεμονεύειν κατά περ ἐν τῷ
30 πρόσθε χρόνῳ. χωρίς τε τούτου τοῦ ἀπηγημένου ἔργου
ἀξιονικότεροι εἰμὲν Ἀθηναίων ταύτην τὴν τάξιν ἔχειν. πολλοὶ
μὲν γὰρ καὶ εὖ ἔχοντες πρὸς ὑμέας ἡμῖν, ἄνδρες Σπαρτιῆται,

---

21 δὴ om. S ‖ τῶν om. ΒΡz, Holder, van H.   22 ἠρόπου C :
ἠροπέου Marc. ‖ φυγέος Β : Phrygis Valla : Κηφέος coni. Paulmier et Stein,
recepi cum van H. : Φηγέος   23 τε : σε R   24 ἐν τοῖσι z ‖
γε Stein : τε ABC : om. reliqui   26 ἀεὶ Β, Holder   29 <ἐς>
ἡμέας Koen, van H. ‖ ἱκνεῖσθαι van H. : ἱκέσθαι C : om. S   30
πρόσθεν az   31 ἀξιονικώτεροι ἦμεν Marc.   32 γάρ τε καὶ z

---

three sons, Temenos, Kresphontes, Aristodemos ; cp. 7. 204, 8. 131, 137 ; also 6.
52. The condition 'lets the cat out of
the bag,' i.e. anticipates the 'Return.'
Diodor. 4. 58 gives fifty years as the limit.
21. προεκρίθη τε . . ἐθελοντής : this
arrangement, a selection of volunteers, is
perhaps necessary to explain why Hyllos
was not faced by the Πελοποννησίων
ἡγεμών—but we are left to discover for
ourselves that this title could not be
applied to Echemos. The 'Peloponnesian
symmachy,' be it observed, is in full
swing a century before the 'Restoration.'
22. Ἔχεμος ὁ Ἠερόπου τοῦ Κηφέος :
Echemos was known to Pindar, Ol. 10.
66 ὁ δὲ πάλᾳ κυδαίνων Ἔχεμος Τεγέαν.
Diodoros l.c. adds nothing to Hdt.
Pausanias, 1. 41. 2, 8. 5. 1, shows some
variation in the traditions : in the former
passage dating the event 'to the reign of
Orestes,' in the latter correcting the
date, and making Echemos son of
Aeropos (son of Kepheus, son of Aleus),
and successor of Lykourgos as king of
Arkadia, husband moreover of Timandra,
daughter of Tyndareus. Pausanias (8.
53. 10) saw at Tegea Ἀλέου οἰκίαν καὶ
Ἐχέμου μνῆμα καὶ ἐπειργασμένην ἐς
στήλην τὴν Ἐχέμου πρὸς τὸν Ὕλλον μάχην.
On Plutarch Thes. 32 cp. c. 73 infra.
Cp. App. Crit.
25. ἄλλα γέρεα : Blakesley infers that

the Tegeatai had a privileged position
in the Spartan symmachy, 'the other
wing,' when the forces were purely
Peloponnesian, and even in time of peace
special privileges in Sparta, to which,
rather than to any personal influence,
he ascribes the weight of Chileus, c. 9
supra.
28. ἄρχειν (varied with ἡγεμονεύειν
above and below) must be doubled for
the sense, or αὐτό supplied. ἱκνέεσθαι
with ἐν 6. 57, without ἐν 2. 36. With
the sense cp. also 6. 84 μᾶλλον τοῦ
ἱκνευμένου.
30. ἀπηγημένου : passive, cp. 1. 207.
31. ἀξιονικότεροι : cp. 7. 187, c. 27
infra.
πολλοὶ μὲν γάρ . . ἀγῶνες ἀγωνίδαται : 1. 66 supplies the commentary on
this statement, at least to some extent.
32. εὖ ἔχοντες from the speaker's
point of view. In praising themselves
the Tegeans are on comparatively safe
ground ; in depreciating the Athenians
the speaker 'gives himself away.' The
want of tact in this speech is quite primitive, or Pelasgian ! These Arkadians
(1) remind the Lakedaimonians that the
Spartan Hegemony is a comparatively
modern invention, (2) glorify themselves
for having kept the 'Herakleids' (=
Dorians) a century out of the Peloponnesos, (3) remind the Spartans of many

ἀγῶνες ἀγωνίδαται, πολλοὶ δὲ καὶ πρὸς ἄλλους. οὕτω ὧν δίκαιον ἡμέας ἔχειν τὸ ἕτερον κέρας <μᾶλλον> ἤ περ 'Αθηναίους· οὐ γάρ σφι ἐστὶ ἔργα οἷά περ ἡμῖν κατερ- 35 γασμένα, οὔτ' ὧν καινὰ οὔτε παλαιά."

Οἱ μὲν ταῦτα ἔλεγον, 'Αθηναῖοι δὲ πρὸς ταῦτα ὑπεκρίναντο 27 τάδε. "ἐπιστάμεθα μὲν σύνοδον τήνδε μάχης εἴνεκα συλλεγῆναι πρὸς τὸν βάρβαρον, ἀλλ' οὐ λόγων· ἐπεὶ δὲ ὁ Τεγεήτης προέθηκε παλαιά καὶ καινὰ λέγειν τὰ ἑκατέροισι ἐν τῷ παντὶ χρόνῳ κατέργασται χρηστά, ἀναγκαίως ἡμῖν ἔχει δηλῶσαι 5 πρὸς ὑμέας ὅθεν ἡμῖν πατρώιον ἐστὶ ἐοῦσι χρηστοῖσι αἰεὶ πρώτοισι εἶναι μᾶλλον ἤ 'Αρκάσι. 'Ηρακλείδας, τῶν οὗτοι

- 33 ἀγῶνας s ‖ ἄλλους : πολλοὺς B   34 δικαιότερον Naber appr. van H. : ἡμέας δίκαιον s ‖ <μᾶλλον> Stein³   35 σφί ἐστι ABR(SV), Holder, van H.   27. 2 σύλλογον τόνδε Naber   4 <καὶ> παλαιά? Stein, prob. van H. ‖ καινὰ : νέα S   5 <καὶ> ἡμῖν? Kallenberg   6 πατρώιον ἐστὶ P : πατρῶιον ἐστὶν Marc. : πατρῷόν ἐστι s   7 μᾶλλον om. S, Gaisford ‖ ἤ <περ> Naber ‖ οὗτοι post φασὶ Pz, om. Marc.

---

a gallant fight successfully waged against them more recently! After such a speech it is almost an inconsequence to be content with second choice! And then to disparage the Athenians, with Marathon in memory, and the heroism of Olympiodoros under their very eyes (c. 21 supra)! But perhaps this last achievement had not taken place when the dispute for precedence arose; the Athenians make no reference thereto.

27. 1. 'Αθηναῖοι δέ. The Athenian reply is judicious and tactful, and exhibits many merits (not including modesty) which were conspicuous by their absence in the speech of 'the Tegean.' The Athenian speaker might have been Aristeides (c. 29 infra); Plutarch (Aristeid. 12) says it was, but puts a different, a shorter and a still more tactful, speech into his mouth, without any Herakleida, Argives, Amazons, or Marathon in it.

2. σύνοδον . . συλλεγῆναι: a σύνοδος may be a political and formal assembly, a periodic meeting; cp. Thuc. 1. 96, etc. In c. 43 infra Ἑλλήνων σύνοδον appears to be polemical; here there is a play on both senses.

In the following antithesis ἔργων might have been more delicate than μάχης and καὶ οὐ than ἀλλ' οὐ. The Athenian orator is a plain - spoken man. The

emphasis placed on μάχη is significant. The Athenians are there not to bandy words with the brethren but to do battle with the barbarian. That is the Athenian cue all along; cp. c. 7 supra.

5. ἀναγκαίως . . ἔχει: cp. 8. 140.

7. μᾶλλον ἤ 'Αρκάσι: the meaning is obvious, yet the phrase is ambiguous, added perhaps because without it the Athenian would be advancing a claim even against the Spartan. Taken strictly the phrase leaves the primacy of the Athenians arguable even against the Spartans. The Spartans may, however, treat the question as purely one between Arkadians and Athenians, ἡμῖν μᾶλλον ἤ 'Αρκάσι πατρώιον ἐστὶ πρώτοισι εἶναι, even though the Athenians, little more than a year before, had been claiming the lead at sea; 8. 3.

'Ηρακλείδας: cp. previous c. The Athenian service to the Herakleids is a service to the ancestors of Pausanias and Euryanax, and to the leaders of the Dorians. 'All Hellenes'—for Hellenes were already Hellenes in those days— drove them out (cp. Diodor. 4. 57, Pausan. 1. 32. 6 etc.). But the speaker can hardly mean to impugn the Hellenism of Athenians or of Herakleids. ἐς τοὺς ἀνικοίατο is in any case a saving clause, though, strictly speaking, it covers Athens.

φασὶ ἀποκτεῖναι τὸν ἡγεμόνα ἐν Ἰσθμῷ, τοῦτο μὲν τούτους,
πρότερον ἐξελαυνομένους ὑπὸ πάντων Ἑλλήνων ἐς τοὺς ἀπι-
10 κοίατο φεύγοντες δουλοσύνην πρὸς Μυκηναίων, μοῦνοι ὑποδεξάμενοι τὴν Εὐρυσθέος ὕβριν κατείλομεν, σὺν ἐκείνοισι μάχῃ
νικήσαντες τοὺς τότε ἔχοντας Πελοπόννησον. τοῦτο δὲ Ἀργείους
τοὺς μετὰ Πολυνείκεος ἐπὶ Θήβας ἐλάσαντας, τελευτήσαντας
τὸν αἰῶνα καὶ ἀτάφους κειμένους, στρατευσάμενοι ἐπὶ τοὺς
15 Καδμείους ἀνελέσθαι τε τοὺς νεκροὺς φαμεν καὶ θάψαι τῆς

---

8 ἐν <τῷ> Ἰσθμῷ ! Kallenberg ‖ τοῦτο μὲν om. ß, Holder   9
πάντων τῶν Cz   10 <ἡμεῖς> μοῦνοι ! Stein⁽²⁾   11 εὐρυσθενέος P :
εὐρυσθένεος Sz ‖ κείνοισι z   15 φαμεν τοὺς νεκροὺς S ‖ τῆς om. z

---

10. **Μυκηναίων**: Eurystheus being
lord of Mykenai (cp. Thuc. 1. 9. 2), τὴν
Εὐρυσθέος ὕβριν κατείλομεν : cp. notes to
previous chapter. According to Diodoros
l.c. Theseus, Hyllos, and Iolaos were in
command and Eurystheus fell by the
hand of Hyllos ; all his sons also perished
in the battle. (This would leave Atreus
in undisturbed possession of Mykenai.)
Iolaos is the son of Iphikles, twin brother
to Herakles ; cp. Pindar *Pyth.* 11. 60
etc.   In *Pyth.* 9. 80 f. it is Iolaos who
deals Eurystheus the death-blow.

12. **τοὺς τότε ἔχοντας** Π. leaves the
withers of Spartan Dorians unwrung,
for *ex hypothesi* they were later comers.
τοῦτο δέ, 'in the second place,'
corresponding with τοῦτο μέν *supra* ; cp.
7. 6. 5 *supra*.

**Ἀργείους τοὺς μετὰ Πολυνείκεος
ἐπὶ Θήβας**. This expedition (ἔλασις) of
Polyneikes and the Argives against
Thebes is the story of the *Septem contra
Thebas* which Aischylos had popularized
in 472 B.C. at Athens and Sophokles
assumes in the action of the *Antigone*,
produced in 440 B.C. (?), in which, however, the heroine anticipates, so far as her
brother is concerned, the pious act here
ascribed to the Athenians. Amphiaraos
was under ground in Boiotia ; cp. 8. 134.
Tydeus too was duly buried in Thebes
according to the *Iliad* 14. 114, which
places the event in the generation before
the Trojan war, 4. 376 ff. Pindar (*Ol.*
6. 15) erects, indeed, funeral pyres to all
the Seven in Thebes. The doctrine that
it was the Athenians who performed the
last rites for the Argive heroes, and that
too by force of arms, supplies the argument to the *Suppliants* of Euripides.
An improved version represented the
same end as effected without violence,
Plutarch, *Theseus* 29 συνέπραξε δὲ καὶ

Ἀδράστῳ τὴν ἀναίρεσιν τῶν ὑπὸ τῇ
Καδμείᾳ πεσόντων, οὐχ ὡς Εὐριπίδης
ἐποίησεν ἐν τραγωδίᾳ μάχῃ τῶν Θηβαίων
κρατήσας, ἀλλὰ πείσας καὶ σπεισάμενος·
οὕτω γὰρ οἱ πλεῖστοι λέγουσι· Φιλόχορος
δὲ καὶ σπονδὰς περὶ νεκρῶν ἀναιρέσεως
γενέσθαι πρώτας ἐκείνας. The rank and
file were buried at Eleutherai, the leaders
at Eleusis, *ibid.* Aischylos had apparently in his *Eleusinioi* represented
Theseus as effecting the arrangement
peacefully, *ibid.*, but Pausan. 1. 39. 2
appears to prove Athenian the view here
followed by Hdt., while the peaceful
solution was a Theban hypothesis ; none
doubted by that time the burial at
Eleusis, where the tombs were on view.
These Eleusinian tombs are here referred
to, and must be part of the fifth-century
argument ; they must have been graves
of the 'Mykenaian' type and age, such
as have been discovered at Eleusis ;
cp. *Ephemeris Archaiologike*, 1898, pp.
29 ff. It would have been too much to
expect the Athenian orator to admit that
in the Mykenaian age Eleusis (to say
nothing of Eleutherai) was quite independent of Athens. The Athenian claims
in regard to the Argive heroes may (I
suppose) be regarded as part of the
Theseian legend, which was cultivated
assiduously in Athens from the days of
Peisistratos onwards. The conflict between this passage and the *Antigone*,
compared with the notorious agreement
between *Ant.* 905 ff. and Hdt. 3. 119,
might support the theory of the prior
composition of Bks. 7–9, even if the
exact date of the production of the
Antigone is not fully ascertained ; cp.
Introduction, §§ 7, 8.

14. **τὸν αἰῶνα** = βίον : cp. 7. 46 *supra*.
15. **Καδμείους** : i.e. the prae-Boiotian
inhabitants of Thebes ; cp. Thuc. 1. 12. 3,

ἡμετέρης ἐν Ἐλευσῖνι. ἔστι δὲ ἡμῖν ἔργον εὖ ἔχον καὶ ἐς
Ἀμαζονίδας τὰς ἀπὸ Θερμώδοντος ποταμοῦ ἐσβαλούσας κοτὲ
ἐς γῆν τὴν Ἀττικήν, καὶ ἐν τοῖσι Τρωικοῖσι πόνοισι οὐδαμῶν
ἐλειπόμεθα. ἀλλ' οὐ γάρ τι προέχει τούτων ἐπιμεμνῆσθαι·

---

17 ἀμαζίδας a ‖ τὰς : τὰς ἀποθήκας τὰς z ‖ θερμόδοντος R   18
ἡρωϊκοῖσι Β   19 ἐλιπόμεθα a : λειπόμεθα Β ‖ προύχει τουτέων z

---

elsewhere by Hdt. (e.g. 5. 57) identified
with 'Phoenicians,' and supposed to
have been driven out by the Argive
Epigonoí (cp. 5. 61).

16. **ἔστι δὲ ἡμῖν ἔργον εὖ ἔχον**: the
third heroic achievement of the Athenians
is their victory over the Amazons who
had invaded Attica from the Thermodon.
εὖ ἔχον, cp. c. 26 *supra*. The connexion
of Attica with the Amazon myth, or
legend, is post-Homeric, or non-Homeric
(*Il.* 3. 184 ff., 6. 186), but is fully
established in the fifth century, and like
the legend of the Seven incorporated
with the Acts of Theseus. Aischylos,
Eumenid. 655 ff., treats the case as
notorious (458 B.C.), and connects the
name of the Areiopagos with the
Amazonian cult of Ares :

πάγον δ' Ἄρειον τόνδ' Ἀμαζόνων ἔδραν
σκηνάς θ' ὅτ' ἦλθον Θησέως κατὰ φθόνον
στρατηλατοῦσαι, καὶ πόλιν νεόπτολιν
τήνδ' ὑψίπυργον ἀντεπύργωσαν τότε,
Ἄρει δ' ἔθυον, ἔνθεν ἐστ' ἐπώνυμος
πέτρα πάγος τ' Ἄρειος.

Pindar had celebrated the wedding of
Theseus and the Amazonian Queen (cp.
Plutarch, *Theseus* c. 78 ; Pausan. 1. 2. 1).
The archaeological evidence (ceramic)
tends, however, to show that the connexion with Theseus is not really
ancient : Herakles, not Theseus, appears
on black figured vases with the Amazons,
and his place is taken by Theseus on
the red figured (cp. Graef *ap.* Pauly-
Wissowa, i. 1773, 1777). The growing
importance and expansion of the Theseus
legend dates from about the middle of the
sixth century. Plutarch, *Thes.* 27, shows
that the Atthidographers (Hellanikos,
Kleidemos, and others) were busy on the
subject, as probably the Logographers,
Mythographers, before them had been ;
and the epic of Theseus (Θησηίς, Aristot.
Poet. 8 = 1451 A, Plut. *op. c.* 28) was
perhaps an earlier work (cp. Bergk, *Gr.
Lit.* ii. (1883) 72) : the *Amazonis*, or
Amazonia, ascribed to Homer by Suidas
sub v. Ὅμηρος, Bergk *l.c.*, perhaps too
sceptically, regards as a literary hypo-

thesis (might not the *Amazonia* be a
section of the *Theseis* ?). The battle of
the Amazons was represented in the great
fresco by Mikon in the *Poikile Stoa* (cp.
Aristoph. *Lysistr.* 678, Pausan. 1. 15. 2),
and Pheidias placed the same subject in
relief upon the shield of the Virgin (E.
Gardner, *Anc. Ath.* 349), and again on the
metopes on the west front of her temple
(*ibid.* 282).

There is nothing surprising in Hdt.,
or even an Athenian orator of 479 B.C.,
taking the story of the Amazonian war
for granted. Hdt.'s other story of the
Amazons (4. 110–117) involves a war of
the Greeks on the Thermodon, and may
be connected with the cycle of Herakles-
legends at least in the first instance
(cp. Pausan. 2. 1. 1) : at any rate in this
place no hint occurs that the Amazons
in Attica were other than the aggressors.
The form **Ἀμαζονίδας** here compared
with **Ἀμάζονες** there emphasizes the
independence both of the sources and of
the composition of the two passages, but
leaves the question of priority open.
(In the *Proem* 1. 1–4 the war with the
Amazons does not rank with the *causes
célèbres* of wars between Europe and
Asia.)

17. **ἀπὸ Θερμώδοντος ποταμοῦ**: the
river here named is the Thermodon by
Themiskyra on the Pontos, 4. 86, cp.
2. 104, albeit there was a stream of the
same name in Boiotia, near Tanagra ; c.
43 *infra*. The Asianic Thermodon, or
its neighbourhood, is in all ancient
authorities from Aischylos to Ammianus
(22. 8. 17) closely associated with the
Amazons, though some authorities (e.g.
Aischylos, *Prom.* 743 cp. 422) regarded
them originally as immigrants thither,
while others (e.g. Ammianus) regarded
the Thermodon as their birth-place.

18. **ἐν τοῖσι Τρωικοῖσι πόνοισι**. The
curtness of this reference to Troy is,
indeed, significant. As a matter of fact
the remarkable thing is what a poor
figure Athens cuts in the Trojan war ;
cp. 7. 161.

19. **προέχει**: *nihil proficit*, Schweig-

20 καὶ γὰρ ἂν χρηστοὶ τότε ἐόντες ὡυτοὶ νῦν ἂν εἶεν φλαυρό-
τεροι, καὶ τότε ἐόντες φλαῦροι νῦν ἂν εἶεν ἀμείνονες. παλαιῶν
μέν νυν ἔργων ἅλις ἔστω· ἡμῖν δὲ εἰ μηδὲν ἄλλο †ἐστὶ
ἀποδεδεγμένον, ὥσπερ ἐστὶ πολλά τε καὶ εὖ ἔχοντα εἰ τεοῖσι
καὶ ἄλλοισι Ἑλλήνων, ἀλλὰ καὶ ἀπὸ τοῦ ἐν Μαραθῶνι ἔργου
25 ἄξιοι εἰμὲν τοῦτο τὸ γέρας ἔχειν καὶ ἄλλα πρὸς τούτῳ,
οἵτινες μοῦνοι Ἑλλήνων δὴ μουνομαχήσαντες τῷ Πέρσῃ καὶ
ἔργῳ τοσούτῳ ἐπιχειρήσαντες περιεγενόμεθα καὶ ἐνικήσαμεν
ἔθνεα ἕξ τε καὶ τεσσεράκοντα. ἆρ' οὐ δίκαιοι εἰμὲν ἔχειν

---

20 ἂν om. z ‖ χρηστοί τε ἐόντες τότε S ‖ ὡυτοὶ C : ὡυτοὶ Pꜱ : ἑωυτοὶ B
‖ φλαυρότερον R   21 ἂν εἶεν repetitum damn. van H.   22 ἐστί :
cf. comment.   23 ἀποδεδειγμένον z ‖ ὥσπέρ ἐστι ABP   26 an
τρομαχήσαντες ? cf. Simonid. Fr. 90   27 <τε> καὶ van H.   28 τε
del. van H. ‖ τεσσαράκοντα B

---

haeuser ; haud praestat, Stein. Op. cc.
4, 22 supra, etc.
20. καὶ γὰρ ἂν . . ἀμείνονες: the
sentiment anticipates any criticism based
on the obscurity of the Athenian record
in the Trojan war. Converted into a
maxim by the historian himself it becomes
a reason for embracing all cities and
societies whether great or small in his
review ; op. 1. 5.
22. εἰ μηδὲν ἄλλο ἐστὶ ἀποδεδεγμένον :
ἐστί is grammatically impossible and
should be ἦν or εἴη (Stein). With ἐστί
just below (the source of the corruptela ?)
subaud. ἀποδεδεγμένα (brachylogy).
24. τοῦ ἐν Μαραθῶνι ἔργου. If this
speech were authentic, we should have to
admit that ten years had been enough
to start the Marathonian legend on a
colossal scale : like the infant Herakles
it strangles snakes in its cradle. The
formula here has three notable points
fully developed. (1) The omission of
the Plataians from the muster-roll of
Marathon, the 'aloneness' of the Athenians in their hour of need : not a very
graceful, or probable, touch on the battle-
field of Plataia, even if the Spartans
could bear to be reminded that they
had been conspicuous by their absence at
Marathon : μουνομαχήσαντες τῷ Πέρσῃ is
meant to emphasize the μοῦνα, not to
represent the battle as a duel between
Athens and the Persian ; for 'the
Persian' is but one of forty-six nations.
τῷ Μήδῳ might have been expected
here. But cp. App. Crit. (2) The
Athenian initiative and forwardness
(ἔργῳ τοσούτῳ ἐπιχειρήσαντες) : the
note which grows into the fiction : πρῶτοι

μὲν γὰρ Ἑλλήνων πάντων τῶν ἡμεῖς ἴδμεν
δρόμῳ ἐς πολεμίους ἐχρήσαντο, πρῶτοι δὲ
ἀνέσχοντο ἐσθῆτά τε Μηδικὴν ὁρέοντες καὶ
τοὺς ἄνδρας ταύτην ἐσθημένους, 6. 112.
(3) "We defeated six-and-forty nations."
The Athenian orator on the field of
Plataia in 479 B.C. is already in possession
of the army-list of Xerxes 7. 60-80,
which enumerates just forty-six ἔθνεα κατ'
ἤπειρον στρατευόμενα. The first alternative that presents itself is to choose
between the authenticity of the speech
and that of the list, as a list of what it
professes to be : either the speech is not
genuine, or the list was made long before
480 B.C. But the list may be made
older than 480 B.C. without guaranteeing
the authenticity of the speech. Are we
in the presence of an Athenian development and gross exaggeration intended to
elevate Marathon above Plataia, and the
defeat of the army of Dareios under
Datis and Artaphrenes at Marathon
above the defeat of the army of Xerxes
under Mardonios and Artabazos at
Plataia ? How came Hdt. by such a
stroke as this ? He certainly did not
mean it as a satire upon Athenian
braggartness. Had he previously written
the story of Marathon, he might have
been saved from such an inconsequence :
this point supports the hypothesis of
the prior composition of Bks. 7-9 ;
cp. Introduction, §§ 7, 8. This view of
Marathon throws Salamis also completely
into the shade : that too was a part of
the anti-Themistoclean tendency which
had long been at work when Hdt. first
composed his history of the war.
28. ἆρα asks the question with some

ταύτην τὴν τάξιν ἀπὸ τούτου μούνου τοῦ ἔργου; ἀλλ' οὐ
γὰρ ἐν τῷ τοιῷδε τάξιος εἵνεκα στασιάζειν πρέπει, ἄρτιοι 30
εἰμὲν πείθεσθαι ὑμῖν ὦ Λακεδαιμόνιοι, ἵνα δοκέει ἐπιτηδεότατον ἡμέας εἶναι ἑστάναι καὶ κατ' οὑστινας· πάντῃ γὰρ
τεταγμένοι πειρησόμεθα εἶναι χρηστοί. ἐξηγέεσθε δὲ ὡς
πεισομένων."

Οἱ μὲν ταῦτα ἀμείβοντο, Λακεδαιμονίων δὲ ἀνέβωσε ἅπαν 35
τὸ στρατόπεδον Ἀθηναίους ἀξιονικοτέρους εἶναι ἔχειν τὸ κέρας
ἤ περ Ἀρκάδας. οὕτω δὴ ἔσχον οἱ Ἀθηναῖοι καὶ ὑπερεβάλοντο
τοὺς Τεγεήτας.

Μετὰ δὲ ταῦτα ἐτάσσοντο ὧδε οἱ ἐπιφοιτῶντές τε καὶ οἱ 28

---

29 μόνου Bβ   30 ἄρτι εἴοιμεν β   31 δοκέῃ z ‖ ἐπιτηδεώτατον
CPz, van H.   32 πάντοι R   37 ὑπερεβάλλοντο SMarc. z   28. 1
ταῦτα om. P: del. van H. ‖ ἐπιφοιτέοντές Stein¹, van H.

---

surprise and indignation (cp. 7. 17
supra): 'is it not right, we should like
to know, for us to have this privileged
position on the strength of this one
achievement even if it stood alone ?'—
But why is no allusion whatever made
to the splendid services of Olympiodoros
and his 300 (cc. 21, 22 *supra*) ? Is the
sequence of events correctly reproduced
by Hdt. ? Did this dispute succeed
that service ? Did the Athenians make
such a speech as is here put into their
mouths ? In any case Hdt. can hardly
be acquitted of inconsequence.

29. ἀλλ' οὐ γὰρ κτλ. Who would
not be glad to believe that the Athenian
spokesman uttered these words, or words
to just this effect, instinct with the
spirit of loyalty, discipline, practical
wisdom, sweet reasonableness, the εἰωθυῖα
πραότης τοῦ δήμου ? Spoken, or unspoken,
they represent the better temper which
governed the policy and action of Athens
during the whole crisis ; cp. 7. 145, 8.
3, 79, 144, c. 7 *supra* ; but 7. 161 is conceived in a less happy vein, like the
earlier passages of this very speech, or
the *ultima ratio* in c. 11 *supra*. The
end is in better keeping with the
practical result. The moral of the
previous boast might have been to
assign not 'the other wing' but the
whole duty of quelling the foe to the
Athenians. If they had once already
all by themselves defeated the six and
forty nations of Asia, why should they
not do it again ? Why had they
worried the Peloponnesians to come to

their aid ? Why even threatened to
make terms with the enemy ?

30. στασιάζειν : cp. 8. 79.
ἄρτιοι : op. c. 48 *infra*.
31. ἵνα : *ubi*, cp. 8. 115.
33. ἐξηγέεσθε δὲ ὡς πεισομένων. The
imperative is a little ambiguous : (1) give
your interpretation, explanation, decision,
verdict ; or (2) give your orders, as
leaders, cp. cc. 11 *supra*, 66 *infra*.
35. Λακεδαιμονίων ἀνέβωσε κτλ.
The Lakedaimonians κρίνουσι (*sic*) βοῇ
καὶ οὐ ψήφῳ, Thuc. 1. 87. 2. Blakesley
thinks the Spartiates were not sorry to
snub the Tegeatai ; but this view (*a*)
takes the story too much *au pied de la
lettre* ; (*b*) is hardly consistent with the
marked preference shown to the Tegeatai
a little later, c. 28 *infra*. Such inconsistencies are frequent in Hdt. and arise
from the *insouciance* with which he uses
various sources not in complete harmony
with one another. The ingenious
harmonist might indeed prove his ingenuity on the present case : here ἅπαν
τὸ στρατόπεδον Λακεδαιμονίων votes the
other wing to the Athenians ; there οἱ
Σπαρτιῆται—outvoted on this occasion
—take the Tegeatai to themselves—a
graceful consolation ! Such harmony is
worse than silence. Hdt. is unconscious
of the dissonance : the Spartiates no
more admitted the Perioikoi and Helots
to vote in the field than 'between Babyka
and Knakion.'

37. ὑπερεβάλοντο : cp. 7. 163, 8.
140.

28. 1. μετὰ δὲ ταῦτα ἐτάσσοντο. For

ἀρχὴν ἐλθόντες Ἑλλήνων. τὸ μὲν δεξιὸν κέρας εἶχον Λακε-

---

2 ἀρχὴν ἐθέλοντες B : ἀρχειν ἐθέλοντες Marc. z

---

reasons above given it is not credible that the Greek forces were ἄτακτοι (6. 93, cp. Thuc. 8. 105. 2—of ships) in the first position. They had reached Erythrai undoubtedly in some order, but necessarily in a marching order (agmen). Before descending to the position marked by the Androkrateion and Gargaphia ('second position') the column had presumably extended itself into line by a deployment westwards (cp. c. 25. 4 supra), and so developed the 'first position' fully along the ὑπωρέη, from Erythrai past Hysiai into the Plataiis (cp. c. 15 supra). In this first position there must have been an order, with a centre (or double centre) and two wings; but whether the Lakedaimonians were as yet on the right or on the left is a disputable problem (cp. c. 21. 1 supra).

The words which here follow, in making a distinction between οἱ ἐπιφοιτῶντες and οἱ ἀρχὴν ἐλθόντες on the Greek side, suggest that in the second position, or just before reaching the second position, the Greeks received considerable reinforcements. It may have been the advent of these reinforcements, in successive contingents (ἐπιφοιτῶντες), that in part emboldened the Greeks to advance to the second position. These reinforcements, or some of them, may have reached the Greek Laager by the direct route from Megara, and may have comprised a large part of the Greek centre. The only divisions of which express mention has been made so far are (1) the Megarians, (2) the Athenians, (3) the Lakedaimonians, (4) the Tegeatai. These are the only ones who figure clearly in the first position, at Erythrai. There are, however, other motifs available for the explanation of the advance of the Greeks from the ὑπωρέη to the Asopos-ridge: had the Persian cavalry, on the Dryoskephalai road, nothing to say to it? cp. c. 39 infra, and Appendix VIII. § 5 (7).

2. τὸ μὲν δεξιὸν κέρας: the right wing consists of 11,500 Hoplites (nominal), viz. 10,000 Lakedaimonians (5000 Spartiatai, 5000 Perioikoi) plus 1500 Tegeatai. To these Hdt. would have us add 40,000 helot ψιλοί (35,000 in attendance on the Spartiates, 7 helots

to each citizen, with 5000 more, one for each 'Lakedaimonian'). Stein treats this proportion as the normal levy, and opines that one of the seven was special body-servant (θεράπων) of the Spartiate hoplite, and the six others members of a regiment under the king's command. But (1) where is there any other evidence of such a proportion as the normal one? (2) When were Spartan armies so well supplied with ψιλοί? (3) What record is there of the services of these ψιλοί in the actual fighting? (4) The request of Pausanias for the Athenian τοξόται, c. 60 infra—no doubt from a tainted source — still emphasizes the defect of the Spartan contingent in light troops, and exploits it, if you like. (5) The phraseology here does not suggest a closed or organized corps of 20,000–30,000 helot ψιλοί, but a distributive number of 35,000 ψιλοὶ θεράποντες. (6) Politically, the idea of an organization of a helot corps of 30,000 ψιλοί at Sparta is well-nigh inconceivable: such a corps would have effected a revolution! Even Pausanias, in his subsequent tampering with the helots, has not got such a basis as that to work on, or we should have heard of it; cp. Thuc. 1. 132. 4. (7) The normal allowance of θεράποντες appears rather to have been one per hoplite, cp. 7. 229 (and 186): the emphasis which is here laid on the number 7 suggests that it is abnormal. (8) If the numerical figures in the text are to stand, other employment must be found for the huge number of helots, and may be found, as an Army Service, engaged in forwarding supplies, cp. c. 39 infra. These reasons are sufficient to disprove the fact and figures here; but they leave Hdt. responsible for an egregious blunder. The only rescue for him would be to challenge the text: are the figures corrupt? The testimonia carry them back to Plutarch (Aristeid. 10) (but neither Diodoros nor Trogus recorded them). This assertion that there were seven helots for every Spartan is made not less than five times in this Book (cc. 10, 28, 29 (bis), 61 implicite): this very iteration rouses suspicion of the fact, if not of the text. Few critics will be so hardy as to expose a five-fold systematic and consistent corruptela!

δαιμονίων μύριοι· τούτων δὲ τοὺς πεντακισχιλίους ἐόντας
Σπαρτιήτας ἐφύλασσον ψιλοὶ τῶν εἰλώτων πεντακισχίλιοι καὶ
τρισμύριοι, περὶ ἄνδρα ἕκαστον ἑπτὰ τεταγμένοι. προσεχέας 5
δὲ σφίσι εἵλοντο ἑστάναι οἱ Σπαρτιῆται τοὺς Τεγεήτας καὶ
τιμῆς εἵνεκα καὶ ἀρετῆς· τούτων δ᾽ ἦσαν ὁπλῖται χίλιοι καὶ
πεντακόσιοι. μετὰ δὲ τούτους ἵσταντο Κορινθίων πεντακισχίλιοι, παρὰ δὲ σφίσι εὕροντο παρὰ Παυσανίεω ἑστάναι Ποτειδαιητέων τῶν ἐκ Παλλήνης τοὺς παρεόντας τριηκοσίους. τούτων 10
δὲ ἐχόμενοι ἵσταντο Ἀρκάδες Ὀρχομένιοι ἑξακόσιοι, τούτων

---

3 τουτέων z   4 εἰλωτέων Βz   6 δέ σφισι C : δέ σφι(ν) ceteri
7 τουτέων z ‖ δὲ Β ‖ ἔσαν z   9 δέ σφισι αCz : δέ σφιν   10, 11, 12
τουτέων (ter) z

Otherwise, either καὶ τρισμύριοι .. τεταγμένοι might go, or rather, in view of c.
10 supra, πεντακισχίλιοι καὶ τρισ-, ἑπτὰ
being reduced to δύο, i.e. ψιλοὶ τῶν
εἰλώτων μύριοι, περὶ ἄνδρα ἕκαστον δύο
τεταγμένοι. There may have been 10,000
or 15,000 Helots on the field at Plataia ;
there will hardly have been 35,000—
40,000. The use of φυλάσσειν here is
remarkable ; cp. 6. 75 ὁ φύλακος, ἦν γὰρ
τῶν τις εἰλωτέων (sic), διδοῖ οἱ μάχαιραν.
5. προσεχέας δὲ σφίσι εἵλοντο. This
statement that the Spartiatai chose the
Tegeatai to stand next them in line of
battle καὶ τιμῆς εἵνεκα καὶ ἀρετῆς, to do
them honour, and because they were
brave men, reads curiously in the light
of the last chapter. The two passages,
though in immediate juxtaposition, are
evidently from wholly different sources.
As σφίσι refers expressly to Σπαρτιῆται,
of whom there were but 5000, Hdt.
appears to say that the 1500 Tegeatai
were posted next the Spartiatai, i.e.
between them and the 5000 Perioikoi ;
but σφίσι may perhaps be generalized
so as to cover the whole force from
Laconia.
8. μετὰ δὲ τούτους. Hdt. is review-
ing the line (acies) from right to left.
The contingents from the Korinthian
to the Megarian next enumerated, and
comprising 18,600 Hoplites, form the
centre of the army (= οἱ πολλοί, c. 52
infra) ; and this centre is again divided,
incidentally, into the right centre, οἱ
ἀμφὶ Κορινθίους, c. 69 infra, comprising
11,300 Hoplites, and the left centre, οἱ
ἀμφὶ Μεγαρέας τε καὶ Φλειασίους, ibid.,
comprising 7300 Hoplites, according to
the muster-roll. (To them succeeds the
left wing, consisting of the Athenians
with the Plataians, 8600 men in all.)

Κορινθίων πεντακισχίλιοι : 5000
Hoplites is an unusually large muster
for Korinth. In 435 B.C. Korinth had
3000 Hoplites ready to send to Korkyra,
Thuc. 1. 27. 2, but only embarked
2000, ib. 29. 1. In 418 B.C. they contributed only 2000 to the great muster
at Phleiûs, Thuc. 5. 57. 2. In the
battle of Korinth, 394 B.C., 3000 Hoplites
from Korinth took part, Xen. Hell. 4.
2. 17.
9. εὕροντο is used in an unusual
sense ; cp. c. 26 supra.
ἑστάναι is the syncopated perfect
infin., cp. 1. 17, Soph. Ant. 640, preceded by τοὺς π. τριηκοσίους. Pausanias
has apparently, at least within certain
limits, the right to determine the order
of battle, and assign the various contingents their stations. This might
square very well with the selection by
'the Spartiates' of the Tegeatai as their
next neighbours, less well with the
story of the Atheno-Tegeatan dispute.
Ποτειδαιητέων. The Korinthians
obtained the grace from Pausanias to
have the 300 Poteidaiatai, who were on
the spot, to stand, or laager, next them.
This is another valiant 300 : how they
came to be at Plataia is not clear.
Poteidaia was, of course, a colony of
Korinth's (Thuc. 1. 56. 2), albeit Hdt.
nowhere happens to say so. The town
has had its own reckoning with the
Persian, cp. 8. 126 ff., and how this
gallant 300 got to Plataia is far from
clear : presumably by sea. The addition of the words τῶν ἐκ Παλλήνης (cp.
7. 123) makes it clear what Poteidaia is
meant.
11. ἐχόμενοι, quasi-geographical rather
than military or tactical ; cp. 7. 108. 8.
Ἀρκάδες Ὀρχομένιοι ἑξακόσιοι.

δὲ Σικυώνιοι τρισχίλιοι. τούτων δὲ εἴχοντο Ἐπιδαυρίων
ὀκτακόσιοι. παρὰ δὲ τούτους Τροιζηνίων ἐτάσσοντο χίλιοι,
Τροιζηνίων δὲ ἐχόμενοι Λεπρεητέων διηκόσιοι, τούτων δὲ

12 δ' R ‖ εἴχοντο del. van H.　　　　13 δὲ om. P ‖ τούτους . . παρὰ δὲ
om. R　　　14 Λεπραιετέων z　　　　14, 15 τουτέων (bis) z

The men of Orchomenos are the only
other Arkadians, besides the Tegeatai,
present on the field, the Mantineians
not having arrived in time; cp. c. 77
infra. In the previous year Ἀρκάδες
πάντες had been at the Isthmos under
Kleombrotos, 8. 72; and besides Tegeatai,
Mantineans, Orchomenians, there had
been 1000 Hoplites ἐκ τῆς λοιπῆς Ἀρκαδίης
in the army of Leonidas, 7. 202.
Ἀρκάδες is here introduced to distinguish
Arkadian Orchomenos from Boiotian;
cp. c. 16 supra. So in Thucyd. 5. 61. 3
Ὀρχομενὸν τὸν Ἀρκαδικόν. (In the
Catalogue Boiotian O. is Μινύειος, Il. 2.
511, Arkadian simply πολύμηλος, ib. 605.)
Six hundred seems a small contingent
from the third city of Arkadia: perhaps
the tardy exit of the Mantineians kept
some of the Orchomenians and other
Arkadians at home. It is not clear
what the constitution of Orchomenos
was at this time. Plutarch Mor. 313
cites Theophilos Πελοποννησιακὰ β' in
a way which might seem to imply that
the βασιλεία lasted into the Peloponnesian war, but the term βασιλεύς is
not quite conclusive (cp. 7. 149): the
constitution was certainly aristocratic,
or oligarchic, in 418 B.C. (cp. Thuc. 5.
61. 4). The name appears as Ἐρχομενος
(Ἐρχομενίων) on the coinage of the
fourth century. Orchomenos asserts, or
reasserts, itself in later times; cp. Head,
H.N. 377 f., and c. 16 supra. The only
contingent here for which a commander's
name is preserved, besides the Spartan,
is the Athenian.

12. Σικυώνιοι τρισχίλιοι. Sikyon
had supplied but 15 ships to the navy-
list of Salamis, 8. 43, and had apparently
been unrepresented in the army of
Leonidas (7. 202), and even in that of
Kleombrotos (8. 72); but Sikyonians
were serving under Leotychidas, cc. 102,
105 infra. Sikyon's contingents are
not as a rule numerically specified (cp.
Thuc. 5. 57. 2), but in 394 B.C. it sent
1500 Hoplites to the support of Sparta,
Xenoph. Hell. 4. 2. 16. (The better
form of the name is probably Σεκυών,
cp. Head, H.N. 345 ff.)

Ἐπιδαυρίων ὀκτακόσιοι. Epidauros had been unrepresented at
Thermopylai (7. 202), but had sent a
contingent to the army of Kleombrotos
(8. 72) as well as to the fleet under
Eurybiades (8. 43), and was probably
represented in the fleet of Leotychidas;
the men ranked as Dorians, cp. 8. 43.
13. Τροιζηνίων χίλιοι. Troizen had
sent men to the army under Kleombrotos
(8. 72) and a small contingent to the
fleet in 480 B.C. (8. 43); in 479 B.C.
they were allowed to have distinguished
themselves at Mykale, c. 105 · infra.
They, too, now counted as Dorians (8.
43), and in 479 B.C. were presumably,
like Korinth, Sikyon, Epidauros, under
oligarchic government; but cp. 8. 41
supra. (The form of the name is
Τροξάνιοι on the Plataian monument;
cp. coinage, Head, p. 371. Τροιζὴν
appears later, e.g. Dittenberger[1] 372.)
14. Λεπρεητέων διηκόσιοι. In 4. 148
Lepreon appears as but one city, or
township of an Hexapolis in the west
Peloponnesos, of 'Minyan,' or at any rate
non-Dorian extraction; cp. 8. 73 Δημίων
δὲ Παρωρεῆται πάντες. The Lepreatis is
the territory of the leading township,
but possibly the 200 Hoplites exhibit
the levy for the whole district. It was,
of course, a bone of contention between
Sparta and Elis; cp. Thuc. 5. 31. 2 etc.
The occurrence recorded by Hdt. in 4.
148 had presumably not taken place, or
was not known to him, when he first
drafted Bk. 9, but Ed. Meyer (G. d.
Alterth. iv. (1901) p. 413) can hardly
be right in referring that passage to the
same occasion as Thuc. l.c. and dating
both well into the 'Attic (i.e. Archidamian) war'; Thuc. records merely an
Eleian raid into Lepreatis, which is
thereupon occupied by a Lakedaimonian
garrison; cp. my note ad l.c. If Meyer
is right that reference would be the
latest, or all but the latest, in Hdt.'s
work, and would confirm the argument
for the priority of Bks. 7-9; in any
case, however, it is prima facie of later
composition than this passage; cp.
Introduction, §§ 7, 8.

Μυκηναίων καὶ Τιρυνθίων τετρακόσιοι, τούτων δὲ ἐχόμενοι 15
Φλειάσιοι χίλιοι, παρὰ δὲ τούτους [ἔστησαν] Ἑρμιονέες τριηκόσιοι. Ἑρμιονέων δὲ ἐχόμενοι ἵσταντο Ἐρετριέων τε καὶ

15 ἐχόμενοι del. van H.   16 ἔστησαν B, Stein¹² (del. Stein³):
ἔστησαν A: ἔστησαν C: ἕστασαν (V): ἕστασαν P: ἕστασαν R(S)z   17
τε om. β

15. **Μυκηναίων καὶ Τιρυνθίων τετρα-κόσιοι.** These ancients, a poor remnant of the 'Perseid' and 'Pelopid' ages, might have 'medized' with a better grace than the Dorian Argives. Their hostility to Argos would seal them to the side of Sparta and of Hellas, of which they might fairly consider themselves the oldest representatives. 'Tiryns' here appears for the first time in the war; 'Mykenai' had sent 80 men to Thermopylai, 7. 202, unless, indeed, those and these alike are 'exiles'? It is hard to see how with Argos neutral, or malevolent, Tiryns and Mykenai could have afforded to send their fighting men to Plataia; but op. c. 12 *supra*. The ruin of Mykenai was still to come or was unknown to Hdt. when he first drafted this passage; cp. 6. 83. (An *obiter dictum* in J. P. Mahaffy's *Survey of Gk. Civilization*, 1897, p. 31, to which Hall's *Oldest Civilization*, 1901, p. 291, directed my attention, treats these Mykenaians and Tirynthians as 'of course exiles' in view of Mahaffy's theory that the destruction (final?) of Mykenai and Tiryns by Argos 'happened in the eighth or early seventh century B.C.' But the names occur upon the Plataian (and Olympian) monuments, and it is not likely that those lists included 'cityless men.' This observation cuts out my own suggestion up above, that these men were exiles from the still existing Mykenai and Tiryns. Mahaffy's prochronism for the destruction of the two cities appears to be partly mixed up with the view that Perseids and Pelopids 'possessed neither the art of writing nor the art of coining,' plus the complementary view that Mykenaians and Tirynthians of the sixth and fifth centuries would have possessed both. Perhaps they did, even though no specimens have come down to us. As to the Perseids and Pelopids, we now know that they could write, and it is hardly safe to assume that they had no coinage or currency. On the whole I should adhere to the dates given in note *ad l.c.* for the destruction of Tiryns and Mykenai. Meyer, *G. d. Alt.* iii. (1901) p. 516, well remarks that a 'Tirynthian' is victor at Olympia Ol. 78=468 B.C. (Olymp. List in *Oxyrhynchos Papyri*, ii. p. 89): *kurz nachher muss die Zerstörung fallen.*

16. **Φλειάσιοι χίλιοι.** The Chiliad from Phleiûs forms the first section of the left centre, which embraces nine distinct contingents, as against eight in the right centre, but numbers only 7300 men as against 11,300. The right wing and right centre are, if the figures be at all trustworthy, very much stronger than the left centre and left wing (22,800 as compared with 15,900). Men of Phleiûs (200) had served under Leonidas (7. 202) and again at the Isthmos in 480 B.C. (8. 72). Phleiûs was accounted a Dorian city (Pausan. 2. 13. 1 f.), and in the fifth century was anti-Argive and a loyal adherent of Sparta's (cp. Thuc. 4. 70. 1, 133. 3, 5. 57. 2 etc.); hence, perhaps, in part the enthusiasm of Xenophon for the men of Phleiûs, though they were conspicuous by their absence in the battle of Korinth in 394 B.C. (*Hell.* 4. 2. 16); but that is to be explained by inner dissensions at the time. The city is described as one of more than 5000 men in 380 B.C., *ib.* 5. 3. 16.

Ἑρμιονέες τριηκόσιοι: men of Hermion (cp. 8. 73) who were 'Dryopians' (*ib.*) had served under Kleombrotos (*ib.* 72) and furnished a small contingent to the fleet at Salamis, 8. 44. These particular 300 do not distinguish themselves. With this contingent the Peloponnesian portion of the forces comes to an end; but the divisions in the army do not follow strictly geographical order, and the two last Peloponnesian items act with the left centre and left wing, which is otherwise all drawn from exo-Peloponnesian states.

17. **Ἐρετριέων τε καὶ Στυρέων ἑξακόσιοι.** Eretria had sent seven and Styra two ships to the fleet at Salamis, 8. 46. The Eretrians were 'Ionians' (*ib.*), and as

Στυρέων ἑξακόσιοι, τούτων δὲ Χαλκιδέες τετρακόσιοι, τούτων
δὲ Ἀμπρακιητέων πεντακόσιοι, μετὰ δὲ τούτους Λευκαδίων
20 καὶ Ἀνακτορίων ὀκτακόσιοι [ἔστησαν], τούτων δὲ ἐχόμενοι
Παλέες οἱ ἐκ Κεφαλληνίης διηκόσιοι. μετὰ δὲ τούτους Αἰγινη-

18 τουτέων (bis) z ‖ τούτων . . τετρακόσιοι om. β   19 ἀμπρα-
κιωτέων β, Holder   20 ἔστησαν α : ἔστησαν Cd : ἔστασαν (V) :
ἔστασαν P : ἔστασαν R(S)z : del. Stein³ ‖ τουτέων z ‖ δὲ ἐχόμενοι z : δὲ
ἐχόμενοι ἵσταντο Marc.

such are one of the two Ionian contingents in the army (excluding the
Athenians); Styra was 'Dryopian' (ib.):
so this third division in the left centre
might have been expected to stand well
beside the second. The names here are
perhaps given in the order of their importance; the Dryopians may have stood
next to each other (Styreans and Her-
mionians), and so too the Ionians from
Eretria and Chalkis.

18. Χαλκιδέες τετρακόσιοι: the men
of Chalkis had supplied, or rather
manned, twenty ships in 480 B.C. (8. 1,
46). At the rate allowed by Hdt. for
Epibatai that might run to 600 men;
but some may have been serving under
Leotychidas, or they may have suffered
in the war. These men of Chalkis must
be natives, not Athenian kleruchs, who,
if serving in the army, would surely be
with the citizens, on the left wing, either
as a distinct corps, or fighting each man
in the ranks of his own tribe (φυλή); cp.
provision in the Salaminian case: [παρὰ
δὲ Ἀθηναίοι]σι τε[λ]εῖν καὶ στρατ[εύεσθ]αι,
Hicks' Manual² No. 4. (It is rather
difficult to believe that kleruchs accustomed to act together as a garrison in
loco would be distributed among the
phylic regiments on the battle-field.
If the 'Chalkidians' here were Athenian
kleruchs they would amount to 1/20 of
the nominal total of the Attic force.)

19. Ἀμπρακιητέων πεντακόσιοι. The
contingent is a considerable one, as
coming ἐξ ἐσχατέων χωρέων, cp. 8. 47,
and with the next might be put down in
part to the credit of Korinth, of which
Amprakia, Leukas, Anaktorion were
colonies; cp. 8. 45. It is the more remarkable that these two contingents (v.,
vi. in the left centre) are not favoured
like the Poteidaiatai above, but placed
among the outsiders.

Λευκαδίων καὶ Ἀνακτορίων ὀκτακόσιοι: probably the contingent from
each state was not equal, but that from

Leukas the larger, or they would have
been separately enumerated. The combination may represent a section, or
division, under one command. For
Leukas cp. 8. 45, 47 and c. 38 infra.
Anaktorion, not elsewhere mentioned by
Hdt. (except c. 31 infra), was a joint
foundation from Korkyra and Korinth
at the mouth of the Amprakian Gulf
(cp. Thuc. 1. 55. 1), and a considerable
bone of contention in the first period of
the Peloponnesian war (of which there
is no hint here).

21. Παλέες οἱ ἐκ Κεφαλληνίης δι-
κόσιοι. Kephallenia is not elsewhere
mentioned by Hdt. Thucydides 2. 30.
2 makes its position clear: κεῖται δὲ ἡ
Κεφαλληνία κατὰ Ἀκαρνανίαν καὶ Λευκάδα
τετράπολις οὖσα, Παλῆς, Κράνιοι, Σαμαῖοι,
Προνναῖοι. Paleis was obviously the
most important member of the Tetrapolis
(cp. Thuc. 1. 27. 2), but were the 200
men here mentioned all from the one
township? Kephallenia was annexed by
Athens in 431 B.C. (Thuc. l.c.), a fact
which Hdt. was in no way bound to
notice, but of which anyway he shows
no consciousness.

It is Stein's suggestion that Hdt. read
ΠΑΛΕΕΣ instead of ΦΑΛΕΙΟΙ on the
inscription at Olympia, described by
Pausanias 5. 23. 1, as the name of the
Eleians is given by Pausanias and that
of the Paleis is not given. This is simply
an inversion of the old suggestion of
P. O. Broendsted (Bursian, G. d. class.
Philol. 1048; cp. Grote, iv. 256 n.
and Rawlinson iv.³ 395, each spelling
the name differently, and both wrongly)
that Pausanias read ΦΑΛΕΙΟΙ for
ΠΑΛΕΕΣ. The old suggestion is much
the better of the two. In Hdt.'s time
the inscription was new and clear; in
the time of Pausanias it was 600 years
old. The name of the Eleians was to
be expected, especially at Olympia, rather
than that of the small Kephallenian
township. Grote adds that the Eleians

τέων πεντακόσιοι [ἐτάχθησαν]. παρὰ δὲ τούτους ἐτάσσοντο
Μεγαρέων τρισχίλιοι. εἴχοντο δὲ τούτων Πλαταιέες ἐξακόσιοι.
τελευταῖοι δὲ καὶ πρῶτοι Ἀθηναῖοι ἐτάσσοντο, κέρας ἔχοντες
τὸ εὐώνυμον, ὀκτακισχίλιοι· ἐστρατήγεε δ' αὐτῶν Ἀριστείδης 25

---

22 πεντηκόσιοι αC ‖ ἐτάχθησαν secl. Stein³ ‖ ἐτάσσοντο secl. van H.
23 τουτέων z   25 δὲ β ‖ αὐτέων z

---

might have altered the name, and that
Plutarch *de m. Hdti = Mor.* 873 seems
to have read the same inscription as
Pausanias.

It remains, however, still to be proved
that Hdt. had read the inscription at
Olympia before writing down this list.
Doubtless an official document of some
kind underlies the list here, but it need
not have been the precise inscription at
Olympia, nor again need Hdt. have
copied that document himself. The list
of Hdt. differs from the list of Pausanias
not merely by the point above specified,
but in others: Pausanias omits Eretrians
and Leukadians, and inserts five names
from the Nesiote region. Again, Hdt.
gives the numbers of the contingents,
which were certainly not on the inscription. There is not the slightest reason
to suppose that Hdt. compiled his army-
list for Plataia at Olympia; it is even
less likely than that he compiled his
navy-list for Salamis at Delphi (cp. 8.
82). The army-list was probably part
of the original draft of the work, not an
addition; cp. further, Introduction, § 10.

Αἰγινητέων πεντακόσιοι: the contingent is not large for Aigina, a state
which had held its own, and something
more, in the recent war with Athens
(cp. 7. 145); but the Aiginetans were no
doubt serving on the fleet, and in any
case the island would not have put a
large force on the mainland.

23. Μεγαρέων τρισχίλιοι: the 3000
Megarians (a contingent six times as
large as the Aiginetan) had already given
a good account of themselves c. 21 *supra*;
and besides this goodly contingent, ἐν
παιδίῳ Βοιωτίῳ οἵτινες ἔτλαν χεῖρας ἐπ'
ἀνθρώπους ἱππομάχους ἰέναι: there were,
if we may trust the same epigram,
Megarians at Mykale (cp. Hicks' *Manual²*
No. 17, where the services of the
Megarians against the cavalry are erroneously restricted to their disaster, c. 69
infra). Like the Aiginetans (8. 46) the
Megarians were Dorians; cp. 5. 76.

Πλαταιέες ἐξακόσιοι. The Plataians would certainly have put every

man they could into the field. The
traditional number of the Plataians at
Marathon is 1000 (cp. Hdt. IV.–VI. ii.
204, 206); fifty years after 479 B.C. they
are minished to 400, Thuc. 2. 78. 8.
Hdt. might here seem to class them with
the Megarians as belonging to the left
centre; but the title of that section in
c. 69 *infra* and the probabilities of the
case alike point to the Plataian contingent being reckoned, with the Athenian,
on the left wing. Was there none on
the right? Cp. c. 72 *infra*.

24. τελευταῖοι δὲ καὶ πρῶτοι Ἀθηναῖοι,
'last,' in reckoning from the right wing,
all along the line to the left; but 'first'
as the army moved westward, or forwards; or head of the column, which
had moved to Erythrai, and then out
on to the ὑπωρέη, before descending into
the second position. This assertion of
the πρωτεῖον of the Athenians comes
from an Atticizing source, and would
hardly have been emphasized at the
Spartan headquarters; the double description τελευταῖοι . . πρῶτοι prepares
the way for the *chassé* in c. 46 below, by
which the last become first and the first
last! 8000 Hoplites, besides some light-
armed troops, is a large contingent,
especially considering the contemporary
service of the fleet, in which the Athenians
were doubtless more largely represented
than any other single state (cp. 8. 131);
but the figure is not incredibly large for
Athens, even in 479 B.C. requiring about
800 men to each phylic regiment, or
τάξις. Cp. the estimate for 431 B.C. in
Thuc. 2. 13. No doubt all ten tribes
were represented in the field; and there
may have been 2000 Athenian Hoplites
at Mykale, or nearly so (50 × 30 = 1500),
as well.

25. Ἀριστείδης ὁ Λυσιμάχου: cp. 8.
79. The occurrence of this name here,
with the patronymic, suggests that the
nomination of this sole Strategos was an
integral part of the document, or the
source, from which Hdt. drew his list,
and also that the source was an
'Atticizing' one. Aristeides is the

29 ὁ Λυσιμάχου. οὗτοι, πλὴν τῶν ἑπτὰ περὶ ἕκαστον τεταγμένων
Σπαρτιήτῃσι, ἦσαν ὁπλῖται, σύμπαντες ἐόντες ἀριθμὸν τρεῖς
τε μυριάδες καὶ ὀκτὼ χιλιάδες καὶ ἑκατοντάδες ἑπτά. ὁπλῖται
μὲν οἱ πάντες συλλεγέντες ἐπὶ τὸν βάρβαρον ἦσαν τοσοῦτοι,
5 ψιλῶν δὲ πλῆθος ἦν τόδε, τῆς μὲν Σπαρτιητικῆς τάξιος
πεντακισχίλιοι καὶ τρισμύριοι ἄνδρες, ὡς ἐόντων ἑπτὰ περὶ
ἕκαστον ἄνδρα, καὶ τούτων πᾶς τις παρήρτητο ὡς ἐς πόλεμον·
οἱ δὲ τῶν λοιπῶν Λακεδαιμονίων καὶ Ἑλλήνων ψιλοί, ὡς εἷς
περὶ ἕκαστον ἐὼν ἄνδρα, πεντακόσιοι καὶ τετρακισχίλιοι καὶ
30 τρισμύριοι ἦσαν. ψιλῶν μὲν δὴ τῶν ἁπάντων <τῶν> μαχίμων
ἦν τὸ πλῆθος ἕξ τε μυριάδες καὶ ἐννέα χιλιάδες καὶ ἑκατον-

---

29. 2 ἔσαν z ‖ συνάπαντες β, Holder, van H. ‖ τρίς β   3 τε om. z
‖ χειλιάδες van H.   4 ἔσαν z   6 ὡς .. ἄνδρα del. Kallenberg
7 τουτέων z   10 ἔσαν z   30. 1 τῶν suppl. Stein   2 καὶ
ἐννέα χιλιάδες om. β ‖ χειλιάδες van H.

---

only general named : the captains or
leaders of all the contingents would have
been included in a document framed at
headquarters. If the name were introduced as a bit of free narrative by Hdt.
it might have been expected above, in
c. 21, when the service of Olympiodoros
must have been mediated through the
Strategos, or in c. 27, where the Strategos
was presumably the spokesman, or else
reserved for c. 44 *infra*, where the
Strategos appears in action. If Aristeides
alone is named it is presumably because
he was Strategos ἡγεμών if not αὐτο-
κράτωρ, and had a constitutional and
permanent lead : the whole college of
Strategoi was not present ; cp. 8. 131,
and Appendix VII. § 4.

29. 1. πλὴν τῶν ἑπτά : this notice of
the 35,000 Helots, who reappear almost
immediately below, is necessitated by
their having been introduced in c. 28
above, where they have been expressly
described as ψιλοί. The object of this
chapter is to estimate the sum total of
Hoplites and ψιλοί. The sum total for
the Hoplites is correct, i.e. corresponds
to the items, which amount to 38,700.

5. ψιλῶν δέ. Hdt. has made a mistake apparently in his estimate of the
light-armed, which he over-estimates
by 800 on his own showing. This
apparent error may have arisen from his
having got totals, not from the addition
of his items, but as *data*, in themselves
correct. The 800 *de trop* may in short
represent an item omitted in his estimate

of details. The narrative in the context
suggests such an omission, for unless the
highly-trained Athenian τοξόται of cc.
22, 60, above and below, are included in
the general total of ψιλοί ὡς εἷς περὶ
ἕκαστον ἐὼν ἄνδρα, they are omitted.
The addition of an allowance of 800 for
these Archers makes Hdt.'s totals correct,
i.e. agree with the items (A. G. Laird,
Notes on Herodotus, 1904).

7. τουτέων πᾶς τις παρήρτητο (pl. p.)
ὡς ἐς πόλεμον. Yet of this huge mass
of light infantry not a single solitary
shot is recorded ; and in the hour of
need the Spartans send to borrow the
Athenian Archers !

8. τῶν λοιπῶν = 33,700 (i.e. 38,700 –
5000 Spartiates). 33,700 + 800 = 34,500,
which is the total given by Hdt. for the
ψιλοί other than the 35,000, seven per
each Spartiate. This includes 5000
Helots for the 5000 Lakedaimonian
Hoplites. The allowance of one ψιλός
per Hoplite is no doubt the normal
Greek average : what is remarkable here
is that Hdt. treats all these θεράποντες as
μάχιμοι, and even more emphatically the
35,000 Helots as all equipped for war.

30. 2. ἕξ τε .. πέντε : 69,500 is an
excess of 800 over the items in Hdt.'s
calculation, as just shown, and the 800
may be the figure for the Athenian
τοξόται, cp. last c. Granting his total for
the ψιλοί the addition of 38,700 Hoplites
gives a grand total of 108,200 men, or, as
Hdt. phrases it, Eleven myriads less
one thousand eight hundred men.   The

τάδες πέντε, τοῦ δὲ σύμπαντος τοῦ Ἑλληνικοῦ τοῦ συνελθόντος
ἐς Πλαταιὰς σύν τε ὁπλίτῃσι καὶ ψιλοῖσι τοῖσι μαχίμοισι
ἔνδεκα μυριάδες ἦσαν, μιῆς χιλιάδος, πρὸς δὲ ὀκτακοσίων 5
ἀνδρῶν καταδέουσαι. σὺν δὲ Θεσπιέων τοῖσι παρεοῦσι ἐξε-
πληροῦντο αἱ ἔνδεκα μυριάδες· παρῆσαν γὰρ καὶ Θεσπιέων
ἐν τῷ στρατοπέδῳ οἱ περιεόντες, ἀριθμὸν ἐς ὀκτακοσίους καὶ
χιλίους· ὅπλα δὲ οὐδ᾽ οὗτοι εἶχον. οὗτοι μέν νυν ταχθέντες
ἐπὶ τῷ Ἀσωπῷ ἐστρατοπεδεύοντο.   10
    Οἱ δὲ ἀμφὶ Μαρδόνιον βάρβαροι ὡς ἀπεκήδευσαν 31
Μασίστιον, παρῆσαν, πυθόμενοι τοὺς Ἕλληνας εἶναι ἐν
Πλαταιῇσι, καὶ αὐτοὶ ἐπὶ τὸν Ἀσωπὸν τὸν ταύτῃ ῥέοντα.

---

3 σύμπαντος στρατοῦ ? Stein : τοῦ ante Ἑλληνικοῦ om. ß, Holder,
van H.   4 ὁπλίτοισι S   5 ἔσαν z : del. van H.   6 ἀνδρῶν
om. ß   8 ἐς om. RS   9 οὐδ᾽ : οὐκ C   10 ἐστρατεύοντο S
31. 1 δ᾽ CPz ‖ ἀμφὶ περὶ C   3 πλαταίῃσι ß ‖ τὸν ταύτῃ ῥέοντα
suspect. habet Kallenberg

full 110,000 was just made up by 1800
Thespians, all that survived of that city,
but they were without arms.

There would be little or no sense in
Hdt.'s adding the 1800 Thespians to the
sum total of μάχιμοι unless they had
served at least as ψιλοί (raising the total
of that branch to 71,300 as against
38,700 Heavies). Panoplies might, however, have been found for them, from the
men slain and wounded in the course of
the fighting in Boiotia ; but perhaps no
Greek state would find panoplies for
another.

Thespiai had lost 700 men at Thermopylai, 7. 222 ; the city had been
subsequently destroyed, the population
having fled into the Peloponnesos, 8. 50.
Are we to understand that except for
these disasters Thespiai might have put
2500 Hoplites into the field at Plataia ?

On the subsequent restoration of
Thespiai cp. 8. 75.

10. ἐπὶ τῷ Ἀσωπῷ : this phrase is of
importance. The second position, as
described in c. 25 supra πλησίον τῆς τε
κρήνης τῆς Γαργαφίης καὶ τοῦ τεμένεος τοῦ
Ἀνδροκράτεος, is here described as ' on the
Asopos.' The river could at least be
seen from the Laager (which would not
be the case from the first position) ; in
other words, the Laager was on the
ridge north of Gargaphia, sloping down
to the river ; but of course the Greeks
could not water from the Asopos proper.
G. B. Grundy, G.P.W. pp. 470 f., argues

that by ' Asopos ' in this passage is to be
understood not the main stream (north
of the position) but one of its tributaries,
A¹, "the brook which has its rise in the
springs of Apotripi." The point is neat,
but does not (me iudice) make any
substantial difference in our conception
of the Greek position. That position is
marked by the Androkrateion, Gargaphia,
and the Asopos ; i.e. it was south of the
main stream, and east of A¹ ; but there
is no need to infer that by the Asopos
here Hdt. definitely means A¹. He
more probably means the main stream in
front ; the river is near enough to define
the position : they had been ἐπὶ τῇ
ὑπωρέῃ, they are now ἐπὶ τῷ Ἀσωπῷ.
Op. next c.

31. 1. ἀμφὶ : cp. c. 69 infra ; or for a
more exact parallel 8. 25 οἱ ἀμφὶ Ξέρξην,
' Xerxes and his men.'

ἀπεκήδευσαν, 'were done with
mourning,' cp. 2. 40 ἀποτύψωνται, 2. 73
ἀποσπειρηθῇ, cp. Thuc. 2. 61. 4 ἀπαλγή-
σαντας δὲ τὰ ἴδια.

2. ἐν Πλαταιῇσι : sc. ἐν τῷ χώρῳ τῷ
Πλαταικῷ, cp. c. 25 supra ; in Plataia,
as the city itself had been destroyed, cp.
8. 50, they could not be.

3. τὸν Ἀσωπὸν τὸν ταύτῃ ῥέοντα :
this expression is a remarkable one,
coming as it does after the Asopos has
just been mentioned without qualification
(c. 30), and after the Persian encampment
has been described as παρὰ τὸν Ἀσωπὸν
ποταμὸν τεταγμένον c. 15 supra. Is τὸν

ἀπικόμενοι δὲ ἀντετάσσοντο ὧδε ὑπὸ Μαρδονίου. κατὰ μὲν
5 Λακεδαιμονίους ἔστησε Πέρσας. καὶ δὴ πολλὸν γὰρ περιῆσαν

4 ἐτάσσοντο Β ‖ διδε P   5 περιῆσαν Matthiae : περίεσαν αCz :
περίεασαν β, Gaisford

ταύτῃ ῥέοντα merely a periphrasis for
ποταμόν ? But why then ταύτῃ ? And
why ἐπὶ τῷ Ἀσωπῷ simpliciter, in c. 30 ?
Is it that the various passages are from
various sources, and that Hdt. does not
very strictly co-ordinate them ? That
may be so, yet hardly explains the
introduction of τὸν ταύτῃ ῥέοντα. The
locative adverb is strictly relative to ἐν
Πλαταιῇσι, and seems to imply that the
Persian moved from the Asopos, where
it was not ἐν Πλ., to the Asopos where it
was. But, even so, a difficulty is left, as
the Laager is described in c. 15 supra as
reaching ἐς τὴν Πλαταιΐδα γῆν. That is,
however, the Laager: here he is speaking
of the line of battle. We must suppose
that Mardonios moves out of his camp
into battle-line, formed up along the
higher course of the Asopos. It is clear
in the sequel that the Persians are on
the left bank of the river. Is Mardonios
aiming to circumvent the Greek position
by turning its left flank, or simply offering battle if they will cross the river ?
G. B. Grundy, G.P.W. p. 470, cp.
Topography p. 19, suggests that the phrase
here in question denotes the main stream
of the Asopos, or even 'the Thespian
Asopos,' as distinguished from the
Plataian Asopos, though he clearly sees
that ταύτῃ refers to ἐν Πλαταιῇσι. If anything but the main stream were here
meant, it would be, not the branch from
Leuktra, but the branch from Plataia, i.e.
A¹. But the contrast is not between
two branches of the river, but between
the main stream, in the neighbourhood
of the Persian camp, and the same main
stream a little higher up, in the neighbourhood of the Greek position.

Stein, who leaves the Persians and the
Persian camp on the right bank of the
river all this time, thinks there must be
a lacuna in the narrative. No doubt
there are many gaps in the narrative,
and many omissions, but Hdt. has
duly taken the Persians across the
Asopos long ago (c. 15 supra), and
Mardonios has not had to cross the river
in order to take up the position here
described.

We may, perhaps, paraphrase the
phrase τὸν Ἀσωπὸν τὸν ταύτῃ ῥέοντα,
'the Asopos, in this part of its course,'

i.e. where it flows through the land of
Plataia : emphasis is perhaps laid on the
ῥέοντα to show that there was water in
the river-bed.

4. ἀντετάσσοντο ὧδε ὑπὸ Μαρδονίου.
This account of Mardonios' battle-array
may be in part at least drawn from a
source (or sources) on the Persian side ;
for example, Hdt.'s friend from Orchomenos (c. 16 supra) ; but it is hardly
based on authoritative and documentary
sources, or it would be fuller and more
precise in regard to numbers, names of
commanders, and so forth : more, in
fact, like the army-list in Bk. 7. Mardonios' men are arranged in five ethnic
divisions, Persians, Medes, Baktrians,
Indians, Sakians (the medized Greeks
not included). If each of these divisions
represents a myriad, he had 50,000 men
under his command (with perhaps an
additional myriad (?) of cavalry) ; if two
myriads, 100,000 ; or with the army
corps of Artabazos, approximately
150,000 : further it is hardly necessary
to go. The infantry and cavalry are
not distinguished from each other in the
description here given. The cavalry
might have been all in front of the
infantry (as at the battle of the Granikos
in 334 B.C.) or on the wings ; it can
scarcely have been in the rear, much
less mixed up with the infantry. As
the Persian forces all freely crossed the
river, the cavalry was probably on the
wings ; and further, the Persian cavalry
was now on the left, and the Boiotio-
Thessalian on the right. Hdt. describes
the divisions of the Persian army with
reference to the ethnic divisions on the
Greek side, already enumerated, but
with the remarkable result of suggesting
a somewhat different ordering of the two
wings and the centre, especially of the
centre and the left wing, the whole
Greek army now falling, like the Persian,
into six corps, four in the centre, two on
the wings, and the constituent items
of these corps—except in the case of the
right wing—being varied as against the
previous army-list. This slight inconsequence again points to a difference in
the sources for the two army-lists at
Plataia.

5. Πέρσας : the 'Persians' properly

πλήθεϊ οἱ Πέρσαι, ἐπί τε τάξις πλεῦνας ἐκεκοσμέατο καὶ
ἐπεῖχον τοὺς Τεγεήτας. ἔταξε δὲ οὕτω· ὅ τι μὲν ἦν αὐτῶν
δυνατώτατον πᾶν ἀπολέξας ἔστησε ἀντίον Λακεδαιμονίων, τὸ
δὲ ἀσθενέστερον παρέταξε κατὰ τοὺς Τεγεήτας. ταῦτα δ'
ἐποίεε φραζόντων τε καὶ διδασκόντων Θηβαίων. Περσέων δὲ 10
ἐχομένους ἔταξε Μήδους· οὗτοι δὲ ἐπέσχον Κορινθίους τε καὶ
Ποτιδαιήτας καὶ Ὀρχομενίους τε καὶ Σικυωνίους. Μήδων δὲ
ἐχομένους ἔταξε Βακτρίους· οὗτοι δὲ ἐπέσχον Ἐπιδαυρίους τε

6 οἱ om. Pz ‖ ἐπεὶ Β ‖ τάξεις C   7 καὶ τοὺς Β, Holder, van H. ‖
οὕτως R ‖ αὐτῶν de Pauw, Stein², Holder, van H. : αὐτοῦ   9 δ': δὲ Β

so called are stationed over against the
Lakedaimonians, who, reckoning only
Hoplites, counted *ex hypothesi* one
myriad. There are besides 40,000 ψιλοί,
whose exact station on the battle-field
is not clearly defined. Greatly to
outnumber these 50,000 the Persians
must have exceeded a fifth of the whole
forces of Mardonios. (That in itself is
not impossible!) If only Hoplites are
considered, a myriad Persians, or at
most two, would serve. If the cavalry
is on the extreme left, Persian footmen
might easily out-flank a myriad Lakedaimonians, drawn up not less than eight
deep, and possibly deeper; but Hdt.,
starting, of course, with a belief in the
immense numerical superiority on the
side of Mardonios, not only makes the
'Persians' overlap the Tegeatai, but
gives them an extra deep formation.

6. **ἐπί τε τάξις πλεῦνας ἐκεκοσμέατο**:
the pluperfect has hardly a strict temporal
force, at least from the point of view of
the objective course of events. πλεῦνας
means not more than the Lakedaimonians
but ' more than he would otherwise have
done,' or 'than was usual.' At Marathon,
where the Athenians, according to Hdt.,
formed up for battle after the Persians,
in order to draw out a line as long as
the Persian, Kallimachos had to diminish
his centre ἐπὶ τάξιας (sic) ὀλίγας 6. 111. In
the present case Mardonios is represented
as drawing up in battle-array after the
Greeks, but he has no apparent desire
to out-flank them, so having men to
spare he deepens his ranks. Oddly
enough, the order was the same on the
Greek side : the wings are much stronger,
and probably much deeper than the
centre ; the tactics of Marathon were
repeated—or the legend of Marathon
was composed in the light of Plataia.

7. **ἐπέσχον τοὺς Τεγεήτας** : Schweig-

haeuser (with whom Sitzler agrees)
takes this phrase to mean, they had the
Tegeatai "stationed over against them "
(*gegenüberstehen*), and inserts a καί, but
cp. κατά just above ; Stein appears to be
correct in rendering the phrase: 'extended so as to cover the Tegeatai '—
who, no doubt, as a matter of fact are
stationed opposite (κατέχουσι) ; in other
words, the part left over (τὸ ὑπέρεχον),
after the Lakedaimonians are fully
covered, covers the Tegeatai. Cp.
Xenoph. *Hell.* 4. 2. 21. The Lakedaimonian and Tegeatan Hoplites, taken
together, form the right (east) wing of
the Greek army, 11,500 strong. This
passage looks as though the Tegeatai
were not standing next the Spartiatai
but next the Perioikoi, cp. c. 28 *supra*,
but the words which follow here are not
magisterial, but a homage to the reputation of Lakedaimonians, Spartiatai
included : the Theban dictation, or
inspiration, is perhaps only inferential.

11. **Μήδους**: the Medes (one, or two
myriads ?) are opposed to and co-extensive
with Korinthians, Poteidaians, Orchomenians, Sikyonians, that is with the
first four divisions, right centre, of the
Greek line, numbering 8900 Hoplites.

13. **Βακτρίους**. The Baktrian division
(including, perhaps, other Iranians, and
numbering one, or possibly two
'myriads'!) has opposite to it, and
extends over, the right middle centre of
the Greeks, and somewhat more; the
Epidaurians, Troizenians, Lepreatai and
Mykeno-Tirynthian contingents taken
together comprise but 2400 Hoplites,
and with the Tirynthians we reach what
afterwards appears as the end of the
right centre (c. 69 οἱ ἀμφὶ Κορινθίους):
the addition of the Phleiasians here,
1000 strong, raises the opponents of the
Baktrian myriad to 3400, but encroaches

καὶ Τροιζηνίους καὶ Λεπρεήτας τε καὶ Τιρυνθίους καὶ
15 Μυκηναίους τε καὶ Φλειασίους. μετὰ δὲ Βακτρίους ἔστησε
Ἰνδούς· οὗτοι δὲ ἐπέσχον Ἑρμιονέας τε καὶ Ἐρετριέας καὶ
Στυρέας τε καὶ Χαλκιδέας. Ἰνδῶν δὲ ἐχομένους Σάκας ἔταξε,
οἳ ἐπέσχον Ἀμπρακιήτας τε καὶ Ἀνακτορίους καὶ Λευκαδίους
καὶ Παλέας καὶ Αἰγινήτας. Σακέων δὲ ἐχομένους ἔταξε ἀντία
20 Ἀθηναίων τε καὶ Πλαταιέων καὶ Μεγαρέων Βοιωτούς τε καὶ

---

14 λεπριήτας **α** : λεπρηίτας Marc. : Λεπραιήτας **z** ‖ τε om. **α**. ‖
τυρινθίους B¹   15 φλιασίους **β**, Stein¹, Holder   18 ἀμβρακιώτας **β**,
Holder ‖ λευκαδίους τε καὶ **β**   19 παλαίας B : παλλέας Marc. ‖
ἀντίον **β**

---

on the first section of the left centre of
c. 69.

16. **Ἰνδούς**: the contingent of the
furthest east was opposed to the Greek
contingents from Hermion, Eretria,
Styra, Chalkis, a group numbering but
1300 Hoplites. If the 'Indian' levy
was reckoned at a myriad, it would
hugely outnumber the force immediately
opposed to it here.

17. **Σάκας**: the Sakai or 'Scyths of
Asia' (cp. 7. 64) are drawn up over
against five Greek ethnic divisions,
Amprakiotes, Anaktorians, Leukadians,
Paleis, Aiginetans, numbering all told
but 2000 Hoplites. The division on
the Persian side represents perhaps a
'myriad'—not necessarily all composed
of Sakai, properly so called ! These five
Greek sections carry us to the extreme
left of the centre, as conceived in c.
28 above, and more certainly in c. 69
below (οἱ ἀμφὶ Μεγαρέας τε καὶ Φλειασίους), except that in the list here given
the Phleiasians have been attached to
the right centre, and the Megarians are
now divorced from the centre altogether,
and apparently reckoned to the left
wing. Such inconsistencies imply that
Hdt. has used various 'Sources,' without
comparing or co-ordinating them, and
has no one clear and consistent conception of the battle-array.

19. **ἀντία Ἀθηναίων τε κτλ.** : cp. ἀντίον
Λακεδαιμονίων above. The variation from
κατά to ἀντία is noticeable and emphatic;
the neuter (s. and pl.) of the adj. is used
adverbially, or as a preposition, cp. 7.
209 ; also with the dative, 7. 236. This
use is not Attic. The plural form is here
perhaps preferred, as the corps opposed
to the Athenians was composed of a

number of Greek contingents. The
order of the names on the Greek side
too is here varied ; proceeding consistently from Mardonios' left to right
they would run, Megarians, Plataians,
Athenians. Again, the formula is
further varied by introducing the names
on the Greek side before the name, or
names, on the Persian. Among other
results, the exact order in which the
various sections of Greeks on the Persian
side stood opposed to the left wing of
the Greeks, including the Megarians,
remains problematic.

20. **Βοιωτούς τε κτλ.** : the extreme
right of Mardonios' line, his right wing
in fact, is composed of medizing Greeks,
to wit, Boiotians, Lokrians, Melians,
Thessalians and Phokians, 1000 strong,
the only figure given for an individual
contingent. Hdt. below estimates the
total of this sixth division at 50,000, an
absurd exaggeration, suggested to him
perhaps by the assumption that each of
the six divisions, like the division of
Artabazos, which is not here brought
into line, consisted approximately of
50,000 men. That would involve an
average twelve thousand each for Boiotia,
Lokris, Malis, Thessaly ! The Boiotians
might have brought 5000–6000 Hoplites
(cp. Thuc. 5. 57. 2, Xenoph. *Hell.* 4. 2.
17) ; the Thessalians will have been
chiefly mounted men ; the Lokrians and
Malians may have raised 1500–2000
Hoplites between them : all told, the
Greek Hoplites on the Persian right
wing will not have numbered more
than one myriad, and they are here
opposed to the Athenians, Plataians and
Megarians, who number together 11,600
men. But there are the Thessalian and

Λοκροὺς καὶ Μηλιέας τε καὶ Θεσσαλοὺς καὶ Φωκέων τοὺς
χιλίους· οὐ γὰρ ὦν ἅπαντες οἱ Φωκέες ἐμήδισαν, ἀλλὰ τινὲς
αὐτῶν καὶ τὰ Ἑλλήνων ηὖξον περὶ τὸν Παρνησσὸν κατειλημένοι, καὶ ἐνθεῦτεν ὁρμώμενοι ἔφερόν τε καὶ ἦγον τήν τε
Μαρδονίου στρατιὴν καὶ τοὺς μετ' αὐτοῦ ἐόντας Ἑλλήνων. 25
ἔταξε δὲ καὶ Μακεδόνας τε καὶ τοὺς περὶ Θεσσαλίην οἰκημένους κατὰ τοὺς Ἀθηναίους. ταῦτα μὲν τῶν ἐθνέων τὰ 32
μέγιστα ὠνόμασται τῶν ὑπὸ Μαρδονίου ταχθέντων, τά περ
ἐπιφανέστατά τε ἦν καὶ λόγου πλείστου· ἐνῆσαν δὲ καὶ

---

21 τε om. βPz, Holder   22 πάντες β ‖ οἱ om. R : οἱ Φωκέες om. SV
23 αὐτέων z ‖ παρνησὸν Marc. z ‖ κατειλημένοι CP : κατειλημμένοι   24
ὁρμεόμενοι P, Stein[1], van H. : ὁρμεώμενοι Cz   26 λακεδαίμονας CMarc.
‖ θεσσαλίην . . ἐθνέων om. R ‖ οἰκεομένους z   32. 2 ὀνόμασται z
3 τε om. CS ‖ ἦσαν RSV corr. : ἤνεσαν Vpr.

Boiotian cavalry to be reckoned with,
on which see c. 32 ad f. infra; as well
as the Makedonians, just below.

21. **Φωκέων τοὺς χιλίους:** the article
is important ; this is that Chiliad which
had shortly before arrived in camp, c.
17 supra, and had covered itself with
dishonour at Thermopylai, 7. 217. It
may fairly be concluded that this regiment had 'medized' there and then.
Not so all the nation : a remnant,
remaining in the land, gained credit for
more patriotism.

23. **τὰ Ἑλλήνων ηὖξον,** sc. πρήγματα,
favoured the Greek side, were for its
growing. Cp. 3. 39 τοῦ Πολυκράτεος τὰ
πρήγματα αὔξετο, 6. 132 τότε μᾶλλον
αὔξετο (sc. ὁ Μιλτιάδης). Cp. also 8. 30
supra.

**περὶ τὸν Παρνησσὸν κατειλη-
μένοι:** cp. 8. 27 κατειλήθησαν ἐς τὸν
Παρνησὸν (sic) οἱ Φωκέες (on another
and previous occasion). Parnassos was
naturally the refuge of the Phokians,
whether from Thessalians, Persians, or
others ; cp. 8. 32. Hdt. may have
varied in spelling; cp. the singular
'Plataia' in 8. 50 supra.

24. **ἐνθεῦτεν ὁρμώμενοι:** cp. 8. 133,
'from that, as their headquarters.'

ἔφερόν τε καὶ ἦγον, 'kept on looting.'
φέρειν would primarily suggest portable
commodities, ἄγειν living beasts, etc.
The assistance rendered by the 'loyal'
Phokians does not appear to have
amounted to very much. A really large
force of confederate Greeks on Parnassos,
in the rear of the Persian position in

Boiotia, might have been of considerable
strategic importance : but perhaps less
than justice is done to the services of
the Phokians.

26. **Μακεδόνας:** the Makedonian contingent was probably in the main
cavalry, which was the chief strength
of Makedonian armies, from the one
Alexander to the other ; though the
great development in this respect is put
down by Thucydides (2. 100. 2) to
Archelaos (413 B.C.), it is doubtful
whether any 'hoplite' organization
existed in the Makedonian army before
Philip II. ; cp. Kaerst ap. Pauly-
Wissowa, ii. 447. There may also have
been some Makedonian ψιλοί. On the
previous service of the Makedonians cp.
8. 34, 140, c. 1 supra.

τοὺς περὶ Θεσσαλίην οἰκημένους.
As Θεσσαλοί have already been specified,
this phrase is to be understood of
'dwellers in the parts about Thessaly,'
other than Thessalians proper, e.g.
'Achaians.' Cp. the list of medizing
Greeks in 7. 132, and more especially
the list of contingents 7. 185 (including
Perrhaiboi, Enienes, Dolopes, Magnetes,
Achaians).

32. 1. **τὰ μέγιστα ὀνόμασται,** that is,
the five divisions named above, Persians,
Medes, Baktrians, Indians, Sakans, were
not exclusively composed of men drawn
respectively from the nations named, but
each division, while containing men of
various nations, has been named from
the greatest and most conspicuous
nationality comprised in it.

ἄλλων ἐθνέων ἄνδρες ἀναμεμιγμένοι, Φρυγῶν τε καὶ Μυσῶν
5 καὶ Θρηίκων τε καὶ Παιόνων καὶ τῶν ἄλλων, ἐν δὲ καὶ
Αἰθιόπων τε καὶ Αἰγυπτίων οἵ τε Ἑρμοτύβιες καὶ οἱ
Καλασίριες καλεόμενοι μαχαιροφόροι, οἵ περ εἰσὶ Αἰγυπτίων
μοῦνοι μάχιμοι. τούτους δὲ ἔτι ἐν Φαλήρῳ ἐὼν ἀπὸ τῶν

---

4 τε om. van H. ‖ Μυσῶν hic pos. ß, Holder, van H.: ap. cet. cum
Θρηίκων locum mutaverat: id conservat Stein   5 θρηικῶν ACP:
θριηικῶν B: θρηκῶν ß   8 ἐὼν ἐν Φαλήρῳ z

---

4. **Φρυγῶν τε καὶ Μυσῶν**: Phrygians
and Mysians may be taken to represent
the Asianic levies. On the Phrygians
cp. 7. 73; on the Mysians op. 7. 74.
Stein⁸ recognizes that the order of the
text in R (ß) is *sachrichtig*; cp. App.
Orit.

5. **Θρηίκων τε καὶ Παιόνων**. Thracians
and Paionians may be taken to represent
European levies drawn from the countries
east of the Axios. On the Thracians cp.
7. 110; Paionians, 7. 113, 124; and on
both 7. 185. (Were these mainly in the
division of Artabazos?)

6. **Αἰθιόπων τε καὶ Αἰγυπτίων**: the
Ethiopians and Egyptians represent the
Libyan levies as a whole. Ethiopians
have been described in the army-list of
Xerxes 7. 69. Egyptians are, however,
a new feature in the land-forces; their
levy and armature have been described,
7. 89, in the navy-list. Their presence
at Plataia calls for explanation, which
Hdt. proceeds to offer, not without
involving himself in some remarkable
discrepancies.

οἵ τε . . μάχιμοι. This note on
the Ἑρμοτύβιες and the Καλασίριες is a
gloss, or a later insertion by the author's
hand, for (i.) it can only refer to the
Egyptians, yet here it must also be
referred to the Ethiopians! (ii.) The
grammar of the whole passage is fault-
less without it, the genitives Αἰθ. τε
καὶ Αἰγ. being strictly co-ordinate with
τῶν ἄλλων etc. and following ἄνδρες.
(iii.) As a note on Αἰγυπτίων the
sentence would have come in much
better in 7. 89. (iv.) The absence of a
reference to 2. 164 ff. is remarkable.
This note appears to be a reminiscence
of that disquisition on the Egyptian
castes (γένεα) in general, and the
warrior caste, or castes, in particular.
Whether gloss, or addition by the
author's hand, this observation points
to the later composition of the Egyptian
Logoi, and the prior composition of the

story of the Persian war, by our author;
but the four reasons above given marks
the sentence rather as a gloss than as
an aut or's addition. Cp. Introduction,
§§ 7-9.h

7. μαχαιροφόροι: cp. 7. 89, where
their arms are much more fully described,
the description ending μαχαίρας δὲ με-
γάλας εἶχον.

8. τούτους δὲ ἔτι ἐν Φαλήρῳ ἐὼν κτλ.
The Egyptian fleet of 200 ships might
have mustered 6000 Epibatai (cp. 7. 184)
while intact; but then, were they
'Egyptians'? Cp. 7. 96. The statement that Mardonios, while still in
Phaleron, debarked these Epibatai for
his own purpose deserves attention.
What becomes of the hasty flight of
the fleet from Salamis (8. 107)? What
becomes of the διάκρισις of the forces
in Thessaly (8. 113)? It might be
argued from the presence of Egyptians
in the forces of Mardonios that the fleet,
or some portion of it, the Egyptian
squadron at least, accompanied the king
on his retirement. The assertion that
Mardonios selected the Egyptian Epibatai
at Phaleron is obviously the translation
into narrative of the reason, which
immediately follows (οὐ γὰρ ἐτάχθησαν
κτλ.), in the light of the supposed
departure of the fleet straight from
Salamis, 8. 107. It is true that, according to *l.c.*, Xerxes before the departure
of the fleet καλέσας Μαρδόνιον ἐκέλευσέ
μιν τῆς στρατιῆς διαλέγειν τοὺς βούλεται,
and to fulfil his engagement. But
nothing is there said of taking any men
from the fleet, and Mardonios himself,
only a few hours before, has been
inveighing against the cowardice of the
Egyptians, etc. (8. 100), in a way hardly
consistent with his including them in
his select force!

The fair inference, however, is not
that there were Egyptians all along in
the land-forces, but that Hdt. in various
contexts preserves various stories and

νεῶν ἀπεβιβάσατο ἐόντας ἐπιβάτας· οὐ γὰρ ἐτάχθησαν ἐς
τὸν πεζὸν τὸν ἅμα Ξέρξῃ ἀπικόμενον ἐς Ἀθήνας Αἰγύπτιοι. 10
τῶν μὲν δὴ βαρβάρων ἦσαν τριήκοντα μυριάδες, ὡς καὶ
πρότερον δεδήλωται· τῶν δὲ Ἑλλήνων τῶν Μαρδονίου
συμμάχων οἶδε μὲν οὐδεὶς ἀριθμόν· οὐ γὰρ ὧν ἠριθμήθησαν·

9 νηῶν Βz   10 ἐς τὰς Marc. z   11 ἔσαν z   12 πρότερόν
μοι z   13 ἠρίθμησαν Β

statements from various sources, often
contradictory or more or less contrary
to each other, without staying to criticize,
to harmonize, to reduce all to self-
consistency.

11. τριήκοντα μυριάδες: 300,000 is the
figure which Hdt. consistently maintains for the fighting men of Mardonios.
This figure, however, in 8. 113 appears
to include the ἱππεῖς. Here the ἱππεῖς
appear not to be included. It also
includes the 60,000 (infantry and cavalry)
of the division of Artabazos, 8. 126.
This division is given as only 40,000
below (c. 66), and though the difference
may be accounted for by the supposed
loss of 20,000 before Poteidaia, and in
Thrace (cp. 8. 126-129), yet Hdt. fails
to subtract these two myriads from the
estimate of Mardonios' forces in this
place.

The army of Mardonios consists of
five divisions, above described, together
with a sixth of 'Greek allies,' which
Hdt. computes at 50,000 men (making
350,000 in all). Probably the division
of Artabazos may be considered here to
be absent, and the five divisions of
barbarians may be taken as each consisting ex hypothesi of 50,000, or 250,000 in
all; that is, each division consists of
five myriads (nominal), each under a
myriarch (and each myriad again is
subdivided into 10 chiliads, nominal,
each led by a chiliarch). The division
perhaps consists of 4 myriads of foot,
and 1 myriad of cavalry. If Artabazos
had really 60,000 men in his division,
he may have had an extra myriad,
perhaps cavalry, for the king's escort;
or the figure may have been reached by
reckoning his division as 50,000 πεζοί,
and adding a myriad ἱππεῖς—in fact,
counting the myriad of cavalry twice
over; the 40,000 men in c. 66 infra
represents his normal number of πεζοί.

But this army of Mardonios, in six
divisions of 50,000 each, viz. 40,000
πεζοί +10,000 ἱππεῖς, is none other than

the original army of Xerxes, the organization of which has been quite clearly, not
quite consciously, indicated in Bk. 7,
where the numbers have been vastly
exaggerated.

Either, then, Mardonios retained the
whole army τὸν ἅμα Ξέρξῃ ἀπικόμενον,
and was in command of a (nominal)
300,000, a very improbable alternative;
or he did indeed only command a selection,
or a section, of the grand army, perhaps
the very division, 50,000 strong, of which
he had been all along in command, while
Artabazos commanded a second division
of equal strength, the army of 479 B.C.
numbering in all 100,000—exclusive of
the European allies; or possibly Mardonios commanded two divisions, which
with the division under Artabazos might
raise the total Asiatic forces in Europe
to 150,000, or thereabouts. See further,
Appendices II. § 5, and VIII. § 2.

ὡς καὶ πρότερον δεδήλωται: the
reference is clearly to Bk. 8, cc. 100, 113,
but the verb is much too strong; εἴρηται
(as elsewhere) would meet the case: a
δήλωσις should have included the items!
The words may be a gloss, especially
without μοι. Cp. App. Crit.

12. τὸν Μαρδονίου συμμάχων: among
the 'allies' of Mardonios must be included the Makedonians, whom Hdt.
perhaps would not deny as 'Hellenes,'
as well as the Boiotians, Lokrians,
Malians, Phokians, Thessalians, and
dwellers in the parts about Thessaly;
cp. c. 31 supra. If these peoples were
allies of 'Mardonios' especially, that
would be a source of strength to him
against Artabazos. But the phrase, perhaps, merely substitutes Mardonios, as
commander-in-chief, for the king; or
the king's subjects might be 'allies' of
Mardonios; cp. 8. 24.

13. οἶδε μὲν οὐδεὶς ἀριθμόν: this would
indeed be a rash statement unless Hdt.
had literary and documentary evidence
to go on. He evidently believes himself to be in control of relatively com-

ὡς δὲ ἐπεικάσαι, ἐς πέντε μυριάδας συλλεγῆναι εἰκάζω. οὗτοι
15 οἱ παραταχθέντες πεζοὶ ἦσαν, ἡ δὲ ἵππος χωρὶς ἐτέτακτο.

33 Ὡς δὲ ἄρα πάντες οἱ ἐτετάχατο κατὰ ἔθνεα καὶ κατὰ
τέλεα, ἐνθαῦτα τῇ δευτέρῃ ἡμέρῃ ἐθύοντο καὶ ἀμφότεροι.

14 ἐπεικάσαι ἐστὶ αC : ἀπεικάσαι ἐστὶ Pz : ἀπεικάσαι ß, Holder   15
ἔσαν z   33. 1 πάντες om. ß, Holder ‖ ἐτέτακτο (πάντες omisso)
Gomperz ‖ κατά τε ἔθνεα ß, Holder, van H. : καὶ τὰ ἔθνεα B

plete sources on the war ; none of his
authorities supplied an exact figure for
the number of the Greek allies of Mardonios, and he is therefore left to conjecture on his own account. Some of
his authorities may also have indulged
expressly in conjectures, but he prefers
his own.

οὐ γὰρ ἂν ἐριθμήθησαν : this statement, given as the reason, is probably
itself an inference from the fact, that
there was no positive tradition on the
subject. οὐ γὰρ ἂν cp. c. 31 *supra*.
Hdt.'s own conjecture of 50,000 is perhaps
relative to the figure already given, at
least implicitly, for each of the other
five divisions of the army of Mardonios.
Hdt. makes no attempt to distribute
the total among the items. The chiliad
of Phokians is the only detailed figure
given. It is not likely that the
Boiotians, Lokrians, Malians, Thessalians,
and dwellers in the parts about Thessaly,
with the Makedonians, put 49,000 men
into the field of Plataia. Hdt. is speaking of fighting men. He only allows
at most 11,600 Hoplites in the Greek
left wing, opposed to this the sixth corps
in the Persian line ; cp. 31 *supra*. A
'myriad' for the Greek allies of Mardonios would be a fair estimate.

15. ἡ δὲ ἵππος χωρὶς ἐτέτακτο : the
pluperfect can hardly be pressed into
meaning that the cavalry had previously
been drawn up and assigned a different
position ; it is only = ἦσαν χωρὶς τεταγμένοι (οἱ ἱππεῖς). Cavalry certainly
formed part of the battle-array. The
words may, however, fairly be taken to
mean that the cavalry had a distinct
position, the infantry being in continuous formation. But all the cavalry was
not in one place. Most probably the
Greek cavalry was on the extreme right,
and the Persian cavalry on the extreme
left of the position. This conjecture is
borne out by the subsequent narrative,
notably the exploit of the Persian
cavalry in c. 39, and that of the Hellenic
c. 69 *infra*. ἡ δὲ ἵππος χωρὶς curiously

anticipates a phrase which became current
in connexion with the legend of Marathon
(cp. Hdt. IV.-VI. ii. 231).

It is not quite clear in this passage
whether Hdt. means to exclude the
cavalry from the numerical computations
just given. *Prima facie* he excludes it
only from the παράταξις. Moreover,
cavalry must surely be included in his
computation of the 50,000 allies. Again,
in 8. 113 the Persian cavalry appears to
be expressly included in the 300,000.
All which considered, it may be concluded that the cavalry is not here to
be reckoned separately, difficult as it
remains on that plan to account for the
figures 60,000 assigned to the *corps
d'armée* under Artabazos 8. 126 (and to
Tigranes c. 69 *infra*, or rather Masistes,
vide notes *in l.*).

33. 1. ἐτετάχατο : their formation in
battle-array had been accomplished—a
fresh development, or stage (ἄρα) ; the
pluperfect is temporal.

κατὰ ἔθνεα καὶ κατὰ τέλεα : both
terms refer alike to the infantry and
to the cavalry ; cp. 7. 81.

2. τῇ δευτέρῃ ἡμέρῃ, i.e. the day after
the one on which the Greeks had advanced and taken up the position near
the Androkrateion and Gargaphia, and
on which Mardonios had moved out,
and somewhat westwards, to face them.
With these words the Journal, or Diary,
of Plataia may be said to begin, but
unfortunately implicit reliance cannot be
placed on the data (cp. Appendix VIII.
§ 2). Both sides (καὶ ἀμφότεροι, you
might not have expected it of the barbarians) had sacrifices offered, with a
view to ascertaining whether they should
deliver the attack ; on each side the
signs were unfavourable to the offensive ;
cp. c. 36 *infra*. Ancient armies approached each other very nearly before
a shot could be loosed, or a blow dealt.
It must often have been necessary to
devise some plan for restraining the
impatience of the men in such close
proximity to the foe from breaking line

Ἕλλησι μὲν Τεισαμενὸς Ἀντιόχου ἦν ὁ θυόμενος· οὗτος
γὰρ δὴ εἴπετο τῷ στρατεύματι τούτῳ μάντις· τὸν ἐόντα
Ἠλεῖον καὶ γένεος τοῦ Ἰαμιδέων [Κλυτιάδην] Λακεδαιμόνιοι 5
ἐποιήσαντο λεωσφέτερον. Τεισαμενῷ γὰρ μαντευομένῳ ἐν

3 Τεισαμενὸς van H., Stein³ : τισαμενὸς (et sic passim) 5 Κλυτιάδου S: Κλυτιάδην del. Valckenaer 6 λεὼ σφέτερον α: νεωστὶ
σφέτερον Naber : πολιήτην σφέτερον Cobet, van H.

and charging forward. The necessity
for a 'sign' could obviously be utilized.
In the present case, with the deep Asopos
bed, not dry either, between them, a
great advantage lay with the side which
could induce the other to cross the
stream.

3. **Τεισαμενὸς Ἀντιόχου.** The proper
name Antiochos was both heroic and
of common occurrence. One of the
Attic tribes (φυλαί) was named the
Antiochis, from an enchorial hero or
ἀρχηγέτης: that Antiochos was a 'Herakleid' (ps.-Demosth. *Epitaph.* 31), and
the name recurs at Athens in the fifth
century (e.g. Xenoph. *Hell.* 1. 5. 11).
It is found also in Makedonia, Thuc.
2. 80. 6 (a source from which it was
destined to spread far and wide), and
occurs throughout Hellas (Messenia,
Pausan. 4. 4. 4 ; Arkadia, Xenoph. *Hell.*
7. 1. 38, etc. etc.). This Eleian (of
whom nothing more is known) is not
included in the list of twenty Antiochi,
antecedent to Antiochos Soter, in Pauly-
Wissowa, i. 2449 f. The name Teisamenos
is first found applied to the son of Orestes,
son of Agamemnon, who succeeded his
father as king of Lakedaimon, and was
driven out by the Herakleids on their
'restoration,' Pausan. 2. 18. 6 ; cp. c.
26 *supra*. A second Teisamenos, son of
Thersandros, son of Polyneikes, appears
among the heroic kings of Thebes ; cp.
4. 147, 6. 52 *supra*. A Trachinian of
the name appears in Thucydides 3. 92. 2
as an envoy to Sparta in the year 427-
426 B.C., and the name was in use at
Athens (cp. *C.I.A.* vol. i. pp. 52, 72,
No. 133, 414-3 B.C.). Of the one here
in question little is known except what
Hdt. records—for Plutarch, *Arist.* 11,
adds nothing, and Pausanias, 3. 11. 5-8,
6. 14. 13, only some details not affecting
the story of Plataia ; e.g. his son's and
grandson's names, Agelochos and Agias.
This Agias was diviner to Lysandros at
Aigospotami (405 B.C.), and the diviner
Teisamenos, who was implicated in the

conspiracy of Kinadon (397 B.C., Xenoph.
Hell. 3. 3. 11), was presumably his son,
or brother.

5. **Ἰαμιδέων** : cp. Pausan. 6. 2. 5 οἱ δ'
Ἰαμίδαι καλούμενοι μάντεις γεγόνασιν ἀπὸ
Ἰάμου· τὸν δὲ εἶναι παῖδα Ἀπόλλωνος καὶ
λαβεῖν μαντικὴν φησὶν ἐν ᾄσματι Πίνδαρος.
The reference is to *Ol.* 6. 43-51. (Perhaps the clan were 'medicine-men,'
cp. ἰάομαι, followers of Apollo ἰατρός, or
παιήων, before they were 'soothsayers.')
The Iamids, though at home perhaps in
Elis, were to be found far and wide
throughout Hellas ; the Pindaric Ode
cited was composed in honour of Agesias,
an Iamid of Syracuse (diviner to Hieron),
whose branch of the family was rooted
in Arkadia (Stymphalos). There were
two other mantic families or clans in
Elis, the Telliadai, cp. c. 37 *infra*, and
the Κλυτιάδαι ; cp. Cicero, *de Div.* 1. 41.
Κλυτιάδην here must be a gloss, and an
error. Blakesley's note is ingenious.
"Κλυτιάδην was originally an alternative, both families claiming Tisamenos :
Κλυτιάδου was an harmonistic improve-
ment in S. or the archetype of S." ; cp.
App. Crit.

6. **λεωσφέτερον** : an *hapaxlegomenon*
absolutely. Two etymologies have been
proposed : (1) λέως, λεῖως, Ion. adv. =
τελέως, 'completely their own' ; cp.
L. & S. (2) λεώς (Attic) = λαὸς *populus*,
popularis. The Ionic form points to (1),
though λεώς is found in Hdt. (e.g. 8.
136). In neither case is the word in
form a laconism. On λεῖως cp. Weir
Smyth, *Ionic*, § 716, p. 614.

γάρ : digressive. Hdt. here inserts
a pure digression on the biography of
Teisamenos, which, though interrupting
the story of Plataia, contains very important matters bearing upon Laconian
law, the history of the *Pentekontaëteris*,
the date of the composition of his own
work, and other matters.

μαντεύεσθαι is used by Hdt. indifferently (a) of the consultant as here,
cp. 8. 36, etc. ; (b) of the diviner, c. 35

Δελφοῖσι περὶ γόνου ἀνεῖλε ἡ Πυθίη ἀγῶνας τοὺς μεγίστους
ἀναιρήσεσθαι πέντε. ὁ μὲν δὴ ἁμαρτὼν τοῦ χρηστηρίου
προσεῖχε γυμνασίοισι ὡς ἀναιρησόμενος γυμνικοὺς ἀγῶνας,
10 ἀσκέων δὲ πεντάεθλον παρὰ ἓν πάλαισμα ἔδραμε νικᾶν
Ὀλυμπιάδα, Ἱερωνύμῳ τῷ Ἀνδρίῳ ἐλθὼν ἐς ἔριν. Λακεδαιμόνιοι δὲ μαθόντες οὐκ ἐς γυμνικοὺς ἀλλ᾽ ἐς ἀρηίους ἀγῶνας

---

7 γόνου: ἀγῶνος sive ἀγώνων ? Krueger   9 τοῖσι γυμνασίοισι z
10 πένταθλον B   11 ἀνδρείωι C ǁ μαθόντες δὲ Λακεδαιμόνιοι z
12 ἀρκίους Marc. z

---

infra, etc.; and even (c) of the god, as
in 1. 65.

ἐν Δελφοῖσι: the notice suggests
a possible source, and, if the story was
picked up by Hdt. in Delphi, the
digression might well belong to the
second draft of the work, and be an
insertion after his visit to Greece. The
last date involved in the story is the
year of the battle of Tanagra, 457 B.C.
See below.

7. **περὶ γόνου**: cp. 5. 92 ἐστάλη ὦν ἐς
Δελφοὺς περὶ γόνου. Schweighaeuser
doubted the reading here. The answer
looks like a bad pun (γόνον, ἀγῶνα).
Teisamenos had a son Agelochos, Pausan.
3. 11. 5.

ἀνεῖλε: ἀναιρέειν edere (*responsum*),
cp. 1. 13 τὸ χρηστήριον (subj.), 2. 52 τὸ
μαντήιον, 6. 69 οἱ μάντιες.

8. **ἀναιρήσεσθαι**: cp. c. 64 *infra*
νίκην ἀναιρέεται καλλίστην, and with
ἀγῶνα per *metonymiam*, 6. 70, 103, cp.
5. 102 (active).

10. **ἀσκέων δὲ πεντάεθλον**: cp. 6. 92
ἀνὴρ πεντάεθλον ἐπασκήσας. The five-
fold contest consisted of 'Jump, Race,
Quoit, Javelin, Wrestling' according to
the epigram ascribed to Simonides, 153
(Bergk iii.⁴ 500):

Ἴσθμια καὶ Πυθοῖ Διοφῶν ὁ Φίλωνος ἐνίκα,
ἅλμα ποδωκείην δίσκον ἄκοντα πάλην,

perhaps in the order of the said penta-
meter. Pausan. 5. 8. 3 dates its introduction at Olympia to Ol. 18.

παρὰ ἓν πάλαισμα ἔδραμε: an odd
combination, 'he only missed running
an Olympic victory in the Pentathlon
by one bout, or fall, in the wrestling.'
One may take ἔδραμε as mere metaphor
('scoring,' cp. 7. 57). παρά, 'exclusive';
cp. Thuc. 7. 2. 4 παρὰ τοσοῦτον ('by so
little') μὲν αἱ Συράκουσαι ἦλθον κινδύνου
(of being surrounded and taken). Teisa-

menos had presumably scored victories
in two out of the five events, but was
thrown twice in the final event by one
of the other competitors. It surely
was never necessary for victory in the
Pentathlon to win all five events: three
out of the five must have scored a win.
Thus it would not always be necessary
to hold all five, cp. Plutarch, *Symp.* 9. 2.
2 ταῖς τρισίν, ὥσπερ οἱ πένταθλοι, περίεστι
καὶ νικᾷ. Cp. also Aischyl. *Agam.* 181
τριακτῆρος οἴχεται τυχών and note *ad l.*
ap. Wecklein, *Orestie* (1888); esp. Pollux,
3. 30 ἐπὶ πεντάθλου τὸ νικῆσαι ἀποτράξαι
λέγουσι. Cp. further the next note.

11. **Ἱερωνύμῳ τῷ Ἀνδρίῳ**: the name
Hieronymos was in use at Athens (cp.
Aristoph. *Ach.* 386, *Eccl.* 201), Elis
(Xenoph. *Anab.* 3. 1. 34), Syracuse
(Diod. 26. 15. 1-2), and elsewhere. The
Andrian too had perhaps claims to a
sacral character. Pausanias (6. 14. 13)
saw a statue of him at Olympia, where
his victory over Teisamenos was memorable; and also (3. 11. 6) mentions that
he was defeated by the Eleian in running
and leaping, though successful in the
wrestling; he omits the disk and the
javelin, in which also he must have been
victorious; cp. the previous note.

The Pentathlon must have been conducted in 'heats,' and the heats in
wrestling, from the nature of the case,
κατὰ λόγον μουνομαχίης, but we need not
conclude that Hieronymos was the only
other competitor on this occasion.

The Olympiad of Teisamenos and
Hieronymos is not specified; it can hardly
have been so recent as the 75th (=480
B.C.), but as Plataia is the first of the
μέγιστοι ἀγῶνες it may have been the
74th = 484 B.C.

Λακεδαιμόνιοι δέ: the overtures
apparently come from the Spartan
side, inspired perhaps by Delphi, or by
friends of the Eleian himself.

φέρον τὸ Τεισαμενοῦ μαντήιον, μισθῷ ἐπειρῶντο πείσαντες
Τεισαμενὸν ποιέεσθαι ἅμα Ἡρακλειδέων τοῖσι βασιλεῦσι
ἡγεμόνα τῶν πολέμων. ὁ δὲ ὁρέων περὶ πολλοῦ ποιευμένους 15
Σπαρτιήτας φίλον αὐτὸν προσθέσθαι, μαθὼν τοῦτο ἀνετίμα,
σημαίνων σφι ὡς, ἤν μιν πολιήτην σφέτερον ποιήσωνται τῶν
πάντων μεταδιδόντες, ποιήσει ταῦτα, ἐπ' ἄλλῳ μισθῷ δ' οὔ.
Σπαρτιῆται δὲ πρῶτα μὲν ἀκούσαντες δεινὰ ἐποιεῦντο καὶ
μετίεσαν τῆς χρησμοσύνης τὸ παράπαν, τέλος δὲ δείματος 20
μεγάλου ἐπικρεμαμένου τοῦ Περσικοῦ τούτου στρατεύματος
καταίνεον μετιόντες. ὁ δὲ γνοὺς τετραμμένους σφέας οὐδ'

---

13 Τεισαμενοῦ abesse malit van H. || σπείσαντες C   15 πολεμίων
Marc. z || ὁρῶν α, Holder   16 προθέσθαι R   17 ποιήσονται R
18 ποιήσειν S, Schaefer   19 δεινά τε ? Stein[2] || ἐποιεῦντο β, Stein[2],
Holder : ἐποίευν τε (δεινά τε ἐποίευν van H.)   20 μετήεσαν Marc.
22 μετιόντες β, Stein[2], Holder, van H. : μετιέντες || οὐδὲ οὕτως α : οὐδὲ ὡς
malit van H.

---

13. **φέρον ἐς**, 'bearing on,' as we say ;
cp. 6. 19 τὸ χρηστήριον ἐς τοὺς Ἀργείους
φέρον.

ἐπειρῶντο πείσαντες : i.e. μισθῷ
πείσαντες ἐπειρῶντο ποιέεσθαι . . ἡγεμόνα
τῶν πολέμων. These words need not be
taken to imply a limitation of the royal
prerogative, least of all in the actual
conduct of war operations. The phrase
comes not from an official Spartan
source, and Xenophon (Lac. Rep. 13)
takes no account of any infringement of
the king's functions in war as ἱερεὺς μὲν
τὰ πρὸς τοὺς θεούς . . στρατηγὸς δὲ τὰ
πρὸς τοὺς ἀνθρώπους. But .the king was
not a μάντις, and this position in the
royal suite was no doubt offered to the
Eleian.

14. **Ἡρακλειδέων** : there were of
course many Herakleids in Sparta beside
the two kings (which accounts for the
genitive), but the introduction of the
word here is curious : it can hardly be
a limitation, an emphatically partitive
genitive, but must rather have been
meant to suggest that the Iamidai and
the Herakleidai were, so to speak, in one
class ; or the Iamids even a step higher,
as co-ordinate with those of the Herakleids
who were actually in the royal office.

15. **ὁρέων** : not so much a case of
literal vision, ὄψις, as of perception by
various channels, cp. μαθών just below.
Hdt. does not always employ the
terminology of sense perceptions with
prosaic literalness or scientific accuracy ;
cp. 8. 12. 6, 88. 9, etc.

περὶ πολλοῦ ποιευμένους: cp. 7.
181, 8. 40 ; also δεινὰ ἐποιεῦντο just below.
16. **Σπαρτιήτας** : i.e. citizens of Sparta.
φίλον προσθέσθαι : cp. 3. 74.
ἀνετίμα, 'kept putting the price
up,' a good imperfect ; the word is rare
in literature (as the language of the
market !), but cp. Pollux 3. 125 ἐπὶ δὲ
τῶν πολλοῦ πιπρασκόντων εἴποις ἂν
ἐπιτιμῶσιν, ἀνατιμῶνται, ἐπιτείνουσι τὰς
τιμάς, ὡς τὸ ἐναντίον ἐπευωνίζουσιν, ἄξια
πιπράσκουσιν.

19. **δεινὰ ἐποιεῦντο καὶ μετίεσαν τῆς
χρησμοσύνης**: the text is in some
doubt ; καὶ μετίεσαν appears to me de
trop, without it τῆς χρ. were plainly 'his
demand.' χρησμοσύνη is a curious word.
Schweighaeuser misunderstood it as =
μαντοσύνη. It has nothing to do with
χρησμός, but was used by Herakleitos
(Bywater, No. xxiv. p. 11) as opposed to
κόρος. Cp. χρηίζειν. The form χρημο-
σύνη is found in Tyrtaios and Theognis ;
cp. L. & S. sub v.

μετίεσαν τῆς χρησμοσύνης must mean
'abandoned their desire, or request'—
relaxed (of) their need—the usual construction being with the accus. rei, but
the gen. being also found ; e.g. Il. 6.
330 ὅν τινά του μεθιέντα ἴδοις στυγεροῦ
πολέμοιο. The occurrence of μετιόντες
just below makes an inelegancy by
'unconscious iteration' : καταίνεον μετιόντες, 'they went after him and agreed,'
consented (imperf.) : though μετιέντες
would be worse.

22. **γνούς** : cp. μαθών, ὁρέων above.

οὕτω ἔτι ἔφη ἀρκέεσθαι τούτοισι μούνοισι, ἀλλὰ δεῖν ἔτι τὸν
ἀδελφεὸν ἑωυτοῦ Ἡγίην γίνεσθαι Σπαρτιήτην ἐπὶ τοῖσι
34 αὐτοῖσι λόγοισι τοῖσι καὶ αὐτός [γίνεται]. ταῦτα δὲ λέγων,
οὗτος ἐμιμέετο Μελάμποδα, ὡς εἰκάσαι βασιληίην τε καὶ

---

23 ἔφη ἔτι z ‖ ἔτι καὶ z   24 αὐτοῦ P : aut τὸν aut ἑωυτοῦ delend.
cens. Krueger, van H. ‖ γενέσθαι z   25 γίνεται del. van H., Stein³

τετραμμένους σφέας, 'their change of
mind'; repeated c. 34 infra, cp. 7. 15
τετραμμένῳ γὰρ δὴ καὶ μετεγνωκότι κτλ.
23. οὕτω .. τούτοισι μούνοισι looks
pleonastic ; cp. ταῦτα οὕτω 8. 119.
ἀρκέεσθαι, pass. 'to be satisfied
with' is observable ; cp. Aristot. Eth. N.
2. 7. 5 = 1107 B ἀρκούμενοι αὐτῷ τούτῳ.
τὸν ἀδελφεὸν ἑωυτοῦ Ἡγίην.
Stein seems to think that the man's
childlessness led him to secure for
his brother (and family) a position in
Sparta. But the Delphian response
περὶ γόνου may have been as favourable
in his case as in that of Eëtion, 5. 92.
Pausanias reports descendants of his in
Sparta (l.c. supra) ; they may, of course,
have been his brother's (or his own by
adoption). The form Hegias is Ionic
(and Attic) for Ἀγίας or Ἀγίας, a name
perhaps identical with Ἄγις. (It cannot
even in this family be connected with
ἅγιος, Ἀγίων, the a in which is short.)
The name recurs in the pedigree, Teisamenos, Agelochos, Agias, Pausan. 3.
11. 5.
24. Σπαρτιήτην, 'a full citizen' ; cp.
πολιήτην σφέτερον and λεωσφέτερον above.
34. 2. οὗτος ἐμιμέετο Μελάμποδα,
'Teisamenos was copying Melampûs.'
The story of Melampûs here is a
digression within a digression, but may
be of the same date in the composition of Hdt.'s work as the story of
Teisamenos ; see, however, below, and
Introduction, § 9. 'Teisamenos did
but follow the example of Melampûs'
(Hdt. is great on plagiarists : so
Kleisthenes of Athens copied his grandfather of Sikyon, 5. 67) 'with a
difference.' ὡς εἰκάσαι βασιληίην τε
καὶ πολιητίην αἰτεομένους (cp. App.
Crit.), 'if we may compare men together
who were demanding respectively kingship and citizenship.' Melampûs was
even more exigeant than Teisamenos.
Melampûs had still reputed descendants in Greece ; a descendant of his
was with Leonidas at Thermopylai, cp.
7. 221. His death perhaps created the

vacancy filled by the Eleian. Hdt. gives
the name of the father of Melampûs
as Amytheon, 2. 49 (i.e. Ἀμυθάων), and
if the patronymic always proved the
earliest notice, that passage would be of
earlier composition than this, and this
digression on Melampûs (probably) of
later composition (third hand) than the
digression on Teisamenos (second hand)
in which it is embedded. Amythaon
apparently belongs (in Homer) to the
south Thessalian cycle ; his mother is
Tyro, his father Kretheus, his brothers
are Aison and Pheres, the Poseidonian
Pelias and Neleus are his uterine brethren ;
Od. 11. 253 ff. A part of Elis was
named Ἀμυθαονία, Steph. B. sub v.
('perhaps the territory of Triphylian
Pylos,' Hirschfeld ap. Pauly-Wissowa i.
2014). Amythaon himself has been
traced to a chthonian source, as 'a
personification of Hades' (cp. Wernicke,
ibid.). Melampûs is the μάντις ἀμύμων
who won the daughter of Neleus 'for
his brother,' Od. 11. 291, a story more
fully set forth Od. 15. 226 ff., where
Pylos is given as his proper home, whence
he passes to Argos, ναιέμεναι πολλοῖσιν
ἀνάσσοντ' Ἀργείοισιν, without the process being further explained — which,
however, hardly proves that 'Homer'
did not 'know' the explanation.
Diodoros 4. 68 gives the story in
rationalized form ; Apollodoros 2. 2. 2
more clearly supplies the part played
by the women, in the first instance the
daughters of Proitos ; Pausanias 2. 18. 4
adds the duration of the dynasties.
Five kings succeeded Bias (in four
generations) and six succeeded Melampûs
(in six generations, down to Amphilochos;
cp. 7. 91 supra), i.e. the dynasty of
Melampûs outlasted that of Bias, while
the native dynasty of the house of
Anaxagoras, son of Argos, outlasted
both the others, but was displaced by
Orestes, son of Agamemnon.
The connexion with the Dionysiac
orgies ascribed to Melampûs in 2. 49
does not at first sight square with the

πολιτηίην αἰτεομένους. καὶ γὰρ δὴ καὶ Μελάμπους τῶν ἐν
Ἄργεϊ γυναικῶν μανεισέων, ὥς μιν οἱ Ἀργεῖοι ἐμισθοῦντο ἐκ
Πύλου παῦσαι τὰς σφετέρας γυναῖκας τῆς νούσου, μισθὸν 5
προετείνατο τῆς βασιληίης τὸ ἥμισυ. οὐκ ἀνασχομένων δὲ
τῶν Ἀργείων ἀλλ᾽ ἀπιόντων, ὡς ἐμαίνοντο πλεῦνες τῶν
γυναικῶν, οὕτω δὴ ὑποστάντες τὰ ὁ Μελάμπους προετείνατο
ἤισαν δώσοντές οἱ ταῦτα. ὁ δὲ ἐνθαῦτα δὴ ἐπορέγεται ὀρέων
αὐτοὺς τετραμμένους, φάς, ἢν μὴ καὶ τῷ ἀδελφεῷ Βίαντι 10
μεταδῶσι τὸ τριτημόριον τῆς βασιληίης, οὐ ποιήσειν τὰ
βούλονται. οἱ δὲ Ἀργεῖοι ἀπειληθέντες ἐς στεινὸν καταινέουσι
καὶ ταῦτα. ὡς δὲ καὶ Σπαρτιῆται, ἐδέοντο γὰρ δεινῶς τοῦ 35

---

34. 3 αἰτεομένους Stein : αἰτεόμενον Reiske, Holder, van H. : αἰτεό-
μενος   4 ἄργειν R ‖ μανασέων z   5 νόσου ßC Marc., Stein²
6 προετείνετο z   7 ἀλλὰ α ‖ πολλῷ πλεῦνες ßz, Holder, van H.
8 προετείνετο C   9 ἤεισαν Marc. ‖ ἐπορέγετο z ‖ ὁρῶν α, Holder
10 ἦν καὶ μὴ ß   11 μεταδώσει RV : μεταδώσειν S   35. 1 ὡς
ABRz : ὃς van H. ‖ καὶ om. ß

---

therapeutic agency here ascribed to him ;
but the diviner may possibly have cast
out Beelzebub by the aid of Beelzebub
on homoeopathic principles.

8. ὑποστάντες, not understanding,
but 'undergoing,' undertaking, agreeing
to ; cp. δίκας ὑποστῆναι c. 94 infra.

προτείνεσθαι (bis) may be used of
a proposal from either side ; cp. 7. 160.

9. ἤισαν δώσοντες, daturi erant, Stein
(or rather datum ibant ?). But here, in
view of ἀπιόντων just before, ἤισαν is
not to be taken as a mere auxiliary,
but means 'they went,' to Pylos, a
second time.

ὁρέων . . τετραμμένους = γνοὺς τετραμμένους c. 33 supra ; otherwise it
might have been taken in a more literal
and physical sense.

10. Βίαντι. Bias is not actually named
in Homer, and the winning of a bride
for 'his brother' (Od. 15. 237) is all
that is ascribed to Melampûs in this
connexion. That Saga is told in Pausan.
4. 36. 3 and more fully by Apollodoros
1. 9. 12 (from which place it appears
that the cunning of 'Blackfoot' was of
more value than the strength of 'Bias').

11. τὸ τριτημόριον τῆς βασιληίης. He
had demanded τὸ ἥμισυ, in the first
instance, for himself ; the other half—
as 'goes without saying'—to be left to
the native king (i.e. Anaxagoras). How
much did he now demand for his

brother ? How much did he keep for
himself ? How much was he asking for
in all ? If he was to have one-half and
his brother one-third, he was asking
now for five-sixths, which is hardly
credible, especially as his demand was
granted. He may have been demanding
still one-half for himself and one-third
of the remaining half for his brother,
i.e. one-sixth of the whole for his brother,
their shares amounting together to two-
thirds of the whole. Schweighaeuser
takes it in this sense. The ancient
authorities all take the division as into
three equal thirds. (So Diodor., Pausan.,
Schol. to Pindar, Nem. 9. 30.) There
is this much to be urged for the second
alternative : (a) nothing is said by Hdt.
of the withdrawal of the previous condition ; (b) it corresponds more nearly
with the relative duration of the two
dynasties, in Pausanias six and four
generations respectively ; (c) the diviner
would presumably keep the lion's share
for himself. (The proportions would
then have been Melampûs one-half,
Anaxagoras one-third, Bias one-sixth.)

12. ἀπειληθέντες ἐς στεινόν : στεινόν
must be properly an adjective ; the
substantive is στεῖνος : cp. c. 13 supra.
For ἀπειλ. cp. 8. 109, and cp. κατειλημένοι c. 31 supra.

35. 1. ὡς = οὕτως, cp. 8. 126. 12 etc.
ἐδέοντο γὰρ δεινῶς τοῦ T., 'for they
were terribly in want of Teisamenos.'

Τεισαμενοῦ, πάντως συνεχώρεόν οἱ. συγχωρησάντων δὲ καὶ
ταῦτα τῶν Σπαρτιητέων, οὕτω δὴ πέντε σφι μαντευόμενος
ἀγῶνας τοὺς μεγίστους Τεισαμενὸς ὁ Ἠλεῖος, γενόμενος
5 Σπαρτιήτης, συγκαταιρέει. μοῦνοι δὲ δὴ πάντων ἀνθρώπων
ἐγένοντο οὗτοι Σπαρτιήτῃσι πολιῆται. οἱ δὲ πέντε ἀγῶνες
οἵδε ἐγένοντο, εἷς μὲν καὶ πρῶτος οὗτος ὁ ἐν Πλαταιῇσι, ἐπὶ
δὲ ὁ ἐν Τεγέῃ πρὸς Τεγεήτας τε καὶ Ἀργείους γενόμενος,
μετὰ δὲ ὁ ἐν Διπαιεῦσι πρὸς Ἀρκάδας πάντας πλὴν Μαντι-

---

2 πάντα Schaefer, van H. : μάντιος, coni. Stein[2]   3 τῶν Σπαρτιητέων del. van H.   7 ἐπεὶ C   8 ἐν τῇ γέῃ R ‖ τε om. ΒΡz
9 ὁ ἐν . . δὲ ὁ om. C

---

2. πάντως has exercised the commentators ; cp. App. Crit.
συνεχώρεον : cp. 7. 161.
3. μαντευόμενος, 'acting in the
capacity of μάντις.' Cp. βουλεύων,
στρατηγῶν, etc.
4. ἀγῶνας τοὺς μεγίστους, repeated
from (the oracle in) c. 33 supra.
Τεισαμενὸς ὁ Ἠλεῖος γεν. Σπ. is
stylistically observable ; it marks the
solemnity of the occasion with a quasi-
heraldic flourish.
5. συγκαταιρέει : cf. ἀναιρέειν in fut.
midd., ibid.
μοῦνοι δὲ δὴ . . πολιῆται. This
remark destroys the sequence, and is
probably a gloss. It would have come
in better after συνεχώρεον οἱ above.
That it is inconsistent with the story of
the Minyai 4. 145 would be no objection
to it, for Hdt. might not have been
acquainted with that story when he
penned this remark, if authentic ;
besides, the Minyai were afterwards
disfranchised ; nor is Hdt. so careful to
avoid inconsistencies. The statement,
however, rules out the case of Tyrtaios
(Plutarch, Mor. 230), the writer perhaps
never having heard of him, or else
considering him a Spartiate von Haus
aus. The exclusiveness of the Spartan
franchise was the ruin of the Spartan
state ; the Lakonic praetorians had as
great an objection to Uitlanders as any
people on record.
7. ὁ ἐν Πλαταιῇσι : that the battle
'in Plataia' (cp. cc. 16, 25 supra) is
the first of the five ἀγῶνες seems to show
that Teisamenos had not long been a
citizen of Sparta in 479 B.C. Cp. c. 33
supra.
ἐπὶ δὲ ὁ ἐν Τεγέῃ : the adverbial
use of ἐπί (local and temporal) is less

common than that of μετά (temporal) ;
τούτῳ may be understood. Cp. 7. 219,
8. 93, 113, etc.
No distinction is drawn in this place
between the relative magnitude or
importance of the five ἀγῶνες, they are
all μέγιστοι perhaps simply as ἄρηοι (cp.
c. 33 supra), but also, perhaps, from any
point of view, even without unduly
depreciating the magnitude and importance of the first, which is here
'first' purely in time.
The battle of Tegea, against the
Tegeatai and Argives, like the two
which succeed it, was an episode in those
πόλεμοι οἰκεῖοι which, according to Thuc.
1. 118. 2, preoccupied the Spartans,
during the period of the growth of the
power of Athens, but of which unfortunately very few details have been preserved for us. Cp. Strabo 377 μετὰ δὲ
τὴν ἐν Σαλαμῖνι ναυμαχίαν Ἀργεῖοι μετὰ
Κλεωναίων καὶ Τεγεατῶν ἐπελθόντες ἄρδην
τὰς Μυκήνας ἀνεῖλον καὶ τὴν χώραν
διενείμαντο. This passage exhibits the
Tegeatai in alliance with Argos, and of
course opposed to Sparta, at the time of
the destruction of Mykenai ; cp. c. 28
supra ; but that was after the outbreak
of the Helot war (Busolt, III. i. 121 n.).
The battle of Tegea probably falls some
years earlier, perhaps while the exiled
Leotychidas was in residence there, 6. 72
supra (and Themistokles already in
Argos ?). It was evidently a victory, but
not a decisive victory, for Sparta, as
it was followed by a second great battle
in Arkadia. Busolt (l.c.) refers the
Epigram of Simonides (Bergk iii. 460,
No. 102) to the Tegeatai who fell in this
fight, and dates the event 473 B.C.
9. ὁ ἐν Διπαιεῦσι : Pausanias (who is
the chief authority) makes Dipaia a

νέων, ἐπὶ δὲ ὁ Μεσσηνίων ὁ πρὸς Ἰσθμῷ· ὕστατος δὲ ὁ ἐν 10
Τανάγρῃ πρὸς Ἀθηναίους τε καὶ Ἀργείους γενόμενος [οὗτος
δὲ ὕστατος] κατεργάσθη τῶν πέντε ἀγώνων.

Οὗτος δὴ τότε τοῖσι Ἕλλησι ὁ Τεισαμενός, ἀγόντων τῶν 36
Σπαρτιητέων, ἐμαντεύετο ἐν τῇ Πλαταιίδι. τοῖσι μέν νυν

10 ὁ ante Μεσσηνίων om. z ‖ τῷ ἰσθμῷ Βα: Ἰθώμῃ Paulmier, Stein¹ ²,
Holder, van H. 11 οὗτος δὲ ὕστατος del. Stein³: οὗτος . . ἀγώνων
secl. Krueger, van H. 36. 1 δὲ S ‖ ἀγὼν R(V) ‖ τῶν om. S

town on the river Helisson (8. 31. 1) in
the Arkadian district of Mainalia (8. 11.
7, cp. c. 11 l. 12 *supra*); it was one of the
townships afterwards absorbed in Megalopolis (8. 27. 3). No details of the battle
have been preserved, but it was a contest between the Spartans and all the
Arkadians (less the Mantineians) and
resulted in a victory for Sparta. The
Argives are this time conspicuous by
their absence; Busolt (III. i. 121 ff.)
conjectures that they were engaged in
the war with Tiryns, places the battle of
Dipaia in 471 B.C., and ascribes the
union of Arkadia to the intrigues of
Themistokles.
Curtius, *Peloponnesos* i. 315, incidentally dates the battle 469 B.C., cp. *Gr. Ges.*
ii.⁶ (1888) 164, 829 (without precise
date). The exact emplacement of Dipaia
(Dipaieis) is disputed, notwithstanding
the fact that the name survives in the
district (village, *Dabia*).
(Polyainos 1. 41 = Xenoph. *Hell.* 7. 1.
28 ff., and has no bearing on this passage.)
10. ὁ Μεσσηνίων ὁ πρὸς †Ἰσθμῷ.
Stein reverts to the reading of the codd.
on the ground that Pausanias must
have read Ἰσθμῷ here, as he attempts to
harmonize this passage with Thuc. 1.
101–3. That is, supposing the text of
Pausanias 3. 11. 8 to run: τέταρτον δὲ
ἠγωνίσαντο πρὸς τοὺς ἐξ Ἰσθμοῦ ἐς Ἰθώμην
ἀποστάντας τῶν Εἱλώτων. That is the
vulgate, and is maintained by Hitzig-
Bluemner as by Schubart, who says:
inepta haec verba (ἐξ Ἰσθμοῦ) *reddidi
Pausaniae e corrupto Herodoti libro* (9.
35) *ea transcribenti.* The ingenious
emendation ἐκ τοῦ σεισμοῦ has been
frequently advocated. Paumier (Pal-
merius) changed the Ἰσθμῷ here to
Ἰθώμῃ. Those who adhere to the MS.
reading are hard bestead to explain it.
Stein⁵ says there was an old Messenian
king named Ἰσθμιος (Pausan. 4. 3. 10)
and that there must have been a place in
Messenia of the name Ἰσθμός. This is

better than Rawlinson and Blakesley,
who think that the Isthmos of Korinth
is intended (which would certainly be
τῷ Ἰσθμῷ): a battle between the Spartans
and Messenians at 'the Isthmos' is
hardly conceivable. The Helot war
broke out in 464 B.C. and lasted ten
years, Thuc. 1. 101–103, Busolt, III. i.
242. Busolt's idea that Μεσσηνίων here
qualifies Ἰσθμῷ and distinguishes it
thereby from the Korinthian Isthmos
appears to be inadmissible. To give
this sense the text should run: ἐπὶ δὲ ὁ
πρὸς Ἰσθμῷ Μεσσηνίων. The text is in
fact corrupt, ὁ Μεσσηνίων not being
co-ordinate with the formula for the
four other ἀγῶνες.

ὁ ἐν Τανάγρῃ: cp. Thuc. 1. 107.
3 ff. For the texts bearing on the
battle cp. Hill, *Sources*, pp. 103 ff. The
date of the battle is 457 B.C. (458–7);
cp. Busolt, III. i. 311 ff. The regent
Nikomedes was in command of the
Lakedaimonians and allies; hence the
presence of Teisamenos. The object of
the expedition was the restoration of
Theban power in Central Greece, as a
makeweight against Athens, but the
expedition was not an unqualified success
from the Spartan point of view. This
battle, as the last of the five ἀγῶνες,
gives us an important term for the date
of Hdt.'s own composition; cp. Introduction, § 9. Teisamenos was not present
at the problematical battle of Oinoa!
(cp. Hill, *op. c.* p. 298).

36. 1. ἀγόντων τῶν Σπαρτιητέων.
The Spartans brought (led) him, not he
them (notwithstanding their wish to
make him their ἡγεμόνα τῶν πολέμων c.
33 *supra*); and as their μάντις he performed that office (ἐμαντεύετο: cp.
μαντευόμενος c. 35 *supra*) for the
Confederates (τοῖσι Ἕλλησι).

2. ἐν τῇ Πλαταιίδι, more correct than
ἐν Πλαταιῇσι c. 35 *supra*; cp. cc. 15,
25 *supra*.

Ἕλλησι καλὰ ἐγίνετο τὰ ἱρὰ ἀμυνομένοισι, διαβᾶσι δὲ τὸν.
37 Ἀσωπὸν καὶ μάχης ἄρχουσι οὔ. Μαρδονίῳ δὲ προθυμεομένῳ
μάχης ἄρχειν οὐκ ἐπιτήδεα ἐγίνετο τὰ ἱρά, ἀμυνομένῳ δὲ καὶ
τούτῳ καλά. καὶ γὰρ οὗτος Ἑλληνικοῖσι ἱροῖσι ἐχρᾶτο, μάντιν
ἔχων Ἡγησίστρατον ἄνδρα Ἠλεῖόν τε καὶ τῶν Τελλιαδέων

---

3 ἱερὰ A   37. 1 προθυομένωι CP, van H. : προθυμένω B
3 οὗτω C ‖ ἐχρέετο Pz : ἐχρέατο aC   4 τελλαδέων B

---

3. καλὰ ἐγίνετο τὰ ἱρά : the imperfect
is significant, and is followed by the
conditions above stated. The phrase is
the best paraphrase of the term καλλι-
ρέειν, cp. c. 19. 5 supra.

ἀμυνομένοισι, 'if and so long as
they acted on the defensive, and
refrained from crossing the Asopos, and
delivering an attack.' The participle
here is equivalent to a conditional
sentence. The Asopos clearly was
between the two armies ; cp. c. 30 supra.
The Hellenic forces had advanced down
from the ὑπωρέη, putting themselves in
battle-array, into ' the second position,'
with the object of inducing the Persian
forces to cross the Asopos, a manœuvre
which they could hardly carry out without some disorder. In their actual
position the Greeks were probably not
directly exposed to the cavalry ; it was
with the barbarian foot that they wished
to engage. To cross the Asopos would
have exposed them to the Persian
cavalry, and would probably have been
absolutely fatal. Teisamenos understood
that well enough.

37. 1. προθυμεομένῳ μάχης ἄρχειν.
This assertion may rest on a genuine
tradition, and the fact remains that
Mardonios did finally begin the decisive
battle. Good reasons for his desire are
not far to seek :—(i.) He was the aggressor,
the invader, and the initiative naturally
lay with him. (ii.) His own reputation
was at stake, and there was opportunity
for great distinction. (iii.) A victory in
the field was desirable, (1) to impress
his allies, (2) to secure his rear and
communications, (3) perhaps to ease the
situation in Asia and especially to recall
the Greek fleet. (iv.) A Persian victory
at Plataia would virtually cancel Salamis,
disrupt the Greek alliance, and probably
lead to the submission of the Hellenes.
(v.) He had succeeded in drawing the
Peloponnesians beyond the Isthmos,
and on to a terrain of his own selection
(cp. c. 13 supra). (vi.) Delay was in

their favour, and they were receiving
reinforcements daily ; thus a quick
decision was desirable from his point of
view. Mardonios, however, evidently
respected his adversaries, and wished to
fight the battle on his own terms. He
was all but as unwilling as the Greeks
themselves to cross the Asopos, at the
point which they had selected for defence
—τὸν Ἀσωπὸν τὸν ταύτῃ ῥέοντα c. 31—
and having drawn them beyond the
Isthmos, and over Kithairon, and even
down to the river bank, he may well
have hoped to induce them to cross the
stream. In the sequel, indeed, he seems
to have attempted to push, or sweep
them over it from behind, by sending his
cavalry round the hills, on which they
were posted, and cutting them off from
their water-supply in the rear. Their
retreat surprised him, far more than
their further advance would have done ;
and finally lured him across the river,
with disastrous results.

2. ἐπιτήδεα, 'suitable thereto,' i.e. to
beginning battle. The adverb is used
c. 7 supra in a more absolute way.

3. Ἑλληνικοῖσι ἱροῖσι ἐχρᾶτο : an
admission which goes to show how
little the Persian war was a religious
crusade against the idolatrous Greeks !
Cp. 8. 109. 15 supra. Mardonios is
especially philhellenic in these respects,
cp. 8. 133.

4. Ἡγησίστρατον : a name of good
omen on either side, and strangely
enough, at this same moment, in full
operation in the Greek fleet, cp. c. 91
infra. Like Teisamenos, the diviner on
the Greek side c. 33 supra, Mardonios'
diviner is an Eleian, but of another
mantic family or clan, the Telliads,
founded or represented by that Tellias
who had wrought the Thessalians woe,
in the service of the Phokians, 8. 27.
There was probably a very pretty rivalry
between the Iamid on the national side
and the Telliad on the Persian.

ἐόντα λογιμώτατον, τὸν δὴ πρότερον τούτων Σπαρτιῆται 5
λαβόντες ἔδησαν ἐπὶ θανάτῳ ὡς πεπονθότες πολλά τε καὶ
ἀνάρσια ὑπ' αὐτοῦ. ὁ δὲ ἐν τούτῳ τῷ κακῷ ἐχόμενος, ὥστε
τρέχων περὶ τῆς ψυχῆς πρό τε τοῦ θανάτου πεισόμενος πολλά
τε καὶ λυγρά, ἔργον ἐργάσατο μέζον λόγου. ὡς γὰρ δὴ ἐδέδετο
ἐν ξύλῳ σιδηροδέτῳ, ἐσενειχθέντος κως σιδηρίου ἐκράτησε, 10
αὐτίκα δὲ ἐμηχανᾶτο ἀνδρηιότατον ἔργον πάντων τῶν ἡμεῖς
ἴδμεν· σταθμησάμενος γὰρ ὅκως ἐξελεύσεταί οἱ τὸ λοιπὸν τοῦ

---

6 <τὴν> ἐπὶ Werfer, van H. ‖ τε om. R 7 ὑπ': πρὸς malit
Kallenberg 8 πησόμενος Marc. z 9 ἐδέετο R(V) 10 ἐσενε-
χθέντος B ‖ κω C 11 δὴ B (αὐτικαδὴ S) ‖ ἀνδρεώτατον Marc.: ἀνδρειό-
τατον ceteri (ἀνδρηιώτατον van H.) ‖ πάντων ἔργον B

---

5. πρότερον τούτων. Hdt. expressly
dates the origin of the feud between
Hegesistratos and the Spartans before
τὰ Πλαταικά, but he does not explain
its origin, nor how Hegesistratos came to
leave Tegea for the Persian camp; nor
what became of him between the battle
of Plataia and his arrest in Zakynthos.
Hdt. possibly starts this story with an
anachronism; the great enmity of the
Spartans for Hegesistratos may only
date from his medism, and his capture
at Plataia, his escape from Sparta, have
been subsequent to that event. If he was
following his father's career in central
Greece, there is no difficulty in understanding how he came to be diviner to
Mardonios. Could he ever have given
the Spartans greater cause of offence?
6. ἔδησαν ἐπὶ θανάτῳ: cp. 3. 119
ἔδησε τὴν (sc. δέσιν) ἐπὶ θ. There
would be some form of trial before
sentence was actually pronounced, or·
carried out (was the Gerousia the
court? Cp. Aristot. Pol. 2. 9. 25=
1270B, 3. 1. 10=1275B, of course under
presidency of the Ephors).
ὡς πεπονθότες . . ὑπ' αὐτοῦ. It
is a weak point in the story that the
injuries inflicted by Hegesistratos upon
the Spartans are not specified. The
conjecture that he had acted as diviner
to the Tegeatai in a war with Sparta
(Stein) assumes that there had just been
such a war, and also that it would have
been lawful to put him to death on such
a charge, which is hardly tenable. A
charge of 'medism' would be another
matter, cp. 7. 214. But his offence was
manifold (πολλά)!

7. ἀνάρσια: c. 110 infra.
ὑπό, with a neuter verb, as often;
cp. 5. 61 ὑπὸ Βοιωτῶν ἀναχωρέουσι, etc.
ἐν τούτῳ τ. κακῷ ἐχόμενος: cp.
ἐν θώματι ἐνέχεσθαι infra, and ἀπορίησι
ἐνέχεσθαι 8. 52. Here, however, the
situation is more definitely material.
ὥστε = ἅτε: cp. 5. 101 ὥστε τὰ
περιέσχατα νεμομένου τοῦ πυρός, 6. 44
ὥστε γὰρ θηριωδεστάτης ἐούσης τῆς
θαλάσσης ταύτης κτλ.
8. τρέχων περὶ τῆς ψυχῆς: cp. 8.
102 δραμέονται περὶ σφέων αὐτῶν, 7.
57 περὶ ἑωυτοῦ τρέχων.
πρό τε τοῦ θανάτου: i.e. he was
prepared to undergo a good deal rather
than die, to escape death; before, instead
of death: on this πρό cp. cc. 139, 157
supra.
9. λυγρός is a decidedly poetical
word.
μέζον λόγου, 'beyond description,'
'too great for words'—as we too say,
when about to describe anything!
10. σιδηροδέτῳ: which explains why
he could not cut the stocks to pieces.
Cp. story of Kleomenes 6. 75, which
may also suggest how Hegesistratos
managed to possess himself of a knife.
σιδήριον: 7. 18 in a somewhat different
sense.
11. πάντων τῶν ἡμεῖς ἴδμεν: a mere
formula; cp. 8. 105, 124, c. 64 infra, etc.
12. σταθμησάμενος (σταθμέομαι, or
-άομαι: on the form σταθμωσάμενος
cp. Veitch, Verbs, sub v.): he might in
this case actually 'measure,' or merely
'calculate'; 'weigh' he could not.
ἐξελεύσεται: of course 'out of the
stocks.'

ποδός, ἀπέταμε τὸν ταρσὸν ἑωυτοῦ. ταῦτα δὲ ποιήσας, ὡς
φυλασσόμενος ὑπὸ φυλάκων, διορύξας τὸν τοῖχον ἀπέδρη ἐς
15 Τεγέην, τὰς μὲν νύκτας πορευόμενος, τὰς δὲ ἡμέρας καταδύνων
ἐς ὕλην καὶ αὐλιζόμενος, οὕτω ὡς Λακεδαιμονίων πανδημὶ
διζημένων τρίτῃ εὐφρόνῃ γενέσθαι ἐν Τεγέῃ, τοὺς δὲ ἐν θώματι
μεγάλῳ ἐνέχεσθαι τῆς τε τόλμης, ὁρῶντας τὸ ἡμίτομον τοῦ
ποδὸς κείμενον, κἀκεῖνον οὐ δυναμένους εὑρεῖν. τότε μὲν οὕτω
20 διαφυγὼν Λακεδαιμονίους καταφεύγει ἐς Τεγέην ἐοῦσαν οὐκ
ἀρθμίην Λακεδαιμονίοισι τοῦτον τὸν χρόνον· ὑγιὴς δὲ γενόμενος καὶ προσποιησάμενος ξύλινον πόδα κατεστήκεε ἐκ τῆς

---

13 αὐτοῦ ? Stein² : del. Krueger, van H. || ὥστε ß, Holder, van H.
16 ὥστε ßP, Stein¹, Holder, van H. || πανδημεὶ ßCPz, Stein   17
θώυματι Pz, Stein¹   18 τε : τότε ß || ὀρέοντας Pz, Stein¹, van H. :
ὀρέωντας C   19 τοῦτο κείμενον z   20 καταφεύγειν R(V)   22
ἐκ : ἐπὶ C

---

18. τὸν ταρσόν would, strictly speaking, be only the flat or fore-part of the
foot, cp. 8. 12, but he must have cut
off rather more than that. Did he not
amputate his foot at the ankle ? And
had he only one foot in the stocks ? Or
did the liberation of one foot enable him
to withdraw the other also ? These
diviners were perhaps not merely
'medicine-men,' but something of
'surgeons' (as well as comparative
anatomists, from their extispications !).

14. διορύξας τὸν τοῖχον : no doubt
merely a mud wall, or built of adobes.
He might use the same knife as he had
used for the operation on his foot.

16. αὐλιζόμενος : sc. ἐν αὐτῇ. For
the verb cp. c. 93 infra.

πανδημὶ διζημένων : there was a
hue and cry raised after him ; πανδημεὶ
does not necessarily imply an expedition
under arms. The verb δίζημαι is of
frequent occurrence in Hdt. and is not
to be confounded with the rarer δίζω,
δίζομαι.

17. τρίτῃ εὐφρόνῃ. Tegea is only
about thirty miles from Sparta, but
Hegesistratos will have had to go a good
deal out of the direct road, travel only
in the dark, and with a bad wound.

τοὺς δέ, as though αὐτὸν μέν had
preceded, which must indeed be understood before γενέσθαι.

18. ἐνέχεσθαι : cp. l. 7 above. Not
quite exact is the co-ordination of the two
points, or causes, of their astonishment,
viz. his hardihood in amputating his
foot, and his success in escaping. τὸ

ἡμίτομον : cp. 7. 39. (But would he
have surprised them less if he had not
left it about ?)

20. ἐοῦσαν οὐκ ἀρθμίην Λακεδαιμονίοισι. Tegea was at war with Sparta
not so very long after τὰ Πλαταιικά : cp.
c. 34 supra, and in some ways, as
already shown, the later feud between
Tegea and Sparta would suit very well the
story of Hegesistratos, except so far as the
words πρότερον τούτων up above may
be held to bar the way. If Tegea was
at war with Lakedaimon before the
Persian invasion, of which no other
record survives, then this feud should
have been noticed in 7. 145 as one of
those composed in 481 B.C. If so, the
reconciliation did not extend to the
Eleian diviner ; the Spartans were already
provided with Teisamenos. Might they
not have had Hegesistratos on easier
terms ? Was Teisamenos himself at all
responsible for their implacable hostility
to the Telliad ?

22. προσποιησάμενος ξύλινον πόδα :
he did not make his wooden foot with
his own hands, but probably employed
a statuary. Artificial limbs were apparently unusual (except as ex voto
offerings).

κατεστήκεε . . πολέμιος : he took
his stand, took up a hostile attitude ;
or simply 'became' ; for the verb cp.
c. 70 infra.

ἐκ τῆς ἰθέης, 'openly,' palam ; sc.
ὁδοῦ or τέχνης : cp. c. 57 infra. Had
he ever pretended friendship for them ?

ἰθέης Λακεδαιμονίοισι πολέμιος. οὐ μέντοι ἔς γε τέλος οἱ
συνήνεικε τὸ ἔχθος τὸ ἐς Λακεδαιμονίους συγκεκυρημένον· ἥλω
γὰρ μαντευόμενος ἐν Ζακύνθῳ ὑπ' αὐτῶν καὶ ἀπέθανε. 25

Ὁ μέντοι θάνατος ὁ Ἡγησιστράτου ὕστερον ἐγένετο τῶν 38
Πλαταιικῶν, τότε δὲ ἐπὶ τῷ Ἀσωπῷ Μαρδονίῳ μεμισθωμένος
οὐκ ὀλίγου ἐθύετό τε καὶ προεθυμέετο κατά τε τὸ ἔχθος τὸ
Λακεδαιμονίων καὶ κατὰ τὸ κέρδος. ὡς δὲ οὐκ ἐκαλλίερεε
ὥστε μάχεσθαι οὔτε αὐτοῖσι Πέρσῃσι οὔτε τοῖσι μετ' ἐκείνων 5
ἐοῦσι Ἑλλήνων (εἶχον γὰρ καὶ οὗτοι ἐπ' ἑωυτῶν μάντιν
Ἱππόμαχον Λευκάδιον ἄνδρα), ἐπιρρεόντων δὲ τῶν Ἑλλήνων

---

23 ἰθείης codd. z ‖ γε ἐς B, Gaisford   24 συγκεχωρησμένον R :
συγκεχωρημένον SV : συγκεκρημένον Reiske, Holder, van H.   38. 1
μέντοι : μὲν νυν B, Holder   2 δ' CPz, van H. ‖ τῷ Μαρδονίῳ z
3 ὀλίγῳ S ‖ προθυμέετο aC (προεθυμεῖτο van H.) ‖ τε τὸ : τὸ BPz ‖ τὸ :
τῶν R   4 ἐκαλλίερει van H.   7 ἐπιρεόντων a, Holder

23. **ἐς τέλος**, 'finally,' 'at last.'
24. **συνήνεικε**: sc. ἐς τὸ ἄμεινον, 'went
well,' was successful; cp. 8. 87 where
the word is used absolutely, as here;
followed in c. 88 by συνήνεικε αὐτῇ ἐς
εὐτυχίην.

†**συγκεκυρημένον**: the passive
form is unique and constitutes a difficulty; it can hardly be right, though
Schweighaeuser ingeniously gets the idea
of 'mutuality' (mutuum odium) out of
it. Eltz thought that the reading of S
was a correction of the true reading
συγκεκρημένον which Reiske conjectured
afterwards; cp. App. Crit.
25. **μαντευόμενος**, 'acting as diviner'
(cp. c. 36. 2 supra), but not necessarily in
battle; it was this assumption of mantic
functions apparently which gave such
great offence in Sparta: that he had
prostituted his art in the service of
Persia might be his chief offence.

ἐν Ζακύνθῳ: what would be the
date of his arrest in Zakynthos! Schoell
dated it to the second summer of the
Peloponnesian war, cp. Thuc. 2. 66, which
would give Hegesistratos indeed a long
life! Busolt, iii. 1. 123, places it with
more probability just after the battle of
Dipaia. Fugitives from Sparta naturally
went west; Demaratos had been overtaken in Zakynthos (6. 70 supra) but
not extradited; Themistokles started in
the same direction, Thuc. 1. 136.

ἀπέθανε: sc. ὑπ' αὐτῶν; cp. l. 7
supra.

38. 2. **ἐπὶ τῷ Ἀσωπῷ**: cp. c. 30
supra. Mardonios and the Greeks are
both 'on the Asopos,' but on different
sides of it.

μεμισθωμένος οὐκ ὀλίγου: there
was nothing peculiar in this circumstance; no doubt all the diviners were
largely remunerated, though to the discredit of Hegesistratos alone is it mentioned that he prostituted the diviner's
office for 'hate and greed.'

4. **οὐκ ἐκαλλίερεε ὥστε μάχεσθαι**: i.e.
οὐκ ἐγίνετο καλὰ τὰ ἱρά, cp. c. 36 supra;
μάχεσθαι must here = μάχην ἄρχειν, otherwise there is a slight discrepancy between
c. 87 ad init. and this place. Perhaps
the signs as divined by Hippomachos
were against fighting simpliciter; while
Hegesistratos modified his divination to
the extent above implied.

6. **ἐπ' ἑωυτῶν**: cp. c. 17 supra.

7. **Ἱππόμαχον Λευκάδιον ἄνδρα**.
Hippomachos of Leukas is the least
distinguished of the diviners, and Hdt.
has nothing to tell of him. His fellow-
citizens are fighting in the ranks of
the confederate Greeks; cp. c. 28 supra.
(The name is not as common as might
be expected, appearing first as that of
a Trojan, Il. 12. 189, and again as one
of the Thirty at Athens in 404 B.C.,
Xenoph. Hell. 2. 3. 2, 2. 4. 19.)

ἐπιρρεόντων: cp. Il. 11. 724
ἐπέρρεον ἔθνεα πεζῶν.

καὶ γινομένων πλεύνων, Τιμηγενίδης ὁ Ἕρπυος ἀνὴρ Θηβαῖος
συνεβούλευσε Μαρδονίῳ τὰς ἐκβολὰς τοῦ Κιθαιρῶνος φυλάξαι,
10 λέγων ὡς ἐπιρρέουσι οἱ Ἕλληνες αἰεὶ ἀνὰ πᾶσαν ἡμέρην καὶ
39 ὡς ἀπολάμψοιτο συχνούς. ἡμέραι δέ σφι ἀντικατημένοισι
ἤδη ἐγεγόνεσαν ὀκτώ, ὅτε ταῦτα ἐκεῖνος συνεβούλευε Μαρδονίῳ.
ὁ δὲ μαθὼν τὴν παραίνεσιν εὖ ἔχουσαν, ὡς εὐφρόνη ἐγένετο,
πέμπει τὴν ἵππον ἐς τὰς ἐκβολὰς τὰς Κιθαιρωνίδας αἱ ἐπὶ

---

8 καὶ <ἀεὶ> γινομένων Naber, Holder : καὶ γινομένων <αἰεὶ> van H.
‖ τιμογενίδης aC(Pz)   9 κιθερῶνος a   10 ἐπιρέουσι a, Holder ‖
αἰεὶ del. van H.   11 ἀπολάμψαιτο B   39. 3 εὐέχουσαν A
4 ἐσβολὰς R : ἐμβολὰς SMarc.

---

8. **Τιμηγενίδης ὁ Ἕρπυος** : this man
appears below, cc. 86, 87, with Attaginos,
as leader of the medizing faction in
Thebes; he doubtless held the post of
'Boiotarch,' cp. c. 16 *supra*. The name
appears as Τιμηγενίδας in Pausan. 7. 10.
2 (who has nothing new to say of
him); the proper form was presumably
Τιμαγενίδας (or Τειμαγενίδας?). The name
Τιμαγέτης is not uncommon, but Timagenidas is only borne by the Theban
traitor. His father's name, Herpys
(Reptile!), is no less unique.
The notion that Mardonios was put
up to employing his cavalry on the
Greek flank and lines of communication
by Timagenidas is probably a popular
fiction. The Persian was, indeed, unworthy of his position, if he had to be
coached in the very rudiments of warfare
by a Boiotian.
9. **τὰς ἐκβολὰς τοῦ Κιθαιρῶνος**. Hdt.
nowhere betrays any clear consciousness
that there was more than one pass over
Kithairon ; but cp. next chapter. The
plural ἐκβολαί is without prejudice, as
Hdt. uses the plural (e.g. 7. 176) of
a single route. ἐσβολή, not ἐκβολή, is,
however, the usual term ; the word here
seems appropriate from the supposed
speaker's point of view. Neither Timagenidas nor Mardonios could have any
pass now in view but the main route
over Kithairon to Eleutherai. The
Eleutherai - Plataia road was merely a
branch of this ; the Plataia-Megara road
was high on the mountain, very rough
and inaccessible for cavalry, and doubtless, like the previously named one,
covered by the Greeks. But in moving
from their first position at Erythrai the
Greeks had opened up the main road
(Thebes - Erythrai - Eleutherai), perhaps
relying upon their supplies coming *via*

Hysiai and Plataia. The Persian cavalry
could now ride freely up the hill past
Erythrai ; and once up there might even
sweep to the west along the road to
Hysiai, to Plataia, and so on. If Mardonios had moved west with a view to
out-flanking the Greek left, he seems
now preparing a diversion on their right.
It is conceivable that the advance of the
Greeks from the position 'at Erythrai'
to the position 'on the Asopos' was
encouraged or enforced by the pressure
of the Persian cavalry. It is even conceivable that Hdt.'s chronology, or
sequence of events, is here at fault, and
that it was this very exploit of the
cavalry, here recorded, which induced
the Greeks to advance down from the
ὑπωρέη on to the Asopos-ridge.
φυλάξαι, 'to occupy in force.'
11. **ἀπολάμψοιτο** : an unusual form ;
cp. 3. 146 ἀπολάμψεσθαι.
39. 1. **ἡμέραι δέ σφι . . ὀκτώ**. *Prima
facie* this means that eight days had
elapsed since the two armies came into
position opposite one another ἐπὶ τῷ
Ἀσωπῷ or in the second position ; cp.
cc. 30, 31 *supra*. The δευτέρη ἡμέρη in
that position has been already noted, c.
33 *supra*. So long a delay as that
without any exchange of hostilities, or
any attempt on the part of the Persian
cavalry either to cut off supplies or to
harass the Greeks in this advanced position, seems improbable. The situation
would be eased if we might substitute
or add the (indefinite) number of days
spent in the first position, and its development. It may, however, fairly be
doubted whether the Diary of Plataia is
to be taken quite seriously in its numbering of days ; cp. Appendix VIII. § 2.
4. **τὰς ἐκβολὰς τὰς Κιθαιρωνίδας αἱ
ἐπὶ Πλαταιέων φέρουσι**, 'the pass over

Πλαταιέων φέρουσι, τὰς Βοιωτοὶ μὲν Τρεῖς κεφαλὰς καλέουσι, 5
Ἀθηναῖοι δὲ Δρυὸς κεφαλάς. πεμφθέντες δὲ οἱ ἱππόται οὐ
μάτην ἀπίκοντο· ἐσβάλλοντα γὰρ ἐς τὸ πεδίον λαμβάνουσι

7 ἐσβαλόντα Β ‖ εἰς R

Kithairon leading in the direction of Plataia.' Only one pass is indicated ; but it is one leading, not to Erythrai, or Thebes, nor to Hysiai, but 'towards Plataia.' Where it leads from Hdt. does not expressly signify ; ultimately no doubt from the Peloponnesos, but by which route ? It is hardly conceivable that exactly the same route is signified by this description as the route by which in c. 19 *supra* the confederate forces marched from Eleusis to Erythrai. But the route to Plataia from Eleusis (and so from Athens, or the Peloponnese) is virtually the same, except in its last stage, where it breaks away to the west before descending the gorge to Erythrai, skirts the further side of the ridge for a short distance, and comes out through a distinct gap, possibly covered by Hysiai, and so down over the ὑπωρέη to Plataia. It may be this loop to the west which is here intended. The Persian cavalry could gain it by riding up the road past Erythrai into the hills, and then turning to the right. That would be the pass leading from Eleutherai (etc.) to Plataia.

The mere words in the text would also apply to the pass leading direct to Plataia from Megara, west of the pass just described ; but that pass was a difficult one, entirely unsuited to cavalry operations, or even to the Greek commissariat service. Stein[5] thinks that *de facto* this was the pass here in question, though he does not identify it with Dryoskephalai. If so Hdt. would have used this term quite wrongly.

The further designations for the pass in question may be held to support the view above adopted.

5. Τρεῖς κεφαλὰς . . Δρυὸς κεφαλάς. The Boiotians had one name for the pass, the Athenians another ; it was a pass then used by Athenians, which rules out the Megara - Plataia pass. Moreover Thucydides proves the point : 3. 24. 1 ἑώρων τοὺς Πελοποννησίους τὴν πρὸς Κιθαιρῶνα καὶ Δρυὸς κεφαλὰς τὴν ἐπ' Ἀθηνῶν φέρουσαν μετὰ λαμπάδων διώκοντας. The Peloponnesians in that case had started from their lines round Plataia. (Even if τὴν ἐπ' Ἀθ. φ. were a

gloss, the argument remains, and the identification of Dryoskephalai with the pass to Megara cannot be entertained. Baehr, note *ad l.*, ascribes this identification to Leake and Vischer, and Leake's map of Plataia, though not his text, lays him open to the charge, of which Vischer, *Erinnerungen* pp. 533, 540, appears innocent, as he certainly identifies the 'Three Heads' pass with the route from Eleutherai. An explanation of the term 'Three Heads' may be found in the supposition that it applied primarily to the meeting-place, or junction of the three roads, from Eleutherai, from Erythrai (Thebes), from Plataia. Goettling suggested that the spot was marked by a *triceps Hermes*, hence the Τρεῖς κεφαλαί : op. Baehr *in l.* Vischer's idea that the name is due to the appearance of three mountain tops (*Kuppen*) from the Boiotian side overhanging the pass is less happy. Why the Athenians preferred the term 'Oak's Heads' is not recorded ; Baehr suggests that it applied to the route from the Athenian side, which wound up through forests of oak (till it reached the top, or 'head' ?).

7. ἐς τὸ πεδίον : this term cannot be quite accurately used in this place, even if ἐσβάλλοντα is given a highly inceptive or imperfect sense ; for the objective of the commissariat train would hardly be τὸ πεδίον.

Five hundred beasts of burden would be a fairly large train : they were no doubt sumpter, not draft animals. They were coming from Peloponnesos, for Attica and Megara could furnish nothing after their devastation, cc. 13, 14 *supra* ; but they were coming, not by the difficult Megara-Plataia route, but by the better road *via* Eleusis and Eleutherai. The attendants may have been Helots, at least in part. The story implies that there was no armed convoy, and no resistance (but some of the *Agogiates* would surely have escaped). The train may have been approaching Plataia at night (see above) to escape notice from the Persians, and it may have been this device, or practice, that was reported to Mardonios by his Theban friends. The terms in which Hdt. records this exploit

ὑποζύγιά τε πεντακόσια, σιτία ἄγοντα ἀπὸ Πελοποννήσου ἐς
τὸ στρατόπεδον, καὶ ἀνθρώπους οἳ εἵποντο τοῖσι ζεύγεσι·
10 ἑλόντες δὲ ταύτην τὴν ἄγρην οἱ Πέρσαι ἀφειδέως ἐφόνευον,
οὐ φειδόμενοι οὔτε ὑποζυγίου οὐδενὸς οὔτε ἀνθρώπου. ὡς δὲ
ἄδην εἶχον κτείνοντες, τὰ λοιπὰ αὐτῶν ἤλαυνον περιβαλόμενοι
παρά τε Μαρδόνιον καὶ ἐς τὸ στρατόπεδον.

40 Μετὰ δὲ τοῦτο τὸ ἔργον ἑτέρας δύο ἡμέρας διέτριψαν,
οὐδέτεροι βουλόμενοι μάχης ἄρξαι· μέχρι μὲν γὰρ τοῦ Ἀσωποῦ
ἐπήισαν οἱ βάρβαροι πειρώμενοι τῶν Ἑλλήνων, διέβαινον δὲ
οὐδέτεροι. ἡ μέντοι ἵππος ἡ Μαρδονίου αἰεὶ προσέκειτό τε
5 καὶ ἐλύπεε τοὺς Ἕλληνας· οἱ γὰρ Θηβαῖοι, ἅτε μηδίζοντες
μεγάλως, προθύμως ἔφερον τὸν πόλεμον καὶ αἰεὶ κατηγέοντο

---

9 οἱ R 11 οὐ om. βκ, van H.: num glossema οὐ . . ἀνθρώπου
deleveris? 12 ἄδην: ἄδε S ‖ αὐτέων z ‖ περιβαλλόμενοι Marc. z (παρα-
βαλόμενοι C) 13 παρά τε om. C: τε om. a 40. 3 ἐπήεισαν
Marc. ‖ πειρεόμενοι van H. 6 προθύμως <τε> ? Stein² ‖ ἐφέροντο
πόλεμον C

---

by the cavalry are not very 'convincing':
the Persians would hardly have killed
the beasts for pure love of slaughter,
like a mad Aias, but presumably captured
as many as possible, with the stores.

10. ἄγρην is rather a sporting word;
cp. 1. 73, 2. 70, 3. 129.

11. οὐ φειδόμενοι . . ἀνθρώπου looks
like a gloss : ἀφειδέως is used without
explanation in l. 163, 207, but I will not
argue from that to the earlier composition
of this passage !

12. ἄδην εἶχον : an adverbial construction, cp. Plato Rep. 541 B. (Schweighaeuser's Lex. treats ἄδη as a subst.)
περιβαλόμενοι : cp. 8. 8.

40. 1. ἑτέρας δύο ἡμέρας : i.e. 9th
and 10th. The ἔργον, or furious
slaughter of slave and beast (not without misplaced irony !) had taken place
on the night of the 8th.

διέτριψαν, 'wasted'—a little hard
upon them, especially on the Persian
cavalry, which, though neither side
wished μάχης ἄρξαι (a pitched battle), did
some useful skirmishing, as is immediately admitted.

2. μέχρι . . τοῦ Ἀσωποῦ ἐπήισαν.
Mardonios apparently drew out his men,
day by day, on the left bank of Asopos,
opposite the Greek Laager, and by sending his cavalry round their position
tried to draw and drive them north
across the Asopos.

5. οἱ γὰρ Θηβαῖοι κτλ. The passage

exhibits a manifest animus against the
Thebans, who were medizing 'wholesale' (μεγάλως). Hdt., following no
doubt a vicious source, Attic or phil-
Attic, represents the Thebans as heading
'Persians and Medes,' until it came to
actual fighting (μέχρι μάχης), and then
leaving it to the 'barbarian' cavalry to do
all the derring deeds (ἀρετάς). In reality
no doubt the Theban, Thessalian and
Makedonian cavalry on the right of the
Persian line rode round the Athenians
on the left wing, even as the Medo-
Persian cavalry on the left rode round
the Lakedaimonians on the Greek right,
and the two may have met about the
springs of Gargaphia ; it is possible,
however, that the Greek left, on higher
ground, or less concerned for Gargaphia,
suffered less from the medizing Greeks
than the Greek right from the Persians.
Only the Thebans are mentioned here :
with Thessalians and Makedonians the
Athenians were afterwards on better
terms.

It is not very likely that the Greeks
had been eight days in the second position
('on the Asopos') before Mardonios
adopted these very obvious tactics ; nor
again very likely that he owed their
adoption to Theban suggestion.

6. ἔφερον τὸν πόλεμον : cp. c. 18
supra.

κατηγέοντο : sc. τῇ ἵππῳ. Cp. c.
104 infra, 7. 183 supra.

μέχρι μάχης, τὸ δὲ ἀπὸ τούτου παραδεκόμενοι Πέρσαι τε καὶ
Μῆδοι μάλα ἔσκον οἳ ἀπεδείκνυντο ἀρετάς.

Μέχρι μέν νυν τῶν δέκα ἡμερέων οὐδὲν ἐπὶ πλεῦν ἐγίνετο 41
τούτων· ὡς δὲ ἑνδεκάτη <σφι> ἐγεγόνεε ἡμέρη ἀντικατημένοισι
ἐν Πλαταιῇσι, οἵ τε δὴ Ἕλληνες πολλῷ πλεῦνες ἐγεγόνεσαν

---

8 μάλιστα Β: καλὰ C   41. 2 τουτέων z || <σφι> Stein(2) s
3 ἐν: ἀλλήλοισι ἐν z

---

7. μέχρι μάχης κτλ. is not inconsistent
with οὐδέτεροι βουλόμενοι μάχης ἄρξαι
above, which plainly refers to a general
or pitched battle.

τὸ δὲ ἀπὸ τούτου παραδεκόμενοι:
in a somewhat different sense 1. 18
παραδεξάμενος παρὰ τοῦ πατρὸς τὸν
πόλεμον προσεῖχε ἐντεταμένως. Still more,
2. 166 τὰ ἐς πόλεμον ἐπασκέουσι μοῦνα
παῖς παρὰ πατρὸς ἐκδεκόμενος. Cp. also
1. 102 παρεδέξατο τὴν ἀρχήν. In all
those cases the predecessor has done
what the successor is doing. ἐκδέκεσθαι
is the commoner verb with Hdt. Cp.
7. 211. 2 (ὑποδέκεσθαι c. 21. 15 al. sens.).

8. μάλα ἔσκον: the verb has the
frequentative form; cp. 7. 119. μάλα is
the positive of μᾶλλον and μάλιστα, and
seems here to have a corrective, adversative, or intensive signification, differenti-
ating still more emphatically the action
of the Persians from that of the Thebans.
It is comparatively rare with verbs: 1.
93 θώματα δὲ γῆ ἡ Λυδίη ἐς συγγραφὴν οὐ
μάλα ἔχει, 1. 134 οἱ δὲ (sc. ἄρχουσι)
μάλα τῶν ἐχομένων, 1. 181 ἐπὶ τούτῳ τῷ
πύργῳ ἄλλος πύργος ἐπιβέβηκε, καὶ ἕτερος
μάλα ἐπὶ τούτῳ, where it very nearly=
αὖθις or πάλιν. Cp. also 7. 11, 186, etc.

ἀρετάς: a significant plural; not
a number of different virtues, but a
number of cases of one virtue (courage):
'derring deeds.' Cp. 1. 176 Λύκιοι δὲ . .
ἐπεξιόντες καὶ μαχόμενοι ὀλίγοι πρὸς
πολλοὺς ἀρετὰς ἀπεδείκνυντο.

41. 1. τῶν δέκα ἡμερέων: viz. the
eight days specified in c. 39 and the two
days specified in c. 40 supra. With
'ten days,' however, we reach the
suspicious Hellenic 'week,' out of which
the previous smaller items may have
been extracted! A good deal had
happened on the eighth, ninth, tenth,
and even on the second (c. 33 supra).
It is hardly credible that from the third
to the eighth (at sundown) the Greeks
had been allowed to occupy their (second)
position absolutely unmolested, or that,

if molested, as on the ninth, tenth,
and twelfth (the eleventh is dropped
by Hdt. from this point of view, and
devoted to the conference between
Mardonios and Artabazos), they could
have held out, without either crossing
the Asopos to do battle, or retreating to
some third position, better protected
from the cavalry. In other words, it is
very unlikely that so many days elapsed
in 'the second position' as Hdt. asserts.

οὐδὲν . . τούτων is a formula; cp.
9. 121, 6. 42.

2. ὡς δὲ ἑνδεκάτη ἐγεγόνεε ἡμέρη,
'when the eleventh day was come' (not
'was past'): sc. the eleventh day on
which the two armies were facing each
other ἐν Πλαταιῇσι, i.e. no doubt
according to Hdt.'s conception 'in the
second position,' ἐν τῇ Πλαταιΐδι, ἐπὶ τῷ
Ἀσωπῷ, cp. cc. 25, 30, 31, 36 supra.
But, even if the chronological index is
to be taken quite strictly, the topographical or enchorial index may admit
of being stretched a little further, so
that ἐν Πλαταιῇσι should not merely
equal ἐν τῇ Πλαταιΐδι, but cover the
ground of all the operations in Boiotia
antecedent to the battle. The word,
indeed, as here used, ἀντικατημένοισι ἐν
Πλαταιῇσι, applies to the Persians
equally with the Greeks, yet the Persians
were on the other side of the Asopos,
which was not even Plataian land.

3. πολλῷ πλεῦνες ἐγεγόνεσαν: this
assertion cannot be taken to mean that
the numbers given above in c. 30 had
by this time been largely exceeded.
Hdt. was bound in his muster-roll to
give the maximal estimates, and the
figures there given must be taken to
cover the accessions here recorded. But
the apparent inconsequence shows that
strict order of time or argument cannot
be assumed in Hdt.'s methods of exposition, and entitles his readers to a
certain liberty of readjustment, whether
in the logical or in the chronological
interest.

καὶ Μαρδόνιος περιημέκτεε τῇ ἕδρῃ, ἐνθαῦτα ἐς λόγους ἦλθον
5 Μαρδόνιός τε ὁ Γοβρύεω καὶ Ἀρτάβαζος ὁ Φαρνάκεος, ὃς ἐν
ὀλίγοισι Περσέων ἦν ἀνὴρ δόκιμος παρὰ Ξέρξῃ. βουλευομένων
δὲ αἵδε ἦσαν αἱ γνῶμαι, ἡ μὲν Ἀρταβάζου ὡς χρεὸν εἴη

4 περιημέκτεε . . Μαρδόνιος om. R 　　 5 γοβρύεω PMarc., Stein :
Γωβρύω van H. : γωβρύεω 　　 6 βουλομένων Β 　　 7 ἔσαν z ‖ μὲν
γὰρ Β ‖ χρεὼν CPz, van H.

4. **Μαρδόνιος περιημέκτεε τῇ ἕδρῃ**:
for the verb cp. 8. 109 ; for the construction rather 4. 154. ἕδρη is a quasi-
military term ; cp. ἀντικατῆσθαι above,
Thuc. 5. 7. 2. But here it means
perhaps little more than 'delay' (δια-
τριβή, cp. διέτριψαν c. 40).

ἐς λόγους ἦλθον, 'had a conversation,' or conference together. The
parties to such a proceeding would be
more or less co-ordinate (like two Roman
consuls commanding different armies) ;
nevertheless, on the present occasion, it
appears that in some way or other the
authority of Mardonios was superior to
that of Artabazos ; moreover the conference is not a private dialogue, but
apparently a council of war, at which
all the chief officers in the army, or
armies, are present—though Hdt. is not
clear or explicit on this point. How
purely rhetorical or stylistic the use of
the patronymic may be is clearly shown
in the present case ; cp. 7. 11 etc. For
Gobryas cp. 7. 2, 5 etc. ; for Pharnakes
8. 126.

5. ἐν ὀλίγοισι : cp. 4. 52.

6. βουλευομένων, not merely the two
Persians just named, but all those
present at the Council, who have two
γνῶμαι laid before them, that of
Artabazos, supported by the Thebans,
and that of Mardonios (which probably
commended itself to his Persian officers).

7. ἡ μὲν Ἀρταβάζου. The plan of
Artabazos is to abandon operations in
the field, to evacuate the fortified camp,
to retire behind the walls of Thebes,
and from there—whither it might be expected the Greek army would follow—to
attempt by bribery and corruption the
realization of the Persian hopes. This
record is remarkable for several reasons.

(i.) It implies that there were serious
misgivings on the Persian side as to the
issue of a battle.

(ii.) It suggests that the forward movement of the Greeks and their occupation
of the second position gave them some

advantage, perhaps threatened the
Persian position more directly than
Hdt. appears to realize. As against
this, however, it seems improbable that
the tradition, so favourable to the
Greeks, and especially to the Athenians,
should have quite forgotten, or missed,
so important a point in their favour.

(iii.) Artabazos cannot be exonerated
from the suspicion of viewing Mardonios
with jealousy, and subordinating the
Persian interest to personal schemes and
rivalries. The story of his subsequent
action or inaction is astounding. The
technical relation between the two
generals is obscure ; see below ; but,
whatever it was, Artabazos comes badly
out of the affair in the sequel, notwithstanding a pretty evident bias in his
favour.

(iv.) The plan proposed by Artabazos,
as far as negotiations, bribery and so
forth are concerned, had already been
tried ; op. notes to c. 4 supra. It is said
to be supported by the Thebans ; it is
indeed their own original idea, cp. c. 2
supra ; but the time has surely gone by
for it now, with the confederate army
in position before them. If there was
a medizing party in the Athenian camp
(Plutarch Arist. 13) there was an Atticizing section on the other side of the
Asopos ! cp. c. 44 infra.

(v.) The idea of retiring into Thebes
is not a sound one, though the proposal
is valuable as implying comparatively
small numbers on the Persian side.
Artabazos might, indeed, have acquired
a respect for Greek fortifications from
his own failure before Poteidaia (8.
126-9), but a siege of Thebes could
hardly have been to the advantage of
the besieged : the Persian cavalry would
have been lost ; the abandonment of
the Persian camp on the Asopos was
morally tantamount to a defeat.

(vi.) Hdt. places this debate on the
11th day. But this date may be merely
a dramatic ruse. The difference of

ἀναζεύξαντας τὴν ταχίστην πάντα τὸν στρατὸν ἰέναι ἐς τὸ
τεῖχος τὸ Θηβαίων, ἔνθα σῖτόν τέ σφι ἐσενηνεῖχθαι πολλὸν
καὶ χόρτον τοῖσι ὑποζυγίοισι, κατ' ἡσυχίην τε ἱζομένους δια- 10
πρήσσεσθαι ποιεῦντας τάδε· ἔχειν γὰρ χρυσὸν πολλὸν μὲν
ἐπίσημον πολλὸν δὲ καὶ ἄσημον, πολλὸν δὲ ἄργυρόν τε καὶ
ἐκπώματα· τούτων φειδομένους μηδενὸς διαπέμπειν ἐς τοὺς
Ἕλληνας, Ἑλλήνων δὲ μάλιστα ἐς τοὺς προεστεῶτας ἐν τῆσι

---

8 ἀναζεύξαντες C   9 Θηβαῖον RV ‖ τέ om. S ‖ ἐνηνέχθαι RS :
συνενηνεῖχθαι Cobet   10 διαπρήσεσθαι C   12 δὲ καὶ ἄργυρόν
CPz ‖ τε om. S : 'τε καὶ ἐκπώματα suspecta' Stein²   13 τουτέων z :
τούτων δὲ β

---

opinion between Artabazos and Mardonios
will not then first have occurred, or
come to light. It was probably of
longer standing. What line had
Artabazos taken when the policy was
originally proposed by the Thebans, c.
3 supra? Hdt. may have crystallized
and misdated a long standing feud and
difference of opinion. Or has Artabazos
and his corps d'armée only just joined
Mardonios? He has had the whole
summer for his march from Poteidaia,
and Mardonios has already offered
battle.

(vii.) At this point there are perhaps
two alternatives recognizable, one or
other of which Artabazos might have
advocated. (a) A tactical stratagem.
Mardonios himself was anxious to draw
the Greeks across the Asopos : why not
retire on Thebes, abandoning even the
camp, with its plate and spoil, for the
nonce, in order to get the Greeks across
the river, and to bring about a general
engagement (cp. Hannibal's ruse, Livy
22. 41 f.)? (b) A strategic coup.
Artabazos may have proposed what he
himself afterwards carried out, retreat,
the evacuation of Boiotia, perhaps of
Greece, the preservation of their two
armies intact for the king's service.
Artabazos has a special loyalty to
Xerxes. Events in Asia (movement of
the Greek fleet, revolt of Babylon, etc.)
may already have been reported at
Persian headquarters in Boiotia. Such
tactics or such strategy Mardonios
rejected : the first might easily prove a
failure ; the second was failure confessed.
The time for political and diplomatic
manoeuvring had gone. Under the
circumstances, with the available
evidences, one's sympathies in this
debate must be with Mardonios.

8. ἀναζεύξαντας : cp. 8. 60 ; but the
verb here governs π. τ. στρατόν, if the
words are genuine.

τὴν ταχίστην : sc. ὁδόν. The phrase
suggests a longer march than just back
to Thebes ; but it may well be taken
with ἀναζεύξαντας and = ὡς τάχιστα.
Still, where was the need of hurry?

τὸ τεῖχος τὸ Θηβαίων. Thebes
was a walled city ; cp. c. 86 infra. If
the whole army was going to find accommodation in Thebes it cannot have
numbered 300,000. Even 150,000 men
would have strained the accommodation !
But perhaps the northern Greeks were
expected to go home ; Artabazos himself
may also have had no intention of remaining
in Boiotia. Thebes might have ac-
commodated 50,000 men — Mardonios'
corps d'armée — as well as its own population.

The statement that there was abundance
of food for man and beast (σῖτος, χόρτος)
will be contradicted, within twenty-four
hours, by Alexander of Makedon, c. 45
infra ; but it is probably true for all
that. Cp. notes ad l.

9. ἐσενηνεῖχθαι is of course pl.p.

10. διαπρήσσεσθαι : obviously of
political intrigue ; the active is used,
not so very differently, c. 94 infra.

13. φειδομένους μηδενός, 'without
stint' (Macaulay), i.e. = ἀφειδέως ; cp.
c. 39 supra.

διαπέμπειν : distributively. Why
suspect the plate? Rather than that
insert πολλά — it was no doubt of gold
and silver. Cp. 3. 148, and c. 80 infra.

14. τοὺς προεστεῶτας : not necessarily
the formally appointed magistrates, or
commanders, but the political leaders ;
προστάται, cp. 5. 23, 49, etc.

15 πόλισι, καὶ ταχέως σφέας παραδώσειν τὴν ἐλευθερίην· μηδὲ
ἀνακινδυνεύειν συμβάλλοντας. τούτου μὲν ἡ αὐτὴ ἐγίνετο καὶ
Θηβαίων γνώμη, ὡς προειδότος πλεῦν τι καὶ τούτου, Μαρδονίου
δὲ ἰσχυροτέρη τε καὶ ἀγνωμονεστέρη καὶ οὐδαμῶς συγγινω-
σκομένη· δοκέειν τε γὰρ πολλῷ κρέσσονα εἶναι τὴν σφετέρην
20 στρατιὴν τῆς Ἑλληνικῆς, συμβάλλειν τε τὴν ταχίστην μηδὲ
περιορᾶν συλλεγομένους ἔτι πλεῦνας τῶν συλλελεγμένων, τά
τε σφάγια τὰ Ἡγησιστράτου ἐᾶν χαίρειν μηδὲ βιάζεσθαι,
42 ἀλλὰ νόμῳ τῷ Περσέων χρεωμένους συμβάλλειν. τούτου δὲ
οὕτω δικαιεῦντος ἀντέλεγε οὐδείς, ὥστε ἐκράτεε τῇ γνώμῃ· τὸ

---

15 προδώσειν Naber   16 ἀνακινδυνεύσειν idem, van H. ‖ συμ-
βαλόντας S ‖ μέν νυν z ‖ ἐγένετο z   18 τε om. B: τε καὶ ἀγνωμονεστέρη om. C ‖ συγγιγνωσκομένη a: συγγινωσκομένου van H.   19
κρέσσονας apr: κρέσσον CV   20 στρατηίην RS   21 πλεῦνας
γίνεσθαι z ‖ συλλεγομένων A¹Pz   22 βιᾶσθαι van H.   23 χρεο-
μένους P, van H.

---

15. **παραδώσειν**: euphemistically for
προδώσειν.

16. **ἡ αὐτὴ ἐγίνετο καὶ Θηβαίων γνώμη**:
(his opinion) was the same as that of
the Thebans—i.e. as expressed above
in c. 2. Hdt. does not mean to say
that the Thebans now expressed their
opinion.

17. **ὡς προειδότος πλεῦν τι**: it is
rather insight than foresight, perhaps,
which the phrase is meant to suggest.
Μαρδονίου δέ: sc. ἡ δὲ γνώμη
Μαρδονίου ἦν (ellipse, or brachylogy).
It follows in *orat. obliq.* Hdt. apparently means to condemn it, as
'stark, obstinate, uncompromising'—i.e.
utterly devoid of reasonableness, of the
spirit of compromise. On ἀγνωμοσύνη cp.
c. 3 *supra*. **πολλῷ κρέσσονα** corresponds
with the figures as given by Hdt. (350,000
v. 110,000), but if true of the real numbers
would somewhat have mitigated the
apparently 'foolish obstinacy' of Mardonios. If tradition had been content
to state the figures of Mardonios' force
more accurately, his obstinacy might
have seemed less reasonable.

20. **συμβάλλειν** may be constructed
with ὡς χρεὸν εἴη or such like, understood out of ἡ γνώμη ἦν, but a looser
construction, or apposition, were no less
idiomatic.
τὴν ταχίστην=ὡς τάχιστα: so.
συμβολήν, ὁδόν, or *sim.*; cp. l. 8 *supra*.

21. **περιορᾶν**: i.e. *pati*, cp. 7. 16.
τά τε σφάγια . . ἐᾶν χαίρειν:
this sentiment sounds, and is intended

to sound, very impious and shocking,
though as coming from a Persian it
might be less offensive than in the
mouth of a Greek; but then, Mardonios
should not have had recourse to Hellenic
divination if he was going to flout it in
this fashion! χ. ἐᾶν, cp. c. 45 *infra*,
4. 112 *supra*.

22. **βιάζεσθαι**: *vim inferre auspiciis*,
Baehr; *permittere ut victimae sibi vim
afferant*, Matthiae: the one taking the
verb as deponent trans., the other as
passive. Both uses are found: Soph.
Antig. 66 βιάζομαι τάδε (pass.), Thuc. 8.
53. 2 τοὺς νόμους βιασάμενοι (as here τὰ
σφάγια). So also with personal object.
In a rather different sense, which might
however work here, Thuc. 4. 11. 4
βιαζομένους τὴν ἀπόβασιν, 7. 72. 3
βιάσασθαι . . τὸν ἔκπλουν. Stein notes
that ἐκβιάζεσθαι would have been clearer.

23. **νόμῳ τῷ Περσέων**: i.e. it was not
the Persian custom to submit military
tactics to the chances of divination.
There is something of a problem here.
Persians were probably as superstitious,
to say the least of it, as Greeks. The
(apparent) absence of the Magi in the
army of Mardonios is remarkable. He
himself is represented as the special
fautor of Greek religion. He here
appears in the character of a 'free-
thinker,' like Claudius Pulcher in 249
B.C. before the battle of Drepana; cp.
Suetonius, *Tib.* 2.

42. 2. **δικαιεῦντος**: a favourite word
with Hdt. =ἀξιοῦν, cp. 8. 126.

γὰρ κράτος εἶχε τῆς στρατιῆς οὗτος ἐκ βασιλέος, ἀλλ᾽ οὐκ
Ἀρτάβαζος. μεταπεμψάμενος ὦν τοὺς ταξιάρχους τῶν τελέων
καὶ τῶν μετ᾽ ἑωυτοῦ ἐόντων Ἑλλήνων τοὺς στρατηγοὺς εἰρώτα 5
εἴ τι εἰδεῖεν λόγιον περὶ Περσέων ὡς διαφθερέονται ἐν τῇ
Ἑλλάδι. σιγώντων δὲ τῶν ἐπικλήτων, τῶν μὲν οὐκ εἰδότων

---

42. 3 ἐκ βασιλέως C: ἐκ βασιλῆος z: om. β, Valla: 'nec fortasse
genuina' van H.   4 τούς τε ταξιάρχους τῶν μετ᾽ ἑωυτοῦ ἐόντων
Ἑλλήνων καὶ malit Stein⁶   5 ἠρώτα CPz   6 εἰδοῖεν z ‖ διαφθερέονται P: διαφθορεῦνται β: διαφθερέοντας Paris. 1635 z: διαφθαρέονται

ὥστε, 'and so,' cp. 7. 118.

τὸ γὰρ κράτος εἶχε κτλ.: the
statement that Mardonios but not (ἀλλ᾽
οὐ) Artabazos was commander-in-chief
of the army by the king's commission
(ἐκ), still leaves the exact relations of
Mardonios and Artabazos an obscure
problem. (a) 8. 126 supra looks as
though Artabazos held a post directly
subordinate to Mardonios, inasmuch as
he was in command of 60,000 of Mardonios' own select soldiers; but that
passage is not convincing, and if 300,000
is really the figure, not for the force of
Mardonios but for the king's grand army
itself (cp. c. 32 supra), the passage must
really tell quite the other way. (b) The
service on which Artabazos is there
engaged points to an independent command, as does also (c) his subsequent
conduct towards Mardonios c. 66 infra,
and (d) the reception which he afterwards enjoys at home; had he been
in a position actually subordinate to
Mardonios his reception could hardly
have been so good. Moreover (e) this
passage itself, closely considered, lends
weight to the supposition that the two
commanders were independent of each
other; Hdt. at any rate has avoided
saying that Artabazos had to take his
orders from Mardonios. Is it not
possible that the exact position of
neither general is fully or clearly stated?
Was the command of Artabazos primarily
a command in Thrace, and the command
of Mardonios a command in Hellas,
south of Olympos? Was Mardonios at
least more than mere 'commander'?
was he governor, or satrap of Hellas,
for the time being? His Greek 'allies'
(cp. cc. 31, 32 supra) were certainly the
king's subjects. It was only their
presence which gave the army of Mardonios its numerical superiority to that
of Artabazos. Mardonios is perhaps to

be thought of as defending his own
province from an Hellenic invasion!

4. μεταπεμψάμενος ὦν: so far as
the two Persian commanders have been
having a private conversation; but that
implication is in itself improbable, and
conflicts with other indications in the
text, viz. (a) the set speech ascribed to
Artabazos; (b) the term βουλευομένων
above; (c) the purely inadequate and
dummy rôle assigned to the ἐπίκλητοι
when now at last summoned; (d) the
obvious probability, and indeed certainty,
that the commander would confer with
his officers. We may fairly conclude
that the Council has really been sitting
through c. 41, or at least that the arguments already given represent speeches
made at the Council, even if the two
chiefs had previously held a private
colloquy.

τοὺς ταξιάρχους τῶν τελέων: the
term τελέαρχοι (cp. τελάρχης) is hardly
found; the 'taxiarchs,' or captains, of
the τέλη, or squadrons, are here apparently the Persian and other native
officers, cp. 8. 67, the ἄρχοντες of the
army-list in Bk. 7, cp. 7. 81, as
distinguished from the Strategoi of the
Greeks, i.e. the Boiotarcha, the Aleuadai,
Alexander of Makedon, Harmokydes
the Phokian, and so forth.

5. εἰρώτα εἴ τι κτλ.: this inquiry by
Mardonios would have been singularly
tactless in form and in substance, if it
had really been addressed to the officers
above indicated, Persian as well as Greek,
summoned ad hoc. 'Know ye any
prediction that we Persians are to be
utterly destroyed here in Hellas?'
Stein⁶ accordingly would emend the
passage, cp. App. Crit. But did Hdt.
reason so closely?

7. τῶν ἐπικλήτων: well rendered by
Macaulay, 'those summoned to council,'
cp. 7. 8, 8. 101. The general, or

τοὺς χρησμούς, τῶν δὲ εἰδότων μὲν ἐν ἀδείῃ δὲ οὐ ποιευμένων
τὸ λέγειν, αὐτὸς Μαρδόνιος ἔλεγε " ἐπεὶ τοίνυν ὑμεῖς ἢ ἴστε
10 οὐδὲν ἢ οὐ τολμᾶτε λέγειν, ἀλλ' ἐγὼ ἐρέω ὡς εὖ ἐπιστάμενος·
ἔστι λόγιον ὡς χρεόν ἐστι Πέρσας ἀπικομένους ἐς τὴν Ἑλλάδα

---

8 ἀδείαι P   9 αὐτός τε B: αὐτός γε Gomperz, Holder ‖ Μαρδόνιος
ἔλεγεν· ἀλλ' ἐγὼ ἐρέω ὡς εὖ ἐπιστάμενος, ἐπεὶ δὴ ὑμεῖς ἢ ἴστε κτλ. S ‖
ἡμεῖς C   11 χρεών CPz ‖ ἐστι: τι B

---

governor, has his ἐπίκλητοι, like the
king. (The word cannot here be evacuated of meaning, or reduced to ἐπικλη-
θέντων or ἐπικλήτων γενομένων.) The
Persians (τῶν μέν) would mostly be
ignorant of the Greek oracles, the Greeks
(τῶν δέ) might know them, but 'did
not consider it safe' (ἐν ἀδείῃ δὲ οὐ
ποιευμένων) to say so.

9. αὐτὸς Μαρδόνιος ἔλεγε: did he
speak in Persian, or in Greek? The
speech ascribed to him still further
complicates the situation. 'There is a
prophecy to the effect that the Persians
after coming to Greece must sack the
temple in Delphi, and thereafter perish
to the last man. We shall not sack the
temple: as far as that is concerned,
then, we are safe enough.' Mardonios
might have gone on to show some
positive cause for expecting a victory;
he has done that (privately!) already to
Artabazos, viz. (1) the Persian army is
superior to the Greek; (2) there is no
time to be lost, for the Greek army is
increasing day by day; (3) it is the
Persian way to assume the offensive, to
deliver the attack.

The present anecdote has very little
to say to the situation at Plataia; it is
not so much part of the story of Plataia,
as part of the Apology of Delphi. It
explains the fact—a fact so very awkward
for Delphi by and by — that Delphi
escaped pillage at the hands of the
Persians. The explanation is good in
itself, but it is completely at variance
with the other and more brilliant explanation and apology already given,
viz. the story of the Persian attack on
Delphi, and the miraculous preservation
of the temple and its contents, 8. 35-39.
Both stories cannot be true, though
both may be false. To suppose that if
the Persians, a year before, had done
their best to plunder Delphi, Mardonios
would have urged this line of argument,
in order to cheer and encourage his
Council of War, is absurd (the rather,

as the Delphic god takes the will for
the deed, 6. 86). But this critique
might only be one point more against
the story in Bk. 8, in itself already
incredible. Is the story here true? It
is improbable. Its apologetic tendency
condemns it. The improbability of the
Persian commander-in-chief urging such
a line of argument in any case remains.
Hdt. himself adds that there was no
such oracle: the oracle cited he refers
to another connexion. Last, not least,
considering the real situation in 480-
79 B.C., there is hardly room or occasion
for such an oracle, much less for such
a scene in the Persian camp as this
anecdote involves; it is, in the truest
sense, a huge anachronism. Delphi, if
not actually on the Persian side, was on
the side of the Greeks who were on the
Persian side, cp. 7. 132. The question
of a Persian sack of Delphi can hardly
have been a real question at the time;
Xerxes and Mardonios were more likely
to be making offerings at Delphi—like
Datis at Delos in 490 B.C., cp. 6. 97—
than plundering the shrine. It may
fairly be concluded that this anecdote,
though not involving physical impossi-
bilities, is not more true, in a strictly
historical sense, than the other.

11. λόγιον is prima facie a prose
utterance (yet op. πεποιημένον in next
c.); the oracle, then, will hardly be a
Delphic response. It cannot, however,
be (as Stein suggests) due to Onomakritos
(cp. 7. 6), for he communicated no
oracle σφάλμα φέρον τῷ βαρβάρῳ. Mardonios might be supposed to have had
it through Mys his commissioner. Cp.
8. 133 ff. Baehr points out that Euripides, Bakch. 1336, has this oracle (or
this anecdote?) in view: ὅταν δὲ Λοξίου
χρηστήριον διαρπάσωσι, νόστον ἄθλιον
πάλιν σχήσουσι (sc. οἱ βάρβαροι). If so,
he has 'harmonized' it with the story
in 8. 35 ff. Here there is no νόστος.

χρεόν ἐστι after ἔστι λόγιον is a
little curious and clumsy: if maintained,

διαρπάσαι τὸ ἱρὸν τὸ ἐν Δελφοῖσι, μετὰ δὲ τὴν διαρπαγὴν
ἀπολέσθαι πάντας. ἡμεῖς τοίνυν αὐτὸ τοῦτο ἐπιστάμενοι οὔτε
ἴμεν ἐπὶ τὸ ἱρὸν [τοῦτο] οὔτε ἐπιχειρήσομεν διαρπάζειν,
ταύτης τε εἵνεκα τῆς αἰτίης οὐκ ἀπολεόμεθα. ὥστε ὑμέων 15
ὅσοι τυγχάνουσι εὔνοοι ἐόντες Πέρσῃσι, ἤδεσθε τοῦδε εἵνεκα
ὡς περιεσομένους ἡμέας Ἑλλήνων." ταῦτά σφι εἴπας δεύτερα
ἐσήμαινε παραρτέεσθαί τε πάντα καὶ εὐκρινέα ποιέεσθαι ὡς
ἅμα ἡμέρῃ τῇ ἐπιούσῃ συμβολῆς ἐσομένης.

Τοῦτον δ᾽ ἔγωγε τὸν χρησμόν, τὸν Μαρδόνιος εἶπε ἐς 43
Πέρσας ἔχειν, ἐς Ἰλλυριούς τε καὶ τὸν Ἐγχελέων στρατὸν
οἶδα πεποιημένον, ἀλλ᾽ οὐκ ἐς Πέρσας. ἀλλὰ τὰ μὲν Βάκιδι
ἐς ταύτην τὴν μάχην [ἐστὶ] πεποιημένα,

---

12 ἁρπαγὴν Β　　　13 οὗτοι τε z　　　14 τοῦτο Stein, van H. :
om. Β, Holder : seclusi　　　15 ταύτηι C　　　17 περισομένους R :
περιεζομένους SV　　18 ἐσήμενε R : ἐσήμηνε SV ‖ εὐρικρενέα Β :
εὔκρινα S　　19 συμβουλῆς R　　43. 2 τῶν Β ‖ ἐγχελέων R :
ἐγχέλεον Β : ἐγχέλεων　　3 τάδε μὲν Β　　4 ἐστὶ post Βακίδι z :
om. C, Gaisford, van H. : secl. Stein², Holder

---

it would show that the original significance of χρεών was virtually forgotten.
But alas for thee, Mardonios! οὔτε ἐς τὸ
μετέπειτα οὔτε ἐς τὸ παραυτίκα νῦν κατα-
προίξεαι ἀποτράπων τὸ χρεὸν γενέσθαι
(cp. 7. 17).

15. ταύτης τε εἵνεκα τῆς αἰτίης
seems to admit that there might be
other grounds for apprehension—which
Mardonios would of course, if this story
were true, have proceeded to remove.
Cp. τοῦδε εἵνεκα just below.

18. εὐκρινέα ποιέεσθαι: apparently
in a physical, not a merely psychical
sense. Our naval order 'to clear the
decks for action' is superficially analogous.
Xenophon, Oikon. 8. 19, makes Ischo-
machos say that 'there should be a
place for everything and everything in
its place,' ὅτι καὶ χύτρας φημὶ εὐρυθμον
φαίνεσθαι εὐκρινῶς κειμένας.

19. ἡμέρῃ τῇ ἐπιούσῃ: i.e. the 12th.
Cp. c. 41 supra.

43. 1. ἐς Πέρσας ἔχειν, 'to apply to
the Persians'; cp. 6. 19.

2. ἐς Ἰλλυριούς τε καὶ τὸν Ἐγχελέων
στρατὸν οἶδα πεποιημένον, 'I know to
have been composed (in verse) with
reference to Illyrians, that is to say,
the Enchelean host.' 'Encheleus' was
apparently (according to Appian, Illyr.
2) the eldest son of Illyrios. The
'Encheleis' are mentioned 5. 61 as a

folk among whom the 'Kadmeians' took
refuge when driven out of Thebes by the
Argives, 'in the days of Laodamas son
of Eteokles.' Pausanias too (9. 5. 3)
represents Kadmos himself as having
retired to dwell among the Illyrian tribe
of Encheleans, leaving the Theban throne
to his son Polydoros. Strabo 326 places
the Ἐγχέλειοι, οὓς καὶ Σεσαρηθίους καλοῦσι, in the Hinterland of Epidamnos
and Apollonia, and adds that ἐν τοῖς
Ἐγχελείοις οἱ Κάδμου καὶ Ἁρμονίας
ἀπόγονοι ἦρχον καὶ τὰ μυθευόμενα περὶ
αὐτῶν ἐκεῖ δείκνυται. Apollodoros (3. 5.
4) gives the story of Kadmos. The
'Encheleis' were at war with the
'Illyrians,' and had an oracular promise
of victory if they took Kadmos and
Harmonia as leaders : they obeyed and
obtained victory. Subsequently, however, Kadmos and Harmonia were meta-
morphosed into serpents. This is the
story utilized by Euripides, where he
shows acquaintance with the oracle as
interpreted by Hdt. in this place; cp.
Bakchai (ed. Sandys) 1330-1339. For
οἶδα here see below.

3. τὰ μὲν Βάκιδι: sc. ἔπη. On
Bakis cp. 8. 20. The μέν here has no
corresponding δέ. So too ταῦτα μέν just
below.

4. ταύτην τὴν μάχην is curious, as
it apparently refers to the battle of
Plataia, still to come.

τὴν δ' ἐπὶ Θερμώδοντι καὶ Ἀσωπῷ λεχεποίῃ
Ἑλλήνων σύνοδον καὶ βαρβαρόφωνον ἰυγήν,
τῇ πολλοὶ πεσέονται ὑπὲρ λάχεσίν τε μόρον τε
τοξοφόρων Μήδων, ὅταν αἴσιμον ἦμαρ ἐπέλθῃ,—
ταῦτα μὲν καὶ παραπλήσια τούτοισι ἄλλα Μουσαίῳ ἔχοντα
10 οἶδα ἐς Πέρσας. ὁ δὲ Θερμώδων ποταμὸς ῥέει μεταξὺ Τανάγρης
τε καὶ Γλίσαντος.

44　Μετὰ δὲ τὴν ἐπειρώτησιν τῶν χρησμῶν καὶ παραίνεσιν
τὴν ἐκ Μαρδονίου νύξ τε ἐγίνετο καὶ ἐς φυλακὰς ἐτάσσοντο.
ὡς δὲ πρόσω τῆς νυκτὸς προελήλατο καὶ ἡσυχίη τε ἐδόκεε

---

5 θερμόδοτον R　　7 πολλὴ **Β** (πολλῇ ap. Gaisf.) || λάχεσί RV
8 ἔσιμον B　　9 τούτοισι om. S || Μουσαίου Bekker　　44. 1
ἐπηρώτησιν C　　2 ἐγένετο Sz　　3 προσελήλατο **Β** || ἡσυχίη τε **Β**,
Stein³ : ἡσυχίηι Β : ἡσυχίη

---

5. λεχεποίῃ of the Asopos is
Homeric : *Il.* 4. 383.

6. σύνοδον : cp. c. 27 *supra*.

ἰυγή is a rare word, found also
ap. Soph. *Philok.* 741 ; cp. verb ἰύζειν
Tr. 784. The Homeric form is ἰυγμός,
Il. 18. 572.

7. ὑπὲρ λάχεσίν τε μόρον τε, 'beyond
what destiny and fate decree.' —
'Lachesis' does not appear in Homer ;
but ὑπὲρ μόρον is Homeric, *Od.* 1. 34.

8. αἴσιμον ἦμαρ : *Homerum quoque
redolet*, Baehr ; cp. *Il.* 8. 72, etc.

9. Μουσαίῳ : cp. 7. 6 *supra*.

10. οἶδα : cp. l. 3 *supra*. The two
are remarkable, the rather as they
hardly refer to exactly the same kind of
knowledge. Had Hdt. in his hands a
ms. copy of the poems and prophecies of
Musaios, or whence his assurance of personal knowledge in this case ? His assertion that the prediction (said to have been)
referred by Mardonios to the Persians in
truth referred not to them but to the
Encheleians is a question of interpretation. Here we may suppose an antecedent visit to Delphi, and even the
correction of a previous error. This
chapter has many marks of being an
insertion, an interpolation : if from the
author's own hand, then not as part of
the first or original draft of the work ;
cp. Introduction, § 9. Two further
points are of special interest in regard
to the λόγιον. (1) It is an 'unfulfilled'
prophecy ; a prophecy, indeed, designed
to defeat its own fulfilment. (2) It
exhibits the possibility and the practice
of transferring predictions from one
event to another as might suit.

ὁ δὲ Θερμώδων κτλ. : the geographical gloss is added to explain the
name in the oracle above. On the river
cp. c. 27 *supra*. Plutarch (*Dem.* 19, cp.
Theseus 27) shows that the 'Sibylline'
verse τῆς ἐπὶ Θερμώδοντι μάχης ἀπάνευθε
γενοίμην could be interpreted of the
battle of Chaironeia, in 338 B.C. On
Tanagra cp. c. 15 *supra*.

11. Γλίσαντος. Glisas appears in
the Catalogue (*Il.* 2. 504) in one line
with Plataia. Its ruins are placed by
Pausanias (9. 19. 2) off the road from
Thebes to Chalkis, seven stades to the
north of Teumesos, under Mount Hypatos.
It was famous as the scene of a battle
between the Argives, i.e. Epigonoi, and
the Thebans (1. 44. 4 etc.). Pausanias
names the Thermodon beside it. Cp.
Strabo 412 Γλίσαντα δὲ λέγει κατοικία
ἐν τῷ Ὑπάτῳ ὄρει . . πλησίον Τευμησσοῦ
. . ᾧ ὑπόκειται τὸ Ἀόνιον καλούμενον
πεδίον.

44. 1. τὴν ἐπειρώτησιν τῶν χρησμῶν :
a curious expression, for 'inquiry about,
or after, the oracles' — referring to
Mardonios' inquiry in c. 42 *supra*. For
the word cp. 6. 67. The παραίνεσις is
also to be found in c. 42 *supra*.

2. νύξ τε . . καὶ . . : a very simple
parataxis, cp. 7. 21.

ἐς φυλακὰς ἐτάσσοντο apparently
applies to both sides, and means practically that they retired to quarters,
bivouacked, instead of continuing in
battle-array, φυλακή being guard-duty,
etc. Cp. also c. 51 *infra*, and here just
below. On the division of the watches
see note to c. 51 below.

3. πρόσω τῆς νυκτὸς προελήλατο : a

εἶναι ἀνὰ τὰ στρατόπεδα καὶ μάλιστα οἱ ἄνθρωποι εἶναι ἐν
ὕπνῳ, τηνικαῦτα προσελάσας ἵππῳ πρὸς τὰς φυλακὰς τὰς 5
Ἀθηναίων Ἀλέξανδρος ὁ Ἀμύντεω, στρατηγός τε ἐὼν καὶ
βασιλεὺς Μακεδόνων, ἐδίζητο τοῖσι στρατηγοῖσι ἐς λόγους
ἐλθεῖν. τῶν δὲ φυλάκων οἱ μὲν πλεῦνες παρέμενον, οἱ δ᾽
ἔθεον ἐπὶ τοὺς στρατηγούς, ἐλθόντες δὲ ἔλεγον ὡς ἄνθρωπος
ἥκοι ἐπ᾽ ἵππου ἐκ τοῦ στρατοπέδου τοῦ Μήδων, ὃς ἄλλο μὲν 10
οὐδὲν παραγυμνοῖ ἔπος, στρατηγοὺς δὲ ὀνομάζων ἐθέλειν φησὶ
ἐς λόγους ἐλθεῖν. οἱ δὲ ἐπεὶ ταῦτα ἤκουσαν, αὐτίκα εἵποντο 45

---

5 τὰς Ἀθηναίων: τῶν Ἀθηναίων Pz   8 δ᾽: δὲ B   10 ἥκει Marc. z
11 ἐθέλειν σφι C: ἐθέλει σφίσιν Marc.: ἐθέλει φησὶ z   45. 1
εἵποντο CPz

---

neuter construction, with a correct
temporal pluperfect: *multum noctis
processerat.* Cp. 2. 121 ὡς δὲ πρόσω ἦν
τῆς νυκτός. Copied by Sallust, *Iug.* 21
ubi plerumque noctis processit. The
whole phrase ὡς δὲ . . ἐν ὕπνῳ is a paraphrase for 'the second watch,' cp. c. 51
infra.

5. τὰς φυλακὰς τὰς Ἀθηναίων: the
feminine φυλακή may be either collective
(cp. ἡ ἵππος) or local; the plural here
suits the latter meaning: the outposts,
vedettes. Cp. l. 2 *supra.*

6. Ἀλέξανδρος ὁ Ἀμύντεω κτλ. If
the patronymic might have been employed here for the sake of clearness and
style, yet the full description added is
rather *de trop,* after the many previous
accounts of Alexander (7. 173-5, 8. 34,
136 ff., cc. 1, 4, 8 *supra*), and points
rather to the independent Attic, or phil-
Attic source, from which this part of
the narrative is obviously derived. The
Makedonians were posted on the Persian
right, opposite the Athenians; cp. c. 31
supra.

7. ἐδίζητο: cp. c. 37 *supra.*

τοῖσι στρατηγοῖσι: in spite of c.
28 *supra* Alexander knows that there is
more than one Strategos in the Athenian
quarters. Stein says, 'probably all ten
were in camp, cp. 6. 103'—but what
then of Xanthippos, and his probable
colleague, or colleagues, on the fleet?
(cp. c. 114 *infra*). And was there no
Strategos left in Salamis?

ἐς λόγους ἐλθεῖν: he wishes to
communicate, to converse with them,
but there is no question of a discussion
or a debate, cp. c. 41 *supra.*

8. τῶν δὲ φυλάκων: the good,
efficient, vigilant, shrewd Athenian
picket! Most of them stay—to keep
an eye on Alexander (whom they did
not recognize), while two or three ran
(ἔθεον) to headquarters with the message.
Probably there was an officer who gave
the proper directions, and the action
was not all quite so spontaneous and
democratic as it reads.

9. ἄνθρωπος is not complimentary
to the king: it suggests a barbarian.
Perhaps οἱ ἄνθρωποι up above has a
special reference to the same side, whose
vigilance Alexander had of course *ex
hypothesi* to avoid; or it might contrast
with the beasts, who were perhaps
awake, but did not matter.

11. παραγυμνοῖ: cp. 8. 19.

στρατηγοὺς δὲ ὀνομάζων: certainly
not all ten of them, but a selection! If
only Hdt. had done as much! The
only Strategoi for this year whom he
names are Aristeides (c. 28 *supra*) and
Xanthippos (c. 114 *infra*). Plutarch
(*Aristeid.* 20) adds for Plataia two
names, Leokrates and Myronides. It is
hardly likely that Aristeides was but
τρίτος αὐτός with so large a force under
arms. The Athenian democratic theory
was that all battles were soldiers' battles,
and that generals did not count for
much, and needed not to be remembered,
unless they were killed. Where was
Themistokles, for example, all this
time? Was he with Xanthippos on the
fleet? Thuc. 1. 90 disproves it. Was
he with Aristeides in the camp? Was
he in Salamis with the women and
children? The Athenians forgot to
say—forgot even to say whether he was
one of the Strategoi this year at all.

45. 1. οἱ δέ: the two, three, or more,
'named' by Alexander. It is not said

ἐς τὰς φυλακάς· ἀπικομένοισι δὲ ἔλεγε Ἀλέξανδρος τάδε.
" ἄνδρες Ἀθηναῖοι, παραθήκην ὑμῖν τὰ ἔπεα τάδε τίθεμαι,
ἀπόρρητα ποιεύμενος πρὸς μηδένα λέγειν ὑμέας ἄλλον ἢ
5 Παυσανίην, μή με καὶ διαφθείρητε· οὐ γὰρ ἂν ἔλεγον, εἰ μὴ
μεγάλως ἐκηδόμην συναπάσης τῆς Ἑλλάδος. αὐτός τε γὰρ
Ἕλλην γένος εἰμὶ τὠρχαῖον καὶ ἀντ᾽ ἐλευθέρης δεδουλωμένην
οὐκ ἂν ἐθέλοιμι ὁρᾶν τὴν Ἑλλάδα. λέγω δὲ ὧν ὅτι Μαρδονίῳ
τε καὶ τῇ στρατιῇ τὰ σφάγια οὐ δύναται καταθύμια γενέσθαι·
10 πάλαι γὰρ ἂν ἐμάχεσθε. νῦν δέ οἱ δέδοκται τὰ μὲν σφάγια
ἐᾶν χαίρειν, ἅμ᾽ ἡμέρῃ δὲ διαφωσκούσῃ συμβολὴν ποιέεσθαι·

---

2 δὴ S   3 τάδε τὰ ἔπεα Β ‖ τίθημι Marc.   5 καὶ om. CPz
‖ οὐ δὲ γὰρ z   7 ἐλευθερίης Marc.   8 ἔλοιμι Β ‖ δὴ Krueger
10 δέ οἱ om. R ‖ μὲν τὰ RV (μὲν om. S ap. Gaisf.)   11 ἅμα Β, Holder,
van H. ‖ διαφωσκούσηι Α² : διαφασκούσηι Α¹Β : διαφαυσκούσῃ reliqui,
Holder ‖ συμβουλὴν Β

---

they had to be roused. Everything is
wide-awake in the Athenian camp.

2. τὰς φυλακάς is practically here
locative, and feminine, cp. cc. 44. 2, 93. 22.

ἔλεγε Ἀλέξανδρος τάδε. Alexander's address is given in orat. recta.
It appears to be made up in essentials
out of Mardonios' in orat. obliq., c. 41
supra ; the change is purely stylistic,
and the one speech doubtless as un-
authentic as the other. If there were
anything to choose, it would not be in
favour of this one. Alexander is the
only speaker at this interview with the
Strategoi ; they supply a passive audience ; it is not a conference, it is a mono-
logue. Alexander may have spo en good
Greek, with a Makedonian brogue : a few
solecisms in his reported language would
have lent it verisimilitude.

3. ἄνδρες Ἀθηναῖοι : strictly correct,
had he been addressing the Boule or
Ekklesia, as in 8. 140. The ἄνδρες
gains point from the ἄνθρωποι in the
previous chapter.

παραθήκην τίθεμαι, ' I deposit,' ' I
entrust,' perhaps without recall ; cp.
6. 73 π. παρατίθενται.

4. ἀπόρρητα ποιεύμενος : sc. τὰ ἔπεα,
'as a solemn secret' ; cp. c. 94 infra.
πρὸς μηδένα λέγειν is exegetical.

ἢ Παυσανίην : Pausanias is here
recognized as the sole commander-in-
chief. The need for this strict secrecy
is not apparent : so long as no one on
his own side knew, Alexander was safe.
When this story came up Pausanias had

been called to his account and was
beyond further inquiry (except by necromancy) ; and as none of the other Greeks
had been told of the matter, owing to
this solemn precaution, it was no use
their saying they had never heard of it !
Thus the story provides its own Apologetics !

6. συναπάσης τῆς Ἑλλάδος, ' of
Hellas collectively': no mere geographical
expression, cp. 7. 157.

αὐτός τε γὰρ Ἕλλην γένος εἰμί : according to the story in 8. 137 and the
judgement of the Hellanodikai 5. 22.
Cp. notes ad ll.c.

7. τὠρχαῖον : i.e. 'originally' ; cp.
1. 56 τὸ ἀρχαῖον, 1. 173 τῶρχαῖον, etc.
Here = τὰ ἀνεκάθεν.

8. (λέγω) δὲ ὧν resumes or emphasizes
the point at which he is driving ; cp.
7. 145.

Μαρδονίῳ τε καὶ τῇ στρατιῇ, ' to
Mardonios and his army.'

9. οὐ δύναται, 'refuse,' 'will not,'
'cannot be got to . . '; cp. 7. 184. A
strictly sacral non possunt.

καταθύμια : cf. 5. 39, of the heart's
desire. An intimate word, warmer than
the καλά, ἐπιτήδεα of c. 37 supra.

10. γάρ, '(for) otherwise.'

δέδοκται : the perfect of absolute
resolution, determination.

11. ἅμ᾽ ἡμέρῃ δὲ διαφωσκούσῃ : i.e.
at dawn of day—the 12th day ; cp.
8. 86 and c. 42 supra ad f.

συμβολὴν ποιέεσθαι : i.e. μάχης
ἄρξαι, or ἄρχειν.

καταρρώδηκε γὰρ μὴ πλεῦνες συλλεχθῆτε, ὡς ἐγὼ εἰκάζω.
πρὸς ταῦτα ἑτοιμάζεσθε. ἢν δὲ ἄρα ὑπερβάληται τὴν συμβολὴν
Μαρδόνιος καὶ μὴ ποιέηται, λιπαρέετε μένοντες· ὀλιγέων γάρ
σφι ἡμερέων λείπεται σιτία. ἢν δὲ ὑμῖν ὁ πόλεμος ὅδε κατὰ 15
νόον τελευτήσῃ, μνησθῆναί τινα χρὴ καὶ ἐμεῦ ἐλευθερώσιος
πέρι, ὃς Ἑλλήνων εἵνεκα οὕτω ἔργον παράβολον ἔργασμαι ὑπὸ
προθυμίης, ἐθέλων ὑμῖν δηλῶσαι τὴν διάνοιαν τὴν Μαρδονίου,
ἵνα μὴ ἐπιπέσωσι ὑμῖν ἐξαίφνης οἱ βάρβαροι μὴ προσδεκο-

---

12 καταρρώδηκε P: καταρρωδήκεε B ‖ συλλεγῆτε B: συναχθῆτε z
13 ἆρα AB   14 καὶ μὴ ποιέηται del. van H.: ποιῆται B, Holder ‖
ὀλίγα S: ὀλίγων ceteri   16 ἐμὲ C   17 ἔργον οὕτω, Holder,
van H.: τοῦτο τὸ ἔργον οὕτω z   19 ἐξαίφνης om. B (οἱ βάρβαροι
ἐξαίφνης P¹) ‖ μὴ cum rasura P: μὴ δὲ Marc.

---

12. καταρρώδηκε γάρ κτλ.: a clear
assertion or admission of the formidable
number of the Greek forces. There was
no need for conjecture about the view of
Mardonios; he has expressly stated it
c. 41 supra (ex hyp. to Artabazos !).
13. ἄρα, 'as is not likely': of the less
probable alternative cp. 7. 10, etc.
14. μὴ ποιέηται: the negative here
seems to coalesce with the verb to form
a single idea, the conditional ἢν being
remote (but not so clearly as in cases
where οὐ might be used).
λιπαρέετε: a word put again into
Alexander's mouth, 5. 19.
ὀλιγέων γάρ σφι ἡμερέων λείπεται
σιτία. If this statement were true, it
would supply another good ground for
the impatience of Mardonios to do battle.
It is contrary, and even contradictory, to
the statement in c. 41 supra, and looks
like either a deliberate lie on the part of
Alexander (hardly in the spirit of the
piece), or an oversight on the part of
Hdt. Rawlinson thought this statement
could not be true. Stein limits it to
'the magazines on the Asopos,' but
admits there was plenty in Thebes.
Blakesley refuted this point of contrast
by anticipation: "With the superiority
in cavalry .. it would have been perfectly easy to maintain uninterrupted
communication between Thebes and the
army in camp."
15. ἢν δὲ .. τελευτήσῃ: an end to the
war acceptable to the Greeks was in
sight; on the Persian side victory was
anything but assured. This is the fifth
clear admission of the fact as recognized
before the event; cp. cc. 41-42 supra.

The 'hedging' of Alexander, as a fact, is
the real evidence.
16. τινά: cp. 8. 109.
ἐλευθερώσιος πέρι: this suggestion that Alexander pleaded beforehand
with the Athenians for deliverance from
the Persian at their hands is in the
true style of Attic afterthought. The
Athenians are the 'liberators' from the
Persian, and not from the Persian alone,
cp. 8. 142. (But in Makedon, or at least
in Thrace, the Spartans are by and by
to bring 'liberty' from the Athenians;
cp. Thuc. 4. 85.)
17. Ἑλλήνων εἵνεκα: Alexander is
moved by the best motives, thinking
mainly of the general interests.
οὕτω Stein takes with παράβολον, cp. 7. 46, where, however, no
word intervenes between οὕτω (bis) on
the one hand and the adjective (and
subst.) on the other.
παράβολον: bold, hazardous,
reckless. Also of persons, Aristoph.
Wasps 192, Diodor. 19. 3. 2 φιλοκίνδυνος
.. καὶ παράβολος ἐν ταῖς μάχαις.
ἔργασμαι ὑπὸ προθ.: cp. c. 37.
18. διάνοιαν (cp. 8. 97): the plan to
attack on the following morning.
19. ἵνα μή κτλ. The concern of
Alexander lest the Greeks should be
taken unawares is a doubtful compliment, and an inconsequence. According
to the context, they had been for ten days
facing the Persians in battle-array, and
anxious that the enemy should cross the
Asopos and attack them; on the morrow
they were to have their wish at last.
ἐξαίφνης is (1) a doubtful form for
ἐξαπίνης, as in 1. 74, 87; (2) omitted in

20 μένοισί κω. εἰμὶ δὲ Ἀλέξανδρος ὁ Μακεδών." ὃ μὲν ταῦτα
εἴπας ἀπήλαυνε ὀπίσω ἐς τὸ στρατόπεδον καὶ τὴν ἑωυτοῦ
τάξιν.

46 Οἱ δὲ στρατηγοὶ τῶν Ἀθηναίων ἐλθόντες ἐπὶ τὸ δεξιὸν
κέρας ἔλεγον Παυσανίῃ τά περ ἤκουσαν Ἀλεξάνδρου. ὃ δὲ
τούτῳ τῷ λόγῳ καταρρωδήσας τοὺς Πέρσας ἔλεγε τάδε.
"ἐπεὶ τοίνυν ἐς ἠῶ ἡ συμβολὴ γίνεται, ὑμέας μὲν χρεόν ἐστι
5 τοὺς Ἀθηναίους στῆναι κατὰ τοὺς Πέρσας, ἡμέας δὲ κατὰ
τοὺς Βοιωτούς τε καὶ τοὺς κατ' ὑμέας τεταγμένους Ἑλλήνων,
τῶνδε εἵνεκα· ὑμεῖς ἐπίστασθε τοὺς Μήδους καὶ τὴν μάχην

---

21 ἀπέλαυνεν β   46. 4 χρεών CPz, van H.   5 τοὺς Ἀθηναίους
abesse malit van H.   6 τε om. αC   7 εἵνεκεν Marc. z || ἐπί-
σταασθαι BR

---

one group of mss.; (3) tautologous and gloss-like in this passage.

20. **εἰμὶ δὲ Ἀλέξανδρος ὁ Μακεδών**: Alexander in thus announcing himself appears to forget that Aristeides and the men of Athens were thoroughly familiar with his appearance, if only from his embassy to Athens in the previous winter; cp. 8. 136 ff. The two stories are of course from independent sources (though both Atticist).

The historical credibility of this interview is not high. Certainly, if any such interview or communication took place between Alexander of Makedon and the Athenian Strategoi, the gist and purport of it were widely different from this report. Possibly there was at Plataia some kind of understanding between the Makedonian and the Athenians. He had been to Athens, or to Salamis, a while before, and may have seen reason to think that Mardonios had anything but an easy task before him. To play off the Greeks and the Persians against each other was the obvious policy of Makedon. The Athenians may have used the opportunity to come to an understanding with the king. He may have had information of the troubles in Asia (revolt of Babylon, etc.). The remarkable success with which, in the subsequent battle, the Athenians dispose of 50,000 men opposed to them, and their comparative immunity during the occupation of 'the second position,' suggest the idea that matters were not pressed against them. For that they may have had to thank Alexander, who was posted on the Persian right.

46. 1. **οἱ δὲ στρατηγοὶ τῶν Ἀθηναίων**: i.e. Aristeides and his colleagues—or so many of them as were present—went to the right wing, the army bivouacking in order of battle. They have cut a very poor figure in the previous interview, acting the part of mere dummies.

2. **Παυσανίῃ**: no account being taken of Euryanax, in spite of c. 10 supra. Pausanias is terror-struck at the report! Not a Laconian touch. His speech, like that of Alexander just before, is given in orat. recta.

4. **ἐς ἠῶ ἡ συμβολὴ γίνεται**: cp. 3. 85 τῆς ἐπιούσης ἡμέρης ὁ ἀγὼν ἡμῖν ἐστί. The present is rhetorical. In this case the argument is double: that the battle is to take place (at dawn) is a reason for the tactical move; that it is not to take place until dawn gives time to execute the proposed manœuvre.

6. **τοὺς . . Ἑλλήνων**: including the Makedonians, whose medism throughout is minimized as much as possible.

7. **τῶνδε εἵνεκα**: the reasons given for the change of front, or exchange of positions, are incredible. The experience of the Μαραθωνομάχαι, as a taunt, might have come very well from a Spartan after the vainglorious boasting of the Athenians in c. 27 supra (cp. notes ad l.), but as a serious argument by a Spartan commander for such a manœuvre as proposed here, it is virtually inconceivable. Nor, on the other hand, could a Spartan have practically ignored the Spartan achievement at Thermopylai as Pausanias here does. True, the Spartans at Thermopylai had all perished (Aristodemos who is at

αὐτῶν ἐν Μαραθῶνι μαχεσάμενοι, ἡμεῖς δὲ ἄπειροί τε εἰμὲν
καὶ ἀδαέες τούτων τῶν ἀνδρῶν· Σπαρτιητέων γὰρ οὐδεὶς
πεπείρηται Μήδων, ἡμεῖς δὲ Βοιωτῶν καὶ Θεσσαλῶν ἔμπειροι 10
εἰμέν. ἀλλ᾽ ἀναλαβόντας τὰ ὅπλα χρεόν ἐστι ἰέναι ὑμέας
μὲν ἐς τόδε τὸ κέρας, ἡμέας δὲ ἐς τὸ εὐώνυμον." πρὸς δὲ
ταῦτα εἶπαν οἱ Ἀθηναῖοι τάδε. "καὶ αὐτοῖσι ἡμῖν πάλαι
ἀπ᾽ ἀρχῆς, ἐπείτε εἴδομεν κατ᾽ ὑμέας τασσομένους τοὺς
Πέρσας, ἐν νόῳ ἐγένετο εἰπεῖν ταῦτα τά περ ὑμεῖς φθάντες 15
προφέρετε· ἀλλὰ ἀρρωδέομεν μὴ ὑμῖν οὐκ ἡδέες γένωνται οἱ
λόγοι. ἐπεὶ δ᾽ ὦν αὐτοὶ ἐμνήσθητε, καὶ ἡδομένοισι ἡμῖν οἱ
λόγοι γεγόνασι καὶ ἕτοιμοι εἰμὲν ποιέειν ταῦτα." ὡς δ᾽ 47

---

8 αὐτέων z ‖ ἐν: ἐπὶ Pz   9 τουτέων z ‖ τῶν ἀνδρῶν (-έων V)
τουτέων B   10 δὲ: τε a   11 ἀλλὰ a ‖ χρεών CPz, van H.
13 εἶπαι z, van H.   15 ταῦτα van H.   16 προσφέρετε Cobet,
van H. ‖ ἀλλὰ γὰρ B, Holder, van H. ‖ γίνωνται RV: γίνονται S   17
ὑμῖν RVz   18 ἕτοιμοι CPz

Plataia, alone excepted, c. 71 infra),
but in so doing had shown how immensely superior they were to the best
Persian troops. The story here is pure
Atticism. Not content with having
bested the Arkadians, the Athenians
must make Sparta too confess her
inferiority. There may have been some
tactical manœuvre on which this fable
was hung (cp. next c.), but as it stands
it is a transparent fiction.

The main contrast throughout the
speech is between the Athenians (ὑμέας
μὲν . . ὑμεῖς . . ὑμέας μέν) and the
Spartans (ἡμέας δὲ . . ἡμεῖς δὲ (bis) . .
ἡμέας δέ).

τοὺς Μήδους καὶ τὴν μάχην
αὐτῶν: 'Medes' here equals or covers
'Persians.' μάχη, 'style of fighting';
cp. 5. 49.

8. ἐν Μαραθῶνι: this homage to
Marathon, beside which Thermopylai is
not worth mentioning, comes with
double effect from a Spartan's lips!

9. ἀδαής with gen. rei, 2. 49, 5. 90;
cp. ἀδαήμων 8. 65; the gen. pers. is
apparently unique. Pausanias uses
ἀνδρῶν, not ἀνθρώπων. The speaker
becomes a little involved in his anxiety
to make the utter inferiority of the
Spartans clear; the second ἡμεῖς δέ is
virtually the δέ with resumed subject, a
false antithesis (the real being Μήδων
μὲν ἄπειροι Βοιωτῶν δὲ ἔμπειροι) but the
running antithesis between ὑμεῖς and
ἡμεῖς helps to determine the phraseology.

Σπαρτιητέων . . Μήδων: this
statement not only ignores the story
of Thermopylai, but implies that any
fighting so far in Boiotia has not been
done by the Spartans; and moreover
that their observation has taught them
nothing of the Persian warfare. How,
then, has their experience of Boiotians
and Thessalians been gained? What
fighting had any dead or living Spartan
done with Boiotians? The only recorded
engagement with Thessalians (5. 63, 64)
was rather an unfortunate precedent!
Of course, if Pausanias really said all
this, it might show how desperately
hard up he was for an excuse.

18. αὐτοῖσι ἡμῖν . . ἐν νόῳ ἐγένετο
εἰπεῖν ταῦτα: i.e. to make the proposal
you have just made. (The formula
carries further, and may serve to hint
that the story stands, almost self-
confessed, an Attic fabrication.) φθάντες
προφέρετε, 'have anticipated us in
proposing.'

πάλαι ἀπ᾽ ἀρχῆς, rather redundant; and the date only goes back
at most ten days.

16. ἀρρωδέομεν μὴ . . οὐκ ἡδέες
γένωνται is not a true case of the double
negative idiom μὴ οὐ, the οὐ in this case
simply coalescing with ἡδέες into a single
idea = ἀηδέες (cp. οὐ φιλίας c. 4 supra).
δ᾽ ὦν, much as in c. 45 supra. καὶ . .
καί, the strong co-ordination, cp. c. 26
supra. ἡδομένοισι ἡμῖν, cp. 8. 101. 10
supra.

ἤρεσκε ἀμφοτέροισι ταῦτα, ἠώς τε διέφαινε καὶ διαλλάσσοντο

47. 2 ἢ ὥστε R ‖ διάλασον R : διάλασσον SV

47. 2. **ἠώς τε διέφαινε καὶ διαλλάσσοντο τὰς τάξις**: the dawn of the twelfth
day, according to the Journal, cp. cc.
41, 44 *supra*. The grammatical *parataxis* is observable, cp. 7. 217 ἠώς τε δὴ
διέφαινε καὶ οἳ ἐγένοντο ἐπ᾿ ἀκρωτηρίῳ τοῦ
ὄρεος. The tenses are important; it
does not appear that the exchange of
positions was ever fully carried out
between the Spartans and Athenians:
dawn broke and found them still engaged
in the manœuvre. **τὸ ποιεύμενον**, too,
is imperfect. (Blakesley's trans. is
misleading: "with the very break of day
they changed their respective positions.")
Hdt. indeed does not expressly say that
the manœuvre was not carried out; he
leaves, however, the impression that it
was not fully carried out, but was
arrested, by the rapid counter-develop-
ment on the Persian side, which showed
Pausanias that his purpose had been
discovered.

This chapter perhaps conceals a great
mystery. Presumably there was an
excuse in fact for the story of the
exchange of positions. Some manœuvre,
some development in the position of
the Greeks took place, which lent colour
to the Athenian version of the affair.
Speeches and motivation with Hdt. are
in a different category to acts and
events: the reported order, the chronological succession of acts and events, is
often less acceptable than the bare acts
or events themselves; they, in turn,
seldom present a complete series, and
frequently undergo a transfiguration, for
better or for worse; but Hdt. is nevertheless not a mere novelist, not even a
mere historical novelist. All this justifies
considerable freedom in the hypothetical
reconstruction of a story, which in its
traditional form is inadequate and incredible; and it makes reconstruction
inevitable. The exchange of positions,
according to Hdt., is to take place on
the twelfth day of the occupation by the
Greeks of the position 'on the Asopos'
marked by the Androkrateion and
Gargaphia. Is it credible that for eleven
days the Greeks occupied this position
unmolested? Why then suddenly on
the twelfth day is the cavalry loosed
upon them, and the position immediately rendered untenable? Again, why
is so much stress laid on the fact that it

was a man on horseback that came to
the Athenian lines on the night of the
eleventh, if the Greek and Persian
armies were then in close contact, only
separated by the Asopos? If the Makedonian came on a horse, it was because
he had a good deal of ground to cover;
in other words, the Greeks were not ἐπὶ
τῷ Ἀσωπῷ on the eleventh, or any of the
preceding days. Hdt. has apparently
antedated the occupation by the Greeks
of the position 'on the Asopos,' that is,
round the Androkrateion, with Gargaphia in their rear; and has under-
estimated and misconceived the 'first
position' and its developments, in front
of Hysiai and Plataiai. It was only on
the twelfth that the Greeks descended
to the 'second' position, i.e. the hills
in front of Gargaphia 'on the Asopos'
—probably counting on the Persians
crossing the river to attack them. In
the process of advancing a tactical
manœuvre, or series of manœuvres, is
performed, which is misunderstood,
parodied, and converted *ad maiorem
gloriam Atheniensium* in this passage
at the expense of the Spartans; exactly
as in a previous passage the move from
the position at Erythrai to the position
at Hysiai had been similarly exploited,
at the expense of the Tegeatai. The
exact nature of the manœuvre may be
a matter of dispute. Hdt. treats the
μετάταξις, or μετακόσμησις, as purely a
question between the two wings, the
centre taking no part in it. In reality
the whole line was doubtless involved.
There was an advance *en échelon*, which
Atticizing tradition interpreted as an
attempt on the part of the Lakedaimonians to get into the Athenian position.
There was perhaps more than that, an
actual development, whereby the Lakedaimonians came to stand where the
Athenians had been standing, on the
extreme left of the line; and again the
Athenians finally, when Gargaphia was
passed, were again standing on the
extreme left of the line. This was the
manœuvre by which the position ἐπὶ τῷ
Ἀσωπῷ was actually occupied. Whether
it had the appearance of an attempt to
outflank the Persians, or not, may be
questioned; such can hardly have been
its real purpose. With their hopeless
inferiority in mounted men the Greeks

τὰς τάξις. γνόντες δὲ οἱ Βοιωτοὶ τὸ ποιεύμενον ἐξαγορεύουσι Μαρδονίῳ. ὁ δ' ἐπείτε ἤκουσε, αὐτίκα μετιστάναι καὶ αὐτὸς ἐπειρᾶτο παράγων τοὺς Πέρσας κατὰ τοὺς Λακεδαιμονίους. 5 ὡς δὲ ἔμαθε τοῦτο τοιοῦτο γινόμενον ὁ Παυσανίης, γνοὺς ὅτι οὐ λανθάνει, ὀπίσω ἦγε τοὺς Σπαρτιήτας ἐπὶ τὸ δεξιὸν κέρας· ὡς δὲ αὕτως καὶ ὁ Μαρδόνιος ἐπὶ τοῦ εὐωνύμου.

Ἐπεὶ δὲ κατέστησαν ἐς τὰς ἀρχαίας τάξις, πέμψας ὁ 48 Μαρδόνιος κήρυκα ἐς τοὺς Σπαρτιήτας ἔλεγε τάδε. " ὦ Λακεδαιμόνιοι, ὑμεῖς δὴ λέγεσθε εἶναι ἄνδρες ἄριστοι ὑπὸ τῶν

---

3 τάξεις CRV ‖ δ' RV   4 δὲ RV   6 τοιοῦτον β ‖ γενόμενον Pz   7, 8 utrum τοὺς Σπαρτιήτας genuina sint an post Μαρδόνιος exciderint τοὺς Πέρσας dubit. van H.   8 ὡς Stein : ὃς van H. : ὡς ‖ δ' CPz ‖ αὕτως καὶ : καὶ αὐτὸς β ‖ <τοὺς Πέρσας> ἐπὶ (van H.), Holder ‖ τὸ εὐώνυμον β, Holder, van H.   48. 1 τάξεις CR ‖ ὁ om. β 2 κήρυκας C   3 λέγεσθαι R

---

would have been courting certain destruction in moving, or attempting to move, on Thebes, by the Plataia-Thebes road. Mardonios draws out his line of battle on the north bank of the Asopos ; he deploys to the west. The medizing Greeks, occupying the extreme west of the Laager, may have been potentially opposite the Greek right for a while, until they pushed up the river westwards, their places being taken by the Medes and Persians. Mardonios has now drawn the Greeks down to the Asopos ; he hopes to draw or drive them across. He gives them no peace all this day : the cavalry ride round the position freely, harass them extremely, and destroy and cut off the water-supply. For but one single day do the Greeks maintain themselves in this position ; they have been disappointed of their expectation that Mardonios would send his infantry across the Asopos to do battle, and they determine to retreat (or to return ?) to the position on 'the island' (c. 51 infra), or the position of which the island was the most prominent feature.

8. ὡς δὲ αὕτως καὶ ὁ Μαρδόνιος : sc. ἦγε τοὺς Πέρσας.

48. 1. τὰς ἀρχαίας τάξις : i.e. the order, or positions, 'originally occupied' before the changes, or attempted changes, recorded in c. 47.

2. κήρυκα .. ἔλεγε τάδε : the exact words of Mardonios' message ! The

speaker must have been a Greek, or a 'diglott.' The herald apparently comes across the river (with a flag of truce ?) to the Spartan quarters ; but the story was never so told in Sparta ! The speech is an Athenian Appendix to the previous Athenian self-glorifications. It contains some sarcastic reflexions on Spartan reputation, and an extremely sporting offer, or challenge, on Mardonios' part. Grote discredits the anecdote ; Rawlinson defends the 'Homeric' (sic!) taunt as quite agreeable to the practice of primitive and specially oriental races (rather contradictory terms), but even he admits that the challenge is less probable. Here again we may fairly conjecture that there was some foundation in fact for the fiction. The object of Mardonios must still have been to induce the Greeks to cross the river. Did he really offer them a free and unmolested passage ? Or did he offer to come across if they would give him time to reform on their side ? Such offers are not made in war à outrance ; but the Persians were cavaliers and sportsmen, and Mardonios may have thought of the Greeks as his own future subjects. (Cp. the Assyrian challenge to Hezekiah, 2 Kings 18. 23.)

3. δή is sarcastic ; cp. l. 115. The first of four such in the speech, to which add ἄρα, νῦν ἄν, δ' ἄν, καί δή, ἀλλά, all of which heighten the effect, to say nothing of the blunter satire in the more material phrases and propositions.

τῇδε ἀνθρώπων, ἐκπαγλεομένων ὡς οὔτε φεύγετε ἐκ πολέμου
5 οὔτε τάξιν ἐκλείπετε, μένοντές τε ἢ ἀπόλλυτε τοὺς ἐναντίους
ἢ αὐτοὶ ἀπόλλυσθε. τῶν δ' ἄρ' ἦν οὐδὲν ἀληθές· πρὶν γὰρ
ἢ συμμεῖξαι ἡμέας ἐς χειρῶν τε νόμον ἀπικέσθαι, καὶ δὴ
φεύγοντας καὶ στάσιν ἐκλείποντας ὑμέας εἴδομεν, ἐν Ἀθηναίοισί
τε τὴν πρόπειραν ποιευμένους αὐτούς τε ἀντία δούλων τῶν
10 ἡμετέρων τασσομένους. ταῦτα οὐδαμῶς ἀνδρῶν ἀγαθῶν ἔργα,
ἀλλὰ πλεῖστον δὴ ἐν ὑμῖν ἐψεύσθημεν. προσδεκόμενοι γὰρ
κατὰ κλέος ὡς δὴ πέμψετε ἐς ἡμέας κήρυκα προκαλεύμενοι
καὶ βουλόμενοι μούνοισι Πέρσῃσι μάχεσθαι, ἄρτιοι ἐόντες
ποιέειν ταῦτα οὐδὲν τοιοῦτο λέγοντας ὑμέας εὕρομεν ἀλλὰ
15 πτώσσοντας μᾶλλον. νῦν ὦν ἐπειδὴ οὐκ ὑμεῖς ἤρξατε τούτου

4 ἐκπλαγεομένων B   6 δὲ a   7 συμμῖξαι libri, Stein[1][2],
Holder ‖ ὑμέας B   8 στάσιν : τάξιν B, Holder ‖ ἐκλιπόντας RV
9 πεῖραν B ‖ ἀντὶ B   10 ταῦτα δὲ z   11 προσδοκώμενοι C   13
μοῦνοι z : μοῦνοι μούνοισι Koen, Holder, van H.   14 τοιοῦτον B ‖
ὑμέας om. B   15 πτώσσοντας SMarc.

The contrast in ἄνδρες : ἀνθρώπων is
intentional. τῇδε, 'in these parts.'
4. ἐκπαγλεομένων : cp. 7. 181. Mardonios was no doubt with Xerxes at
Thermopylai, cp. 7. 209, and had heard
Demaratos' testimonials to his countrymen! The reputation of the Spartans
ὡς ἀπολεόμενοί τε καὶ ἀπολέοντες (l.c.)
was unshaken in Greece down to
425 B.C. ; cp. Thuc. 4. 40. 1. (The
notion that this speech dates after that
disillusionment will not do ; the point,
the irony of the passage, lies in its
barbarous insolence.)
6. τῶν δ' ἄρ' ἦν οὐδὲν ἀληθές. Mardonios, like the Athenians throughout,
ignores the lesson of Thermopylai. But
that story had not yet reached the
classic development which it exhibits
in Bk. 7 supra, a form which illustrates
the effects of dialectic on the genesis of
tradition, partly in answer to the charge
of blundering, and partly, no doubt, in
answer to other Athenian criticisms.
ἄρα gives a touch of ironic surprise, and
the irony is also continued in the tense.
7. συμμεῖξαι : of hostile congress, cp.
8. 94, so that ἐς χειρῶν τε νόμον ἀπικέσθαι (cp. 8. 89) is somewhat tautologous.
ἡμέας : us and you ?
καὶ δή = ἤδη : cp. 8. 94. 11 supra.
8. στάσιν = τάξιν : cp. c. 21 supra.
ἐν Ἀθηναίοισί τε τὴν πρόπειραν
ποιευμένους : the phrase betrays the
source. For πρ. ποιεῖσθαι cp. Thuc. 3.

86. 4 πρόπειράν τε ποιούμενοι εἰ σφίσι
δυνατὸ εἴη τὰ ἐν τῇ Σικελίᾳ πράγματα
ὑποχείρια γενέσθαι. Here the Athenians
would remember that they had already
furnished a πρόπειρα at Erythrai, c. 21
supra, to say nothing of Marathon c. 46
supra. Athenian tradition fully exploited this motif ; cp. Plutarch, Aristeid.
16.
9. ἀντία δούλων τῶν ἡμετέρων :
pleasant hearing, or reading, for Thebans,
and other medizers ! ἀντία, plural ; cp.
c. 31 supra.
11. ἐν ὑμῖν, 'in your case.'
12. κατὰ κλέος, ob vestram gloriam,
Baehr ; cp. c. 38 supra.
προκαλέεσθαι, ' to challenge '
(Homeric, but also legal Attic).
13. ἄρτιοι : cp. c. 27 supra.
14. εὕρομεν : cp. c. 28 supra. The
tense is observable ; we might render it
in the perfect, 'we have found' ; so too
ἤρξατε just below.
15. πτώσσοντας : like timid birds ;
an Homeric word and metaphor passim,
e.g. Il. 7. 129. Oddly enough Tyrtaios
(a Spartan !) uses it without any suggestion of fear : 11. 36 (Bergk ii.[4] 17)
ὑμεῖς δ' ὦ γυμνῆτες, ὑπ' ἀσπίδος ἄλλοθεν
ἄλλος πτώσσοντες μεγάλοις βάλλετε χερ-
μαδίοις.
νῦν ὦν : here too the speaker
comes to the point ; cp. c. 45 supra.
ἐπειδὴ .. ἀλλά : cp. c. 42 supra
ἐπεί .. ἀλλ' ἐγὼ ἐρέω.

τοῦ λόγου, ἀλλ' ἡμεῖς ἄρχομεν. τί δὴ οὐ πρὸ μὲν τῶν
Ἑλλήνων ὑμεῖς, ἐπείτε δεδόξωσθε εἶναι ἄριστοι, πρὸ δὲ τῶν
βαρβάρων ἡμεῖς, ἴσοι πρὸς ἴσους ἀριθμὸν ἐμαχεσάμεθα; καὶ
ἢν μὲν δοκέῃ καὶ τοὺς ἄλλους μάχεσθαι, οἳ δ' ὧν μετέπειτα
μαχέσθων ὕστεροι· εἰ δὲ καὶ μὴ δοκέοι ἀλλ' ἡμέας μούνους 20
ἀποχρᾶν, ἡμεῖς δὲ διαμαχεσώμεθα· ὁκότεροι δ' ἂν ἡμέων
νικήσωσι, τούτους τῷ ἅπαντι στρατοπέδῳ νικᾶν." ὁ μὲν 49
ταῦτα εἴπας τε καὶ ἐπισχὼν χρόνον, ὥς οἱ οὐδεὶς οὐδὲν
ὑπεκρίνατο, ἀπαλλάσσετο ὀπίσω, ἀπελθὼν δὲ ἐσήμαινε
Μαρδονίῳ τὰ καταλαβόντα. ὁ δὲ περιχαρὴς γενόμενος καὶ
ἐπαερθεὶς ψυχρῇ νίκῃ ἐπῆκε τὴν ἵππον ἐπὶ τοὺς Ἕλληνας. 5

---

16 ἄρξομεν B || τί δὴ οὐ ὧν R: τί δὴ ὧν V: τὸ δὴ ὧν S   17
ἐπεὶ vel ἐπείπερ malit van H.   18 μαχεσόμεθα S, Wesseling, Gaisford
19 δοκήι aC: δοκεῖς Marc.   20 ὕστερον B   21 διαμαχεσόμεθα Bz
49. 2 οἱ om. C   3 ὑπεκρίνετο B, Holder, van H. || ἐσήμηνε B   5
ἐπαρθεὶς libri

---

16. τί δὴ οὐ . . ἐμαχεσάμεθα; this
'Attic' form of challenge, 'mostly with
the aorist,' is only found in this one
place in Hdt. (Stein). Cp. Madvig,
§ 111, R. c ; 141, R. 3.
17. δεδόξωσθε: cp. 7. 135, 8. 124 ;
the perfect is both more magniloquent
and also slightly suggestive of a *temps
passé*. It is time they did something
κατὰ κλέος δή.

πρὸ δὲ τῶν βαρβάρων ἡμεῖς. Hdt.
gives himself, his source, his herald, and
Mardonios away in this phrase ; it is a
sheer impossibility. When Plautus uses
barbarus for Roman it is by the mouth
of a *dramatis persona* who would use
the word naturally, as even in his
prologues: 'Demophilus scripsit, Marcus
vortit barbare !' *Trinum.* 19, *Asin.* 10.
If this grated on a Roman ear, it was
after all a comedy. Here the noble
Persian commander by the mouth of
his herald taunting the premier Greeks
writes himself down—just at a Greek's
valuation ! That the messenger in the
Persai of Aischylos does the like (187,
225, 337) emphasizes the unhistorical
character of this speech put by Hdt.
into the mouth of Mardonios.
18. ἴσοι πρὸς ἴσους. Xerxes had
among his guards men prepared to
engage three Greeks at a time, 7. 103 ;
in his own playful vein he had suggested
to Demaratos that as a Spartan king he
should be prepared to tackle a score
of Persians. Mardonios proposes the
strictest λόγον μουνομαχίης. Such pro-

posals in the eyes of the Spartans of
the fifth century might be magnificent
but were not war ; cp. Thuc. 5. 41. 3.
19. ἢν μὲν δοκέῃ .. εἰ δὲ καὶ μὴ δοκέοι:
the first gives the more probable, the
second the less probable alternative.

οἳ δ' ὧν seems to combine (1) δέ
with resumed subject, (2) δέ *in apodosi*,
(3) δ' ὧν as a significant admission.
ἡμεῖς δέ combines (1) and (2).

21. ἀποχρᾶν: cp. c. 94 *infra*. νικᾶν,
'be victors' ; cp. cc. 69, 100 *infra*.
49. 2. ἐπισχὼν χρόνον, 'after pausing
a while' ; cp. 5. 16, 1. 175, and c. 93
infra.

οὐδεὶς οὐδὲν ὑπεκρίνατο. The
Athenian or phil-Attic concocters of the
story did not venture to devise a reply
for the Spartans, who could only have
referred Mardonios to Thermopylai for
proof of their mettle ; that was their
πρόπειρα. This haughty silence (for the
story now begins in the hands of Hdt.
to round somewhat to the Spartan side)
recalls the indifference of the Spartans
at Thermopylai to the curious Persian
scout, 7. 208.

4. τὰ καταλαβόντα: sc. ἑαυτόν: cp.
cc. 93, 104 *infra*.

ὁ δὲ περιχαρὴς κτλ. : "an Hellenic
view of Mardonios' sentiments, with no
foundation of truth," Blakesley. περιχ.
3. 35.

5. ἐπαερθεὶς ψυχρῇ νίκη: for the
participle cp. 5. 81, 6. 132, 7. 38. ψ. ν.,
inani victoria, cp. 6. 108.

ἐπῆκε τὴν ἵππον ἐπὶ τοὺς Ἕλληνας.

ὡς δὲ ἐπήλασαν οἱ ἱππόται, ἐσίνοντο πᾶσαν τὴν στρατιὴν
τὴν Ἑλληνικὴν ἐσακοντίζοντές τε καὶ τοξεύοντες ὥστε ἱπποτοξόται τε ἐόντες καὶ προσφέρεσθαι ἄποροι· τήν τε κρήνην
τὴν Γαργαφίην, ἀπ᾽ ἧς ὑδρεύετο πᾶν τὸ στράτευμα τὸ
10 Ἑλληνικόν, συνετάραξάν <τε> καὶ συνέχωσαν. ἦσαν μὲν

---

6 ἐσινέοντο Β   7 ἐστοξεύοντες Β, Holder, van H. ‖ ὥσγε Marc. :
ὥστε καὶ Β ‖ ἱπποτόξαι V   8 τε om. ΒC ‖ εὔποροι z   9 γαρ-
σαφίην S   10 <τε> (van H.), Stein³ ‖ ἔσαν z

If little or nothing has been heard of the
Persian cavalry for twelve days, it must
be because the Greeks were in a position
where the cavalry could not get at them,
or else because the services of the cavalry
have been suppressed. The cavalry,
however, had at least cut the Greek
lines of communication by Dryoskephalai, c. 39 supra. If they had
not also already destroyed Gargaphia,
and rendered the Greek position at
Gargaphia untenable, it must be because
that position had not been occupied by
the Greeks until this very day, to wit,
the twelfth. On this day the Greeks
were reduced to the necessity of advancing across the Asopos, or else retiring
and giving up the position.

6. ἐσίνοντο πᾶσαν τὴν στρατιήν: the
Persian cavalry, and perhaps the Boiotian, Thessalian, Makedonian, could
now ride completely round the Greek
position, and especially could harass the
Greeks in the rear. The horsemen
evidently did not attempt to ascend the
hill-slopes and sides, but swept safely
through the trough in the hills, in which
Gargaphia and its neighbouring wells
lay, and lie. A detachment of Lakedaimonians may have been posted near the
wells, in the vain attempt to save them :
these men must have been beaten back
northwards on to the 'Asopos Ridge.'
What were the hosts of ψιλοί about on
the Greek side? They should, were
they in being, have kept the Persian
cavalry off. It is this situation which
makes it difficult to believe in the
69,500 Greek ψιλοί of c. 30 supra, or
even a tithe of that number.

7. ὥστε ἱπποτοξόται τε ἐόντες καὶ
προσφέρεσθαι ἄποροι: ὥστε = ἄτε, cp. c.
37 supra. With προσφ. ἄπ. cp. ἄποροι
προσμίσγειν 4. 46. The meaning is
evidently that it was difficult to come to
close quarters with them. Blakesley
renders "impossible to bring to close
fight "—as though προσφέρεσθαι were

passive, or, if not, as·if αὐτούς were to
be understood. The verb is better taken
as middle, or deponent, ἐς αὐτοὺς or
αὐτοῖς being understood, the construction being the personal instead of the
neuter : ἄπορον ἦν προσφέρεσθαι ἐς αὐτούς
(αὐτοῖς), ' it was impossible to come to
close quarters with them.'
The difficulty affects hoplites, not
ψιλοί, τοξόται, ἀκοντισταί, σφενδονῆται,
κτλ., who should have shot down the
horses and men, eminus, at least if they
had been decently trained ; but they
were probably πτώσσοντες among the
hoplites ! On the superiority of the
Persian still at the end of the fifth
century cp. Xenoph. Anab. 3. 3. 7.
ἱπποτοξόται: a form of service
afterwards familiar in Athens (cp. Thuc.
2. 13. 8), though a corps of 200 could
not hope to effect very much. The
Persian cavalry, Hdt. says (7. 84), had
the same equipment as the infantry
(described in 7. 61) including bows and
arrows, and short spears, i.e. throwing
spears, javelins. Rawlinson argues from
Arrian 1. 15 (the Granikos) and 3. 15
(Arbela) that in Alexander's day the
favourite weapon of the Persian cavalry
was the javelin (jereed). Cp. c. 17 supra.
8. τήν τε κρήνην τὴν Γαργαφίην: cp.
c. 25 supra for its identity and position.
The statement here that the whole
Greek force under arms (στράτευμα, not
στρατόπεδον) depended on this one source
for water-supply might have warned
Hdt. that the position could hardly
have been occupied for twelve days !
What? 110,000 men, for twelve days,
watered from one spring? It would
needs have been a copious one. Now at
any rate in the course of a few hours the
Persian cavalry renders it quite useless—
as they could have done on any one of
the preceding eleven days !
10. συνετάραξαν καὶ συνέχωσαν: the
first verb describes the condition of the
water-supply after the Persian cavalry

ὧν κατὰ τὴν κρήνην Λακεδαιμόνιοι τεταγμένοι μοῦνοι, τοῖσι
δὲ ἄλλοισι Ἕλλησι ἡ μὲν κρήνη πρόσω ἐγίνετο, ὡς ἕκαστοι
ἔτυχον τεταγμένοι, ὁ δὲ Ἀσωπὸς ἀγχοῦ· ἐρυκόμενοι δὲ τοῦ

---

11 μοῦνοι τεταγμένοι z ‖ τοῖσι . . τεταγμένοι om. B   12 ἄλλησι
Marc. ‖ ἐγένετο z   13 ἀπὸ τοῦ CPz

---

has been riding over it and through it ;
the second the absolute dilapidation of
the troughs, basin, stone-work, and so
forth (cp. c. 13 *supra*)·which they must
have dismounted to effect. Pausan. 9. 4.
2 has little independent value, but may
be just worth quoting : τὴν δὲ κρήνην τὴν
Γαργαφίαν Μαρδόνιοι καὶ ἡ ἵππος συνέχεεν
ἡ Περσῶν, ὅτι τὸ Ἑλλήνων στράτευμα τὸ
ἀντικαθήμενόν σφισιν ἀπ᾽ αὐτῆς ἔπινεν·
ὕστερον μέντοι τὸ ὕδωρ ἀνεσώσαντο οἱ
Πλαταιεῖς.

ἦσαν μὲν ἂν . . Λακεδαιμόνιοι :
ὧν marks the gravity of the situation.
That Lakedaimonians and Lakedaimonians alone (μοῦνοι) were posted
opposite, or ' over against ' the fountain,
suggests several inferences. (1) The
main body of the Lakedaimonians form
the Greek right wing, stationed apparently on the high ground immediately
north of the spring, or well (Grundy's
'Gargaphia') ; but (2) doubtless a detachment would have been on guard in
the immediate vicinity of the water. If
so, that detachment cannot have maintained its ground.

If *Apotripi* be Gargaphia, the Greek
left would have to be moved a little,
but only a little, westward. In reality
the centre probably watered from *Apotripi*, which no doubt was equally
destroyed by the Persian cavalry. The
centre was posted immediately in and
about the Androkrateion (the Church of
St. John).

The left wing may have been expected
to get its water from the stream A¹
running down from *Apotripi* into the
Asopos proper, or failing that from
Apotripi.

11. τοῖσι δὲ ἄλλοισι Ἕλλησι : i.e.
the right centre (οἱ ἀμφὶ Κορινθίους c.
69), the left centre (οἱ ἀμφὶ Μεγαρέας τε
καὶ Φλειασίους *ib.*) and the left wing
(Athenians and Plataians). The Tegeatai are probably lumped with the
Lakedaimonians above.

12. ἡ μὲν κρήνη πρόσω ἐγίνετο : πρόσω
is the antithesis of ἐγγύς, op. Plato,

Protag. 356. There is no need to expand
ἡ κρήνη into ἡ εἰς τὴν κρήνην ὁδός (Sitzler),
but the next words, ὡς ἕκαστοι ἔτυχον
τεταγμένοι, introduce an element of
relativity or comparison into πρόσω, to
which the imperfect ἐγίνετο is also
adapted : the well was not equi-distant
from all ; it was not near to any, but it
was further from some (the Athenians)
than from others (the centre), according
to their places in the line of battle.

13. ὁ δὲ Ἀσωπὸς ἀγχοῦ : ἀγχοῦ=ἄγχι
=ἐγγύς. Used with a dat. 3. 85 ἀγχοῦ
τῇ ἵππῳ. The assertion that the Asopos
was near any of the Greeks, or any of
the Greeks near the Asopos, is puzzling.
The whole position, indeed, has been
described above, c. 30, as ἐπὶ τῷ Ἀσωπῷ,
but that is relatively to the previous
position ἐπὶ τῇ ὑπωρέῃ, and not from
the point of view of the actual water-
supply. The Greek position along the
tops of the Asopos Ridge was not, from
the army-service point of view, near the
Asopos, if by Asopos is meant the main
stream (as in c. 30, and *passim*). Hdt.
has here probably made a mistake,
owing to his ignorance of the ground :
that the parts of the army which were
not near Gargaphia were near the Asopos
may be a blind inference from the
general (and not, broadly speaking, incorrect) description of their position as
ἐπὶ τῷ Ἀσωπῷ. It is possible, however,
that Dr. G. B. Grundy's suggestion (for
a phrase ;in c. 31 *supra*, *q.v.*) is here
applicable, and that ' Asopos' is here
used of stream A¹, though not with
conscious knowledge or discrimination
on the historian's part. The Greek left,
in particular the Athenians, were certainly in the vicinity of this streamlet,
but were no doubt unable to use it ὑπό
τε τῶν ἱππέων καὶ τοξευμάτων. They may
erroneously have spoken of it as the
Asopos, or the Plataian Asopos ; but
Hdt., had he known the real state of the
case, would surely have distinguished
expressly between the main stream and
this comparatively insignificant affluent.

ⁱⁱ ἐρυκόμενοι : passive ; cp. 5. 15.

Ἀσωποῦ οὕτω δὴ ἐπὶ τὴν κρήνην ἐφοίτων· ἀπὸ τοῦ ποταμοῦ
15 γάρ σφι οὐκ ἐξῆν ὕδωρ φορέεσθαι ὑπό τε τῶν ἱππέων καὶ
50 τοξευμάτων. τούτου δὲ τοιούτου γινομένου οἱ τῶν Ἑλλήνων
στρατηγοί, ἅτε τοῦ τε ὕδατος στερηθείσης τῆς στρατιῆς καὶ
ὑπὸ τῆς ἵππου ταρασσομένης, συνελέχθησαν περὶ αὐτῶν τε
τούτων καὶ ἄλλων, ἐλθόντες παρὰ Παυσανίην ἐπὶ τὸ δεξιὸν
5 κέρας. ἄλλα γὰρ τούτων τοιούτων ἐόντων μᾶλλον σφέας
ἐλύπεε· οὔτε γὰρ σιτία εἶχον ἔτι, οἵ τε σφέων ὀπέωνες

---

14 ἐφοιτέων C: ἐφοίτεον Pz, Stein[1], van H.   15 ὕδωρ om. B
50. 1 γενομένου Marc.   3 αὐτέων τε τουτέων z   4 Παυσανίην
ἐπὶ om. z   5 ἄλλα A[2]SMarc.: ἀλλὰ ‖ τουτέων z ‖ μᾶλλον σφέας AB,
Stein[2]: μᾶλλόν σφεας   6 ἐπελύπεε CP ‖ τέ σφεων vulgo ‖ ὀπέωνες R:
ὀπαῶνες S: ὀπάονες Schaefer

---

14. οὕτω δή : here not temporal but modal, or even causal.

15. ὑπό : cp. c. 45. 17 supra.

50. 1. τούτου δὲ τοιούτου γινομένου, 'such coming to be the state of the case,' 'things getting to this pass' (cp. 5. 109)—a somewhat vague phrase, repeated below in more positive or substantial form, τούτων τοιούτων ἐόντων, but explained as referring to the two serious incommodities, (1) the ruin of the water-supply, (2) the harassing fire from the cavalry. Nor was this all! (3) The army was without rations, and (4) completely cut off from its base: (3) and (4) were vexing them all the more (μᾶλλον σφέας ἐλύπεε) owing to the sudden development of (1) and (2)! The admissions made in this chapter are notable; but the logical and chronological sequences are not acceptable.

οἱ τῶν Ἑλλήνων στρατηγοί : other than Pausanias (and Euryanax), who no doubt summoned them to the Council of War, which is held on the right wing. The position of the Greek force is highly precarious. The question before the Council must have been whether to advance and cross the Asopos, or to retreat. The third alternative, remaining where they are, is impossible.

6. οὔτε γὰρ σιτία εἶχον ἔτι. This had been probably one of the chief reasons for their advance to the] position on the Asopos Ridge, in which they were offering battle to the Persian, if only he would come across the Asopos with his infantry. Mardonios had perhaps turned them out of their position at Hysiai by seizing and occupying Dryoskephalai, and forced them to come down to the Asopos and offer battle ; he is still, no doubt, even hoping to draw or drive them across the Asopos. Hdt., who keeps the Greeks twelve days on the Asopos Ridge, for eleven of which they are absolutely unmolested and allowed to water freely from Gargaphia, now at last admits that battle or retreat is a necessity, owing to the complete break-down of the commissariat ; that break-down being due to the complete command attained by the Persian cavalry of the main route to the rear of the Greek forces. The difficult Plataia-Megara pass remains indeed open ; and it is just upon that they resolve to fall back, for even that pass was no use to them in their present position.

οἵ τε σφέων ὀπέωνες ἀποπεμφθέντες ἐς Πελοπόννησον : the ὀπέωνες = the ψιλοὶ τῶν εἱλωτέων, περὶ ἄνδρα ἕκαστον ἑπτὰ τεταγμένοι (c. 28 supra) and the ψιλοί, ὡς εἷς περὶ ἕκαστον ἐὼν ἄνδρα (c. 30 supra), whatever their total numbers. The Peloponnesian portion of them has been sent away, to bring up supplies (ὡς ἐπισιτιεύμενοι, cp. 7. 176), to manage the ἐπισίτησις of their masters, and cannot get back, the Greek army being completely isolated in its present position by the Persian cavalry.

This passage goes to show that the only ὀπέωνες, or ψιλοί, in camp, or with the army, at this crisis, would be those in attendance on the Athenians, Megarians, Plataians. The presumption is, however, that the Athenian and Megarian ὀπέωνες were also absent (though the Athenian τοξόται were of course on the spot, cp. c. 60 infra). The army was practically a purely hoplite force at this moment.

ἀποπεμφθέντες ἐς Πελοπόννησον ὡς ἐπισιτιεύμενοι ἀπεκεκληίατο
ὑπὸ τῆς ἵππου, οὐ δυνάμενοι ἀπικέσθαι ἐς τὸ στρατόπεδον.
βουλευομένοισι δὲ τοῖσι στρατηγοῖσι ἔδοξε, ἢν ὑπερβάλωνται 51
ἐκείνην τὴν ἡμέρην οἱ Πέρσαι συμβολὴν ποιεύμενοι, ἐς τὴν

7 ἀπεκεκληίατο Dindorf, Stein, Holder : ἀποκεκληίατο van H. : ἀπο-
κεκλέατο Β**z** : ἀπεκεκλέατο   8 ὑπό: ἀπὸ C ‖ ἀπικέεσθαι R   51. 2
κείνην **z** ‖ μὴ ποιεύμενοι **β**, Holder, van H.

But, perhaps, we should allow still the regulation attendant on each hoplite.

7. **ἀπεκεκληίατο**, 'were utterly and had for some time previously been shut off,' from returning. *Ionice pro* ἀποκεκλεισμένοι ἦσαν, Schweighaeuser (but cp. Veitch, *Gk. Verbs* s.v. κλείω). Cp. ἀποκληισθέντες τῆ ὀπίσω ὁδοῦ 3. 55, in a somewhat different connexion.

8. **ὑπό**: cp. c. 37 *supra*. The Persian cavalry completely dominates the situation. On the night of the 8th (c. 39 *supra*) they have seized *Dryoskephalai*, the junction of the Eleutherai-Erythrai and Eleutherai-Hysiai-Plataia roads, in the rear of the Greek position, at Hysiai. The Persians have, of course, maintained their hold on that position. In consequence the Greeks are cut off from their base (except by the difficult Plataia-Megara route), and on the 11th (no doubt) come to the determination to go down to a position ἐπὶ τῷ Ἀσωπῷ, and offer battle to the Persian. This manoeuvre is carried out upon the 12th (perhaps not without some loss) and Mardonios moves into position opposite them, with the Asopos still between, c. 47 *supra*.

Still, neither side will cross the river ; but all that day, the 12th, the Greeks are harassed by the cavalry, cut off from the water-supply on all sides, cut off from their bases, not merely *via* Erythrai and Hysiai, but even *via* Plataia ; the rations they have with them are giving out —battle or retreat becomes an absolute necessity.

51. 1. βουλευομένοισι δὲ τοῖσι στρατηγοῖσι ἔδοξε: a council of war never fights ; but this time the council was right. The two alternatives for the Persians are here presented by tradition— (*a*) that the Persians should come across the river and attack them (διαβῆναι τὸν Ἀσωπὸν καὶ μάχης ἄρξαι); (*b*) that the Persians should not do so, but postpone for that day, or indefinitely, delivering the attack (ἢν ὑπερβάλωνται . . οἱ Πέρσαι συμβολὴν ποιεύμενοι). Here συμβολὴν

ποιέεσθαι has nothing to say to the cavalry skirmishing which was going on, but of course means to bring on a general engagement, to deliver the attack, μάχης ἄρξαι. The participial construction is noticeable. Only one course is treated as open to the Greeks, viz. to retreat. But there was another, viz. to advance, to cross the Asopos, to assume the offensive. That was what Alexander did at the Granikos ; but then, Alexander's army was not composed simply of hoplites. To have crossed the Asopos must have meant annihilation to the army of Pausanias. He had no cavalry. He had practically no ψιλοί, or none worth counting. Crossing the stream would have broken the Greek ranks. Once across the Persian cavalry could have ridden round and round them on the comparatively level and open plain. On a smaller scale the situation would have anticipated Arbela, with no cavalry, no light infantry, no developed tactics, no Alexander, on the Greek side ; the issue would have been the annihilation of the Greek army, the hot victory of Mardonios. The Asopos stream was a Rubicon indeed ; the Greek determination to remain south of it was their salvation ; Mardonios crossed it to his ruin. Had he crossed on the 12th the result would have been the same. The Council of War was only summoned by Pausanias (and Euryanax) when it became fairly obvious that the Persian infantry was not coming across, and that the present position was untenable.

2. **ἐς τὴν νῆσον ἰέναι**: this was to retreat (perhaps to the position previously occupied). A third alternative besides advancing and retreating was logically possible, viz. to stay where they were, and as they were, in hopes the Persian might still deliver an attack. But why should he grant to-morrow what he refuses to-day? Or how are they to remain, without water, without rations? Where is the island to be located? And how? The measurements given

νῆσον ἰέναι. ἣ δὲ ἐστὶ ἀπὸ τοῦ Ἀσωποῦ καὶ τῆς κρήνης
τῆς Γαργαφίης, ἐπ᾽ ᾗ ἐστρατοπεδεύοντο τότε, δέκα σταδίους
5 ἀπέχουσα, πρὸ τῆς Πλαταιέων πόλιος. νῆσος δὲ οὕτω ἂν εἴη
ἐν ἠπείρῳ· σχιζόμενος [ὁ] ποταμὸς ἄνωθεν ἐκ τοῦ Κιθαιρῶνος

---

3 δ᾽ ἔστιν R   4 γαρσαφίης S ‖ ἐπ᾽ ᾗ Β: ἐς τὴν z: ἐπ᾽ ἦν   5
ἔχουσα Β ‖ νῆσος .. ἐς τώυτό del. Krueger ‖ δ᾽ ἂν Β   6 ὁ secl. Stein²,
Holder, van H.

---

by Hdt. are not the most important
evidence in determining the site. His
measurements are only round numbers,
approximative, in decimals. The important factors are :—(i.) The island was
πρὸ τῆς Πλαταιέων πόλιος. (ii.) The island
was formed not by the Asopos, or its
tributaries, but by the Oëroë. These
two factors were, indeed, used by Leake
and Vischer in fixing the island away
to the west, beyond the main road from
Plataia to Thebes. (iii.) The strategic
and tactical necessities of the case must
be met. From this point of view the
objections to Leake's location are over-
powering. On such an island the Greeks
(a) would still have been exposed to the
attacks of the Persian cavalry, (b) would
not have been in a better position as
regards supplies. The island must be
sought up on the ὑπωρέη, and it must be
backed by the only remaining pass
through which the Greeks could draw
supplies, viz. the difficult Plataia-Megara
route; and there must be a water-supply.
The position proposed by Dr. Grundy
meets these requirements : (i.) it is in
front of Plataia (and perhaps also Hysiai?);
(ii.) it is formed by the Oëroë ; (iii.) it is
inaccessible to cavalry, backed by the
route to Megara, and well supplied with
water (Oëroë, Vergutiani spring) ; and
also (iv.) accords rather better with the
measurements given by Hdt., such as
they are, than the position assigned by
Leake and Vischer. Cp. G. B. Grundy,
G. P. W. pp. 480 ff.

3. ἣ δὲ ἐστὶ τοῦ Ἀσωποῦ κτλ. :
how vague are the distances as expressed
by Hdt. in stades is shown by his
pairing the Asopos and Gargaphia
together as 'ten stades' from the
'island.' Unless Gargaphia and the
Asopos are identical they can hardly
have been so exactly the same distance
from a third point. Again, if by 'the
Asopos' were here meant the main
stream, we should either have to fall
back on Leake's location of the island,

or to confess that Hdt.'s measurement
is valueless. If the Asopos here = A¹,
it approximates sufficiently to Gargaphia
to allow Hdt.'s measure to pass, and to
refer to Dr. Grundy's 'island,' as above.

κρήνη is a fountain, with artificial
pipes, outlet, and so forth, as distinct
from φρέαρ, a well, 1. 68 (cp. 4. 120) and
πηγή, a spring, source, 1. 189, 7. 26.

4. ἐπ᾽ ᾗ ἐστρατοπεδεύοντο τότε : the
apparent exclusion of the Asopos from
the purview of the Hellenic Laager is
curious ; but (a) the singular of the
relative may have been determined by
the proximity of the feminine antecedent ; (b) the council was being held
on the right wing of the Greek position,
and the right wing was in immediate
proximity to the fountain ; (c) the
Asopos just above has been defined as
more or less near the position of the
Greek contingents, and so perhaps comes
to be omitted here (as in c. 25) ; (d)
the grammatical construction might be
strained, so as to carry back and cover
the Asopos too, κατὰ σύνεσιν.

5. πρὸ τῆς Πλαταιέων πόλιος : the
'island' between O² and O³ was eminently 'in front of the city of the
Plataians' to any one approaching
Plataia by the road from Athens ; it
might also, however, though less
appropriately, be so described from the
point of view of the position occupied
by the Greek forces 'on Gargaphia.'

νῆσος δὲ οὕτω ἂν εἴη ἐν ἠπείρῳ :
the adverb οὕτω here = ὧδε, referring to
what follows ; cp. 8. 98. 4 (109. 12,
140. 34).

6. σχιζόμενος, being rent (in twain),
'dividing itself' ; cp. 7. 31, 219, 8. 34 ;
also 2. 17. Hdt. evidently conceives
the Oëroë as first starting in a single
channel, or stream, then parting into two
and re-uniting, so as literally to form
an island ; cp. 2. 17 μέχρι μὲν νυν
Κερκασώρου πόλιος ῥέει ἐὼν ὁ Νεῖλος,
τὸ δὲ ἀπὸ ταύτης τῆς πόλιος σχίζεται
τριφασίας ὁδούς. Such (i.e. διφασίας

ῥέει κάτω ἐς τὸ πεδίον, διέχων ἀπ' ἀλλήλων τὰ ῥέεθρα ὅσον
περ τρία στάδια, καὶ ἔπειτα συμμίσγει ἐς τωὐτό. οὔνομα δέ
οἱ Ὠερόη· θυγατέρα δὲ ταύτην λέγουσι εἶναι Ἀσωποῦ οἱ
ἐπιχώριοι. ἐς τοῦτον δὴ τὸν χῶρον ἐβουλεύσαντο μετανα- 10
στῆναι, ἵνα καὶ ὕδατι ἔχωσι χρᾶσθαι ἀφθόνῳ καὶ οἱ ἱππέες

7 ὅσον περὶ Marc. : ὅσον τε Krueger : ὅσον ἐπὶ ? Stein²   8 τοῦτο β
9 οἱ pr. loc. : ὁ RV   10 μεταστῆναι SV

ὁδοὺς σχίζεται) is not the case with
the Oëroë, and probably never was.
Hdt. is not writing from autopsy, or
even from a cartographical survey!
But such an eminent and conspicuous hill or
mound between two streams, as *Ridge 4*
now is, might easily be named an
'island' though not quite strictly
speaking surrounded by water. Even
the 'Pelopo-nesos' is only a peninsula;
cp. 'Chersonese,' etc.

7. **ἐς τὸ πεδίον**: if Hdt. meant by
these words to imply that 'the island'
was down on 'the plain,' he would be
giving further evidence of his ignorance
of the ground. But need the phrase be
so closely pressed? The river in any
case is flowing down to the flat land.
διέχων, 'holding apart . .'; cp.
προέχειν c. 4 *supra*. **τὰ ῥέεθρα** may
here mean 'channels,' cp. 7. 130, and
L. & S. *sub v.* ῥεῖθρος, but ῥέει above and
συμμίσγει just below rather suggest
'streams'; and dry channels would not
have been enough for the Greeks on this
occasion.
ὅσον περ τρία στάδια: the measurement given is very exact (ὅσον περ,
cp. ὅκως περ c. 120 *infra*), but only
in one direction! How, then, is the
distance of 3 stades reckoned, in latitude
or in longitude? Is the island 3 stades
long, or 3 stades broad? Unless the
island were a rectangle, a square, it
would seem that it must be its length
that is given, and rectangular it could
not be. On the other hand, a plot of
land only 3 stades long (and probably
not 3 stades wide) would have been far
too small to receive the army. Not
indeed that the whole forces need have
been actually on 'the island' in the
strictest sense. Dr. Grundy's island is
considerably less than 3 stades wide,
and indefinitely more than 3 stades
long, but the actual mound might be
about 3 stades long, which is perhaps
what Hdt. would have said, had he
measured, or even seen, the ground
before writing.

9. **Ὠερόη**. Oëroë is a word of four
syllables, and more than that! 'The
men of those parts' in Hdt.'s time
regarded Oëroë as 'a daughter of Asopos.'
Hdt. need not have gone to Plataia
to learn that. He might have met
an ἐπιχώριος elsewhere. Thersander of
Orchomenos (c. 16 *supra*) might have
been his informant; or he might have
read the statement in a geographical or
mythological work; but it was probably
the last thing a Plataian would have
admitted. What was the sense of calling
Oëroë a daughter of Asopos? Much the
same as of saying that Thebe and Aigina
were daughters of Asopos (cp. 5. 80).
There is policy in it; the Oëroë region
is claimed as part of the Παρασωπίς (cp.
c. 15 *supra*). If this myth were intended
for science, the hydrography is against it.
Oëroë, the identity of which is certain,
belongs to a different land-system to
that of the Asopos, and sheds its waters
to the west, down into the bay of
Kreusis, not eastward to the Euboian sea.
The names of rivers are seldom
feminine in Greek. Wesseling remarked
that Oëroë is not included in the twelve
daughters of Asopos by Diodoros 4. 72;
cp. Apollod. 3. 11. 5. Only two of the
names, Πειρήνη, Ἀσωπίς, could apply to
springs, or streams. The latter perhaps
might be the Oëroë (but that the Asopos
with twelve daughters is the Phleiasian
or Sekyonian, cp. c. 15. 13 *supra*).

10. **ἐβουλεύσαντο μετανασστῆναι**, 'they
resolved after deliberation to migrate';
cp. μετανίστημι in Thuc. 1. 12. 1, 3.
114. 3; also the substantive μεταναά-
στασις 1. 2. 1, 2. 16. 1.
Three motives for this move are given:
(1) need of water-supply; (2) avoidance
of the cavalry; (3) the relief of the
commissariat-train, which was cooped
up on Kithairon. All three reasons are
so much homage to the dominance of
the Persian cavalry, as is also further
the determination to carry out the move
under cover of night.

11. **ἵνα . . ἔχωσι . . καὶ . . μὴ**

σφέας μὴ σινοίατο ὥσπερ κατιθὺ ἐόντων· μετακινέεσθαι δὲ
ἐδόκεε τότε ἐπεὰν τῆς νυκτὸς ἦ δευτέρη φυλακή, ὡς ἂν μὴ

12 δὲ Stein³ : τε

σινοίατο : a more immediate and a more
remote, a more certain and a less certain,
purpose or result, are indicated by the
modal variation, cp. ἢν μὲν δοκέῃ . . εἰ
δὲ καὶ μὴ δοκέοι c. 48 supra.

12. ὥσπερ κατιθὺ ἐόντων, "as they
did when they were directly exposed to
them" (Blakesley); "as now, when
they were right opposite" (Macaulay);
"as when it was drawn up right in their
front" (Rawlinson). κατιθύ, or κατ᾽ ἰθύ,
can hardly mean anything but 'right
opposite.' To what subject is ἐόντων to
be referred : ἱππέων out of ἱππέες, or
σφέων out of σφέας ! The material
result, or argument, will be the same in
either case—which perhaps accounts for
the formal ambiguity. The argument
is obscure. A. If Hdt. means that the
cavalry was making frontal attacks upon
the Greeks in their position (II.) 'on
the Asopos,' the lie of the land is prima
facie against him. It is not likely that
the cavalry crossed the Asopos in front
of the Greek position, and charged up
the hill, halting and discharging their
missiles, and then retired to a safe
distance ; for (a) this would require that
bridges should have been laid across the
river in many places, a proceeding of
which there is no record ; (b) this frontal
attack would have no connexion with the
destruction of Gargaphia and the water-
supply in rear of the Greek position.
B. If Hdt. means that frontal attacks
by the cavalry were more to be dreaded
than attacks on flank, or on rear (κατὰ
νότου), he would be saying what is
manifestly absurd, and in contradiction
with his own context. The frontal
attacks at Erythrai failed ; the flank
and rear attacks by the Persian cavalry
upon the Greek positions since the
advance from Erythrai have been successful. C. Is it possible that ὥσπερ κατιθὺ
ἐόντων here practically means that the
Greeks were completely surrounded, and
open to direct attack on all sides, though
Hdt. himself may have repeated the
phrase of his authority, or source,
imperfectly and without fully understanding it ! The actual fact was as
suggested. In the position 'on the
Asopos,' the position associated with
the Androkrateion and Gargaphia, the
Persian cavalry could attack the Greeks
on all sides, more or less. The destruction of Gargaphia proves that the
cavalry ranged freely behind the Greek
position ; the same fact is proved by the
admission that the Greek connexions were
cut, and that supplies could not reach
them. In such a situation the Greeks
cannot have maintained a formation on
a single front, facing Asopos (north).
The Greek army must necessarily have
formed either in two lines back to back
(φάλαγξ ἀμφίστομος Arrian Tact. 29) or
in a hollow square, or parallelogram,
round the Androkrateion ; otherwise the
Persian Hippotoxotai would have shot
them down from the rear. (Though the
south side of the 'Asopos Ridge' is
steeper than the north slope, it is not
inaccessible.) Especially the detachment
told off to guard Gargaphia must have
had such a formation. It is possible
that the expression ὥσπερ κατιθὺ ἐόντων
covers these facts. The Nesos was
practically quite inaccessible for cavalry.
D. Last, and least likely : the words
might, ungrammatically, have reference
to the new position about to be taken—
they are in any case more or less
incorrect—or may represent words in
Hdt.'s source originally intended to
mean that in the new position, ἅτε
κατιθὺ ἐσομένων (sc. ἀμφοτέρων τῶν
στρατ.), only frontal, and therefore less
formidable, attacks will be possible.
The grammatical obstacle to this interpretation is threefold : (1) the genitive
absolute remains objectionable, as on
every hypothesis ; (2) ὥσπερ has to be
made = ὥστε, ἅτε ; (3) the present participle has to be taken as loosely equivalent
to a future participle. These objections,
fatal to this interpretation of the words
as they stand, do not convince me that
the phrase, as originally used by Hdt.'s
authority, may not have had reference
to the new position to be occupied, viz.
the νῆσος.

13. δευτέρη φυλακή. The Romans
certainly divided the night into four
vigiliae ; cp. Caesar, B.G. 1. 40, and
Lewis & Short, sub v. vigilia. The
Greek division is not so clear. Pollux 1.
70 is the main authority and might be
taken to limit it to three (περὶ πρώτας

ἰδοίατο οἱ Πέρσαι ἐξορμωμένους καί σφεας ἑπόμενοι ταράσσοιεν
οἱ ἱππόται. ἀπικομένων δὲ ἐς τὸν χῶρον τοῦτον, τὸν δὴ ἡ 15

---

14 ἐξορμεομένους Pz, Stein[1], van H. : ἐξορμεωμένους CMarc., Gaisford

---

φυλακὰς καὶ δευτέρας καὶ τρίτας). Suidas sub v. φυλακή· τὸ τέταρτον μέρος τῆς νυκτός· τετραχῆ γὰρ διῄρηται, has been assumed to be referring to the Roman system exclusively ; but I think it more probable that the Greek system was practically identical with the Roman : thus in Pollux l.c. I. νυκτὸς ἀρχή, περὶ πρώτην νύκτα, νυκτὸς ἀρχομένης = prima nocte, prima vigilia. II. περὶ πρῶτον ὕπνον = nocte concubia (Tac. Ann. 1. 89), secunda vigilia. III. μεσούσης νυκτός, μέσων νυκτῶν = nocte media, tertia vigilia. IV. περὶ ἀλεκτρυόνων ᾠδάς, ἀλεκτρυόνων ᾀδόντων, ὑπὸ τὸν ᾠδὸν ὄρνιθα = gallicínium, noctis gallicinio. The words καὶ δευτέρας καὶ τρίτας in Pollux l.c. are out of place, and should not prejudice the question. The 'second watch' is very elaborately paraphrased in c. 44 supra, ubi v., and 'the first watch' perhaps in 7. 215, ubi v. The exact length of the watch depended on the length of the night between sunset and sunrise, but was roughly two to three hours. The 'watches' in Ev. Marc. 13. 35 (ἢ ὀψὲ ἢ μεσονυκτίον ἢ ἀλεκτοροφωνίας ἢ πρωΐ) seem to exclude the prima. Is it not some confirmation of this fourfold division of the night, that the five terms in 4. 181 by which the time of day is marked give likewise a fourfold division ? Obviously in the present case 'the first watch' was not dark enough for the intended movement of the Greeks : they meant to start about 10 P.M. apparently.

14. ἐξορμωμένους, 'starting,' in the act of moving out of position ; cp. 7. 37, and esp. 7. 215 ὁρμέατο . . ἐκ τοῦ στρατοπέδου.

ταράσσοιεν : as they had been doing most of the day ; cp. c. 50 τῆς στρατιῆς ὑπὸ τῆς ἵππου ταρασσομένης etc. The confusion (ταραχή) was only confounded (συνετάραξαν) in the case of the fountain, c. 49 supra, or perhaps in the immediate vicinity of the fountain. There is here fresh admission of the efficiency of the Persian cavalry.

15. ἀπικομένων δὲ ἐς τὸν χῶρον τοῦτον : genitive absolute and participle keep up the mystery of the preceding crux, ἐόντων supra ; the aorist here must be

conditional, i.e. virtually future : in the dative (with ἐδόκεε) it would, of course, record their actual arrival at the island ; in the genitive, it only continues the report of the council's decisions, to the effect that, 'on arrival at the island, they should still, under cover of night, despatch a division to Kithairon, etc. etc.' Whether this report be correct is, of course, another question.

τὸν δὴ ἡ Ἀσωπὶς [Ὠερόη] περισχίζεται. There is no difficulty in a verb, neuter or passive, compounded with περί taking the accusative (cp. περιρρέω, περιρρήγνυμι). The peculiarity here, however, arises from the preposition apparently having a sense in connexion with τὸν χῶρον τοῦτον, which is not strictly compatible with the meaning of the verb. Thus περὶ τὸν ἡ Ἀσωπὶς σχίζεται would mean simply that at this point the Asopis divides, or is split, into two streams ; cp. Plato, Tim. 21 R ἔστι τις κατ' Αἴγυπτον, ᾗ δ' ὅς, ἐν τῷ Δέλτα, περὶ δ κατὰ κορυφὴν σχίζεται τὸ τοῦ Νείλου ῥεῦμα, Σαϊτικὸς ἐπικαλούμενος νομὸς κτλ. σχίζεσθαι περί τι marks a point, not a region ; but here the idea of 'surrounding' seems suggested : the νῆσος is not a point, or a κορυφή, on which the Asopis splits, but an oblong figure, or χῶρος, which it surrounds. Had περιρρέειν been the verb here, no one would have felt a difficulty. Thus 7. 214 περιηγησάμενοι τὸ ὄρος τοῖσι Πέρσῃσι : 1. 84 περιενειχθέντος τοῦ λέοντος τὸ τεῖχος : 4. 180 παρθένον . . περιάγουσι τὴν λίμνην do not clear this case, the difficulty lying not in the περί but in the σχίζεται. If Hdt. had written σχιζομένη or σχισθεῖσα περιρρέει, instead of ῥέουσα περισχίζεται, the phrase would have been unimpeachable. Hdt. is here a little befogged in his phraseology (like the man who 'boiled an icicle' instead of 'oiling a bicycle,' yet not so badly as that !) ; cp. c. 55 infra. Polybios, 3. 42. 7, shows a much clearer head : οἱ ποιησάμενοι τὴν πορείαν ἀντίοι τῷ ῥεύματι . . παραγενόμενοι πρὸς τινα τόπον, ἐν ᾧ συνέβαινε περί τι χωρίον νησίζον περισχίζεσθαι τὸν ποταμόν, ἐνταῦθα κατέμειναν (Hannibal's crossing of the Rhone).

Ἀσωπὶς [Ὠερόη] περισχίζεται ῥέουσα ἐκ τοῦ Κιθαιρῶνος, ὑπὸ τὴν νύκτα ταύτην ἐδόκεε τοὺς ἡμίσεας ἀποστέλλειν τοῦ στρατοπέδου πρὸς τὸν Κιθαιρῶνα, ὡς ἀναλάβοιεν τοὺς ὀπέωνας τοὺς ἐπὶ τὰ σιτία οἰχομένους· ἦσαν γὰρ ἐν τῷ Κιθαιρῶνι 20 ἀπολελαμμένοι.

---

16 nomen seclusi ‖ σχίζεται S ‖ ἐκ τοῦ Κιθαιρῶνος del. Gomperz, Holder   18 ὀπάονας R : ὀπαῶνας S   19 ἔσαν z

---

16. ὑπὸ τὴν νύκτα ταύτην: i.e. apparently 'before daybreak'; yet ὑπὸ νύκτα is generally taken to mean 'about nightfall,' towards night, as night comes on. The temporal indication must qualify not ἐδόκεε (for the date of which see above) but ἀποστέλλειν.

17. ἐδόκεε repeats the ἐδόκεε just above; but the change to the imperfects, after ἐβουλεύσαντο and ἔδοξε, in the report of the proceedings of one and the same council, looks as though (1) the precise time of departure, (2) the operations projected for the ἀπόστολος στρατός (so to speak, cp. τοὺς ἡμίσεας ἀποστέλλειν infra), were less clearly, less definitely resolved, expressed, understood, than the previous question of retreat, and retreat to the 'island' as a new halting-place. Anyway, these imperfects introduce resolutions which were very imperfectly realized.

τοὺς ἡμίσεας ἀποστέλλειν τοῦ στρατοπέδου πρὸς τὸν Κιθαιρῶνα: a most curious statement: it was resolved, or was in a way to be resolved, that after the whole army had reached the island, the half of the army should be further despatched to Kithairon, in order to convoy, relieve, the attendants who had gone away to fetch supplies (cp. c. 50 supra). Which half of the army was to be despatched on this service ? To what part of Kithairon was it to go ? Was it really proposed to bisect the army ? One half would have comprised (presumably) either (a) the right wing and right centre, 22,800 men ; or (b) the left wing and left centre, 15,900 men ; or (c) the two wings together, 20,100 men ; or (d) the right and left centre, 18,600 men. Cp. the tactical disposition and figures as given and annotated c. 28 supra. There is no clear indication which of these four alternatives is intended. But as in the sequel the whole centre moves back far beyond the two wings, while the two wings attempt to form up in one, though unsuccessfully, it is best to understand by τοὺς ἡμίσεας in this passage the right and left centre (cp. cc. 52, 69 infra) (or else, one half only of the centre ?). The whole plan, then, is apparently that the two divisions of the centre should retire πρὸς τὸν Κιθαιρῶνα, while the right and left wings, i.e. the Lakedaimonians with the Tegeatai and the Athenians with the Plataians, should concentrate back on to the island. To what point on Kithairon was the centre to retire ? Were they to go back on to the Plataio-Megarian pass, and to protect and convoy the ὀπέωνες and the σιτία down the pass, and to the island ? The Persian cavalry was in command and possession of Dryoskephalai and the two routes, or passes, therefrom on to the plain, or the ὑπωρέη. Was the centre to attempt the recovery, or the reopening of the loop from 'Three Heads' to Plataia ? The centre was to be detached upon a service apparently which was the less hazardous ; they were to retire first, they were to retire furthest, they were to retire in a compact body, leaving the two wings in the dark to find or keep touch of each other, and to concentrate back on to the island, from their isolated positions at the two extremities of the existing line. It showed some confidence in the virtues of the centre to charge them with that service, as they might have gone clean off (like Artabazos on the other side ?) from the battle-field : in the sequel they did good service. One thing is manifest : Hdt. has not fully conceived the precise meaning of the traditions which he reports ; but, as often, the report is sufficiently full and faithful to yield the facts to a critical reconstruction.

18. ἀναλάβοιεν : a remarkable use of this flexible word ; cp. 7. 231, 8. 109.

19. ἦσαν γὰρ ἐν τῷ Κιθαιρῶνι ἀπολελαμμένοι, 'they were on Kithairon unable to make further progress.' ἀπολαμβάνειν : cp. c. 38 supra, etc. Hdt. uses perf. pass. ἀπολέλαμμαι (not ἀπεί-

Ταῦτα βουλευσάμενοι κείνην μὲν τὴν ἡμέρην πᾶσαν προσ- 52
κειμένης τῆς ἵππου εἶχον πόνον ἄτρυτον· ὡς δὲ ἥ τε ἡμέρη
ἔληγε καὶ οἱ ἱππέες ἐπέπαυντο, νυκτὸς δὴ γινομένης καὶ
ἐούσης τῆς ὥρης ἐς τὴν συνέκειτό σφι ἀπαλλάσσεσθαι, ἐνθαῦτα
ἀερθέντες οἱ πολλοὶ ἀπαλλάσσοντο, ἐς μὲν τὸν χῶρον ἐς τὸν 5
συνέκειτο οὐκ ἐν νόῳ ἔχοντες, οἳ δὲ ὡς ἐκινήθησαν ἔφευγον

---

52. 1 ἐκείνην β ‖ προκειμένης (C)RS   2 ἔχον z   3 νυκτός τε
vel νυκτός τε δὴ ? Stein[1]   4 θεούσης aC ‖ τὴν δὴ β, Holder, van H.
5 ἀπαλλάσσοντο om. Marc. ‖ ἐς ὃν aC   6 ὡς : ἐς C

λήμμαι). ἦσαν is here more than a
mere auxiliary, and ἦσαν ἀπολελαμμένοι
more than merely ἀπελελάμφατο(?). Hdt.
does not specify upon what part of
Kithairon the supply train was arrested,
or cut off, or prevented from advancing
—by the Persian cavalry, or the fear
thereof. He nowhere shows any clear
knowledge of a pass direct from Plataia
to Megara.

52. 1. ταῦτα βουλευσάμενοι.. πᾶσαν:
the natural inferences from this sequence
were that the Council took place early,
and that the cavalry assaults continued
for the whole day after. But that
inference would be inconsistent with cc.
49, 50 *supra* where the Council is only
summoned τούτων τοιούτων ἐόντων, or at
least τούτου δὲ τοιούτου γινομένου. 'All
the day' means (*a*) 'all the rest of that
day,' or (*b*) simply 'all day,' to signify
that after the Council, as before, the
ταραχὴ ὑπὸ τῶν ἱππέων continued. The
day is still the 12th, which dawned in
c. 47 *supra*. There has been nothing
to justify the insertion of one or more
days between the dawn there and the
night here. κείνην, indeed, places the
πόνον ἄτρυτον and the βουλήν upon the
same day. ἄτρυτος is a poetic word,
with a intensive; Pindar, *Pyth.* 4. 174,
has the same phrase, ἄτρυτος πόνος, but
not in quite the same sense (πέμπε δ'
Ἑρμᾶς χρυσόραπις διδόμους υἱοὺς ἐπ' ἄτρυτον
πόνον).

2. ἥ τε ἡμέρη ἔληγε, 'towards evening
on the 12th.' λήγειν here of time, as of
space 7. 216; cp. 4. 39. Xenoph. *Anab.*
7. 6. 6 has αὕτη μὲν ἡ ἡμέρα οὕτως ἔληξε.
οἱ ἱππέες ἐπέπαυντο: sc. προσκείμενοι, or
προσβάλλοντες, or ταράσσοντες τὴν στρατιήν, as they have been doing all day.
The use of the pluperfect after the
imperfect is noticeable; the cavalry
attacks came to an end before the daylight. But Hdt. uses a material aux-

iliary, and not the pure pluperfect (προσ-
εβεβλήκεσαν, or possibly προσεβεβλέατο,
cp. 6. 24) to signify the cesser of the
attacks.

3. νυκτὸς δὴ γινομένης would serve to
mark the first watch, νυκτὸς ἀρχή, καὶ
περὶ πρώτην νύκτα, καὶ νυκτὸς ἀρχομένης
καὶ περὶ πρώτας φυλακάς, Pollux, 1. 70,
cp. c. 51 *supra*.

4. ἐούσης τῆς ὥρης ἐς τὴν συνέκειτο:
i.e. δευτέρης φυλακῆς c. 51 *supra*, sc.
περὶ πρῶτον ὕπνον Pollux *l.c.*, cp. c. 44
supra. The word ὥρη here comes very
near to our word 'hour,' τὸ δυωδεκατὸν
μέρος τῆς ἡμέρης (sive νυκτός), cp. 2. 109.

**5. ἀερθέντες οἱ πολλοὶ ἀπαλλάσ-
σοντο:** the participle and the subject
both strike a depreciatory, a dyslogistic,
a sarcastic note, which is immediately
followed by still more damnatory clauses.
ἀερθέντες (αείρειν, αίρειν) is used in 1.
165, 170 (also in 4. 150 βαρὺς αείρεσθαι)
in a technical way of sea-faring, starting
on a sea-voyage, νηυσί perhaps, or
ἱστίοις, being understood; or even τὰ
ἱστία, cp. 8. 56, 94. Here, then, 'the
masses' or 'the mass' of the army
departs under full sail! (This might be
an Athenian touch.) οἱ πολλοί here
presumably corresponds exactly to τοὺς
ἡμίσεας in c. 51 *supra*. They are not,
strictly speaking, in the majority: the
whole centre numbers 18,600 as compared with 20,100 for the two wings;
as compared with either wing alone,
however, and especially the left (8600),
the centre has a large plurality.

ἐς τὸν συνέκειτο repeats with a
touch of persiflage the ἐς τὴν συνέκειτο
just above; the construction is, of
course, neuter. (Contr. προσκειμένης
higher up. Hdt. is not over careful to
avoid such inconcinnities, or 'unconscious iterations.')

6. οὐκ ἐν νόῳ ἔχοντες marks their
duplicity (like the Spartans c. 54), 'hav-

ἄσμενοι τὴν ἵππον πρὸς τὴν Πλαταιέων πόλιν, φεύγοντες δὲ
ἀπικνέονται ἐπὶ τὸ "Ηραιον· τὸ δὲ πρὸ τῆς πόλιος ἐστὶ τῆς

8 ἡραῖον RS ‖ δὴ β ‖ τῆς: τῶν Marc.

---

ing no intention'—not having it in
their minds, sc. ἀπαλλάξασθαι (or even
ἀπικέσθαι) to the *rendezvous*, the appointed place; i.e. no doubt in the
view of Hdt. himself, as of his source,
the island. But the previous chapter
shows that the division, or divisions,
here in question were to retire πρὸς τὸν
Κιθαιρῶνα—much further than the island.
They probably did exactly what had
been agreed upon at the Council of War.
οἱ δέ: the subject repeated with
the δέ which might more usually go
with the verb, to emphasize their action:
'but they . .' Cp. 7. 51.
δὲ ἐκινήθησαν ἔφευγον, 'were no
sooner in movement than they took to
their heels, leaving to their joy the
Persian cavalry far behind!'
The representation of this ἀπάλλαξις
(cp. c. 13 *supra*) as a φυγή (*bis*) is the
clearest indication of the *animus* of
Hdt.'s source, and of his own simplicity,
in reproducing his authority.
7. πρὸς τὴν Πλαταιέων πόλιν: the
city of Plataia was no doubt in ruins
(cp. 8. 50 *supra*), though its site and its
remains might offer some cover (on the
morrow) from the dreadful Persian
cavaliers. The story, however, goes on
to relate that in the course of their
flight (φεύγοντες δέ), and before they
actually reached the (ruins of) the city
of Plataia, they arrived at the temple
of Hera (perhaps in ruins too), and
there, in front of the temple, they
halted, with the utmost precision!
Had they been in 'flight' they would
not have stopped there, nor do fugitives
pile arms and take laager: they throw
their arms away, and bolt. The division
which halted (presumably according to
orders) at the Heraion, perhaps comprised only the left centre, οἱ ἀμφὶ Μεγαρέας τε καὶ Φλειασίους c. 69 *infra*, 7300
strong; at the Heraion the left centre
was perhaps in a better position ἀνα-
λαβεῖν τοὺς ὁπέωνας, cp. c. 51 *supra*.
Further, the right centre, in this case,
οἱ ἀμφὶ Κορινθίους c. 69 *infra*, 11,300
strong, may either have gone higher up
Kithairon, in order to bring forward the
σιτία, or have been posted on the road
leading from Plataia to Dryoskephalai,
to protect both the rear of the forces on

the island and the flank of the baggage-
train, coming down the pass from
Megara. In that position they may
subsequently have had some fighting
to do.
8. τὸ "Ηραιον: the temple of Hera
was in front of the πόλις, i.e. the Akropolis of the Plataians, 20 stades from
the fountain of Gargaphia. The site of
the Heraion has been fixed with high
probability by the excavations of Mr.
Henry S. Washington; see *Papers of the
American School at Athens*, vi. (1897),
pp. 40–54. Its position is almost in
the very centre of the plateau of Plataia,
the southern end of which alone constituted the πόλις even in 429 B.C.
Even at that date there were perhaps
no other buildings on the site. The
restored Plataia of Makedonian, Roman,
and later times covered the whole
plateau, as the extant remains of the
city-walls demonstrate (cp. *Papers of
the A.S.A.* v. (1892) pp. 253 ff.), and
must have enclosed the *Heraion*, the
site of which, in 479 B.C., was certainly
outside the city-walls, lower down on
the larger northern portion of the table.
Any one from the north side would
describe the site as πρὸ τῆς πόλιος, and
the Plataians themselves, or any one
following their terminology, would use
the same language (cp. 8. 53), which
would also be not unsuitable from the
point of view of the supposed 'fugitives'
in this story. It is very doubtful, however (to my mind), whether the Heraion
was standing in the year 479 B.C., or
even at the time when Hdt. was writing.
The Persians had probably destroyed it
in 480 B.C. (cp. 8. 50). If so, it was in
ruins at the time of the battle. At the
second destruction of Plataia by the
Thebans, in 426 B.C., it is not recorded
that they destroyed the Heraion, but it
is recorded that they built a great inn,
or khan, round a courtyard 200 feet
square (for the reception of pilgrims),
dedicating it and its furniture to Hera,
καὶ νεὼν ἑκατόμπεδον λίθινον ᾠκοδόμησαν
αὐτῇ Thuc. 3. 68. 3. This was probably
the very temple (ναός) which Pausanias
(9. 2. 7) found within the restored and
enlarged city of his time, θέας ἄξιος
μεγέθει τε καὶ ἐς τῶν ἀγαλμάτων τὸν κόσμον.

Πλαταιέων, εἴκοσι σταδίους ἀπὸ τῆς κρήνης τῆς Γαργαφίης
ἀπέχον· ἀπικόμενοι δὲ ἔθεντο πρὸ τοῦ ἱροῦ τὰ ὅπλα. καὶ οἱ 53
μὲν περὶ τὸ Ἥραιον ἐστρατοπεδεύοντο, Παυσανίης δὲ ὁρῶν
σφεας ἀπαλλασσομένους ἐκ τοῦ στρατοπέδου παρήγγελλε καὶ

---

9 γαρσαφίης S　　　　　53. 2 ἱρὸν β ‖ ὁρέων CPz, Stein[1], van H.
3 παρήγγελε z

But though a *Hekatompedon*, and built
on or over the foundations discovered by
Mr. Washington, the restored temple
was perhaps not so long as the earlier
(sixth century) building, to judge by the
measurements. It is not likely that the
Thebans destroyed a temple which had
been restored since the Persian war; nor is
any account of a temple in such a position
made by Thucydides in his stories of the
siege in 429-7 B.C. Probably the Heraion
had not been restored, but was purposely
left in ruins, as an eternal protest
against the Persian spoiler (and his
Greek allies ; hence the Theban restoration of 426 B.C.). The temple built by
the Plataians out of the spoil of the
battle of 479 B.C. was a temple to
Athene (the Thebans did not destroy
that), Plutarch, *Aristeid.* 20, Pausan. 9.
4. 1. Hdt. in this connexion too shows
no sign of having visited Plataia before
writing his account of the battle.

9. εἴκοσι σταδίους : these distances
in decimals are quite unconvincing, but
might pass for rough estimates, say,
2½ miles. By mere map measurement
the Heraion is about 15 stades from
Apotripi, and 18 from Dr. Grundy's
Gargaphia, and would be a good 20
stades from the Greek position round
the Androkrateion. Why is Gargaphia
here specified as the *terminus a quo* ?
that was rather the Spartan post and
point of departure. ἀπέχειν, intrans.
with acc. of distance, is of course a
sufficiently common construction, cp. 1.
179 ἄλλη πόλις ἀπέχουσα ὀκτὼ ἡμερέων
ὁδὸν ἀπὸ Βαβυλῶνος, 3. 26 ἀπέχουσι δὲ
ἑπτὰ ἡμερέων ὁδὸν ἀπὸ Θηβέων.

10. ἔθεντο πρὸ τοῦ ἱροῦ τὰ ὅπλα,
'they piled arms in front of the temple'
—an admission in itself sufficient to
disprove the insinuation of φυγή. The
Greek centre, or perhaps only the left
centre, must now be conceived as posted
περὶ τὸ Ἥραιον, on the lower or northern
end of the Plataian plateau, with the
heavy shields piled πρὸ τοῦ ἱροῦ. In this
position they are unassailable by cavalry ;
they are in proximity to water (at least

four springs or brooks in the immediate
vicinity of the plateau, cp. *Papers
A.S.A.* v. 1892, p. 269) ; they are
covering to a greater or less extent the
road from Plataia to Megara. They are
also apparently on the extreme left of
the 'third' Greek position, which is to
be when the whole manœuvre shall
have been successfully carried out. But
they are not actually convoying the
baggage-train, ὀπέωνες and σιτία, nor in
any way covering the line from Plataia
to Dryoskephalai, through which the
Persians might possibly circumvent the
supplies. That particular duty may
have been entrusted to the right centre ;
cp. note to l. 7 above.

53. 2. Παυσανίης δὲ ὁρῶν. Hdt.
speaks as though Pausanias himself had
not issued, or agreed to, the order for
retirement ; as though οἱ πολλοί were
stampeding out of laager, or station ; as
though in consequence he issued orders
to the Lakedaimonians to retreat. ὁρῶν,
however, need not be pressed against
Hdt., cp. c. 34. 9 *supra* (=μαθών). Pausanias could hardly have 'seen' the movement, in the literal sense of the word.

3. παρήγγελλε καὶ τοῖσι Λακεδαιμονίοισι : the Spartan method of the
παράγγελσις has been immortalized by
Thucydides, 5. 66. 8: βασιλέως γὰρ
ἄγοντος ὑπ' ἐκείνου πάντα ἄρχεται, καὶ
τοῖς μὲν πολεμάρχοις αὐτὸς φράζει τὸ δέον,
οἱ δὲ τοῖς λοχαγοῖς, ἐκεῖνοι δὲ τοῖς πεντη-
κοντῆρσιν, αὖθις δὲ οὗτοι τοῖς ἐνωμοτάρχαις,
καὶ οὗτοι τῇ ἐνωμοτίᾳ. καὶ αἱ παραγ-
γέλσεις, ἤν τι βούλωνται, κατὰ τὰ αὐτὰ
χωροῦσι καὶ ταχεῖαι ἐπέρχονται· σχεδὸν
γάρ τι πᾶν πλὴν ὀλίγου τὸ στρατόπεδον
τῶν Λακεδαιμονίων ἄρχοντες ἀρχόντων εἰσί,
καὶ τὸ ἐπιμελὲς τοῦ δρωμένου πολλοῖς
προσήκει. On the present occasion,
however, as the whole movement had
been discussed and determined in the
Council of War hours before (cp. c. 51
supra), one must suppose that all the
necessary orders had already been given,
at least to the officers. Pausanias may
still have had to give the word for the
actual moment of departure.

τοῖσι Λακεδαιμονίοισι ἀναλαβόντας τὰ ὅπλα ἰέναι κατὰ τοὺς
5 ἄλλους τοὺς προϊόντας, νομίσας αὐτοὺς ἐς τὸν χῶρον ἰέναι ἐς
τὸν συνεθήκαντο.   ἐνθαῦτα οἱ μὲν ἄλλοι ἄρτιοι ἦσαν τῶν
ταξιάρχων πείθεσθαι Παυσανίῃ, Ἀμομφάρετος δὲ ὁ Πολιάδεω
λοχηγέων τοῦ Πιτανητέων λόχου οὐκ ἔφη τοὺς ξείνους φεύ-

---

6 ἔσαν z   7 ταξιαρχέων β : ταξιηρχέων z ‖ Ἀμομφάρετος δὲ om. C
8 λοχηγετέων z : om. Marc. ‖ Πιτανήτεω Koen, Holder, van H.

---

4. ἀναλαβόντας τὰ ὅπλα : the shields
were piled, but of course there must
have been some men under arms, if only
those on the watch.

ἰέναι κατὰ τοὺς ἄλλους can hardly
have been the precise form of the commander's order, but rather gives the
effect of the order, as the writer conceived that effect. With the expression
cp. c. 89 infra, κατὰ πόδας ἐμεῦ ἐλαύνων.

5. νομίσας αὐτοὺς . . ἐς τὸν συνεθήκαντο, 'for he believed the others to be
going to the place agreed upon,' i.e.,
according to Hdt., the island : συνεθήκαντο, sc. ἰέναι. The 'agreement' had
been made at the Council of War, c. 51
supra. Hdt. describes (i.e. follows an
authority which conceived) the movements of the Greek army in the field of
battle as the results of compacts, agreements, bargains, argument, persuasion,
but not of definite orders, originating
from headquarters or the commander-in-
chief.   In any case the result of his
παράγγελμα to the 'Lakedaimonians'
(10,000 strong) must have been to set
Λακεδαιμονίων ἅπαν τὸ στρατόπεδον in
motion, unless indeed the order was
addressed only to a portion of the forces.

6. οἱ μὲν ἄλλοι . . τῶν ταξιάρχων :
not ταξιαρχέων. ταξίαρχος is the usual
Attic form of the word. The term is
not a Spartan one at all. All but one
of these good Spartan officers, whatever
their proper title, were willing and
ready (ἄρτιοι, cp. c. 27 supra) to obey
their commander ! No very astonishing
circumstance in an army where πειθαρχία
was so sedulously enforced as in the
Spartan (cp. Xenophon, Lac. Rep. 8).

7. Ἀμομφάρετος δὲ ὁ Πολιάδεω :
Amompharetos is hardly a mere Ehren-
name (Stein) ; a Spartan of the name
appears as one of the five arbitrators in
the early Megaro-Athenian dispute about
Salamis, Busolt ii.² (1895) 248 ; cp.
Plutarch, Solon 10. The younger might
be a grandson, or descendant, of the elder
Amompharetos. But those are the only

two known wearers of the name. The
(father's) name Poliades is found elsewhere, but not again at Sparta.   If
Pape - Benseler sub v. is correct in
deriving it from Athene Πολιάς, the
Spartan might have been named by his
father in compliment to Athens ; cp.
the case of the Spartan Σάμιος 3. 55.
Was there even perhaps an Athenian
ξενία or προξενία in the family !

8. λοχηγέων, 'occupying the rank
of a Lochagos,' or commander of a
Lochos, a strictly Spartan office and
command.   But the exact duty and
rank of a Lochagos are not so clear. In
Xenophon Rep. Lac. 11. 4 a λόχος is
one-quarter of a μόρα, and there are six
μόραι in the army, each apparently under
the command of a Polemarchos.   That
would give a total of 24 Lochoi. In an
army of 5000 that total allows about
292 men to the Lochos.   But Xenophon
is writing in the fourth century, when a
Spartan army in the field never approached a strength of 5000.   The
numerical strength of Spartan divisions
varied with the levy probably.   The
Spartan Mora destroyed in the Korinthian war numbered 600 men, Xenoph.
Hell. 4. 5. 11-12. If it consisted of
four Lochoi, the Lochos was numbering
150 men, but there may have been six
Lochoi of 100 men each in it. Thucydides,
writing of the battle of Mantineia (418
B.C.), with the air of an eye-witness,
expressly notices the difficulty of ascertaining the exact number of men in a
Spartan force.   He uses the term λόχος
apparently for the division commanded
by a Polemarch (perhaps only under
exceptional circumstances), and makes
the army of Agis on that occasion
consist of 7 Lochoi, exclusive of the
Skiritai 600 strong.   It is obvious that
the Lochos in that passage corresponds
to the Mora of Xenophon, a term not
employed by Thucydides (cp. Hell. 2.
4. 31, earliest case) ; the number 7
remains a problem, which Arnold in-

ξεσθαι οὐδὲ ἑκὼν εἶναι αἰσχυνέειν τὴν Σπάρτην, ἐθώμαζέ

9 ἐθώυμαζέ Pz, Stein[1]

---

geniously solves by the hypothesis that the army really consisted of six divisions, together with the corps of Βρασίδειοι and Νεωδαμώδεις. (Gilbert, *Gr. Staatsalt.* i.[2] 77, 1893, apparently identifies this corps with the Skiritai, and gives up the number of *Lochoi* as hopeless.) In the *Lochos* at Mantineia there were four πεντηκοστύες, each consisting in turn of four ἐνωμοτίαι. If the numerical strength of the *Pentekostys* necessarily and always corresponded to its name, that would give but 200 men to the *Lochos*, and (roughly) but 12 to the *Enomotia*; but on the possibility of variations in the numbers of men composing the various subdivisions, Arnold's note to Thucydides *in l.* (of which G. Gilbert, for example, took no account) is still worth consulting. The normal number of the *Enomotia* is not really quite certain, it may have been 15 (cp. Gilbert, *op. c.* 75, n. 4), it may have been 24, besides the captain, as Arnold supposes; but it is certain that the tactical organization of the Spartan army underwent modification not merely between the time of Thucydides and of Xenophon, but between the time of Herodotos and of Thucydides; nor is it to be supposed that the indications of the narrative in Hdt. will correspond exactly with the traditions of the Lykurgean system. An army of 5000 men might very well consist of 5 *Lochoi* of 1000 men each; and as a matter of fact 5 is the number of *Lochoi* suggested by some of the authorities for the older period (say, sixth century), cp. Gilbert, *op. c.* p. 76. A *Lochos* of 1000 men would probably have been subdivided into 10 companies of 100 each, possibly 'double *Pentekostyes*,' such as Arnold speaks of (possibly even, though to my thinking less probably, also called *Lochoi* as he suggests). Amompharetos is emphatically not one of the 'Polemarchs' (cp. 7. 173), but may have been in command of 1000 men. He was no mere 'centurion,' or the story that follows could hardly have been told about him.

τοῦ Πιτανητέων λόχου. Thucydides, still in this respect employing the same terminology as Hdt., goes out of his way to assert that it was an error to say that there was, 'or ever had been,' a Πιτανάτης λόχος (cp. just below) in the Spartan army, 1. 20. 3. Whether Thucydides is contraverting the source from which Hdt. gets this story, or, as seems likely enough, Hdt. himself, the express assertion of the Athenian on this matter is final, if rightly understood. But what does Thucydides exactly mean? Not that the Spartan army was not organized κατὰ λόχους, for that would contradict his own text elsewhere, but either that the λόχοι had not territorial designations, or that no λόχος derived its designation from Πιτάνη (cp. 3. 55). The recorded names of *Lochoi* are territorial, at least in part, e.g. Μεσοάτης (cp. Gilbert, *op. c.* p. 76 n. 3); so that we may conclude in favour of the latter alternative. If Amompharetos was a δημότης of Pitana, a Πιτανάτης, and commanded one of the *Lochoi* in the Spartan army, an Athenian source might very probably speak of the division under his command as the Πιτανάτης λόχος, especially if, as above argued, the family of this Pitanate was likely to be known and popular in Athens.

Hdt. himself calls Πιτάνη a δῆμος, rather an Atticism than a Laconism, 3. 55. Pausanias (3. 16. 9) seems to put Pitane and Mesoa in juxtaposition (οἱ) ἐκ Μεσόας τε καὶ Πιτάνης θύοντες τῇ Ἀρτεμίδι: and the mistake censured by Thucydides may lie in calling the Μεσοάτης λόχος the Πιτανάτης. Pitana itself was evidently a considerable place: Pausanias (3. 14. 2) mentions a λέσχη Κροτανῶν in the vicinity of the Royal Tombs of the Agiadai, adding εἰσὶ δὲ οἱ Κροτανοὶ Πιτανατῶν μοῖρα. This makes Pitane in the west end of Sparta: the Artemis above named is Artemis Issoria, Pausan. *l.c.* (cp. Wide, *Lakonische Kulte*, 1893, p. 109). Close by were the tombs of Leonidas and Pausanias the Regent, and the monument to the 300 who fell at Thermopylai (cp. 7. 224).

The story of Amompharetos may well belong to the first draft of Hdt.'s work. It is a superficial inference that Hdt. got this story of Amompharetos in Pitane, during his visit to Sparta: the story is plainly not a Spartan story, it is almost as plainly an Athenian. There is nothing in the story to show that

10 τε ὁρῶν τὸ ποιεύμενον ἅτε οὐ παραγενόμενος τῷ προτέρῳ λόγῳ.
ὁ δὲ Παυσανίης τε καὶ ὁ Εὐρυάναξ δεινὸν μὲν ἐποιεῦντο τὸ
μὴ πείθεσθαι ἐκεῖνον σφίσι, δεινότερον δὲ ἔτι, κείνου ταῦτ᾽
ἀναινομένου, ἀπολιπεῖν τὸν λόχον τὸν Πιτανήτην, μὴ ἢν
ἀπολίπωσι ποιεῦντες τὰ συνεθήκαντο τοῖσι ἄλλοισι Ἕλλησι,

10 ὀρέων Stein¹², van H.　　　12 δ᾽ ἔτι αCz ‖ ἐκείνου B ‖ ταῦτα
νενωμένου B, Wesseling, Gaisford　　13 πιτανίτην C

Hdt. had been in Sparta before writing it down, rather the reverse. If Hdt. afterwards made friends in Pitane it was perhaps because he took introductions from Athens; but he either did not discover his mistake about the Πιτανάτης λόχος, or he failed to correct it, If the emperor Caracalla (211-217 A.D.) before starting for the east sent for a bodyguard from Sparta and called it the Πιτανάτης λόχος (Herodian 4. 8. 3), that only shows how hard an error dies which has once attained classic expression in literature. If Photius, Lex. sub v. Πιτάνη, has φυλὴ καὶ τόπος τῆς Λακωνικῆς, that is because in the Roman period the name had been adopted for a local tribe; cp. C.I.G. 1425-6.

τοὺς ξείνους: cc. 11 supra, 55 infra.
9. ἐὰν εἶναι: cp. 7. 164.
10. ὁρῶν τὸ ποιεύμενον: cp. l. 2 supra. Amompharetos could hardly 'see' in the dark; he no doubt received certain orders (probably to stay where he was, or to cover the retreat).

ἅτε οὐ παραγενόμενος τῷ προτέρῳ λόγῳ: the πρότερος λόγος in this case is the Council of War in cc. 50 f. supra. The phrase does not necessarily imply that there was any fresh council or discussion now taking place. If Amompharetos was really absent from the previous Council it was not because he was not a sufficiently high officer to be present, but for some other reason. Stein suggests that he was in command of an important outpost; but which? And had he retired from it? The army had been ex hypothesi all together, and in battle-array. How also does Amompharetos now come to be back in the Laager? A statement of this sort, explanatory or rather assertorial of his absence from the Council, is very suspicious; it is argumentative, and apologetic, to meet the obvious objection to the story, that Amompharetos must have known all

about the intended movement from having been present at the Council earlier in the day. (It is just conceivable that a Spartan Lochos, under Amompharetos, or some other, might have been posted in or about the church of St. Demetrion; but the position would have been a dangerously isolated one, as the detachment could not have kept touch of the forces on the Asopos Ridge, with the Persian cavalry riding up and down the valleys or combes between the ridges; or he might have been holding or trying to hold Gargaphia: in which case he had retired before the strangers already.)

11. ὁ δὲ Παυσανίης τε καὶ ὁ Εὐρυάναξ: why Euryanax (c. 10 supra) here suddenly comes by his apparent rights it is not easy to say; down below, c. 55, he even takes precedence. Does this 'Attic' story tend to discredit both Spartan commanders at the expense of Amompharetos? The Spartan commanders were shocked at his insubordination, but still more horrified at the idea of abandoning him to his fate.

δεινὸν ποιέεσθαι, a mental process, or condition; cp. 7. 1.
12. κείνου ταῦτ᾽ ἀναινομένου: i.e. so long as Amompharetos refused to retire: ἀναλαβόντας τὰ ὅπλα ἰέναι .. ἐς τὴν νῆσον. The verb ἀναίνομαι is common in Homer, and not unknown even in Attic prose. (Cp. App. Crit.)
13. τὸν λόχον τὸν Πιτανήτην: see above.

ἢν ἀπολίπωσι: sc. τὸν λόχον.
14. ποιεῦντες τὰ συνεθήκαντο τ. ἄλ. Ἕλλησι, 'in carrying out their agreement with all the other Greeks.' But the centre, if the Spartans had only known it, had, as already recorded, been guilty of a gross and dastardly breach of faith; the only other Greeks, therefore, now worth considering are—as the reader knows—the Athenians.

ἀπόληται ὑπολειφθεὶς αὐτός τε Ἀμομφάρετος καὶ οἱ μετ' 15
αὐτοῦ. ταῦτα λογιζόμενοι ἀτρέμας εἶχον τὸ στρατόπεδον τὸ
Λακωνικόν, καὶ ἐπειρῶντο πείθοντές μιν ὡς οὐ χρεὸν εἴη
ταῦτα ποιέειν. καὶ οἱ μὲν παρηγόρεον Ἀμομφάρετον μοῦνον 54
Λακεδαιμονίων τε καὶ Τεγεητέων λελειμμένον, Ἀθηναῖοι δὲ
ἐποίευν τοιάδε· εἶχον ἀτρέμας σφέας αὐτοὺς ἵνα ἐτάχθησαν,
ἐπιστάμενοι τὰ Λακεδαιμονίων φρονήματα ὡς ἄλλα φρονεόντων

16. ἀτρέμας εἶχον τὸ στρατόπεδον τὸ
Λ. As the order to march had already
been issued, the *modus operandi* here is
not quite clear. Either the order to
march had not yet taken effect, and was
countermanded; or the van, or a
portion of the line, had indeed started,
and was arrested by a message from
headquarters. It is, of course, not
impossible that the army was falling
back *en échelon*, Lochos by Lochos; and
that the 'Mesoate' Lochos, or the
Lochos under the command of the
Pitanate Amompharetos, being at the
extremity of the Spartan wing, was the
last to retire. The process would be a
pretty slow one, carried out, as it was
being carried out, in the dark; and daylight might overtake them (c. 56 *infra*)
before the whole manœuvre had been
fully executed.

ἀτρέμας ἔχειν: cp. 7. 8.

17. ἐπειρῶντο πείθοντες: c. 26 *supra*.

54. 2. Ἀθηναῖοι δέ. The previous
chapter has witnessed the Greek centre
in full 'flight'—to the Heraion: *ex
hypothesi* a disgraceful 'breach of contract.' The Spartans have equally
broken faith, by not retreating at all,
so far: the commanders being involved
in a dispute with a refractory *Lochagos*,
whom they would not abandon, with
his men, to fate. μοῦνον . . λελειμμένον
just here is a rhetorical exaggeration:
the participle, passive and perfect in
form, must be middle and present, or
imperfect, in sense; cp. 7. 153. The
tense at least marks his obstinacy.
Meanwhile what of the Athenians?
Were they keeping their contract, were
they true to their word? The story
goes on to admit (it is an Athenian
story) that they were forsworn; but,
then, they had a good excuse — the
notorious duplicity of their neighbours!

3. εἶχον ἀτρέμας σφέας αὐτοὺς ἵνα
ἐτάχθησαν. These good democrats act
as one man, and do not require,
apparently, orders, like the Spartans,
just up above. Or is the story tender
to the fame of Aristeides, the commander-
in-chief, and so refrains from directly
implicating him! ἵνα, *ubi*, cp. Index.
The aorist is practically = a pluperfect.

4. ἐπιστάμενοι τὰ Λακεδαιμονίων
φρονήματα. The participle ἐπιστάμενοι
is used purely from the Athenian point
of view, nor does it necessarily involve
more than 'belief,' cp. 8. 132 *supra*. With
φρονήματα cp. 8. 144, and c. 7 *supra*.
It would be unfair to Hdt. to cite him
as endorsing or accepting even, as his
own, the utterance of Athenian prejudice which follows: to wit, that Lakedaimonians were men who thought one
thing and said another, men w ose
words, agreements, promises, pledges,
could not be relied on as representing
their intentions, much less their conduct, when the time for action arrived.
Lakedaimonian perfidy was a popular
topic at Athens: Aristophanes (who
had another axe to grind) satirizes the
commonplace, cp. *Acharn.* 300 ff., *Peace*
1063 ff. Blakesley compared the Roman
view of *Punica fides* and continental
opinion of 'perfidious Albion': one
might perhaps add Albion's opinion of
certain continental states. Rawlinson
more innocently observed that the sore-
ness caused by recent disappointment
(in 479 B.C.) might have produced, at
Athens, a distrust of the Spartans.
Stein's observation that Hdt. in this
passage stands *ganz auf athenischer Seite*
is more to the point, but hardly carries
us quite far enough. Hdt. himself is
probably as innocent as Rawlinson in
the matter; but if the Athenian story
goes out of its way to charge the Spartans

5 καὶ ἄλλα λεγόντων. ὡς δὲ ἐκινήθη τὸ στρατόπεδον, ἔπεμπον
σφέων ἱππέα ὀψόμενόν τε εἰ πορεύεσθαι ἐπιχειρέοιεν οἱ
Σπαρτιῆται, εἴτε καὶ τὸ παράπαν μὴ διανοεῦνται ἀπαλλάσσε-
55 σθαι, ἐπειρέσθαι τε Παυσανίην τὸ χρεὸν εἴη ποιέειν. ὡς δὲ
ἀπίκετο ὁ κῆρυξ ἐς τοὺς Λακεδαιμονίους, ὥρα τε σφέας κατὰ
χώρην τεταγμένους καὶ ἐς νείκεα ἀπιγμένους αὐτῶν τοὺς

---

5 δ' α   6 ἐπιχειροῖεν α, Holder   7 τοπαράπαν Pz   8
χρεὼν CPz, van H.   55. 2 τε σφέας R : τέ σφεας   3 αὐτέων z

---

with duplicity, it is because the Athenian
source has some perfidy, or incompetence,
or failure on the Athenian side to excuse
or to disguise.

5. ὡς δὲ ἐκινήθη τὸ στρατόπεδον
refers back to ὡς ἐκινήθησαν in c. 52
supra. The movement of the centre
had, of course, for the time being, placed
the Athenians in isolation on the left
wing.

6. ἱππέα. The Athenians had no
proper cavalry at this time (cp. c. 21 l. 15
supra), but they may have had mounted
aides-de-camp or κήρυκες. The Spartan
commander has apparently a mounted
aide-de-camp too ; c. 60 infra. The
double construction ἔπεμπον ὀψόμενον
and (ἔπεμπον) ἐπειρέσθαι is noticeable :
ἐπειρέσθαι apparently refers to one only
of the two alternatives covered by
ὀψόμενον, so that ἐπειρησόμενον would
have conveyed a different and inappropriate sense. The temptation is strong
to read εἴ τε for τε εἰ, as that would
soften the strict co-ordination between
participle and verb ; cp. a somewhat
similar case c. 6 supra. The variation
εἰ πορεύεσθαι ἐπιχειροῖεν (opt. for the
less probable alternative) and εἰ (τε) . .
μὴ διανοεῦνται ἀπαλλάσσεσθαι (for
the move to be expected) is observable ;
cp. 8. 106 ὅσα . . ἔχοι . . ὅσα ποιήσει).
The second construction is, of course,
different from the εἰ μὴ ἀμυνεῦσι of the
partially parallel passage in c. 6 supra.

8. ἐπειρέσθαι τε κτλ.: and in that
case 'to ask Pausanias what they ought to
do'—on the whole, these good Athenians
are still ready to take their directions
from the commander-in-chief ; cp. c. 27
supra ad f. ἐξηγέεσθε ὡς πεισομένων.
They cannot trust the Spartan's word,
but they are ready to obey the Spartan's
orders ! It is as though, in some way
or other, the Spartans would take a
mean advantage of the Athenians, in

getting these to go, while they themselves remained at their post ! That is
an idea belonging to the Athenian theory
of the Persian war, which represented
it as a race between Athens and Sparta,
which should first crush out the invader
—a race in which Marathon for ever
secured the prize of valour for Athens !
(Cp. Hdt. IV.-VI. vol. ii. p. 194.)

Perhaps this (mounted man) episode
is only a reply to, or refutation of, the
(Spartan) assertion that in the stress of
battle the Spartans had sent to ask for
assistance, which the Athenians failed
to render, c. 60 infra. If there is any
truth in it, that truth may underlie the
question τὸ χρεὸν εἴη ποιέειν, 'what are
we to do ?' The Athenians were in
difficulties, but not on account of the
retreat of the centre, if it be true that a
general retreat had been agreed on, and
ordered ; for they could not yet know
that the centre had not retreated but
fled (even if that was true !). But in
what difficulties were the Athenians !
Perhaps the message was to the effect
that the centre was retreating so slowly
that the Athenians had not yet been
able to start, and to request Pausanias to
hurry the centre's movements. Cp. l. 14.

55. 2. ὥρα τε : the τε is not in its
logical place (τεταγμένους τε), unless it
were meant to suggest a zeugma, καὶ
(ἤκουε), or such. The herald (κῆρυξ =
ἱππεύς) 'saw,' or found them, κατὰ
χώρην, cp. 8. 73, 108. The Spartans
were in proper array (τεταγμένους). It
was, of course, still night. He saw, or
heard, the first men among them openly
quarrelling. τοὺς πρώτους, not apparently first in order of march, but first in
order of rank ; not, however, referring
to 'Euryanax and Pausanias,' who
appear to be on one side, but to them
on the one part and Amompharetos on
the other.

πρώτους. ὡς γὰρ δὴ παρηγορέοντο τὸν Ἀμομφάρετον ὅ τε
Εὐρυάναξ καὶ ὁ Παυσανίης μὴ κινδυνεύειν μένοντας μούνους 5
Λακεδαιμονίων, οὔ κως ἔπειθον, ἐς ὃ ἐς νείκεά τε συμπεσόντες
ἀπίκατο καὶ ὁ κῆρυξ τῶν Ἀθηναίων παρίστατό σφι ἀπιγμένος.
νεικέων δὲ ὁ Ἀμομφάρετος λαμβάνει πέτρον ἀμφοτέρῃσι τῇσι
χερσὶ καὶ τιθεὶς πρὸ ποδῶν τῶν Παυσανίεω ταύτῃ τῇ ψήφῳ
ψηφίζεσθαι ἔφη μὴ φεύγειν τοὺς ξείνους, λέγων τοὺς βαρ- 10
βάρους. ὃ δὲ μαινόμενον καὶ οὐ φρενήρεα καλέων ἐκεῖνον,
πρός τε τὸν Ἀθηναίων κήρυκα ἐπειρωτῶντα τὰ ἐντεταλμένα
λέγειν ὁ Παυσανίης ἐκέλευε τὰ παρεόντα σφι πρήγματα,
ἐχρήιζέ τε τῶν Ἀθηναίων προσχωρῆσαί τε πρὸς ἑωυτοὺς καὶ

---

4 παρηγόρεον ΒPz, Holder   5 καὶ om. C   6 Λακεδαιμονίων
Paris. fr., Schaefer, Wesseling, Gaisford, Stein², Holder, van H.: Λακεδαιμονίους ‖ οὔκων ? Stein¹: οὔκουν Paris. fr.   7 ἀπικέατο Pz ‖ ὁ om.
Marc.   9 τῶν : τὸν Β : τοῦ Paris. fr.   10 λέγων : ξείνους λέγων Β,
Holder : ξείνους λέγων τοὺς βαρβάρους del. Werfer, Naber, van H. : aut
ξείνους legendum aut λέγων τοὺς βαρβάρους tollenda censeo   11 μαινό-
μενόν <τε> van H. ‖ οὐ : ὡς Β : om. Marc. ‖ καλέων . . ἐπειρωτῶντα om. R
12 πρός τε del. Krueger, van H. : τραπόμενός τε πρὸς coni. Stein² ‖ τὸν :
τῶν S ‖ ἀθηναῖον a ‖ κήρυκα τραπόμενος coni. Stein¹ ‖ ἐπειρωτῶντα codd.
(ἐπηρωτῶντα C), Stein², Holder : ἐπειρωτέοντα Stein¹, van H.   13 ὁ
Παυσανίης del. Krueger, van H.   14 ἐχρῆζέ RSMarc. z : ἐχρηξε V ‖
τε om. Β ‖ καὶ ποιέειν . . ἑωυτοὺς om. R

---

4. παρηγορέοντο: in the previous
chapter the same word is used in the
active ; the imperfect remains in full
force. A further variation is obtained
by the substitution of μούνους ('he and
his men') for μοῦνον there.
6. ἐς νείκεά τε συμπεσόντες ἀπίκατο
καὶ . . παρίστατό σφι ἀπιγμένος.
There is here (a) a simple and obvious
parataxis ; cp. c. 47 supra. (b) But why
συμπεσόντες and ἀπιγμένος ? Why not
ἐς νείκεά τε ἀπίκατο (cp. ἐς νείκεα ἀπιγμένους just above) καὶ ὁ κῆρυξ ἀπῖκτο,
or ἀπιγμένος ἦν, or ἐστί, or even ἀπίκετο ?
Well, there are limits to the baldness
of phraseology tolerable to Hdt., though
he is not over-careful to avoid verbal
repetitions and clash. (c) But συμπεσόντες with ἀπίκατο seems de trop ; the
phrase here is ἐς νείκεα ἀπίκατο (cp. ἐς
ν. ἀπιγμένους). In 3. 120 ἐκ λόγων ἐς
νείκεα συμπεσεῖν is not 'from words to
come to blows,' but 'to fall a-quarrelling
in the course of conversation.' Here
too συνέπεσον without ἀπίκατο would
have done. The participle here is used
(I cannot but think) with a confused

sense of anticipating the 'coincidence,'
the 'synchronism,' recorded in the bare
parataxis. Hdt. is not invariably lucid
in point of expression ; cp. c. 51 supra,
7. 152 (confusion in οἰκήια κακά).
8. πέτρον . . ψήφῳ: in marked contrast : 'boulder,' and 'pebble.'
11. ὃ δὲ κτλ. The agitation of the
scene seems to communicate itself to the
narrative of the historian. ὃ is, of course,
Pausanias ; ἐκεῖνον is Amompharetos.
The τε in πρός τε is perhaps merely displaced, and co-ordinates the sentence
ἐκέλευε τά κτλ. with ἐχρήιζέ τε κτλ. The
displacement has led to a reintroduction
of the subject ὁ Παυσανίης.
οὐ φρενήρεα: non compotem sui ;
cp. 3. 25.
12. τὰ ἐντεταλμένα: sc. τί χρεόν ἐστι
ποιέειν ; τί ἡμῖν ποιητέον ; c. 54 ad f.
13. τὰ παρεόντα σφι πρήγματα, 'the
business (trouble) on which they were
engaged,' or 'in which they were involved.'
14. προσχωρῆσαί τε πρὸς ἑωυτοὺς
καὶ ποιέειν περὶ τῆς ἀπόδου τά περ ἂν
καὶ σφεῖς. So far as this request in-

56 ποιέειν περὶ τῆς ἀπόδου τά περ ἂν καὶ σφεῖς. καὶ ὃ μὲν
ἀπαλλάσσετο ἐς τοὺς Ἀθηναίους· τοὺς δὲ ἐπεὶ ἀνακρινομένους
πρὸς ἑωυτοὺς ἠὼς κατελάμβανε, ἐν τούτῳ τῷ χρόνῳ κατήμενος
ὁ Παυσανίης, οὐ δοκέων τὸν Ἀμομφάρετον λείψεσθαι τῶν
5 ἄλλων Λακεδαιμονίων ἀποστειχόντων, τὰ δὴ καὶ ἐγένετο,
σημήνας ἀπῆγε διὰ τῶν κολωνῶν τοὺς λοιποὺς πάντας·
εἵποντο δὲ καὶ Τεγεῆται. Ἀθηναῖοι δὲ ταχθέντες ἤισαν τὰ

56. 2 [ἀνα]κρινομένους van H.   5 ἀποστιχόντων αΒ ‖ καὶ om. Β
6 κωλῶν S   7 ἤισαν ΑΒ : ἦσαν C : om. Marc.

volves any modification of the original
decision of the Council of War to retire,
c. 51 *supra*, the modification may simply
amount to this, that, whereas by the
original plan the two wings were to
concentrate independently on the Island,
by this modification they were to effect
an earlier junction, the delay in the
movement of the centre having altered
the conditions unfavourably. But this
interpretation is not inevitable. The
formula above may simply represent the
original plan for concentration back on
to the Island by the two wings. If that
plan had broken down now, its collapse
may have been due, not to the insub-
ordinate obstinacy of Amompharetos
(which Athenians might regard as heroic)
nor to the 'flight' of the centre, but to
the failure of the Athenians to start
soon enough, perhaps because prematurely engaged on the left. περ, 'exactly';
ἑωυτούς perhaps because 'Euryanax and
Pausanias' have been mentioned; or
else = Σπαρτιήτας, and to avoid σφέας
with σφεῖς immediately following. Its
use is quite in keeping with this *oratio
non nihil turbata* (Baehr).

56. 2. τοὺς δὲ . . ἠὼς κατελάμβανε:
the dawn of the 13th, op. c. 52 *supra*;
the very day of battle, or of the supreme
battle. ἀνακρινομένους, 'quarrelling';
the verb is apparently used with this
meaning only in this one passage; the
subst. ἀνάκρισις in 8. 69 may be compared
though used in a different sense; but cp.
App. Crit. ἑωυτούς here seems = ἀλλήλους.

3. ἐν τούτῳ τῷ χρόνῳ might better
be taken of the point of dawn than of
the much enduring night, now over.
κατήμενος: perhaps not literally
'sitting,' cp. c. 72 *infra*, but 'without
moving.'

4. οὐ δοκέων . . λείψεσθαι: nothing
has been recorded in the story previously
to justify this belief that Amompharetos
will not remain behind.

5. ἀποστειχόντων is a rather grand
and poetical word; the simple verb is
never used in prose.

6. σημήνας: sc. τῇ σάλπιγγι, op. 8.
11 (c. 42 *supra*, the case is not so clear).
The operations at night had doubtless
been carried out with all possible silence
and secrecy; but it was now daylight,
and the movement of the Greek forces
no doubt observed; there could be no
reason for not employing the usual
signals.

ἀπῆγε διὰ τῶν κολωνῶν: the statement is precise to the effect that Pausanias was retiring; what are the κολωνοί
in question? Presumably the ridges
descending from Kithairon, as is more
fully indicated in the next chapter.
Unfortunately Hdt. does not specify
the point of the compass towards which
Pausanias was moving.

7. εἵποντο: as the Tegeatai had been
standing to the west of the Spartans,
if they really 'followed' them now, the
Spartans would have moved first, and
presumably in an easterly direction
(however otherwise qualified); but it is
possible that εἵποντο is not to be pressed,
and that the Spartans really bring up
the rear. The action of Amompharetos
looks like that. If so, the retreat was
probably in a SW. direction. But see
further, below.

Ἀθηναῖοι δέ κτλ. Neither is the
movement and direction of the Athenians
indicated or described so precisely as
could be wished.

ταχθέντες points to the movement
being in accordance with orders, presumably the orders of Pausanias; τεταγμένοι would signify that they were in
actual battle-array (as no doubt they
were). Stein cps. c. 104 *infra*, and 7.
121, 169, 8. 7, 18.

ἤισαν τὰ ἔμπαλιν ἢ Λακεδαιμόνιοι.
In 7. 58 the king's fleet goes from
Abydos τὰ ἔμπαλιν πρήσσων τοῦ πεζοῦ

ἔμπαλιν ἢ Λακεδαιμόνιοι · οἱ μὲν γὰρ τῶν τε ὄχθων ἀντείχοντο
καὶ τῆς ὑπωρέης τοῦ Κιθαιρῶνος φοβεόμενοι τὴν ἵππον,
Ἀθηναῖοι δὲ κάτω τραφθέντες ἐς τὸ πεδίον. Ἀμομφάρετος δὲ 57

---

9 ὑπωρείης libri   10 τραφέντες B : στραφθέντες C

(i.e. ἢ ὁ πεζός), which Hdt. explains as
meaning in that case that the fleet was
going west while the army was going
east; i.e. he does not there mean that the
fleet went on water while the army went
on land; the point of difference is purely
one of direction, of orientation. Yet in
the present passage Stein maintains that
τὰ ἔμπαλιν denotes not a difference of
direction, but simply and solely the
difference of the surface over which the
two bodies were moving; this appears
an improbable and inadequate explanation, not in accordance with the meaning
of ἔμπαλιν, with the other clear instance
in Hdt., or finally, with the context here.
For here Hdt. says not merely that the
Spartans were moving διὰ τῶν κολωνῶν
(τῶν τε ὄχθων καὶ τῆς ὑπωρέης τοῦ Κιθαιρῶνος ἀντεχόμενοι) and the Athenians ἐς
τὸ πεδίον (not by the way διὰ τοῦ πεδίου,
or κατὰ τὸ πεδίον); he also expressly
describes the Athenians as τραφθέντες
or κάτω τραφθέντες (sc. ἦσαν ἐς τὸ
πεδίον).

There has, therefore, been a turn, a
wheel, in the line, in the orientation of
the Athenians. Whether there has also
been a turn in the orientation of the
Lakedaimonians Hdt. does not say.
What amount of wheel would constitute
or justify the use of τὰ ἔμπαλιν may be
a question; the words obviously might
be used of a movement, or double movement, much short of being in contrary
directions. In the present case Hdt.
need not mean that Athenians and
Spartans were moving in diametrically
opposite directions, starting, as it were,
back to back; he may mean no more
than that 'they were moving in anything but the same direction.' Whether
he is right or not is a widely different
question. If Spartans and Athenians
were under orders to fill up the gap and
concentrate, while at the same time retiring, 'on the Island,' that movement
might have been effected by the wings
falling back, Lochos by Lochos, from the
east and the west ends of the previous
line to a common point south, or south-
west, of the position at starting; and even
such a manœuvre, with reference to the

termini a quibus, might be described as
movements τὰ ἔμπαλιν. But the movement here predicated of the Athenians
may go far beyond this. By τὸ πεδίον
might be understood not merely the
trough of Gargaphia and Α¹, but the
more genuine plain north of Plataia. If
so, the movement of the Athenians was
westward, more or less by south, and its
object may have been to balk the
approach of the medizing Greeks on the
Persian right, with whom the Athenians
are presently engaged. Had the Greeks
previously been in a hollow square, or
with a φάλαγξ ἀμφίστομος round the
church of St. John (Androkrateion), then
the Athenians, to the north, might have
wheeled round, till they were facing
west, or even south-west, while the
Spartans may have either remained,
facing south (by west) as they had been
all the previous day, or may even have
turned, have been obliged to turn, until
they were facing east, or north-east.

8. τῶν τε ὄχθων ἀντείχοντο. It is
not by any means self-evident what
actual ground is here denoted by the
ὄχθοι, cp. 8. 52, 4. 203 (not ὄχθαι, 'river-
banks'), to which the Lakedaimonians
were 'holding on,' clinging, keeping
close, or anxious to do so: are they
identical with τῆς ὑπωρέης τοῦ Κιθαιρῶνος?
Are the Spartans already thereon, and
wishing to stay thereon, or are they
striving to get thereonto? Are the
ὄχθοι generally the ridges running down
from Kithairon to the Asopos, as distinguished from τὸ πεδίον? Or are they
the ridges north of the trough in which
Gargaphia was situate?—in fact, the
'Asopos Ridge' and 'Long Ridge' of
Dr. Grundy's map?

9. φοβεόμενοι τὴν ἵππον: the Lakedaimonians are 'afraid of the cavalry'
according to this story, and that is given
as the reason for their line of retreat: a
genuinely Attic touch. Oddly enough,
when it comes to action, the Lakedaimonians, who are on more or less high
ground, are apparently assaulted by the
cavalry, while the Athenians are not
expressly recorded to have encountered
any cavalry below! (cp. c. 67 infra).

ἀρχήν γε οὐδαμὰ δοκέων Παυσανίην τολμήσειν σφέας ἀπολιπεῖν, περιείχετο αὐτοῦ μένοντας μὴ ἐκλιπεῖν τὴν τάξιν·
προτερεόντων δὲ τῶν σὺν Παυσανίῃ, καταδόξας αὐτοὺς ἰθέῃ,
5 τέχνῃ ἀπολείπειν αὐτόν, ἀναλαβόντα τὸν λόχον τὰ ὅπλα ἦγε
βάδην πρὸς τὸ ἄλλο στῖφος· τὸ δὲ ἀπελθὸν ὅσον τε δέκα
στάδια ἀνέμενε τὸν Ἀμομφαρέτου λόχον, περὶ ποταμὸν Μολόεντα

57. 2 γε Schweighaeuser, Stein, van H. : τε (del. Krueger)　　　4
καταδόξαντες Β : κάρτα δόξας Marc. ‖ θείη Β : ἰθείῃ ceteri : ἰθέῃ μὴ τέχνῃ
coni. Madvig, adm. Holder　　5 ἀπολιπεῖν ΒΡ ‖ τὸν λόχον om. ᶻ
6 ἄλλο om. Β ‖ στίφος CR　　7 παρὰ Marc. ‖ μοόεντα Β : μελόεντα
Marc.

57. 2. ἀρχήν γε οὐδαμὰ δοκέων, 'originally at least never dreaming (that
Pausanias would go so far as to abandon
them).' ἀρχήν, 7. 220, 8. 128. οὐδαμά
might more logically have gone with
τολμήσειν. The γε serves here in contrast
to προτερεόντων δέ : but cp. App. Crit.
3. περιείχετο .. μὴ ἐκλιπεῖν : the construction is peculiar, as περιέχεσθαι
(mid.) naturally takes a genitive, even as
ἀντέχεσθαι just above ; cp. 7. 39, 160 ;
8. 60. αὐτοῦ is of course a local adverb,
'on the spot.' περιέχεσθαι as a passive,
and in a strictly physical sense in 8. 10,
79, 80 supra, here is plainly middle, but
is it purely psychological in sense ? cp.
the various renderings : (a) "he was urgent
with them that they should stay and not
leave him," L. & S. ; "he stuck to it that
they should stay there and not leave
their post," Macaulay ; "setzte sich
darauf dass sie (alle)," Krueger ; "be-
harrte darauf hier zu bleiben," Baehr ;
(b) "remained firm in his resolve," Rawlinson ; "hielt sich an den Gedanken,
dass sie," Sitzler. As the statement is
qualified by ἀρχήν, and the mentality of
Amompharetos is set forth in δοκέων,
and his contrasted action is purely
physical (ἦγε), I do not hesitate to take
περιείχετο as belonging to the external
order and descriptive of the action, i.e.
utterance of the man : 'he kept on
insisting that they should stay where
they were, and not desert their post,' as
in the (a) group (but L. & S. give rather
a paraphrase than a translation).
4. προτερεόντων δὲ τῶν σὺν Παυσανίῃ, 'as Pausanias and his men were
getting further and further off . ., convinced (καταδόξας) that they were really
abandoning him, he led his Lochos, after
the men had taken up their shields, at
a slow step towards the main body.'

προτερέειν, op. c. 66 infra ; καταδόξας,
cp. 8. 69.
ἰθέῃ τέχνῃ : cp. c. 37 supra.
5. αὐτόν is remarkable : it is generally
referred to the man = ἑωυτόν ; it might
more correctly refer to τὸν λόχον.
Krueger renders it "ihn und seinen
Lochos."
6. βάδην, contrasted with δρόμῳ ; cp.
c. 59 infra, Xenophon Anab. 4. 6. 25,
Hell. 5. 4. 53.
στῖφος : cp. c. 70 infra. This
'main body' is awaiting 'the Lochos of
Amompharetos' (sic) at a distance of 10
stades ; i.e. exactly the distance given
above, c. 51, as the distance separating
the Island, to which the Council of War
had agreed and determined to retreat,
from the position of the Greek forces at
Gargaphia ; yet the Lakedaimonians are
not at the Island, as the next words go
on to say !
7. περὶ ποταμὸν Μολόεντα. There is
no third river, beside the Asopos with
its tributaries, and the Oëroë with its
tributaries, to which the name Μολόεις
can be applied : it follows that the name
must be applied to some stream belonging to one or other of the two systems.
No ancient authority clearly indicates
the right identification ; modern travel-
lers and commentators are divided on
the subject. Thus the Moloeis has been
identified with O[1] (so by Vischer, p. 547,
cp. Bursian, Geogr. v. Griechenl. i. 247),
while Dr. Grundy, who adopted A[5] in
his Topography of the Battle of Plataia,
1894, p. 33, in his Great Persian War,
1901, p. 495, now prefers A[6]. These
(O[1], A[6]) are respectively the two most
considerable affluents, the one of Oëroë,
the other of Asopos ; Ridge 2, forming
the watershed east and west, lies between
them. Thus, as far as the R. Moloeis

ἱδρυμένον Ἀργιόπιόν τε χῶρον καλεόμενον, τῇ καὶ Δήμητρος

8 ἀργίοπτόν Marc.

goes, the geographical indication comes to much the same thing, and might point to Ridge 2 as the halting-place of Pausanias.

8. **Ἀργιόπιόν τε χῶρον καλεόμενον.** The Ἀργιόπιος χῶρος, possibly τὸ Ἀργιόπιον, is not elsewhere mentioned. A nymph Argiope is known to Pausanias (4. 33. 3), but she belongs to Parnassos, not to Kithairon: more in place here were Argiope, wife of Agenor, and mother of Kadmos; Pherekydes, *Frag.* 40. She is a water-nymph, for she is a daughter of Neilos: her name should perhaps be Ἀγριόπη rather than Ἀργιόπη. (Cp. Hyginus, *Fab.* vi. ed. Th. Muncker, 1681.) In any case, the Argiopion rather leans towards Oëroë. The attempt to connect the 'place' with a 'White Rock' (W. Irving Hunt, *Papers of Am. Sch. at Athens,* v. 1892, p. 276) is not satisfactory; cp. Grundy, p. 495; nor need Pape now be cited as authority for that etymological effort. Dr. Grundy was divided (in 1894) between 'Long Ridge' and 'Plateau'; he has now decided for the latter. But Ridge 2, the watershed between Oëroë and his own Moloeis, has clearly as good a right as either.

Δήμητρος Ἐλευσινίης ἱρόν. One of the indications, which make it difficult to believe that Hdt. had been over the ground, is the fact that there were at least two temples of Eleusinian Demeter within the area of the operations he is describing, viz. (1) at Plataia, Pausanias 9. 4. 2; (2) at Hysiai, Plutarch, *Aristeid.* 11. To these Dr. Grundy adds (3) one at Erythrai, on the strength of the discovery of inscribed stones on the traditional site of Erythrai, *Topography* (1894), p. 34. (The ναός at Skolos, Pausan. 9. 4. 3, and the ἄλσος at Potniai, Pausan. 9. 9. 1, which would raise the *Demetria* to five in number, may be ignored for present purposes.) Of these three temples, the Plataian, if it were inside the city, on no possible theory of the battle could be employed to define the position of the Spartans; nor would a site in Plataia in any sense accord with the other indications so far as they have been provisionally identified above, viz. the river Moloeis and the Argiopion, or Ἀργιόπιος χῶρος. But if it were outside

the city, though in Plataian territory, the case would be altered. See further, below.

The third, the Erythraian *Demetrion,* was located high up the ὑπωρέη, considerably more than 10 stades from either Gargaphia, and, what is still more against it, would indicate that the Spartans were making back to Erythrai, and to the first position (I^A), from which they had advanced originally, and where the Greeks had been especially open to attack from the Persian cavalry, and also in want of water. These considerations rule out the Erythraian shrine in this place.

There remains the Hysiatan, which, from the position of Hysiai and its territory, would necessarily in some sense lie between the Demetrion of Plataia west, and that of Erythrai east. Such a position obviously suits the general requirements of the story, as well as the provisional identifications of the Argiopion and the river Moloeis above. The question remains of the exact site of the Hysiatan Demetrion. Was it actually in the town of Hysiai, i.e. high up on the ὑπωρέη, in front of the middle pass, on the road from Plataia to Athens, where it entered the mountain; or was it lower down the slopes, in Hysiatan territory ?

Plutarch, *Arist.* 11, describes it as τῶν Ὑσιῶν πλησίον, ὑπὸ τὸν Κιθαιρῶνα. It was near Hysiai, therefore, not inside Hysiai; it was 'close under Kithairon' —a description which might be applied to any spot south of Asopos, especially by a visitor coming from the north (Thebes or Chaironeia). It is not probable that there were two temples of Eleusinian Demeter in the Hysiatis. If then, as Dr. Grundy has ingeniously suggested (*Topography*, p. 33; *Persian War*, pp. 495 f.), the modern church of St. Demetrion marks the site of an ancient temple of Demeter, that would be the Hysiatan Demetrion, outside and to the north below the city.

But this identification will not suit at all either Plutarch or Herodotus. In Plutarch the Demetrion marks the position near Hysiai to which the Athenians advanced in the first instance, a position high up on the ὑπωρέη and

Ἐλευσινίης ἱρὸν ἧσται. ἀνέμενε δὲ τοῦδε εἵνεκα, ἵνα ἢν μὴ
10 ἀπολείπῃ τὸν χῶρον ἐν τῷ ἐτετάχατο ὁ Ἀμομφάρετός τε καὶ
ὁ λόχος, ἀλλ' αὐτοῦ μένωσι, βοηθέοι ὀπίσω παρ' ἐκείνους.
καὶ οἵ τε ἀμφὶ τὸν Ἀμομφάρετον παρεγίνοντό σφι καὶ ἡ

9 ἶστα R: ἶσται S (Gaisf.): ἴϛαι V: ἐστι coni. Krueger ‖ εἵνεκεν B
10 ἀπολείπηι αPMarc.: ἀπολίπῃ ceteri, van H. ‖ δι αCMarc.   11
βοηθέει Marc.   12 παρεγένοντό z

nowhere near the church of St.
Demetrion. In Hdt. the Demetrion
here marks the position to which the
Spartans retreated, 10 stades back, from
Gargaphia: that might very well coincide with the original position of the
Athenians on the extreme left of the
Greek position, which was now become
the extreme right of the position; but
it is nowhere near the church of St.
Demetrion. Thus, if Dr. Grundy is
right, Plutarch and Hdt. are wrong in
relation to the Demetrion.

Mr. W. Irving Hunt, op. c. p. 276,
places the Plataian Demetrion "on high
ground south-east of Plataia at a point
where are now the foundations of a large
Byzantine church." He further defines
the position as "about six minutes' walk
east of the spring Vergoutiani." This
position might do for the Plataian
Demetrion, but Plutarch professes to be
dealing with the Hysiatan; Mr. Hunt
has not marked the difference. It
appears to me that Dr. Grundy has
really hit upon the position of the
Hysiatan Eleusinion; but that it was the
Plataian Eleusinion (if Mr. Hunt is
right in regard to its site), of which
Plutarch ought to have spoken in that
passage, and Hdt. in this. It is quite
obvious that if the church of St.
Demetrion marks the site of the Hysiatan
Demetrion, that site, and that edifice, can
have nothing to say to the former
position of the Athenians (Plutarch) nor
to the latter position of the Lakedaimonians (Hdt.). The wonder recorded by Hdt., c. 62 below, if occurring
in the Persian rout, however, might
suit with the site of the church. The
cause of all the confusion is Hdt.'s
ignorance that there could be more
than one Demetrion in question. By a
somewhat unusual infelicity Hdt. here
applies ἰδρυμένον to the army (στῖφος)
and uses the term ἧσται of the temple
(ἱρόν). ἡμένον, or κατημένον of the army,
ἴδρυσται of the temple, would have been
more natural. Buttmann (ap. Baehr)

even said that ἧσθαι for ἱδρῦσθαι was
inadmissible: cp. c. 51 supra (περισχίζεται
ῥέουσα). (If ἱδρυμένον was to be used of
the man, and ἡμένον of the temple,
Amompharetos, rather than Pausanias,
would seem to be the proper man. As
far as the word goes it might here agree,
not with τό (sc. τὸ ἄλλο στῖφος) but with
τὸν Ἀμομφαρέτου λόχον, in which case it
would be easier to identify the Demetrion
with the church of Demetrion. But
the argument demands that Pausanias'
position should be the one described;
the position of Amompharetos is ex
hypothesi near Gargaphia, and this
would be a curiously late point at which
to be describing it; cp. c. 53 supra.)

9. ἀνέμενε δὲ τοῦδε εἵνεκα: the fact
that he waited for Amompharetos, or at
any rate halted and was afterwards
joined by Amompharetos, is much more
likely to be true (in accordance with a
constant canon of Herodotean criticism)
than the reason given for the fact, the
motivation. The statement here made
that, if only Amompharetos had carried
his obstinate insubordination a little
further, Pausanias would have yielded
and returned to support him, is very
little short of absurd. The obvious
hypothesis is that Amompharetos, like
every other good Spartan, was strictly
obeying orders; that his λόχος was the
last to move because such was his
commander's will; that it was really
told off to cover the movement backwards. The words ἐν τῷ ἐτετάχατο ὁ Ἀμ.
τε καὶ ὁ λόχος unconsciously support
that view, but Hdt. unfortunately does
not further define this χῶρος (unless
ἱδρυμένον above be taken to agree with
λόχον).

12. οἵ τε ἀμφὶ . . καὶ ἡ ἵππος: a
parataxis. Amompharetos and his men
joined them just as the whole Persian
cavalry attacked them. This statement
is somewhat puzzling. The Spartans
have retired from their previous position
10 stades backwards, to avoid the
cavalry (φοβεόμενοι τὴν ἵππον) and on to

ἵππος ἡ τῶν βαρβάρων προσέκειτο πᾶσα. οἱ γὰρ ἱππόται
ἐποίευν οἷον καὶ ἐώθεσαν ποιέειν αἰεί, ἰδόντες δὲ τὸν χῶρον
κεινὸν ἐν τῷ ἐτετάχατο οἱ Ἕλληνες τῇσι προτέρῃσι ἡμέρῃσι, 15
ἤλαυνον τοὺς ἵππους αἰεὶ τὸ πρόσω καὶ ἅμα καταλαβόντες
προσεκέατό σφι.

Μαρδόνιος δὲ ὡς ἐπύθετο τοὺς Ἕλληνας ἀποιχομένους ὑπὸ 58
νύκτα εἶδέ τε τὸν χῶρον ἔρημον, καλέσας τὸν Ληρισαῖον
Θώρηκα καὶ τοὺς ἀδελφεοὺς αὐτοῦ Εὐρύπυλον καὶ Θρασυδήιον
ἔλεγε " ὦ παῖδες Ἀλεύεω, ἔτι τί λέξετε τάδε ὁρῶντες ἔρημα ;
ὑμεῖς γὰρ οἱ πλησιόχωροι ἐλέγετε Λακεδαιμονίους οὐ φεύγειν 5

---

14 εἰώθεσαν S ‖ ἀεὶ α, Holder ‖ δὲ del. Krueger　　15 ἐκεῖνον
Marc. z ‖ ᾧ CPMarc. z　　16 ἀεὶ α, Holder　　58. 2 τε om. β ‖
ληρισσαῖον β　　3 θρασυδαῖον β : θρασύδηον Marc. : Θρασύδιον z　　4
ἀλεύετω B ‖ ἔτι τι Krueger : τί ἔτι van H. : τί om. CMarc. ‖ ὁρέοντες
Marc. z, Stein[1], van H. : ὁρέωντες C ‖ ἐρῆμα CPMarc. z　　5 λέγετε CPz

---

higher ground. How can the whole
cavalry be attacking them ? The vagueness of the statement is further exhibited
by what immediately follows. Hdt.
says that in thus attacking them the
cavalry was only doing what it had been
doing all along on the previous days.
In c. 40 supra a similar generalization
occurs ; but, if we look for details in
confirmation, none is forthcoming. On
the contrary, it appears that for upwards
of a week the Greeks had enjoyed
immunity from the cavalry (c. 39 supra).
The vague generalities in c. 40 and here
look like a priori or inferential saving
clauses, while in fact the Greeks in
Position I² had enjoyed immunity from
the cavalry, and it was very much that
position which the Spartans were now
attempting to regain.

15. κεινόν : vacant, vacated.
58. 1. ἀποιχομένους, 'to be gone
away,' to have departed ; this fact he
learnt by report, from his scouts, etc.
(ἐπύθετο), and then satisfied himself by
his own eyes (εἶδε) that the position
previously occupied by the Greeks had
been vacated. ἔρημον = κεινόν previous
c. That Mardonios then proceeded to
waste time in summoning (καλέσας) the
Aleuadai to his side, in order to crow
over them and Artabazos, is a story of
another colour.

ὑπὸ νύκτα, 'under cover of night,'
is not usually retrospective, cp. 8. 71,
c. 51 supra ; c. 60 infra makes the case
here plain.

2. τὸν Ληρισαῖον Θώρηκα. Thorax

of Larisa has appeared, c. 1 supra, but
without his brothers. He was, doubtless,
the most important of the three.

3. Εὐρύπυλον καὶ Θρασυδήιον.
Eurypylos is an eminently heroic and
Homeric name, little used, apparently,
in historic times, Il. 2. 677 (of Kos) ;
ib. 736, cp. Plato, Rep. 405D, 408A (of
Thessaly) ; Od. 11. 520 (of Mysia), etc.
Of this particular one nothing more is
narrated. Thrasydaios, on the contrary,
is a name not found in legend or saga,
but associated with several historic
characters : (1) The Theban, in whose
honour Pindar composed the obscure
Epinikion, Pyth. 11 (the theories which
date this ode to Pyth. 28 = 478 B.C.
overlook the improbability of the appearance of a Theban at that celebration).
(2) The son and successor of Theron of
Akragas, cp. 7. 165 f., Diodor. 11. 48.
6, 53. 1. These two would both have
been contemporaries of the Thessalian.
(3) Xenoph. Hell. 3. 2. 27 ff. mentions
an Eleian προστάτης τοῦ δήμου of the
name (anno 400 B.C.). Of the Thessalian
in the text nothing more is known.

4. παῖδες Ἀλεύεω : cp. 7. 130 =
Ἀλευάδαι 7. 6, 172. The name Aleuas
is very rare in the historic period, but
is found in two Boiotian inscripp., C.I.G.
1564, 1580, referring to an Orchomenian.

5. πλησιόχωροι : that the speaker
should regard the Thessalians and
Spartans as ' neighbours ' would suggest
to a Greek hearer, or reader, the large
scale upon which the Persian was wont
to think and operate ; cp. 3. 89. No

ἐκ μάχης, ἀλλὰ ἄνδρας εἶναι τὰ πολέμια πρώτους· τοὺς
πρότερόν τε μετισταμένους ἐκ τῆς τάξιος εἴδετε, νῦν τε ὑπὸ
τὴν παροιχομένην νύκτα καὶ οἱ πάντες ὁρῶμεν διαδράντας·
διέδεξάν τε, ἐπεί σφεας ἔδεε πρὸς τοὺς ἀψευδέως ἀρίστους
10 ἀνθρώπων μάχῃ διακριθῆναι, ὅτι οὐδένες ἄρα ἐόντες ἐν
οὐδαμοῖσι ἐοῦσι Ἕλλησι . . ἐναπεδεικνύατο. καὶ ὑμῖν μὲν
ἐοῦσι Περσέων ἀπείροισι πολλὴ ἔκ γε ἐμεῦ ἐγίνετο συγγνώμη,

---

6 ἀλλ' ΒΡ   8 ὁρέομεν Pz, Stein[1], van H. : ὁρέωμεν CMarc. ‖
διαδράντες C   11 Ἕλλησι del. Naber, Holder : lacunam ind. Stein[3]
12 γε: τε Β

---

statement in regard to Spartan heroism has been recorded of the Aleuads; Mardonios ought to have addressed his remarks to Demaratos (cp. 7. 102, 209, 284); that he does not do so is some evidence that the Spartan exile was not with him. To believe that Mardonios represented the Spartan retirement as a φυγή would at once lower our opinion of him as a general.

6. τὰ πολέμια: the accusative 'of reference'; cp. Index.

πρώτους: not in time but in rank, quality, etc. Cp. c. 53 supra.

7. μετισταμένους: the story in cc. 46, 47 supra. That movement is nowhere said to have been fully carried out. It was not in fact what Hdt. and his sources supposed; cp. notes ad ll.

8. οἱ πάντες ὁρῶμεν, 'we all see'; there is a contrast with εἴδετε just above; Mardonios himself had not perceived the μετάταξις, it had been reported to him, not indeed by the Aleuadai (as might seem to be here implied) but by the Boiotians; cp. c. 47 supra. καὶ διαδράντας, 'that they have scattered and fled'; cp. 8. 60.

9. διέδεξαν: cp. 7. 172; the third τε is a climax.

ἔδεε, without any suggestion of the supernatural; cp. 7. 9, 144; contr. 8. 53, and c. 109 infra.

10. ἀνθρώπων: perhaps without prejudice.

μάχῃ διακριθῆναι: cp. 7. 206. Differently, 7. 219, 8. 18.

οὐδένες ἄρα ἐόντες ἐν οὐδαμοῖσι ἐοῦσι Ἕλλησι . . ἐναπεδεικνύατο: durius sane dictum ab Herodoto, Baehr; see below. οὐδένες as a normal plural 3. 26 οὐδένες ἄλλοι οὐδὲν ἔχουσι εἰπεῖν. For the obvious meaning here Blakesley compares Soph. Ai. 1135 τοὺς μηδένας.

It is even frequent in Euripides, Androm. 700, Ion 594, Iph. Aul. 371 βαρβάρους τοὺς οὐδένας. The neuter τὸ μηδέν with even more effect for less force, 8. 106.

ἄρα suggests surprise, here as arising from an expectation at last overcome. Cp. Index.

11. οὐδαμοῖσι: after οὐδένες perhaps οὐδέοι might have been expected, but οὐδαμοί is the more usual pl. The chief difficulty in the passage lurks in ἐναποδείκνυσθαι, to which three different renderings have been given: (a) ostentari, 'to show off,' 'to cut a fine figure,' etc., merely because the Greeks at large, like themselves, were nobodies. Portus (b) supplying ἔργα, ἀρετάς, or τι, cp. c. 67 infra; so Stein. If merely τι is supplied (and the τι can be supplied from the immediate context below), this works out very nearly as = (a); if ἔργα, it makes too much of a concession; in either case the omission of the object is obscure. (c) Taking the verb as meaning simply monstrare, demonstrare; so Baehr: commonstrarunt illi satis se vel inter eos, qui nihili sunt, Graecos, nullo loco esse censendos. This sentiment, as one degree less insulting to his Greek allies, whom Mardonios is addressing, might be preferable, but there is nothing in the Greek corresponding to vel which is essential to the rendering. On the whole, then, (a) seems preferable.

12. ἐοῦσι Περσέων ἀπείροισι: nearly as absurd and refutable, in application to the Thessalians, as to the Spartans themselves, c. 46 supra, each story ignoring any previous fighting by land. The Thessalians, indeed, had not fought against the Persians, but they had seen the Persians fight—with the Spartans.

ἐπαινεόντων τούτους τοῖσί τι καὶ συνηδέατε· Ἀρταβάζου δὲ
θῶμα καὶ μᾶλλον ἐποιεύμην τὸ καὶ καταρρωδῆσαι Λακεδαιμονίους καταρρωδήσαντά τε ἀποδέξασθαι γνώμην δειλοτάτην, 15
ὡς χρεὸν εἴη ἀναζεύξαντας τὸ στρατόπεδον ἰέναι ἐς τὸ Θηβαίων
ἄστυ πολιορκησομένους· τὴν ἔτι πρὸς ἐμεῦ βασιλεὺς πεύσεται.
καὶ τούτων μὲν ἑτέρωθι ἔσται λόγος· νῦν δὲ ἐκείνοισι ταῦτα
ποιεῦσι οὐκ ἐπιτρεπτέα ἐστί, ἀλλὰ διωκτέοι εἰσὶ ἐς ὃ καταλαμφθέντες δώσουσι ἡμῖν τῶν δὴ ἐποίησαν Πέρσας πάντων 20
δίκας." ταῦτα εἴπας ἦγε τοὺς Πέρσας δρόμῳ διαβάντας τὸν 59

---

13 συνηιδέατε Α²P ante corr.: συνηιδέαται aCPcorr.: συνηδέαται Bε:
συνηδέατε Marc.: συνηδέετε Schaefer: συνήδειτε van H. (συνήδέιτε typ.
errore)   14 θῶμα aCMarc., Stein², Holder, van H.: θώϋμα B: θῶυμα
|| καὶ post. loc. om. B, van H. || καταρρωιδῆσαι P   15 καταρρωιδή-
σαντά P || τε: δὲ Krueger   16 χρεὸν aB, Stein, Holder: χρεὼν   18
τουτέων z   20 ἐποιήσαντο z   59. 1 τὸν om. z

---

18. **ἐπαινεόντων τούτους**: the sequence
after ὑμῖν is not strictly correct; cp. c.
51 *supra*, 8. 69. The occasion is not
recorded; cp. l. 5 above. **τοῖσί τι καὶ
συνηδέατε**, sc. 'just among yourselves.'
The reference is not to Thermopylai,
cp. l. 20.

Ἀρταβάζου δέ: the genitive may
be explained as after τὸ καταρρωδῆσαι,
θῶμα being in apposition to the subst.
infin.; but in any case the accus.
καταρρωδήσαντα comes in as a grammatical *non sequitur*. The full report
of the opinion of Artabazos, already
given c. 41 *supra*, makes its repetition
here *in extenso* the more remarkable,
especially as there is here a direct
reference back (ἐποιεύμην imperf.) to
that passage. πολιορκησομένους here
is more explicit than the former report,
and the substitution of ἄστυ for πόλιν
discredits the project all the more.

17. **τὴν ἔτι πρὸς ἐμεῦ βασιλεὺς πεύσεται**: the irony of this promise, or
prediction, in the story is keen; what
actually happened was that Artabazos
reported to the king the folly and the
fate of Mardonios. The same tone is
maintained in the next sentence: καὶ
τούτων μὲν ἑτέρωθι ἔσται λόγος, i.e. of
all that, account shall be taken when I
go home. λόγος, *ratio* rather than *oratio*.
There is a slight logical confusion in
the use of μέν and δέ in this connexion.
The contrast is between ἑτέρωθι and νῦν,
not between τούτων and νῦν or even
ἐκείνοισι. If that natural antithesis
had been observed, it would have been

more logical to contrast νῦν μέν with
ἑτέρωθι δέ . .

19. **ποιεῦσι** is strictly present, or
imperf., 'engaged in performing . .'

ἐπιτρεπτέα does not agree with
ταῦτα (acc.), and the singular might be
clearer. Is the plural used to emphasize
the divisions of the Hellenes (διαδράντας
supra)?

καταλαμφθέντες: the normal
Herodotean form; cp. 5. 21.

20. **δώσουσι . . δίκας** is hardly consistent with their having done nothing!
And δή emphasizes their malefactions!
The reference is certainly not to 7. 184 ff.
but rather to Thermopylai, and ironically
to the story 8. 114, and is thus altogether
inconsistent with the contempt for the
Spartans expressed just above.

59. 1. ἦγε τοὺς Πέρσας. Here, if
anywhere, the battle begins; but the
cavalry have, according to c. 57 *supra*,
already opened the ball. Mardonios
himself is mounted, cp. c. 63 *infra*,
but he is evidently leading infantry.
'Persians' here used specifically, as
distinguished from the rest of the
barbarians; cp. just below, and cc. 31,
47 *supra*.

δρόμῳ, 'at the double'; cp. c. 57
supra βάδην, and especially 6. 112.

διαβάντας τὸν Ἀσωπόν, 'after
they (had) crossed the Asopos'—words
which show clearly (if anything in a
narrative by Hdt. can be really conclusive), that the Persians had been
beyond the Asopos, the river between
them and the Greeks, so far as the

Ἀσωπὸν κατὰ στίβον τῶν Ἑλλήνων ὡς δὴ ἀποδιδρησκόντων,
ἐπεῖχέ τε ἐπὶ Λακεδαιμονίους τε καὶ Τεγεήτας μούνους· Ἀθηναίους γὰρ τραπομένους ἐς τὸ πεδίον ὑπὸ τῶν ὄχθων οὐ

2 τῶν : τὸν ? Kallenberg

---

main positions, and the στρατόπεδα, the armies at rest, were concerned.

How the Persians got across the Asopos Hdt. does not specify; it cannot have been all boarded over; there may have been some bridges, or planks, in use; but for all that appears they scrambled across as best they could. The passage of the Asopos, which they had steadily declined, so long as the Greeks were in battle - array on the other side, is now undertaken apparently under the idea that the Greeks are in full retreat, perhaps for their several homes; the extreme left wing is invisible to Mardonios. He may even believe that it has made good its escape; at least he may safely leave it to the tender mercies of the Thebans and his own right. He sights easily enough the glint of Greek weapons at the Heraion, and up beyond, in the gap of the road to Megara, in the gap of the road to Athens; while in the nearer foreground are the Spartans, with their commander, apparently in full retreat, and isolated from the other Greek divisions. His cavalry is riding un-opposed up the road to Erythrai, as it has been free to do ever since the Greek deployed from that position.

2. κατὰ στίβον : cp. 4. 122, 140, 5. 102. Not to be taken here as implying that the Lakedaimonians were invisible to their pursuers; the whole context implies the reverse.

ὡς δὴ ἀποδιδρησκόντων : such was the idea in the minds of the Persians, but it has no justification in fact.

The motivation is here to be accepted not so much on the ground that Greeks in the Persian ranks, or Persian sources themselves, might afterwards have reported Mardonios' motives to that effect; but rather on the ground that to obtain a satisfactory theory of the battle, we must suppose that the object, or a part of the object of the Greeks, in retiring, was to entice Mardonios across the river, in effecting which object the Greek commanders will have given their movement as much as possible the appearance of a 'flight.'

3. ἐπεῖχέ τε : cp. διέδεξάν τε c. 58.

The verb projected with this copula appears to be emphatic. ἐπεῖχε is variously taken (a) as psychical, animum attendit, sese direxit, cp. 6. 96, Baehr; (b) as physical, sc. τοὺς Πέρσας, i.e. duxit Stein; (c) intrans. (Sitzler), which is really = Baehr's sese direxit. In any case Mardonios with his Persians, followed by the whole mass of the barbarian infantry, made after the Greek right wing, which was apparently in complete isolation.

Ἀθηναίους γάρ : the particle explains the μούνους just before. The movement of the Athenians appears here less fully developed than in c. 56 supra (τραπο-μένους as against τραφθέντες .. ἐς τὸ πεδίον); but the last three words there may rather be taken with the verb ἧσαν repeated, or understood from the context. We are there, however, on the Greek side, here with the Persians; and it by no means follows that the action of the Persians, as here recorded, was not antecedent to the position above reached in the description of the manœuvres of the Greeks.

4. ὑπὸ τῶν ὄχθων οὐ κατέρα : he could not see the Athenians on their way down on to the plain by reason of the ridges (ὄχθοι). There is the same ambiguity here as in c. 56 supra. Are the ὄχθοι in each case the same? Are not the ὄχθοι here the ridges close to the river (almost in fact ὄχθαι)? To adduce (with Ross and Baehr) this statement, perhaps in itself true enough, as evidence that Hdt. had with his own eyes inspected the battle-field, is a fine instance of half-methods. The statement is a clear example of the dialectical production or evolution of tradition. Why did not Mardonios attend to the Athenians? Because he could not see them. Why could he not see them? By reason of the ὄχθοι—and so forth. The statement may, of course, have come to Hdt. ready made in his source. Though perhaps true, it is not an adequate explanation of the Persian general's action, for he was bound to acquaint himself at once with the pro-ceedings of the Greek left wing; and what were the Aleuadai about to receive

κατώρα. Πέρσας δὲ ὁρῶντες ὁρμημένους διώκειν τοὺς Ἕλληνας 5
οἱ λοιποὶ τῶν βαρβαρικῶν τελέων ἄρχοντες αὐτίκα πάντες
ᾔειραν τὰ σημήια, καὶ ἐδίωκον ὡς ποδῶν ἕκαστοι εἶχον, οὔτε
κόσμῳ οὐδενὶ κοσμηθέντες οὔτε τάξι. καὶ οὗτοι μὲν βοῇ 60
τε καὶ ὁμίλῳ ἐπήισαν ὡς ἀναρπασόμενοι τοὺς Ἕλληνας·
Παυσανίης δέ, ὡς προσέκειτο ἡ ἵππος, πέμψας πρὸς τοὺς

---

5 ὀρέοντες Stein[1], van H. ‖ ὁρμημένους α : ὡρμημένους   6 ἄπαντες Β
(sic Holder : sed αὐτίκα πάντες om. S)   7 ᾔειραν Stein, van H. : ἦιραν α :
ἦραν reliqui, Holder ‖ ἕκαστος ΒMarc. z, Holder, van H. ‖ ἦκον Β   8
τάξει Β   60. 2 ἐπῆσαν BMarc. ‖ ἀρπασόμενοι RS(V)

---

his rebuke so meekly in c. 58 *supra*, or where were the Thebans, the Makedonians ! had he issued no orders to his own right wing !

5. ὁρμημένους διώκειν, 'in full pursuit of.' διώκειν is treated as a 'telic' infinitive ; but the 'purpose' is really fully contained, or supplied by the verb ὁρμᾶσθαι as in 7. 4 ὁρμᾶτο στρατεύεσθαι, or c. 61 *infra* ὁρμέατο βοηθέειν, and the infinitive might be regarded not as having in itself telic, i.e. purposive force, but as being an ordinary limiting or definitive idea ; in other words, as belonging not to the 'subjective' but to the 'objective' order. This view may equally prevail, even if ὁρμημένους be taken in a physical sense, of the actual motion.

6. οἱ λοιποὶ τῶν βαρβαρικῶν τελέων ἄρχοντες. If the army of Mardonios had really numbered 300,000 non-Hellenes, the officers here designated would have been the thirty myriarchs named in the army-list in 7. 61 ff., with allowance for deaths, promotions, etc. In fact they are the myriarchs of the Medes, Baktrians, Indians, Sakai, the four remaining τέλη which, with his own 'Persians,' were comprised in the *corps d'armée* ; cp. c. 31 *supra*. The whole of the other *corps d'armée* under Artabazos is already on its way to Thrace ! cp. c. 66 *infra*.

7. ᾔειραν τὰ σημήια, 'raised the signals' (for battle, pursuit, or what not). In a Roman army the first sign of battle was the scarlet flag raised at headquarters ; the trumpet - sound followed. Cp. Caesar, *B.G.* 2. 20. 1. Greek armies had apparently a very similar procedure ; cp. Thuc. 1. 49, 63, 4. 42, 111, 7. 34, 8. 95 (Baehr). Something of the kind must have been in vogue in all armies, with any organization to speak of ; cp. 7. 128 (on the fleet).

Xenophon, *Kyrop.* 8. 5. 13, may be describing rather Greek than Persian organization, but the differences in this respect were probably not great.

ὡς ποδῶν ἕκαστοι εἶχον : ποδῶν ἔχειν, 'to be off for feet,' i.e. to be furnished with ; ἔχειν τινος εὖ, κακῶς, or absolutely ; cp. 8. 107, and almost this very phrase 6. 116. ἕκαστοι, i.e. each set, Medes, Baktrians, Indians, Sakai—it was a race among them to overtake the Greeks.

οὔτε κόσμῳ . . οὔτε τάξι : κόσμος is the general expression or the whole results of νοῦς : τάξις is the particular position in the battle-array ; cp. 8. 86. The statement here of the chaos and the disorder of the Persian pursuit is perhaps exaggerated : the crossing of the river and river-banks would tend to bring about a certain amount of confusion.

60. 1. βοῇ τε καὶ ὁμίλῳ : *cum clamore ac tumultu*, Baehr. βοή is the 'battle-cry.' ὅμιλος in Homer is the 'ruck' as compared with the leaders. In Thuc. 4. 125. 2 τὸν ψιλὸν ὅμιλον as compared with τοὺς ὁπλίτας, cp. 4. 112. 3. But Thucydides (e.g. 2. 65. 4 contemptuously), Hdt. 5. 23, and 3. 81 (contemptuously) use it without reference to fighting (cp. 1. 88) ; and so too Homer, etc.

2. ἀναρπασόμενοι : cp. 8. 78.

3. Παυσανίης δέ. The narrative, the scene, changes to the Greek side ; the time, or at least the situation, also goes back to a point reached, or anticipated, in c. 57 *supra ad f.*, ὡς προσέκειτο ἡ ἵππος. This point was there put early in the morning. If the Persian cavalry was really attacking the Lakedaimonians in any position accessible to cavalry, Pausanias and his men were likely to be having a bad time ; but the Spartans

Ἀθηναίους ἱππέα λέγει τάδε. "ἄνδρες Ἀθηναῖοι, ἀγῶνος·
5 μεγίστου προκειμένου ἐλευθέρην εἶναι ἢ δεδουλωμένην τὴν
Ἑλλάδα, προδεδόμεθα ὑπὸ τῶν συμμάχων ἡμεῖς τε οἱ
Λακεδαιμόνιοι καὶ ὑμεῖς οἱ Ἀθηναῖοι ὑπὸ τὴν παροιχομένην
νύκτα διαδράντων. νῦν ὦν δέδοκται τὸ ἐνθεῦτεν τόδε ποιητέον
ἡμῖν, ἀμυνομένους [γὰρ] τῇ δυνάμεθα ἄριστα περιστέλλειν

4 ἱππέα: ἄνδρα Marc.   5 ἐλευθερίην id.   6, 7 οἱ Λακεδαιμόνιοι
et οἱ Ἀθηναῖοι abesse malit van H.   8 δέδεκται (palam est) Cobet,
van H. || τοενθεῦτεν Pz || τόδε Stein³ : τὸ α etc. Stein¹ ² : om. β, Holder,
van H.   9 ἡμῖν βPcorr. z : ὑμῖν || γὰρ secl. Stein³

were now 10 stades up the ὑπωρέη, above the Moloeis, on the Argiopion: how could the cavalry come by them? Is the cavalry attack on the Lakedaimonians in this place anything more than a transfer of the sufferings of the previous day, c. 49 supra? If more, did any Lochos suffer except perhaps that of Amompharetos? Was not the bulk of the Persian cavalry engaged elsewhere?

4. ἱππέα. It is doubtful, at best, whether the Spartans had any mounted men or aides-de-camp; he is perhaps only the double of the ἱππεύς in c. 54 supra. This man might have been one of τῶν καλουμένων ἱππέων, cp. 8. 124, but he would have had a good deal of ground to cover a-foot, if he had really been despatched in the circumstances here supposed.

ἄνδρες Ἀθηναῖοι. Is this the proper formula from Pausanias to Aristeides, or has the story-teller (or source) the fear of the Demos before his eyes? Cp. c. 45 supra. This is not the only or the greatest improbability in the message.

ἀγῶνος μεγίστου προκειμένου. Pausanias knows that the supreme hour is come.

5. ἢ δεδουλωμένην (the permanent state, rather than the single act?) seems to add the less likely alternative; cp. 7. 104 ἐπικρατέειν ἢ ἀπόλλυσθαι. A perfectly open question has co-ordinate ἢ . . ἢ, cp. 7. 11.

6. προδεδόμεθα . . διαδράντων: Pausanias (a) wastes time by telling the Athenians what they know only too well already—if the story in c. 55 supra (cc. 52-57) had been true, as there related; (b) repeats the very words of Mardonios above, addressed to the Aleuadai, ὑπὸ τὴν παροιχομένην νύκτα (καὶ οἱ πάντες ὁρῶμεν) διαδράντας. There is, however, some virtue in the word

διαδράντων here; for it supports the hypothesis that the Greek centre had not all retired on precisely the same point, but that at this moment the Greek forces are at four distinct positions: the Lakedaimonians on the Argiopion, the right centre at the Island, or thereabouts, the left centre at the Heraion, and the Athenians apparently 'on the plain.'

8. νῦν ὦν comes to the point; cp. c. 48 supra.

δέδοκται perhaps only means 'it is perfectly clear,' without reference to any antecedent agreement, or formal resolution; yet none of the passages quoted by Stein, in support of a simple constat, is quite convincing; 4. 68 δέδοκται τοῖσι πρώτοισι τῶν μαντίων αὐτοῖσι ἀπόλλυσθαι points to law or enactment, 6. 109 δέδοκται τὰ πείσονται παραδεδομένα to a decree or resolution, 8. 110 πρότερον δεδογμένος εἶναι σόφος is perhaps merely anachronistic, cp. 8. 124; c. 87 infra δέδοκται τοῖσι Ἕλλησι is a decision, an actual resolution taken. Cp. also c. 45 supra. Even in this case there seems no adequate reason for weakening the force of the term and the tense, c. 55 supra. Pausanias has actually summoned the Athenians to his side: that arrangement was probably part of the δόγμα imperfectly recorded c. 51 supra βουλευομένοισι δὲ τοῖσι στρατηγοῖσι ἔδοξε κτλ. The eventuality of the Lakedaimonians and the Athenians finding themselves isolated by the retirement of the centre had been foreseen and provided for; dimly and unconsciously this fact is here involved in the formula. The γὰρ in the next sentence is superfluous.

9. περιστέλλειν: 2. 90 περιστείλαντας ὡς κάλλιστα θάψαι (αὐτόν), cp. 6. 30, passages exhibiting a more primary use of the verb than the present one,

ἀλλήλους. εἰ μέν νυν ἐς ὑμέας ὅρμησε ἀρχὴν ἡ ἵππος, χρῆν 10
δὴ ἡμέας τε καὶ τοὺς μετ' ἡμέων τὴν Ἑλλάδα οὐ προδιδόντας
Τεγεήτας βοηθέειν ὑμῖν· νῦν δέ, ἐς ἡμέας γὰρ ἄπασα
κεχώρηκε, δίκαιοι ἐστὲ ὑμεῖς πρὸς τὴν πιεζομένην μάλιστα
τῶν μοιρέων ἀμυνέοντες ἰέναι. εἰ δ' ἄρα αὐτοὺς ὑμέας καταλελάβηκε ἀδύνατόν τι βοηθέειν, ὑμεῖς δ' ἡμῖν τοὺς τοξότας 15

10 ἡμέας Marc. ‖ ὅρμησε (CP), Stein[1] ‖ χρῆν AB   11 μετ' ἡμέας z
15 βωθεῖν van H. ‖ τούς <γε> Naber, van H.

especially with accus. of the person. With neuter or inanimate objects it is common: τοὺς νόμους 2. 147, cp. τὸν νόμον 3. 31, τὸ τοιοῦτο περιστέλλειν 3. 82, πόλισμα 1. 98. Theokritos 15. 75 ἄμμε περιστέλλων (ἐν καλῷ εἴης) seems to be the nearest parallel to the present case.

10. εἰ μὲν νυν . . ἡ ἵππος. This argument, or appeal, admits that the Athenians, though apparently 'on the plain,' were not attacked by the cavalry —while the Lakedaimonians, who were on the ὑπωρέη, φοβεόμενοι τὴν ἵππον c. 56, were being attacked, ex hypothesi, by the cavalry. This hypothesis seems absurd. It is no use saying that Pausanias is merely speaking of the 'Persian' cavalry; he makes no distinction, and cavalry is cavalry. What was the Theban, the Thessalian, the Makedonian cavalry about all this time, even if there were no Persians, Medes, Baktrians, Indians, or Scyths on 'the plain'? Either the Athenians were in a position where they could not be attacked by cavalry, or the cavalry on the right wing had arranged not to attack them.

ὅρμησε: the active, intransitive, of actual or physical motion.

The exception made in favour of the Tegeatai is probably more Attic than Laconic, cp. c. 26. All the rest of the Greeks are 'traitors,' have betrayed the cause of Hellas (τὴν Ἑλλάδα, sc. γῆν, συμμαχίην). The Athenians recognize only themselves, the Spartans and Tegeatai, as having had any hand in this victory, and they depreciate the services even of the Spartans and Tegeatai as much as possible. Just here, they are on the defensive.

ἀρχήν: cp. 8. 128.

χρῆν δή: far more emphatic is the apodosis without ἄν, denoting a duty unconditionally; cp. Madvig, § 118.

12. ἄπασα κεχώρηκε: again an admission that the Athenians were free

from cavalry assaults. (Strictly speaking, ' the whole cavalry' would include that of the medizing Greeks.)

13. δίκαιοι ἐστί: the personal and idiomatic construction; cp. c. 27 (Athenian speech).

τὴν πιεζομένην μάλιστα τῶν μοιρέων seems to suggest that the Lakedaimonians were, at this moment, the division of the Greek forces that was being most hard pressed. The plural genitive μοιρέων emphasizes the fact of this division, a tactical not an accidental result. The word μοῖρα, however, cannot be pressed as a technical term in the mouth of a Spartan; even if the word μόρα was already in use at Sparta (which is doubtful; cp. notes c. 53 supra), this story is not a Spartan story, and the word is of frequent occurrence in Hdt. For a parallel to the present case cp. 4. 120. With πιέζειν cp. 8. 142.

14. εἰ δ' ἄρα αὐτ. ὑμ. καταλελάβηκε ἀδύνατόν τι βοηθέειν, 'if (as we hardly suppose) anything has occurred to you making it impossible to assist us.' ἀδύνατον τι idem valet ac ἀδυνασία τις, Schweighaeuser; so too Stein (who well cps. 1. 61, 6. 138 δεινόν τι=δέος; 7. 101 ἡδύ τι=ἡδονή). ἄρα, c. 58 supra.

15. ὑμεῖς δ': the resumed subject (virtually) with the δέ in apodosi, cp. 7. 51, etc.

τοὺς τοξότας ἀποπέμψαντες χάριν θέσθε: a polite request, not to say command; the archers had not been sent yet: 'oblige us by the despatch of your Archers.' The Athenian corps of Archers has just been mentioned incidentally in c. 22, but not included in the army-list, or numbering of the forces, cp. notes to c. 29 supra; it was apparently 800 strong. The request for the loan of them ill sorts with the supposition that the Spartans had 40,000 ψιλοὶ μάχιμοι, πᾶς τις παρηρτημένος ὡς ἐς πόλεμον l.c.; it also implies or assumes that the Athenians themselves were not

ἀποπέμψαντες χάριν θέσθε. συνοίδαμεν δὲ ὑμῖν ὑπὸ τὸν
παρεόντα τόνδε πόλεμον ἐοῦσι πολλὸν προθυμοτάτοισι, ὥστε
61 καὶ ταῦτα ἐσακούειν." ταῦτα οἱ Ἀθηναῖοι ὡς ἐπύθοντο,
ὁρμέατο βοηθέειν καὶ τὰ μάλιστα ἐπαμύνειν· καί σφι ἤδη
στείχουσι ἐπιτίθενται οἱ ἀντιταχθέντες Ἑλλήνων τῶν μετὰ
βασιλέος γενομένων, ὥστε μηκέτι δύνασθαι βοηθῆσαι· τὸ γὰρ
5 προσκείμενον σφέας ἐλύπεε. οὕτω δὴ μουνωθέντες Λακεδαιμόνιοι καὶ Τεγεῆται, ἐόντες σὺν ψιλοῖσι ἀριθμὸν οἱ μὲν
πεντακισμύριοι Τεγεῆται δὲ τρισχίλιοι (οὗτοι γὰρ οὐδαμὰ

---

16 ὑμῶν χάριν Paris. 1634 ‖ θέσθαι B (C cum ε supersc.) ‖ σύνιδμεν
Mehler, Cobet, van H. ‖ ὑμῖν χάριν Marc. 　　　61. 2 ὁρμέατο α :
ὡρμέατο ‖ βοηθεῖν C : βωθεῖν van H. 　　3 στίχουσι aCR 　　　4
βασιλῆος z ‖ ὥστε καὶ B 　　5 προκείμενον Rz ‖ προσκείμενόν σφεας
(CP), Stein¹, Holder, van H. 　　7 τρισχείλιοι van H.

---

in want of the Archers at this crisis, or
should not have been. χάριν θέσθαι, cp.
c. 107 infra.

16. συνοίδαμεν δὲ ὑμῖν κτλ. This
interesting testimonial to the unparalleled
zeal of Athens was hardly 'made in
Sparta,' though it is put into the mouth
of a Spartan. The phraseology again
reproduces the speech of Mardonios :
ἐπαινεόντων τούτους τοῖσί τι καὶ συνηδέατε
c. 58.

ὑπὸ τὸν π. τ. πόλεμον : cp. ὑπὸ
τὴν παροιχομένην νύκτα above.

17. ὥστε . . ἐσακούειν, 'so as to give
heed to this our petition,' i.e. οὕτω
πολλὸν προθυμότατοι ἐστὲ ὥστε expressing
a result, not an intention or purpose.
For the present infinitive we might have
expected the aorist infinitive, or (with a
different sense) the future indicative !
The construction preferred suggests
perhaps a more continuous and immediate
sequence (though not, of course, the
actual fact, as present indicative might
do ; the sequence remains an ideal one).
ἐσακούειν c. 9 supra ; Baehr here supplies
ἡμῖν, Sitzler ἡμῶν. The dat. pers. is
expressed 1. 214 (or might be taken
elegantly as 'ethical') ; the gen. is
found, e.g., Soph. Ai. 789 τοῦδ' εἰσάκουε
τἀνδρός.

61. 1. οἱ Ἀθηναῖοι : they act en
masse as above addressed, ἄνδρες Ἀθ.

2. ὁρμέατο βοηθέειν : cp. ὁρμημένους
διώκειν c. 59. The pl.p. ὁρμέατο marks
the depth, or intensity, of their emotion,
or the instantaneous rapidity of their
action. The position of ταῦτα is emphatic.
τὰ μάλιστα, 8. 97. ἤδη στείχουσι : the

Athenians are actually on the way to
the support of the Lakedaimonians, or
to effect a juncture with them, but
fail to carry out their intention, or this
manœuvre, in consequence of being
attacked, or intercepted, by the medizing Greeks, or some of them. στείχειν,
cp. c. 56 supra.

3. οἱ ἀντιταχθέντες = οἱ ἀντιτεταγμένοι
c. 31 supra. The description of οἱ
ἀντιταχθέντες as a part of (the) Greeks
τῶν μετὰ βασιλέος γενομένων is rather
curious at this point ; in c. 31 they are
described as τοὺς μετ' αὐτοῦ (i.e. Μαρδονίου) ἐόντας Ἑλλήνων.

4. τὸ προσκείμενον : collective for οἱ
προσκείμενοι, cp. τὸ ἀσθενέστερον c. 31.

5. οὕτω δή, not of time so much
as of causation. μουνωθέντες, 'without
support' : the Athenians could still fall
back on Marathon, where, μοῦνοι Ἑλλήνων
δὴ <προ>μαχήσαντες τῷ Πέρσῃ, they
had defeated forty-six nations, c. 27
supra ; whereas at Plataia there was but
one, the Persian, opposed to the Spartans
and Tegeans, c. 31 supra.

7. πεντακισμύριοι : i.e. 5000 Spartiate
hoplites, 5000 Lakedaimonian hoplites,
35,000 helots in attendance on the
Spartiates, 5000 in attendance on the
Lakedaimonians, in accordance with
the calculations in cc. 29, 30 supra.
But the calculation for the ψιλοί at least
has been disallowed ; cp. notes to ll.c. ;
and perhaps the total number of hoplites
ought to be reduced by a quarter, if
not by a half.

τρισχίλιοι : i.e. 1500 hoplites,
1500 ψιλοί, ibid. The reassertion of

ἀπεσχίζοντο ἀπὸ Λακεδαιμονίων), ἐσφαγιάζοντο ὡς συμβαλέοντες Μαρδονίῳ καὶ τῇ στρατιῇ τῇ παρεούσῃ. καὶ οὐ
γάρ σφι ἐγίνετο τὰ σφάγια χρηστά, ἔπιπτόν τε αὐτῶν ἐν 10
τούτῳ τῷ χρόνῳ πολλοὶ καὶ πολλῷ πλεῦνες ἐτρωματίζοντο·
φράξαντες γὰρ τὰ γέρρα οἱ Πέρσαι ἀπίεσαν τῶν τοξευμάτων

10 ἔπιπτόν τε Schaefer, van H., Stein³: ἔπιπτον δὲ (δ' a: δι' C)
12 γέρα Apr.β ‖ τῶν om. z

these numbers at this point is remarkable : no allowance is made for losses
previous. There was little or no excuse
for the request to the Athenians for the
ταξόται. And what a host the right
wing was, compared with the Athenians,
here, or at Marathon !

8. ἀπεσχίζοντο, middle, 'separated
from': if the Athenians owed anything
to the Plataians, e.g. at Marathon, the
Spartans owed still more to the Tegeatai
at Plataia !

ἐσφαγιάζοντο ὡς συμβαλέοντες
Μαρδονίῳ. This statement comes
abruptly and with a shock: it proves
that the Spartans were contemplating
not merely battle, and self-defence, but
the assumption of the offensive (συμβάλλειν = μάχην ἄρχειν, cp. cc. 41, 45
supra). It suggests that the retirement
of the Lakedaimonians was purely a
reculer pour mieux sauter; it shows that
everything was proceeding en règle in
the Spartan position, Teisamenos (cc.
33, 36 supra) inspecting the sacrifices in
order to determine by their aid, and
possibly on a sign from Euryanax, or
Pausanias, the right moment for the
charge. On the verb σφαγιάζεσθαι cp.
c. 72 infra.

9. καὶ τῇ στρατιῇ τῇ παρεούσῃ.
These words refer presumably to the
Persian forces with Mardonios, and
imply that only a portion of his army
was in action. (a) The corps of Artabazos was not there, c. 66 infra. (b)
The Medes, Baktrian, Indian, Sakan
corps were apparently coming on pêle-
mêle, anyhow, c. 59 supra. (c) The
medizing Greeks, so far as they were
taking any part in the action at all (cp.
c. 67 infra), were fully engaged with
the Athenians (just above) and perhaps
with other Greek corps. (d) The Persian
cavalry, which has been reported above,
c. 60, as engaged with the Lakedaimonians, but which now seems to be
doing nothing against them, was perhaps
engaged elsewhere (possibly against the

Greek centre, or right centre, upon the
Plataia-Athens road, cp. note to c. 52. 7).
The army of Mardonios appears to be far
less in being than the Greek forces themselves, each division of which, at least,
is still a compact unit.

οὐ γάρ σφι ἐγίνετο τὰ σφάγια
χρηστά: sc. μάχης ἄρχουσι, συμβολὴν
ποιευμένοις, or such like. χρηστά is
perhaps superfluous; cp. c. 36 supra.

10. ἔπιπτον, 'were being killed,' as
distinguished from those who were
merely wounded: they were all alike
sitting on the ground (cp. c. 72 infra)
and probably crouching under their
shields (cp. c. 48 supra), as they had,
no doubt, been doing the greater part
of the previous day.

ἐν τούτῳ τῷ χρόνῳ here at least
covers some time in duration; cp. c.
56 supra. The proportion of wounded
to killed is unfortunately not stated: in
an ordinary conflict between two heavy-
armed Greek forces it was probably not
great; but in the present case no doubt
it was unusually large (πολλῷ πλεῦνες):
only 91 Spartiates at most were killed,
cp. c. 70 infra.

12. φράξαντες γὰρ τὰ γέρρα οἱ
Πέρσαι. The use of the γέρρον (cp. 7.
61) proves that the Persians here in
action are infantry. The exact nature
of the contrivance here described is in
some doubt. Rüstow supposed that
each Persian fixed his long light wicker
shield in the ground by means of a
point below: such 'a wall of shields'
would, of course, offer but a slight protection against the push of the hoplites.
Others (cp. Baehr ad l., and esp. Stein
ad l.) suppose 'that the Persians had
devised a new plan against the Greeks:
συνεφόρησαν τὰ γέρρα ἕρκος εἶναι σφίσι
c. 99 infra. Yes, no doubt at Mykale,
where the Persians were acting throughout on the defensive; but not here at
Plataia (or rather, in front of Hysiai !)
where they were advancing to the attack.
In this case, at most, the individual

[πολλά] ἀφειδέως, οὕτω ὥστε πιεζομένων τῶν Σπαρτιητέων καὶ
τῶν σφαγίων οὐ γινομένων ἀποβλέψαντα τὸν Παυσανίην πρὸς
15 τὸ "Ηραιον τὸ Πλαταιέων ἐπικαλέσασθαι τὴν θεόν, χρηίζοντα
62 μηδαμῶς σφέας ψευσθῆναι τῆς ἐλπίδος. ταῦτα δ' ἔτι τούτου

---

13 πολλά 'interpolatum videtur' van H.: seclusi   15 ἡραῖον R,
Gaisford, Palm ‖ χρήίζοντα Α: χρήζοντα CMarc.: χρήζοντα z   16
σφέας z

---

soldier fixed his shield in the ground,
in line with his neighbours, so that
there was a front, a screen, a fence of
shields (φράγμα 8. 52, φραγμὸς 7. 36,
142), hence φράξαντες here. (The helots
may have been throwing stones.)
13. ἀφειδέως: cp. c. 39 supra; here
in a somewhat different sense, largiter,
copiose, cp. 1. 163, 207 (Schweighaeuser).
πιεζομένων: cp. πιεζομένην c. 60
supra; the Spartans are acting still
strictly on the defensive—they are, in
fact, apparently doing nothing, still
unable χρήσασθαι τῇ χειρί (c. 72 infra).
14. τῶν σφαγίων οὐ γινομένων: Baehr
says, χρηστῶν hic optime carebit oratio.
Why, then, not everywhere? Cp. 7.
134, and cc. 41 supra, 62 infra. The
sign they are awaiting is the sign in
favour of their rising up and going for
the Persians.
ἀποβλέψαντα τὸν Παυσανίην.
Did Pausanias 'raise his eyes' (Rawlinson)? Did he look 'up' to the Heraion?
Was he on lower ground? Or did he do
more than 'look away to,' 'fix his eyes
upon' the Heraion? The upward look
is not essential to ἀποβλέπειν 7. 135
(cp. ἀναβλέπειν, though not as in 2.
111). For what reason did Pausanias
fix his gaze on the Heraion? Ex
hypothesi in order the better to invoke
the goddess. What did he see? Could
he see the Greek left, or left centre, in
front of the temple, c. 52 supra? Could
he see any signal? If there was such a
signal given, what intimation did it
convey? Or was he directing a signal
to that quarter? (Op. c. 69. 6 infra.)
15. τὸ "Ηραιον τὸ Πλαταιέων. Was
it really the Heraion he looked to?
Was there more than one Heraion in
the neighbourhood? There were at least
three temples of Eleusinian Demeter,
though Hdt. only mentions one of them
(cp. c. 57 supra); there was (so far as
known) only one temple of Hera, though
Hdt. so carefully specifies its Plataian
possessive. It was doubtless the principal
temple of the district; but strategically

more may have been going on at the
temple of Demeter, the Plataian one,
at this moment, just as later at the
Hysian; cp. c. 57 supra. (There was
an Heraion at Koroneia, Pausan. 9. 34.
3, apparently the only other one in
Boiotia.)
ἐπικαλέσασθαι, to invoke, summon
to his aid; cp. 8. 64; here, probably,
in audible tones.
16. μηδαμῶς σφέας ψευσθῆναι τῆς
ἐλπίδος. This is the very εὐχή of Pausanias. What was the ἐλπίς, for the
fulfilment of which he prayed? Was it
merely victory as such? Or not rather
such a 'sign' as would justify his assuming the offensive? In either case
the commander is fully in favour of
doing battle; for he is surely not hoping
simply to make good his retreat! But
the intimate connexion between the
εὐχή and the ἐλπίς, between the εὐχή and
the σφάγια χρηστά, and the coincidence
of these with the transition from 'passive
resistance' to active and offensive tactics,
compel us to believe that at this point
the situation on the field of battle was
such that gods and men, on the Greek
side, believed the hour was come to
deliver the attack, to charge home upon
the foe, behind his fence of shields.
Perhaps two or three things had
happened, e.g. (a) the Persian infantry
had been drawn across the Asopos in
disorder, and were now massed, at
short range, behind the feeble barrier of
the γέρρα, like sheep for the slaughter,
before the Argiopion, and the Plataian
temple of Demeter; (b) the Persian
cavalry was, perhaps, far off, or quite
out of fighting range, and held in check,
so far as the road in the rear was concerned, by the right centre in the
Plataia-Athens Pass, or thereabouts;
(c) from the left came word, or sign,
that there was nothing to fear in that
quarter; the Thebans alone, of the
king's Greek allies, showing fight.
(Blakesley long ago (1854) boldly said
that the hope of Pausanias was to bring

ἐπικαλεομένου προεξαναστάντες πρότεροι οἱ Τεγεῆται ἐχώρεον
ἐς τοὺς βαρβάρους, καὶ τοῖσι Λακεδαιμονίοισι αὐτίκα μετὰ
τὴν εὐχὴν τὴν Παυσανίεω ἐγίνετο θυομένοισι τὰ σφάγια
χρηστά· ὡς δὲ χρόνῳ κοτὲ ἐγένετο, ἐχώρεον καὶ οὗτοι ἐπὶ 5
τοὺς Πέρσας, καὶ οἱ Πέρσαι ἀντίοι τὰ τόξα μετέντες. ἐγίνετο
δὲ πρῶτον περὶ τὰ γέρρα μάχη. ὡς δὲ ταῦτα ἐπεπτώκεε,
ἤδη ἐγίνετο ἡ μάχη ἰσχυρὴ παρ' αὐτὸ τὸ Δημήτριον καὶ
χρόνον ἐπὶ πολλόν, ἐς ὃ ἀπίκοντο ἐς ὠθισμόν . . . τὰ γὰρ

62. 2 ἐπικαλευμένου z ‖ πρότερον B　　　4 ἐγένετο α (Holder), AB,
Stein⁽¹⁾, (van H.): minus recte, ut videtur　　5 ἐγένετο Schaefer, Gaisford,
Stein² (AB, Stein⁽²⁾): ἐγίνετο Stein¹ (S ap. Gaisf.)　　6 ἀντίοι ἔστασαν ?
Stein　　7 γέρα S　　8 ἡ om. B, Holder　　9 ἐσὸ AB ‖ ὠθησμόν
Cpr.P ‖ lacunam indic. Stein³

the whole army of the enemy to action
at close quarters : " the problem for
Pausanias was to keep his troops perfectly in hand . . until the onset of the
enemy became so general that they
would no longer have it in their power
to avoid a pitched battle," i.e. upon
Pausanias' own terms.)

62. 2. προεξαναστάντες πρότεροι οἱ
Τεγεῆται. The source, or sources, followed by Hdt. for the battle itself are
not too favourable to the Spartans, and
apparently prefer to give the Tegeatai
what credit is going ; cp. c. 70 infra.
It may, of course, be that the men of
Tegea were first on the move ; if so, it
was by order of Pausanias, for some
tactical reason of the moment ; but it is
more probable that Spartans and Tegeatai
advanced together.

πρότεροι is redundant, cp. 4. 145.
προεξαναστῆναι, cp. 8. 59, indicates
that they were sitting or lying down ;
cp. c. 72 infra.

ἐχώρεον ἐς τοὺς βαρβάρους : like
the Athenians at Marathon ; but the
δρόμῳ ἰεντο of 6. 112 quite surpasses this
advance ! The ἐχώρεον ἐς and the
ἐχώρεον ἐπί just below mark a distinction
without much difference. χρόνῳ κοτέ
marks, perhaps, the impatience of the
waiters rather than the actual length of
time : contr. χρ. ἐπὶ πολλόν just below.

6. οἱ Πέρσαι ἀντίοι τὰ τόξα μετέντες, 'the Persians put away their bows
and stood their ground to meet them,'
having recourse to their other weapons,
short spears, daggers (7. 61). What
exactly they did with the bows is not
clear ; perhaps they actually flung them
away : μετιέναι πολλὰ τῶν δακρύων, c. 16
supra, is to let them drop. Cp. 3. 128

μετῆκάν οἱ τὰς αἰχμάς, after which the
δορυφόροι had recourse to their ἀκινάκας.
The μάχη περὶ τὰ γέρρα which now
ensues is really πρῶτον in relation to
what follows ; but the preceding episode,
while the Persians are showering shots
on the Spartans from behind the fence
of shields, is an essential part of the
battle-piece. ἤδη just below practically
= δεύτερον.

7. ἐπεπτώκεε more literally than
ἔπιπτον above, but still a mild way of
putting it : Stein renders niedergeworfen
waren.

8. ἰσχυρή is of course predicative.
παρ' αὐτὸ τὸ Δημήτριον. Hdt.
knows only of one Demetrion in the
region, cp. c. 57 supra ; there were two,
if not three, that might come into the
account. It is here a problem not
merely which Demetrion is in question,
but what space, what change of place, if
any, here intervenes between the μάχη
περὶ τὰ γέρρα and the μάχη ἰσχυρὴ παρ'
αὐτὸ τὸ Δημήτριον. The shields had been
overthrown ; their owners probably
perished or fled. There may be a considerable amount of ground traversed
between the γέρρα and the Δημήτριον
here in question, and the bulk of the
men who struggled with the Spartans,
under the temple walls, may not be the
same men who had stood their ground,
higher up the hills, behind the γέρρα.
The Demetrion here in question may be
the ' Hysiatan,' and its site may still be
marked by the church of St. Demetrion,
though the Spartan position up by the
Moloeis may have been about, or in front
of, the Plataian Demetrion.

9. ὠθισμόν. One might have thought
that there would have been ' pushing '

10 δόρατα ἐπιλαμβανόμενοι κατέκλων οἱ βάρβαροι. λήματι μέν
νυν καὶ ῥώμῃ οὐκ ἥσσονες ἦσαν οἱ Πέρσαι· ἄνοπλοι δὲ ἐόντες
καὶ πρὸς ἀνεπιστήμονες [ἦσαν] καὶ οὐκ ὅμοιοι τοῖσι ἐναντίοισι
σοφίην, προεξαΐσσοντες [δὲ] κατ' ἕνα καὶ δέκα καὶ πλεῦνές
τε καὶ ἐλάσσονες συστρεφόμενοι, ἐσέπιπτον ἐς τοὺς Σπαρτιήτας
63 καὶ διεφθείροντο. τῇ δὲ ἐτύγχανε αὐτὸς ἐὼν Μαρδόνιος, ἀπ'
ἵππου τε μαχόμενος λευκοῦ ἔχων τε περὶ ἑωυτὸν λογάδας

10 λήματι PMarc. : λήμματι   11 ἥσσονες ἔσαν z ‖ οἱ πέρσαι Β,
om. α (Holder)   12 πρὸς secl. Krueger ‖ ἦσαν secl. van H., Kallenberg,
Holder, Stein³ : ἦσαν οἱ Πέρσαι R (Stein⁽¹⁾) ‖ ὅμοιοι CPMarc. z ‖ ἀντίοισι Β,
Schaefer ('male' van H.)   12, 13 καὶ et σοφίην del. Sitzler ‖ δὲ secl.
Stein³ (virgula pro puncto post σοφίην posita) ‖ καὶ ante πλεῦνές om. Β
14 ἐλάττονες CMarc.   63. 1 μαρδόνιος ἐὼν Marc.

before the γέρρα were overthrown. So
no doubt there had been : Hdt. seems to
use ὠθισμός for fighting at the closest
quarters (without special reference to its
etymological sense), cp. 7. 225, 8. 78.

In this particular case, if the battle
has shifted down the ridge, and is now
going forward beside the Demetrion (as
above located), the fugitive Persians
would probably be met by swarms advancing to the assault, or support, none
too regularly, and escape would be
doubly difficult. But we cannot be
sure that the words which follow do not
describe the scene immediately on the
overthrow of the γέρρα. Stein, indeed,
marks a lacuna after ὠθισμόν on the
ground that the next sentence is not in
logical or natural sequence of the argument or narrative : the now-exposed
barbarians seized on and tried to break
the large heavy spears of the Spartans—
no doubt in vain.

10. λήματι μέν νυν κτλ. This generous
tribute to the valour or spirit (λῆμα 7.
99) and bodily strength (ῥώμη 1. 31) of
the Persians is rather out of place in the
very midst of a description of the actual
engagement ; at any rate it interrupts a
narrative which has already become
involved in some obscurity, and when
resumed, just below, grows still more
unintelligible.

11. ἄνοπλοι, without ὅπλα, i.e. the
shields (and other heavy arms associated
therewith). There was a great inferiority
of armature on the Persian side for
fighting at close quarters : nothing
could have compensated for that (other
things, strength and courage, being
equal) but superior tactics, skill, ad-

dress ; but ἐπιστήμη, but σοφίη were
also on the side of the Greeks ; cp. 7.
211.

13. προεξαΐσσοντες : the προ- is here
local, not temporal. The tactics described are almost unintelligible of a
retreating force. Single combatants, or
small groups, separate themselves from
the main body and rush forward, out of
the ranks, form or rally in bands (συστρεφόμενοι, cp. c. 18 supra), some larger
some smaller, charge the Spartans, and
are annihilated.

Perhaps the obscurity arises from Hdt.
not distinguishing clearly between those
Persians who were in retreat and the
various forces hurrying up to their
support.

63. 1. τῇ δὲ ἐτύγχανε αὐτὸς ἐὼν
Μαρδόνιος : a more explicit local definition of the exact position of Mardonios
in the battle would be worth a good
deal for the reconstruction of the piece.
Was he παρ' αὐτῷ τῷ Δημητρίῳ, and, if
so, which Demetrion ! Was he really
at the head of his troops, and himself
leading the assault (cp. c. 59 supra) !
Or was he, where he should have been,
in a position to co-ordinate and direct
his whole forces !

ἀπ' ἵππου τε μαχόμενος λευκοῦ :
the specific mention, and memory, of the
fact that Mardonios was mounted on a
white horse might seem to imply that
those about him were unmounted, or at
least not mounted on white horses.
(His mount was perhaps a Nesaian ; cp.
8. 40.)

2. λογάδας Περσέων τοὺς ἀρίστους
χιλίους : the reference to 8. 113 is not
quite direct or obvious, but is generally

Περσέων τοὺς ἀρίστους χιλίους, ταύτῃ δὲ καὶ μάλιστα τοὺς
ἐναντίους ἐπίεσαν. ὅσον μέν νυν χρόνον Μαρδόνιος περιῆν,
οἱ δὲ ἀντεῖχον καὶ ἀμυνόμενοι κατέβαλλον πολλοὺς τῶν 5
Λακεδαιμονίων· ὡς δὲ Μαρδόνιος ἀπέθανε καὶ τὸ περὶ ἐκεῖνον
τεταγμένον ἐὸν ἰσχυρότατον ἔπεσε, οὕτω δὴ καὶ οἱ ἄλλοι
ἐτράποντο καὶ εἶξαν τοῖσι Λακεδαιμονίοισι. πλεῖστον γὰρ
σφέας ἐδηλέετο ἡ ἐσθὴς ἔρημος ἐοῦσα ὅπλων· πρὸς γὰρ
ὁπλίτας ἐόντες γυμνῆτες ἀγῶνα ἐποιεῦντο. ἐνθαῦτα ἥ τε δίκη 64

---

3 δὴ z   5 οἱ δὲ C, Stein², Holder : οἱ δὲ α, Stein¹, van H. : οἶδεν
R(V) ‖ κατεβάλλοντο edd. vett. (Gaisf.) ‖ τῶν : τοὺς R   7 ἐὼν Apr.B :
om. Marc. ‖ οἱ ἄλλοι om. C   9 ἐρῆμος CPMarc. z   10 ἐόντας B
(Gaisf.) ‖ γυμνῆται Ask. : γυμνῆτας B ‖ ἀγῶνας B : τὸν ἀγῶνα Iacobitz

---

taken to signify τὴν ἵππον τὴν χιλίην
there specified, though not described as
λογάδας. In 7. 40 ἱππόται χίλιοι ἐκ
Περσέων πάντων ἀπολελεγμένοι form the
head of the marching column ; and a
second chiliad of cavalry, similarly
described, precedes the Immortals (apparently) ; besides these two chiliads of
select cavalry there are two chiliads of
select infantry, αἰχμοφόροι. The chiliad
here mentioned might be any one of
these four chiliads, and the mere fact
that Mardonios himself is mounted
hardly decides the question.

3. ταύτῃ δὲ καὶ μάλιστα τοὺς ἐναντίους
ἐπίεσαν : sc. οἱ Πέρσαι. The statement
is astonishing for two reasons : (a) the
aorist ἐπίεσαν instead of the imp.
ἐπίεζον, especially after the number of
antecedent imperfects, is a puzzle ; (b)
the statement describes the action of an
advancing, an attacking party, not the
action of a retreating party, and the
Persians were already in retreat in
the previous chapter. But the sequence
of events in the narrative may be inaccurately chronologized. This sentence
(τῇ δὲ ἐτύγχανε . . ἐπίεσαν) emphasizes the
rôle of Mardonios in the battle, and
may hark back to a point already passed
by the general narrative in the previous
chapter. This suggestion might account,
perhaps, for the occurrence of the
anomalous aorist : it is virtually equivalent to a pluperfect in time.

4. ὅσον μέν νυν χρόνον M. περιῆν :
the actual time may be synchronous
with the χρόνον ἐπὶ πολλόν of c. 62,
during which ἐγίνετο ἡ μάχη ἰσχυρὴ παρ'
αὐτὸ τὸ Δημήτριον. The corresponding
sentence begins ὡς δὲ Μαρδόνιος ἀπέθανε
(when Mardonios had been killed).

οἱ δὲ ἀντεῖχον is the apodosis with δέ ;
the action described is that of men subject themselves to assault rather than
attacking. The difficulty may be solved
by the supposition above, that there was
a temporary rally of the Persians παρ'
αὐτὸ τὸ Δημήτριον, where Mardonios
himself sat on horseback, surrounded
doubtless by his staff and bodyguard,
which is here distinctly acting on the
defensive (ἀντεῖχον, ἀμυνόμενοι).

6. τὸ περὶ ἐκεῖνον τεταγμένον : neut.
abst. for concrete = οἱ περὶ αὐτὸν τεταγμένοι,
cp. α. 61 supra. There is nothing to
suggest that this body is cavalry, rather
the reverse. ἔπεσε, was cut to pieces,
or fell mortally wounded each in his
place ; cp. ἔπιπτον c. 61 supra.

7. οὕτω δή : the narrative, having
started afresh with Mardonios, now
arrives again at the point previously
reached, in general terms, in c. 62 ad f.
The τροπή here (ἐτράποντο) must be in
immediate sequence to the ὠθισμός there,
and the observation on the Persians'
ἐσθής here is exactly parallel to the reflexion there upon their inferiority in
arms and skill.

9. ἐδηλέετο, 'contributed to their
destruction' ; the effect is, however,
not positive, but negative, privative.
γυμνῆτες, 'light-armed foot-soldiers,'
a word not elsewhere used by Hdt., but
cp. Tyrtaios, 11. 35, quoted c. 48 supra.

64. 1. ἥ τε δίκη τοῦ Λεωνίδεω. At
this point Hdt. treats the battle as over,
the victory as won, and goes off on a
number of side issues, oracular, portentous, biographic, anecdotal, to wit, the
fulfilment of a Delphic utterance ; the providential preservation of the Demetrion
from defilement ; the fate of Mardonios,

τοῦ φόνου τοῦ Λεωνίδεω κατὰ τὸ χρηστήριον τοῖσι Σπαρτιήτῃσι ἐκ Μαρδονίου ἐπετελέετο, καὶ νίκην ἀναιρέεται καλλίστην
ἁπασέων τῶν ἡμεῖς ἴδμεν Παυσανίης ὁ Κλεομβρότου τοῦ
5 Ἀναξανδρίδεω· τῶν δὲ κατύπερθέ οἱ προγόνων τὰ οὐνόματα
εἴρηται ἐς Λεωνίδην· ὡυτοὶ γάρ σφι τυγχάνουσι ἐόντες.
ἀποθνήσκει δὲ Μαρδόνιος ὑπὸ Ἀειμνήστου ἀνδρὸς ἐν Σπάρτῃ
λογίμου, ὃς χρόνῳ ὕστερον μετὰ τὰ Μηδικὰ ἔχων ἄνδρας

64. 2 τὸ τοῖσι ß   3 γενόμενον excidisse susp. Kallenberg ‖ ἐπι-
τελέετο ß, Schaefer, Gaisford   5 τῶν . . . ἐόντες suspecta habeo   6
οὗτοι αCMarc.   7 αἰμνήστου α : ἀριμνήστου ß, Plutarch. Aristid. 19,
Holder, van H. : cf. c. 72 infra ‖ ἀνδρὸς ἐόντος ἐν Marc.   8 χρόνον id.

and that of the man who slew him ; the
glory of Pausanias.

2. κατὰ τὸ χρηστήριον : the reference
is clear, though not explicit, to the
anecdote 8. 114 supra, which of course
was an anachronism ; given the death of
Mardonios at Plataia by the hands of a
Spartan (!), and the 'prediction' was inevitable. This whole chapter (with the
possible exception of a couple of sentences)
reads like an insertion by Hdt. into the
first draft of his history, and may
perhaps be put down to his 'second
hand' ; cp. Introduction, § 9.

3. νίκην ἀναιρέεται κτλ. Hdt. treats
the victory as a fait accompli, as though
the whole battle had been simply
between Mardonios with his Persians on
the one side and Pausanias with his
Spartans or Lakedaimonians on the
other ; the centre, the left wing, are
treated here as negligible quantities :
this treatment can hardly be Attic, or
phil-Attic tradition, or theory, but it
might very well be 'Delphic,' cp.
Thucyd. 1. 132. 2, or picked up at Delphi
by Hdt. himself, or his authorities. On
the formula καλλίστην . . τῶν ἡμεῖς
ἴδμεν cp. 8. 105. 3. Is it not a metrical
tag ? (τῶν ἡμέες ἴδμεν).

νίκην ἀναιρέεσθαι reportare victoriam
6. 103, cp. c. 33 supra (ἀγῶνας), Ὀλυμπιάδα 6. 70 etc. The express recognition
of the personal merits or service of
Pausanias (to the exclusion of Euryanax)
in this passage is remarkable : Plataia is
his victory, the most ideal (καλλίστην)
victory on record—Marathon, Salamis
not excepted ! The use of the patronymic,
here raised to the third power, ἐκ
τριγονίας, is also remarkable : plainly and
purely for rhetorical effect.

5. τῶν δὲ . . ἐόντες is, however, an
addition with somewhat an unfortunate

effect ; if genuine, it is a very clear
reference back to 7. 186 : such a bathos
can hardly belong to the first draft of
the description of the great battle ; the
language reads, however, like authentic
Hdt. κατύπερθε, cp. 5. 28. οἱ, possessive,
or perhaps 'ethical' dat. ἐς Λεωνίδην,
either 'down to Leonidas,' or 'with
reference to Leonidas,' à propos of
Leonidas. (As Leonidas could not be
included, the latter seems the preferable
rendering.)

6. ὡυτοὶ . . ἐόντες, not ταὐτὰ . .
ἐόντα. Rawlinson, doubtless feeling the
literary and stylistic flaw of this passage,
translates it very loosely : 'I omit to
recount his other ancestors, since they
are the same with those of Leonidas.'

7. ἀποθνήσκει . . ὑπό : cp. c. 37
supra.

Ἀειμνήστου ἀνδρὸς ἐν Σπάρτῃ
λογίμου. It is unfortunate that there is
any uncertainty in the exact form of the
proper name, though 'Aeimnestos' and
'Arimnestos' come to much the same
sense ; cp. c. 72 infra. (Some persons
with an inability to give value to the
rho would pronounce the two forms in-
distinguishably.) Blakesley very acutely
suggested that this ἀνὴρ ἐν Σπάρτῃ
λόγιμος was not himself a Spartiate ; for
(i.) Plutarch (de or. def. 5, Mor. 412)
says Mardonios was killed by a stone,
and a Spartiate would not be throwing
stones (but cp. c. 55 supra !) ; (ii.)
Thucydides (3. 52. 5) has a Plataian,
one 'Lakon, son of Aeimnestos,' and
an ἀνὴρ ἐν Σπάρτῃ λόγιμος would be
very likely to have a son named Λάκων.
(But what, then, of his service in the
Messenian war ? see below.)

8. ὃς χρόνῳ ὕστερον κτλ. is certainly
a reference to events in the Pentekontae-
tris, and appears to be a reference to the

τριηκοσίους συνέβαλε ἐν Στενυκλήρῳ πολέμου ἐόντος Μεσσηνίοισι πᾶσι, καὶ αὐτός τε ἀπέθανε καὶ οἱ τριηκόσιοι. ἐν δὲ **65**
Πλαταιῆσι οἱ Πέρσαι ὡς ἐτράποντο ὑπὸ τῶν Λακεδαιμονίων,
ἔφευγον οὐδένα κόσμον ἔς <τε> τὸ στρατόπεδον τὸ ἑωυτῶν

---

9 συνέβαλλε C ‖ μεσσηνίοισι ΒC: Μεσσηνίοισί τε z   10 πᾶσι:
ἀποστᾶσι Naber   65. 2 πλαταίησι a: πλαταίησι(ν V) Β ‖ ἐτρά-
πησαν z   3 <τε> coni. Stein¹, adm. van H., Stein³ ‖ ἑωυτὸν Β

'third' Messenian war (464-454 B.C.).
The reference is obscure. Hdt. does not
clearly indicate that the war is between
the Lakedaimonians and Messenians ; he
does not describe the character or nature
of the corps of 300 men under Aeimnestos ; he does not say on which side
Aeimnestos was fighting ; he gives no
details or circumstances in regard to
the engagement. This is, in short, one
of the obscurest references to contemporary events in the whole work. Hdt.,
however, does not say that Aeimnestos
was a Spartan, nor that the men under
his command were Spartans. Blakesley
says : "no doubt Aeimnestos commanded
the garrison which was intended to maintain military possession of the country."
But that seems to me very doubtful :
how came a Plataian by such an appointment ? Rather we might suppose that
the Plataian, with a contingent of his
fellow-citizens, 300 strong, was (*pace*
ἰδίᾳ in the following) with the Athenian
contingent in the Messenian war ; cp.
Thuc. 3. 54. 5 καὶ ὑμῖν, ὦ Λακεδαιμόνιοι,
ἰδίᾳ, ὅτεπερ δὴ μέγιστος φόβος περιέστη
τὴν Σπάρτην μετὰ τὸν σεισμὸν τῶν ἐς
Ἰθώμην Εἱλώτων ἀποστάντων τὸ τρίτον
μέρος ἡμῶν αὐτῶν ἐξεπέμψαμεν ἐς ἐπι-
κουρίαν· ὧν οὐκ εἰκὸς ἀμνημονεῖν (Δάκων
son of Αἱλιμνηστος is speaking, 427 B.C.).
ἔχων, 'commanding.'
9. τριηκοσίους: if this was τὸ τρίτον
μέρος the full number of Plataians at that
time would be 900. In c. 28 *supra* there
are 600 with the Athenians on the left ;
that may be ⅔ (and ⅓ may be with the
Spartans, cp. c. 72 *infra*, or the number
of Plataians in 464 B.C. may somewhat
have risen. In 429 B.C. it had fallen
again, op. *l.c.*).
συνέβαλε: i.e. συμβολὴν ἐποίησε,
cp. c. 41 *supra*.
Στενυκλήρῳ: the old Dorian, or
quasi-Dorian, capital of Messenia (cp.
Strabo 361), where Kresphontes had built
his palace, and established a residence
(cp. Pausan. 4. 3. 7), situate on a plain

(Pausan. 4. 33. 4) in the midst of the
land, a natural meeting-place for the
Messenians (Paus. 4. 6. 6)—in fact, the
centre of the upper of the two plains into
which hollow Messenia naturally divides;
cp. Curtius, *Peloponnesos* ii. 125 f. It was
an unwalled place, however, and has
left no remains *in situ*, *ib.* 136.
65. 1. ἐν δὲ Πλαταιῆσι, 'to return
to Plataia,' the name of the city for
the land ; cp. c. 16 *supra*. Even so,
there may be an inaccuracy. The actual
scene of the Persian repulse was perhaps
rather in the confines of Hysiai than in
the land of Plataia proper ; though the
position occupied at the Androkrateion
and Gargaphia had no doubt been ἐν τῇ
Πλαταιίδι, cp. c. 25 *supra*.
2. ἐτράποντο Baehr takes as imperf.
passive, but renders *in fugam conversi
sunt*; Stein (more accurately) *in fugam
vertebantur*.
3. οὐδένα κόσμον: cp. 8. 117. The
Persians may have advanced originally
in good order; not so, however, the
rest of the βαρβαρικὰ τέλη, cp. c. 59
supra.
τὸ στρατόπεδον τὸ ἑωυτῶν appears
to be distinguishable from τὸ τεῖχος τὸ
ξύλινον to this extent, that the στρατόπεδον was considerably larger than the
τεῖχος, cp. c. 15 *supra*. But Stein's
theory that the τεῖχος was on the south
side of the Asopos and the στρατόπεδον
on the north side of the Asopos, and,
(apparently) quite distinct and separate,
is hardly satisfactory. The distinction
between the στρατόπεδον and the τεῖχος
is perfectly sound and intelligible, even
if both were on the same side of the
river and locally continuous with each
other ; it is a distinction analogous to
that between ἡ πόλις and τὸ ἄστυ. Again,
the addition of the words τὸ ἐποιήσαντο
ἐν μοίρῃ τῇ Θηβαΐδι cannot possibly mean
that the τεῖχος was on Theban territory
while the στρατόπεδον was not ! And
if that were the meaning, then the
στρατόπεδον would have to be placed

καὶ ἐς τὸ τεῖχος τὸ ξύλινον τὸ ἐποιήσαντο ἐν μοίρῃ τῇ
5 Θηβαΐδι. θῶμα δέ μοι ὅκως παρὰ τῆς Δήμητρος τὸ ἄλσος
μαχομένων οὐδὲ εἷς ἐφάνη τῶν Περσέων οὔτε ἐσελθὼν ἐς τὸ
τέμενος οὔτε ἐναποθανών, περί τε τὸ ἱρὸν οἱ πλεῖστοι ἐν τῷ
βεβήλῳ ἔπεσον. δοκέω δέ, εἴ τι περὶ τῶν θείων πρηγμάτων

---

5 θῶνμα Pz, Stein¹ ‖ περὶ τῆς z   7 περὶ τὸ ἱρόν· οἱ δὲ πλεῖστοι ßPz
('fortasse rectius si π. τ. ἱ. ut gloasema deleveris' van H.) ‖ τῷ fortasse
delend. cens. Kallenberg

---

south of the river, and the τεῖχος north,
whereas Stein places the τεῖχος south,
and the στρατόπεδον north.

In my opinion the camp (στρατόπεδον)
and the fort (τεῖχος) were continuous;
the camp was on the left (north) bank
of the Asopos, along the road from
Erythrai to Thebes; the fortified portion
of the camp may have been projected
across the river on to the south bank,
so that a part of the river flowed right
through the fortification, or at least a
tête de pont may have been fortified to
the south of the river on the said road.
This τεῖχος was an ἔρυμα to the στρατός
in any case, and a κρησφύγετον in case
of disaster; cp. c. 15 supra. It probably
contained the quarters of all the combatants, and assuredly of the Persians
and picked troops.

4. ἐν μοίρῃ τῇ Θηβαΐδι: μοῖρα here is
as strictly topical as it ever can be; cp.
8. 23 τῆς Ἑλλοπίης μοίρης δὲ τῆς
Ἱστιαιήτιδος τὰς παραθαλασσίας χώρας
πάσας ἐπέδραμον, 5. 57 οἴκεον δὲ τῆς
χώρης ταύτης (sc. τῆς γῆς τῆς νῦν Βοιωτίης
καλεομένης) ἀπολαχόντες τὴν Ταναγρικὴν
μοῖραν. There is nothing to restrict the
word here to one side of the Asopos, least
of all the south side. ἡ Θηβαῒς μοῖρα is
all the portion of Boiotia in the dominion
of Thebes; it cannot be distinguished
from ἡ Θηβαῒς γῆ nor from οἱ τῶν Θηβαίων
χῶροι (cp. c. 15 supra). But, at least
as against Plataia and Hysiai, the Asopos
was its boundary, 6. 108.

5. θῶμα δέ μοι: the cause of this
marvel Hdt. explains just below as a
direct divine interposition to bring about
the given result. On the supposition
that the Demetrion in question is marked
by the church of St. Demetrion Dr.
Grundy explains the fact by the lie of
the ground: the Persians in rushing back
to their laager and camp would naturally
avoid the delay of climbing up the hill,
on the top of which the Demetrion was
situate, and would naturally rush along

the lower slopes and stream valleys (A⁴,
A⁵) either side the 'Long Ridge.' This
plausible suggestion remains equally
valid whether the routed fugitives were
mounted or on foot. But it is possible
that Mardonios himself had occupied
this hill during the battle, in order to
survey the action; and Hdt. (or his
source) would have had small excuse
for wonder if the area had not been
within the field of battle. At an earlier
stage in the proceedings the Demetrion
may have been held by the Spartans
(Amompharetos? cp. c. 53 supra). Hdt.
does not say that no Greeks fought or
fell within the enclosure. See also next
note.

τῆς Δήμητρος τὸ ἄλσος: this grove
(cp. 7. 197) is a new feature in the
Herodotean landscape and may very
suitably be imagined growing round the
church of St. Demetrion, upon the hill-
top, which is of decidedly conical formation. Hdt. apparently conceives this
point as the very centre and stress of
the fight, as οἱ πλεῖστοι, sc. τῶν Περσέων,
fell in the immediate vicinity of the
Holy Place, though upon unconsecrated
ground (ἐν τῷ βεβήλῳ, cp. Thuc. 4. 97.
3). As the Persians are here in flight
the slaughter among them may well
have been great, but we can scarcely
feel quite sure that the case of the
Persians was quite as Hdt. reports, no
doubt bona fide; the statement is so
exactly what would afterwards have
been believed and said ad maiorem Deae
gloriam.

8. δοκέω δέ: an expression of uncertainty; cp. οὐ δοκέω 7. 186, and
δόκησιν δὲ δεῖ λέγειν 7. 185—a proceeding
unobjectionable in purely human matters,
such as the number of the Persian forces,
but perhaps not advisable περὶ τῶν θείων
πρηγμάτων. This reserve is not an expression of incredulity on Hdt.'s part,
but seems to arise rather from a belief
in the vindictive nature of the gods, and

δοκέειν δεῖ, ἡ θεὸς αὐτή σφεας οὐκ ἐδέκετο ἐμπρήσαντας τὸ
ἱρὸν τὸ ἐν Ἐλευσῖνι ἀνάκτορον.   10

Αὕτη μέν νυν ἡ μάχη ἐπὶ τοσοῦτο ἐγένετο. Ἀρτάβαζος 66
δὲ ὁ Φαρνάκεος αὐτίκα τε οὐκ ἠρέσκετο κατ᾽ ἀρχὰς λειπο-
μένου Μαρδονίου ἀπὸ βασιλέος, καὶ τότε πολλὰ ἀπαγορεύων

---

9 δοκεῖν A, van H. ‖ ἐδέξατο CPMarc. z ‖ τὸ ἱρὸν del. Valckenaer,
Holder, van H.   10 ἐλευσῖνοι R ‖ ἀνακτόριον BPcorr. z : del. Bredow
66. 1 τοσοῦτον Bz   2 ἀρέσκετο z ‖ καταρχὰς ABRz ‖ λιπομένου z
3 ὑπὸ van H. ‖ βασιλῆος z

---

an apprehension that such speculations
might be visited with a nemesis : οὐ γὰρ
ἐᾷ φρονέειν μέγα ὁ θεὸς ἄλλον ἢ ἑωυτόν
7. 10.

9. σφεας οὐκ ἐδέκετο, 'rejected them,'
refused them entrance. δέκεσθαι, sc. as
ἱκέτας, or ἐπὶ ξεινίῃ. Would the Greeks
have spared the lives of any Persians
found in the Holy Place, or simply have
taken them out and slain them ἐν τῷ
βεβήλῳ ? Hdt. does not go so far as to
say that Demeter interfered directly to
procure the victory of the Greeks, any
more than Hera, c. 61 supra. The story
of the war is comparatively free from
the miracle manifest, apart from the
Delphic apology (8. 35 ff.). Cp. Introduction, § 11.

ἐμπρήσαντας . . τὸ ἐν Ἐλευσῖνι :
this outrage has not been expressly recorded before ; cp. cc. 13, 14 supra.
Mardonios has put the saddle on the
wrong horse, c. 42 supra. It is not
clear whether the destruction at Eleusis
was in 480 B.C. (8. 50), or in the present
year (c. 14 supra). Baehr defends both
ἱρόν and ἀνάκτορον in this passage.
Valckenaer had condemned τὸ ἱρὸν,
Bredow ἀνάκτορον. Hdt. nowhere else
uses the word. Euripides applies it to
(1) Delphic temple of Apollo, Andr.
1157 ; (2) Tauric temple of Artemis, Iph.
T. 41, 66 ; (3) Trojan temples, Troad.
15 : Pausanias, 2. 14. 4, of a part of the
Demetrion at Keleai, near Phleiûs. In
Athenaeus first, apparently, we get the
word used with a special or restricted
reference to Eleusis : 213 τὸ σεμνὸν ἀνάκτορον τοῖν θεοῖν, cp. 167. Dr. Frazer has
suggested that it designated the Great
Hall of Initiation (τὸ τελεστήριον), cp. n.
to Pausan. l.c. But Pollux, 1. 9, still
has ἀνάκτορον (seemingly as an adj.) for
the ἄδυτον or any χωρίον ἄβατον τοῦ ἱεροῦ,
i.e. of any temple. ἀνάκτορον is, of
course, the house of the ἄναξ (or ἄνασσα).

66. 1. αὕτη . . ἐπὶ τοσοῦτο ἐγένετο,
'in this battle nothing further took place,'
i.e. the battle between the Spartans and
the Persians, which is here treated as
though it were whole and complete in
itself. To the Persian combatants must
be added the other non-Hellenic divisions, which have also been represented
as taking part in ' this battle,' cp. c. 59
supra. Hdt.'s method of treating the
conflict between the Persians and
Spartans as one battle, and the conflict
between the Athenians and Thebans as
another, corresponds probably more or
less to differences in his sources ; while
some failure in his sources may help to
account for his inadequate treatment of
the fortunes of the centre. Moreover,
Hdt. here makes an effort to mark the
exact point in the struggle at which
Artabazos took his departure (when
the battle had reached this point, Artabazos—ἐποίησε τοιάδε).   With him,
perhaps, departed the Makedonians and
others in the Persian right wing, which
he probably commanded.

Ἀρτάβαζος . . ὁ Φαρνάκεος : the
patronymic is so little called for by the
occasion, that it may better be supposed
a repetition from the source of the
eccentric story which ensues.

2. αὐτίκα . . κατ᾽ ἀρχάς, 'from the
very first' ; cp. for the expression 7. 88,
and for the situation referred to 8. 115,
126.   The use of ἀπό instead of ὑπό is
remarkable ; cp. 7. 102, 5. 2, etc.

3. καὶ τότε : not the point reached in
the narrative, in the immediate context,
but a much earlier one, viz. in c. 41
supra (a backward reference).

πολλὰ ἀπαγορεύων οὐδὲν ἤνυε recalls the formula put into the mouth of
a Persian in the story of Thersander,
c. 16 supra : πολλὰ φρονέοντα μηδενὸς
κρατέειν.

οὐδὲν ἤνυε, συμβάλλειν οὐκ ἐῶν· ἐποίησέ τε αὐτὸς τοιάδε ὡς
5 οὐκ ἀρεσκόμενος τοῖσι πρήγμασι τοῖσι ἐκ Μαρδονίου ποιευ-
μένοισι. τῶν ἐστρατήγεε ὁ Ἀρτάβαζος (εἶχε δὲ δύναμιν οὐκ
ὀλίγην ἀλλὰ καὶ ἐς τέσσερας μυριάδας ἀνθρώπων περὶ ἑωυτόν),
τούτους, ὅκως ἡ συμβολὴ ἐγίνετο, εὖ ἐξεπιστάμενος τὰ ἔμελλε
ἀποβήσεσθαι ἀπὸ τῆς μάχης, ἦγε κατηρτημένως, παραγγείλας

---

6 ὁ om. aC, Holder   7 τέσσαρας ACR(V) ‖ αὐτὸν B   8
ἐγένετο B   9 συμβήσεσθαι S ‖ ἀπὸ τῆς μάχης delenda suspic. Kallenberg ‖ ἦγε BPz : ἦϊε ‖ κατηρτημένως a, Stein, Holder : κατηρτισμένως B,
van H.: κατηρτημένος CPMarc.: κατηρτισμένος z, Krueger, Baehr: κατηρτη-
μένους ? Blakesley : κατηρτισμένους ? van H.

---

4. **συμβάλλειν οὐκ ἐῶν**, prohibiting,
arguing against, 'trying to prevent a
general engagement,' cp. c. 41 *supra*;
μηδὲ ἀνακινδυνεύειν συμβάλλοντας.

ἐποίησέ τε: the τε marks the
climax (after the two items marked by
the previous τε and καί, cp. c. 58 *supra*).

5. **ἀρεσκόμενος**: passive (not middle,
as in 6. 128). The active is used with
accus. of the person, as well as with the
dative (3. 142), so 3. 34, 4. 78, and
7. 160.

ἐκ, instead of ὑπό, cp. 7. 175 ; cp.
c. 64 *supra*.

The *asyndeton* which follows may
help to mark the laboured character of
the apology for Artabazos, which is far
from coherent or close in its argument.
As Stein points out, Hdt. (or rather,
perhaps, his source) is anxious to explain
and justify the treacherous conduct of
Artabazos ; while Blakesley regards the
difficulty as arising from an "Hellenic
interpretation" of a proceeding which
the Greeks did not understand : he even
accepts the suggestion of 8. 126 that the
reputation of Artabazos was raised by
his conduct at Plataia, that is, the skill
with which he brought off his division.
It is quite possible that the action,
position, and proceedings of Artabazos
have not been correctly envisaged by
Greek tradition, and that, imperfect
information having created a problem,
apologetics were called in to reconcile
the facts of the subsequent career of
Artabazos with his supposed conduct at
Plataia. But if Artabazos was really at
Plataia with 40,000 men, no amount of
insight or foresight, of wit or wisdom,
could conceal or excuse his shameful
treachery to Mardonios, and thereby to
the Persian cause. However, the Greek
idea that he was in Boiotia, or within

reach of Mardonios at the time of the
battle, may be erroneous. It is this idea
which creates the problem.

6. **εἶχε**, 'was in command of . .'
δύναμιν, cp. 4. 155. The 40,000 men of
this passage may be reconciled with the
60,000 of 8. 126 by the supposition
that Artabazos had lost 20,000 in the
siege of Poteidaia and his other operations ; but the harmony is our own
doing. We are in the presence of more
or less independent stories, and, it may
be, of independent estimates of the
numbers under Artabazos' command.
Each figure represents a division of
50,000, or one-sixth of the Grand Army ;
but, perhaps, in the one case a myriad
of cavalry has been added, and in the
other case subtracted, or not included.
The position assigned to Artabazos in
tradition makes him only a little inferior
to Mardonios, and discounts the larger
estimate for the latter's army. Moreover, 40,000 is just about the figure
for the Makedonian and Hellenic contingent, minus the Thebans (cp. next c.),
a coincidence which suggests that, if
present at the battle of Plataia, he
was in command of the right wing,
including the Makedonians, medizing
Greeks, etc. Their attitude and conduct
may help to explain his.

7. **ἀνθρώπων**, as frequently; cp. Index.

8. **εὖ ἐξεπιστάμενος**: the verb is
doubly reinforced, and denotes real
knowledge. Artabazos was one προειδὼς
πλεῦν τι, c. 41 *supra*, and his conduct
itself (according to the story) secures the
fulfilment of his previsions and predictions. **ἀπό** here = ἐκ, **ὅκως** = ὡς.

9. **κατηρτημένως**. Stein prefers the
participial adverb, and understands it as
meaning *wohl vorbereitet*, *in wohl über-
legter Weise*, i.e. with all due prepara-

κατὰ τὠυτὸ ἰέναι πάντας τῇ ἂν αὐτὸς ἐξηγέηται <καὶ> ὅκως 10
ἂν αὐτὸν ὁρῶσι σπουδῆς ἔχοντα. ταῦτα παραγγείλας ὡς ἐς
μάχην ἦγε δῆθεν τὸν στρατόν. προτερέων δὲ τῆς ὁδοῦ ὁρᾷ
καὶ δὴ φεύγοντας τοὺς Πέρσας· οὕτω δὴ οὐκέτι τὸν αὐτὸν
κόσμον κατηγέετο, ἀλλὰ τὴν ταχίστην ἐτρόχαζε φεύγων οὔτε
ἐς τὸ ξύλινον οὔτε ἐς τὸ Θηβαίων τεῖχος ἀλλ' ἐς Φωκέας, 15
ἐθέλων ὡς τάχιστα ἐπὶ τὸν Ἑλλήσποντον ἀπικέσθαι. καὶ 67
δὴ οὗτοι μὲν ταύτῃ ἐτράποντο· τῶν δὲ ἄλλων Ἑλλήνων τῶν

10 κατὰ τοῦτο Β: κατ' αὐτὸ Pz ‖ ἐξηγέηται Βz: ἐξηγῆται reliqui,
Holder, van H. ‖ <καὶ> Stein³   11 ἂν om. Β ‖ ὁρέωσι z, Stein¹,
van H.   12 προτερέως C: προτερεύων z ‖ ὁρᾷ Stein³: ὁρᾶι aC: ὥρα Β,
Stein¹ ³, Holder, van H.   15 εἰς R ‖ ξύλινον τεῖχος S, Bekker, Palm
et τεῖχος post Θηβαίων retinentes ‖ ἀλλὰ a   67. 2 ἄλλων secl.
van H.

tion and reflexion on his part, deliberately, of set purpose. But the words
οὕτω δὴ οὐκέτι τὸν αὐτὸν κόσμον κατηγέετο
below point to the meaning of the word
here, whatever its form, as having a
more material reference to the order and
appearance of the men being led : 'well-
hung, well-adjusted, well-ordered.' The
verb καταρτάω = virtually = καταρτίζω
is curious, and in any case rare ; cp. 3.
80 and App. Crit. Krüger has κατηρτισμένος with active or transitive force ;
nachdem er sie geordnet hatte, 'after
putting them in battle-array' (or marching array); κατηρτισμένους (Kampf-bereit,
Sitzler) is of course to be taken as
passive.

10. κατὰ τὠυτὸ ἰέναι . . τῇ ἂν αὐτὸς
ἐξηγέηται κτλ. Such directions might be
given by the leader of a company, but
are absurd as the general orders of the
commander of a corps d'armée. κατὰ
τὠυτὸ may mean 'in the same way'
(merely anticipating ὅκως . . σπουδῆς),
or 'in the same direction' (merely anticipating τῇ . . ἐξηγέηται), or it might be
taken to cover both, or possibly it might
have the sense of keeping together, not
breaking ranks (cp. πάντας). They are
to march all together, they are to follow
him, and not to exceed or fall short of
his pace or speed (σπουδή, cp. c. 89
infra. Mardonios had led his men
δρόμῳ, c. 59 supra ; Artabazos probably
was leading his βάδην) ; and they can
do all that by keeping their eyes on him
(ὁρῶσι). Hdt. treats the march of
50,000 men as though it were the
excursion of a small mountaineering

party. The apologist may say that the
general's orders were issued to his
officers, myriarchs, chiliarchs ; even so,
they are irrational.

11. ὡς ἐς μάχην . . δῆθεν : apparently he led them at first in battle-array,
and presumably in the direction of
Plataia ; but what was his starting-point ?
Was he on the Asopos, in command of
the right ? Or was he at Thebes, in
command of reserves ? Or was he even
further away ? He had been marching
some time before the rout of the Persians
came to his knowledge (ὁρᾷ).

12. προτερέων, cp. c. 57 supra. καὶ
δή = ἤδη, c. 48 supra.

13. οὐκέτι τὸν αὐτὸν κόσμον κατηγέετο.
He apparently changed from battle-
array into marching order, substituting
the agmen for the acies, and (ἐτρόχαζε)
'wheeled' round (or perhaps only
'wheeled along,' i.e. ran, cp. Xenoph.
Anab. 7. 3. 46), fled to Phokis, with a
view to reaching the 'Hellespont.' He
had previously advocated their falling
back on τὸ τεῖχος τὸ Θηβαίων, c. 41.
Hellespont may here be used in the
largest sense ; he made for Byzantion
c. 89.

67. 2. τῶν δὲ ἄλλων . . ἐθελοκακεόντων. 'The other Greeks' are in
contrast to the Boiotians, and must be
taken to cover the Makedonians, and to
number, on Hdt.'s own showing, at least
40,000 ! cp. c. 32 supra.

τῶν μετὰ βασιλέος : cp. c. 61
supra. The action, or inaction, of these
'Hellenes' is most remarkable, and
Hdt. seems to make curiously little of

μετὰ βασιλέος ἐθελοκακεόντων, Βοιωτοὶ Ἀθηναίοισι ἐμαχέσαντο
χρόνον ἐπὶ συχνόν· οἱ γὰρ μηδίζοντες τῶν Θηβαίων, οὗτοι
5 εἶχον προθυμίην οὐκ ὀλίγην μαχόμενοί τε καὶ οὐκ ἐθελοκα-
κέοντες, οὕτω ὥστε τριηκόσιοι αὐτῶν οἱ πρῶτοι καὶ ἄριστοι
ἐνθαῦτα ἔπεσον ὑπὸ Ἀθηναίων. ὡς δὲ ἐτράποντο καὶ οὗτοι,
ἔφευγον ἐς τὰς Θήβας, οὐ τῇ περ οἱ Πέρσαι καὶ τῶν ἄλλων
συμμάχων ὁ πᾶς ὅμιλος, οὔτε διαμαχεσάμενος οὐδενὶ οὔτε τι
68 ἀποδεξάμενος, ἔφευγον. δηλοῖ τέ μοι ὅτι πάντα τὰ πρήγματα

---

3 βασιλέως R : βασιλῆος z   4 ἐπὶ συχνόν om. R   5 ἔχον z ‖
μαχόμενοί ΒP : μαχεόμενοί   6 αὐτέων z   8 οὐ τῇ περ Stein,
Holder : οὐ τῇπερ Bekker, van H. : οὐκ ῇ ‖ post Πέρσαι interpunx. Holder,
van H., plerique   9 διαμαχεσάμενοι Krueger ‖ οὐδὲν R   10 ἀπο-
δεξάμενός τι Pz : ἀποδεξάμενοι Krueger   68. 1 τε ἐμοὶ Β

---

it. On his own showing some 40,000 of
Mardonios' allies are useless, or worse
than useless, in the supreme hour.
None of the Greeks on the Persian side,
with the exception of the Thebans,
showed any fight ; the whole right wing,
with that one exception, was *hors de
combat*. This arrangement left a fairly
easy field for the Athenians. Was there
not already an understanding to this
effect ? The omission of any explicit
notice of the Makedonians at this point
is remarkable. The action of Artabazos
and his section of the army can hardly
be divorced from the action, or inaction,
of these medizing Greeks.

3. **Βοιωτοὶ Ἀθηναίοισι ἐμαχέσαντο.**
This situation is apparently treated
almost as a separate μάχη. Βοιωτοί
might cover more than Θηβαῖοι. The
golden shields dedicated by the Athenians
at Delphi ἀπὸ Μήδων καὶ Θηβαίων
(Aischines *in Ctesiph.* 116), if genuine,
may represent the political position of the
Thebans as heads of Boiotia at the time,
but perhaps rather expresses the intensity of anti-Theban feeling at Athens.
The very next words here show that even
in Thebes the Thebans were divided.

4. **οἱ μηδίζοντες τῶν Θηβαίων** implies
the presence of others ; so too Thucyd.
3. 63. 3 f. (in a Theban speech).

6. **τριηκόσιοι αὐτῶν** : a favourite,
perhaps a conventional figure. **οἱ πρῶτοι
καὶ ἄριστοι** has a strong political flavour
about it, though the immediate question
is one of pure fighting.

7. **ἔπεσον ὑπό** : cp. c. 37 *supra*.

καὶ οὗτοι, 'as well as the Persians.'
Can we be quite sure that the fight
between the Athenians and the Thebans

out-lasted the fight between the Spartans
and the Persians ? The tardy arrival of
the Athenians at the ξύλινον τεῖχος (c. 70
infra) might be easily accounted for
otherwise, by a greater distance to cover,
by an initial doubt how far to pursue,
and so on. Yet it is possible that the
retreat, or flight, of the Thebans on the
Persian right wing was determined not
so much by the valour of the Athenians,
as by the victory of the Spartans over
the other wing. That consideration is
obscured by the way in which Hdt. has
isolated the operations upon the right
from those upon the left, to say nothing
of the retreat of Artabazos and his
myriads !

8. **οὐ τῇ περ οἱ Πέρσαι** : by a different
road to that taken by the Persians.
No doubt the Thebans retreated along
the direct road from Plataia to Thebes,
while the Persians recrossed the Asopos
(as far as possible) by the bridge on the
other road, from Erythrai to Thebes.

τῶν ἄλλων συμμάχων can hardly
reinclude the medizing Greeks, who
have been already accounted for, nor yet
the men under the command of Artabazos,
but rather refers to the nations, other
than the Persians proper, included in the
forces of Mardonios, cp. c. 31 *supra*;
the βαρβαρικὰ τέλη of c. 59 *supra*.
ἄλλων is idiomatic ; neither the Persians
nor the Thebans are here referred to as
σύμμαχοι.

9. **ὅμιλος** : cp. c. 60 *supra*.

διαμάχεσθαι ought to mean 'to
fight to a finish,' op. c. 48 *supra*. **ἀπο-
δέξασθαί** (N.B. middle) τι, cp. c. 27
supra.

68. 1. **δηλοῖ** Schweighaeuser, followed

τῶν βαρβάρων ἤρτητο ἐκ Περσέων, εἰ καὶ τότε οὗτοι πρὶν ἢ
καὶ συμμεῖξαι τοῖσι πολεμίοισι ἔφευγον, ὅτι καὶ τοὺς Πέρσας
ὤρων. οὕτω τε πάντες ἔφευγον πλὴν τῆς ἵππου τῆς τε
ἄλλης καὶ τῆς Βοιωτίης· αὕτη δὲ τοσαῦτα προσωφέλεε τοὺς 5
φεύγοντας, αἰεί τε πρὸς τῶν πολεμίων ἄγχιστα ἐοῦσα ἀπέρ-
γουσά τε τοὺς φιλίους φεύγοντας ἀπὸ τῶν Ἑλλήνων.

Οἱ μὲν δὴ νικῶντες εἵποντο τοὺς Ξέρξεω διώκοντές τε καὶ 69
φονεύοντες. ἐν δὲ τούτῳ τῷ γινομένῳ φόβῳ ἀγγέλλεται τοῖσι

---

2 ἤρτητο Β   3 συμμεῖξαι van H., Stein³ || ὅτε coni. Stein¹ ²
4 ὤρων Β : ἑώρων   6 ἀπείργουσά libri : corr. Stein   69. 1 τε
om. Pz   2 φόνωι Α² : πόνῳ Wesseling, 'fortasse recte' van H.

---

by Stein, takes as impersonal, cp. 2.
117. Blakesley objects to its impersonality and translates, 'it proves to
me that . .,' a translation not incompatible with impersonality. In fact
δηλοῖ should be more significant than
δῆλόν ἐστι, but there is no expressed
subject for it. τε seems to have a
cumulative force, cp. c. 66 supra.

2. ἤρτητο ἐκ, 'depended on.' The
pluperfect can hardly be pressed into
meaning that all that is now a thing of
the past, cp. 6. 109 ταῦτα ὧν πάντα ἐς
σὲ νῦν τείνει καὶ ἐκ σέο ἤρτηται, 1. 125, 3.
19. τὰ πρήγματα, 7. 10. 34 f. supra.

οὗτοι cannot refer to the same body
of men as the οὗτοι just above; but
whether it refers to οἱ ἄλλοι Ἕλληνες οἱ
μετὰ βασιλέος or to τῶν ἄλλων συμμάχων
ὁ πᾶς ὅμιλος, or more vaguely includes
both, is not quite clear. The first
reference is rather remote, the second
rather pointless, inasmuch as Hdt. is
here dealing with the action on the right
wing of Mardonios' army. The clearest
point would be made by the omission
of c. 67, in which case οὗτοι would refer
to Artabazos and the men under his
command, as do the words καὶ δὴ οὗτοι
μὲν ταύτῃ ἐτράποντο. Possibly c. 67 is
an insertion by the author, and was not
in the original draft of the battle-piece;
it is intended to recall the Athenians
to mind. If that is the case, the next
sentence too is probably an addition
(οὕτω τε . . τῶν Ἑλλήνων). Cp. Introduction, § 9.

3. συμμεῖξαι, of hostile congress,
c. 48 supra.

4. ὤρων : sc. φεύγοντας.

πάντες ἔφευγον. In c. 63 supra

the Persians have been routed, and in
c. 65 have fled ἐς τὸ τεῖχος τὸ ξύλινον.
In c. 66 Artabazos and his men have
fled ἐς Φωκέας. In c. 67 the Thebans
have fled ἐς τὰς Θήβας, and ὁ πᾶς ὅμιλος
have followed the Persians.

πλὴν τῆς ἵππου : the cavalry generally, on both wings, may have covered
the retreat, or 'flight,' to some extent;
but the Persian left wing does not
appear to profit much by its cavalry,
while the Boiotian cavalry does appear
as actively and efficiently engaged. The
Persian camp is reached and captured,
while the Thebans make good their retreat to Thebes. τῆς τε ἄλλης καί here
may be rather perfunctory. The disappearance of the Persian cavalry on
the left wing is something of a problem:
did it ride off with Artabazos?

5. τοσαῦτα refers to what follows
(=τοσάδε), viz. the cavalry kept close
to the enemy and screened the men who
were in flight. ἀπέργουσα τοὺς φιλίους
ἀπὸ τῶν Ἑλλήνων might rather have
been ἀπέργουσα τοὺς Ἕλληνας ἀπὸ τῶν
φιλίων. With πρὸς τῶν π. cp. 8. 87.

69. 1. οἱ . . νικῶντες, 'the victors'
—primarily the Lakedaimonians; cp.
the message reported just below.

τοὺς Ξέρξεω : i.e. the barbarians
(the term hardly includes τοὺς μετὰ
βασιλέος Ἕλληνας). Mardonios is no
more; but the phrase is perhaps merely
conventional, and hardly chosen expressly with that reference.

2. ἐν δὲ τούτῳ . . φόβῳ, 'at the
beginning of this rout.' ἐν, temporal, cp.
c. 60 supra.

φόβος=φυγή, "the only sense in
Homer" (L. & S.).

ἄλλοισι Ἕλλησι τοῖσι τεταγμένοισι περὶ τὸ Ἥραιον καὶ
ἀπογενομένοισι τῆς μάχης, ὅτι μάχη τε γέγονε καὶ νικῷεν οἱ
5 μετὰ Παυσανίεω· οἱ δὲ ἀκούσαντες ταῦτα, οὐδένα κόσμον
ταχθέντες, οἱ μὲν ἀμφὶ Κορινθίους ἐτράποντο διὰ τῆς ὑπωρέης

---

3 ἄλλοισι om. R ‖ περὶ τὸ ἥραιον (ἱραῖον R) τεταγμένοισι Β　　4
τε om. Marc.　　5 παυσανίεωι Β　　6 ὑπωρείης Β

---

3. τοῖσι . . περὶ τὸ Ἥραιον: cp. c.
52 supra; it is admitted here too that
they were τεταγμένοι. The whole centre,
both right and left, is here apparently
involved; see below.

4. ἀπογενομένοισι τῆς μάχης: qui
pugnas non interfuerunt (Baehr). In 2.
85, 136, 3. 111, 5. 4 ἀπογίνεσθαι means
'to die.'

μάχη τε γέγονε καὶ νικῷεν οἱ μετὰ
Παυσανίεω, 'a battle has taken place,
Pausanias and his men being victorious.'
The combination of moods and tenses
in this message is remarkable; the
indicative and optative in somewhat
similar fashion 8. 100 δώσει δίκην . .
καὶ οἱ κρέσσον εἴη, 8. 111 ἦσαν ἄρα αἱ
Ἀθῆναι μεγάλαι τε καὶ εὐδαίμονες, αἱ καὶ
θεῶν χρηστῶν ἥκοιεν εὖ. The present
optative here is remarkable: even in
this context, with the antecedent
perfect, it could hardly be imperfect
(γέγονε can hardly mean merely 'has
begun'). Just about the same moment,
or a little later in the day, ex hypothesi,
substantially the same news was spread
through the army on the strand at
Mykale, c. 100 infra; but here οἱ μετὰ
Π. is emphatic, and does not include
the Athenians.

5. οὐδένα κόσμον ταχθέντες: a
suspicious assertion, reducing them
almost to the level of the barbarians
in c. 59 supra.

6. οἱ μὲν ἀμφὶ Κορινθίους: Schweighaeuser, Krueger, Baehr, and others,
have interpreted this merely of the
Korinthians, and so the corresponding
phrase below merely of the Megarians
and Phleiasians. This interpretation is
neither grammatically nor materially
tenable. The phrase means 'the
Korinthians and those with them,' and
plainly covers 'the right centre' as
enumerated in c. 28 supra, comprising
some 11,300 hoplites, in six (or eight)
divisions, from the Korinthians on the
extreme left (next the Lakedaimonians
and Tegeatai) to the Mykenaians and
Tirynthians on the right, i.e. just at
the very middle of the Greek line.

This body, the right centre, is here
dimly reported as betaking itself from
the Heraion, where it had been duly
disposed and drawn up in order (of
battle), through, or over, the skirts of
the mountain and the ridgeland, by
the way leading up to the temple of
Demeter.

This notice at first sight suggests that
they are going to the help of Pausanias
in the position of the Lakedaimonians
as described in cc. 56, 57 supra. But
Pausanias is ex hypothesi already
victorious, and does not need their
assistance; and in fact nothing more is
heard of this body of men and their
ill-starred movement, οὐδένα κόσμον
ταχθέντες, started without waiting for
any orders

There is the same ambiguity here as
elsewhere in regard to the exact extent
of the ὑπωρέη, in regard to the identity
of the κολωνοί, in regard to the precise
one of three Demetria which may have
been involved in the movement; perhaps
also as to the exact point of time at
which this movement of the right centre
took place. It is curious, too, that no
message reaches this body of men
summoning them (like the Athenians
c. 60 supra) to the aid of Pausanias.
(But cp. note to c. 61. 14 supra.) The
precise sequence and chronology of the
orders, messages, movements in various
parts of the field of battle are not coher-
ently presented by Hdt. Perhaps the
division of the Greek army forming the
right centre had been detached and
deployed on to the road from Plataia to
Athens (Dryoskephalai) for the purpose
of holding it against the Persian cavalry,
and was actually so engaged, while the
Lakedaimonians were resisting the onset
of the Persian infantry, lower down the
slope, or had even already put the
Persians to flight. In any case the line
of march here indicated for the right
centre is uphill from Plataia, and its
objective cannot be marked by the
present church of St. Demetrion, the
site of which is far below the Heraion.

καὶ τῶν κολωνῶν τὴν φέρουσαν ἄνω ἰθὺ τοῦ ἱροῦ τῆς
Δήμητρος, οἱ δὲ ἀμφὶ Μεγαρέας τε καὶ Φλειασίους διὰ τοῦ
πεδίου τὴν λειοτάτην τῶν ὁδῶν. ἐπείτε δὲ ἀγχοῦ τῶν πολεμίων
ἐγίνοντο οἱ Μεγαρέες καὶ Φλειάσιοι, ἀπιδόντες σφέας οἱ τῶν 10
Θηβαίων ἱππόται ἐπειγομένους οὐδένα κόσμον ἤλαυνον ἐπ'
αὐτοὺς τοὺς ἵππους, τῶν ἱππάρχεε Ἀσωπόδωρος ὁ Τιμάνδρου,
ἐσπεσόντες δὲ κατεστόρεσαν αὐτῶν ἐξακοσίους, τοὺς δὲ λοιποὺς
κατήραξαν διώκοντες ἐς τὸν Κιθαιρῶνα.

Οὗτοι μὲν δὴ ἐν οὐδενὶ λόγῳ ἀπώλοντο· οἱ δὲ Πέρσαι 70
καὶ ὁ ἄλλος ὅμιλος, ὡς κατέφυγον ἐς τὸ ξύλινον τεῖχος,

---

7 τὸν κολωνὸν Marc. ‖ ἄνω om. B   10 ἀποδιδόντες z ‖ τῶν om. B,
Holder   11 ἐπηγομένους Marc.   12 τοὺς ἵππους secl. van H.
13 κατεστώρεσαν B ‖ αὐτέων z   14 κατήρραξαν Marc. z   70. 1
post λόγῳ excidisse ὄντες vel γενόμενοι suspic. van H.

---

8. οἱ δὲ ἀμφὶ Μεγαρέας τε καὶ
Φλειασίους. The left centre, comprising the Megarians, Phleiasians, and those
in their division, a force of 7300
hoplites, op. c. 78 *supra*. Of them it
might have been said that they ἦσαν τὰ
ἔμπαλιν ἢ οἱ ἀμφὶ Κορινθίου (cp. c. 56
supra). As the right centre has moved,
apparently E., or SE., to support, or
cover, the right wing, so the left centre
moves N., or NW., to support the left
wing : διὰ τοῦ πεδίου τὴν λειοτάτην
τῶν ὁδῶν, words which seem to carry a
disparaging reflexion with them ! Of
course for the left centre to advance
down hill, on to the plain, over which
the road from Plataia to Thebes ran, to
the support of the Athenians, who were
evidently in difficulties (cp. c. 61 *supra*),
was a gallant enough proceeding ; but
the Athenians do not appear to have
been very grateful therefor.

10. ἀπιδόντες : op. 8. 37.

12. τῶν ἱππάρχεε : cp. c. 20 *supra* ;
the τῶν should be referred to ἱππόται.

Ἀσωπόδωρος ὁ Τιμάνδρου. Of
Timandros the father nothing more is
known, but this Asopodoros may well
be the father of that Herodotos, of
Thebes, in whose honour Pindar composed an Epinikion, *Isth.* 1. The family,
which was, of course, aristocratic and
medizing, had some connexion with
Orchomenos (*op. c.* 35) ; op. c. 16 *supra*.
To these circumstances may be due the
remembrance of the exploit here recorded.

13. κατεστόρεσαν αὐτῶν ἐξακοσίους.
This heavy loss, and the consequent

flight of the left centre ἐς τὸν Κιθαιρῶνα,
can hardly have taken place after the
victory of the Athenians over the
Boiotians already recounted in c. 67
supra ; it was more probably its antecedent, or concomitant, at least in part ;
in other words, the support afforded to
the Athenians, on the extreme left, by
the left centre, enabled them to claim a
success over the Thebans.

70. 1. ἐν οὐδενὶ λόγῳ, (as) 'of no
account,' op. 7. 14, 57 (ἐν οὐδενὶ λόγῳ
ποιέεσθαι). Hdt. cannot have seen the
monument at Megara, erected in honour
of those who had fallen in the Persian
war, with an epigram, in whole or part
ascribable to Simonides (though of
doubtful authenticity), containing a
distich especially referable to the courage
of the Megarians in facing the cavalry
at Plataia ; op. c. 21 *supra* ; Hauvette,
de l'authenticité etc. pp. 7-8, 92-94 ;
C.I.G. 1. 1051. The silence, or rather
this explicit statement, of Hdt. might be
added to the *raisons extrinsèques* against
the authenticity of the epigram, or even
against its existence in the time of Hdt.
But such an argument ascribes too
scientific a standard to Hdt.'s methods,
and though the inscription is certainly
late, the verses are certainly early.

οἱ δὲ Πέρσαι καὶ ὁ ἄλλος ὅμιλος.
The narrative returns to the fortunes of
the Persian left, the Greek right, cp.
c. 65 *supra*. The ἄλλος is idiomatic
('besides,' 'as well') : even in their
flight the Persians proper are not to be
classed with ὁ ὅμιλος, ὁ πᾶς ὅμιλος of
c. 67 *supra*.

ἔφθησαν ἐπὶ τοὺς πύργους ἀναβάντες πρὶν ἢ τοὺς Λακεδαιμονίους ἀπικέσθαι, ἀναβάντες δὲ ἐφράξαντο ὡς ἠδυνέατο ἄριστα
5 τὸ τεῖχος· προσελθόντων δὲ τῶν Λακεδαιμονίων κατεστήκεέ σφι
τειχομαχίη ἐρρωμενεστέρη. ἕως μὲν γὰρ ἀπῆσαν οἱ Ἀθηναῖοι,
οἱ δ᾽ ἠμύνοντο καὶ πολλῷ πλέον εἶχον τῶν Λακεδαιμονίων
ὥστε οὐκ ἐπισταμένων τειχομαχέειν· ὡς δέ σφι Ἀθηναῖοι

---

4 ἐφράζοντο Β   5 Ἀθηναίων Stein[(2)3], van H.: cp. comment.
6 ἐπῆεσαν Β   7 οἶδε Β ‖ ἔχον z ‖ τῶν Ἀθηναίων Stein[(2)] (preli err.)
8 οἱ Ἀθηναῖοι Marc. z

---

3. **ἔφθησαν ἐπὶ τοὺς πύργους ἀναβάντες**: for the gramm. construction cp.
7. 142, c. 113 *infra*. This is the first
(and last) appearance of the πύργοι on
the ξύλινον τεῖχος. The defenders, at
least the combatants among them, took
their stand apparently not upon or below
the wall, but above on these towers,
from which they hurled weapons, stones,
etc., against the assailants, no doubt.

4. **ἐφράξαντο**: φράξαι, φράξασθαι
means properly 'to fence,' fortify, cp. 8.
51 and 7. 142 ἡ γὰρ ἀκρόπολις τὸ πάλαι
τῶν Ἀθηναίων ῥηχῷ ἐπέφρακτο. (φράξαντες, 8. 7, 'blocked'.) But the exact
nature of the operation here recorded
is obscure. The time was past for
'strengthening' their wall by additional
fortifications, nor would the ascent of
the towers be the natural preliminary
to such work. φράσσειν can hardly be
watered down so as merely to = φυλάσσειν,
but might perhaps be translated, 'put
into a posture of defence.'

5. **προσελθόντων δὲ τῶν Λακεδαιμονίων**. There is a certain clumsiness
and obscurity in the way the τειχομαχίη
is described. First, the Persians and
the rest of the barbarian rout made good
their escape into τὸ ξύλινον τεῖχος, and
before the arrival of the 'Lakedaimonians'
ascended the towers, and put the fort
into a posture of defence. (It is not a
case where pursuers and pursued entered
together: either their lighter equipment
or the intervention of the cavalry, c. 68
supra, enables the barbarian infantry to
outstrip its pursuers. But were not a
good many of the barbarians shut out
of the fortification? And the pursuers
were also retarded by the slaughter,
c. 69 *supra*.) Next, the Lakedaimonians
arrived at the fortification, and for a
while were unable to effect an entrance;
and there took place a τειχομαχίη. But
cp. App. Crit. and next note.

6. **ἐρρωμενεστέρη**. If the vulgate
reading above is maintained the comparative can only be a rhetorical elegance,
unless indeed it means that the fighting
was too much for the Lakedaimonians,
'more than they could cope with.'
Stein takes σφι to refer not to the
Persians only, but to both sides, Persians
and Greeks. He also has substituted
Ἀθηναίων for Λακεδαιμονίων. This
emendation is not convincing. If
adopted, the next sentence will hark
back to explain the situation antecedent
to the arrival of the 'Athenians' already
recorded (cp. c. 61 *supra* φράξαντες γάρ
κτλ., following ἔπιπτον κτλ.). κατεστήκεε is, of course, not simply = ἦν or
ἐγίνετο, but ἐρρωμενεστέρη may be part of
the predicate.

7. **οἱ δέ**: i.e. δέ *in apodosi* (cp. 7.
51), the ἕως μέν just before being
answered by ὡς δέ below. οἱ = οἱ Πέρσαι.

πολλῷ πλέον εἶχον, 'were getting
the better of'; cp. πλέον ἔχειν 4. 3, and
οὐδὲν ἔλασσον εἶχον c. 102 *infra*.

8. **ὥστε = ἅτε**, cp. c. 37 *supra*. Rawlinson instances the failures of the Spartans
to subdue Eira, Ithome, Pylos: the story
of the siege of Plataia (429-7 B.C.) is no
less eminent a case. But the Athenians
were not so very much better: the siege
of Poteidaia lasted two years (432-30
B.C.); no assault on Syracuse occurred
during the Athenian siege (414-13 B.C.).
The defence of stone walls had always
the advantage, in the absence of heavy
machines and engines: fire or starvation were the chief hopes of the besiegers
(cp. Thucydides, his essay in Poliorketica
2. 75-78). The Athenian reputation
was more or less established at the time
of the third Messenian war (Thuc. 1.
102. 2), and may have been enhanced in
the assaults on Samos (440-39 B.C.)
where some engines were perhaps employed, without much success (Plutarch,

προσῆλθον, οὕτω δὴ ἰσχυρὴ ἐγίνετο <ἡ> τειχομαχίη καὶ
χρόνον ἐπὶ πολλόν. τέλος δὲ ἀρετῇ τε καὶ λιπαρίῃ ἐπέβησαν 10
Ἀθηναῖοι τοῦ τείχεος καὶ ἤριπον· τῇ δὴ ἐσεχέοντο οἱ Ἕλληνες.
πρῶτοι δὲ ἐσῆλθον Τεγεῆται ἐς τὸ τεῖχος, καὶ τὴν σκηνὴν
τὴν Μαρδονίου οὗτοι ἦσαν οἱ διαρπάσαντες, τά τε ἄλλα ἐξ
αὐτῆς καὶ τὴν φάτνην τῶν ἵππων ἐοῦσαν χαλκέην πᾶσαν καὶ
θέης ἀξίην. τὴν μέν νυν φάτνην ταύτην τὴν Μαρδονίου 15
ἀνέθεσαν ἐς τὸν νηὸν τῆς Ἀλέης Ἀθηναίης Τεγεῆται, τὰ δὲ

9 <ἡ> Stein³   11 ἤρειπον Marc. z   12 εἰσῆλθον Marc.
13 τὴν: τοῦ βz

Perikles 27, cp. Diodor. 12. 28. 3 ; the
authority was merely Ephoros, and it is
clear that the city was not captured by
force) ; but it looks as if their reputation
was based rather on the defensive aptitude of their own city, long walls, and
fortified harbour than on the brilliance
of their record in assaulting others.
The Lakedaimonians not having any
walls of their own of course could not
τειχομαχέειν. Cp. Thucyd. 1. 90. 2.
The case of 'wooden walls' was vastly
different ; cp. 8. 52 supra.

ἐς δέ σφι Ἀθηναῖοι προσῆλθον.
A fresh stage is reached on the arrival
of the Athenians ; the ἰσχυρὴ τειχομαχίη
now set up hardly enforces the τειχομαχίη
ἐρρωμενεστέρη recorded just above. The
sequel shows that the claim made for
the Athenians is untenable : it is the
Tegeatai who effected a breach (perhaps
even before the arrival of the Athenians).

10. ἀρετῇ τε καὶ λιπαρίῃ : cp. c. 21
supra, where the Megarians claim credit
for this combination in a defensive
position, a case to which the first term
would more naturally apply. The
question here is of scaling the wall
(ἐπέβησαν τοῦ τείχεος) and effecting a
breach.

11. ἤριπον : sc. αὐτό, or even αὐτοῦ.
In either case the use of the 2nd aorist
with transitive sense is remarkable ;
cp. App. Crit. Hdt. has the 1st aor.
ἐρεῖψαι in 1. 164, but cp. L. & S. sub v.

12. πρῶτοι δὲ ἐσῆλθον Τεγεῆται : this
statement is hardly reconcileable with
the immediately preceding context ;
those who first scaled the wall and
effected a breach must also have been
the first to enter the fort, and vice versa ;
if the Tegeatai were the first to enter,
the Tegeatai doubtless effected a breach
for themselves. The latter is the more
probable alternative ; the former is

discounted by the Attic bias in Hdt.'s
source or sources for the story of Plataia,
and by the obvious anomaly in this
record.

τὴν σκηνὴν τὴν Μαρδονίου : the
tent, or pavilion, of Mardonios was
probably in or near the centre of the
fortified camp, and the fact that the
Tegeatai pillaged it would not seem to
throw any light upon their place of
entrance. The tent was, perhaps, the
same tent as Xerxes had used ; cp. c. 82
infra.

15. θέης ἀξίην : that Hdt. had himself
seen this bronze manger (φάτνη) cannot
be inferred from this description or
phrase ; cp. c. 25 supra ; but he might
have added this sentence or two upon
the manger and its destination after his
visit to the Peloponnesos. It has a
somewhat parenthetical air, and might
very well be 'second-hand.' Cp. Introduction, § 9.

16. τῆς Ἀλέης Ἀθηναίης. This
goddess and her temple at Tegea are
mentioned elsewhere, 1. 66, and in such
a wa as rather to suggest autopsy
(morey directly than anything in the
present passage). The temple as it
existed in Hdt.'s day was burnt down
in the year 395-4 B.C., and the splendid
temple described by Pausanias 8. 45 ff.
was a later edifice ; but, though it still
contained the fetters of the Spartans
(8. 47. 2), Pausanias makes no mention
of the manger of Mardonios. If the
Tegeatai really found the φάτνη τῶν
ἵππων in the σκηνή of Mardonios, the
white charger (c. 63 supra) must have
been stabled in rather close proximity
to his rider's quarters. On the further
contents of the pavilion cp. c. 82 infra.

Alea as a title of Athene is perhaps to
be connected with the Arkadian town of
the same name mentioned by Pausanias

ἄλλα ἐς τώυτό, ὅσα περ ἔλαβον, ἐσήνεικαν τοῖσι Ἕλλησι. οἱ
δὲ βάρβαροι οὐδὲν ἔτι στῖφος ἐποιήσαντο πεσόντος τοῦ τείχεος,
οὐδέ τις αὐτῶν ἀλκῆς ἐμέμνητο, ἀλύκταζόν τε οἷα ἐν ὀλίγῳ
20 χώρῳ πεφοβημένοι τε καὶ πολλαὶ μυριάδες κατειλημέναι
ἀνθρώπων. παρῆν τε τοῖσι Ἕλλησι φονεύειν οὕτω ὥστε

---

17 ἐσηνείκαντο β   18 στῖφος R Marc.   19 οὐδέ Stein : οὔτε ‖
τις : τῆς Β ‖ αὐτέων z   20 χώρῳ : χρόνῳ ΒCpr. z, del. Krueger, van H.
‖ κατειλημέναι P, Schweighaeuser : κατειλλημμέναι R : κατειλλημέναι V :
κατειλημμέναι α etc.

(8. 23. 1), containing a sanctuary of
Athene Alea, a goddess worshipped also
in Mantineia (*ib.* 8. 9. 6). The cult
was not confined actually to historic
Arcadia ; Pausanias saw a wooden image
of Athene Alea on the road from Sparta
to Therapne (3. 19. 7), and Xenophon
(*Hell.* 6. 5. 27) mentions a ἱερὸν τῆς
Ἀλέας apparently in the same place at
the time of the first Theban invasion
of Lakonia (369 B.C.). Tegea was undoubtedly the most important centre of
the cult in historic times ; ' Aleus' was
reckoned the city's founder (Pausan.
8. 45. 1), but Pausanias seems to distinguish clearly between the sanctuary
of Athene Poliatis at Tegea and that of
Athene Alea (*ib.* 8. 47. 5).
17. ἐς τώυτό . . ἐσήνεικαν τοῖσι
Ἕλλησι : i.e. they brought into the
common stock ; it is not quite clear
whether τοῖσι Ἕλλησι is an ethical dative
(*pro bono publico*) or loosely constructed
with τώυτό, into the same place, or the
common heap, to which all the rest of
the Greeks brought their spoils. There
seems to be some little feeling of jealousy
over the possession by the Tegeatai of the
bronze manger, and a hint that they
had secreted it. The probability is that
they were allowed to retain it as a special
reward for having been first into the
Persian camp.
18. στῖφος : cp. c. 57 *supra.*
πεσόντος τοῦ τείχεος : the fortification 'fell' as soon as a breach had
been made in the wall.
19. ἀλκῆς ἐμέμνητο : an Homeric
reminiscence, e.g. *Il.* 5. 112. Cp.
Baehr.
ἀλύκταζον : an *hapaxlegomenon,*
apparently connected with ἀλύω (poetic),
'to be distraught,' frantic. Cp. ἀλα-
λύκτημαι *Il.* 10. 94 (as if from ἀλυκτέω).
20. κατειλημέναι : a conj. of Schweighaeuser, "undoubtedly a true one,"

Blakesley ; it is in fact the reading of
P ! cp. App. Crit.
21. ἀνθρώπων : cp. c. 44 *supra.*
παρῆν τε : the climactic τε, cp. c.
66. 4 *supra.* παρῆν, cp. 8. 20, like παρεόν
6. 137, 7. 24, etc., 'it was in their
power . .' The 'many myriads' are
immediately precised as 30–4 = 260,000
units, of whom less than 3000 survive !
Such butchery is practically inconceivable. If we accept 3000 as about the
number of the survivors, the figures for
Mardonios' forces would have to be indefinitely reduced ; but the one extreme
is hardly more to be trusted than the
other. It is observable that the *corps
d'armée* under Artabazos is here again
included strictly in the original total
of Mardonios' army, consistently with
8. 126 ; but this involves Hdt. in an
inconsistency, for he here seems to take
no account of the fact that Artabazos
had started with 60,000. He also seems
to allow nothing for the losses in previous
skirmishes. Hdt.'s statement is tantamount to saying that 99 per cent
were slain, for of (300,000–40,000) only
(3000–*x*) escaped. The estimate might
be rationalized down to meaning that
of the 300,000 men, taken by Hdt. as
the estimate of the forces left with
Mardonios, and still acceptable as an
estimate for the total land-forces of
Xerxes (τοὺς Ξέρξεω c. 69 *supra*), only
43,000 returned to Asia from the
campaign of 479 B.C. If that was
less than half the forces entrusted to
Mardonios and Artabazos the losses
would still have been enormous, and
might justify Aischylos and his 'heaps
of corpses' (θῖνες δὲ νεκρῶν *Pers.* 821 ff.).
Diodoros 11. 32 puts the Persian losses
in the battle of Plataia at upwards
of 100,000 (probably only Ephoros'
rationalism) ; Ktesias 26 the Persian
losses from Salamis to Plataia at 120,000.

τριήκοντα μυριάδων στρατοῦ, καταδεουσέων τεσσέρων τὰς ἔχων
Ἀρτάβαζος ἔφευγε, τῶν λοιπέων μηδὲ τρεῖς χιλιάδας περιγενέσθαι. Λακεδαιμονίων δὲ τῶν ἐκ Σπάρτης ἀπέθανον οἱ
πάντες ἐν τῇ συμβολῇ εἶς καὶ ἐνενήκοντα, Τεγεητέων δὲ 25
ἐκκαίδεκα, Ἀθηναίων δὲ δύο καὶ πεντήκοντα.

Ἠρίστευσε δὲ τῶν βαρβάρων πεζὸς μὲν ὁ Περσέων, ἵππος 71

22 μυριαδέων C Marc.　　　23 ἔφυγε Marc.　　　25 συμβουλῆι C
‖ καὶ om. B

The one tolerably certain fact in the whole story is the escape of Artabazos with not less than 40,000 men.

24. Λακεδαιμονίων δὲ τῶν ἐκ Σπάρτης: a remarkable periphrasis for Σπαρτιητέων. No account is taken apparently of the Perioikoi, much less of mere Helots ; cp. c. 85 *infra*. The figures which follow have a precise and an authentic air, but apparently refer merely to those who fell in the final and decisive engagement (ἐν τῇ συμβολῇ) of the thirteenth day. In c. 61 *supra* πολλοί have been killed, and in c. 63 the Persians κατέβαλλον πολλοὺς τῶν Λακεδαιμονίων—here only 91 'Spartiates' are accounted for ' in all ' (οἱ πάντες). The proportionate losses are interesting : the Spartans lose not quite 2 per cent (91 out of 5000) ; the Tegeatai just over 1 per cent (16 out of 1500) ; the Athenians considerably under 1 per cent (52 out of 8000) ; the totals, however, are only nominal, especially for the last engagement. No account at all is taken of the right and left centre, to say nothing of the ψιλοί, such as they were. Plutarch (*Aristeid.* 19) gives the sum total (οἱ πάντες) of those who fell upon this occasion as 1360, whereas the figures here amount to 159 only. Plutarch adds, on the authority of Kleidemos, the curious statement that the 52 Athenians were all of one tribe, the Aiantis. If 52 Athenians of one tribe had been slain, we might have to multiply roughly by ten to reach the sum total, though one or other tribe of course might have been specially hard hit on the occasion. At Marathon 192 Athenians were admitted to have fallen (6. 117), considerably more than the total loss here reported for Plataia. There is something radically wrong in these figures, though doubtless they repose on some monuments, or inscriptions, carelessly copied, or misunderstood.

71. 1. ἠρίστευσε δὲ κτλ. There should

follow here the record of the formal ἀριστήια, or awards of valour ; as in 8. 11, 17 for Artemision, in 8. 93, 123 for Salamis etc., and in c. 105 *infra* for Mykale. But the record here is not of any formal and express award, for (*a*) the merits of the barbarians are included (cp. however 8. 17) ; (*b*) Hdt. himself expressly indicates that he has no official authority for his awards. There is in fact here a *casus omissus*, which generates a problem, for assuredly Greeks failed not in the case of Plataia to discuss and award the *Aristeia*, as for the other battles of the war ; nor is it credible that Hdt. should unwittingly have passed over the record, or tradition, of the formal award : he must have omitted it deliberately. Plutarch (*Aristeid.* 20 and *de malign. Hdti* 42, 10 = *Mor.* 873) makes good the omission. The Athenians and Spartans nearly came to blows over the question of the award (τὸ ἀριστεῖον) : the question was referred to the confederates. Theogeiton of Megara suggested the award of the prize to some third city, Kleokritos of Korinth proposed that Plataia should be that city, Aristeides at once accepted the suggestion on behalf of Athens, and Pausanias on behalf of Lakedaimon. Eighty talents were assigned to the Plataians, out of which they built the temple of Athene, which was still up-standing in the days of Plutarch (cp. note to c. 70 *supra*) : the Lakedaimonians, however, erected a trophy on their own account, and the Athenians one likewise separately. This story has intrinsic probability, and the chief argument against it is the silence of Hdt. here, and the silence of Thucydides in the Plataian Apology, 3. 53-59. But the *argumentum e silentio* seldom is conclusive. The story in question was little to the credit either of Sparta or of Athens, and was probably a sore subject at both places. The Athenian Thucydides may have ignored it from patriotism, or

δὲ ἡ Σακέων, ἀνὴρ δὲ λέγεται Μαρδόνιος· Ἑλλήνων δέ,
ἀγαθῶν γενομένων καὶ Τεγεητέων καὶ Ἀθηναίων, ὑπερεβάλοντο
ἀρετῇ Λακεδαιμόνιοι. ἄλλῳ μὲν οὐδενὶ ἔχω ἀποσημήνασθαι
5 (ἅπαντες γὰρ οὗτοι τοὺς κατ' ἑωυτοὺς ἐνίκων), ὅτι δὲ κατὰ
τὸ ἰσχυρότερον προσηνείχθησαν καὶ τούτων ἐκράτησαν. καὶ
ἄριστος ἐγένετο μακρῷ Ἀριστόδημος κατὰ γνώμας τὰς ἡμετέρας,
ὃς ἐκ Θερμοπυλέων μοῦνος τῶν τριηκοσίων σωθεὶς εἶχε ὄνειδός
<τε> καὶ ἀτιμίην. μετὰ δὲ τοῦτον ἠρίστευσαν Ποσειδώνιός

71. 2 ἡ: ὁ Β ‖ λέγεται del. Cobet, van H.   3 ὑπερέβαλον Marc.
4 <τὸ> ἄλλῳ ἡ van H.   5 πάντες Β   6 ἰσχυρότατον ΒΡz,
Holder ‖ προσηνέχθησαν Β ‖ τουτέων z   8 ἔχε z   9 <τε>καὶ
coni. Stein¹², recep. van H., Stein³ ‖ τούτων a

made his dramatic mouthpiece ignore it
from fact. It is harder to explain the
silence or the ignorance of Hdt.: he takes
part definitely with the Lakedaimonians:
has he deliberately suppressed the story
in the Lakedaimonian interest? It does
not help us in this connexion to infer
(with Grote and Rawlinson) that no
formal decision was made; their inference
eases the Thucydidean problem, but not
the Herodotean: our author was bound
to have told the story of the dispute,
even if there was no formal award. He
prefers to divide the honours of the day
between the Koryphaioi (6. 98), for
Plataia to Lakedaimon, for Mykale to
Athens. Pindar, Pyth. 1. 77, hints
that Plataia was a Spartan victory;
Aischylos, Pers. 816 f., might seem to
recognize the claims of the Δωρὶς λόγχη,
and Diodoros 11. 33. 1 records a definite
award to Sparta and to Pausanias (cp.
c. 64 supra); but Attic prejudice is
most fully represented in the Menexenos
240 f. where τὰ ἀριστεῖα τῷ λόγῳ are
awarded to the Μαραθωνομάχαι, τὰ
δευτερεῖα to τοῖς περὶ Σαλαμῖνα καὶ ἐπ'
Ἀρτεμισίῳ ναυμαχήσασι, while τὸ ἐν
Πλαταιαῖς ἔργον, κοινὸν ἤδη τοῦτο Λακεδαιμονίων τε καὶ Ἀθηναίων, holds but the
third place, and of the respective credit
of the two states the speaker is discreetly
silent. This may represent an early,
the earliest, Attic tendency. Nothing
other states might do should ever be
admitted to have eclipsed 'the trophies
of Miltiades'! The legend of Marathon
had ten years' start of the story of
Plataia, and doubtless received a strong
stimulus from the idealized 'victory of
Pausanias' (cp. c. 27 supra).

ὁ Περσέων: i.e. the Persian
infantry, as distinguished from Medes,

Baktrians, Indians, Sakans, which was
directly opposed to the Spartans; cc. 31,
47, 59 supra.

2. ἡ Σακέων: the Sakai or Scyths
(cp. 7. 64) oddly enough are not enumerated among the nations furnishing
cavalry to the army of Xerxes, 7. 84–86,
unless they are masquerading there as
Κάσπιοι.

ἀνὴρ δέ: the word here in pregnant
sense. λέγεται looks a little superfluous,
but perhaps is intended to insinuate a
doubt; in any case the λόγος must be a
Greek one.

3. ὑπερεβάλοντο ἀρετῇ Λακεδαιμόνιοι.
This is a very definite award by the
historian himself, as against the
Athenians and Tegeatai, and a fortiori
against all the rest. ὑπερβάλλεσθαι, cp.
8. 123. The award further stultifies the
story told c. 46 supra, and the reason
given for the award confirms the importance of the ἐθελοκακία on the part of the
medizing Greeks admitted in c. 67 supra.
The asyndeton in giving the reason
makes it look almost like an argument
inserted to answer a challenge or
criticism: the ὅτι δέ (sc. πλὴν ὅτι, or
τῷδε δέ, ὅτι) in apposition to ἄλλῳ μέν
is observable.

6. προσφέρεσθαι is primarily of
attacking, cp. c. 49 supra.

τούτων: sc. τοῦ ἰσχυροτέρου, i.e.
τῶν Περσέων.

7. ἐγένετο, 'proved himself': this is
the historian's own private judgement
(κατὰ γνώμας τὰς ἡμετέρας, cp. 4. 53) in
opposition to Spartan opinion. The
absence of a cross reference back to 7.
232, and the full and sufficient description
of Aristodemos here, are observable: ὃς
ἐκ . . ἀτιμίην is rather gloss-like; cp. l.c.

9. Ποσειδώνιός τε καὶ Φιλοκύων:

τε καὶ Φιλοκύων καὶ Ἀμομφάρετος ὁ Σπαρτιήτης. καίτοι 10
γενομένης λέσχης ὃς γένοιτο αὐτῶν ἄριστος, ἔγνωσαν οἱ
παραγενόμενοι Σπαρτιητέων Ἀριστόδημον μὲν βουλόμενον
φανερῶς ἀποθανεῖν ἐκ τῆς παρεούσης οἱ αἰτίης, λυσσῶντά τε
καὶ ἐκλείποντα τὴν τάξιν ἔργα ἀποδέξασθαι μεγάλα, Ποσει-
δώνιον δὲ οὐ βουλόμενον ἀποθνήσκειν ἄνδρα γενέσθαι ἀγαθόν· 15
τοσούτῳ τοῦτον εἶναι ἀμείνω. ἀλλὰ ταῦτα μὲν καὶ φθόνῳ ἂν

---

10 ὁ σπαρτιήτης αC : σπαρτιήτης ceteri : Σπαρτιῆται Krueger, Holder :
' an fuit ὁ Πιτανήτης ?' Stein : seclusit van H.   11 αὐτέων ѕ   12
μὲν : δὲ Marc.   13 αἰτίης : ἀτιμίης Cobet, van H. (tacite)   14 ἐκλιπόντα ß, Holder, van H. ‖ μεγάλα ἀποδέξασθαι ß   16 ἀμείνωι R

---

there was not much to choose apparently
between this pair ; they are mentioned
again c. 85 *infra*. The men to whom
the ἀριστήια are awarded had all fallen
in the fight. The addition of ὁ Σπαρτιήτης to the name of Amompharetos
might suggest that Poseidonios and
Philokyon were not 'Spartiatai,' but
Perioikoi : did Hdt. himself, indeed, write
ὁ Σπαρτιήτης ? It seems unlikely that the
Spartans, even in a *Lesche*, would put
Perioikoi above citizens in honour : the
burial arrangements, rightly understood,
point the same conclusion ; cp. c. 85
infra. This Poseidonios is not elsewhere
mentioned : Poseidon was worshipped in
Sparta and throughout Lakonia ; cp. S.
Wide, *Lakonische Kulte*, 1893, pp. 31–47.
Philokyon also as an historical person is
otherwise unknown ; the name is significant of sporting tendencies, in favour at
Sparta.

10. **Ἀμομφάρετος †ὁ Σπαρτιήτης.** On
Amompharetos cp. cc. 53 *supra*, 85
infra. Hdt. can hardly have written ὁ
Σπαρτιήτης here ; cp. App. Crit.

11. **γενομένης λέσχης,** 'on the
occurrence of a discussion.' λέσχη is
hardly official, or authoritative, but
rather informal discussion ; cp. 2. 32,
and ἔλλεσχος 1. 153, περιλεσχήνευτος 2.
135. Blakesley's note *ad l.* is worth
consulting, but he seems guilty of an
hysteroproteron in deriving the idea of the
conversation or the meeting from the
place of resort, the 'seat in a warm
situation,' which was no doubt the scene
of many a λέσχη. *Od.* 18. 329 has the
word in the locative sense, and the local
or material sense is predominant in
Attic and Delphic usage (Pausan. 10. 25),
but it is hardly possible that location is
the primary sense of a derivative of
λέγω, and that 'assembly,' 'conversa-

tion,' 'talk,' are only secondary, and a
function of the place.

δς appears to be used for τίς or
ὅστις, cp. τὸ χρεὸν εἴη c. 55 *supra*, and 6.
37 τὸ θέλει τὸ ἔπος εἶναι, 6. 124 δς μέντοι
ἦν ὁ ἀναδέξας κτλ.

αὐτῶν may refer to the three men
above named.

οἱ παραγενόμενοι : those present,
i.e. (who had been) present (at the
battle) ? Or, (who were) present (at the
discussion) ? The former meaning is
compatible with the latter fact. Was
Hdt. himself present ? And where did
the discussion take place ?

13. **ἐκ τῆς παρεούσης οἱ αἰτίης,** 'in
consequence of the blame attaching to
him.' ὁ τρέσας apparently had been
allowed to resume his place in the ranks ;
or was Aristodemos at Plataia *extra
ordinem* ? Had he any choice but
ἐκλείπειν τὴν τάξιν ? λυσσᾶν is rare ; cp.
Plato, *Rep.* 829 c, 586 c, of ἔρων : here
used in its earlier Homeric sense of
battle-rage (only in *Iliad*). With his
desperate courage may be compared that
of his fellows at Thermopylai 7. 223
παραχρεώμενοί τε καὶ ἀτέοντες. Philokyon
and Amompharetos are apparently nowhere beside him.

16. **ταῦτα μὲν καὶ φθόνῳ ἂν εἴποιεν.**
Was Aristodemos Hdt.'s own hero ?
Was it the Halikarnassian himself who
put in a plea at the discussion for the
due recognition of his heroism, was
worsted in the argument, and now
explains away his own defeat by ascribing φθόνος (*inter alia*) to the other
speakers ? φθόνος is no doubt a *vera
causa* in Greek life and literature (cp. 7.
237), but it is not always rightly
invoked, nor does it appear self-evident
why Spartiates should be more jealous
of Aristodemos than of the others.

εἴποιεν· οὗτοι δὲ τοὺς κατέλεξα πάντες, πλὴν Ἀριστοδήμου,
τῶν ἀποθανόντων ἐν ταύτῃ τῇ μάχῃ τίμιοι ἐγένοντο· Ἀριστόδημος δὲ βουλόμενος ἀποθανεῖν διὰ τὴν προειρημένην
20 αἰτίην οὐκ ἐτιμήθη.

72 Οὗτοι μὲν τῶν ἐν Πλαταιῇσι ὀνομαστότατοι ἐγένοντο.
Καλλικράτης γὰρ ἔξω τῆς μάχης ἀπέθανε, ἐλθὼν ἀνὴρ
κάλλιστος ἐς τὸ στρατόπεδον τῶν τότε Ἑλλήνων, οὐ μοῦνον
αὐτῶν Λακεδαιμονίων ἀλλὰ καὶ τῶν ἄλλων Ἑλλήνων· ὅς,
5 ἐπειδὴ ἐσφαγιάζετο Παυσανίης, κατήμενος ἐν τῇ τάξι ἐτρω-

---

17 εἴποιμεν αC Marc. ‖ πάντες B : πάντας   18 τῶν ἀποθανόντων ..
ἐν Πλαταιῇσι ut glossema tollenda suad. Krueger : mihi quidem verba
βουλόμενος ἀποθανεῖν vix genuina videntur   72. 1 πλαταίῃσι α :
πλαταίῃσιν B   3 τότε om. Marc. ‖ οὐ .. Ἑλλήνων om. B ‖ μόνων
RSVcorr. : μόνον Vpr. z   4 αὐτέων z ‖ Ἑλλήνων del. Gomperz, van H.
5 τάξι Pz : τάξει

Probably the Spartiates put aside the case of Aristodemos altogether; with them the only candidates for honours were the others: Poseidonios, Philokyon, Amompharetos. Hdt. has not made this quite clear, his own γνῶμαι running counter.

17. τοὺς κατέλεξα: a reference back to the immediate context, cp. 7. 99.

18. Krueger suspected the words τῶν ἀποθανόντων ἐν ταύτῃ τῇ μάχῃ as a gloss on the words τῶν ἐν Πλαταιῇσι below: cp. App. Crit.

τίμιοι ἐγένοντο were made 'honourables,' were 'ennobled' or given titles: a strictly official act, or process of glorification, canonization, but only perhaps performed for the departed, and involving (1) a public funeral, (2) a monument, (3) offerings at the tomb ὥσπερ ἥρωι. (So too Stein, who cps. 3. 55, which is hardly to the point, and 5. 67.) A lower form of the same act, or process, was the ἐπαίνεσις, which was conferred upon the living; cp. Thuc. 2. 25. 2 πρῶτος τῶν κατὰ τὸν πόλεμον ἐπῃνέθη ἐν Σπάρτῃ (sc. ὁ Βρασίδας).

19. διὰ τὴν προειρημένην αἰτίην: i.e. for the aforesaid reason, for the reason I have given; αἰτίη being used in a somewhat different sense to that above, ἐκ τῆς παρεούσης οἱ αἰτίης. βουλόμενος ἀποθανεῖν is like a gloss, and would be on Hdt.'s part an admission weakening his own verdict.

72. 1. ὀνομαστότατοι: in the positive 8. 89, 6. 114; in the comparative 6. 126. τῶν ἐν Πλαταιῇσι seems = τῶν ἐν τῇ μάχῃ ἀποθανόντων: cp. note above.

2. Καλλικράτης γάρ gives the reason for his not being one of the ὀνομαστότατοι —he died, perforce, a passive death, ἔξω τῆς μάχης, without having been able to strike a blow. It seems a restricted idea of the μάχη which regards Kallistratos as hors du combat; yet he was not actually slain in the ranks but apparently carried to the rear, and he was unable to strike a blow cominus: the passive virtues, and even the passive states of active virtues (e.g. courage) were less highly esteemed in Sparta than with us. The name Kallikrates is not an uncommon one. Plutarch, Agesilaos 35, mentions a Spartan of his own time so named, a descendant of the man, Antikrates, who had dealt Epameinondas his death-blow. Who would not fain believe that Kallikratidas, the typical Spartan of the old school (Xenophon, Hell. 1. 6. 1–36) towards the end of the fifth century, was a relative of the Plataian hero, who was remembered for his good looks and his last bon mot!

3. κάλλιστος .. τῶν τότε Ἑλλήνων: like Nireus to Ilion, Il. 2. 673; like Philippos of Kroton to Segesta, 5. 47. Size was an element in the Hellenic conception of κάλλος, whether male or female (cp. 3. 1 κάρτα μεγάλη τε καὶ εὐειδής, 5. 12 μεγάλη τε καὶ εὐειδέα, 1. 60 Phye); cp. the description of Xerxes 7. 187, κάλλεός τε εἵνεκα καὶ μεγάθεος. Plutarch, Aristeid. 17, specifies the size as well as the beauty of Kallikrates.

5. ἐπειδὴ ἐσφαγιάζετο Παυσανίης: cp. c. 61 supra; ἐπεί is used with the

ματίσθη τοξεύματι τὰ πλευρά. καὶ δὴ οἱ μὲν ἐμάχοντο, ὁ δ'
ἐξενηνειγμένος ἐδυσθανάτεέ τε καὶ ἔλεγε πρὸς Ἀείμνηστον
ἄνδρα Πλαταιέα οὐ μέλειν οἱ ὅτι πρὸ τῆς Ἑλλάδος ἀποθνήσκει, ἀλλ' ὅτι οὐκ ἐχρήσατο τῇ χειρὶ καὶ ὅτι οὐδέν ἐστί οἱ
ἀποδεδεγμένον ἔργον ἑωυτοῦ ἄξιον προθυμευμένου ἀποδέξασθαι. 10
Ἀθηναίων δὲ λέγεται εὐδοκιμῆσαι Σωφάνης ὁ Εὐτυχίδεω, 73

---

6 ὁ δὲ Β   7 ἐξεινηνεγμένος z ‖ τε om. Β ‖ ἀείμνηστον SVz :
ἀρίμνηστον ceteri, Stein, Holder, van H., cf. c. 64 supra   8 μέλλειν
ΒΒ Marc. ‖ ἀποθνῄσκει van H., Stein³ : ἀποθνῄσκει (ἀποθνῄσκειν C)   9
χερὶ z

---

imperf. c. 56 supra. The verb is a
'deponent' (L. & S.), but why not
'middle,' as σφαγιάζω is found in
Aristophanes (bis) Birds 569 f. (σφαγια-
ζομένῳ passive) and in later writers (cp.
σφαγιασθέντι 7. 180 supra)?

κατήμενος ἐν τῇ τάξι. The
hoplites sat on the ground in the battle-
array, crouching under their shields, to
avoid the arrows and other missiles, cp.
cc. 61, 62 (especially προεξαναστάντες).
Wesseling refers to Plutarch Aristeid.
17 ὡς δὲ θυόμενος οὐκ ἐκαλλιέρει προσέταξε
τοῖς Λακεδαιμονίοις τὰς ἀσπίδας πρὸ τῶν
ποδῶν θεμένους ἀτρέμα καθέζεσθαι. The
idea that the shields were put out
of use for the time is hardly to be
entertained. The passages quoted from
Euripides, Suppl. 357, 664, 674 (παρ'
ὅπλοις ἧσθαι, ἐφ' ὅπλοις ἧσθαι, or ἧσθαι
simpliciter), are not really to the point,
as they do not describe a tactical position.
More to the point were Tyrtaios, 11.
35 (ὑπ' ἀσπίδος ἄλλοθεν ἄλλος πτώσσοντες),
but that it applies only to γυμνῆτες, cp.
c. 48 supra.

6. τὰ πλευρά: cp. c. 22 supra, an
accusative 'of reference' or limitation ;
a plural of extent or abstraction (it
takes a plurality of ribs to make one
side). On which side he was wounded
Hdt. does not say ; probably the right.

ἐμάχοντο: the μάχη is in progress,
though Kallikrates dies ἔξω τῆς μάχης,
having been carried to the rear ; or
perhaps the imperfect is used to denote
their ability and mind for battle, as
compared with his disqualification. καὶ
δή, concessive, cp. cc. 6, 8, 48 supra.

7. ἐξενηνειγμένος: he was carried out
of the ranks by his helot, with or
without assistance ; cp. the narrative
of the destruction of the Spartan mora
in 390 B.C., Xenoph. Hell. 4. 5. 14 οἱ δὲ
Λακεδαιμόνιοι ἐπεὶ ἠκοντίζοντο καὶ ὁ μέν

τις ἐτέτρωτο ὁ δὲ καὶ ἐπεπτώκει, τούτους
μὲν ἐκέλευον τοὺς ὑπασπιστὰς ἀραμένους
ἀποφέρειν εἰς Λέχαιον· καὶ οὗτοι μόνοι τῆς
μόρας τῇ ἀληθείᾳ ἐσώθησαν (ὑπασπισταί,
i.e. γυμνῆτες, i.e. helots).

ἐδυσθανάτεε, 'was dying hard,'
i.e. kept death at bay for some time ;
cp. Plato Rep. 406 B δυσθανατῶν δὲ ὑπὸ
σοφίας εἰς γῆρας ἀφίκετο (anticipated
just before in μακρὸν τὸν θάνατον αὑτῷ
ποιήσας). How long the struggle lasted
in the case of Kallikrates is not stated.

Ἀείμνηστον ἄνδρα Πλαταιέα.
This can hardly be any other than the
ἀνὴρ ἐν Σπάρτῃ λόγιμος who had the
credit of dealing Mardonios his death-
wound, cp. c. 64 supra, perhaps one
with ὁ στρατηγὸς τῶν Πλαταιέων of
Plutarch Aristeid. 11. How the dying
Kallikrates comes to be conversing with
him ἔξω τῆς μάχης is not very clear.
Were there Plataians attached to the
staff of Pausanias, or working with the
Spartans (as well as those with the
Athenians) ; or had the Plataians been
shifted wholesale to the right wing ; or
did the interview between Aeimnestos
and the dying man take place after the
battle ?

8. πρό, 'on behalf of . .' = ἕνεκα,
ὑπέρ. Cp. c. 22 supra.

9. οὐκ ἐχρήσατο τῇ χειρί: cp. 3. 78
ὁρέων δέ μιν ἀργὸν ἐπεστεῶτα ὁ Γοβρύης
εἴρετο ὅ τι οὐ χρᾶται τῇ χειρί.

73. 1. Ἀθηναίων δέ. The interest is
shifted to the left wing, of which very
little has been recorded in the actual
battle, cp. cc. (60), 61, 67, (70). A different source is doubtless here in evidence,
though the introduction of the verb
λέγεται is not reassuring as to its
reliability. εὐδοκιμῆσαι is, of course,
less than ἀριστεῦσαι, which is used of
the same man in the next chapter.

Σωφάνης ὁ Εὐτυχίδεω: an old

ἐκ δήμου Δεκελεῆθεν, Δεκελέων δὲ τῶν κοτε ἐργασαμένων
ἔργον χρήσιμον ἐς τὸν πάντα χρόνον, ὡς αὐτοὶ Ἀθηναῖοι
λέγουσι. ὡς γὰρ δὴ τὸ πάλαι κατὰ Ἑλένης κομιδὴν Τυνδαρίδαι

73. 2 ἐκ : ἐὼν Koen, Holder, van H. ‖ δεκελῆθεν ΒΡ Marc. z : δὲ κεκλῆθεν
C ‖ κοτὲ Bekker : ποτε libri   4 τοπάλαι Pz

acquaintance, as the work of Hdt. now
stands ; cp. 6. 92, where his deme but
not his patronymic is given ; cp. further
c. 75 *infra*, where his biography is
enlarged. The father's name, Euty-
chides, is commoner at Athens and
elsewhere than the son's (cp. Pape-
Benseler, *sub vv.*), but nothing more
appears to be recorded of this particular
man. Greek onomatology rang a score
of changes on the significant compounds
εὐ-τυχ-. The wish was father to the
name.

2. **ἐκ δήμου Δεκελεῆθεν.** The first
two words were superfluous in official
Attic. The *demotikon* is given as Δεκελεύς
here and in 6. 92. Δεκελειεύς *ap*. Steph.
B. *sub v.*, also Δεκελειᾶθεν and Δεκε-
λειόθεν. On the position of Dekeleia
cp. c. 15 *supra*. It belonged to the (VIII)
Hippothontis (cp. *l.c.*) and was perhaps
the chief deme in the Mesogaian or
Land-Trittys of that tribe, though this
point does not appear to have been as yet
established epigraphically (cp. Judeich
ap. Pauly-Wissowa ii. 2229 f. ; Milch-
höfer, *ib.* iv. 2425).

Δεκελέων δὲ τῶν κοτε κτλ. The
genitive may be in rough apposition to
Δεκελεῆθεν or to δήμου, or constructed
with Σωφάνης, or even regarded as a
correction or limitation of Ἀθηναίων, or,
in fine, of no very strict construction at
all ! The digression or excursus into
the mythical history of Attica is rather
forced, and looks like an insertion, but
how far the insertion extends is not
obvious. Insertions may even have been
made here at more than one time ; thus
the last sentence of the chapter (οὗτω
ὥστε . . ἀπέχεσθαι) is manifestly to be
dated after the outbreak of the Peloponnesian war, but may be a separate
addition. There are, in fact, traces in
this passage of all three drafts, or stages,
in the composition of Hdt.'s work, viz.
the original basis, which would naturally
record the ἀριστήια on the Athenian
side ; the addition of a note on the
mythical antecedents of Dekeleia ;
thirdly, the little appendix upon the
sparing of Dekeleia by the Spartans.

The first would belong to the earliest
draft ; the second might have resulted
from Hdt.'s first visit to Athens ; the
third is plainly an addition to be dated
after 431 B.C. Cp. Introduction, § 9.

3. **ἐς τὸν πάντα χρόνον,** 'for ever,' 'to
all time' ; contrast c. 13. 6 *supra*.

ὡς αὐτοὶ Ἀθηναῖοι λέγουσι, 'as
even Athenian (writers) themselves admit.' The mythic origins of the privileges enjoyed by the Dekeleians at Sparta
had doubtless been made the subject of
research and investigation by native
writers before Hdt. penned this passage ;
cp. Introduction, § 10.

4. **τὸ πάλαι** here goes back to a time
before the Trojan war.

κατὰ Ἑλένης κομιδήν : *ad recu-
perandam Helenam*, Baehr. Helene is,
of course, Homeric Helen, Ἀργείη Ἑλένη
Il. 2. 161, sister of Kastor and Poly-
deukes, *Il.* 3. 237 f., daughter of Tyndareus and Leda, *Od.* 11. 299 ff., unless
indeed Zeus himself was her sire, *Od.* 4.
219, 227, cp. 569. The adventure here
involved is not recorded in Homer, but
it was perhaps represented on the Chest
of Kypselos (Pausan. 5. 19. 3, Dio
Chrysost. *Or*. 11. 325 R, Dindorf-Teubner
i. 179), and was familiar to the Lyric
poets ; cp. Alkman, Fr. 13 = Pausan. 1.
41. 4, Stesichoros 27 = Pausan. 2. 22. 6,
Pindar, Fr. 258 = Pausan. 1. 41. 5 ; and
the story is told by Diodor. 4. 63,
Plutarch, *Thes.* 31–34, Pausan. 1. 17. 5
(in part). Theseus and Peirithous stole
Helena, a lovely girl of ten years, as she
danced before the altar of Artemis
Orthia in Sparta ; they drew lots for
her, Theseus won, and put her for safety
in Aphidna with his mother Aithra.
During his absence (to help Peirithous
to carry off Persephone !) the sons of
Tyndareus invaded Attica, and recovered
their sister. Aithra was carried off by
them into captivity, which may account
for her figuring as attendant on Helena
in the *Iliad*.

Τυνδαρίδαι. This patronymic does
not occur in *Iliad* or *Odyssey*, but makes
its appearance (like Διὸς κοῦροι) in the
Hymns, e.g. 17, 33. (Does the name

ἐσέβαλον ἐς γῆν τὴν Ἀττικὴν σὺν στρατοῦ πλήθεϊ καὶ ἀν- 5
ίστασαν τοὺς δήμους, οὐκ εἰδότες ἵνα ὑπεξέκειτο ἡ Ἑλένη,
τότε λέγουσι τοὺς Δεκελέας, οἱ δὲ αὐτὸν Δέκελον ἀχθόμενόν
τε τῇ Θησέος ὕβρι καὶ δειμαίνοντα περὶ πάσῃ τῇ Ἀθηναίων
χώρῃ, ἐξηγησάμενόν σφι τὸ πᾶν πρῆγμα κατηγήσασθαι ἐπὶ
τὰς Ἀφίδνας, τὰς δὴ Τιτακὸς ἐὼν αὐτόχθων καταπροδιδοῖ 10

5 πλήθεϊ AB   6 ἡ om. C   7 καὶ τοὺς z ‖ δεκελεὸν B   8 ὕβρει
C Marc. ‖ δημαίνοντα C   10 ἀφνίδας B ‖ τὰς δή τοι κακὸς Marc.

contain that conjunction of -νδ-, the
supposed minor-Asiatic equivalent for
-nt-, -nth-, Kretschmer, 293 ff.? (L. & S.
appear to connect it with (Lat.) tund-o
etc.).)

5. **ἀνίστασαν τοὺς δήμους,** 'were
upsetting, depopulating, ravaging, the
demes.' There is no material anachronism in the assumption that the Demoi
were in existence in the days of Theseus,
for the Demoi are the oldest institutions
in historic Attica; yet the phraseology
here, as elsewhere in Hdt. (cp. 1. 60
bis), is rather post-Kleisthenean (cp. 5.
69) than 'Theseian.' Theseus, indeed,
was already accounted the author of the
Attic synoikismos (cp. Thuc. 2. 15),
but Thucydides is careful to represent
the Thesean synoikism as a purely
political centralization, the units in which
had been themselves πόλεις. Diodoros
l.c. has τῶν δὲ Ἀθηναίων ἀγανακτούντων
ἐπὶ τῷ γεγονότι φοβηθεὶς ὁ Θησεὺς ὑπεξ-
έθετο τὴν Ἑλένην εἰς Ἀφίδναν, μίαν τῶν
Ἀττικῶν πόλεων. (That the description
may not square with the hypothetical
synoikism need not distress us.)

6. **ἵνα,** ubi : cp. Index.

7. **τότε** is, of course, 'at the date of
Theseus.'

λέγουσι . . οἱ δέ shows that
there were already conflicting variants on
the tradition; an extreme illustration
is supplied by Plutarch (Thes. 32) who
substitutes Ἀκάδημος and the Ἀκαδήμεια
for Δέκελος and Δεκέλεια. Δέκελος is, of
course, the eponymous hero of the deme.
Stein connects his name with δεικνύναι
indicare, index. and sees in this etymology the origin of the rôle played by
Δέκελος or the Δεκελεῖς.

8. **τῇ Θησέος ὕβρι** : primarily the
adventure with Peirithous itself; cp.
the passage cited from Diodoros above;
in the second place, perhaps more generally the high-handed tyranny of Theseus,
his attack on local liberties, and so on.
The phrase is hardly of Attic origin, and

perhaps betrays Hdt.'s Anti-Ionism (cp.
Hdt. IV.-VI. ii. 214). In the version
followed by Plutarch the Tyndaridai are
working in the interests of Menestheus,
the earliest demagogue on record (c.
32). So too in Pausanias 1. 17. 5 στρα-
τεύουσιν ἐς Ἀφίδναν οἱ Τυνδάρεω παῖδες,
καὶ τήν τε Ἀφίδναν αἱροῦσι καὶ Μενεσθέα
ἐπὶ βασιλείᾳ κατήγαγον.

**δειμαίνοντα περὶ πάσῃ τῇ Ἀθη-
ναίων χώρῃ** : this solicitude on the part
of the local leader, or hero, for 'the
whole Athenian land' presupposes the
unification of Attica, or at least a
synoikism on a large scale, and a solidarity of interests; but the variant cited
above from Pausanias might suggest
that what Dekelos really wished to avoid
was being subjected to Menestheus and
the central power! In reality Dekelos
here plays the chief rôle, and the political
turn given to the legend there is probably
afterthought. **περί** with dat. causal,
especially common with verbs denoting
fear, courage, hope, etc.

9. **ἐξηγησάμενόν σφι . . κατηγήσασθαι.** Hdt. is not over-careful to
avoid such stylistic incongruities; cp.
Index s.v. Iterations.

10. **τὰς Ἀφίδνας.** Strabo 397 gives
Ἀφίδνα (λέγουσι δὲ καὶ πληθυντικῶς
Ἀφίδνας) as one of the twelve original
city-states of Attica, on the authority
of Philochoros. Steph. Byz. makes
Aphidna a deme of the Leontis, apparently a slip for Aiantis (cp. Milchhoefer
ap. Pauly-Wissowa i. 2719), and mentions
the suggestive fact that there was an
Aphidna in Lakonia. The position of
the Attic deme is identified on and
round Kotroni, in the neighbourhood
of Marathon; but Aphidna probably
belonged to the Mesogaian Trittys of
the Aiantis, and may have given its
name thereto; it was one of the largest
and most important demes in Attica
(cp. Milchhoefer, Demenordnung, 1892,
p. 8) and was fortified in the time of

Τυνδαρίδῃσι. τοῖσι δὲ Δεκελεῦσι ἐν Σπάρτῃ ἀπὸ τούτου τοῦ
ἔργου ἀτελείη τε καὶ προεδρίη διατελέει ἐς τόδε αἰεὶ ἔτι
ἐοῦσα, οὕτω ὥστε καὶ ἐς τὸν πόλεμον τὸν ὕστερον πολλοῖσι
ἔτεσι τούτων γενόμενον Ἀθηναίοισί τε καὶ Πελοποννησίοισι,
15 σινομένων τὴν ἄλλην Ἀττικὴν Λακεδαιμονίων, Δεκελέης ἀπ-
74 έχεσθαι. τούτου τοῦ δήμου ἐὼν ὁ Σωφάνης καὶ ἀριστεύσας
τότε Ἀθηναίων διξοὺς λόγους λεγομένους ἔχει, τὸν μὲν ὡς ἐκ

11 ἐν Σπάρτῃ post ἔργου z   12 προεδρίηι Β : προεδρείη Marc.
15 σινεομένων Β   74. 1 τοῦ om. Α¹

Demosthenes (de Cor. 38), and probably
from time immemorial. It appears again
in Hdt. as the deme of Kallimachos the
polemarch at Marathon, 6. 109, and of
the insignificant Timodemos, 8. 125.

Τιτακός is unmistakably the
eponymous hero of the neighbouring
deme Τιτακίδαι, and in this story of his
betrayal of Aphidnai Milchhoefer (Demenordnung p. 34) sees indications (1)
of local jealousies, (2) of the former inclusion of Titakidai in Aphidnai. The
little deme, together with Thyrgonidai
and Perrhidai (all members of the
Aphidna-Trittys), may have occupied
the modern villages of Kapandriti, Masi
and Tsiurka.

11. τοῖσι δὲ Δεκελεῦσι ἐν Σπάρτῃ:
doubtless the Dekeleians reall held
privileges in Sparta, which had yprigin-
ated in legendary days, before the coming
of the Dorians, and were continuously
maintained, though perhaps not very
often exercised, in historic Sparta. ἀπό,
'from the date of . .,' rather temporal
than causal.

12. ἀτελείη τε καὶ προεδρίη: two
privileges frequently combined (cp. 1.
54); the former term denotes financial,
economic, freedom from taxation, dues,
etc., which might be complete or partial
(cp. 3. 67); the latter term denotes
precedence (front seat) at public festivals,
games, etc.; cp. L. & S. sub vv. (The
latter could only be a personal privilege, conferred upon individuals or
communities; the former might be
attached to property, irrespective of the
particular owner; cp. the ἀτελὲς χωρίον
on Hymettos, Ἀθην. πολ. 16. 6.)
Demosthenes, Lept. 105, says that the
Lakedaimonians (and Thebans) οὐδενὶ
τῶν παρ' ἑαυτοῖς διδόασι τοιαύτην οὐδεμίαν
τιμήν (sc. ἀτελείαν). That is an obvious
exaggeration: ἔστι γὰρ αὐτοῖς νόμος τὸν
μὲν γεννήσαντα τρεῖς υἱοὺς ἄφρουρον εἶναι

τὸν δὲ τέτταρας ἀτελῆ πάντων, Aristot.
Pol. 2. 9. 18 = 1270 Β.

ἐς τόδε αἰεὶ ἔτι ἐοῦσα. As the
text now stands the date here indicated
comes down to the out-break of the war
noted in the next following sentence;
but, if the latter is an addition, these
words may have stood originally as denoting a date fifteen to twenty years
earlier. We have here also traces of the
stratification in Hdt.'s composition, which
explains the appearance of the later,
or latest references in the portion earliest
drafted; cp. Introduction, § 9, and next
note.

13. οὕτω ὥστε κτλ. As the privileges
of the Dekeleians in Sparta must have
been suspended by war, this passage
(Stein too observes) would have the air
of an addition, while grammatically the
οὕτω has no proper reference to what
precedes. The war here mentioned is
plainly the 'ten years' war' which
broke out in 431 B.C., and the special
favour shown to Dekeleia is hardly less
plainly to be dated to the first invasion,
in which Archidamos laid waste the
Thriasian plain, and all the parts of
Attica north of the city, and retired via
(Dekeleia) Oropos and Boiotia, Thuc. 2.
18-23. ἐς τὸν πόλεμον is hardly so clear
as ἐν τῷ πολέμῳ, or κατὰ τὸν πόλεμον
(cp. 7. 137) would have been, and is
perhaps only a carelessness produced by
the proximity of ἐς τόδε just before (cp.
c. 64 supra).

15. τὴν ἄλλην Ἀττικήν looks like
an exaggeration; the whole of the south
of Attica was ravaged in the second
invasion, 430 B.C., Thuc. 2. 55, 57.

74. 1. ἀριστεύσας: cp. c. 73 ad init.
2. διξοὺς λόγους λεγομένους ἔχει: sc.
ὁ Σωφάνης: for λόγον ἔχειν (to be
reported) cp. 5. 66. Stein suggests as
the source of these 'Märchen' Skolia
in honour of the popular Marathono-

τοῦ ζωστῆρος τοῦ θώρηκος ἐφόρεε χαλκέη ἀλύσι δεδεμένην
ἄγκυραν σιδηρέην, τὴν ὅκως πελάσειε ἀπικνεόμενος τοῖσι
πολεμίοισι βαλλέσκετο, ἵνα δή μιν οἱ πολέμιοι ἐκπίπτοντες 5
ἐκ τῆς τάξιος μετακινῆσαι μὴ δυναίατο· γινομένης δὲ φυγῆς
τῶν ἐναντίων δέδοκτο τὴν ἄγκυραν ἀναλαβόντα οὕτω διώκειν.
οὗτος μὲν οὕτω λέγεται, ὁ δ' ἕτερος τῶν λόγων τῷ πρότερον
λεχθέντι ἀμφισβατέων λέγεται, ὡς ἐπ' ἀσπίδος αἰεὶ περι-
θεούσης καὶ οὐδαμὰ ἀτρεμιζούσης ἐφόρεε ἄγκυραν, καὶ οὐκ ἐκ 10
τοῦ θώρηκος δεδεμένην σιδηρέην. ἔστι δὲ καὶ ἕτερον Σωφάνεϊ 75
λαμπρὸν ἔργον ἐξεργασμένον, ὅτι περικατημένων Ἀθηναίων
Αἴγιναν Εὐρυβάτην τὸν Ἀργεῖον ἄνδρα πεντάεθλον ἐκ προ-

---

3 ἀλύσει αCSV   4 ἀπικνεομένοισι τοῖσι V: ἀπικνευμένοισι
τῆσι R: ἀπικνεόμενος <ἐς μάχην> τοῖσι Ι Stein⁽²⁾   5 βαλλέσκετο Pz,
Stein², van H.: βαλέσκετο   6 κινῆσαι Marc.   7 ἐδέδοκτο Β,
Holder: ἐδέδοκτό <οἱ> van H.   8 οὗτος: οὕτω B ‖ ὁ δ'.. λέγεται
om. B   9 ἀμφισβητέων ΒPz   10 οὐδαμᾶ Rz ‖ ἐπίσημον ἄγκυραν Β,
Holder, van H.: ἄγκυραν εἰκασμένην sive μεμιμημένην (ἐπίσημον omisso)
coni. Stein² ³   75. 1 σωφάνει AB   2 ἐξειργασμένον Marc. ‖
ὅτε Β, Krueger, Holder, van H.   3 εὐρυβάντην Marc.: εὐρυβιάδην Β ‖
ἀρεῖον C ‖ προβλήσιος Β

---

maches. (It is not expressly recorded
that Sophanes was at Marathon, but
he may certainly be credited therewith.)
Such Skolia may have contained expressions or allusions, of which the διξοὶ
λόγοι here reported are prosaic interpretations.

(a) According to the one, Sophanes
used to carry, slung (δεδεμένην ἐκ) from
the belt of his cuirass on a bronze chain,
an iron anchor; this he would throw,
when he approached the enemy (and it
would, no doubt, stick in the ground),
in such a way that the enemy could not
make him budge, though they might
charge him; then, when the adversaries
were put to flight, his plan was to pick
up his anchor and so be after them.
This is not a very credible story, and
it is contradicted by the other.

(b) He had upon his shield an anchor
as a device, or emblem; and his shield
was in perpetual motion, never at rest.
In which case there was a contrast
between the man's emblem and his
action.

It is possible that the latter and
simpler story was at the root of the
other, or that some jest on the anchor
and its bearer generated the more prosaic
and less credible interpretation.

7. δέδοκτο: sc. αὐτῷ.

οὕτω: i.e. to take up his anchor
before attempting to pursue.

9. ἀμφισβατέων: cp. the subst. 8. 81.

10. ἀτρεμιζούσης: the form ἀτρεμέειν
7. 8, 8. 68 supra; but ἀτρεμίζειν 7. 18.
It must have been the man, not his
shield, that was so restless. The
Karians had the credit of such inven-
tions; cp. 1. 171.

75. 1. ἔστι δὲ .. ἐξεργασμένον. The
position of ἔστι shows that it is not a
mere auxiliary, nor is the form of construction merely equivalent to a perfect
passive. The λαμπρὸν ἔργον, though
wrought, and wrought out, in the past,
is conceived of as existing in the present:
it is for ever.

2. περικατημένων, 'blockading':
perfect in form, but present, or imperfect, in sense. The verb is used here
as in 8. 111 of an island-city, but the
operations are in part at least on land.

3. Εὐρυβάτην τὸν Ἀργεῖον. The story
is told, and that more fully, in 6. 92,
though without cross-reference either
here or there; the present is probably
the older passage. Had the other been
composed first, the further notes on
Sophanes would have been there added
(unless it were supposed that the passage was composed before his death!
Even so, a reference to his anchor might

κλήσιος ἐφόνευσε. αὐτὸν δὲ Σωφάνεα χρόνῳ ὕστερον τούτων
5 κατέλαβε ἄνδρα γενόμενον ἀγαθόν, Ἀθηναίων στρατηγέοντα
ἅμα Λεάγρῳ τῷ Γλαύκωνος, ἀποθανεῖν ὑπὸ Ἠδωνῶν ἐν Δάτῳ
περὶ τῶν μετάλλων τῶν χρυσέων μαχόμενον.

---

4 τουτέων z   7 μαχεόμενον z : om. B

have been expected). Cp. Introduction,
§§ 7, 8.

πεντάεθλον : cp. c. 33 *supra*.

ἐκ προκλήσιος ἐφόνευσε : cp. 5. 1 ;
i.e. 'he challenged (or answered a
challenge) to single combat and slew . .'
The fuller story in 6. 92, from the
Aiginetan war (487–488 B.C.), reports
that Eurybates was Strategos of the
1000 Argive volunteers who fought for
Aigina, and that he slew three Athenians
in single combat before succumbing to
Sophanes, a record which on the one
hand enhances, on the other diminishes,
the achievement of Sophanes ; the
Argive pentathlete may have been
pretty well done-up before he reached
his round with Sophanes.

4. **χρόνῳ ὕστερον τούτων** : i.e. subsequent to the Persian war ; op. c. 73
supra ; the exact date is not so certain.

5. **κατέλαβε** is impersonal ; cp. cc. 93,
104 *infra*.

**Ἀθηναίων στρατηγέοντα ἅμα
Λεάγρῳ τῷ Γλαύκωνος,** 'Leagros son of
Glaukon' was no doubt the father of
'Glaukon son of Leagros' (Thuc. 1. 51.
4 ; cp. *C.I.A.* i. 179, Hicks² No. 53),
who commanded at Sybota in 432 B.C.,
as he had previously done in the Samian
war, Androtion *Fr.* 44 a. Nearly half
a score Athenians of the name of
Glaukon can be identified (op. Pape-
Benseler *sub v.*), but nothing more is
known of the eldest one here named.

6. **ἀποθανεῖν ὑπὸ Ἠδόνων ἐν Δάτῳ.**
Stein identifies this disaster with the
defeat recorded by Thucydides 1. 100. 3
(cp. 4. 102. 2) synchronously with the
revolt and blockade of Thasos, and
dated by Busolt, III. i. 202, very
precisely to the late summer of 465 B.C.
Thucydides, however, without mentioning Daton makes Drabeskos the scene
of the disaster. Stein suggests that
Hdt. has confounded the objective, or
goal, of the expedition, viz. Daton, with
the scene of the Athenian defeat, viz.
Drabeskos, which is to be placed on the
road to Datos, or Daton. Drabeskos
is, indeed, the less problematic spot
geographically ; its position is ascertained
"on the road from Herakleia Sintica

to Philippi" (Forbiger, *Alt. Geogr.* iii.
1070), or at any rate to the north, and
inland from Philippi (cp. mod. *Drama*).
If the Athenians were defeated at
Drabeskos on their way to Datos, or
Daton, they were fetching a considerable
compass from Amphipolis and the
Strymon. Busolt (*l.c.*, following Henzen)
regards Daton, at least in Hdt.'s time,
as the name not of a town but of a
district (that too seems to be Stein's
first idea) ; the reconciliation between
Hdt. and Thuc. in this case being
effected by the supposition that Hdt.
names the region and Thuc. the exact
scene, or the township nearest to the
scene, of the disaster. Cp. Strabo 331
(7. fr. 36) παρὰ δὲ τὴν παραλίαν τοῦ
Στρυμόνος καὶ Δατηνῶν πόλις Νεάπολις
καὶ αὐτὸ τὸ Δάτον, εὔκαρπα πεδία καὶ
λίμνην καὶ ποταμοὺς καὶ ναυπήγια καὶ
χρυσεῖα λυσιτελῆ ἔχον, ἀφ' οὗ καὶ παροι-
μιάζονται Δάτον ἀγαθῶν ὡς καὶ ἀγαθῶν
ἀγαθίδας. This passage places the town
of Daton on the coast, hard by Neapolis ;
but though this Neapolis appears on
the Attic tribute-lists of the fifth
century (Νεάπολις ἐν Θράκῃ, N. παρ'
Ἀντισάραν, Νεοπολῖται οἱ παρὰ Θάσον)
Daton is never mentioned. Neapolis
was, in fact, at that period the port for
the district of Datos ; the town of
Daton was only founded c. 360 B.C. by
the Thasians, when they took possession
of Krenides, under the leadership of the
exiled Athenian Kallistratos (Busolt,
op. c. 197 note 5). The identification
of Daton with Krenides, the later
Philippi (Appian *B. C.* 4. 105 οἱ δὲ
Φίλιπποι πόλις ἐστὶν ἡ Δάτος ὠνομάζετο
πάλαι, καὶ Κρηνίδες ἔτι πρὸ Δάτου. So
too Harpokration *s.v. Δατός* (*sic*) on the
authority of Ephoros and Philochoros ;
cp. Diodor. 16. 3. 7), is hardly reconcilable with Strabo's statement
above quoted ; but Strabo must give
way to Harpokration's authorities ; least
of all should Datos have been identified
with Neapolis (as by Leake, *N.G.* iii.
224). On the Edonians cp. 7. 110.

ἀποθανεῖν ὑπό : cp. c. 37.

7. **περὶ τῶν μετάλλων τῶν χρυσέων.**
The whole region was argentiferous

Ὡς δὲ τοῖσι Ἕλλησι ἐν Πλαταιῆσι κατέστρωντο οἱ 76
βάρβαροι, ἐνθαῦτά σφι ἐπῆλθε γυνὴ αὐτόμολος· ἡ ἐπειδὴ
ἔμαθε ἀπολωλότας τοὺς Πέρσας καὶ νικῶντας τοὺς Ἕλληνας,
ἐοῦσα παλλακὴ Φαρανδάτεος τοῦ Τεάσπιος ἀνδρὸς Πέρσεω,
κοσμησαμένη χρυσῷ <τε> πολλῷ καὶ αὐτὴ καὶ <αἱ> ἀμφίπολοι 5
καὶ ἐσθῆτι τῇ καλλίστῃ τῶν παρεουσέων, καταβᾶσα ἐκ τῆς
ἁρμαμάξης ἐχώρεε ἐς τοὺς Λακεδαιμονίους ἔτι ἐν τῇσι φονῇσι
ἐόντας, ὁρῶσα δὲ πάντα ἐκεῖνα διέποντα Παυσανίην, πρότερόν
τε τὸ οὔνομα ἐξεπισταμένη καὶ τὴν πάτρην ὥστε πολλάκις
ἀκούσασα, ἔγνω τε τὸν Παυσανίην καὶ λαβομένη τῶν γουνά- 10

76. 1 πλαταίῃσι α : πλαταίῃσι β   4 φαρναδάτεος β   5 <τε>
Stein⁽²⁾³, van H. ‖ <αἱ> Reiske, Holder, van H., quod mihi quoque
placitum inserui   6 ἐκ τῶν z   7 ἁρμαμάξης B ‖ φωνῆσιν Marc.
8 ἐόντας om. αC Marc. ‖ ὀρέουσα Stein¹

and auriferous; cp. 7. 112. The mines
at Krenides-Philippi were only fully
exploited by Philip; cp. Diodor. 16. 8.
ὁ τὰ δὲ κατὰ τὴν χώραν χρύσεια μέταλλα
παντελῶς ὄντα λιτὰ καὶ ἄδοξα ταῖς κατα-
σκευαῖς ἐπὶ τοσοῦτον ηὔξησεν ὥστε δύνασθαι
φέρειν αὐτῷ πρόσοδον πλέον ἢ ταλάντων
χιλίων.
76. 1. ἐν Πλαταιῆσι: probably the
actual conflict between the Lakedaimonians and Persians took place on the
soil of Hysiai (cp. c. 62 supra); but (a)
the Athenians were doubtless fighting
on Plataian ground, (b) the island
position was Plataian ground, (c) the
'second position' of the Greeks was on
Plataian ground (c. 25 supra), (d)
Plataia was a much more important
place than Hysiai or Erythrai, the
former of which at least was accounted
Attic ground, cp. 5. 74, and perhaps
subordinate to Plataia, cp. 6. 108 (but
cp. also Plutarch Aristeid. 11). Thus,
all things considered, the battle and
the operations generally seem naturally
associated with the name of Plataia,
albeit, in the reconstruction of the
battle-piece as a whole, Erythrai, Hysiai,
Plataia, and their respective territories,
have to be carefully distinguished; cp.
cc. 15, 19, 25 supra.
κατέστρωντο, as in 8. 53; cp. c.
69 supra.
3. νικῶντας, 'victors'; cp. c. 69
supra.
4. παλλακή: opposed to κουριδίη γυνή
1. 84.
Φαρανδάτεος τοῦ Τεάσπιος.
Pharandates had been ἄρχων, i.e. myri-

arch, of the Mares and Kolchoi in the
army of Xerxes, 7. 79. He was evidently
an Achaimenid (Teaspes), though Hdt.
does not expressly say so; and his
mother, too, was perhaps a sister of
Dareios; cp. 4. 43.
6. τὰν παρεουσέων: not to disparage
her travelling wardrobe, or to suggest
that she had still better at home, but
rather to emphasize its splendour.
7. ἁρμάμαξα: cp. 7. 41, 8. 88.
ἐχώρεε: on foot.
ἔτι ἐν τῇσι φονῇσι ἐόντας, 'still
engaged on the work of slaughter
φοναί is Homeric and poetical; the
singular is not in use.
8. διέπων: as in 6. 107, 5. 22.
πρότερόν τε . . ἀκούσασα, 'as she
was previously well acquainted with
his name and country (father-land),
having heard them again and again'—
her father having been on terms of
ξεινίη with Pausanias; see just below.
9. πάτρη, cp. 6. 126, 'land,' not
'lineage' (as in Il. 13. 354, cp. the use
in Pindar=gens, Rumpel, Lex. Pind. sub
v.). Hdt. has the more usual form
πατρίς, 8. 61, for fatherland; he uses
πατρή for lineage, cp. 3. 75, 2. 143, and
the lady addresses Pausanias not as 'son
of Kleombrotos' (c. 78. 4), but as king
of 'Sparta.' ὥστε=ἅτε: cp. c. 70 supra.
10. ἔγνω, without ever having seen
him before, from now seeing him in
authority. He was probably young;
cp. c. 10 supra.
λαβομένη τῶν γουνάτων: as a
ἱκέτις, cp. Od. 6. 310 μητρὸς ποτὶ γούνασι
χεῖρας | βάλλειν ἡμετέρης ἵνα νόστιμον

των ἔλεγε τάδε. "ὦ βασιλεῦ Σπάρτης, ῥῦσαί με τὴν ἱκέτιν
αἰχμαλώτου δουλοσύνης. σὺ γὰρ καὶ ἐς τόδε ὤνησας, τούσδε
ἀπολέσας τοὺς οὔτε δαιμόνων οὔτε θεῶν ὄπιν ἔχοντας. εἰμὶ
δὲ γένος μὲν Κῴη, θυγάτηρ δὲ Ἡγητορίδεω τοῦ Ἀνταγόρεω.
15 βίῃ δέ με λαβὼν ἐν Κῷ εἶχε ὁ Πέρσης." ὁ δὲ ἀμείβεται

---

11 βασιλεὺς C ‖ ῥῦσαί B, Stein², Holder, van H.: λῦσαί   12
δουλωσύνης R: δουλωσύνην C ‖ ἐς del. Krueger, van H.   15 βίῃ B
‖ ἐν Κῴ z: ἐκ κῶ B: ἐν κῶ ceteri: del. Kallenberg

ἦμαρ ἴδηαι, 7. 142 ἀμφὶ δ' ἄρ' Ἀρήτης
βάλε γούνασι χεῖρας Ὀδυσσεύς. C.
Sittl, Die Gebärden der Gr. u. Röm.
1890, 163. In order to perform such a
gesture the suppliant would have to
kneel or prostrate himself.

11. ὦ βασιλεῦ Σπάρτης. Thus this
lady of Kos inaugurates the error which
dies so hard ; cp. c. 5 supra. She
doubtless knew better, but thought there
was nothing to lose by a little exaggeration : was the fatal ambition of Pausanias
born in this moment ? But after all
βασιλεύς was not the technical term at
Sparta, but βαγός or ἀρχαγέτης, cp.
Gilbert, Gr. Staatsalt. i.² 47.

ῥῦσαί με τὴν ἱκέτιν: the article
is idiomatic, with the appositive, "as
regularly with personal pronouns"
(Sitzler), cp. ὑμέας . . τοὺς Ἀθηναίους c.
46 supra.

12. αἰχμαλώτου δ., a very strong
genitive : from, out of, 'slavery as a
prisoner of war.' In c. 90 infra ἐκ is
expressed. The lady was not a prisoner
of war to the Persians ; but she is asking
not to be treated as a prisoner of war by
the Greeks.

ἐς τόδε, 'so far,' of time ; cp. c.
73 supra ; or perhaps of action, as explained in the next sentence.

13. τοὺς οὔτε δαιμόνων οὔτε θεῶν
ὄπιν ἔχοντας: ὅπις 8. 143 in a similar
connexion (on the lips of Aristeides ?).
The charge is, of course, unjust, even as
respects 'the gods of Greece' ; cp. l.c.
supra ; but allowance in this case may
be made for a lady whose situation is
not free from ambiguity.

δαίμονες, as distinct from θεοί, are
not merely deities of lower rank, but
perhaps distinctly 'deified dead' ; so the
departed Dareios, Aischyl. Pers. 620, the
departed Alkestis, Eurip. Alk. 1003.
Cp. Hesiod, Wks. 121 αὐτὰρ ἐπειδὴ

τοῦτο γένος <sc. τὸ χρύσεον> κατὰ γαῖα
κάλυψεν, τοὶ μὲν δαίμονές εἰσι Διὸς μεγάλου διὰ βουλὰς ἐσθλοί, ἐπιχθόνιαι,
φύλακες θνητῶν ἀνθρώπων.

14. γένος μὲν Κῴη : the γένος here is
locative rather than genetic. Kos was
at this time under the government of
Artemisia, cp. 7. 99, in succession to the
righteous Kadmos, 7. 164. She ought
to have given her own name.

Ἡγητορίδεω τοῦ Ἀνταγόρεω.
Of these Koans, Hegetoridas (a truly
aristocratic name) and his father Antagoras, nothing more appears to be known.
Plutarch, Aristeid. 23, mentions an
Antagoras of Chios as one of the leaders
in the movement for the transfer of the
hegemony from Sparta to Athens, and
actually heading an attack on Pausanias.
Polyainos 2. 33 has an anecdote of a
Hegetoridas of Thasos, who was instrumental in bringing about the surrender
of the island to Athens.

15. βίῃ δέ με . . εἶχε ὁ Πέρσης.
'The Persian' might have a more extended sense than Pharandates. Perhaps
the lady had been kidnapped in her
youth or infancy. It is not easy to
see what Pharandates or the Persians
generally would be doing in Kos ; it is
not even certain that Kos had joined in
the 'Ionic' revolt, or we might suppose
that the daughter of Pharandates had
been carried off then ; but cp. 7. 164
supra. The βίῃ might qualify both the
participle and the verb (ἔχειν, cp. 8. 136.
4, and 8. 68. 12), but the lady of course
may be overstating the case.

ὁ δὲ ἀμείβεται. The reply and
the conduct of Pausanias proves him a
cavalier sans reproche. This anecdote
of the Koan Anonyma is the first of a
series, in which the moral contrast
between Hellenism and Barbarism is
enforced and illustrated by incidents
from the battle-field of Plataia.

τοισίδε. "γύναι, θάρσεε καὶ ὡς ἱκέτις καὶ εἰ δὴ πρὸς τούτῳ
τυγχάνεις ἀληθέα λέγουσα καὶ εἰς θυγάτηρ Ἡγητορίδεω τοῦ
Κῴου, ὃς ἐμοὶ ξεῖνος μάλιστα τυγχάνει ἐὼν τῶν περὶ ἐκείνους
τοὺς χώρους οἰκημένων." ταῦτα δὲ εἴπας τότε μὲν ἐπέτρεψε
τῶν ἐφόρων τοῖσι παρεοῦσι, ὕστερον δὲ ἀπέπεμψε ἐς Αἴγιναν, 20
ἐς τὴν αὐτὴ ἤθελε ἀπικέσθαι.

Μετὰ δὲ τὴν ἄπιξιν τῆς γυναικός, αὐτίκα μετὰ ταῦτα 77
ἀπίκοντο Μαντινέες ἐπ' ἐξεργασμένοισι· μαθόντες δὲ ὅτι
ὕστεροι ἥκουσι τῆς συμβολῆς, συμφορὴν ἐποιεῦντο μεγάλην,
ἄξιοί τε ἔφασαν εἶναι σφέας ζημιῶσαι. πυνθανόμενοι δὲ τοὺς

---

16 τοισίδε Stein : ὧδε Β : τοῦσδε ceteri || θάρσει libri, Holder, van H.
|| τοῦτο Β   17 εἰς Β : εἰ α : εἶ ceteri   18 κείνους Β   19 οἰκεο-
μένων z || μέν <μιν> Bekker, van H.   21 ἠθέλησεν Marc. || ἀπικέσθαι
om. Β, Holder, van H.   77. 1 μετὰ ταῦτα del. Krueger, van H.
3 ὕστεροι Marc. z, Stein², van H. : ὕστερον || συμβουλῆς ΒC   4 aut
ἀξίους aut σφεῖς requirit van H. || εἶναι ἔφασαν Β

---

18. ξεῖνος μάλιστα. On ξεινία op. 7.
116 supra.

τῶν περὶ ἐκ. τ. χ. οἰκημένων :
cp. 7. 102 for the same phrase.

20. τῶν ἐφόρων τοῖσι παρεοῦσι,
perhaps two in number; op. Xenoph.
Respub. Lac. 13. 5 πάρεισι δὲ καὶ τῶν
ἐφόρων δύο, οἳ πολυπραγμονοῦσι μὲν
οὐδέν, ἢν μὴ ὁ βασιλεὺς προσκαλῇ·
ὁρῶντες δὲ ὅ τι ποιεῖ ἕκαστος πάντας σω-
φρονίζουσιν, ὡς τὸ εἰκός. The fact that
we do not find the presence of Ephors
noted in the narratives of the fifth
century does not prove that they were
not present, but there are occasions upon
which they are rather conspicuous by
their absence, e.g. with Leotychidas at
Mykale, with Pausanias at Byzantion,
with Agis at Dekeleia (cp. Thuc. 8. 5.
3). Rawlinson, indeed, would date the
regular practice described by Xenophon
only to the year 403 B.C., cp. Hell. 2. 4.
36. But the present instance makes the
practice look older, though it may not
have affected the Navarchy.

ἐς Αἴγιναν. Hdt. does not say
that there was any special facility for
crossing from Aigina to Kos, but we
may charitably suppose that the lady
wished to return to her father's house,
as, from the way Pausanias speaks,
Hegetoridas must be still alive.

77. 1. μετὰ δὲ τὴν ἄπιξιν : for ἄπιξις
(arrival, advent) op. c. 17 supra. Hdt.
is very exact in dating the next episode,
so as to emphasize the advent of the
Mantineians as too late, ἐπ' ἐξεργα-

σμένοισι, cp. 8. 94, 4. 164. The Koan
lady had reached the Lakedaimonians
while they were still ἐν τῇσι φονῇσι.

αὐτίκα μετὰ ταῦτα, a standing
formula, cp. Index.

2. ἀπίκοντο Μαντινέες : this is their
first appearance since Thermopylai, to
which they sent a force equal to the
Tegeatan, cp. 7. 202. They are not
included in the army-list above, c. 28 ;
the force here in question will have
numbered probably 1000—1500 hoplites.

3. ὕστεροι τῆς συμβολῆς, 'too late
for the engagement'; σ.. cp. c. 70 supra.
If the Mantineians (and Eleians) arrive
too late to take part in the great encounter, were they on other service—for
example, guarding the convoy from the
Peloponnesos, cp. c. 51 supra, or perhaps
engaged, and retarded, by the Persian
cavalry ? The name of the Mantineians
is not on the τρικάρηνος ὄφις (cp. 8. 82,
and c. 81 infra), though that of the
Eleians is.

συμφορὴν ποιέεσθαι : cp. 8. 10, 69.
2 supra, l. 9 infra.

4. ἄξιοί τε ἔφασαν εἶναι σφέας ζημιῶσαι : ἄξιοι is the idiomatic personal
construction ; cp. 8. 65. 11 (αὐτός). The
sentence would be clearer perhaps without
σφέας, leaving ζημιῶσαι as an epexegetical infinitive : as the object is expressed
in σφέας, a subject must be understood,
sc. τοὺς Ἕλληνας, τὸν στρατηγόν, or what
not.

τοὺς Μήδους : here used generally

5 Μήδους τοὺς μετὰ Ἀρταβάζου φεύγοντας, τούτους ἐδίωκον
μέχρι Θεσσαλίης· Λακεδαιμόνιοι δὲ οὐκ ἔων φεύγοντας διώκειν.
οἳ δὲ ἀναχωρήσαντες ἐς τὴν ἑωυτῶν τοὺς ἡγεμόνας τῆς
στρατιῆς ἐδίωξαν ἐκ τῆς γῆς. μετὰ δὲ Μαντινέας ἧκον
Ἠλεῖοι, καὶ ὡσαύτως οἱ Ἠλεῖοι τοῖσι Μαντινεῦσι συμφορὴν
10 ποιησάμενοι ἀπαλλάσσοντο· ἀπελθόντες δὲ καὶ οὗτοι τοὺς
ἡγεμόνας ἐδίωξαν. τὰ κατὰ Μαντινέας μὲν καὶ Ἠλείους
τοσαῦτα.

---

9 ἠλεῖοι PR ‖ ἠλεῖοι BR ‖ μαντιεῦσι C   11 τὰ om. B ‖ ἠλείους PR

---

as = τοὺς βαρβάρους, and not in the specific sense of c. 81 *supra*.

5. ἐδίωκον, 'they were for pursuing,' they offered to pursue—a truly laughable offer on the part of these Mantineian hoplites. The indefinite or even the distant pursuit of a fugitive enemy was against Spartan custom, cp. 8. 108, and Blakesley understands the next sentence as a parenthesis intended to record not a particular prohibition on this occasion, but that general rule: the imperfect οὐκ ἔων hardly supports that view.

On the return of the Mantineians to their home τοὺς ἡγεμόνας τῆς στρατιῆς ἐδίωξαν ἐκ τῆς γῆς. The verb ἐδίωξαν (exiled) after the ἐδίωκον (pursued, or were for pursuing) just before makes a very unfortunate pun, albeit the contrast of the tenses is grammatically effective; perhaps it is only an "unconscious iteration." τοὺς ἡγ. τῆς στ. as a periphrasis for τοὺς στρατηγούς—if that be its significance—is remarkable. Perhaps the ἡγεμονία is emphasized as the offence was one of omission, incurred by the way. Possibly, however, there was a political background to the prosecution. Arkadia, or single states in Arkadia, may have been divided on the question of 'Medism,' cp. 8. 26. In the immediate sequel Mantineia sides with Sparta, or at least preserves a benevolent neutrality, when all the rest of Arkadia rises against her; cp. c. 35 *infra*. Mantineia was early and normally democratic; cp. 4. 161; but the discredit, which the ἡγεμόνες incurred in the Persian war, and the penalties meted out to them, may have brought about a temporary modification of the government of Mantineia (not without Lakonian approval). It does not follow that the leaders were really to blame. The injustice of the Athenian democracy (probably humaner than the Arkadian) towards unfortunate

commanders is notorious; and the comic story in Thuc. 5. 60 of the treatment of Thrasylos, Strategos of Argos, by the Argive democracy in 418 B.C., has much the same moral.

8. μετὰ δὲ Μαντινέας ἧκον Ἠλεῖοι: naturally, as they had further to come. The Eleians had not even sent a contingent to Thermopylai. Yet their name appears upon the Delphian tripod; *I.G.A.* 70; Hill's *Sources*, i. 1; Hicks², No. 19 (5th Coil, No. 27). As the Eleians are not represented in the navy-lists of Artemision and Salamis, nor in the army-list c. 28 *supra*, the occurrence of their name on the monument is problematic (but they at least sent a contingent to the army under Kleombrotos in 480 B.C.; cp. 8. 72). Stein ascribes it to their influence with Sparta; but why then did not Sparta reward the Mantineians also? cp. also notes in Hicks *l.c.* and note to Παλέες in c. 28 *supra*. ὡσαύτως: 7. 86, etc.

9. συμφορὴν ποιησάμενοι: one of the chief grounds of this woe would be that they could have no lot in the Plataian booty, but there was also the loss of honour. The Eleians had a way of being rather behindhand; Thuc. 5. 75. 5. The subsequent exile of their ἡγεμόνες may have a political significance, as in the case of the Mantineians above.

11. τὰ κατὰ Μαντινέας μὲν καὶ Ἠλείους: this story, or rather the brief note to the discredit of the two Peloponnesian democracies, might provoke the suspicion that there was some kind of understanding between them and Argos, not favourable to Sparta, and the recognition of the Spartan ἡγεμονία. But the service of the Mantineians at Thermopylai, the service of the Eleians at the Isthmos, and the arrival of both, even if belated, on the field of Plataia, have to be put in the other scale.

Ἐν δὲ Πλαταιῇσι ἐν τῷ στρατοπέδῳ τῶν Αἰγινητέων ἦν **78**
Λάμπων Πυθέω, Αἰγινητέων <ἐὼν> τὰ πρῶτα· ὃς ἀνοσιώτατον ἔχων λόγον ἵετο πρὸς Παυσανίην, ἀπικόμενος δὲ σπουδῇ
ἔλεγε τάδε. " ὦ παῖ Κλεομβρότου, ἔργον ἔργασταί τοι
ὑπερφυὲς μέγαθός τε καὶ κάλλος, καί τοι θεὸς παρέδωκε 5
ῥυσάμενον τὴν Ἑλλάδα κλέος καταθέσθαι μέγιστον Ἑλλήνων
τῶν ἡμεῖς ἴδμεν. σὺ δὲ καὶ τὰ λοιπὰ τὰ ἐπὶ τούτοισι
ποίησον, ὅκως λόγος τέ σε ἔχῃ ἔτι μέζων καί τις ὕστερον
φυλάσσηται τῶν βαρβάρων μὴ ὑπάρχειν ἔργα ἀτάσθαλα
ποιέων ἐς τοὺς Ἕλληνας· Λεωνίδεω γὰρ ἀποθανόντος ἐν 10

---

78. 1 πλαταίῃσι **a** : πλαταίῃσιν **B**   2 ὁ πυθέω **B** : ὁ Πύθεω z ‖
ἐὼν add. Stein², Holder, van H. ‖ τὰ πρῶτα φέρων z   3 λόγον ἔχων z
‖ ιετο A : ἵετο ceteri (ap. Stein) : ἵκετο SV   7 τὰ λοιπὰ del. Cobet,
van H.   8 μείζων **a**   10 ποιέειν **B**

Plutarch, in the *de malign. Hdti*, takes
no exception to this record; but has
the whole truth been told in the case ?
The story does not come from Mantineian
and Eleian sources, or we should have
had more particulars, and perhaps something to the good credit of the States.
What is related—καὶ φθόνῳ ἂν εἴποιεν.

**78. 1. ἐν τῷ στρατοπέδῳ τῶν Αἰγι-
νητέων:** there were but 500 Aiginetan
hoplites, all told, cp. c. 28 *supra*; as
they were posted next to the Megarians,
they may have been literally ἐν Πλαταιῇσι at this time; but cp. c. 76 *supra*.
They should have been ἐν τῷ Κιθαιρῶνι,
cp. c. 69 *ad f.*

2. Λάμπων Πυθέω: to be distinguished from the Athenian, c. 21 *supra*,
and the Samian, c. 90 *infra*, of the same
name; but this Aiginetan Lampon, son
of Pytheas, may be identified (as by K.
O. Müller, *Aeginetica* 126) with Lampon,
father of Pytheas and Phylakides, whose
victories Pindar celebrates in *Nem.* 5,
Isth. 4 and 5. The Pytheas, son of
Ischenoos, captured off Skiathos, 7. 181
supra, and liberated at Salamis, 8. 92,
can hardly be identical with the father
of Lampon, but he may be of the same
house, the Ψαλυχιάδαι, or Ψαλυχίδαι,
Pindar, *Isth.* 5 (6). 63.

τὰ πρῶτα: as in 6. 100. On this
occasion Lampon may have been Strategos
of the Aiginetans.

ἀνοσιώτατον ἔχων λόγον, 'with a
most impious (shocking) proposal.'

3. ἵετο, 'came full speed'; repeated
in ἀπικόμενος σπουδῇ.

σπουδῇ: cp. cc. 1, 66 *supra*, etc.

4. ὦ παῖ Κλεομβρότου: cp. c. 76 l. 9.

5. ὑπερφυές, 'supernatural,' 'colossal,'
in a bad sense 8. 116; here in a good.

μέγαθός τε καὶ κάλλος: generally
of corporeal beauty; cp. c. 72 *supra*.
Pausanias' work was a καλλίστη νίκη,
c. 64 *supra*. The accusative is "of
reference." Cp. Index.

τοι . . ῥυσάμενον is not strict
grammar; cp. c. 58. 13, 15 *supra*.

θεὸς παρέδωκε: cp. 7. 18, 5. 67.
The god would probably be Zeus.

6. κλέος καταθέσθαι: 7. 220.

μέγιστον . . τῶν ἡμεῖς ἴδμεν: the
formula (cp. 8. 105 *supra*) is here especially interesting, as used, not by the
historian *propria persona*, but by one of
his puppets. The use is hardly quite accurate : the τῶν is presumably masculine,
referring to Ἑλλήνων, though the reference to κλέος might be eased by the use
of that word in the plural (κλέα ἀνδρῶν
Il. 9. 189, *Od.* 8. 73); but πάντων is
here desiderated in either case. The
fame of Leonidas (who is named just
below) is here given a distinct set-back;
but with posterity the failure of Thermopylai has ever outshone the success
at Plataia; cp. Leopardi's *All' Italia*.

7. ἐπὶ here nearly =πρός; cp. 7. 236
(or 'after').

8. λόγος . . σε ἔχῃ: λόγος here comes
near to κλέος, δόξα : cp. λ. ἀγαθός 7. 5. 11.

τις =πᾶς τις.

9. φυλάσσηται . . μὴ ὑπάρχειν: an
idiomatic negative; we should say, 'be-
ware of beginning . .' In point of form
this sentence is identical with the
phraseology in 7. 5 ἵνα λόγος τε κτλ., but
the idiomatic μή is there dropped.

ἀτάσθαλα: cp. c. 116 *infra*.

Θερμοπύλησι Μαρδόνιός τε καὶ Ξέρξης ἀποταμόντες τὴν
κεφαλὴν ἀνεσταύρωσαν· τῷ σὺ τὴν ὁμοίην ἀποδιδοὺς ἔπαινον
ἕξεις πρῶτα μὲν ὑπὸ πάντων Σπαρτιητέων, αὖτις δὲ καὶ πρὸς
τῶν ἄλλων Ἑλλήνων· Μαρδόνιον γὰρ ἀνασκολοπίσας τετιμω-
79 ρήσεαι ἐς πάτρων τὸν σὸν Λεωνίδην." ὁ μὲν δοκέων χαρίζεσθαι
ἔλεγε τάδε, ὁ δ᾽ ἀνταμείβετο τοισίδε. "ὦ ξεῖνε Αἰγινῆτα, τὸ
μὲν εὐνοέειν τε καὶ προορᾶν ἄγαμαί σευ, γνώμης μέντοι
ἡμάρτηκας χρηστῆς· ἐξαείρας γάρ με ὑψοῦ καὶ τὴν πάτρην
5 καὶ τὸ ἔργον, ἐς τὸ μηδὲν κατέβαλες παραινέων νεκρῷ λυμαί-

---

12 ἐσταύρωσαν **B**　　13 ὑπὸ τῶν Σπαρτιητέων πάντων z　　14
ἀνασκολοπήσας B ‖ τετιμωρήσεαι Suevern, Stein, Holder : τετιμώρησαι (cp.
Cobet *Mnemos.* XII. 388 : post τετιμώρησαι (quod servat) lacunam indicat
van H. cp. *Mnemos.* XIII. 166) · 　79. 2 δὲ **B** ‖ τοισίδε Holder, van H. :
τοῖσιδε Marc., Stein : τοίσι δὲ C : τοῦσδε　　3 εὐνοεῖν BPz, Holder, van H.
‖ πρώραν B ‖ σου **a**　　4 ἐξάιρας **a** : ἐξάρας z : ἐξάρας　　5 κατ-
έβαλλες ? Stein[1]

---

11. **Μαρδόνιός τε καὶ Ξέρξης** : there
is nothing in the story as told 7. 238
to implicate the living Mardonios in
the outrage ; but there is, of course, no
direct inconsistency in Hdt.'s allowing
Lampon to discredit the dead Mardonios,
though we are hardly justified in arguing,
as we might do in the case of a more
careful writer, that he himself acquits
Mardonios. More probably he has
followed his source in each case, without
noting the potential inconsistency ; perhaps the anecdote in 8. 114 suggested
that Mardonios was concerned in the
case.

12. **τῷ** is ambiguous : grammatically
it might seem to belong to Λεωνιδέω,
but naturally it seems to refer to **Μαρδόνιος**. Taking τὴν ὁμοίην as=δίκην,
or τὴν ὁμ. χάριν, or τίσιν, it would,
however, make good sense to refer the
relative to Λεωνίδεω. The introduction
of the name **Μαρδόνιον γάρ** just below
also favours this interpretation, and
especially the expression in c. 79 below,
Λεωνίδη δὲ τῷ με κελεύεις τιμωρῆσαι κτλ.

ἀποδιδοὺς is strictly conditional :
perhaps the tense, as compared with
ἀνασκολοπίσας just below, also favours
the reference of τῷ to Leonidas, not to
Mardonios.

ἔπαινον ἕξεις . . ὑπό. On the
ἐπαινετοί cp. c. 71 *supra* ; the phrase
here is hardly used in the technical
sense. ὑπό as ἐπ. ἐξ. = ἐπαινεθήσεαι
(Stein) ; cp. c. 75. 6 *supra*.

14. **ἀνασκολοπίζειν**, ' to impale ': cp.

for the subst. c. 97 ; for the verb, and
the barbarous practice, 1. 128, 3. 159, 4.
43, 202. ·

τετιμωρήσεαι : cp. App. Crit., the
future perfect, passive ; doubly remarkable in respect both of the voice and of
the tense ; though passive in form, it
must here be middle in sense, "thou
wilt have taken vengeance in respect
to Leonidas" (so too τετιμώρημαι in
some cases ; cp. L. & S.). The active
and passive of the verb are used in the
next chapter. The normal construction
of the verb is τινί (pers.), or ὑπέρ τινός
τινα (pers.), τινός (rei), or τί. With the
use of ἐς here cp. ἐς Λεωνίδην c. 64 *supra.*

15. **πάτρων** : Kleombrotos, the father
of Pausanias, being brother of Leonidas ;
cp. c. 10 *supra.*

79. 1. **χαρίζεσθαι** : *gratificari*, 6. 130.

3. **προορᾶν** : in regard to the future
fame of Pausanias.

ἄγαμαι : perhaps not without a
slight touch of irony or persiflage ; cp.
4. 46, 157, 6. 76, 8. 144.

4. **καὶ τὴν πάτρην καὶ τὸ ἔργον.** On
the strong co-ordination cp. c. 26 *supra.*
On πάτρη cp. c. 76 *supra.* In the speech
of Lampon reference has been made to
Kleombrotos and to Leonidas, but hardly
to Sparta, as a state or fatherland (except
in the words ἔπαινον ἕξεις πρῶτον μὲν ὑπὸ
πάντων Σπαρτιητέων). The accusatives
are "of reference" ; cp. c. 72 *supra.*

5. **ἐς τὸ μηδὲν κατέβαλες** : sc. ἐμέ.
With τὸ μηδέν cp. 8. 106.

νεσθαι, καὶ ἢν ταῦτα ποιέω, φὰς ἄμεινόν με ἀκούσεσθαι· τὰ
πρέπει μᾶλλον βαρβάροισι ποιέειν ἤ περ Ἕλλησι, καὶ ἐκείνοισι
δὲ ἐπιφθονέομεν. ἐγὼ δ' ὢν τούτου εἵνεκα μήτε Αἰγινήτῃσι
ἄδοιμι μήτε τοῖσι ταῦτα ἀρέσκεται, ἀποχρᾷ τέ μοι Σπαρτιήτῃσι
ἀρεσκόμενον ὅσια μὲν ποιέειν, ὅσια δὲ καὶ λέγειν. Λεωνίδῃ 10
δέ τῷ με κελεύεις τιμωρῆσαι, φημὶ μεγάλως <τε> τετιμω-
ρῆσθαι, ψυχῇσί τε τῇσι τῶνδε ἀναριθμήτοισι τετίμηται αὐτός
τε καὶ οἱ ἄλλοι οἱ ἐν Θερμοπύλῃσι τελευτήσαντες. σὺ μέντοι

---

6 ποιέωι B: ποιέῳ z　　7 βαρβάροισι μᾶλλον Β ‖ κἀκείνοισι Β,
Holder, van H: κἀκείνοισι z　　9 ἄδοιμι A: ἄδοιμι B ‖ ταὐτὰ Bekker,
Holder, van H. ‖ ἀποχρᾷ S ‖ τέ V (ap. Holder), Stein³: τε S (ap. Gaisford): δέ a etc., Stein¹², Holder, van H.: δέ τέ R: (δ' ἐμοὶ Gaisford)
11 <τε> Stein³　　12 τε: γε Gomperz, van H. ‖ τῇσι om. Marc. z

---

6. ἄμεινον . . ἀκούσεσθαι: cp. 8. 93,
also c. 107 infra (the active is usual).

τὰ πρέπει μᾶλλον βαρβάροισι
ποιέειν ἤ περ Ἕλλησι: this sentence
gives the two-edged moral of the anecdote,
cutting the barbarians and the Aiginetan
to boot ; while Pausanias again emerges
as the chevalier sans reproche ; cp. c.
76 supra. πρέπει is strictly relative ; cp.
8. 68, 114. In the latter passage may
be found an undesigned commentary or
complement to the present anecdote :
the recompense made by Mardonios, as
prophesied, was in a double sense οἴας
ἐκείνοισι (sc. Ἕλλησι) πρέπει.

8. ἐπιφθονέομεν: non tam invidiae
quam odii significatione, Baehr : 'we
grudge it them even,' we think none
the better of them therefor. With καὶ
ἐκείνοισι δέ cp. 2. 44 καὶ δοκέουσι δέ μοι,
4. 105 καὶ ὀμνῦσι δὲ λέγοντες. The καί is
emphatic.

δ' ὢν, 'however that may be.'
Cp. Index.

τούτου εἵνεκα, 'as far as that is
concerned'; or, if it depends on that.

μήτε Αἰγινήτῃσι ἄδοιμι : the
animus of the anecdote is very plainly
revealed in this pious wish ; the
Aiginetans one and all were to be
damnified, otherwise there seems no
very obvious reason for making them responsible for the unholy propositions of
their fellow-citizen. The animus here
evinced is presumably Attic, and of long
standing (cp. 7. 145) ; and such stories
would have been greedily swallowed in
Athens about the time of the first
Peloponnesian war and the reduction of
Aigina (462-457 B.C.). It seems, then,
unnecessary to bring this passage down

to the final expulsion of the Aiginetans
in 431 B.C. (cp. 6. 91), much less with
H. B. Wright, Campaign of Plataea
(1904) p. 79 (following Knapp), to see in
it a justification of the massacre of 424
B.C. See further, Introduction, § 9.

ἀνδάνω with personal subject is unusual.

9. ἀποχρᾷ: cp. 8. 130, also 7. 148 ;
with an expressed subject c. 94 infra.

11. τῷ . . τιμωρῆσαι, 'to avenge
whom,' in the normal construction.
The perf. pass. neut. construction which
follows implies the government of an
accusative rei by the active. Cp.
previous chapter, note to l. 14.

12. ψυχῇσί τε . . τετίμηται : as by a
sacrifice, hecatomb on hecatomb. The
animistic idea underlying this magnificent utterance is not perfectly clear.
What has become of 'the countless souls
of these men here,' and where now are
'those who met their end at Thermopylai' (οἱ ἐν Θερμοπύλῃσι τελευτήσαντες) ? The antithesis between αἱ ψυχαί
and τῶνδε might recall the Homeric
antithesis between the πολλὰς ἰφθίμους
ψυχὰς ἡρώων sent to Hades and the ἡρῶας
αὐτούς left lying on the earth, a prey for
dogs and vultures (Il. ad init.). The
souls of Leonidas and his men must
surely be down there too: the barbarians'
souls are sent to bear them company,
and to wait upon them, in strict conformity with animistic beliefs. Such a
sacrifice upon a smaller scale Achilles
performed at the tomb of Patroklos (cp.
Il. 23. 19 ff.) ; and the battle of Plataia,
from this point of view, was a superb
ἀγὼν ἐπιτάφιος in honour of Leonidas
and his fellows.

ἔτι ἔχων λόγον τοιόνδε μήτε προσέλθῃς ἔμοιγε μήτε συμβου-
15 λεύσῃς, χάριν τε ἴσθι ἐὼν ἀπαθής."

80 Ὁ μὲν ταῦτα ἀκούσας ἀπαλλάσσετο. Παυσανίης δὲ κήρυγμα
ποιησάμενος μηδένα ἅπτεσθαι τῆς ληίης, συγκομίζειν ἐκέλευε
τοὺς εἵλωτας τὰ χρήματα. οἱ δὲ ἀνὰ τὸ στρατόπεδον σκιδνάμενοι εὕρισκον σκηνὰς κατεσκευασμένας χρυσῷ καὶ ἀργύρῳ,
5 κλίνας τε ἐπιχρύσους καὶ ἐπαργύρους, κρητῆράς τε χρυσέους
καὶ φιάλας τε καὶ ἄλλα ἐκπώματα· σάκκους τε ἐπ' ἀμαξέων
εὕρισκον, ἐν τοῖσι λέβητες ἐφαίνοντο ἐνεόντες χρύσεοί τε καὶ
ἀργύρεοι· ἀπό τε τῶν κειμένων νεκρῶν ἐσκύλευον ψέλιά τε
καὶ στρεπτοὺς καὶ τοὺς ἀκινάκας ἐόντας χρυσέους, ἐπεὶ ἐσθῆτός
10 γε ποικίλης λόγος ἐγίνετο οὐδείς. ἐνθαῦτα πολλὰ μὲν κλέπτοντες
ἐπώλεον πρὸς τοὺς Αἰγινήτας οἱ εἵλωτες, πολλὰ δὲ καὶ ἀπεδείκνυσαν, ὅσα αὐτῶν οὐκ οἷά τε ἦν κρύψαι· ὥστε Αἰγινήτῃσι

---

14 ἔτι om. Marc. ‖ ἔμοιγε: ἐμὲ R ‖ συμβουλεύῃς PMarc. z　　　15 τε
ἴσθι z: ἴσθι τε　　　80. 2 ἐκέλευσε Β　　4 χρυσῷ <τε> van H.
6 καὶ φιάλας Βz, Stein², Holder, van H.: φιάλας ‖ ἄλλα: ἄλλα καὶ C ‖
σάκκους: θάκους C: 'An σάκους?' van H.　　7 ἐόντες Β　　8 ψέλλιά
Marc. z　　9 ἀκινάκεας S, Wesseling, Gaisford　　10 ἐγέντετο SV ‖
οὐδὲ εἷς Β, Holder, van H.　　11 οἱ om. R　　12 αὐτέων Βz

---

15. χάριν τε ἴσθι: the τε is cumulative, 'and indeed'; cp. c. 70. χάριν εἰδέναι
3. 21. Cp. χάριν ἔχειν 7. 120. With
the 'sentiment' cp. the Athenian remark
to Alexander, 8. 143 ad f.

80. 2. μηδένα ἅπτεσθαι τῆς ληίης: no
one was to touch the spoil, in order that
it might be duly collected and divided.
As implied above, c. 70, the Tegeatai
disregarded this order, unless indeed
its issue was subsequent to their plunder
of the tent of Mardonios, or unless the
implication in that passage is unjust.

3. τοὺς εἵλωτας: but surely not to the
number of 40,000, c. 29 supra.

ἀνά: passim per . .
τὸ στρατόπεδον: sc. Περσέων.
σκιδνάμενοι: cp. 8. 23.

5. ἐπιχρύσους: i.e. 'gilt,' cp. 1. 50.
In the following inventory of treasure
κρητῆρας are large mixing bowls;
φιάλας smaller vessels, primarily for
pouring, cp. 8. 54 (χεῖ, FUD, cp. Curt.
Gr. Etym.² p. 186); ἐκπώματα drinking
vessels; ἄλλα being idiomatic, 'as well,'
cp. 3. 55. 5 supra. The Persians were
hard drinkers, cp. 1. 133.

7. λέβητες: cauldrons, or pots, not
primarily connected with drinking; why
these were already packed in baize or

bags (σάκκους) ready for departure, and
the others not so, is obscure.

8. ψέλια, στρεπτούς: cp. 8. 113.
Possibly only the 'Persians' were so
decorated. τοὺς ἀκινάκας, 'their
swords,' referring, as the article shows,
especially to the notorious 'Persian'
weapon; cp. 7. 54. The hilt and sheath
might have been of gold, or covered
therewith: or were the blades dama-
scened?

9. ἐπεί, in an adversative sense,
implying a suppressed sentence ('of
mere clothing I say nothing,' or sim.);
cp. L. & S. sub v. B. 4.

10. λόγος ἐγίνετο οὐδείς, 'no account
was (being) taken'—embroidered robes,
etc., were at a discount. λόγος, cp. 4.
135.

11. πρὸς τοὺς Αἰγινήτας: not necessarily the 500 hoplites, or the survivors
of them (cp. cc. 28, 69 supra); but the
animus of the story is obvious; see
previous chapter.

ἀπεδείκνυσαν, duly reported or
'accounted for'; cp. 8. 35.

12. ὥστε . . ἐγένοντο: a transparent
scandal, perhaps of Attic origin, which
Hdt. could hardly have thus accepted,
or endorsed, had he known as much

οἱ μεγάλοι πλοῦτοι ἀρχὴν ἐνθεῦτεν ἐγένοντο, οἳ τὸν χρυσὸν
ἅτε ἐόντα χαλκὸν δῆθεν παρὰ τῶν εἱλώτων ὠνέοντο. συμφορή- 81
σαντες δὲ τὰ χρήματα καὶ δεκάτην ἐξελόντες τῷ ἐν Δελφοῖσι

---

14 εἱλώτεων R: εἱλωτέων s

---

about the Aiginetans when he first
penned this passage as he afterwards
came to know ; cp. 2. 178 etc. It is
very unlikely that this scandal is to be
dated (as Stein suggests) after the
expulsion of the Aiginetans from their
island in 431 B.C. Aiginetan wealth
and greatness was a thing of the past
after 457 B.C., but the scandal in regard
to their origin does not necessitate even
the inference that they were no more
when it circulated ; rather indeed the
reverse : φθόνος dealt with the living
present ; cp. 7. 236 and note to
previous chapter, l. 8.

13. ἀρχήν, 'originally,' cp. Index.
The plural πλοῦτοι, perhaps because the
wealth was not ἐν τῷ κοινῷ, but distributed in several holdings (not like the
Latin divitiae, fortunae, bona, opes,
etc.) ; cp. Plato Rep. 618 B. The article,
as with ἀκινάκας above.

ἐνθεῦτεν : neither temporal nor
local, but causal ; cp. Thuc. 1. 5. 1 τὸν
πλεῖστον τοῦ βίου ἐντεῦθεν ἐποιοῦντο,
Aristot. Eth. N. 5. 3. 6=1131 a 23
ἐντεῦθεν αἱ μάχαι καὶ τὰ ἐγκλήματα ὅταν
κτλ.

οἵ, 'for they . . ' exchanged
on the χρύσεα χαλκείων principle : ἅτε
ἐόντα χαλκὸν δῆθεν. With the innocence
of the helots (who, however, in this case
were only robbers robbed) Wesseling
and many commentators since have
compared what Philippe de Comines, 5.
2, has to say of the Helvetians and their
treatment of the spoil after the defeat of
Charles the Bold at Granson, A.D. 1476.
The anecdote in Hdt. may be intended
not merely to discredit the Aiginetans
but to raise a laugh at the expense of
Sparta, with its iron money and so on.
As a matter of fact the glint of gold was
as recognizable in Sparta as anywhere
in the Greek world (cp. 1. 69, 3. 148,
5. 51); if there was any pilfering on
the field, and selling of stolen goods, no
doubt the thieves sold cheap, not so
much because they did not know the
difference between gold and brass, as
because they had to get rid of stolen
goods as quickly as possible.

81. 2. δεκάτην ἐξελόντες. Stein

conceives the tithe (or the tithes) as
composed not of actual spoils, but of
values. That being so, the spoils must
have been valued, and even sold, before
the tithe was actually handed over ;
unless we suppose that a rough estimate
and division of spoil was made, and the
tithes then converted into money. In
either case, however, some time will
have elapsed before this operation was
complete, and it was hardly completed
on the field of Plataia. Three gods are
mentioned, three sacred places, as
recipients and receptacles ; but it is not
clear whether one-tenth of all the spoil
was divided among the three gods (in
which case each would have received in
reality a thirtieth of the whole : Larcher's
view), or whether, as seems more
probable, each of the three divinities
received a full tithe (Baehr and others).
Here again, however, there is an unresolved obscurity ; it might be argued that
only Delphi obtained the full tithe (the
Amphiktyonic shrine being of greatest
pan-Hellenic importance) ; that a tithe
of what remained (i.e. $\frac{1}{10}$ of $\frac{1}{10}$) was
given to Olympia, the Peloponnesian
centre, while to the Isthmos went a
tithe of the remainder ($\frac{10 : 9 : 8\frac{1}{10}}{100}$ being
thus the proportionate shares). But that
arrangement looks rather complicated !

τῷ ἐν Δελφοῖσι θεῷ. If a tithe of
the spoil of Plataia was on the battle-
field set apart and consecrated to the god
in Delphi, the victors can scarcely have
held the god, or his ministers, guilty of
medism.

Plutarch, Aristeid. 11, shows the
lengths to which the Rettung of
Delphi could be carried : according to
that story the god in Delphi had
dictated the very spot for the Greek
victory, and that in response to an
Athenian inquiry !

Of the material reality and historic
authenticity of the Anathema at Delphi
there cannot be a shadow of doubt ; but
the precise date at which it was made,
or provided for, the exact method by
which the expenses were defrayed, are
doubtful points. The list of states upon

θεῷ, ἀπ' ἧς ὁ τρίπους ὁ χρύσεος ἀνετέθη ὁ ἐπὶ τοῦ τρικαρήνου
ὄφιος τοῦ χαλκέου ἐπεστεὼς ἄγχιστα τοῦ βωμοῦ, καὶ τῷ ἐι;
5 Ὀλυμπίῃ θεῷ ἐξελόντες, ἀπ' ἧς δεκάπηχυν χάλκεον Δία
ἀνέθηκαν, καὶ τῷ ἐν Ἰσθμῷ θεῷ, ἀπ' ἧς ἑπτάπηχυς χάλκεος

---

81. 4 ὄφεος z ‖ ἐφεστεὼς B   6 ἀνέθηκε B

---

the τρικάρηνος ὄφις still legible proves
that the monument was not merely a
memorial of Plataia (even if offered from
the spoil of that battle exclusively), for
names occur upon it which were not
represented at Plataia.

The monument consisted of two parts,
as here described: (a) the golden λέβης
or κρατήρ, elevated upon (b) a pillar,
having the appearance of a three-headed
serpent wound round a column. Thucydides, 1. 132. 2, does not accurately distinguish the two parts, but speaks of the
whole offering as ὁ τρίπους. The golden
bowl was melted down by the Phokians
in the Sacred War, Pausan. 10. 13. 5.
The (gilt) bronze pillar upon which it
stood was carried off to Constantinople
by the founder, where it was discovered
in the Atmeidan by O. T. Newton in
1855 and the inscribed names deciphered,
as frequently since. Cp. Otto Frick, Das
plataeische Weihgeschenk, Leipzig, 1859;
Fabricius D.A.I. 1. 176 ff.; Hicks,
Manual,² No. 19, etc. But especially
Frazer, Pausanias v. 299-307, where the
modern literature is fully given; cp.
also 8. 82 supra, Introduction § 10,
Appendix I.

This monument has perhaps the
longest and most continuous literary
history in antiquity of any objet d'art,
having been noticed by Hdt. (bis),
Thucydides (1. 132. 2, 3. 57. 2), ps.-
Demosth. (c. Neaer. § 97), C. Nepos
(Pausan. 1), Diodoros (11. 33. 2), Plutarch
(de malig. Hdti 42 = Mor. 873), Pausanias
(10. 13. 5), Ael. Aristeides (iii. 290 B
ed. Cantero, 1604), Suidas (sub v.
Παυσανίας).

4. ἄγχιστα τοῦ βωμοῦ. The altar
here mentioned is identical with the
altar 'dedicated by the Chians' mentioned in 2. 135, and stood in front of
the temple, where its remains have been
found; cp. Pausanias 10. 14. 7 (Frazer,
v. 309).

The base of the 'Plataian' monument
has also been found (cp. Frazer, v. 299).
The particularity of the description here
is not quite conclusive evidence that
Hdt. had visited Delphi, and seen the

'Tripod' before writing the passage, for
the immediate context contains evidence
of his having consulted written authorities
in regard to the allocation of the spoils,
and he does not here specify the connexion of the Chians with t e altar, as
in 2. 135, a passage in which h'autopsy"
is much more evident than here. But
it need not therefore be denied for the
present chapter, which might very well
be an addition to the original draft of
the work, to be dated after his (first)
visit to Greece; cp. Introduction, § 9.

τῷ ἐν Ὀλυμπίῃ θεῷ: i.e. Zeus.
Pausanias, 5. 23. 1-2, describes the bronze
figure, adds that it was dedicated by
the Greeks who fought at Plataia, and
gives the list of cities which took part
'in the battle,' from an inscription on
the right side of the base. The names
of the islanders from Keos, Melos, Tenos
again throw some doubt on the question
whether the list was rigidly limited to
the combatants at Plataia. This inscription has not been recovered; and
we are therefore dependent for its contents on the report of Pausanias, not in
all respects above suspicion. Cp. Introduction, § 10. For the size of the
statue (15 feet) upon the testimony of
Hdt. cp. further Frazer, Pausanias
iii. 630 f.

6. τῷ ἐν Ἰσθμῷ θεῷ: i.e. Poseidon.
A dedication to Poseidon from the spoils
of Plataia seems hardly called for, and
supports the view that these offerings
and monuments had reference to the
whole war; the suggestion is fortified
by the observation that no special
dedications are recorded for Artemision
and Mykale, the latter of which at least
must have been reckoned a victory.
(Was this offering connected with it?)
Hdt. however (8. 121) has recorded a
dedication at Delphi after Salamis,
which may have been identical with the
Apollo, 'from the spoils of Artemision
and Salamis,' mentioned by Pausanias
10. 14. 5. The dedication at the Isthmos
is quite lost sight of subsequently;
cp. 8. 121 supra. The substitution of
ἐγένετο for ἀνετέθη may be merely a

Ποσειδέων ἐξεγένετο, ταῦτα ἐξελόντες τὰ λοιπὰ διαιρέοντο, καὶ
ἔλαβον ἔκαστοι τῶν ἄξιοι ἦσαν, καὶ τὰς παλλακὰς τῶν
Περσέων καὶ τὸν χρυσὸν καὶ τὸν ἄργυρον καὶ τἆλλα χρήματά
τε καὶ ὑποζύγια. ὅσα μέν νυν ἐξαίρετα τοῖσι ἀριστεύσασι 10
αὐτῶν ἐν Πλαταιῆσι ἐδόθη, οὐ λέγεται πρὸς οὐδαμῶν, δοκέω
δ' ἔγωγε καὶ τούτοισι δοθῆναι· Παυσανίῃ δὲ πάντα δέκα
ἐξαιρέθη τε καὶ ἐδόθη, γυναῖκες ἵπποι τάλαντα κάμηλοι, ὡς
δὲ αὔτως καὶ τἆλλα χρήματα.

7 ἐγένετο Β   8 ἦσαν om. Marc. : ἔσαν z ‖ παλακὰς C   9 τὸν
ἄργυρον ΒΡz : ἄργυρον ‖ τἆλλα coni. Stein¹, rec. van H., Stein³ : ἄλλα
11 αὐτέων ΒCz ‖ πλαταίῃσι α : πλαταίῃσιν Β   12 δ' : δὲ Β   13 τε
καὶ ἐδόθη om. Β, Holder, van H. ‖ τάλαντα : ἄρματα ? Stein ‖ ὡς ΡΒz
14 τὰ ἄλλα Β

stylistic variation, but in fact Hdt. does not expressly say that the bronze Poseidon was ever actually erected: Pausanias in describing the Isthmos (2. 1. 7 etc.), though he mentions several images of Poseidon, does not attempt to identify any of them with the one here in question.

7. τὰ λοιπὰ διαιρέοντο: it appears just below that another δεκάτη (possibly of what was left) was reserved for the commander-in-chief, Pausanias, and if we allow the Helots 10 per cent for their pilferings, above recorded, it appears that of all the spoil only one-half would remain for division among all the various states concerned, and their commanders, or to furnish the rewards of valour.

8. ἔλαβον ἔκαστοι τῶν ἄξιοι ἦσαν. On what principle the distribution was effected is not indicated: was it the relative size of the contingents (κατὰ τὸν στρατιωτῶν ἀριθμὸν Diodor. 11. 33. 1)? Or this simple principle may have been combined with a consideration of services rendered, the proportion of dead, and so forth. Nor is it clear who made the awards, whether the whole council of war, or the Hegemonic state (cp. c. 27 supra), or the commander-in-chief. It is unlikely that the awards gave complete satisfaction to every one, cp. c. 70 supra. On the plural ἔκαστοι cp. 7. 1. 7 etc.

9. τἆλλα: the ἄλλα is idiomatic, 'besides'; cp. c. 80 supra.

10. τοῖσι ἀριστεύσασι: according to Hdt. there had been, and was, no award to any state collectively, cp. c. 71 supra, or at least he could not discover any; he might seem here, therefore, to be re-

ferring to individuals, but it is likely that individuals, ἀριστεύσαντες, would have been rewarded out of the share of their state and not out of the common or undivided booty: the case of the commander-in-chief would stand on a different footing.

11. οὐ λέγεται πρὸς οὐδαμῶν. As Rawlinson points out, this phrase indicates that Hdt. consulted authors, i.e. written authorities; cp. Introduction, § 10. Their silence was perhaps a part of the conspiracy of silence on the whole question of the ἀριστεῖα, cp. c. 71 supra.

12. καὶ τούτοισι as well as to the gods and the commander-in-chief. These would have been the Plataians if the story in Plutarch, Aristeid. 20, be true. Plutarch, indeed, not only records the extra allowances to the Plataians, but names the temple (dedicated to Athene) which was built therefrom.

πάντα δέκα. Rawlinson renders "ten specimens of each kind of t ing," which gives a rather curious and hardly adequate result when you come to details. Stein has (cp. 4. 88) "alles zehnfach," i.e. ten times as much of each and everything as he would have had on an ordinary occasion, 'a tenfold portion': the case was evidently an extraordinary one. How much exactly his portion amounted to does not appear, but it will probably have been not less than another tithe of the spoil—though that exact meaning can hardly be got out of the expression here.

13. γυναῖκες, as though the men had all been slain: this was not, however, the case, as the next anecdote shows. For τάλαντα Stein suggests ἄρματα.

82　　Λέγεται δὲ καὶ τάδε γενέσθαι, ὡς Ξέρξης φεύγων ἐκ τῆς
Ἑλλάδος Μαρδονίῳ τὴν κατασκευὴν καταλίποι τὴν ἑωυτοῦ.
Παυσανίην ὢν ὁρῶντα τὴν Μαρδονίου σκηνὴν χρυσῷ τε καὶ
ἀργύρῳ καὶ παραπετάσμασι ποικίλοισι κατεσκευασμένην, κε-
5 λεῦσαι τούς τε ἀρτοκόπους καὶ τοὺς ὀψοποιοὺς κατὰ ταὐτὰ
καθὼς Μαρδονίῳ δεῖπνον παρασκευάζειν. ὡς δὲ κελευόμενοι
οὗτοι ἐποίευν ταῦτα, ἐνθαῦτα τὸν Παυσανίην ἰδόντα κλίνας τε
χρυσέας καὶ ἀργυρέας εὖ ἐστρωμένας καὶ τραπέζας τε χρυσέας
καὶ ἀργυρέας καὶ παρασκευὴν μεγαλοπρεπέα τοῦ δείπνου,
10 ἐκπλαγέντα τὰ προκείμενα ἀγαθὰ κελεῦσαι ἐπὶ γέλωτι τοὺς

---

82. 2 παρασκευὴν Athenaeus p. 138 ‖ καταλίπει C　　3 ὁρέοντα
P Marc. z, Stein¹ : ὁρέωντα C ‖ σκηνὴν Schweighaeuser, Stein³ : κατασκευὴν
4 ποικίλῃσι C ‖ κατασκευασμένην ASV, Schaefer, Gaisford : παρασκευα-
σμένην C　　5 ἀρτοπόπους Cobet : 'volgatam tuetur inscr.' van H.
6 καθὼς : καὶ Schaefer : ὡς καὶ ? Stein : del. Abicht, Gomperz, van H. ‖
κατασκευάζειν B　　8 εὖ . . ἀργυρέας om. B¹Sz ‖ τε post χρυσέας B
10 γέλωτα S

κάμηλοι have not been mentioned since
7. 125 (except for 7. 184. 20), and ave
played no part in the campaign. They
cannot have been much used in Greece,
and no doubt quickly died out, for
camels were evidently a curiosity there
early in the fourth century B.C., cp.
Xenoph. Hell. 3. 4. 24 (though they are
to be seen there to-day : Itea, 17.4.'05).
The horses may have been used to
improve the Hellenic breeds, perhaps
helped to mount the first Athenian
cavalry, and reappear on the frieze of
Pheidias in their descendants.

ὣς δ' αὗτως = ὡσαύτως δέ, i.e. πάντα
δέκα, tenfold (8. 21. 5).

82. 1. λέγεται δέ κτλ. : probably by
some author, or λογογράφος ; cp. c. 81
supra, οὐ λέγεται πρὸς οὐδαμῶν. The
specification indicates a doubt of the
truth of the following story, which is
indeed not prima facie very probable,
and carries too obvious a tendency and
moral.

Ξέρξης φεύγων. Xerxes is seldom
allowed to leave Hellas except 'in flight.'
Here the exaggeration serves to make
the bequest of his κατασκευή to Mardonios more probable. The κατασκευή
might certainly include the σκηνή (above
described, c. 70, as of Mardonios) ;
the παραπετάσματα, hangings, curtains,
tapestries, as well as παρασκευή lower
down, support that view ; but if the
Tegeatai had sacked it on entering the

camp, how could Pausanias have seen it
in the good order implied by the present
story ? According to Plutarch, Perikles
13 (cp. Pausanias 1. 20. 4), the Oideion
was said to have been a copy of the
king's tent (εἰκὼν καὶ μίμημα τῆς βασιλέως
σκηνῆς). Vitruvius 5. 9 represents the
roof as constructed from the masts and
spars of the Persian ships, and names
Themistokles as the (first?) erector. (On
the subsequent fate of the building
cp. Frazer, Pausan. l.c. ; E. Gardner,
Ancient Athens, pp. 394-5.) That looks
as though the king's pavilion had fallen
into the hands of the Athenians, a conclusion hardly compatible with c. 70
above. Or did the adoption of that
pattern cover a protest or claim ?

5. ἀρτοκόπους . . ὀψοποιούς : cp.
Xenoph. Hell. 7. 1. 38 (report of the
Arkadian Antiochos to the Myriad, 367
B.C.) ὅτι βασιλεὺς ἀρτοκόπους μὲν καὶ
ὀψοποιοὺς καὶ οἰνοχόους καὶ θυρωροὺς
παμπληθεῖς ἔχοι, ἄνδρας δὲ οἳ μάχοιντ' ἂν
Ἕλλησι, πάνυ ζητῶν οὐκ ἔφη δύνασθαι
ἰδεῖν. Hdt. makes ἀρτοκόπος feminine
in 1. 51. The males had not all been
put to the sword at Plataia ; cp. c. 81
supra (γυναῖκες). ὀψοποιός is not a pastry-
cook (μάγειρος, at least originally) but
a cook for ὄψα, q.v.

6. καθώς is anomalous ; cp. App. Crit.
It occurs ap. Athenaeum 138 c, in quoting
this very passage.

10. ἐκπλαγέντα, whether of fear, or

ἑωυτοῦ διηκόνους παρασκευάσαι Λακωνικὸν δεῖπνον. ὡς δὲ
τῆς θοίνης ποιηθείσης ἦν πολλὸν τὸ μέσον, τὸν Παυσανίην
γελάσαντα μεταπέμψασθαι τῶν Ἑλλήνων τοὺς στρατηγούς,
συνελθόντων δὲ τούτων εἰπεῖν τὸν Παυσανίην, δεικνύντα ἐς
ἑκατέρην τοῦ δείπνου παρασκευήν, "ἄνδρες Ἕλληνες, τῶνδε 15
εἵνεκα ἐγὼ ὑμέας συνήγαγον, βουλόμενος ὑμῖν τοῦδε τοῦ
Μήδων ἡγεμόνος τὴν ἀφροσύνην δέξαι, ὃς τοιήνδε δίαιταν ἔχων
ἦλθε ἐς ἡμέας οὕτω οἰζυρὴν ἔχοντας ἀπαιρησόμενος." ταῦτα
μὲν Παυσανίην λέγεται εἰπεῖν πρὸς τοὺς στρατηγοὺς τῶν
Ἑλλήνων. ὑστέρῳ μέντοι χρόνῳ μετὰ ταῦτα καὶ τῶν 83
Πλαταιέων εὗρον συχνοὶ θήκας χρυσοῦ καὶ ἀργύρου καὶ τῶν
ἄλλων χρημάτων. ἐφάνη δὲ καὶ τάδε ὕστερον ἔτι τούτων

---

14 τουτέων BCz ‖ εἶπαι z, van H. ‖ τὸν Παυσανίην secl. van H. ‖
ἐς om. B 15 τὴν παρασκευὴν B, Holder, van H. 16 ὑμέας ἐγὼ
Marc. ‖ ἡμῖν B ‖ τοῦδε τοῦ : τοῦ τοῦ V : τοῦ RS, Holder, van H. 17
Μήδου S : (ἡγεμόνος deleto) Schaefer, Palm : βασιλῆος z ‖ δεῖξαι libri
18 οὕτως B 19 παυσανίης RS ‖ εἶπαι z, van H. 83. 3 ἐφάνη . .
ἐτάφη (c. 84) ut spuria secl. Krueger ‖ τάδε ὕστερον ἔτι τούτων <ἐπὶ>
Stein³ : τόδε ὕστερον τούτων ἐπὶ Stein² : τόδε ὕστερον ἐπὶ τούτων libri
(τουτέων z), Stein¹ : τόδε ὕστερον ἔτι τούτων. Abresch, Wesseling, Holder,
van H.

---

astonishment, as here, is more usually
constructed with the dative; cp. 7. 226,
4. 4, etc.

ἐπὶ γέλωτι, of the end or object
in view; cp. 6. 67. Pausanias should
be credited with a more serious purpose;
but the anecdote is a contribution to
"the comic Nemesis"; cp. 8. 24. 4 supra.

τοὺς ἑωυτοῦ διηκόνους, including
the hereditary cooks (6. 60), whose pro-
ductions were not likely to be triumphs
of the culinary art. Athenaeus (4. 16 ff.)
139 follows up his citation of this passage
by numerous quotations on various forms
of Lakonian banquets, the κοπίς, the
αἶκλον, the φειδίτια (e.g. ἔστι δ' ἡ κοπὶς
δεῖπνον, μάζα, ἄρτος, κρέας, λάχανον ὠμόν,
ζωμός, σῦκον, τράγημα, θέρμος).

12. θοίνη : food, banquet, 1. 119.
τὸ μέσον, 'the interval,' 'the difference'; cp. Index, and 1. 126.

13. τῶν Ἑλλήνων τοὺς στρατηγούς :
he might have been going to entertain
them, and perhaps he was, to a banquet
à la Perse. The subsequent career of Pausanias seems to suggest that the Persian
cooks made a speedy convert; but here
Pride—the Pride of Poverty—prevents
his fall. No wonder Hdt. doubts the
story (λέγεται again), but it was too good

a one to throw over. It is apparently
an addition, at second or third hand,
for it interrupts the natural sequence of
cc. 81, 83. Cp. Introduction, § 9.

18. ὀιζυρός (only here in Hdt.) is a
common Homeric epithet of πόλεμος, γόος,
νύξ, and βροτοί (human beings, most frequently): 'miserable,' woeful, pitiable.
A harder epithet could scarcely have
been used of the poverty-stricken Laconic
fare.

83. 1. ὑστέρῳ μέντοι . . χρημάτων. This
sentence has nothing to say to the immediately preceding sentence, or chapter;
nor does it fit on very well to c. 81. It
would follow most naturally immediately
on c. 80 supra; that is to say, in view
of the previous notes, c. 81 looks like
an addition 'of the second hand,' and
c. 82 like an addition of the second, or
third hand. μέντοι after μέν instead of
δέ: cp. 6. 86 ποιέετε μὲν . . ὁκοῖον μέντοι
κτλ.

2. θήκας, 'deposits'; the Helots not
having been able to dispose of all their
thefts to the Aiginetans, had buried
many of them in the ground. (The
Helots may not have been the only
thieves and depositors.)

3. ἐφάνη δέ κτλ. Krüger damned the

<ἐπὶ> τῶν νεκρῶν περιψιλωθέντων τὰς σάρκας· συνεφόρεον
5 γὰρ τὰ ὀστέα οἱ Πλαταιέες ἐς ἕνα χῶρον· εὑρέθη κεφαλὴ οὐκ
ἔχουσα ῥαφὴν οὐδεμίαν ἀλλ' ἐξ ἑνὸς ἐοῦσα ὀστέου, ἐφάνη δὲ
καὶ γνάθος κατὰ τὸ ἄνω [τῆς γνάθου] ἔχουσα ὀδόντας μουνοφυέας ἐξ ἑνὸς ὀστέου πάντας τούς τε προσθίους καὶ γομφίους,
84 καὶ πενταπήχεος ἀνδρὸς ὀστέα ἐφάνη. ἐπείτε δὲ Μαρδονίου
δευτέρῃ ἡμέρῃ ὁ νεκρὸς ἠφάνιστο, ὑπὸ ὅτευ μὲν ἀνθρώπων
τὸ ἀτρεκὲς οὐκ ἔχω εἰπεῖν, πολλοὺς δὲ τινὰς ἤδη καὶ

5 ὀστᾶ C　　6 οὐδεμίην z ‖ ἀλλὰ Marc. z　　7 κατὰ Stein[(1)2],
van H.: καὶ ‖ ἐπάνω ßPz ‖ τῆς γνάθου del. Stein[(1)2], Holder, van H. ‖
ὀδόντας secl. van H. ‖ μουνοφυέας . . ὀδόντας (vel προσθίους) om. B[1]:
μονοφυέας ß　　8 προσθίους Stein[(1)2 3]: ὀδόντας ‖ τοὺς γομφίους z
9 πεντεπήχεος a　　84. 1 ἐπεὶ δὲ ß: ἐπεί γε δὴ malebat Stein[1 3]:
'locus et lacunosus et corruptus' Stein[2]　　2 ἠφάνισται Paris. 1635 z |
ὑπ' C Marc.: ὑπό RSV ‖ τευ ß: ὅτεω z ‖ ἀνθρώπου S　　3 ἀτρεκέως ß ‖
εἶπαι z, van H. ‖ ἤδη om. S

rest of this and the next chapter. The
matter is quite to Hdt.'s mind on such
occasions, cp. 3. 12, but these curiosities
of the battle-field may be additions
of his own; on the other hand, the fate of
Mardonios' corpse must have been a
primary problem.

ὕστερον τούτων: not strictly after
the discovery of the hidden treasures by
Plataians, but simply 'after the war';
cp. c. 75 supra.

4. <ἐπὶ> τῶν νεκρῶν περιψιλωθέντων
τὰς σάρκας: the plural σάρκας perhaps
with reference to the numbers of different dead, but Homer habitually uses the
plural, even as ὀστέα. The accusative
is "of reference"; cp. c. 72 supra. ἐπὶ
with the genitive here, 'upon the corpses,'
can hardly be temporal, though that
would give one of the quaintest dates
on record ('at, or by, the time the dead
bodies were cleaned bare of flesh'); nor
even local (the dead bodies having been
gathered into one place), but perhaps
more generally 'in the case of' (cp. App.
Crit.). Hdt. does not say that he had
himself seen these curiosities. 1. The
skull without a single suture (ῥαφή).
2. The jaw (upper) with all the teeth of
a piece. γομφίος (sc. ὀδούς), regular word
for 'molars' (προσθίος 'front'). (Plutarch Pyrrh. 3 makes a similar statement
of Pyrrhus; Pliny 7. 69 of the son of
Prusias of Bithynia.) 3. The bones of
a man five cubits high (the tallest of
the Persians wanted four fingers of that
height, 7. 117 supra).

84. 1. ἐπείτε δέ: there is no apodosis
to this protasis, whether formal or
material. Stein suggested ἐπεί γε δή
on the assumption that the giant corpse,
just mentioned, had been mistaken for
that of Mardonios; but Hdt. would
scarcely have left so much to be understood, and the grammatical confusion of
the passage may arise from the amount
of 'retractation,' not fully carried through,
in the whole of this context. This little
c. is altogether significant for the sources
and composition problems of Hdt.'s work.
Cp. Introduction, § 10.

2. δευτέρῃ ἡμέρῃ: i.e. the day after
the battle, or the 14th; the night of
the day of battle has not been indicated:
the nearest thing thereto is the evening
meal ordered in c. 82, if indeed that
anecdote belongs to the same day. The
dawn of the day of battle has been recorded in c. 56 supra.

ὁ νεκρὸς ἠφάνιστο, 'the corpse of
Mardonios was nowhere to be found . .'
The scandal against Lampon of Aigina,
cc. 78 f. supra, assumed the recovery of
the body as a matter of course. The
pl.p. may be taken as strictly temporal.

3. τὸ ἀτρεκὲς οὐκ ἔχω εἰπεῖν. Hdt.
can hardly have seen the monument to
Mardonios on the road from Eleutherai
to Plataia mentioned by Pausanias 9.
2. 2, evidently with some hesitation and
doubt, due to this very passage in Hdt.

ἤδη . . ἤκουσα: as in 7. 55.
Though Hdt. uses ὁράω of perceptions
not strictly visual (cp. c. 53 supra, and

παντοδαποὺς ἤκουσα θάψαι Μαρδόνιον, καὶ δῶρα μεγάλα οἶδα
λαβόντας πολλοὺς παρὰ Ἀρτόντεω τοῦ Μαρδονίου παιδὸς 5
διὰ τοῦτο τὸ ἔργον· ὅστις μέντοι ἦν αὐτῶν ὁ ὑπελόμενός τε
καὶ θάψας τὸν νεκρὸν τὸν Μαρδονίου, οὐ δύναμαι ἀτρεκέως
πυθέσθαι, ἔχει δὲ τινὰ φάτιν καὶ Διονυσοφάνης ἀνὴρ Ἐφέσιος
θάψαι Μαρδόνιον. ἀλλ᾽ ὃ μὲν τρόπῳ τοιούτῳ ἐτάφη.

Οἱ δὲ Ἕλληνες ὡς ἐν Πλαταιῇσι τὴν ληίην διείλοντο, 85
ἔθαπτον τοὺς ἑωυτῶν χωρὶς ἕκαστοι. Λακεδαιμόνιοι μὲν

6 αὐτέων C Marc. z ‖ ὑπονοούμενος B   7 τοῦ μαρδονίου Marc.
8 φάτις S ‖ διονυσοφάνης B Marc. : διονυσιοφάνης   9 τρόπῳ τοιούτῳ :
πρὸς ὁτευδήποτε van H.   85. 1 πλαταίῃσι a : πλαταίησι B ‖
διείλαντο B

6. 69 ὁρέων δέ με κατομνυμένην κτλ.), he
probably uses ἀκούω with definite reference to audible, oral information (not
as we, who speak of 'hearing' by letter,
etc. The curious passage 1. 124, 125
comes dangerously near our colloquial
usage: τὸ βυβλίον . . λαβὼν ἐπελέγετο,
τὰ δὲ γράμματα ἔλεγε τάδε . . ἀκούσας
ταῦτα ὁ Κῦρος κτλ.). The use of οἶδα just
below contrasts not with the uncertainty
of hearsay, as though the οἶδα (εἰδέναι)
had necessarily some other source, but
merely assures us of Hdt.'s personal conviction (cp. 7. 214 οἴδαμεν, 1. 5, 20 etc.),
not but what he might have seen the
δῶρα, or some of them, or some of the
persons who received them, or even
Artontes himself, though he never saw
the corpse, or even the tomb, of Mardonios.
5. Ἀρτόντεω: to be distinguished
from the father of Bagaios 3. 124, though
possibly of the same house, and named
after him. Nothing more is known
of Artontes the son of Mardonios; but
as in 492 B.C. Mardonios was young and
lately married to Artozostra, the daughter
of Dareios (cp. 6. 43), Stein ingeniously
conjectures that Artontes may have had
an official post in Asia Minor about
460 B.C. or later, when these applications
were made to him, and his piety so
cruelly exploited. Pausanias (9. 2. 2)
makes all the successful applicants
'Ionians,' but he may have nothing
more to draw on than this story in Hdt.
This passage may obviously quite well
belong to the earliest draft of Hdt.'s work.
Cp. de Mardonii morte Nipperdey ad
Nep. Arist. 2. 1; Müller ad Aristod. 2.
5 (F.H.G. v. p. 5); Enmann, die Quellen

des Trogus, Dorpat, 1880, p. 23; Krumbholz, p. 26.
6. ὅστις μέντοι ἦν: that none of the
applications was really genuine or honest,
that the body was never identified and
buried, are alternatives which Hdt. does
not even consider. He assumes that
some one secretly got the body away
(ὑπελόμενος) and buried it. Another
and more discreditable alternative has,
indeed, been disposed of cc. 78 f. above.
The pro lem evidently exercised Hdt.
a good deal (οὐ δύναμαι ἀτρεκέως πυθέσθαι).
That 'burial' was not perhaps quite the
proper rule for Persians Hdt. half knows,
cp. 1. 140, but the 'Magian' use may
not have been as yet universal among
'Persians.' Cp. also 7. 10 ad f.
8. ἔχει δὲ τινὰ φάτιν: cp. διξοὺς λόγους
λεγομένους ἔχει c. 74 supra, the reverse
construction to λόγος ἔχει (cp. c. 78
supra) or φάτις μιν ἔχει 7. 3.   φάτις perhaps comes nearer than any single word
in Hdt. to 'oral report,' mere hearsay,
written down by him for the first time;
cp. 7. 3, 189, 8. 94; Introduction, § 10.
Διονυσοφάνης: of this Ephesian
nothing is known but what Hdt.
tells us. How an Ephesian, how other
'Ionians' ame to be on the battle-field
of Plataia is anything but obvious: on
which side were they supposed to be
fighting? Were they prisoners, or slaves?
or merchants? or diviners?
85. 1. διείλοντο, ἔθαπτον: the sequence
of tenses seems to warrant the conclusion,
strange as it may appear that the Greeks
postponed the burial of their own dead
to the division of the spoil.
2. χωρὶς ἕκαστοι: each set, each state,
its own apart from those of the others.

τριξὰς ἐποιήσαντο θήκας· ἔνθα μὲν τοὺς ἰρένας ἔθαψαν, τῶν
καὶ Ποσειδώνιος καὶ Ἀμομφάρετος ἦσαν καὶ Φιλοκύων τε

3 ἔνθα .. Καλλικράτης secl. Sitzler ‖ ἰρένας Valckenaer, Stein, van H.:
εἰρένας de Pauw, ΛΕΞΕΙΣ : ἰρέας AB : ἰρέας Holder : ἱερέας Marc. : ἰρέας
reliqui ‖ τῶν καὶ : τῶν B Marc.   4 ποσειδόνιος R ‖ ἦσαν post Ποσειδώνιος S : ἔσαν z

Pausanias 9. 2. 5 locates the tombs on
the road, after the junction of the routes
from Eleutherai and from Megara, and
just at the entrance to the city : κατὰ
δὲ τὴν ἔσοδον μάλιστα τὴν ἐς Πλάταιαν
τάφοι τῶν πρὸς Μήδους μαχεσαμένων εἰσί.
Such is the precision of the actual
Periegete ; but even he has not quite
accurately described the tombs themselves : τοῖς μὲν οὖν λοιποῖς ἐστὶν Ἕλλησι
μνῆμα κοινόν. If this is correct, the
statement of Hdt. below in regard to
the tombs of the Tegeatai, of the
Megarians and Phleiasians, to say nothing
of the alleged kenotaphs, must be
incorrect.   Blakesley suggests that
Pausanias mistook the barrow of the
Helots for 'the common sepulture of
all the Greeks.' Or was it the Megaro-
Phleiasian ? Pausanias proceeds: Λακεδαιμονίων δὲ καὶ Ἀθηναίων τοῖς πεσοῦσιν
ἰδίᾳ τέ εἰσιν οἱ τάφοι, καὶ ἐλεγεῖά ἐστι
Σιμωνίδου γεγραμμένα ἐπ' αὐτοῖς. Pausanias unfortunately does not quote the
epigrams ; for possible texts cp. Hauvette,
sur l'authenticité etc., Nos. 28, 29. Dr.
Frazer is doubtless right in declining
to see in the rock-cut graves, a little
SE. of the plateau of the city, any
remains of the θῆκαι, χώματα, or πολυ-
άνδρια which contained the bodies of
the slain in 479 B.C., Pausanias, v.
p. 15.

Λακεδαιμόνιοι μέν. The Lakedaimonians made them three graves, or
tombs, τριξὰς θήκας, or as Dr. Frazer
l.c., harmonizing Pausanias with Hdt.,
suggests, a triple grave, a common
receptacle for three groups of dead men.
That is, indeed, very probably what
they did ; but Hdt. speaks of three
τάφοι for the Lakedaimonians, in each
of which a separate group is deposited,
and, though the τάφοι may not be χωρίς,
they appear to be quite distinct. If
Hdt. is mistaken on this point, it is
not the only mistake he makes in this
passage. τριξός, as in 4. 192.

3. τοὺς ἰρένας : a conjecture by
Valckenaer for ἰρέας, but a certain one.
The Λέξεις contains the word εἰρήν (cp.

Stein ed. maj. ii. 465), but this is the
only place in the text where it can
occur ; the burial of ἰρέες by themselves
is inadmissible, and who were the ἰρέες ?
So great an error in Greek or Spartan
institutions Hdt. could not incur. The
ἰρήν (ἰρην, εἰρην, ἰραν, Fἰραν) was the
Spartiate warrior from twenty to thirty
years of age, Plutarch, Lyk. 17 ; cp.
G. Gilbert, Gr. Staatsalt. i.[2] 70 ; but it
is not credible that Spartan citizens of
that age occupied high military or civil
posts, nor is it credible that Poseidonios,
Amompharetos, Philokyon (cp. c. 71
supra), and Kallikrates (cp. c. 72 supra)
were merely ἰρανες, least of all Amompharetos. Neither is it to be admitted
(with L. & S. sub v.) that the word in
this passage denotes 'officers of all
ranks'; the glosses in Hesychios (ἰρένες·
οἱ ἄρχοντες ἡλικιωτῶν and εἰρηνάζει·
κρατεῖ) do not go beyond Plutarch l.c.
οὗτος οὖν ὁ εἰρην εἰκόσι ἔτη γεγονὼς ἄρχει
τε τῶν ὑποτεταγμένων ἐν ταῖς μάχαις καὶ
κατ' οἶκον ὑπηρέταις χρῆται πρὸς τὸ
δεῖπνον. (Plutarch may be following
'Aristotle' Λακ. πολιτεία.) Rawlinson's
assertion that 'at the age of twenty the
Spartiate acquired the right to speak
in the Assembly and to have a
command' is a bit of constitutional lore
due to combining the pseudo-etymology
(εἰρην from ἐρέω) in Etym. Mag. with
the misunderstanding of the gloss of
Hesychios above cited. It appears that
Hdt., though he employs the technical
term ἰρένες, has not understood it when
he puts the ἰρένες in one grave, 'the rest
of the Spartiates' in another, and the
Helots in a third. That arrangement,
indeed, takes no account of the 'Lakedaimonians,' or Perioikoi. Probably the
three trenches, or mounds, covered (i.)
Spartiates—a majority of whom would
be ἰρανες, (ii.) Lakedaimonians, (iii.)
Helots. Of the first, ninety-one had
fallen, c. 70 supra ; the figures for the
others are not given. The error shown
in the passage makes it unlikely that
Hdt. derived this passage from a Spartan
source, least of all one in Sparta itself.

καὶ Καλλικράτης. ἐν μὲν δὴ ἑνὶ τῶν τάφων ἦσαν οἱ ἰρένες, 5
ἐν δὲ τῷ ἑτέρῳ οἱ ἄλλοι Σπαρτιῆται, ἐν δὲ τῷ τρίτῳ οἱ
εἵλωτες. οὗτοι μὲν οὕτω ἔθαπτον, Τεγεῆται δὲ χωρὶς πάντας
ἀλέας, καὶ Ἀθηναῖοι τοὺς ἑωυτῶν ὁμοῦ, καὶ Μεγαρέες τε καὶ
Φλειάσιοι τοὺς ὑπὸ τῆς ἵππου διαφθαρέντας. τούτων μὲν δὴ
πάντων πλήρεες ἐγένοντο οἱ τάφοι· τῶν δὲ ἄλλων ὅσοισι καὶ 10
φαίνονται ἐν Πλαταιῇσι ἐόντες τάφοι, τούτους δέ, ὡς ἐγὼ
πυνθάνομαι, ἐπαισχυνομένους τῇ ἀπεστοῖ τῆς μάχης ἑκάστους
χώματα χῶσαι κεινὰ τῶν ἐπιγινομένων εἵνεκεν ἀνθρώπων,

5 ἦσαν: ἐτάφησαν? Stein(2) || ἰρένες Valckenaer etc.: εἰρένες ut supra:
ἰρέες AB: ἰρέες Holder: ἱερέες Marc.: ἰρέες ceteri   7 οὕτω μὲν οὗτοι
ἔθαφθεν B || πάντας ἔθαψαν Bz   8 ἀλέας AB: ἀλέας Marc. || τοὺς
ἑωυτῶν ὁμοῦ om. B   9 τουτέων C Marc. z   10 τῶν . . τάφοι om. B:
citat Plutarch. Mor. 872 || ὅσοισι Krueger, Stein³: ὅσοι   11 πλαταίῃσι
AB || δὴ z   12 ἀπαισχυνομένους aC: ἀπεσχοινισμένους Marc. ||
ἀποεστοῖ R (B ap. Holder: ἀποστοῖ τῆς μάχης ἐγένοντο S ap. Gaisford):
ἀπεστύϊ coni. Valckenaer || ἑκάστη Marc.   13 κοινὰ Paris. 1635 z ||
ἐπιγεινομένων aC || εἵνεκα z

7. **Τεγεῆται.** The Tegeatai buried
their sixteen (c. 70 *supra*) all together,
in a separate place, and grave, probably
next the Lakedaimonians (cp. c. 28
supra). Pausanias does not notice the
Tegean grave.

8. **Ἀθηναῖοι** had fifty-two slain (c. 70
supra). One might have expected them
to have buried their dead down on the
plain, where, presumably, they had
fallen (c. 67 *supra*), but Pausanias *l.c.*
appears to put the grave in the
neighbourhood of the Spartan. (Could
he have made a mistake?) Stein sees
in Thucydides 2. 34. 5 an intentional
contradiction of this passage in Hdt.
Krüger proposed to reconcile the two
by supposing that the Athenian tomb
at Plataia was a kenotaph; Baehr
boldly regards Thucydides as in the
wrong.

Μεγαρέες τε καὶ Φλειάσιοι. This
formula denotes the left centre of the
Greek army (cp. c. 69 *supra*), and
probably only one grave or *Polyandrion*
is here indicated, in which those of the
right centre, who fell in conflict with
the Thebans, were interred, to the
number of 600; cp. c. 69 *supra*. That
figure is not, indeed, convincing. It
should perhaps be taken to represent
the total losses of the Greeks other than
the figures for the Lakedaimonians,
Tegeatai, and Athenians, in fact to
cover also the losses of the right centre

of the Greek army (which Hdt. appears
to think was not engaged at all). If
so, then this tumulus is the first of the
τάφοι described by Pausanias, the μνῆμα
κοινόν for all the Greeks (i.e. the whole
centre), distinguished from the separate
τάφοι for the Lakedaimonians and for the
Athenians.

10. **τῶν δὲ ἄλλων**: sc. Ἑλλήνων.

11. **φαίνονται ἐν Πλαταιῇσι ἐόντες,**
'are to be seen at Plataia,' i.e. in the
land of Plataia (cp. c. 16 etc.). It does
not follow that Hdt. had seen them
before writing; indeed, what ensues
is based on hearsay, or correspondence
(πυνθάνομαι, ἀκούω); and, if Hdt. had
been writing from his own personal
inspection and remembrance, the imperfect tense would have been more
naturally employed (ἐφαίνοντο).

τούτους δέ: a true δέ in apodosi;
τούτους is better referred to τάφοι than
to τῶν ἄλλων, and taken as in virtual
opposition to χώματα, ἑκάστους (the
several states) being subject of the verb.
There is still a slight confusion in the
construction, which is in *oratio obliqua*,
the ὡς in ὡς ἐγὼ πυνθάνομαι notwithstanding.

12. **ἀπεστοῖ** = ἀπουσίᾳ. Hesychios
gives the form ἀπεστύϊ as well as
ἀπεστύ, Ionic forms. Cp. εὐεστώ 1. 85.
τῆς μάχης, on the 13th.

13. **τῶν ἐπιγινομένων ἕνεκεν,** 'for the
sake of (deceiving) posterity'!

ἐπεὶ καὶ Αἰγινητέων ἐστὶ αὐτόθι καλεόμενος τάφος, τὸν ἐγὼ
15 ἀκούω καὶ δέκα ἔτεσι ὕστερον μετὰ ταῦτα δεηθέντων τῶν
Αἰγινητέων χῶσαι Κλεάδην τὸν Αὐτοδίκου ἄνδρα Πλαταιέα,
πρόξεινον ἐόντα αὐτῶν.
86 Ὡς δ᾽ ἄρα ἔθαψαν τοὺς νεκροὺς ἐν Πλαταιῆσι οἱ
Ἕλληνες, αὐτίκα βουλευομένοισί σφι ἐδόκεε στρατεύεσθαι ἐπὶ

---

14 τὸν: τῶν R(V)   15 τῶν om. βPz, Holder   16 ἀλεάδην
αC Marc.   17 πρόξενον β ‖ ὄντα C ‖ ἑωῦτῶν z   86. 1 δὲ R(V)
‖ πλαταίῃσι α: πλαταίῃσιν R(V)   2 βουλομένοισί σφιν C ‖
στρατεύειν αC

---

14. καὶ Αἰγινητέων: a particular case
but an unfortunate one to have selected,
as upon Hdt.'s own showing the
Aiginetans, being included in the left
centre, οἱ ἀμφὶ Μεγαρέας τε καὶ Φλειασίους,
were at least engaged with the Theban
cavalry on the 13th. Cp. cc. 69, 28
supra. If they erected subsequently
a kenotaph (χῶμα κεινόν or τάφος κεινός),
it might be because their actual dead
had been interred in the common grave,
the 'Megaro-Phleiasian' grave, or κοινὸν
μνῆμα, and they wished, as time went
on, to commemorate their own separately.
A similar consideration would account
for any other kenotaphs on the field.

ἐγὼ ἀκούω: not very convincing
evidence, nor very critically received by
Hdt. The use of the present is perhaps
rhetorical, or is he writing in Athens,
where he would be hearing such things
said? Cp. Introduction, § 10.

15. καὶ δέκα ἔτεσι ὕστερον μετὰ ταῦτα,
'as much as ten years subsequently
after the war' (καὶ etiam); i.e. in
469 B.C. For μετὰ ταῦτα cp. c. 83 supra.
(Plutarch de malig. Hdti 42=Mor. 873
paraphrases ἔτεσι δέκα ὕστερον τῶν Μηδι-
κῶν.) As the dative of time marks a
point, the date here given must be
meant to be exact.

16. Κλεάδην τὸν Αὐτοδίκου: only
mentioned again in Plutarch l.c. quoting
this passage. The name Kleades is
known at Sparta and Argos; the name
Autodikos only elsewhere at Athens
(cp. Pape-Benseler sub vv.). As πρό-
ξεινος of the Aiginetans this Plataian
might not be a very popular person in
Athens, whence Hdt. directly or indirectly 'heard' this scandal. Plutarch
l.c. makes one of his bitter points
against Hdt. à propos of these kenotaphs; yet, like most of his arguments,
it is wide of the mark. The 'trophies

and colossi' on which the names were
inscribed were commemorative of the
war rather than of the particular battle
of Plataia (on the 13th); moreover, as
above shown, there might be kenotaphs
on the field of battle in honour of
warriors buried elsewhere. On the
προξενία cp. 8. 136, 143.

86. 1. ἄρα: if the word is to suggest
an element of the unexpected, the note
of admiration may in this case arride
the place of sepulture, to most even of
the Greek dead a foreign land; cp. 1.
30. But what became of the 237,000
corpses, more or less, of the enemies,
with which Hdt. has bestrown the field
in c. 70 supra: are they covered by this
notice? In which case the surprise
might extend to the numbers.

2. αὐτίκα βουλευομένοισί σφι ἐδόκεε:
here is the record, or the hint, of a
deliberation, a council, which issues in a
resolution to 'visit' Thebes. Ought the
record in Plutarch Aristeid. 21 of the
treaty of Plataia, or the revision of the
confederate articles and the institution
of the Eleutheria, to be inserted here?
Grote (iv. 282) seems to date it to "a
general and solemn meeting, held at
Plataia after the victory," but also
apparently dates that meeting after the
surrender of Thebes. Plutarch omits
the Theban incident altogether, and
there is no room below for any other
congress or meeting at Plataia after the
surrender of Thebes. If, then, the
meeting which carried the psephism of
Aristeides was held at Plataia, it would
be the meeting here imperfectly reported;
but perhaps the psephism of Aristeides,
if ever carried at all, was carried at a
congress at the Isthmos, for which room
may be found in c. 88 infra. Grote
defends the authenticity of the psephism
of Aristeides, but the story, as told by

τὰς Θήβας καὶ ἐξαιτέειν αὐτῶν τοὺς μηδίσαντας· ἐν πρώτοισι
δὲ αὐτῶν Τιμηγενίδην καὶ 'Ατταγῖνον, οἳ ἀρχηγέται ἀνὰ
πρώτους ἦσαν· ἢν δὲ μὴ ἐκδιδῶσι, μὴ ἀπανίστασθαι ἀπὸ τῆς 5
πόλιος πρότερον ἢ ἐξέλωσι. ὡς δέ σφι ταῦτα ἔδοξε, οὕτω
δὴ ἐνδεκάτῃ ἡμέρῃ ἀπὸ τῆς συμβολῆς ἀπικόμενοι ἐπολιόρκεον
Θηβαίους, κελεύοντες ἐκδιδόναι τοὺς ἄνδρας· οὐ βουλομένων
δὲ τῶν Θηβαίων ἐκδιδόναι, τήν τε γῆν αὐτῶν ἔταμνον καὶ
προσέβαλλον πρὸς τὸ τεῖχος. καὶ οὐ γὰρ ἐπαύοντο σινόμενοι, 87
εἰκοστῇ ἡμέρῃ ἔλεξε τοῖσι Θηβαίοισι Τιμηγενίδης τάδε.

3, 4 αὐτέων z (bis): ἀστέων prior. l. Koen   4 αὐτῶν abesse malit
van H. ‖ ἀτταγῖνον P   5 ἔσαν z ‖ ἀπὸ . . ἐξέλωσι om. β   7
ἐνδεκάτηι C   9 τῶν Θηβαίων 'abesse poterat' van H. ‖ αὐτέων z
10 προσέβαλον S Marc.   87. 1 σινεόμενοι β

Plutarch, is not confirmed by Thucydides
2. 71, for (a) nothing is there said of the
renewal or extension of the military
confederacy ; (b) the privileges accorded
the Plataians are granted by Pausanias
at a meeting of the allies in the Agora
of Plataia. This grant might very well
have been made at the meeting here
recorded. Grote hardly showed his
normal sagacity in accepting the story of
the psephism of Aristeides and at the
same time rejecting the story of the
quarrel over the Aristeia (which certainly
ill squares with it!).

3. **ἐξαιτέειν αὐτῶν τοὺς μηδίσαντας.**
If the story told in 7. 132 of the vow in
the previous year against the medizers
were true, the resolution now formally
taken, to demand the extradition of the
traitors among the Thebans, would
appear both mild and superfluous : a
reason the more for doubting the truth
of that story. But again, this resolution
recognizes very clearly the existence of
two parties in Thebes, the medizing
party being evidently the Equestrians,
not the Hoplites ; cp. c. 69 supra and 7.
223.

The reading ἀστέων out of αὐτέων for
αὐτῶν is attractive : a second αὐτῶν
(sc. τῶν μηδισάντων) comes immediately,
and there is no proper personal antecedent
for αὐτῶν here. Cp. App. Crit.

4. **Τιμηγενίδην** : cp. c. 38 supra.
'Ατταγῖνον : cp. c. 16 supra. The
absence of the patronymics in this place
seems to show that the previous descriptions of the men are present to the
author's mind, though there is no express
reference back to the earlier passages.
Hdt. writes for a reading public ; and

all three passages apparently belong to
the first draft of his work.

ἀρχηγέται ἀνὰ πρώτους. The use
of ἀνά is not easy to parallel, and
πρώτους is awkward after ἐν πρώτοισι just
before, and slightly tautologous with
ἀρχ-ηγέται, i.e. ἡγέται ἀνὰ πρώτους, or ἐν
πρώτοις. The term ἀρχηγέται is a word
of exceptional dignity applicable to
gods (Thuc. 6. 3), heroes ('Αθ. πολ. 21.
6), kings (Plutarch, Lyk. 6), and founders
(Pind. Ol. 7. 143) ; so too Inscripp.
How comes Hdt. to apply it to these
Theban traitors ? Did he get it of
Thersander ? cp. c. 16 supra. It is an
hapaxlegomenon in Hdt., though the
verb is used 2. 123.

6. **πρότερον ἢ ἐξέλωσι** : sc. αὐτήν.
The subjunctive without ἄν is observable ;
cp. c. 117 infra, also 7. 8 οὐ πρότερον
παύσομαι πρὶν ἢ ἕλω τε καὶ πυρώσω τὰς
'Αθήνας, c. 93 infra οὐ πρότερόν τε
παύσεσθαι τιμωρέοντες ἐκείνῳ πρὶν ἢ δίκας
δῶσι. Cp. also c. 87 just below.

7. **ἐνδεκάτῃ ἡμέρῃ.** Is this the 23rd
or the 24th reckoning continuously ?
The answer depends on whether ἀπό is
exclusive or inclusive. It might naturally be the former ; but the δευτέρη
ἡμέρῃ in c. 84 supra is the day after the
battle. In any case we have here merely
another of Hdt.'s weeks, or 'ten-days' ;
cp. c. 8 supra and the next chapter
here. The 11th day begins a fresh week.

συμβολῆς, c. 77 supra, etc.

ἐπολιόρκεον Θηβαίους : the tense
is strictly imperfect, 'they made as
though to besiege—they were for besie-
ging . .' Θηβαίους = τὰς Θήβας.

87. 2. **εἰκοστῇ ἡμέρῃ** : probably not
of the siege, but ἀπὸ τῆς συμβολῆς as just

" ἄνδρες Θηβαῖοι, ἐπειδὴ οὕτω δέδοκται τοῖσι Ἕλλησι, μὴ
πρότερον ἀπαναστῆναι πολιορκέοντας ἢ ἐξέλωσι Θήβας ἢ
5 ἡμέας αὐτοῖσι παραδῶτε, νῦν ὦν ἡμέων εἵνεκα γῆ ἡ Βοιωτίη
πλέω μὴ ἀναπλήσῃ, ἀλλ' εἰ μὲν χρημάτων χρηίζοντες πρόσχημα ἡμέας ἐξαιτέονται, χρήματά σφι δῶμεν ἐκ τοῦ κοινοῦ
(σὺν γὰρ τῷ κοινῷ καὶ ἐμηδίσαμεν οὐδὲ μοῦνοι ἡμεῖς), εἰ δὲ
ἡμέων ἀληθέως δεόμενοι πολιορκέουσι, ἡμεῖς ἡμέας αὐτοὺς ἐς
10 ἀντιλογίην παρέξομεν." κάρτα τε ἔδοξε εὖ λέγειν καὶ ἐς
καιρόν, αὐτίκα τε ἐπεκηρυκεύοντο πρὸς Παυσανίην οἱ Θηβαῖοι

---

3 οὕτω: οὔτε S   4 πρὶν ἢ z   5˙ ἡμέας παραδότε B ‖
Βοιωτίηι B   6 πλέω om. S ‖ ἀνατλήσῃ z ‖ εἰ: ἡ B: ἢν B ‖ χρήι-
ζοντες P: χρήζοντες R(V): χρήζοντες z   7 ἐξαιτέωνται B   8 οὐ
δὴ μοῦνοι ἡμέες z   9 ἀληθῶς Marc. ‖ ἡμεῖς <δὲ> Krueger, van H. ‖
ἑωυτοὺς z ‖ εἰς R(V), Holder   10 εὖ om. Marc.

---

above; it would then be the 10th day
of the siege, the last day of the 'week,'
which begins with the 11th day just
above. (It would be the 33rd day
of the whole journal—if the figures were
to be treated as quite exact; cp. cc. 84,
56, 52, 47, 44, 41, *supra*.)

3. οὕτω refers here to what follows
and = ὧδε. Cp. Index.

δέδοκται τοῖσι Ἕλλησι: a formal
δόγμα, repeated from c. 86 above.

5. νῦν ὦν in *apodosi* is unusual.

ἡμέων εἵνεκα, 'for our sakes,' or
'so far as we are concerned . .'

γῆ ἡ Βοιωτίη: treated as equivalent
to τὴν γῆν αὐτῶν just above.

6. πλέω μὴ ἀναπλήσῃ, "dehortative
conjunctive in 3rd person" (Stein); cp.
7. 107 μὴ νῦν οὕτω γένηται.

πρόσχημα (cp. 4. 167) might be
appositive to ἡμέας but is better understood as an adverbial accusative, contrasted with ἀληθέως just below; cp.
πρόφασιν 5. 33, also ἀρχήν, τέλος, etc.

7. ἐκ τοῦ κοινοῦ . . σὺν τῷ κοινῷ
are used in different senses, which might
be preserved by using our word 'commonwealth.' For the first sense cp. 7. 144;
for the second 8. 135. The juristic
principle here asserted by this oligarchic
traitor is of considerable interest, viz.
that the individual citizen cannot be
held responsible for the common fault,
the crime or error of the community,
even though he himself be its author or
proposer. It is a plausible maxim,
which easily lends itself to sophistry;
its employment shows a considerable
development of political reflexion. In

the present case we are not informed
whether there had been a formal vote of
ἄνδρες Θηβαῖοι in favour of medism, or
whether the public medism is treated *de
facto*; there was at any rate an opposition,
and an opposition, which, if the Theban
speaker *ap*. Thuc. 3. 62. 3 is to be
trusted, was numerically a majority,
though impotent. On this ground
Pausanias 9. 6. 2 acquits the Commons:
τῆς δὲ αἰτίας ταύτης δημοσίᾳ σφίσιν οὐ
μέτεστιν, ὅτι ἐν ταῖς Θήβαις ὀλιγαρχία
καὶ οὐχὶ ἡ πάτριος πολιτεία τηνικαῦτα
ἴσχυεν. He adds that if the Persians had
invaded Hellas in the days of Peisistratos,
the Athenians would have incurred the
reproach of medism. The rider is disputable; but in any case the Athenians,
among whom the convenient principle
of the political scapegoat was only
too well understood, would have made
short work of the arguments of a
Timagenidas.

9. ἡμέων ἀληθέως δεόμενοι, 'because
they really want to get hold of us'—or
perhaps, 'if the demand for us is the
true cause of the siege.'

ἐς ἀντιλογίην παρέξομεν, 'we will
give ourselves up to be tried' (Blakesley);
or rather, to reply to the charge. No
doubt a juristic trial is contemplated;
ἀντιλογίη in itself only means 'contradiction,' cp. 8. 77, but it comes to be
used for reply, defence to objections
or charges, controversy, discussion; cp.
Thuc. 1. 31. 4, 1. 78. 1, 2. 87. 3. On the
showing of this passage the surrender
of the men should have been conditional.
Cp. next chapter *ad f*.

θέλοντες ἐκδιδόναι τοὺς ἄνδρας. ὡς δὲ ὡμολόγησαν ἐπὶ 88
τούτοισι, Ἀτταγῖνος μὲν ἐκδιδρήσκει ἐκ τοῦ ἄστεος, παῖδας
δὲ αὐτοῦ ἀπαχθέντας Παυσανίης ἀπέλυσε τῆς αἰτίης, φὰς τοῦ
μηδισμοῦ παῖδας οὐδὲν εἶναι μεταιτίους. τοὺς δὲ ἄλλους
ἄνδρας τοὺς ἐξέδοσαν οἱ Θηβαῖοι, οἱ μὲν ἐδόκεον ἀντιλογίης 5
τε κυρήσειν καὶ δὴ χρήμασι ἐπεποίθεσαν διωθέεσθαι· ὁ δὲ ὡς

---

88. 2 ἀττατῖνος Apr.P || ἐκ : ἐπὶ C   3 αὐτοῦ om. B   5 τοὺς :
οὓς αC Marc.   6 κηρήσιν R : κηρύσειν Marc. || ἐπεπύθεον α : ἐπεπόθεον
C Marc. : ἐπεπείθεσαν Paris. 1635 z || διώσασθαι B : σωθήσεσθαι Cobet,
van H. ('nisi forte mavis διώσεσθαι τὴν αἰτίην simileve quid' idem): δια-
δύσεσθαι ? Stein⁵ || ὁ δὲ ὡς βPz, Stein¹, van H. : ὡς δὲ

---

88. 1. ὡμολόγησαν ἐπὶ τούτοισι.
The terms upon which (ἐπὶ) Thebes surrendered cannot have been confined to
the extradition of Timagenidas, Attaginos,
and a few others; the depression of
Thebes for the next twenty years could
hardly be accounted for on that hypothesis. The ὁμολογία must have included further terms: the break-up of
the Boiotian confederacy, the 'autonomy'
of the Boiotian cities, the overthrow of
Theban hegemony, possibly some revision
of the Theban constitution itself, possibly
a fine. Nothing exhibits the position
of affairs during the period so well as
the coinage of Boiotia; cp. B. Head,
Coins of Boiotia (1881) pp. 20 ff., *Hist.
Num.* (1887) pp. 291 ff., while the occasion and rationale of the Spartan expedition of 457 B.C. (cp. c. 35 *supra*)
supplies an argument *e contrario*.

3. Παυσανίης ἀπέλυσε: another
tribute to the magnanimity of the
Spartan general, unqualified by any
insinuation of bribery or corruption. In
thus distinguishing between the guilt
of various members of one family, and
refusing to hold the children responsible
for the father's crimes, Pausanias exhibits
an advance upon the good old morality
of the fable *ex hypothesi* related by his
contemporary Leotychidas at Athens
some ten years earlier; cp. 6. 86. Baehr
extols *Pausaniae animum vere sublimem
et a . . superbia . . alienum.* Blakesley
remarks that Attaginos was at large,
and therefore formidable, and suspects
Pausanias of medism already ! We may
be content to note the hint of a growing
consciousness of individual responsibility, proper to an age of reflexion and
liberty.

4. τοὺς δὲ ἄλλους ἄνδρας: the omission of their number and names, the
anomaly of the grammatical construction,
the violence of the proceeding itself, all
point to an unresolved problem behind
this passage. The anacoluthon may be
softened by referring οἱ μέν to οἱ Θηβαῖοι,
but the historical situation is not thereby
lightened.

5. ἐδόκεον ἀντιλογίης τε κυρήσειν,
'were expecting to be put on trial,' or,
to be called upon for a defence; Blakesley
renders ἀντ. "pleadings on each side."
The τε should naturally follow the verb,
and relates to καὶ δὴ . . ἐπεποίθεσαν.
The 2nd perf. πέποιθα serves as
"present middle" (Veitch, *Gk. Verbs
sub v. Il.* 4. 325 etc. "rare in Attic
prose," *Thuc.* 2. 42. 4 ἐλπίδι μὲν τὸ
ἀφανὲς τοῦ κατορθώσειν ἐπιτρέψαντες,
ἔργῳ δὲ περὶ τοῦ ἤδη ὁρωμένου σφίσιν
αὐτοῖς ἀξιοῦντες πεποιθέναι), and the pl.p.
as an imperfect.

6. διωθέεσθαι: the word has caused
the commentators trouble; the use of
the present is anomalous, and there is no
clear object expressed. For suggested
emendations cp. App. Crit. Baehr
supplies τὴν αἰτίην out of the preceding,
i.e. *crimen pecuniis amoliri.*
The verb διωθέεσθαι is used 4. 102
(τὸν Δαρείου στρατὸν ἰθυμαχίῃ διώσασθαι)
simply as a strengthened form of ὠθέεσθαι
(cp. c. 25 *supra*), and so in Demosthenes
21. 124 (διεωσάμην . . ψευδῆ λόγον καὶ
συκοφαντίαν), but also 'to push through,'
to push apart, to break one's way through,
as in c. 102 *infra* διωσάμενοι γὰρ τὰ
γέρρα. Might it not here be used, without an object, in an absolute way: 'to
push their way through,' 'to pull
through' (as we say), i.e. to get off !
(The anomaly of the present is eased a
little by referring οἱ μέν to οἱ Θηβαῖοι,
who then believed the men were making their escape by means of bribery.)

παρέλαβε, αὐτὰ ταῦτα ὑπονοέων τὴν στρατιὴν τὴν τῶν συμμάχων ἅπασαν ἀπῆκε καὶ ἐκείνους ἀγαγὼν ἐς Κόρινθον διέφθειρε. ταῦτα μὲν τὰ ἐν Πλαταιῇσι καὶ Θήβῃσι γενόμενα.

89 Ἀρτάβαζος δὲ ὁ Φαρνάκεος φεύγων ἐκ Πλαταιέων καὶ δὴ

7 τὴν τῶν : τῶν Marc.   9 πλαταίῃσι **a** : πλαταίῃσι R : πλαταίῃσιν V ‖ γινόμενα z   **89**. 1 καὶ δὴ : καὶ δὴ καὶ Marc., Gaisford

ἐς παρέλαβε : sc. αὐτούς, i.e. τοὺς ἄνδρας παραλαβών.

7. αὐτὰ ταῦτα ὑπονοέων, 'suspecting (cp. ὑπονοήσαντες c. 99 *infra*) their intentions,' or 'just that very course.'

τὴν στρατιὴν . . ἅπασαν ἀπῆκε. Pausanias may have disbanded, or dismissed to their homes, from Thebes, the Athenians, and perhaps the Aiginetans, and one or two other contingents; but it is very unlikely that the rest of the allied forces will have been disbanded at Thebes, or before reaching the Isthmos. There appears to be a tendency in this passage, i.c. in the source followed by Hdt. for the story, to make Pausanias himself wholly and solely responsible for the execution of (Timagenidas and) the anonymous Theban *dévoués* (was Asopodoros, c. 69 *supra*, among them? was Leontiades, 7. 233?). They are not tried by a Spartan court (like the Plataians for 'atticism' in 427 B.C., Thuc. 3. 52–68), nor brought before a jury of the allies; Pausanias puts them to death out of hand. This appears to be a very arbitrary proceeding, just such as might be ascribed to him after his fall, at a time when various parties might be glad to wash their hands, at his expense, of anti-Theban conduct. Blakesley goes a long step further in damning the memory of Pausanias: he accepts this story just as it stands, for the facts, and suggests, as the explanation, that Pausanias had been already intriguing with the Persians, and "put the Theban oligarchs to death in order to conceal the evidence which they might have given against him, had they been brought to trial." But then Blakesley (with Ktesias)also believed that the battle of Plataia took place before the battle of Salamis, and was quite a small and trifling affair (virtually, indeed, a defeat for the Greeks). It is at least possible that the Theban prisoners were duly, or at least *pro forma*, put upon their trial at the Isthmos, and that this was indeed one of the conditions of their surrender (ἡμεῖς ἡμέας αὐτοὺς ἐς ἀντιλογίην παρέ-

ξομεν) : Pausanias merely executed the sentence of the court.

8. ἐς Κόρινθον=ἐς τὴν Κορινθιάδα, cp. c. 17 *supra*, probably an inaccuracy for ἐς τὸν Κορινθίων Ἰσθμόν cp. 7. 195. There was probably a meeting, perhaps a final meeting, of the allies, at which the awards were made, offerings voted, immunities conferred, and the alliance perhaps reconstituted; cp. 8. 123 and c. 85 *supra*.

89. 1. Ἀρτάβαζος δὲ ὁ Φαρνάκεος. This narrative is resumed from c. 66 *supra*. Hdt.'s partiality for the patronymic in the case of 'Artabazos son of Pharnakes' is remarkable; he gives it in 7. 66, 8. 126, 9. 41, 66, and here, five times in all; in fact there are only three places, and those all in this Book, viz. cc. 58, 70, 77, where the name is introduced in anything like a fresh connexion without it: the first place is in a speech by Mardonios; in the other two, where the historian writes *propria persona*, the reference to the immediate context is so slight and so obvious (τὰς sc. μυριάδας τὰς ἔχων Ἀρτάβαζος ἔφευγε, τοὺς μετὰ Ἀρταβάζου φεύγοντας) that the introduction of the patronymic would have been a stylistic absurdity. There may be a polemical purpose in this curious iteration: was there another Artabazos with whom 'the son of Pharnakes' was liable to be confounded? For example, the Artabazos who figures in Diodoros as successful against the Athenians in the Egyptian war (11. 74. 6, 77. 4), and again as admiral in the Kyprian war (12. 3. 2) and negotiating the 'Peace of Kallias' (12. 4. 5); cp. 7. 151 *supra*. Or is not that indeed the very same man? Otherwise who or what was his father, and his father's father? The name Φαρνάκης has been regarded as a variant for Φαρνούχης (or *vice versa*); cp. Rawlinson, iii.³ p. 549. Was the father of Artabazos the high-placed hipparch who died by a fall from his horse at Sardes? cp. 7. 88. The names Pharnakes and Pharnabazos afterwards recur in the satrapy of Daskyleion; cp. 8. 126

πρόσω ἐγίνετο. ἀπικόμενον δέ μιν οἱ Θεσσαλοὶ παρὰ σφέας
ἐπί τε ξείνια ἐκάλεον καὶ ἀνειρώτων περὶ τῆς στρατιῆς τῆς
ἄλλης, οὐδὲν ἐπιστάμενοι τῶν ἐν Πλαταιῆσι γενομένων. ὁ δὲ
Ἀρτάβαζος γνοὺς ὅτι, εἰ ἐθέλει σφι πᾶσαν τὴν ἀληθείην τῶν 5

2 ἐγένετο β ‖ παρά σφεας B   3 ἐπεί R(V) ‖ ξένια α ‖ ἀνειρώτευν
Marc., Stein[1] (Ask. V, Gaisford): ἀνηρώτευν CPz   4 πλαταίῃσι α:
πλαταίῃσι R(S)V ‖ γινομένων α Marc.   5 ἐθέλει ABCSV: ἐθέλοι ‖
ἀληθηίην z ‖ τῶν ἀγώνων del. van H.

supra. Pharnabazos 'son of Pharnakes,' 413–388 B.C. (Thuc. 8. 6. 1), was succeeded by Ariobarzanes (Xenoph. Hell. 5. 1. 28, cp. 1. 4. 7), and he in turn by an Artabazos; Krumbholz, op. c. p. 73. Another Ariobarzanes 'son of Artabazos' appears with his father among the most loyal followers of the last Dareios (cp. Arrian, 3. 21. 4, 23. 7, etc.). The names Pharnakes, Pharnabazos, Artabazos, Ariobarzanes all belong, ll.c., apparently to one house, or clan, and that, one highly placed and esteemed in the Persian Empire (cp. Judeich ap. Pauly-Wissowa, sub v.). There is a gap in the succession at Daskyleion between 470 B.C. or thereabouts and 430 B.C. Was it filled by 'Pharnabazos' the father of Pharnakes II.? The name Pharnabazos does not occur in Hdt.

φεύγων ἐκ Πλαταιέων. Hdt. has been suspected of special relations with the family of Artabazos, cp. 8. 126 supra, but he never represents his retreat as anything but a φυγή. In that respect, unless it be in the softer verb at the close of this very chapter, ἀπενόστησε, he may have done his supposed patron less than justice. The 'flight' of Artabazos from 'Plataia' may be little more historical than the 'flight' of Xerxes from Athens. The story, as told in this chapter, is full of intrinsic improbabilities. The rôle assigned to Artabazos helped to explain two awkward facts, awkward especially to medizing Greeks afterwards: (a) the defeat of Mardonios, and their own; (b) the escape of 40,000 men, who might have been stopped, and offered as an atonement to the patriotic league. The historical element in the quarrels of Mardonios and Artabazos is problematic, and in view of the licence of Greek historiography a critic may be pardoned if he suspect at times that Artabazos never was on the field of Plataia at all. Cp. Appendix VIII. § 5 (19). ἐκ Πλαταιέων could not mean at most

more than ἐκ τῆς Πλαταιίδος: cp. c. 16 supra.

καὶ δή here = ἤδη: cp. Index.

2. πρόσω, 'far on his way' by the time the Thebans surrendered, or Pausanias had put an end to them at 'Korinth.'

οἱ Θεσσαλοί: the first absurdity, for 'the sons of Aleuas' had been in the camp of Mardonios, cp. c. 58 supra, and had probably supported the view of Artabazos and the Thebans against Mardonios; cp. c. 41 supra. In any case it is not likely that Artabazos, with some 40,000 Persians, regained Thessaly ahead of the Aleuads and the Thessalian cavalry; or that on his arrival no news of τῶν ἐν Πλαταιῆσι had reached Thessaly. It does not really help to interpret οἱ Θεσσαλοί here as representing a different party, an opposing faction or element, the bulk of the population, and so on, as compared with the Aleuads and aristocracy; there were doubtless in Thessaly, as in Phokis, as in Boiotia, as in the Peloponnese, as possibly in Athens itself (cp. Plutarch, Aristeid. 13), two parties, two rival interests on the Persian question, but it remains an absurdity to attribute to either the ignorance here predicated of οἱ Θεσσαλοί.

3. ἐπὶ ξείνια ἐκάλεον, 'invited to a banquet,' cp. c. 16 supra.

καί, 'at which they ..'

τῆς στρατιῆς τῆς ἄλλης: i.e. the army of Mardonios (not their own men); cp. ὁ μετ' αὐτοῦ στρατός, and αὐτὸς Μαρδόνιος καὶ ὁ στρατὸς αὐτοῦ just below.

5. εἰ ἐθέλει: cp. εἰ ἐθελήσει 1. 32.

πᾶσαν τὴν ἀληθείην τῶν ἀγώνων εἰπεῖν: that is unfortunately what no one has done, not even Hdt. himself. Artabazos least of all could afford to do so, if Hdt.'s record of him is true. The plural recognizes a number of ἀγῶνες at Plataia; or are they inquiring about the previous campaign too?

ἀγώνων εἰπεῖν, αὐτός τε κινδυνεύσει ἀπολέσθαι καὶ ὁ μετ'
αὐτοῦ στρατός· ἐπιθήσεσθαι γάρ οἱ πάντα τινὰ οἴετο πυνθα-
νόμενον τὰ γεγονότα· ταῦτα ἐκλογιζόμενος οὔτε πρὸς τοὺς
Φωκέας ἐξηγόρευε οὐδὲν πρός τε τοὺς Θεσσαλοὺς ἔλεγε τάδε.
10 "ἐγὼ μέν, ὦ ἄνδρες Θεσσαλοί, ὡς ὁρᾶτε, ἐπείγομαί τε κατὰ
τάχος ἐλῶν ἐς Θρηίκην καὶ σπουδὴν ἔχω, πεμφθεὶς κατά τι
πρῆγμα ἐκ τοῦ στρατοπέδου μετὰ τῶνδε· αὐτὸς δὲ ὑμῖν
Μαρδόνιος καὶ ὁ στρατὸς αὐτοῦ, οὗτος κατὰ πόδας ἐμεῦ

---

6 εἶπαι z, van H.   7 αὐτὸν Marc. || οἴετο Βz : ὠίετο α : ὠίετο C :
ὠίετο P : ᾤετο Marc. : secl. Cobet, van H.   8 τοὺς om. S Marc.   9
ἐξαγόρευε C Marc., Gaisford || οὐδεὶς C   10 κατὰ τάχος Stein[1] ²,
Holder : τὴν ταχίστην Stein¹, van H. : κατὰ τὴν ταχίστην Marc. z : κατὰ
ταχίστην A(RV ?): κατὰ ταχίστηι B : καταταχίστην CP : κατατάχιστα S
(Gaisf.)   11 ἐλθὼν Ask. : ἐλθεῖν z || θρήκην R(S)V   13 αὐτοῦ
om. Marc. || ἐμεῦ om. Β : μου z : μευ Krueger

---

8. οὔτε πρὸς τοὺς Φωκέας ἐξηγόρευε
οὐδέν : i.e. while marching through
Phokis, as he must have done to get to
Thessaly. This statement is evidently
an afterthought (but that hardly con-
verts ἐξηγόρευε into a pluperfect !). It
is also an absurdity. There were 1000
Phokians in the camp of Mardonios, c.
17 supra ; they would not have allowed
Artabazos to get such a start of them.
Had they done so, the remainder of the
nation at home, on Parnassos, who
ἐνθεῦτεν ὁρμώμενοι ἔφερόν τε καὶ ἦγον τὴν
τε Μαρδονίου στρατιὴν καὶ τοὺς μετ' αὐτοῦ
ἐόντας Ἑλλήνων c. 31 supra, would hardly
have allowed Artabazos free passage,
much less entertained him, or invited
his reports ! However, to them he held
his peace ; to the Thessalians he told a
lie. It is, however, also perhaps an
absurdity to suppose, or imply, that
there was any force at the disposal of
the Phokians which could have barred
the retreat of Artabazos.

10. ὦ ἄνδρες Θεσσαλοί : he talks as
though he were addressing a public
meeting. His speech incidentally furnishes three curious examples of the
use of κατά (κατὰ τάχος—κατά τι πρῆγμα
—κατὰ πόδας). His haste is expressed
thrice over : ἐπείγομαι· κατὰ τάχος ἐλῶν·
σπουδὴν ἔχω : he makes little of his
40,000 companions (μετὰ τῶνδε).

11. ἐς Θρηίκην : why to Thrace ? Why
not to Makedonia ? Why does he
advertise the Thessalians that his bourne
is Thrace, instead of specifying his nearer
objective, unless it be that Artabazos

had really a special mission in Thrace,
was, in fact, governor of the province ?
The vague reference to his mission, the
suppression of his object (κατά τι πρῆγμα),
is not the least of the absurdities in the
story ; Artabazos would have had the
sense to lie with more circumstance, if
lying had been necessary, or the
Thessalians would have asked for details.
But this story presents one of those
monologues which are all alike suspicious,
cp. c. 58 supra.

πεμφθείς seems to imply the
subordination of Artabazos to Mardonios,
cp. c. 42 supra, and is in so far unfavourable to the son of Pharnakes, who
indeed, on his own showing, is 'a slight
unmeritable man, meet to be sent on
errands !'

12. ὑμῖν : a pretty 'ethical' dative ;
the announcement that Mardonios with
his army is close at hand (or at heel) is
a fresh absurdity : the said commander
and army after spending the previous
winter in Thessaly had gone south with
a manifest object ; the Thessalians would
have known, or asked, how far that
object had been accomplished. The
more, however, the actual numbers of the
force of Mardonios are reduced, the less
absurd this item becomes. Per contra,
this whole anecdote is hardly consistent
with the view that the army numbered
about 300,000—except, indeed, so far as
Hdt. throughout operates with myriads
and millions as though they were
emancipate from the conditions of space
and time ; cp. 7. 60.

ἐλαύνων προσδόκιμος ἐστί. τοῦτον καὶ ξεινίζετε καὶ εὖ
ποιεῦντες φαίνεσθε· οὐ γὰρ ὑμῖν ἐς χρόνον ταῦτα ποιεῦσι 15
μεταμελήσει." ταῦτα δὲ εἴπας ἀπήλαυνε σπουδῇ τὴν στρατιὴν
διὰ Θεσσαλίης τε καὶ Μακεδονίης ἰθὺ τῆς Θρηίκης, ὡς ἀληθέως ἐπειγόμενος, καὶ τὴν μεσόγαιαν τάμνων τῆς ὁδοῦ. καὶ
ἀπικνέεται ἐς Βυζάντιον, καταλιπὼν τοῦ στρατοῦ τοῦ ἑωυτοῦ

---

14 καὶ om. Paris. 1635 z ‖ καὶ om. C 15 ποιοῦντες Marc. 16
ἀπέλαυνε Bz 17 Θρήκης R(S)V 18 μεσόγεαν R ‖ τέμνων S ‖
καὶ om. Marc.

---

14. ξεινίζετε (7. 27) (as ye are enter-
taining me).

15. ἐς χρόνον = ὕστερον : cp. 3. 72
ἄμεινον ἐς χρόνον ἔσται.

ταῦτα ποιεῦσι, conditional : ἢν
τοῦτον καὶ ξεινίζητε καὶ εὖ ποιεῦντες
φαίνησθε. ταῦτα ποιεῦσι and εὖ ποιεῦντες
(just before) of course are not identical.
σπουδῇ : cp. l. 11 supra.

17. Μακεδονίης here appears en route,
and signalizes another absurdity, for
absurdity may lie in an assumption,
and an assumption be made by omission.
What then of Alexander and the
Makedonians at this crisis ? (Was he
not, like the Aleuadai so far, in Artabazos'
company ?) Demosthenes, 23. 200, says
that 'Perdikkas' king of Makedonia
destroyed τοὺς ἀναχωροῦντας ἐκ Πλαταιῶν
τῶν βαρβάρων and completed 'the king's'
disaster τέλειον τἀτύχημα (ποιήσας) τῷ
βασιλεῖ, and was given πολιτεία by the
Athenians in consequence (ps.-Dem.
13. 24). Perhaps the only serious
mistake Demosthenes here makes is in
calling the Makedonian 'Perdikkas'; but
the passage says nothing of Artabazos,
and might be true even if Alexander
saw Artabazos and his 40,000 safely
through Makedonia, and no less true if
Artabazos had never taken his 40,000
southwards across the Axios at all !

ἰθὺ τῆς Θρηίκης, 'straight for
Thrace,' genitive of the direction off
which the movement is estimated. The
construction is frequent in Homer and
Hdt., e.g. 4. 89 ἰθὺ τοῦ Ἴστρου, 6. 95 ἰθὺ
τοῦ τε Ἑλλησπόντου καὶ τῆς Θρηίκης.
But ἰθὺς ἐπὶ Θεσσαλίης 5. 64, ἰθέως ἐπὶ
τὸν Ἑλλήσποντον 8. 108 (where the adverb
may perhaps be taken in a temporal
signification).

ὡς ἀληθέως ἐπειγόμενος re-empha-
sizes the point humorously : 'that he
was in a hurry was true enough.'

18. τὴν μεσόγαιαν τάμνων τῆς ὁδοῦ :
i.e. marching not by the coast, but by a
shorter or more direct route, further
inland ; cp. 7. 124. It is not clear for
what portion of the route of Artabazos
the remark holds good ; doubtless from
Therme to Akanthos, cp. l.c. ; but further
east likewise an inland course may have
been followed, from Akanthos to Doriskos
for example ; cp. 7. 121. At Doriskos
(cp. 7. 106) Artabazos would learn that
the bridges on the Hellespont were
threatened, or were in fact destroyed,
cp. c. 114 infra (if he did not know it
already), and that Sestos was being
blockaded, if not actually in the hands of
the Hellenes. To get to Byzantion he
would therefore give the Hellespont and
Thrakian Chersonese a wide berth,
though he might have made for
Perinthos in the first instance (cp. 7. 25).

19. ἀπικνέεται ἐς Βυζάντιον. Hdt.
unfortunately does not date the arrival
of Artabazos at Byzantion, but it must
have been before the capture of Byzantion
by Pausanias in 478-7 B.C. (Thuc. 1. 94.
2), and he had again evacuated it, or we
should have heard more definitely of his
having been among those, βασιλέως
προσήκοντές τινες καὶ ξυγγενεῖς οἳ ἑάλωσαν
ἐν αὐτῷ (Thuc. 1. 128. 5). Besides, he
reappears very soon as satrap of Daskyleion (Thuc. 1. 129). This is, oddly
enough, the first and only mention of
Byzantion by Hdt. in these Books ; it
figures more largely in his 'second
volume,' cp. 4. 87, 144, 5. 26, 103, 6. 5,
26, 33 (probably after he had seen the
city, cp. Hdt. IV.-VI. i. p. xcv.) ;
it is not mentioned in Bks. 1, 2, 3, an
accident arising, perhaps, from the
nature of their contents, or from the
circumstances of their composition.

τοῦ στρατοῦ τοῦ ἑωυτοῦ : this
force had originally consisted of 60,000
men, 8. 126 ; it is reported at 40,000

20 συχνοὺς ὑπὸ Θρηίκων κατακοπέντας κατ᾽ ὁδὸν καὶ λιμῷ
συστάντας καὶ καμάτῳ· ἐκ Βυζαντίου δὲ διέβη πλοίοισι.
οὗτος μὲν οὕτω ἀπενόστησε ἐς τὴν Ἀσίην.

90   Τῆς δὲ αὐτῆς ἡμέρης τῆς περ ἐν Πλαταιῆσι τὸ τρῶμα ἐγένετο, συνεκύρησε γενέσθαι καὶ ἐν Μυκάλῃ τῆς Ἰωνίης . . . . ἐπεὶ

---

20 θρηκῶν R(S)V ‖ τε κατακοπέντας βz, Holder, van H.   21
βυζαντείου R   22 οὗτος S, Stein², Holder, van H. : οὕτως RV : αὐτὸς
90. 1 πλαταίῃσι a : πλαταίῃσι R(S)V   2 συνεκήρυσε z ‖ <τὸ> ἐν
Krueger, van H. ‖ μυκάλλῃ S ‖ lacunam indic. Stein³ ‖ ἐπειδὴ γὰρ βPz,
Holder

---

before the battle of Plataia (δύναμιν οὐκ
ὀλίγην c. 66 supra) without any attempt
to explain the discrepancy. It is
presumably still further reduced in this
passage, unless, indeed, the 20,000 very
inadequately accounted for by the operations at Olynthos and Poteidaia (8 l.c.)
cover the total losses of Artabazos during
his command in Europe.

20. ὑπὸ Θρηίκων κατακοπέντας κατ᾽
ὁδόν. Hdt. does not charge or honour
the Makedonians or their king with
inflicting an losses on Artabazos: that
was reservedyfor Attic tradition; cp. l.c.
supra. If Artabazos lost no men in
Phokis, Thessaly or Makedonia, it
argues that he had few if any men with
him while passing through those regions,
or else that the populations of those
regions were friendly. Losses in Thrace,
from actual hostilities of a guerrilla
kind, from failure of supplies, and from
exhaustion, his forces may have experienced; but the moderation of this
record, in contrast with the story of the
flight of Xerxes in the previous year (8.
115–117), is observable, and tends to
discredit the accounts of the annihilation
of la Grande Armée. Probably the
experiences of the various forces, in
various years, during the retreats through
Thrace, have not been very carefully
distinguished by Greek tradition.

λιμῷ συστάντας καὶ καμάτῳ: fame
conflictatos (Baehr; cp. 7. 170 (more
naturally of a garrison besieged)), et
laboribus. κάματος (κάμνω), an Homeric
and poetical word for labour, and its
resultant fatigue.

21. διέβη πλοίοισι: he would only
want one boat for his own crossing; the
plural refers to his army; cp. πλοίῳ
διαβαίνειν 1. 186. The Persians with
Xerxes in the previous year, according
to 8. 117 τῇσι νηυσὶ διέβησαν ἐς Ἄβυδον,

that of course was on the Hellespont in
the narrower sense (cp. c. 66 supra),
which was now closed to Artabazos by the
Greeks at Sestos. The warships were
no longer in those waters; but it is
perhaps curious that Artabazos, with
40,000 men, more or less, makes no
attempt to raise the siege of Sestos; c.
118 infra. Hdt. does not specify the
point opposite Byzantion at which
Artabazos and his men landed: did
he not as yet know the geography of
the Bosporos (4. 85), or is the omission
simply taken over inadvertently from
his source? Byzantion must have been
a notorious place and position at any
and every date possible for Hdt.'s
composition. Captured by Pausanias in
478–7 B.C. from the Persians (Thuc. 1.
94. 2), and from Pausanias by the
Athenians (ib. 1. 131. 1) a year or two
later (cp. Busolt, III. i. 96), when the
city became a contributing member of
the Athenian Alliance, with the high
assessment of fifteen talents (normal
quota 1500 Dr. or upwards; cp. Hill's
Sources c. ii., C.I.A. i. passim), Hdt.
may have visited the city after the
thirty years' truce (cp. Hdt. IV.–VI. i.
pp. xciii., xcv.), and probably long
after the composition of this passage:
the fruits of that visit are to be seen
at large in The Scythian Logoi (4. 1–144).

90. 1. τῆς δὲ αὐτῆς ἡμέρης. On this
synchronism cp. cc. 100, 101 infra.

τὸ τρῶμα: just as in 5. 121, 6.
132. The relative τῆς may be in the
same construction as ἡμέρης: the genitive
of time is a partitive genitive; 'in the
course of the same day' (Madvig, § 66).
Cp. c. 94. 12 infra, and Index.

2. συνεκύρησε γενέσθαι: the verb is
used with an expressed subject, 8. 87.
The construction is obviously incomplete;
cp. App. Crit.

γὰρ δὴ ἐν τῇ Δήλῳ κατέατο οἱ Ἕλληνες οἱ ἐν τῇσι νηυσὶ
ἅμα Λευτυχίδῃ τῷ Λακεδαιμονίῳ ἀπικόμενοι, ἦλθόν σφι ἄγγελοι
ἀπὸ Σάμου Λάμπων τε Θρασυκλέος καὶ Ἀθηναγόρης Ἀρχε- 5
στρατίδεω καὶ Ἡγησίστρατος Ἀρισταγόρεω, πεμφθέντες ὑπὸ
Σαμίων λάθρῃ τῶν τε Περσέων καὶ τοῦ τυράννου Θεομήστορος
τοῦ Ἀνδροδάμαντος, τὸν κατέστησαν Σάμου τύραννον οἱ
Πέρσαι. ἐπελθόντων δὲ σφέων ἐπὶ τοὺς στρατηγοὺς ἔλεγε

---

3 καθέατο ß : ἐκατέατο z　　5 τε ὁ ß ‖ θρασυκλέος α Marc. : θρασι-
κλέους C : Θρασυκλῆος z ‖ ἀρχιστρατίδεω ß　　7 θεομήτορος Α, Ask. :
θεομνήτορος ß (ν supersc. V)　　8 τύραννον σάμου ß ‖ οἱ Πέρσαι om.
Ask.

---

3. **ἐν τῇ Δήλῳ κτλ.** The record of
the naval operations, treated throughout
as absolutely independent of the land-
campaign in central Greece, is resumed
from 8. 132. **κατέατο** here can hardly
refer to winter-quarters (pace Stein), for
the advance to Delos is expressly dated
after the advent of spring, 8. 131, 132.
No doubt the expression ἐν τῇ Σάμῳ
κατημένοι 8. 130 is used of a portion of
the Persian fleet wintering in Samos;
but the winter there does not turn on
the word κάτημαι but on the context.
The word suggests (relative) inactivity,
as in a siege, or blockade; cp. Thuc.
4. 124. 4 ὁ Περδίκκας ἐβούλετο προιέναι
ἐπὶ τὰς Ἀρραβαίου κώμας καὶ μὴ καθῆσθαι
(cp. ἀντεκαθέζοντο ib. 2); id. 2. 20. 3
πεῖραν ἐποιεῖτο περὶ τὰς Ἀχαρνὰς καθή-
μενος εἰ ἐπεξίασιν (of Archidamos in
summer !); 2. 101. 2 καθημένου δ' αὐτοῦ
περὶ τοὺς χώρους τούτους (of Sitalkes, in
winter, certainly, but not in winter-
quarters !).

4. **Λευτυχίδῃ τῷ Λακεδαιμονίῳ** : the
addition appears both superfluous and
bald after the full pedigree, 8. 131.
Leotychidas' father's name was probably
not familiar to foreigners; Hdt. may
have taken over the title from his
source.

ἄγγελοι ἀπὸ Σάμου : this embassy
contrasts with the Chian embassy described 8. 132. It consists of only three
men (instead of six), but they have an
indubitable commission (πεμφθέντες ὑπὸ
Σαμίων), and they not merely invoke
the navarch to liberate Ionia but bring
assurances of an Ionian revolt from the
Persians. In both cases there is the
same connexion between the tyrannis
and the Persian supremacy; Strattis of
Chios, Theomestor of Samos, are alike
immersed in medism.

5. **Λάμπων . . Θρασυκλέος.** Of this
Samian Lampon nothing more is recorded. The name is a common one;
Hdt. mentions an Athenian c. 21 supra,
an Aiginetan c. 78 supra—three in this
Book ! Cp. notes ad ll.c. Thrasykles
of Samos only figures here. The best
known bearer of the name is an
Athenian; cp. Thuc. 5. 19. 2, 24. 1, 8.
15. 1, 17. 3, 19. 2.

Ἀθηναγόρης Ἀρχεστρατίδεω. The
Samian Athenagoras is merely a name.
Thucydides mentions two others, name-
sakes—a prominent Syracusan, 6. 35;
a Rhodian, 8. 6. 'Archestratides' is
less common a name than Archestratos
(which it implies), but appears at Athens
(e.g. the Archon 577-6 B.C.).

6. **Ἡγησίστρατος　　　　Ἀρισταγόρεω.**
Hegesistratos proves the ring-leader and
bird of good omen. He is one of three
men of the name mentioned by Hdt.;
cp. cc. 37-41 supra (the Telliad) and 5.
94 (a son of Peisistratos). This name
comes very near the preceding (Archestratides), and the patronym 'Aristagoras'
is not very different in sense from
Athenagoras (perhaps the two pairs
were related ?) but of more frequent
occurrence. Hdt. alone mentions four
men of the name : (1) the tyrant of
Kyme 4. 138, 5. 37; (2) the tyrant of
Kyzikos 4. 138; (3) the tyrant of Miletos
5. 30, etc. etc.; (4) the Samian here, of
whom nothing more is known.

7. **Θεομήστορος τοῦ Ἀνδροδάμαντος** :
cp. 8. 85 supra; he had not enjoyed the
tyranny very long ! The absence of
any express reference back to the
previous passage is observable; the
sources are probably different here and
there. (The article is hardly referential.)

9. **ἐπελθόντων . . ἐπὶ τοὺς στρατηγούς.** ἐπέρχεσθαι, 'to come forward for

10 Ἡγησίστρατος πολλὰ καὶ παντοῖα, ὡς ἦν μοῦνον ἴδωνται
αὐτοὺς οἱ Ἴωνες ἀποστήσονται ἀπὸ Περσέων, καὶ ὡς οἱ
βάρβαροι οὐκ ὑπομενέουσι· ἢν δὲ καὶ ἄρα ὑπομείνωσι, οὐκ
ἑτέρην ἄγρην τοιαύτην εὑρεῖν ἂν αὐτούς· θεούς τε κοινοὺς
ἀνακαλέων προέτραπε αὐτοὺς ῥύσασθαι ἄνδρας Ἕλληνας ἐκ
15 δουλοσύνης καὶ ἀπαμῦναι τὸν βάρβαρον. εὐπετές τε αὐτοῖσι
ἔφη ταῦτα γίνεσθαι· τάς τε γὰρ νέας αὐτῶν κακῶς πλέειν

12 ὑπονέουσιν C ‖ ἄρα AB ‖ οὐκ ὑπομενέουσι C   13 ἂν om. β
14 προέτραπε(ν) libri   16 νῆας αὐτέων z ‖ πλώειν van H.

the purpose of speaking,' 'to address';
cp. c. 7 *supra*. The scene here is laid in
the Synedrion of Strategoi, over which
Leotychidas is presiding at Delos, as
Eurybiades at Salamis in the previous
year; cp. 8. 49 *supra*.

10. **παντοῖα** does not seem to be very
complimentary to the speech of Hegesistratos; cp. 7. 10 *supra*. The report
imitates the 'variousness,' for it is made
up of (1) a double conditional assertion,
(*a*) positive and (*b*) negative, each limb
constructed with ὡς and indicative (fut.)
but nevertheless in the oblique (αὐτοὺς
not ὑμέας); (2) a conditional, in strict
oratio obliqua, i.e. accus. and infinitive;
(3) a narrative report (ἀνακαλέων προέτραπε κτλ.) which again indirectly reproduces the speaker; (4) a resumption
of the *oratio obliqua* with ἔφη (the *recta*
might well have been introduced here !)
in (*a*) a simple assertion of fact, or
opinion, (*b*) a rather complex conditional
sentence, with the idiomatic subject of
the apodosis in the nominative (αὐτοί τε
κτλ.).

11. **οἱ Ἴωνες ἀποστήσονται**: if they
will merely show themselves at Samos
'the Ionians will revolt'—the speaker
could hardly, perhaps, answer for more
than his own island. Was this promise
kept ? Cp. c. 99 *infra*.

οἱ βάρβαροι οὐκ ὑπομενέουσι: the
Persian fleet is at Samos 8. 130 *supra*.
This prediction proved correct, c. 96
infra. The alternative proposed is the
seizure of the king's fleet in the Samian
harbour; that would be a 'haul,' the
like of which they could never make
again.

12. **ἄρα**: a particle suggesting surprise,
improbability, etc.; cp. 8. 135 *supra*,
and Index.

13. **ἄγρην** is generally the chase, the
hunting, e.g. 1. 73, absolutely, 3. 129
θηρῶν, 2. 70 ἄγραι πολλαὶ καὶ παντοῖαι,
'many various ways of catching' (τῶν

κροκοδείλων). Here, not the hunting
but the 'quarry,' not the chase but the
'catch,' a usage originally perhaps poetic
(e.g. Aischyl. *Eumen.* 148, Sophokl. *Ai.*
64, Eurip. *Fr.* 521), literally of a draught
of fishes, *Ev. Luc.* 5. 9.

θεούς τε κοινοὺς ἀνακαλέων. On
the κοινοὶ θ. cp. 8. 144 *supra*. ἀνακαλεῖν
in Aischyl. *Pers.* 621 is to call up the
dead; here rather, to call up to, 'to
invoke,' the immortals; cp. Soph. *O.K.*
ἀνακαλοῦμαι ξυμμάχους ἐλθεῖν θεούς. Cp.
5. 93 τοὺς αὐτοὺς ἐπικαλέσας θεούς. Or,
perhaps, 'recalling' (to the minds of
the hearers), appealing to . . (Cp. the
description of Chryses imploring Apollo,
Plat. *Rep.* 394 A τάς τε ἐπωνυμίας τοῦ
θεοῦ ἀνακαλῶν.)

14. **προέτραπε αὐτούς**: sc. τοὺς Ἕλληνας. The verb is used more curiously
in 1. 31. In Aristot. *Eth. N.* 3. 5. 7 =
1113 B it is used in contrast to κωλύειν.
With this passage cp. Thuc. 8. 63. 3
αὐτῶν τῶν Σαμίων προυτρέψαντο τοὺς
δυνατωτάτους ὥστε πειρᾶσθαι μετὰ σφῶν
ὀλιγαρχηθῆναι, 5. 16. 3 χρόνῳ δὲ προ-
τρέψαι τοὺς Λακεδαιμονίους φεύγοντα αὐτὸν
. . καταγαγεῖν. Thuc., as it happens,
like Hdt., uses the word twice only,
once in the act., once in the mid. voice.

**ῥύσασθαι ἄνδρας Ἕλ. ἐκ δουλο-
σύνης**: the speech of Hegesistratos has
a curious resemblance to the speech
of Aristagoras at Sparta in 498 B.C.,
5. 49, given in *oratio recta*. Did Hegesistratos consciously reproduce Aristagoras?
Or does the similarity of the two situa-
tions explain the coincidence ? Or did
Hdt. mould the one passage on the
other, that one, perhaps, on this ?

15. **εὐπετές**. Is this word used
adverbially, or must εἶναι be supplied ?
The proper adverb is found 8. 68. 18
supra, *et al.*, the substantive construction
5. 97.

16. **αὐτῶν**: sc. τῶν βαρβάρων.

κακῶς πλέειν, 'were ill-found for

καὶ οὐκ ἀξιομάχους κείνοισι εἶναι. αὐτοί τε, εἴ τι ὑποπτεύ-
ουσι μὴ δόλῳ αὐτοὺς προάγοιεν, ἕτοιμοι εἶναι ἐν τῆσι νηυσὶ
τῆσι ἐκείνων ἀγόμενοι ὅμηροι εἶναι. ὡς δὲ πολλὸς ἦν 91
λισσόμενος [ὁ ξεῖνος] ὁ Σάμιος, εἴρετο Λευτυχίδης, εἴτε
κληδόνος εἵνεκεν θέλων πυθέσθαι εἴτε καὶ κατὰ συντυχίην
θεοῦ ποιεῦντος, " ὦ ξεῖνε Σάμιε, τί τοι τὸ οὔνομα ;" ὁ δὲ
εἶπε "Ἡγησίστρατος." ὁ δὲ ὑπαρπάσας τὸν ἐπίλοιπον λόγον, 5
εἴ τινα ὅρμητο λέγειν ὁ Ἡγησίστρατος, εἶπε "δέκομαι τὸν
οἰωνὸν τὸν Ἡγησιστράτου, ὦ ξεῖνε Σάμιε. σὺ δὲ ἡμῖν ποίεε
ὅκως αὐτός τε δοὺς πίστιν ἀποπλεύσεαι καὶ οἱ σὺν σοὶ
ἐόντες οἵδε, ἦ μὲν Σαμίους ἡμῖν προθύμους ἔσεσθαι συμ-

---

18 προαγάγοιεν B ‖ ἕτοιμοι CP Marc. z ‖ ἐν τῆσι νηυσὶ ante ἕτοιμοι z
19 κείνων a   91. 2 ὁ ξεῖνος ὁ Σάμιος del. Gomperz, Holder : ὁ ξεῖνος
tantum Stein³ : ὁ ante Σάμιος om. CP ‖ ἤρετο C ‖ ὁ λευ⟨λεω R⟩τυχίδης B
3 κληδόνος z : κλεηδόνος Merzdorf ‖ εἵνεκα RS ‖ καὶ om. B   4 θεοῦ
ποιεῦντος del. Gomperz, Holder ‖ τὸ om. B, Holder ‖ ὄνομα van H.   5
ὑφαρπάσας a   6 ὅρμητο SV, Gaisford, Stein², Holder, van H. : ὥρμητο
7 τὸν ἡγησίστρατον B : del. Valckenaer, Holder, van H. : non male
8 ἀποπλώσεαι van H.   9 μὴν Bz ‖ προθύμως z

---

sea'; cp. 8. 42 supra, referring as much
to the crews as to the hulls.

17. κείνοισι: sc. τοῖς Ἕλλησι.

αὐτοί τε: in oratio recta the
sentence would run: αὐτοί τε, εἴ τι
ὑποπτεύετε μὴ δόλῳ ὑμέας προάγωμεν,
ἕτοιμοι ἐσμὲν ἐν τῆσι νηυσὶ τῆσι ὑμετέρῃσι
ἀγόμενοι ὅμηροι εἶναι.

18. δόλῳ: cp. 8. 140 supra.

91. 1. πολλός: cp. 7. 158 supra.

3. κληδόνος εἵνεκεν: i.e. for the sake
of getting an omen from it; cp. c. 101
infra, and 5. 72. κληδών is no ordinary
sound, or rumour, but a significant, a
portentous voice. The king was surely
acquainted with the name of the orator
addressing the Council, before the
speaking began.

κατὰ συντυχίην θεοῦ ποιεῦντος:
τύχη, συντυχίη, are beyond direct human
control or agency, but not independent
of the divine agency, cp. θείη τύχη 4. 8,
not substantially different from θ. πόμπη
4. 152; cp. also 5. 92, where the τύχη is
clearly providential.

5. ὁ δὲ ὑπαρπάσας κτλ.: cp. 5. 50 ὁ
δὲ ὑπαρπάσας τὸν ἐπίλοιπον λόγον τὸν ὁ
Ἀρισταγόρης ὥρμητο (sic) λέγειν : one or
other passage is a copy—probably that
of this? cp. c. 90 supra.

6. δέκομαι τὸν οἰωνόν. If δέκεσθαι in

itself meant to accept as ominous, then
τὸν οἰωνόν here would be de trop; cp. 8.
115 supra. οἰωνός is also once used in
Thucydides, 6. 27. 3 τοῦ τε γὰρ ἔκπλου
οἰωνὸς ἐδόκει εἶναι κτλ. Cp. Π. 12. 243 εἷς
οἰωνὸς ἄριστος ἀμύνεσθαι περὶ πάτρης.
Blakesley well cites the parallel anecdote
of L. Paullus, quum ei, bellum ut cum
rege Perse gereret, obtigisset. He came
home that evening to find his little
daughter in the depths. "Quid est,"
inquit, "mea Tertia? quid tristis es?"
"Mi pater (inquit), Persa periit." Tum
ille arctius puellam complexus "Accipio,"
inquit, "mea filia, omen": erat autem
mortuus catellus eo nomine. Cicero de
Divin. 1. 46.

7. σὺ δὲ ἡμῖν κτλ., 'but do thou,
prithee, contrive, before you sail away, to
pledge yourselves . .' The apparent is
not the real predicate; the position of
αὐτός τε . . πίστιν secures the phrase
predicative force; the words καὶ οἱ σὺν
σοὶ ἐόντες οἵδε is hardly in construction.

9. ἦ μὲν Σαμίους . . συμμάχους: the
formula ἦ μέν (ἦ μήν, ἦ μάν, all three
Homeric), of oath-taking, occurs generally
in oratio recta, but also, as here, in
obliqua, after verbs of swearing, etc.
(πίστιν δούς), cp. 4. 154, 5. 93. The
Samians alone are here nominated:
what of the 'Ionians' c. 90 supra?

92 μάχους." ταῦτά τε ἅμα ἠγόρευε καὶ τὸ ἔργον προσῆγε·
αὐτίκα γὰρ οἱ Σάμιοι πίστιν τε καὶ ὅρκια ἐποιεῦντο συμμαχίης πέρι πρὸς τοὺς Ἕλληνας. ταῦτα δὲ ποιήσαντες οἱ
μὲν ἀπέπλεον· [μετὰ σφέων γὰρ ἐκέλευε πλέειν τὸν Ἡγησί-
5 στρατον, οἰωνὸν τὸ οὔνομα ποιεύμενος·] οἱ δὲ Ἕλληνες
ἐπισχόντες ταύτην τὴν ἡμέρην τῇ ὑστεραίῃ ἐκαλλιερέοντο,
μαντευομένου σφι Δηιφόνου τοῦ Εὐηνίου ἀνδρὸς Ἀπολλωνιήτεω,
93 Ἀπολλωνίης δὲ τῆς ἐν τῷ Ἰονίῳ κόλπῳ. τούτου τὸν πατέρα

92. 1 προῆγεν B   3 τοὺς om. C Marc. || οἱ μὲν : an ' οἱ μὲν δύο ?'
Bekker, van H. : (οἱ μὲν Stein¹³ : οἱ μὲν ἄλλοι coni. Stein²)   4
ἀπέπλωον van H. || μετὰ . . ποιεύμενος secl. Stein⁸ || μετά σφεων PRz |
ποιέειν z : πλώειν van H. || τὸν Ἡγησίστρατον om. B   7 μαντευο-
μένους R(S)V || δηϊοφόνου C   8 ἰωνικῶ B   93. 1 incipit verbis
οἱ δὲ Ἕλληνες supra, Stein², Holder, van H. || τούτου : τοῦ B, Holder

92. 1. ταὐτά τε ἅμα κτλ.: for the
parataxis cp. 8. 5, c. 98 supra, and 3.
135 ταῦτα εἶπε καὶ ἅμα ἔπος τε καὶ ἔργον
ἐποίεε—a still more forcible parataxis.
προσῆγε, sc. τούτοις, or τῷ ἔπει.
2. αὐτίκα γὰρ οἱ Σάμιοι κτλ. If
authentic, and true, this statement is of
high historical importance as (a) dating
the admission of the Samians, and of
the Samians alone, into the Hellenic
Symmachy before the battle of Mykale ;
(b) representing the matriculation into
the Symmachy as effected by the king-
navarch, without reference to any
further authority (except perhaps the
Synedrion of admirals). The exact
scope of the Symmachy is not here
defined, but it could hardly be one
restricted in its object to the liberation
of Samos from the Persians and the
tyrant ; it appears to be the general
alliance, πρὸς τὸν Πέρην (7. 145) or ἐπὶ
τῷ Μήδῳ Thuc. 1. 102. 4. Or did they
only bind themselves, συμμαχίης πέρι, to
become full members of the Symmachy
as soon as they were free ? Cp. c. 106
infra.
3. οἱ μὲν . . ποιεύμενος. The end of this
chapter at least looks very unsatisfactory.
οἱ μέν as it stands covers all the Samians,
and if Hegesistratos is to be detained,
and the last sentence is to be retained,
οἱ μέν must be amended, or supplemented,
but the detention of Hegesistratos is
inconsistent with the permission or
command above ποίεε ὅκως ἀποπλεύσεαι.
If τὸν οἰωνόν is retained in c. 91, οἰωνὸν
τὸ οὔνομα ποιεύμενος here is intolerable.
Cp. App. Crit.
6. ἐπισχόντες. Why this pause ?

(8. 23, 66, 113, c. 49 supra, et al.).
Mardonios had doubtless evacuated
Attica by this time ; the fleet was presumably in communication with the
army in Attica, or in Boiotia. They
obtained favourable omens for proceeding
no doubt at the right strategic point.
ταύτην τὴν ἡμέρην : the acc. of
duration of time ; Madvig, § 30. τῇ
ὑστεραίῃ, the dat. of point of time, ib.
§ 45. Cp. c. 90 ad init. and Index.
ἐκαλλιερέοντο : a strong imperfect ;
for the word cp. 7. 134 supra. μαντευομένου, as in c. 36 supra.
7. Δηιφόνου τοῦ Εὐηνίου. The
name 'Deiphonos' apparently occurs
only in this passage ; like other and
commoner compounds of δήιος (δάιος,
δάις) it has a distinctly archaic ring
(well suited to a seer). Εὐήνιος—also
unique as a personal name—is apparently
the adj. of Εὔηνος, a river, or river-god,
of Aitolia: Hesiod, Theog. 345 ; Thucyd.
2. 83. 3, etc. Its other (and earlier ?)
name was Λυκόρμας, cp. ps.-Plutarch
Mor. 1011 (ed. Didot, v. 86). It is the
central river of 'old' Aitolia, and
Kalydon was on its bank ; Strabo 451
describes its course ; its modern name is
Phidari (Baedeker, Greece, p. 29), and it
debouches east of Mesolonghi.
8. Ἀπολλωνίης δὲ τῆς ἐν τῷ Ἰονίῳ
κόλπῳ. Steph. Byz. enumerates 25 cities
of this name, some of them duplicates
(Rawlinson). Hülsen ap. Pauly-Wissowa
ii. 112 ff. enumerates 32 cities, islands,
castles or places, which bore the name
at one time or other. This observation
concerns rather the popularity of Apollon
than the matter in hand. The two

κατέλαβε Εὐήνιον πρῆγμα τοιόνδε. ἔστι ἐν τῇ Ἀπολλωνίῃ
ταύτῃ ἱρὰ ἡλίου πρόβατα, τὰ τὰς μὲν ἡμέρας βόσκεται παρὰ

---

2 Εὐήνιον: 'nonne melius abest ?' Kallenberg: secl. Holder: Εὐήνιον
κατέλαβε transp. Stein[2]   3 τὰ: ᾶ β

chief foundations were undoubtedly
Apollonia on the Euxine (4. 90, 93
supra), and the one here in question.
It was south of Epidamnos (cp. Thuc. 1.
26. 2), in proximity to the river Aous
(see below). Strabo 316 ἐφ' ᾧ 'Ἀπολλωνία
πόλις εὐνομωτάτη κτίσμα Κορινθίων καὶ
Κορκυραίων (Κορκυραίων τε καὶ Κορινθίων
κτίσις Skymnos, 440), τοῦ ποταμοῦ μὲν
ἀπέχουσα σταδίους δέκα τῆς θαλάττης δὲ
ἑξήκοντα. Thuc. l.c. makes it simply
a Korinthian foundation (cp. Plutarch
Mor. 552 f, who puts the foundation in
the reign of Periander, i.e. before 585 B.C.
The Olympian dedication (Pausan. 5.
22. 3) made Phoibos himself the founder.
The coinage (silver, of five periods, but
not going back before the fourth century
B.C., cp. B. Head, Hist. Num. p. 265)
well illustrates the importance of
Apollonia, especially in the Roman
period, when the city was one of the W.
termini of the Egnatian way, Dyrrachium
(Epidamnos) being the other, Strabo
322. It played a considerable part in
the civil war (cp. Caesar, B. C. 3. 1,
Cicero, Phil. 11. 26); at Apollonia in 44
B.C. Octavius received the news of his
uncle's death, and started to recover his
inheritance and to refound the Empire.
ἐν τῷ Ἰονίῳ κόλπῳ: the usual
designation of this Apollonia, e.g.
Pausanias 5. 22. 3 'Ἀπολλωνιᾶται οἱ ἐν
τῷ Ἰονίῳ: cp. Aelian, V. H. 13. 16.
Strabo 424 has ἡ πρὸς Ἐπιδάμνῳ, Steph.
B. ἡ κατ' Ἐπίδαμνον. Cp. Thuc. 1. 24. 1
Ἐπίδαμνός ἐστι πόλις ἐν δεξιᾷ ἐσπλέοντι ἐς
τὸν Ἰόνιον κόλπον· προσοικοῦσι δ' αὐτὴν
Ταυλάντιοι βάρβαροι, Ἰλλυρικὸν ἔθνος.
On the Ionian gulf cp. 7. 20 supra (ὁ Ἰ.
πόντος). Strabo 316 ad f. places ἡ ἀρχὴ
τοῦ στόματος τοῦ Ἰονίου κόλπου καὶ τοῦ
Ἀδρίου at the Keraunian mountains
south of Apollonia and of Panormos,
the port of Orikon; the 'mouth' is
common to the 'Ionian' and 'Adrian,'
the difference being that, properly speaking, the inner part of the sea is the
'Adrian,' and the outer, or lower, the
'Ionian' (cp. 4. 33, 5. 9, 1. 163).
93. 2. κατέλαβε: cp. cc. 60 supra,
104 infra, τὰ καταλαβόντα c. 49 supra.
3. ἱρὰ ἡλίου πρόβατα. 'Phoibos'
himself was their founder (cp. Pausan.

5. 22. 3), the city bore the Apolline
name, the fusion of Φοῖβος Ἀπόλλων
with Ἥλιος is therefore a fait accompli
in Apollonia; and this perhaps is the
oldest evidence of the amalgamation, in
cult and myth. The πρόβατα here are
apparently sheep, or goats (cp. τὰ
λεπτὰ τῶν προβάτων 8. 137 supra), as
they are raided by wolves. The animals
associated with Helios are chariot-horses
(ὑπὸ δ' ἄρσενες ἵπποι, Hom. Hymn. 31.
14), and, still earlier, oxen and sheep
(Od. 12. 127 ff. Ἠελίοιο βόες καὶ ἴφια
μῆλα, ἑπτὰ βοῶν ἀγέλαι, τόσα δ' οἰῶν
πώεα καλά, 50 in each herd, or flock,
350 in all, tended by the nymphs,
Phaethusa and Lampetie, day and night!).
Apollon is almost certainly in origin a
truly pastoral deity (and, especially as
Λύκιος, Λύκειος, Λυκέργος, the guardian
of the sheep; as also Κάρνειος, Νόμιος,
Ἀρισταῖος, etc.).
βόσκεται: middle, pascuntur (the
active 6. 39, also 1. 44, in quasi-meta-
phorical sense). Cp. Hom. Hymn. ad
Apoll. 412 f. Ταίναρον ἔνθα τε μῆλα
βαθύτριχα βόσκεται αἰεὶ Ἠελίοιο ἄνακτος.
παρὰ [< Χῶνα >] ποταμόν. "There
can be no doubt that the river intended
is the Aous, or Viosa, which flows from
the central part of Pindus, called Lacmon
by the ancients (Hecat. Fr. 72, Soph.
ap. Strab. vi. 391), and empties itself
into the Adriatic a little south of the
site of Apollonia" (Rawlinson). Χῶνα
is restored by Stein from the Canons of
Theognostos 794 (cp. Cramer, Anecd.
Oxon. ii. (135) p. 131 Χών, Χωνός, ὄνομα
ποταμοῦ ἐξ οὗ καὶ ἡ Ἤπειρος Χωνία
παρὰ Ἡροδότῳ). But it is Χωνία, not
Χών, which this passage records for Hdt.
The Epeirote 'Chonia' no doubt represents 'Chaonia,' which got its name from
the Χάονες (cp. Thuc. 2. 68. 9, 80. 1, 5,
81. 3-6), and not from a river Χών, for
whose real existence the Canons of
Theognostos are not evidence. If such
a river anywhere existed, it would perhaps
be in South Italy, where the 'Chaones'
reappear as 'Chones,' cp. note to 7. 170.
13 supra. The grammarian is wrong in
citing Hdt. as authority for 'Chonia';
and he has apparently invented 'Chon'
to account for Chonia.

[<Χῶνα>] ποταμόν, ὃς ἐκ Λάκμονος ὄρεος ῥέει διὰ τῆς
5 Ἀπολλωνίης [χώρης] ἐς θάλασσαν παρ' Ὥρικον λιμένα, τὰς
δὲ νύκτας ἀραιρημένοι ἄνδρες οἱ πλούτῳ τε καὶ γένεϊ δοκιμώ-
τατοι τῶν ἀστῶν, οὗτοι φυλάσσουσι ἐνιαυτὸν ἕκαστος· περὶ
πολλοῦ γὰρ δὴ ποιεῦνται Ἀπολλωνιῆται τὰ πρόβατα ταῦτα
ἐκ θεοπροπίου τινός· ἐν δὲ ἄντρῳ αὐλίζονται ἀπὸ τῆς πόλιος
10 ἑκάς. ἔνθα δὴ τότε ὁ Εὐήνιος οὗτος ἀραιρημένος ἐφύλασσε.
καί κοτε αὐτοῦ κατακοιμήσαντος φυλακὴν παρελθόντες λύκοι
ἐς τὸ ἄντρον διέφθειραν τῶν προβάτων ὡς ἑξήκοντα. ὁ δὲ
ὡς ἐπήϊσε, εἶχε σιγῇ καὶ ἔφραζε οὐδενί, ἐν νόῳ ἔχων

---

4 Χῶνα e Theognosti canon. 794 inser. Stein, Holder, van H. : cancellos
posui ‖ λακμόνος B : Λάκμωνος z, van H. ‖ οὔρεος CPMarc. z, van H.
5 Ἀπολλωνιήτιδος Valla (per apolloniatem agrum) ‖ χώρης om. Marc. : secl.
Stein² ‖ ὥρικον Marc. : ὥρηκον R   6 ἀναιρημένοι C   7 ἕκαστον
Apr. : ἕκαστοι C   8 γὰρ : τε B ‖ δὴ om. CMarc.   9 ἀπὸ del.
Cobet, van H.   10 ἀφαιρημένος R(S)V   11 κατακοιμίσαντος
primo scr. sed statim correct. S(Gaisford)V, Reiske, Holder, van H. ‖ τὴν
φυλακὴν BPz, Holder, van H.   13 ἐπήϊσε ABC : ἐπῆσαν Marc. :
ἐποίησεν S ‖ ἔφραξε(ν) B ‖ ἐνίῳ S

---

4. **Λάκμονος ὄρεος**: Steph. B. sub
v. Λάκμων, ἄκρα τοῦ Πίνδου ὄρους, ἐξ
ἧς ὁ Ἴναχος καὶ Αἴας ῥεῖ ποταμός· ὡς
Ἑκαταῖος ἐν πρώτῳ. Strabo 271, 316
(quoting Hekataios) gives the form
Λάκμος : τὸν δ' Ἄωον Αἴαντα καλεῖ
Ἑκαταῖος καί φησιν ἀπὸ τοῦ αὐτοῦ τόπου
τοῦ περὶ Λάκμον, μᾶλλον δὲ τοῦ αὐτοῦ
μυχοῦ, τόν τε Ἴναχον ῥεῖν εἰς Ἄργος
πρὸς νότον καὶ τὸν Αἴαντα πρὸς ἑσπέραν
καὶ πρὸς τὸν Ἀδρίαν.

διὰ τῆς Ἀπολλωνίης: the name
of the city for the country ; cp. ἐς
Ἀθήνας = ἐς Ἀττικήν c. 17 supra, ἐς
Θήβας, ibid. etc.

5. **παρ' Ὥρικον λιμένα**. Steph. Byz.
sub v. Ἑκαταῖος λιμένα καλεῖ τῆς Ἠπείρου
τὴν (sic) Ὥρικόν, ἐν τῇ Εὐρώπῃ· μετὰ
δὲ Βουθρωτὸς πόλις, μετὰ δὲ Ὥρικὸς
λιμήν. Orikos, or Oricum (so with the
Latins, e.g. Caesar B. C. 3 passim), now
is Ericho ; no stream rising on Lakmon
flows out anywhere near it. The geography of Hdt. is at fault, and probably
at second hand ; this passage, though it
deals with the West, is probably not a
result of his own western voyage, but
belongs to the first draft of the Book.

6. **ἀραιρημένοι ἄνδρες**: cp. 7. 118
supra.

οἱ **πλούτῳ τε καὶ γένεϊ δοκι-**
μώτατοι: cp. Aristot. Pol. 6 (4). 4. 5 =
1290 B ἐν Ἀπολλωνίᾳ τῇ ἐν τῷ Ἰονίῳ

.. ἐν ταῖς τιμαῖς ἦσαν οἱ διαφέροντες
κατ' εὐγένειαν καὶ πρῶτοι κατασχόντες
<τὴν ἀποικίαν> ὀλίγοι ὄντες πολλῶν.

7. **περὶ πολλοῦ** .. **ποιεῦνται**: cp.
6. 104, 7. 181, 8. 40 supra.

9. **ἐκ θεοπροπίου τινός**, 'in consequence of a certain prophetic (or divine)
utterance'—ἐκ is here rather causal than
temporal. θεοπρόπιον is an Homeric
word, much used by Hdt. for an oracular
response ; so θεοπρόπος is with him
always used for 'consultants' of an
oracle. Just below the Apolloniates are
found consulting both at Dodona and at
Delphi.

ἀπὸ .. **ἑκάς**: cp. 3. 41 ὡς δὲ ἀπὸ
τῆς νήσου ἑκὰς ἐγένετο ..

10. **τότε**: the time above referred to
in κατέλαβε πρῆγμα τοιόνδε.

11. **κατακοιμήσαντος φυλακήν**: the
accusative may be of temporal duration,
or, more generally, of limitation ; the
verb is used in a transitive sense 8. 134
supra.

παρελθόντες λύκοι ἐς τὸ ἄντρον.
Evenios was asleep outside, and the
wolves got past him into the cave ; cp.
3. 72 ὑμεῖς δὲ ἴστε φυλακὰς τὰς κατε-
στεώσας ἐούσας οὐδὲν χαλεπὰς παρελθεῖν :
cp. 3. 77. Here one might have expected
παρεσελθόντες.

13. **ὡς ἐπήϊσε**, 'when he perceived
(it).' The verb occurs in a still more

ἀντικαταστήσειν ἄλλα πριάμενος. καὶ οὐ γὰρ ἔλαθε τοὺς
Ἀπολλωνιήτας ταῦτα γενόμενα, ἀλλ᾽ ὡς ἐπύθοντο, ὑπαγαγόντες 15
μιν ὑπὸ δικαστήριον κατέκριναν, ὡς τὴν φυλακὴν κατακοιμή-
σαντα, τῆς ὄψιος στερηθῆναι. ἐπείτε δὲ τὸν Εὐήνιον
ἐξετύφλωσαν, αὐτίκα μετὰ ταῦτα οὔτε πρόβατά σφι ἔτικτε
οὔτε γῆ ἔφερε ὁμοίως καρπόν. πρόφαντα δέ σφι ἔν τε
Δωδώνῃ καὶ ἐν Δελφοῖσι ἐγίνετο, ἐπείτε ἐπειρώτων [τοὺς 20

---

15 γινόμενα B ‖ ἀλλ᾽ ὡς : ὡς δὲ S : ἀλλά κως ? Stein[1 2] ‖ ὑπάγοντες B
16 ὑπὸ : εἰς τὸ Paris.1635 : ἐς τὸ z ‖ κατέκριναν om. B ‖ κατακοιμίσαντα R,
Reiske, Holder, van H. : sed verba ὡς .. κατακοιμίσαντα susp. habet van H.
18 τὰ πρόβατα S   19 καρπόν om. B, Holder ‖ πρόφαντα : πρόβατα B
20 ἐγένετο B ‖ ἐπείτε Reiske : ἔπειτα ‖ ἔπειτα . . ἔφραζον del. Krueger :
τοὺς προφήτας et οἱ δὲ αὐτοῖσι ἔφραζον del. Stein, Holder, van H. ‖ ἐπει-
ρώτευν Marc., Gaisford, Stein[1] : ἐπηρώτευν CP : ἐπερώτευν z

---

generalized sense in 3. 29 ἐπατοντες σιδηρίων, 'sensible of steel.'

εἶχε σιγῇ, 'kept quiet,' silent, rather than rem clam tenebat or tacuit (the normal construction of ἔχειν with adverb, cp. Index). σιγῇ, as 8. 66, 74, still more 7. 287 (cp. also 2. 140). σιγὴν ἔχειν 1. 86, literally.

ἐν νόῳ ἔχων, 'intending . .'
15. ταῦτα γενόμενα, 'what had happened.'

ὑπαγαγόντες μιν ὑπὸ δικαστήριον : cp. 6. 104 ὑπὸ δ. αὐτὸν ἀγαγόντες, 6. 136 θανάτου ὑπαγαγὼν ὑπὸ τὸν δῆμον Μιλτιάδεα, 6. 72 ὑπὸ δικαστήριον ὑπαχθείς.

17. τῆς ὄψιος στερηθῆναι : on the principle that the punishment should fit the crime. ὄψις = ὄμματα, as in Aristot. Hist. An. 8. 19. 7 λευκὴν ἔχοντες τὴν ὄψιν. Polybius goes further : 3. 79. 12 ἐστερήθη τῆς μιᾶς ὄψεως. ὄψις is also used for the chose vue (as we say, a 'sight'), cp. 7. 15, 8. 54 supra, 3. 65. The two extremely concrete meanings correspond to the two primary and more abstract meanings of ὄψις, viz. the faculty of seeing, 4. 81, and the aspect or appearance, 7. 47.

18. ἐξετύφλωσαν is logically a pluperfect of time.

αὐτίκα μετὰ ταῦτα, 'immediately thereupon.'

οὔτε πρόβατα κτλ. : cp. 6. 139 οὔτε γῆ καρπὸν ἔφερε οὔτε γυναῖκές τε καὶ ποῖμναι ὁμοίως ἔτικτον καὶ πρὸ τοῦ. This was, of course, the result of a curse (cp. 3. 65, the blessing and the curse of Kambyses on the Persians). Here the γυναῖκες are not included. (Economi-

cally this might only make things worse —though the Greek god, or historian, was hardly thinking of that.)

19. πρόφαντα δέ σφι ἔν τε Δωδώνῃ καὶ ἐν Δελφοῖσι ἐγίνετο, 'it was foreshown to them at Dodona and at Delphi.' πρόφαντος occurs also 5. 63 (and twice in Sophokl. Trach. 1159, 1163). The city had doubtless been founded under Delphic auspices, cp. c. 93 supra Dodona fills a larger place in the earlier Books of Herodotos, esp. 2. 52, a passage which proves a personal visit by the historian to the place. It is here mentioned purely en passant, and no doubt taken over from the source, whatever it was, of the story of Evenios ; and there is nothing in the notice to suggest that this passage was penned after Hdt.'s visit—rather the reverse ; nothing in fact to lead us to date the composition of this passage other than early in the genesis of the work.

Strabo 327-8 treats at length of Dodona ; Steph. Byz. devotes his longest article thereto. The Dodona in question here is, of course, the Thesprotian (cp. 4. 33), or oldest Greek oracle, which had seemingly been eclipsed by Delphi, though the tribes and cities of the neighbourhood naturally resorted thereto. It was destined to something like a revival at a later time, when Delphi was in difficulties, and during the Roman period, when all this district rose in importance. The method, or methods, of divination practised at Dodona are obscure ; upon the whole subject cp. Carapanos, Dodone et ses ruines, Paris, 1878.

προφήτας] τὸ αἴτιον τοῦ παρεόντος κακοῦ, [οἳ δὲ αὐτοῖσι
ἔφραζον] ὅτι ἀδίκως τὸν φύλακον τῶν ἰρῶν προβάτων Εὐήνιον
τῆς ὄψιος ἐστέρησαν· αὐτοὶ γὰρ ἐπορμῆσαι τοὺς λύκους, οὐ
πρότερόν τε παύσεσθαι τιμωρέοντες ἐκείνῳ πρὶν ἢ δίκας δῶσι
25 τῶν ἐποίησαν ταύτας τὰς ἂν αὐτὸς ἕληται [καὶ δικαιοῖ]·
τούτων δὲ ἐπιτελεομένων αὐτοὶ δώσειν Εὐηνίῳ δόσιν τοιαύτην
94 τὴν πολλούς μιν μακαριεῖν ἀνθρώπων ἔχοντα. τὰ μὲν
χρηστήρια ταῦτά σφι ἐχρήσθη, οἱ δὲ Ἀπολλωνιῆται ἀπόρρητα
ποιησάμενοι προσέθεσαν τῶν ἀστῶν ἀνδράσι διαπρῆξαι. οἱ
δέ σφι διέπρηξαν ὧδε· κατημένου Εὐηνίου ἐν θώκῳ ἐλθόντες

---

22 ἰρῶν om. C ‖ Εὐήνιον susp. habet Kallenberg   23 ἐς τοὺς C
24 παύσασθαι Β ‖ τιμωρέοντας R(S)V ‖ ἐκείνῳ om. S ‖ δώσειν ABCSV
25 ἕλοιτο Marc. ‖ ἕληται καὶ secl. Cobet, Holder, van H. ‖ καὶ δικαιοῖ
secl. Blakesley, Stein²   26 τουτέων z ‖ ἐπιτελεομένων Stein⁽²⁾ ³ : τελεο-
μένων Stein¹, Holder, van H.: τελεουμένων Marc. ‖ δόσιν εὐηνίῳ δώσειν R :
δώσειν εὐηνίῳ δίκην Marc.   94. 3 προσέθεσαν Cobet, van H., Stein³ :
προέθεσαν ‖ ἀστέων z ‖ ἀνδράσι <τρισὶ> Gomperz   4 ὧδε P

---

21. τὸ αἴτιον, 'the cause'; this use
of the word is observable. Cp. 7. 125.
τοὺς προφήτας is inconsistent with 2. 55
and with 8. 36. Stein suggests that
the corrector misunderstood αὐτοί and
followed the lead of πρόφαντα. But
see below.

22. φύλακον: the form is constant in
Hdt. (φύλαξ is found 1. 41, in a somewhat different sense.)

23. αὐτοὶ γὰρ ἐπορμῆσαι τοὺς λύκους:
the plural (αὐτοί) is remarkable, as associa-
ting Zeus and Apollon in the joint
action, Dodona and Delphi in a common
utterance; a curious collaboration, an
improbable coincidence, is suggested by
these Responses, which is not much eased
by remembering that there was a Ζεὺς
Λυκαῖος as well as an Ἀπόλλων Λύκειος in
the Greek Pantheon. Even Kroisos was
not favoured to this extent (1. 46–49)
unless indeed we are to infer that
Apollon and Amphiaraos exactly coincided on that occasion. Are we to
suppose collusion, genuine inspiration,
or false report, as the source of this
coincidence? Or is the record an in-
exact one; did the one oracle merely
confirm the other, as if, for example, the
Apolloniates might have inquired first
at Dodona, and then, dissatisfied with
the reply, have gone to Delphi only to
get it reaffirmed there? (Cp. the action
of Agesipolis at Olympia and Delphi in
388 B.C. (390?) Xenoph. Hell. 4. 7. 2.)
αὐτοί must, of course, refer to the gods,

whether we keep τοὺς προφήτας above or
not. The proposal to cut out τοὺς
προφήτας on the ground that it is inconsistent with 2. 55 (of Dodona) and
with 8. 36 (of Delphi) is vitiated by the
assumption that Hdt. is a careful and
self-consistent writer. But further, a
προφήτης is mentioned for Delphi in 8.
37, and in 2. 55 we have to reckon not
merely with the three female προμάντιες
or ἰρεῖαι, but with οἱ ἄλλοι Δωδωναῖοι
(cp. 4. 33); while Homer shows that
originally men (the Σελλοί) were the
prophets, or priests, of the god in Dodona,
and Strabo 402 declares that to the end
Βοιωτοῖς μόνοις ἄνδρας προθεσπίζειν ἐν
Δωδώνῃ. The ἰρεῖαι anyway had not
everything their own way. Possibly if
Hdt. had been in Dodona before writing
this passage he would have expressed
himself differently: the failure to specify
the Πυθίη for Delphi might in any case
be merely a bit of careless composition.

24. τιμωρέοντες ἐκείνῳ. The verb is
used of bringing aid to the living 7. 169,
or vengeance to the dead 7. 144, etc.
This long prose Response badly wants
reducing to verse!

25. ταύτας: the pronoun seems to
refer to the future, the compensation
still to be specified.

26. δόσειν δόσιν, cognate accus.

94. 2. ταῦτα is virtually predicative.
ἐχρήσθη, 7. 144 supra.
ἀπόρρητα ποιησάμενοι, c. 45 supra.

4. ἐν θώκῳ: no doubt in a public

οἱ παρίζοντο καὶ λόγους ἄλλους ἐποιεῦντο, ἐς ὃ κατέβαινον 5
συλλυπεύμενοι τῷ πάθεϊ· ταύτῃ δὲ ὑπάγοντες εἰρώτων τίνα
δίκην ἂν ἕλοιτο, εἰ ἐθέλοιεν Ἀπολλωνιῆται δίκας ὑποστῆναι
[δώσειν] τῶν ἐποίησαν. ὃ δὲ οὐκ ἀκηκοὼς τὸ θεοπρόπιον
εἵλετο εἴπας εἴ τίς οἱ δοίη ἀγρούς, τῶν ἀστῶν ὀνομάσας τοῖσι
ἠπίστατο εἶναι καλλίστους δύο κλήρους τῶν ἐν τῇ Ἀπολ- 10
λωνίῃ, καὶ οἴκησιν πρὸς τούτοισι τὴν ᾔδεε καλλίστην ἐοῦσαν
τῶν ἐν πόλι· τούτων δὲ ἔφη ἐπήβολος γενόμενος τοῦ λοιποῦ
ἀμήνιτος εἶναι, καὶ δίκην οἱ ταύτην ἀποχρᾶν γενομένην. καὶ
ὃ μὲν ταῦτα ἔλεγε, οἱ δὲ πάρεδροι εἶπαν ὑπολαβόντες "Εὐήνιε,
ταύτην δίκην Ἀπολλωνιῆται τῆς ἐκτυφλώσιος ἐκτίνουσί τοι 15
κατὰ θεοπρόπια τὰ γενόμενα." ὃ μὲν δὴ πρὸς ταῦτα δεινὰ
ἐποίεε, τὸ ἐνθεῦτεν πυθόμενος τὸν πάντα λόγον, ὡς ἐξαπατη-

6 συλλυπούμενοι S ‖ εἰρώτεον Marc., Stein¹: ἠρώτων C: ἠρώτεον Pz
8 δώσειν secl. Stein²   12 πόλει aC: τῇ πόλει Marc.: τῃ πόλι z
‖ τουτέων z ‖ ἔφη abesse malit van H. ‖ ἐπίβολος BS   13 <ἂν>
ἀμήνιτος van H., Holder   15 τοι: τε CS   16 κατὰ τὰ z, van H. ‖
γινόμενα B   17 ἐποίεε, τὸ: Stein², van H. (ἐποίει, τὸ): ἐποιέετο

place, an exedra, or what not; cp. 1.
181, 6. 63.

5. λόγους ἄλλους ἐποιεῦντο, 'conversed (were conversing) about other
(indifferent) matters . .'

ἐς ὃ: donec.

κατέβαινον συλλυπεύμενοι τῷ πάθεϊ,
'they came round (down) to expressing
sympathy with his case'; cp. 1. 90
λέγων δὲ ταῦτα κατέβαινε αὐτὸς παραιτεό-
μενος κτλ.: cp. 1. 116, 118 ὣς οἱ ἐπαλιλ-
λόγητο κατέβαινε λέγων ὡς κτλ.   πάθος,
of course, the loss of his eyes.

6. ὑπάγοντες: in a different sense to
ὑπαγαγόντες c. 98 supra; here, 'drawing him on' furtively, or little by little;
cp. ἐξαπατηθείς infra. ὑποστῆναι, to
undertake; cp. c. 84 supra.

8. τὸ θεοπρόπιον = τὰ χρηστήρια supra.

10. καλλίστους δύο κλήρους τῶν ἐν τῇ
Ἀπολλωνίῃ: these two allotments must
have been ἐν τῇ χώρῃ. The 'dwelling'
(οἴκησις) was no doubt ἐν (τῇ) πόλι.

12. ἐπήβολος: cp. 8. 111 supra.

τοῦ λοιποῦ: sc. χρόνου, cp. 8.
143. 11 and c. 90. 1 supra.

13. ἀμήνιτος: μῆνις, generally of supernatural wrath, is here applied by the
diviner to his own feeling, which, no
doubt, is conceived as having a touch of
the uncanny about it. (The ι is long.)

ἀποχρᾶν: satisfacere, cp. c. 48
supra.

14. πάρεδροι = παριζόμενοι: cp. 5. 18

γυναῖκας ἐσάγεσθαι παρέδρους (i.e. παρα-
κατεθευμένας), or 6. 65 πάρεδροι ἐόντες =
παριζόμενοι.

ὑπολαβόντες, took him up, or took
up the conversation, as frequently; 7.
101, etc. (λόγον).

15. τῆς ἐκτυφλώσιος: with gen. cp.
δίκας τῶν 1. 8 supra. ἐκτύφλωσις is a
hapaxlegomenon.

16. τὰ θεοπρόπια = τὰ χρηστήρια supra.

δεινὰ ἐποίεε: cp. App. Crit., but
he very probably 'made a great ado,' a
great fuss, not merely took it sorely to
heart. The active is good here; cp. 2.
121, δεινὰ ποιέειν 7. 1 supra.

17. τὸν πάντα λόγον, 'the whole
story,' i.e. the real facts. He had been
tricked (ἐξαπατηθείς). The trick is
indicative of a relatively low standard
of morality, which keeps the pledge in
the letter, and breaks it in the spirit,
and is characteristic of a certain type of
culture, or education, which unites a
scrupulous conscience with a good deal
of essential dishonesty; cp. 4. 154, 201,
etc. etc. In this case, however, there
was a difficulty: had Evenios known
the whole story, he might have been
sorely tempted into extravagant demands.
The gods plainly condoned the trick,
and consoled the diviner with a gift
which brought him honour, and doubtless
proved extremely profitable to him and
his descendants.

θείς· οἱ δὲ πριάμενοι παρὰ τῶν ἐκτημένων διδοῦσί οἱ τὰ
εἵλετο. καὶ μετὰ ταῦτα αὐτίκα ἔμφυτον μαντικὴν εἶχε, ὥστε
95 καὶ ὀνομαστὸς γενέσθαι. τούτου δὴ ὁ Δηίφονος ἐὼν παῖς
τοῦ Εὐηνίου ἀγόντων Κορινθίων ἐμαντεύετο τῇ στρατιῇ. ἤδη δὲ
καὶ τόδε ἤκουσα, ὡς ὁ Δηίφονος ἐπιβατεύων τοῦ Εὐηνίου οὐνόματος ἐξελάμβανε ἐπὶ τὴν Ἑλλάδα ἔργα, οὐκ ἐὼν Εὐηνίου
5 παῖς.
96 Τοῖσι δὲ Ἕλλησι ὡς ἐκαλλιέρησε, ἀνῆγον τὰς νέας ἐκ τῆς
Δήλου πρὸς τὴν Σάμον. ἐπεὶ δὲ ἐγένοντο τῆς Σαμίης πρὸς

---

18 κεκτημένων C   20 καὶ om. Marc. || οὐνομαστὸν S : οὐνομαστὸς z
95. 1 δὴ ὁ om. Β   2 τοῦ Εὐηνίου suspect. hab. van H. || ἀγαγόντων
Β, van H.   3 ὁ om. Β || ἐπιβατεύων post Εὐηνίου Marc. : ἐπιβατέων
Β¹R(S)V || ὀνόματος R(S)VPMarc., van H.   4 ἐπὶ : ἐπιὼν Reiske ||
ἔργῳ Ask.   96. 1 νῆας z

---

18. οἱ δέ: sc. οἱ Ἀπολλωνιῆται.

19. μετὰ ταῦτα αὐτ.: cp. c. 77. 1 supra.
ἔμφυτον μαντικήν: this was the
δόσις promised by Zeus and Apollon, c.
93 ad f. This talent of divination as
ἔμφυτος was (a) not acquired from a
human master, (b) hereditary, transmis-
sible. Cp. Demosth. de Cor. 208 οὐκ ἦν
ταῦθ' ὡς ἔοικε τοῖς τότε Ἀθηναίοις πάτρια
. . οὐδ' ἔμφυτα.
εἶχε, 'became possessed of.'
Wesseling well cps. Od. 22. 347 αὐτο-
δίδακτος δ' εἰμί, θεὸς δέ μοι ἐν φρεσὶν
οἴμας παντοίας ἐνέφυσεν.

95. 1. ἐὼν παῖς. Hdt. appears to
prefer the view that Deiphonos was
true son to Evenios; but there was a
doubt on the subject: why? Was
Deiphonos too old to be the son of
Evenios, or to have been born after the
date of Evenios' acquisition of μαντική?
The date of the events just related is
not indicated by Hdt., but the sceptical
doubt as to his paternity may have been
based upon chronological grounds. The
doubt may have been started by rivals,
diviners, Athenian or other.

2. ἀγόντων Κορινθίων, Apollonia
being a Korinthian colony; cp. c. 93
supra.
ἤδη δὲ . . ἤκουσα: the same
formula 7. 55 supra, introducing an
alternative not credited by the historian
himself. The passage here looks like an
addition, perhaps of later date.

3. ἐπιβατεύων τοῦ Εὐηνίου οὐνόματος.
Cf. 3. 63 ἐπιβατεύων τοῦ Σμέρδιος οὐνόματος, with a slight difference, the Mage
calling himself Smerdis, Deiphonos call-

ing his father Evenios, or Evenios his
father. In either case, however, there
is the usurpation of a name, the usurper
taking advantage of a name to get (or
give himself) 'a lift'; cp. also 6. 65
ἐπιβατεύων τοῦ ῥήματος.

4. ἐξελάμβανε : as Blakesley (after
Schweighaeuser) observes, ἐκλαμβάνειν
elocare may be the correlative of ἐκδοῦναι
locare; he 'undertook,' was undertaking,
to perform works (ἔργα), sc. of divination.
ἐπὶ τὴν Ἑλλάδα: the preposition
is curious, suggesting 'against,' which
would here be senseless; Schweighaeuser
(Lexicon) defends it, and explains passim
per Graeciam: ἀνὰ would be more usual,
but Stein cites Homer, Od. 16. 63 πολλὰ
βροτῶν ἐπὶ ἄστεα δυνηθῆναι, etc. etc. (cp.
4. 417 ὅσσ' ἐπὶ γαῖαν ἑρπετὰ γίγνονται) ;
cp. ἐπὶ πολλόν 8. 107 supra.

96. 1. ὡς ἐκαλλιέρησε: sc. τὰ ἱρά, cp.
c. 19 supra. Doubtless in the fleet also
the victims had been slow to reveal the
favourable sign until the moment for
advance was come, not earlier than the
evacuation of Attica by Mardonios surely;
cp. c. 13 supra.
ἀνῆγον τὰς νέας: cp. 8. 76 supra ;
the move from Delos to Samos marks
the assumption of the offensive by the
Greeks at sea, even more decisively than
the move into Boiotia the assumption
of the offensive by land; c. 19 supra.

2. πρὸς τὴν Σ., of motion, but not
hostile motion, to . .
ἐγένοντο τῆς Σαμίης πρὸς †Καλα-
μίσοισι: they reached (came to rest at)
Kalamisa in Samian territory; Athenaeus
572 f. Ἄλεξις δ' ὁ Σάμιος ἐν δευτέρῳ Ὥρων

Καλαμίσοισι, οἱ μὲν αὐτοῦ ὁρμισάμενοι κατὰ τὸ Ἡραιον τὸ
ταύτῃ παρεσκευάζοντο ἐς ναυμαχίην, οἱ δὲ Πέρσαι πυθόμενοι
σφέας προσπλέειν ἀνῆγον καὶ αὐτοὶ πρὸς τὴν ἤπειρον τὰς 5
νέας τὰς ἄλλας, τὰς δὲ Φοινίκων ἀπῆκαν ἀποπλέειν. βουλευο-

3 λαμίοισιν ß : Καλάμοισι Larcher, Gaisford, Holder, van H., ex
Athenaeo p. 572 F ‖ ὁρμισάμενοι z : ὡρμισάμενοι Marc. : ὁρμησάμενοι ceteri
‖ ἡραῖον R　　4 ὡς ἐς z ‖ πυθόμενοι σφέας B, Stein² : πυθόμενοί σφεας
Stein¹, Holder, van H.　　6 νῆας z ‖ ἀποπλώειν van H.

<῾Ωρων> Σαμιακῶν τὴν ἐν Σάμῳ Ἀφροδί-
την, ἣν οἱ μὲν ἐν Καλάμοις καλοῦσιν, οἱ δὲ
ἐν Ἕλει, Ἀττικαί φησὶν ἑταῖραι ἱδρύσαντο αἱ
συνακολουθήσασαι Περικλεῖ ὅτε ἐπολιόρκει
τὴν Σάμον. This is the only passage
where a name resembling what is here
in evidence occurs associated with Samos.
It suggests three conclusions: (a) that
the name of the place was Κάλαμοι, 'the
Reeds' (cp. the variant Ἕλος); (b) that
it was a natural place for an enemy's
fleet to attempt a landing at; (c) that
the temple here referred to was not an
Heraion but an Aphrodision, though
not, of course, one founded as late as
440-39 B.C. The origin and foundation
of the temple, described by Alexis, is
not convincing, though dedications, anathemata, there may have been from the
occasion and the persons described.

3. τὸ Ἡραιον τὸ ταύτῃ: the expression seems to suggest that 'the Heraion
in this place' is distinguished from an
Heraion in some other. There may, of
course, have been more than one Heraion
in Samos; but there appears to be no
independent evidence to prove the
existence of more than one. If the
great Heraion (3. 60) be here intended,
the addition of the words τὸ ταύτῃ is
rather perplexing. (Could they signify
not the Heraion of Kalamoi in contrast
with another Heraion also in Samos,
but simply the Samian Heraion as
distinguished from the Argive, the
Olympian, or any other?) The position
of the Heraion would seem suitable to
the story in this chapter. The temple
was on the sea-coast, at some distance
from the city, and on a flat plain; cp.
H. F. Tozer, Islands of the Aegean
(1890) p. 175.

5. ἀνῆγον . . πρὸς τὴν ἤπειρον: the
ἀνάπλους is reckoned as from Samos; in
relation to the mainland it was a κατά-
πλους. It appears presently that the
Persians went SE. as for Miletos, not
NE. as for Ephesos. They were well

served by their intelligence department,
and had timely notice of the advance of
the Greek fleet from Delos.

6. τὰς δὲ Φοινίκων ἀπῆκαν ἀποπλέειν.
Hdt. apparently means that while the
rest of the Persian fleet retired on the
mainland, close by, the Phoenician
squadron or contingent was sent to sail
right away—exactly whither he does
not indicate. Others supply the omission
—home. This statement in any form
is a major crux. That the Phoenician
fleet was clean dismissed to save it from
a battle, and in the presence of the
enemy, is scarce credible. If it was at
Samos in the spring of 480 B.C. it would
have retired on the mainland and helped
to defend the fortified camp on Mykale;
or, if detached from the rest of the
fleet, it would have been employed on
some special service—an advance on the
Kyklades, left exposed by the Greeks,
or more probably to operate upon the
rear of the Greek force, or to attack the
ships, after the greater part of the Greek
forces had been drawn on to the mainland, and induced to debark.

Hdt. can hardly be understood as
meaning that the Phoenician ships had
been dismissed (ἀπῆκαν aorist pluperfect!)
in the winter ("schon im Winter," Stein)
home. That may have been the case;
but if so, Hdt. does not know it.

Domaszewski has suggested that the
Phoenician (and Egyptian) fleets were
really all the time on service off Thrace,
Makedon, Thessaly, protecting the coasts,
and attending to the commissariat of
Mardonios. But Hdt. does account for
the 'Egyptians' (c. 32 supra); and if
the Phoenicians were in the Thrakian
sea, why did they not support or cover
Sestos? Or how did they get away?
If the Phoenicians are withdrawn from
the Persian fleet at Samos, and the
Egyptians likewise, what remains?
Very little except Greek vessels, or
quasi-Greek (Kypriote), whose loyalty

μένοισι γάρ σφι ἐδόκεε ναυμαχίην μὴ ποιέεσθαι· οὐ γὰρ ὧν
ἐδόκεον ὅμοιοι εἶναι. ἐς δὲ τὴν ἤπειρον <ἀνῆγον>, ὅκως ἔωσι
ὑπὸ τὸν πεζὸν στρατὸν τὸν σφέτερον ἐόντα ἐν τῇ Μυκάλῃ,
10 ὃς κελεύσαντος Ξέρξεω καταλελειμμένος τοῦ ἄλλου στρατοῦ

---

8 ὅμοῖοι CP Marc. z : valde suspect. habet van H. ‖ <ἀνῆγον> Stein³ :
ἀπέπλεον β, Stein¹ ², Holder : ἀπέπλωον van H. : om. αC Marc.   9
στρατὸν σφέτερον Marc. ‖ μυκάλλῃ S

---

to Persia certainly could not be trusted
at this juncture. Had the Phoenicians
been present, yet the Persian admirals
would hardly have risked a sea-battle in
Greek waters, even with the memory of
Lade to back them. Cp. Appendix VII.
§ 1. Hdt.'s rationale or motivation for
the retirement upon the mainland, and
the dismissal of the Phoenician contingent, is presumably an inference from
the facts, but a not unreasonable inference ; the Persian admirals felt they
were not equal to fighting a battle at
sea with the Greeks (ὅμοιοι=ἀξιόμαχοι) ;
and they desired to obtain the cover
(ὑπό, cp. 8. 92 supra) and coöperation
of the large land-army, which was holding Ionia. But Hdt. fails to explain
why the Persians were not ἀξιόμαχοι at
sea (absence of the Phoenicians, etc.,
suspect loyalty of the Ionians, etc.);
and he certainly credits them with no
ulterior intention or hope of luring the
Greeks on to the mainland, into the
clutches of the corps d'armée.

9. ἐν τῇ Μυκάλῃ. Mykale has been
described c. 90 supra simply as τῆς
Ἰωνίης (assuming the text to be there
complete, at least so far as this point
is concerned). The mention of Mykale
in 7. 80 is merely en passant, and does
not prejudice the problem of composition
in any way. It is more significant that
no geographical description of Mykale
occurs in this Book, whereas such a
description is given in Bk. 1. 148 (ἡ δὲ
Μυκάλη ἐστὶ τῆς ἠπείρου ἄκρη πρὸς ζέφυρον
ἄνεμον κατήκουσα Σάμῳ καταντίον): how
is such a sequence to be reconciled with
the hypothesis that these Books (7-9)
are the earliest portion of Hdt.'s work
drafted by him, and in particular that
Bk. 9 is of older composition than
Bk. 1 ? The answer is not really difficult.
(a) Mykale was a locality famous in
this story, and Hdt. has not paused to
describe it expressly ; at the same time
incidentally the topography of the place
is here in evidence. (b) The passage in

Bk. 1 occurs in an eminently descriptive passage, where a topographical note
was obviously in order. (c) Hdt. had
probably in writing the early Books of
his history a western, or at least a
larger, audience more distinctly in view
than when he first sat down to write
the annals of the great invasion ; it is
to this wider public that the large
amount of geography in Bks. 1-4 is
addressed. (d) The whole context in
1. 148 forbids the supposition that in
describing Mykale there he has the
battle of 479 B.C. in view ; and equally
in this place the total absence of any
back reference to 1. 148 is noticeable.
As far as this story was concerned he
was content originally with the simple
indication τῆς Ἰωνίης c. 90 supra ; that,
indeed, would have been superfluous if
he had had 1. 148 in view. (e) It is
also observable that in 6. 16 Mykale is
mentioned as requiring no description
whatever. The explanation there is
probably not that he has the description
in 1. 148 in view, but that he is following an Ionian source in the account of
the Ionian revolt, and that the source
took Mykale for granted. Mykale is,
however, here both expressly and
incidentally more fully described than
there ; though that passage now precedes
this in the opus.

10. κελεύσαντος Ξέρξεω, 'by order
of Xerxes' ; the particularity of this
statement is remarkable. It exhibits,
of course, the king as commander-in-
chief, but does not specify the precise
point of time at which this order
had been issued. Was it part of a
general plan, devised or sanctioned by
the king, during his first residence at
Sardes, in 481-80 B.C. ? Or was it
an afterthought, dictated (possibly by
personal apprehension) during his second
residence in Sardes, after his return,
his 'flight' from Europe ? Ionia cannot have been denuded of troops when
Xerxes advanced into Europe ; and the

Ἰωνίην ἐφύλασσε· τοῦ πλήθος μὲν ἦν ἐξ μυριάδες, ἐστρατήγεε
δὲ αὐτοῦ Τιγράνης κάλλεϊ καὶ μεγάθεϊ ὑπερφέρων Περσέων.
ὑπὸ τοῦτον μὲν δὴ τὸν στρατὸν ἐβουλεύσαντο καταφυγόντες
οἱ τοῦ ναυτικοῦ στρατηγοὶ ἀνειρύσαι τὰς νέας καὶ περιβαλέ-
σθαι ἕρκος ἔρυμά <τε> τῶν νεῶν καὶ σφέων αὐτῶν κρησφύ- 15
γετον. ταῦτα βουλευσάμενοι ἀνήγοντο. ἀπικόμενοι δὲ παρὰ 97
τὸ τῶν Ποτνιέων ἱρὸν τῆς Μυκάλης ἐς Γαίσωνά τε <ποταμὸν>

---

11 ἰωνίην τε R || πλήθεος Β   12 κάλλει AB : κάλλεῖ τε z, van H.
|| μεγέθει a   13 ὑπὸ : ἐπὶ z   14 οἱ τοῦ ναυτικοῦ στρατηγοὶ
om. S || νῆας z   15 ἔρημα S || τε add. Stein, van H. || καί σφεων AB :
κέσφεων R || αὐτέων z   97. 1 παρὰ τῶν Ποτνιέων τὸ ἱρὸν ? Kallen-
berg   2 μυκάλλης S || γέσωνά R : γέσονά Marc. || τε : τε ποταμὸν ?
Stein² : verbum inserui, cf. comment. infra

---

words καταλελειμμένος τοῦ ἄλλου στρατοῦ are more than compatible with the
view that this force had been left behind
the main force, when the latter passed
over the bridge in 480 B.C., though the
words are generally interpreted (as Hdt.
perhaps understood them) as meaning
'retained after the rest of the forces,
which had returned from Europe, were
dismissed (like the Phoenicians!) to their
own homes.'

11. ἓξ μυριάδες: 60,000 as the (nominal)
strength of the *corps d'armée* in Ionia is
an eminently luciferous item, and confirms other suggestions in regard to the
organization of the Persian forces. This
army, or *corps d'armée*, presumably comprises six Myriads, under six Myriarchs,
perhaps five of infantry, and one of
cavalry; and it exactly tallies, in
number, with the army of Artabazos 8.
126 *supra*. Cp. Appendix II. § 5.

12. Τιγράνης. This Tigranes is the
ἀνὴρ Ἀχαιμενίδης who one year before,
if 7. 62 is to be trusted, was ἄρχων of
the Medes. (Cp. also 8. 26.) He had
still perhaps his Medes with him (but
cp. 8. 113, and c. 31 *supra*). He is now
ὁ τοῦ πεζοῦ στρατηγός, i.e. in supreme
command of a *corps d'armée*, by promotion; he is killed in the ensuing
action c. 102 *supra*. Hdt. himself takes
no account of the previous mention, or
mentions, of him (so independent is
story of story, and source of source). In
describing Tigranes as <ἀνὴρ> κάλλεϊ
καὶ μεγάθεϊ ὑπερφέρων Περσέων Hdt. has
also perhaps forgotten his own previous
eulogy of Xerxes 7. 187 *supra*. ὑπερφέρων : cp. 8. 138 *supra*.

15. ἔρυμα· κρησφύγετον : cp. c. 15
supra.

97. 1. ἀνήγοντο: middle, and so without τὰς νέας : cp. c. 96 *ad init.*

2. τὸ τῶν Ποτνιέων ἱρόν. The term
πότνια is found applied to many a goddess
together with the name proper, cp. 8. 77
supra, but as here, absolutely, to Demeter
and Kore only, Sophokl. *O. K.* 1050.
(The πότνιαι δεινῶπες *ib.* 84 are plainly
the Eumenides; but πότνιαι there is
not absolute.) Perhaps, then, the temple
here mentioned was dedicated to the
Mother and Child; though it cannot be
identical with the Δήμητρος Ἐλευσινίης
ἱρόν, presently to be mentioned. There
was an old Boiotian town named Ποτνιαί,
Pausan. 9. 8. 1, between the Asopos and
Thebes, where the Mother and the Maid
were worshipped (with remarkable rites).
The passage in Pausanias is unfortunately
corrupt, but the town-name may naturally
be connected with this title of the god-
desses in question. There would be
nothing curious in finding a Boiotian title
(i.e. a prae-Boiotian or old Ionian title
from Boiotia) reproduced on Mykale;
Mykale was the centre of the worship
of Helikonian 'Potidan' (cp. 1. 148).

Γαίσωνά τε <ποταμὸν> καὶ Σκολοπόεντα. The Gaison was the stream on
which Priene was situate, Ephoros *Fr.* 91
(=Athenaeus 311 e), apparently forming,
or emptying into a lake, ἡ Γαισωνὶς λίμνη,
between Priene and Miletos (Athen. *l.c.*,
Pliny 5. 31. 3 *Gessus amnis*). Rawlinson, remarking that Hdt. "never introduces the name of a river without either
calling it a river or prefixing the article,"
wants to make Gaison a town.

Σκολοπόεις does not occur elsewhere.
Many commentators (Schweighaeuser,
Larcher, *et al.*) have taken it (as well as
Gaison) for a river-name. Stein points

καὶ Σκολοπόεντα, τῇ Δήμητρος Ἐλευσινίης ἱρόν, τὸ Φίλιστος
ὁ Πασικλέος ἱδρύσατο Νειλεῳ τῷ Κόδρου ἐπισπόμενος ἐπὶ
5 Μιλήτου κτιστύν, ἐνθαῦτα τάς τε νέας ἀνείρυσαν καὶ περι-
εβάλοντο ἔρκος καὶ λίθων καὶ ξύλων, δένδρεα ἐκκόψαντες
ἥμερα, καὶ σκόλοπας περὶ τὸ ἔρκος κατέπηξαν, καὶ παρε-

---

3 ἐστὶ(ν) ἱρόν β　　4 Πασικλῆος z ‖ νειλέω R(S)V ‖ ἐπισπομένου
a Marc.　　5 κτιστὴν R Marc. z ‖ τε om. Marc. ‖ νῆας z ‖ περιβάλλοντο S
6 καὶ ante λίθων om. S　　7 παρὰ Marc. ‖ κατέκοψαν Rᵗ

---

out that the name was derived from the σκόλοπες mentioned below; it is no doubt a place-name, marking the position of the Persian fortification. If so, the name must be later than 479 B.C., though Hdt. gives no hint thereof, and seems to imply that the name was as old as t e foundation of Miletos.

3. Δήμητρος Ἐλευσινίης ἱρόν: an indirect omen, had the Greeks but known it, of the coming victory; cp. c. 101 infra.

τὸ Φίλιστος ὁ Πασικλέος ἱδρύσατο. Pasikles recurs at Athens (and elsewhere) as a personal name, in the fourth century B.C. and after. The father of Philistos is not otherwise celebrated. The name Φίλιστος recurs before the end of the fifth century B.C. as that of the Syracusan historian, who witnessed the siege of Syracuse (414–13 B.C.), Plutarch, Nik. 19.

4. Νειλεῳ τῷ Κόδρου: 5. 65 and 1. 147 incidentally confirm this founder, without actually mentioning his name; Νηλεύς is, however, the form of the name apparently implied in 5. 65 (for the father of Nestor; it is not likely that the son of Kodros should have spelt his name differently). Marm. Par. 27 has Νε[ι]λεὺς ᾤκισ[ε Μίλητον καὶ τὴν] ἄλ[λη[ν] ἅ[πα]σ[αν Ἰων]ίαν (anno 1087 B.C.). (F. Jacoby, ed. 1904, reads Νη[λ]εύς.) Both forms obtain indifferently in mss. The grave of Neleus was to be seen on the road to Didymi, Pausan. 7. 2. 6. Kodros was the son of Melanthos (1. 147), of Pylian and 'Neleid' extraction (5. 65), king of Athens (5. 76), in which capacity he resisted the Dorian invasion successfully; the legend of Kodros and his 'devotion' is fully developed in Lykurgos, c. Leocrat. 84–87, and was probably, although Hdt. does not expressly mention it, at least as old as the age of Peisistratos, who claimed kinship with the Neleids and Melanthids; cp. 5. 65.

ἐπὶ Μιλήτου κτιστύν. This notice

of the foundation of Miletos, and of the temple of Eleusinian Demeter, the former by Neileus, or Neleus, son of Kodros, the latter by his companion Philistos, son of Pasikles, is presumably taken from the work of some logograph on κτίσεις, κτίσιες, or κτιστύες. Such a work was ascribed afterwards to one Kadmos of Miletos: ὃς πρῶτος κατὰ τινας συγγραφὴν ἔγραψε καταλογάδην, μικρῷ νεώτερος Ὀρφέως. συνέταξε δὲ κτίσιν Μιλήτου καὶ τῆς ὅλης Ἰωνίας ἐν βιβλίοις δ′ (Suidas sub v.). To Charon of Lampsakos was also ascribed a work κτίσεις πόλεων ἐν βιβλίοις β′. (The reference to 'Books' shows that these works had been at least 'edited' much later than the dates of their ostensible authors: but then so were the ΛΟΓΟΙ of Hdt.) A sample of this kind of work, or of work founded thereon, may be seen in the accounts of the Ionian settlements, that of Neleus, or Neileus, at Miletos included, in Strabo 632–33 (citing 'Pherekydes') and Pausanias 7. 2.

The form κτιστύς belongs to a class of nouns common in Ionic prose, but confined in Attic to poetry; cp. Weir Smyth, Gk. Dialects (Ionic) § 497. 1, viz. nouns terminating in -τύς. The list given by Smyth may be supplemented from Baehr's note in l. (after Valckenaer). Hdt. 5. 6 has ληιστύς, 4. 75 καταπλαστύς.

6. ἔρκος καὶ λίθων καὶ ξύλων: some emphasis is lent to λίθων by the form of conjunction καὶ—καί. The τεῖχος of Mardonios on the Asopos (c. 15 supra) had probably no stones; here they would be easily procurable from Mykale and the seashore. ἔρκος, as in 6. 134, or c. 99 infra; differently 7. 85 supra.

δένδρεα ἐκκόψαντες ἥμερα: this was distinctly 'an unfriendly act' (cp. c. 15 supra), the rather in this case as Mykale was well-wooded (ὄρος εὔθηρον καὶ εὔδενδρον Strabo 636).

7. σκόλοπας, 'stakes,' 'pales'; very common for this purpose in Homer, Il.

σκευάδατο ὡς πολιορκησόμενοι καὶ ὡς νικήσοντες· [ἐπ᾿ ἀμφότερα
ἐπιλεγόμενοι γὰρ παρεσκευάζοντο.]

Οἱ δὲ Ἕλληνες ὡς ἐπύθοντο οἰχωκότας τοὺς βαρβάρους 98
ἐς τὴν ἤπειρον, ἤχθοντο ὡς ἐκπεφευγότων ἀπορίη τε εἴχοντο
ὅ τι ποιέωσι, εἴτε ἀπαλλάσσωνται ὀπίσω εἴτε καταπλέωσι ἐπ᾿
Ἑλλησπόντου. τέλος δ᾿ ἔδοξε τούτων μὲν μηδέτερα ποιέειν,
ἐπιπλέειν δὲ ἐπὶ τὴν ἤπειρον. παρασκευασάμενοι ὦν ἐς 5
ναυμαχίην καὶ ἀποβάθρας καὶ ἄλλα ὅσων ἔδεε, ἔπλεον ἐπὶ
-ῆς Μυκάλης. ἐπεὶ δὲ ἀγχοῦ τε ἐγίνοντο τοῦ στρατοπέδου

---

8 glossema delebam: amplius emendavit Stein⁵, hoc scilicet modo: ἐπ᾿
ἀμφότερα γὰρ ἐπιλεγόμενοι παρεσκευάζοντο καὶ ὡς πολιορκησόμενοι καὶ ὡς
νικήσοντες: καὶ ὡς . . παρεσκευάζοντο del. Krueger: γὰρ παρεσκευάζοντο
del. Stein², Holder, van H.: ἐπ᾿ ἀμφότερα ἐπιλεγόμενα AC: ἐπ᾿ ἀμφότερα·
ἐπιλεγόμενοι ceteri   9 παρεσκευάδατο z   98. 2 ἐν (ἀπορίῃ) β,
Holder, van H. || ἤχοντο R   3 ὅ om. β: τι om. Marc. || ἀπαλλάσσονται
Marc.   4 δὲ R(S)V, Holder || τουτέων z || μὲν: δὲ R || μηδ᾿ ἕτερα R
6 τὰ ἄλλα β, Holder || ὅσον R || ἔπλεεν R Marc.: ἔπλωον van H. || ἐπὶ τὴν
Μυκάλην vel ἐπὶ Μυκάλης malit Kallenberg   7 μυκάλλης S || ἐπείτε
δὲ vel ἐπεὶ δὲ δὴ? van H.

---

8. 343, 15. 1 (διά τε σκόλοπας καὶ τάφρον
ἔβησαν), Od. 7. 44 τείχεα μακρὰ ὑψηλά,
σκολόπεσσιν ἀρηρότα. Cp. l. 3 supra.

παρεσκευάδατο: the temporal force
can hardly be insisted on in this
pluperfect. The passage is, however,
corrupt, and Stein's later emendation
would eliminate this word and leave
παρεσκευάζοντο (less forcible). Cp. App.
Crit. I prefer to regard ἐπ᾿ ἀμφότερα . .
παρεσκευάζοντο as the gloss: the Persians
were not prepared for an alternative
(ἐπ᾿ ἀμφότερα), nor is a true alternative
presented; they wish to stand a siege,
and to issue therefrom victorious. The
glossator has misunderstood the situation. The resolution of the Persian
admirals to stand a siege can hardly be
explained except by their distrust of the
(Ionian) forces under their command,
and also by the absence of the corps
d'armée, and their expectation that it
would come to their relief. They had,
of course, under their command, the
Medo-Persian Epibatai, 8. 180 supra.

9. ἐπιλεγόμενοι, if it stands, may be
interpreted by ἐπιλεξάμενος, not in 8.
136 but in 5. 30.

98. 2. ἤχθοντο ὡς ἐκπεφευγότων: sc.
τῶν βαρβάρων. The construction is not
quite regular; cp. 8. 109 ἐκπεφευγότων
περιημέκτεον.

ἀπορίῃ τε εἴχοντο ὅ τι ποιέωσι,
'were in doubt (at a loss) what to do';
the agendum is conceived of as future,
the antecedent imperfect notwithstanding, hence the subjunctives. Three
courses were open to them: (i.) to return
to Delos, (ii.) to steer for the Hellespont,
(iii.) to follow the Persians to the mainland at Mykale. The first is merely a
logical alternative; the second might
have drawn the Persian fleet after them,
but was obviously rather speculative.
The third course was under the circumstances the obvious one to take, and
hardly required very much deliberation,
especially if, as appears, they were still
counting upon a sea-engagement. The
ἐπίπλοος is distinctly militant and
hostile: ἐπὶ τὴν ἤπειρον. The actual
πλόος is merely geographical, ἐπὶ τῆς
Μυκάλης.

6. ἀποβάθραι reappear in Thuc. 4. 12.
1 as 'landing-gangways'; here they
must have been intended in the first
instance for boarding the Persian ships.

7. ἐπεὶ δὲ ἀγχοῦ τε . . καὶ οὐδὲς . . :
a common form of parataxis; cp. 8. 37.
ἐπαναγόμενος, 'putting out to sea
against them.' παρακεκριμένον, cp. 8.
70. 2: in acie stantem, Baehr. ἐγχρίμψας, a not uncommon word with Hdt.
and elsewhere transitive; cp. 2. 60 τὴν
βᾶριν τῇ γῇ, also 2. 93, 3. 85, 4. 113.

καὶ οὐδεὶς ἐφαίνετό σφι ἐπαναγόμενος, ἀλλ' ὡρῶν νέας
ἀνελκυσμένας ἔσω τοῦ τείχεος, πολλὸν δὲ πεζὸν παρακεκριμένον
10 παρὰ τὸν αἰγιαλόν, ἐνθαῦτα πρῶτον μὲν ἐν τῇ νηὶ παραπλέων,
ἐγχρίμψας τῷ αἰγιαλῷ τὰ μάλιστα, Λευτυχίδης ὑπὸ κήρυκος
προηγόρευε τοῖσι Ἴωσι λέγων "ἄνδρες Ἴωνες· ὅσοι ὑμέων
τυγχάνουσι ἐπακούοντες, μάθετε τὰ λέγω· πάντως γὰρ οὐδὲν
συνήσουσι Πέρσαι τῶν ἐγὼ ὑμῖν ἐντέλλομαι. ἐπεὰν συμμί-
15 σγωμεν, μεμνῆσθαι τινὰ χρὴ ἐλευθερίης μὲν πάντων πρῶτον,
μετὰ δὲ τοῦ συνθήματος Ἥβης. καὶ τάδε ἴστω καὶ ὁ μὴ
ἀκούσας ὑμέων πρὸς τοῦ ἀκούσαντος." [ὠυτὸς δὲ οὗτος ἐὼν
τυγχάνει νόος τοῦ πρήγματος καὶ ὁ Θεμιστοκλέος ὁ ἐπ'

8 σφιν ἐφαίνετο β: ἐγένετό σφι Marc. ‖ νῆας z   9 παρακεκρυμ-
μένον S   11 ἐγκρίψας Cz ‖ ταμάλιστα Pz   12 ὅσοι β, Holder,
van H., Stein³: οἱ   13 μάθε R ‖ πάντες Marc.   14 συμμισγῶμεν
RSV   15 πάντων om. Ask.   16 Ἥρης Roscher, Holder   17
ἐσακούσας αC: ἐπακούσας Bekker, Holder, van H. ‖ ἐπακούσαντος β,
Holder, van H. ‖ ὠυτὸς . . Ἕλλησι secl. Krueger, van H., Stein³ ‖ οὗτος:
τούτου coni. Stein⁽²⁾   18 τυγχάνει: ἐτύγχανε requir. Krueger, van H.
‖ πρήγματος: ῥήματος aut κηρύγματος? Stein ‖ ὁ om. R ‖ Θεμιστοκλῆος z

11. **ὑπὸ κήρυκος**, 'by the voice of a
herald,' instrumental ; but not quite
parallel with ὑπὸ μαστίγων 7. 22, 56.

12. **τοῖσι Ἴωσι**, who probably furnished
and manned the major part, if not the
whole, of the Persian fleet on this
occasion, the Epibatai excepted ; cp. c.
97 supra.

14. **ἐπεὰν συμμίσγωμεν**: Hdt. characteristically makes nothing of the determination of the Greeks to effect a landing.
They had advanced against the mainland
only in the expectation of fighting a
ναυμαχίη. The resolution to force a
landing in the actual presence of a
hostile force, in possession of the shore,
is far more remarkable. This was more
than the Persians themselves had
attempted at Marathon, and certainly
more than they could have effected.
The Persians at Mykale were in a
position to dispute the attempted landing
of the Greeks (cp. the situation at Pylos
in 425 B.C., Thucyd. 4. 11 ff.), and their
failure to do so is best explained by their
distrust of the Ionians. συμμίσγειν, as in
8. 22. 12, 4. 127, 6. 14, etc., of hostile
encounter.

15. **τινὰ χρή**: cp. 8. 109. 19 καί τις
οἰκίην κτλ.

16. **τοῦ συνθήματος Ἥβης**: σύνθημα is
any preconcerted signal (cp. 8. 7. 10), or
even the mere prearrangement itself (cp.

5. 75 ἀπὸ συνθήματος, 6. 121 ἐκ σ.). Here
it is the 'password' (Ἥβης in apposition). Why Ἥβη should have been
the mot d'ordre is not self-evident : there
was no apparent local association to
suggest it, but it need not be changed
into Ἥρης, out of compliment to
the Samians. Hebe is, indeed, in
attendance upon Here, Iliad 5. 721 f.,
and on Ares, ib. 905, and in Hesiod,
Theog. 922, 952, is daughter of Zeus
and Here (and sister of Ares). Moreover, she is the bride of Herakles in
heaven, Od. 11. 603, and so might well
have charms for a Herakleid on earth.
μετὰ δέ is, of course, adverbial : the
genitives are regular, with μεμνῆσθαι,
cp. 8. 62. 9 (but the accus. is found 7.
18. 9, 10).

τάδε ἴστω καὶ ὁ μὴ ἀκούσας ὑμέων:
there is something of the nature of an
Irish 'bull' in this imperative ; but
Leotychidas means ὁ ἀκούσας, not ὁ μὴ
ἀκούσας, to act on the suggestion, and to
pass the word.

17. **ὠυτὸς δὲ . . τοῖσι Ἕλλησι.** The
passage is clumsy in expression, and
particular words are scarcely correct.
Stein⁵ now brackets the whole as a
gloss, or imitation of 8. 22 supra;
presumably after Krueger.

18. **νόος**: cp. 7. 162 and c. 120 infra,
notwithstanding which, the co-ordina-

Ἀρτεμισίῳ· ἡ γὰρ δὴ λαθόντα τὰ ῥήματα τοὺς βαρβάρους
ἔμελλε τοὺς Ἴωνας πείσειν, ἡ ἔπειτα ἀνενειχθέντα ἐς τοὺς 20
βαρβάρους ποιήσειν ἀπίστους τοῖσι Ἕλλησι.]

Λευτυχίδεω δὲ †ταῦτα ὑποθεμένου δεύτερα δὴ τάδε ἐποίευν 99
οἱ Ἕλληνες· προσσχόντες τὰς νέας ἀπέβησαν ἐς τὸν αἰγιαλόν.
καὶ οὗτοι μὲν ἐτάσσοντο, οἱ δὲ Πέρσαι ὡς εἶδον τοὺς Ἕλληνας
παρασκευαζομένους ἐς μάχην καὶ τοῖσι Ἴωσι παραινέσαντας,
τοῦτο μὲν ὑπονοήσαντες τοὺς Σαμίους τὰ Ἑλλήνων φρονέειν 5
ἀπαιρέονται τὰ ὅπλα. οἱ γὰρ ὦν Σάμιοι ἀπικομένων Ἀθηναίων
αἰχμαλώτων ἐν τῇσι νηυσὶ τῶν βαρβάρων, τοὺς ἔλαβον ἀνὰ

20 ἐπείτε B, Koen : del. Krueger : ἐκεῖθεν ? Stein¹ ² ‖ ἀνενειχθέντα :
ἀνενειχθῇ Koen 21 τοῖσι Ἕλλησι secl. Abicht, Stein², Holder
99. 1 λεωτυχίδεω a ‖ δὴ om. z 2 προσσχόντες RP Marc. z ‖ τὰς νῆας z :
del. van H. 6 ὦν : ἀν R

tion here of νόος τοῦ πρήγματος or
κηρύγματος and ὁ Θεμιστοκλέος (νόος) is
a little manqué. So, too, ἔπειτα ἀνενειχθέντα as a reproduction of ἐπείτε
ἀνενειχθῇ 8. 22 is poor, and ἀπίστους
active, for the passive there, very
suspicious. τυγχάνει should be ἐτύγχανε
(Krueger). οὗτος might better be τούτου.
Cp. App. Crit. ; prodit interpolatorem
sermonis imperitia, van H.

99. 1. ταῦτα ὑποθεμένου : cum hocce
consilium dedisset, Baehr.

δεύτερα δή seems de trop, but serves
to separate the action of the Hellenes
from the suggestions of Leotychidas.

2. προσσχόντες τὰς νέας ἀπέβησαν ἐς
τ. αἰγ. Hdt. records this remarkable
operation without apparently the slightest
apprehension of its military magnitude
or significance. To debark on the
shore in the presence of an army
numerically superior (even if the ἐξ
μυριάδες of c. 96 were not within hail),
and in possession of a fortified camp,
was surely a very brilliant achievement.
Hdt. seems to regard it as something
quite en règle, and keeps the Persians
quietly looking on, as if they could
never think of attempting to interfere.
The inactivity of the Persians at this point
is inexplicable except on the supposition
that they despaired of the Ionians.

3. ὡς εἶδον . . παρασκευαζομένους . .
παραινέσαντας : there is a double
awkwardness in the sentence, the zeugma
in εἶδον, and the hysteroproteron in the
order of the participles, only partially
corrected by the difference of tense.
' On seeing the Hellenes making them

ready to battle (after landing), and that
they had addressed an appeal to the
Ionians (before landing), the Persians
took two precautions.'

5. τοῦτο μέν. 'In the first place'
they disarm the Samians on a suspicion
of Hellenic leanings. The suspicion is
indeed an old one, for it is based upon
an act of the previous winter, or autumn :
and does the ὅπλων ἀπαίρεσις only take
place now, at this point, after the landing of the Greeks at Mykale ? ὑπονοέων : c. 88 supra. τὰ Ἑλ. φρονέειν :
cp. 7. 102 supra.

6. οἱ γὰρ ὦν Σάμιοι κτλ. This
memorable little digression records a
service of the Samians to Athens, which
must have taken place months before.
The king's ships had reached Samos in
the previous autumn, 8. 130 supra ; the
Samians had redeemed 500 Attic
prisoners, and had sent them home to
Athens (ex hypothesi reoccupied) after
duly providing them for the journey,
or voyage (ἐπισιτίσαντες).

This note is somewhat startling. It
presupposes an open sea between Samos
and Athens. Had the 500 Athenians
accompanied the Samian ambassadors in
c. 90 supra, or preceded them ? Such
a pledge of good-will comes in for scant
appreciation ! There is doubtless some
truth in the anecdote ; but is it correctly
chronologized ? Were these Athenian
prisoners liberated before the arrival of
the Hellenes in Samos, c. 96 supra ?
Were they really redeemed, or had they
been sold into slavery, in Samos, and
liberated on the approach, or arrival of
the Greek fleet ?

τὴν Ἀττικὴν λελειμμένους οἱ Ξέρξεω, τούτους λυσάμενοι
πάντας ἀποπέμπουσι ἐποδιάσαντες ἐς Ἀθήνας· τῶν εἵνεκεν
10 οὐκ ἥκιστα ὑποψίην εἶχον, πεντακοσίας κεφαλὰς τῶν Ξέρξεω
πολεμίων λυσάμενοι. τοῦτο δὲ τὰς διόδους τὰς ἐς τὰς κορυφὰς
τῆς Μυκάλης φερούσας προστάσσουσι τοῖσι Μιλησίοισι φυλάσσειν ὡς ἐπισταμένοισι δῆθεν μάλιστα τὴν χώρην· ἐποίευν
δὲ τοῦτο <τοῦδε> εἵνεκεν, ἵνα ἐκτὸς τοῦ στρατοπέδου ἔωσι.
15 τούτους μὲν Ἰώνων, τοῖσι καὶ κατεδόκεον νεοχμὸν ἄν τι ποιέειν
δυνάμιος ἐπιλαβομένοισι, τρόποισι τοιούτοισι προεφυλάσσοντο
οἱ Πέρσαι, αὐτοὶ δὲ συνεφόρησαν τὰ γέρρα ἔρκος εἶναι σφίσι.

---

8 οἱ : ὑπὸ B   9 ἐς τὰς Sz   10 ἔχον z   11 ἐς κορυφὰς z
12 μυκάλλης S   13 ἐποίευν . . ἔωσι del. Gomperz   14 τοῦτο
τοῦδε Krueger, Stein², Holder, van H. : τούτου   15 καὶ om. R ‖
νεοχμὸν C   17 γέρα S ‖ σφίσι Stein, Holder, van H. : σφι(ν)

---

10. ὑποψίην εἶχον, 'were suspected. .,'
objects of suspicion; cp. αἰτίην εἶχον
5. 70, etc.

11. τοῦτο δέ. The second precaution
taken by the Persians is the removal of
the Milesians from the camp, on the
plea that they are best qualified to guard
the passes on Mykale. Precaution and
plea are perplexing. The charge of
the passes over Mykale interposes a
suspected force between the Persians
and Sardes, and the camp between that
force and Miletos. Are the facts or
the motives here rightly reported ? If
there were no Milesians in the Persian
camp at Mykale, was it because the
Persians had dismissed them ? Or were
there 'Milesians' and 'Milesians' ? If
the Persians entrusted to Milesians the
guard of the passes, that would rather
point to a confidence in their loyalty !
And who are these Milesians ? According to 6. 19 f. the Milesians had been
annihilated and the remnant expatriated
in 494 B.C., i.e. fifteen years previously ;
their places had been taken by Persians
and Karians, the former as landlords,
the latter as labourers. Was there
already a new agrarian question in
Miletos (cp. 5. 29) ? Or is the situation
of 494 B.C. grossly exaggerated ? In
any case it is significant of Hdt.'s
methods that he betrays no misgiving
on this point. Possibly when he first
composed this passage he was unac-
quainted with the story told in 6. 19,
or at least had not incorporated it in
his own work—the last three Books
being of earlier composition.

τὰς διόδους τὰς ἐς τὰς κορυφὰς . .
φερούσας: the occupation of these passes
might be for the purpose of preventing
the Greeks from attacking the camp in
the rear, or to obtain touch with Ephesos
and the road to Sardes, in case a retreat
became necessary.

Mykale (as seen from the south on a
fine April morning) is a grand mountain
range, culminating in twin κορυφαί, east
and west (4130 ft. and 3966 ft. in height
respectively), with a gentle slope down
to the western point, where the promontory becomes involved in the outline of
Samos.

15. τοῖσι καὶ κατεδόκεον. This dative
is puzzling. The normal construction
is with accus. and infinitive. Valckenaer
wished to insert ἐνεόν. Baehr takes
δοκέειν = existimare, κατά in comp. contra
aliquem, the dative being constructed
with verbs compounded with κατά
(though never anywhere else with κατα-
δοκέειν). Stein explains the dative as
used by analogy with συνειδέναι (and
compares κατακρίνειν τινί τι 2. 133, 17.
146. 6). Kuehner, Gr. Gr. § 568. 1, ap.
Baehr renders : sic glaubten bei ihnen,
dass sie Neuerungen machten. νεοχμόν:
cp. c. 104. 7 infra, νεοχμοῦν 4. 201, 5. 19.

16. δυνάμιος ἐπιλαβομένοισι, "if
occasion offered," Rawlinson ; "if they
found the occasion," Macaulay. δύναμις
as 'potentiality,' possibility, is remarkable in Hdt. The participle is here
conditional. With the phrase cp. προφάσιος ἐπιλαβέσθαι 3. 36, 6. 49 ; also
Plato Rep. 360 D εἴ τις τοιαύτης ἐξουσίας
ἐπιλαβόμενος κτλ.

Ὡς δὲ ἄρα παρεσκεύαστο τοῖσι Ἕλλησι, προσήισαν πρὸς 100
τοὺς βαρβάρους· ἰοῦσι δέ σφι φήμη τε ἐσέπτατο ἐς τὸ
στρατόπεδον πᾶν καὶ κηρυκήιον ἐφάνη ἐπὶ τῆς κυματώγης

---

100. 1 παρεσκεύαστο Reiske, van H., Stein³: παρεσκενάδατο ‖ προσίη-
σαν BParis. 1635 z: προσίεσαν S: προσείησαν Marc.   3 κηρύκιον CP

προεφυλάσσοντο, 'took precautions against beforehand,' cp. 7. 176 *supra*; in the active more naturally of place, (νέα) τὴν προφυλάσσουσαν ἐπὶ Σκιάθῳ 8. 92 *supra*.

17. αὐτοὶ δὲ . . σφίσι. The exact relation of this ἕρκος of γέρρα to the ἕρκος καὶ λίθων καὶ ξύλων in c. 97 *supra* is problematical. The former is the fortified camp, from which all suspicious characters have been removed (or rendered innocuous); the 'rampart of shields' actually reappears in c. 102 *infra*; and we may suppose that here the Persians are drawn up, outside their camp, and have fixed their shields in the ground to act as a screen; but if they have advanced out beyond their fortified camp, all the more inexplicable does it appear that they should have allowed the Greeks to effect a landing without dispute, while the Greeks at their leisure landed, and drew up in battle-array, and then advanced to the attack. On the γέρρα cp. c. 61 *supra*.

100. 2. φήμη τε ἐσέπτατο . . καὶ κηρυκήιον ἐφάνη. The *Fama* is plainly in Hdt.'s belief supernatural, as he explains; of the κηρυκήιον, a more material τεκμήριον, he takes no further account. What became of this κηρυκήιον? How many persons saw it? Was it the supernatural bearer of the supernatural message? Alas! that so much should be made of the impalpable φήμη and nothing said of the subsequent history of the ocular sign! This omission is a weak spot in the story, in the argument; and nowadays, in a world of telepathy, crystal-gazing, subliminal selves, and other scientific enchantments, which explain the φήμη to perfection, one is bound to take cognisance of the total disappearance of the material evidence.

A φήμη which Hdt. treats as in no way supernatural had run right through the medizing Greek army in Boiotia a few weeks before, cp. c. 17 *supra*; it had proved a fraud; had it turned out

to be true, it might have been regarded as divine.

Diodoros 11. 35 (Ephoros), cp. Polyain. 1. 33, completely rationalizes the story of this φήμη, regarding it as a ruse by Leotychidas; Larcher and Thirlwall approve. A somewhat similar case was the fraud of Agesilaos in 394 B.C., which no doubt helped him to win the battle of Koroneia (Xenoph. *Hell.* 4. 3. 10–14), when he announced the defeat of the Lakedaimonian fleet off Knidos to his army as a victory; but he had received actual despatches, and had no need to pretend a synchronism. If a few days' interval occurred between the victory in Boiotia and the victory in Ionia the φήμη is simple enough. If there was a real synchronism between the battles of Plataia and Mykale, then one of three or four alternatives can alone be true: either (a) the φήμη was a fraud, a ruse, a γενναῖον ψεῦδος at the moment, which afterwards proved to be true to fact; or (b) it was in truth supernormal, whether you explain it by direct divine interposition or by abnormally heightened human feeling; or (c) thirdly, it is an element of afterthought, a product of tradition, an embellishment of the facts, possibly traceable to excited hopes and feelings of the actual day, but without the adequate or full basis of fact asserted by the pious tradition. There is so much of this kind of thing in the story of the war that it does not appear unreasonable to ascribe the φήμη *motif*, though it rings out more precisely and positively than any other, to the same creative faculty. There was some Homeric precedent for it, though the word φήμη does not occur in the *Iliad* at all (*pace* Aischines § 141, cp. D. B. Monro, *Odyssey XIII.-XXIV.* p. 427), for the ὄσσα ἐκ Διός (*Od.* 1. 282) is its precursor. The word εἰσέπτατο occurs *Il.* 21. 494 of the flight of a bird, to which is likened the motion of a goddess (Artemis).

κείμενον· ἡ δὲ φήμη διῆλθέ σφι ὧδε, ὡς οἱ Ἕλληνες τὴν
5 Μαρδονίου στρατιὴν νικῷεν ἐν Βοιωτοῖσι μαχόμενοι. δῆλα δὴ
πολλοῖσι τεκμηρίοισι ἐστὶ τὰ θεῖα τῶν πρηγμάτων, εἰ καὶ
τότε, τῆς αὐτῆς ἡμέρης συμπιπτούσης τοῦ τε ἐν Πλαταιῇσι
καὶ τοῦ ἐν Μυκάλῃ μέλλοντος ἔσεσθαι τρώματος, φήμη τοῖσι
Ἕλλησι τοῖσι ταύτῃ ἐσαπίκετο, ὥστε θαρσῆσαί τε τὴν
10 στρατιὴν πολλῷ μᾶλλον καὶ ἐθέλειν προθυμότερον κινδυνεύειν.
101 καὶ τόδε ἕτερον συνέπεσε γενόμενον, Δήμητρος τεμένεα Ἐλευσινίης παρὰ ἀμφοτέρας τὰς συμβολὰς εἶναι· καὶ γὰρ δὴ ἐν

4 δίδε CP : ἤδε ? Krueger   5 δὲ Β   7 αὐτῆς del. Krueger
|| συμπίπτοντος Reiske, van H., Stein³ || τε : τ' R(S)V || πλαταίῃσι α :
πλαταίῃσι R(S)V   8 μυκάλλῃ S || φήμη δὲ Β   9 τοῖσι om.
Marc.   101. 2 παρὰ : 'expectes παρὰ Δήμητρος κτέ ? van H. : πάρα
Dobree

4. ἡ δὲ φ. διῆλθέ σφι ὧδε : sc. τὸ
στρατόπεδον. The exact terms of the
φήμη are very nearly identical with the
message (ἀγγελίη) which had reached
the Greeks at the Heraion in front of
Plataia that same day, ὅτι μάχη τε
γέγονε καὶ νικῷεν οἱ μετὰ Παυσανίεω c.
69 supra. The imperf. pres. νικῷεν here
of the fait accompli (cp. γεγονέναι νίκην
c. 101 infra) is remarkable ; Xenoph.
Hell. 4. 3. 1 has νικῷεν (but 4. 3. 10 ὅτι
ἡττημένοι εἶεν) ; Stein compares νικᾶν in
c. 48 supra, and interprets 'are victors'
(Sieger seien). The use of νικᾶν there
absolutely is easier than νικῷεν here
with a direct object. Might it be one
of Hdt.'s imperfects, of an action the
result of which is abiding, or continuous ?
The passage in Xenophon shows that
we need not read νενικῷεν here. ἐν
Βοιωτοῖσι is purely geographical.

5. δῆλα δὴ . . τὰ θεῖα τῶν πρηγμάτων :
"many things prove to me that the gods
take part in the affairs of men," Rawlinson ; "now by many signs is the divine
power seen in earthly things," Macaulay.
But the passage involves a classification
of 'things,' into τὰ θεῖα and τὰ μὴ θεῖα,
rather than the general assertion of the
existence of "a divinity that shapes our
ends, rough hew them as we will." Cp.
c. 65 supra. Hdt. is here a 'dualist' :
far from the formula of Thales, πάντα
πλήρη θεῶν, but close to 'common sense,'
or 'popular philosophy,' as we know it.
Hdt.'s argument is not very closely
expressed ; the particular instance (εἰ
καὶ τότε) cannot prove the general
(πολλοῖσι τεκμηρίοισι). But the formal
statement here is not the real statement.

The true predicate lies in τὰ θεῖα : what
is plain, by many infallible proofs,
among them par exemple the particular
case quoted, is the fact that some things
are θεῖα, that 'miracles do happen'—
though, of course, most happenings are
quite ordinary and natural. (There are
even degrees in the class, cp. 7. 137
τοῦτό μοι ἐν τοῖσι θειότατον φαίνεται
γενέσθαι, 8. 65 θεῖον τὸ φθεγγόμενον, 8. 94
θεῖον τὸ πρῆγμα.) Cp. Introduction,
§ 11.

7. τῆς αὐτῆς ἡμέρης συμπιπτούσης :
the expression is somewhat clumsy—a
day cannot coincide with itself—but the
meaning is plain : the day, or date, of
the action at Plataia and the date of
the action just about to take place at
Mykale was identically the same ; but
it was 'the actions,' not 'the day,'
which coincided. συμπίπτοντος or συμ-
πιπτόντων would certainly be clearer
(cp. App. Crit.) : but is Hdt. always quite
clear in thought or expression ? τρῶμα :
cp. c. 90 supra. ταύτῃ : sc. ἐν Μυκάλῃ.

101. 1. τόδε ἕτερον συνέπεσε γενόμενον, 'a second coincidence occurred
as follows.' The expression again is not
quite accurate : it takes two items to
make a coincidence, and only one item
is here expressed. Again, the coincident
'occurrences' are the 'existence' of two
shrines of Demeter, one at Plataia and
one at Mykale ; but, strictly speaking,
the existence of the shrines is not the
occurrence, but rather the battles by
the shrines.

2. συμβολάς, of 'hostile meeting,' as
in 4. 159, 6. 120, 7. 210, etc.

τῇ Πλαταιίδι παρ' αὐτὸ τὸ Δημήτριον ἐγίνετο, ὡς καὶ πρότερόν μοι εἴρηται, ἡ μάχη, καὶ ἐν Μυκάλῃ ἔμελλε ὡσαύτως
ἔσεσθαι. γεγονέναι δὲ νίκην τῶν μετὰ Παυσανίεω Ἑλλήνων 5
ὀρθῶς σφι ἡ φήμη συνέβαινε ἐλθοῦσα· τὸ μὲν γὰρ ἐν
Πλαταιῆσι <τρῶμα> πρωὶ ἔτι τῆς ἡμέρης ἐγίνετο, τὸ δὲ ἐν
Μυκάλῃ περὶ δείλην. ὅτι δὲ τῆς αὐτῆς ἡμέρης συνέβαινε
γίνεσθαι μηνός τε τοῦ αὐτοῦ, χρόνῳ οὐ πολλῷ σφι ὕστερον
δῆλα ἀναμανθάνουσι ἐγίνετο. ἦν δὲ ἀρρωδίη σφι, πρὶν τὴν 10
φήμην ἐσαπικέσθαι, οὔτι περὶ σφέων αὐτῶν οὕτω ὡς τῶν

---

3 ἐγένετο P Marc. : οὗ ἐγένετο z   4 εἴρητο P ‖ μυκάλλῃ S ‖
ἔσεσθαι ὡσαύτως B   7 πλαταίῃ B ‖ <τρῶμα> Stein(2) 3, van H.
8 μυκάλλῃ S   9 μηνός τε τοῦ αὐτοῦ suspecta habeo   10 πρινὴ
R(S)V : πρὶν ἢ Holder, van H.   11 αὐτέων z ‖ τῶν Ἑλλήνων : τῶν
ἐκεῖ Ἑλλήνων coni. Stein¹ : τῶν ἄλλων Ἑλλήνων Krueger, Stein(2), van H.

---

3. ὡς καὶ πρότερόν μοι εἴρηται : a
definite cross-reference back to cc. 57,
62, 65 supra.

5. γεγονέναι δὲ νίκην : this appears as
equivalent to νικᾶν c. 100 supra ; cp.
also c. 69 supra.

6. ὀρθῶς σφι ἡ φήμη συνέβαινε
ἐλθοῦσα, 'the rumour which (had)
reached them turned out to be true,' or
'they discovered the truth of the rumour
which had reached them.' The exact
force of συνέβαινε here is disputable : its
repetition just below, and in a slightly
different sense, is by no means un-Herodotean.

7. πρωὶ ἔτι τῆς ἡμέρης. The adv.
πρωί is not found elsewhere in Hdt.
Homer (Il. 8. 530 etc.), Xenophon (Hell.
1. 1. 30 ἑκάστης ἡμέρας πρῲ καὶ πρὸς
ἑσπέραν) and other good writers use it =
mane, explained by Theophrastos Fr. 6.
1. 9 as the forenoon, from ἀνατολή to
μεσημβρία. But it is also used more
generally, cp. Thuc. 4. 6. 1, etc. ἔτι is
not = ἤδη but used with comparative
force.

8. περὶ δείλην, 'about evening,' cp.
8. 6, 9, a passage which proves that the
term admits of degrees. Here, in opposition to πρωί, it may mean merely p.m.

ὅτι δὲ τῆς αὐτῆς ἡμέρης συνέβαινε
γίνεσθαι. Hdt.'s predication again is not
quite clear. The grammatical subject
of συνέβαινε may be τὸ ἐν Μυκάλῃ (sc.
τρῶμα), or the two (sc. ἀμφότερα, or τὰ
τρώματα), δῆλα perhaps favouring this
view : συνέβαινε γίνεσθαι is, however,
a simple and constant form for an
occurrence, or event, taking place.

9. μηνός τε τοῦ αὐτοῦ is a very frigid

addition. Or would Hdt., then, have
regarded it as possible for two events to
take place on the same day in different
months? But it is a thousand pities
that he did not happen to give us the
Attic date, by month, and day of the
month, for the victory. If it had taken
place in Boëdromion, and about the
time of the Eleusinia, would not tradition have more clearly emphasized the
festive date?

The actual and precise day is given
by Plutarch Aristeid. 19 as Boëdromion 4
= Panemos 27, but in Camillus 19 and
Mor. 349 F as Boëdromion 3 < = Panemos
26 >, a curious discrepancy. In any case
the date may be that of the Charisteria,
not of the battle. Hdt.'s data do
not enable us to fix the date of the
final battle at Plataia with precision.
Busolt, Gr. Gesch. ii.² (1895) 726, 742,
places Plataia 'at the beginning of
August,' and Mykale 'about the middle
of August,' denying the synchronism.
I should be inclined to admit the
synchronism, or an approximate synchronism, and to place the battles
somewhat later, early in September ; cp.
Appendix VII. § 6, VIII. § 2 (i.). The
fact that other striking synchronisms
are less trustworthy, cp. 7. 166 supra,
does not entirely discredit this one.
What is damaging to Hdt.'s credit
as historian is the insistence on the
synchronism, as a mere wonder, to the
complete exclusion of its significance
from a strategic point of view.

11. οὔτι περὶ σφέων αὐτῶν : this
generous self-oblivion might at least
attest the sense that strategically the

Ἑλλήνων, μὴ περὶ Μαρδονίῳ πταίσῃ ἡ Ἑλλάς. ὡς μέντοι
ἡ κληδὼν αὕτη σφι ἐσέπτατο, μᾶλλόν τι καὶ ταχύτερον τὴν
πρόσοδον ἐποιεῦντο. οἱ μὲν δὴ Ἕλληνες καὶ οἱ βάρβαροι
15 ἔσπευδον ἐς τὴν μάχην, ὥς σφι καὶ αἱ νῆσοι καὶ ὁ Ἑλλήσποντος ἄεθλα προέκειτο.

102   Τοῖσι μὲν νυν Ἀθηναίοισι καὶ τοῖσι προσεχέσι τούτοισι
τεταγμένοισι, μέχρι κου τῶν ἡμισέων, ἡ ὁδὸς ἐγίνετο κατ'
αἰγιαλόν τε καὶ ἄπεδον χῶρον, τοῖσι δὲ Λακεδαιμονίοισι καὶ
τοῖσι ἐπεξῆς τούτοισι τεταγμένοισι κατά τε χαράδραν καὶ
5 ὄρεα. ἐν ᾧ δὲ οἱ Λακεδαιμόνιοι περιήισαν, οὗτοι οἱ ἐπὶ τῷ

---

13 κληδὼν z : κληηδὼν Merzdorf ‖ σφι : τοι Marc. ‖ τι : τοι Marc.
14 Cf. comment. infra   102. 2 κου : κατὰ Paris. 1635 z ‖ ἡμισέων
Cz : ἡμίσεων ‖ ἡ om. CS   3 δὲ om. C   4 χαράνδραν C : χαράδρην Pz   5 οὔρεα CP Marc. z, van H.

---

decisive blow in this campaign could not be struck by the fleet, nor could a check, or even a disaster to the fleet, matter so much. περί is used with the genitive similarly 8. 36 σφέων αὐτῶν πέρι ἐφρόντιζον. For ἀρρωδίη cp. ibid.

τῶν Ἑλλήνων, 'the Greeks at home'—ἡ Ἑλλάς includes themselves.

12. μὴ περὶ Μαρδονίῳ πταίσῃ ἡ Ἑλλάς : with the dative περί has primarily a locative force, and does not lose it even when locality ceases to be the prominent interest ; the metaphor here (πταίσῃ) may be of shipwreck, but πρός is the preposition more generally in use. Cp. Plato, Rep. 553 Β ἔπειτα αὐτὸν ἴδῃ ἐξαίφνης πταίσαντα ὥσπερ πρὸς ἕρματι πρὸς τῇ πόλει. The wrecking of Hellas on Mardonios might have been accomplished by battle, or by bribery, cp. c. 2 supra.

13. ἡ κληδών : cp. c. 91 supra ; here the word = ἡ φήμη, cp. c. 100 supra.

ταχύτερον : θᾶσσον is not found in Hdt., nor ταχύτατα.

τὴν πρόσοδον, of a hostile advance, advance to the attack, as in 7. 223 (differently 6. 46). There is predicative force in the position of αὕτη.

14. καὶ οἱ βάρβαροι ἔσπευδον : this assertion is of something quite new ; hitherto the barbarians have not been anxious to fight. Now, however, they have drawn the Greeks to land, they have a fortified camp behind them, they have a corps d'armée somewhere about, if c. 96 supra is to be trusted, and they have apparently advanced and fixed their γέρρα as a ἕρκος before them (c. 99

supra) ; they still remained on the defensive though eager for the fray. Is the text here correct ? Nothing corresponds to οἱ μὲν δὴ Ἕλληνες—οἱ δὲ βάρβαροι with a contrasted verb to ἔσπευδον might originally have concluded the chapter.

15. ὥς σφι καὶ αἱ νῆσοι καὶ ὁ Ἑλλήσποντος ἄεθλα προέκειτο, 'inasmuch as (seeing that) the islands and the Hellespont were the prizes at stake for them.' ὡς . . προέκειτο is remarkable : ὡς = ἐπεί (one might have expected ὡς with participle, gen. abs.).

The Greeks and Persians at Mykale could hardly have taken this view of the case unless they had been already acquainted with the defeat of Mardonios. Were the Persians equally informed, by the φήμη, or by an ἀγγελίη from Leotychidas, which, of course, they would not have believed ; or, in fact, had sufficient time elapsed for the news to have reached Sardes as well as Samos ? The islands would be those in proximity to Asia : the Kyklades were already free.

102. 1. προσεχέσι : for the word cp. c. 28 supra. The construction here with τεταγμένοισι is quasi-adverbial ; cp. ἐπεξῆς τεταγμένοι infra ; the Korinthians, Sikyonians and Troizenians are intended, but the names are here withheld ; they, with the Athenians, formed the left half, or flank, of the army. As they walk over the lower ground it seems that the Greeks have landed east of the Persian encampment.

5. ἐν ᾧ : sc. χρόνῳ. ἔτι is perhaps a corruption, or remainder of a lost word

ἑτέρῳ κέρεϊ [ἔτι] καὶ δὴ ἐμάχοντο. ἔως μέν νυν τοῖσι
Πέρσῃσι ὀρθὰ ἦν τὰ γέρρα, ἠμύνοντό τε καὶ οὐδὲν ἔλασσον
εἶχον τῇ μάχῃ· ἐπεὶ δὲ τῶν Ἀθηναίων καὶ τῶν προσεχέων
ὁ στρατός, ὅκως ἑωυτῶν γένηται τὸ ἔργον καὶ μὴ Λακεδαιμονίων,
παρακελευσάμενοι ἔργου εἴχοντο προθυμότερον, ἐνθεῦτεν ἤδη 10
ἑτεροιοῦτο τὸ πρῆγμα. διωσάμενοι γὰρ τὰ γέρρα οὕτω φερόμενοι ἐσέπεσον ἀλέες ἐς τοὺς Πέρσας, οἳ δὲ δεξάμενοι καὶ
χρόνον συχνὸν ἀμυνόμενοι τέλος ἔφευγον ἐς τὸ τεῖχος.
Ἀθηναῖοι δὲ καὶ Κορίνθιοι καὶ Σικυώνιοι καὶ Τροιζήνιοι
(οὗτοι γὰρ ἦσαν ἐπεξῆς τεταγμένοι) συνεπισπόμενοι συνεσέ- 15

6 κέραϊ βz ‖ ἔτι del. Schaefer, Stein², Holder : ante περιήισαν retrax.
Steger, van H. : αν ἔτυχον προτερέοντες καὶ δή ! 7 ὀρθὰ Stein²,
Holder, van H. : ὄρθρια S : ὄρθια ‖ γέρα S ‖ οἱ δ᾽ ἠμύνοντο ! Krueger
8 ἐπεί τε δὲ S ‖ τῶν ante προσεχέων om. S 9 γένοιτο z 11
γὰρ : δὲ β ‖ γέρα S ‖ οὕτω Naber, Gomperz, Holder, Stein³ : οὗτοι
12 ἐπέπεσον Marc. ‖ αλέες A : ἀλέες B ‖ καὶ om. C 13 ἀμυνάμενοι
van H. 15 οὗτοι β, Holder, Stein³ : οὕτω ‖ ἔσαν z ‖ οἱ ἐπεξῆς β ‖
ἐπισπόμενοι Cobet, van H. ‖ συνέπιπτον β

(ἐτιμωρέοντο, or ἔτυχον προτερέοντες).
Stein takes καὶ δή as it stands to be=
ἤδη.

6. ἔως . . τὰ γέρρα : the shields have
been erected in c. 99 ad f.

7. οὐδὲν ἔλασσον εἶχον : cp. c. 70
supra (πλέον εἶχον). Only Persians
appear engaged.

8. τῶν Ἀθηναίων καὶ τῶν προσεχέων
ὁ στρατός : treated as quite a distinct
and separate unit, or rather army, or
corps d'armée ; the names are still withheld.

9. ὅκως ἑωυτῶν . . καὶ μὴ Λακεδαιμονίων : the negative μή shows that this
is given as in the minds of the
Athenians ; it is, indeed, a genuine
motif of Athenian legend and oratory,
and in the hands of Isokrates (cp. Hdt.
IV.–VI. ii. 194 f.) became a guide
to the reconstruction of the past. It
betrays, or suggests, the character of the
source from which Hdt. has drawn the
story of Mykale : Athenian, or phil-
Athenian.

10. παρακελευσάμενοι, 'encouraging
each other with shouts,' cp. 8. 15. ἔργου
εἴχοντο, cp. 8. 11 supra.
ἤδη, 'at once.'

11. ἑτεροιοῦτο τὸ πρῆγμα, 'the affair
took a fresh turn, aspect' ; cp. 7. 225
supra.
διωσάμενοι γὰρ τὰ γέρρα : this
phrase marks the second stage in the

struggle ; they pushed their way through
the rampart of Persian shields—or
pushed the shields apart, so as to open
a way for themselves—and then charged
(φερόμενοι) en masse (ἀλέες) on the
Persians behind the shields, who had
doubtless been plying them with arrows.
διωθέεσθαι in a more general sense, c. 88
supra.

12. οἳ δέ : the δέ is demonstrative,
or emphatic ; the sentence might otherwise have been relative.

13. χρόνον συχνὸν ἀμυνόμενοι τέλος
ἔφευγον = χρ. σ. ἠμύνοντο τέλος δὲ ἔφευγον.
A rather lax use of the present, or imperfect, participle.

14. Ἀθηναῖοι δὲ καὶ Κορίνθιοι καὶ
Σικυώνιοι καὶ Τροιζήνιοι : at last, when
the victory is won, the other contingents
on the left wing are expressly named,
besides the Athenians.

15. ἦσαν . . τεταγμένοι : how little
this construction is a mere temporal
pluperfect appears from this passage ;
they were, what they had been all along,
ranged ἐπεξῆς Ἀθηναίοισι, in the given
order (οὕτω).
συνεπισπόμενοι συνεσέπιπτον :
they entered the fortified camp en masse
(i.e. without breaking from one another),
and at the same time as the Persians,
whom they were pursuing, i.e. pursuers
and pursued all entered together. συνεσέπιπτον, by the way, throws some light

πίπτον ἐς τὸ τεῖχος. ὡς δὲ καὶ τὸ τεῖχος ἀραίρητο, οὔτ᾽ ἔτι
πρὸς ἀλκὴν ἐτράποντο οἱ βάρβαροι πρὸς φυγήν τε ὁρμέατο
οἱ ἄλλοι πλὴν Περσέων· οὗτοι δὲ κατ᾽ ὀλίγους γινόμενοι
ἐμάχοντο τοῖσι αἰεὶ ἐς τὸ τεῖχος ἐσπίπτουσι Ἑλλήνων. καὶ
20 τῶν στρατηγῶν τῶν Περσικῶν δύο μὲν ἀποφεύγουσι, δύο δὲ
τελευτῶσι· Ἀρταΰντης μὲν καὶ Ἰθαμίτρης τοῦ ναυτικοῦ
στρατηγέοντες ἀποφεύγουσι, Μαρδόντης δὲ καὶ ὁ τοῦ πεζοῦ
103 στρατηγὸς Τιγράνης μαχόμενοι τελευτῶσι. ἔτι δὲ μαχομένων
τῶν Περσέων ἀπίκοντο Λακεδαιμόνιοι καὶ οἱ μετ᾽ αὐτῶν, καὶ
τὰ λοιπὰ συνδιεχείριζον. ἔπεσον δὲ καὶ αὐτῶν τῶν Ἑλλήνων
συχνοὶ ἐνθαῦτα ἄλλοι τε καὶ Σικυώνιοι καὶ στρατηγὸς Περίλεως.

---

16 καὶ om. Paris. 1635 z || οὔτέ τι P Marc.: οὔτε τι z　　　　17 καὶ
πρὸς ante ἀλκὴν R (ap. Stein¹) || καὶ πρὸς ante φυγὴν β (ap. Holder) ||
ὁρμέατο P Marc.　　　18 κατ᾽ ὀλίγον S: κατὰ λόγους B　　　21 Ἰθρα-
μίτρης z　　　103. 2, 3 αὐτέων (bis) z　　　3 τῶν om. RSV　　　4
Σικυώνιοι καὶ: Σικυωνίων coni. Stein, adsc. van H. || περίλεος βz

---

upon its correlate συνεξέπιπτον as in 5.
22.

16. ὡς δὲ καὶ τὸ τεῖχος ἀραίρητο
marks the third stage in the combat, or
rather its culmination. The pluperfect
is hardly temporal, for the fighting is not
yet all over. πρὸς ἀλκὴν τρέπεσθαι (cp.
ἀλκῆς μεμνῆσθαι c. 70 supra) is just the
opposite of ἐς φυγὴν τρέπεσθαι, cp. c. 63
supra, 8. 91, etc.

17. οἱ βάρβαροι: did no Greeks strike
a blow on this occasion upon the Persian
side ? Cp. c. 103. 8 infra. πρὸς φυγήν τε ὁρμέατο: so in
Thuc. 4. 14. 1 τῶν ἀνδρῶν ἐς φυγὴν
ὡρμημένων, of actual or literal physical
movement.

18. κατ᾽ ὀλίγους γινόμενοι, "forming
into small knots," Blakesley; the preposition has distributive force, op. 8. 113
supra ἐξελέγετο κατ᾽ ὀλίγους.

19. τοῖσι αἰεὶ . . ἐσπίπτουσι might
seem hardly consistent with συνεπισπόμενοι συνεσέπιπτον above (the imperfect notwithstanding) ; but that phrase
was obviously rhetorical, this is both
more accurate and more 'elegant.'

21. Ἀρταΰντης: cp. 8. 130 supra, c.
107 infra.

Ἰθαμίτρης: cp. 8. 130 supra.

22. Μαρδόντης: cp. 8. 130 supra ;
his fate suggests that he was especially
in command of the Persian Epibatai.

23. Τιγράνης: cp. c. 96 supra. His
death is really the first clear intimation
in the story of the actual presence at

Mykale of any of the six myriads, of
which he is there put in command : is
it sufficient to convince us that any part
of the corps d'armée was present, or
engaged in the battle, or that the battle
was more than an engagement between
the Greek forces, from the fleet, and the
Medo-Persian Epibatai from the king's
fleet—the only portion of the navy,
probably, which could be trusted to
show fight, especially on land ? Athenian
or phil-Attic tradition has exaggerated
the battle of Mykale into a grand piece
to match the synchronous battle in
Boiotia ; cp. c. 106 infra. Tigranes, if
killed on this occasion, was perhaps in
command of the Persian Epibatai ; cp.
c. 96 supra.

103. 1. ἔτι δέ. It is only at the
fourth stage of the fight that the Lakedaimonians and their half of the army
arrive on the scene, and help to finish
the remnant (τὰ λοιπὰ συνδιεχείριζον).
Hdt. does not employ the simpler forms
χειρίζειν or διαχειρίζειν, nor any one else
the double compound.

4. συχνός = πολλός, πολύς : cp. c. 102
supra, et passim.

Περίλεως: the name Perilaos was
common and widespread ; i.e. there is
nothing specially Sikyonian, or even
Peloponnesian about it. (Cp. Pape-
Benseler, sub v.) Nothing more is recorded of this man : the absence of a
patronymic suggests that Hdt. did not
get this item from an inscription, least

τῶν τε Σαμίων οἱ στρατευόμενοι ἐόντες τε ἐν τῷ στρατοπέδῳ 5
τῷ Μηδικῷ καὶ ἀπαραιρημένοι τὰ ὅπλα, ὡς εἶδον αὐτίκα κατ'
ἀρχὰς γινομένην ἑτεραλκέα τὴν μάχην, ἔρδον ὅσον ἐδυνέατο
προσωφελέειν ἐθέλοντες τοῖσι Ἕλλησι· Σαμίους δὲ ἰδόντες οἱ
ἄλλοι Ἴωνες ἄρξαντας οὕτω δὴ καὶ αὐτοὶ ἀποστάντες ἀπὸ
Περσέων ἐπέθεντο τοῖσι βαρβάροισι. Μιλησίοισι δὲ προσε- 104
τέτακτο μὲν <ἐκ> τῶν Περσέων τὰς διόδους τηρέειν σωτηρίης

---

5 τε : δὲ ß, Holder, van H. ‖ συστρατευόμενοι Cobet, van H. ‖ ἐνεόντες
Ask. ‖ τε om. Rz   6 καταρχὰς ABPz   7 ὑπεραλκέα ß ‖ ἔρδον P,
Stein, Holder : ἔρδον AB : ἔρδον ‖ ἠδυνέατο SV(Gaisf.)   104. 1
μιλήσιοι SR : μηλίσιοι V   2 μὲν om. ß ‖ ἐκ suppl. Valckenaer, Stein²,
van H. : πρὸς Cobet, Holder ‖ τηρεῖν libri, Holder, van H. : corr. Stein

---

of all in Sikyon. Samian or Athenian tradition may have preserved the bare name of the only general who fell on this occasion.

5. τῶν τε Σαμίων : this great, though somewhat vague, service of the Samians is very lightly and easily introduced ; in fact Hdt. has nothing concrete or definite to report on their behalf. οἱ στρατευόμενοι, cp. 7. 61 supra. ἐν τῷ στρατοπέδῳ, not necessarily ἐν τῷ τείχει, cp. c. 15 supra. But what of the Samians on the Greek side, of whom there should now have been some ? Or were there as yet no Samians serving ? Cp. c. 92 supra.

6. ἀπαραιρημένοι τὰ ὅπλα, 'deprived of their heavy arms,' cp. c. 99 supra. ἀπαιρέειν takes double acc., cp. 8. 3 supra.

αὐτίκα κατ' ἀρχάς: cp. 7. 88 supra ; it would go better here with ἔρδον.

7. ἑτεραλκέα : cp. 8. 11 supra.

ἔρδον ὅσον ἐδυνέατο: the first verb is rather epic (cp. 7. 33 supra). What did they 'do' ? They might have set fire to the camp ? or they might have pulled it partially to pieces ; or they might have 'done sacrifice' : but this testimonial lacks precision.

8. προσωφελέειν with the dative Stein regards as 'poetical' ; it is used with the acc. c. 68 supra in a more precise or definite context.

οἱ ἄλλοι Ἴωνες : not including the Milesians, as the next c. shows. There were thus Ionians besides the Samians and the Milesians serving with the Persians ; they would be the crews of the ships.

9. ἄρξαντας : i.e. αὐτίκα κατ' ἀρχὰς ἔρδοντας ὅσον ἐδυνέατο.

ἀποστάντες ἀπὸ Περσέων : this phrase is hardly to be taken in the physical sense, suggested by the immediate context, viz. stood off, separated from the Persians there and then, but rather in the political sense : threw off their allegiance to Persia. The absence of the article and the last sentence of the next c. support this view. Cp. c. 90 supra.

10. ἐπέθεντο τοῖσι βαρβάροισι. This attack on the barbarians goes beyond anything explicitly recorded of the Samians in the context, but it still leaves something to be desired, in the way of concrete definiteness. Rawlinson ad l. remarks that "Hdt. is never very favourable to the Ionian Greeks and may have given them on this occasion less credit than they deserved." Euge ! Diodoros (Ephoros) is kinder ; cp. Appendix VII. § 7 (c), 2. Had Hdt. written the story of Mykale before his visit to Samos, where the fame of that island grew dearer to him (cp. 3. 60) ? And did he leave what he had written unrevised ?

104. 1. Μιλησίοισι δὲ προσετέτακτο : the pluperfect is in strict time ; cp. c. 99 supra ; but the two reasons already given, and here more explicitly repeated, are inconsistent with each other. If the Persians removed the Milesians to prevent their creating a disturbance, a mutiny, or at least some trouble in the camp, they distrusted their loyalty. If they distrusted their loyalty, they did not entrust to them the custody of the passes, or expect them to act as their

εἵνεκά σφι, ὡς, ἢν ἄρα σφέας καταλαμβάνῃ οἷά περ κατέλαβε,
ἔχοντες ἡγεμόνας σῴζωνται ἐς τὰς κορυφὰς τῆς Μυκάλης.
5 ἐτάχθησαν μέν νυν ἐπὶ τοῦτο τὸ πρῆγμα οἱ Μιλήσιοι τούτου
τε εἵνεκεν καὶ ἵνα μὴ παρέοντες τῷ στρατοπέδῳ τι νεοχμὸν
ποιέοιεν· οἱ δὲ πᾶν τοὐναντίον τοῦ προστεταγμένου ἐποίεον,
ἄλλας τε κατηγεόμενοί σφι ὁδοὺς φεύγουσι, αἳ δὴ ἔφερον ἐς
τοὺς πολεμίους, καὶ τέλος αὐτοί σφι ἐγίνοντο [κτείνοντες]
10 πολεμιώτατοι. οὕτω δὴ τὸ δεύτερον Ἰωνίη ἀπὸ Περσέων
ἀπέστη.

105 Ἐν δὲ ταύτῃ τῇ μάχῃ Ἑλλήνων ἠρίστευσαν Ἀθηναῖοι
καὶ Ἀθηναίων Ἑρμόλυκος ὁ Εὐθοίνου ἀνὴρ παγκράτιον

---

3 ἀρά ΑΒ   4 σῴζωνται van H., Stein³: σώιζονται C: σῴζωνται
α, Stein¹², Holder: σώζονται βPpr. Marc. z ‖ (μυκάλλης S ?)   6 τε:
γε α: om. β ‖ εἵνεκα Marc.z ‖ ἐν τῷ β, Holder, van H.   7 τὸ
ἐναντίον β   8 δὴ ἔφερον z: διέφερον   9 αὐτοῖς R ‖ κτείνοντες
del. Gomperz, Holder, van H., Stein³   10 ἰωνίη τὸ δεύτερον β
(τοδεύτερον S)   105. 1 ἀρίστευσαν Marc.   2 εὐθοίνου CPz:
εὐθόνου α: εὐθύνου β, Valla, Gaisford

---

guides to safe places of retreat, in case
of a disaster occurring, such as actually
occurred.

3. ἄρα here, as frequently, may be
taken to suggest the unexpected. The
historian speaks propria persona in οἷά
περ κατέλαβε: ἢν καταλαμβάνῃ being of
course future in force. νεοχμόν (l. 6) is
repeated from c. 99.

7. οἱ δέ: the demonstrative (article),
with δέ, resumes the subject of the
sentence, and so lends it additional
emphasis. Cp. note to 7. 51. 3, etc.

8. αἳ δή: the relative, emphasized.

ἔφερον ἐς, 'led into,' among;
φέρειν ἐς in metaph. sense c. 33 supra.
But cp. App. Crit.

10. τὸ δεύτερον Ἰωνίη ἀπὸ Περσέων
ἀπέστη, 'Ionia threw off the Persian
yoke for the second time.' (Cp. cc. 103,
90 supra.) This statement involves an
implicit reference to the first or former
revolt, and so might seem to take the
record given in Bk. 5 for granted. But
the fact of that revolt was no doubt
notorious; Hdt. might even have found
the revolt of 479 B.C. already noted as
the δευτέρη ἀπόστασις, and it is not even
necessary to suppose this little sentence
(or the words τὸ δεύτερον) a gloss, or an
insertion of the second draft by the
author, in order to reconcile it with the

theory of the prior composition of Bks.
7-9. Cp. Introduction, §§ 7, 8.

105. 1. ἠρίστευσαν Ἀθηναῖοι, 'the
Athenians obtained the meed of valour.'
Cp. 8. 17 supra for the formula.

2. Ἑρμόλυκος ὁ Εὐθοίνου. The father's
name is corrupt in the best mss.;
cp. App. Crit. εὐθύνου looks like a correction of εὐθόνου. Euthynos is a commoner name at Athens than ' Euthoinos,'
which is, however, found on Inscripp.
' Hermolykos ' is mentioned again as
pankratiast with a statue on the Akropolis (Pausan. 1. 23. 10). Whether this
Hermolykos son of Euthoinos was any
relation to Hermolykos son of Diitrephes,
who dedicated a statue of his father (cp.
Pausanias 1. 23. 3), apparently the
general Diitrephes well known from
Thucydides (7. 29. 1, 8. 64. 1), is a much
debated question; cp. Frazer, Pausanias
ii. 275 f., 289; Hitzig-Bluemner, Pausanias (1896), notes ad ll.c.

παγκράτιον ἐπασκήσας, 'who (had)
practised (successfully! ἐπι-) as a pankratiast.' The pankration, a combination
of boxing (πυγμή) and wrestling (πάλη),
was first introduced at Olympia in 648
B.C., Ol. 33, Pausan. 5. 8. 8; cp. Clinton,
Fasti i. p. 198; and victories in the
pankration are celebrated in several of
Pindar's Epinikia: e.g. Nem. 2, 3, 5,
Isth. 3, 4, 5, 6, 7.

ἐπασκήσας. τοῦτον δὲ τὸν Ἑρμόλυκον κατέλαβε ὕστερον
τούτων, πολέμου ἐόντος Ἀθηναίοισί τε καὶ Καρυστίοισι, ἐν
Κύρνῳ τῆς Καρυστίης χώρης ἀποθανόντα ἐν μάχῃ κεῖσθαι 5
ἐπὶ Γεραιστῷ. μετὰ δὲ Ἀθηναίους Κορίνθιοι καὶ Τροιζήνιοι
καὶ Σικυώνιοι ἠρίστευσαν.

Ἐπείτε δὲ κατεργάσαντο οἱ Ἕλληνες τοὺς πολλοὺς τοὺς 106
μὲν μαχομένους τοὺς δὲ καὶ φεύγοντας τῶν βαρβάρων, τάς
<τε> νέας ἐνέπρησαν καὶ τὸ τεῖχος ἅπαν, τὴν ληίην προεξ-
αγαγόντες ἐς τὸν αἰγιαλόν, καὶ θησαυρούς τινας χρημάτων
εὗρον· ἐμπρήσαντες δὲ τὸ τεῖχος καὶ τὰς νέας ἀπέπλεον. 5
ἀπικόμενοι δὲ ἐς Σάμον οἱ Ἕλληνες ἐβουλεύοντο περὶ ἀνα-

---

4 τουτέων z   6 γεραίστω R(S)V   106. 2, 3 τάς <τε>
van H., Stein³ : τὰς   3, 5 νῆας (bis) z   4 καὶ <γὰρ> van H.
5 τό <τε> van H. ‖ ἀπέπλωον idem   6 περὶ τῆς Marc. ‖ ἀναστάσεος z

3. κατέλαβε ὕστερον τούτων : for the
verb cp. cc. 93, 104 supra, 'overtook.'
The general date places the event in the
Pentekontaëteris, but unfortunately without a precise year. The war between
'the Athenians' and the Karystians
is, however, presumably that one commemorated by Thuc. 1. 98. 3 about
472 B.C.; cp. Busolt, Gr. G. iii. (1897) 140.

4. ἐν Κύρνῳ : this Kyrnos in Euboia,
in the territory of Karystos, is not elsewhere mentioned. The nominal coincidence with the island Corsica (cp. 7. 165
supra) was not perhaps accidental. On
Karystos cp. 8. 121 supra. On Geraistos,
8. 7 supra.

6. Κορίνθιοι . . Τροιζήνιοι . . Σικυώνιοι : the order of merit differs slightly
from their order in battle-array c. 102
supra, but all contingents on the left
wing obtained prizes. The right (Lakedaimonians, etc.) was quite left in the
shade. This story is hardly of Spartan
origin.

106. 1. ἐπείτε . . κατεργάσαντο, cum
interfecissent (Baehr). They seem to
have taken no prisoners on this occasion.

3. τὴν ληίην προεξαγαγόντες, 'though
not until they (had) brought (led) out
the spoil.' It was apparently alive, at
least some of it. Thuc. 2. 94. 3 ἀνθρώπους
καὶ λείαν λαβόντες.

4. καὶ θησαυρούς . . εὗρον is not in
strict construction. Stein regards it as
an addition from the author's hand ; cp.
Introduction, § 9. χρήματα apparently
=money, but might cover plate.

5. ἀπέπλεον. Obviously the Greek
forces at Mykale had not defeated, had

not even encountered, the corps d'armée
accredited to Tigranes c. 96 supra ; had
they done so, the road to Sardes was
once more open to them. The battle
of Mykale was evidently a πρόσκρουσμα
βραχὺ τοῖς βαρβάροις, a raid, a brilliant
raid no doubt, but not a great victory,
and the Greeks at once retired, before
the Persian land-forces came up, and
abandoned the mainland to its fate.

6. περὶ ἀναστάσιος τῆς Ἰωνίης. At
Samos, after their return from Mykale,
the Hellenes, i.e. the naval Synedrion,
cp. c. 90 supra, discussed the question
of 'the evacuation of Ionia.' This was
an old idea, started by Bias of Priene,
if 1. 170 may be trusted ; some of the
Ionians (in 546 B.C.) τὴν δουλοσύνην οὐκ
ἀνεχόμενοι ἐξέλιπον τὰς πατρίδας (1. 169).
Again in 494 B.C. a few voluntarily
(6. 17) and still more against their will
(6. 20) had left their homes for ever. A
migration en masse had recently been
recommended to Athens by the Delphic
oracle (7. 140 supra), and brought within
the range of practical politics by Themistokles (8. 62 supra). There was thus
a good deal in the recent experience of
the Greeks, not to speak of the migra-
tions and colonizations of earlier days,
to make a wholesale flitting no absurd
or unpractical idea. For the use of
ἀνάστασις cp. Thuc. 2. 14. 2 (of the
flitting of the Athenians from the country
into the city 431 B.C.), 7. 75. 1 τοῦ στρατεύματος (of the break-up and departure
before Syracuse in 413 B.C.), 1. 133 ad f.
ἐκ τοῦ ἱεροῦ (of the retirement from the
temple by a suppliant). Cp. 4. 115

στάσιος τῆς Ἰωνίης, καὶ ὅκῃ χρεὸν εἴη τῆς Ἑλλάδος κατοικίσαι
τῆς αὐτοὶ ἐγκρατέες ἦσαν, τὴν δὲ Ἰωνίην ἀπεῖναι τοῖσι
βαρβάροισι· ἀδύνατον γὰρ ἐφαίνετό σφι εἶναι ἑωυτούς τε
10 Ἰώνων προκατῆσθαι φρουρέοντας τὸν πάντα χρόνον, καὶ
ἑωυτῶν μὴ προκατημένων Ἴωνας οὐδεμίαν ἐλπίδα εἶχον χαίροντας
πρὸς τῶν Περσέων ἀπαλλάξειν. πρὸς ταῦτα Πελοποννησίων
μὲν τοῖσι ἐν τέλεϊ ἐοῦσι ἐδόκεε τῶν μηδισάντων ἐθνέων τῶν
Ἑλληνικῶν τὰ ἐμπολαῖα ἐξαναστήσαντας δοῦναι τὴν χώρην
15 Ἴωσι ἐνοικῆσαι, Ἀθηναίοισι δὲ οὐκ ἐδόκεε ἀρχὴν Ἰωνίην

---

7 ὅπῃ α: ὅπη BC: ὅποι PMarc. z || χρεὼν CPz, van H. || κατοικῆσαι Bz
8 ἔσαν z: εἴησαν ? Stein[2] || ἀπεῖναι β: ἀφεῖναι   9 ἑωυτούς τε secl.
van H.   10 φρουρέων R(S)V   11 οὐδὲ μίαν AB: οὐδεμίην z ||
ἔχον z   13 τέλεϊ AB: τέλεσι z   14 ἐμπολαῖα Stein[2]: 'num forte
ἐπίπλοα ?' van H.: ἐμπόλια αC Marc.: ἐμπόρια || ἐπαναστήσαντας β

---

supra φέρετε ἐξαναστέωμεν ἐκ τῆς γῆς
τῆσδε.

7. **ὅκῃ .. τῆς Ἑλλάδος .. τῆς αὐτοὶ
ἐγκρατέες ἦσαν.** If Ionia was to be
evacuated and abandoned to the 'barbarians,' some place for the Ionians
would have to be found on Hellenic
soil. This problem appears to take the
control or possession of Hellas proper
(or the greater part of it) for granted;
it assumes the truth of the φήμη of the
day before (a night will presumably have
intervened); or has the φήμη (of c. 100)
by this time been officially confirmed
by despatches to Samos? Or may this
deliberation be taken as an undesigned
confession that the victory in Boiotia
had been fully reported to the Greeks
at Samos or ever they advanced on
Mykale? Ἑλλάς here comes very nearly
to 'Greece' in our sense of the word.
ἐγκρατής is used similarly 8. 49 supra.
The imp. indic. ἦσαν is remarkable;
= εἰσί l.c.

10. **προκατῆσθαι:** as in 8. 36 supra,
and cp. also 7. 172.

τὸν πάντα χρόνον, 'for ever,' c.
73. 3.

11. **μή** as in a conditional sentence
(participial).

**χαίροντας πρὸς τῶν Περσέων ἀπαλ-
λάξειν,** 'will get off with impunity (go
unpunished) at the hands of Persia.'
Cp. 3. 69 οὗτοι μὲν .. δεῖ χαίροντα
ἀπαλλάσσειν. The negative is more
usually combined with χαίρων, e.g. 3. 29
ἀτάρ τοι ὑμεῖς γε οὐ χαίροντες γέλωτα
ἐμὲ θήσεσθε, Xenoph. Anab. 5. 6. 32
διαστασθέντες δ' ἂν .. οὔτε χαίροντες ἂν
ἀπαλλάξαιτε.

12. **Πελοποννησίων μὲν τοῖσι ἐν τέλεϊ
ἐοῦσι:** primarily Leotychidas, the
Spartan king and navarch, and in the
second line the captains of the Korinthians, Sikyonians, Troizenians. Two
points raise suspicion: (i.) Could the
king or the Synedrion have decided
off-hand so immense and far-reaching a
question? (ii.) Would the Dorian states
at least have desired to reinforce the
'Ionian' element in Central Hellas, and
in Peloponnese itself, by supporting
such a proposal? οἱ ἐν τέλεϊ as in 3. 18,
Thuc. 1. 10. 4 ἔξω τῶν βασιλέων καὶ τῶν
μάλιστα ἐν τέλεϊ, 5. 47. 9 οἱ τὰ τέλη
ἔχοντες (official term at Elis; 1. 58. 1 τὰ
τέλη τῶν Λακεδαιμονίων, cp. 4. 15. 1, etc.

13. **ἐδόκεε:** a strict imperfect; the
δοκέον did not become a δόγμα.

τῶν μηδισάντων ἐθνέων τῶν Ἑλ.:
a preliminary list of them has been
given 7. 132 supra, but the list is not
complete, omitting the Argives (cp. 8.
73) and some islanders (Andros, the
Karystians, etc.).

14. **τὰ †ἐμπολαῖα† ἐξαναστήσαντας.**
The ἐξανάστασις in this case was hardly
to be accomplished without violence.
ἐμπολαῖα is a conjectural emendation;
cp. App. Crit. = ἐμπόρια. But the adj.
ἐμπολαῖος is not common, and would
mean (in the neuter) not 'markets,'
but rather 'commodities.'

δοῦναι .. ἐνοικῆσαι: exactly as
in Thuc. 2. 27. 2 ἐκπεσοῦσι δὲ τοῖς
Αἰγινήταις οἱ Λακεδαιμόνιοι ἔδοσαν Θυρέαν
οἰκεῖν. (Exegetical and telic, or
gerundive.)

15. **ἀρχήν,** 'at all'—in the first
instance; they moved in fact the

γενέσθαι ἀνάστατον οὐδὲ Πελοποννησίοισι περὶ τῶν σφετερέων
ἀποικιέων βουλεύειν · ἀντιτεινόντων δὲ τούτων προθύμως, εἶξαν
οἱ Πελοποννήσιοι. καὶ οὕτω δὴ Σαμίους τε καὶ Χίους καὶ
Λεσβίους καὶ τοὺς ἄλλους νησιώτας, οἳ ἔτυχον συστρατευόμενοι τοῖσι Ἕλλησι, ἐς τὸ συμμαχικὸν ἐποιήσαντο, πίστι τε 20

---

16 Πελοποννησίους Schweighaeuser, Holder, van H. : 'An deest προσ-
ήκειν ?' Stein² ‖ σφετέρων libri, Holder, van H.   17 ἀποικίων β ‖
τουτέων z   19 <καὶ ἠπειρώτας καὶ>νησιώτας Schwartz : νησιώτας
<καὶ τοὺς ἠπειρώτας> Steup : sed cf. Busolt III. i. 39 ‖ στρατευόμενοι β
20 ἐσεποιήσαντο Krueger, Stein³ ‖ πίστει C Marc. ‖ τε om. αC

---

previous question, and had also a formal
or constitutional objection to urge, viz.
against interference between a metropolis
and its colonies. The metropolitan
claim of Athens had been recognized
and urged from the other side as early
as 498 B.C., cp. 5. 97—and probably
dated back at least to the days of
Peisistratos (cp. c. 97 *supra*), but
perhaps only referred to Miletos, and
some of the mainland towns at first.
It was, of course, a part of the basis of
the Delian symmachy just afterwards,
and was then perhaps more widely
extended ; cp. next note.

18. καὶ οὕτω δή : there might perhaps
seem to be a *non sequitur* in these
words, which throws doubt, not upon
the fact here stated so much as upon
the previous report of the debate in the
Synedrion at Samos (cc. 90, 91). If
Peloponnesians were not to be allowed
βουλεύειν περὶ τῶν ('Αττικῶν) ἀποικιέων—
and yielded the point—the matriculation
of the 'Samians' and 'Chians' (which
appear on the *Marmor Par.* 27 as
colonies from Athens) might seem to
be inconsistent therewith. But was
the Ionian settlement in Samos rightly
ascribed to Athens? The Ionians of
Samos were ultimately traced back to
Epidauros ; cp. Pausan. 7. 4. 2 (op.
Δωριέες (sic) 'Επιδαύριοι Hdt. 1. 146).
The case of Chios is even more obscure ;
according to the native historian, Ion, a
contemporary of Hdt.'s, the island was
peopled by Abantes from Euboia (cp. Hdt.
1. 146), and by immigrants from Histiaia ;
their 'Ionization' they owed to a king
Hektor, in the third generation after ;
but Ion failed to account for the Chians
being reckoned Ionians (οὐ μέντοι ἐκεῖνό
γε εἴρηκε καθ' ἥντινα αἰτίαν Χίοι τελοῦσιν
ἐς 'Ίωνας, Pausan. 7. 4. 10). Possibly
Samos and Chios, at least in 479 B.C.,

were not yet accounted 'Athenian'
colonies ; and even the passage in Hdt.
1. 146-7 distinguishes among the Ionians
between οἱ . . ἀπὸ τοῦ πρυτανηίου τοῦ
'Αθηναίων ὁρμηθέντες καὶ νομίζοντες γεν-
ναιότατοι εἶναι 'Ιώνων and the rest.
(The passage in c. 147 making the
Apaturia the test of Ionism admits
that the Ephesians and Kolophonians
did not observe it ; but the passage is
very like a gloss.) The Athenians
might protest against any intervention
between themselves and their settlements abroad, and yet allow the enrol-
ment of Samos and Chios in the Hellenic
alliance without a murmur, having (at
this time at least) no metropolitan claim
over these islands any more than over
the Aiolian Lesbos. But the whole
story of the deliberations is, of course,
highly suspicious ; the proposed ἀνάστασις would have meant a civil war,
and the admirals could hardly have
settled such a question.

19. καὶ τοὺς ἄλλους νησιώτας cannot
refer to the islands enumerated in 8. 46
supra, for they already belonged to the
Symmachy ; the Greeks at Mykale, at
Samos, at the Hellespont (cp. c. 114
infra) had Samians, Chians, Lesbians,
and a good many other 'nesiotes' with
them, συστρατευόμενοι τοῖσι Ἕλλησι (sic),
who are completely ignored in the
narrative of the actual operations, and
only come into account in this highly
suspicious passage on diplomatic and
constitutional points. 'The Islands'
were understood to be half the prize of
Mykale, c. 101 *supra*.

20. ἐς τὸ συμμαχικὸν ἐποιήσαντο,
'admitted them as members of the
alliance' : τὸ σ.=τοὺς συμμάχους. Hdt.
has συμμαχίην . . ἐποιήσατο 1. 77,
πόλιας . . ὑπ' ἑωυτοῖσι ἐποιήσαντο 5.
103. Cp. Thuc. 3. 3. 4 τοὺς ἄνδρας . .

καταλαβόντες καὶ ὁρκίοισι <ἢ μὲν> ἐμμενέειν τε καὶ μὴ
ἀποστήσεσθαι. τούτους δὲ καταλαβόντες ὁρκίοισι ἔπλεον τὰς
γεφύρας λύσοντες· ἔτι γὰρ ἐδόκεον ἐντεταμένας εὑρήσειν.
οὗτοι μὲν δὴ ἐπ' Ἑλλησπόντου ἔπλεον.

107　　Τῶν δὲ ἀποφυγόντων βαρβάρων ἐς τὰ ἄκρα τῆς Μυκάλης
κατειληθέντων, ἐόντων οὐ πολλῶν, ἐγίνετο - κομιδὴ ἐς Σάρδις.
πορευομένων δὲ κατ' ὁδὸν Μασίστης ὁ Δαρείου παρατυχὼν
τῷ πάθεϊ τῷ γεγονότι τὸν στρατηγὸν Ἀρταΰντην ἔλεγε πολλά
5 τε καὶ κακά, ἄλλα τε καὶ γυναικὸς κακίω φὰς αὐτὸν εἶναι
τοιαῦτα στρατηγήσαντα, καὶ ἄξιον εἶναι παντὸς κακοῦ τὸν
βασιλέος οἶκον κακώσαντα. παρὰ δὲ τοῖσι Πέρσῃσι γυναικὸς
κακίω ἀκοῦσαι δέννος μέγιστος ἐστί. ὁ δὲ ἐπεὶ πολλὰ

---

21 ἢ μὲν add. Krueger, van H., Stein³ || ἐμμενέειν Stein, Holder :
ἐμμένειν vel ἐμμενεῖν　　22 ἀπονοστήσεσθαι SVz　　24 ἑλλήσποντον S ||
ἔπλωον van H.　　107. 1 ἄκρα τε ß, Holder, Kallenberg || μυκάλλης S
2 ἐγένετο R·|| σάρδεις R　　5 τε καὶ om. Marc. || εἶναι om. Marc.　　7
βασιλῆος z　　8 πολλά <τε καὶ κακὰ> ? Krueger, van H.

ἐς φυλακὴν ἐποιήσαντο, 8. 1. 3 τὰ τῶν
ξυμμάχων ἐς ἀσφάλειαν ποιεῖσθαι. But
cp. App. Crit. The statement here may
be reconciled with the statement in c.
92 supra by supposing that at Delos
Hegesistratos and his two companions
only bound themselves to do their best
to bring the Samians into the alliance ;
but the harmony is a little strained—
especially considering that the allies
have been to Samos once already (c. 96)
in the interval.

πίστι τε . . καὶ ὁρκίοισι, as in
c. 92 supra.

21. ἐμμενέειν τε καὶ μὴ ἀποστήσεσθαι:
this formula seems to presuppose a
ξυμμαχία ἐς ἀεί, ἐς τὸν πάντα χρόνον.
The right of ἀπόστασις is surrendered.
The formula and the story may have
been useful 'precedents' for the Delian
alliance, which no doubt was equally
unlimited in time (cp. Ἀθ. πολ. 23. 5).

22. ἔπλεον τὰς γεφύρας λύσοντες.
Rawlinson (ad l.) suggests that the
destruction of the bridges (8. 117) must
have been already known (by Lesbians,
for example) and that Hdt. has misconceived the motive of the move to
the Hellespont, which was "only to
reconnoitre." The Greeks will have
aimed at more than that—promoting
revolt, cutting off remnants, and so on.
But is it so certain that they knew the
bridges were no more, or might not be
restored ?

107. 1. ἀποφυγόντων· κατειληθέντων·
ἐόντων : this string of participles is not
elegant, but ἀποφ. is little more than
an adjective ; it might very well be
dispensed with. κατειληθέντων here
seems to mean 'crowded,' 'confined,'
'cooped up'; cp. 5. 119, 8. 27, cc. 31,
70 supra (κατειλημένοι). If there were
so few of them, one would have thought
Mykale roomy enough for them.

τὰ ἄκρα τ. Μ.=τὰς κορυφὰς τ. Μ.
cc. 104, 99 supra.

2. κομιδὴ : cp. 8. 108 supra.

3. Μασίστης ὁ Δαρείου : he was full
brother to Xerxes, cp. 7. 82 supra, and
had been one of the six generals, or
field-marshals, of the army in 480 B.C.
It is odd to find him here a casual
attaché of the naval forces, or of the
corps d'armée in Ionia : nor is he ! For
he has a bodyguard, οἱ δορυφόροι οἱ
Μασίστεω infra ; was he, not Tigranes,
the real commander of the six myriads,
c. 96 supra ! If so, he was not present
at the disaster which had just taken
place (τῷ πάθεϊ τ. γ.) but was probably
coming to the support of the encampment at Mykale, and naturally fell foul
of Artayntes (c. 102 supra).

5. γυναικὸς κακίω : cp. c. 20 supra.

6. τὸν βασιλέος οἶκον : cp. 8. 102
supra, 5. 31.

8. ἀκοῦσαι, 'to be called . .'

δέννος : the verb δεννάζειν occurs
twice in Sophokles, Antig. 759, Aias

ἤκουσε, δεινὰ ποιεύμενος σπᾶται ἐπὶ τὸν Μασίστην τὸν
ἀκινάκην, ἀποκτεῖναι θέλων. καὶ μιν ἐπιθέοντα φρασθεὶς 10
Ξειναγόρης ὁ Πρηξίλεω ἀνὴρ Ἁλικαρνησσεὺς ὄπισθε ἑστεὼς
αὐτοῦ [Ἀρταΰντεω], ἁρπάζει μέσον καὶ ἐξαείρας παίει ἐς τὴν
γῆν· καὶ ἐν τούτῳ οἱ δορυφόροι οἱ Μασίστεω προέστησαν.
ὁ δὲ Ξειναγόρης ταῦτα ἐργάσατο χάριτα αὐτῷ τε Μασίστῃ
τιθέμενος καὶ Ξέρξῃ, ἐκσῴζων τὸν ἀδελφεὸν τὸν ἐκείνου· καὶ 15
διὰ τοῦτο τὸ ἔργον Ξειναγόρης Κιλικίης πάσης ἦρξε δόντος
βασιλέος. τῶν δὲ κατ᾽ ὁδὸν πορευομένων οὐδὲν ἐπὶ πλέον
τούτων ἐγένετο, ἀλλ᾽ ἀπικνέονται ἐς Σάρδις·

---

9 ποιησάμενος z   10 ἀκινάκεα z ‖ ἀποκτεῖναι θέλων del. van H.:
θέλων om. S ‖ φθὰς z   11 ὁ Πρηξίλεω om. R: πρηστίλεω Ask. ‖
ἁλικαρνησεὺς BC ‖ ὄπισθεν R(S)VP Marc., Holder   12 Ἀρταΰντεω
del. Stein² ‖ ἐξαείρας Bredow, Stein, Holder, van H.: ἐξαίρας a: ἐξάρας z:
ἐξάρας   13 οἱ poster. loc. om. β Marc. z, Holder   14 χάριτας Marc.:
χάριν van H.   15 θέμενος Marc. ‖ ἐκσῴζων van H., Stein³: ἐκσώζων
16 Κιλικίης: Λυκίης Krueger ‖ ἦρξε Κιλικίης πάσης P: πάσης ἦρξε
Κιλικίης z   17 βασιλῆος z ‖ πορευομένων βαρβάρων βz ‖ ἐπὶ Werfer,
Schweighaeuser, Stein², Holder, van H.: ἔτι   18 ἐγένετο τούτων
CP Marc. z (τουτέων z) ‖ ἀλλὰ Marc. ‖ σάρδεις Marc.

243, and in Euripides, *Rhes.* 925. It
is found previously also in Theognis 1211.
The substantive (reproach, taunt) is rare.

ἐπὶ πολλὰ ἤκουσε, 'when he had
heard more than enough . .'

9. δεινὰ ποιεύμενος, 'in a rage . .'

σπᾶται ἐπὶ . . τὸν ἀκινάκην,
'draws his native sword upon Masistes,'
as we say. On ἀκινάκης cp. 7. 54 *supra*.

10. φρασθεὶς (*ubi animadvertit*) seems
less forcible than the Aldine φθὰς
(*praevertens*), but both would be *de trop*.

11. Ξειναγόρης ὁ Πρηξίλεω. Prexileos,
or Praxilas, is a very uncommon name,
and nothing more is known of this
Halikarnassian (Praxilla of Sikyon,
Pausan. 3. 13. 5, is also unrivalled).
Xeinagoras, or Xenagoras, is less rare.
Of this man nothing more is known
than is here by Hdt. recorded, but the
record is significant: (*a*) There were
Greeks with the Persian forces after
Mykale: this man, to be sure, would be
a subject of Artemisia (less probably an
exile, or adventurer). (*b*) His appointment as 'syennesis' of Kilikia is remarkable, and probably the first instance
of the investiture of a Greek subject
with a Persian governorship. (*c*) This
fact (which belongs to the history of
the *Pentekontaëteris*) may be regarded as
more certain than the cause or occasion
alleged by Hdt. for it. (*d*) Nevertheless

as himself a Halikarnassian Hdt. will
have had special interest and information
in regard to this fellow-citizen.

The predecessor of Xeinagoras in
Kilikia was Syennesis, or the *syennesis*,
son of Oromedon, mentioned 7. 98 *supra*,
who according to Aischyl. *Pers.* 326 lost
his life at the battle of Salamis, leaving
presumably no son to succeed him.
This Halikarnassian may have founded
a dynasty in Kilikia: the next governor
of Kilikia known to history is the
'syennesis' of the *Anabasis*; cp. *l.c.*
supra. (Rawlinson ventures to say that
"Xeinagoras can only have occupied a
subordinate position": thus indirectly
charging Hdt. in this case with a serious
and apparently wilful exaggeration of
his fellow-citizen's greatness. Krueger's
emendation shifts the venue to Lykia.)

12. ἁρπάζει μέσον: cp. Terent. *Ad.* 3.
2. 18 *sublimem medium arriperem et
capite pronum in terram statuerem*.

ἐξαείρας is here quite literally
intended; cp. Xenoph. *Kyr.* 2. 4. 14
συναρπάσας ἐξῆρε, Aristoph. *Knights*
1359 ἄρας μετέωρον εἰς τὸ βάραθρον
ἐμβαλῶ (Valckenaer).

14. ταῦτα ἐργάσατο χάριτα . . τιθέμενος: χάριν τίθεσθαι, cp. c. 60 *supra*:
an inverted predication (=ταῦτα ἐργαζό-
μενος χάριν ἐτίθετο).

17. οὐδὲν ἐπὶ πλέον τούτων: a mere

108   'Εν δὲ τῇσι Σάρδισι ἐτύγχανε ἐὼν βασιλεὺς ἐξ ἐκείνου

108. 1 'Εν : ἐπὶ Β ‖ σάρδησιν R Marc.

confession of ignorance ! For the formula cp. c. 41 *supra*. One would like to know what happened to Artayntes.

108. There follows here, by way of digression (cc. 108–113), a story of the King's Amour, or the Death of Masistes, which exhibits Hdt. at his best. A story could hardly be better told, or present more artfully the elements of a domestic tragedy, of a palace intrigue, started in passion and jealousy, culminating in torture, rebellion, death. One great defect the story, indeed, has from the moral point of view : it is the innocent who suffer, or who suffer most ; the guilty king, the jealous and cruel queen, come off scot free. Two considerations may slightly relieve this objection from an aesthetic standpoint : Artaynta, the daughter of Masistes, has a good deal to answer for : she is the root of the mischief. Again, 'rebellion is as the sin of witchcraft,' and Masistes and his sons die with arms in their hands against the king. But it cannot be said that Hdt. makes anything of these *motifs*. As a historian he might plead (though it is not his way !) that the facts were as he stated them, painfully immoral, and aesthetically distressing. As a moralist he might plead that the true moral lay outside the story, in the suggestion of all that Hellas had been spared by the successful resistance to the Oriental despot, which had made such tragedies, possible in tyrants' houses, for ever impossible in Hellas ! And, again, that he thus dismisses Xerxes, to go to his own place, the scorn and derision of all good men, with his lawless passions and his slavish submission to 'the law of the Medes and Persians,' his childish vanities (ἡσθεὶς περιβάλλεται) and his prodigal pleasures (ἡσθεὶς δὲ καὶ ταύτῃ), his humorous caprices (speeches to Masistes) and his capricious wrath (θυμωθείς). The dramatic narrative falls into five acts.

(i.) The scene in Sardes : Xerxes' passion for his brother Masistes' wife : her faithfulness and virtue ! and the king's ruse to win her, by wedding his son Dareios to her daughter.

(ii.) The scene shifts to Susa : the king's still fouler transfer of his affections from his brother's wife to his son's wife, Artaynta.

(iii.) The fatal gift : the robe of Amestris the queen : her jealousy and error : destruction to the wife of Masistes, the mother of Artaynta !

(iv.) The king's birthday feast : the queen's request : the despot's involuntary humiliation.

(v.) The catastrophe : wreck of the house of Masistes. (Masistes rejects the king's overtures : the mutilation of his wife : the rebellion, and its defeat.)

It is an omission that Artaynta does not expressly share the fate of her family.

This story might almost rank with the Hebrew story of *Esther* as an illustration of life at the Persian court. But, except for the external reference above indicated, it lacks the national and popular setting, the political purpose, and therewith the ethical contents, which ennoble the Jewish tale. The Greek interest in this tale is purely reflexive. No Greek, whether man or woman, figures in this drama : the virtues of the wife of Masistes are purely domestic ; her husband as the ἀνὴρ ἀγαθός, good man, husband, father, and yet rebel withal, prepared to work 'no end of ill' to the king, his brother, unites to some extent the rôles of Mordecai and Haman ; the king himself cuts no great figure in either tale, but here he is less of a puppet and more of a curse, while behind and over all rises the terrible figure of Amestris, 'a fury slinging flame,' a barbarian fiend incarnate. (If Ahasuerus = Xerxes, Esther would = Amestris. But that cannot be, "if we accept the stories which Hdt. tells of Amestris," and which the Jews tell of Esther.)

1. ἐν δὲ τῇσι Σάρδισι : cp. 8. 117 *supra* ; it is, however, a question whether Xerxes was in Sardes at this time, and not rather engaged, in upper Asia, in the reduction of the revolted satrapy of Babylon ; cp. C. F. Lehmann, 'Xerxes und die Babylonier,' *Wochensch. f. Klass. Philologie*, 1900, 959–965, Ed. Meyer, *G.d.A.* iii. p. xiv. ; Appendix VII. § 2.

ἐτύγχανε ἐών marks a coincidence, which is not causally related to the antecedents, or rather concomitants. Xerxes, as we are here given to understand, spent the winter of 480–79 B.C., and at least the whole of the ensuing

τοῦ χρόνου, ἐπείτε ἐξ Ἀθηνέων προσπταίσας τῇ ναυμαχίῃ
φυγὼν ἀπίκετο. τότε δὴ ἐν τῇσι Σάρδισι ἐὼν ἄρα ἤρα τῆς
Μασίστεω γυναικὸς ἐούσης καὶ ταύτης ἐνθαῦτα. ὡς δέ οἱ
προσπέμποντι οὐκ ἐδύνατο κατεργασθῆναι, οὐδὲ βίῃ προσεφέρετο 5
προμηθεόμενος τὸν ἀδελφεὸν Μασίστην· τὠυτὸ δὲ τοῦτο εἶχε
καὶ τὴν γυναῖκα· εὖ γὰρ ἐπίστατο βίης οὐ τευξομένη·
ἐνθαῦτα δὴ Ξέρξης ἐργόμενος τῶν ἄλλων πρήσσει τὸν γάμον
τοῦτον τῷ παιδὶ τῷ ἑωυτοῦ Δαρείῳ, θυγατέρα τῆς γυναικὸς
ταύτης καὶ Μασίστεω, δοκέων αὐτὴν μᾶλλον λάμψεσθαι ἢν 10
ταῦτα ποιήσῃ· ἁρμόσας δὲ καὶ τὰ νομιζόμενα ποιήσας
ἀπήλαυνε ἐς Σοῦσα· ἐπεὶ δὲ ἐκεῖ τε ἀπίκετο καὶ ἠγάγετο ἐς

---

2 ἀθηναίων BCRSVz   3 δὴ RS(V): δὲ ‖ ἄρα del. Cobet, Holder,
van H. ‖ ἔρα β: 'an ἠράσθη ?' Stein   5 βίῃ Stein²: βίην ‖ προσέφερε β, Holder, van H.   6 προμνθεόμενος Marc. ‖ ἀδελφὸν Marc.
Priscian 18. 283: τοῦ ἀδελφεοῦ van H. ‖ Μασίστην del. van H. ‖ ταυτὸ C
‖ ἔχε z: 'an ἔσχε ?' Stein¹   7 εὖ τε γὰρ β, Holder ‖ ἠπίστατο Marc. ‖
τεξομένη B¹   8 πρήσει C   10 λάμψασθαι C   12 ἐκεῖ τε αC:
ἐκεῖσε β etc.: ἐκεῖσέ τε van H., Holder

---

summer, in Sardes, presumably awaiting
the issue of the campaign in Greece.
Aischylos (*Persai*) makes Xerxes return
direct from Athens to Susa.

3. φυγών accepts the representation
of the king's return as a φυγή.

τότε δή: at the time of the battle
of Mykale ; or perhaps more generally
throughout the period from his return to
the battle of Mykale.

ἄρα: cp. c. 104. 8 *supra*. ἄρα ἤρα
looks unfortunate. Stein compares the
position of ἄρα here and in c. 9 *supra*
and in 4. 134 (i.e. construes it with ἐν
τῇσι Σάρδισι ἐών ?).

τῆς Μασίστεω γυναικός: that this
lady is anonymous in the story does not
make for its credit. Was she possibly,
like her daughter, an Ἀρταΰντη, and
possibly again a relative, a sister, of
the Artayntes who has figured above ?
Masistes apparently throughout has only
one wife. She had not accompanied her
lord on the march to Greece (cp. 7. 187),
but had probably come down to meet
him on his return to Sardes with Xerxes.

5. προσπέμποντι: sc. ἀγγέλους. The
subject of ἐδύνατο may be ἡ γυνή (van H.
takes it to be τὸ ἐπεθύμει).

6. προμηθεόμενος, 'out of respect
for . .'; a genitive might be expected.

εἶχε, 'supported,' 'upheld.'

7. εὖ γάρ κτλ., 'for she well knew
that violence would not be employed
against her.'

8. ἐργόμενος is middle ; cp. 7. 197. 21
supra.

τὸν γάμον τοῦτον refers to the
following θυγατέρα. The verb πρήσσει
has, perhaps, a suggestion of intrigue :
he indeed was hoping still to get hold of
the mother (λάμψεσθαι=λήψεσθαι : cp.
Smyth, *Ionic* § 130, p. 136).

9. Δαρείῳ: this Dareios was the
eldest son, and on the assassination of
his father in 465 B.C. was falsely accused
of the crime, and executed by his
youngest brother Artaxerxes ; Ktesias,
Pers. 29 ; Gilmore, p. 158 f.   Had all
this happened when this story was first
contrived ?

12. ἐς Σοῦσα: the scene shifts to the
capital ; cp. 8. 99, 7. 151 *supra*, and 5.
54.

ἠγάγετο: the middle is generally
used of the bridegroom, here of the
father-in-law. This word marks the
actual marriage ; the practices (πρήσσει)
and the performances of the usual rites (τὰ
νομιζόμενα ποιήσας), at Sardes previously,
only amounted to a betrothal (ἁρμόσας).
The crown-prince lives apparently in his
father's palace, even after his marriage :
is this improbable ?

ἑωυτοῦ Δαρείῳ τὴν γυναῖκα, οὕτω δὴ τῆς Μασίστεω μὲν
γυναικὸς ἐπέπαυτο, ὃ δὲ διαμειψάμενος ἦρά τε καὶ ἐτύγχανε
15 τῆς Δαρείου μὲν γυναικὸς Μασίστεω δὲ θυγατρός· οὔνομα δὲ
109 τῇ γυναικὶ ταύτῃ ἦν Ἀρταΰντη. χρόνου δὲ προϊόντος
ἀνάπυστα γίνεται τρόπῳ τοιῷδε. ἐξυφήνασα Ἄμηστρις ἡ
Ξέρξεω γυνὴ φᾶρος μέγα τε καὶ ποικίλον καὶ θέης ἄξιον
διδοῖ Ξέρξῃ. ὃ δὲ ἡσθεὶς περιβάλλεταί τε καὶ ἔρχεται παρὰ
5 τὴν Ἀρταΰντην. ἡσθεὶς δὲ καὶ ταύτῃ ἐκέλευσε αὐτὴν αἰτῆσαι
ὅ τι βούλεταί οἱ γενέσθαι ἀντὶ τῶν αὐτῷ ὑπουργημένων·
πάντα γὰρ τεύξεσθαι αἰτήσασαν· τῇ δὲ κακῶς γὰρ ἔδεε πανοικίῃ γενέσθαι, πρὸς ταῦτα εἶπε Ξέρξῃ "δώσεις μοι τὸ ἄν σε
αἰτήσω;" ὃ δὲ πᾶν μᾶλλον δοκέων κείνην αἰτῆσαι ὑπισχνέετο

14 <ἐρῶν> ἐπέπαυτο? van H.　　15 μὲν om. Marc. || μασίστεωι B
109. 2 ἐξυφήνασα Gaisford　　3 φᾶρος BR Marc. z || ποικίλῳ Marc.
4 πρὸς Ask.　　5 ταύτῃ: αὐτὴ B || ἐκέλευε Iacobitz　　6 ὃ βού-
λεται R || οἱ om. aC Marc. (S) || οἱ . . ὑπουργημένων om. S(Gaisf.) || ὑποργη-
μένων RV　　7 αἰτήσασα Marc.　　8 εἶπαι z || ἐάν B　　9 πάντα
B: πᾶν <ἄν> Madvig || ἐκείνην Sz || αἰτήσεσθαι B: αἰτήσειν Cobet, van H.
|| ὑπισχνέεται B: ὑπισχνεῖτο van H.

13. οὕτω δὴ . . ἐπέπαυτο: this pluperfect is plainly rhetorical, and not
used of strict temporal sequence. ὃ δέ:
the subject is re-expressed, and the δέ
attached, for the sake of emphasis; cp.
c. 106. 7 supra.
14. διαμειψάμενος ἦρα, 'transferred
his affections': perhaps the δια- (in
comp.) marks the completeness of the
change, ἦρά τε καὶ ἐτύγχανε the
rapidity of his success. For τυγχάνειν
cp. 5. 23 (ἔτυχε), and τευξομένη supra,
τεύξεσθαι c. 109 infra.
16. Ἀρταΰντη: the mere identity of
name with Artayntes, c. 107 supra, is
not, of course, sufficient to prove any
connexion between the house of Masistes
and that of his colleague and foeman;
but the name is of ill-omen for the house
anyway—and perhaps for that reason
the daughter of Masistes bears it.
109. 1. χρόνου δὲ προϊόντος: an
interval occurs. ἀνάπυστα γίνεται: cp.
c. 64 ἔδεε δὲ ὡς ἔοικε ἀνάπυστα γενόμενα
ταῦτα καταπαῦσαι Δημάρητον τῆς βασιληίης. The moment of 'discovery' is
fateful.
2. Ἄμηστρις ἡ Ξέρξεω γυνή: she
hardly requires the description after 7.
61, 114 supra; but this passage is, of
course, independent of those, the second,
indeed, of which is of later composition

than this (and the former, perhaps, a
gloss).
3. φᾶρος . . θέης ἄξιον: the hardiest
advocate of the extension of Hdt.'s
autopsy, and first-hand authority in
general, will hardly venture to argue
from this phrase that Hdt. had actually
seen this plaid or pall: why then press
the phrase elsewhere? Cp. cc. 25, 70
supra.
4. ἡσθεὶς . . ἡσθείς: such are a
despot's 'pleasures'! Cp. note to c.
108 supra. There is some humour,
perhaps, in the repetition.
6. ἀντὶ τῶν αὐτῷ ὑπουργημένων, 'in
return for her services to him'; cp.
ὑπουργέειν 8. 110, χρηστὰ ὑπουργέειν 8.
143, ὑπουργήσειν 7. 38 (of the despot
himself).
7. τεύξεσθαι is absolute ('shall obtain
her request'). πάντα with αἰτήσασαν,
'whatever she asked,' even if she asked
everything.
τῇ δὲ κακῶς γὰρ ἔδεε πανοικίῃ
γενέσθαι: the δέ is of course misplaced
(unless we were to read ἢ δέ). πανοικίῃ
7. 39. ἔδεε κακῶς γενέσθαι is the coldest
of fatalistic formulae; cp. 5. 33. It does
not clearly appear what the fate of this
woman was.
9. πᾶν μᾶλλον δοκέων κτλ.: cp. 7.
38 supra.

καὶ ὤμοσε. ἡ δὲ ὡς ὤμοσε ἀδεῶς αἰτέει τὸ φᾶρος. Ξέρξης 10
δὲ παντοῖος ἐγίνετο οὐ βουλόμενος δοῦναι, κατ' ἄλλο μὲν
οὐδέν, φοβεόμενος δὲ Ἄμηστριν, μὴ καὶ πρὶν κατεικαζούσῃ
τὰ γινόμενα οὕτω ἐπευρεθῇ πρήσσων· ἀλλὰ πόλις τε ἐδίδου
καὶ χρυσὸν ἄπλετον καὶ στρατόν, τοῦ ἔμελλε οὐδεὶς ἄρξειν
ἀλλ' ἡ ἐκείνη. Περσικὸν δὲ κάρτα ὁ στρατὸς δῶρον. ἀλλ' 15
οὐ γὰρ ἔπειθε, διδοῖ τὸ φᾶρος, ἡ δὲ περιχαρὴς ἐοῦσα τῷ
δώρῳ ἐφόρεέ τε καὶ ἀγάλλετο. καὶ ἡ Ἄμηστρις πυνθάνεταί 110
μιν ἔχουσαν· μαθοῦσα δὲ τὸ ποιεύμενον τῇ μὲν γυναικὶ ταύτῃ
οὐκ εἶχε ἔγκοτον, ἡ δὲ ἐλπίζουσα τὴν μητέρα αὐτῆς εἶναι
αἰτίην καὶ ταῦτα ἐκείνην πρήσσειν, τῇ Μασίστεω γυναικὶ
ἐβούλευε ὄλεθρον. φυλάξασα δὲ τὸν ἄνδρα τὸν ἑωυτῆς 5

10 ὄμοσε **a** (bis ?) ‖ φάρος BR Marc. z   11 ἐγένετο CPz   12
φοβούμενος **B** ‖ δὲ om. C ‖ ἄμιστριν C ‖ καὶ om. **B** ‖ κατεικαζούσῃ z, Stein,
van H. : κατεικαζούσης Schweighaeuser : κατεικάζουσα Marc. ‖ ἐπορεύθη BC ‖ πόλεις Cd   13 γενόμενα
Marc. ‖ ἐπορεύθη BC ‖ πόλεις Cd   15 ὁ στρατὸς κάρτα **B** : ὁ στρατὸς
(ante κάρτα) del. van H.   16 φάρος R Marc. z   17 ἐγάλλετο R :
ἠγάλλετο P Marc. z   110. 2 ἔχουσα C ‖ ταύτῃ : αὐτῇ **B**   3 ἔχε z

10. ἀδεῶς, 'confidently,' sure of the result.

11. παντοῖος ἐγίνετο : cp. 7. 10. 30.

13. ἐπευρεθῇ : his detection would follow upon (ἐπ-) her previous (πρὶν) suspicions, strong (κατ-) suspicions : the dative participle κατεικαζούσῃ is observable : a dat. of the agent, instead of ὑπό with genitive ; cp. Madvig § 38 g (p. 37) —where the instances leave much to be desired.

πρήσσων refers here to decided malpractices ! Cp. c. 108.

πόλις : cp. the assignment of the city of Anthylla to the wife of the Satrap of Egypt for 'shoe-money,' 2. 98 ; the assignations to Themistokles, Thuc. 1. 138. 5, etc.

ἐδίδου, 'offered,' kept offering, a strong imperf. ; cp. 8. 114 supra.

14. ἄπλετον : a standing epithet of χρυσός ; cp. 1. 14, 50, 215, 3. 106 (also with οἰμωγή 6. 58, 8. 99, c. 24 supra, ὕδωρ 8. 12, ἅλες 4. 53)—'gold beyond the dreams of avarice,' gold galore.

στρατόν seems the least likely to appeal to a lady : what would she do with it ? Perhaps it is only introduced for the sake of the next learned remark. Or were Persian princesses too titular colonels at times ?

16. διδοῖ, 'is giving,' 'gives,' seems a little weak after the ἐδίδου just above :

a perfect or pluperfect here would do nicely.

110. 1. πυνθάνεται : by hearsay.

2. μαθοῦσα : by native wit ; she did not, however, quite get at the facts.

τὸ ποιεύμενον : cp. c. 22 supra.

τῇ μὲν . . οὐκ εἶχε ἔγκοτον : she did not (presumably) suspect the intrigue between Xerxes and Artaynta (the younger), their son's bride, but thought perhaps that his visits to the daughter covered an intrigue with the mother, and that the mother had bestowed the φᾶρος on the daughter. She therefore planned the destruction of the wife of Masistes. The curtain descends upon the third act of this tragedy.

3. ἔγκοτον : 8. 29 supra.

ἡ δέ, 'but she . .' ; the resumed subject annexes the particle, cp. c. 109. 13 supra.

ἐλπίζουσα : rather 'believing' than 'hoping,' cp. Index, sub v.

4. ταῦτα ἐκείνην πρήσσειν, 'that she was at the bottom of the whole business' —'intrigue.' The ἐκείνην is no more, strictly speaking, necessary than the ἡ just before, but its introduction makes for emphasis and lucidity. πρήσσειν as above.

5. φυλάξασα δὲ . . προτιθέμενον, 'she waited her own husband's holding a royal feast,' i.e. a royal feast held by her own husband Xerxes. φυλάσσειν, cp.

Ξέρξην βασιλήιον δεῖπνον προτιθέμενον· τοῦτο δὲ τὸ δεῖπνον
παρασκευάζεται ἅπαξ τοῦ ἐνιαυτοῦ ἡμέρῃ τῇ ἐγένετο <ὁ>
βασιλεύς· οὔνομα δὲ τῷ δείπνῳ τούτῳ περσιστὶ μὲν τυκτά,
κατὰ δὲ τὴν Ἑλλήνων γλῶσσαν τέλειον· τότε καὶ τὴν
10 κεφαλὴν σμᾶται μοῦνον βασιλεὺς καὶ Πέρσας δωρέεται.
ταύτην δὴ τὴν ἡμέρην φυλάξασα ἡ Ἄμηστρις χρηίζει τοῦ
Ξέρξεω δοθῆναί οἱ τὴν Μασίστεω γυναῖκα. ὁ δὲ δεινόν τε
καὶ ἀνάρσιον ἐποιέετο τοῦτο μὲν ἀδελφεοῦ γυναῖκα παρα-
δοῦναι, τοῦτο δὲ ἀναιτίην ἐοῦσαν τοῦ πρήγματος τούτου·
111 συνῆκε γὰρ τοῦ εἵνεκεν ἐδέετο. τέλος μέντοι ἐκείνης τε
λιπαρεούσης καὶ ὑπὸ τοῦ νόμου ἐξεργόμενος, ὅτι ἀτυχῆσαι
τὸν χρηίζοντα οὔ σφι δυνατόν ἐστι βασιληίου δείπνου προ-

---

7 ἐν ἡμέρῃ β, Holder, van H. ‖ ἐγίνετο A ‖ ὁ βασιλεύς β : articulum
om. Stein, Holder, van H.　　8 τικτά S　　9 τὴν om. β ‖ τέλειον :
τέλεον Holder, van H. ‖ ('τὴν om. R' Stein¹ ?)　　10 τοὺς πέρσας S :
Πέρσαις z　　11 χρηίζει P : χρήζει Marc. : χρήξει β (ap. Holder :
δέεται S ap. Gaisf.) : χρήζει z　　15 ἕνεκεν Marc.　　111. 1 μέντοι
γε β, Holder ‖ κείνης C ‖ τε om. C　　3 χρηίζοντα P : χρήζοντα R(β ?)
Marc. : χρήζοντα z, Gaisford

---

1. 48 φυλάξας τὴν κυρίην τῶν ἡμερέων.
δεῖπνον προτίθεσθαι, of the king ; cp.
ξείνια προθεῖναι 7. 29.
7. τῇ ἐγένετο <ὁ> βασιλεύς, 'on the
king's birthday' : a strong ἐγένετο, cp.
1. 133 τῇ ἕκαστος ἐγένετο. (Not a mere
Accession celebration, on the day when he
became king !) <ὁ> βασιλεύς, sc. ὁ ἀεὶ β.
1. 133 illustrates the importance of birthday feasts among the Persians, who were
no pessimists (like Thrakians, cp. 5. 4).
8. τυκτά : tachi ; not from τυκτός.
The interesting philological note, even if
from Hdt.'s own pen, will not convince
any one that Hdt. was deeply versed in
Persian ; cp. 8. 85 supra.
9. τὴν κεφαλὴν σμᾶται : cp. 4. 73
σμησάμενοι τὰς κεφαλάς (ἐκσμᾶν 3. 148).
The meaning here must be that on his
birthday and on his birthday alone (τότε
μοῦνον) the king appears without his
tiara, or crown (Stein), his hair glisten-
ing with the oil of gladness.
12. δεινόν τε καὶ ἀνάρσιον ἐποιέετο,
'thought it shocking and monstrous'
(ἀνάρσιον c. 37 supra), for two reasons :
τοῦτο μέν, to hand over his brother's
wife to certain torture and death (he
knew what was in store for her) ; τοῦτο
δέ, she being innocent in the whole affair.

15. συνῆκε γὰρ τοῦ εἵνεκεν ἐδέετο.
'he knew with what object she was
making the request of him.' There had
probably been previous words on the
subject between Amestris and Xerxes.
συνῆκα is the Attic form (Ep. ξυνέηκα).
ἐδέετο, cp. 8. 3.
111. 2. λιπαρεούσης : c. 45 supra.
ὑπὸ τοῦ νόμου ἐξεργόμενος : cp.
ἀναγκαίῃ ἐξέργομαι 7. 96, 139 supra. As
to the νόμος, Xerxes was not equal to the
occasion, or his sages and councillors
would have come to the rescue ; cp. the
Response of the Royal Justices 3. 31,
τῷ βασιλεύοντι Περσέων ἐξεῖναι ποιέειν τὸ
ἂν βούληται. The two cases are not,
indeed, precisely the same ; but the
moral is that the king was not bound
by any law. Besides, τὸν χρηίζοντα
(masc.) might have given them a loop-
hole !
ἀτυχῆσαι, 'to fail' ; the opposite
of τυχεῖν, cp. c. 108 supra.
3. σφι : sc. τοῖσι Πέρσῃσι.
δυνατόν : fas, 7. 149 supra. 'O
Kate, nice customs curtsy to great kings'
(Henry V. v. ii. 293). But Custom
still was king o' the king of kings ! Cp.
3. 38.

κειμένου, κάρτα δὴ ἀέκων κατανεύει, καὶ παραδοὺς ποιέει
ὧδε· τὴν μὲν κελεύει ποιέειν τὰ βούλεται, ὁ δὲ μεταπεμψά- 5
μενος τὸν ἀδελφεὸν λέγει τάδε. "Μασίστα, σὺ εἶς Δαρείου
τε παῖς καὶ ἐμὸς ἀδελφεός, πρὸς δ' ἔτι τούτοισι καὶ εἶς ἀνὴρ
ἀγαθός· γυναικὶ δὴ ταύτῃ τῇ νῦν συνοικέεις μὴ συνοίκεε,
ἀλλά τοι ἀντ' αὐτῆς ἐγὼ δίδωμι θυγατέρα τὴν ἐμήν. ταύτῃ
συνοίκεε· τὴν δὲ νῦν ἔχεις, οὐ γὰρ δοκέει ἐμοί, μὴ ἔχε 10
γυναῖκα." ὁ δὲ Μασίστης ἀποθωμάσας τὰ λεγόμενα λέγει
τάδε. "ὦ δέσποτα, τίνα μοι λόγον λέγεις ἄχρηστον, κελεύων
[μοι] γυναῖκα, ἐκ τῆς μοι παῖδές τε νεηνίαι εἰσὶ καὶ θυγατέρες,
τῶν καὶ σὺ μίαν τῷ παιδὶ τῷ σεωυτοῦ ἠγάγεο γυναῖκα, αὐτή
τέ μοι κατὰ νόον τυγχάνει κάρτα ἐοῦσα· ταύτην με κελεύεις 15
μετέντα θυγατέρα τὴν σὴν γῆμαι; ἐγὼ δὲ βασιλεῦ μεγάλα
μὲν ποιεῦμαι ἀξιεύμενος θυγατρὸς τῆς σῆς, ποιήσω μέντοι

---

5 διδε P ‖ μεταμειψάμενος Marc.   6 σὺ <γὰρ> coni. Stein(2),
recep. van H.   8 δὲ Β Marc. z ‖ νυν ΑΒ   9 ἀλλά . . συνοίκεε
om. R ‖ θυγατέρα δίδωμι S   10 δοκέεις R ‖ μοι Β ‖ μήκετι? van H.
11 ἀποθωνμάσας Pz, Stein¹   12 λόγον μοι A   13 μοι αCPz etc.
Stein¹: με Β, Stein², Holder, van H.: secl. Stein³ ‖ τε post νεηνίαι ΒPz,
Stein¹, Holder ‖ εἰσὶ τρεῖς z   14 καὶ om. Β ‖ μία R(Β ?): μίην z ‖
τῷ poster. l. om. C Marc. ‖ ἠγάγετο R(Β ?): ἤγαγες Marc. ‖ αὕτη CPz
15 τυγχάνει κατὰ νόον C ‖ με om. CP: μὲν R(Β ?)   16 μετέντα Β:
μεθέντα ‖ τὴν om. Β ‖ σὴν: σεωυτοῦ z, van H. ‖ μέγα Β, Holder, van H.
17 ἀξόμενος Marc.

---

4. κατανεύει, frequent in Homer, but
rare in prose (Plato, Rep. 350 E, seems
to use the word literally. Here it may
be used metaphorically, 'assents').

ποιέει ὧδε . . ὁ δέ: the curtain
rises upon the last act of the tragedy;
the desperate effort of Xerxes to make
things right with his brother, the bar-
barities of Amestris in her revenge, the
splendid crime of Masistes, and the doom
that just anticipates his treasonable
success. ὁ δέ, cp. c. 108. 13 supra.

5. ποιέειν after ποιέει is rather thin.

6. Δαρείου: i.e. the son of Hystaspes.
(Atossa is not mentioned, but cp. 7. 82.)

7. εἶς ἀνὴρ ἀγαθός: more, perhaps,
than he could say for all his brothers.
Masistes could scarcely have returned
the compliment with truth.

9. δίδωμι θυγατέρα τὴν ἐμήν, 'I offer
you my daughter,' in marriage; she is,
therefore, niece to Masistes. Such near
marriages were not illegal even in Sparta
(cp. 7. 239 supra), much less in poly-
gamous Persia.

10. ἔχεις· ἔχε, 'have to wife'; cp. 7.
61. 13.
δοκέει, 'seems good.'

11. ἀποθωμάσας, 'when he had recovered from his astonishment'; cp. 8.
65 supra.

12. ἄχρηστον: a meiosis, 'injurious,'
inexpedient.

14. αὕτη τέ μοι κατὰ νόον . . ἐοῦσα: cp.
the story of Anaxandridas 5. 39, who
was allowed to retain his first wife.
Masistes might be puzzled in Persia to
know why marrying the king's daughter
should involve putting away his first
wife (and might have suspected Xerxes
of too personal an interest in the matter);
but even in the Harem there is a chief
wife or sultana, and this fact is perhaps
taken for granted in the story.

16. γῆμαι, of the bridegroom (γήμα-
σθαι, of the bride; e.g. 4. 117).

μεγάλα μὲν ποιεῦμαι, 'account it
greatness,' 'am highly honoured'; the
plural is observable, cp. 1. 119 μεγάλα
ποιησάμενος.

τούτων οὐδέτερα. σὺ δὲ μηδαμῶς βιῶ πρήγματος τοιοῦδε
δεόμενος· ἀλλὰ τῇ τε σῇ θυγατρὶ ἀνὴρ ἄλλος φανήσεται
20 ἐμεῦ οὐδὲν ἧσσων, ἐμέ τε ἔα γυναικὶ τῇ ἐμῇ συνοικέειν." ὁ
μὲν δὴ τοιούτοισι ἀμείβεται, Ξέρξης δὲ θυμωθεὶς λέγει τάδε.
"οὕτω τοι, Μασίστα, πέπρηκται· οὔτε γὰρ ἄν τοι δοίην
θυγατέρα τὴν ἐμὴν γῆμαι, οὔτε ἐκείνῃ πλεῦνα χρόνον συνοι-
κήσεις, ὡς μάθῃς τὰ διδόμενα δέκεσθαι." ὁ δὲ ὡς ταῦτα
25 ἤκουσε, εἴπας τοσόνδε ἐχώρεε ἔξω "δέσποτα, οὐ δή κού με
112 ἀπώλεσας;" ἐν δὲ τούτῳ τῷ διὰ μέσου χρόνῳ, ἐν τῷ Ξέρξης
τῷ ἀδελφεῷ διελέγετο, ἡ Ἄμηστρις μεταπεμψαμένη τοὺς
δορυφόρους τοῦ Ξέρξεω διαλυμαίνεται τὴν γυναῖκα τοῦ
Μασίστεω· τούς τε μαζοὺς ἀποταμοῦσα κυσὶ προέβαλε καὶ

---

18 τουτέων z ‖ οὐδέτερον B ‖ τοιούτου R(S ?)V   20 ἧσσω z : ἔσσων
Schaefer, van H. ‖ συνοικεῖν R(S)V, van H.   21 τούτοισιν ἀμείβετο B
22 οὕτω τοι : οὕτω δή τοι z ‖ δοίην ἔτι R(S ?)V, Holder, van H. : δώιην a :
δώην CP Marc.   23 γῆμαι : γυναῖκα B, Holder, van H. ‖ ἔτι πλεῦνα B :
24 ὡς pr. l. om. Marc. ‖ ἤκουσε ταῦτα B   25 κώ Schaefer, van H.
26 ἀπώλεσας ; Stein : volgo punctum ponitur   112. 1 ἐν δ B   2
ἀδελφῶ Marc. ‖ ἄμηστρις Ask. hic et alibi   3 τοῦ : τοὺς Krueger ‖ τοῦ :
τὴν Ba, Holder, van H.   4 μασίστεωι B ‖ μαστοὺς B

---

18. μηδαμῶς βιῶ . . δεόμενος, 'do not
press (insist on) thy request.'

22. πέπρηκται : ita sane (οὕτω) actum
est de te (Baehr) ; igitur hoc profecisti
(Schweighaeuser) ; deine Sache steht jetzt
so (Stein, taking οὕτω to refer to what
follows).

24. ὡς μάθῃς τὰ διδόμενα δέκεσθαι,
'that you may learn to accept what is
offered to you.' This must be almost
a proverbial expression ; cp. 8. 26, 137
supra.

25. εἴπας τοσόνδε ἐχώρεε ἔξω, 'all he
said before going out was . .'

οὐ δή κού με ἀπώλεσας; 'can it be
thou hast undone me?' The v.l. κω
gives a good sense : nondum sane me
perdidisti (Baehr) ; 'thou hast not yet
taken my life' (Rawlinson), i.e. there is
still fight left in me ; I am not at the
end of my resources (of course with a
period, not an interrogative) ; this well
accords with the sequel.

112. 1. ἐν δὲ τούτῳ κτλ. : the second
pitiless scene in this act of the tragedy :
non tamen intus | digna geri promes in
scaenam, multaque tolles | ex oculis, quae
mox narret facundia praesens (Hor. de
A. p. 182 ff.). What a meeting between

the faithful wife and her fond husband !
What vows of vengeance by the stalwart
sons, what tears and lamentation of the
daughters, over the mother's dying bed !
What self-reproaches of the guilty one
before her self-inflicted end ! It is in
a way strange that no Greek playwright
ever utilized the material lying to his
hand in the pages of Hdt.

3. διαλυμαίνεται : the simple verb
λυμαίνεσθαι is common, cp. 8. 28 supra ;
the prep., of course, strengthens it. The
perfect part. infra is passive.

4. τούς τε μαζούς : cp. 4. 202. If the
ἀποταμοῦσα is taken to extend down as
far as χείλεα, and the ἐκταμοῦσα as
applying only to γλῶσσαν, there is
grammatically an asyndeton ; probably
the καί after προέβαλε connects that verb
with ἀποπέμπει and ἐκταμοῦσα 'governs'
ῥῖνα, ὦτα, χείλεα as well as γλῶσσαν.
But the sentence is unsightly from every
point of view. It sounds barbarous,
savage, unhellenic enough ; but it curiously resembles the threat of Antinoos
to Iros, Od. 18. 84 ff. πέμψω σ' ἠπει-
ρόνδε, βαλὼν ἐν νηὶ μελαίνῃ, | εἰς Ἔχετον
βασιλῆα, βροτῶν δηλήμονα πάντων, ὅς κ'
ἀπὸ ῥῖνα τάμῃσι καὶ οὔατα νηλέι χαλκῷ, |
μήδεά τ' ἐξερύσας δώῃ κυσὶν ὠμὰ δάσασθαι.

ῥῖνα καὶ ὦτα καὶ χείλεα καὶ γλῶσσαν ἐκταμοῦσα ἐς οἰκόν 5
μιν ἀποπέμπει διαλελυμασμένην. ὁ δὲ Μασίστης οὐδέν κω 113
ἀκηκοὼς τούτων, ἐλπόμενος δέ τί οἱ κακὸν εἶναι, ἐσπίπτει
δρόμῳ ἐς τὰ οἰκία. ἰδὼν δὲ διεφθαρμένην τὴν γυναῖκα, αὐτίκα
μετὰ ταῦτα συμβουλευσάμενος τοῖσι παισὶ ἐπορεύετο ἐς
Βάκτρα σύν τε τοῖσι ἑωυτοῦ υἱοῖσι καὶ δή κου τισὶ καὶ 5
ἄλλοισι ὡς ἀποστήσων νομὸν τὸν Βάκτριον καὶ ποιήσων τὰ
μέγιστα κακῶν βασιλέα· τά περ ἂν καὶ ἐγένετο, ὡς ἐμοὶ

6 μιν om. Marc.   113. 1 κω om. Marc.   2 δέ τί : δ' ἔτι
R(β) ‖ οἱ R   5 βάκτραν C ‖ που Marc.   6 νόμον CR Marc.
7 κακὸν Marc. ‖ βασιλῆα z

113. 2. ἀκηκοὼς . . ἐλπόμενος: the
former participle is clearly stronger
than ἀκούσας, the latter is clearly not
'hoping.'
3. διεφθαρμένην, 'utterly ruined' (but
not necessarily 'dead'); cp. 1. 34
οὕτερος μὲν διέφθαρτο, ἦν γὰρ δὴ κωφός,
38 τὸν γὰρ δὴ ἕτερον διεφθαρμένον τὴν
ἀκοὴν οὐκ εἶναί μοι λογίζομαι. But
obviously the miserable woman could
not long survive such treatment.
αὐτίκα μετὰ ταῦτα introduces the
last scene (shifted to Baktria), where,
after conspiring with his sons, Masistes
raises the flag of revolt in his satrapy,
and falls, his brave boys fighting
round him, at the head of an army of
devoted adherents, in battle against the
all too loyal subjects of the feeble tyrant.
5. Βάκτρα, the city of Balkh, capital
of the Βάκτριος νομός, or Baktrian satrapy
(3. 93), of which he was governor (ὕπαρχος
τῶν Βακτρίων = Βακτριανῶν l.c.). The
city is mentioned 6. 9 (as a sort of
ultima Thule of the Persian Empire
from the Greek point of view; but cp.
4. 204). On the Baktrians cp. 7. 64
supra, where the Σάκαι are associated with
them, as here.
7. τά περ ἂν καὶ ἐγένετο, but did
not, for Xerxes took measures to crush
him. Hdt. implies that Masistes did
not reach Baktra, or the Baktrian land,
but was overtaken on the way thither,
and came to an end. The mention of
his army, however (καὶ τὴν στρατιὴν τὴν
ἐκείνου), seems hardly consistent with
that view, which is also not in itself
probable; Masistes and his sons would
have reached Baktria long before the
army collected and sent against them by
Xerxes. Hdt. is led into the inconsistency and error apparently by his own

notion (ὡς ἐμοὶ δοκέω) that, if Masistes
had once succeeded in raising a revolt
in Baktria, he would have wrought the
king no end of woe; in other words, the
ease with which Masistes was suppressed
convinced Hdt. that he had not actually
raised a rebellion in Baktria, and as the
Baktrians were devoted to Masistes, he
cannot have reached Balkh, or he would
have raised a rebellion.
Probably Masistes, as satrap of Baktria,
did raise the province, and fell fighting
at the head of the eastern levies of the
empire. The gruesome story just related
was an attempt to explain the cause of
the revolt in terms acceptable to Hellenic
romance. There may have been a set of
more political factors at work. There
was a constant possibility in the Achaimenid Empire of a rupture between the
eastern and western halves, the Iranian
highland, and the older centres and areas
of secular civilization. The weakness of
Xerxes, and the ignominious failure of
the European expedition, were calculated
to provoke disloyalty. Masistes, his
brother, was but re-enacting the rôle of
Bardiya, the son of Kyros the Great;
Xerxes, or his servants, succeeded, as
Kambyses, or again as Dareios had succeeded, in reasserting the unity of the
empire. Masistes, who like Xerxes himself united both strains in the Achaimenid pedigree (cp. 7. 11 supra), was a
very formidable Pretender, and a far
better man evidently than his brother.
Rawlinson (ad l.) seems to underestimate
the possibilities of a Baktrian secession,
or Home-rule movement, though he is
justified in correcting the excesses of
Blakesley in the other direction. The
loyalty of the Baktrians to Dareios and
their general loyalty to the Achaimenid

δοκέειν, εἴ περ ἔφθη ἀναβὰς ἐς τοὺς Βακτρίους καὶ τοὺς
Σάκας· καὶ γὰρ ἔστεργόν μιν καὶ ἦν ὕπαρχος τῶν Βακτρίων,
10 ἀλλὰ γὰρ Ξέρξης πυθόμενος ταῦτα ἐκεῖνον πρήσσοντα,
πέμψας ἐπ᾽ αὐτὸν στρατιὴν ἐν τῇ ὁδῷ κατέκτεινε αὐτόν τε
ἐκεῖνον καὶ τοὺς παῖδας αὐτοῦ καὶ τὴν στρατιὴν τὴν ἐκείνου.
κατὰ μὲν τὸν ἔρωτα τὸν Ξέρξεω καὶ τὸν Μασίστεω θάνατον
τοσαῦτα ἐγένετο.

114　Οἱ δὲ ἐκ Μυκάλης ὁρμηθέντες Ἕλληνες ἐπ᾽ Ἑλλησπόντου
πρῶτον μὲν περὶ Λεκτὸν ὅρμεον, ὑπὸ ἀνέμων ἀπολαμφθέντες,
ἐνθεῦτεν δὲ ἀπίκοντο ἐς Ἄβυδον καὶ τὰς γεφύρας εὗρον δια-
λελυμένας, τὰς ἐδόκεον εὑρήσειν ἔτι ἐντεταμένας, καὶ τουτέων
5 οὐκ ἥκιστα εἵνεκεν ἐς τὸν Ἑλλήσποντον ἀπίκοντο. τοῖσι μέν
νυν ἀμφὶ Λευτυχίδην Πελοποννησίοισι ἔδοξε ἀποπλέειν ἐς τὴν

---

8 δοκέει z : δοκεῖ van H.　　9 τέ μιν Β Marc. z, Holder, van H.　　11
κτείνει Β : κατέκτειναν z　　12 πέδας z || ωὐτοῦ z　　114. 1 ἐπὶ Marc.
2 ὅρμεον αSV : ὥρμεον || ὑπὸ ἀνέμων om. Marc.　　4 τουτέων z, Stein³ :
τούτων　　5 ἕνεκα z　　6 λευτυχίδεα Β Marc. z

House (based upon the *argumentum a
silentio*) might not prevent their prefer-
ring a Masistes to a Xerxes. The failure of
Masistes in the end may have been due to
the fact that the flower of the Baktrians
had been culled by Mardonios (cp. 8.
118 *supra*), and their bones were now
enriching the plain of Boiotia. The
exact date of Masistes' attempt is
problematic ; but it falls, no doubt, into
the *Pentekontaëteris*.

114. 1. ἐκ Μυκάλης : in c. 106 *supra*
the Greeks have been conveyed from
Mykale back to Samos, and have started
from Samos for the Hellespont. Moreover, it was only at Samos (according
to that passage) that they had decided
on their policy.

ὁρμηθέντες, of physical motion
(cp. 7. 37. 6, 7).

2. Λεκτόν : the position of Lekton is
more nearly indicated by Thucydides
8. 101. 3. It is the SW. corner of the
Troad, the extreme projection of Mount
Ida (as is implied even in Homer, *Il.* 14.
283-4), now Cape Baba, or Sta. Maria—
the most westerly point of the continent
of Asia.

ὅρμεον, though from another verb,
is not very happy in juxtaposition. Cp.
ὅρμεον . . ὁρμώμενοι 7. 22. 3, 4.

ἀπολαμφθέντες, *intercepti* (Valla) ;
cp. 2. 115. Wesseling compares Livy
37. 37 Eumenes rex, conatus primo

ab Hellesponto reducere classem in
hiberna Elaeam, adversis deinde ventis
quum aliquot diebus superare Lecton
promontorium non potuisset, in terram
egressus . . in castra Romana (ad caput
Caici amnis) cum parva manu contendit.
But Eumenes (in 190 B.C.) was going
from the Hellespont to the Caicus ; the
Greeks in 479 B.C. from Samos to the
Hellespont. Violent north, or west,
winds would have held them up :
would wind from any quarter but the
south have hindered Eumenes? (Perhaps
the west? {γεφύρου τε καὶ νότου εἵνεκα 7.
36 *supra.*)

3. Ἄβυδον : cp. 8. 130, etc. As to
the bridges, and the pol'cy of going to
the Hellespont, cp. c. 106 *supra.*

6. ἔδοξε, 'Leotychidas and his Peloponnesian following decided . .' ἀμφί, cp.
c. 69 *supra* ; with ἔδοξε contr. ἐδόκεε
c. 106 *supra.* Stein (*ad l.*) understands
Thuc. 1. 90 to represent Leotychidas
and the Peloponnesians as going straight
home from Samos ; but the case is not
quite clear. Thucydides does not,
indeed, expressly record the removal
to the Hellespont ; but neither does
he expresaly say that it was Samos
wherefrom the Peloponnesians returned ;
he merely says, the Peloponnesians
returned, the Athenians remained. On
this point there is no contradiction
between Hdt. and Thuc.

Ἑλλάδα, Ἀθηναίοισι δὲ καὶ Ξανθίππῳ τῷ στρατηγῷ αὐτοῦ
ὑπομείναντας πειρᾶσθαι τῆς Χερσονήσου. οἱ μὲν δὴ ἀπέπλεον,
Ἀθηναῖοι δὲ ἐκ τῆς Ἀβύδου διαβάντες ἐς τὴν Χερσόνησον
Σηστὸν ἐπολιόρκεον. ἐς δὲ τὴν Σηστὸν ταύτην, ὡς ἐόντος 115
ἰσχυροτάτου τείχεος τῶν ταύτῃ, συνῆλθον, ὡς ἤκουσαν παρεῖναι
τοὺς Ἕλληνας ἐς τὸν Ἑλλήσποντον, ἔκ τε τῶν ἀλλέων τῶν
περιοικίδων, καὶ δὴ καὶ ἐκ Καρδίης πόλιος Οἰόβαζος ἀνὴρ
Πέρσης, ὃς τὰ ἐκ τῶν γεφυρέων ὅπλα ἐνθαῦτα ἦν κεκομικώς. 5
εἶχον δὲ ταύτην ἐπιχώριοι Αἰολέες, συνῆσαν δὲ Πέρσαι τε καὶ

8 χερρονήσου CP   9 διαβαλόντες β, Holder ‖ χερρόνησον CP
115. 3 ἀλλέων Stein : ἄλλων ‖ τῶν om. S, Ask.   4 δὴ καὶ : δὴ β ‖
οἰάβαζος β   6 ἔχον z

7. Ἀθηναίοισι δὲ καὶ Ξανθίππῳ, 'the
Athenians and their strategos, Xanthippos,' decided to remain and attempt
the recovery of the Chersonese. Hdt.
does not make clear, what Thuc. l.c.
expressly records, that the new allies—
οἱ ἀπ' Ἰωνίας καὶ Ἑλλησπόντου ξύμμαχοι,
ἤδη ἀφεστηκότες ἀπὸ βασιλέως—remained
with the Athenians and assisted them.
Xanthippos is here named for the first
time since 8. 131 (but without his patronymic) ; not much credit is given him
for the victory of Mykale.

αὐτοῦ: not quite strictly 'on the
spot,' for they move across to Sestos ;
it refers perhaps rather to 'the Hellespont' than to 'Abydos.'

8. ὑπομένειν has four meanings or
uses in Hdt. (a) 'To remain behind,'
as here ; cp. τὸ ὑπομένον ἐν Σπάρτῃ 7.
209. (b) 'To await, sustain, an attack,'
a defensive attitude ; cp. 4. 3 οὐκ ὑπομενέουσι (as enemies, cp. 7. 101, 120, and
c. 23 supra). (c) Simply 'to await'
(as a friend), 3. 9 ὑπέμενε ἐνθαῦτα τὸν
Καμβύσεω στρατόν (as friends). (d)
Absolutely, 'to abide,' to survive ; 4.
149 οὐ γὰρ ὑπέμειναν τὰ τέκνα.

9. τὴν Χερσόνησον: the Chersonese
'on the Hellespont' last mentioned 7.
58 (cp. 7. 33. 3, where it should have
been noted that the name had occurred
previously c. 22. 3 without further
specification, a fact pointing to the
independence of the two passages).
Thucydides speaks of it always, like Hdt.
here, simply as 'the Chersonese.' Our
oldest authority for the designation ἡ
Θρακία Χερρόνησος appears to be Strabo
92, etc. Cp. 6. 33 supra.

10. Σηστόν: last mentioned in 7. 78 ;
cp. 7. 33. It was an old possession of the

Athenians ; cp. 4. 143, and 6. 34, etc.
Sestos was, or was to be made, φρούριον
καὶ φυλακὴ τοῦ παντὸς Ἑλλησπόντου (cp.
Thuc. 8. 62. 3).

115. 1. ταύτην: there was only one
Sestos ; the demonstrative is purely
stylistic, referring to the previous
nomination.

ὡς ἐόντος, 'it being . .' as a
matter of fact (cp. ὡς οὐ παρεόντος αὐτοῦ
8. 69 supra) ; the gender is determined
by τείχεος.

2. συνῆλθον: sc. οἱ περίοικοι (cp. τῶν
περιοικίδων), or, more probably, ἄνδρες
Πέρσαι, out of ἀνὴρ Πέρσης below, just
as ἀλλέων sc. πολίων out of πόλιος. But
has a word or two dropped out before
καὶ δὴ καί? (Cp. cc. 101. 14, 102. 6
supra.)

4. Καρδίης: cp. 7. 58 supra.
Οἰόβαζος: on this name cp. 7. 68
supra.

5. ἐνθαῦτα ἦν κεκομικώς: is this expression merely equivalent to ἐνθαῦτα
ἐκεκομίκει? If so, why not ἐκεῖσε instead
of ἐνθαῦτα? The substantive or auxiliary
verb has at least affected the adverb !
But ἐνθαῦτα ἦν is a complete statement
in itself, save that τὰ [ἐκ] τῶν γεφυρέων
ὅπλα demands a governing verb. Moreover, ἐνθαῦτα might = ἐν Καρδίῃ if ἦν κ.
simply = ἐκεκομίκει. In fine ἦν κεκομικώς
is not a mere temporal pluperfect, used
indifferently with the thematic form, or
the aorist ; it records an action, past
indeed, but of still abiding effect. In
this case perhaps even something more:
'he was in Sestos whither he had conveyed the ropes.'

6. ταύτην: sc. τὴν Σηστὸν ταύτην
supra. 'Aiolians of the locality' were
in actual possession of the town, but

116 τῶν ἄλλων συμμάχων συχνὸς ὅμιλος. ἐτυράννευε δὲ τούτου
τοῦ νομοῦ Ξέρξεω ὕπαρχος Ἀρταΰκτης, ἀνὴρ μὲν Πέρσης,
δεινὸς δὲ καὶ ἀτάσθαλος, ὃς καὶ βασιλέα ἐλαύνοντα ἐπ'
Ἀθήνας ἐξηπάτησε, τὰ Πρωτεσίλεω τοῦ Ἰφίκλου χρήματα

---

116. 1 τοῦ νομοῦ τούτου B　　　3 δεινός τε BC : 'an δεινὸς δέ τε !'
Kallenberg, van H. ‖ βασιλῆα z

---

the garrison included Persians and a
good crowd of allies 'as well' (ἄλλων,
cp. 8. 55. 5).

ἐπιχώριοι Αἰολέες: i.e. Aiolians on
the European side, in distinction to
those of Aiolis proper (cp. 7. 95 supra).
Ainos (7. 58) was an 'Aiolian' town, like
Sestos (also Alopekounesos, Skymn. 705).

116. 1. ἐτυράννευε δὲ τούτου τοῦ νομοῦ.
This νομός, a European, a Thrakian
province, is not reckoned in the list of
satrapies 3. 89–94 (which is ex hypothesi
valid for the year 520 B.C.), but it must
have been constituted by Dareios about
512 B.C. (cp. 4. 143 and 7. 105 supra),
though it may have been temporarily
lost during the Ionic Revolt (498–493 B.C.)
and only recovered shortly before
Marathon (cp. 6. 40, 41, 104). The
verb looks as though it might carry a
'dyslogistic' intention here ("richtiger
ἐπετρόπευε," Stein, as in 7. 78). The
satrap was specifically Ξέρξεω ὕπαρχος,
having been actually appointed by him;
he is described in 7. 35 as Σηστοῦ
ὕπαρχος, Sestos being no doubt the
residence of the governor. This variation is one of several observations in
this case, which prove once more with
how much insouciance Hdt. works from
various sources in different contexts.

2. Ἀρταΰκτης might never have been
mentioned before! In 7. 33 supra his
fate has already been related—and this
passage consequently discounted. In 7.
78 he has figured as one of the ἄρχοντες
in the army-list, and his patronymic is
there supplied (ὁ Χεράσμιος). The first
passage is probably a late insertion.
The army-list is, of course, sui generis.
The present passage may well be of
the original draft of the Book, i.e. of
older composition than 7. 33.

3. δεινὸς δὲ καὶ ἀτάσθαλος: not what
might have been expected of a Persian!
ἀτάσθαλος 7. 35, 8. 109 supra. He was
also something of a humourist, to judge
by the sequel. ὃς καί oddly enough
reappears 7. 33.

βασιλέα ἐλαύνοντα ἐπ' Ἀθήνας: not
much reliance is to be placed on this

chronological index, nor indeed upon the
anecdote which it introduces; but the
phrase clearly betrays the Attic or
Atticizing source of the story, making
Athens the goal of the king's march.

4. ἐξηπάτησε . . ὑπελόμενος: an inverted predication; in reality, after and
by deceiving the king he filched away the
objects of value. It is not necessarily
implied that otherwise Xerxes would
have taken them himself: rather, (that)
the king was the natural patron and
protector of the shrine. There is a
comical contradiction between Blakesley
and Rawlinson at this point:

B. ii. 402.	R. iv.³ 462.
"The contrast be-tween the reckless pro-ceedings of Artayctes and the tenderness of Xerxes for religious institutions of exactly the same character as the Protesilaos - wor-ship (see 7. 43) is not to be overlooked."	"It harmonised with the general designs of Xerxes, who had no real tenderness for the Greek religion, but sought to depress and disgrace it in every possible way (vide supra 8. 33, 35, 53 etc.)."

In fact both observations are somewhat
beside the mark, and ascribe too conscious
and politic an attitude to Xerxes in the
question of Religion and Greek Religion.
A good deal of the apparent evidence on
the subject is afterthought and reflexion,
which glorified the war by lending it a
religious or quasi-religious halo; cp.
note to 8. 109. 15.

Πρωτεσίλεω τοῦ Ἰφίκλου. Protesilaos led to Troy the men of Phylake,
Pyrasos, Iton, Antron, Ptelion, leaving
a wife and half-built house behind him
in Phylake. First of all Achaians he
leaped ashore, and was felled in the very
act by a Dardan, Iliad (2. 695–702).
At home in Phylake he was worshipped
(as a hero): Πρωτεσίλα, τὸ τεὸν δ' ἀνδρῶν
Ἀχαιῶν ἐν Φυλάκᾳ τέμενος συμβάλλομαι,
Pindar, Isth. 1. 58. And in the Thrakian
Chersonese his tomb (τάφος) was to be
seen, close to Elaiûs; cp. Thuc. 8. 102
3 τὸ ἱερὸν τοῦ Πρωτεσιλάου, Strabo 595
τὸ Πρωτεσιλάειον. Pausanias (1. 34.
2) appears to class him with Trophonios

<τὰ> ἐξ Ἐλαιοῦντος ὑπελόμενος. ἐν γὰρ Ἐλαιοῦντι τῆς 5
Χερσονήσου ἐστὶ Πρωτεσίλεω τάφος τε καὶ τέμενος περὶ
αὐτόν, ἔνθα ἦν χρήματα πολλὰ καὶ φιάλαι χρύσεαι καὶ
ἀργύρεαι καὶ χαλκὸς καὶ ἐσθὴς καὶ ἄλλα ἀναθήματα, τὰ
Ἀρταΰκτης ἐσύλησε βασιλέος δόντος. λέγων δὲ τοιάδε Ξέρξην
διεβάλετο. "δέσποτα, ἔστι οἶκος ἀνδρὸς Ἕλληνος ἐνθαῦτα, 10
ὃς ἐπὶ γῆν σὴν στρατευσάμενος δίκης κυρήσας ἀπέθανε·
τούτου μοι δὸς τὸν οἶκον, ἵνα καί τις μάθῃ ἐπὶ γῆν τὴν σὴν
μὴ στρατεύεσθαι." ταῦτα λέγων εὐπετέως ἔμελλε ἀναπείσειν
Ξέρξην δοῦναι ἀνδρὸς οἶκον, οὐδὲν ὑποτοπηθέντα τῶν ἐκεῖνος 15
ἐφρόνεε. ἐπὶ γῆν δὲ τὴν βασιλέος στρατεύεσθαι [Πρωτεσίλεων]

---

5 <τὰ> Stein[(1)(2)8] || ἐλεοῦντος aBz || ὑφελόμενος : corr. Wesseling,
Koen : αἰτήσας B, Holder || ἐλεοῦντι aBz 6 χερρονήσου CP Marc.
7 ἔην z . 9 βασιλῆος z || Ξέρξεα z 10 διεβάλλετο B Marc. :
διέβαλε coni. Stein[(2)], prob. van H. || οἶκός ἐστιν B 11 γῆν τὴν
σὴν B, Holder, van H. || στρατευόμενος PRz || <τῆς> δίκης coni. Stein[(2)],
recep. van H. 12 τις καὶ B 14 λέγων om. Marc. 15
Ξέρξεα z || δοῦναί <οἱ τοῦ>? Stein[1] : δοῦναι ἀνδρὸς οἶκον secl. van H.
16 ἐφρόνει van H. || βασιλῆος z || στρατεύσασθαι? Stein[2] : adsc. van H. ||
Πρωτεσίλεων secl. Stein[8]

(cp. 8. 188 *supra*) and Amphiaraos (*ibid.*),
as all three heroes who have been
apotheosized (that is of the very
essence of Polytheism, cp. A. Lyall,
Asiatic Studies, pp. 20 ff.). Stein (note
ad l.) asserts that he was (*ohne Zweifel*)
a pre-Hellenic deity, in the Chersonese,
identified, for some reason or other, with
the Greek hero. Our own Wordsworth
has made his ghost the subject of a
pseudo-antique conversation in one of
his best-known poems (*Laodamia*), the
motifs of which he may have taken from
Hyginus' *Fabulae* 103, 104. Those fables,
especially the second, point to an
orgiastic, or mysterious cult, proper to
women, and perhaps at home in Thrace,
which might in part at least explain the
worst charges against Artayktes ; cp.
infra. Iphiklos is the father of Protesilaos
and Podarkes (*Iliad l.c.*) and himself
the son of Phylakos (*ibid.* 13. 698), the
founder of Phylake. According to the
myth in *Od.* 11. 281-297 he was the
owner of beeves, that Neleus was bent
on getting stolen, and the would-be
cattle-lifter was caught and kept a year
in bonds by the might of Iphiklos.
These things may be in part an allegory ;
cp. note to c. 93. 3 *supra*.

5. Ἐλαιοῦντος : cp. 7. 22 *supra*.

The shrine was evidently a wealthy one
(τὰ χρήματα, objects of value, cp. 8.
35. 8).

6. ἐστὶ . . ἦν : a designed contrast,
the 'tomb' and 'temenos' existing in
Hdt.'s own day (as in Thucydides', 8.
102. 3), the objects of value having been
carried off by Artayktes. Below, a ἱρόν
and an ἄδυτον are further implied.

10. διεβάλετο = ἐξηπάτησε just above ;
the active is used generally in this sense ;
cp. 8. 110 *supra*, 5. 50, 97.

11. δίκης κυρήσας does not imply
actual judicial proceedings.

12. τις, as in 8. 109.

15. ἀνδρός is of course emphatic ;
Artayktes, δεινὸς καὶ ἀτάσθαλος, had
implicitly denied the divinity and the
heroism of Protesilaos. Xerxes would
not have granted him his request had
he known that the tomb of a hero, the
temple of a god, was in question.
ὑποτοπηθέντα is from the deponent
ὑποτοπέομαι, cp. 6. 70.

16. ἐπὶ γῆν δὲ τὴν βασιλέος στρατεύεσθαι. Hdt. considers it in no way
necessary to explain further or account
for Protesilaos : his name and story were
familiar to all Hellenes. The Persian
assumption of an immemorial sovranty
over Asia is well illustrated *supra* 7. 11

ἔλεγε νοέων τοιάδε· τὴν Ἀσίην πᾶσαν νομίζουσι ἑωυτῶν εἶναι
Πέρσαι καὶ τοῦ αἰεὶ βασιλεύοντος. ἐπεὶ δὲ ἐδόθη, τά <τε>
χρήματα ἐξ Ἐλαιοῦντος ἐς Σηστὸν ἐξεφόρησε καὶ τὸ τέμενος
20 ἔσπειρε καὶ ἐνέμετο, αὐτός τε ὅκως ἀπίκοιτο ἐς Ἐλαιοῦντα ἐν
τῷ ἀδύτῳ γυναιξὶ ἐμίσγετο. τότε δὲ ἐπολιορκέετο ὑπὸ
Ἀθηναίων οὔτε παρεσκευασμένος ἐς πολιορκίην οὔτε προσ-
117 δεκόμενος τοὺς Ἕλληνας, ἀφύκτως δέ κως αὐτῷ ἐπέπεσον. ἐπεὶ
δὲ πολιορκεομένοισί σφι φθινόπωρον ἐπεγίνετο, καὶ ἤσχαλλον
οἱ Ἀθηναῖοι ἀπό τε τῆς ἑωυτῶν ἀποδημέοντες καὶ οὐ δυνάμενοι
ἐξελεῖν τὸ τεῖχος, ἐδέοντό τε τῶν στρατηγῶν ὅκως ἀπάγοιεν
5 σφέας ὀπίσω, οἱ δὲ οὐκ ἔφασαν πρὶν ἢ ἐξέλωσι ἢ τὸ
Ἀθηναίων κοινόν σφεας μεταπέμψηται· οὕτω δὴ ἔστεργον τὰ
118 παρεόντα. οἱ δὲ ἐν τῷ τείχεϊ ἐς πᾶν ἤδη κακοῦ ἀπιγμένοι
ἦσαν, οὕτω ὥστε τοὺς τόνους ἔψοντες τῶν κλινέων ἐσιτέοντο.
ἐπείτε δὲ οὐδὲ ταῦτα ἔτι εἶχον, οὕτω δὴ ὑπὸ νύκτα οἴχοντο

17 νοέων: ποιέων B ‖ ἅπασαν R(S ?)V   17, 18 πέρσαι εἶναι Pz ‖
ἐπείτε ? van H. ‖ <τε> add. Stein³   19 ἐλεοῦντος aBz   20
ἐλεοῦντα aBz   23 ἀφυλάκτω (-ῳ) B, Holder, van H. ‖ δέ: τέ B
117. 1 ἐπείτε ? van H.   2 πολιορκέουσί Schweighaeuser, Krueger
‖ ἐπεγένετο B ‖ καὶ om. B, secl. van H. ‖ ἤσχαλλον Acorr.B: ἤσχαλον
Apr.BCz   3 τε om. S   4 ἀπαγάγοιεν Bz   5 σφέας libri,
Stein², Holder: σφεας Stein¹, van H.   6 κοινὸν σφέας z   118. 1
δ' ARz ‖ ἐς: ἀμφὶ τὸν ἀρταύκτεα ἐς Bz ‖ ἤδη: δὴ B   2 ἔσαν z ‖
οὕτως ABR ‖ ἔψοντες R: ἐψῶντες Marc.   3 ἔχον z ‖ δὴ om. B ‖
οἴχοντο B, Krueger, Stein², Holder, van H.: οἴχονται

Πέλοψ ὁ Φρύξ, ἐὼν πατέρων τῶν ἐμῶν
δοῦλος κτλ. Cp. 1. 4 τὴν γὰρ Ἀσίην καὶ
τὰ ἐνοικέοντα ἔθνεα οἰκηιεῦνται οἱ Πέρσαι.
17. ἔλεγε νοέων, 'in saying this he
meant as follows.'
18. αἰεί, 'for the time being,' 'from
time to time,' cp. 2. 98, 168 τοῖσι
αἰεὶ δορυφορεῦσι, c. 102 supra τοῖσι αἰεὶ
ἐσπίπτουσι.
20. ἔσπειρε καὶ ἐνέμετο, αὐτός τε κτλ.,
he cultivated and grazed it. Blakesley
interprets to mean merely that Artayktes
converted the demesne and temple into
a paradise and seraglio. The cult of
Protesilaos was perhaps especially an
orgiastic one for women. Cp. p. 823 a
supra.
21. τότε δέ: cp. c. 114 supra.
23. ἀφύκτως δέ κως: like fate, like
Nemesis. Baehr doubts ἀφύκτως without sufficient reason: the adj. is found
in Simonides, Pindar, Aischyl., Soph.,
Plato, etc. Cp. App. Crit.
117. 2. πολιορκεομένοισί σφι φθινόπωρον ἐπεγίνετο: the verb is passive;

the persons are the men in Sestos;
the autumn (Stein observes) began
September 18 (early rising of Arkturos).
φθινόπωρον: 4. 42; Thuc. 2. 31. 1.
ἤσχαλλον: aegre ferebant, 3. 152.
4. τῶν στρατηγῶν. Xanthippos was
not in sole command; this was perhaps
the first instance of the forces of the
democracy being employed through the
winter and on foreign service: 'the
generals' had perhaps a holy horror of
Themistokles, who was certainly in
Athens; cp. Thuc. 1. 90. 3.
5. πρὶν ἢ ἐξέλωσι: if conditional, ἄν
might be expected; if merely temporal,
the infinitive. μεταπέμψηται, 'recall.'
6. οὕτω δή marks the apodosis.
στέργειν: differently, c. 113 supra.
118. 1. ἐς πᾶν ἤδη κακοῦ ἀπιγμένοι
ἦσαν: cp. 7. 118 ἐς π. κ. ἀπίκατο οὕτω
ὥστε . . ἐγίνοντο. But ἀπιγμένοι ἦσαν
here is not perhaps a mere equivalent to
ἀπίκατο there. The phrase here is more
extensive (e.g. ἤδη). Cp. c. 115 supra.
2. τόνους: purely concrete, and no

ἀποδράντες οἵ τε Πέρσαι καὶ ὁ Ἀρταΰκτης καὶ ὁ Οἰόβαζος,
<τὸ> ὄπισθε τοῦ τείχεος καταβάντες, τῇ ἦν ἐρημότατον τῶν 5
πολεμίων. ὡς δὲ ἡμέρη ἐγένετο, οἱ Χερσονησῖται ἀπὸ τῶν
πύργων ἐσήμηναν τοῖσι Ἀθηναίοισι τὸ γεγονὸς καὶ τὰς πύλας
ἄνοιξαν. τῶν δὲ οἱ μὲν πλεῦνες ἐδίωκον, οἱ δὲ τὴν πόλιν
εἶχον. Οἰόβαζον μέν νυν ἐκφεύγοντα ἐς τὴν Θρηίκην Θρήικες 119
Ἀψίνθιοι λαβόντες ἔθυσαν Πλειστώρῳ ἐπιχωρίῳ θεῷ τρόπῳ
τῷ σφετέρῳ, τοὺς δὲ μετ᾽ ἐκείνου ἄλλῳ τρόπῳ ἐφόνευσαν.
οἱ δὲ ἀμφὶ τὸν Ἀρταΰκτην ὕστεροι ὁρμηθέντες φεύγειν, καὶ
ὡς κατελαμβάνοντο ὀλίγον ἐόντες ὑπὲρ Αἰγὸς ποταμῶν, ἀλεξό- 5

---

4 ὁ ante Οἰόβαζος om. αP Marc.   5 <τὸ> Stein(2) 3 ‖ ὄπισθεν
R(S 1)V ‖ τοῦ ἦν ἐρημότατος R ‖ τῶν om. z   7 ἐσημήναντο R   8
πλεῦνες om. P⁴ Marc.   9 ἔχον z: ἔσχον? Krueger   119. 1 ἐκφυ-
γόντα S, Holder, van H. ‖ θρήικην θρήκες R(S)V   3 ἄλλῳ τρόπῳ del.
Gomperz   4 ἀρταΰντην C ‖ ὕστερον SC ‖ καὶ om. z, van H.: secl.
Holder   5 ὀλίγοι S ‖ ποταμοῦ Sz ‖ ἀλεξάμενοι S

---

doubt of leather=ἱμάντας (5. 25). Cp.
Aristoph. Lys. 923, Ekk. 533 (cp. 7. 36).

5. ὄπισθε τοῦ τείχεος: on the side of
the wall away from the Athenian lines,
which did not surround the city. τῶν
πολεμίων, sc. τῶν Ἀθηναίων. Could this
turn occur in an Attic source?

6. οἱ Χερσονησῖται: the inhabitants
of the Chersonese ἀπὸ τασέων τῶν πολίων,
cp. 4. 137, 6. 38, 39. (The names of
upwards of forty places are recoverable,
cp. Pauly-Wissowa iii. 2247 f. Of these
about nine are found in Hdt., viz. Ἀγορή
7. 58, Αἰγὸς ποταμοὶ c. 119 infra,
Ἐλαιοῦς c. 116 supra, etc., Ἕλλης τάφος
7. 58, Καρδίη c. 115 supra, etc., Λευκὴ
ἀκτή 7. 25, Μάδυτος 7. 33, c. 120 infra,
Πακτύη 6. 36, Σηστὸς c. 114 supra, etc.)

9. εἶχον, 'mounted guard on ..,' a
very strong ἔχειν.

119. 1. Θρήικες Ἀψίνθιοι: these were
old enemies of the Δόλογκοι Θρήικες, the
occupants of the Chersonese (cp. 6. 34),
and the wall from Kardia to Paktye was
built by Miltiades I. to keep them out
(ib. 36). Steph. B. sub v. Αἶνος gives
Ἀψινθος as another name; cp. 7. 58
supra. Blakesley well describes them as
the Perioikoi of Ainos; cp. Strabo, 331
fr. 58, ἡ μὲν γὰρ Αἶνος κεῖται κατὰ τὴν
πρότερον Ἀψινθίδα νῦν δὲ Κορπιλικὴν
λεγομένην, ἡ δὲ τῶν Κικόνων ἐφεξῆς
πρὸς δύσιν. The word Apsinthos, or
Apsinthioi, belongs to the group of proper
names in -nth- of which Korinthos,
Zakynthos, Perinthos (in Thrace) are

only the best known examples; cp.
Oberhummer, Akarnanien (1887), p. 58.
The termination appears on the Asianic
side in names formed with -nd- (cp.
Kretschmer, op. c. 293 ff.). Whatever
be the positive significance of this
observation, it confirms the opinion that
the whole group of names belongs to a
non-Greek, a prae-Hellenic population.

2. ἔθυσαν Πλειστώρῳ ἐπιχωρίῳ θεῷ:
this Thrakian deity is perhaps the
Thrakian Ares of 5. 7. Their method of
human sacrifice (τρόπῳ τῷ σφετέρῳ)
will have differed from the rite as
practised by the Tauroi (4. 103), and
perhaps resembled that of the Getai, in
the cult of Salmoxis (4. 94). Cp.
further 7. 114. The companions of
Oiobazos were put to death in another
fashion, and also not as a religious
sacrifice.

4. οἱ δὲ ἀμφὶ τὸν Ἀ., 'Artayktes
and his followers,' cp. c. 114 supra.

ὁρμηθέντες, of physical motion;
cp. ibid.

5. κατελαμβάνοντο ὀλίγον ἐόντες ὑπὲρ
Αἰγὸς ποταμῶν, 'were overtaken while
they were a little way beyond Aigospotamoi.' The participle is not strictly
necessary, and suggests itself therefore
as predicative. 'They were not far
beyond Aigospotamoi when they were
overtaken.' Xenophon Hell. 2. 1. 21
describes the place as 'opposite Lampsakos.' Rawlinson will not allow that
Aigospotamoi was more than an open

μενοι χρόνον ἐπὶ συχνὸν οἱ μὲν ἀπέθανον οἱ δὲ ζῶντες
ἐλάμφθησαν. καὶ συνδήσαντες σφέας οἱ Ἕλληνες ᾖγον ἐς
Σηστόν. μετ' αὐτῶν δὲ καὶ Ἀρταΰκτην δεδεμένον αὐτόν τε καὶ
120 τὸν παῖδα αὐτοῦ. καὶ τεῳ τῶν φυλασσόντων λέγεται ὑπὸ
Χερσονησιτέων ταρίχους ὀπτῶντι τέρας γενέσθαι τοιόνδε· οἱ
τάριχοι ἐπὶ τῷ πυρὶ κείμενοι ἐπάλλοντό τε καὶ ἤσπαιρον
ὅκως περ ἰχθύες νεοάλωτοι. καὶ οἱ μὲν περιχυθέντες ἐθώμαζον,
5 ὁ δὲ Ἀρταΰκτης ὡς εἶδε τὸ τέρας, καλέσας τὸν ὀπτῶντα τοὺς
ταρίχους ἔφη " ξεῖνε Ἀθηναῖε, μηδὲν φοβέο τὸ τέρας τοῦτο·
οὐ γὰρ σοὶ πέφηνε, ἀλλ' ἐμοὶ σημαίνει ὁ ἐν Ἐλαιοῦντι
Πρωτεσίλεως ὅτι καὶ τεθνεὼς καὶ τάριχος ἐὼν δύναμιν πρὸς
θεῶν ἔχει τὸν ἀδικέοντα τίνεσθαι. νῦν ὦν ἄποινά μοι τάδε

---

7 ἐλάμφθησαν S ‖ ἦγαγον Β, Holder, van H. ‖ ἐς : ἐπὶ Marc.　　　8
αὐτέων z ‖ δεδεμένον secl. van H.　　　120. 1 τῶν τεῳ malit van H.
2 χερρονησιτέων C : χερσονησιωτέων z : (χερσονηγιτέων R ?) ‖ ταρίχου R ‖
τέρας τε Β　　　3 ἔσπαιρον (SV) Marc. z : ἔσπερον R　　　4 οἱ ἰχθύες Β ‖
νεάλωτοι Βz, Holder, van H. ‖ ἐθώυμαζον Β, Stein¹　　　6 φοβέετο τὸ R :
τὸ om. S　　　7 ἐλεοῦντι Βz　　　8 πρωτεσίλεος AB　　　9 σινέεσθαι Β ‖
μοι de Pauw, Stein, van H. : οἱ

---

roadstead even in 405 B.C. But the
coinage appears to prove the contrary ;
cp. Head, Hist. Num. p. 222 ; and perhaps the plural form of the word might
support the correction. Xen. l.c., Diodor.
13. 105, Strabo 287, Plutarch. Lys. 9.

7. ἐλάμφθησαν, 'were captured' ; cp.
c. 114. 2 supra. (The aorist of the
simple verb has a fuller sense than the
imperfect of the verb in composition
just above.)

συνδήσαντες, 'after binding, or
chaining them together,' one to another.

οἱ Ἕλληνες perhaps covers οἱ
Ἀθηναῖοι καὶ οἱ σύμμαχοι whose presence
has not been expressly recognized.

120. 1. λέγεται ὑπὸ Χερσονησιτέων :
the express notice of the source is perhaps a disclaimer of responsibility for
the story of the τέρας (ter).

2. ταρίχους (ῑ) : cp. 4. 53 etc. The
neuter form of this word (cp. L. & S.)
predominates in Attic : Hdt. uses it
only as masculine.

3. ἐπάλλοντό τε καὶ ἤσπαιρον : for
πάλλεσθαι cp. 7. 140 supra ; ἀσπαίρειν,
cp. 8. 5 supra (an Ionic word).

4. ὅκως, 'as'—comparative. Contr.
the uses of ὅκως above, c. 116 ὅκως ἀπίκοιτο, c. 117 ὅκως ἀπάγοιεν (ἐδέοντο).

νεοάλωτοι appears to be an

hapaxlegomenon. Everything turns on
this. That kippers should dance when
laid on the fire is not in itself miraculous.

περιχυθέντες : probably guards or
soldiers lying round the fire ; cp. 3. 12.

7. σοί, ' for thy benefit ' ; dat. eth.

ὁ ἐν Ἐλαιοῦντι : it was indeed
wonderful that Protesilaos in Elaiûs
should reveal a sign in Sestos. He here
appears as not a god himself, but a
hero, dead and kippered, but with
power, by help of the gods, to avenge
his wrongs ! (δύναμιν πρὸς θεῶν ἔχει, but
cp. τῷ θεῷ just below). τίνεσθαι, a
τίσις clearly in order. The speech of
Artayktes so far might read as a fresh
evidence of his δεινότης and ἀτασθαλίη—
even though the verb ταριχεύειν is used
by Hdt. himself (2. 86 ff.), apparently
without the least comic reference, for
mummification. It will hardly follow
from this passage that the τάφος at
Elaiûs actually contained a mummy :
Artayktes speaks metaphorically.

9. ἄποινα : cp. 6. 79. ἐπιθεῖναι :
Artayktes acts as judge and jury in
his own case (cp. δίκην ταύτην ἐπέθηκε 1.
120, ταύτην τὴν ζημίην ἐπέθηκαν 1. 145).
He offers a fine, 100 talents, instead of
the objects of value robbed from the
temple (what of them ! had they been

ἐθέλω ἐπιθεῖναι, ἀντὶ μὲν [χρημάτων] τῶν ἔλαβον ἐκ τοῦ ἱροῦ 10
ἑκατὸν τάλαντα καταθεῖναι τῷ θεῷ, ἀντὶ δ᾽ ἐμεωυτοῦ καὶ τοῦ
παιδὸς ἀποδώσω τάλαντα διηκόσια Ἀθηναίοισι περιγενόμενος."
ταῦτα ὑπισχόμενος τὸν στρατηγὸν Ξάνθιππον οὐκ ἔπειθε· οἱ
γὰρ Ἐλαιούσιοι τῷ Πρωτεσίλεῳ τιμωρέοντες ἐδέοντό μιν
καταχρησθῆναι, καὶ αὐτοῦ τοῦ στρατηγοῦ ταύτῃ νόος ἔφερε. 15
ἀπαγαγόντες δὲ αὐτὸν ἐς τὴν ἀκτὴν ἐς τὴν Ξέρξης ἔζευξε τὸν
πόρον, οἱ δὲ λέγουσι ἐπὶ τὸν κολωνὸν τὸν ὑπὲρ Μαδύτου
πόλιος, <πρὸς> σανίδας προσπασσαλεύσαντες ἀνεκρέμασαν·
τὸν δὲ παῖδα ἐν ὀφθαλμοῖσι τοῦ Ἀρταΰκτεω κατέλευσαν.
ταῦτα δὲ ποιήσαντες ἀπέπλεον ἐς τὴν Ἑλλάδα, τά τε ἄλλα 121
χρήματα ἄγοντες καὶ δὴ καὶ τὰ ὅπλα τῶν γεφυρέων ὡς
ἀναθήσοντες ἐς τὰ ἱρά. [καὶ κατὰ τὸ ἔτος τοῦτο οὐδὲν ἐπὶ
πλέον τούτων ἐγένετο.]

---

10 ἐπιχθῆναι αC: ἐπαχθῆναι Marc. (οἱ . . καταθεῖναι? van H.) ‖
μὲν γὰρ Marc. ‖ χρημάτων secl. Stein³: τῶν ἔλαβον χρημάτων? Stein⁽²⁾
11 ἀντὶ δ᾽ om. R   12 ἀποδώσω τάλαντα abesse malit van H. ‖
Ἀθηναίοισι om. S   13 ὑποσχόμενος Marc. z: ὑπισχνόμενος S   14
ἐλεούσιοι β: Ἐλεούντιοι z ‖ Πρωτεσιλάῳ z   15 ὁ νόος z, van H.
18 πόλεος z ‖ πρὸς Dobree, Stein², Holder, van H. ‖ σανίδα z, Dobree,
van H.: σανίδι Reiske   19 τοῦ: αὐτοῦ an τοῦσι? Kallenberg
121. 3, 4 glossema notavi ‖ ἐπὶ Werfer, Stein², Holder, van H.: ἔτι
‖ πλέον om. C ‖ τουτέων z

---

recovered and restored!), and 200
talents to be paid (ἀποδώσω) to the
Athenians as ransom for son and self.
13. τὸν στρατηγὸν Ξάνθιππον: the
offer must have been conveyed to
Xanthippos by the guard. Artaÿktes
apparently could speak Greek. The
men of Elaiûs, τῷ Π. τιμωρέοντες, cp. 8.
144. 11, demanded his execution (καταχρησθῆναι pass., cp. καταχρήσασθαι mid.
1. 82 etc.), and the general himself inclined to the same view (νόος ἔφερε, cp.
8. 100 ἐφερέ οἱ ἡ γνώμη).
17. οἱ δὲ λέγουσι: no variant is
recognized in 7. 38 supra. The absence
of a cross reference is significant. It
is remarkable that the exact scene of
the crucifixion was in dispute; but that
doubt did not extend to the crucifixion
itself. On the ἀκτή cp. l.c. Artaÿktes
was crucified, 7. 33 adds ζῶντα, which
is plainly the sense of this passage. The
fate of his son (cp. c. 4 supra) is comparatively merciful; but these executions
do not exhibit the εἰωθυῖα πραότης of
the Demos. The victims were perhaps

handed over to the Ἐλαιούσιοι, or the
Χερσονησῖται, though Hdt. writes as
though the Athenians present were the
executioners.
121. 1. ἐς τὴν Ἑλλάδα: the term here
seems used with a very definite and
concrete geographical reference; cp. c.
101 supra.
2. χρήματα: the spoils, chiefly from
Mykale—where they had found θησαυρούς
τινας χρημάτων c. 106 supra.
καὶ δὴ καί: cp. 8. 132. 10 supra.
τὰ ὅπλα τῶν γεφυρέων: presumably
the great cables described in 7. 36 supra.
They must have been fetched from
Kardia, where they had been deposited
by Oiobazos c. 115 supra. Their fresh
destination is not quite clear; the
temples of Athens were in ruins, but the
city was being rebuilt, Thuc. 1. 89. 3.
3. κατὰ τὸ ἔτος τοῦτο: the year here
indicated could only be either the Attic
civil year, or the campaigning year, from
spring to spring, such as Thucydides
employs after its introduction by Hdt.
in the history of this very war; cp. 7.

122　Τούτου δὲ τοῦ Ἀρταΰκτεω τοῦ ἀνακρεμασθέντος προπάτωρ
Ἀρτεμβάρης ἐστὶ ὁ Πέρσῃσι ἐξηγησάμενος λόγον τὸν ἐκεῖνοι
ὑπολαβόντες Κύρῳ προσήνεικαν λέγοντα τάδε. " ἐπεὶ Ζεὺς
Πέρσῃσι ἡγεμονίην διδοῖ, ἀνδρῶν δὲ σοὶ Κῦρε, κατελὼν

---

122. 2 ἐστιν ἀρτεβάρης S ‖ τὸν λόγον R　　3 λέγον R　　4
<ἐθνέων μὲν> Πέρσῃσι van H. ‖ σὺ S cod. Pal. 152 ‖ κατελὼν Ἀστυάγην
del. Gomperz

37, 8. 131 (cp. also the history of the
Triennium, Bk. 6). This consideration
makes it plain that Hdt. has here in
view the campaigning year 479–78 B.C.
But there are nevertheless two questions
which remain: (a) the date of the return
of the Fleet from the Hellespont to
Athens ; (b) the date of the next expedition, under Pausanias, to Kypros, Thuc.
1. 94. Is there not a reference thereto
in this passage ?
(a) According to Rawlinson ἐπιχειμάσαντες in Thuc. 1. 89. 2 means not that
they passed the winter before Sestos
(διαχειμάζειν), but that they just reached
winter before taking it ; cp. ἐπιπολιοῦ-
σθαι, ἐπισερκάζειν (inceptives), and ἐπι-
as dimin. in composition with adj.
(ἐπίπικρος, etc.). It is possible that the
Athenian fleet reached home before our
New Year (though that cannot be Hdt.'s
new ἔτος) ; and the remark here would
be in that case correct, though rather
otiose.
(b) The expedition under Pausanias
certainly did not start before the spring
of 478 B.C., i.e. after Hdt.'s ' New Year.'
The interpretation of ἐπιχειμάσαντες in
Thuc. l.c. as involving the whole winter
dated the return of the Athenians to the
spring, and led to the start of Pausanias
being pushed on into the summer,
possibly even over the Athenian New
Year. The revision of the meaning of
ἐπιχειμάσαντες allows an earlier and
normal date for the expedition of 478
B.C., and leaves of course this chronological note of Hdt.'s, if it be indeed his,
correct, but again otiose.
I doubt the authenticity of this sentence. It has all the air of being inserted
by some one with the history of the
Pentekontaëteris before him. It could not,
indeed, prove the work of Hdt. to be
unfinished, or incomplete ; but it lends
perhaps some colour to that misconception. Remove it and the story of the
war as told by Hdt. attains a finer
climax, apart from the colophon, or
concluding anecdote, in c. 122. The

last item in the annals of the war, that
great *Biennium* (or Τριετηρίς), is the
dedication of the cables which had bound
Europe to Asia, and paved the way for
the barbarous invader of Hellas. The
sentence has all the air of a gloss, and
it not merely spoils the splendid climax
ἐς τὰ ἱρά, but separates unduly the
closing anecdote from the peg upon
which it depends, the name and fate of
Artayktes.
122. 2. Ἀρτεμβάρης must have been
father of Cherasmis ; and he might just
perhaps have been the Artembares whose
son (Cherasmis ?) Kyros had bullied 1.
114, somewhere about 570 B.C., though
the exigencies of that anecdote require
Artembares to have been a ' Mede.'
Artayktes, the governor of Sestos, is
not a young man in 479 B.C. His father
might have been a boy with Kyros nearly
a century before (two generations will
sometimes exceed a century). The whole
anecdote here is, however, full of inconsequence. The scene is placed just
after the overthrow of Astyages (κατελὼν
Ἀστυάγην) ; but the Kyros of this
anecdote is plainly *le bon père*, and the
ἔτος εὖ εἰρημένον ascribed to him ought
plainly to be thought of as his legacy
and testament to the ' Persians.'
ἐστὶ ὁ . . ἐξηγησάμενος, ' is (was)
the real author of a proposal . .' ; cp. 5.
31 σὺ ἐς οἶκον τὸν βασιλέος ἐξηγητὴς γίνεαι
πρηγμάτων ἀγαθῶν. The construction
ἐστὶ (ὁ) ἐξ. of course gives no colour to
the construction of the substantive verb
with aorist participle. ὑπολαβόντες here
' took up and . .' as we might say ; cp.
3. 146, and contr. 7. 101.
3. Κύρῳ προσήνεικαν. Blakesley too
ingeniously interprets ' attributed to
Cyrus,' and his remarks upon the barbarism of Artembares are directed to
the wrong address. The words obviously
mean ' reported to Kyros.'
Ζεὺς : cp. 7. 40 *supra*.
4. ἡγεμονίην : sc. ἐθνέων, cp. 1. 95.
κατελὼν Ἀστυάγην (*N.B.* not κατε-

Ἀστυάγην, φέρε, γῆν γὰρ ἐκτήμεθα ὀλίγην καὶ ταύτην 5
τρηχέαν, μεταναστάντες ἐκ ταύτης ἄλλην σχῶμεν ἀμείνω.
εἰσὶ δὲ πολλαὶ μὲν ἀστυγείτονες πολλαὶ δὲ καὶ ἑκαστέρω,
τῶν μίαν σχόντες πλέοσι ἐσόμεθα θωμαστότεροι. οἰκὸς δὲ
ἄνδρας ἄρχοντας τοιαῦτα ποιέειν· κότε γὰρ δὴ καὶ παρέξει
κάλλιον ἢ ὅτε γε ἀνθρώπων τε πολλῶν ἄρχομεν πάσης τε 10
τῆς Ἀσίης;" Κῦρος δὲ ταῦτα ἀκούσας, καὶ οὐ θωμάσας τὸν
λόγον, ἐκέλευε ποιέειν ταῦτα, οὕτω δὲ αὐτοῖσι παραίνεε
κελεύων παρασκευάζεσθαι ὡς οὐκέτι ἄρξοντας ἀλλ᾿ ἀρξομένους·
φιλέειν γὰρ ἐκ τῶν μαλακῶν χώρων μαλακοὺς γίνεσθαι

---

5 Ἀστυάγεα z ‖ γὰρ om. S   6 τρηχέαν B: τρηχέην ceteri ‖ σχῶμεν
B, Krueger, Stein², Holder, van H.: ἔχωμεν   7 καὶ om. B ‖ ἑκαστέρωι
aP: ἑκατέρω CSV   8 μίην z ‖ ἔχοντες B, Holder: σχῶντες C ‖ πλείοσι
aC Marc. ‖ θωυμαστότεροι SV, Stein¹: θωμαϋστότεροι R ‖ οἰκὸς BP: εἰκὸς
9 ἄνδρας ἔχοντας R(B ?) ‖ κότερα B   10 ὅτε: οὔτε B   11 θωμάσας
R(V)z: Stein¹   12 παραίνεε S: παρήνεε   13 κελεύων del. Cobet,
van H. ‖ ἀρξαμένους C   14 μαλακοὺς ἄνδρας γίνεσθαι B, Holder,
van H.: μαλακοὺς γίνεσθαι a etc., Stein¹²

λόττι). As Astyages had been the re-
presentative of the Median ἀρχή the
Persians and Artembares regard themselves now as masters of all Asia; cp.
7. 8 *supra*. That position was not really
attained until Lydia and Babylon at
any rate had been conquered too. In
Bk. 1 the conquest of Lydia, the overthrow of Kroisos, make Kyros master
of all Asia (cp. 1. 130, also 1. 71). This
anecdote is from a different (and less
philo-Lydian) source.

5. **φέρε**: an adverbial imperative,
'come!' L. & S. *sub v.* ix. 2.

γῆν .. ὀλίγην καὶ ταύτην τρηχέαν:
cp. χώρην ἔχοντες τρηχέαν 1. 71. Hdt.
himself nowhere (not even in 3. 97)
describes Persis proper in any detail.
As a general description of the land this
phrase here is sufficiently accurate, and the
later Greek writers endorse it; cp. Plato,
Laws 695, Arrian, *Anab.* 5. 4. 5. For
modern descriptions cp. Curzon, *Persia*
2 vv. (1892); Sykes, *Ten Thousand Miles
in Persia* (1902); Rawlinson, *Ancient
Monarchies* iv. (1867); Duncker, *Hist. of
Antiq.* Bk. vii. c. i. (E.T. vol. v. pp. 3 ff.,
1881); Perrot and Chipiez, *Art in Persia*,
E.T. (1892) pp. 2-8; Reclus, *Universal
Geogr.* E.T. vol. ix. c. iv.; *Ency. Brit.*
xviii. 561, etc. etc. Cp. note l. 18 *infra*.

6. **μεταναστάντες .. σχῶμεν**, 'let us
emigrate .. and seize ..' So σχόντες

just below, cp. 7. 164. 5, and Index for
the strong ἔχειν.

7. **ἀστυγείτονες**, adjectivally, and
without stress on the first word in composition; cp. 6. 99.

8. **πλέοσι**, *pluribus hominibus* (Baehr);
in mehr Stücken (Stein). This idea for
a wholesale and voluntary migration
expresses, no doubt, (*a*) a current notion,
cp. 8. 140, 62, etc., (*b*) a genuine *vera
causa* at the back of many movements
of populations and peoples, cp. 7. 20,
etc. But the position here is slightly
different. The Persians are supposed
already to have dominion over all Asia;
they can take tribute and gifts from all
their subjects without evacuating their
own land. Cp. note l. 18 *infra*.

11. **Κῦρος δὲ .. ἐκέλευε ποιέειν ταῦτα**:
Kyros is, of course, conceived as speaking
ironically: 'do as you propose and
become subjects instead of rulers.'
αὐτοῖσι παραίνεε κελεύων is a resumptive
parenthesis. οὕτω δὲ as part of his
speech = ταῦτα δὲ ποιήσαντας.

13. **οὐκέτι ἄρξοντας ἀλλ᾿ ἀρξομένους**:
the same antithesis (in a more restricted
sense) 7. 162 *supra*.

14. **φιλέειν γὰρ .. τὰ πολέμια**. The
relation between 'Physics and Politics'
occupied a large space in the minds of
Greek thinkers. Hdt.'s own work is

15 <ἄνδρας>· οὐ γάρ τι τῆς αὐτῆς γῆς εἶναι καρπόν τε
θωμαστὸν φύειν καὶ ἄνδρας ἀγαθοὺς τὰ πολέμια. ὥστε
συγγνόντες Πέρσαι οἴχοντο ἀποστάντες, ἑσσωθέντες τῇ γνώμῃ

15 <ἄνδρας> Stein³ ‖ τι : τοι V Marc. z, Holder　　　16 θωυμαστὸν Βκ
17 οἱ πέρσαι S

saturated with the assumption of a connexion between race and place, between climate and institutions. His interest in the varieties of humankind makes him the father of Anthropology, as his sense of the unity and continuity of human adventure and experience makes him the 'father of history.' Hence his descriptions of the land and river of Egypt as a prelude to his account of the people, their manners and institutions; and so too with Skythia and the Skythians, Libya and the Libyans, the ends of the earth, and the more familiar coasts of the Aigaian. Hdt. has in a remarkable degree the sense of the relativity of human institutions; it is a part of the sophistical illumination of the age, just begun. It had done something to correct the exaggerated notion of the omnipotence of the *Nomothetes*. It attains formal expression in the work of his great contemporary Hippokrates of Kos, *de aëre aquis et locis* (*Hippocr. opera*, vol. i. ed. Kvehlewein, 1895), and the philosophy of the reaction, with its practical concern for the ideal city-state, does not fail to realise that for the πόλις κατ' εὐχήν a site, a climate, a race κατ' εὐχήν must also be posited. Thucydides (more clearly than Hdt.) mediates the action of physics on politics through the economic conditions (as in his *Archaiologia*): this profounder analysis was not lost in the sequel; Aristotle, for example, not only generalizes (or preserves the generalization) on the relation between τροφή and βίος (*Politics* 1. 8 = 1256 a), but traces in a fashion the merits of the Greek nation to its happy position between the barbarous extremes of cold and heat, of Europe and Asia (*Pol.* 4 (7). 7 = 1327 b). It stands to reason that the lesser differences between one Greek folk and another might be in part traceable to differences in the physico-geographical environment; and as a matter of fact the popular philosophy of Greece early ascribed the superiority of the Attic race to the advantages of its climate, traced the genesis of political parties to features in the Attic landscape—

the shore, the plain, the mountain— or ascribed the development of the democracy (somewhat superficially) to the growing importance of the sea, and sea-power, in the life of the city. Livy (38. 17) puts a speech into the mouth of Cn. Manlius (Ȧ.U.C. 565) on the Gallograeci, which might be taken as a commentary on this text; but in general the Roman conqueror believed in race (*fortes creantur fortibus*), and under the cosmopolitan rule of Rome, whether imperial or pontifical, much of the sense of the relativity of human institutions passed out of consciousness, to be rediscovered and reintroduced with the revival of Greek letters and the return to nature. The idea is now a commonplace of every history of civilisation, or philosophy of history; but an initial place in the bibliography of the subject must always be reserved for Montesquieu's *Esprit des Lois*, 1748 (Livres xiv.–xviii.), as also for Buckle's *Hist. of Civilization in England* (1857), c. ii. The *regnum hominis*, much as it has advanced in our own day, has not yet succeeded in completely emancipating Man from the physico-geographical conditions of polity; climate, soil, structure, position, and even physical aspect, are permanent though modifiable factors in the life and character of the race.

17. συγγνόντες . . ἀποστάντες, ἑσσωθέντες: the piling of these participles is a little clumsy. With the first cp. συγγνούς abs. 7. 13 *supra* (*melius edocti*, Stein); or συγγινώσκων (οἱ) λέγειν ἀληθέα 4. 43 (Baehr). The ἀπόστασις here is merely a retirement from the Presence. The defeat (ἧσσα) is purely dialectical, and precedes or coincides with the σύγγνοια.

18. ἀρχαίην τε εἵλοντο λυπρὴν οἰκέοντες. As history, this statement is hardly correct; the 'Persian folk' may have remained in Persis proper, but the nobles certainly came down into the richer and civilized portions of the empire to a considerable extent; and the dynasty resided as a rule less in Pasargadai (Persia proper) than in Susa (Elam)

πρὸς Κύρου, ἄρχειν τε εἵλοντο λυπρὴν οἰκέοντες μᾶλλον ἢ
πεδιάδα σπείροντες ἄλλοισι δουλεύειν.

ΗΡΟΔΟΤΟΥ ΙΣΤΟΡΙΩΝ Θ | XXHHΠΙ ΑΒ: ἡροδότου ἱστοριῶν
ἐνάτη C: ἡροδότου ἱστοριῶν θ. R: τέλος ἡροδότου ἱστοριῶν θ.' Marc. :
ἡροδότοιο βίβλος κλεινοῖο πέρας λάβεν ὡδί S

or Ekbatana (Media), or Babylon. As geography, the description of Persis proper is unduly severe ; though *Fars* might compare ill with Babylonia, or even Susiana (cp. E. Meyer, *G. d. Alterth.* iii. (1901) p. 18). As argument, the conclusion looks, at first sight, oddly infelicitous for the last word of a record, which has exhibited in unsparing colours the attempt of the Persians to extend their empire over Hellas, an attempt ending in failure and flight, the prelude to further loss and forfeiture. But something else is in Hdt.'s mind. *Mutato nomine fabula narratur.* He is too delicate to dictate to the Greeks, or it may be to the Athenians ; but the lesson is there for those who have ears to hear. It is at once the rationale of the Greek success, and a call to future expansion. The men λυπρὴν οἰκέοντες, the nurslings of poverty (7. 102) and hard fare (9. 82)—theirs is the victory, and theirs the empire, if they will : what the Persians had done in the days of Kyros, why should not the Greeks do in the days of Kimon, or of Perikles ?

Such a moral belongs to a period long before the Peloponnesian war, and fits in well with the many other evidences that the story of the Great Invasion of 480–79 B.C. was composed early in the period of Hdt.'s literary labours. This anecdote, which conveys, in dramatic form, the rationale and the moral of the war, no doubt in the first instance was

designed as the conclusion of Bks. 7, 8, 9, though it now serves as the hardly less appropriate colophon to the whole work. It is an anecdote which is hardly consistent with the representation of Kyros in Bk. 1, and especially of his end : it seems to belong to one of those other cycles of stories on the later years of Kyros which Hdt. rejected when he came to deal with the passing of Kyros as itself an integral portion of his work (cp. 1. 214 *ad f.*).

It might even have been this finale to his work, as originally conceived and drafted, which led Hdt. back to the investigations, τόν τε Κῦρον ὅστις ἐὼν τὴν Κροίσου ἀρχὴν κατεῖλε, καὶ τοὺς Πέρσας ὅτεῳ τρόπῳ ἡγήσαντο τῆς 'Ασίης, which now bulk so large in Bk. 1. And thus, indeed, to use Rawlinson's simile, 'the tail of the snake is curved round into his mouth' in the completed work of Hdt., which forms a whole now, with a clear Beginning, Middle, and End. Historically and artistically the work is complete and concluded, though not, indeed, equally or evenly finished throughout : a phenomenon which the prior genesis of the latest portion, and the subsequent addition of the earlier, introductory, and discursive parts, go some way to explain. Blakesley, who, while recognizing the earlier composition of the last three Books, nevertheless holds the work to be incomplete, questions the authenticity of this chapter.

END OF VOL. I PART II

Printed by R. & R. CLARK, LIMITED, *Edinburgh.*

Lightning Source UK Ltd.
Milton Keynes UK
UKHW021844281118
333125UK00010B/479/P